INTELLIGENCE

THE SECRET WORLD OF SPIES
An Anthology

Fifth Edition

Edited with Introductions by

Loch K. Johnson
UNIVERSITY OF GEORGIA
SCHOOL OF PUBLIC AND INTERNATIONAL AFFAIRS

James J. Wirtz
NAVAL POSTGRADUATE SCHOOL

NEW YORK   OXFORD
OXFORD UNIVERSITY PRESS

Oxford University Press is a department of the University of Oxford.
It furthers the University's objective of excellence in research,
scholarship, and education by publishing worldwide.

Oxford   New York
Auckland   Cape Town   Dar es Salaam   Hong Kong   Karachi
Kuala Lumpur   Madrid   Melbourne   Mexico City   Nairobi
New Delhi   Shanghai   Taipei   Toronto

With offices in
Argentina   Austria   Brazil   Chile   Czech Republic   France   Greece
Guatemala   Hungary   Italy   Japan   Poland   Portugal   Singapore
South Korea   Switzerland   Thailand   Turkey   Ukraine   Vietnam

For titles covered by Section 112 of the US Higher Education
Opportunity Act, please visit www.oup.com/us/he for the
latest information about pricing and alternate formats.

Published in the United States of America by
Oxford University Press
198 Madison Avenue, New York, NY 10016
http://www.oup.com

Library of Congress Cataloging-in-Publication Data
Names: Johnson, Loch K., 1942-, editor. | Wirtz, James J., 1958-, editor.
Title: Intelligence : the secret world of spies : an anthology / edited with
   introductions by Loch K. Johnson, University of Georgia School of Public
   and International Affairs, James J. Wirtz, Naval Postgraduate School.
Description: Fifth Edition. | New York : Oxford University Press, [2018]
Identifiers: LCCN 2018032411 (print) | LCCN 2018033653 (ebook) | ISBN
   9780190854836 (ebook) | ISBN 9780190854829 (paperback : acid-free paper)
Subjects: LCSH: United States. Central Intelligence Agency. | Intelligence
   service. | Intelligence service--United States. | National security. |
   National security--Government policy--United States. | Spies.
Classification: LCC JK468.I6 (ebook) | LCC JK468.I6 I467 2019 (print) | DDC
   327.1273--dc23
LC record available at https://lccn.loc.gov/2018032411

Printing number: 9 8 7 6 5 4 3 2 1
Printed by LSC Communications, Inc., United States of America

This book is dedicated to the memories of
Michael Handel, Naval War College,
Harry Howe Ransom, Vanderbilt University,
and H. Bradford Westerfield, Yale University,
early leaders in the field of Intelligence Studies.

BRIEF CONTENTS

CONTENTS

v

ABOUT THIS BOOK

The fifth edition of *Intelligence: The Secret World of Spies* provides a comprehensive set of readings in the field of intelligence studies. Loch K. Johnson and James J. Wirtz's anthology spans a broad array of topics, from how the United States gathers and interprets information collected around the world to comparisons of the American intelligence system with the secret agencies of other nations. The readings are written by renowned experts, and each article is prefaced by a brief, framing introduction written by the editors.

Among the wide range of materials included in this text are: the meaning of strategic intelligence; methods of intelligence collection; intelligence analysis; the danger of intelligence politicization; relationships between intelligence officers and the policymakers they serve; covert action; counterintelligence; accountability and civil liberties; the implications of the major intelligence failures in 2001 and 2002 regarding, respectively, the terrorist attacks against the United States and the faulty estimates about weapons of mass destruction in Iraq; the controversy over highly classified documents leaked by insiders within the intelligence agencies in recent years; and intelligence as practiced in other nations.

This edition also contains valuable pedagogical features, including thirty-three articles on intelligence by leading experts (nine of which are new to this edition); ten thorough, chapter-length introductory essays by Johnson and Wirtz, which serve as "road maps" for the reader; brief synopses of each article; author profiles; charts and figures on intelligence organization and leadership; discussion questions following each chapter; a glossary; and a select bibliography.

PREFACE

As the references at the end of this anthology indicate, several fine texts on intelligence have been published in the past few years. Missing, though, has been a set of readings to accompany them. We have tried to fill that gap with this collection of outstanding articles on intelligence. To help orient those who use this book, we have added essays of our own to introduce each set of readings. Selecting the pieces for this anthology proved difficult, because space limitations forced us to exclude many first-rate articles. We believe, however, that the articles included in this volume will provide the reader with a good introduction to the breadth of this fascinating and relatively new field of scholarly inquiry.

NEW TO THIS EDITION

The nine new articles added to this edition fill previous gaps and take into account the latest events and research findings in the field. For example, Adrian Wolfberg's look at the *President's Daily Brief,* a highly classified document rarely written about by outsiders; an examination, offered by a group of British experts, on the place of social media intelligence; provocative articles on intelligence analysis; essays on the notorious Edward J. Snowden leaks, and on the intelligence challenge posed by the terrorist group known as ISIS; and a probe into the state of Soviet intelligence during the grave Cuban missile crisis of 1962, along with looks inside the intelligence organizations in a major European nation (Germany). The book covers a wide range of additional topics, from the history of intelligence in the United States to how the nation gathers and interprets information collected around the world. It also includes comparisons of the American intelligence system with the secret agencies of other nations.

Among other specific subjects examined in the anthology are the meaning of national security intelligence; methods of intelligence collection; intelligence analysis; the danger of intelligence politicization; relationships between intelligence officers and the policymakers they serve; covert action; counterintelligence; accountability and civil liberties; the implications of major intelligence failures in 2001 and 2003 regarding, respectively, the terrorist attacks against the United States and the prediction that Iraq possessed unconventional weaponry; insights into an ongoing domestic spying controversy involving the National Security Agency (NSA); and intelligence as practiced in other nations.

ACKNOWLEDGMENTS

The editors would like to thank the authors and publishers whose work we reprint for allowing us to showcase their outstanding research. We also express our appreciation to the reviewers who gave the draft of the fifth edition a thorough critique and offered many useful suggestions. They include Michael Poznansky (University of Pittsburgh), and John D. Woodward, Jr. (Boston University). We also thank the Freedom House and the U.S. Senate for allowing us to draw on our earlier writings for them in the preparation of a couple of the introductory essays in this volume. We acknowledge our debt to Rebecca Eversole and Scott Oney for proofreading; to William J. Daugherty (Armstrong Atlantic State University), Allen Dupont (Young Harris College), Bruce Farcau (Valencia Community College), Gardel Feurtado (The Citadel), George C. Fidas (The George Washington University), Glenn Hastedt (James Madison University), Ann Marie Kinnell (University of Southern Mississippi), Ken Kitts (Marion University), David Lorenzo (Virginia Wesleyan College), Pete Peterson (University of San Diego), Edward Schatz (Southern Illinois University), J. David Singer (University of Michigan), Stephan Sloan (University of Oklahoma), Frank J. Smist, Jr. (Rockhurst University), John D. Stempl (University of Kentucky), and Michael Turner (Alliant International University) for their guidance on article selection; to Andy Blitzer, Alison Ball and Brad Rau for production assistance, and to acquisitions editor Jennifer Carpenter for her steady encouragement and enthusiasm for the project.

Loch K. Johnson
James J. Wirtz

ABOUT THE EDITORS

Loch K. Johnson is the Regents Professor of Public and International Affairs, as well as a Josiah Meigs Distinguished Teaching Professor, at the University of Georgia; senior editor of the international journal *Intelligence and National Security*; and author of several books on U.S. American foreign policy and national security, including recently *Spy Watching: Intelligence Accountability in the United States* (Oxford, 2018); *National Security Intelligence: Secret Operations in Defense of the Democracies* (Polity, 2017); *American Foreign Policy and the Challenges of World Leadership: Power, Principle, and the Constitution* (Oxford, 2015); and *The Threat on the Horizon: An Inside Account of Intelligence Reform between the End of the Cold War and 9/11* (Oxford, 2011). He has won the Certificate of Distinction from the National Intelligence Study Center; the Studies in Intelligence Award from the Center for the Study of Intelligence; the Distinguished Professor Award from the Intelligence Section of the International Studies Association; and the V.O. Key Prize from the Southern Political Science Association. He has served as secretary of the American Political Science Association and president of the International Studies Association, South. Johnson was special assistant to the chair of the Senate Select Committee on Intelligence in 1975–1976; staff director of the House Subcommittee on Intelligence Oversight in 1977–1979; and special assistant to Les Aspin, chair of the Aspin-Brown Commission on Intelligence, in 1995.

Born in Auckland, New Zealand, Professor Johnson received his PhD in political science from the University of California, Riverside. At the University of Georgia, he has won the Josiah Meigs Prize, the university's highest teaching honor, as well as the Owens Award, its highest research honor. He also led the founding of the new School of Public and International Affairs at the University in 2001. Professor Johnson has been a Visiting Fellow at Oxford University (2003) and at Yale University (2005). In 2009, he was named a Phi Beta Kappa Visiting Scholar; in 2012, he was selected as the inaugural recipient of the Southeast Conference Professor of the Year Award; in 2014 he was named "Distinguished Scholar" by the Intelligence Studies Section of the International Studies Association; in 2015, he received the Lifetime Achievement Award from the International Association for Intelligence Education in Washington, DC; and in 2017 he was presented the Alumni Association Faculty Service Award at the University of Georgia.

James J. Wirtz is Dean of the School of International Graduate Studies at the Naval Postgraduate School, Monterey, California. He is the author of *The Tet Offensive: Intelligence Failure in War* (Cornell University Press, 1991, 1994) and has co-edited several books, including *Strategic Denial and Deception* (Transaction, 2002) and *Balance of Power: Theory and Practice in the 21st Century* (Stanford, 2004). He is section chair of the Intelligence Studies Section of the

International Studies Association and the President of the International Security and Arms Control Section of the American Political Science Association. He is general editor of the book series Initiatives in Strategic Studies: Issues and Policies, published by Palgrave Macmillan.

A native of New Jersey, Professor Wirtz earned his degrees in political science from Columbia University (M.Phil. 1987, PhD 1989), and the University of Delaware (MA 1983, BA 1980). He was a John M. Olin Fellow at the Center for International Affairs, Harvard University, and a Visiting Professor at the Center for International Security and Cooperation, Stanford University.

ABOUT THE CONTRIBUTORS

Richard J. Aldich is Professor of International security and Director of the Institute of Advanced Study at the University of Warwick, UK.

Aspin-Brown Commission, led by former Secretaries of Defense Les Aspin and Harold Brown, was established in 1994 and presented its report on the state of U.S. intelligence in 1996.

David M. Barrett is Professor of Political Science at Villanova University.

Bruce D. Berkowitz, a former fellow at the Hoover Institute, is the author of several books and articles on U.S. intelligence.

Richard K. Betts is Leo A. Shifrin Professor of War and Peace Studies in the Department of Political Science at Columbia University and author of *American Force* (2013).

Robert D. Blackwill served as Special Assistant to the President and Senior Director for European and Soviet Affairs on the National Security Council staff from 1989–1990 and, more recently, as adviser to President George W. Bush on Iraq.

James Burch is an officer in the U.S. Navy and has served with the National Security Agency.

Frank Church, Democrat of Idaho, led the 1975–1976 Senate inquiry into allegations of CIA abuses and served as chairman of the Senate Foreign Relations Committee.

Percy Cradock served as chairman of the British Joint Intelligence Committee from 1985 to 1992.

Jack Davis served as a career CIA analyst.

Raymond L. Garthoff is a senior fellow (emeritus) at the Brookings Institution in Washington, DC.

Michael Grow is Associate Professor Emeritus of History at Ohio University and the author of *U.S. Presidents and Latin American Interventions: Pursuing Regime Change in the Cold War* (2008).

Glenn Hastedt received his PhD in political science from Indiana University, is chair of the Justice Studies Department at James Madison University, and is the author of *American Foreign Policy: Past, Present, Future*, 6th ed. (2005) and many articles on intelligence.

Michael Herman is a former intelligence practitioner in the United Kingdom. His publications since his retirement have included the influential *Intelligence Power in Peace and War* (1996). His principal academic association has been with Nuffield College at Oxford University, where he is active as the Founder Director of the Oxford Intelligence Group. He is an Honorary DLitt of Nottingham University.

Frederick P. Hitz, inspector general of the CIA from 1990 to 1998, is a lecturer at the University of Virginia School of Law.

Arthur S. Hulnick served as Associate Professor of International Relations at Boston University, a veteran of U.S. Air Force Intelligence and the CIA, and author of *Keeping Us Safe* (2004).

Robert Jervis is Adlai E. Stevenson Professor of International Politics at Columbia University, former president of the American Political Science Association, and the author of many books and articles on international relations and intelligence.

Loch K. Johnson is the Regents Professor of Public and International Affairs at the University of Georgia and senior editor of the international journal *Intelligence and National Security.*

Kean Commission, led by Thomas H. Kean and Lee H. Hamilton, and known as well as the 9/11 Commission or more formally as the National Commission on Terrorist Attacks upon the United States, was a national committee of inquiry that investigated the terrorists attacks against New York City and Washington, DC, in 2001 and reported its findings in 2004.

Wolfgang Krieger is Professor of History Emeritus at the University of Marburg, Germany

Mark M. Lowenthal, author of *Intelligence: From Secrets to Policy,* 5th ed. (2012), has served as deputy assistant secretary for functional analysis in the State Department's Bureau of Intelligence Research, as staff director of the House Permanent Select Committee on Intelligence, and assistant director of Central Intelligence for analysis and production at the CIA. He is currently the President and CEO, The Intelligence & Security Academy, LLC.

Frederic F. Manget is retired from the Office of Legal Affairs at the CIA.

Stephen Marrin is an Associate Professor at James Madison University and a former CIA analyst.

Rose McDermott is Professor of Political Science at Brown University.

Phyllis Provost McNeil is a former CIA intelligence officer, U.S. Naval officer, and director of the Federal Executive Programs at the Kennedy School of Government, Harvard University, who served on the staff of the Aspin-Brown Commission in 1995–96 and wrote the intelligence history section of its final report.

Stephen C. Mercado is an analyst in the CIA's Directorate of Science and Technology.

Carl Miller is the research director of the Centre for the Analysis of Social Media (CASM) at Demos in London, where he writes about social media.

Christopher Moran is a British Academy Postdoctoral Fellow at the Unversity of Warwick, UK.

Sir David Omand is former UK Security and Inelligence Coordinator and Permanent Secretary in the Cabinet Office.

Paul R. Pillar is on the faculty of the Security Studies Program at Georgetown University and, concluding a long career in the CIA, he served as National Intelligence Officer for the Near East and South Asia from 2000 to 2005.

Mark Phythian is Professor of Political Science at the University of Leicester, UK, and co-editor of the journal *Intelligence and National Security.*

Paul J. Redmond is a former Chief of Counterintelligence at the CIA.

Joshua Rovner is on the faculty at American University in Washington, D.C.

Elke Schwarz is Lecturer in Politics and International Relations at the University of Leicester, UK.

Senate Select Committee on Intelligence is the U.S. Senate's intelligence oversight committee, founded in 1976.

Daniel Snow received an MBA degree from the Marriott School of Management at Brigham Young University and has published on economic espionage.

Stan A. Taylor, a professor of political science at Brigham Young University, has served as a staff member of the Senate Select Committee on Intelligence (1976–1979) and has co-authored *America the*

Vincible: U.S. Foreign Policy for the Twenty-First Century (1994).

Gregory F. Treverton served on the staff of the Church Committee and as vice chairman of the National Intelligence Council, and is currently with RAND in Santa Monica and on the faculty at the University of Southern California.

Wesley K. Wark is Director of the Security and Policy Institute, University of Ottawa, Canada.

James M. Wirtz is Dean of the School of International Graduate Studies at the Naval Postgraduate School, Monterey, California.

Adrian Wolfberg is Chairman of Defense Intelligence, Department of National Security and Stratgegy, U.S. Army War College.

Amy B. Zegart is on the faculty at the Hoover Institute, Stanford University.

I

INTELLIGENCE STUDIES

AN INTRODUCTION

Hamlet: ". . . we defy augury. There is a special providence in the fall of a sparrow. If it be now, 'tis not to come—if it be not to come, it will be now—if it be not now, yet it will come—the readiness is all . . ."

—SHAKESPEARE, *Hamlet*, 5.2.217

Americans have mixed attitudes when it comes to intelligence and intelligence agencies. Some are fascinated with the image of the secret agent, spy, or covert operator who moves easily across international boundaries, uses the latest high-tech gadgetry, frequents only the trendiest resorts, and spends his or her time with glamorous members of the opposite sex. Intelligence professionals happily cultivate this image. A Central Intelligence Agency (CIA) identification card and a well-crafted story about secret operations has gotten more than one CIA mail clerk off the hook for speeding in some country village. Some see intelligence agencies as rogue elephants, giant bureaucracies beyond public scrutiny or the control of elected officials. From this perspective, intelligence agencies are threats to democratic institutions because they can be hijacked by conspiratorially minded politicians to undertake some nefarious scheme.

Given that public accountability is central to democracy, some wonder whether intelligence organizations that undertake secret operations, deal with secret information, and produce restricted reports are compatible with government based on democratic principles. Others never think at all about intelligence organizations or prefer to believe that intelligence agencies possess unlimited information about all significant threats to national security. Every so often, however, a tragic event shatters the complacency of this third group, which of course includes its share of government officials. This leads to much recrimination and a hunt for those responsible for the latest intelligence failure.

Today we live in the Information Age, in a world undergoing an information revolution. The Internet and desktop computers allow millions of people to access and manipulate unlimited amounts of data and to transmit information to a global audience at virtually no cost. This type of capability was available only to large government organizations (for example, the CIA) just a few short decades ago. As the al-Qaeda terrorist attacks against the United States in September 2001 demonstrate, we also live in an age when intelligence—the ability to make sense out of this endless stream of data—is at a premium. The information revolution is affecting everyone, including intelligence analysts and the way they gather, analyze, and disseminate intelligence reports and estimates. But the full impact of the

1

Information Age on intelligence agencies remains a matter of debate. With more state and non-state actors acquiring the communications, transportation, and weaponry needed to influence world events, intelligence agencies face the challenge of trying to stay ahead of these actors before they can wreak havoc on U.S. interests. The Information Age has actually placed even greater pressure on the U.S. intelligence community to sift through this torrent of information to detect new threats to the United States and its interests. New questions also have emerged about the limits of intelligence and the definition of privacy as personal information is digitized and shared across the World Wide Web.

DEFINING INTELLIGENCE

So what exactly is intelligence? Scores of definitions are available. Some are simple; Thomas F. Troy, for instance, defines intelligence as "knowledge of the enemy" (Troy 1991–1992, 433). And some definitions, like the one offered by The Economist, are a bit more convoluted. According to this respected periodical, intelligence is

> the painstaking collection and analysis of fact, the exercise of judgment, and clear and quick presentation. It is not simply what serious journalists would do if they had time; it is something more rigorous, continuous, and above all operational . . . that is to say related to something that somebody wants to do or may be forced to do. (quoted in Troy 1991–1992, 442)

Many definitions of intelligence begin with Sherman Kent's description of the concept. Kent, an early theorist and practitioner of intelligence, defined it as *knowledge*, as *organization*, and as an *activity*. This definition allowed him to describe the way intelligence services collect and analyze information, the finished intelligence product that agencies provide to policymakers, and the way intelligence services are organized (Kent 1949). Mark Lowenthal, a contemporary intelligence theorist and practitioner, borrowed a page from Kent's work when he devised this succinct description of the three dimensions of intelligence:

> Intelligence as process: Intelligence can be thought of as the means by which certain types of information are required and requested, collected, analyzed, and disseminated, and as the way in which certain types of covert action are conceived and conducted.

> Intelligence as product: Intelligence can be thought of as the product of these processes, that is, as the analyses and intelligence operations themselves. Intelligence as organization: Intelligence can be thought of as the units that carry out its various functions. (Lowenthal 2006, 9)

We offer a twist to Lowenthal's definition by adding the phrase *national security* to the term *intelligence* to suggest that the readings we have collected focus on issues of great importance and are the stuff of national policy debate. *National security intelligence* contributes to the processes, products, and organizations used by senior officials to create and implement national foreign and defense policies. National security intelligence thus provides warning of immediate threats to vital national security interests and assesses long-term trends of interest to senior government officials. National security intelligence is of political importance because it can shape the course and conduct of U.S. policy.

INTERDISCIPLINARY APPROACH

In the essays that follow, our contributors address intelligence in the three ways described by Kent and Lowenthal. Sometimes they address intelligence as a process: Parts II and III, for example, address key facets of the "intelligence cycle," a commonly accepted way to divide the process of producing intelligence. Sometimes they write about intelligence as a product. References abound, for instance, to finished intelligence (research reports and analysis) and current intelligence (daily news summaries such as the *National Intelligence Daily*). The contributors also discuss the impact of organization on intelligence—that is, the way the structure of national intelligence and the relationship between and within intelligence organizations shapes intelligence processes and products.

Three academic disciplines have focused on the study of intelligence, and essays from each of these schools are contained in this volume. Political scientists are primarily interested in intelligence as a process. Drawing on the fields of psychology, organizational theory, security studies, and international relations, they explore the challenges inherent in developing accurate and timely estimates of current and future events. Historians provide compelling accounts of intelligence failures, explaining how the road to surprise, paved with what in hindsight appears to be clear indications of trouble, was missed or misinterpreted by analysts or ignored by policymakers. Scholars of public policy focus on the management, and oversight of secret organizations in a democratic setting. They are particularly interested in striking a balance between the need for secrecy in intelligence matters to preserve and enhance national security and the need for citizens in a democracy to know about the activities of their government.

Because each of these schools borrows freely from the others, they generally use the same concepts, terminology, and history in their research. Their work also is cumulative in the sense that it incorporates earlier findings and reflects points of consensus in the literature on intelligence. The essays we have chosen suggest that despite different approaches and formal training, those writing about intelligence are forming a distinct and relatively coherent field of scholarly endeavor: a true interdisciplinary approach to the study of intelligence.

The essays we have selected reflect the way scholars organize their research in the field of intelligence studies. Part I offers an overview of the evolution of the U.S. intelligence community, as well as a look at the current literature on intelligence and a wide-ranging conversation on key intelligence issues. Parts II and III contain readings that address critical functions of the intelligence cycle (collection and analysis), which inevitably leads to a discussion of intelligence failures and surprise. Parts IV and V deal with intelligence dissemination (another critical aspect of the intelligence cycle), the general relationship between the intelligence community and policymakers and intelligence politicization, and the deliberate or inadvertent corruption of intelligence estimates. Parts VI and VII discuss the paramilitary (covert action) and security (counterintelligence) operations conducted by the U.S. intelligence community, activities of increasing importance to policymakers in the aftermath of the September 11 terrorist attacks on the Pentagon and the World Trade Center. The essays in Part VIII probe the issue of intelligence oversight and the problems that arise when secret organizations are devoid of safeguards in a democracy. Part IX looks at the circumstances surrounding the major intelligence failures associated with the 9/11 terrorist attacks in the United States, along with the faulty intelligence analysis in 2002 concluding that Iraq possessed weapons of mass destruction. It also examines twenty-first-century controversies over domestic spy operations conducted by the National

Security Agency (NSA) apparently undertaken to overcome weaknesses revealed in the aftermath of the 9/11 attacks. Part X offers a brief look at intelligence organizations in other countries.

THE U.S. INTELLIGENCE COMMUNITY

Although some intelligence agents live in foreign capitals, work the diplomatic cocktail circuit, undertake daring operations, and are known to most of the world by an assumed name, most intelligence managers and analysts spend their careers at a desk and become experts on a few subjects. Their job is to scrutinize and make sense of the deluge of information provided by national collection systems—everything from agent reports to pictures taken by spy satellites.

Some analysts work with information collected from people who know or have access to sensitive information. This human source intelligence is known as HUMINT. The Central Intelligence Agency and the Defense HUMINT Service, which is part of the Defense Intelligence Agency, are the organizations within the U.S. intelligence community that collect the majority of human intelligence. Analysts also work with signals intelligence (SIGINT), which is information obtained from intercepted communications, radar emissions, or data transmissions. The National Security Agency is the primary collector of SIGINT. Geospatial intelligence (GEOINT—formerly known as imagery intelligence, or IMINT) is information gathered chiefly by the National Geospatial-Intelligence Agency, through the use of spy satellites and reconnaissance aircraft. GEOINT sometimes offers real-time electro-optical, radar, or infrared images of specific areas of interest. Measurement and signature intelligence (MASINT) consists of data that describe distinctive physical characteristics of a specific event such as measuring the contents of a rocket plume or the size of a nuclear explosion. The Defense Intelligence Agency and the armed forces collect MASINT. Intelligence analysts also focus on open-source intelligence (OSINT)—information gathered from newspapers, magazines, the Internet, and other public sources around the world. Indeed, OSINT is the starting point when analysts try and piece together the "jigsaw puzzle" pieces that will give policymakers an accurate picture of world affairs.

Analysts also participate in the interagency process: that is, the way mid-level officials from across the U.S. government make and implement policy.

They are members of specific expert communities who have a professional or academic interest in a given area of study. Most intelligence work has little to do with physical exertion and everything to do with mental activity.

Once information is collected, it is disseminated to a variety of organizations to produce "all-source" finished intelligence. These analyses are at the heart of the "data fusion process" because they are intended to combine all relevant information to provide a coherent and accurate depiction of the topic at hand. All-source analyses of long-term interest are generally referred to as "intelligence estimates," although the intelligence community also provides all-source intelligence on topics of immediate concern.

Three civilian organizations provide the majority of strategic all-source intelligence estimates to national policymakers. The National Intelligence Council (NIC) consists of about twenty national intelligence officers who are experts on specific issues or regions. Working for the Director of Central Intelligence, they supervise the production of major intelligence reports, often referred to as National Intelligence Estimates (NIEs). The National Foreign Intelligence Board, which comprises senior representatives drawn from across the intelligence community, approves the estimates produced by the NIC, thereby generating a "community-wide" position on a particular subject. The Directorate of Intelligence (DI) is where the majority of all-source analysis is conducted within the CIA. Organized into offices that cover geographic regions and specific political, military, or economic issues, analysts produce current intelligence and undertake long-term research efforts, such as NIEs. The third organization that produces all-source intelligence is the State Department's Bureau of Intelligence and Research (INR). Organized into bureaus covering regional and issue areas, its analysts supply finished intelligence to the secretary of state and other State Department officials. It produces the *Morning Summary*, which is provided daily to the secretary of state.

The Department of Defense also maintains a vast network of organizations that produce finished intelligence, which deals mostly with foreign militaries. The DIA provides finished intelligence on military issues to the secretary of defense, the Office of the Secretary of Defense, and the Joint Chiefs of Staff. Additionally, each of the military services maintains specialized intelligence capabilities. The U.S. Army runs the National Ground Intelligence Center. It produces all-source analysis on foreign armies and security forces. The Intelligence Center of the Office of Naval Intelligence gathers information about foreign surface ships, submarines, and undersea weapons and monitors the capabilities of foreign sensor systems and ocean surveillance systems. The National Air Intelligence Center is the Air Force's analytical organization that monitors foreign air forces and space programs. The Marine Corps Intelligence Activity provides finished intelligence to guide acquisition decisions for the Marines and to plan military operations. Each of the unified commands (such as the U.S. Central Command, or CENT-COM) runs a Joint Intelligence Center that produces intelligence directly related to military activities in the unified command's area of responsibility.

Other government departments and agencies operate specialized intelligence bureaus. The Department of Energy's Office of Intelligence, for instance, collects open-source information and produces classified and unclassified estimates dealing with foreign energy and technology programs. The DOE is especially concerned with monitoring international programs that could lead to the further proliferation of nuclear weapons. The Treasury Department also maintains a small intelligence bureau that monitors international economic, financial, and security affairs.

Domestic counterintelligence activities are primarily the responsibility of the Federal Bureau of Investigation's National Security Division. The FBI investigates and monitors foreign efforts to spy against the U.S. government and industry. It also conducts operations against hostile intelligence services operating within the United States. Recently, the bureau has been under pressure to place less emphasis on investigating terrorist activities within the United States with an eye toward criminal prosecution and to take more direct action to capture or interdict terrorists before they can strike.

THE READINGS

Our first essay is drawn from the final report of the Aspin-Brown Commission (1996). Prepared by Commission staff member Phyllis Provost McNeil, the essay offers an overview of the U.S. intelligence community's evolution. Then Adrian Wolfberg adds to the introductory history lessons with a look at how the *President's Daily Brief* (PDB) is prepared in the United States.

1. THE EVOLUTION OF THE U.S. INTELLIGENCE COMMUNITY—AN HISTORICAL OVERVIEW

PHYLLIS PROVOST McNEIL

Written by an Aspin-Brown Commission staff member, this essay reviews the long and colorful history of successes, failures, scandals, and reforms that have shaped America's secret agencies.

The function of intelligence as an activity of the U.S. Government is often regarded as a product of the Cold War. Indeed, much of what is known today as the Intelligence Community was created and developed during the Cold War period. But intelligence has been a function of the Government since the founding of the Republic. While it has had various incarnations over time, intelligence has historically played a key role in providing support to U.S. military forces and in shaping the policies of the United States toward other countries.

THE EARLY YEARS OF THE REPUBLIC

During the Revolutionary War, General George Washington was an avid user of intelligence as well as a consummate practitioner of the intelligence craft. Records show that shortly after taking command of the Continental Army in 1775, Washington paid an unidentified agent to live in Boston and surreptitiously report by use of "secret correspondence" on the movements of British forces. Indeed, Washington recruited and ran a number of agents, set up spy rings, devised secret methods of reporting, analyzed the raw intelligence gathered by his agents, and mounted an extensive campaign to deceive the British armies. Historians cite these activities as having played a major role in the victory at Yorktown and in the ability of the Continental Army to evade the British during the winters at Valley Forge.

In a letter to one of his officers written in 1777, Washington wrote that secrecy was key to the success of intelligence activities:

The necessity of procuring good intelligence is apparent and need not be further urged—All that remains for me to add is, that you keep the whole matter as secret as possible. For upon Secrecy, success depends in most Enterprises of the kind, & for want of it, they are generally defeated, however, well planned. . . . [letter to Colonel Elias Dayton, 26 July 1777]

Washington was not the only one to recognize the importance of intelligence to the colonials' cause. In November of 1775, the Continental Congress created the Committee of Secret Correspondence to gather foreign intelligence from people in England, Ireland, and elsewhere on the European continent to help in the prosecution of the war.

Washington's keen interest in intelligence carried over to his presidency. In the first State of the Union address in January 1790, Washington asked the Congress for funds to finance intelligence operations. In July of that year the Congress responded by establishing the Contingent Fund of Foreign Intercourse (also known as the Secret Service Fund) and authorizing $40,000 for this purpose. Within three years, the fund had grown to $1 million, about 12 percent of the Government's budget at the time. While the Congress required the President to certify the amounts spent, it also allowed him to conceal the purposes and recipients of the funds. (In 1846, this latter provision was challenged by the House of Representatives, but President Polk, citing national security grounds of protection of sources, refused to turn over more specific information on the use of the Fund to the Congress.) Judging by the paucity of the historical record, interest in intelligence as a tool of the Executive appears to have waned in succeeding Administrations, although occasional lapses in performance sometimes produced controversy. During the War of 1812, for example, military intelligence failed to discover that British troops were advancing on Washington until they were 16 miles from the Capital. The Secretary of War had refused to believe that the British would invade Washington, and military intelligence reported from this perspective.

Intelligence regained prominence during the Civil War. Both the Union and Confederate leadership valued intelligence information, established their own spy networks, and often railed at the press for providing intelligence to the other side. The Confederate forces established the Signal and Secret Service Bureau with the primary charter of obtaining northern newspapers. On the Union side, the Departments of the Navy, State, and War each maintained an intelligence service. Union codebreakers decoded Confederate messages and learned that the plates for Confederate currency were being manufactured in New York. In June of 1861, the first electronic transmission of information was sent from an aerial reconnaissance platform—in this case, a balloon—directly to President Lincoln on the ground. Two months later, Union forces established a Balloon Corps. Although disbanded after two years, it succeeded in detecting a large concentration of Confederate troops preparing to attack at Fair Oaks, Virginia.

In 1863, the first professional intelligence organization was established by the Union forces, the Bureau of Military Intelligence. Headed by the Commander of the Army of the Potomac, General Joseph Hooker, the Bureau prepared evaluations of the Confederate Army's strength and activities based on sources that included infiltrations of the Confederacy's War and Navy Departments. It was considered the best run intelligence operation of the Civil War. Yet, Hooker's ineffective use of intelligence (reportedly he was inundated with information) was largely responsible for the Confederate victory at Chancellorsville. Similarly, it has been suggested that Lee's defeat at Gettysburg was partially attributable to his lack of intelligence on the strength and deployment of Union forces.

The Bureau of Military Intelligence was disestablished at the end of the war. A byproduct of its dissolution was the Secret Service, established in 1865 to combat counterfeiting.

A PEACETIME ROLE FOR INTELLIGENCE

Prior to the 1880s, intelligence activities were devoted almost exclusively to support of military operations, either to support deployed forces or to obtain information on the views or participation of other countries in a particular conflict. In March 1882, however, the first permanent intelligence organization—the Office of Naval Intelligence—was created within the Department of the Navy to collect intelligence on foreign navies in peace-time and in war. Three years later, a similar organization—the Military Intelligence Division—was created within the Army to collect foreign and domestic military data for the War Department and the Army.

The Administration of Theodore Roosevelt saw perhaps the most active use of intelligence for foreign policy purposes by any President until that time. Historians note that Roosevelt used intelligence operatives to incite a revolution in Panama to justify annexing the Panama Canal. In 1907, the President also relied on intelligence that showed the military build-up of the Japanese as justification to launch the worldwide cruise of the "Great White Fleet" as a display of U.S. naval force.

For the most part, however, the early part of the twentieth century was marked not by an expanded use of intelligence for foreign policy purposes, but by an expansion of domestic intelligence capabilities. The Justice Department's Bureau of Investigation (the forerunner of the FBI) was established in 1908 out of concern that Secret Service agents were spying on members of Congress. By 1916, the Bureau had grown from 34 agents focusing primarily on banking issues to 300 agents with an expanded charter that included internal security, Mexican border smuggling activities, neutrality violations in the Mexican revolution, and Central American unrest. After war broke out in Europe, but before the United States joined the Allied cause, the Bureau turned its attention to activities of German and British nationals within our borders.

WORLD WAR I

At the time the United States entered the war, it lacked a coordinated intelligence effort. As a champion of open diplomacy, President Woodrow Wilson had disdained the use of spies and was generally suspicious of intelligence. His views on the subject appeared to change, however, as a result of a close association developed with the British intelligence chief in Washington.

In fact, British intelligence played a major role in bringing the United States into World War I. Public revelations of German intelligence attempts to prevent U.S. industry and the financial sector from assisting Great Britain greatly angered the American public. Subsequently, British intelligence presented Wilson with the decryption of German diplomatic and naval traffic showing a German effort to entice the Mexican government into joining Germany against the United States in return for Texas, Arizona, and New Mexico if Germany won the war. Later declassified and disclosed to the public, this intercepted communication, known as the "Zimmerman Telegram," infuriated Wilson and added support to his address before a joint session of Congress in 1917 urging that the U.S. declare war on Germany.

In June of 1917, the first U.S. signals intelligence agency was formed within the Army. Known as "MI-8," the agency was charged with decoding military communications and providing codes for use by the U.S. military. In 1919, at the end of the war, the agency was transferred to the State Department. Known as the "Black Chamber," it focused on diplomatic rather than military communications. In 1921, the Black Chamber celebrated perhaps its most significant success by decrypting certain Japanese diplomatic traffic. The intelligence gained from this feat was used to support U.S. negotiators at a Washington conference on naval disarmament. Yet, despite such successes, President Hoover decided that the State Department's interception of diplomatic cables and correspondence could not be tolerated. Apparently agreeing with the alleged, yet oft-quoted statement of his Secretary of State, Henry Stimson, that "Gentlemen do not read each other's mail," Hoover returned the agency to a military orientation under the Army Signal Corps.

Other intelligence entities remained in existence after the end of WWI but saw their resources cut substantially. An exception to this general trend was the Justice Department's Bureau of Investigation, which saw a marked expansion of its mission and workforce. In 1924, J. Edgar Hoover was named director of the Bureau [renamed the Federal Bureau of Investigation (FBI) in 1935]. The FBI's charter was broadened particularly in the years leading to World War II, when concerns for U.S. internal security were mounting in the face of German aggression in Europe. The FBI was made responsible for investigating espionage, counterespionage, sabotage, and violations of the neutrality laws. It was also during this period that the first effort was made to coordinate the activities of the various intelligence elements of the Government. An Interdepartmental Intelligence Coordinating Committee was created for this purpose, but because the Committee lacked a permanent chair and participating agencies were reluctant to share information, it had limited impact.

WORLD WAR II AND ITS AFTERMATH

The years immediately before the United States entered World War II saw American interest in developments in Europe and the Pacific intensify dramatically, prompting both formal and informal efforts to gather and analyze information. President Franklin Roosevelt relied heavily on American and British friends traveling abroad to provide him with intelligence on the intentions of other leaders. One such friend was William J. Donovan, an aficionado of intelligence and a veteran of World War I, whom Roosevelt sent to Europe in 1940 to gather information on the stability of Britain and again in the spring of 1941 to gather information on Italian Dictator Mussolini, among other matters. Upon his return, Donovan lobbied hard for the creation of a centralized, civilian intelligence apparatus to complement that of the military.

In July 1941, in response to Donovan's urging, Roosevelt appointed Donovan as Coordinator of Information (COI) to form a non-military intelligence organization. The Coordinator of Information was to "collect and analyze all information and data which may bear upon the national security" for the President and those he designated. The Coordinator was given the authority, "with the approval of the President," to request data from other agencies and departments, but was specifically admonished not to interfere with the duties and responsibilities of the President's military and naval advisers. FBI Director J. Edgar Hoover, fearing a loss of authority to the new Coordinator, secured the President's commitment that the Bureau's primacy in South America would not change.

Borrowing heavily from the British intelligence model, Donovan created a special staff to pull together and analyze all national security information and empaneled an eight-member review board, drawn from academia, to review analysis and test its conclusions. In concert with the Librarian of Congress, COI Donovan organized the Division of Special Information at the Library, to work with Donovan's analytical staff and to coordinate scholarship within the Library and in academia. In theory, the Division was to provide unclassified information to Donovan's staff, who would combine it with classified information to produce an analysis that would be reviewed by the special board before presentation to the President. Although in practice the process did not operate precisely as planned, the concept of centralized analysis was established.

The surprise attack on Pearl Harbor by the Japanese on December 7, 1941, brought America into the war and revealed a significant failure on the part of the U.S. intelligence apparatus. As subsequent investigations found, intelligence had been handled in a casual, uncoordinated manner, and there had been insufficient attention to certain collection requirements. The lack of coordination among agencies, principally the Army and the Navy, resulted in a failure to provide timely dissemination of relevant information to key decisionmakers. Moreover, intelligence analysts had grossly underestimated Japanese capabilities and intentions, revealing a tendency to misunderstand Japanese actions by looking at them with American cultural biases. After the war, the resolve of America's leaders "never again" to permit another Pearl Harbor largely prompted the establishment of a centralized intelligence structure.

America's entrance into World War II created an immediate need for intelligence to support the warfighter. While the Army and the Navy maintained their own intelligence capabilities, none were prepared to provide the kind of support needed.[1] To bolster this effort, the Office of Strategic Services (OSS) was created in June 1942, under the recently established Joint Chiefs of Staff to succeed the Coordinator of Information. William Donovan remained in charge of the reorganized unit. In addition to assuming the analytical role of its predecessor, the OSS was chartered to carry out clandestine operations against the Axis powers on a worldwide scale. It was not, however, readily accepted by the Joint Chiefs of Staff (JCS), who remained skeptical of the value of OSS activities, and the new unit faced strong competition from the FBI and the Army's intelligence organization.

Usually glamorized as the dashing operations arm of the U.S. Army (with its well-known espionage exploits with the Resistance in Europe), the OSS's contribution to intelligence production has gone largely unnoticed. It was, however, one of the seven major intelligence producers and was an important training ground for a generation of intelligence analysts, as well as operatives. Decidedly different than

the British system, the OSS established the tradition of putting analysts and operatives in the same organization. The difficulties, however, that the OSS had in establishing itself within the JCS structure reaffirmed Donovan's belief that the peacetime successor to the OSS should be a civilian organization directly responsible to the President. In 1944, Donovan started campaigning for this model.

In the meantime, substantial intelligence capabilities were created in the military services to support the war effort. Army intelligence operations were supervised by the Military Intelligence Division of the Army General Staff. Its operating arm, the Military Intelligence Service (MIS), was created in 1942 and carried out collection activities around the world, including agent operations, signals interception, and photo reconnaissance. MIS also provided intelligence analysis to U.S. and allied commands. At the same time, intelligence elements were assigned directly to operating forces in the field. These intelligence units collected and analyzed tactical signals intelligence, interpreted photos, and performed ground reconnaissance missions. Aerial reconnaissance missions were run by the Army Air Corps. To provide counterintelligence support, including the debriefing of prisoners and defectors, the Army Counterintelligence Corps was established in 1942 with both domestic and overseas missions.

Army signals intelligence analysts succeeded in breaking and exploiting the code systems used by the Imperial Japanese Army, producing intelligence which many believe shortened the war in the Pacific. In England, after the U.S. joined the war, Army teams participated in the work begun by the Polish and continued by the British to decode German military communications encrypted with the Enigma cipher machines. The intelligence produced by this effort, codenamed "ULTRA," gave the Allies unparalleled insight into the workings of the German military and shortened the war in Europe.

Within three days of the devastating and embarrassing attack on Pearl Harbor, the Navy's Combat Intelligence Unit at Pearl Harbor was busy trying to crack the Japanese Fleet code, JN25. By April 1942, enough information was known to allow the American Pacific Fleet to deal the first blow without visual sighting of the Japanese Fleet at the Battle of Coral Sea. By May 1942, Navy cryptanalysts succeeded in cracking the Japanese code. This significant naval intelligence capability, on par with the British and Polish decryption of the German code, allowed the Americans to defeat the Japanese at the Battle of

Midway and to countermeasure the Japanese during the rest of the war in the Pacific.

Also in the Pacific theater, an Allied Translator and Interpreter Section, composed of 2,000 American Nisei soldiers, interrogated Japanese prisoners and exploited captured documents. Since the OSS did not operate in the South Pacific Theater, special human source intelligence capabilities were established, using Australian and Philippine guerrilla forces as well as a special Army long-distance reconnaissance team known as the Alamo Scouts.

Similarly, the Marine Corps developed and deployed the Navajo Code Talker Program in May 1942. By 1945, operating in both theaters of the War, 400 Native American Navajo members of the Corps were encoding, transmitting, and decoding English messages in the complex language of the Navajo Indians. The Code Talkers have been credited with playing a significant role in the Marine Corps victory on Iwo Jima. So successful was this method of encryption and communication that it was employed in the Korean and Vietnam conflicts.

Toward the end of the war, the Administration was left to decide what to do with these intelligence capabilities. A vigorous and heated debate ensued between those who favored the Donovan idea of an independent, civilian intelligence organization reporting directly to the President and those who favored retention and control of intelligence by the military. The State Department, among others, weighed in heavily against the Donovan approach.

In September 1945, while the debate continued, President Truman, acting on a recommendation from his Budget Director, abolished the OSS by Executive Order and divided its functions between the War and State Departments. State received the research and analysis function, combining it with the existing analytical office to form the Interim Research and Intelligence Service (IRIS). The War Department formed the Strategic Services Unit (SSU) out of the clandestine side of the OSS. President Truman had unrealized hopes that the State Department would take over the coordination of intelligence for the Government.

At about the time the OSS was being disbanded, a study commissioned by Navy Secretary James Forrestal and chaired by private businessman Ferdinand Eberstadt was published. While the report dealt principally with the issue of military unification, it also recommended coordination of the intelligence function through the establishment of a National Security Council (NSC) and a Central Intelligence Agency (CIA). The NSC would coordinate the civilian and military national security policy for the President. The CIA, under the auspices of the NSC, would serve "to coordinate national security intelligence." While the military generally supported the recommendation calling for centralized coordination of "national security" intelligence, it was unwilling to give up its own collection programs and analytical capabilities.

THE CENTRAL INTELLIGENCE GROUP

While the recommendations of the Eberstadt study were to influence significantly the content of what eventually became the National Security Act of 1947, they were not immediately implemented. However, President Truman decided to settle the question of whether there should be a centralized civilian intelligence organization.

Reflecting his dissatisfaction with what he perceived to be the haphazard nature of intelligence collection, his desire to have one authoritative source for intelligence advice, and, above all, his desire to avoid another Pearl Harbor, President Truman issued an executive directive on 22 January 1946 establishing a National Intelligence Authority, a Central Intelligence Group (CIG) "under the direction of a Director of Central Intelligence" (DCI), and an Intelligence Advisory Board. The latter body comprised civilian and military heads of intelligence agencies who were to advise the DCI. The National Intelligence Authority, comprising the Secretaries of War, State, Navy, and the President's personal representative, was charged with planning, developing, and coordinating the intelligence effort. Finally, the CIG (a small interdepartmental group—not an independent agency) was responsible for coordinating, planning, evaluating, and disseminating intelligence and overtly collected information. Funding and staffing of the CIG were provided by other departments and agencies which retained control over their own intelligence efforts.

The first DCI, Rear Admiral Sidney Souers (who wrote the intelligence section of the Eberstadt study), reluctantly accepted the appointment and stayed in the position only six months. Under his tenure, the CIG played a limited analytical role due to Souers' reluctance to challenge the analytical product of the State Department's IRIS. But the IRIS was soon decimated by congressional budget cutting, and most of its positions were dispersed throughout the Department and to other agencies. In all, 600 positions were transferred from the IRIS to the National Intelligence Authority, the CIG, and the military services. This left the Department with a skeleton analytic group, thus limiting its mission to providing intelligence support only to the policymakers within the Department of State.[2]

The second DCI, Lieutenant General Hoyt Vandenberg, proved more aggressive than his predecessor, gaining authority for the CIG to hire personnel and acquire its own administrative support, as well as expanding clandestine collection, research and analysis, and the overall size of the organization. At the behest of the President, the first national estimate, on Soviet intentions and capabilities, was produced in 1946 during Vandenberg's tenure.

At the time Vandenberg became DCI, in June of 1946, legislation was being drafted in the Congress and in concert with the Truman Administration to provide for the unification of the military establishment under a Secretary of Defense. Inasmuch as the CIG would need an annual appropriation to continue in existence, Vandenberg saw an opportunity to incorporate legislative language creating an independent central intelligence agency with several features modeled on the existing charter of the CIG. Within a month of assuming the duties of DCI, Vandenberg submitted a proposal describing this new entity, with the support of the Truman Administration, which consisted basically of the pertinent language from the 1946 presidential directive and language that had been previously published in the Federal Register.

THE NATIONAL SECURITY ACT OF 1947

In the ensuing congressional debate on the Vandenberg proposal, several issues emerged about the role of the DCI.

One was whether the DCI should be a civilian or military officer. Some argued that if the DCI were an active duty military officer, he would be subject to the control of his parent service. On the other hand, the military was recognized as the principal consumer of intelligence and controlled most of the resources devoted to it. The legislation ultimately provided that the President could appoint either a civilian or a military officer as the DCI, but if a military officer were appointed, he would be removed from the control of his parent service.

Another issue was whether the DCI should be a member of the National Security Council that was being established by the bill as the White House focal point for national security matters. Navy Secretary James Forrestal argued strongly against this proposal saying that the Council would be too large

to accomplish its business and that the new DCI would have ready access without formal membership. His argument was persuasive and the DCI's proposed membership on the NSC was dropped.

A third issue was the relationship of the DCI to other agencies, in particular, the FBI. The draft proposal provided that the new Central Intelligence Agency would serve as the focal point within the Government where intelligence would be gathered and evaluated. As such, the CIA would necessarily require access to information collected by other agencies. The military agreed to this coordinating role for the CIA so long as the military was able to maintain its own collection and analytical capabilities to support military operations. The FBI, however, insisted on limiting the CIA's access to FBI files only if written notice was given first and only if access was "essential to the national security."

On July 27, 1947, President Truman signed into law the National Security Act of 1947, creating a postwar national security framework. A National Security Council was created to coordinate national security policy. The Act created the position of Secretary of Defense and unified the separate military departments (the Army, the Navy, and the newly created Air Force) under this position. The Act also established the Joint Chiefs of Staff to serve as the principal military advisers to the President and the Secretary of Defense. Finally, a Central Intelligence Agency was established with the Director of Central Intelligence as its head. At the time of its creation, the CIA was the only agency charged with a "national" intelligence mission.

The statutory language regarding the authorities and functions of the new Central Intelligence Agency was left intentionally vague. In part this reflected the bureaucratic sensitivities involved in specifying in the law the DCI's roles and missions in regard to other agencies, and, in part, the desire to avoid wording that other governments might find offensive. Thus, there was no mention of "espionage" or "spying" in the statute, nor was there any wording to suggest that covert actions (i.e., secret operations to influence political conditions in other countries) were part of the new agency's charter. Rather, the CIA was authorized to perform "services of common concern" to other intelligence agencies as may be determined by the National Security Council and to perform "such other functions and duties related to intelligence affecting the national security as the National Security Council may from time-to-time direct." (The NSC did, in fact, issue directives in 1947 and 1948, providing specific authority for CIA's operational and analytical functions.)

The 1947 Act also included an express prohibition on the CIA's having any "police, subpoena, law-enforcement powers, or internal security functions," reflecting the congressional and public desire to ensure that they were not creating a U.S. "Gestapo" and to preserve the FBI's primacy in domestic matters. The law also made the DCI responsible for "protecting intelligence sources and methods from unauthorized disclosure."

THE EARLY YEARS OF THE CIA

The early years of the CIA appear to have been difficult ones as the Agency attempted to establish itself within the Government, amid growing concern about Communist gains in Eastern Europe and Soviet expansionism.

Rear Admiral Roscoe Hillenkoetter was DCI at the time the CIA was created. He organized the Agency into two principal divisions: one dealing with intelligence operations and the other with analysis. The analytical arm, in response to policymaker interest, prepared and disseminated short-term intelligence pieces. DCI Hillenkoetter found it difficult, however, to force other agencies to participate in the development of longer papers despite the language of the 1947 Act. The emphasis on producing short-term pieces, on the other hand, was often seen as intruding on the role of other producers such as the State Department, the military departments, and the FBI. There was also conflict on the operational side. The Government considered initiating psychological warfare operations overseas to counter Soviet expansionism, but the NSC preferred that the State Department, rather than the CIA, be responsible for them. It was only when the Secretary of State vigorously objected to this role for the Department that it was assigned to the CIA.

In January 1948, less than a year after the CIA was created, the National Security Council, exercising its oversight role under its Executive Secretary Sidney Souers,[3] asked three private citizens to examine comprehensively the CIA's "structure, administration, activities, and interagency relations." Allen Dulles, William Jackson and Matthias Correa, three New York lawyers with experience in intelligence, submitted their highly critical report in January 1949. Although the NSC found the criticism of DCI Hillenkoetter and the CIA "too sweeping," it nevertheless accepted the report's basic findings: CIA was not coordinating intelligence activities in the Government; the correlation and evaluation functions were not well organized, and other members of the fledgling Intelligence Community were not fully included in the estimates process; and the DCI lacked sufficient day-to-day contact with the work of CIA. The Dulles-Jackson-Correa report called upon the DCI to exert "forthright leadership," and to actively use existing coordination bodies, such as the Intelligence Advisory Committee (IAC) comprising the leaders of the military and civilian intelligence agencies. For example, the report urged that the final coordination of intelligence estimates be done through IAC, to establish estimates as "the most authoritative statement[s] available to policymakers."

The Dulles-Jackson-Correa report also made the point that coordination and planning could only be effective with a strong DCI and CIA. It therefore recommended that the DCI reorganize his office to include on his immediate staff the heads of CIA's main components. The report also stated that the CIA would benefit from civilian leadership and recommended that if another military DCI was appointed, he should resign his military commission "to free him from all service ties and from rotations that would preclude the continuity needed for good intelligence work."[4]

Also during 1948, the Congress established "The Commission on Organization of the Executive Branch of the Government." Chaired by former President Herbert Hoover, the Commission established a sub-group to look at national security organizations, including CIA. This group, headed by New York businessman Ferdinand Eberstadt,[5] concluded that the basic organizational arrangements for national security were sound, but there were problems in carrying out the function. The CIA was specifically criticized for not being properly organized to assimilate all information concerning scientific developments abroad, to estimate the significance of these developments, and to give direction to collectors. Concern was also expressed that the CIA was not being given access to all available information within the Government. The fear that other countries might develop nuclear weapons led the Eberstadt group, with some urgency, to state:

> Failure properly to appraise the extent of scientific developments in enemy countries may have more immediate and catastrophic consequences than failure in any other field of intelligence.

In its November 1948 report, the Hoover Commission mission called for "vigorous efforts" to improve CIA's internal structure and the quality of its product, especially in scientific and medical intelligence. A senior-level "evaluation board or section" within CIA was proposed to work solely on intelligence evaluations. Finally, the Commission urged positive efforts to foster "relations of mutual confidence" between CIA and its consumers.[6]

Lieutenant General Walter Bedell Smith, who succeeded Hillenkoetter as DCI soon after the outbreak of the Korean War, took the initial steps to implement the recommendations of the Hoover and the Dulles-Jackson-Correa reports. Among his first steps was to recruit Allen Dulles, an OSS veteran, as Deputy Director for Plans, and to establish a Board of National Estimates chaired by William Langer of Harvard University.

In 1949, Congress enacted additional legislation for the CIA providing its Director with certain administrative authorities necessary for the conduct of clandestine intelligence activities that were not available to government agencies generally. In particular, the new law permitted the DCI to expend appropriated funds for procuring goods and services to carry out the Agency's functions without having to comply with the cumbersome procurement rules applicable to other government agencies. It also permitted the Agency to expend appropriated funds based solely on a voucher signed by the DCI.

1950S AND 1960S: THE DEVELOPMENT OF THE INTELLIGENCE COMMUNITY

The decades of the 1950s and 1960s saw an expansion and an intensification of the Cold War as well as an expansion in the size and responsibilities of U.S. intelligence agencies to cope with its challenges.

THE 1950S

Acting on the recommendations of a commission of senior officials headed by George Brownell, President Truman, by classified memorandum, established the National Security Agency (NSA) in October 1952 in recognition of the need for a single entity to be responsible for the signals intelligence mission of the United States. Placed within the Department of Defense, NSA assumed the responsibilities of the former Armed Forces Security Agency as well as the signals intelligence responsibilities of the CIA and other military elements. In 1958, the National Security Council issued directives that detailed NSA's mission and authority under the Secretary of Defense.

CIA meanwhile made important strides. Its analytical efforts during the Korean War established the Agency as a key player in the defense and foreign policy areas. On the operational side, the National Security Council reissued its 1948 directive on covert action to achieve peacetime foreign policy objectives in 1955, reemphasizing that implementation responsibility was with the CIA. In 1954, President Eisenhower approved the concept of a high-flying reconnaissance aircraft to fly above the Soviet air defense systems. Due largely to CIA's special procurement authorities and ability to carry out the mission in secret, the President established the effort as a joint CIA-Air Force program. The ability of the program to develop and field the U-2 (by 1955) earlier than planned and below the original cost estimate was a clear success for the participants. Before the end of the decade photos provided by the U-2 figured prominently in defense planning.

In 1954, Congress once again sought to examine the organization and efficiency of the Executive Branch and revived "The Commission on Organization of the Executive Branch of the Government." With former President Hoover again at the helm, the "Second Hoover Commission" formed a sub-group headed by General Mark Clark to study the agencies of the Intelligence Community.[7]

The Clark task force recommended that the CIA be reorganized internally to focus better on its primary missions, and that the DCI appoint a "Chief of Staff" or executive officer to run the day-to-day operations.[8] It also called for a permanent "watchdog" commission to oversee the CIA, comprising members of the House and Senate and distinguished private citizens appointed by the President.[9] A year later, in 1956, President Eisenhower established the Presidential Board of Consultants on Foreign Intelligence Activities (later renamed the President's Foreign Intelligence Advisory Board by President Kennedy). Shortly after it was formed, the Board issued a critical review of the DCI's management of the Intelligence Community. Later, in 1957, on the Board's recommendation, President Eisenhower established the United States Intelligence Board as the single forum for all intelligence chiefs to provide advice to the DCI on intelligence activities.

In 1957, spurred by the Soviet launch of Sputnik, the CIA and the Air Force began planning for the first photo reconnaissance satellite. Publicly referred to as "the Discoverer Weather System" and recently declassified as "CORONA," the system was successfully operational by 1962.

THE 1960S

The decade of the 1960s was marked by significant technological advances, further expansion of the Intelligence Community, and the first tentative efforts of a DCI to exert control over it. But, as far as the public was concerned, it started with the notable failure of the CIA at the Bay of Pigs. An invasion of Cuban expatriates, trained by the CIA, launched an invasion of Cuba in the spring of 1961 with the intent of ousting the Castro regime. Without U.S. military assistance, the invasion crumbled. The reputation of the Agency suffered significantly.

In August of the same year, Secretary of Defense McNamara created the Defense Intelligence Agency (DIA) to consolidate and to coordinate the production of intelligence analysis by each of the military services and to serve as the principal source of intelligence support to the Secretary and his staff, as well as to the Joint Chiefs of Staff and the unified commands. DIA opened a new production center in 1963, but the military departments continued to maintain their own analytical capabilities. In 1965, DIA was given responsibility for administering the newly-created Defense Attaché system, consisting of uniformed military personnel serving in embassies and collecting, by overt means, information useful to the military.

In the meantime, there were substantial advances in U.S. technical collection capabilities. Photographs taken by the U-2 were a large factor in the successful resolution of the Cuban missile crisis in 1962. The first photo reconnaissance satellite was launched the same year. The first high altitude, high speed reconnaissance aircraft, the SR-71, was built and tested by the CIA a short while later. While these technical collection efforts had been ongoing for several years in both CIA and the Air Force, they were formally consolidated, pursuant to a national security directive, in 1961 within the National Reconnaissance Office (NRO).

While the fact of its existence remained classified, the NRO was designated a separate operating agency of the Department of Defense, reporting to the Secretary of Defense albeit with the DCI retaining a role in selecting key personnel as well as substantial control over the budget, requirements, and priorities of the organization. Using the special procurement authorities of the DCI, the NRO was able expeditiously to procure and to operate satellite collection systems for the Intelligence Community.

In addition to the NSA, DIA, and NRO, each of the military services maintained substantial intelligence organizations, both at the departmental level and at the tactical level. These organizations typically collected information and provided analysis regarding the weapons systems, tactics, and capabilities of foreign counterpart forces. This information and analysis were used to support the weapons acquisition process in each service, to support force development and contingency planning, and were incorporated into training programs.

The growth of intelligence efforts within the Department of Defense served to accentuate the relative lack of the DCI's role over the rest of the Community. In July 1961, the President's Foreign Intelligence Advisory Board proposed to the President that the DCI be separated from the CIA and head-up an Office of Coordination in the White House. President Kennedy did not endorse the recommendation but in January 1962 issued a letter to his new DCI John McCone stating:

> As head of the Central Intelligence Agency, while you will continue to have overall responsibility for the Agency, I shall expect you to delegate to your principal deputy, as you may deem necessary, so much of the detailed operation of the Agency as may be required to permit you to carry out your primary task as Director of Central Intelligence.

In 1963, DCI McCone established a National Intelligence Programs Evaluation Staff to review and evaluate Community programs and cost-effectiveness. Later in the decade, DCI Helms set up a National Intelligence Resources Board to review all community programs and budgets, and to referee community disputes.[10]

But the burgeoning U.S. military involvement in the Vietnam War, the efforts to block Communist expansion in Laos and to deal with conflicts in the Middle East (notably the Arab-Israeli Six-Day War of 1967), effectively precluded serious efforts by the DCIs to assert greater control over the Intelligence Community.

THE 1970S: THE DECADE OF TURMOIL AND REFORM

The decade of the 1970s began with serious efforts to institute DCI control over the Intelligence Community, but they were eventually undermined by a series of sensational disclosures in the media, followed by unprecedented investigations of the Intelligence Community within the Executive Branch and by the Congress. During the latter half of the decade, new reforms were adopted and new oversight mechanisms put into place. While the intelligence functions of the Government continued, Congress began to take a much more active role in determining their cost and overseeing their execution.

In December 1970, President Nixon directed Deputy Director of the Office of Management and Budget James Schlesinger to recommend how the organizational structure of the Intelligence Community should be changed to bring about greater efficiency and effectiveness. The Schlesinger report, completed in March 1971, found, among other things, that intelligence functions were fragmented and disorganized; collection activities were unnecessarily competitive and redundant; intelligence suffered from unplanned and unguided growth; intelligence activities were too costly; and, because analytical products were provided on such a broad range of topics, they often suffered in quality. The report called for basic reform of the management structure with a strong DCI who could bring intelligence costs under control and improve analytic quality and responsiveness. Among other things, the study recommended that the DCI put together a consolidated budget for the Intelligence Community and oversee its execution.

Following-up on the recommendations in November 1971, President Nixon issued a directive calling for improvement in the intelligence product and for more efficient use of resources. The DCI was made responsible for "planning, reviewing, and evaluating all intelligence programs and activities and in the production of national intelligence." The Nixon directive reconstituted the United States Intelligence Board to assist the DCI, and set up the Intelligence Committee[11] of the NSC to coordinate and to review intelligence activities. It also established an Intelligence Resources Advisory Committee, comprising representatives from the State and Defense Departments and OMB, to advise the DCI on the consolidated intelligence budget. In March 1972, DCI Helms created a special "Intelligence Community Staff" to assist him in the daily execution of his Community responsibilities.

None of these changes had a substantial impact at the time, however, because the Government became largely preoccupied with the Watergate affair in 1973 and 1974. There was only tangential involvement by the CIA in Watergate primarily through the activities of former employees, and in the preparation of a psychological profile of Daniel Ellsberg.[12] The press, however, motivated to some extent by the distrust generated by Watergate, increasingly began to report critically on intelligence activities. Press articles covered allegations of collection efforts undertaken against U.S. citizens during the Vietnam era, attempts to assassinate foreign leaders or destabilize communist regimes, and efforts to raise the remains of a Soviet submarine off the floor of the Pacific.

In December 1974, in reaction to reports of CIA's support to the non-Communist resistance forces in Angola, Congress passed an amendment to the Foreign Assistance Act, known as the "Hughes-Ryan amendment," which for the first time required that the President report any covert CIA operations in a foreign country (other than for intelligence collection) to the relevant congressional committees (which, at that time, included the armed services committees, foreign relations committees, and appropriations committees in each house of Congress).

The various media revelations also led to official investigations in both the Executive branch and the Congress:

A. THE ROCKEFELLER COMMISSION

The Commission on CIA Activities Within the United States, chaired by Vice President Rockefeller, was created by President Ford on 4 January 1975, to determine whether CIA employees had engaged in illegal activities in the United States. The inquiry was later expanded to include the CIA's foreign intelligence charter and to make suggestions for operational guidelines. In June 1975, the Commission issued its report which, among other things, confirmed the existence of a CIA domestic mail opening operation; found that in the late 1960s and early 1970s the Agency had kept files on 300,000 U.S. citizens and organizations relating to domestic dissident activities; found that President Nixon tried to use CIA records for political ends; and concluded that the CIA had no involvement in President Kennedy's assassination. The Commission also found "that the great majority of the CIA's domestic activities comply with its statutory authority." In looking to the future, the Commission called for a joint congressional oversight committee and a stronger executive oversight mechanism; consideration by the Congress to disclose "to some extent" CIA's budget; and appointment of two confirmed deputy directors, one to manage the CIA and one to advise the DCI on military matters. The Commission further recommended that the DCI serve no more than 10 years.

B. THE CHURCH COMMITTEE

Twenty-three days after the Rockefeller Commission was empaneled, the Senate announced its own investigatory body, the Committee to Study Government Operations with Respect to Intelligence Activities (also known as the Church Committee after its Chairman). Handling one of the largest investigations ever undertaken by the Senate, the Church Committee was charged with looking at CIA domestic activities; covert activity abroad, including alleged assassinations of foreign leaders; alleged abuses by the Internal Revenue Service and the FBI; alleged domestic spying by the military; and the alleged interceptions of the conversations of U.S. citizens by the National Security Agency. The Committee's inquiry lasted for almost a year, resulting in a six-volume report, released in April 1976. The Committee recommended, among other things, that the President consider separating the DCI from the CIA; that the authorities of the DCI over elements of the Intelligence Community be enhanced; that statutory charters be established for CIA, DIA, and NSA; that the National Foreign Intelligence Budget be published; and that clandestine support to repressive regimes that disregarded human rights be prohibited by law. The Committee lauded several reforms (including a ban on assassination) already implemented by President Ford.

C. THE PIKE COMMITTEE

The House counterpart to the Church Committee was the Select Committee on Intelligence to Investigate Allegations of Illegal or Improper Activities of Federal Intelligence Agencies. Impanelled in February 1975, the committee was also known by the name of its Chairman, Congressman Otis Pike. The Pike Committee's report was voted down by the House in January 1976, and was never officially issued. Portions, however, were leaked to a New York newspaper, the *Village Voice*.

D. THE MURPHY COMMISSION

In June 1975, around the time that the Rockefeller Commission was completing its inquiry into intelligence improprieties, another congressional commission, the Commission on the Organization of the Government for the Conduct of Foreign Policy, was culminating a three-year study which included an examination of the organization and performance of the Intelligence Community. Headed by veteran diplomat Robert Murphy,[13] the Commission recommended that the DCI be given greater status

in the White House and the Intelligence Community; that the DCI delegate his responsibility for running the CIA to a deputy; that the DCI occupy an office geographically closer to the White House to better enable him to carry out his role as presidential adviser; and that the CIA change its name to the Foreign Intelligence Agency.[14] The Commission also recommended that covert action should be employed only where it is clearly essential to vital U.S. purposes and only after a careful process of high level review. It further urged that the NSC's Committee on Intelligence be actively used as the principal forum to resolve the differing perspectives of intelligence consumers and producers, and "should meet frequently for that purpose."

REFORM AND OVERSIGHT

Even as the Church and Pike Committees were continuing their investigations, the Executive branch undertook extensive efforts to bring about reform.[15]

In the summer of 1975, President Ford ordered the implementation of 20 of the 30 recommendations of the Rockefeller Commission, to include measures to provide improved internal supervision of CIA activities; additional restrictions on CIA's domestic activities; a ban on mail openings; and an end to wiretaps, abuse of tax information, and the testing of drugs on unsuspecting persons. Ford did not agree to public disclosure of the intelligence budget, however, nor did he readily agree to a separate congressional oversight committee.

President Ford issued the first Executive Order on intelligence on 18 February 1976 (E.O. 11905),[16] before either the Church or Pike investigating committees had reported. For the first time, a description of the Intelligence Community and the authorities and responsibilities of the DCI and the heads of other intelligence agencies, were specified in a public presidential document. The order also set up a Committee on Foreign Intelligence as part of the National Security Council, chaired by the DCI and reporting directly to the President, as the focal point for policy and resource allocation on intelligence.[17] A number of restrictions on intelligence agencies were also instituted, including a ban on assassinations as an instrument of U.S. policy. To monitor compliance with the Order, a new Intelligence Oversight Board was established within the Executive Office of the President.

Both congressional investigating committees recommended in their final reports that permanent follow-on committees be created to provide oversight of the intelligence function and to consider further legislative actions as might be necessary.

The Senate acted first in May 1976, creating the Select Committee on Intelligence. The House followed suit a little over a year later, creating the Permanent Select Committee on Intelligence. Both committees were made responsible for authorizing expenditures for intelligence activities (although the Senate was limited to "national" intelligence, whereas the House mandate included both "national" and "tactical" intelligence activities), and for conducting necessary oversight. The resolutions creating both committees recognized that they would be kept "fully and currently informed" of intelligence activities under their purview. Both committees were added to the list of those to receive notice of covert actions under the Hughes-Ryan amendment. The Senate committee also was given responsibility for handling the confirmation proceedings when the DCI and the Deputy DCI were nominated by the President.

While efforts were made in succeeding months to let emotions over intelligence activities subside and to establish more "normal" relationships between the Legislative and Executive branches, the hiatus was relatively short-lived. In 1977, the Senate Committee reexamined the question whether the aggregate intelligence budget should be released publicly. This issue would continue to be debated for the next two decades. The statement of newly-appointed DCI Turner that he had no problem with the release of this figure aroused protests from those who believed disclosure could assist hostile intelligence services in deciphering U.S. intelligence activity.

In August 1977, DCI Turner prompted a more substantial controversy by announcing his intention to reduce the CIA's Directorate of Operations by 800 people. The first reductions occurred on 31 October 1977 (called the "Halloween Massacre" within CIA) when 200 officers were fired. Critics of the DCI charged that he was destroying the CIA's human source collection capability in favor of technical collection programs run by the Department of Defense. (Some in Defense, on the other hand, perceived Turner as attempting to take over those programs.)

On 24 January 1978, President Carter issued a new Executive Order on intelligence which reaffirmed the DCI's Community-wide authority over priorities, tasking, and the budget; contained additional restrictions on collection techniques, participation in domestic activities, and human experimentation; and reiterated the ban on assassinations. Intelligence agencies were specifically required to promulgate procedures to govern the collection of information on U.S. citizens and persons admitted to the U.S. for permanent residence.

Notwithstanding the new presidential order, both congressional committees proceeded to consider bills in 1978 which would have dramatically overhauled the Intelligence Community. Following the suggestions of the Church Committee as well as incorporating various aspects of the Executive branch reforms, the Senate committee developed a comprehensive bill entitled the "National Intelligence Reorganization and Reform Act of 1978." The bill called for the creation of a "Director of National Intelligence" with broader powers than the DCI to serve as head of the Intelligence Community. The Director of National Intelligence would have retained leadership of CIA[18] with the authority to delegate this responsibility to a Deputy or Assistant Director at the President's discretion. The bill also contained a long list of restricted or banned activities, provided specific missions and functions for each element of the Intelligence Community, stipulated rigorous review and notification procedures for covert action and clandestine collection, and instituted numerous requirements for reporting to Congress.

While the Carter Administration initially supported the attempt to draft "charter" legislation, it ultimately withdrew its support in the face of growing concern that the intelligence function would be hamstrung by having too much detailed regulation in statute. After extended negotiations with the two intelligence committees, the Administration agreed to a measure limited to establishing the ground rules for congressional oversight. The Intelligence Oversight Act of 1980 provided that the heads of intelligence agencies would keep the oversight committees "fully and currently informed" of their activities including "any significant anticipated intelligence activity." Detailed ground rules were established for reporting covert actions to the Congress, in return for the number of congressional committees receiving notice of covert actions being limited to the two oversight committees.

Congress also passed, with the support of the Carter Administration, the Foreign Intelligence Surveillance Act of 1978, providing for a special court order procedure to authorize electronic surveillance for intelligence purposes, activities that had previously been conducted based upon a claim of constitutional authority of the President.

Finally, in response to continued criticism from the congressional committees over the usefulness of national intelligence estimates, a new mechanism for the development of estimates was established. DCI Colby, in 1973, had established the National Intelligence Officer system in lieu of the Board of Estimates. He had appointed the first six NIOs in an effort to make intelligence more responsive to policymaking. By the end of the decade, DCI Turner formed the NIOs into the National Intelligence Council. Reporting to the DCI, the Council comprised a Chairman and eight National Intelligence Officers, who were considered the senior analysts of the Intelligence Community within their respective areas of expertise. As such, they would supervise the preparation of estimates, ensure quality control, and present the results of their work to policymakers as required.

1980S: A DECADE OF GROWTH AND SCANDAL

The beginning of the decade saw the election of a President, Ronald Reagan, who had made the revitalization of intelligence part of his campaign. Intelligence budgets were increased, and new personnel were hired. The vast majority of rules and guidelines adopted during the Ford and Carter Administrations remained in place. However, by the middle of the decade, the U.S. experienced a series of spy scandals, and the first serious breach of the oversight arrangements with the Congress. While the organization of the Intelligence Community remained stable during the decade, it was a period of burgeoning growth and activity.

During the 1980 presidential election, intelligence became a targeted campaign issue. The Republican Party platform contained a plank asserting that the Democrats had impaired the efficiency of the Intelligence Community and had underestimated the Soviet's military strength. President Reagan came into office promising to improve intelligence capabilities by upgrading technical systems and strengthening counterintelligence.

To make good on these promises, Reagan appointed William Casey, a veteran of the OSS, as DCI, and announced that the DCI, for the first time, would hold cabinet rank. With this presidential mandate, Casey sought and received higher budgets for intelligence and instituted an unprecedented period of personnel growth across the Intelligence Community.

On 4 December 1981, almost a year into his Administration, President Reagan issued his Executive Order on intelligence (E.O. 12333). It generally reaffirmed the functions of intelligence agencies (as outlined in the previous order) and continued most of the previous restrictions, but it set a more positive tone than its predecessor, and gave the CIA greater latitude to gather foreign intelligence within the United States and to provide assistance to law enforcement. The Executive Order also provided a new NSC structure for reviewing intelligence activities, including covert actions.[19]

Meanwhile, the congressional intelligence committees demonstrated a willingness to provide legislative authority sought by the Intelligence Community. In 1980, the Classified Information Procedures Act was passed to protect classified information used in criminal trials. In 1982, following the public revelation of the names of certain CIA officers that appeared to result in the murder of one officer, the Congress passed a new law making it a crime to reveal the names of covert intelligence personnel. In October 1984, Congress exempted certain operational files of the CIA from disclosure under the Freedom of Information Act. However, legislative proposals offered in 1984 calling for a fixed term for the DCI and Deputy DCI and requiring that they be career intelligence officers, were not passed.

The 1986 Goldwater-Nichols Act, which reorganized the Department of Defense and shifted authority from the military departments to the Joint Chiefs and theater commands, also had an impact on intelligence. The Defense Intelligence Agency and Defense Mapping Agency were specifically designated as combat support agencies, and the Secretary of Defense, in consultation with the DCI, was directed to establish policies and procedures to assist the National Security Agency in fulfilling its combat support functions. The Act also required that the President submit annually to Congress a report on U.S. national security strategy, including an assessment of the adequacy of the intelligence capability to carry out the strategy.

1985: THE YEAR OF THE SPY

Beginning in 1985, the Intelligence Community experienced an unprecedented rash of spy cases that led to numerous recommendations for change.

The defection of former CIA officer Edward Lee Howard in the spring of 1985 was followed by the arrests of John A. Walker, Jr. and Jerry A. Whitworth, Navy personnel with access to highly sensitive information; CIA employees, Sharon Scranage and Larry Wu-Tai Chin; former NSA employee, Ronald W. Pelton; FBI agent, Richard Miller; and an employee of Naval intelligence, Jonathan J. Pollard.

The Walker-Whitworth, Pelton, and Howard cases dealt especially serious blows to U.S. intelligence. As the year drew to a close, a Marine guard at the U.S. Embassy in Moscow confessed to having passed information to the Soviets and was charged with allowing Soviet personnel to enter the chancery building. It was further disclosed that the U.S. had determined its new chancery in Moscow had been thoroughly bugged during its construction. Coming in close succession, these disclosures shocked the public and the Congress.

Various efforts were taken within the Executive branch to identify and correct shortcomings in counterintelligence and security. The Secretary of Defense commissioned a special inquiry into Defense policy and practice. The Secretary of State commissioned a review of embassy security, including the vulnerability of U.S. diplomatic establishments to electronic penetration. The CIA undertook an internal review of counterintelligence and its procedures for handling defectors.

The congressional intelligence committees also investigated these problems and prepared lengthy reports recommending change. In 1988, the Senate committee asked a group of distinguished private citizens, led by New York businessman Eli Jacobs, to review the progress that had been made in counterintelligence and to provide recommendations for further improvements. Their report was provided in 1989, but did not result in any legislation being enacted at the time. This was due in part to the fall of the Berlin Wall, and dramatic changes taking place in the Soviet Union, which lessened the intensity of focusing on problems with spies.

THE IRAN-CONTRA AFFAIR AND ITS AFTERMATH

In November 1986, Congress learned that representatives of the Reagan Administration, contrary to the announced policies of the Government, had sold arms to the Government of Iran in return for its assistance in securing the release of U.S. hostages held in Lebanon. Initiated by members of the NSC staff, the operation was accomplished with the assistance of some officers of the CIA and the Defense Department pursuant to a retroactive covert action "finding" signed by President Reagan in January 1986, which had never been reported to the Congress. It was also disclosed that the NSC staff members involved in the sales had overcharged the Iranians for the weapons and had used the proceeds to support the anti-Communist rebels, the "Contras," in Nicaragua at a time when such assistance was prohibited by law. The veracity of public statements made by the President and other senior officials with knowledge of the episode appeared in doubt. CIA and other intelligence agencies were quickly drawn into the controversy, which collectively became known as the Iran-Contra affair.

A special prosecutor was appointed to look into possible criminal activity, and investigations ensued in both the Executive branch and the Congress. In December 1986, the President commissioned a Special Review Board, chaired by former Senator John Tower. Three months later, the Tower Board found that the Iran and Contra operations were conducted outside of regularly established channels and that intelligence oversight requirements had been ignored. The Board also faulted President Reagan's management style. While not recommending organizational changes *per se*, the Board urged that a better set of guidelines be developed for approving and reporting covert action. The Board also recommended that Congress consider merging the two intelligence committees into a single joint committee.

In early 1987, the House and Senate formed separate investigating committees, but later agreed to form a Joint Committee for purposes of interviewing witnesses and holding hearings. After months of intense public hearings, a majority of the Committee issued a lengthy account of its work in the fall of 1987. It recommended, among other things, that a statutory Inspector General be created at the CIA and that the legal requirements for reporting covert actions to the congressional oversight committees be tightened.

Lawrence Walsh, the special prosecutor appointed in January 1987, carried on his investigation of the Iran-Contra affair for almost seven years, and brought criminal prosecutions against the key NSC figures involved, some CIA employees, and a former Secretary of Defense. President Bush later issued pardons to six of those charged.

Legislation creating a statutory Inspector General for the CIA was enacted in 1989. Although the Inspector General reported to the DCI, he could be removed only by the President. Among other things, the law required that the Inspector General submit semi-annual reports to the congressional intelligence committees, summarizing problems that had been identified and corrective actions taken.

Legislative efforts to tighten the covert action reporting requirements did not succeed for several more years. In 1988, with the election of President George Bush, a former DCI, Congress received assurances that the experience of Iran-Contra would not be repeated and that appropriate consultations would occur on future covert actions. These assurances did not put the matter to rest as far as the committees were concerned, but did serve to dampen congressional fervor to legislate precise time requirements for reporting.

1990–1995: THE END OF THE COLD WAR AND RETRENCHMENT

The three years following the election of President Bush saw profound changes in the world that had enormous impacts on the Intelligence Community. In the fall of 1989, the Berlin Wall came down and Germany began the process of reunification. The Communist regimes of Eastern Europe gave way to democratic rule. In August 1990, Iraq invaded Kuwait. Shortly thereafter, the Soviet Union began to break apart with many former Soviet Republics declaring independence. In early 1991, the U.S. together with NATO allies (and the agreement of the Soviet Union) invaded Kuwait to oust the occupying Iraqi forces with a fearsome display of modern weaponry. Later in the year, Communist rule ended in Russia.

Some began to question whether an intelligence capability was needed any longer; others urged significant retrenchment. Leaders within the Intelligence Community began streamlining their agencies and reorienting toward new missions, with a greater focus on transnational threats. Congress pushed them along by proposing a new Intelligence Community structure, and mandating across-the-board reductions in personnel.

The period ended with a shocking new spy case at the CIA and renewed calls for reform.

THE GULF WAR

The Gulf War of 1991, brief though it was, had profound repercussions for U.S. intelligence. Never had so much information been conveyed so quickly from intelligence systems to warfighters with such devastating effect. The accuracy of U.S. precision guided weapons astounded the world. The war also highlighted the need for the United States to expand its own efforts to link intelligence systems with combat systems and to train military personnel to use these systems effectively. The U.S. recognized that the future of warfare was apt to be battles fought at a distance between opposing forces, placing a premium on the availability of intelligence on the nature and disposition of hostile forces.

Yet the Gulf War also demonstrated problems with intelligence. Initially, the Intelligence Community was not well prepared to support military operations in this locale, but given time in the fall and winter of 1990 to put together a capability, the job was done. The Joint Intelligence Center was established during the war with representation from the key intelligence agencies and provided a model of providing crisis support to military operations. Indeed, a permanent National Military Joint Intelligence Center was established shortly after the conflict at the Pentagon and later at all unified commands. Still, the war illuminated problems in disseminating imagery to the field as well as the limitations of U.S. human intelligence capabilities. In addition, a substantial problem arose with competing CIA and military assessments of the damage caused by allied bombing.

THE GATES TASK FORCES

In 1991, after a wrenching confirmation process which provided the first public examination of the analytical process at the CIA, DCI Robert Gates undertook a comprehensive reexamination of the post-Cold War Intelligence Community. The recommendations of 14 separate task forces produced significant change: analysis would be made more responsive to decisionmakers; a formalized requirements process would be established for human source intelligence collection; new offices were created at the CIA to coordinate the use of publicly available ("open source") information and to improve CIA support to the military. The staff of the DCI, which supported him in his Community role, was strengthened. And, after much negotiating about which entities to include, a new Central Imagery Office, under the joint control of the DCI and the Secretary of Defense, was established to coordinate imagery collection and to establish uniform standards for the interpretation and dissemination of imagery to the field.

BOREN-MCCURDY LEGISLATION

While the Gates task forces were at work, legislation was introduced by the respective Chairmen of the Senate and House intelligence committees to restructure the Intelligence Community. The bills called for the creation of a Director of National Intelligence with authority over the intelligence budget as well as authority to transfer personnel temporarily from one intelligence agency to another. The DNI would continue to establish requirements and priorities for intelligence collection and serve as the President's intelligence adviser. In this regard, the analytical element of the CIA would be transferred under the control of the DNI, leaving the remainder of the CIA to be administered by a separate agency director. The legislation also proposed a National Imagery Agency to coordinate imagery tasking, collection, processing, and dissemination.

Given the actions taken by DCI Gates to implement the results of his task forces, however, the committees did not push for enactment of their alternative proposals. Instead they opted to codify and to clarify the existing statutory framework that had been largely unchanged since 1947. The Intelligence Organization Act of 1992 (enacted as part of the Intelligence Authorization Act for 1993) for the first time defined the Intelligence Community by law, enunciated the three roles of the DCI, set forth the authorities and responsibilities of the DCI in relation to other elements of the Intelligence Community, and articulated the responsibilities of the Secretary of Defense for the execution of national intelligence programs. Among other things, the Secretary was required to consult with the DCI prior to appointing the Directors of the NSA, the NRO,[20] and the DIA.

Congress continued to debate whether the intelligence budget should be declassified. In 1991 and 1992, Congress passed non-binding "Sense of Congress" resolutions urging the President to make public the aggregate funding for intelligence. President Bush declined to do so, as did President Clinton in 1993.

THE VICE PRESIDENT'S
NATIONAL PERFORMANCE REVIEW

In 1993, as part of the Clinton Administration's overall effort to "reinvent" government, a team from the Vice President's National Performance Review looked at the Intelligence Community and suggested that several actions be taken to consolidate activities and build a sense of Community in order to be more efficient and to better serve customers. The review found that the Community was too often drawn apart by the competition for new programs and budget allocations and recommended rotational assignments among agencies as a means of promoting a broader, more collegial perspective.

The review's recommendation that the Intelligence Oversight Board be merged into the President's Foreign Intelligence Advisory Board was accomplished by Executive Order in September 1993.

THE AMES SPY CASE

In February 1994, Aldrich H. Ames, a CIA employee with almost 30 years' experience in operations, was charged with spying for the Soviet Union since at least 1985. During this period, he was alleged to have disclosed virtually all of the CIAs active Soviet agents, many of whom were later executed or imprisoned. In May, Ames and his wife pled guilty and were sent to prison.

The ensuing investigations by the CIA Inspector General and by the congressional intelligence committees reported that Ames had exhibited serious personal problems and a penchant for exorbitant spending which should have brought him under security scrutiny. The investigations also highlighted problems in coordinating counterintelligence cases between the FBI and the CIA. Notwithstanding the seriousness of Ames' disclosures and the numerous shortcomings on the part of CIA officers, DCI Woolsey meted out what were perceived as relatively mild disciplinary measures. The confidence of the public and the Congress in the CIA appeared considerably eroded.

In the fall of 1994, new legislation was enacted to improve counterintelligence and security practices across the Intelligence Community, and, in particular, to improve the coordination between the FBI and CIA. In addition, the President created a new bureaucratic framework for handling counterintelligence matters, to include the placement of FBI counterintelligence specialists within the CIA.

THE CREATION OF A NEW COMMISSION

Even before the Ames case provided the immediate impetus, the congressional intelligence committees anticipated that the Executive branch would conduct a comprehensive review of the Intelligence Community. When this failed to materialize, the Senate committee, and, in particular, its Vice Chairman, Senator John Warner, developed legislation to establish a commission to study the roles and capabilities of intelligence agencies in the post-Cold War era, and to make recommendations for change. The legislation was approved in October 1994, as part of the Intelligence Authorization Act for 1995.

QUESTIONS FOR FURTHER DISCUSSION

1. Which do you think was a more important factor leading to the establishment of the CIA in 1947: the Pearl Harbor attack, President Truman's management style, or the rising threat of the Soviet Union? Why?
2. When did the CIA become a "key player" in the U.S. government, according to the author?
3. What were the most important developments in the evolution of U.S. intelligence since World War II?
4. What were the CIA's most important successes and failures prior to the creation of the Aspin-Brown Commission in 1994?

ENDNOTES

1. Former Secretary of State Dean Rusk recalled the 1941 state of the U.S's intelligence effort in testimony before a Senate subcommittee: "When I was assigned to G-2 in 1941, well over a year after the war had started in Europe, I was asked to take charge of a new section that had been organized to cover everything from Afghanistan right through southern Asia, southeast Asia, Australia, and the Pacific. Because we had no intelligence organization that had been giving attention to that area up to that time, the materials available to me when I reported for duty consisted of a tourist handbook on India and Ceylon, a 1924 military attache's report from London on the Indian Army, and a drawer full of clippings from the *New York Times* that had gathered since World War One. That was literally the resources of the G-2 on that vast part of the world a year after the war in Europe started."
2. In 1957, this group was renamed the Bureau of Intelligence and Research.
3. The same Sidney Souers who had been appointed the first DCI by President Truman in January 1946. Souers served as Executive Secretary of the NSC from 1947 to 1950.
4. Although NSC 50 was issued to implement the report's recommendations, DCI Hillenkoetter did not take follow-up action on its numerous recommendations.
5. The same person who proposed the creation of the National Security Council and the CIA in a 1945 report to Navy Secretary Forrestal.
6. The depth and importance of this problem was revealed when President Truman announced that the Soviets had detonated a nuclear device in September 1949. The CIA's only coordinated estimate on the urgent question of when the Soviets would have a nuclear weapon gave three incorrect predictions: 1958, 1955, and 1950–1953,

and none of the predictions was accepted by all departments.

7. In its 1955 report, the Second Hoover Commission recognized for the first time the existence of an "intelligence community" within the Government, naming the NSC, CIA, NSA, FBI, Department of State, Army, Navy, Air Force, and the Atomic Energy Commission as its members.
8. Allen Dulles, who had been elevated to DCI in 1953, did not appoint a Chief of Staff, due to his active interest in the operation of the CIA. Instead, he appointed General Lucien Truscott as his deputy to resolve jurisdictional disputes between CIA and the military services, in an attempt to increase his community coordination capabilities.
9. In 1956, the House and Senate Armed Services Committees, and the Senate Appropriations Committee established intelligence subcommittees, and the House Appropriations Committee formed a "special group" under its chairman.
10. The United States Intelligence Board, previously established in the 1950s to serve as the DCI's primary advisory body, was used unevenly by DCIs depending on their interests in Community management.
11. The Intelligence Committee, chaired by the National Security Advisor, consisted of the Attorney General, the Under Secretary of State, the Deputy Secretary of Defense, the Chairman of the Joint Chiefs of Staff, and the DCI.
12. CIA officials refused the White House request that the CIA be used to cover-up the Watergate affair.
13. In 1976, Murphy was appointed by President Ford as the first chairman of the newly-formed Intelligence Oversight Board, and as a member of PFIAB.
14. The principal author of these conclusions was reportedly William Casey, later to become DCI.
15. It should also be noted that DCI Colby appointed a study group within CIA, headed by James Taylor, which issued an internal report in October 1975: "American Intelligence: A Framework for the Future." The Taylor study asserted that intelligence needed to become more efficient and effective, and more compatible with our democracy. The study suggested refining the current intelligence system and focused on the role of the DCI, including the relationship with the Secretary of Defense and the Intelligence Community, arguing that the DCI needed more influence over both substantive judgments and resource management. The report noted that the DCI's responsibilities, but not his authorities, had grown considerably since 1947. The study recommended separating the DCI from CIA (which would be

run by its own director), and appropriating funds to the DCI who would allocate them to program managers.

16. This order and succeeding orders issued by President Carter (E.O. 12036,1978) and President Reagan (E.O. 12333,1981) listed the following members of the Intelligence Community: CIA, NSA, DIA, DOD reconnaissance offices, INR/State, intelligence elements of Army, Navy, Air Force, Marines, FBI, Treasury, and DOE (then known as the Energy Research & Development Administration). Staff elements of the DCI were added in the Carter and Reagan orders.

17. The other members of the CFI were the Deputy Secretary of Defense for Intelligence and the Deputy Assistant to the President for National Security Affairs. The CFI reported directly to the NSC.

18. Those who thought the DNI must retain a direct management role over the CIA argued that separating the DNI from the CIA would deprive the Director of a strong institutional base and would subject him to more pressure from the policymakers.

19. Neither President Bush nor President Clinton issued executive orders on intelligence that supersede E.O. 12333. It remains in effect.

20. In 1992, as the legislation was under consideration, the President declassified the fact of the NRO's existence.

From Phyllis Provost McNeil, Aspin-Brown Commission, "The Evolution of the U.S. Intelligence Community—An Historical Perspective," *Preparing for the 21st Century: An Appraisal of U.S. Intelligence, Report of the Commission on the Roles and Capabilities of the United States Intelligence Community* (March 1, 1996), Appendix A: A1–A25.

2. THE PRESIDENT'S DAILY BRIEF: MANAGING THE RELATIONSHIP BETWEEN INTELLIGENCE AND THE POLICYMAKER

ADRIAN WOLFBERG

Because it serves the needs of the "chief consumer," developing and delivering the *President's Daily Brief (PDB)* takes on enormous importance for the U.S. intelligence community. In this account of how *PDB* briefers go about their business, the author explores how the *PDB* serves as a means for the White House to communicate its interests to analysts, but also how the brief itself shapes policy agendas in Washington.

When we think about the information the president and other national security policymakers need in today's complex and ambiguous world, two considerations come to mind: first, ensuring that they have access to the information they need when they need it, and second, ensuring that they receive advice on what decision to make based on that information. The intelligence community provides the former, and policy advisers provide the latter.[1] As the adage goes, never shall the twain meet, as facts are the purview of the intelligence community, while beliefs are the purview of politicians.[2] However, these two communities—intelligence and policy—regularly come into intimate contact with each other through the *President's Daily Brief* (PDB), a highly classified and agenda-informing document consisting of a set of short articles contained in a "briefing book" authored by intelligence analysts working in the intelligence community and under the auspices and direction of the Office of the Director of National Intelligence (ODNI).

The intelligence community has the daily task of providing the *PDB* to the president and about two dozen senior policymakers in Washington, DC, to enhance their situational awareness of threats to national security. Policymakers then consider this threat information when making decisions in meetings of various groups, such as the National Security Council (whose members are the president, vice president, and selected cabinet officers), Principals Committee (cabinet officer–level members), and Deputies Committee (members are the deputies to a cabinet officer), as part of the interagency national security process.

The briefing book consists not only of the set of short articles written for the president and approved by the ODNI but also additional articles placed "behind the tab," which satisfy the unique information needs of each policymaker who receives the *PDB*. In almost all cases, an employee of the intelligence community—an intelligence officer working in a full-time capacity as the "*PDB* briefer"—delivers the *PDB* to the policymaker. The *PDB* briefer does not author the articles but does select the behind-the-tab articles.

It is the *PDB* briefer who, on a daily basis, crosses into the world of policy, not to reinforce or dispute policy but to support the policymaking process.[3] Because the *PDB* briefers spend face-to-face time with policymakers, a unique type of highly personal and trusting relationship between the intelligence community and policymakers develops, a relationship that not only takes place during but also extends beyond the duration of their face-to-face encounter. Through this relationship, the *PDB* briefer adds meta-information—information about information not included in the *PDB* contents, that is, policy-relevant organizational and background information deemed necessary by the *PDB* briefer to help the policymaker. This interpersonal, trust-laden service to policymakers, called *sensegiving*, lies obscured and is not obvious from casual observation because it is neither purely intelligence nor purely policy.[4] Sensegiving is defined here as a process that is used by the *PDB* briefer to contextualize and adapt complex and technical information, thus assisting the policymaker in making the most use of intelligence, but does not include advice on what actions to take.

While sensegiving has previously been studied in superior-to-subordinate contexts—that is, when executives and managers use it to help their employees—in this very different context, sensegiving occurs in a reverse direction, from subordinate to superior, during routine yet intimate one-on-one, high-stakes information exchanges. The *PDB* briefer is not part of the policymaker's formal organization and therefore is not located within the policymaker's reporting chain of command; rather, the *PDB* briefer is someone of lower rank who is related to someone of much higher authority, trusted to help the superior make sense of the *PDB* information within the unique, personalized decision-making needs of the policymaker's political landscape. Understanding the *PDB* briefer's role in providing sensegiving service to the policymaker is therefore an appropriate focus for research, for three reasons.

First, the *PDB* has for decades been one of the most sought-after items produced for policymakers within the national security community.[5] Second, in 2015, the Central Intelligence Agency (CIA) declassified and publicly released about 2,500 *PDBs* from the John F. Kennedy and Lyndon B. Johnson administrations, affording political scientists and historians the unique opportunity to read firsthand the barrage of complex information faced by the most senior national security policymakers day after day.[6] Third, empirical research on sensegiving has been limited to the superior-to-subordinate direction, mostly in organizational change contexts.[7] Only a few of these studies were conducted in government contexts, focusing on leadership behavior.[8] Because few, if any, studies have focused on the reverse, that is, subordinate-to-superior sense-giving—such as briefer to policymaker—and given the *PDB* briefers' politically sensitive placement, operating across the worlds of intelligence and politics, such a study would be quite valuable and would offer a key contribution to the study of a unique phenomenon within national security policymaking.

Therefore, the critical sensegiving service provided by the *PDB* briefers and their contributions deserve systematic exploration. Specifically, how and why the *PDB* briefer conducts this sensegiving service is the research question for this study. The article begins with a history of the *PDB*. Then it sheds light on the context of the *PDB* briefer's interaction with the policymaker, introduces the need for sensegiving to the policymaker, explains the research method used to reveal how and why sensegiving occurs and its results, reflects on sensegiving within the evolution of the *PDB*, and concludes with practitioner and theoretical implications for sensegiving within the national security arena.

HISTORY OF THE PDB

The intelligence community has evolved its *PDB* support to the national security policy community. Originally, the CIA produced the *PDB* and its predecessor publications, but with the passage of the Intelligence Reform and Terrorism Prevention Act of 2004, responsibility for *PDB* production shifted from the CIA to the ODNI.[9] However, even though the ODNI became responsible for the *PDB*, the *PDB* briefers and the *PDB* management team continue to work from their offices at CIA headquarters in Langley, Virginia.

Support began decades ago with an assumption that it was necessary to minimize policy influence for the sake of protecting analytical objectivity.[10] The intelligence community has been walking a fine line ever since between, on the one hand, not getting too close to the policymaker so that the intelligence does not lose objectivity and, on the other hand, not getting close enough to the policymaker, resulting in intelligence becoming irrelevant to the needs of policymakers and therefore losing value.[11] Over time, the intelligence community has attempted to move from a relationship framed by separation toward one of closeness, a shift that intelligence professionals, more broadly, have advocated.[12] In general, the intelligence community believes it should establish and maintain the trust of the policymaker by using its ability to contextualize information so the policymaker can understand the implications of intelligence data within the threat environment, but it should not recommend policy.[13]

The *PDB* originated in 1946 during the Harry S. Truman administration. President Truman wanted to be personally notified of the most important intelligence on a daily basis following his brief tenure as vice president and his dissatisfaction with the lack of situational awareness.[14] In response, in January 1946, the CIA predecessor organization, the Central Intelligence Group, published the *Daily Summary* for him, and so began the product that would evolve into the *PDB*.

In February 1951, the *Current Intelligence Bulletin* replaced the *Daily Summary*.[15] It was not until the Kennedy administration that the next turn occurred. In June 1961, the CIA created an additional daily publication in response to what President Kennedy wanted, the *President's Intelligence Checklist*, whose first issue contained seven pages of text and maps.[16] In December 1964, President Johnson wanted something different, so the CIA replaced the *Checklist* with the *PDB*.[17] The *PDB* contained, on average, about 20 pages of information for President Gerald Ford, 15 pages for President Jimmy Carter, and 10 to 12 pages for President Bill Clinton.[18]

Inside the *PDB* are articles that the intelligence community believes meets the threshold of the president's interest, especially topics that will likely be addressed in major media outlets.[19] *PDB* articles can also presage topics in an upcoming National Intelligence Estimate, a lengthy assessment of a foreign threat that reflects the judgment of the intelligence community. As an example of *PDB* content, in the 18 January 1969 issue, 10 short articles were included: one on South Vietnam, three on the Soviet Union, and one each on Peru, Venezuela, Jordan, Kuwait, Berlin, and Canada.[20] The lead item was a short article on the status of discussions between South Vietnamese vice president Nguyen Cao Ky and American ambassador Henry Cabot Lodge Jr. One of the articles on the Soviet Union discussed the test firing of a new short-range missile from a Soviet nuclear attack submarine; it also included a terrestrial-based photo of the submarine entering the White Sea three days prior to missile launch, a map of the test firing location, and an overhead image of the submarine at its berthed location in Litsa Bay. Another Soviet article reported on the return to Earth of the *Soyuz 5* manned spacecraft, which had completed the first-ever docking of two manned spacecraft (the other being *Soyuz 4*) and the transfer of the Soviet crew between the two. The articles on Jordan and Kuwait generally addressed the degree to which these two governments supported terrorist organizations and their activities.

All versions of the *PDB* began with a small distribution but expanded beyond the initial intended audience. The *Bulletin* was given to seven individuals—the president, the secretary of state, the secretary of defense, the chairman of the Joint Chiefs of Staff, and the three service chiefs—but grew to 13 by 1967.[21] The *Checklist* started out with one individual—the president—and expanded to 17 by 1964: the president, the secretary of defense plus two others from the office of the secretary of defense, the secretary of state plus four subordinates, the chairman of the Joint Chiefs of Staff and two staff members, the secretary of the treasury, and the attorney general.[22] The *PDB* started with seven at the start of President George W. Bush's administration and grew to 20 by 2008.[23]

Presidents Truman, Eisenhower, Kennedy, and Johnson did not read the *Bulletin*; instead, their White House staff or advisers read it and then summarized it for the president.[24] Presidents Kennedy (for the *Checklist*), Johnson, Nixon, Ford, Carter, and Reagan did read the *PDB*, typically in front of a White House policy adviser.[25] President George H.W. Bush was the first sitting president to read the *PDB* in the presence of a career intelligence officer, the *PDB* briefer, who was seated near the president, a practice that continued through President George W. Bush's administration.[26] President George W. Bush was the first president to conduct "deep dives," taking topics from the *PDB* and scheduling in-depth follow-up discussions directly with the intelligence experts, typically in the presence of other key policymakers.[27] President Barack Obama made some changes during his first administration: reading the *PDB* by himself first, then having an ODNI senior executive as the briefer join him later; beginning in 2012, he received the *PDB* digitally on a mobile device instead of print media.[28]

The *PDB* briefer's daily schedule begins by waking up by about 1:00 a.m.; arriving to work each day on the seventh floor of CIA headquarters in Langley, typically between 2:00 and 3:00 a.m.; reading and preparing for the briefing later that morning; meeting the intelligence analysts who author the *PDB* articles (called "pre-briefers") at about 5:00 a.m.; typically heading out by 6:30 a.m. or earlier to meet policymakers in their offices; returning by 9:30 a.m. for an all-*PDB* briefer feedback session with the *PDB* management at Langley; then completing administrative work, communicating with analysts and managers, cleaning up and preparing for the next day, and departing CIA headquarters typically by 1:00 or 2:00 p.m.; and arriving at home by 3:00 p.m.[29]

THE *PDB* BRIEFER-POLICYMAKER CONTEXT

The purpose of the intelligence information in the *PDB* is to help policymakers create better policy within the national security arena.[30] As such, the *PDB* often sets the agenda for the president's daily discussions with his or her closest advisers.[31] The presence of the *PDB* briefer is important to both the intelligence and policymaker communities because it implies that the intelligence is essential and that policymakers' feedback will be captured and incorporated.[32] For the *PDB*, whose primary customer is the president, it is essential that the contents meet the presidential threshold of attention. However, it is hard for *PDB* briefers to get accurate feedback from policymakers.[33] There are two primary reasons for this: first, policymakers read the *PDB*, which is a solitary activity, and second, the harder of the two, the social conditions separating briefer and policymaker are extreme.

First, sitting in front of someone who is reading and trying to figure out whether the *PDB* meets his or her needs is a psychological challenge. Readers try to understand complex information with as few words as possible, and busy executives have little time to spend reading—both incentives to keep the narrative short.[34] And then there are the technical aspects of how the information is constructed, the nuances of the data and assembly process, and the inferences created by the author.[35] Finally, the nature of reading itself, because it is a solitary act and not a social interaction with another person, means the reader is left to his or her own interpretation, without the observer, such as a *PDB* briefer, knowing how or why the reader's views are forming or changing.[36]

The *PDB* briefer has a very different worldview than the policymaker. The intelligence officer sees his or her purpose as being a source of valuable information for policy formation, whereas the policymaker wants to find information to support his or her policy or to refute someone else's policy.[37] Differences in worldview create key tensions for the policymaker: intelligence often leaves the situation muddy, whereas clarity is needed to bolster the policymaker's confidence; intelligence may come across as so clear that it restricts policymaker's options; intelligence may contradict the policymaker's policies; the policymaker may be so busy integrating other, less technical, more compatible sources and types of information that focusing on intelligence information is not a priority; intelligence may come after a policymaker has made up his or her mind and therefore is too late to influence policy; intelligence may contain different assumptions about the world than those of the policymaker; or uncertainties stated in intelligence may force contingency thought planning about second- or third-order effects, which is

well beyond the need for simplicity within the policymaker's arena.[38] However, even though these tensions exist, in the moment of their face-to-face encounter and as a result of their repeated and daily one-on-one interactions, *PDB* briefers and policymakers exchange information of value.[39]

Second, the *PDB* briefer's temporary yet recurring journey into the policymaker's world is affected by at least two intense social forces: the tremendous power distance between briefer and policymaker and the intensity of dealing with senior policymaker personalities. The power distance between two people is the difference in authority; when the difference in authority is great, so, too, is the power distance.[40] When the distance is great, access to those with power is both highly improbable and, if acquired, highly unpredictable because of a lack of common ground.[41] Studies of the personalities of presidents of the United States, which likely are applicable to other senior policymakers, show that individuals can vary dramatically in how they process information—using internal versus external informational cues or being comfortable versus less comfortable with ambiguous information—and how they interact personally with others—being introverted versus extroverted, dominating versus accommodating, or having a positive or negative outlook about the job.[42]

When combined, these psychological factors—the solitary nature of reading and differences in worldview—along with the social factors—power distance and intensity of personality—make it imperative for the policymaker to trust the *PDB* briefer. It is only by gaining and maintaining the policymaker's trust that the *PDB* briefer is able to provide a sensegiving service, adding information that the policymaker needs in order to use the *PDB*.

SENSEGIVING

Policymakers place a high value on having access to information that helps them make sense of what they read, see, and hear because they are constantly negotiating the game of influence in their policymaking terrain with their peers, superiors, and subordinates.[43] Prior to national security meetings, most policymakers need the information contained within the *PDB* adapted for the language and meaning processes they know. The *PDB* briefer has unique access, giving him or her the opportunity to simultaneously under-stand the intelligence information contained within the *PDB* and the policymaker's personal cognitive and processing needs. One important result is that *PDB* briefers are able to increase policymakers' situational awareness of how other policymakers involved with the interagency national security process think about the *PDB* content, a key political competency for predicting and compensating for how policymakers will react.[44] The policymaker does not usually do the adapting of the *PDB* information because this ability to contextualize intelligence-based threat information is not a typical competency for most policymakers.[45] This is where *PDB* briefers' rare access comes into play: their low-key, personalized, and trusted sensegiving service to policymakers aids the policymakers in making sense of the threat information within their cognitive terms and political landscape.[46] The research method used to study this sensegiving service is discussed next.

RESEARCH METHOD

The research is based on interviews with 14 intelligence officers conducted during 2011; the intelligence officers had been *PDB* briefers between 2007 and 2010.[47] The policymakers they briefed were in office during the last two years of the second George W. Bush administration and the first two years of the first Obama administration. The 14 *PDB* briefers stated that they briefed a total of 24 policymaker positions during these four years, ranging from the president to an undersecretary in various departments. Because almost all *PDB* briefers who were interviewed—with the exception of those briefing the president and vice president—briefed more than one policymaker during any one day, the number of policymaker positions briefed by the 14 briefers was 37. As briefer tour lengths were far less than the total time the interviewed *PDB* briefers worked collectively, some briefers supported the same position because one briefed the position during the Bush administration and the other during the Obama administration, for example. Some briefers through replacement tours of duty during the same administration briefed the same policymaker. As a result, the actual number of unique individual policymakers briefed by the 14 briefers was 27. Table 2.1 summarizes this information.

TABLE 2.1 NATIONAL SECURITY POLICYMAKERS BRIEFED BY PDB BRIEFERS, 2007–2010

24 National Security Positions that were Briefed	Of the 14 Briefers Interviewed, the Number who Briefed these Positions	Of these, Number of Unique Policymakers Briefed
President of the United States	2	1
President's Chief of Staff	1	1
Deputy National Security Advisor (NSA)	1	1
Deputy NSA for Homeland Security and Counterterrorism	1	1
Deputy NSA for Strategic Communications	1	1
Director, National Economic Council	2	1
Vice President of the United States	3	2
Vice President's National Security Advisor	1	1
Chairman of the Joint Chiefs of Staff	1	1
Vice Chairman of the Joint Chiefs of Staff	3	2
Secretary of Defense	1	1
Deputy Secretary of Defense	2	2
Under Secretary of Defense for Policy	1	1
Under Secretary of Defense for Intelligence	2	1
Secretary of State	1	1
Deputy Secretary of State	1	1
US Ambassador to the United Nations	1	1
Secretary of Treasury	2	1
Deputy Secretary of Treasury	2	1
Under Secretary of Treasury for Terrorism	2	1

Continued

TABLE 2.1 *Continued*

Secretary of Homeland Security	2	1
Deputy Secretary of Homeland Security	2	1
Under Secretary of Homeland Security for Intelligence and Analysis	1	1
Under Secretary of Homeland Security for National Protection	1	1
TOTAL BRIEFED	**37**	**27**

Source: Interview data from the 14 PDB briefers.

Using grounded theory as the analytic methodology to analyze the interview data, 251 initial interpretative codes were associated with the interviewees' statements, consolidated into 11 codes during the second phase of focused coding and further consolidated into four theoretical codes during the third phase of coding.[48] The four codes were "information to help the policymaker make sense of information in the *PDB*"; "feedback information from the policymaker"; "creating a trusting relationship with the policymaker"; and "threats to the mutual trusting relationship with policymaker."

Because *PDB* briefer sensegiving involves the social construction of information—where two or more people interact with each other to develop new information—an interpersonal communications-related framework was deemed suitable to guide the analysis. In particular, relational communication theory is designed to explain the ways two people communicate.[49] The theory consists of two parts. First, the communication of meaning between two people simultaneously occurs at two levels: cognitive and relational.[50] Second, when communicating with each other, individuals self-regulate the exchange of cognitive and relational meanings through feedback loops; one type of feedback loop changes the relationship usually for the better to increase the opportunity for improving the relationship, while the other type stabilizes the relationship because of the risk of the relationship getting worse.[51] Recent psychological evidence reinforces this theory of communication.[52]

The data analysis identified two sensegiving components within the *PDB* briefer-to-policymaker context. Sensegiving consists of the provision of information and the existence of mutual trust. Not only do information and trust occur simultaneously, but also they affect each other. Trust is an antecedent of the value of information, but if trust is broken, that puts its benefit at risk and therefore can be an obstacle to sensegiving. Information helps create and reinforce trust, but if the information is not valued, that puts trust at risk and therefore can also be an obstacle to sensegiving. The *PDB* briefer is constantly balancing all four effects of sensegiving: the benefits of and obstacles to information and the benefits of and obstacles to trust. Next, the effects of information are discussed, followed by the effects of trust.

EFFECTS OF INFORMATION: BENEFITS AND OBSTACLES

BENEFITS OF INFORMATION: HELPING POLICYMAKERS MAKE SENSE OF INFORMATION

Briefers create value through their sensegiving. They provide additional politically relevant meta-information, or "information about information," by knowing why policymakers want critical organizational information, where they acquire the information they need to satisfy policymakers' needs, and how they contextualize threat information effectively to policymakers.

Policymakers Want Critical Organizational Information

Briefers describe three types of organizational information that policymakers seek but are not included in the *PDB*. First, policymakers want to know what *PDB*-related information the president of the United States is thinking about or focusing on.

> (Briefer 9, designated B9) Like North Korea, is in the office holder's book because the President sees it, but not so much highlighted. I asked the office holder if I highlight too much, was I talking too much or including too many products behind the tab. I asked the office holder twice, for example, "do you want me to include Libya?" The office holder said, "I want to see what the President is paying attention to and by seeing all the articles in the PDB, it helps me see his landscape. It helps me in competing with what I want but have no control over."

Second, policymakers want to know what peer policymakers think about *PDB*-related information because having that knowledge gives policymakers a strategic advantage when national security issues are discussed or decided on during various interagency meetings, such as National Security Council, Principals Committee, or Deputies Committee meetings.

(B7) I found it useful to know if the other office holder found something in the PDB useful and if my office holder did not but the other did. My office holder would want to know what the other office holder was interested in. The knowledge of a particular intelligence question or interest then would come up at a PC [Principals Committee] meeting, and my office holder would know the nuances of the topic.

The third reason is that they want to be prepared for other perspectives on *PDB*-related information that might come up from their staff, peers, and superiors, and if those perspectives cannot be assessed or validated directly, they appreciate it when the briefer provides an independent view —the intelligence community view—about a topic.

(B3) One day I passed the office holder in the West Wing. The office holder took me into the office and closed the door. The office holder said, "This is what I understand how things are in . . . so what do you think?" I reached into my book bag but the office holder stopped me and said, "I know you have a paper in there, but I want to know what you think." I knew the office holder was looking for reassurances from intelligence so I mentally reviewed the intelligence I had read recently and said, "I appreciate the question and the answer is . . . " I gave the office holder the position of the Intelligence Community. The office holder said, "That was good. I just wanted to hear from someone outside my staff."

Where Briefers Get Additional Information

Briefers seek out information to increase the policymaker's knowledge related to a topic prior to a decision meeting, a visit from a domestic or foreign official, or travel to a domestic or foreign location. Briefers do this in at least four ways.

The predominant way is during the daily meeting that starts at 9:30 a.m., when the available *PBD* briefers who have completed their daily briefings get together in one room to share with each other what policymakers are thinking. What one *PDB* briefer says about the policymaker he or she supports becomes useful information for other *PDB* briefers who are listening.

(B6) I realized that the key portion of the feedback session was the first segment. Then, only the PDB briefers were in the room and one or two senior managers of the PDB program. The analysts had not come in the room yet. It was a very frank discussion. I could hear exactly how the office holders reacted to articles. If there was a discussion of a sensitive issue, you can hear the explicit discussion. You get the real low-down of what is going on, if the office holder's reaction was notable. It provided insight into the workings of the administration, it helped with esprit de corps of the briefers, it was the only time we could freely share what only we were going through. It was a place to talk about a context that only we experienced, and it helped me provide context around the issues that my office holders might be working on.

The second way is the rapport the *PBD* briefers establish with the administrative and operational support staff assigned to a policymaker in order to collect information that identifies the policymaker's focus of attention. Examples of the types of information collected are topics of interest, upcoming scheduled visits or meetings, and the attendees. These support personnel are in the reporting chain of command of the policymaker, often work near or adjacent to the policymaker's office, and have frequent but short contact with the policymaker. However, because of the *PDB* briefer's dedicated time, typically spanning 15 to 20 continuous minutes with the policymaker, and the intimate nature of their interaction during that time, the *PDB* briefer can provide as much benefit to the support personnel in terms of useful knowledge as the support personnel can provide to the *PDB* briefer.

(B14) I heard all the discussions about the office holder's meeting schedule, the office holder's travel schedule, issues coming up, policy decisions the office holder made during the staff meeting, how action oriented the office holder was, the office holder's priorities, including daily priorities, short term priorities, and long-term priorities.

(B11) There is a lot of mystery behind the PDB. The White House . . . office . . . needed a little visibility and I needed insight into what they needed. After the briefing, I would go to them and let them know what the office holder was interested in. They were very appreciative of my input because even though they were providing three inputs a day to the office holder, they never had any interaction with the office holder. They just put together a list of hot items and fed them forward. I was the only one who actually got feedback so I was helping them so they could help the office holder better.

The third way the *PDB* briefers get additional information is by talking one on one with other *PDB* briefers who may share useful information. With the time crunch preparing each morning for the brief, when briefers spend two to three hours sometime between 2:00 and 5:00 a.m., it is almost impossible for the briefer to know everything that might be helpful to a policymaker, so establishing close ties with coworking *PDB* briefers is an advantage some are able to pursue.

(B7) The PDB briefers who sat closest to me on the 7th floor were the ones I talked with the most. I would talk one-on-one with these PDB briefers. They would show me what they put behind the tab and I would show them what I put. They gave me a nickname, the ". . ." because I would get and find stuff they didn't. We bonded that way between PDB briefers.

(B13) I have very good collaboration with the other PDB briefers. I would ask what they are doing as far as selection of products. If I used a product that a PDB briefer gave to an office holder, I would tell my White House office holder that the product was provided to that office holder.

Fourth, almost all briefers brief two or more policymakers, and many are able to talk with a subordinate policymaker who is willing to discuss what information his or her superior needs.

(B6) I interacted with the subordinate office holder. That office holder would be a good source of knowledge about what the secretary was interested in.

(B9) The subordinate office holder is the office holder's point person into the National Security Council and subordinate office holder is an adviser to the office holder. So, I keep close tabs with the subordinate because the subordinate has all of the office holder's policy issues, meetings with foreign leaders, cyber topics, and policy core issues like counterterrorism.

How Briefers Accomplish Sensegiving of Threat Information

Briefers realize that policymakers are very busy people and that intelligence information is only one of many kinds of information—originating from many types of individuals—coming to the policymaker. Briefers employ at least three techniques to help ensure the policymaker makes sense of the threat information they convey.

The first technique—called "going beyond the article"—involves the recognition by the briefer that the additional information he or she provides has to not only connect the policymaker to something in the *PDB* but also add context, interpretation, and/or details tailored to the cognitive and processing needs of the policymaker.

(B3) The office holder wanted stuff beyond the article. That means the office holder wanted articles that could have branches and sequels. These would be opportunities to have a conversation that could extend the value of just reading the article. When I sensed that the office holder was willing to go beyond the article, that is when I would start the conversation.

(B12) The briefing has to carry further than what is on paper, it has to advance the story. I have to provide more background and context. I also quizzed the pre-briefer for what was really relevant to the office holder in their articles. I have my game plan, in a way. It is whatever can carry the story farther so that the office holder could ask the team what they can do.

The second technique—the "storyline"—involves the briefer's recognition that because time has elapsed since the last time a threat item was included in the *PDB*, the introduction of additional information has to be connected to what the policymaker knew and understood the last time he or she was briefed. The story has to meet the policymaker's threshold for paying attention. Every successive reintroduction of a story, especially when time has elapsed in terms of days, weeks, or months, has to appear as if the old item is still fresh in the policymaker's consciousness, as if the elapsed time was just a few minutes.

(B11) You become familiar with the storyline. After a while it is about advancing the story for the office holder. The PDB was either advancing the story, or bringing something new. Some issues were hard-wired like the Middle East.

(B14) All the stories were continuous threads but some were more reoccurring than others. For example, if there was a story that was more strategic like how leadership in Pakistan or Afghanistan was thinking, that would have a developing story and I would only brief those when something new was building on the developing story.

The third technique—the "tee-up"—involves verbally introducing a topic by adding context in a sentence or two before the policymaker begins to read the *PDB* article. There is usually a reason why a tee-up is needed, normally because the *PDB* article may not explicitly contain an important point that the briefer believes the policymaker should know.

(B12) Sometimes an article came out in the PDB because of production timing. The office holder would be confused by that, and ask, "Why is this piece in the book?" It was a matter of story development. Yes, it was arbitrary. But it kept them from being totally captured to the inbox. For the blind spot, we looked for new topics. They required more tee-up, we had to sell the piece. Sometimes I had to annotate in the margins of the PDB so that when the office holder read it the office holder would have some context already and not be confused, often reading the PDB while the office holder was eating breakfast.

OBSTACLES TO INFORMATION: ATTENDING TO POLICYMAKER INTENTIONAL AND UNINTENTIONAL FEEDBACK

While the foregoing describes the benefits of information, briefers also experience two kinds of potential obstacles: the challenges of responding satisfactorily to policymakers' verbal requests directed at the briefer, and the uncertainty in interpreting policymakers' nonverbal behavior.

Verbal Feedback from Policymakers to Briefers

Briefers can receive verbal feedback from policymakers while sitting with them during briefing sessions. Briefers generally receive three types of requests from policymakers.

One type is a request by policymakers to use the *PDB* as a venue to raise to the president what they feel are important issues that would be otherwise difficult for them personally to raise within a sometimes contentious interagency process. Getting a topic written for the *PDB* raises the visibility of that topic to the president.

(B14) The office holder has a keen interest in. . . . So I would brief anything to do with. . . . There were times the office holder would say, "Put this in the PDB." I would then come back to the 0930 feedback session and report this. And they would say, "oh no, here comes another request for. . . ." After all, it's competing with other articles. I have

seen my office holder use the PDB as a marketing strategy to raise the visibility of issues my office holder was committed to, like. . . . The office holder's approach was always multipronged. The approach was to integrate departmental interests. The office holder knew one way to get that done was through raising the issue through the PDB because then the President would be exposed to it and he would ask questions, and the departments that needed to be involved would do so.

The briefer mitigates obstacles to meeting such a request by balancing the ease of being in the presence of policymakers, who have tremendous power distance from them, with the need for the briefer to coexist within the hierarchical *PDB* and intelligence community structure in which they officially are subordinated. The briefer tactfully relays the policymaker's request using the voice of positional authority of the policymaker.

Another type of request asked of *PDB* briefers is to better understand the quality of the information presented in the *PDB*. Policymakers want to know about the intelligence sources of the information. The sources are often from human intelligence or signals intelligence collection. The briefer knows that knowledge about foreign threats is rarely complete, rarely available to be answered in the way a puzzle has a definitive answers. Intelligence problems are more mysterious and therefore are conducive to the necessary art of framing.[53] Knowledge about sources provides a way for policymakers to frame the quality of the information, an especially important competency for policymakers motivated by the investigations of the 11 September terrorist attacks of 2001 and the reforms prompted by the Intelligence Reform and Terrorism Prevention Act of 2004.

(B5) With the office holder and the subordinate office holder, they are getting the feed every day. Both office holders knew the sources like an analyst would. They could weigh the source. I was very surprised how many times I get questions about sources. I thought they would not care about details on sources, how intimately familiar they were with sources; I was told that even the President recognized particular sources. Why are office holders interested in sourcing? It provides a sense of confidence in the reports. It tells them how close the source of the intelligence was to the information. The office holder was also interested in the history of the source. How reliable has the source been?

Because the briefers are not the authors of *PDB* articles and usually do not have expertise about the specific human intelligence sources used in an article, they mitigate this potential obstacle either by making use of intelligence-related material made available to them as part of their briefing preparation in order to answer the question on the spot, or they let the policymaker know they do not know the answer and promise to get the information to the policymaker at a later time after discussing the issue with the intelligence analysts who authored the article.

A third type of request asks for additional analytical information about a *PDB* article. While briefers meeting with policymakers on a daily basis tend to provide them with an understanding of what intelligence capabilities more or less can or cannot do and what else the intelligence community generally knows or does not know, it is usually policymakers with a greater understanding of intelligence, typically those longer into their term of office, who are the ones who ask more meaningful questions.[54]

(B6) When I did not have the answer, I generated a tasking when I got back to headquarters. I always had a dialogue with the office holder and the subordinate office holder when I was going to task their questions to make sure I understood exactly what their questions were. Sometimes, their question was for extra data, and sometimes it was for a more complex analysis that for a variety of reasons that I said the PDB article was not designed to accommodate.

As discussed earlier, briefers do not author the *PDB* articles and may not be experts in the topic. To mitigate the potential obstacle of not being able to provide additional analytical knowledge during the briefing, briefers make formal requests to the intelligence community. Policymaker questions become "tasks" within the *PDB* management system, which means an intelligence analyst in the intelligence community is assigned the responsibility of providing an answer to the *PDB* briefer.

Nonverbal Feedback from Policymakers to Briefers

Briefers observe nonverbal behavior from policymakers while sitting with them during briefing sessions. Nonverbal behavior includes the gesturing, posturing, finger touching and positioning, facial expressions, and eye movements by policymakers while reading the *PDB*. A policymaker's use of nonverbal behavior can be unintentional, yet the briefer may attach significance to it even though the policymaker is not aware of such meaning.[55] Briefers attach great meaning to policymakers' nonverbal behavior in three ways.

First, briefers become an accepted part of the policymaker's surroundings, and policymakers let their personalities show, which includes the changeability in their mood.

(B1) I gave the office holder the morning briefing at the office holder's residence. I would arrive before the office holder came downstairs. I sat in the chair waiting for the office holder. When the office holder started down the stairs, I stood up and said "good morning." Depending on how the office holder answered, would determine how I talked to the office holder the rest of the day. If, say, the office holder would talk on and on in response to my "good morning," then I knew it was good. If the office holder was not chipper but was real quiet, then I was quiet also. It was very important to watch nonverbal communication as cues to the office holder's mood. I got good at it.

When a briefer enters the area where the policymaker is located for the briefing—an office, a home residence, a car, or an airplane—the briefer mitigates the potential of not considering his or her mood by paying an exceeding amount of attention to the mood of the policymaker to gauge whether the timing is right to provide additional information during the briefing session. Detecting and acting accordingly in response to the policymaker's mood is one of the most important competencies for the briefer.

Once the mood is established, then the briefer monitors the policymaker's nonverbal behaviors while he or she is reading the *PDB*, which provides cues to when additional information can be conveyed.

(B4) You are trying to crack the code. Everybody thinks that when you say you are giving a brief, you are talking, like how you see it on television, someone standing behind a podium talking to an audience. But that is not the case with the PDB. The nonverbal cues are critical because the PDB is meant to be read. There is really not a lot of opportunity to brief in the normal sense of what people think of talking.

The briefer mitigates the potential of not being aware of what the policymaker is concentrating on by sitting near the policymaker, close enough to watch how and where the policymaker's eyes, hands, and fingers physically track the narrative of the *PDB* content.

Lastly, after the briefer finishes monitoring the nonverbal behavior, the briefer also has to interpret what it means in such a way that it can be meaningfully fed back as input to the intelligence analysts who wrote the *PDB* article, which is also part of the briefer's responsibility.

> (B7) The biggest frustration I had was more about coming back after the briefings. The analysts were upset if I didn't get feedback. But because the office holder and the subordinate office holder were readers, that was hard. I had to explain that the office holder was a reader and that you (the analyst) were lucky if they read the article. That is why I created those categories to give some detail, to differentiate how they read an article if they read it. I also looked at the amount of time they spent on a page. You could see eye movement of the page, or if they turned the page, or if they got to the bottom of the page. I categorized their body language in a way that would provide feedback to the PDB authors and management into four categories: "was not read," "was read," "was read but skimmed," and "was read and appreciated."

Sometimes, because reading the PDB is a solitary act, when there is little dialogue between briefer and policymaker, these nonverbal behaviors are the main source of feedback to the intelligence analyst and the *PDB* management. *PDB* briefers mitigate the potential of not making use of what becomes an important source of nonverbal feedback by categorizing the extent to which the policymaker pays attention to a *PDB* article.

Next, the trust component of sensegiving is discussed in detail.

EFFECTS OF TRUST: BENEFITS AND OBSTACLES

BENEFIT OF TRUST: CREATING MUTUAL TRUST WITH THE POLICYMAKER

A trusting relationship is important for both briefer and policymaker, but for different reasons: for the briefer, it is to feel the policymaker values him or her, while for the policymaker, it is to be comfortable and to trust the briefer. Briefers, in addition, provide types of incidents that demonstrate why a policymaker needs a trusting relationship with a briefer.

Why Briefers Need a Trusting Relationship with the Policymaker

Briefers have a professional need to be of value to the policymaker. The briefer feels his or her value must be consistent with the level of important matters of state surrounding the policymaker's setting, which means the briefer has to span a tremendous power distance between the two. To the outside observer, the spanning of great power distances must seem unreal, but to the briefer, his or her relational trust component overrides the distance and actually determines the value of the information component.

> (B9) I want to offer something more than what is in the PDB. What is in the PDB is often bare bones, just the facts. If I am to provide a service instead of just a courier, I need to have a discussion and provide some kind of context for things that are in the office holder's primary bin of interest.

> (B4) If they have to ask for it, by the time you get it to them, it is too late. I saw my value as anticipating what the office holder needed. When I was giving the brief, my mission was for the office holder to consume data and have the context needed to understand it. And to ascertain what the office holder needs to make the office holder's job easier. When I sit down with the PDB, I am focused on the individual. I am engaging the individual in order to provide support for the institution.

Why Policymakers Need a Trusting Relationship with the Briefer

Briefers said that policymakers have two main reasons for wanting a trusting relationship with them.

First, at a minimum, the policymaker needs to have a level of comfort— feeling at ease—in the presence of the briefer. If there is unease, the briefer will likely not be invited back.

> (B11) Over time, the office holder got more comfortable with me. Probably it was harder to develop a rapport. I know for a fact that the office holder was comfortable with me. I was told that by one of the staff.

Second, once comfort is established, the policymaker can begin to trust the briefer, trust being the expectation that what the briefer says he or she will do, he or she actually will do. Briefers understand that trust by the policymaker means that what is heard or seen by the briefer will be carefully guarded.

(B1) Office holders establish trust with you. During the first few months of my tenure as briefer, the office holder would only make comments in reaction to the articles in the PDB that were directly related to the content in the articles. I knew that trust had been established when the office holder gave me information from others. For example, while thinking about an article while reading, the office holder might say to me "I had lunch with . . . who had a different point of view." When the office holder revealed that kind of information to me, I knew I was trusted.

Evidence that Policymakers Need a Trusting Relationship with the Briefer

Briefers discuss three types of incidents when they feel trust is demonstrated by the policymaker.

The first type involves the briefer feeling part of a team with the policymaker.

(B5) The office holder had just gotten back from two weeks of leave. I come in and the office holder says, "Good morning, how was your leave?" Of course, I was not on leave. I was doing my briefings. The office holder said on Monday you have to recharge your soul, "When was the last time you took leave?" On Friday, the office holder asked me what are my leave plans and said "I will call your supervisors and tell them to get you leave." The following week, the office holder brought it up again and pressed me. On some level, the office holder cared for me. Caring is part of the familiarity. The office holder values people who are close. The office holder asked me if I could stay on as the briefer until . . . but could have said, "I want you to stay." But the office holder asked in a way that was very cognizant of my life as a briefer, one that I had done it for two years. The office holder asked in a way I could say no.

The second shows what it is like when trust is established.

(B2) The relationship I had as briefer with the office holder was like the glue that let the knowledge get to the office holder. The office holder knew that analytic products were watered down by consensus. The office holder would ask how it was watered down, who and what were the dissenting views because not all that kind of dissenting information is put into print. The office holder would like it when I could give the inside story of the analysis disagreements. One day, I told the office holder about the disagreements but that I would only be willing to share that with the office holder if the office holder did not attribute me as the source because if it ever got out that I snitched on the analysts, I would lose my integrity. I directly asked the office holder if this could be kept private. I said, "Don't out me." The office holder said, "You can trust me."

The third case is quite interesting. Sometimes after trust is established, an incident happens between the briefer and policymaker to break that trust. This third case is an example of when trust is reestablished.

(B3) One day, the office holder said, "What else do you have for me?" I gave the office holder the behind-the-tab articles but after three articles, the office holder fell asleep. I went into a cold sweat. I immediately thought this incident would impact my future access to the office holder and I wasn't sure what to do. The office holder awoke after two minutes; I just stood there for those two minutes. It was just the two of us in the room. The office holder saw me upon awakening. I ended the briefing real quickly, like within three minutes. After that, I was not invited back to give the office holder a briefing. But after one month, the office holder called me back to start the briefings again. I believe the reason I was called back was that no rumors were heard around the White House. In other words, I kept my mouth shut.

OBSTACLES TO TRUST: MITIGATING ANY THREATS TO TRUST

Threats to the briefer's trusting relationship with the policymaker are of utmost concern to the *PDB* briefer because without trust, the briefer cannot provide sensegiving service to the *policymaker*. Without trust, there is no benefit to the information. Threats originate from three sources: the *PDB* editing process, the analyst who authors the *PDB* article, and the *PDB* briefer.

Quality of the *PDB* Articles

All briefers see the quality of the articles as a reflection of themselves. They are sales men and women, selling the intelligence product, one they have not authored. The biggest and strongest concern they have is that the *PDB* editing process sometimes omits the most compelling part of the article.

(B12) Oftentimes, the most important part of the story was not present in the story. This was evident during the pre-briefer session with the analysts. Some pre-briefers made it very easy to understand what was important about the article. Others made it hard for me to figure out what was important. While for other pre-briefers, it was impossible to tell. Occasionally, the author may even say, "I don't agree with the piece." It could be that the editing and review processes had so changed what the author said, that the author disagrees what is now said.

When this happens, briefers mitigate this obstacle by adding their own oral narrative when briefing the policymaker to compensate so that the compelling part can be voiced, a decision the briefer makes independent—without consultation—of the *PDB* management system and yet depends on the briefer's assessment of the informational and processing needs of the policymaker at the time of the briefing.

Another concern briefers have, although less serious a threat, are readability problems and grammar errors within the *PDB* articles.

(B6) I also read the PDB for quality control purposes. You cannot believe that after so many layers of review how many mistakes there are. There are typos, grammatical errors, missing words, and sentences that do not make sense. What I did, as all the PDB briefers did when they found errors, was to take the article back to the production center to have them correct it.

Briefers mitigate this obstacle by having the errors corrected by the *PDB* production team.

The Analyst Who Wrote the PDB Article

For many briefers, coming back to headquarters and meeting with analysts is one of the most stressful parts of their job. Briefers talk about three problem areas they have to manage.

The first and most important to the briefers is not revealing to the analyst all the feedback they get from the policymaker in order to protect the policymaker's trust in them.

(B1) The President's Support Staff would leave the room and the authors of the articles that were included in the PDB were invited into the room and sat behind the briefers. The briefers discussed how each of the office holders reacted to the articles, if any comments were made. I would explain the feedback by my office holder but I had to protect what was said. You had to develop trust with the

office holder. Bad comments would not make their way back to the author. I would paraphrase comments that the office holder said so that the author could not attribute anything negative made by the office holder.

(B4) You had to guard very carefully this feedback, only for those in the circle of trust. I had to protect the relationship. It is key to the access and what to talk about. The only people that I could share what was said were other PDB briefers. If the office holder talks with . . . , you don't talk about their conversation. You just give them the information they asked for, not the inside baseball.

Holding back this kind of feedback is a balancing act for the briefer. On the one hand, briefers know what it is like—as they have served as intelligence analysts—to want feedback from their customers, but on the other hand, briefers are protectors of policymaker's trust and know that such feedback cannot be fully disclosed. Briefers mitigate this obstacle by providing some feedback but not anything so direct and nothing that can be associated with any policymaker. The briefers are the gatekeepers of this intimate kind of policymaker feedback into the intelligence system, and it is an important competency they must master.

A second concern is how the briefer is going to deal with cases in which the policymaker knows more than what the analyst writes about.

(B12) The office holder was so well informed. The office holder had conversations throughout the day with many types of people. And the office holder got inputs from staff. I assumed the office holder was more knowledgeable than what the PDB article said.

(B14) The office holder has met many foreign leaders. The office holder would challenge the way the PDB authors characterized the leaders whom the office holder knew. The office holder knew more about some of these foreign leaders than the analysts.

Briefers say that many policymakers know more about people and issues through their personal involvement through years of professional contact, yet intelligence analysts write about such people and issues for these same policymakers who may know more than the analysts. Policymakers are reluctant to give negative feedback to the analyst in such cases; while the policymaker may do so in front of the briefer, the briefer mitigates this obstacle by not revealing such feedback to the analyst. The briefer knows that the policymaker is concerned that negative feedback may have the unintended effect of reducing access to topics in which the analyst is an expert and the policymaker may need in the future.

The third concern involves the difference between the feedback policymakers give and what analysts expect as feedback. Briefers say that analysts are concerned with the quality of their presentation and the structure of their argument, whereas the policymaker is concerned with whether the article influences his or her policy position.

> (B7) If the office holder had a critical comment, I would go to the analyst's manager because the analyst would usually personalize it and think it was about them. Handling the critical comment required tact because if the office holder did not like the content for reasons they stated, it had nothing to do with the author. I would let the manager then deal with the author. The manager got it.

Analysts can take feedback about their writing quality and logic very emotionally and personally, especially when the audience is a senior policymaker. Analysts typically do not understand that the policymaker views the knowledge in a *PDB* article by whether it does or does not support his or her policy position. Briefers mitigate this obstacle by giving their feedback to someone in a management role supervising the analyst because managers—having little or no personal involvement in the article—are better positioned to objectively hear the needs of the policymaker.

The *PDB* Briefer's Own Missteps

Briefers discuss two areas of interaction with policymakers where they—the briefers—are the very instigators of threats to the trust they want to protect. The briefers' own missteps are the greatest threats to trust with policymakers.

Briefers are constantly judging whether they are eliminating the power separation from the policymaker from their consciousness in fear that they might cross the line into an improper professional relationship.

> (B2) One day, there was article in the PDB about . . . talking about the tension between Democracy and Islam. I knew the office holder's

comfort zone and assumptions about Islam. The office holder talked about a Middle-East expert who had written about. . . . , and I said [the scholar] was not very current. The office holder then said that [the scholar] was coming to dinner. I offered an opposing analysis off the cuff. The office holder did not embrace my comments. I said, "It is just another data point." The office holder said, "It's interesting and I'll bring it up with him." I thought this was not a good sign and that I had overstepped my boundary.

> (B6) What is the inner circle? They have their senior advisors who have easy access to them all of the time, who the office holder relies upon. The PDB has aspects of the inner circle. If I called down to the office holder's staff that I needed to see the office holder only for five minutes to talk about a critical issue, they would get me in. But you don't want to play that card too often. You don't want to cry wolf. I did that one time. There was a lasting impact. For about a week, the office holder did not want me to brief, and when the office holder did see me, it was different.

Briefers are drawn into the policymaker's "inner circle" by the desire to be on the inside, where the action is.[56] Briefers mitigate this obstacle to trust by constantly being reflexively aware of a professional line they must not cross, no matter how tempting it is, and they are almost always able to catch themselves in the act if they find themselves doing so.

The other area of the briefer's concern is the tendency to move toward a close emotional, interpersonal relationship with the policymaker and the need to fight the tendency.

> (B13) The delivery was great. It was so conversational. But both these office holders were disarming. They were very senior people; they had a lot of authority. There were not intelligence types. They talk about their personal life. You have to watch what you say because they will take it as the official intelligence position and their being disarming makes it easy to fall into that. I caught myself once and pulled myself back. They use very colorful language. You have to maintain a professional stance. Its okay for them to say whatever they want. But not okay for you.

> (B3) I never saw my relationship with the office holder as friendship because I knew the office holder was political. But when you have an

emotional connection with the office holder, you see the person as a real person, not as a position of authority.

Briefers find themselves, amplified by their close proximity to and high degree of intimacy with policymakers, in a close, familiar relationship with them. Briefers are aware of the possible negative consequences of being too friendly, yet know they cannot be unfriendly. They walk a thin line between emotional closeness and distance by being constantly and reflexively aware of themselves, by being cognizant of the politically sensitive situation they are in, and having other briefers available—who understand the unique context no one else in the world is experiencing—to support them by sharing their concerns and learning from each other.

Figure 2.1 summarizes the components and effects—the how and why, respectively—of *PDB* briefers engaging in sensegiving to policymakers, specifically, the interrelated components of information and trust as well as the interrelated effects of their benefits and obstacles. *PDB* briefers create, protect, and maintain trust with the policymaker in order to assess and provide customized meta-information needs—critically needed, contextualized information related to but not included in the *PDB*—to help the policymaker make use of intelligence information within the policymaking process.

FIGURE 2.1 Components and Effects of Sensegiving. *Source:* Analysis of interview data from the 14 PDB briefers.

ENTER THE AGE OF SENSEGIVING

How did the *PDB* briefer's sensegiving come into existence? The *PDB* is the official daily product of a large, federated system of 17 intelligence agencies (including the ODNI), each a rule-based, authority-driven organization, like most government agencies, whose primary purpose is to marshal people, systems, and processes to maximize the output of their product or service. This is the nature of hierarchical organizations; it is the nature of the beast—the official system.

Sometimes, leaders of national security organizations realize— proactively or reactively, intentionally or not—that their official system is not designed to meet all of the needs of those they serve. Rather than attempt the difficult task of redesigning the organization to satisfy a new need, they construct a supplemental organization—like *PDB* briefers—to handle such responsibilities that sits alongside yet outside the official system but may require different norms, rules and procedures, division of labor, and levels of authority. Official systems tend to be hierarchical, whereas *PDB* briefers tend to operate non-hierarchically, having few levels of authority, few divisions of labor, highly networked inside and outside, where individuals achieve influence by solving problems and have fewer rules and different norms.[57] *PDB* briefers are aware they behave in these nonhierarchical ways. These characteristics of *PDB* briefers are indicative of a *parallel organization*; the nonhierarchical system of *PDB* briefers is connected in parallel to, in order to supplement, the hierarchical official system of the intelligence community.[58] Members of parallel organizations, such as *PDB* briefers, enjoy a freedom of movement and a freedom from reporting, a unique type of independence that is not typically found in an official hierarchical system.

Even though, as noted, President George H.W. Bush was the catalyst for the creation of a full-time briefer for a sitting president, thus creating a parallel organization to the intelligence community, it was not until the George W. Bush administration—following the September 11 terrorist attacks of 2001 and the resulting Intelligence Reform and Terrorism Prevention Act of 2004—that escalation in the emphasis and value of intelligence to policymakers occurred.[59] In response to this escalation, sensegiving emerged as a necessary service for *PDB* briefers to help policymakers attend to the use of intelligence during this difficult and rare time in recent American history—when America was attacked on its own soil—by contextualizing it within the policymaker's decision-making cycle. Sensegiving helps ensure knowledge is not wasted.

Figure 2.2 shows the 70-year evolution of the *PDB*-based policymaker and intelligence community relationship, as discussed earlier in the history of the *PDB* section of this article, stepping through four distinct "ages," from one originally based on separation between these two worlds to one now based on a parallel organization with *PDB* briefer sensegiving: the age of little feedback (1946–1964); the age of indirect feedback (1964–1988); the age of direct feedback, when fulltime *PDB* briefers were created as a parallel organization (1988–2001); and the age of sensegiving by *PDB* briefers (2001–present).

How can sensegiving survive and flourish? Sensegiving in national security parallel organizations is a double-edged sword. On the beneficial side, official systems survive, in part, because they create parallel organizations, ones that act nonhierarchically in order to satisfy a sensegiving service that the official system is not designed to perform. On the detrimental side, most individuals within official systems cannot see into parallel organizations and are not able to understand the sensegiving service to clients or its value to the official system.

There are three dilemmas that make it difficult for intelligence community members, the official system, to understand *PDB* briefer sensegiving: first, sensegiving occurs in a subordinate-to-superior direction, quite the opposite of the normative

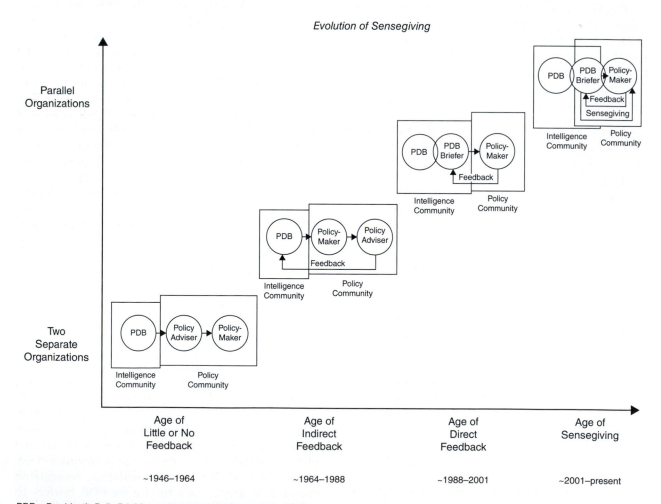

PDB = President's Daily Brief (or predecessor in the case of pre-1964)

FIGURE 2.2 *Evolution of Sensegiving. Source:* Literature review and results of this study.

superior-to-subordinate direction that is usually found in official systems; second, sensegiving takes place by bridging the worlds of policy and intelligence, not a typical competency found within the official system; and third, sensegiving across dramatically different organizational boundaries thrives in nonhierarchical conditions, quite the opposite condition as that found in official systems.

Official systems using parallel organizations require individuals—both in the intelligence community and with *PDB* briefers—to consciously acknowledge these dilemmas. The *PDB* briefers interviewed for this study were able to put these dilemmas into perspective; they possessed the emotional calmness and maturity necessary to handle apparent contradictions within their work life.[60] But it likely does not work to the same degree for those from the intelligence community in their relationship with *PDB* briefers because of the dilemmas stated earlier. This double-edged sword breeds a tension that must be continually managed in order for sensegiving to flourish.

CONCLUSION

This article brings the *PDB* briefer sensegiving service to national security policymakers to the forefront and, by making it transparent, presents six contributions, practical and theoretical.

First, scholars now have access to the subordinate-to-superior contextualizing service that intelligence officers—playing the role of *PDB* briefers—have in the policymaking process. What *PDB* briefers add through sensegiving is more than the narrative available in the *PDB*. Sensegiving is based on reciprocal trust with policymakers, providing policymakers contextually relevant information to help them understand the value and implications of intelligence within their policymaking process.

Second, intelligence community professionals managing and employed in the official system can better understand the contextualizing service that sensegiving and parallel organizations contribute to the success of the official system. To conduct sensegiving activities, *PDB* briefers operate in a very different, nonhierarchical way than the official systems from whence they came; *PDB* briefers operate in a context that is independent and self-regulated, characteristic of a parallel organization as they operate outside of but alongside the official intelligence community system, yet essential to the success of the official system. Therefore, the success of the

parallel organization (and the national security system at large) is not only dependent on the *PDB* briefer relationship with the policymaker, but also on appropriate stakeholders within the official system who understand the *PDB* briefer role as subordinate-to-superior sensegivers.

Third, sensegiving can be recognized as a valuable competency. In subordinate-to-superior contexts crossing between different organizational worlds, as occurs with *PDB* briefers and policymakers, the intelligence community can improve the design of *PDB* briefer job descriptions, selection criteria of applicant material and interviews, and initial orientation and ongoing training. The components and effects of sensegiving identified in Figure 1 could be the basis for developing sensegiving into a competency: providing meta-information to policymakers to help them effectively use the *PDB* in their policymaking process; detecting and interpreting policymaker reactions to the *PDB* and responding as needed; establishing a trusting relationship with the policymaker so that meta-information needs are detected and become valuable to the policymaker; and detecting and mitigating threats to that trust. Sensegiving, as a professional competency for the role of *PDB* briefer, could lead the way for recognizing the value of sensegiving in other subordinate-to-superior national security and policy contexts.

Fourth, this article raises the question of whether a parallel organization must first be in place to bridge two worlds—in our case, of intelligence and national security policymaking—before sensegiving can emerge in subordinate-to-superior contexts. It was the case for the *PDB* briefer, but it is not known how generalizable this context is. Regarding generalizability, in the Department of Defense, a group of employees serve as briefers within a parallel organization—the Executive Support Office—and its official system, the Defense Intelligence Agency, interfacing with policymakers within the Department of Defense. These briefers provide a briefing product analogous to the *PDB* to department officials and provide sensegiving to the unique needs of defense officials. In the Department of Homeland Security, we might expect a similar capability in law enforcement fusion centers—where intelligence analysts from various organizations are collocated to share information across levels and sectors of government—that uses analysts, serving as briefers, to provide sensegiving service to state and local public safety policymakers, private sector partners, and the federal government. These two departments would be appropriate contexts for future national security research on sensegiving.

Fifth, this article also raises the question of why and when sensegiving emerges in national security policymaking domains. Is the reason the nature of a specific context that needs contextualizing services, the occurrence of a catalyst such as an event like the September 11 terrorist attacks, a combination of both, or something else? The question becomes especially relevant for other national security and public safety contexts beyond that of *PDB* briefer sensegiving to policymakers. One notable study specifically focused on sensegiving triggers, but neither within a national security or policymaking context nor from within a parallel organization, and included both managers and employees; the study found that sensegiving emerged when individuals felt an issue had important consequences for themselves and others in their organization and when they felt their leaders lacked competency in that issue.[61] Sensegiving research on triggers in national security and parallel organization contexts is suggested.

Sixth, this article focused exclusively on the process of sensegiving within the *PDB* context because the purpose of the research question was to bring to light knowledge about this relatively unknown phenomenon. However, a future research question, given what we now know about the process of subordinate-to-superior sensegiving, could address sensegiving under different security threat and policy conditions. For the threat condition, the *PDB* could contain articles during a national crisis as well as those of a routine nature. The example from the 1969 *PDB* discussed earlier is suggestive that this may be the case: one article involved diplomatic discussions about the Vietnam War, while another article discussed the latest Soviet manned spacecraft developments. Similarly, for different policy conditions, there might be decision-making contexts in which the *PDB* includes a topic for which a presidential policy already exists, but it may also include a topic for which policy does not yet exist. From a policy perspective, knowing whether and how sensegiving might be different for national security situations in crisis from those not in crisis, and in situations when policy does or does not already exist, would be especially relevant and important topics.

In summary, sensegiving is needed by policymakers to make sense of and use the *PDB* during policymaking processes, such as those that occur prior to, during and after National Security Council, Principals Committee, and Deputies Committee meetings. *PDB* briefers use sensegiving to provide a contextualizing service to policymakers, which requires establishing and maintaining a very close and trusting relationship with policymakers in order for *PDB* briefers to anticipate, detect, and react to the meta-information needs of policymakers—information about information—such as politically relevant organizational information as well as the contextualization of threat information not included in the *PDB*. Yet, at the same time, *PDB* briefers also establish and maintain a very close and trusting relationship with intelligence analysts who author articles in the *PDB* and the managers who oversee the production of the *PDB*. Hence, *PDB* briefers connect two very different information-intensive worlds by managing the emotional relationship within each and between them.

QUESTIONS FOR FURTHER DISCUSSION

1. How is the *PDB* used as a means of communication among senior government officials?
2. Why do *PDB* briefers focus on gaining the trust of their audience?
3. What pitfalls lurk in the sustained interactions and relationships between policymakers and intelligence officers surrounding the production and delivery of the *PDB*?
4. Should the President and Principals simply read the *PDB* without routine interaction with a briefer? Should they just have just an oral briefing, if they wish, instead of the expectation that they will actually read part or all of the *PDB*?

ENDNOTES

1. Alexander L. George, *Bridging the Gap: Theory and Practice in Foreign Policy* (Washington, DC: United States Institute of Peace Press, 1993), 132–134.
2. Thomas L. Hughes, "The Fate of Facts in the World of Men," *Proceedings of the American Society of International Law at Its Annual Meeting* 63 (1969): 233–245.
3. Robert Jervis, "Why Intelligence and Policymakers Clash," *Political Science Quarterly* 125 (Summer 2010): 185–204.
4. Dennis A. Gioia and Kumar Chittipeddi, "Sensemaking and Sensegiving in Strategic Change Initiation,"

Strategic Management Journal 12 (September 1991): 433–448.

5. John L. Helgerson, *Getting to Know the President: Intelligence Briefings of Presidential Candidates, 1952–2004*, 2nd ed. (Washington, DC: Center for the Study of Intelligence, 2012), 190–191.

6. Central Intelligence Agency, "CIA Releases Roughly 2,500 Declassified President's Daily Briefs," 16 September 2015, accessed at https://www.cia.gov/news-information/press-releases-statements/2015-press-releases-statements/cia-releases-declassified-presidents-daily-briefs.html, 22 December 2015.

7. Sally Maitlis, "The Social Processes of Organizational Sensemaking," *Academy of Management Journal* 48 (February 2005): 21–40; Linda Rouleau, "Micro-Practices of Strategic Sensemaking and Sensegiving: How Middle Managers Interpret and Sell Change Every Day," *Journal of Management Studies* 42 (November 2005): 1413–1441; and Sally Maitlis and Thomas B. Lawrence, "Triggers and Enablers of Sensegiving in Organizations," *Academy of Management Journal* 50 (February 2007): 57–84.

8. Jean M. Bartunek, R.M. Krim, R. Necochea, and M. Humphries, "Sensemaking, Sensegiving, and Leadership in Strategic Organizational Development," *Advances in Qualitative Organizational Research* 2 (1999): 35–71; and Deirdre Dixon, "Staying Alive: The Experience of *In Extremis* Leadership" (PhD diss., Case Western Reserve University, Cleveland, OH, 2014), accessed at https://etd.ohiolink.edu/!etd. send_file?accession=case1396607108&disposition=inline, 27 March 2017.

9. Intelligence Reform and Terrorism Prevention Act of 2004, Pub. L. No. 108-458, 118 Stat. 3638 (2004).

10. Hughes, "The Fate of Facts in the World of Men," 236; Hans Heymann, Jr., "The Intelligence-Policy Relationship," *Studies in Intelligence* 28 (Winter 1984): 57–66; Robert M. Gates, "An Opportunity Unfulfilled: The Use and Perceptions of Intelligence at the White House," *Washington Quarterly* 12 (Winter 1989): 35–44; and Jack Davis, "The Kent-Kendall Debate of 1949," *Studies in Intelligence* 35 (Summer 1991): 37–50.

11. Sherman Kent, *Strategic Intelligence for American World Policy* (Princeton, NJ: Princeton University Press, 1949); Heymann, "The Intelligence-Policy Relationship"; Richard K. Betts, "Policy-Makers and Intelligence Analysts: Love, Hate or Indifference?," *Intelligence and National Security* 3 (January 1988): 184–189; L. Keith Gardiner, "Dealing with Intelligence-Policy Disconnects," *Studies in Intelligence* 33 (Summer 1989):

1–10; Robert M. Gates, "Guarding against Politicization," *Studies in Intelligence* 36 (Winter 1992): 5–13; Jervis, "Why Intelligence and Policymakers Clash"; Arthur S. Hulnick, "Intelligence Producer-Consumer Relations in the Electronic Era," *International Journal of Intelligence and Counter-intelligence* 24 (Winter 2011–2012): 747–756; Dennis C. Wilder, "An Educated Consumer Is Our Best Customer," *Studies in Intelligence* 55 (June 2011): 23–31; and Stephen Marrin, "Rethinking Analytic Politicization," *Intelligence and National Security* 28 (February 2013): 32–54.

12. David D. Gries, "New Links between Intelligence and Policy," *Studies in Intelligence* 34 (Summer 1990): 1–6; John E. McLaughlin, "New Challenges and Priorities for Analysis," *Defense Intelligence Journal* 6 (Fall 1997): 11–21; John McCreary and Richard A. Posner, "The Latest Intelligence Crisis," *Intelligence and National Security* 23 (June 2008): 371–380; Josh Kerbel and Anthony Olcott, "Synthesizing with Clients, Not Analyzing for Customers," *Studies in Intelligence* 54 (December 2010): 11–27; Thomas Fingar, *Reducing Uncertainty: Intelligence Analysis and National Security* (Stanford, CA: Stanford University Press, 2011), 52; and Wilder, "An Educated Consumer Is Our Best Customer."

13. Kerbel and Olcott, "Synthesizing with Clients," 18; and Helgerson, *Getting to Know the President*, 185.

14. Helgerson, *Getting to Know the President*, 7.

15. Ibid., 9.

16. Ibid., 49.

17. Ibid., 58.

18. Loch K. Johnson, "Glimpses into the Gems of American Intelligence: *The President's Daily Brief* and the National Intelligence Estimate," *Intelligence and National Security* 23 (June 2008): 330–370.

19. Johnson, "Glimpses into the Gems of American Intelligence," 336.

20. Central Intelligence Agency, "The President's Daily Brief," 18 January 1969, accessed at http://www.foia.cia.gov/sites/default/files/document_conversions/1827265/DOC_0005976569.pdf, 22 December 2015.

21. G. Fred Albrecht, *A History of the Central Intelligence Bulletin* (Washington, DC: Central Intelligence Agency, 1967), 18–19, CIA Freedom of Information Act release to Dr. William Burr, accessed at http://nsarchive.gwu.edu/NSAEBB/NSAEBB116/albrecht.pdf, 22 December 2015.

22. Helgerson, *Getting to Know the President*, 57.

23. Ibid., 168.

24. Albrecht, *A History of the Central Intelligence Bulletin*, 1–2.

25. Helgerson, *Getting to Know the President*.

26. Ibid., 127.

27. Ibid., 169.

28. Walter Pincus, "Measuring a President's Approach on Foreign Policy, *Washington Post*, 16 January 2012, accessed at https://www.washingtonpost.com/world/national-security/measuring-a-presidents-approach-on-foreign-policy/2012/01/14/gIQANYv13P_story.html, 22 December 2015; Colin Clark, "Inside the President's Daily Briefing; DNI Moves with Care to Tablets," *Breaking Defense*, 21 April 2014, accessed at http://breakingdefense.com/2014/04/inside-the-presidents-daily-briefing-dni-moves-with-care-to-tablets/, 22 December 2015.

29. Johnson, "Glimpses into the Gems of American Intelligence"; Pincus, "Measuring a President's Approach on Foreign Policy"; and Adrian Wolfberg, "Communication Patterns Between the Briefer and the Policymaker," *International Journal of Intelligence and Counterintelligence* 27 (Fall 2014): 509–528.

30. Jervis, "Why Intelligence and Policymakers Clash"; and Johnson, "Glimpses into the Gems of American Intelligence."

31. Johnson, "Glimpses into the Gems of American Intelligence"; and Pincus, "Measuring a President's Approach on Foreign Policy."

32. Gardiner, "Dealing with Intelligence-Policy Disconnects."

33. Wolfberg, "Communication Patterns between the Briefer and the Policymaker."

34. Walter Lipmann, *Public Opinion* (New York: Harcourt, Brace and Co., 1922), 30.

35. James G. March and Herbert A. Simon, *Organizations* (New York: John Wiley, 1958), 168.

36. Wolfgang Iser, *The Act of Reading: A Theory of Aesthetic Response* (Baltimore: Johns Hopkins University Press, 1978), 166–167.

37. Hughes, "The Fate of Facts in the World of Men."

38. Hughes, "The Fate of Facts in the World of Men"; Heymann, "The Intelligence-Policy Relationship"; Betts, "Policy-Makers and Intelligence Analysts"; Gardiner, "Dealing with Intelligence-Policy Disconnects"; and Jervis, "Why Intelligence and Policymakers Clash."

39. Richard J. Kerr and Peter Dixon Davis, "Ronald Reagan and the President's Daily Brief," *Studies in Intelligence* 42 (Winter 1998–1999): 51–56; and Wolfberg, "Communication Patterns between the Briefer and the Policymaker."

40. Geert Hofstede, "The Cultural Relativity of Organizational Practices and Theories," *Journal of International Business Studies* 14 (Fall 1983): 75–89.

41. Geert Hofstede, "Motivation, Leadership, and Organization: Do American Theories Apply Abroad," *Organizational Dynamics* 9 (Summer 1980): 42–63.

42. James D. Barber, *The Presidential Character: Predicting Performance in the White House*, 4th ed. (Englewood Cliffs, NJ: Prentice Hall, 1992); Charles E. Snare, "Windows of Opportunity: When and How Can the Policy Analyst Influence the Policymaking During the Policy Process," *Review of Policy Research* 14 (September 1995): 407–430; and Steven J. Rubenzer, Thomas R. Faschingbauer, and Deniz S. Ones, "Assessing the U.S. Presidents Using the Revised NEO Personality Inventory," *Assessment* 7 (December 2000): 403–420.

43. Karl E. Weick, *Sensemaking in Organizations* (Thousand Oaks, CA: Sage, 1995), 14; Mirko Noordegraaf, "Professional Sense-Makers: Managerial Competencies amidst Ambiguity," *International Journal of Public Sector Management* 13 (July 2000): 319–332; and Matthew N. Beckmann, *Pushing the Agenda: Presidential Leadership in the U.S. Lawmaking, 1953–2004* (New York: Cambridge University Press, 2010), 37.

44. Beckmann, *Pushing the Agenda*, 37.

45. Noordegraaf, "Professional Sense-Makers."

46. While sensegiving characterizes *what* service *PDB* briefers provide, the reason for and method of *how* they do it are analogous to "informing" behaviors. The phenomenon of informing comes from the management literature; see, for example, Alistair Preston, "Interactions and Arrangements in the Process of Informing," *Accounting, Organizations and Society* 11 (1986): 521–540; Heath Colebach, Sam Horrocks, and Jeff Smith, "Executive Models of Informing—An Empirical Study," *Journal of Information Technology Theory and Application* 3 (2001): 21–32; and Matthew Hall, "Accounting Information and Managerial Work," *Accounting, Organizations and Society* 35 (2010): 301–315. Informing begins with the delivery of an organization's officially produced document—a product by the *official system*—to a decision maker. The purpose of the document is to provide the decision maker with information the organization believes the decision maker needs and wants, but in actuality, it does not provide all of what decision makers consider critical and essential information. As a result, the decision maker needs the information contextualized by acquiring additional information.

Empirical studies within management settings have shown that decision makers initiate the process of informing by talking with others, observing others, and sharing informal documentation with others—socially constructing information—to glean additional understanding. The reason decision makers initiate their own informing process is that they need to increase their understanding of the context of the official information and how to interpret the meaning of information for future decisions they cannot anticipate. See Martha S. Feldman and James G. March, "Information in Organizations as Signal and Symbol," *Administrative Science Quarterly* 26 (1981): 171–186; Preston, "Interactions and Arrangements in the Process of Informing"; and Hall, "Accounting Information and Managerial Work."

47. Fourteen currently employed intelligence officers with *PDB* briefer experience were interviewed between March and June 2011. Eleven were men and three were women. Their average federal employment tenure as intelligence officers prior to their selection as a *PDB* briefer was 18.4 years, with a standard deviation of 6.2 years. The length of a *PDB* briefer's tour varies, but the average for the 14 briefers was 17.3 months, with a standard deviation of 4.5 months. They were highly educated: of the 14, eight had a master's degree, one a doctorate, and the remaining five bachelor's degrees. Most degrees were in the social sciences. To find briefers to interview, the author knew one former *PDB* briefer through his personal social network and used a snowball approach to invite a briefer to introduce him to another. No *PDB* briefer who was asked declined to be interviewed. Each, in fact, looked forward to telling their story—an intense experience that was difficult to share with anyone not having the same experience—because they felt it had never been told. Each briefer was asked one question: "Please tell me about a typical day as a *PDB* briefer from the time you woke up to go to work until the time you left work." Most interviews lasted 90 minutes, and two lasted almost two hours. The briefers were guaranteed anonymity as well as anonymity of their association with a named policymaker or policymaker's position. Therefore, every attempt has been made here to ensure that briefers' identities or associations to policymakers have been protected. All gender references made by briefers in quotations presented in the article have been replaced with the gender-neutral phrase "the

office holder." There was no audio or video recording of the interviews since they all took place in secure government buildings. Only handwritten notes and verbatim quotations were taken. On any one day between 2007 and 2010, 15 *PDB* briefers were on duty. The 14 briefers interviewed for this study represent about 20 percent of the entire number of *PDB* briefers on duty during this time period, a large proportion of a sample to participate in qualitative research.

48. Kathy Charmaz, *Constructing Grounded Theory: A Practical Guide through Qualitative Analysis* (Thousand Oaks, CA: Sage, 2006), chap. 3.

49. L. Edna Rogers, "Relational Communication Theory," in Leslie A. Baxter and Dawn O. Braithwaite, eds., *Engaging Theories in Interpersonal Communication: Multiple Perspectives* (Los Angeles, CA: Sage, 2008), 335–336.

50. Gregory Bateson, "Information and Codification: A Philosophical Approach," in Jurgen Ruesch and Gregory Bateson, eds., *Communication: The Social Matrix of Psychiatry* (New York: W.W. Norton, 1951), 168–211.

51. Paul Watzlawick, Janet B. Bavelas, and Don D. Jackson, *Pragmatics of Human Communication: A Study of Interactional Patterns, Pathologies, and Paradoxes* (New York: W.W. Norton, 1967), 28–32.

52. Daniel Kahneman, *Thinking, Fast and Slow* (New York: Farrar, Straus and Giroux, 2011), 1–30.

53. Adrian Wolfberg, "Full-Spectrum Analysis: A New Way of Thinking for a New World," *Military Review* 86 (July/August 2006): 35–42; and Gregory F. Treverton, "Risks and Riddles," *Smithsonian Magazine*, June 2007, 98–102.

54. Wilder, "An Educated Consumer Is Our Best Customer," 23–24.

55. Mark L. Knapp and Judith A. Hall, *Nonverbal Communication in Human Interaction*, 5th ed. (Boston, MA: Wadsworth, 2002), 94.

56. See C.S. Lewis, "The Inner Ring," Memorial Lecture, King's College, University of London, 1944, accessed at http://www.lewissociety.org/innerring.php, 20 March 2016, for an insightful analysis of the natural temptation to be inside the "inner circle," or what Lewis called the "inner ring."

57. Dale E. Zand, "Collateral Organization: A New Change Strategy," *Journal of Applied Behavioral Science* 10 (January 1974): 63–89.

58. Zand, "Collateral Organization"; Barry A. Stein and Rosabeth M. Kanter, "Building the Parallel Organization: Creating Mechanisms for Permanent Quality of Work Life," *Journal of Applied Behavioral Science* 16

(July 1980): 371–388; and Thomas F. Hawk and Dale E. Zand, "Parallel Organization: Policy Formulation, Learning, and Interdivision Integration," *Journal of Applied Behavioral Science* 50 (September 2014): 307–336.

59. Robert Jervis, *Why Intelligence Fails: Lessons from the Iranian Revolution and the Iraq War* (Ithaca, NY: Cornell University Press, 2010), 184.

60. Wendy K. Smith and Marianne W. Lewis, "Toward a Theory of Paradox: A Dynamic Equilibrium Model of Organizing," *Academy of Management Review* 36 (April 2011): 381–403.

61. Maitlis and Lawrence, "Triggers and Enablers of Sensegiving in Organizations," 76–77.

From Adrian Wolfberg, "Intelligence and the President's Daily Brief," *Political Science Quarterly* 132/2 (2017): 225-258. Reproduced with permission.

II

INTELLIGENCE COLLECTION

Hamlet: "If thou art privy to thy country's fate
Which happily foreknowing may avoid,
O speak!"

—Shakespeare, *Hamlet*, 1.1.134–136

Professional intelligence officers often think of their primary mission of information collection and analysis in terms of an "intelligence cycle" (see Figure II.1). The CIA defines the cycle as "the process by which information is acquired, converted into intelligence, and made available to policymakers" (CIA 1983, 17). The first phase in the cycle is planning and direction—that is, the identification of what kinds of information need to be collected ("requirements"), which agencies will do the collecting, and what means ("tradecraft" or modus operandi) will be used. These are questions for senior management, and the top senior manager in the U.S. intelligence community is the Director of National Intelligence (DNI), whose office is located at Liberty Crossing in northern Virginia near Arlington.

Once these decisions about planning and direction are made—and they are driven chiefly by a sense of threats to the United States—the collection of information begins by way of machines (surveillance satellites, for example) and human agents. Then the acquired information is processed. This processing step can involve the translation of materials into English if originally in a

foreign tongue or, say, the enlargement of photographs taken by satellite or U-2 cameras. Once the material is in a format an analyst can work with, the job is to make sense of the information,

FIGURE II.1 A depiction of the intelligence cycle. *Source: Fact Book on Intelligence*, Office of Public Affairs, Central Intelligence Agency (October 1993): 14.

bringing insight to "raw" data—what we mean by *analysis* (or what the British call *assessment*). Finally, the evaluated information must be disseminated in a timely manner to policy officials in the White House and elsewhere. It must be accurate and relevant to the current issues of the day, as well as free of bias.

The purpose of the intelligence cycle is to provide policymakers with useful knowledge to assist them in weighing decision options. As the CIA puts it, "Intelligence is knowledge and foreknowledge of the world around us—the prelude to Presidential decision and action" (CIA 1983, 17). The seemingly simple sweep of the cycle, as depicted in Figure II.1, is in fact a complicated series of interactions among, on the one hand, intelligence officers and their organizations (the producers of information) and, on the other hand, policymakers (the consumers of information). As information moves from aerial surveillance platforms or agents ("assets") in the field back to the CIA and other intelligence agencies in the United States and then on to policy councils, many things can go wrong. As discussed in the articles contained in this part of the book, the collection phase alone is replete with challenges, beginning with decisions about which nations or groups the United States wishes to target for gathering information.

TARGETING

From the vantage point of an astronaut in space, the world may seem small, and it is indeed becoming smaller, in a sense, as advancing technology brings about a decrease in communications and travel time between continents. Yet from the vantage point of an intelligence agency, the world remains vast, with nearly 200 sovereign nations and a wide galaxy of groups, factions, and cells spread across the globe—a fragmentation greatly accentuated by the end of the Cold War and the splintering of the bipolar world of that era. No nation—not even one like the affluent United States—can hope for perfect transparency into all these nations and factions. Priorities must be set. So nations and groups with intelligence organizations engage in "threat assessment" calculations, establishing a list of places and people that are especially threatening or that present an opportunity to advance national interests. These targets are ranked from high to low priority—say, from the high of the al-Qaeda terrorist organization to the low of Japanese fishing boats

off America's shores suspected of harvesting illegal quotas of salmon. This assessment—which can lead to heated debate among policymakers and intelligence managers—is important, for it becomes a blueprint for spending priorities with respect to intelligence collection.

During the Cold War (1947–1991), the United States had one preeminent intelligence target: the Soviet Union and its Communist allies. This target accounted for upward of 70 percent of the U.S. intelligence budget (which tends to run at about 10 percent of the overall defense budget in any given year). The intelligence budget reached a high point of some $30 billion during the Reagan administration, when the president declared the U.S.S.R. an "evil empire" and directed the intelligence agencies to ratchet up a covert war against global Communism (especially in Nicaragua and Afghanistan). Today, the world has grown more complex, and intelligence targeting is more diffuse and even more expensive: costing more than $44 billion, according to newspaper accounts. As President Bill Clinton's first director of central intelligence, R. James Woolsey, observed, the Soviet dragon had been slain, but "we live now in a jungle filled with a bewildering variety of poisonous snakes" (Woolsey 1993).

Throughout the Clinton years, the primary target was not a single nation or group but a more generic global threat: the proliferation of weapons of mass destruction (WMD), or so-called NBC (nuclear, biological, chemical) weapons that could destroy thousands—even millions—of people in a brief interlude of horror. The events of September 11, 2001, had a profound effect on reassessing America's threat status, as the perpetrators of the catastrophic attacks against New York City and the Pentagon catapulted their organization, al-Qaeda (and its patron, the Taliban regime in Afghanistan), to Intelligence Priority No. 1. Stunning events of violence can quickly change America's sense of threat, leading to a rapid reorientation of intelligence resources toward new requirements and "tasking."

Often such events seem to come out of the blue, as did the Japanese attack against Pearl Harbor and the September 11 attacks—but in both of these instances there were early warnings that were missed, ignored, or lost in the labyrinths of the intelligence bureaucracy. Sometimes the failure to anticipate danger is not so much related to mistakes in intelligence collection as it is to the inability or unwillingness of policymakers to take action on the information they have been provided. In 1995, the

CIA warned the Clinton administration of "aerial terrorism" in which airplanes might be used by terrorists to destroy skyscrapers in the United States or abroad, but policymakers did little to enhance airport security (Johnson 2002).

As they examine collected information, intelligence officials and policymakers can also suffer a failure of imagination as to what it means. "The danger is not that we shall read the signals and indicators with too little skill," Thomas C. Schelling (1962) noted, looking back at the Pearl Harbor attack. "The danger," he continued, "is in a poverty of expectations—a routine obsession with a few dangers that may be familiar rather than likely"—in sum, a "great national failure to anticipate."

Rwanda provides a memorable example of how unanticipated disasters can leap quickly from the bottom to the top of America's international threat-assessment priorities. In 1993, a genocidal civil war suddenly erupted in this African nation. "When I became Secretary of Defense [in 1993], I served several months without ever giving Rwanda a thought," recalled Les Aspin of the Clinton administration. "Then for several weeks, that's all I thought about. After that, it fell abruptly off the screen again and I never again thought about Rwanda" (quoted in Johnson 2002, 20). The list of "shooting stars" or "flavors of the month," as intelligence professionals sometimes refer to these sudden crises, has included in recent decades such places as Grenada, Panama, Yugoslavia, and Somalia. All too often, the United States has had inadequate information about these locations, having focused its intelligence resources on more obvious threats from "rogue nations" such as North Korea and Iran.

TYPES OF INTELLIGENCE

SUBSTANTIVE INTELLIGENCE

Policymakers and intelligence professionals must decide, too, what substantive types of intelligence should be collected: military, political, economic, or cultural. Respectively, *military intelligence* might involve a concentration on the worldwide flow of weapons of mass destruction or, more narrowly, on the efficiencies of North Korean missile fuel. *Political intelligence* can run the gamut from gathering information on presidential candidates in a French national election to sorting out the plethora of party factions in the Russian *duma*. For *economic intelligence*, U.S. officials may want to have information on the likely strategies of the Organization of Petroleum Exporting Countries (OPEC) or on the degree to which Afghanistan in the wake of the Taliban regime has a chance of building a viable economic infrastructure. Regarding *cultural intelligence*, officials may want to know the extent to which high vodka consumption is ravaging Russian society or the destabilizing effects of the AIDS epidemic on the leadership in countries (such as Zaire) that are heavily afflicted by this global pandemic.

Among these choices, the military dimension has been in the forefront of considerations about the funding of intelligence collection. In the United States, about 85 percent of the intelligence dollar is spent on the military intelligence agencies (although these agencies do collect some information relevant to the other substantive areas). Critics of intelligence collection in the United States have complained that the tasking is tilted too much toward support to military operations (SMO, in Pentagonese)—especially protecting the war fighter in the foxhole or at sea, or the pilot in the cockpit of a fighter plane—at the expense of support to diplomatic operations (SDO), that is, gathering "diplomatic intelligence" (political, economic, and cultural information) that might help prevent the outbreak of war in the first place.

"The traditional idea of intelligence is the spy who provides the enemy's war plans," noted a CIA memorandum written during the Cold War. Yet, as the memo correctly argued, despite the pressures toward SMO:

> Intelligence is concerned not only with war plans, but with all the external concerns of our government. It must deal with the pricing debates of OPEC and the size of this year's Soviet crop. . . . It is concerned with Soviet strength along the Sino-Soviet boarder, with the intricacies of Chinese politics, with the water supply in the Middle East, with the quality of Soviet computers and its impact on our own export controls, with the narcotics trade in Southeast Asia, even with the struggle for control of Portuguese Timor. (Senior CIA analyst, declassified by the Church Committee, 1975a)

CURRENT AND RESEARCH INTELLIGENCE

Officials must also decide whether they seek information about what happened yesterday and what is likely to happen today and tomorrow (*current intelligence*), such as answers to the questions, "What is the threat against the U.S. embassy in country X?" and

"Where will Al Qaeda strike next?," or information of a deeper kind that provides a longer perspective and more nuanced understanding of world affairs (*research intelligence*, addressing such questions as, "How does the Japanese public view North Korean missile developments?" and "What is the future of democracy in Egypt?"). Most officials desire current intelligence, and they want precision—not vague warnings about a possible attack somewhere, sometime. This kind of information can be hard to obtain and can often be wrong. Research intelligence poses its own set of difficulties inherent to any deep probe into a topic, including the costs of time and money required to carry out the research. Further, research intelligence is often unread by busy policymakers who shun lengthy, footnoted tomes. Yet, in-depth intelligence is vital for a more meaningful understanding of world events. Unfortunately, it is being given short shrift as increasingly resources are directed toward current intelligence, anticipating and trying to answer questions that flare up in the daily inboxes of harried policymakers.

SECRETS AND MYSTERIES

An added dimension of intelligence collection is the distinction made by intelligence professionals between secrets and mysteries. *Secrets* are empirical facts that, with luck and perseverance, the United States might be able to acquire—steal, if necessary—such as information about the number of Chinese nuclear submarines, their range, and the location of their docking sites. *Mysteries* are the more imponderable questions faced by intelligence officers and policymakers, such as the likely longevity of the current Chinese leadership, or how the BREXIT vote in 2016—the British decision to leave the European Union—will transform London's relations with Paris. No one really knows the answers to mysteries; their importance, though, warrants grappling with possible outcomes regardless, and a well-trained analyst can often come up with helpful insights for policymakers to consider as they contemplate the future. The collection phase of the intelligence cycle concentrates on unearthing secrets, leaving the sifting of tea leaves about mysteries to analysts steeped in the history and culture of foreign lands.

COLLECTION METHODS

After deciding what kind of information is required to assist foreign policy decision making, officials ask the intelligence agencies to gather the desired data.

Here we enter the domain of the "ints"—that is, the various intelligence methods used for collecting information around the world (Berkowitz & Goodman 2000; Lowenthal 2003; Shulsky & Schmitt 1993).

OSINT

The most mundane of the ints, though in some ways the most important, is simply tapping into public sources of information—open-source intelligence, or OSINT. Authorities report that about 80 percent of all the information found in intelligence reports during the Cold War was based on data acquired by traditional library research, such as digging through Soviet and Chinese newspapers. Today the OSINT figure is even higher, approaching 95 percent, as Russian, Chinese, and other formerly closed societies have become more open. The Internet has also taken on importance as a wellspring of information, and television and radio stations (along with periodicals, newspapers, and social media) are proliferating around the globe. Ironically, in spite of these burgeoning open sources, intelligence analysts often eschew publicly available data in favor of the more titillating and exotic information that comes to their desks from overseas clandestine sources—even though they are trained to search open sources first, then they turn to clandestine sources to fill in the missing pieces of the puzzle.

On the clandestine side of intelligence collection, the ints (as introduced in the introduction to Part 1) include GEOINT, SIGINT, MASINT, and, last but not least, HUMINT. These acronyms, widely used by intelligence professionals, stand for geospatial intelligence, signals intelligence, measurement and signature intelligence, and human intelligence.

GEOINT

Imagery, or geospatial intelligence (GEOINT), refers to photography—the snapshots taken by reconnaissance airplanes such as the U-2 or unmanned drones such as the Global Hawk, as well as by surveillance satellites that revolve around the earth at altitudes ranging from a few hundred miles to over 200,000 miles in deep space (either in polar orbit, sweeping around the earth, or in geosynchronous orbit, hovering over a particular country or region). Today, the photographs from satellites do not even have to be developed; they are sent digitally to U.S. ground stations and fed quickly to policymakers and warriors who need the information in as close to real time as possible. The picture resolution is impressive, capable of distinguishing a football from a jackrabbit.

GEOINT (until recently known as IMINT, or imagery intelligence) is much sought after and appreciated by policymakers when it can display irrefutable evidence about an adversary's hostile actions against the United States, as when the U.S. ambassador to the United Nations, Adlai E. Stevenson, was able during the 1962 Cuban missile crisis to convince American and world opinion of Soviet provocation in the Western hemisphere by laying on the table clear U-2 photos of Russian missiles in Cuba. More recently, in 2003 Secretary of State Colin Powell used satellite photographs to argue the U.S. case that Iraq still possessed chemical weapons capabilities and had permitted the establishment of a terrorist training camp within its nation—although in this instance, confirmation of the intelligence reports proved elusive.

Imagery is hardly a panacea, even though it attracts the lion's share of the U.S. intelligence budget. (Just the launching of a Greyhound bus–sized intelligence satellite can cost $1 billion.) For starters, half the world is covered with clouds at any moment, and, naturally, darkness is a hindrance as well (although the United States has made great strides in developing cameras that can overcome these obstacles to some extent). More difficult to deal with has been the tidal wave of images flowing back to the United States, cloudy weather and nocturnal conditions notwithstanding— some four hundred images a day. A shortage of photo interpreters means that only a small fraction of these pictures are carefully studied, although the rise of Artificial Intelligence (AI) and computational power will eventually allow analysts to sift through unimaginable amounts of data.

Further, adversaries have grown skilled at hiding their activities, as demonstrated by the surprise nuclear tests in India during 1994 (Johnson 2001). Indian officials had determined exactly when U.S. satellite cameras would be passing over their nuclear testing facility near Pokharan in the Rajasthan Desert. In synchrony with these flights (every three days), Indian nuclear scientists camouflaged their activities. Ironically, U.S. officials had explicitly informed the Indian government about the timing of U.S. satellite coverage for South Asia, in hopes of impressing on them the futility of trying to conceal test activity. Even without this unintended assistance, however, the Indians could have calculated the cycles for themselves, as even amateur astronomers can track the orbits of spy satellites. (Because of their very large collection arrays, GEOINT and SIGINT satellites are easily observed with the naked eye). The Indians also adroitly used deception techniques to fool intelligence photo interpreters. For instance, ground cables normally moved into place for a nuclear test were nowhere to be seen in U.S. satellite photographs of the site; the Indians had devised less visible ignition techniques. The Indians also stepped up activities at their far-removed missile-testing range in an attempt to draw the attention of spy cameras away from the nuclear testing site.

In 2002, when U.S. troops first entered eastern Afghanistan's rugged Shah-i-Kot Valley as part of Operation Anaconda in search of al-Qaeda terrorists and their Taliban hosts, the military command had at its disposal the best GEOINT platforms available: satellites, reconnaissance airplanes, and Predator drones. Nonetheless, "despite these high-tech systems, the intelligence estimate failed to accurately portray the enemy's size, location, principal weapons and course of action," noted *New York Times* reporter Sean Naylor (2003, A13).

GEOINT has other liabilities. Satellite and U-2 cameras are unable to see through roofs into buildings or basements where chemical and biological weapons may be manufactured. Even large-scale nuclear weapons programs can be hidden from the prying cameras, as the North Koreans have demonstrated by locating their nuclear weapons operations in deep underground caverns. Moreover, while the spy cameras can provide some idea of an adversary's military capabilities, they have nothing to say about the intentions of these adversaries.

SIGINT

To supplement imagery, nations also rely on the gathering of signals intelligence, especially the electronic communications that travel between telephones and personal computers. At the United Nations in 2003, Secretary Powell also played the transcripts of confidential telephone conversations between Iraqi officials to demonstrate further that they were trying to deceive UN inspectors and the world. Once again, however, we run into the problem of information overload, as a firehose of SIGINT transcripts from around the world overwhelms the ability of U.S. translators and analysts to keep up with the torrent. According to a recent estimate (Millis 1998), only about 10 percent of all SIGINT transcripts are examined by analysts. An intercepted September 10, 2001, telephone conversation between al-Qaeda terrorists indicating that a major attack would occur against the United States the next day ("Tomorrow is zero hour") was not translated until September 12, the day after the attacks.

In addition, adversaries have learned to use deception against SIGINT just as they do against GEOINT. Reportedly, in 2002 Bin Laden handed his cell phone to his bodyguard and had him travel away from where the al-Qaeda leader was heading in his escape from Afghanistan, thereby drawing U.S. intelligence officers in the wrong direction. People tell lies over the telephone, too; intercepts cannot be taken at face value but are sometimes a source of disinformation. Further, the current switch in technology from airwave transmissions of telephone conversations to underground optic fibers ("light pipes") has significantly complicated the science of intercepting telephone conversations. Still, SIGINT has had its moments of success and is highly valued by policymakers, as when intercepted communications in an African nation recently saved the lives of a U.S. ambassador and his family on their way to a local airport by tipping them off to a planned ambush by an indigenous rebel faction. The ambassador altered his travel route, and he and his family escaped the trap.

In 2005, SIGINT became controversial inside the United States when the *New York Times* revealed that the George W. Bush administration had bypassed legal warrant procedures for conducting national security wiretaps (required by the Foreign Intelligence Surveillance Act of 1978), and again in 2013 when a major leak of classified material by a government contractor, Edward J. Snowden, showed that the National Security Agency was engaging in the widespread collection of "metadata" on the source and duration of telephone calls and Internet communications made by virtually all American citizens, and was monitoring the personal cell phone of the German chancellor.

MASINT

Weapons systems, such as ballistic missiles and nuclear warheads, give off emissions as they are being tested, and factories produce gases and waste products. Measurement and signature intelligence can provide information about these and other forms of weapons systems and can add significantly to America's understanding of an adversary's military preparedness. It can also reveal what is being made inside a factory: normal pharmaceuticals or lethal chemical or biological substances.

HUMINT

The oldest form of spying (and some say the world's second oldest profession) is the use of human intelligence—the cloak-and-dagger agents of James Bond fame. These spies are not Americans but rather local assets recruited by U.S. intelligence officers, who then serve as their "case officers." To avoid the kinds of concealment and deception against GEOINT and SIGINT as practiced by the Indians and the North Koreans, the United States would like to have an asset inside the Indian test bunkers or within the North Korean caverns. A well-placed asset might also be able to ascertain whether a suspicious factory is making aspirin or sarin (a chemical nerve agent)—a distinction that distant satellites and U-2s are unable to make. Particularly helpful in today's world would be having an asset in attendance at a terrorist cell's strategy session. Afterward, using rapid electronic communications from a palm-held computer to a satellite and down to his CIA case officer, the spy could secretly transmit the plans for a terrorist attack against the United States, its allies, or its overseas interests.

These wishes are difficult to fulfill, since access to North Korean caverns or terrorist strategy sessions is, to say the least, difficult. North Korea has sophisticated security systems, and successful terrorist cells painstakingly vet their recruits—especially those who have access to critical plans. Beyond questions of access, spies can be highly unreliable. Sometimes they fabricate reports just to justify their stipend from the CIA. Of 200 asset reports on missile sightings in Cuba during the crisis of 1962, only six proved accurate (Powers 1979, 447). Sobering, too, is the fact that all of America's assets in Cuba and East Germany during the Cold War turned out to be double agents, loyal not to their CIA case officers but to their own Communist governments (Gates 1996, 560).

Spies are often the most venal individuals in a society, with dubious histories of human rights abuses—perhaps even with criminal records as murderers. Though sometimes necessary for America's security, assets are unlikely to be boy scouts or nuns (as realists like to chide those squeamish about the business of espionage). The employment of unsavory characters by the United States raises serious ethical questions, however, about the extent to which the United States should be in alliance with drug dealers, liars, thieves, and assassins—even if they can occasionally provide useful information.

Despite the controversies and drawbacks associated with the use of human assets, the United States has had some notable HUMINT successes. Prior to the missile crisis, for example, the Soviet military intelligence officer Colonel Oleg Vladimirovich

Penkovsky provided valuable information about Soviet missiles, including operational manuals. These data, including drawings of missile bases in the U.S.S.R., helped CIA analysts discern the presence of Soviet ballistic missiles in Cuba.

ALL-SOURCE FUSION

None of these collection methods are perfect. At best, each may provide some pieces to the puzzle that the intelligence agencies have been asked to solve. The objective is to use them all and hope for a synergism among them—an "all-source fusion," in intelligence lingo—that will provide policymakers with a more comprehensive understanding of the world and especially of our adversaries. As the United States has become more sophisticated in its TECHINT capabilities (a term often used by intelligence professionals in reference to the more technical "ints": GEOINT, SIGINT, MASINT), the nation's collection successes have continued to improve, and the country is generally regarded as the most effective gatherer of intelligence in the world— even in the face of a rising ability of nations and groups to evade surveillance and despite the striking failure of the intelligence agencies to warn the American people of the September 11 attacks.

The weakest link in the collection chain has been HUMINT, and in the aftermath of the 9/11 tragedy and the mistakes about WMDs in Iraq in 2002, the United States is now engaged in a crash program to improve this part of the equation by hiring new case officers, assets, analysts, managers, and translators who understand the language and culture of places such as Afghanistan, Iraq, and Pakistan, a part of the world largely ignored throughout most of the Cold War. Another weakness has been the lack of adequate sharing of information among the intelligence agencies and with policy officials—a defect that will require significant organizational and cultural changes throughout the government, further complicated by the creation in 2003 of a poorly defined Department of Homeland Security that has been plagued in its early days with management and organizational confusion throughout the government. Although a poorly defined Department of Homeland Security got off to a slow start following its creation in 2003, it is making progress in facilitating both law enforcement and foreign intelligence sharing across federal, state, local, and tribal governments and agencies.

THE READINGS

The articles that follow describe the process of intelligence collection. Arthur S. Hulnick, an accomplished practitioner and student of intelligence, begins this section with a discussion of how reality deviates from the idealized description of intelligence production depicted by the intelligence cycle. Instead of a cycle, Hulnick suggests that the production of finished intelligence occurs along two ongoing and parallel processes involving collection and analysis and that structured collaboration between policymakers and analysts is rare. Intelligence support to ongoing law enforcement, counterterrorism, and counterintelligence operations is characterized by other patterns of interaction that have little to do with a "cycle." Hulnick suggests that it is time to develop new concepts to describe the process of creating finished intelligence.

Our second essay describes human source intelligence—the stuff of spy novels and movies— placing it in strategic context over the last half-century. As Frederick P. Hitz notes, the nature and effectiveness of HUMINT is influenced not only by the target environment where agents must operate but also by changing political attitudes toward espionage and covert action. The domestic and international setting is not always conducive to the conduct of human source intelligence, and collection shortcomings are often punctuated by some notable foreign policy failures and lapses in national security. Hitz highlights the latest challenge facing intelligence managers: penetrating the new threat posed by non-state actors.

Although open-source information is sometimes dismissed by intelligence professionals who point to espionage or technical intelligence as the best way to pry into another society, Stephen C. Mercado highlights in the third essay the important role played by open-source information. Data gathered from open sources can be used to target more precise collection activities or to place information gathered using clandestine means in a broader context. Mercado warns his audience, however, that the skills required to be an accomplished open-source analyst need to be cultivated. Without language skills and an understanding of other cultures, it is difficult to exploit the wealth of data made available by the information revolution.

Our final essay, written by Sir David Omand, Jamie Bartlett, and Carl Miller, provides an introduction to the latest intelligence collection method: social media intelligence (or SOCMINT).

3. THE INTELLIGENCE CYCLE

ARTHUR S. HULNICK

Although just about every book on intelligence offers the intelligence cycle as a model for the production of finished intelligence, insiders know that the model is at best a stylized version of reality. It captures the functions that more or less have to occur to produce intelligence, but it has little to do with how policymakers, intelligence managers, and analysts go about accomplishing those tasks. In this chapter, a scholar with an insider's perspective suggests that the notion of a "cycle" is misleading when it comes to describing how intelligence is actually produced.

No concept is more deeply enshrined in the literature than that of the "intelligence cycle." I studied the intelligence cycle as an undergraduate in Sherman Kent's book on strategic intelligence and then later when I attended the U.S. Air Force Intelligence School in 1957.[1] In 1965, in the training courses required by the Central Intelligence Agency (CIA), I studied it yet again. When it came time to start writing about intelligence, a practice I began in my later years in the CIA, I realized that there were serious problems with the intelligence cycle.[2] It is really not a very good description of the ways in which the intelligence process works. Additionally, it ignores two main parts of intelligence work, counterintelligence and covert action. There is an alternative view.

THE FIRST STEP

Let us start at the beginning and look at what is wrong. The notion that policy makers, or intelligence consumers, as they are sometimes called, provide guidance to intelligence managers to begin the intelligence process is incorrect. Policy consumers do sometimes indicate their main concerns to intelligence managers, but often they assume that the intelligence system will alert them to problems, or provide judgments about the future. Consumers will sometimes tell intelligence managers what they are worried about, or the direction in which they intend to take policy—but not always.

Still, it is usually not too difficult for intelligence managers to learn what policy makers are up to, but the managers often have to take the initiative to obtain the information. If intelligence managers at various levels are in touch with their policy counterparts, this sharing of information may work quite well. Over the years, intelligence managers have tried to systematize this process by asking policy officials to provide specifics on their concerns. In the Carter administration, for example, a system of National Intelligence Topics (NITs) was created as a way of soliciting guidance for intelligence. Later, they were called Key Intelligence Questions (KIQs). In some cases, when policy consumers failed to submit NITs or KIQs, managers had to resort to sending policy officials a list of topics, asking them to cross out the ones they thought were not necessary, or adding those they wanted to add to the list. Even then, the lists were sometimes ignored.

In the end, intelligence managers have to make decisions about the subjects that ought to be covered. Often, this is driven by world events. But, none of this provides guidance for intelligence collection. The guidance comes from within the system. Secretary of Defense Donald Rumsfeld, in the George W. Bush administration, is reported to have once said that "we don't know what we don't know," but that is usually not the case. Intelligence managers often know what gaps exist in the intelligence database, derived from intelligence collectors, and analysts. Filling the gaps is what drives the intelligence collection process, not guidance from policy makers. Thus, the first step in the intelligence cycle is incorrect in reality.

THE SECOND STEP

The second step is equally incorrect. Collection managers cannot wait for guidance in regard to gaps in the intelligence data base to begin the collection process. The gaps will be filled once the collection process is under way. For example, in running espionage operations, commonly called HUMINT (for human intelligence), it may take months or years to find a person who has access to the information needed and is willing to be recruited as a spy. The same may be true for technical collection sensors. Satellites in space, which make up many of the sensor platforms, are not nearly as flexible as managers would wish. Thus, anticipating the intended targets cannot be overlooked. For example, during the British confrontation with Argentina over the Falkland Islands, the United States could not help the British with space imagery because the satellite, programmed to observe the Soviet Union at that time, only passed over the Falklands at night.

Of course, with the use of unmanned aerial vehicles, imagery collection has become more easily refocused on targets of opportunity, but the unmanned aircraft may still not be in the right place when they are needed. Even open source intelligence (OSINT), which has been given new life in recent years because of the proliferation of information on the Internet, requires planning to ensure access to needed material. Intelligence managers need sophisticated software to mine the data because there is so much of it.

THE REAL DRIVERS

For all these reasons, intelligence managers, and not policy officials, are the real drivers of the intelligence collection process. Clearly, intelligence moves from collection to analysis, as the intelligence cycle holds, but analysts do not always need new intelligence material to understand world events. The data base is already so large that a competent analyst could write about most events without any more than open sources to spur the process. The incremental addition of new intelligence from human sources or technical sensors may modify the analytic process but rarely drives it.

The job of the analyst is, in part, to evaluate raw material and put it in perspective. The analyst receives intelligence material from a variety of sources, including media reports, official reports from other government agencies, as well as reports from the intelligence collection process. In my experience as a practicing analyst in the military and in the CIA, raw reports from human sources or technical sensors are sometimes fragmentary, biased, contradictory, or just plain wrong. In order to analyze the data, the analyst compares the new material with the existing data base and previous analysis. Hanging a finished product—whether it is current reporting or a longer range estimate—on one source usually does not work well. This is apparently what happened in the case of the estimate on weapons of mass destruction (WMD) in Iraq that helped trigger the invasion of that country. The estimate was based, in part, on the reporting of one rather poor and unreliable source. The estimate turned out to be quite wrong, as we now know.[3]

OPERATING IN PARALLEL

A better way of looking at the relationship of intelligence collection and intelligence analysis is to think of the two processes as operating in parallel rather than sequentially. The two processes are coequal in terms of utility. It is important to note as well that raw reporting from the collection process, set up into standardized formats, usually goes to policy officials as well as to analysts at about the same time. Though this may not always be true in other intelligence systems, it is certainly true in the United States. Whereas senior policy officials may not see a great deal of the raw reporting, there are usually watch centers at the various policy agencies that screen the raw reporting and send forward the most interesting ones.

Unfortunately, as I have already noted, some of this raw intelligence may be incomplete, contradictory, or just wrong. Policy officials sometimes take the reporting as having been judged and evaluated. Thus, I have heard officials say that the CIA has reported an event, when in fact what the officials have seen is an unevaluated agent report passed along to them by their watch centers. It is not possible to stop this flow of raw reporting. As Bob Gates, the former Director of the CIA once noted to me, once the spigot is opened, it is not possible to close it, even though allowing consumers to have raw reporting at about the same time as the analysts receive them creates some serious problems for the analysts. Collection managers often take a different view. They believe they are doing a great service to the policy community by providing this raw reporting. If the intelligence cycle really worked, the circulation of raw reports to policy officials would not happen.

A MAJOR PROBLEM

Since intelligence collection and intelligence analysis operate in parallel and should be co-equal, one would expect that there would be a great deal of information sharing between the two. Regrettably, this is not always the case. Because of restrictions of information sharing, psychological barriers, fears of compromising sources, and security concerns, the intelligence collection process and the intelligence analytic process not only operate in parallel, they are sometimes quite independent of each other. This is a major problem.

When I first joined the CIA, I was assigned on a temporary basis to an office in the Directorate of Plans (DDP), later renamed the Directorate of Operations (DO), and in 2005, renamed yet again as the National Clandestine Service (NCS). My job was to deal with incoming reports from the field. When an interesting report came in one day, I asked my boss if we should alert the relevant analyst about it. He rejected the idea, saying that our job was to send reports like it to the White House, and not to the Directorate of Intelligence, since analysts were not worth the attention. I was shocked. Later, when I became an analyst, I did my best to establish good relations with my operational colleagues, but there were issues.

BARRIERS TO COMMUNICATION

In those days there were physical barriers, manned by armed guards, to prevent analysts and operations officers from visiting each other's offices. Later, the physical barriers were removed, but the psychological ones remained. Operations people feared that somehow analysts would mishandle reports from the field and reveal the identity of clandestine sources. Analysts mistrusted operations officers because they were thought to be devious and untrustworthy. This mistrust was kindled in part because analysts in those days tended to be introverts who found the extroverted personality of the typical operations officers to be abrasive. Operations people tended to think that the introverted analysts were "wimps."

Over the years these stereotypes have largely been overcome, but recent efforts to increase communication between analysts and operators by colocating them have not always been successful. Agency managers have pushed analysts to take tours overseas with field stations, but it is more difficult for an operations officer to serve a tour as an analyst.

Similar issues may not arise in other intelligence agencies unless they have co-equal collection and analysis components.

The Defense Intelligence Agency (DIA), for example, was immune to this sort of "stovepipe" problem because it was mostly an analytic rather than collection agency. As Defense HUMINT grows, perhaps the same problem will arise. The National Security Agency (NSA) and the National Geospatial Intelligence Agencies (NGIA) are devoted mostly to collection, but they tend to be tightly compartmentalized, creating a different kind of "stovepipe" problem. In theory, all the intelligence agencies should share raw data and coordinate analysis, but for a variety of reasons they do not always do so. This was one of the main critiques of both the 9/11 Commission and the commission investigating the intelligence failure surrounding the estimate on WMD.

A MIXED BAG

There is a tendency among intelligence agencies to hold back the most sensitive and exciting reports until the agency's leaders have been able to deliver the reports to senior policy officials, thus highlighting the skill and cleverness of their people and "scoring points" with the officials. One effort to spur interagency communications has been the establishment of centers, where all the agencies have representation and where their representatives can easily talk with their counterparts, even informally, to discuss events and incoming intelligence. The establishment of these centers has been something of a mixed bag. We know from the 9/11 investigations that the then-existing counterterrorism center (CTC) was not a place where all information was shared.[4]

Now, efforts at intelligence reform have "morphed" the CTC into a National Counterterrorism Center (NCTC), controlled by the new Director of National Intelligence (DNI). Will that spur the agencies into more easily sharing their best and most sensitive data? It would be nice to think so, but experience shows that this does not always happen, even at the highest level.

THE FINAL STAGES

In the final stages of the intelligence cycle finished intelligence, broken down into a variety of products, emerges from the analytic process. It is supposed to be delivered to policy officials—the literature refers to this delivery as dissemination—and then policy officials either make decisions or create further requirements and the cycle starts over again. This, too, is a distortion of what really happens. Much of this depends on the kind of intelligence product that is being delivered. These products include warning intelligence, in which consumers are alerted to "breaking news," current intelligence to update consumers on world events on which they already have some knowledge, in-depth studies on particular situations or issues, and forecasts of the future, the estimate. All products are received and used in a different way, but none of them really drive the policy process.

Warning intelligence is supposed to alert policy officials to breaking world situations, especially those for which they may have to take action. Both intelligence managers and policy consumers hate surprise. It is embarrassing for intelligence when the system misses an event about which it should have had information. For example, the CIA failed to detect the fact that the Indian government planned to conduct a nuclear test in 1998. Later investigations revealed that this was both a collection and an analysis failure. The CIA had no assets it could tap in India at that time, and the Indian analyst at the CIA had somehow missed the fact that the Indian prime minister had declared his intention to hold the tests. Despite the fact that there was little the U.S. government could do to stop the tests, policy officials were nonetheless outraged at this failure.[5]

Even greater outrage was directed at the entire intelligence community for its failure to detect the 9/11 terrorist attack on the United States. This has been exhaustively examined and has led to the restructuring of the intelligence system. Yet, there is considerable evidence that there was little that might have been done to avert the disaster. But, it illustrates the point that policy officials expect the intelligence system to be all-knowing, all-seeing, and always correct. As Richard Betts pointed out many years ago, intelligence failure is probably inevitable.[6]

Warning of crisis should come early enough so that policy officials can have time to develop some kind of considered response. Unfortunately, the warning may come so late that it is really an alert that the crisis has already begun. Using a system that is composed of warning centers at major military commands, tied in to warning centers at all the intelligence agencies and in policy departments in Washington, and taking advantage of the proliferation of twenty-four-hour TV and Internet outlets, the warning network rarely misses the start of a crisis, and it is then able to reach out to decision makers quite rapidly. When the decision makers ask intelligence officers how they should respond to the crisis, typically intelligence officers decline to provide advice, thus staying clear of the policy process.

THE MOST USEFUL PRODUCT

Current or daily intelligence is the most ubiquitous of all types of intelligence products, delivered at all levels and usually first thing in the morning. It is designed to supplement the media, based on the assumption that policy officials have already gotten their media inputs from newspapers or television news. It is the most popular of all intelligence products because current intelligence is an "easy read," short, and to the point. For those policy officials who only have ten or fifteen minutes a day to absorb intelligence products—and consumer surveys consistently show that this is about all the time policy officials have for such things—current intelligence is rated as the most useful product from the intelligence community. The idea of this product is to summarize events, explain how they fit into some context, and suggest what might happen next. It is a very journalistic methodology.

Unlike warning intelligence that may lead to policy action, as the intelligence cycle suggests, current intelligence hardly ever leads to policy decisions—and it is not meant to do so. Instead, it gives generalists at senior levels a chance to find out about events outside their main areas of responsibility. Specialists often complain that the daily intelligence flow does not provide the level of detail they would need to make policy, but the current intelligence products are not designed for specialists. In fact, it would be quite likely that specialists would have seen a great deal of the raw intelligence data that lay behind the current intelligence product anyway.

During the 9/11 investigation, much was made of the fact that one daily publication, the *President's Daily Brief* (PDB), had on August 6, 2001, reported the possibility that terrorists might use commercial aircraft as cruise missiles to attack commercial or government buildings within the United States.[7] Critics of the president took this to have been a warning the president and his senior staff had missed, but normally the PDB would not have been the kind of intelligence product used for warning. The warning would have been delivered in a much more specific document devoted entirely to the subject. Intelligence managers have never expected the PDB or similar publications to be more than educational in nature. Certainly, these publications do not drive the intelligence process.

IN-DEPTH STUDIES

The same might be said for the myriad in-depth intelligence studies churned out by the analytic components. These studies have proliferated in recent years, although they were rarely attempted at the beginning of the Cold War. These studies are designed to provide in-depth analysis on specific subjects and are meant more for policy officials at working levels rather than senior decision makers, who rarely have the time to read them. These studies help in forcing analysts to come to grips with a specific subject, provide useful information to consumers within the intelligence system, and support policy makers as they design policy initiatives.

The production of these studies grew over the years as a way of giving analysts a vehicle for attacking a problem in more depth than was possible in a daily or weekly publication, and without the fuss and bureaucracy involved in producing the more formal national estimate. Policy officials sometimes request these in-depth studies, along the lines suggested by some versions of the intelligence cycle, but in many cases, the studies are produced because analysts are directed by intelligence managers to write them, or analysts themselves believe they should be written. When Robert M. Gates took over the Directorate of Intelligence (DI) at the CIA during the early days of the Reagan administration, he decreed that analysts should produce at least two of these in-depth studies every year. Gates was fond of pointing out that the DI produced about 5,000 of these studies one year. It was not clear, however, how many of them were actually read.

In recent years, these studies have been more carefully tailored to the needs of policy officials. The same might be said for the Defense Intelligence Agency products, which are geared to military needs, or those coming from the State Department's intelligence and research unit, which has always focused its analysis on foreign policy issues. The fourth category of product, the estimate, is the one most likely to drive the policy process, at least in theory. But the reality is often different.

THE REALITY OF ESTIMATES

The estimate is a creature of the Cold War, but has its roots in World War II. It is supposed to be a forecast of the future that decision makers can use to build policy, just as the intelligence cycle proposes. The estimate is supposed to be drawn by analysts from all the producing agencies, coordinated by the analysts among themselves to reach an agreed forecast, with dissenting views included. Then, it is blessed by the agency leaders; is signed off at the top; is sent to the president, the National Security Council, and staffs; and serves as the basis for policy discussions. There are actually cases where this has happened, where decision makers have waited for the intelligence community's views as embodied in the estimate, but these cases are rare.

The reality is that policy officials often know what they want to do even before they receive the estimate and hope that this product will confirm in some way the wisdom of the path they have already chosen. When the estimate conflicts with their views, policy consumers may dismiss it as uninformed, useless, or even obstructionist. When it agrees with what they think they already know, then they may see it as confirming, irrelevant, or again useless. Although one would think that policy makers would want to know when they were heading in the wrong direction, this is not usually the case. Policy consumers do not welcome intelligence that is nonconfirming, perhaps because the large egos that brought them into positions of power do not permit admissions of ignorance.

THE WMD CASE

There is no better example of what can go wrong in the estimates process than the recent experience with the problems related to Iraq and Saddam Hussein's alleged possession of weapons of mass destruction. We now know how the intelligence system politicized the estimate to meet the needs of the George W. Bush administration. The estimate on WMD was flawed from the beginning. It was based on the reporting of only a few unreliable sources. Then, analysts made several faulty assumptions about the weapons Saddam Hussein had had or used before the first Gulf War. Finally, policy officials used the estimate to convince both Americans and other nations that Saddam was about to develop nuclear weapons. All of this was wrong.[8]

According to James Risen, intelligence officials in both the collection and analysis arms of the CIA, as well as those in other agencies, knew the sources were poor and the conclusions wrong, but they could not fight senior managers who wanted to satisfy the political needs of the White House. Even more corrupting, it appears that Secretary of Defense Rumsfeld, fearing that the estimate would not support the already planned invasion of Iraq, sent his own officials, neither of them intelligence officers, to find the "correct" information.[9] All these steps were perversions of the estimates process. One can only hope that such antics will not take place in the future.

For all the reasons cited, it seems clear to me that trying to learn how intelligence works by using the intelligence cycle model will lead to misunderstandings about what really happens in the intelligence world. Collection and analysis are really parallel processes. The key to their effective functioning lies in the extent to which there is good communication between the two processes. There needs to be, as well, good communication between intelligence managers and policy consumers throughout the intelligence process. At the same time, however, intelligence managers must stand up to policy officials when they seek to make the intelligence judgments conform to political needs.

INTELLIGENCE AND POLICY

In the early days of the Cold War, the founders of the CIA debated the extent to which intelligence should be close to policy. Sherman Kent, a Yale professor who went on to establish the national estimates system in the CIA, and one of the early thinkers about the intelligence process, believed as did "Wild Bill" Donovan and others, that if intelligence became enmeshed in the policy process, it would lose its value. Kent argued that the best way to avoid politicization of intelligence was to remain distant and aloof. Later, Roger Hilsman, one of the intelligence chiefs at the State Department, took a different view. Hilsman thought that intelligence had to be close to policy to remain relevant.[10] The experiences of the Bush era suggest that Kent may have been right all along.

Nonetheless, other studies have shown that there must be good communication between policy consumers and intelligence managers if intelligence is to be on target and meet the needs of decision makers. At the same time, intelligence managers have to stand up to efforts by policy officials to skew intelligence judgments when the conclusions are at variance with the political proclivities of partisan officials. No one said this would be easy. It is a constant challenge to provide "truth to power." Intelligence must deliver the unvarnished bottom line. Policy officials can go elsewhere for politicized information if they wish, but at their own peril.

LOOKING AT COUNTERINTELLIGENCE

Leaving aside the collection and analysis processes in intelligence, one cannot understand the entire intelligence system without looking at counterintelligence. Counterintelligence is largely defensive in nature, and it is not part of the traditional intelligence cycle—although some writers have tried to adapt the cycle into a counterintelligence model.[11] In my view, counterintelligence follows an entirely different and unique path, with a model of its own. It is certainly worth studying because counterintelligence is a major function of intelligence, consists of both active and passive components, and has become as controversial as any aspect of the intelligence function in government.

In its earliest forms, counterintelligence usually meant counterespionage, stopping enemy, adversary, or even friendly spies from stealing a country's own secrets. Of course, the target country might very well be carrying out espionage against the enemies, adversaries, or friends at the same time as it tries to defend against similar sorts of spying. Thus, stealing secrets for one's country is good and necessary; having one's secrets stolen is dangerous and despicable. U.S. intelligence officers, for example, are rewarded for their successes in gathering information from their targets, even though some of what they do may be illegal in the countries they target. At the same time, other U.S. intelligence officers are heralded for their ability to root out foreign spies and are castigated when they fail to do so. After all, espionage is illegal in the United States and must be stopped.

MORE DIVERSE

Today, counterintelligence has become much more diverse than just stopping spies. It now means countering terrorism, narcotics flows, global organized crime, and subversion. Whatever the threat, however, the patterns of intelligence activity in fighting all of them are similar. It has nothing to do with the intelligence cycle. Instead, there is a counterintelligence methodology that is unique.

First, in countering national security threats, counterintelligence units must identify and locate the evildoers. This might be foreign intelligence operatives working for a hostile intelligence service, a terrorist cell, a unit of a crime "army," or a group of narcotics pushers. There are several proven intelligence methods for identifying the "bad guys," including the use of: penetrations, or "moles," to get on the inside of the groups or services; surveillance, either physical or technical; informants; and intelligence derived from captured or detained individuals. All have both positive and negative aspects.

Based on the Cold War experience, we know that it is possible to recruit officials of a foreign intelligence service to turn coat and betray some of the activities of their operatives. There are several known cases where the United States was able to place a mole inside a foreign service, and there were a number of U.S. intelligence officers—such as Aldrich Ames, John Walker, and Robert Hanssen—who gave away U.S. secrets to the Soviets. The FBI seemed quite capable of recruiting penetrations of crime groups such as the Sicilian Mafia. Penetrating a terrorist cell is far more difficult and dangerous. Terrorist cells are usually made up of a handful of people, all of whom may be bonded by family or religious ties. Even if a terrorist cell member wanted to become a "double agent," the first hint of disloyalty to the cell could result in death.

Physical or electronic surveillance is another proven method of identifying counterintelligence targets. Overseas, this kind of surveillance can be mounted against potential targets as a result of decisions by intelligence managers. In the United States, however, the rules are more strict. Counterintelligence officials would, in most circumstances, be required to go through a legal process and obtain a warrant before employing surveillance against a U.S. citizen, a resident alien, or a U.S. person. This issue became front page news early in 2006 when the *New York Times* revealed that President George W. Bush had authorized surveillance of communications without warrant, arguing that Congress had given the president the authority to do so.[12] The issue may not be resolved until a court case is brought, or new legislation is passed defining the parameters of surveillance use domestically.

USING INFORMANTS

Informants can be very useful in identifying counterintelligence targets. Informants are not recruited agents, but rather people who see something amiss and report their suspicions to authorities. In hostage situations, informants may be able to point out where unusual activity is taking place. For example, prior to 9/11, flight school managers reported to the Federal Bureau of Investigation (FBI) their concerns about Middle Eastern men seeking flight training only to steer aircraft, rather than learn to take off

and land. Unfortunately, FBI senior officials refused to grant field agents permission to interview the informants, claiming that there was no probable cause to do so.[13]

Informants can also cause a lot of wasted effort. During the sniper crisis in Washington, DC, in 2002, in which two men were able to terrorize the area by random attacks on innocent targets, requests for information resulted in more than 100,000 inputs, of which 40,000 were worth investigating.[14] People who have experience in fielding informant reports note that often the reports are used to denounce spouses, parents, or unpleasant neighbors, and provide no useful intelligence. Nonetheless, informants can prove to be helpful in identifying bad guys.

INTELLIGENCE FROM INTERROGATION

After 9/11 a good deal of controversy arose over the use of intelligence gained from the interrogation of detainees, either overseas or here at home. In the wake of 9/11 some men of Middle Eastern Muslim extraction, who were not U.S. citizens, were required to register with the federal government. Some of these people had irregularities in their visas, had overstayed their stay in the United States, or were in the United States illegally. They were detained in somewhat harsh conditions and in some cases, badly mistreated. It did not appear, however, that much effort was made to find out if any of them had ties to terrorism.

At the same time, as the United States geared up to take down the Taliban government in Afghanistan, some Taliban fighters or people associated with Al Qaeda were captured, turned in by informants, or sold to the United States, by Afghan warlords. These people, dubbed "enemy combatants" by the Bush administration, were shipped to the Guantanamo Naval Base in Cuba, where U.S. authorities said U.S. legal rules did not apply to them. These people were interrogated using what some described as harsh methods, or even torture, according to press reports.

After the United States invaded Iraq in 2003, more detainees were captured on the battlefield. These fighters were imprisoned in Iraq at some of Saddam Hussein's former prisons, including the infamous one at Abu Ghraib. It was at this location that the worst abuses took place. Apparently, unschooled, unscreened, untrained guards were turned loose to abuse the prisoners in the mistaken belief that this would "soften them up" for interrogation.

All of these situations involving detainees were handled badly.

Long experience has taught that there are effective ways to interrogate prisoners, using methods that do no harm to the subjects while producing useful intelligence. Unfortunately, those lessons were not applied effectively in the post-9/11 situations. The literature on interrogation methods, on training interrogators, on handling subjects should have been readily available to anyone involved in trying to extract intelligence from detainees. Anyone who has been involved in intelligence style interrogations knows that torture is ineffective and counterproductive, as well as abhorrent and illegal. Since those experiences, the rules have been changed to exclude such behavior by U.S. officials.

A good interrogation may yield only bits and pieces of information, but if intelligence collectors are careful, they may be able to piece together a broader picture from a series of subjects. The main aim, of course, is to try to learn something about the cells, or units, that the subjects have come from, especially about their plans for future operations.

STOPPING THE BAD GUYS

After the "bad guys" have been identified, then a decision has to be made about the kinds of operations that will be mounted to stop whatever kind of plan or activity might be under way against U.S. interests. This creates a dilemma. Usually, intelligence officers will press to extend or broaden the collection effort to make sure that all the bad guys have been identified and located. At the same time, law enforcement officials are eager to bring the bad guys to justice. This creates a serious problem, often described as the "cops and spies" dilemma.[15]

The divisions between law enforcement and intelligence in the United States have deep roots. Unlike many other industrialized countries, the United States does not have a domestic intelligence service, such as the MI-5 in Great Britain, or the DST in France. Instead, the United States has relied for many years on the FBI—which is really a law enforcement organization—to gather counterintelligence and then act to bring lawbreakers to justice. In other countries, the domestic intelligence services collect and analyze counterintelligence in parallel with counterpart foreign intelligence organizations, which work beyond the country's borders. When suspected criminal behavior is uncovered, the domestic intelligence services may turn to national police organizations to carry out law enforcement operations against the suspects.

INTELLIGENCE VERSUS LAW ENFORCEMENT

In the United States, however, where no domestic intelligence service has existed, there have been both legal and procedural barriers between the national intelligence services, whose focus has been almost exclusively abroad, and the FBI, which has always had a role in domestic counterintelligence. Traditionally, counterintelligence collected abroad was passed to the FBI, which then determined, usually in consultation with the Justice Department, whether there was probable cause to open a criminal investigation. This would be used to gather evidence that could be brought if a court case arose. This was different from the gathering and analysis of intelligence data, which traditionally was not treated or handled as evidence.

Because of cover considerations and the need to protect the identity of intelligence officers, intelligence managers did not want their people to have to appear in court, and wanted as well to protect the sources and methods used to collect intelligence. The FBI was under no such strictures, but the evidence they gathered had to be backed by appropriate warrants and protected according to legal standards. The Aldrich Ames case is a perfect example of how this system used to work.

A joint CIA and FBI team was able to track down Ames and identify him as a Soviet mole in the CIA. Then, the FBI obtained a warrant under the Foreign Intelligence Surveillance Act (FISA) to be certain that they had the right target. Once that was done, a second FBI team, with a criminal warrant, took over the investigation and gathered evidence that might be used to prosecute Ames. In the end, Ames agreed to a plea bargain and the case never came to court, but it illustrates how a firewall was in place to separate the counterintelligence investigation from the criminal one.[16]

TAKING DOWN BARRIERS

Since 9/11 some of the barriers between intelligence and law enforcement have been weakened, but the cops and spies dilemma still exists. Under the new rules, the FBI may levy requirements on the U.S. intelligence services to collect information specific to their domestic needs. It is not yet clear if such intelligence would be used as evidence in court cases. More likely, the FBI would ask that intelligence be gathered to support its newly created National

Security Branch, which combines the FBI's older counterterrorism and counterintelligence units with its newer intelligence bureau, created after 9/11.

At the same time, the CIA and the FBI have drawn more closely together with a strong push from Congress. FBI agents have been assigned to the CIA for counterintelligence purposes for many years, and more recently, to fight terrorism. CIA officers are reportedly working closely with FBI field offices where antiterrorism task forces have been created. While this may break down traditional barriers between the two agencies, there is still some resentment among CIA officers about the growing role of FBI attachés serving abroad, and FBI concerns about the reluctance of CIA officers to share information.

THE COUNTERINTELLIGENCE MODEL

So, when one looks at the pattern of counterintelligence functions, it does not look at all like the intelligence cycle. Instead, it may be seen as follows:

IDENTIFICATION
PENETRATION
EXPLOITATION
INTERDICTION
CLAIM SUCCESS

In this pattern, exploitation is the process of learning as much as possible about the bad guys before moving against them. Interdiction means either arresting the law breakers or pre-empting their operations. Though political leaders often talk about bringing the enemy to justice, suggesting that they would be arrested and taken to trial, convicted, and punished in the fight against terrorism, pre-emption may be the preferred course of action, especially overseas. In one case, for example, a U.S. *Predator* with a missile on board was reportedly used to strike a terrorist leader in Yemen, killing him and his associates while they were driving in the desert.[17] One might argue that this was punishment before trial, or alternatively, that this was necessary to prevent the terrorist from leading a strike against the United States.

The downside of pre-emption is that sometimes innocent victims are slain along with the intended targets. That was apparently what happened when the Bush administration launched a missile from a drone aircraft against Ayman al-Zawahiri, Osama bin Laden's deputy, early in 2006. The missile killed 17 people, according to press reports, but not the intended target, who later broadcast an attack on Mr. Bush, equating him with Adolf Hitler. Despite the failure to kill Al-Zawahiri, the Bush administration later said that the attack had indeed killed an important terrorist leader and was worth the cost.[18]

EXPLOITATION BEFORE INTERDICTION

In the counterintelligence model, exploitation comes before interdiction, meaning that as much intelligence should be gathered before the case or operation is turned over to law enforcement. Of course, in cases in which there is pressure to stop the enemy or adversary, exploitation may come before the intelligence is fully gathered. For example, in the case of the "Lackawanna Six," exploitation was cut short because of the need for political leaders to show that they were cracking down on terrorism. The Six were Yemeni immigrants living outside Buffalo, New York, who went to Afghanistan before 9/11 in the misguided belief that training with the Talilban fighters was going to be something of a lark.[19]

When they discovered that the Taliban were really training terrorists, the Yemeni immigrants returned to the United States. After 9/11, they turned themselves in to authorities to explain what they had done. They were quickly arrested, and eventually jailed. No one at the time seemed to realize that at least one or two of them might have been sent back to Afghanistan as double agents to penetrate Al Qaeda. Even an effort to learn more about their experiences was cut short by the pressure to achieve quick convictions to show that the government was moving swiftly against terrorism.

CLAIMING SUCCESS

Finally, in the last step of the counterintelligence process, authorities often make public claims of success, a rare step in intelligence work. Normally, intelligence managers try very hard to keep successes secret so that they might be repeated. An oft-quoted CIA saying is, "The secret of our success is the secret of our success."[20] In cases in which intelligence has been gathered successfully, it is critical to protect sources and methods. In counterintelligence, however, the claim of success, made when the case has ended, could be used to convince the public that the government is ever watchful and actually doing something with the billions of dollars spent on intelligence. During his tenure as FBI director, J. Edgar Hoover made a fine art out of going public with counterintelligence success. His senior agents all received training in public relations and the FBI was made to look good, even when serious mistakes had been made.[21]

Whereas intelligence is usually carefully hidden (except for the counterintelligence cases), intelligence failure quickly becomes public. This is a serious problem for intelligence managers. In the early days of the CIA there was no public affairs function even to deal with the public or the media. When Admiral Turner became director, however, he instituted a Public Affairs Office, much to the chagrin of many old-timers. Since then, the CIA has had to wrestle with the appropriate response when media queries arise. This is especially true when a spy case, such as the capture of Aldrich Ames, becomes public knowledge, or when a covert action surfaces.

More forthcoming CIA directors, such as George Tenet, have had the Public Affairs Office respond generously to media questions. Under the successor regime of Porter Goss as CIA director, however, the CIA seemed to return to a more conservative approach. In such cases, it would not be uncommon for the media to receive the standard answer to questions about intelligence. This says that the CIA "can neither confirm nor deny allegations of intelligence activity," which is little more forthcoming than "no comment." Nonetheless, enterprising reporters, such as Bill Gertz of the *Washington Times* and James Risen of the *New York Times*, seem to be quite successful in learning about inside stories at the CIA and other intelligence agencies.

DEFENSIVE COUNTERINTELLIGENCE

There are defensive measures in counterintelligence that do not fit into either the traditional intelligence cycle or the model just described. These measures are often lumped together as various aspects of security. They include careful background checks on prospective employees, including the use of polygraph interviews to verify the information candidates submit on their applications, and continuing monitoring of employees throughout their careers. Facilities used for intelligence and other governmental functions are extensively guarded and patrolled, monitored with alarm and surveillance devices, and protected by barrier entry devices to keep out unwanted visitors.

Some facilities have protective systems in roadways and parking areas that can be activated to stop suicidal vehicle bombers. Buildings may be shielded electronically to prevent an adversary's use of listening devices or electronic surveillance to intercept and steal secrets. Most important, employees are trained in security awareness, so that they can report anything that seems to be a threat. They are taught to protect the secrets with which they have been entrusted, and this responsibility lasts even after they leave their employment.

For example, those of us who were once inside the system and signed secret agreements are obligated to submit their published materials, including this Chapter, to their agencies for review before they are given to their editors and publishers. This is not censorship, but rather a system to ensure that no secret information is inadvertently released. Some CIA authors have taken advantage of this system to include blacked-out passages in their books, demonstrating that they really were prepared to release sensitive information but were stopped by the review process. This tends to sell more books and can be a clever marketing ploy.

THE COVERT ACTION FUNCTION

The last function of intelligence—and again one not included in the intelligence cycle—is that of covert action, or special operations. This activity is not really intelligence in its traditional role of gathering and analyzing information, but rather the use of intelligence resources to carry out the national security policy of the state using surreptitious methods. Intelligence agencies around the globe carry out such operations because they have the necessary secret facilities and personnel. All through the Cold War, it was covert action that drew most of the attention and most of the criticism of American intelligence.

General Jimmy Doolittle, one of the notable heroes of World War II, after taking a hard look at intelligence in the immediate postwar period, concluded that the United States would have to be more clever, more tricky, and more devious than our Communist adversaries if we were to overcome their bid for world domination. He stated that Americans would just have to accept this "repugnant" policy.[22] When the CIA became involved in trying to overthrow governments in Guatemala, Iran, Indonesia, and Cuba, and was severely criticized in some quarters for having done so, it became clear that there were limits to what the American people were prepared to accept.

Much has been written about the nature and limits of covert action, and there seems no need to repeat that here.[23] Though covert action does not fit into the intelligence cycle, there is a pattern to this function worth outlining. This pattern is similar to other aspects of policy development and implementation, except that covert action is supposed to be secret and to disguise the role of the United States.

POLICY FORMULATION

The pattern of policy formulation looks a bit like the intelligence cycle, but in reality it is quite different. In the first step of the policy process policy officials within the national security bureaucracy recognize and identify a problem they must address. Theoretically, the identification of the problem comes from intelligence, but in reality policy officials often see this at about the same time as intelligence officials because both receive the incoming data at about the same time, as explained earlier.

In the next step policy officials begin to seek options for dealing with the problem, assuming some role for the United States is necessary. At this point, one of the options might well be a covert action. We know from long experience with covert action that it only makes sense as an adjunct to policy and should not be the policy itself.[24] Thus, the choice of using covert action remains with decision makers and is not chosen by intelligence. The conventional wisdom in some circles during the Cold War was that intelligence managers decided to mount covert actions independent of policy officials. (This notion that the CIA was a "rogue elephant" running amok was debunked during the famous investigations of intelligence held by Senator Frank Church in the 1970s. Church learned that all CIA covert actions had been directed in some way by the White House and funded in secret by members of Congress.[25])

Finally, decision makers at the top choose the option they desire and direct its implementation. In the case of covert action, this requires that the president issue a written finding that the covert action is needed. Then the appropriate intelligence official must brief the Intelligence Oversight Committees of Congress, in secret, about the policy "on a timely basis." Congress has often pressed presidents to issue the findings before the option is implemented, but presidents have usually chosen to ignore this, claiming that it infringes on their freedom of action.[26]

The pattern looks like this:

PROBLEM RECOGNITION
OPTION CREATION
OPTION SELECTION
IMPLEMENTATION

Intelligence analysis should feed into the process at all stages, but we know that the options that policy officials choose are driven by many things. Intelligence is not always at the top of the list.

CONSEQUENCES OF COVERT ACTION

Covert action has both short- and long-term consequences. This is true of all kinds of policy choices, but because covert action is kept secret, the normal debate about policy choices takes place among a relatively small group of people. The result is that short-term solutions, which may seem attractive at the time they are chosen, may prove to have unintended consequences in the long run. There are too many examples to cover here, and the literature on covert action is voluminous. It is sufficient to say that U.S. governments rarely think about the long-term consequences of policy choices and, in that regard, covert action is no different from more open kinds of policies.

There is a long tradition in intelligence that intelligence officers do not offer policy recommendations to decision makers. Though this may be true for the delivery of finished intelligence products, it is not so in regard to covert action. As Dr. James Steiner, a former CIA officer, has pointed out, in covert action, especially in war on terrorism, the attempt to be policy-neutral does not apply.[27] For many years, a senior CIA officer has been assigned to the White House staff to help work out the details of covert action when policy makers decide to have such operations.

This officer's role is to make sure that requested covert actions are feasible and supportable. Thus, the officer is as much a policy maker as an intelligence official.[28]

It is argued elsewhere in this chapter that one way to address the short-term versus the long-term consequences of covert action is to set up a center, much like other interagency centers in U.S. intelligence. This center, however, should include both intelligence and policy officials. Its goal would be to analyze how a covert action might work and what its impact would be. The intelligence officers assigned to such a center should come from both the analytic and the operational units of the CIA. Traditionally, covert action has been kept compartmentalized within operations units, without the benefit of analytic inputs.

It seems pretty clear that presidents will always want to have the option of using some form of covert action against enemies and adversaries. No presidents in living memory, even those who were suspicious of covert action, have ever said that they would not use it. Therefore, the intelligence agencies that might be involved in such operations—primarily the CIA in the present U.S. intelligence community—must be prepared to be tasked to carry out covert action, and must maintain the capability to do so.

A FLAWED VISION

I suspect that, despite my preaching about alternatives to the traditional intelligence cycle, it will continue to be taught both inside government and elsewhere. Nonetheless, it would be encouraging to think that those so deeply wedded to the flawed concept of the intelligence cycle would, in the course of studying this volume, realize that there is an alternative to the traditional view of how intelligence works. Perhaps they might even consider it for discussion. Yet we know that people tend to look for confirming rather than disconfirming data. They will seek to defend the intelligence cycle, rather than consider the alternatives. Nonetheless, the intelligence cycle is a flawed vision, and thus poor theory. One need only ask those who have toiled in the fields of intelligence.

QUESTIONS FOR FURTHER DISCUSSION

1. What is the greatest shortcoming in using the notion of a "cycle" to describe the production of finished intelligence?
2. If intelligence production actually consists of a series of parallel processes, at what point do those processes meet to produce analysis of interest to policymakers?
3. Do you think that operational intelligence breaks down any meaningful distinction between intelligence producers and consumers?
4. Can you devise a better model to capture what really goes on in the production of finished intelligence?

ENDNOTES

1. Sherman Kent, *Strategic Intelligence for American World Policy* (Princeton: Princeton University Press, 1966). I studied an earlier version published in 1948.
2. See, for example, Arthur S. Hulnick, "The Intelligence Producer-Policy Consumer Linkage: A Theoretical Approach," *Intelligence and National Security* 1 (May 1986).
3. James Risen, *State of War: The Secret History of the CIA and the Bush Administration* (New York: Free Press, 2006).
4. The 9/11 Commission Report (New York: W.W. Norton, 2003), pp. 339–60.
5. Arthur S. Hulnick, *Fixing the Spy Machine: Preparing American Intelligence for the 21st Century* (Westport, CT: Praeger, 1999), p. 59.
6. Richard K. Betts, "Analysis, War, and Decision: Why Intelligence Failures Are Inevitable," *World Politics* 31 (1978).
7. Arthur S. Hulnick, *Keeping Us Safe: Secret Intelligence and Homeland Security* (Westport, CT: Praeger, 2004), p. 16.
8. Risen, *State of War.*
9. Hulnick, *Keeping Us Safe,* pp. 85–86.
10. Roger Hilsman, *Strategic Intelligence and National Decision* (Glencoe, IL: Free Press, 1956).
11. "CSIS and the Security Intelligence Cycle," available at http://www.csis-scrs.gc.ca (accessed 1 April 2004).
12. Risen, *State of War,* pp. 39–60.
13. 9/11 Report.
14. Arthur S. Hulnick, "Indications and Warning for Homeland Security: Seeking a New Paradigm," *International Journal of Intelligence and CounterIntelligence* 18 (Winter 2005–6).
15. Hulnick, *Keeping Us Safe,* pp. 103–18.
16. See, for example, Pete Earley, *Confessions of a Spy: The Real Story of Aldrich Ames* (New York: G.P. Putnam's Sons, 1997).
17. Hulnick, *Keeping Us Safe,* p. 72.
18. Craig Whitlock and Walter Pincus, "Qaeda Deputy Mocks Bush," *Washington Post,* 31 January 2006.
19. Hulnick, *Keeping Us Safe,* pp. 126–127.
20. Hulnick, *Fixing the Spy Machine,* p. 81.
21. Ronald Kessler, *The Bureau: The Secret History of the FBI* (New York: St. Martin's Press, 2002).
22. Harold M. Greenberg, "The Doolittle Commission of 1954," *Intelligence and National Security* 20 (December 2005), pp. 687–694.
23. See, for example, Abram Shulsky and Gary Schmitt, *Silent Warfare* (Washington, DC: Brassey's, 2002).
24. James E. Steiner, "Restoring the Red Line Between Intelligence and Policy on Covert Action." *International Journal of Intelligence and CounterIntelligence* 19 (Spring, 2006), pp.: 156–65.
25. See, for example, Rhodri Jeffreys-Jones, *The CIA and American Democracy,* 3rd ed. (New Haven, CT: Yale University Press, 2003).
26. Christopher Andrew, *For the President's Eyes Only* (New York: HarperCollins, 1995).
27. Steiner, op. cit.
28. Hulnick, *Fixing the Spy Machine,* pp. 82–83.

4. HUMAN SOURCE INTELLIGENCE

FREDERICK P. HITZ

Human source intelligence—espionage—is the most controversial mission undertaken by the intelligence community. In this overview, Frederick Hitz describes the controversies, successes, failures, and personalities that shaped the practice of human intelligence over the last sixty years. As the threat of transnational terrorism continues to loom on the strategic horizon, HUMINT will continue to be in high demand within the law enforcement and intelligence communities.

When President Truman signed The National Security Act of 1947 into law, creating the Central Intelligence Agency (CIA), he believed not that he was creating a new espionage organization for the United States, but rather that he was greatly improving the manner in which important national intelligence would find its way to his desk. Earlier he had disestablished the Office of Strategic Services (OSS), the wartime foreign intelligence collection and analytical entity, declaring that he did not want an American Gestapo in peacetime. By 1947, he had changed his mind on the need for a civilian intelligence organization for three principal reasons. First, and most important, the lessons of the 1941 Pearl Harbor attack strongly suggested the need for greater early warning of a future surprise attack on the United States. Second, he needed a centralizing intelligence organization that would gather and analyze all the intelligence reports headed for the Oval Office and attempt to make something coherent out of them so he would not have to do it himself. It is not clear that he wanted the new organization to go out and collect intelligence information on its own, as this had been tasked primarily to the Armed Services and to the Federal Bureau of Investigation (FBI). Third, he was convinced by Secretary of the Navy James Forrestal and others in his Cabinet that the U.S.S.R. would become a problem now that the Nazis were defeated, and that he needed a window into Stalin's thinking and imperial ambitions, especially in Western Europe. The Cold War was beginning.

The CIA got off to a slow start. Its early directors were military men who had a limited idea of the co-ordinating role the CIA was intended to play and were aware of the bureaucratic sharks circling them, representing the parochial interests of the military departments, the FBI, and the State Department, all of which wanted to maintain their direct access to the president on intelligence matters. Two events conspired to change this modest approach. George F. Kennan penned his famous "Long Telegram" from Moscow, alerting Washington in 1946 to Stalin's imperialist designs on that part of Europe not already under Soviet control, and recommending a policy of "containment" by the United States. At the very least, this would require affirmative action by the United States in funding democratic political parties, labor unions, student groups, and cultural organizations in Italy, France, and Western Germany to oppose the Communist elements seeking to dominate these entities. In addition, to be most effective, the hand of the United States should remain hidden. The military were not the appropriate weapon to oppose clandestine Soviet infiltration and the State Department rejected the assignment, so the fledgling CIA got the job. Luckily, there was language in the 1947 Act creating the CIA that directed it to perform, with the authorization of the president, vice-president, and secretaries of defense and state acting as the National Security Council, "such other functions and duties related to intelligence affecting the national security as the National Security Council may from time to time direct." Thus was created the covert action responsibility of the CIA that grew enormously from 1948 to 1952 under the leadership of Frank Wisner. Wisner's so-called Office of Policy Coordination (OPC) was lodged ostensibly in the Department of State, but in reality it was an operational element of the CIA.

The second major development was the arrival on the scene of two savvy Directors of Central Intelligence (DCI). Air Force Lieutenant General Hoyt S. Vandenberg and retired Army General Walter Bedell Smith (who had been Eisenhower's wartime chief of staff) knew what the organization required to move up to the big leagues and were prepared to fight for it. Vandenberg was responsible for securing for future DCIs the requisites to do their job. The National Security Acts of 1947 and 1949 that he had lobbied for (and that had also shown the handiwork of an outside commission appointed by President Truman in 1949 that included Allen Dulles) gave the DCI unparalleled authority in Washington. They gave Vandenberg and his successors as DCI the power to: hire and fire his subordinates; spend money on their own say-so without further justification; short-circuit the federal government's cumbersome procurement authorities in order to perform the intelligence mission; and act across the range of intelligence collection, analysis, and dissemination responsibilities. The scope of authority was to include activities from classic espionage, to special operations (covert action), to all-source analysis, to briefing the president's National Security Council. In short, Vandenberg got the CIA, and the DCI especially, off to a running start before he returned to the Air Force. Bedell Smith took the new organization the rest of the way.

Bedell resuscitated the CIA's estimative intelligence, a function that had earned its stripes during the wartime OSS period but had lain dormant upon the OSS's demise. Estimative intelligence looks out to the future, attempting to foresee problems of concern to the president that may be coming down the line. With Truman's go-ahead, Bedell created a Board of National Estimate reporting to the DCI, led by the same Harvard history professor, William Langer, who had put it together for General Donovan during World War II. Professor Langer managed to convince a number of wise men from the nation's best universities to work for him and Bedell, tasking them with tracking the future course of the Cold War rivalry with the U.S.S.R.

DCI Smith also made it clear that covert action and special operations existed in a chain of command extending from the DCI, and in coordination with the other espionage capability that the DCI oversaw for the president, the Office of Special Operations (OSO). He thus contrived to bring Wisner's OPC into the CIA in fact.

The OSO's responsibility was to gather foreign intelligence information by secret means (i.e., classic espionage). It was often stumbling over or wandering into operations conducted by the OPC, because the foreign actors who stole the secrets were often the same ones who could manage the propaganda or organize the political meetings for the OPC. This is an important historical point. If the CIA did not take the field to secretly oppose Soviet propaganda, backdoor electioneering, and subversion in Western Europe, several of the United States' most important allies might have been in jeopardy. Furthermore, intelligence activity that connoted "action" was very much in the American character. It drew many adherents in the early CIA both because there was a perceived need (as the constant stream of national security directives from the president and National Security Council attested) and because, if successful, you could see the results. At the same time, the slow, painstaking process of recruiting spies to report on happenings behind the Iron Curtain and in the Soviet Union itself had to be undertaken. In the late 1940s and 1950s this was difficult and dangerous work, new to Americans of whom very few spoke the relevant languages, Russian, Polish, Czech, and Hungarian. It required a patience and professionalism in terms of tradecraft that the OPCers sometimes overlooked or made fun of. The spy recruiters and handlers (of whom DCI-to-be Richard Helms was a prominent representative) were dubbed "the prudent professionals" and were not as esteemed or promoted as quickly as the OPC "action" types. Bedell tried to end all that by making of the OSO and OPC one clandestine service, directed by one chief, Allen Dulles, who reported to him. Over time it worked. The two skill sets became a little more interchangeable, although DCI Smith noted in his farewell remarks to President Truman that he thought the CIA was expending far too little effort with too meager results in acquiring intelligence penetrations of the Soviet Union.

Bedell was, of course, succeeded by DCI Allen Dulles, who jumped on the Eisenhower administration's desire to contain the Soviet Union by mounting covert action programs rather than confronting it with U.S. military force. As Supreme Commander, Allied Forces, Europe, in World War II, General Eisenhower had been a consumer of Britain's ENIGMA German code-breaking successes and knew both the role and the limitations of intelligence. As president, he believed strongly that the Soviet worldwide advance had to be stopped, if not rolled back, and covert action operations seemed a cheap and relatively low-risk way to do it. Enamored of early successes in overthrowing regimes in Iran (1953) and Guatemala (1954), the president and his advisors at the CIA grew accustomed to pushing the envelope in operations, overlooking close shaves and longer term backlash.

However, this extraordinary progress in spying on the U.S.S.R. and containing its influence during the Eisenhower years encountered several highly public setbacks as well. The revelation in May 1960, initially denied by President Eisenhower, that the Soviets had shot down a U-2 surveillance aircraft flying over Soviet territory, disrupted the Paris summit. The plan to secretly train Cuban exiles to land on Cuban soil to overthrow the Castro regime—later adopted by President Kennedy, and put into practice half-heartedly in an indefensible location at the Bay of Pigs—abruptly ended a run of successes by the CIA. Kennan's X article had alerted Washington to the bitter adversities ahead in confronting as politically hardened a foe as the Soviets; so it was naturally only a matter of time before a handful of poorly conceived or blighted operations gave the CIA an enduring notoriety and taint abroad, and dispelled the aura of the Agency's infallibility around Washington. The Bay of Pigs disaster triggered the replacement of Allen Dulles by John McCone, whose signal innovation as DCI was to put the analytical consensus within his own Agency under intense personal scrutiny.

The tattered doctrine of plausible deniability, however, still held an occasionally disproportionate allure for Kennedy and later presidents. After a national wake-up on the shores of Cuba's Bay of Pigs, JFK raised CIA's operational arm from the ashes, only to shoot for the moon all over again in *Operation Mongoose*, which saw the Agency embark on a rash of sometimes frantic missions to overthrow a now-entrenched Fidel Castro.

Despite the evident hazards of the profession, presidents relied substantially on CIA spies in Berlin to counter Soviet pressure there. The Eisenhower Kennedy years were the beginning of the era of America's greatest technical intelligence successes as well, with spies and electronics working hand-in-glove in Berlin and elsewhere; with the construction of the U-2 high-altitude photo-reconnaissance aircraft; and with the refinement beginning in the 1960s of overhead satellite surveillance, eventually able to communicate images and intercepted electronic signals to Washington in real time. Nonetheless, it was on Cuba, in the October missile crisis in 1962, that U.S. intelligence showed that it had arrived at a position of sufficient maturity in its collection systems to be able to support President Kennedy with intelligence from all three principal collectiori branches: SIGINT, IMINT, and HUMINT. The U-2 flyovers were the first to supply photographs of Soviet medium and intermediate-range ballistic missiles being transported to, unloaded, and installed in Cuba. Signals intercepts pointed to a heavy buzz of communications around the part of the island where the missiles were being installed, and human sources witnessed the transfer of mysterious long tubes on highways too small to accommodate them. Although there were many details that human sources were unable to provide, our principal spy, Oleg Penkovsky, from his vantage point at the pinnacle of Soviet military intelligence, reported on the ranges and characteristics of the IRBMs and MRBMs which were being installed. He also revealed that General Secretary Khrushchev was way out in front of his Politburo in thus challenging the United States so close to its home territory.

The fact that President Kennedy had Penkovsky's insights into Khrushchev's overexposure, confirming the observations of his own former ambassador to the U.S.S.R. Llewelyn Thompson, meant that JFK was prepared to give up the strategic advantage of a surprise attack on the installation and, in a masterstroke of statecraft, give General Secretary Khrushchev an opportunity to escape from the corner into which he had painted himself. In my view, this was the apex of U.S. intelligence support to the president during the Cold War.

After October 1962 prosecution of the Vietnam War became the overriding national security concern of Presidents Kennedy, Johnson, and Nixon. The CIA built up its presence in South Vietnam and collected useful human intelligence, from captured Vietcong and North Vietnamese prisoners especially, that permitted it to report consistently that the Government of South Vietnam (GOSVN) was unlikely to prevail in the war unless it took a more active role in the fighting and was able to win over greater support in the Vietnamese countryside. The CIA's rejection of the validity of high body counts that were held by American millitary intelligence to signal attrition in the North Vietnamese capacity to wage the war is reminiscent of today's intelligence controversy about the import of the nonexistence of weapons of mass destruction (WMD) in Iraq.

In the case of Vietnam, the CIA more or less stuck to its guns that North Vietnam was not being defeated in 1968 despite its loss of manpower, whereas it was "dead wrong" in its assessment of the existence of chemical and biological weapons stores in Iraq in 2003, according to the Silberman-Robb Presidential Commission Report. In both cases the requirement of good, on-the-ground, contemporaneous human source reporting was critical to CIA intelligence judgments. In Vietnam we had it, whereas in Iraq we did not. Silberman-Robb found that the critical National Intelligence Estimate of October 2002 on Iraqi WMD was based on unilateral spy reporting that dated from 1991 and UN weapons inspection reporting that dated to 1998. There was no direct, on-the-ground HUMINT after that before the outbreak of the war. Over the decades, the NIE process had taken on its share of taxing intelligence puzzles, but it was clearly compromised and out of date in this one.

It is ironic that, as today, the great blows to the quality and competence of CIA human source reporting in the 1970s were delivered during a Republican presidency, on the watch of a national security establishment that valued and to some extent depended on good intelligence for its activist foreign and defense policy. Although Richard Nixon privately disparaged the Ivy Leaguers at Langley whom he believed had favored his opponent in the 1960 presidential race against JFK, he needed good intelligence on Vietnam to support the Paris peace talks Secretary of State Henry Kissinger was conducting with the North Vietnamese, and also his overtures to China. Indeed, when it looked as if an unabashed Marxist, Salvador Allende, was poised to win the Chilean presidential election of 1970, it was to the CIA that President Nixon turned, improperly bypassing the rest of his foreign policy establishment and the U.S. Congress to mount a coup against a democratically elected Latin American leader.

Watergate and the Nixon resignation turned the tide against this manifestation of executive imperialism, while the CIA caught a fair measure of popular and congressional backlash. Investigative reporter Seymour Hersh wrote a series of articles in the *New York Times* in December 1974 setting forth the ways in which the CIA (and the FBI) had illegally spied on American anti-Vietnam War protesters, opened people's mail, tested hallucinogenic substances on unwitting subjects, and otherwise acted

outside the bounds of an already broadly demarcated charter without the knowledge of Congress or the American people.[1]

Congressional reaction was swift and severe. The U.S. Senate and House of Representatives each convened investigating committees to hold extensive public hearings on CIA abuses. Senator Frank Church, a Democrat from Idaho who was running for president, tried to lock then-DCI William Colby into admissions that the Agency had attempted to assassinate several world leaders such as Fidel Castro, Patrice Lumumba of the Congo, Rafael Trujillo of the Dominican Republic, and Salvador Allende, without a president's authorization, claiming that the CIA was a "Rogue Elephant." In the end, the Church Committee was unable to substantiate these allegations. There was some assassination plotting at the CIA, directed by presidents, but none was shown to have been carried out successfully.

However, the Senate's inquiry caused President Ford to create a blue ribbon panel headed by Vice-President Rockefeller to look into the matter and to preempt Congress's certain desire to legislate restrictions on U.S. intelligence activity. Thus was born the effort to establish greater executive and legislative branch oversight of the intelligence community. President Ford promulgated Executive Order 11905 in February 1976, which banned assassination of foreign political leaders by U.S. intelligence operatives or their surrogates, among other restrictions. The order contained a number of additional dos and don'ts that were binding on the intelligence community, and it was reissued by Ford's successors, Carter and Reagan, in substantially the same form. After several years of trying to pass legislation establishing more comprehensive and binding charters for intelligence community agencies such as the FBI, CIA, NSA, and NRO, real-world dangers posed to the United States by the Soviet Union caused the public and Congress to regain some equilibrium on the subject of further restraining U.S. intelligent gathering capabilities, and the effort was dropped. Congress settled for one paragraph in the Intelligence Authorization Act of 1980. It required the DCI and the president to keep Congress "fully and currently informed" of all intelligence activities, including covert action, consistent with the president's constitutional authorities and the DCI's duty to protect "sources and methods from unauthorized disclosure."

Congress believed it could settle for this paragraph instead of the several-hundred-page charter bill, because it had established in 1975 and 1976 permanent oversight committees of the House and Senate to review intelligence community programs and operations, just as every other department and agency in the executive branch is reviewed.

Some argue that since the creation of the House Permanent Select Committee on Intelligence (HPSCI) and the Senate Select Committee on Intelligence (SSCI), with rotating memberships after seven years service, the CIA has never been the same aggressive collector of human intelligence that it was during the height of the Cold War. I disagree. The world had changed by 1975. Although the Soviets still maintained a nuclear arsenal pointed at America's heartland, it was on the downhill side of the slope economically and politically. It had an aging leadership and an increasing inability to provide for the needs and wants of its people. The United States was receiving more volunteers as spies from the Soviet Union, as its high-ranking cadres became increasingly gloomy about the country's future prospects. In the United States Vietnam had exploded the postwar consensus surrounding U.S. foreign policy, and a stronger demand for oversight and accountability for all of America's overseas activities had emerged.

When this era of intelligence reform ended, the full-time housecleaners who worked at Langley and the FBI had managed to stay out of the headlines for the most part. Spying against private citizens clearly violated the 1947 Act but made for no more than a sideshow when compared to spy-hunting inside the U.S. government. Light almost never shines on this most sensitive area of surveillance, counterespionage, but in this domain of intelligence work especially, tumult has been virtually inseparable from tradecraft. Penetrations and double-crosses can be expected in the competition among major intelligence services, but the integrity of intelligence operations rests on how well very fragmentary and circumstantial clues about possible security breaches can be read. Moles were often uncovered only years after their work got started. Indeed, when the Cold War did end abruptly, counterespionage work was not ready to wind down but was putting itself in high gear, as Americans were making inroads into the former Warsaw Pact services, shedding light on turncoats here at home.

American intelligence contended with a number of notorious penetrations in the Cold War, and most spectacular of these was the early discovery that the Soviets had recruited the top British liaison official in America, Kim Philby. Philby had until then been regarded as one of MI6's best men—a man in line to be its next director, a brilliant and affable character, and a mentor to many of Langley's rising stars. The United States had depended heavily on him personally for many of our early postwar efforts in Europe. Philby had been in a position to alert Moscow to many of the biggest and most sensitive intelligence exploits under way: the development of the atomic bomb and the VENONA project, through which the NSA was attempting to break encrypted communications from the Soviet embassy and the New York consulate during World War II. But he could not prevent the NSA from discovering an old code-name, Homer, referring to a British mole in the U.K. embassy in Washington. Homer was one member of the entire Cambridge Five spy ring, another of whom was quickly tied to Philby, as a friend boarding at Philby's home. In 1951, Philby's official career effectively ended. But it took another decade's worth of revelations for his career as a double-agent to be sufficiently understood to put him in criminal jeopardy, whereupon he defected.

James Jesus Angleton, the CIA's master spy-hunter, was one among many of Philby's former friends on whom his treachery left a lasting impression. Angleton's occupation at the CIA was actually not widely known. He was simply, "the Ghost of Langley," the man who showed up unannounced at the DCI's office for an immediate, private audience with the boss. A classics major and poet at Yale who moved in the same circles as T.S. Eliot and Ezra Pound, Angleton was picked toward the beginning of his career to run the counterintelligence operation in Rome, during the crucial 1947 elections that kept the Italian Communist Party out of power. Angleton's early career also solidified CIA liaison operations with other services, including those of Britain and Israel. And he worked alongside the Mafia during his Rome posting. The Mafia had operated on behalf of the OSS in wartime Italy, and had helped to perfect some of the more lethal aspects of the CIA's tradecraft.

Angleton's cunning instincts came to the attention of Allen Dulles, who asked him in 1954 to head the CIA's counterspy operations. By 1959, Angleton had unearthed Jack Dunlap as a mole in the NSA who had reached high-level "no inspection" clearances. But in retrospect, though the Philby affair had ignited Angleton's imagination, it had not furnished the CIA with the kind of tradecraft lessons that would shed a much clearer light on future penetration controversies. In 1961 Angleton seemed to be nearing more breakthroughs, having been given personal charge of debriefing a defecting KGB major,

Yuri Golitsyn, but Golitsyn became increasing problematic for the CIA over time. In addition to the key information he did betray, he was willing to speculate endlessly about other penetrations of U.S. intelligence, and spun out theories that Angleton showed himself ready to embrace. Among the most troubling questions he raised was the identity of the mole Sasha, a code-name that sparked the most tortuous inquisition that the Agency would ever launch: These investigations had such disproportionate impact on work at the Agency that their records remain completely restricted to this day. And Golitsyn insisted with some vehemence to CIA officers, after each subsequent defector surfaced, that anyone to follow him would almost certainly be a plant, blunting the CIA Counterintelligence Staff's instincts. The name of one of those subsequent defectors, Yuri Nosenko, was much later cleared of being a Soviet double agent, but Nosenko fell afoul of his own glaring penchant for fabrication, and at first cast the most severe suspicions upon himself. Working on Angleton's behalf, J. Edgar Hoover's FBI went to extremes to try to extract a confession from Nosenko but were ultimately unsuccessful. Meanwhile, Nosenko had languished in solitary confinement for three years. In the aftermath, Hoover judged Angleton poisonously misguided, and the debacle helped to drive a permanent wedge between the FBI and CIA, from which neither agency extricated itself until after September 11.

Angleton put at least fifty intelligence officers under surveillance during his career, and removed at least sixteen from the service. Problems at the CIA became more severe as his views darkened into clinical paranoia over the course of the 1960s. The only personal trust Angleton was ultimately able to sustain was in his closest circle. Meanwhile he elaborated plots with Golitsyn's help. As facts became hunches, and his hunches increasingly bordered on the absurd, he came into permanent conflict with the Agency's leadership. Finally, he could not find a distinction between political loyalty and personal allegiance to his theories. He was barred from direct contact with Golitsyn in 1968 by DCI Dick Helms, and ushered into retirement in 1974 by DCI Bill Colby, while the Hersh revelations of domestic spying were in the headlines. His Counterintelligence Staff was diminished from 300 to 80.

The counterespionage underworld that defends against other powerful foreign intelligence agencies is a reality in which things remain extraordinarily indeterminate. A myriad of conceivable avenues might lead to operational betrayal. Angleton's version of

reality was to adopt the premise that the most successful Soviet campaigns were those of knowingly false information—disinformation—that could operate at a great remove from the Agency's headquarters. Penetrations were less important than the false tracks onto which the CIA could be lured. But in truth the kinds of judgment calls are immensely difficult that spy-hunters must make to arrive at breakthroughs in cases of penetration. Major revelations might never come down the road. And surveillance might fail to turn up any mole at all. Moreover, in the life-or-death stakes of the Cold War, there was always the potential that too broad or intrusive a mole-hunt would leave more self-inflicted damage to CIA operations than unearthing a mole would stanch. Nevertheless, crucial countermeasures still had to be taken, and in counterespionage it was often the effort to run down trails of minor lifestyle and procedural misconduct that kept operations secure.

Philby was the result of a relatively spectacular breakthrough, but the Aldrich Ames and Robert Hanssen penetrations during the 1980s and 1990s remained almost entirely invisible for years after the investigations got rolling. Ames and Hanssen did their damage over a period of time when CIA attitudes about lifestyle and procedural misconduct had remained too lax for too long. The Agency lost the distinction between operations in the outside world and the life of discipline required inside. Most espionage operations are carried out in the gray areas of administrative procedure; but over the years, these moles built microcosms of that mission right in the offices that they ran at the CIA and FBI. Like all other skilled professions, intelligence officers have to accept a high level of personal autonomy in those they rely upon; but the basics of tradecraft, on-time reporting, and drug and alcohol-free behavior are important too. Over the long haul, the maintenance of strict operational routine and personal integrity goes a fair ways toward assuring the success of the intelligence community in its operational mission.

Within the CIA, the chaos that followed Operation CHAOS (the controversial CIA domestic mail-opening program revealed in 1974) lasted well into the Carter presidency and the tenure of DCI Stansfield Turner. President Carter put the CIA back on the offensive in his changing attitude to the Sandinistas in Nicaragua, and the covert action he instigated to oppose the Soviet takeover of Afghanistan in 1979. Still, it remained for Ronald Reagan to initiate an across-the-board revitalization of both U.S. defense and intelligence resources that would reverse the post–Vietnam War drawdown and counter ongoing outbreaks of Soviet aggression. President Reagan authorized a covert action to train and reinforce the *contra* resistance to the Marxist Sandinista revolution of 1979 in Nicaragua, and a second covert program to build up the *mujahedeen* factions opposing the Soviet-controlled government in Afghanistan. At the same time, he initiated a research program to intercept incoming missiles in space. The Kremlin began to believe the United States was trying for a first-strike capability against the U.S.S.R. and initiated a worldwide intelligence alert called Project Ryan to report on indicators confirming such an effort. At the same time, old age and sickness were removing Soviet premiers at a record rate. In March 1985 a completely new figure ascended to power in the Kremlin, Mikhail Gorbachev, who was focused on curtailing Soviet commitments to defend communism everywhere (the Brezhnev Doctrine) and reforming the economy to provide a better response to the needs of the Soviet people. Meanwhile the Reagan administration was having a difficult time keeping the U.S. Congress on board for the operation to support the *contras*. After the second amendment curtailing CIA support for the *contras* passed Congress—and was signed into law by the president because it was attached to an omnibus and year-end appropriations bill—some members of the administration on the National Security staff and in the CIA concocted a scheme to sell embargoed weaponry to Iran in exchange for information about terrorists who had abducted Americans in the Middle East, using the proceeds from the sales to supply weapons illegally to the *contras*. The Iran-Contra scheme finally blew up in the press in fall 1986, sending the Reagan White House and William Casey's CIA into a tailspin.

It took the appointment in 1987 of Judge William Webster as DCI, a former Director of the FBI and U.S. Court of Appeals judge, to restore legitimacy and integrity to CIA operations after the Iran-Contra fiasco. Meanwhile, CIA covert operators got congressional approval to supply Stinger missiles to the Afghans *mujahedeen*, a policy that proved pivotal to driving the Soviets out of Afghanistan. As unintentionally transparent as the Nicaraguan covert action was to the world, so the cooperation by the CIA with the Pakistani intelligence service to supply armaments to Afghani and Arab guerillas in Afghanistan was painted as a state secret within the boundaries of "plausible deniability." The Soviets knew where the weaponry, especially the Stingers, was coming from,

but they were in no position to do much about it, despite the concerns of Pakistan's nervous chief of state, Mohammed Zia-ul-Haq.

To date, the Afghan covert action has been the last big successful clandestine political operation mounted by the CIA in which the U.S. hand did not show to an impermissible degree. By and large, the CIA officers involved kept their promise to Pakistan's rulers that they would physically stay out of Afghanistan and work through the Pakistani intelligence service, the ISI. The advent of both round-the-clock cable news programming and instant worldwide communications via the Internet have successfully impinged upon the United States's ability to maintain the necessary secrecy of a major covert political operation. This was made manifest in the administration of President George H.W. Bush, when the president, despite his tour of duty as DCI and his appreciation for the role of intelligence, turned instead to the American military to deal with both Manuel Noriega in Panama in 1989 and Saddam Hussein in the first Gulf War in 1991. When President Clinton sought to make use of covert action in overthrowing Saddam in the mid-1990s, he found it was impossible. Congress had gained an appetite for micromanaging an operation that could have high domestic stakes, and the CIA had too few covert assets to bring it off.

By the same token, viewed in retrospect, in the mid-1980s it would turn out that the United States had suffered unprecedented high-level penetrations of its intelligence services, through the handiwork of Aldrich Ames in the CIA and Robert Hanssen in the FBI. Ames began his espionage for Soviet handlers in March 1985 in order to get $50,000 to buy himself out of debt. He was a thirty-year spy in the CIA's operations directorate who had specialized in Soviet matters, arriving at a senior level even though he had a mediocre record—which included numerous episodes of alcohol abuse, security violations, and a chronic inability to get his financial accountings and contact reports about meetings with Soviet officials in on time. In short, Ames probably should never have been permitted to be on the front line, meeting and assessing Soviet officials one-on-one. But he was. And he used his position and his knowledge of how both the Soviet and U.S. intelligence systems operated to betray, over a period of nine years, every agent working for the United States against the U.S.S.R.; details of numerous U.S. operations against the Soviets; and the names of his colleagues who were engaged in the effort. Ames's betrayal led to the certain execution of ten U.S. spies and probably more, along with the compromise of hundreds of U.S. intelligence operations. The arrest of Aldrich Ames in 1994 provoked a wave of disillusionment and dismay in the American public, and among the congressional oversight committees, that such a sloppy and seemingly inept spy could betray so much over such a long period, not only without being caught, but without the CIA having mounted a serious effort to track him. The damage to the Agency's reputation was nothing short of devastating.

For the FBI, no less damaging was the tale of Robert Hanssen, a dour misfit who had used his superior information technology skills to eventually burrow into the deepest corners of the Bureau's counterintelligence operations against the U.S.S.R. Hanssen managed to turn over vast amounts of operational detail and names of U.S. agents to the Soviets in an on again–off again career of espionage that began in the late 1970s and continued until his arrest in February 2001. Hanssen's case was a tougher one to crack than Ames's because Hanssen had been careful never to meet with his Soviet handler, conducting all his business with the Soviets through dead drops in a park near his home in Northern Virginia. Furthermore, Hanssen had compromised many of the same spies named by Ames or by Edward Lee Howard, another CIA turncoat of the period; so it took an analysis of operations that had gone sour that could not have been compromised by Ames or Howard, and also the help of a Soviet source, before Hanssen's own activities could be distinguished and an arrest finally made.

At the same time that these spy wars were taking place between the Soviet and U.S. intelligence services, the CIA was beginning to enjoy real success in running Soviet and Bloc volunteer spies who were supplying vast amounts of useful intelligence information about Soviet and Warsaw Pact war-fighting plans in Europe, and Soviet military research and development (R&D). In the former case, Ryszard Kuklinski, a high-ranking member of the Polish General Staff, passed the CIA all of the Warsaw Pact plans that crossed his desk from 1972 until his defection in 1981; and in the second case, Adolph Tolkachev provided his U.S. case officer with the latest Soviet military R&D on stealth technology and air defense missilery from the late 1970s until 1985, saving the U.S. taxpayer millions of dollars in unnecessary defense expenditure. These successful Soviet spy volunteer recruitments at the end of the Cold War, and others like them, proved the value of a vigorous human source collection program at

the time that the Soviet regime was under severe internal stress.

The need for espionage did not disappear with the dismantling of the Berlin Wall in 1989 and the dismemberment of the U.S.S.R. in 1991. The successor Russian government kept its intelligence officers in the field and the West at bay on a number of important issues. Yet, over time, the threats targeted by American intelligence agencies began to shift. As authoritarian regimes calcified or collapsed over the decade of the 1990s—frequently ex–Cold War client governments—the new threats would become proliferating weapons of mass destruction and emerging nonstate terrorist factions, exemplified by Osama bin Laden and Al Qaeda.

In a series of bold and ever more sophisticated attacks, beginning with that on the Khobar Towers, a U.S. Air Force billet in Saudi Arabia in 1997; followed by the bombings of U.S. embassies in Dar es Salaam and Nairobi in 1998; and the attack on the *U.S.S. Cole* in 2000, this affluent Saudi veteran of the *mujahedeen* effort against the Soviets in Afghanistan, Osama bin Laden, showed he was capable and desirous of inflicting unacceptable damage on the United States in order to drive it out of the Muslim holy places of the Middle East. His organization, known as Al Qaeda, or the Franchise, had in 1991 volunteered to lead the Islamic effort to force Saddam Hussein to leave Kuwait, but his offer was overlooked by the Saudi royals. Subsequently in exile in the Sudan, and after 1995 in Afghanistan as a guest of the Taliban regime, Osama preached Islamic unity and defiance in opposing the West's continued military basing in the region and the support it was giving to autocratic and selfish rulers in Saudi Arabia, Egypt, and the Gulf who were doing nothing to provide for their populations. The CIA, in particular in the U.S. intelligence community, became alarmed at the growing strength, sophistication, and appeal of Osama's rhetoric against the United States' role in the Middle East, which targeted it as the "far enemy." After President Clinton's weak and ineffective response to the African embassy bombings, the CIA established a task force to track Osama and Al Qaeda, but it was never able to deliver the knockout punch on his compound in Afghanistan or stop his continuing deadly momentum during the Clinton years, even though then-DCI George Tenet "declared war" on Al Qaeda in an attempt to bring focus to American intelligence's counterterrorist strategy.

In 2001 the CIA began receiving heightened liaison reporting from U.S. allies in Europe and the

Middle East that Al Qaeda was planning something big. But where—in the region or against a U.S. installation overseas—was unknown. This was becoming Osama's trademark: long months of preparation and then a sudden strike. But just like the U.S. government's previous experience with a massive surprise attack on U.S. territory at Pearl Harbor, we were not prepared nor really expecting an attack in the continental United States. September 11, 2001, was an unforeseen and life-shattering wake-up call on the capacity of nonstate, religious-inspired terrorism to threaten stable societies like the United States and our European allies. It took President George W. Bush minutes to declare that the United States was involved in a war against terror and that all the military and intelligence resources of the United States would be deployed to win it.

What were those intelligence resources? In late 2001, in what condition did the intelligence community find itself to take on Osama bin Laden, Al Qaeda, and the challenge of religious-based international terror? With the passing of the Cold War, the CIA had been downsized and had in addition witnessed the dramatic departure of large numbers of expert spy handlers and analysts whose skills had been shaped by the challenge of the Soviet Union, and who did not have much interest in and familiarity with the milieu of terrorism, drugs, crime, and weapons proliferation, issues which would be the meat and potatoes of Presidential Decision Directive 35 that set the blueprint for intelligence community targeting after the Cold War ended. So they retired, and took with them their knowledge of spy tradecraft and of foreign languages. On top of that, as the 9/11 post-mortems would show, the intelligence agencies had grown into mature bureaucracies without much initiative, imagination, or creativity. They faced a target that operated in the shadows of nation-states but wasn't one; that had low overhead and a tight network of collaborators that it deployed with iron-handed discipline; and that possessed one unassailable attribute: Many of its adherents were willing to commit suicide for the cause, and would strap on a bomb just to take civilian bystanders with them.

Other problems beset the intelligence agencies in 2001 as well. A division between domestic and international spheres of terrorism no longer existed. A plot that could begin in a Hamburg mosque or a Madrid suburb could be planned for immediate execution in New York or Washington. The divided responsibilities between the FBI and CIA that historical accident and concern about domestic civil liberties had spawned

in the aftermath of World War II were hindrances in the 21st century to the kind of instant information sharing and teamwork that cell phones and Internet access in the hands of our terrorist attackers demanded. Compartmentalization and "need to know" take on sinister meanings when the effect is to deny intelligence to a sister agency equally charged with the responsibility to preempt a terrorist act.

Some of the more egregious barriers to intelligence sharing and teamwork between the intelligence agencies were struck down in the USA-PATRIOT Act passed in October 2002, and in the Intelligence Reform Bill, passed in December 2004. Now, wiretap permissions, when granted, run to the individual who is the target of the surveillance, not the instrument by which he intends to communicate. Grand jury testimony in terrorist cases can be shared among the law enforcement and intelligence entities having an interest in the matter. The Foreign Intelligence Surveillance Act (FISA) has been amended to include among the parties against whom the U.S. government may seek authorization for electronic surveillance from the special Foreign Intelligence Surveillance Court not just spies but terrorists as well; and the standard for authorizing surveillance has been broadened to encompass those as to whom terrorism is "a principal purpose" of their activity and not "the" purpose. There are additional sections in the 2001 Act that beef up the anti–money laundering provisions of federal statute and enhance the "sneak and peek" possibilities open to law enforcement, as well as enable more Internet intrusion of suspected terrorists. It is possible that some of the more aggressive portions of the USA-PATRIOT Act may be modified somewhat to include a greater measure of accountability.

The intended changes included in the Intelligence Reform Act of 2004 date back to the Church Committee era but trespassed on more turf, and would only see the light of day three years after September 11, with some of the most intense bureaucratic lobbying of any intelligence bill. In the Act, there has been a concerted effort to remedy one of the principal perceived deficiencies in the performance of the intelligence agencies prior to 9/11, namely the absence of "an attending physician" who could treat the patient as a whole and be responsible for the work of all the specialists racing around performing tests on the patient on their own. That metaphor, used by the 9/11 Commission to sway Congress and the president, was the premise behind creating the new position of Director of National

Intelligence (DNI). The DNI was intended to be the intelligence czar, a Cabinet officer holding both managerial and budgetary authority over the entire intelligence community. He would also be the president's principal intelligence adviser.

When the dust settled after passage of the Act, the DNI's lines of command were not as clear as the Commission hoped for. The Defense Secretary and the Department of Defense (DOD) continue to share many of the DNI's management and budgetary authorities relating to the intelligence agencies under the command of the DOD. The DOD intelligence agencies—NRO, NSA, DIA, and NGA—account for 80 percent of the intelligence budget. There is also the matter of information sharing, which the Act seeks to encourage by requiring the DNI to have a subordinate responsible for creating an information sharing environment in the intelligence community.

The 2004 Act also treats the intelligence community's self-inflicted wounds represented the failures to warn of the 9/11 attacks and to accurately account for the weapons of mass destruction stockpiled by Saddam Hussein since 1991—believed ready for dispersal to terrorists by Saddam at some point if the UN embargo of Iraq was not lifted. The existence of Iraqi WMD was one of the principal reasons cited by the Bush administration for preparing to go to war against Iraq. A seemingly authoritative National Intelligence Estimate (NIE) circulated by the CIA in October 2002 detailed the supposed holdings of chemical and biological weapons by the Iraqi Ba'athist regime, and the efforts of the regime to make nuclear weaponry advances. Furthermore, United Nations testimony drawn from the NIE by Secretary of State Colin Powell in February 2003, on the eve of the Iraq War, was used to sweep aside Allied opposition to the invasion. It has become painfully clear since that Saddam suspended his WMD programs after 1991 to get out from under the UN-sponsored embargo. There were no WMD stockpiled in Iraq prior to the war, as Saddam had destroyed them.

What made the U.S. intelligence community's views on Iraqi WMD so objectionable was not that they held such preconceptions (most other knowledgeable intelligence services held identical views—the UK, Russia, Germany, France, and Israel), but that the NIE sought to justify the weapons' existence on outdated and unconfirmed reporting. The proprietary data dated from 1991; reports from UN inspectors stopped in 1998; and assessments rested heavily on unilateral sources like "Curveball"

whose credibility was in question. The analytical tradecraft employed by the CIA on the critical NIE was fatally deficient.

At the same time, the president's decision to spread the war from Afghanistan to Iraq sounded alarm bells for quite a few veteran intelligence officers within the ranks. A number of these in-house critics believed the move into Iraq would instantly squander goodwill that the American government had gained in the Islamic world as a result of the September 11 attacks. Some intelligence officers subscribed to the view, later corroborated in the post–invasion Iraq Survey Group's two reports, that the inspections broken off in 1998 and the sanctions in place after had already boxed in Saddam.

Moreover, although DCI George Tenet had gained the confidence of the hawks on the president's war cabinet, both Vice President Cheney and Defense Secretary Donald Rumsfeld made it known in the press that they harbored deep distrust of the CIA's analysis of Iraq. The Defense Secretary had steered the 1998 Rumsfeld Commission that took the CIA to task to sharpen its poor nonproliferation reporting, against a backdrop of two missed calls at the Agency in five years—Saddam Hussein's startling WMD advances up to the 1990 Gulf War, and India's clandestine nuclear tests in 1996. The vice president possessed quite the opposite disposition, misappropriating even dubious raw intelligence leads to hype the imminent threat from the Ba'athist regime. Analysts at Langley found themselves frozen out of most White House planning. The war cabinet opened a small ad hoc shop within the Defense Department to cherry-pick intelligence reporting from across the community, to be seeded in the media to reinforce two bogus claims: (1) that Iraq's Ba'athists had entered into an active pact with bin Laden's network, and that (2) the Ba'athists were on the verge of going nuclear. The Secretary was known to scorn the DIA's Iraq analysis as well, and he overruled pointed warnings issued by the Army Chief of Staff that the U.S. military could not occupy the country without a contingent of 300,000 soldiers. Amidst rising tensions and mounting controversy over Saddam's alleged possession of nuclear weaponry, Tenet balked too, sending a formal request to the Department of Justice to begin a criminal investigation to identify the source of a leak of a CIA operative's identity (a career officer who was unwittingly dragged into the dispute over the war's strained *casus belli*) even though it was sufficiently clear that the leaker would have to have been a senior White House official.

As the war wore the military down until it was an occupation in disarray, disgruntlement surfaced publicly. First, Richard Clarke, the former counter-terrorism czar at the National Security Council made searing statements against the administration at the 9/11 Commission hearings, and then the departing National Intelligence Officer for the Middle East, Paul Pillar spoke out:

> If the entire body of official intelligence analysis on Iraq had a policy implication, it was to avoid war—or, if war was going to be launched, to prepare for a messy aftermath. What is most remarkable about prewar U.S. intelligence on Iraq is not that it got things wrong and thereby misled policymakers; it is that it played so small a role in one of the most important U.S. policy decisions in recent decades.[2]

The overlord at the D1A for Iraq planning, Spider Marks, told a reporter at the *Times* that prewar misjudgments had been made in many quarters, not just in the Cabinet leadership. "We lost our finger on the pulse of the Iraqi people and built intelligence assessments from a distance."[3] Out in Langley, the CIA has been under a pall.

The blunt consensus in the 9/11 Commission report and on Capitol Hill in the Intelligence Reform Act of 2004 to downgrade the CIA was probably not ill-advised. The Agency now has the leeway to be loyal at arm's length during domestic imbroglios, and in principle it has a new referee in the DNI. This has hardly been an auspicious time, however, to watch the demoralization at the CIA, with constant leaking of sensitive intelligence information and the hemorrhaging of experienced intelligence officers into lucrative private-sector security jobs or retirement. Where does that now leave the CIA and the intelligence community, who bear the preponderant responsibility to inform the president about terrorists and their targets *before* these attacks occur? Future performance alone will provide the answer. The intelligence community has weathered its share of crises in the past. Yet there are some systemic reasons to be concerned.

To start with, the intelligence agencies allowed their capabilities to attenuate markedly during that ten-year period between the disintegration of the Soviet Union and September 11, 2001. There are still too few intelligence officers who have studied and understand Arabic civilizations or who have lived in the Middle East at some point in their careers. Moreover, many of the collection techniques of the Cold War have been rendered obsolete by cell phones, the Internet, and other aspects of changing technology. The CIA cannot continue to operate as it did in the pre-Iraq period, largely excluded from the hard targets that the United States is up against. Where it has no physical presence, the Agency has historically relied for HUMINT primarily on defectors, detainees, legal travelers, opposition groups, and foreign government liaison services, but these sources divulge their secrets at some distance in time and space from the ongoing developments inside the target they are reporting on. Getting inside the adversary's organization is thus a higher priority than it was even in the Cold War. Yet even though the Directorate of Operations budget is now more than double its pre-September 11 levels, an estimated 80–90 percent of intelligence information about Al Qaeda still comes in as SIGINT.[4] The whereabouts, goals, and tactics of terrorists are thus available only imprecisely and intermittently.

In the HUMINT area, American intelligence is still behind other services in having linguists who speak the hard languages of the Middle East, Central Asia, or Southeast Asia. In addition, this assignment is becoming less appealing to spy runners from the standpoint of safety and quality of life. Increasingly, CIA operatives will bring back key intelligence only by acting with the flexibility, the skills, and the cover it takes to run operations unlinked with an official installation—under nonofficial cover. Consequently, the problems spies face conducting espionage will be more dangerous. Families, too, will be divided, as many overseas tours in areas of prime concern to the intelligence agencies are not safe for young children.

Furthermore, there has been an especially rocky post-Tenet transition for the current Director of the Central Intelligence Agency (DCIA), former Congressman Porter Goss. Mr. Goss has been criticized for bringing a number of hostile and inexperienced congressional staffers with him to Langley, making for even more precipitous erosion from the ranks among senior officers with substantial field experience. This will hinder the CIA's ability to take full advantage of the uptick in personnel recruitment, because so many experienced officers appear to be leaving. Goss announced that rebuilding the operations directorate would be the overriding priority of his tenure, but an irony thus far has been the number of critics comparing the present impasse to DCI Stansfield Turner's first year, marked by some of the most severe confrontations and mishandled purges the Directorate had ever experienced. By the end of

2005, Goss had lost one Directorate of Operations head, two deputy directors, and more than a dozen department, division, and station heads.[5]

An equally fundamental point is that Americans are not the "good guys" any more in many areas of the Middle East. This sounds simplistic, yet much of U.S. intelligence success during the mature stages of the Cold War occurred because Soviet and Soviet Bloc officials volunteered to work for the American or British intelligence services as a way to oppose the corruption and misery of their own lives behind the Iron Curtain. That motivation appears less prevalent in the Middle East today. The United States is perceived as a threatening, non-Islamic outside force, only interested in the region's petroleum resources. Perhaps President Bush's hard push for democratic governments in the region will alter this attitude. It will be a hard sell.

The upshot of pervasive suspicions in the region about American aims is that, to be successful, the CIA and the other intelligence community HUMINT collectors will have to work indirectly, and multilaterally, through the good offices of friendly intelligence services, the operational channels called intelligence liaison. Since September 11 the CIA has been doing that in a major way, trading superior resources and technology for on-the-ground intelligence information about terrorist threats. The CIA has built a formalized network of over two dozen liaison offices, and DOD has gotten into the game as well, with less formal and even lower profile liaison and reconnaissance missions for the special forces. These DOD operations do not fill the need for nonofficial cover and penetrations, but they do have a tactical yield.

The difficulty liaison relationships present, however, is that we are no longer in complete control of the spy operation. Our liaison intermediaries will influence both whom we target and how we manage the take. The result is bound in many cases to be a dilution of the product and a diminished timeliness. But the most worrisome deficiency will be a lack of confidence that one is getting the full picture, with the ongoing potential to leave the United States vulnerable and the region unstable. It is worth remembering the lessons of the Pakistani ISI's control over our access to the *mujahedeen* during the 1980s and 1990s in Afghanistan, or the heavily slanted read of the opposition that the Shah's SAVAK presented the CIA in Iran's prerevolutionary decades. Nevertheless, liaison operations account so far for nearly all

of the 3,000 suspected terrorists who have been captured or killed outside the Iraq theater.[6]

Disruptions in these liaison relationships comes with the territory, but the CIA's experiences in Latin American counternarcotics operations have provided a number of relatively useful lessons for working with less corruptible, more trustworthy elite units in the more questionable partnerships with foreign services. Porter Goss has rightly pronounced himself wary of leaning too far toward liaison operations. There are, however, elements of liaison operations that cannot be replaced by CIA HUMINT work. The first of these is legal access: To carry out targeted killings in a foreign country, it becomes prudent to give and receive assurances from other sovereign governments. Kidnapping also is best avoided wherever the local service is willing to kick down the door for us. And shutting down nearly endlessly reroutable financing pipelines to terrorists requires a willingness to do so on the part of many sovereign partners simultaneously.

The intelligence community's technical collection programs may not be in much better shape than its HUMINT. Signals intelligence gathering is hindered by inadequate translation capabilities, while a wary target will be more willing to communicate by word of mouth, cleft stick, and carrier pigeon, than by telephone or more modern means. From an operational standpoint, the fallout from the brouhaha over warrantless surveillance by the NSA of communications from potential terrorists abroad with individuals in the United States that arose in early 2006 may further limit the gathering of useful intelligence. Actually, it appears that most Al Qaeda instructions are moving through Arabic websites on the Internet, which intelligence services worldwide are not yet recovering or translating in a comprehensive or timely fashion.

When all is said and done, counterterrorism and counterproliferation intelligence gathering follows a new paradigm. It is less about classic espionage than persistent tracking of terrorists and their potential weapons by good detective work and perceptive mining of reams of open sources. This is no longer back-alley skulking in a trench coat. It is down-and-dirty police investigative work, tracing radicals and their bomb-making materials, and recruiting informants to watch mosques and radical meeting sites. That is why in the United States it is so important for the CIA to work well with the FBI, with Customs, with Immigration and Naturalization, and with local police first responders. Intelligence gathering in the 21st century is now less about James Bond or George Smiley than it is a Frankenstein composite of law enforcement, spies and forensics.

QUESTIONS FOR FURTHER DISCUSSION

1. Have legislative initiatives overly constrained the U.S. practice of human source intelligence?
2. Should the CIA and U.S. military intelligence agencies abandon altogether the secret recruitment of foreign assets ("agents"), who are often doubled against the United States? Should the United States at least refuse to recruit a foreign asset suspected, or known, to have violated human rights in the past—perhaps even murdered someone?
3. Should human intelligence play a greater role in homeland security?
4. Is human intelligence just a conduit for deceptive information?

ENDNOTES

1. Seymour Hersh, "Huge CIA Operation Reported in U.S. Against Antiwar Forces. Other Dissidents During Nixon Years," *New York Times.* December 22, 1974; Hersh, "President Tells Colby to Speed Report on CIA," *New York Times*, December 24, 1974; Hersh, "3 More Aides Quit in CIA Shake-Up," *New York Times*, December 30, 1974.
2. Paul R. Pillar, "Intelligence, Policy, and the War in Iraq," *Foreign Affairs* 85 (March/April 2006), pp. 15–27, at 16.
3. Michael R. Gordon, "Catastrophic Success: Poor Intelligence Misled Troops About Risk of Drawn-Out War," *New York Times*, October 20, 2004.
4. Dana Priest, "Foreign Network at Front of CIA's Terror Fight," *Washington Post*, November 18, 2005.
5. Dafna Linzer, "A Year Later, Goss's CIA Is Still in Turmoil," *Washington Post*, October 19, 2005.
6. Ibid.

5. OPEN-SOURCE INTELLIGENCE

STEPHEN C. MERCADO

Open-source intelligence is a hot-button issue inside the intelligence community; many intelligence professionals do not believe it constitutes real intelligence. In the view of this intelligence professional, however, data gleaned from open sources can place other types of information in context.

Our age's increasingly voluminous open-source intelligence (OSINT) sheds light on issues of the day for all-source analysts, covert collectors, and policymakers, but have we done enough to exploit its potential? My short answer is "No," and here's why I think so.

Collecting intelligence these days is at times less a matter of stealing through dark alleys in a foreign land to meet some secret agent than one of surfing the Internet under the fluorescent lights of an office cubicle to find some open source. The world is changing with the advance of commerce and technology. Mouse clicks and online dictionaries today often prove more useful than stylish cloaks and shiny daggers in gathering intelligence required to help analysts and officials understand the world. Combined with stolen secrets, diplomatic reports, and technical collection, open sources constitute what one former deputy director of intelligence termed the "intricate mosaic" of intelligence.[1]

Today's commercial and technical advances are only the latest developments in a collection discipline whose pioneers began developing the field in the late 1930s. Building on early work at Princeton University to monitor foreign shortwave radio, the Foreign Broadcast Intelligence Service (FBIS) in 1941 began to turn radio into a primary intelligence source during World War II.[2] The government did not neglect the printed word either. The Interdepartmental Committee for the Acquisition of Foreign Periodicals (IDC) gathered Axis publications through a global collection network.

The men and women who labored in the OSINT fields of the day produced products that compared well in quantity and quality to those of other agencies that stamped their documents "SECRET." Dr. Charles B. Fah, writing in mid-1942 as chief of the Far Eastern Section, Office of Strategic Services (OSS), praised the output of FBIS as "indispensable in our work" and "the most extensive single source available" on developments in Japan and occupied Asia. The OSS itself fared less well, failing to establish an agent network in Japan and reporting the fabrications of an Italian "con man" in Rome as its most valuable source on developments in Tokyo.

Publications also held up well against classified reports. John King Fairbank, the Harvard sinologist who led his field in the postwar era, recounted how, after reading an inaccurate and "unintelligent" British report on Japanese shipbuilding, he advised Col. William Donovan that better intelligence on the issue would be found in "scrutinizing the Japanese press." The OSS director evidently found Dr. Fairbank's brief compelling, for he sent the young academic, literate in Chinese and Japanese, to China to help organize a publications procurement program.[3]

NAVIGATING COLD WAR WATERS

After the guns of the Second World War fell silent, intelligence officers expert in open sources continued to help analysts and officials navigate the murky waters of the Cold War. For example, analysts in FBIS, whose acronym by then stood for the *Foreign*

Broadcast Information Service, and the Foreign Document Division (FDD) led the CIA in detecting the developing estrangement between Moscow and Beijing. FBIS and FDD officers began discerning signs of the Sino-Soviet split from their readings of propaganda material in the early 1950s. In contrast, some CIA officers from the covert side of the house erred, along with many observers elsewhere, in dismissing as disinformation the open evidence well into the next decade.[4]

Throughout the Cold War, in fact, OSINT constituted a major part of all intelligence on the Soviet Union, China, and other adversaries. OSINT on the Soviet Union, for example, grew from modest beginnings to become the leading source. In the closing years of World War II, intelligence officers searched German, Japanese, and Russian documents in the Army's Special Documents Section and the joint Army-Navy Washington Document Center for clues to Soviet technical capabilities. By the late 1950s, the CIA and Air Force had discovered a "wealth of information" in the increasing flow of books and periodicals from the Soviet Union.[5] By the early 1960s, one insider wrote that "In aggregate, open sources probably furnish the greater part of all information used in the production of military intelligence on the Soviet Union."[6] By the decade's end, another wrote of the "tidal wave of publicly printed paper" that both supported and threatened "to swamp" the Intelligence Community. He also offered an example of OSINT's value: "Intense scrutiny of the North Vietnamese press and radio has been an essential intelligence element in support of [the] US effort" in the Indochina conflict.[7]

It is worth noting in passing that all powers exploited OSINT during World War II and the Cold War. Indeed, our adversaries used technical information from open sources in the United States and other advanced industrial nations to monitor foreign developments and to save time and money on their own projects. The US aerospace publication *Aviation Week,* dubbed "Aviation Leak" for its scoops, was a perennial favorite. The journal was among the US technical periodicals that East German intelligence, among others, translated to monitor current developments in aerospace.[8]

By the Cold War's end, commercial and technical changes had made evident the value of OSINT. Radio, the cutting edge in the 1930s, remained a key source in the Second World War and the years thereafter. When Soviet tanks rolled into Budapest in 1956, for example, intelligence officers in Washington kept current through radio reports. One veteran of the CIA's Directorate of Operations (DO), referring to Moscow's suppression of the Hungarian uprising, wrote: "It is a well-known phenomenon in the field of intelligence that there often comes a time when public political activity proceeds at such a rapid and fulminating pace that secret intelligence, the work of agents, is overtaken by events publicly recorded."[9] Some 30 years later, intelligence officers at Langley and government leaders across the Potomac watched, glued to their television sets, as CNN broadcast the fall of the Berlin Wall.[10]

The world today abounds in open information to an extent unimaginable to intelligence officers of the Cold War. When the Soviet Union sent the first man into space in 1961, secretive officials revealed little and lied even about the location of the launch site. In contrast, television reports, Internet sites, and newspaper articles heralded China's first manned flight into orbit in 2003. Even intelligence services have emerged from the shadows to some extent. Two journalists caused a stir in 1964 by writing a landmark book on the US Intelligence Community. Today, former case officers recount their clandestine careers.[11]

OSINT, OSINT EVERYWHERE . . .

The revolution in information technology, commerce, and politics since the Cold War's end is only making open sources more accessible, ubiquitous, and valuable. Simply put, one can gather more open intelligence with greater ease and at less cost than ever before. The explosion in OSINT is transforming the intelligence world with the emergence of open versions of the covert arts of human intelligence (HUMINT), overhead imagery (IMINT), and signals intelligence (SIGINT).

The Intelligence Community has seen open sources grow increasingly easier and cheaper to acquire in recent years. The Internet's development and commercial innovation has given us Web sites, "amazon.com," and countless other vendors. During the Second World War, Dr. Fairbank traveled far and at great expense to gather Japanese publications in China and send them to Washington. Today, anyone, anywhere, can order Japanese media with a click of the mouse from amazon.co.jp or other online merchants and receive the orders by express air shipment. In the "old days," not so long ago, academics and analysts made the pilgrimage to Maryland to browse the shelves of Victor Kamkin's unmatched store for Soviet publications. In the present, one can go online from the comfort of home to www.kamkin.com to buy from the half-million Russian titles in stock or to place a custom order.

Moreover, the IT revolution extends beyond the printed word. More and more local radio and television broadcasts, for example, are found on the World Wide Web. Monitors no longer need to sit close to the broadcast source. Nor do they always need an expensive infrastructure of antennas and other equipment to listen to radio or watch television.

Beyond the usual public media, OSINT is expanding into the areas of HUMINT, IMINT, and SIGINT. In the words of one advocate with experience in both the government and private sector, "OSINT now pervades all of the collection disciplines." He notes that one can gather intelligence today by overtly tasking collectors to elicit information, ordering commercial satellite imagery, and using software to conduct traffic analysis.[12]

IMINT, for example, is becoming such a commercial commodity as to be in danger, in the view of one intelligence expert, of ceasing to be an "INT." Japan offers a fine demonstration of media exploitation of commercial IMINT. A major magazine known for its focus on North Korea, for example, prominently and frequently displays commercial imagery of such sites as the nuclear facilities at Yongbyon and the alleged residences of leader Kim Chong-il. Journalists combine the IMINT with published defector information, leaks, and other sources to analyze issues. As an example of open IMINT closer to home, the Federation of American Scientists (FAS) used Space Imaging photographs of a DPRK missile site to argue in 2000 that P'yongyang's missile threat was far less than Washington had claimed. Whatever the merits of the FAS argument, the case underscores the opening of the covert INTs.[13]

Even so, OSINT is no replacement for covert collection. Rather, open sources increasingly enhance secret collection programs. The CIA, NGA, NSA, and other actors on the classified side all benefit from the growing volume of open data serving them as collateral information. Too, OSINT allows covert collectors to marshal limited resources for the most intractable problems. Digital Globe and Space Imaging will never replace NGA, for example, but government acquisition of their commercial imagery for basic requirements can relieve NGA of mundane tasks and permit it focus on higher priorities.

In addition to their influence on collection disciplines, open sources have long played a major role in covert action. Imperial Japan, for example, employed the German, Alexander von Siebold, to influence foreign opinion in Tokyo's favor. The agent launched the journal *Ostasien* (East Asia) in 1899 with Japanese backing, contributed favorable articles to the European media, and otherwise worked to shape views on Japan. He also monitored the media, submitting his "Baron von Siebold's Report on the Press" to inform the Japanese of foreign developments and opinion.[14] In the Cold War, covert organs of the major powers disseminated news and views through front organizations to win hearts and minds. Open sources still constitute the core of political covert action today, except that overt organizations are often conducting the campaigns.[15]

SURROUNDING TARGETS HARD AND SOFT

Not only are open sources increasingly accessible, ubiquitous, and valuable, but they can shine in particular against the hardest of hard targets. OSINT is at times the "INT" of first resort, last resort, and every resort in between.

To some, this assertion may represent an overselling of OSINT. Arthur Hulnick, a former CIA officer who went on to teach at Boston University has written about OSINT's importance: "Neither glamorous nor adventurous, open sources are nonetheless the basic building block for secret intelligence." He has also noted how OSINT, whether conveyed via FBIS or CNN, provides early warning. He has even estimated that open sources may account for "as much as 80 percent" of the intelligence database in general. Nevertheless, Hulnick has suggested that OSINT would probably be far less useful against such tough cases as North Korea.[16]

However, open sources may often be more useful in penetrating closed borders than open societies. Because OSINT is intelligence derived from open sources, fewer sources mean greater coverage is possible with a limited number of monitors. Take the two Koreas, for example. The Democratic People's Republic of Korea (DPRK), with perhaps the world's most authoritarian government, is a relatively easy OSINT target. North Korea has only two major daily newspapers: *Nodong Sinmun* and *Minju Choson*, the newspapers of the ruling party and the government, respectively. There is no opposition newspaper in the capital and no lively provincial media to offer competing opinions or expose wrongdoing. The

Republic of Korea (ROK), on the other hand, has a boisterous press, comprising over a dozen newspapers centered in Seoul, with views spanning the full spectrum of political opinion. Each day brings a flood of government statements, corporate press releases, editorials, scoops, and scandals. In relative terms, monitoring P'yongyang's media is like sipping through a straw; following Seoul's open sources is like drinking from a fire hose.

P'yongyang media, while controlled, constitute a valuable resource to anyone seeking to understand the DPRK. More than mere propaganda, as Dr. Wayne Kiyosaki, an expert literate in Korean and well-versed in the media, argued in his study of DPRK foreign relations, P'yongyang's communications are a tool of mass indoctrination. As such, they provide "a barometer of priorities."[17] Dr. Adrian Buzo, a former Australian diplomat with the rare experience of residing in P'yongyang, has seconded the value of DPRK media as a "continuing record of the regime's priorities, of its ideological concerns, and of key personnel changes." Warning readers against the common trap in the West of dismissing the media "out of hand," he has advised that "Sustained exposure to the DPRK media is an essential requirement for the would-be analyst, both in itself and as an essential check on the reportage of the DPRK's adversaries."[18]

Finally, continuing with the DPRK as an example, US analysts and policymakers often have little beyond OSINT upon which to base their judgments. The State Department has no embassy in P'yongyang. Few foreigners reside in the capital; even fewer live in the provinces. Opportunities to make contact with the rare North Koreans who reside or travel abroad have been poor. Only the trusted few may make an international telephone call, send a fax, exchange e-mails, or surf the Internet. Such restrictions reduce covert collection opportunities. The open record for HUMINT is telling. Ambassador Donald Gregg, an "Asia hand" whose DO career included a stint in Seoul, has described the DPRK as "one of the longest-running intelligence failures in the history of US espionage."[19]

Other nations fare no better. One would expect the Japanese, former colonial overlords of Korea for more than 30 years, to accomplish more covert collection against their neighbors than their writings suggest. Tsukamoto Katsuichi, a retired army general with experience as defense attaché in Seoul, has confessed: "No country is as opaque as the DPRK (North Korea). Almost no information leaks out of there. Therefore, we have no choice but to make our judgments based on the little announced in the official newspaper *(Nodong Sinmun)* and radio broadcasts (Korea Central News Agency), as well as a limited number of visitor accounts."[20] A former officer of the Public Security Intelligence Agency (PSIA), Japan's, equivalent to the FBI, has also written that analysis of "published materials" is "central" to analyzing the DPRK, given the absence of nearly all else. Such OSINT, he has written, is "more important and indispensable than is generally imagined."[21]

. . . BUT FEW TO SAIL THE SEA

> Today, open source has expanded well beyond "frosting" and comprises a large part of the cake itself. It has become indispensable to the production of authoritative analysis.
>
> —*John Gannon, former Chairman, National Intelligence Council*[22]

With open sources so accessible, ubiquitous, and valuable, one would expect to see OSINT occupying a commensurately large space within the Intelligence Community. This is not the case. Too many people still reject OSINT as intelligence. Worse, too few are able to gather and exploit open sources. Worst of all, the Intelligence Community assigns only a handful of those capable people to the task.

Too many people still mistake secrets for intelligence. The enduring popularity of the fictional James Bond bears much of the blame, perhaps, for the misperception outside of the Intelligence Community that a tuxedo, pistol, and charm are the main tools of intelligence gathering. Even some insiders err in believing intelligence to be identical with covert sources and methods. The following opinion of a retired DO officer is typical: "Despite frequent references to 'open source intelligence,' within the CIA this term is somewhat of an oxymoron. By definition, intelligence is clandestinely acquired information—stolen, to put it bluntly. Information from a magazine, a television broadcast, or someone's newsletter may be valuable, but it is not intelligence."[23]

More than 40 years after Sherman Kent, the CIA's father of intelligence analysis, persuasively argued that intelligence is knowledge, some still confuse the method with the product. Sadly, such confusion is widespread. As one DPRK watcher noted: "Much of the best political intelligence comes from careful culling of public sources, like reading reports in the North Korean media, but within the intelligence community this source is not considered as reliable as more esoteric technical means, like satellite photography and communications intercepts, or spies."[24] However, as a staff director of the House Permanent Select Committee on Intelligence (HPSCI) once explained to a deputy director of operations, "We don't give you brownie points for collecting intelligence by the hardest means possible."[25]

A few examples should suffice to support Kent's definition of intelligence:

- An intelligence officer would likely have received high marks for stealing a map of the Khabarovsk area of the Soviet Far East in 1988. Drawn at a scale of 1:10,000 and running to 80 pages, the map of the General Staff's Military Topographic Headquarters would have taken a classified stamp and stayed within a secure vault, available only to those with a need to know. The map, published in 1998 and advertised as the first of this scale declassified in Russia, is for sale today.[26]
- Stanislav Levchenko, a KGB officer working under cover as a reporter in Japan, defected to the United States in 1979. In 1983, a Japanese journalist conducted more than 20 hours of interviews with him, during which the former operative named agents and discussed tradecraft. The resulting book and Levchenko's press conferences were, according to a US intelligence officer, more revealing than his CIA debriefing.[27]
- On 7 June 1942, the day after the US "miracle" at Midway due to the top-secret breaking of Japanese communications, the *Chicago Tribune* trumpeted on its front page that the US Navy had known of Japanese plans "several days before the battle began." A Japanese officer reading that newspaper probably would have grasped that the naval codes were insecure.[28]

Information openly acquired, whether open from the start (say, a telephone book), declassified, or leaked, is intelligence when assessed and disseminated appropriately.[29] History abounds with examples of OSINT collection by intelligence officers:

- Military attachés have long attached magazine photographs of aircraft, ships, and tanks to their classified reports.
- Japan's Kempeitai in wartime Shanghai gathered the writings of Agnes Smedley and Edgar Snow in the course of collecting intelligence on the Chinese Communist Party.[30]

- Various services culled intelligence from the pages of the Soviet military daily *Krasnaya Zvezda* (Red Star), including the wartime Imperial Japanese Army's Harbin Special Services Agency and the postwar US Intelligence Community.[31]

Beyond the persistent dismissal of open sources as intelligence, the US Intelligence Community suffers from America's general indifference to foreign languages and ideas. Any intelligence agency reflects the society from which it comes. Americans, living in a vast country and speaking a language that has become the world's *lingua franca*, show little interest in learning other languages or, indeed, knowing what those outside their borders think. The result is an Intelligence Community recruiting officers from among a relatively small pool of Americans who, through immigration or education, possess the expertise in foreign languages and area studies required for collecting open sources.

Knowing foreign languages is the key to exploiting OSINT. An account with LexisNexis and a subscription to the *Wall Street Journal* are hardly sufficient. English is declining from the world's dominant language to merely "first among equals."[32] Even the Internet fails the monolingual American. Chinese is slated to surpass English as the Internet's leading language in the near future.[33] Domain names, once issued only in English or other languages with Roman letters, increasingly appear in Arabic, Chinese, Farsi, Korean, and other non-alphabet languages. Put simply, English is best for monitoring nations where English is used. But what intelligence challenges confront the United States in Australia, Britain, Canada, Ireland, or New Zealand? On the contrary, languages with which Americans are least familiar are precisely those of countries of greatest concern: Arabic (Iraq), Chinese (China), Farsi (Iran), Korean (DPRK), and Pashto (Afghanistan), to name only some examples.

Although facing such challenges, the United States lacks the education base upon which to develop tomorrow's intelligence officers. Relatively few Americans pursue a foreign language from secondary school through the university level. Worse, most university language students still study the Romance tongues or German in courses designed chiefly to produce professors of literature. The Intelligence Community must then compete with the private sector for the handful of competent linguists graduating from university.

The bleak alternative is to start adults on crash courses at the Defense Language Institute (DLI) or elsewhere on some of the world's most difficult languages.

On a related issue, an indifference to foreign languages and even foreign sources in translation diminishes the OSINT value of the US mass media. American journalists on the whole have been ignorant of the countries on which they have reported. Most who have covered the nuclear dispute between P'yongyang and Washington, for example, cannot read a Korean restaurant menu, let alone the pages of *Nodong Sinmun*. Worse, as one observer noted of an earlier period of crisis: "Reporters did not routinely read translations of the North Korean news by the Foreign Broadcast Information Service. Nor did they avail themselves of information circulating among outside experts by e-mail and fax."[34] The resulting level of reporting has been so poor that one prominent academic who can read Korean wrote recently of having to turn to P'yongyang's "tightly controlled press" for information on Washington-P'yongyang relations.[35]

The reluctance of US publishers to introduce foreign books in translation further lessens the flow of open sources available to Americans. For example, ROK movie star Ch'oe Un-hui and her former husband, the director Sin Sang-ok, gained extraordinary access to Kim Chong-il after he kidnapped them in 1978 in a bid to upgrade P'yongyang's film industry; they worked for him until their escape in 1986. Their account of the Dear Leader, complete with photographs, appeared in 1988 in Seoul and Tokyo. They were for years the only outsiders who had known Kim and written of their experience, but no American publisher saw fit to issue the book in translation. The same is true of numerous books in recent years, from other insiders, including the architect of DPRK ideology and Kim's private sushi chef.[36]

An example closer to home is that of Dr. Emmanuel Todd's *After the Empire: The Breakdown of the American Order*. Published originally in 2003 in French, the book appeared the same year in various languages, including German, Italian, Japanese, Korean, and Spanish. The belated appearance a year later of the American edition of a book regarding what a prominent academic—who had forecast in 1976 the eventual fall of the Soviet Union—sees as Washington's futile struggle to maintain a global hegemony stands as an indictment of the US publishing industry.[37]

Compounding the problem of insufficient foreign information reaching the United States, the decline of area studies since the Cold War's end has reduced the pool of able applicants prepared to exploit foreign information in the vernacular. Russian studies, for example, have suffered grievously in funding and enrollment. Many graduates have found that US businesses prefer to send monolingual accountants to Moscow to teaching a Russian expert accounting. Area experts seeking university tenure find positions going to political scientists churning out papers on "rational choice" regarding countries they know hardly at all. Students attending courses of area studies today are more often seeking their ethnic roots than preparing to join the Intelligence Community. For example, a German professor teaching Korean political economy at a time of high military tension between Washington and P'yongyang found that around three quarters of his students at Columbia University were Asians or Asian-Americans. He wrote, "I was astonished by the relative lack of interest in Korea among American students, especially in such a tense situation as at present, when only deep knowledge about modern Korea can help prevent potentially disastrous policy decisions."[38]

All of this would be bad enough, but even worse is the fact that only a handful of capable officers with language and area skills are casting their nets into the global sea of open sources for intelligence. The results have been catastrophic. In the words of one former DO officer who has argued that "covert collectors should not be blamed" for missing Osama Bin Laden: "It is virtually impossible to penetrate a revolutionary terrorist organization, particularly one structured and manned the way al-Qa'ida is. The responsibility falls on the intelligence community's overt collectors and analysts." He suggests that the information was out there, but that analysts were simply not reading the relevant foreign media. The same lack of OSINT exploitation, he asserts, was also behind Washington's failure to comprehend the rise to power of Ayatollah Khomeini in Iran a quarter century ago.[39] Two senior CIA officers warn that things are likely to grow worse. They note how "knowledge of culture, history, and language will be even more critical as the amount of open source material increases." They also admit that, "Inadequate American foreign language skills are a mismatch for the exponential growth in foreign language materials."[40]

BUILDING A NEW "CRAFT" OF INTELLIGENCE

"The collection of foreign intelligence is accomplished in a variety of ways, not all of them either mysterious or secret. This is particularly true of overt intelligence, which is information derived from newspapers, books, learned and technical publications, official reports of government proceedings, radio and television. Even a novel or play may contain useful information about the state of a nation."

—*Allen Dulles, The Craft of Intelligence*[41]

The words of the former director of central intelligence (DCI) seem even more true today than when he published them over 40 years ago, but the Intelligence Community needs to build a better ship to sail the sea of open sources. FBIS, the largest and best equipped of the disorganized collection of offices engaged in OSINT, is too small a craft with too few hands to navigate the waters and harvest the catch. Analysts, by and large, lack the knowledge of foreign languages, media expertise, and time to do their own fishing.

WHAT IS TO BE DONE?

First, the DCI should increase the number of language officers at FBIS. Officers with knowledge of foreign languages, countries, and media are necessary to gather and analyze open sources, as photo interpreters are required to make sense of satellite imagery. The sea of open sources is arguably as large as that of covert communications, so one could argue that there should be as many open source officers surfing the Web as there are signals intelligence officers breaking secure communications. Required are college scholarships for students literate in Chinese and other innovative means of enlarging the pool of future OSINT officers.

Second, the Intelligence Community should take steps to turn the motley group of OSINT units into an organized fleet, with FBIS as the flagship. At a minimum, the Intelligence Community would do well to designate FBIS as the coordinator for OSINT. An enhanced FBIS could build on its expertise, its databases, and its longstanding role of serving the entire Intelligence Community by coordinating the output from the various embassy press translation units, military gray literature collectors, and such. An alternate, and more ambitious, plan would be to build a central agency for open intelligence based on

FBIS. The new organization would be for OSINT what the DO is for HUMINT, National Reconnaissance Office is for IMINT, and the National Security Agency is for SIGINT.[42]

Third, the Intelligence Community must organize its own technical resources and tap those of the private sector to exploit the latest information technology for OSINT collection, analysis, production, and dissemination. OSINT collectors, all-source analysts, and others would benefit from smarter search engines, enhanced machine-assisted translation software, and better tools for incorporating audio and video streams into intelligence reports.

Above all, the Intelligence Community requires a sustained approach to open sources. As with other collection disciplines, one cannot conjure OSINT programs out of thin air. Assembling a substantial number of officers competent in Arabic, Chinese, Farsi, Korean, and other languages and expert in fishing in the OSINT seas, then giving them the sources and methods to do their work, would be no small feat.

QUESTIONS FOR FURTHER DISCUSSION

1. Is open-source intelligence a lost art that is only now being rediscovered by the intelligence community?
2. Why are some intelligence professionals resistant to the idea of open-source intelligence?
3. What skills are needed to become a practitioner of open-source intelligence?
4. Is the information revolution making open-source information more valuable?

ENDNOTES

1. Russell Jack Smith, *The Unknown CIA: My Three Decades with the Agency* (Washington, DC: Pergamon-Brassey's, 1989), 195.
2. Information on the Princeton Listening Center, launched in 1939, is available at http://libweb.princeton.edu:2003/libraries/firestone/rbsc/finding_aide/plc.html. For a history of FBIS during the Second World War, see Stephen C. Mercado, "FBIS Against the Axis, 1941–1945," *Studies in Intelligence,* Unclassified Edition no. 11 (Fall-Winter 2001): 33–43.
3. For Dr. Fah's comment, see Mercado, 41. On the Italian "confidence trickster" who fooled James Jesus Angleton and other OSS officers, see David Alvarez, *Spies in the Vatican: Espionage and Intrigue from Napoleon to the Holocaust* (Lawrence: University Press of Kansas,

2002), 248–53. Regarding Dr. Fairbank's role in OSS, see John King Fairbank, *Chinabound: A Fifty-Year Memoir* (New York: Harper Colophon, 1983), 174–75.

4. The downgrading of the "I" in FBIS from "Intelligence" to "Information" reflects the mistaken notion that only stolen secrets count as intelligence. CIA counterintelligence officers, under the leadership of James Jesus Angleton, were among those in Washington who continued to dismiss the growing evidence of the Sino-Soviet split well into the 1960s. On how OSINT officers led the way in understanding the breakup of "monolithic communism," see Harold P. Ford, "Calling the Sino-Soviet Split," *Studies in Intelligence*, Winter 1998–99, Unclassified Edition: 57–71. On Angleton, see also Harold P. Ford, "Why CIA Analysts Were So Doubtful About Vietnam," *Studies in Intelligence*, Unclassified Edition No.

5. J. J. Bagnall, "The Exploitation of Russian Scientific Literature for Intelligence Purposes," *Studies in Intelligence* (Summer 1958): 45–49. Declassified article.

6. Davis W. Moore, "Open Sources on Soviet Military Affairs," *Studies in Intelligence* (Summer 1963-declassified article): 101.

7. Herman L. Croom, "The Exploitation of Foreign Open Sources," *Studies in Intelligence* (Summer 1969-declassified article): 129–30.

8. Joseph Becker, "Comparative Survey of Soviet and US Access to Published Information," *Studies in Intelligence* (Fall 1957-declassified article): 43; John O. Koehler, *Stasi: The Untold Story of the East German Secret Police* (Boulder, CO: Westview Press, 1999), 110. Becker's article includes a reference to Soviet reading of *Aviation Week*.

9. Peer de Silva, *Sub Rosa: The CIA and the Uses of Intelligence* (New York: Times Books, 1978), 120.

10. Antonio J. Mendez, with Malcolm McConnell, *The Master of Disguise: My Secret Life in the CIA* (New York: William Morrow & Co., 1999), 337. On the monitoring of television in the Cold War, see Maureen Cote, "Veni, Vidi, Vid-Int," *Studies in Intelligence*, Fall 1990. Unclassified.

11. See David Wise and Thomas B. Ross, *The Invisible Government* (New York: Random House, 1964). Notable insider accounts of recent years include Duane "Dewey" Clarridge, *A Spy for All Seasons* (New York: Simon & Schuster, 1997) and Robert Baer, *See No Evil* (New York: Crown, 2002).

12. Mark M. Lowenthal, "OSINT: The State of the Art, the Artless State," *Studies in Intelligence* 45, no. 3 (2001): 62.

13. On IMINT ceasing to be an "INT," see Gregory F. Treverton, *Reshaping National Intelligence for an Age of Information* (New York: Cambridge University Press, 2001), 87. A Japanese magazine notable for its prominent use of commercial IMINT on DPRK pol-mil issues is *SAPIO*, which advertises itself as an "international intelligence magazine." See *SAPIO*, 8 January 2003, for example, for use of Digital Globe imagery of alleged residences of Kim Chong-il. Regarding the FAS dispute, see *New York Times*, 11 January 2000.

14. Foreign Ministry Diplomatic Records Office and Nihon Gaikoshi Jiten Editorial Committee, eds., *Nihon Gaikoshi Jiten* [Dictionary of Japanese Diplomatic History] (Tokyo: Yamakawa Shuppansha, 1992), 361. A British historian of Japanese diplomatic history has also written of "indications" that Von Siebold went beyond OSINT for the Japanese Foreign Ministry and Army. Ian Nish, "Japanese Intelligence and the Approach of the Russo-Japanese War," in Christopher Andrew and David Dilks, eds., *The Missing Dimension: Governments and Intelligence Communities in the Twentieth Century* (Urbana: University of Illinois Press, 1984), 19.

15. Frederick L. Wettering, "(C)overt Action: The Disappearing 'C,'" *International Journal of Intelligence and CounterIntelligence* (Winter 2003–2004), 566–67.

16. Arthur S. Hulnick, *Fixing the Spy Machine: Preparing American Intelligence for the Twenty-First Century* (Westport, CT: Praeger, 1999), 8, 40–41.

17. Wayne S. Kiyosaki, *North Korea's Foreign Relations: The Politics of Accommodation, 1945–75* (New York, Praeger, 1976), x–xi. Dr. Kiyosaki, a graduate in Korean of the Defense Language Institute who later honed his media insights at FBIS, knew of what he wrote.

18. Adrian Buzo, *The Guerrilla Dynasty: Politics and Leadership in North Korea* (Boulder, CO: Westview Press, 1999), 284–85. On the value of DPRK media in charting personnel changes in P'yongyang, it is worth noting that the standard reference works, such as the annual *North Korea Directory* of Japan's impressive Radiopress and the online biographic compilations of the ROK's National Intelligence Service (www.nis.go.kr) are based on media monitoring. For one journalist's recognition of the value of following P'yongyang's media, see Gordon Fairclough, "To See North Korea, Keep Your Eyes Peeled on the Official Press," *Wall Street Journal*, 19 February 2004:1.

19. Donald P. Gregg, "A Long Road to P'yongyang," *The Korea Society Quarterly*, Spring 2002: 7.

20. Tsukamoto Katsuichi, "Kitachosen josei to Higashi Ajia no anzen hosho," *Securitarian*, July 1995: 22. General Tsukamoto, who began his career as a commissioned officer of the Imperial Japanese Army and

finished it as commander of the Ground Self-Defense Force's Western Army, has written several books on Korean security issues.

21. Noda Hironari (pseud.), *CIA supai kenshu: Am Koan Chosakan no taikenki* [CIA Spy Training: One PSIA Officer's Account] (Tokyo: Gendai Shokan, 2000): 169–170. It is interesting to note that PSIA changed its English name, but not its acronym, in 2003, replacing "Investigation" with "Intelligence."

22. John Gannon, "The Strategic Use of Open-Source Information," *Studies in Intelligence* 45, no. 3 (2001): 67.

23. Thomas Patrick Carroll, "The Case Against Intelligence Openness," *International Journal of Intelligence and CounterIntelligence* (Winter 2001–2002): 561.

24. Leon V. Sigal, *Disarming Strangers: Nuclear Diplomacy With North Korea* (Princeton, NJ: Princeton University Press, 1998), 234.

25. Sherman Kent, *Strategic Intelligence for American World Policy* (Princeton, NJ: Princeton University Press, 1949). There is no more succinct definition of intelligence than the title of Part I: "Intelligence Is Knowledge." For the HPSCI staff director's remark, see Mark M. Lowenthal, "Open Source Intelligence: New Myths, New Realities," *Defense Daily Online*, reprinted in *The Intelligencer* (Winter 1999): 7.

26. This and many other declassified Russian maps have been advertised on line at East View Information Services of Minneapolis, MN (www.eastview.com).

27. Levchenko's interviews, which appeared in abbreviated form in a series running in the Japanese weekly magazine *Shukan Bunshun* over five weeks in mid-1983, were issued later that year as a book. Shukan Bunshun, ed. *Refuchenko wa shogen suru* [Levchenko Testifies] (Tokyo: Bungei Shunju, 1983). Haruna Mikio, a former Washington bureau chief of Japan's Kyodo News Agency with extensive contacts in the US Intelligence Community, wrote that an unidentified CIA officer was "surprised" at how much more detailed he found Levchenko's public revelations. See Haruna Mikio, *Himitsu no fairu: CIA no tainichi kosaku* [Secret Files: The CIA's Operations Against Japan] (Tokyo: Shinchosha Bunko, 2003), volume 2, 483. Whatever the accuracy of Haruna's purported source, Levchenko's Japanese book is more revealing than the one he published in the United States: *On the Wrong Side: My Life in the KGB* [Washington: Pergamon-Brassey's, 1988).

28. "Navy Had Word of Jap Plan to Strike at Sea," *Chicago Tribune*, 7 June 1942. On the "miraculous" character of the victory, see Gordon Prange et al., *Miracle at Midway* (New York: McGraw-Hill, 1982).

29. Intelligence officers have long worried about the damage done through the leaks of classified intelligence and even the gathering of published information by adversaries. Leaks are an old problem. See, for example, Allen Dulles, *The Craft of Intelligence* (New York: Harper & Row, 1963), 241–43. On leaks today, see James B. Bruce, "The Consequences of Permissive Neglect," *Studies in Intelligence* 47, no. 3 (2003, Unclassified). Becker, "Comparative Survey," 35, noted in 1957 Soviet exploitation of US open sources and the repeated failures of the US Government from the 1940s to find a solution to the problem.

30. Tsukamoto Makoto, *Arujoho shoko no shuki* [Memoirs of an Intelligence Officer] (Tokyo: Chuo Bunko, 1998), 195. Agnes Smedley (*China's Red Army Marches*, 1934) and Edgar Snow (*Red Star Over China*, 1938) were prolific American writers with extraordinary access to Chinese communists.

31. Nakano Koyukai, ed., *Rikugun Nakano Gakko* [Army Nakano School] (Tokyo: Nakano Koyukai, 1978), 176, and Moore, "Open Sources," 104.

32. David Graddol, "The Future of Language," *Science* 303 (27 February 2004): 1329–31.

33. The prediction on Chinese Internet was made at a conference of the World Intellectual Property Organization, according to the *Financial Times*, 7 December 2001.

34. Sigal, *Disarming Strangers*, 221.

35. Bruce Cumings, *North Korea: Another Country* (New York: New Press, 2004), 47–48.

36. The architect of North Korea's Chuch'e philosophy, Hwang Chang-yop, has written a number of books, including *Na nun yoksa ui chilli rulpoatta: Hwang Chang-yop hoegorok* [I Saw the Truth of History: Memoirs of Hwang Chang-yop] (Seoul: Hanul, 1999). A Japanese sushi chef in Kim's service, publishing under the pseudonym Kenji Fujimoto, wrote *Kin Seinichi no ryorinin* (Tokyo: Shinchosha, 2003). These are two of many insider accounts likely never to see the light of day in the United States.

37. Emmanuel Todd, *After the Empire: The Breakdown of the American Order* (New York: Columbia University Press, 2004), *Après l'empire: Essai sur la décomposition du système américain* (Paris: Gallimard, 2003) and *La Chute finale: Essai sur la décomposition de la sphère sovietique* (Paris: Robert Laffont, 1976).

38. Constantine Pleshakov, "Russian Studies: A Sinking Academic Atlantis," *Japan Times*, 15 March 1995:17. Dr. Ruediger Frank of Humboldt-Universität zu Berlin noted the general lack of interest in "An Interview with a Visiting Lecturer," *Annual Report 2002–2003*, Weatherhead East Asian Institute, Columbia University, 21.

39. Robert D. Chapman, "The Muslim Crusade." *International Journal of Intelligence and CounterIntelligence* (Winter 2002–2003): 613–14.

40. Aris A. Pappas and James M. Simon, Jr., "The Intelligence Community: 2001–2015," *Studies in Intelligence* 46, no. 1 (2002): 45. For a view of how deficiencies in foreign languages hurt covert collection, see Matthew M. Aid, "All Glory Is Fleeting: SIGINT and the Fight Against International Terrorism," *Intelligence and National Security* 18, no. 4 (Winter 2003): 100–102.

41. Allen Dulles, *The Craft of Intelligence* (New York: Harper & Row, 1963), 55. For a similar view, see Robert D. Steele, *The New Craft of Intelligence: Personal, Public, Political* (Oaktoh, VA: OSS International Press, 2002). For those interested in a concrete example of literature serving as a guide to intelligence, see how poems in the DPRK literary journal *Choson Munhak* [Korean Literature] signaled the preparation of Kim Chong-il to succeed his father. Morgan E. Clippinger, "Kim Chong-il in the North Korean Mass Media: A Study of Semi-Esoteric Communication," *Asian Survey* (March 1981): 291.

42. Creating a central OSINT agency is far from a novel idea. The proposal surfaced, for example, in *Studies in Intelligence* in 1969. See Croom, "Exploitation," 135.

6. INTRODUCING SOCIAL MEDIA INTELLIGENCE (SOCMINT)

SIR DAVID OMAND, JAMIE BARTLETT AND CARL MILLER

We introduce the latest member of the intelligence family. Joining IMINT, HUMINT, SIGINT and others is 'SOCMINT'—social media intelligence. In an age of ubiquitous social media it is the responsibility of the security community to admit SOCMINT into the national intelligence framework, but only when two important tests are passed. First, that it rests on solid methodological bedrock of collection, evidence, verification, understanding and application. Second, that the moral hazard it entails can be legitimately managed. This article offers a framework for how this can be done.

INTRODUCTION

On Thursday 4 August 2011, Mark Duggan was shot and killed by a police officer in Tottenham. By the morning of the 6th, social media channels showed burgeoning hostility, peppered with explicit threats against the police. From the 7th, social media information indicated the possible spread of disorder to other parts of London, then England. Over the next few days, content indicating criminal intent or action ratcheted in huge numbers through both open-source social networking, such as Twitter, and closed system networks, such as the BlackBerry Messaging Service and closed groups such as chat forums. Similarly, huge numbers of messages appeared trying to provide information to the police, either about an outbreak of disorder or the identities of the people behind it.[1]

In the aftermath, the police acknowledged that they had been insufficiently equipped to deal with intelligence gathering via social media. One intelligence professional said it was like 'searching the British Library for a page in a book without an index to refer to'.[2] Social media did not fit into their systems of receiving, corroborating, prioritizing and disseminating information, and therefore was not properly acted on. Her Majesty's Chief Inspector of Constabulary noted: 'With some notable individual exceptions, the power of this kind of media (both for sending out and receiving information) is

not well understood and less well managed'.[3] He concluded that 'the police have much to learn about social media, and the quickly shifting modern communications of today'.[4]

Since then, Government has reacted. The Metropolitan Police has established a social media hub, in time for the London Olympics. A number of police forces in the UK and elsewhere are believed to be trialling various types of automated social media collection and analysis to collect information to help criminal investigations and gauge the 'temperature' of communities they are working with.[5] Police forces have used Flickr to crowd source identifications of suspects from photographs. In the UK, the Ministry of Defence's Cyber and Influence Science and Technology Centre has released a number of calls for research to develop capabilities including 'cyber situational awareness', 'influence through cyber' and 'social media monitoring and analysis: crowd sourcing'.[6] Underlying these developments is significant planned public investment in the capabilities that will allow the authorities to continue to access communications data and access under warrant where necessary the content of internet communications including social media. In the UK, new legislation has been proposed to ensure law enforcement agencies maintain the ability to tackle crime and terrorism as criminals use modern technology and new ways of communicating in the digital space to plan and commit crime.

This rapid growth of interest by law enforcement in intelligence derived from social media (which we term SOCMINT) prompts questions about the methodological and ethical framework within which it will be used. Public acceptability lies at the heart of any form of intelligence collection, and this can only be secured if SOCMINT is properly used and properly authorized. This article suggests a framework for how this can be achieved.

THE AGE OF SOCIAL MEDIA

We live in the age of social media. Facebook, Twitter, Google + and LinkedIn are all examples of the rapid transfer of people's lives—interactions, identities, arguments and views—onto a new kind of public and private sphere; a vast digital social commons. This transfer is happening on an unprecedented scale. On Facebook alone, 250 million photos are added per day,[7] as are 200 million tweets on Twitter.[8] There are four billion video views per day on YouTube.[9]

As people transfer more of their lives onto social media platforms, they become an increasingly significant public space, and therefore of interest to, and used by, public bodies. Understanding the content of social media presents an opportunity for public bodies better to understand, and respond to, the public they serve. Public health experts are learning to scan tweets and search requests to identify pandemics earlier than traditional methods.[10] US psychologists believe Facebook contains valuable indicators of mental health, and indeed the social media profiles of a number of participants in school shootings, such as the suspect in the Ohio School Shooting, TJ Lane, seem to show some indicative content.[11] The United Nations believes that tapping into social media can help tackle global unemployment and food insecurity.[12]

Social media spaces are also now significantly relevant to security and public safety. Facebook has been used to try to hire hitmen, groom the targets of paedophiles, violate restraining orders, steal identities and fatally cyberbully victims.[13] Al-Qaeda's Somali affiliate Al-Shabaab runs a twitter account, whilst pirates operating in the Gulf of Aden use blogs, Twitter and Facebook to plan and coordinate with each other.[14] The Daily Mail reported that 12,300 alleged offences were linked to Facebook in 2011.[15]

When society develops and adopts new methods of communication and organization—such as social media—public institutions, including the police and intelligence services, have a responsibility to react and adapt. The explosion of social media is the latest in a long line of disruptive technological innovations, and now requires a response from the authorities in turn.

THE OPPORTUNITY OF SOCMINT

Measuring and understanding the visage of millions of people digitally arguing, talking, joking, condemning and applauding is of wide and tremendous value to many fields, interests and industries. A family of 'big data' approaches already exists to make sense of social media. Known as social media analytics, these tools constitute a broad church, ranging from advertisers listening to social media 'buzz' to track attitudes surrounding their brands and companies monitoring their social media reputation, to mapping 'social graphs' of relationships between people, to drawing 'wisdom of the crowd' solutions to emergency situations, to conducting linguistic analysis of forum posts and network analysis of Twitter users. Fledgling academic efforts have used social media to inform investments into hedge funds.[16]

Looking at the current SOCMINT technologies now on the horizon—as well as the threats we now face—the following capabilities could for example contribute in the future to public security:

- *Crowd-sourced information.* This could help ensure a better flow of information between citizens and the government, especially in times of emergency.[17] With access to social media, passive bystanders can become active citizen journalists, providing and relaying information from the ground. The report by Her Majesty's Inspectorate of Constabulary into the riots notes, for example, a messaging service on West Midlands Police's website, which allowed citizens to post messages and questions, allowing the police to build up a picture of the situation on the ground in real-time, as well as allowing people to identify pictures of suspects uploaded to the site.[18] Tapping into the 'wisdom of the crowds' is already of great, demonstrated value. For example, the open-source platform Ushahidi has allowed large groups of people to provide collective testimony on everything from the earthquake in Haiti to blocked roads in Washington, DC.[19]

These applications, impressive as they are, are only the beginning, and the stronger the techniques to make sense of information of this kind, scale and dynamism, the more effective the responses, from providing snow ploughs to drinking water, that can be made.

- *Research and understanding.* Research based on social media could contribute to our understanding of a number of phenomena. This could include the thresholds, indicators and permissive conditions of violence; pathways into radicalization; an analysis of how ideas form and change; and investigation of the socio-technical intersections between online and offline personae. Beneath the tactical and operational level, a background of more generic and distanced understanding is important for security work. For instance, the British counter-terrorism strategy aims to reduce the threat from terrorism so that people can go about their normal lives, freely and with confidence, and it is understood that the long-term way to do this is through tackling the underlying social, ideational and political causes of terrorism.

In addition, the rise in use of social media, together with the rapid development of analytics approaches, now provides a new opportunity for law enforcement to generate operational intelligence that could help identify criminal activity, indicate early warning of outbreaks of disorder, provide information and intelligence about groups and individuals, and help understand and respond to public concerns. Some of this access will come from 'open source' information derived from Twitter and other social media content authorized for public access. Some, however, will require legal authorization to override privacy settings and encryption of communications. We can group the advantages of such operational exploitation in terms of:

- *Near real-time situational awareness.* This is the ability to collect and cluster social media and output in a way that indicates and describes unfolding events. Analysis of Twitter has shown that, while the majority of Twitter traffic only occurred after an event had been reported by a mainstream news outlet, 'bursts' of tweets indicating a significant event often pre-empt conventional reporting.[20] Social media traffic analysis could allow for a more rapid identification of emerging events than traditional reporting mechanisms. With the application of geo-location techniques this could lead, for example, to a constantly evolving map showing spikes in possible violence-related tweets, facilitating a faster, more effective, and more agile emergency response.

- *Insight into groups.* This would include the ability to better understand activities and behaviour of certain groups already of interest to police or intelligence agencies. Given the appropriate legal authorization, the police could use SOCMINT to spot new, rapidly emerging 'hot topics' that spring up within group-specific conversations and how the group reacts to a specific, perhaps volatile, event. Through these and other techniques, SOCMINT might indicate the overall levels of anger within a group, and their key concerns and themes that animate intra-group discussions. At a higher level of specificity, information can also be identified and extracted regarding when a group is planning demonstrations or flashmobs, which could lead to violence or increasing community tensions; football fans planning 'meets', which could cause major economic disruption; groups planning counter-demonstrations, which could change the kind of policing required to maintain public order.

- *Identification of criminal intent or criminal elements in the course of an enquiry both for the prevention and prosecution of crime.* Similarly, law enforcement could use the warranted surveillance of social media use by individuals suspected of involvement in a crime or criminal conspiracy, the cross referencing of such individuals' accounts, the identification of accomplices, the uncovering of assumed identities, the identification of criminal networks that operate through social media sites, and the provision of social media content suspected of being evidence of a crime to the Crown Prosecution Service.

Such potential suggests that SOCMINT will merit a significant place in the national intelligence framework. However, whenever a new form of technology emerges, it takes some time before legitimate and rigorous systems of capture, analysis and interpretation are developed. There are a number of key challenges that need to be addressed before SOCMINT can be fully exploited in the interest of national and public security. It is to these challenges, and their suggested solutions, that we turn next.

THE CHALLENGES OF SOCMINT: NECESSITY AND LEGITIMACY

The full promise of SOCMINT as a law enforcement tool in addition to its use as an open source of information must be tempered against the reality that the methods employed to protect society rest ultimately on some form of public acceptability and involvement. Britain's National Security Strategy recognizes that security and intelligence work in general is predicated not only on the public's consent and understanding but also on the active partnership and participation of people and communities. Serious and recognized damage to security occurs when the state's efforts are not accepted or trusted.[21]

Public acceptability can be secured and maintained through two important public demonstrations. First, that the collection of intelligence is able to make an effective and necessary contribution toward safety and security; second, that this contribution is being proportionately and appropriately balanced against other desirable public goods—such as the right to private life. In sum, intelligence activity must effectively contribute to a public good but not detract from or threaten any others in ways that are not recognized and appropriately managed. These are the challenges of necessity and legitimacy.

NECESSITY

The first demonstration that the use of SOCMINT must make is that it works. If it did not have a reasonable prospect of contributing towards public safety there would be no moral, or indeed financial, argument for it to be collected or used. If SOCMINT is not efficacious, it risks harm to suspects who turn out to be innocent, risks of collateral damage to others to whom a duty of care is owed, and the risk of confounding otherwise sound intelligence efforts.

The 'success' of intelligence is not the information or even secrets that it collects, but the value it adds to decision-making. Indeed, the justification for creating SOCMINT (or any intelligence) capabilities and applying them, with all the recognized hazards this entails, is that it contributes to the public good of safety and security. It is therefore morally imperative that SOCMINT operations present a reasonable chance that they will yield actionable, useable intelligence that contribute to consequential decisions, such as deploying emergency services to the right place at the right time.

For information to be considered successful 'intelligence' it needs to meet certain thresholds of how it is gathered, evidenced, corroborated, verified, understood and applied. Different sources and kinds of information have developed signature ways of meeting this challenge. For example, open-source intelligence (OSINT) triangulates reliable sources; human intelligence (HUMINT) might consider the track record of the agent; imagery intelligence (IMINT) needs to pay attention to the technical characteristics of the collection platform; and signals intelligence (SIGINT) would need to understand the context of the language used. All source intelligence assessments try to get an overall picture on the basis of these different types and reliability of contribution.

SOCMINT has its own characteristics that can be seen by examining how SOCMINT fits into the traditional intelligence cycle, in particular the functional steps of collection, processing and analysis, and dissemination.

Data Access

One of the difficulties of SOCMINT which it shares with much of modern SIGINT is not a paucity of data, often the key problem in the collection of Cold War secret intelligence, but a deluge. The term 'access' is preferred over 'collection' to indicate that in the internet we are dealing with a very different process from that of traditional intelligence gathering. During the week of the August 2011 riots, for example, millions of riot-related tweets were sent, consisting of news stories, rumours, reactions and indications of criminal intent.[22] Knowing what data ought to have been accessed and analyzed—sorting the wheat from the chaff—is the critical consideration. Selection and filtering tools (including such techniques as semantic search) are available and have, for example, been extensively used in signals intelligence and in email searches and legal discovery and will be needed for social media analysis by law enforcement of their targets.

Rather different problems arise for the analyst when trying to distil general meaning from large open data sets. One useful way to approach this challenge is to draw on how traditional quantitative disciplines deal with overwhelmingly large data sets. Most turn to the statistical technique of sampling, wherein a manageable amount of data is collected that represent the unmanageably large 'population' being researched. The reliability and validity of inferences or extrapolations made on this basis depend on the quality, especially representativeness, of the sample collected. Over the past century, statisticians have developed techniques that allow small data sets to be representative, and therefore permit more general conclusions to be drawn—particularly through the use of randomized sampling. Simply put, however, inferences and conclusions can only be reasonably drawn if one knows how the sample was constructed and the data collected, and what this means about the inferences that are then made.

The broad problem is that social sciences have not developed an approach to robustly sample social media data sets. Only a very limited amount of work has been done to develop different types of sampling for automated systems of data collection.[23] More attention has been paid to methodologies that produce a large sample (something that computational approaches are good at delivering), rather than methodologies that produce a representative one (something social sciences are good at delivering). Moreover, the emerging, highly technical and computer science-driven developments in social media sampling practices, including 'forest-fire' (wherein links and nodes 'burn' outward from a random seed to create the sample), useractivity and location-attribute-based techniques, have had very little uptake within the social science community.

Very little research based on social media data sets acknowledges the sampling frame applied, and how this might limit or bias the results that are drawn. Typical data acquisition strategies within the small but growing field of academic work of remain 'samples of convenience' or 'incidental sampling', which means the most readily available or easily accessible—rather than the most representative—are collected.[24] For obvious reasons this type of sampling limits the strength of conclusions drawn. One prominent example is the recent *Reading the Riots* collaboration involving the Guardian, a number of British universities, freelance journalists and community researchers. The project gathered 2.6 million tweets about the August 2011 riots and drew a number of conclusions, including that there were very few examples of Twitter being used to express or encourage criminal activity. However, the data set of tweets was collected using around 150 'hashtag clouds', which means only tweets that included an identifying hashtag, such as #londonriots, were collected and analyzed. It is possible, however, that people who use a hashtag when tweeting are not representative of all tweets about the riots; for example, they might be less likely to talk about criminal activity because hashtags are usually employed by users to disseminate tweets to a wider audience. In statistics, this is known as 'missing at non-random data', which means certain data might be systemically absent as a result of the sampling method. This is considered a serious problem when drawing conclusions, because when people are absent from a data set for a reason other than chance, they share a related and likely important trait (or traits) that could have a substantial impact on the research findings.

Unlike in traditional social science research, technical considerations might also affect the quality of sample. For example, in the case of Twitter, the publicly available application programme interface is limited to 150 requests per hour, going up to 20,000 when it is 'whitelisted'. While this can capture an enormous data set by traditional social science standards, it can only capture a small amount, and not an automatically representative sample, of the total number of tweets. Researchers can gain access to larger proportions of the tweet-feed. The 'firehose' gives access to all tweets, the *gardenhose* gives 10 per cent, and the 'spritzer' gives 1 per cent. Unfortunately, precisely how these different access levels affect the quality of the data, and what sorts of systemic bias they might hide, are not fully known—and very rarely stated.

For the interests of public policy, including security strategies, what are especially required are data acquisition plans that allow online phenomena to be related to offline behaviour. Demographic representativeness is key for this. The people who use social media such as Twitter and Facebook tend to be younger, richer, more educated and more urban than the population in general.[25] Additionally, when looking at demography, it is not only the general population that is important, but also the community that accounts for the information that is gathered. Online social content is subject to the enduring influence of the Pareto principle of the 'vital few' that 80 per cent of the user-generated content for any given site will tend to come from a highly productive 20 per cent of users.[26] A 2010 study of Twitter found this to be broadly true: 22.5 per cent of users accounted for around 90 per cent of all activity.[27]

Processing and Analysis

As described in the previous section, drawing meaning from open social media data presents great challenges for the intelligence analyst. Many of the technologies that have been developed in the private sector by the advertising and public relations sectors have been moulded by the metrics traditions and to suit the needs of these industries. They aim to gain a general understanding of attitudes toward a product or whether a new advertising campaign is creating a 'buzz'. Security and intelligence efforts, however, demand modes of analysis that can deliver levels of confidence that these technologies cannot, yet, deliver.

Because social media data sets are so large, a number of broadly computational approaches have been developed to infer and extract 'meaning' automatically, without the routine presence of a human analyst. The most important approach is a variant of artificial intelligence—'machine learning'—where algorithms are taught to recognize patterns and therefore meaning within pieces of information that human beings need therefore never see. Machine learning has a number of important applications, from identifying clusters and anomalies in large data sets to the extraction of semantic information from text. A particularly important application is 'sentiment analysis', where an algorithm looks for certain qualities and properties in a piece of text that it considers to correlate statistically with an emotion or 'sentiment'. Once human input has defined what sentiments are being searched for, and what textual examples of these sentiments are, the algorithm is able, with varying degrees of specificity and accuracy, to classify enormous volumes of data automatically on the same basis. Sentiment analysis has been applied for a number of aims, from measuring Twitter users' feelings towards political parties to predicting the future of box office revenues.[28] In the future we may see sentiment analysis used by the police to gauge the mood of demonstrators and the possibility of criminal violence erupting.

The ability to extract automatic meaning from unstructured data such as tweets opens many research opportunities, and social researchers can now contemplate handling bodies of information, and compiling sample sets, on a previously unmanageable scale. However, a crucial consequence of the rise of machine learning approaches within social media analytics is that we are currently much better at counting examples of online human behaviour than critically explaining why they are and what it might mean.

To make this sort of sense of any form of communication, context is critical. A central tenet of all semiotics and linguistics is that language is textured: the intent, motivation, social signification, denotation and connotation of any utterance is mutable and dependent on the context of situation and culture. The accuracy of any interpretation depends on a very detailed understanding of the group or context that is being studied. For example, most groups of people use vernacular and group-specific language that a generic or standardized sentiment lexicon or thesaurus would often misinterpret.

However, because automatic data collection is required to process the sheer volume of data now available, many of the contextual cues—the thread of a conversation, information about the speaker, the tone of the utterance and the information about the speaker—are often lacking in analysis of social media data. Therefore utterances have to be abstracted out of the wider situational, contextual and cultural picture—what we would call their 'naturalistic setting'. The act of 'scraping' a social media platform—such as collecting tweets or Facebook posts—like filtered selection in signals intelligence usually does not by itself provide the utterance's position in a social network (such as whether they were talking to their friend) or a conversational network (such as whether the utterance was a heated rebuttal in an argument). Again, these are issues that have been faced by signals intelligence agencies in the internet age and where analytic experience and judgment have been shown to be key.

Context is also shaped by the norms and mores of the medium we are using. A number of studies are beginning to identify norms, rules and behaviours that dictate communication via social media that differ in significant ways to how people might communicate offline. Some studies for example argue for an 'online disinhibition effect'—that the invisible and anonymous qualities of online interaction lead to disinhibited, more intensive, self-disclosing and aggressive uses of language.[29] Identification with groups or movements has also changed. Traditional forms of membership to a group or a movement are relatively intense, often involving subscription fees and membership lists. For many online groups, however, a single click of a mouse is sufficient to express some form of affiliation. This is a more ephemeral, looser and possibly less involved form of affiliation. Indeed, a recent study of 1300 Facebook fans of the English Defence League found that only three-quarters considered themselves 'members' of the group, and only one-quarter of those had ever actually been on a march.[30]

Taken together, these phenomena constitute the rapid emergence of distinct social media subcultures, which are developing new understandings, social mores and uses of language in clearly distinct ways.[31] Indeed, a new branch of sociology—digital sociology—is devoted to understanding these sociocultural consequences of the internet and the new ways it is being used.

When context is not considered, there can be profound consequences and potential for misinterpretation. In 2010, Paul Chambers declared to his 650 Twitter followers his intention of 'blowing [Robin Hood] airport sky high!!'[32] Undoubtedly in jest, his initial conviction for the 'menacing use of a public communication system' under the Communications Act 2003 has attracted wide public criticism and was overturned on appeal. Jonathan Bennett, the district judge, noted the 'huge security concerns' within the context of the times in which we live, but perhaps not the Twitter-specific situational and cultural context of the utterance.[33] In a similar case, Leigh Van Bryan and Emily Bunting were denied entry to America after tweeting 'free this week for a quick gossip/prep before I go and destroy America? x'.[34]

Although there are no simple solutions to these difficulties, some steps forward are possible. First, big data computational tools must become more 'human-sized'—sympathetic to the human subject they wish to measure. Statistical analytical methods, such as sentiment analysis, must involve analysts and experts who understand the norms and behaviours of the groups involved. Second, any analysis of social media data sets should always be based on an understanding of the medium itself: the specific online culture, language and behaviour. Project Raynard is a good and relatively recent of an intelligence programme that stresses the importance of first establishing norms in online environments before looking for deviations from the norm.[35] Most important is that any organization using SOCMINT must recognize the analytical and interpretative limitations of the field, how they reflect on the kind of insight that can be drawn, and the kind of decisions that can be made on the basis of those limitations.

Dissemination

The effective use of intelligence from internet sources including social media data sets also depends on it getting to the right people quickly, securely and presented in a format that makes sense to strategic and operational decision-makers. Depending on the purpose of the SOCMINT, this may range from a footnoted, caveated and in-depth strategic analysis paper, to the operational use of single-screen, real-time visualizations of data available on portable devices.[36]

Several challenges will need to be addressed. First, SOCMINT dissemination must reflect the general difficulties in using SOCMINT: its complexity, scale, dynamism and—given the problems outlined above relating to both access and interpretation—any presentation of data needs to be presented with new procedures and caveats.

Second, SOCMINT dissemination must slot into existing intelligence channels—police, emergency service response, the Security Service, the Joint Terrorism Analysis Centre, Cabinet Office Assessments Staff and so on. However, this requires specific training for gold, silver and bronze commanders and additional training for frontline officers who could benefit from the daily use of such intelligence but who are not today regarded as direct intelligence customers.

Third, SOCMINT dissemination and retention must comply with the highest standards of information assurance. Existing controls must be applied to ensure the safekeeping of SOCMINT data accessed under warrant and regulating their dissemination, including overseas. The unregulated dissemination of SOCMINT data would risk jeopardizing public confidence in this form of intelligence. More generally, whether lost, insecurely held, or subject to hostile access, as government increases the amount of personal information it holds, the potential for various data compromises, and the harm it might cause to public confidence, will inevitably grow.

Fourth, the effective application of data visualization techniques will be required to render complex and often interlinked intelligence in a way that is intuitively comprehensible, but conserves the networked nature of the information. More experience of using such SOCMINT data analysis techniques by law enforcement in particular is needed in order to draw up detailed rules and regulations for its safe management.

Validation and Use

The way SOCMINT can add value relates to how the operators—such as frontline police officers—will actually use the information, and how they ought to interpret and act on it (such as deploying reserve forces in the build up to a march). In addition to the many methodological hurdles that stand in the way of the responsible interpretation of data, the social media being monitored is itself prone to contain misleading information of a polemical nature, which may involve the recirculation of selective half-truths, mistakes and outright distortions. Validation of SOCMINT intelligence is therefore an important function for the social media analyst.

One risk that must be accounted for when considering validating SOCMINT data is the risk of engineering the 'observation effect': the tendency of individuals to change their behaviour if they believe they are being observed. In 2009, the LSE's Policy Engagement Network warned of this 'effect' in a briefing paper responding to the then-government's Interception Modernisation Programme. The report feared that when the public became aware that communications data were being collected and collated, there would be a risk that 'it will generate a chilling effect on the individual's right to free expression, association and might dissuade people from participating in communications transactions'.[37] On the other hand, previous predictions such as the decline of communications intelligence due to the ready availability of hard encryption have not proved correct, and similarly it is unlikely that changes in public behaviour as a result of knowledge of social media monitoring will significantly limit the effectiveness of social media and online communications data as sources of intelligence.

Related to this issue is the problem of 'gaming'—the deliberate use of this media as a means of misleading or confusing an observer, in this case the law enforcement agencies. In the context of intelligence work, this problem is not new, although experience such as the Allied deception operations in the Second World War illustrates the care with which deception operations have to be planned if they are not to backfire on the originator. The nature of SOCMINT may make attempts at deception more likely given the ubiquity of social media, its widespread use and the democratization of computer coding and technical know-how. In a recent example, a leaked cache of emails allegedly belonging to Bashar al-Assad indicated that an aide, Hadeel al-Assad, posted pro-regime commentary under an assumed Facebook identity that was mistaken as genuine and given international coverage by CNN.[38]

For these reasons, there must be a thorough (yet sufficiently rapid) process to ensure that an item of SOCMINT can, as far as possible, be validated before it reaches the final user. The validation of SOCMINT is ideally done further up the 'food chain' from the functions of access and processing of data when all sources of intelligence, including open source material, can be brought to bear.

As with other intelligence sources, this validation process must take the form of a reporting framework that rates the 'confidence' in any piece of freestanding piece of SOCMINT. By pointing out potential vulnerabilities and biases in the acquisition and analysis of the information, we may gauge the importance of the information collected and caveat the conclusions that may be drawn.

We must also be able to relate SOCMINT to other kinds of evidence to produce an overall picture—the equivalent of an 'all-source assessment'. The value of SOCMINT relative to other forms of intelligence must be evaluated and the ways in which various types of intelligence can be used in tandem needs to be investigated. The crucial points here are the exact application of SOCMINT in a given circumstance and its 'strength' in relation to other forms of intelligence. To complicate the issue, both will of course vary according to the situation ranging from identifying broad societal-level trends on the one hand and the context of a riot or crowd control on the other.

A number of strategies will be useful to create processes to validate SOCMINT. More methodologically mature forms of offline research can be conducted in parallel to SOCMINT projects to allow the results to be compared. For example, it would be especially useful to establish rules about how online phenomena maps onto offline behaviour. Retrospective analysis can also be used to quantify SOCMINT accuracies and diagnose instances where accuracy was confounded. In addition to the specific validation responsibilities placed on the agency that collected the intelligence, there needs to be a very general up-skilling of all the branches of government that might be involved in this work. It will be impossible to use this medium without analysts, police officers or judges who understand its norms and mores. Ultimately, the value of SOCMINT can only really be understood through using it. Understanding will slowly emerge as SOCMINT is trialled—we must expect varying degrees of success in different contexts.

In general, the origin of the main risks in using information from social media arises from a lack of interaction between the humanities and the statistical and computational disciplines. Those disciplines best equipped to understand and explain human behaviour—the social and behavioural sciences, political science, psephology, anthropology and social psychology—have not kept pace in relating this insight to the big-data approaches necessary to understand social media. Conversely, these very same big-data approaches that form the backbone of current SOCMINT capabilities have not used sociology to employ the measurements and statistics they use to the task of meaningfully interpreting human behaviour.

Taken together, the methodological steps forward point towards a fundamental evolution in the capabilities available to exploit social media. If SOCMINT is to be methodologically robust enough to base decisions on and change policy, it must rest on a new, applied, academic inter-discipline: social media science. This would embody a more meaningful and intensive fusion of the computational, technological and humanities approaches. Only through this fusion can data-led explanations of human behaviour also be humanistic explanations of human behaviour. This will require new relationships with industry and academia, and concerted, long-term investment to build technological, methodological and presentational capabilities.

LEGITIMACY

The second important condition of SOCMINT use is that it be legitimate. Broadly speaking, all security and intelligence work rests on a delicate balance between three classes of public goods: the maintenance of national security including public order and public safety; citizens' right to the rule of law, liberty and privacy; and the overall economic and social wellbeing of the nation and its citizens. To be legitimate, any use of SOCMINT similarly has to recognize where it risks harm to a public good, and balance this against any contribution it makes to another.

In most circumstances these three classes of public goods should be mutually reinforcing: security promotes inward investment and market confidence promoting economic wellbeing and social harmony that in turn supports the maintenance of security. There are times however when choices have to be made. Within a rights-based approach, the only justification for one public good to be hazarded is the provision of another. Yet social media is a potentially disruptive phenomenon that is already affecting and in some cases redefining how these three classes of public goods can be attained, for the following reasons:

- *Fungibility and heterogeneity.* SOCMINT cuts across several categories and can be in more than one category at a time. The broad scanning of tweets has similarities to mass surveillance such as the deployment of CCTV in crowded places. The close following of an individual's Facebook page during the course of an investigation has similarities to *de visu* surveillance as 'authorizable' by a senior police officer. Accessing encrypted BlackBerry messaging by cracking the security PIN is an interception of communications under RIPA 2000 for which a warrant would be required.

- *Generality.* When used for intrusive investigation there may be no named suspect or telephone number to target and the output may be general rather than specific to an individual (such as noting an increase in social media communications in a specific area where demonstrations are taking place).

- *Scalability.* Many of the automated techniques can be scaled up from the collection of hundreds to millions of pieces of social media data easily and cheaply. The scale may be difficult to pin down in advance.

- *Flexibility.* The scope of many 'scraping' technologies (for instance, the keywords they scan for) can be changed easily. This means they can easily be redirected away from their original mission and function, which may be justified operationally by tactical changes on the ground.

- *Invisibility.* Like other forms of covert surveillance, the operation of SMA techniques will normally not be visible to the social media users themselves and will override what they may assume are their privacy settings.

- *Broader public concerns with digital surveillance.* SOCMINT must be understood within the context of public concerns about digital surveillance driven by the broad rise in information systems that have vast capacities to capture, stockpile, retrieve, analyze, distribute, visualize and disseminate information. Concerns arise in the proliferation of surveillance opportunities in this data-rich environment, and the consequences of collateral intrusion, the possibility of data compromise, and a general implication of suspicion of wrongdoing entailed by the widespread collection of information.[39]

As with other forms of intelligence, public concerns over privacy must be managed. Privacy itself is an elusive concept. Article 8 of the European Convention of Human Rights enshrines the right to respect for 'a person's private and family life, his home and correspondence'. Respecting privacy can mean that data are kept confidentially, gathered anonymously, used in a self-determined way (the principle of 'informed consent'), and that people are able to see them and correct errors, or, of course, that no data are gathered at all.

Many broad and fundamental changes in society are nonetheless transforming what privacy means to people and social media use in particular challenges clear-cut distinctions of what is private and what is not. McKinsey Global Institute has calculated that 30 billion pieces of content are shared on Facebook each month, many of them personal.[40] This sharing of such a large amount of voluntarily uploaded personal data, and the number of people and institutions to whom these data are accessible, is unprecedented; depending on the user-selected privacy settings employed, personal information added to Facebook can be viewed by all of Facebook's 845 million other users. Far from being incidental, this move towards the widespread dissemination of personal information is fundamental to the ethos of social networking sites. Facebook's privacy settings inform users that the ability to share information 'allows us to provide Facebook as it exists today', while Twitter states more explicitly that 'most of the information you provide to us is information you are asking us to make public'.[41] Indeed as a result of these changing behaviours, Mark Zuckerberg, Facebook's CEO, declared that privacy is 'no longer a social norm'.[42] Most of us accept that both private and public bodies—from Tesco through its Clubcards to Amazon, Oyster and Google—learn and record a vast amount about us daily. In a Eurobarometer poll, a bare majority of UK respondents considered photos of themselves to be personal data, less than half considered 'who your friends are' to be personal data, 41 per cent thought that details of the websites they visit were personal data, and only 32 per cent thought their tastes and opinions were personal data, yet in contrast, large majorities regard financial data as personal.[43] However, although research suggests that users recognize disclosing personal information is an increasingly important part of modern life, the majority have concerns about what this means.[44] In a 2008 European Commission Poll, around 80 per cent of people agreed that 'people's awareness about personal data protection in the UK is low'.[45]

Attitudes towards privacy—especially broad, generic and in-principle attitudes—are notoriously hard to measure objectively. Broad behavioural norms, such as the amount of information we now share, suggest the concept is in a state of flux, where its boundaries of definition are being fundamentally redrawn. The debate will continue to rage about where these redrawn boundaries on the possession, sharing and use of personal information, now lie—indeed what privacy is.[46]

The crucial implication for the use by government of different types of SOCMINT is that the framework for recognizing and managing incursions into privacy is struggling to keep pace with changing social attitudes and habit. There are many ways the state can collect and use information about people, while different systems exist for carrying this out. Each system identifies and limits potential harm from accessing private information. When the state conducts clinical research, for example, consent is requested and anonymity often guaranteed; when the state draws on the research of others we apply fair usage and ascribe credit to the individuals concerned. When the state obtains biometric information such as a DNA sample from a suspect, consent is not required but restrictions are applied to the retention of material. When the state carries out surveillance, the activity is usually covert and individual consent is irrelevant. Instead, to deal with concerns of privacy and intrusiveness, society's consent is needed, expressed through enabling legislation. Whilst enabling legislation differs between states, they are predicated on an association between the level of harm on the one hand, and a series of steps to mitigate harm (including ways of establishing authorization, accountability, and necessity) on the other. With the concept of privacy now so mutable, the calculation of this particular kind of moral hazard is difficult.

Economic and Social Wellbeing

The internet as a free and open space—of course within reasonable limits—provides an immense economic and social benefit. Government activity is intended to protect prosperity, not undermine it. As the British Foreign Secretary William Hague commented in 2011 'nothing would be more fatal or self-defeating than the heavy hand of state control on the internet, which only thrives because of the talent of individuals and of industry within an open market for ideas and innovation[47] On the other hand, the risk must be recognized that the unregulated large-scale collection and analysis of social media data by business and government alike (even if open source) risks undermining confidence in, and therefore the value of, this space. The idea that the economic and social benefit of the internet is premised on its openness and freedom of government control is not new. From the early 1990s, a powerful argument and vision has existed about what the internet is for and what it should be like: an opportunity to evolve past the nation-state system into post-territorial, self-governing communities who operate under their own floating social contracts of consent-through-use. John Perry Barlow's famous Declaration of Cyberspace Independence declared to the 'weary giants of flesh and steel' that cyberspace was developing its own sovereignty and 'you are not welcome among us'[48]

We believe that it is important to distinguish, as we have tried to do in this article, between open-source, non-intrusive SOCMINT and closed-source, intrusive SOCMINT. Any legitimizing and enabling framework for the collection and use of SOCMINT must therefore begin by distinguishing between what is a form of intrusive surveillance and what is not. This recognizes that there are times when we can legitimately seek control of what information we give away and how it is used, but there are also times when individual control must be over-ridden. The circumstances where this can happen are based on collective decisions and assent about the state's authority.

The key concept relevant to making this distinction is whether the user controls the use of their data through consent. For SOCMINT to be non-intrusive and open-source, it should not be able to identify individuals, be used as a means of criminal investigation, or puncture the privacy wishes of the user.

Any Government use of open SOCMINT should be put on the same footing as private companies and academia, with conditions relating to anonymity and data protection. For open SOCMINT, then, harm is conceived not as intrusion into someone's private space, nor the wider issues of trust and implied suspicion (since neither of these would happen within open SOCMINT), but by the loss of control over the information through use beyond what can be reasonably expected. Reasonable expectation can be protected through a characteristic openness of

how or when this kind of SOCMINT is conducted. All such collection, retention, and sharing policies are publicized and justified and the reason why the information is collected is publicized.

Intrusive SOCMINT is more straightforward since most states already have a legislative framework for regulating intrusive intelligence gathering, for example for the purposes of national security and the prevention and detection of crime (in the case of the UK such authority is provided in the Regulation of Investigative Powers Act 2000). The application of such legislation can be codified for intrusive SOCMINT to cover the powers of access required and the procedures to be followed at a legal and operational level. What is important is that there is public acceptance of the arrangements based on recognition that at the heart of an enduring, effective settlement for state surveillance rest sound ethical principles. We suggest an adaptation of the set of principles earlier suggested for the intelligence community by Sir David Omand in his book, *Securing the State*.[49]

Principle 1: There Must Be Sufficient, Sustainable Cause

This first and overarching principle forces the big picture to be taken into account: the overall purposes that could justify the acquisition by a public body of capabilities to gather, understand and use social media data. There is a danger that a series of SOCMINT measures—each in themselves justifiable—together creep towards an undesirable end point: a publicly unacceptable level of overall surveillance; the possession of a dangerous capability; and the overall damage to a medium that is of obvious intrinsic value beyond security. Just because it can be done does not mean that it should be done.

Application of the principle of requiring sufficient, sustainable cause is therefore necessary to ensure that SOCMINT remains within the boundaries required to deliver social, economic, security and law enforcement benefits to the public, resisting bureaucratic empire building, finding ways to employ spare capacity or simply the *banalization* of the technology available from commercial suppliers.

Principle 2: There Must Be Integrity of Motive

This principle refers to the need for integrity throughout the whole 'intelligence' system, from the statement of justification for access, accessing the information itself, through to the objective analysis, assessment and honest presentation of the results.

The justification for seeking SOCMINT in individual cases must in particular be clear and not mask other motives on the part of the investigating officers. Intelligence is by its nature usually incomplete and fragmentary, and can be wrong or subject to deception. In presenting intelligence to end-users the limitations and caveats must be made clear. Nor must the decision to use (or not to use) SOCMINT, or the conclusions drawn from it, be influenced by local or national political considerations or media pressure.

Principle 3: The Methods Used Must Be Proportionate and Necessary

There is a well-established principle in law enforcement that the extent of harm likely to arise from any specific action being taken should be proportionate to the harm that it is being sought to prevent. In assessing proportionality, the extent of intrusion has to be assessed. That would mean a lower threshold for covertly monitoring material that the user has not restricted than in cases where they had only a limited list of friends who had access, or where they used a system such as BlackBerry that required a PIN.

Principle 4: There Must Be Right Authority, Validated by External Oversight

There is a general principle that there must be an audit trail for the authorization of actions that may carry moral hazard with an unambiguously accountable authority within a clear chain of command. Having an adequate paper trail (or its electronic equivalent) for key decisions is essential for confidence of staff and politicians, and for the operation of investigations and redress in any cases of suspected abuse of powers. We believe this principle should apply to SOCMINT as well as to any other intelligence operation. This is an important way in which proportionality and accountability is realized in practice.

Principle 5: Recourse to Secret Intelligence Must Be A Last Resort if More Open Sources Can Be Used

Because of the moral hazards of all intrusive secret intelligence gathering methods, those authorizing such operations should ask whether the information could reasonably be expected to be obtained through other means, ranging from fully open sources to information freely volunteered from within the community. Applying this general principle to SOCMINT, less intrusive forms should be preferred to more intrusive covert forms. SOCMINT should be based wherever possible on the clearest possible mandate of informed consent. The most preferred route is to access explicitly 'consenting' information from the online community, for example crowdsourced information that has been explicitly volunteered on a particular Facebook wall or hashtag. Recourse to covert intelligence gathering, including via exploitation of social media, should be confined to cases where the information is necessary for the lawful purpose of the operation and cannot reasonably be expected to be gained by other means.

Overall, these principles maintain a series of crucial associations: as the type of surveillance becomes increasingly intrusive so three vital and increasingly narrow conditions are imposed onto it: the agencies that can conduct it, who must authorize it, and the reasons why the surveillance can be legitimately conducted. This is vital to balance the possible good of the collection and use of SOCMINT with the possible harm. Measuring intrusion, however, is far from straightforward. People often share what would usually be considered private things about their lives in ways that are unprecedentedly public, sometimes with unexpected or unrealized consequences. The scale of intrusion entailed by SOCMINT access varies greatly. To gather and analyze a suspect's open tweets looks similar to the surveillance of someone in public, whilst to gather and analyze someone's Facebook messages seems closer to reading their private correspondence. We do not yet have a conceptual framework of what should in future constitute privacy in social media use and the consequent sorts of harms associated with breaching that privacy.

CONCLUDING REMARKS

The opportunities that the explosion of social media use offers are remarkable. SOCMINT must become a full member of the intelligence and law enforcement family. At the heart of this process are the twin demonstrations of necessity and legitimacy.

To meet the challenge of necessity, a new, applied academic discipline—social media science—must be developed. This requires new relationships with industry and academia, and concerted, long-term investment to build technological, methodological and presentational capabilities. Those disciplines best equipped to understand and explain human behaviour—the social and behavioural sciences, political science, psephology, anthropology and social psychology—must be made to interweave with the big data approaches necessary to understand social media. Only through this fusion can data-led explanations of human behaviour also be humanistic explanations of human behaviour.

But technology and capability is only half the picture. To meet the challenge of legitimacy, the public must broadly understand and accept why, when and with what restrictions SOCMINT is undertaken. Any Government that wishes to conduct SOCMINT must adopt an explicitly articulated approach grounded in respect for human rights and the associated principles of accountability, proportionality and necessity.

QUESTIONS FOR FURTHER DISCUSSION

1. Should intelligence or law enforcement officials monitor social media to act on potential threats in real time?
2. How does one distinguish between a joke and a legitimate threat in the "Twitter- sphere"?
3. Is it possible to manipulate social media for purposes of denial and deception?
4. What can you accomplish with social media intelligence that you could not accomplish with good old-fashioned intelligence tradecraft?

ENDNOTES

1. Her Majesty's Inspectorate of the Constabulary (HMIC), *The Rules of Engagement: A Review of the August 2011 Disorders* (London: Crown Copyright 2011) especially pp.36–9.
2. Ibid., p.31.
3. Ibid., p.30.
4. Ibid.
5. 'Facebook Crimes Probed by Humberside Police', *Hull Daily Mail*, 24 August 2011, <www.thisishullandeast riding.co.uk/Facebook-crimes-probed-Humberside-Police/story-131 91231-detail/story.html> (accessed 17 April 2012); see also Westminster City Council's 'Your Choice' programme: *Choose Life, Not Gangs: Problem Kids Told to Clean Up or Face the Consequence* (City of Westminster, 29 September 2011), <www.westminster. gov.uk/press-releases/2011–09/choose-life-not-gangs-problem-kids-told-to/> (accessed 17 April 2012).
6. Ministry of Defence and Centre for Defence Enterprise, Cyber and Influence Science and Technology Centre, *CDE Call for Research Proposals*, 1 November 2011, <www.science. mod.uk/controls/getpdf.pdf?603> (accessed 17 April 2012).
7. 'The Value of Friendship', *Economist*, 4 February 2012, <http://www.economist.com/node/21546020> (accessed 17 April 2011).
8. Twitterblog, *200 Million Tweets a Day*, 30 June 2011, <http://blog.twitter.com/2011/06/200-million-tweets-per-day.html> (accessed 17 April 2012).
9. YouTube, *Statistics*, <www.youtube.com/t/press_statistics> (accessed 17 April 2012).
10. A. Signorini, A.M. Segre and P.M. Polgreen, 'The Use of Twitter to Track Levels of Disease Activity and Public Concern in the US During the Influenza A H1N1 Pandemic', *PLoS ONE* 6/5 (2011) pp.1–10.
11. J. Hoffman, 'Trying to Find a Cry of Desperation Amid the Facebook Drama', *New York Times*, 23 February 2012, <www.nytimes.com/2012/02/24/us/facebook-posts-can-offer-clues-of-depression.html?_r=3> (accessed 17 April 2012); 'T.J. Lane Facebook Photos: Suspect Faces Charges in Chardon High School Shooting (Slideshow)', *Huffington Post*, 28 February 2012, <www.huffingtonpost.com/2012/02/28/tj-lane-facebook-photos_n_1307836.html#s736080&title=TJ_Lane_Facebook> (accessed 17 April 2012).
12. For instance the UN Global Pulse Programme, *UN Unveils Initial Findings on Uses of Real-time Data for Development Work* (UN News Centre, 8 December 2011), <www.un.org/apps/news/story.asp?NewsID=40667& Cr=global&Cr1=pulse> (accessed 17 April 2012).
13. Criminal Justice Degrees Guide, *20 Infamous Crimes Committed and Solved on Facebook*, <http://mashable. com/2012/03/01/facebook-crimes/> (accessed 1 July 2012).
14. Diego Laje, '#Pirate? Tracking Modern Buccaneers Through Twitter', *CNN*, 15 March 2012, <http://edition.cnn.com/2012/03/15/business/somalia-piracy-twitter/index.html> (accessed 1 June 2012).
15. Jack Doyle, 'A Facebook Crime Every 40 Minutes', *Daily Mail*, 4 June 2012, <http://www.dailymail.co.uk/news/article-2154624/A-Facebook-crime-40-minutes-12-300-cases-linked-site.html> (accessed 1 June 2012).
16. T.O. Sprenger and I.M. Welpe, *Tweets and Trades: The Information Content of Stock Microblogs*, 1 November 2010, <http://papers.ssrn.com/sol3/papers.cfm?abstract_id=1702854> (accessed 17 April 2012).
17. Twitter was used by pupils as an *ad hoc* emergency broadcasting system during the Ohio school shooting. See L. Dugan, 'Twitter Used as an Impromptu Broadcast System During Ohio School Shooting', *Media Bistro*, 28 February 2012, <www.mediabistro.com/alltwitter/twitter-used-as-impromptu-emergency-broadcast-system-during-ohio-school-shooting_b19030> (accessed 1 June 2012).

18. HMIC, *The Rules of Engagement*, p. 31.

19. J. Howe, 'The Rise of Crowdsourcing', *Wired*, June 2006, <www.wired.com/wired/archive/14.06/crowds.html> (accessed 17 April 2012).

20. 'Reading the Riots: Investigating England's Summer of Disorder' [interactive], *Guardian*, <www.guardian.co.uk/uk/interactive/2011/aug/24/riots-twitter-traffic-interactive> (accessed 17 April 2012).

21. Cabinet Office, *A Strong Britain in an Age of Uncertainty: The National Security Strategy* London: HMSO 2010) p.5.

22. R. Proctor, F. Vis and A. Voss, 'Riot Rumours: How Misinformation Spread on Twitter During a Time of Crisis', *Guardian*, 7 December 2011, <www.guardian.co.uk/uk/interactive/2011/dec/07/london-riots-twitter> (accessed 17 April 2012).

23. See for instance J. Leskovec, J. Kleinberg and C. Faloutsos, 'Graph Evolution: Densification and Shrinking Diameters', *ACM Transactions on Knowledge Discovery from Data* 1/1 (2007) <www.cs.cmu.edu/~jure/pubs/powergrowth-tkdd.pdf> (accessed 16 April 2012); J. Leskovec and C. Faloutsos, 'Sampling from Large Graphs' in T. Ellassi-Rad (chair), *Proceedings of the 12th ACM SIGKDD International Conference on Knowledge Discovery and Data Mining, 2006* (Philadelphia: KDD 2006), <www.stat.cmu.edu/~fienberg/Stat36-835/Leskovec-sampling-kdd06.pdf> (accessed 16 April 2012).

24. See, for instance, B. O'Connor, R. Balasubramanyan, B.R. Routledge and N.A. Smith, 'From Tweets to Polls: Linking Text Sentiment to Public Opinion Time Series', *Proceedings of the AAAI Conference on Weblogs and Social Media* (Washington, DC: AIII Press 2010). The authors collected their sample using just a few keyword searches.

25. For information Twitter and Facebook demographics see, 'Infographic: Facebook vs. Twitter Demographics', *Digital Buzz Blog*, 21 December 2010, <www.digitalbuzzblog.com/infographic-facebook-vs-twitter-demographics-2010-2011/> (accessed 16 April 2012).

26. See C. Shirky, *Here Comes Everybody: The Power of Organizing Without Organizations* (New York: Penguin 2008).

27. 'Twitter Statistics for 2010', *Sysomos*, December 2010, <www.sysomos.com/insidetwitter/twitter-stats-2010/> (accessed 16 April 2012).

28. J. Weng, Y. Yao, E. Leonardi and F. Lee, 'Event Detection in Twitter', *HP Laboratories*, 6 July 2011, <www.hpl.hp.com/techreports/2011/HPL-2011-98.html> (accessed 17 April 2012); S. Asur and B.A. Huberman, 'Predicting the Future With Social Media', *HP Laboratories*, 29 March 2010, <www.hpl.hp.com/research/scl/papers/socialmedia/socialme-dia.pdf> (accessed 17 April 2012).

29. J. Suler, 'The Online Disinhibition Effect', *Journal of Cyberpsychology and Behaviour* 7/3 (2004) pp.321–6. See also J. Suler, *The Psychology of Cyberspace: The Online Disinhibition Effect*, <http://users.rider.edu/~suler/psycyber/disinhibit.html> (accessed 17 April 2012).

30. J. Bartlett and M. Littler, *Inside the EDL* (London: Demos 2011).

31. 'Twitterology High and Low', *The Economist*, 31 October 2011, <www.economist.com/blogs/johnson/2011/10/technology-and-language?fsrc=scn%2Ftw%2Fte%2Fbl%2Ftwitterolo gyhighandlow> (accessed 16 April 2012).

32. 'Robin Hood Airport Tweet Bomb Joke Man Wins Case', *BBC News*, 27 July 2012, <www.bbc.co.uk/news/uk-england-19009344> (accessed 16 April 2012).

33. 'Jack of Kent' (David Allen Green), *Paul Chambers: A Disgraceful and Illiberal Judgment*, 11 May 2010, <http://jackofkent.blogspot.com/2010/05/paul-chambers-disgraceful-and-illiberal.html> (accessed 16 April 2012).

34. A. Parker, 'US Bars Friends over Twitter Joke', *Sun*, 30 January 2012, <www.thesun.co.uk/sol/homepage/news/4095372/Twitter-news-US-bars-friends-over-Twitter-joke.html> (accessed 16 April 2012).

35. Intelligence Advanced Research Projects Agency, *Broad Agency Announcement: Reynard Program*, 16 June 2009 <http://www.iarpa.gov/solicitations_reynard.html> (accessed 12 June 2012).

36. For instance, in deprived areas of Berlin, civil servants have increasingly used portable devices connected to database records when visiting care homes for the elderly and hospitals. These devices give constant, mobile access to databases, enabling public servants to understand the needs of individuals and families, track their previous contact and check for problems and underlying issues that may have been recorded by other agencies. See J. Millard, 'eGovernance and eParticipation: Lessons from Europe in Promoting Inclusion and Empowerment', paper presented to UN Division for Public Administration and Development Management (DPADM) workshop 'e-Participation and e-Government' (Budapest, Hungary, 27–28 July 2006), <unpan1.un.org/intradoc/groups/public/documents/UN/UNPAN023685.pdf> (accessed 23 January 2012).

37. Briefing on the Interception Modernisation Programme, *Policy Engagement Network Paper 5* (2009), p.56.

38. 'Shopping Amid a Massacre: Leaked E-mails from Syria's Regime', *CNN International*, 16 March 2012, <http://edition.cnn.com/2012/03/15/world/meast/syria-al-assad-e-mails/index.html?iphoneemail> (accessed 16 April 2012).

39. For a description of many of these trends, see Information Commissioner's Office, *Information Commissioner's Report to Parliament on the State of Surveillance* (November 2010).

40. S. Sengupta, 'Zuckerberg's Unspoken Law: Sharing and More Sharing', *New York Times*, 23 September 2011, <http://bits.blogs.nytimes.com/2011/09/23/zuckerbergs-unspoken-law-sharing-and-more-sharing/> (accessed 17 April 2012).

41. Twitter, *Privacy Policy*, <http://twitter.com/privacy/previous/version_2> (accessed 17 April 2012); Facebook, *Data Use Policy*, <www.facebook.com/about/privacy/your-info> (accessed 17 April 2012).

42. B. Johnson, 'Privacy No Longer a Social Norm, Says Facebook Founder', *Guardian*, 11 January 2011, <www.guardian.co.uk/technology/2010/jan/11/facebook-privacy> (accessed 17 April 2012).

43. *Attitudes on Data Protection and Electronic Identity in the European Union: Special Eurobarometer 359* (Brussels: European Commission 2010).

44. See D. Boyd and E. Hargittai, 'Facebook Privacy Settings: Who Cares?', *First Monday* 15/8 (2010).

45. European Commission, *Data Protection in the European Union: Citizens' Perceptions* (2008), <http://ec.europa.eu/public_opinion/flash/fl_225_en.pdf> (accessed 17 April 2012).

46. For recent deliberative research into people's conceptions of privacy, see P. Bradwell, *Private Lives: A People's Inquiry into Personal Information* (London: Demos 2010), <www.demos.co.uk/files/Private_Lives_-_web.pdf> (accessed 17 April 2012).

47. M. Hick, 'Hague: Governments Must Not Censor Internet', *Huffington Post*, 1 November 2011, <www.huffingtonpost.co.uk/2011/11/01/william-hague-government-internet-censor ship_n_1069298.html> (accessed 17 April 2012).

48. J.P. Barlow, *A Declaration of the Independence of Cyberspace*, 8 February 1996, <https://projects.eff.org/~barlow/Declaration-Final.html> (accessed 17 April 2012).

49. D. Omand, *Securing the State* (London: Hurst & Co 2010).

Sir David Omand, Jamie Bartlett & Carl Miller (2012) "Introducing Social Media Intelligence (SOCMINT)", *Intelligence and National Security*, 27:6, 801–823, DOI:10.1080/02684527.2012.716965.Reprinted with permission of the publisher.

III

INTELLIGENCE ANALYSIS

Hamlet: "There are more things in heaven and earth Horatio,
Than are dreamt in your philosophy."
—SHAKESPEARE, *Hamlet*, 1.5.167–169

The hardest and most unforgiving task in the intelligence cycle is analysis. It is difficult because the fundamental problem facing intelligence analysts is that all information is inherently ambiguous. Most raw data about the world around us reaches us without any indication about its importance, its inherent meaning, or what it portends for the future. It is up to analysts to place this information in its historical context, in the context of current events, or in an appropriate analytical framework to uncover its meaning and significance so that policymakers or senior military officers can respond appropriately. Yet analysts sometimes lack the appropriate theoretical or historical framework to identify signals, lack accurate information about what is about to happen, and must deal with noise—misleading or superfluous information about coming events (Wohlstetter 1962). In fact, the dominant view among observers is that failures of intelligence are inevitable and that when they occur, important signals are always found in the intelligence pipeline that embarrass analysts and lead to much acrimony about the latest intelligence failure.

To avoid surprise, intelligence analysts often have to use old information to predict the future.

Information about ship movements or what happened at some clandestine meeting, for example, might reach them hours or even weeks after actual events, but analysts have to use this rather dated information to gain insight into an even more distant future. In a sense, they are in a race to use old information to predict what is about to unfold before events catch them by surprise. The target of intelligence analysts always has a head start in the race, and sometimes analysts fail to close the information gap before it is too late. The history of surprise is in fact replete with warnings that were *almost* issued in time: A message warning of the possibility of hostile Japanese action, for instance, reached the U.S. Navy commander at Pearl Harbor just as the attackers headed for home. Intelligence analysts thus face a deadline, but they can never be quite sure how much time they have left before their effort to develop an accurate estimate of the future is literally overtaken by events.

On the rare occasions when they obtain clear indications of what is about to happen, analysts also have to be wary. Opponents often use denial (efforts to hide their true intentions or operations) and deception (inaccurate information about current operations and intentions) to mislead analysts. Denial and deception can take many forms. Sometimes it is best to hide information from the prying eyes of reconnaissance satellites or agents on the ground so that accurate information fails to reach analysts. Sometimes intelligence targets will try to blend into their surroundings to try to make themselves appear innocuous. This is a good way to hide, because intelligence agencies lack the resources to monitor people, organizations, or states that appear to be engaged in routine and nonthreatening kinds of activities. Deception can also take the form of exaggerating one's capabilities in the effort to ward off attack or coerce opponents who might alter their policies because they mistakenly believe that they are in a weak military or diplomatic position. Denial and deception thus create a host of problems for analysts. When things sound too good to be true, analysts should suspect deception because they face an opponent who would like to do nothing more than put their minds at ease while carrying out some nefarious scheme. When things become too quiet, analysts should suspect that collection systems might be failing to alert them to potential problems. For intelligence analysts, no news, or the fact that events seem to be going according to plan, is not necessarily good news.

Analysts also have to deal with the fact that the actions of some opponents might defy logic or be fundamentally irrational in that they fail to further the known objectives of the state or non-state actor in question. Governments, militaries, bureaucracies, and terrorist syndicates have multiple decision centers, factions, and interests, and it is often difficult to harness all these individuals and organizations into unified and purposive behavior. Analysts might be correct in predicting what action an opponent should take, but they might turn out to be wrong when the opponent lacks the organizational or political wherewithal to carry out the predicted action. In other words, even if analysts discover what another state or non-state actor intends to do, they cannot say categorically that it will occur, because the other party might not be able to implement its plan.

States or non-state actors who seek to surprise their opponents often do so out of desperation. They generally lack the military, diplomatic, or economic resources to achieve their objectives without the force multiplier offered by surprise. They want to present their opponents with a *fait accompli*, then hope they will reach a negotiated settlement before

their opponents rally to reverse the gains obtained from using surprise. The fact that state and non-state actors can launch what amounts to a reckless gamble creates real problems for intelligence analysts. States and non-state actors wishing to achieve surprise are engaged in an extraordinarily risky enterprise, which often, with good reason, looks implausible to intelligence analysts. Prior to the Cuban missile crisis, for example, analysts at the CIA predicted that the Soviet Union would not place offensive missiles in Cuba, because such an action would prompt a strong reaction from the United States and prove to be counterproductive. In effect, analysts recognized the possibility that the Soviets might place offensive missiles in Cuba, but they dismissed this course of action as implausible because it entailed too much risk from the Soviet perspective (Wirtz 1998).

The risk inherent in the effort to gain the element of surprise, according to Michael Handel, creates a paradox that works against intelligence analysts: "The greater the risk, the less likely it seems, and the less risky it becomes. In fact, the greater the risk, the smaller it becomes" (Handel 1977, 468). So even when intelligence analysts detect signals of what is about to happen, they often dismiss these signals as too fantastic to be credible. Or even worse, they find it impossible to convince senior officials that the opponent is about to launch what appears to be a harebrained operation. It might be impossible to improve on the Bard, but this might be a good way to think about the challenge of intelligence analysis. There are, in fact, more things in life than we can dream of; the opponent is likely to pick one of them and to try to hide it from us, and analysts will have extraordinary difficulty convincing senior officials that something bad is about to happen.

IMPEDIMENTS TO ACCURATE ANALYSIS

Only the most creative and diligent minds can succeed as analysts. Good analysts have to be able to step outside the conventional military, diplomatic, and bureaucratic wisdom of their day to see vulnerabilities and opportunities that others might be tempted to exploit. They also face real-time constraints when it comes to generating their analysis. Estimates have to be accurate and delivered to officials or military officers in time to be used effectively.

Over the years, scholars and intelligence professionals have worked hard to understand general challenges in the process of intelligence analysis and the specific kinds of problems that can trip up analysts. Often, these studies come in the aftermath of spectacular events, and they tend to focus on the problems that seem to have contributed to the latest failure of intelligence. After Pearl Harbor, for instance, it appeared that a lack of "all-source" intelligence might have contributed to intelligence failure, so the CIA was created to guarantee that at least one organization would have access to all of the data collected by the U.S. intelligence community. Despite the episodic attention that intelligence analysis receives, scholars and practitioners seem most concerned about problems that are idiosyncratic to intelligence analysis and about the constraints created by the limits of human cognition and organizational pathologies.

IDIOSYNCRATIC CHALLENGES

Although intelligence analysis shares many similarities with journalism or academic research, several aspects of turning raw data into finished intelligence are unique and create special problems for analysts. A host of these idiosyncratic challenges exist. Probably the best-known challenge is the "cry wolf" syndrome. Analysts have to be careful about repeatedly issuing warnings that fail to materialize, because policymakers are likely to stop heeding alerts if they turn out to be false alarms. Responding to warnings also is not without costs. Forcing an opponent to respond repeatedly to false alarms is a good way to create operational, financial, and political strains that soften it up for the real initiative. The "ultra" syndrome, named after the intelligence obtained from decrypted Nazi radio communications in World War II, occurs when analysts become overly dependent on highly valuable intelligence gained from a credible and reliable source. At a critical moment, however, the source might fail to produce important information for any number of reasons, and analysts might be caught without other sources or methods to track important developments. Alternatively, analysts might take the absence of information from a credible source as evidence that nothing important is going on, a judgment that can lull them into a false sense of security even when other indicators suggest that trouble is brewing (Kam 1988).

Because developing estimates of what is going to happen in the future is so difficult and unforgiving, analysts and the intelligence production process can fall into routines that are reassuring but prove to be highly counterproductive. Intelligence reports that are supposed to provide insight into future events can sometimes become reports on what has happened in the recent past or compilations of reports about past activities. Instead of offering a glimpse into the future, finished intelligence can take on a historical quality by summarizing events over the last few days or weeks. This "historical intelligence" often carries greater weight than more speculative intelligence about the future, because it is grounded in real evidence about past events. Information about what *has* happened is far more credible to the reader than information about what *might* happen.

A similar type of problem emerges when intelligence estimates become a matter of routine, involving the repeated assertion of key analytical judgments without recognition of either the passage of time or changing circumstances. Intelligence estimates having to do with the development of weapons systems often fall into this trap. For instance, in the years immediately following World War II, it was widely assumed that the Soviet Union would need about five years to acquire an atomic bomb. This estimate was repeated in 1946, 1947, 1948, and 1949—the year that the Soviets actually detonated their first nuclear device. Apparently analysts lost track of the fact that the five-year window at the heart of their analysis was not a moving target but was instead pegged to 1945. The "five-year window" actually is rather common in intelligence estimates—especially in predictions of how long it might take for a state or non-state actor to develop chemical, biological, or nuclear weapons and associated delivery systems—because it allows analysts to draw attention to a problem without setting in motion difficult political, economic, or military actions to deal with it. By predicting something that might happen in the relatively distant future, one can still claim that a warning was given, without forcing policymakers to act immediately to solve the problem.

THE LIMITS OF HUMAN COGNITION

Humans everywhere share one thing that transcends culture, history, and politics: human cognition and psychology. Whether they are leaders or led, highly educated or poorly educated, world travelers or stay-at-home country bumpkins, they all share the same cognitive biases and patterns of perception. Analysts, however, must struggle to overcome their own psychological precepts if they are going to avoid cognitive pitfalls that often bedevil the analytic process.

First, people generally do not realize that their initial perception of the world occurs without much conscious awareness. Although cognitive psychologists might cringe at this explanation, our minds use what amounts to a pattern-recognition program to help order the world around us and to bring a reality we recognize to our conscious mind (Heuer 1999). Without this precognition, we would be condemned to forever revisit first principles, to spend all our time just interpreting our sensory perceptions. If this situation were to occur, it would be extraordinarily difficult for us to learn or to generalize across various experiences and events. But because this precognition is extremely powerful, it can be dangerous from the analyst's perspective. If his or her mind places incoming data into the wrong pattern, the analyst will find it difficult to reinterpret the data in a more useful way or in a way that better corresponds to reality.

Second, how we interpret events or others' actions is often shaped by a series of cognitive biases. When others do something that has a negative effect on us, we tend to see them as evil people who intended to harm us, but when we do something that has a negative impact on others, we tend to see ourselves as having no choice in the matter, as being boxed in by circumstances. This thinking pattern is known as the *fundamental attribution error.* Similarly, people tend to take too much credit for the good things that happen and take too little blame when bad things happen. These biases complicate analytical work, because they prevent analysts from recognizing weaknesses that can be exploited by opponents or ways their own country is contributing to a deteriorating international situation. People also tend to interpret information in terms of what is on their mind when they receive the information or what comes to mind when they hear the information. Individuals interpret the world around them not based on the collected wisdom of humankind but in terms of living memory and experience, especially the vivid events that happen in their lives. This phenomenon is known as the *availability principle.* Thus, the life experiences and educational background of analysts is critical to the process of producing finished intelligence, because analysts have to compare incoming information with the historical and theoretical knowledge they possess to generate a useful estimate.

The key point to remember about the impact of human cognition on intelligence analysis is that the human mind tends to fill in the missing pieces of information, sometimes in ways that are difficult for analysts to recognize. For instance, *mirror imaging* often is a problem for analysts. That is, it generally is difficult for them to see the world from another person's perspective, especially when their differences with the person are created by a lack of shared cultural or historical perspective. But in the absence of clear information about what motivates others, analysts will "mirror image" by projecting their own values and motivations onto others in an effort to interpret these others' behavior. Analysis based on mirror imaging rarely is productive, because it tends to place data in a wrong analytical framework, which easily produces misleading estimates.

ORGANIZATIONAL PATHOLOGIES

Because most intelligence analysis takes place in an institutional setting, bureaucracy itself can have a negative impact on the process of creating finished intelligence. Analysts can become preoccupied with defending institutional turf by keeping analysts from other organizations from undertaking work that replicates or contradicts their estimates. Organizations have a keen interest in preventing others from encroaching on their mission and issue domain, because they are interested in preserving their slice of the budgetary pie. Defending an organization's past positions on a given issue can also get in the way of honest estimates of a developing situation; it is difficult to admit that past estimates might have been inaccurate, because such an admission would call into question the usefulness of current intelligence products.

Organizations also have to create the proper working atmosphere to encourage analysts to take risks and to think "outside the box," to use a popular phrase. Although a full discussion of the issue of intelligence politicization must wait for Part IV, we should mention here that organizations must send a message to their rank and file that those who make bold predictions will not suffer negative consequences if their estimates fail to materialize. Intelligence organizations must cultivate independent thinkers, even if they sometimes ignore bureaucratic decorum to make their opinions known. Indeed, if signals can always be found somewhere in the intelligence production process in the aftermath of an analytic failure, more often than not an "intelligence dissenter" can be found in the organization, someone who bucked the conventional wisdom and predicted accurately what was about to happen. An organization that can empower these dissenters so that their views obtain a fair hearing can greatly improve its performance. Of course, too much free thinking can produce disorder, acrimony, and a failure to reach a conclusion or consensus that policymakers might put to good use (Odom 2003). Striking a balance between consensus and healthy debate is a never-ending struggle for those who manage the production of finished intelligence.

Intelligence organizations are also prone to specific bureaucratic problems related to the process of intelligence production. Secrecy and compartmentalization lie at the heart of intelligence analysis; after all, this is what distinguishes secret organizations from other organizations (newspapers, television networks, Internet sites) that disseminate information to government officials, military officers, and the general public. Secrecy can impede analysis, because as information becomes increasingly sensitive, the number of analysts who have the necessary clearances to view the information diminishes. Moreover, finished intelligence based on highly sensitive sources often is distributed only to a limited number of individuals; these restrictions can have negative consequences if the people who can put the information to good use are not given access to finished intelligence.

Compartmentalization also is an effort to restrict the dissemination of information within intelligence organizations. If a hostile agent penetrates an organization by becoming a trusted agent or operative, compartmentalization prevents that person from gaining access to all the secrets kept by an agency. But compartmentalization impedes the efforts of analysts to develop a comprehensive intelligence estimate. If various analysts are allowed to look at only a small piece of the intelligence puzzle, will they know who else holds the other critical pieces, or will they ever be able to figure out the whole picture from just a few pieces of information?

THE READINGS

The articles that follow provide a sense of the difficult challenges faced by intelligence analysts. Few articles shape an entire intellectual endeavor, but "Analysis, War, and Decision," by Richard K. Betts of Columbia University, made that type of contribution to the field of intelligence analysis. The careful reader will detect that many of the themes raised in this opening essay are expressed forcefully and clearly in Betts's analysis. In describing the cognitive, idiosyncratic, and bureaucratic challenges faced by analysts, Betts states that it is not possible to use organizational reforms to overcome all of these problems simultaneously, because making progress in resolving one type of problem only makes other problems worse. Eliminating false alarms, for example, only makes it more likely that analysts will fail to respond to signals of real danger. Betts's article is probably best known for his bold judgment, made at the outset of the piece, that intelligence failures are inevitable and that despite the resources invested and the reforms undertaken, it is realistic to expect only marginal improvements in the performance of intelligence organizations. But his article also offers an outstanding overview of the problems that can creep up as analysts try to place raw intelligence in some useful context and convince policymakers that they should act on their estimates.

In a candid description of not only what life is like for a senior policymaker but also how intelligence can contribute to policymaking itself, Ambassador Robert D. Blackwill explains to CIA officer Jack Davis how analysts from the Office of European Analysis (EURA) supported him as he represented U.S. interests in various forums. Blackwill's description of eighteen-hour workdays and an inability to pay attention to anything not related to the immediate problem in his inbox should change the minds of those who think the life of a senior official is glamorous. "A Policymaker's Perspective on Intelligence Analysis" also describes how Blackwill found finished intelligence directed toward a general audience of no particular value and how he cultivated personal and professional relationships to obtain outstanding staff and analytical support from EURA. Blackwill tells a rare story in the literature on the nexus between intelligence and policy, a story of an outstanding intelligence success. Even though it appears mundane, it really is no small accomplishment. Blackwill describes the bureaucratic obstacles that had to be overcome and the personal sacrifices that had to be made by analysts to create a useful exchange between intelligence professionals and policymakers.

Next, in "Intelligence Analysis and American Foreign Policy," Stephen Marrin maintains that strategic intelligence analysis has only marginal influence on the making of American foreign policy.

7. ANALYSIS, WAR, AND DECISION:
WHY INTELLIGENCE FAILURES ARE INEVITABLE

RICHARD K. BETTS

The history of diplomatic and military affairs is riddled with instances when intelligence analysts failed to provide timely warning of what was about to unfold. Betts presents a strong explanation of why intelligence failures are inevitable, as well as insights into the myriad challenges that analysts must overcome to offer useful estimates of future events. In arguing that the nature of intelligence analysis prevents all but modest improvements in the performance of intelligence organizations, Betts offers a compelling argument that continues to serve as the conventional wisdom on the limits of intelligence reform and analysis.

Military disasters befall some states, no matter how informed their leaders are, because their capabilities are deficient. Weakness, not choice, is their primary problem. Powerful nations are not immune to calamity either, because their leaders may misperceive threats or miscalculate responses. Information, understanding, and judgment are a larger part of the strategic challenge for countries such as the United States. Optimal decisions in defense policy therefore depend on the use of strategic intelligence: the acquisition, analysis, and appreciation of relevant data. In the best-known cases of intelligence failure, the most crucial mistakes have seldom been made by collectors of raw information, occasionally by professionals who produce finished analyses, but most often by the decision makers who consume the products of intelligence services. Policy premises constrict perception, and administrative workloads constrain reflection. Intelligence failure is political and psychological more often than organizational.

Observers who see notorious intelligence failures as egregious often infer that disasters can be avoided by perfecting norms and procedures for analysis and argumentation. This belief is illusory. Intelligence can be improved marginally, but not radically, by altering the analytic system. The illusion is also dangerous if it abets overconfidence that systemic reforms will increase the predictability of threats. The use of intelligence depends less on the bureaucracy than on the intellects and inclinations of the authorities above it. To clarify the tangled relationship of analysis and policy, this essay explores conceptual approaches to intelligence failure, differentiation of intelligence problems, insurmountable obstacles to accurate assessment, and limitations of solutions proposed by critics.

I. APPROACHES TO THEORY

Case studies of intelligence failures abound, yet scholars lament the lack of a theory of intelligence.[1] It is more accurate to say that we lack a positive or normative theory of intelligence. Negative or descriptive theory—the empirical understanding of how intelligence systems make mistakes—is well developed. The distinction is significant because there is little evidence that either scholars or practitioners have succeeded in translating such knowledge into reforms that measurably reduce failure. Development of a normative theory of intelligence has been inhibited because the lessons of hindsight do not guarantee improvement in foresight, and hypothetical solutions to failure only occasionally produce improvement in practice. The problem of intelligence failure can be conceptualized in three overlapping ways. The first is the most reassuring; the second is the most common; and the third is the most important.

1. FAILURE IN PERSPECTIVE

There is an axiom that a pessimist sees a glass of water as half empty and an optimist sees it as half full. In this sense, the estimative system is a glass half full. Mistakes can happen in any activity. Particular failures are accorded disproportionate significance if they are considered in isolation rather than in terms of the general ratio of failures to successes; the record of success is less striking because observers tend not to notice disasters that do not happen. Any academician who used a model that predicted outcomes correctly in four out of five cases would be happy; intelligence analysts must use models of their own and should not be blamed for missing occasionally. One problem with this benign view is that there are no clear indicators of what the ratio of failure to success in intelligence is, or whether many successes on minor issues should be reassuring in the face of a smaller number of failures on more critical problems.[2] In the thermonuclear age, just *one* mistake could have apocalyptic consequences.

2. PATHOLOGIES OF COMMUNICATION

The most frequently noted sources of breakdowns in intelligence lie in the process of amassing timely data, communicating them to decision makers, and impressing the latter with the validity or relevance of the information. This view of the problem leaves room for optimism because it implies that procedural curatives can eliminate the dynamics of error. For this reason, official post mortems of intelligence blunders inevitably produce recommendations for reorganization and changes in operating norms.

3. PARADOXES OF PERCEPTION

Most pessimistic is the view that the roots of failure lie in unresolvable trade-offs and dilemmas. Curing some pathologies with organizational reforms often creates new pathologies or resurrects old ones;[3] perfecting intelligence production does not necessarily lead to perfecting intelligence consumption; making warning systems more sensitive reduces the risk of surprise, but increases the number of false alarms, which in turn reduces sensitivity; the principles of optimal analytic procedure are in many respects incompatible with the imperatives of the decision process; avoiding intelligence failure requires the elimination of strategic preconceptions, but leaders cannot operate purposefully without some preconceptions. In devising measures to improve the intelligence process, policy makers are damned if they do and damned if they don't.

It is useful to disaggregate the problem of strategic intelligence failures in order to elicit clues about which paradoxes and pathologies are pervasive and therefore most in need of attention. The crucial problems of linkage between analysis and strategic decision can be subsumed under the following categories:

1. Attack Warning

The problem in this area is timely prediction of an enemy's immediate intentions, and the "selling" of such predictions to responsible authorities. Major insights into intelligence failure have emerged from catastrophic surprises: Pearl Harbor, the Nazi invasion of the U.S.S.R., the North Korean attack and Chinese intervention of 1950, and the 1973 war in the Middle East. Two salient phenomena characterize these cases. First, evidence of impending attack was available, but did not flow efficiently up the chain of command. Second, the fragmentary indicators of alarm that did reach decision makers were dismissed because they contradicted strategic estimates or assumptions. In several cases hesitancy in communication and disbelief on the part of leaders were reinforced by deceptive enemy maneuvers that cast doubt on the data.[4]

2. Operational Evaluation

In wartime, the essential problem lies in judging the results (and their significance) of interacting capabilities. Once hostilities are under way, informed decision making requires assessments of tactical effectiveness—"how we are doing"—in order to adapt strategy and options. In this dimension, the most interesting insights have come from Vietnam-era memoirs of low-level officials and from journalistic muckraking. Again there are two fundamental points. First, within the context of a glut of ambiguous data, intelligence officials linked to operational agencies (primarily military) tend to indulge a propensity for justifying service performance by issuing optimistic assessments, while analysts in autonomous non-operational units (primarily in the Central Intelligence Agency and the late Office of National Estimates) tend to produce more pessimistic evaluations. Second, in contrast to cases of attack warning, fragmentary tactical indicators of *success* tend to override more general and cautious strategic estimates. Confronted by differing analyses, a leader mortgaged to his policy tends to resent or dismiss the critical ones, even when they represent the majority view of the intelligence community, and to cling to the data that support continued commitment.[5] Lyndon Johnson railed at his Director of Central Intelligence (DCI) at a White House dinner:

> Policy making is like milking a fat cow. You see the milk coming out, you press more and the milk bubbles and flows, and just as the bucket is full, the cow with its tail whips the bucket and all is spilled. That's what CIA does to policy making.[6]

From the consensus-seeking politician, this was criticism; to a pure analyst, it would have been flattery. But it is the perspective of the former, not the latter, that is central in decision making.

3. Defense Planning

The basic task in using intelligence to develop doctrines and forces for deterrence and defense is to estimate threats posed by adversaries, in terms of both capabilities and intentions, over a period of several years. Here the separability of intelligence and policy, analysis and advocacy, is least clear. In dealing with the issue of "how much is enough" for security, debates over data merge murkily into debates over options and programs. As in operational evaluation, the problem lies more in data mongering than in data collecting. To the extent that stark generalizations are possible, the basic points in this category are the reverse of those in the previous one.

First, the justification of a mission (in this case, preparedness for future contingencies as opposed to demonstration of current success on the battlefield) prompts pessimistic estimates by operational military analysts; autonomous analysts without budgetary axes to grind, but with biases similar to those prevalent in the intellectual community, tend toward less alarmed predictions.[7] Military intelligence inclines toward "worst-case" analysis in planning, and toward "best-case" analysis in operational evaluation. (Military intelligence officials such as Lieutenant General Daniel Graham were castigated by liberals for *under*estimating the Vietcong's strength in the 1960's but for *over*estimating Soviet strength in the 1970's.) Air Force intelligence overestimated Soviet air deployments in the "bomber gap" controversy of the 1950s, and CIA-dominated National Intelligence Estimates (NIE's) underestimated Soviet ICBM deployments throughout the 1960's (overreacting, critics say, to the mistaken prediction of a "missile gap" in 1960).[8]

Second, in the context of peacetime, with competing domestic claims on resources, political leaders have a natural interest in at least partially rejecting military estimates and embracing those of other analysts who justify limiting allocations to defense programs. If the President had accepted pessimistic CIA operational evaluations in the mid-1960's, he might have withdrawn from Vietnam; if he had accepted pessimistic military analyses of the Soviet threat in the mid-1970's, he might have added massive increases to the defense budget.

Some chronic sources of error are unique to each of these three general categories of intelligence problems, and thus do not clearly suggest reforms that would be advisable across the board. To compensate for the danger in conventional attack warning, reliance on worst-case analysis might seem the safest rule, but in making estimates for defense planning, worst-case analysis would mandate severe and often unnecessary economic sacrifices. Removing checks on the influence of CIA analysts and "community" staffs[9] might seem justified by the record of operational evaluation in Vietnam, but would not be warranted by the record of estimates on Soviet ICBM deployments. It would be risky to alter the balance of power systematically among competing analytic components, giving the "better" analysts more status. Rather, decision makers should be encouraged to be more and less skeptical of certain agencies' estimates, *depending on the category of analysis involved.*

Some problems, however, cut across all three categories and offer a more general basis for considering changes in the system. But these general problems are not very susceptible to cure by formal changes in process, because it is usually impossible to disentangle intelligence failures from policy failures. Separation of intelligence and policy making has long been a normative concern of officials and theorists, who have seen both costs and benefits in minimizing the intimacy between intelligence professionals and operational authorities. But, although the personnel can be segregated, the functions cannot, unless intelligence is defined narrowly as the collection of data, and analytic responsibility is reserved to decision makers. Analysis and decision are interactive rather than sequential processes. By the narrower definition of intelligence, there have actually been few major failures. In most cases of mistakes in predicting attacks or in assessing operations, the inadequacy of critical data or their submergence in a viscous bureaucracy were at best the proximate causes of failure. The ultimate causes of error in most cases have been wishful thinking, cavalier disregard of professional analysts, and, above all, the premises and preconceptions of policy makers. Fewer fiascoes have occurred in the stages of acquisition and presentation of facts than in the stages of interpretation and response. Producers of intelligence have been culprits less often than consumers. Policy perspectives tend to constrain objectivity, and authorities often fail to use intelligence properly. As former State Department intelligence director Ray Cline testified, defending his analysts' performance in October 1973 and criticizing Secretary Kissinger for ignoring them:

> Unless something is totally conclusive, you must make an inconclusive report . . . by the time you are sure it is always very close to the event. So I don't think the analysts did such a lousy job. What I think was the lousy job was in bosses not insisting on a new preparation at the end of that week [before war broke out] . . . the reason the system wasn't working very well is that people were not asking it to work and not listening when it did work.[10]

II. BASIC BARRIERS TO ANALYTIC ACCURACY

Many constraints on the optimal processing of information lie in the structure of authority and the allocation of time and resources. Harold Wilensky argues persuasively that the intelligence function is hindered most by the structural characteristics of hierarchy, centralization, and specialization.[11] Yet it is precisely these characteristics that are the essence of any government. A related problem is the dominance of operational authorities over intelligence specialists, and the trade-off between objectivity and influence. Operators have more influence in decision making but are less capable of unbiased interpretation of evidence because they have a vested interest in the success of their operations; autonomous analysts are more disinterested and usually more objective, but lack influence. Senior generalists at the policy level often distrust or discount the judgments of analytic professionals and place more weight on reports from operational sources.[12] In response to this phenomenon, the suggestion has been made to *legislate* the requirement that decision makers consider analyses by the CIA's Intelligence Directorate (now the National Foreign Assessment Center) before establishing policy.[13] Such a requirement would offer no more than wishful formalism. Statutory fiat cannot force human beings to value one source above another. "No power has yet been found," DCI Richard Helms has testified, "to force

Presidents of the United States to pay attention on a continuing basis to people and papers when confidence has been lost in the originator."[14] Moreover, principals tend to believe that they have a wider point of view than middle-level analysts and are better able to draw conclusions from raw data. That point of view underlies their fascination with current intelligence and their impatience with the reflective interpretations in "finished" intelligence.[15]

The dynamics of decision are also not conducive to analytic refinement. In a crisis, both data and policy outpace analysis, the ideal process of staffing and consultation falls behind the press of events, and careful estimates cannot be digested in time. As Winston Churchill recalled of the hectic days of spring 1940,

> The Defence Committee of the War Cabinet sat almost every day to discuss the reports of the Military Coordination Committee and those of the Chiefs of Staff; and their conclusions or divergences were again referred to frequent Cabinets. All had to be explained or reexplained; and by the time this process was completed, the whole scene had often changed.[16]

Where there is ample time for decision, on the other hand, the previously mentioned bureaucratic impediments gain momentum.[17] Just as information processing is frustrated by constraints on the time that harried principals can spend scrutinizing analytic papers, it is constrained by the funds that a government can spend. To which priorities should scarce resources be allocated? The Schlesinger Report of 1971, which led to President Nixon's reorganization of U.S. intelligence, noted that criticisms of analytic products were often translated into demands for more extensive collection of data, but "Seldom does anyone ask if a further reduction in uncertainty, however small, is worth its cost."[18] Authorities do not always know, however, which issues require the greatest attention and which uncertainties harbor the fewest potential threats. Beyond the barriers that authority, organization, and scarcity pose to intelligence lie more fundamental and less remediable intellectual sources of error.

1. AMBIGUITY OF EVIDENCE

Intelligence veterans have noted that "estimating is what you do when you do not know,"[19] but "it is inherent in a great many situations that after reading the estimate, you will still not know."[20] These observations highlight an obvious but most important obstacle to accuracy in analysis. It is the role of intelligence to extract certainty from uncertainty and to facilitate coherent decision in an incoherent environment. (In a certain and coherent environment there is less need for intelligence.) To the degree they reduce uncertainty by extrapolating from evidence riddled with ambiguities, analysts risk oversimplifying reality and desensitizing the consumers of intelligence to the dangers that lurk within the ambiguities; to the degree they do not resolve ambiguities, analysts risk being dismissed by annoyed consumers who see them as not having done their job. Uncertainty reflects inadequacy of data, which is usually assumed to mean *lack* of information. But ambiguity can also be aggravated by an *excess* of data. In attack warning, there is the problem of "noise" and deception; in operational evaluation (particularly in a war such as Vietnam), there is the problem of overload from the high volume of finished analyses, battlefield statistics, reports, bulletins, reconnaissance, and communications intercepts flowing upward through multiple channels at a rate exceeding the capacity of officials to absorb or scrutinize them judiciously. (From the CIA alone, the White House received current intelligence dailies, Weekly Reports, daily Intelligence Information Cables, occasional Special Reports and specific memoranda, and analyses from the CIA Vietnam Working Group.) Similarly, in estimates for defense planning, there is the problem of innumerable and endlessly refined indices of the strategic balance, and the dependence of assessments of capabilities on complex and variable assumptions about the doctrine, scenarios, and intentions that would govern their use.

Because it is the job of decision makers to decide, they cannot react to ambiguity by deferring judgment.[21] When the problem is an environment that lacks clarity, an overload of conflicting data, and lack of time for rigorous assessment of sources and validity, ambiguity abets instinct and allows intuition to drive analysis. Intelligence can fail because the data are too permissive for policy judgment rather than too constraining. When a welter of fragmentary evidence offers support to various interpretations, ambiguity is exploited by wishfulness. The greater the ambiguity, the greater the impact of preconceptions.[22] (This point should be distinguished from the theory of cognitive dissonance, which became popular with political scientists at the time it was being rejected by psychologists.)[23] There is some inverse relation between the importance of an assessment (when uncertainty is high) and the likelihood that it will be accurate. Lyndon Johnson could reject pessimistic NIE's on Vietnam by inferring more optimistic conclusions from the reports that came through command channels on pacification, interdiction, enemy casualties, and defections. Observers who assume Soviet malevolence focus on analyses of strategic forces that emphasize missile throw weight and gross megatonnage (Soviet advantages); those who assume more benign Soviet intentions focus on analyses that emphasize missile accuracy and numbers of warheads (U.S. advantages). In assessing the naval balance, Secretary of Defense Rumsfeld focused on numbers of ships (Soviet lead), and Congressman Les Aspin, a critic of the Pentagon, focused on total tonnage (U.S. lead).

2. AMBIVALENCE OF JUDGMENT

Where there are ambiguous and conflicting indicators (the context of most failures of intelligence), the imperatives of honesty and accuracy leave a careful analyst no alternative but ambivalence. There is usually *some* evidence to support any prediction. For instance, the CIA reported in June 1964 that a Chinese instructor (deemed not "particularly qualified to make this remark") had told troops in a course in guerrilla warfare, "We will have the atom bomb in a matter of months."[24] Several months later the Chinese did perform their first nuclear test. If the report had been the only evidence, should analysts have predicted the event? If they are not to make a leap of faith and ignore the data that do not mesh, analysts will issue estimates that waffle. In trying to elicit nuances of probability from the various possibilities not foreclosed by the data, cautious estimates may reduce ambivalence, but they may become Delphic or generalized to the point that they are not useful guides to decision. (A complaint I have heard in conversations with several U.S. officials is that many past estimates of Soviet objectives could substitute the name of any other great power in history—Imperial Rome, 16th-century Spain, Napoleonic France—and sound equally valid.) Hedging is the legitimate intellectual response to ambiguity, but it can be politically counterproductive, if the value of intelligence is to shock consumers out of wishfulness and cognitive insensitivity. A wishful decision maker can fasten onto that half of an ambivalent analysis that supports his predisposition.[25] A more objective official may escape this temptation, but may consider the estimate useless because it does not provide "the answer."

3. ATROPHY OF REFORMS

Disasters always stimulate organizational changes designed to avert the same failures in the future. In some cases these changes work. In many instances, however, the changes persist formally but erode substantively. Standard procedures are constant. Dramatic failures occur only intermittently. If the reforms in procedure they have provoked do not fulfill day-to-day organizational needs—or if, as often happens, they complicate operations and strain the organization's resources—they fall into disuse or become token practices. After the postmortem of North Korea's downing of a U.S. EC-121 monitoring aircraft in 1969, there was, for several months, a great emphasis on risk assessments for intelligence collection missions. Generals and admirals personally oversaw the implementation of new procedures for making the assessments. Six months later, majors and captains were doing the checking. "Within a year the paperwork was spot-checked by a major and the entire community slid back to its old way of making a 'quick and dirty' rundown of the JCS criteria when sending in reconnaissance mission proposals."[26] The downing of the U-2 over the Soviet Union in 1960 and the capture of the intelligence ship *Pueblo* in 1968 had been due in part to the fact that the process of risk assessment for specific collection missions, primarily the responsibility of overworked middle-level officers, had become ponderous, sloppy, or ritualized.[27] At a higher level, a National Security Council Intelligence Committee was established in 1971 to improve responsiveness of intelligence staff to the needs of policy makers. But since the subcabinet-level consumers who made up the committee were pressed by other responsibilities, it lapsed in importance and was eventually abolished.[28] A comparable NSC committee that *did* serve tangible day-to-day needs of consumers to integrate intelligence and policy—the Verification Panel, which dealt with SALT—was more effective, but it was issue-oriented rather than designed to oversee the intelligence process itself. Organizational innovations will not improve the role of intelligence in policy unless they flow from the decision makers' views of their own needs and unless they provide frequent practical benefits.

None of these three barriers are accidents of structure or process. They are inherent in the nature of intelligence and the dynamics of work. As such, they constitute severe constraints on the efficacy of structural reform.

III. THE ELUSIVENESS OF SOLUTIONS

If they do not atrophy, most solutions proposed to obviate intelligence dysfunctions have two edges: in reducing one vulnerability, they increase another. After the seizure of the *Pueblo*, the Defense Intelligence Agency (DIA) was reprimanded for misplacing a message that could have prevented the incident. The colonel responsible developed a careful microfilming operation in the message center to ensure a record of transmittal of cables to authorities in the Pentagon. Implementing this check, however, created a three-to-four hour delay—another potential source of failure—in getting cables to desk analysts whose job was to keep reporting current.[29] Thus, procedural solutions often constitute two steps forward and one step back; organizational fixes cannot transcend the basic barriers. The lessons of Pearl Harbor led to the establishment of a Watch Committee and National Indications Center in Washington. Although this solution eliminated a barrier in the communication system, it did not prevent the failure of timely alert to the Chinese intervention in Korea or the 1973 October War, because it did not eliminate the ambiguity barrier. (Since then, the Watch Committee has been replaced by the DCI's Strategic Warning Staff.) DIA was reorganized four times within its first ten years; yet it continued to leave most observers dissatisfied. The Agranat Commission's review of Israel's 1973 intelligence failure produced proposals for institutional reform that are striking because they amount to copying the American system of the same time—which had failed in exactly the same way as the Israeli system.[30] Reform is not hopeless, but hopes placed in solutions most often proposed—such as the following—should be circumscribed.

1. ASSUME THE WORST

A common reaction to traumatic surprise is the recommendation to cope with ambiguity and ambivalence by acting on the most threatening possible interpretations. If there is *any* evidence of threat, assume it is valid, even if the *apparent* weight of contrary indicators is greater. In retrospect, when the point of reference is an actual disaster attributable to a mistaken calculation of probabilities, this response is always justifiable, but it is impractical as a guide to standard procedure. Operationalizing worst-case analysis requires extraordinary expense, it risks being counterproductive if it is effective (by provoking enemy countermeasures or pre-emption), and it is likely to be ineffective because routinization will discredit it. Many Israeli observers deduced from the 1973 surprise that defense planning could only rest on the assumption that no attack warning will be available, and that precautionary mobilization should always be undertaken even when there is only dubious evidence of impending Arab action.[31] Similarly, American hawks argue that if the Soviets' intentions are uncertain, the only prudent course is to assume they are seeking the capability to win nuclear war.

In either case, the norm of assuming the worst poses high financial costs. Frequent mobilizations strain the already taut Israeli economy. Moreover, countermobilization can defeat itself. Between 1971 and 1973, the Egyptians three times undertook exercises similar to those that led to the October attack; Israel mobilized in response, and nothing happened. It was the paradox of self-negating prophecy.[32] The Israeli Chief of Staff was sharply criticized for the unnecessary cost.[33] The danger of hypersensitivity appeared in 1977, when General Gur believed Sadat's offer to come to Jerusalem to be a camouflage for an Egyptian attack; he began Israeli maneuvers in the Sinai, which led Egypt to begin maneuvers of its own, heightening the risk of accidental war.[34] To estimate the requirements for deterrence and defense, worst case assumptions present an open-ended criterion. The procurement of all the hedges possible for nuclear war-fighting—large increments in offensive forces, alert status, hardening of command-control-and-communications, active and passive defenses—would add billions to the U.S. defense budget. Moreover, prudent hedging in policy should be distinguished from net judgment of probabilities in estimates.[35]

Alternatively, precautionary escalation or procurement may act as self-fulfilling prophecies, either through a catalytic spiral of mobilization (à la World War I) or an arms race that heightens tension, or doctrinal hedges that make the prospect of nuclear war more "thinkable." Since evidence for the "action-reaction" hypothesis of U.S. and Soviet nuclear policies is meager, and arms races can sometimes be stabilizing rather than dangerous, the last point is debatable. Still, a large unilateral increase in strategic forces by either the United States or the Soviet Union would, at the least, destroy the possibility of gains desired from SALT. A surprise attack or defeat makes the costs of *under*estimates obvious and dramatic; the unnecessary defense costs due to *over*estimates can only be surmised, since the minimum needed for deterrence

is uncertain. Worst-case analysis as a standard norm would also exacerbate the "cry wolf" syndrome. *Unambiguous* threat is not an intelligence problem; rather, the challenge lies in the response to fragmentary, contradictory, and dubious indicators. Most such indicators turn out to be false alarms. Analysts who reflexively warn of disaster are soon derided as hysterical. General William Westmoreland recalled that the warnings that had been issued before the 1968 Tet Offensive were ignored. U.S. headquarters in Saigon had each year predicted a winter-spring offensive, "and every year it had come off without any dire results . . . . Was not the new offensive to be more of the same?"[36]

Given the experience of intelligence professionals that most peace-time indicators of suspicious enemy activity lead to nothing, what Colonel who has the watch some night will risk "lighting up the board" in the White House simply on the basis of weak apprehension? How many staffers will risk waking a tired President, especially if they have done so before and found the action to be needless? How many distracting false alarms will an overworked President tolerate before he makes it clear that aides should exercise discretion in bothering him? Even if worst-case analysis is promulgated in principle, it will be compromised in practice. Routinization corrodes sensitivity. Every day that an expected threat does not materialize dulls receptivity to the reality of danger. As Roberta Wohlstetter wrote of pre-Pearl Harbor vigilance, "We are constantly confronted by the paradox of pessimistic realism of phrase coupled with loose optimism in practice."[37] Seeking to cover all contingencies, worst-case analysis loses focus and salience; by providing a theoretical guide for everything, it provides a practical guide for very little.

2. MULTIPLE ADVOCACY

Blunders are often attributed to decisionmakers' inattention to unpopular viewpoints or to a lack of access to higher levels of authority by dissident analysts. To reduce the chances of such mistakes, Alexander George proposes institutionalizing a balanced, open, and managed process of debate, so that no relevant assessments will be submerged by unchallenged premises or the bureaucratic strength of opposing officials.[38] The goal is unobjectionable, and formalized multiple advocacy certainly would help, not hinder. But confidence that it will help systematically and substantially should be tentative. In a loose sense, there has usually been multiple advocacy in the U.S. policy process, but it has not prevented mistakes in deliberation or decision. Lyndon Johnson did not decide for limited bombing and gradual troop commitment in Vietnam in 1965 because he was not presented with extensive and vigorous counterarguments. He considered seriously (indeed solicited) Under Secretary of State George Ball's analysis, which drew on NIE's and lower-level officials' pessimistic assessments that any escalation would be a mistake. Johnson was also well aware of the arguments by DCI John McCone and the Air Force from the other extreme—that massive escalation in the air war was necessary because gradualism would be ineffective.[39] The President simply chose to accept the views of the middle-of-the-road opponents of *both* Ball and McCone.

To the extent that multiple advocacy works, and succeeds in maximizing the number of views promulgated and in supporting the argumentive resources of all contending analysts, it may simply highlight ambiguity rather than resolve it. In George's ideal situation, the process would winnow out unsubstantiated premises and assumptions about ends-means linkages. But in the context of data overload, uncertainty, and time constraints, multiple advocacy may in effect give all of the various viewpoints an aura of empirical respectability and allow a leader to choose whichever accords with his predisposition.[40]

The efficacy of multiple advocacy (which is greatest under conditions of manageable data and low ambiguity) may vary inversely with the potential for intelligence failure (which is greatest under conditions of confusing data and high uncertainty). The process could, of course, bring to the surface ambiguities where false certainty had prevailed; in these cases, it would be as valuable as George believes. But if multiple advocacy increases ambivalence and leaders do *not* indulge their instincts, it risks promoting conservatism or paralysis. Dean Acheson saw danger in presidential indecisiveness aggravated by debate: " 'I know your theory,' he grumbled to Neustadt. 'You think Presidents should be warned. You're wrong. Presidents should be given confidence.' "[41]

Even Clausewitz argued that deference to intelligence can frustrate bold initiative and squander crucial opportunities. Critics charged Henry Kissinger with crippling U.S. intelligence by refusing to keep analysts informed of his intimate conversations with foreign leaders.[42] To do so, however, would have created the possibility of leaks and might thereby have crippled his diplomatic maneuvers. It is doubtful that Nixon's initiative to China could have survived prior debate, dissent, and analysis by the bureaucracy.

It is unclear that managed multiple advocacy would yield markedly greater benefits than the redundancy and competitiveness that have long existed. (At best it would perfect the "market" of ideas in the manner that John Stuart Mill believed made liberalism conducive to the emergence of truth.) The first major reorganization of the American intelligence community in 1946–1947 emphasized centralization in order to avert future Pearl Harbors caused by fragmentation of authority; the latest reorganization (Carter's 1977 extension of authority of the Director of Central Intelligence over military intelligence programs) emphasized centralization to improve efficiency and coherence. Yet decentralization has always persisted in the overlapping division of labor between several separate agencies. Recent theorists of bureaucracy see such duplication as beneficial because competition exposes disagreement and presents policy makers with a wider range of views. Redundancy inhibits consensus, impedes the herd instinct in the decision process, and thus reduces the likelihood of failure due to unchallenged premises or cognitive errors. To ensure that redundancy works in this way, critics oppose a process that yields coordinated estimates—negotiated to the least common denominator, and cleared by all agencies before they are passed to the principals. George's "custodian" of multiple advocacy could ensure that this does not happen. There are, of course, trade-off costs for redundancy. Maximization of competition limits specialization. In explaining the failure of intelligence to predict the 1974 coup in Portugal, William Hyland pointed out, "if each of the major analytical components stretch their resources over the same range, there is the risk that areas of less priority will be superficially covered."[43]

The problem with arguing that the principals themselves should scrutinize numerous contrasting estimates in their integrity is that they are constantly overwhelmed by administrative responsibilities and "action items"; they lack the time to read, ponder, and digest that large an amount of material. Most intelligence products, even NIE's, are never read by policy makers; at best, they are used by second-level staffers as background material for briefing their seniors.[44] Consumers want previously coordinated analyses in order to save time and effort. In this respect, the practical imperatives of day-to-day decisions contradict the theoretical logic of ideal intelligence.

3. CONSOLIDATION

According to the logic of estimative redundancy, more analysis is better than less. Along this line of reasoning, Senate investigators noted critically that, as of fiscal year 1975, the U.S. intelligence community still allocated 72 percent of its budget for collection of information, 19 percent for processing technical data, and less than 9 percent for production of finished analyses. On the other hand, according to the logic of those who focus on the time constraints of leaders and the confusion that results from innumerable publications, quantity counteracts quality. The size of the CIA's intelligence directorate and the complexity of the production process "precluded close association between policy makers and analysts, between the intelligence product and policy informed by intelligence analysis."[45] For the sake of clarity and acuity, the intelligence bureaucracy should be streamlined.

This view is consistent with the development of the Office of National Estimates (ONE), which was established in 1950 and designed to coordinate the contributions of the various organs in the intelligence community for the Director of Central Intelligence. DCI Walter Bedell Smith envisioned an operation of about a thousand people. But William L. Langer, the scholar Smith imported to organize ONE, wanted a tight group of excellent analysts and a personnel ceiling of fifty. Langer prevailed, and though the number of staff members in ONE crept upwards, it probably never exceeded a hundred in its two decades of existence.[46] Yet ONE could not eliminate the complexity of the intelligence process; it could only coordinate and integrate it for the production of National Intelligence Estimates. Other sources found conduits to decision makers (to Cabinet members, through their own agencies, or to the President through the National Security Council). And some policy makers, though they might dislike the cacophony of multiple intelligence agencies, were suspicious of the consolidated NIE's, knowing that there was pressure to compromise views in order to gain agreement. Over time, the dynamics of bureaucracy also blunted the original objectives of ONE'S founder. From a cosmopolitan elite corps, it evolved into an insular unit of senior careerists from the CIA. The National Intelligence Officer system that replaced ONE reduced the number of personnel responsible for coordinating NIE's, but has been criticized on other grounds such as greater vulnerability to departmental pressures. Bureaucratic realities have frustrated other attempts to consolidate the intelligence structure. The Defense Intelligence Agency was created in 1961 to unify Pentagon intelligence and reduce duplicative activities of the three service intelligence agencies, but these agencies regenerated themselves; in less than a decade they were larger than they had been before DIA's inception.[47]

The numerous attempts to simplify the organization of the analytic process thus have not solved the major problems. Either the streamlining exercises were short-lived, and bureaucratization crept back, or the changes had to be moderated to avoid the new dangers they entailed. Contraction is inconsistent with the desire to minimize failure by "plugging holes" in intelligence, since compensating for an inadequacy usually requires *adding* personnel and mechanisms; pruning the structure that contributes to procedural sluggishness or complexity may create lacunae in substantive coverage.

4. DEVIL'S ADVOCACY

Multiple advocacy ensures that all views held by individuals within the analytic system will be granted serious attention. Some views that should receive attention, however, may not be held by anyone within the system. Virtually no analysts in Israel or the United States believed the Arabs would be "foolish" enough to attack in 1973. Many observers have recommended institutionalizing dissent by assigning to someone the job of articulating apparently ridiculous interpretations to ensure that they are forced into consideration. Establishing an official devil's advocate would probably do no harm (although some argue that it may perversely facilitate consensus-building by domesticating true dissenters or providing the illusory comfort that all views have been carefully examined;[48] worse, it might delude decision makers into believing that *uncertainties* have been resolved). But in any case, the role is likely to atrophy into a superfluous or artificial ritual. By the definition of the job, the devil's advocate is likely to be dismissed by decision makers as a sophist who only makes an argument because he is supposed to, not because of its real merits. Institutionalizing devil's advocacy is likely to be perceived in practice as institutionalizing the "cry wolf" problem; "There are limits to the utility of a 'devil's advocate' who is not a true devil."[49] He becomes someone to be indulged and disregarded. Given its rather sterile definition, the role is not likely to be filled by a prestigious official (who will prefer more "genuine" responsibility); it will therefore be easier for policy makers to dismiss the arguments. In order to avert intelligence failures, an analyst is needed who tells decision makers what they don't want to hear, dampening the penchant for wishful thinking. But since it is the job of the devil's advocate to do this habitually, and since he is most often wrong (as would be inevitable, since otherwise the conventional wisdom would eventually change), he digs his own grave. If the role is routinized and thus ritualized, it loses impact; but if it is not routinized, there can be no assurance that it will be operating when it is needed.

Despite the last point, which is more important in attack warning than in operational evaluation or defense planning, there is a compromise that offers more realistic benefits: *ad hoc* utilization of "real devils." This selective or biased form of multiple advocacy may be achieved by periodically giving a platform within the intelligence process to minority views that can be argued more persuasively by prestigious analysts outside the bureaucracy. This is what the President's Foreign Intelligence Advisory Board and DCI George Bush did in 1976 by commissioning the "Team B" critique of NFE's on Soviet strategic objectives and capabilities. Dissenters within the intelligence community who were skeptical of Soviet intentions were reinforced by a panel of sympathetic scholars, with a mandate to produce an analysis of their own.[50] This controversial exercise, even if it erred in many of its own ways (as dovish critics contend), had a major impact in promoting the reexamination of premises and methodology in U.S. strategic estimates. The problem with this option is that it depends on the political biases of the authorities who commission it. If it were balanced by a comparable "Team C" of analysts at the opposite extreme (more optimistic about Soviet intentions than the intelligence community consensus), the exercise would approach regular multiple advocacy, with the attendant limitations of that solution. Another variant would be intermittent designation of devil's advocates in periods of crisis, when the possibility of disaster is greater than usual. Since the role would then be fresh each time, rather than ritualized, the advocate might receive a more serious hearing. The problem here is that receptivity of decision makers to information that contradicts preconceptions varies inversely with their personal commitments, and commitments grow as crisis progresses.[51]

5. SANCTIONS AND INCENTIVES

Some critics tribute intelligence failures to dishonest reporting or the intellectual mediocrity of analysts. Suggested remedies include threats of punishment for the former, and inducements to attract talent to replace the latter. Other critics emphasize that, will or ability aside, analytic integrity is often submerged by the policy makers' demands for intelligence that suits them; "the NIE sought to be responsive to the evidence, not the policy maker."[52] Holders of this point of view would institutionalize the analysts' autonomy. Unobjectionable in principle (though if analysts are totally unresponsive to the consumer, he will ignore them), these implications cannot easily be operationalized without creating as many problems as they solve.

Self-serving operational evaluations from military sources, such as optimistic reports on progress in the field in Vietnam or pessimistic strategic estimates, might indeed be obviated if analysts in DIA, the service intelligence agencies, and command staffs were credibly threatened with sanctions (firing, nonpromotion, reprimand, or disgrace). Such threats theoretically could be a countervailing pressure to the career incentives analysts have to promote the interests of their services. But, except in the most egregious cases, it is difficult to apply such standards without arbitrariness and bias, given the problem of ambiguity; it simply encourages an alternative bias or greater ambivalence. Moreover, military professionals would be in an untenable position, pulled in opposite directions by two sets of authorities. To apply the sanctions, civil authorities would have to violate the most hallowed military canon by having civilian intelligence officials interfere in the chain of command. In view of these dilemmas, it is easier to rely on the limited effectiveness of redundancy or multiple advocacy to counteract biased estimates.

Critics concerned with attracting better talent into the analytic bureaucracy propose to raise salaries and to provide more high-ranking positions (supergrades) to which analysts can aspire. Yet American government salaries are already very high by academic standards. Those who attribute DIA's mediocrity (compared to CIA), to an insufficient allocation of supergrades and a consequent inability to retain equivalent personnel are also mistaken; as of 1975 the difference in the grade structures of DIA and CIA had been negligible.[53] And the fact that CIA analysts cannot rise to a supergrade position (GS-16 to 18) without becoming administrators is not convincing evidence that good analysts are underpaid; GS-15 salaries are higher than the maximum for most tenured professors.

Non-military analysts, or high-ranking soldiers with no promotions to look forward to, have fewer professional crosspressures to contend with than military intelligence officers. But an analyst's autonomy varies inversely with his influence, and hortatory injunctions to be steadfast and intellectually honest cannot ensure that he will be; they cannot transcend political realities or the idiosyncrasies of leaders. Richard Helms notes that "there is no way to insulate the DCI from unpopularity at the hands of Presidents or policy makers if he is making assessments which run counter to administrative policy. That is a built in hazard of the job. Sensible Presidents understand this. On the other hand they are human too." Integrity untinged by political sensitivity courts professional suicide. If the analyst insists on perpetually bearing bad news, he is likely to be beheaded. Helms himself succumbed to policy makers' pressures in compromising estimates of the MIRV capabilities of the Soviet SS-9 missile in 1969, and the prospects for Cambodia in 1970.[54] The same practical psychological constraints are reflected in an incident in which Chief of Naval Operations Elmo Zumwalt, who had already infuriated Nixon and Kissinger several times with his strategic estimates, was determined to present yet another unwelcome analysis; Secretary of Defense Schlesinger dissuaded him with the warning, "To give a briefing like that in the White House these days would be just like shooting yourself in the foot."[55]

6. COGNITIVE REHABILITATION AND METHODOLOGICAL CONSCIOUSNESS

The intertwining of analysis and decision and the record of intelligence failures due to mistaken preconceptions and unexamined assumptions suggest the need to reform the intelligence consumers' attitudes, awareness, and modes of perception. If leaders were made self-conscious and self-critical about their own psychologies, they might be less vulnerable to cognitive pathologies. This approach to preventing intelligence failure is the most basic and metaphysical. If policy makers focused on the methodologies of competing intelligence producers, they would be more sensitive to the biases and leaps of faith in the analyses passed to them.

> In official fact-finding ... the problem is not merely to open up a wide range of policy alternatives but to create incentives for persistent criticism of evidentiary value.[56]

Improvement would flow from mechanisms that force decision makers to make explicit rather than unconscious choices, to exercise judgment rather than engage in automatic perception, and to enhance their awareness of their own preconceptions.[57]

Unlike organizational structure, however, cognition cannot be altered by legislation. Intelligence consumers are political men who have risen by being more decisive than reflective, more aggressive than introspective, and confident as much as cautious. Few busy activists who have achieved success by thinking the way that they do will change their way of thinking because some theorist tells them to. Even if they could be forced to confront scholarly evidence of the dynamics of misperception it is uncertain that they could consistently internalize it. Preconception cannot be abolished; it is in one sense just another word for "model" or "paradigm"—a construct used to simplify reality, which any thinker needs in order to cope with complexity. There is a grain of truth in the otherwise pernicious maxim that an open mind is an empty mind. Moreover, the line between *perception* and *judgment* is very thin, and consumers cannot carefully scrutinize, compare, and evaluate the methodologies of competing analyses, for the same prosaic reason (the problem of expertise aside) that impedes many proposed reforms: they do not have the *time* to do so. Solutions that require principals to invest more attention than they already do are conceptually valid but operationally weak. Ideally, perhaps, each principal should have a Special Assistant for Rigor Enforcement.

Although most notable intelligence failures occur more often at the consuming rather than the producing end, it is impractical to place the burden for correcting those faults on the consumers. The most realistic strategy for improvement would be to have intelligence professionals anticipate the cognitive barriers to decision makers' utilization of their products. Ideally, the Director of Central Intelligence should have a theoretical temperament and personal skills in forcing unusual analyses to the attention of principals; he might act as George's "custodian" of the argumentation process. To fulfill this function, the DCI should be not only a professional analyst and an intellectual (of the twelve DCI's since 1946, only James Schlesinger met those criteria, and he served for only three months), but also a skilled bureaucratic politician. These qualifications seldom coincide. The DCI's coordinating staff and National Intelligence Officers should be adept at detecting, making explicit, and exposing to consumers the idiosyncrasies in the assessments of various agencies— the *reasons* that the focus and conclusions of the State Department's Bureau of Intelligence and

Research differ from those of DIA, or of naval intelligence, or of the CIA. For such a procedure to work, the consumers would have to favor it (as opposed to negotiated consensual estimates that would save them more time). There is always a latent tension between what facilitates timely decision and what promotes thoroughness and accuracy in assessment. The fact that there is no guaranteed prophylaxis against intelligence failures, however, does not negate the value of incremental improvements. The key is to see the problem of reform as one of modest refinements rather than as a systematic breakthrough.

IV. LIVING WITH FATALISM

Organizational solutions to intelligence failure are hampered by three basic problems: most procedural reforms that address specific pathologies introduce or accent other pathologies; changes in analytic processes can never fully transcend the constraints of ambiguity and ambivalence; and more rationalized information systems cannot fully compensate for the predispositions, perceptual idiosyncrasies, and time constraints of political consumers. Solutions that address the psychology and analytic style of decision makers are limited by the difficulty of changing human thought processes and day-to-day habits of judgment by normative injunction. Most theorists have thus resigned themselves to the hope of marginal progress, "to improve the 'batting average'—say from .275 to .301—rather than to do away altogether with surprise."[58]

There is some convergence in the implications of all three ways of conceptualizing intelligence failures. Mistakes should be expected because the *paradoxes* are not resolvable; minor improvements are possible by reorganizing to correct *pathologies,* and despair is unwarranted because, seen *in perspective,* the record could be worse. Marginal improvements have, in fact, been steadily instituted since World War II. Although many have indeed raised new problems, most have yielded a net increase in the rationalization of the system. The diversification of sources of estimates of adversaries' military power has grown consistently, obviating the necessity to rely exclusively on military staffs. The resources and influence of civilian analysts of military data (principally in the CIA's Office of Strategic Research but also in its Directorate of Science and Technology) are unparalleled in any other nation's intelligence system. At the same time, the DCI's mechanism for coordinating the activities of all agencies—the Intelligence Community Staff—has

grown and become more diverse and representative, and less an extension of the CIA, as more staffers have been added from the outside. In 1972, a separate Product Review Division was established within the staff to appraise the "objectivity, balance, and responsiveness" of intelligence studies on a regular basis. It has conducted postmortems of intelligence failures since then (the Yom Kippur War, the Cyprus crisis of 1974, the Indian nuclear test, and the seizure of the *Mayaguez).*[59] (Previously, postmortems had been conducted by the analysts who had failed, a procedure that hardly guaranteed objectivity.)

Within the Pentagon, capabilities for estimates relevant to planning were enhanced with the establishment of an office for Net Assessment, which analyzes the significance of foreign capabilities in comparison with U.S. forces. (CIA, DIA, and NIE's only estimate foreign capabilities.) Civilian direction of military intelligence was reinforced by an Assistant Secretary of Defense for Intelligence after the 1970 recommendation of the Fitzhugh Commission, and an Under Secretary for Policy in 1978. Experiments in improving communication between producers and consumers have been undertaken (such as, for example, the testing of a Defense Intelligence Board in late 1976). The dominance of operators within the intelligence community has also waned—especially since the phasing out of paramilitary operations in Southeast Asia and the severe reductions in size and status of CIA's covert action branch that began in 1973. Dysfunctions in the military communications system, which contributed to crises involving intelligence collection missions in the 1960's (the Israeli attack on the U.S.S. *Liberty* and North Korea's seizure of the *Pueblo)* were alleviated (though not cured) by new routing procedures and by instituting an "optimal scanning system" in the Pentagon.[60] Statistical analyses of strategic power have become progressively more rigorous and comprehensive; as staffs outside the executive branch—such as the Congressional Budget Office—have become involved in the process, they have also become more competitive.[61]

Few of the changes in structure and process have generated more costs than benefits. (Some critics believe, however, that the abolition of the Office and Board of National Estimates and their replacement with National Intelligence Officers was a net loss.) But it is difficult to prove that they have significantly reduced the incidence of intelligence failure. In the area of warning, for instance, new sophisticated coordination mechanisms have recently been introduced, and since the institution at the time of the 1974 Cyprus crisis of DCI "alert memoranda"—"brief notices in a form which cannot be overlooked"[62]—no major warning failure has occurred. But the period of testing is as yet too brief to demonstrate that these adaptations are more effective than previous procedures. In the area of operational evaluation, it is clear that there was greater consciousness of the limitations and cost-ineffectiveness of aerial bombardment during the Vietnam War than there had been in Korea, due largely to the assessments made by the offices of Systems Analysis and International Security Affairs in the Pentagon and Secretary of Defense McNamara's utilization of CIA estimates and contract studies by external analytic organizations.[63] Yet this greater consciousness did not prevail until late in the war because it was not consensus; Air Force and naval assessments of bombing effectiveness contradicted those of the critical civilian analysts. Nor has the elaboration and diversification of analytical resources for strategic estimates clearly reduced the potential for erroneous planning decisions. Determination of the salience and proper weight of conflicting indicators of strategic power and objectives or of the comparative significance of quantitative and qualitative factors is inextricable from the political debate over foreign policy: uncertainties always remain, leaving the individual's visceral fears or hopes as the elements that tilt the balance of judgment.

Although marginal reforms may reduce the probability of error, the unresolvable paradoxes and barriers to analytic and decisional accuracy will make some incidence of failure inevitable. Concern with intelligence failure then coincides with concern about how policy can hedge against the consequences of analytic inadequacy. Covering every hypothetical vulnerability would lead to bankruptcy, and hedging against one threat may aggravate a different one. The problem is thus one of priorities, and hedging against uncertainty is hardly easier than resolving it. Any measures that clarify the cost-benefit trade-off's in policy hedges are measures that mitigate the danger of intelligence failure.

One reasonable rule in principle would be to survey the hypothetical outcomes excluded by strategic premises as improbable but not impossible, identify those that would be disastrous if they *were* to occur, and then pay the price to hedge against them. This is no more practicable, however, than the pure form of worst-case analysis, because it requires willingness to bear and inflict severe costs for

dubious reasons. Escalation in Vietnam, after all, was a hedge against allowing China to be tempted to "devour" the rest of Southeast Asia. The interaction of analytic uncertainty and decisional prudence is a vicious circle that makes the segregation of empirical intelligence and normative policy an unattainable Platonic ideal.

In the simplest situation, the intelligence system can avert policy failure by presenting relevant and undisputed facts to non-expert principals who might otherwise make decisions in ignorance. But these simple situations are not those in which major intelligence failures occur. Failures occur when ambiguity aggravates ambivalence. In these more important situations—Acheson and Clausewitz to the contrary—the intelligence officer may perform most usefully by *not* offering the *answers* sought by authorities, but by offering *questions*, acting as a Socratic agnostic, nagging decision makers into awareness of the full range of uncertainty, and making the authorities' calculations harder rather than easier. Sensitive leaders will reluctantly accept and appreciate this function. Most leaders will not; they will make mistakes, and will continue to bear the prime responsibility for "intelligence" failures. Two general values (which sound wistful in the context of the preceding fatalism) remain to guide the choice of marginal reforms: anything that facilitates dissent and access to authorities by intelligence producers, and anything that facilitates skepticism and scrutiny by consumers. The values are synergistically linked; one will not improve the use of intelligence without the other. (A third value, but one nearly impossible to achieve, would be anything that increases the time available to principals for reading and reflection.)

Intelligence failures are not only inevitable, they are natural. Some are even benign (if a success would not have changed policy). Scholars cannot legitimately view intelligence mistakes as bizarre, because they are no more common and no less excusable than academic errors. They are less forgivable only because they are more consequential. Error in scholarship is resolved dialectically, as deceptive data are exposed and regnant theories are challenged, refined, and replaced by new research. If decision makers had but world enough and time, they could rely on this process to solve their intelligence problems. But the press of events precludes the luxury of letting theories sort themselves out over a period of years, as in academia. My survey of the intractability of the inadequacy of intelligence, and its inseparability from mistakes in decision, suggests one final conclusion that is perhaps most outrageously fatalistic of all: tolerance for disaster.

QUESTIONS FOR FURTHER DISCUSSION

1. Why is it so difficult to strike the correct balance in undertaking intelligence reforms?
2. Why is it impossible to overcome many of the problems faced by intelligence analysts?
3. Who in the intelligence community should play the role of "devil's advocate"?
4. How might net assessment contribute to better intelligence analysis?

ENDNOTES

1. For example, Klaus Knorr, "Failures in National Intelligence Estimates: The Case of the Cuban Missiles," *World Politics,* XVI (April 1964), 455, 465–66; Harry Howe Ransom, "Strategic Intelligence and Foreign Policy," *World Politics,* XXVII (October 1974), 145.

2. "As that ancient retiree from the Research Department of the British Foreign Office reputedly said, after serving from 1903–50: 'Year after year the worriers and fretters would come to me with awful predictions of the outbreak of war. I denied it each time. I was only wrong twice.'" Thomas L. Hughes, *The Fate of Facts in a World of Men—Foreign Policy and Intelligence Making* (New York: Foreign Policy Association, Headline Series No. 133, December 1976), 48. Paradoxically, "successes may be indistinguishable from failures." If analysts predict war and the attacker cancels his plans because surprise has been lost, "success of the intelligence services would have been expressed in the falsification of its predictions," which would discredit the analysis. Avi Shlaim, "Failures in National Intelligence Estimates: The Case of the Yom Kippur War," *World Politics,* XXVIII (April 1976), 378.

3. Compare the prescriptions in Peter Szanton and Graham Allison, "Intelligence: Seizing the Opportunity," with George Carver's critique, both in *Foreign Policy,* No. 22 (Spring 1976).

4. Roberta Wohlstetter, *Pearl Harbor: Warning and Decision* (Stanford: Stanford University Press 1962); Barton Whaley, *Codeword Barbarossa* (Cambridge: The M.I.T. Press 1973); Harvey De Weerd, "Strategic Surprise in the Korean War," *Orbis,* VI (Fall 1961); Alan Whiting, *China Crosses the Yalu* (New York: C1 Macmillan 1960); James F. Schnabel, *Policy and Direction: The First Year* (Washington, D.C.: Department of the Army 1972), 61–65, 83–85, 274–78; Michael I.

Handel, *Perception, Deception, and Surprise: The Case of the Yom Kippur War* (Jerusalem: Leonard Davis Institute of International Relations, Jerusalem Paper No. 19, 1976); Shlaim (fn. 2); Abraham Ben-Zvi, "Hindsight and Foresight: A Conceptual Framework for the Analysis of Surprise Attacks," *World Politics,* XXVIII. (April 1976); Amos Perlmutter, "Israel's Fourth War, October 1973: Political and Military Misperceptions," *Orbis,* XIX (Summer 1975); U.S. Congress, House, Select Committee on Intelligence (hereafter cited as HSCI], *Hearings, U.S. Intelligence Agencies and Activities: The Performance of the Intelligence Community,* 94th Cong., 1st sess., 1975; Draft Report of the House Select Committee on Intelligence, published in *The Village Voice,* February 16, 1976, pp. 76–81.

5. David Halberstam, *The Best and the Brightest* (New York: Random House 1972); Morris Blachman, "The Stupidity of Intelligence," in Charles Peters and Timothy J. Adams, eds., *Inside the System* (New York: Praeger 1970); Patrick J. McGarvey, "DIA: Intelligence to Please," in Morton Halperin and Arnold Kanter, eds., *Readings in American Foreign Policy: A Bureaucratic Perspective* (Boston: Little, Brown 1973); Chester Cooper, "The CIA and Decision-Making," *Foreign Affairs,* Vol. 50 (January 1972); Sam Adams, "Vietnam Cover-Up: Playing War With Numbers," *Harper's,* Vol. 251 (June 1975); Don Oberdorfer, *Tet!* (Garden City, N.Y.: Doubleday 1971). For a more detailed review, see Richard K. Belts, *Soldiers, Statesmen, and Cold War Crises* (Cambridge: Harvard University Press 1977), chap. 10.

6. Quoted in Henry Brandon, *The Retreat of American Power* (Garden City, N.Y.: Doubleday 1973), 103.

7. Betts (fn. 5), 160–61, 192–95. On bias within CIA, see James Schlesinger's comments in U.S., Congress, Senate, Select Committee to Study Governmental Operations with Respect to Intelligence Activities [hereafter cited as SSCI], *Final Report, Foreign and Military Intelligence,* Book I, 94th Cong., 2d sess., 1976, 76–77.

8. *Ibid.,* Book IV, 56–59; William T. Lee, *Understanding the Soviet Military Threat: How CIA Estimates Went Astray* (New York; National Strategy Information Center, Agenda Paper No. 6. 1977), 24–37; Albert Wohlstetter: "Is There a Strategic Arms Race?" *Foreign Policy,* No. 15 (Summer 1974); Wohlstetter, "Rivals, But No Race," *Foreign Policy,* No. 16 (Fall 1974); Wohlstetter, "Optimal Ways to Confuse Ourselves," *Foreign Policy,* No. 20 (Fall 1975). There are exceptions to this pattern of military and civilian bias: see *ibid.,* 185–188; Lieutenant General Daniel Graham, USA (Ret.), "The Intelligence Mythology of Washington," *Strategic*

Review, IV (Summer 1976), 61–62, 64; Victor Marchetti and John Marks, *The CIA and the Cult of Intelligence* (New York: Knopf 1974), 309.

9. The U.S. intelligence *community* includes the CIA, Defense Intelligence Agency (DIA), National Security Agency, the intelligence branches of each military service, the State Department Bureau of Intelligence and Research, the intelligence units of the Treasury and Energy Departments, and the FBI. Before 1973, coordination for national estimates was done through the Office of National Estimates, and since then, through the National Intelligence Officers. The Intelligence Community Staff assists the Director of Central Intelligence in managing allocation of resources and reviewing the agencies' performance.

10. HSCI, Hearings (fn. 4), 656–57.

11. Wilensky, *Organizational Intelligence* (New York: Basic Books 1967), 42–62, 126.

12. *Ibid., passim* The counterpoint of Cooper (fn. 5) and McGarvey (fn. 5) presents a perfect illustration.

13. Graham Allison and Peter Szanton, *Remaking Foreign Policy: The Organizational Connection* (New York: Basic Books 1976), 204.

14. Quoted in SSCI, *Final Report* (fn. 7), I, 82.

15. *Ibid.,* 267, 376; SSCI, *Staff Report, Covert Action in Chile 1963–1973,* 94th Cong., 1st sess., 1975, 48–49. The Senate Committee deplored the tendency of decision makers to focus on the latest raw data rather than on refined analyses, a practice that contributed to the intelligence failure in the 1974 Cyprus crisis. SSCI, *Final Report* (fn. 7), I, 443. But the failure in the October War was largely due to the *reverse* phenomenon: disregarding warning indicators because they contradicted finished intelligence that minimized the possibility of war. HSCI Draft Report (fn. 4), 78; Ben-Zvi (fn. 4), 386, 394; Perlmutter (fn. 4), 453.

16. Churchill, *The Gathering Storm* (Boston: Houghton Mifflin 1948), 587–88.

17. "Where the end is knowledge, as in the scientific community, time serves intelligence; where the end is something else—as in practically every organization but those devoted entirely to scholarship—time subverts intelligence, since in the long run, the central institutionalized structures and aims (the maintenance of authority, the accommodation of departmental rivalries, the service or established doctrine) will prevail." Wilensky (fn. 11), 77.

18. Quoted in SSCI, *Final Report* (fn. 7), I, 274.

19. Sherman Kent, "Estimates and Influence," *Foreign Service Journal* XLVI (April 1969), 17.

20. Hughes (fn. 2), 43.

21. "The textbooks agree, of course, that we should only believe reliable intelligence, and should never cease to be suspicious, but what is the use of such feeble maxims? They belong to that wisdom which for wane of anything better scribblers of systems and compendia resort to when they run out of ideas." Carl von Clausewitz, *On War,* ed. and trans. by Michael Howard and Peter Paret (Princeton: Princeton University Press 1976), 117.

22. Robert Jervis, *The Logic of Images in International Relations* (Princeton: Princeton University Press 1970), 132; Jervis, *Perception and Misperception in International Politics* (Princeton: Princeton University Press 1976), chap. 4; Floyd Allport, *Theories of Perception and the Concept of Structure* cited in Shlaim (fn. 2), 358. Cognitive theory suggests that uncertainty provokes decision makers to separate rather than integrate their values, to deny that inconsistencies between values exist, and even to see contradictory values as mutually supportive. John Steinbruner, *The Cybernetic Theory of Decision* (Princeton: Princeton University Press 1974), 105–8.

23. See William J. McGuire, "Selective Exposure: A Summing Up," in R. P. Abelson and others, eds., *Theories of Cognitive Consistency* (Chicago: Rand McNally 1968), and Irving L. Janis and Leon Mann, *Decision Making: A. Psychological Analysis of Conflict, Choice, and Commitment* (New York: Free Press 1977), 213–14.

24. CIA Intelligence Information Cable, "Remarks of the Chief of the Ranking Military Academy and Other Chinese Leaders on the Situation in South Vietnam," June 25, 1964, in Lyndon B. Johnson Library National Security Files, Vietnam Country File [hereafter cited as LBJL/NSF-VNCF], Vol. XII, item 55.

25. See for example, U.S. Department of Defense, *The Senator Gravel Edition: The Pentagon Papers* (Boston: Beacon Press 1971) [hereafter cited as Pentagon Papers], Vol. II, 99; Frances Fitzgerald, *Fire in the Lake* (Boston: Atlantic-Little, Brown 1972), 364; Special National Intelligence Estimate 53–64, "Chances for a Stable Government in South Vietnam," September 18, 1964, and McGeorge Bundy's covering letter to the President, in LBJL/NSF-VNCF, Vol. XIII, item 48.

26. Patrick J. McGarvey, *CIA: The Myth and the Madness* (Baltimore: Penguin 1974), 16.

27. David Wise and Thomas B. Ross, *The U-2 Affair* (New York: Random House 1962), 56, 176, 180; Trevor Armbrister, *A Matter of Accountability* (New York: Coward-McCann 1970), 116–18, 141–45, 159, 187–95; U.S. Congress, House, Committee on Armed Services, *Report, Inquiry Into the U.S.S. Pueblo and EC-121 Plane*

Incidents [hereafter cited as *Pueblo and EC-121 Report*], 91st Cong., 1st sess., 1969,1622–24,1650–51; U.S. Congress, House, Committee on Armed Services, *Hearings, Inquiry Into the U.S.S. Pueblo and EC-121 Plane Incidents* [hereafter cited as *Pueblo and EC-121 Hearings*], 91st Cong., 1st sess., 1969, 693–94, 699–700, 703–7, 714, 722, 734, 760, 773–78, 815–16.

28. SSCI, *Final Report* (fn. 7), I, 61–62; HSCI Draft Report (fn. 4), 82.

29. McGarvey (fn. 26), 16.

30. Shlaim (fn. 2), 375–77. The proposals follow, with their U.S. analogues noted in parentheses: appoint a special intelligence adviser to the Prime Minister (Director of Central Intelligence) to supplement the military chief of intelligence; reinforce the Foreign Ministry's research department (Bureau of Intelligence and Research); more autonomy for non-military intelligence (CIA); amend rules for transmitting raw intelligence to research agencies, the Defense Minister, and the Prime Minister (routing of signals intelligence from the National Security Agency); restructure military intelligence (creation of DIA in 1961); establish a central evaluation unit (Office of National Estimates). On the U.S. intelligence failure in 1973, see the HSCI Draft Report (fn. 4) 78–79.

31. Shlaim (fn. 2), 379; Handel (fn. 4), 62–63.

32. *Ibid.*, 55.

33. Shlaim (fn. 2), 358–59. The Israeli command estimated a higher probability of attack in May 1973 than it did in October. Having been proved wrong in May, Chief of Staff Elazar lost credibility in challenging intelligence officers, complained that he could no longer argue effectively against them, and consequently was unable to influence his colleagues when he was right. Personal communication from Michael Handel, November 15, 1977.

34. *Washington Post*, November 27, 1977, p. A17.

35. Raymond Garthoff, "On Estimating and Imputing Intentions," *International Security*, II (Winter 1978), 22.

36. Westmoreland, *A Soldier Reports* (Garden City, N.Y.: Doubleday 1976), 316. See the postmortem by the President's Foreign Intelligence Advisory Board, quoted in Herbert Y. Schandler, *The Unmaking of a President* (Princeton: Princeton University Press 1977), 70, 76, 79–80.

37. Wohlstetter (fn. 4), 69.

38. George, "The Case for Multiple Advocacy in Making Foreign Policy," *American Political Science Review*, Vol. 66 (September 1972). My usage of the term multiple advocacy is looser than George's.

39. Henry F. Graff, *The Tuesday Cabinet* (Englewood Cliffs, N.J.: Prentice-Hall 1970), 68–71; Leslie H. Gelb with Richard K. Berts, *The Irony of Vietnam: The System Worked* (Washington, D.C.: Brookings, forthcoming), chap. 4; Ball memorandum of October 5, 1964, reprinted as "Top Secret; The Prophecy the President Rejected," *Atlantic Monthly*, Vol. 230 (July 1972); McCone, memorandum of April 2,1965, in LBJL/NSF-VNCF, Troop Decision Folder, item 14b.

40. Betts (fn. 5), 199–202; Schandler (fn. 36), 177. George (fn. 38), 759, stipulates that multiple advocacy requires "no major maldistribution" of power, influence, competence, information, analytic resources, and bargaining skills. But, except for resources and the right to representation, the foregoing are subjective factors that can rarely be equalized by design. If they are equalized, in the context of imperfect data and time pressure, erroneous arguments as well as accurate ones will be reinforced. Non-expert principals have difficulty arbitrating intellectually between experts who disagree.

41. Quoted in Steinbruner (fn. 22), 332.

42. Clausewitz (fn. 21), 117–18; HSCI, *Hearings* (fn. 4), 634–36; William J. Barnds, "Intelligence and Policy-making in an Institutional Context," in U.S. Commission on the Organization of the Government for the Conduct of Foreign Policy [hereafter cited as Murphy Commission], *Appendices* (Washington, D.C.: G.P.O., June 1975), Vol. VII, 32.

43. HSCI, *Hearings* (fn. 4), 778.

44. SSCI, *Final Report* (fn. 7), IV, 57; Roger Hilsman, *Strategic Intelligence and National Decisions* (Glencoe, I11.: Free Press 1956),40. During brief service as just a low-level staff member of the National Security Council, even I never had time to read all the intelligence analyses relevant to my work.

45. SSCI, *Final Report* (fn. 7), I, 344, and IV, 95 (emphasis deleted).

46. Ray S. Cline, *Secrets, Spies, and Scholars* (Washington, D.C.: Acropolis 1976), 20.

47. Gilbert W. Fitzhugh and others, *Report to the President and the Secretary of Defense on the Department of Defense, By the Blue Ribbon Defense Panel* (Washington D.C.; G.P.O., July 1970), 45–46.

48. Alexander George, "The Devil's Advocate: Uses and Limitations," Murphy Commission, *Appendices* (fn. 42), II, 84–85; Jervis, *Perception and Misperception* (fn. II), 417.

49. *Ibid.*, 416.

50. U.S. Congress, Senate, Select Committee on Intelligence, Report, *The National Intelligence Estimates A-B Team Episode Concerning Soviet Capability and Objectives,* 95th Cong., 2d sess., 1978; *New York Times,* December 36, 1976, pp. 1, 14; *Washington Post,* January 2, 1977, pp. A1, A4.

51. George H. Poteal, "The Intelligence Gap: Hypotheses on the Process of Surprise," *International Studies Notes,* III (Fall 1976), 15.

52. Cline (fn.46), 140.

53. SSCI, *Final Report* (fn. 7), I, 352. A valid criticism is that military personnel systems and promotion standards penalized intelligence officers, thus encouraging competent officers to avoid intelligence assignments. This situation was rectified in the service intelligence agencies by the early 1970's, but not within DIA. *Ibid.* Betts (fn. 5), 196–97.

54. SSCI, *Final Report* (fn. 7), 1, 77–81. See also U.S., Congress, Senate, Committee on Foreign Relations, *Hearings, National Security Act Amendment,* 92d Cong., 2d sess. 1972, 14–24.

55. Zumwalt, *On Watch* (New York: Quadrangle 1976), 459.

56. Wilensky (fn. 11), 164.

57. Jervis, *Perception and Misperception* (fn. 22), 181–87.

58. Knorr (fn. I), 460.

59. SSCI, *Final Report* (fn. 7), I, 276, and IV, 85; U.S., Congress, House, Committee on Appropriations, *Hearings, Supplemental Appropriations for Fiscal Year 1977,* 95th Cong., 2d sess., 1977, *515–621* ; *Washington Post,* February 15, 1977, p. A6; Paul W. Blackstock, "The Intelligence Community Under the Nixon Administration," *Armed Forces and Society,* I (February 1975), 238.

60. Joseph C. Goulden, *Truth Is the First Casualty* (Chicago: Rand McNally 1969), 101–4; Phil G. Goulding, *Confirm or Deny* (New York: Harper & Row 1970), 130–33, 269; *Pueblo and EC-I21 Hearings* (fn. 27), 646–47, 665–73, 743–44, 780–82, 802–3, 865–67, 875, 880, 897–99; *Pueblo and EC-121 Report* (fn. 27), 1654–1656, 1662–67; Armbrister (fn. 27), 196ff, 395; U.S. Congress, House, Committee on Armed Services, Report, *Review of Department of Defense Worldwide Communications: Phase I,* 92d Cong., 1st sess., 1971, and *Phase II,* 2d sess., 1972.

61. See, for example, James Blaker and Andrew Hamilton, *Assessing the NATO/Warsaw Pact Military Balance* (Washington, D.C.: Congressional Budget Office, December 1977).

62. SSCI, *Final Report* (fn. 7), I, 61; Thomas G. Belden, "Indications, Warning, and Crisis Operations," *International Studies Quarterly,* XXI (March 1977), 192–93.

63. *Pentagon Papers,* IV, 111–12, 115–24, 217–32. CIA critiques of bombing results begin even before the Tonkin Gulf crisis. CIA/OCI, Current Intelligence Memorandum, "Effectiveness of T-28 Strikes in Laos," June 26, 1964; CIA/DDI, Intelligence Memorandum, "Communist Reaction to Barrel Roll Missions," December 29, 1964. But ambivalence remained even within the CIA, which occasionally issued more sanguine evaluations—e.g., CIA Memorandum for National Security Council, "The Situation in Vietnam," June 28, 1965 (which McGeorge Bundy called directly to the President's attention), and CIA/OCI, Intelligence Memorandum, "Interdiction of Communist Infiltration Routes in Vietnam," June 24, 1965. (All memoranda are in LBJL/NSF-VNCF, Vol. I, item 5, Vol. III, items 28, 28a, 28b, Vol. VI A, items 4, 5, 8.) See also *Pentagon Papers,* IV, 71–74. See also the opposing assessments of the CIA, the civilian analysis in the Pentagon, and the Joint Chiefs in NSSM-I (the Nixon Administration's initial review of Vietnam policy), reprinted in the *Congressional Record,* Vol. 118, part 13, 92d Cong., 2d sess., May 10, 1972, pp. 16749–836.

From Betts, Richard K., "Analysis, War and Decision: Why Intelligence Failures Are Inevitable." *World Politics* 31:1 (1978): 61–89. Reprinted with the permission of Cambridge University Press.

8. A POLICYMAKER'S PERSPECTIVE ON INTELLIGENCE ANALYSIS

ROBERT D. BLACKWILL AND JACK DAVIS

As Robert D. Blackwill reveals in this interview with CIA analyst Jack Davis, the life of a senior policy official in the U.S. government—in this case, an ambassador—can be overwhelming. Policymakers must focus on the pressing issues of the day, leaving little time to study broad-gauged intelligence reports. What officials need, and what Blackwill sought out, was a team of analysts who were willing to respond directly to his requests for information. Blackwill offers the reader a glimpse into the lives of policymakers and analysts as they interact.

Sherman Kent, in *Strategic Intelligence for American World Policy*, his path-breaking effort to join intelligence doctrine and practice for post-World War II America, concluded that:

> There is no phase of the intelligence business which is more important than the proper relationship between intelligence itself and the people who use its products. Oddly enough, this relationship, which one would expect to establish itself automatically, does not do this. It is established as a result of a great deal of conscious effort . . .[1]

Despite guidance from Kent and numerous subsequent authors, the terms of engagement between intelligence analyst and policymaker are still ill-defined doctrinally and thus practiced as much to suit the immediate preferences of the players on both sides of the relationship as to meet the fundamental demands of sound policymaking. The quest to join sage principle—*what should work*—to solid practice—*what does*—is more important than ever in post-Cold War America, as resources for intelligence support of policymaking are cut back more rapidly than responsibilities.

The original pillar of Ambassador Blackwill's doctrinal views on intelligence and policy was self-interest—his effort to make the relationship work for him personally under trying conditions. He served as Special Assistant to the President and Senior Director for European and Soviet Affairs, National Security Council Staff, during 1989–90, a tumultuous period that witnessed the collapse of the Soviet Union and the reshaping of Europe. The more lasting pillar is his concern for the national interest—a belief that the United States can ill afford prevailing patterns of ineffective ties between experts on events overseas and policymakers in Washington.

SOME KEY POINTS

The Ambassador's framework for defining the requirements for sound intelligence-policy relations consists of four key points:

- Roughly 90 percent of what passes for national security analysis in the US Government, including structured study of events overseas, is done by intelligence analysts.
- The national interest requires that this effort be effectively joined to the policymaking process.
- The officials who carry most of the day-to-day burden of policymaking on key issues are so besieged by time-consuming responsibilities that decisions on how much to stay informed on events overseas and in what way are narrowly based on self-interest in managing the pressures and getting the job done.
- Intelligence professionals have to carry nearly all the burden to convince each key policy official that they are committed to servicing his or her analytic needs via customized expert support.

Thus, to meet their responsibilities in promoting the national interest, intelligence professionals have to become expert not only on substantive issues but also on serving the self-interest of policy professionals by providing specialized analytic support.

A SHAKY START

I first met the Ambassador in November 1987, when he was teaching in the CIA-funded Kennedy School Seminar on Intelligence and Policy. He seized the attention of the class of some 30 Directorate of Intelligence (DI) division chiefs and managers from elsewhere in the Intelligence Community by asserting that as a policy official he never read DI analytic papers. Why? "Because they were nonadhesive." As Blackwill explained, they were written by people who did not know what he was trying to do and, so, could not help him get it done:

> When I was working at State on European affairs, for example, on certain issues I was the Secretary of State. DI analysts did not know that—that I was one of a handful of key decision-makers on some very important matters. Why bother to read what they write for a general audience of people who have no real responsibility on the issue.

More charitably, he now characterizes his early periods of service at the NSC Staff and in State Department bureaus as ones of "mutual ignorance":

> DI analysts did not have the foggiest notion of what I did; and I did not have a clue as to what they could or should do.

An unpromising start. Yet during his 1989–90 NSC Staff tour, Ambassador Blackwill—by the lights of DI analysts working with him on European affairs—raised analyst-policy relations to an exemplary level. Time after time, the DI's Office of European Analysis (EURA) provided much-needed intelligence support under stringent time constraints. In a tribute with resonance in the hometown of the Washington Redskins, Blackwill called the EURA crew his "analytic hogs," opening up holes in the line for him to run through. At least one EURA analyst considers this period "the most exciting and meaningful" of his career.

The balance of this article consists of the Ambassador's replies to my questions.

FROM MUTUAL IGNORANCE TO MUTUAL BENEFIT

Q: What caused your apparent change of mind about the utility of DI analysis?

A: I had started to rethink my position even before our 1987 classroom encounter. As chief negotiator for the MBFR talks,[2] I worked closely for the first time with Agency analysts—those assigned to the US delegation. They regularly came up with information and interpretations that helped me sharpen my approach to the individual negotiating issues. When I gave them a special task, they delivered to suit my schedule, even if it meant considerable inconvenience to them.

One more matter important to negotiators, and to heavily engaged policymakers generally. Unlike other intelligence people I had worked with in the past, including those from State, my informal talks about possible US tactical initiatives with CIA analysts from the Arms Control Intelligence Staff did not end up in the *Washington Post*.

My understanding of the role of intelligence was also broadened by my work at Kennedy School. In addition to the CIA seminar, I collaborated with Professors Ernest May and Richard Neustadt on a course called "Assessing Other Governments." Here, the importance of country expertise, of language skills, of perspective and a sense of history were underscored by well-documented case studies. Then there was the survival factor. I knew soon after [President] Bush's election in November 1988 that I was to be selected for the NSC Staff job on both Europe and the USSR. This meant longer hours and more pressures for me than ever before. Frankly, I was concerned about forgetting what my 10-year-old daughter looked like. So I sat down in Cambridge and planned how I was going to interact with Executive Branch colleagues, with Congress, with the press—and with intelligence. I decided that in my own self-interest I had to arrange to get as much support as practical from Agency analysts.

Q: Why Agency analysts?

A: You mean besides the fact there are many more of them in my areas of responsibility than in the other intelligence outfits? My experience at State convinced me that INR [Bureau of Intelligence and Research] works for the Secretary. I suppose it is the same at Defense. I judged that Agency analysts would be much more likely to provide close and continuous support to an NSC Staff director.

Back to State. From my White House perspective, the State Department almost never met a deadline it could not miss. Then there is also the confidentiality factor. As I said earlier, your musings about possible policy initiatives are not leaked to the press by the DCI to shoot down your policy.

The most important consideration is that Agency analysts are better informed about individual countries than anyone else in the [US] Government. And I judged they had the wit—the historical perspective I spoke of—to interpret this information for my benefit and the President's benefit. I just had to determine whether they had the professional interest and enterprise to be responsive to my overtures.

Let me expand on one point. Intelligence analysts—essentially DI analysts—do 90 percent of the analysis by the USG on foreign affairs. Policy officials, even those with academic backgrounds, are too busy with more pressing matters.

In some administrations, the most heavily engaged and influential policy officials on any given issue spend 90 percent of their time assessing their policy competitors in Washington. I am talking here about getting ready to leverage competing Administration officials, not just Congress. Busy decision-makers concentrate what little time they have for foreign policy analysis on narrowly focused aspects of key agenda issues— often how to deal effectively with their foreign counterparts. Let me tell you any policy official who can do his own research on all aspects of an issue, cannot be very important—because he is not fully engaged in the coalition-building and power-leverage games essential for getting serious policy work done in Washington.

And there is no second team. If Agency analysts do not do the work of keeping up with developments overseas that the decisionmakers need to know about, it does not get done. It was in my self-interest to see if I could get those analysts working for me, to help me keep up with a broad range of developments I could not possibly follow on my own.

WHAT WORKS, AND WHAT DOES NOT

Q: You have mentioned self-interest a couple of times.

A: Let me explain. The policymakers who count the most—those five to 10 on any issue who have the most power for getting anything done, decided,

implemented—work much harder than intelligence analysts. During 1989–90, I was often at my desk from 7 in the morning till 10 at night. Others at the NSC Staff, Brent Scowcroft and Bob Gates for instance, started even earlier.[3] Unlike analysts we had no evening tennis games. No weekends.

Even with these hours, as I indicated, I needed help to stay informed. But it had to be the right kind of help. I could not afford to read intelligence papers because this or that intelligence agency was entitled to produce them. It did not matter to me how much work the Agency had put into its products, or how polished they were in scholarly terms. In fact, I could not afford the time to read intelligence papers written by personal friends and colleagues. I could only read intelligence products tailored to help me get through my substantive schedule. There was no other rational choice.

Q: The old issue of "adhesive analysis."

A: You asked, so let me unload here. During my [1989–90] NSC tour, the Agency was still putting out gobs of analytic products that I never read. During the two years I did not read a single [National Intelligence] estimate. Not one. And except for Gates, I do not know of anyone at the NSC who did. The reason, at least for me, is simple. There was no penalty to be paid for not reading an NIE. It did not cost you anything in terms of getting done the most important policy things you had to get done.

The same goes for your other general audience papers. I got them, but I did not read them. I am sure somebody did or you would not bother to put them out. Let me grant without hesitation that there is a lot you put out for good reason that has nothing to do with policymakers at my level. I think however that you ought to consider the cost-benefit ratios of producing papers that are read mostly by specialists at the desk level at State and Defense, or by policy officials with general interest but no direct say on an issue.

Q: What about the NID [*National Intelligence Daily*]? I've heard a number of NSC Staff members praise its utility over the years.

A: Of course, I was interested in the PDB [*President's Daily Brief*] because President Bush read it. As for the NID, I would spend, literally, 60 seconds a day on it. This was a defensive move. I wanted to know in advance what would likely be leaked to the press by readers in Congress. Other than that, there was, again, no cost to me, no penalty, from not having read the NID.

Q: What did you read, aside from what you commissioned directly from DI analysts?

A: Despite what you hear about policymakers not having time to read, I read a lot. Much of it was press. You have to know how issues are coming across politically to get your job done. Also, cables from overseas for preparing agendas for meetings and sending and receiving messages from my counterparts in foreign governments. Countless versions of policy drafts from those competing for the President's blessing. And dozens of phone calls. Many are a waste of time but have to be answered, again, for policy and political reasons.

Q: Let's turn to what you commissioned from DI analysts.

A: One more minute, please, on what I did not find useful. This is important. My job description called for me to help prepare the President for making policy decisions, including at meetings with foreign counterparts and other officials. One thing the Agency regularly did was send me memos on the strategic and tactical agendas of foreign officials; in effect, what they wanted from the United States. Do you think that after I have spent long weeks shaping the agenda, I have to be told a day or two before the German foreign minister visits Washington why he is coming?

O.K. What did I want from analysts? I want their reading of what is going on in the domestic affairs of country "X" or "Y"—countries the President is planning to visit to advance foreign policy or countries from which we are going to receive important visitors to discuss problems and bilateral strategy, or countries on which, for one reason or another, we feel a need to get US policy into better shape.

What is going on domestically in these countries that could have an impact on how the President's counterparts and my counterparts will behave? What pressures are they under at home? Although I knew the national security issues cold, I could not become expert on all important issues affecting Germany or France or Italy at the national level, much less at the provincial or state levels. DI analysts knew this, and they helped me bone up on what I needed to understand to nuance and sharpen the US approach.

You also have to consider that President Bush, as a political animal, was naturally interested in the domestic politics of other leaders, even when there was no pressing bilateral business on the table.

Q: We variously call this "opportunity analysis," or "value-added analysis." Sometimes we call it "targeted tactical analysis."

A: I never put a label on it. Your terms are all good ones. Incidentally, the MacEachin metaphor you told me, about scouts and coaches, is also useful.[4] Yes, intelligence analysts should help key policymakers make the best game plan by telling them what they do not know or appreciate sufficiently. Regarding my own needs, this was mostly, as I said, on the domestic politics of the countries I was dealing with.

Whatever label you put on it, the service I got on Europe from EURA was superb and invaluable. As you know, when I traveled to Europe, EURA analysts prepared a daily cable for me on key developments. They got it to me first thing in the morning European time, which means they worked late into the night in Washington to get it done. I appreciated that immensely. Once a senior State Department colleague joined me for breakfast in Brussels as I was reading my very own newsletter. He studied it with great interest and asked me where it came from. I chose not to give him a clear answer.

EURA people met without exception whatever deadlines I set for informal memos while I was in Washington. They also were responsive and quick with some major projects I laid on with little advance notice. My only problem with their written work is sometimes the text had gone through too many levels of review and began to read like a NID article. If I wanted a NID article, I could read one. What I wanted was the analyst's unvarnished response to my questions. After I made this point, the incidence of overpolished papers diminished.

Q: What about briefings?

A: Yes, because you get a chance to ask questions, briefings can be more helpful than memos. Here, too, I got first-rate customized service. Whenever I asked for briefings in my office, the analysts who came were both informed and responsive. Really terrific people.

Again, I was mostly interested in domestic affairs in this and that country. From time to time, though, I would ask the analysts in my office what the response of a European government would be to the policy initiatives the President was considering or that I was thinking of recommending to the President. Their unrehearsed responses here were also useful. I always hesitated to put such requests into writing for fear of leaks to the press. I learned you can trust DI analysts. They were well informed. Ready to help. And they kept their traps shut.

Q: That sounds like a good advertisement for DI analysts.

A: You bet. They were expert on their subjects. They were responsive to my needs. And they did not leak my confidences to the press.

POLITICIZATION NOT AN ISSUE

Q: Did your NSC Staff colleagues resent your close ties to DI analysts?

A: Not that I was aware of. The people who worked for me, rather than being resentful, made use of EURA support on their own.

Q: What about this kind of closeness pushing analysts across the line into policymaking?

A: Again, I saw no problem with EURA analysts. When I asked, they provided advice on tactics to support an established policy. They were good at that too. But the EURA people did not get into policy prescription. And where it did happen on occasion with others, when intelligence people started recommending policy, I pushed them back.

Q: What about telling you what you wanted to hear, or avoiding bad news?

A: Not a problem. I wanted their help in avoiding setbacks as well as for advancing policy goals. If there were negative developments I had to know about, they let me know. We had trust going both ways.

I would like to continue with this for a minute. I know during the Gates confirmation hearings [for DCI during 1991] the media were full of charges of analysts writing to please policymakers. My experience was different. I would argue that at least in my experience close professional relationships encouraged frankness—not politicization. But I know it does not always turn out that way.

Just as top policy aides have got to deliver bad news to the President when called for, intelligence people have got to have the intellectual courage to tell key policy officials that something is not working, or is not going to work. It is tough, really tough, to stop a policy failure based on

ignorance of the ground truth. Intelligence analysts have got to rise to this challenge. I am not talking about shouting it from the rooftops. NSC directors are especially resentful when Congress is told bad news before they have a chance to think about it. But limited distribution memos should work. Private briefings might be even better, since that gives the policy official a chance to ask questions.

Often it is important to decisionmakers to know how to get to the least bad outcome, to limit the damage. I think options papers work very well here, especially if they are delivered after bad news forces key policymakers to focus on an issue. Somalia is a good example. The analysts could table a paper or lay on a briefing outlining three possible outcomes six months down the road, and what opportunities, leverage, and so forth the United States has to influence the outcome.

INTELLIGENCE AND POLICY TRIBES

Q: Why do not more overworked policy officials lean on Agency analysis the way you did?

A: I guess some do, though I do not personally know of any case quite like mine with EURA. The absence of a pattern of effective relations probably reflects a combination of professional differences and mutual ignorance about what really makes the relationship work.

I am not the only policy official who decided that too many intelligence products still are non-adhesive. They are, or were when I last served, too long and complex. Analysts love words and complexities; it is one of their strengths. Good policymakers are driven by the need to take action. They need problems broken down, simplified. You and I have been through this before, and you can probably make a better list of tribal differences than I can. The key still is getting close enough to the individual policymaker to find out what he needs.

Policymakers do not as a rule know what intelligence analysts can do for them. They read Estimates, think pieces, the NID, and say, in effect, "What does this have to do with *my* problems"? They do not see it as their job to teach analysts how to be helpful. Besides, they would not have the time.

Q: How did your counterpart NSC Staff senior directors stay informed, and, for that matter, others in the Bush administration who were the kinds of key hands-on policy officials you think the Agency should cultivate?

A: The only honest answer is, I do not really know. I was too busy with my own affairs. But I seriously doubt that any of them [during 1989–90] received the kind of customized support from the Agency that I am talking about.

Q: This seems to bother you.

A: Yes. As a citizen and taxpayer it sure does. I am talking here about the national interest. Let's go back to my statement that the Intelligence Community does 90 percent of foreign affairs analysis in the USG.

Policy choices are made and policy actions are taken whether or not the expertise of analysts is brought to bear. But how can anyone argue that we should pay for this expertise and not make use of it?

I do not mean to say it is all the analysts' fault, but I am fully prepared to argue that if an analyst's work does not have an impact on policymaking as a process, including in the long run, he or she is taking pay under false pretenses. A lot that you do is useful to someone. You have to make it more useful to those who count.

Let me say this: the Agency's understanding of the world is probably needed more today than ever. The world and the challenges the United States faces are changing so rapidly. Also, the new [Clinton] administration does not seem to have yet defined its policy approach. The costs of tribal tensions between analysts and -policymakers— mutual ignorance, really—may be rising.

AT A LOWER LEVEL

Q: Much of what you have had to say relates to officials at your level, the NSC senior director and departmental assistant secretaries and above. What about one level down—deputy assistant secretaries, office directors?

A: I would say, much the same. Find out who counts—the five or 10 midlevel officials who have the most influence on more senior decisionmakers—and cultivate close relations with them. Trade customized support for access to the real agenda, and so forth.

A PROGRAM FOR THE DI

Q: How would you combine your various recommendations for Agency analysts into a program?

If you were advising the DCI or DDI, what measures would you propose to enhance the effectiveness of relations between analysts and policy decisionmakers?[5]

A: Thank you for letting me know in advance this question was coming. It is a good question, and I have given it considerable thought. Let's see if the seven measures I have sketched out add up to a program.

1. Identify the 30 or so senior policy officials who count—those who really carry weight with administration Cabinet officers on key foreign policy issues. These officials, usually assistant secretaries in policy departments or special assistants to the President on the NSC Staff, regularly set the thinking of NSC principals on major policy decisions. As a rule, these are the assessors of foreign governments, or the analysts of last resort. To contribute to sounder policymaking, intelligence analysts have to reach this group. Remember, the list of policy notables has to be carefully worked out and kept up to date, because office titles do not always reflect real policy weight.

2. Approach the policy officials who count as if they were motivated solely by self-interest. Their self-interest has to be worked on because they are just too busy to allow either institutional considerations or personal friendships to determine their attitude toward intelligence analysts.

3. Learn as much as you can about each senior official. Study them as carefully as you do foreign leaders. For example, read everything they have written on the subjects in their policy portfolios. Check them out through mutual contacts.

4. Take the initiative to establish ties. This is an essential obligation of intelligence managers, because policy officials will rarely seek them out.

   • For new appointees, send a letter asking for an appointment and spelling out your areas of expertise and the services you are ready to extend.

   • For serving officials, anticipate a major pending visit or event and offer to send over your analysts for a briefing on any one of several related aspects. For example, if the prime minister from Denmark is to visit the President, the DI manager should signal that he will bring over his Denmark analyst to fill the policymaker in on any gaps in understanding in time for the latter to prepare briefing memos for his or her principal, be it the Secretary of State or the President.

- Whenever DI managers know of travel plans by a key policy official, offer to send over country analysts who can fill in the official's knowledge on areas of his choice.
- Have the DCI set up luncheon meetings in town (CIA Headquarters is just too inconvenient), at which analysts and their managers can establish their credentials as entrepreneurial experts.

5. Customize intelligence papers and briefings to solidify the relationship. Many policy officials, overwhelmed by the volume both of their activities and of seemingly important information, will welcome specialized newsletters. They will welcome even one-page summaries of key events overseas that provide the kind of information and analysis they want at the time of day or week they prefer to set aside for keeping up with developments. For the same reason—fear of being overwhelmed—many will welcome customized briefings and memos relating to their policymaking responsibilities on matters on which the DI country analyst is much better informed than they can be or than anyone else in the government. Give them something they will really miss if they do not get it.

6. Place the best and most promising analysts on tours in the policy world. The Agency could offer, free of charge, 50 first-rate people to policy officials around town. Intelligence officers can learn something about how to use intelligence resources effectively by reading about policymaking. You can learn some more by periodic visits to a policymaker's office. But the best way to learn about a different bureaucracy is just the same as the best way to learn about any alien tribe—go live with them for a couple of years.

7. Reward those managers and analysts who are successful in gaining and maintaining access. As a rule, once a win-win relationship takes hold, momentum will keep it going. Once the policy official knows the intelligence unit can and will deliver support when it is needed, he

will provide in exchange access to the real policy agenda. But policy officials come and go, and the Agency has to take care of those with talent at starting over again with newcomers who, as almost always will be the case, will not seek you out.

FINAL THOUGHTS

Q: How do you stay informed on events overseas these days, while working again at Kennedy School?

A: My main current interest is Russian politics and military affairs. I have been spending one week per month in Russia, dealing directly with the General Staff. While at Harvard, I spend a couple of hours each morning on the Internet. It is amazing how much good information and worthwhile commentary is out there for those with the interest and the time. While at the NSC, I had the interest but not the time.

Internet, CNN, increasing visits by all sorts of Americans. The competition for the DI analyst is becoming much stronger. This means you are going to have to work much harder to find a comparative advantage. How do you get more expertise—living there, of course, language, and history?

I worry a bit about this. Just as you cannot rely on quality alone to get your job of informing policy done, you cannot rely only on access. In fact, marketing without a quality product to deliver is worse than passivity.

Q: Final question. At the end of a long day, which is it, working for more expertise, or for more access?

A: The answer, I suppose, is more efficiency. I imagine a textbook breakdown would have the analysts spending 40 percent of their time on collection and other activities for building expertise, 30 percent on analysis and writing—putting things together, and 30 percent on assuring impact on the policymaking process. I never managed an analytic unit, and this is just a guess. I do not think you are anywhere near the last 30 percent.

One final thought occurs to me. Managers in particular should spend enough time establishing and keeping up effective links to the policymaking world that they begin to feel guilty about not having enough time for their other duties. It is that important.

QUESTIONS FOR FURTHER DISCUSSION

1. Why are policymakers often dissatisfied with the analysis they receive from the intelligence community?
2. Why is it difficult for policymakers to obtain useful analysis and information from intelligence analysts?
3. Should policymakers view the intelligence community as an extension of their own staff?
4. Will the "information revolution" help analysts build constructive relationships with policymakers?

ENDNOTES

1. Princeton University Press (1949), p. 180.
2. Mutual and Balanced Force Reduction negotiations between NATO and the Warsaw Pact.
3. Scowcroft was Special Assistant to the President for National Security Affairs. Robert M Gates, subsequently Director of Central Intelligence, was then Deputy Special Assistant.
4. Douglas A. MacEachin, currently CIA's Deputy Director for Intelligence, uses the scout-coach metaphor for analyst-policymaker relations to underscore that it is the scout's responsibility to help the coach prepare to win the game and not to predict the outcome of the game before it is played.
5. This question was communicated in a letter sent in October 1991 and answered in an interview in November 1991. The DI has been moving in the recommended direction for several years. When the interviewer showed an outline of Blackwill's program to DDI Douglas MacEachin (October *1993*) he said, "I guess Bob [Blackwill] and I agree."

Reprinted with permission from Jack Davis, "A Policymaker's Perspective on Intelligence Analysis," *Studies in Intelligence* 38 (1995): 7–15.

9. WHY STRATEGIC INTELLIGENCE ANALYSIS HAS LIMITED INFLUENCE ON AMERICAN FOREIGN POLICY

STEPHEN MARRIN

Why does strategic intelligence analysis have limited influence on American foreign policy? The prevailing explanation is that policymakers have political or policy commitments and cognitive biases that prevent their acceptance and use of discordant intelligence analysis in policymaking. But this explanation—while accurate in some cases—is incomplete because it has embedded in it normative expectations of influence derived from idealized conceptions of the intelligence and policy process. Intelligence analysis is frequently disregarded, this paper contends, because it is a duplicated step in the decision-making process and supplements but does not supplant policy assessment. As a number of historical cases show, many intelligence analyses will confirm policy assessments and be redundant or will provide different interpretations that compete in the policy process for influence. Frequently policymakers will choose their own interpretation over that of intelligence analysis for any number of legitimate reasons, making the intelligence analysis appear as if it were disregarded (even if it were taken into account in the policy planning process). The findings of this chapter provide scholars with important insights into the limits of intelligence analysis in the foreign policy process as well as opportunities to provide policy recommendations increasing its positive impact on policy.

Strategic intelligence analysis frequently does not influence the creation and implementation of American foreign policy. This is contrary to an expectation that intelligence analysis should matter in the making of foreign policy and national security. Better intelligence analysis should lead to better policy. Ideally, independent and objective intelligence analysts provide the information and assessments that decision-makers use to make the best possible decisions.

Yet strategic intelligence analysis appears to have had limited influence on national security decision-making. As former senior intelligence official and Temple University historian Richard Immerman suggests, in terms of foreign policy "instances of the formulation of national security policy, or grand strategy, hinging on intelligence collection and analysis are few and far between—if they exist at all."[1] Former National Intelligence Officer Paul Pillar has also made a similar argument on the irrelevance of intelligence to great decisions.[2] Their conclusions are not new, however.

For decades, there have been questions about the degree to which strategic intelligence influences policy. In 1953, Roger Hilsman, then a professor at Columbia University and later director of the State Department's Bureau of Intelligence and Research, observed that decision-makers frequently made decisions without asking for or using intelligence assessments.[3] In 1960 Benno Wasserman said that "despite its voluminous labours, intelligence does not . . . influence policy greatly" because decision-makers frequently do not read or accept the intelligence analysis they are provided with.[4] In 1966 Sherman Kent, the most important foundational figure in the development of American intelligence analysis, also pointed out that "no matter how right we are . . . (policymakers) will upon occasion disregard the thrust of our findings."[5] In the decades since, many others have referenced the frequent irrelevance of strategic intelligence analysis to national security decision-making.[6]

Intelligence analysts can become frustrated when their analysis does not have the influence or impact that they think it should. In 1953 Roger Hilsman observed that an intelligence analyst "is not only frustrated when he decides that policy is made without benefit of the information supplied by intelligence, but bewildered and indignant as well."[7] Hilsman quotes one frustrated official who said that contrary to the way things should work, "policy was made without intelligence or was only supplemented by intelligence. Intelligence people always had to analyze what had already happened, or merely to give support for policy decisions that were already made. Intelligence did nothing but hack work and research. In practice, the thing was all backwards."[8]

Strategic intelligence analysis has had less influence on American foreign policy than many would expect, and the literature on American foreign policy contains the frustration of intelligence analysts whose work was not accepted by policymakers: Samuel Adams on the order of battle assessments during the Vietnam War; Melvin Goodman on Cold War assessments regarding the Soviet Union; and Paul Pillar on his assessments before the Iraq War.[9] Forgotten by scholars, in 1974 Ray Cline—then the recently retired director of the US State Department's Bureau of Intelligence and Research—eviscerated both Henry Kissinger and the Nixon administrations for their failure to rely on intelligence analysis in their decision-making.[10] Obviously frustrated and disappointed, Cline titled the article "Policy without Intelligence."

Taken in the aggregate, these incidents indicate that there is an unresolved dilemma that lies at the core of the American intelligence and foreign policy process. Strategic intelligence analysis, which many think should be the foundation for decision-making, is frequently not relied upon in the making of decisions. Yet many scholars, practitioners, and even the general public persist in retaining this belief that intelligence analysis should play a central role in the making of American foreign policy.

To suggest that strategic intelligence analysis frequently does not influence policy is not to argue that strategic intelligence analysis never influences policy. In fact, strategic intelligence analysis has influenced policy for the better in some situations.[11] But it happens less frequently than many would expect and seems to happen even less frequently on the most important national security decisions. So why does strategic intelligence analysis have limited influence on American foreign policy?

COMPETING EXPLANATIONS

Explanations for the lack of intelligence analysis influence on policy suggests that it is due to the combination of political commitments and cognitive biases at the highest levels of national policymaking that hinder or otherwise prevent intelligence analysis from influencing policy. Scholars referencing the limited influence of intelligence analysis on policy rely upon these explanations, including Richard Immerman, Robert Jervis, Joshua Rovner, and Paul Pillar.[12]

There is some evidence to support the contention that politics and cognitive bias affect some foreign policy decisions. As former CIA officer Harold Ford explains, policymaking is not based on orderly reason; instead "all kinds of forces go into their making of policy, not excluding timidity, ambition, hubris, misunderstandings, budgetary ploys, and regard for how this or that policy will play in Peoria."[13] The CIA itself said as much when it observed that "national estimates have played only a modest role in the formulation of policy" because "national security policy is not directly driven by facts, analyses, and judgments, and knowledge does not lead to action in any simple way. What also come into play are competing bureaucratic pressures, a wide range of domestic considerations, the concepts, perceptions and stereotypes held by the policy makers themselves, and a host of essentially political inputs."[14]

But the predominant explanation for policymaker disregard of intelligence analysis is insufficient because it cannot account for the extent to which it arises as a problem across space, time, and different subject matter domains. The limited influence that intelligence analysis has had on decisions is noticeable over an extended period of time in many different countries, as well as in other fields such as law enforcement and business, the prevailing explanation—which is essentially an idiosyncratic one dependent on the prevailing mindset of the policymaker—does not seem sufficient to account for the scope of the problem.[15] So why does intelligence analysis frequently not matter in all these different contexts?

This paper contends that the primary problem is not with the policymakers who disregard intelligence analysis but rather with how scholars have been conceptualizing the intersection of intelligence analysis and decision-making. Scholars appear to be assuming that intelligence analysis should influence policy and then explain why decision-makers were not influenced by the intelligence analysis. But why should intelligence analysis influence policymaking in the first place?

Instead of asking "why do decisionmakers not accept intelligence analysis?" better questions to ask are "how is strategic intelligence analysis used by decisionmakers?" and "why should decisionmakers accept intelligence analysis as better than their own analysis?" Answers to these questions show that the privileging of intelligence analysis in the policy process that exists in the current problem specification is based on normative expectations derived from idealized conceptions of the intelligence and policy process. In the end, intelligence analysis will inevitably have limited influence on policymaking because it is a duplicative step in the policy process.

POLICYMAKERS ARE ANALYSTS, TOO

Intelligence analysis is frequently disregarded because the analysis of a situation is a duplicated step in the decision-making process and supplements but does not supplant policy assessment. Yet this is not the impression most scholars have of the intelligence and policy process.

The prevailing conceptualization of the relationship between intelligence and policy is best illustrated using the intelligence cycle, which is a simplified heuristic to describe the different steps in intelligence production. The intelligence cycle starts with information requirements levied on intelligence collection capabilities, the collection and processing of the raw intelligence and transmission of this material to analysts who decipher its meaning and relay their understandings to the decision-makers, who levy additional requirements. While there is some criticism of the intelligence cycle for being an over-simplification of the process, it is the predominant framework used to understand and explain intelligence production. For that reason it is frequently used as the foundation for the Standard Model of the intersection of intelligence analysis and decision-making that is dominant in the intelligence and security studies literature.[16]

The intelligence cycle differentiates between intelligence and decision-making functions, implying that intelligence organizations collect and analyze intelligence, and decisionmakers make decisions based on the information and assessments provided. The reason intelligence and policy functions are separated in this ideal relationship is to ensure that decision-makers get the objective, unbiased information and interpretation they need to make the best possible decisions. As Paul Pillar observed, "The proper relationship between intelligence gathering and policymaking sharply separates the two functions. The intelligence community collects information, evaluates its credibility, and combines it with other information to help make sense of situations abroad that could affect U.S. interests."[17] Decisionmakers then use this intelligence analysis in making decisions. The role of intelligence analysis is conceived either as a way of reducing uncertainty, or helping to ensure that power is applied more effectively and efficiently.[18]

For those employing normative expectations derived from this idealized conception of the relationship, when decisions are made that disregard intelligence analysis in favor of other sources, including ideological or partisan ones, controversy and criticism erupts as it is taken as indicative of a corrupted decision-making process. In 1949 Sherman Kent implied as much when he suggested that decision-makers should not disregard intelligence analysis because if they do they would be turning their backs on "the two instruments by which western man has, since Aristotle, steadily enlarged his horizon of knowledge—the instruments of reason and scientific method."[19] This expectation that policymakers should use intelligence analysis can be found in more contemporary evaluations that identify policymaker "neglect" of intelligence analysis as one of the primary pathologies of intelligence-policy.[20]

But a different conceptualization of the intelligence and policy process emphasizes the ways in which each process overlaps the other. Ernest May and Philip Zelikow developed a model for evaluating the intersection of intelligence analysis and policymaking that summarizes decision-making as the process of evaluating international events and issues that have the potential to affect national interests (what's going on?), the analysis and evaluation of this information (so what?), and the ability to create and implement effective policies (what is to be done?).[21] In this three-step process, intelligence organizations perform a delegated function by either finding out what is going on (collection and analysis), or determining what it means (analysis answering the "so what" question), or both. Contrary to conventional portrayals, decision-makers do not just make decisions after receiving finished intelligence analysis. Instead, they engage in all three steps, focusing their attentions on what to do about the situation at hand.

This reconceptualization of the intelligence and policy process shows that the analytic function is duplicated in both domains. If intelligence analysis were the primary locus of analysis and assessment, then policymaker disregard of intelligence analysis would be potentially significant. But the assessment function is duplicated in both the intelligence and policy domains. As Sherman Kent observed, there is "no universal law which obliges policy, plans, and operations to accept and use (intelligence analysis) findings."[22] Over 50 years later, former CIA officer Jack Davis observed that policymakers can "reach, publicize, and act upon" their own judgments, which may different from those of intelligence agencies precisely because intelligence analysis "is an input to and not a substitute for policy analysis."[23]

Why should policymakers base their decisions on intelligence analysis and assessment in the first place? The normative expectation that intelligence analysis should be accepted by decision-makers is based on assumptions that intelligence analysis is more accurate because analysts have more and better information and are more expert than policymakers and that accuracy or truth can be achieved through intelligence agencies' ability to accumulate, aggregate, and expertly interpret information independent of policy preferences. But on closer examination, each of these assumptions is problematic.

POLICYMAKERS ALSO HAVE INFORMATION AND EXPERTISE

Intelligence analysts do not necessarily have more or better information than decisionmakers do. For example, decision-makers have access to raw intelligence—in fact, according to former senior CIA manager Martin Petersen, "the same stuff intelligence analysts are reading"[24]—as well as the finished intelligence analysis. In 1989 Robert Gates suggested that the creation of the White House Situation Room in the early 1960s had severely degraded the influence of current intelligence analysis for the president in a way that had yet to be fully appreciated.[25] More than twenty years later, decision-maker access to raw intelligence continues to marginalize the contributions of intelligence analysts. In addition, policymakers acquire a lot of information through non-intelligence channels including friends, broader networks, and other contacts in government, academia, and business.[26] Sometimes these other sources provide information that is more accurate than that provided by intelligence agencies. Very little of the information acquired by policy officials is shared with the intelligence community. As a result, on strategic issues it can be difficult for the intelligence analyst to provide decision-makers with better information than they already have access to.

Also, if intelligence analysts had more expertise than policymakers, then that might also provide sufficient justification for arguing that they produce more accurate assessments on a regular basis. But on a closer examination, this does not hold up to scrutiny either. While the literature sometimes portrays decision-makers as political generalists and the intelligence analysts as knowledgeable experts, with the inference being that the generalist should defer to the knowledge and expertise of the experts, the reality is that strategic national security policymakers frequently have considerable knowledge and expertise of their own and they trust their own judgments. Robert Jervis has said that "one reason why policy-makers paid little attention (to intelligence analysis) was that they thought their own general knowledge of the situation provided an adequate basis for their decisions. As one senior State Department official put it, "A policy maker usually has some expertise of his or her own, after all. I use the intelligence community as a resource for factual information, but I don't need it for opinions. I have my own."[27] Or, as three CIA officers put it, "Policy people regard themselves as having certain expertise and ample sophistication. They are accustomed to interpreting, analyzing, and projecting, as well as planning, deciding, and operating. . . . Intelligence that attempts to do for them what they believe they can accomplish competently themselves generally is less well received."[28]

In fact, policymakers sometimes have more expertise than intelligence analysts. As former CIA analyst Richard Russell says, "It is not uncommon for policy makers to be more expert than most CIA managers and analysts."[29] Or as former CIA analyst Harold Ford says, "Senior policy-makers often know much more about given foreign questions than do the experts preparing intelligence for them."[30] As a result, as Robert Gates has observed, "On more than a few occasions, policymakers have analyzed or forecast developments better than intelligence analysts."[31]

Why should policymakers accept the judgments of intelligence analysts when they conflict with their own? Before one can criticize decisionmakers for rejecting intelligence analysis one has to establish that they should have deferred to intelligence analysts' judgments in the first place. But that case has not yet been made.

POLICYMAKERS CAN PRODUCE GOOD ANALYSES DIFFERENT FROM INTELLIGENCE ANALYSTS

If accuracy or truth could be achieved through independent accumulation and aggregation of information, then that might also suggest that better information combined with more knowledge leads to more accurate assessment. But this assumption, too, has difficulty withstanding scrutiny.

The embedded assumption here is based on the portrayal of intelligence assessment as primarily inductive in nature, where facts lead to judgment in a simple and demonstrable way. The primary source of this empirical, inductive analytic model is Sherman Kent himself. Kent's underlying assumption was that there was one and only one correct interpretation to every set of data and that the job of the intelligence analyst was to interpret the information available in order to come up with that one correct interpretation.[32]

The problem with Kent's assumption is that intelligence assessments are not derived solely from the data; facts do not speak for themselves. They have to be interpreted, and that requires some form of conceptual framework to organize the information and derive inferences from it.[33] This is important because it means that intelligence analysts can arrive at different answers to the same question. As Richards Heuer, one of the CIA's foremost analytic methodologists, has observed, research in cognitive psychology indicates that analysts do not fit information together into pictures the way someone putting together a puzzle might do. Instead, "analysts typically form a picture first and then select the pieces to fit."[34] Under these conditions, different interpretations are possible depending "at least as much upon the conceptual framework employed to analyze the data as it does upon the data itself."[35]

This also explains how decision-makers can arrive at assessments that are different from those of intelligence analysts. In the case of policymakers, the deductive frameworks used to interpret the significance of events are frequently driven by world views or perspectives that are grounded in a particular political philosophy. Policymakers use these as

filters accept or reject the intelligence assessments they are provided with.

Some observers appear to believe that politics or ideology should not shape policy interpretations, or that such interpretations are less legitimate than those made by intelligence analysts. But policymakers are inherently political decisionmakers, responsible to the people through elections. If one believes in democracy as a form of government, one also believes that the democratic impulse as operationalized in the political process should be incorporated into the decision-making process as well. One could make the argument that political predispositions and perspectives should be the driving force behind the assessment of national security situations, to include the intelligence collected about them. Senior CIA analyst Fulton Armstrong acknowledges this directly when he says that "the policymakers and the political processes that empower them . . . determine what is in the national interest" and as a result "our system encourages a political competition to define problems as well as solutions."[36]

Political preferences and values implicitly shape the intelligence analysts' evaluation of the problem as well, and this can limit the degree to which intelligence analysis is incorporated into policy. In 1949, Yale University professor Willmoore Kendall argued that the functional differentiation between intelligence analysts and decision-makers would mean that the analysts would become "mere research assistants to the George Kennans" precisely because the independent and objective role would prevent them from being able to provide decision-makers with the kinds of knowledge that "determines the 'pictures' they have in their heads of the world to which their decisions relate."[37] Kendall's conclusions are similar to Richard Betts's later observation that the strict separation between intelligence analysis and decision-making may be "an unrealistic application of 'pure science' norms to areas where fact and value are inseparable and judgment must preside."[38]

INTELLIGENCE ANALYSIS INCREASES UNCERTAINTY AND COMPLICATES POLICYMAKING

An additional problem for policy receptivity to or acceptance of intelligence analysis is that, in the context of duplicated assessment, intelligence analysis increases uncertainty and complicates policymaking. Contrary to portrayals of intelligence analysis as reducing uncertainty, Robert Jervis has suggested that strategic intelligence analysis may actually increase decision-maker uncertainty.[39] Increasing decision-maker uncertainty may, in fact, be what the founders of the US intelligence community wanted intelligence analysis to accomplish in the first place.

In Sherman Kent's 1949 argument for the creation of strategic intelligence analysis as a separate career field, he acknowledged that the acquisition and interpretation of information could be done by policy staffs and that policymakers would prefer this.[40] But the risk of relying on policy staff for evaluating intelligence was that they would, to use a term developed decades later, provide "intelligence to please" that was consistent with the biases and preferences of the decision-maker. To prevent this outcome, Kent argued strongly that intelligence analysis should be independent of policy.

The purpose of independent intelligence analysis is to provide the inconvenient facts and unwanted interpretations that challenge reigning assumptions, presumptions, and preferences. As Kent put it, the job of intelligence analysis "is to see that the doers are generally well-informed; its job is to stand behind them with the book opened at the right page, to call their attention to the stubborn fact they may be neglecting."[41] Or, according to Roger Hilsman, "by having one man collect facts without thinking of policy and another use the facts to make policy, one at least guarantees that the policy man will have to face the unpleasant facts that do not support his policy. . . . Thus the policy man who has become wedded to an incorrect policy can be faced with the unpleasant facts which he has ignored and be made to see the one right solution."[42] In other words, the purpose of independent intelligence analysis is to increase decision-maker uncertainty rather than reduce it.

The implicit assumption was that policymakers would—or should—adjust policy for the better when confronted with intelligence assessments that challenged their interpretations and policies. This appears to be what Sherman Kent expected to happen when he argued that strategic intelligence analysts should be as independent from policy as possible. Sherman Kent did not say that decision-makers actually use these inconvenient facts and unwanted interpretations in their deliberative and decision-making processes; instead, he said that they should use them. In a particularly strong rhetorical flourish for 1949, he says that policymakers

should not reject their intelligence analysis or else they risk the failures of Hitler by turning their backs on reason and the scientific method.[43]

But history has shown that on receiving intelligence analysis that is inconvenient or unwanted, policymakers are more likely to reject or ignore the intelligence analysis than change policy. The literature does not provide any evidence indicating that intelligence analysis influences policymaker judgment when provided with unwelcome analyses. Instead, it indicates that they will disregard or ignore the analysis in favor of other assessments.

As Robert Gates points out, in his experience having supported five presidential administrations, "the usual response of a policymaker to intelligence with which he disagrees or which he finds unpalatable is to ignore it."[44] Gates does not say they ignore it sometimes. Nor does he say they ignore it frequently. Instead, he says they ignore it as a matter of course; that ignoring inconvenient intelligence analysis is the usual state of affairs.

Some might argue that policymaker rejection of intelligence analysis is evidence of a corrupted—or at least inefficient or ineffective—decision-making process. But this conclusion would not be justified as there is not yet any evidence that policy assessment in general is any less accurate than intelligence analysis.

Examples of policymakers making more correct assessments of situations can be found in their rejection of inaccurate warning. Intelligence analysts in general—irrespective of the more specialized dedicated warning function—have an incentive to provide warning of harm to national security resulting from the downside risk or negative consequence of both action and inaction. Policymakers frequently and appropriately discount or disregard these warnings, as acting on them would lead to expensive policy failures. As Erik Dahl says, "In some cases . . . intelligence might be wrong, and the result of policymaker receptivity could be the failure of policy or even disaster. Mark Lowenthal has pointed out that in some cases military leaders do well by failing to pay attention to intelligence (that is, by being unreceptive)."[45]

This kind of correct rejection of inaccurate intelligence analysis is only infrequently captured in the literature; yet it provides a significant counterpoint to the charge that ignoring intelligence analysis produces policy failure. While specific instances can be identified where policymaker disregard of intelligence analysis led to policy failures, there are many other instances in which policymakers rejected intelligence analysis warnings that—if acted upon—would have led to other kinds of policy failures. The rejection of the inconvenient fact or unwanted interpretation in and of itself is not evidence of a flawed decision-making process.

HOW POLICYMAKERS USE INTELLIGENCE ANALYSIS

Taken all together, this means that intelligence analyses frequently do not matter in terms of policy analyses. Viewed from the perspective of decision-makers, intelligence analysis serves as a check on their judgment; if it confirms what they already think of a situation, then it is both confirmatory and redundant.[46] But if the intelligence analysis provides a new interpretation or assessment, then the decision-makers must decide whether to use that different interpretation or assessment as a way to revise their own analysis. The policymakers' subsequent receptivity to this different interpretation or assessment can be highly variable.[47]

Frequently policymakers will choose their own interpretation over that of intelligence analysts for any of a wide variety of legitimate reasons, making the intelligence analysis appear as if it were ignored. In only a subset of cases does the conventional explanation apply; that intelligence analysis is rejected due to inappropriate policymaker commitments to policy preferences and biases. In contrast to those who might view policymaker disregard of intelligence analysis as one of the pathologies of intelligence-policy relations, this duplication suggests that it really may be the normal state of affairs in foreign policy decision-making.

When the evaluative and assessment process is deficient at the level of policy, intelligence analysis can make a positive contribution to policy. When policymakers might have misunderstood something that they did not have the time to assess, intelligence analysis can make a positive contribution to policy. When policy assessment is shaped by motivated bias, intelligence analysis may come to a different answer. But what matters here is not the actual analysis itself but the differential between the intelligence analysis and the assessment or assessments made by the decision-makers themselves. The place to start understanding the impact that intelligence analysis has on a decision is not with the intelligence available or the analysis of it but rather decision-maker understandings of what is happening, why it is happening, and what they are planning to do about it.

EXPLAINING HISTORICAL CASES OF INTELLIGENCE AND FOREIGN POLICY

Strategic intelligence analysis has a role to play in national security decision-making, but it is a much more limited role than the conventional explanation implies. The reason for this much more limited role is because legitimate differences of interpretation frequently lead decision-makers discount the evaluation embedded in intelligence assessments. This is borne out through study and evaluation of historical cases.

PERSIAN GULF WAR (1990–1991)

In the case of the Persian Gulf War, strategic intelligence analysis had limited influence mostly because it was consistently incorrect and disregarded in favor of more accurate policy analysis. Specifically, intelligence analysis first incorrectly assured policymakers that Iraq would not invade Kuwait via a 1989 NIE, which "said that Iraq would not attack any of its neighbors for two to three years."[48] Then, while warning of Iraqi troops massing on the Kuwaiti border during the summer of 1990, intelligence assessments incorrectly suggested that the Iraqi presence was an effort to put pressure on Kuwait for negotiating purposes and that they would not invade.[49] Just before the invasion, National Intelligence Officer for Warning, Charlie Allen, warned that an invasion might be imminent; however, this warning was not provided early enough to implement policies that would deter or prevent it.[50] Even after the Iraqi invasion of Kuwait, US intelligence analysts believed that war was not forthcoming. Instead, in late 1990 they suggested that Iraq would withdraw from Kuwait rather than engage with invading US forces.[51]

None of this intelligence analysis had much of an influence on American foreign policy. In this case, Paul Wolfowitz—the Undersecretary of Defense for Policy during the Gulf War—has said that the December 1989 NIE on Saddam Hussein's intentions did not "influence policy one way or the other."[52] Instead, he says that by October or November 1989 policymakers were already debating how to respond to a possible Iraqi invasion of Kuwait and Saudi Arabia. The reason they did this was not based on intelligence assessments but was instead part of a strategic planning process with "a five-to-ten year time frame and recognizing the reasonable range of uncertainty about what could happen." Later intelligence analyses were subsequently disregarded in favor of the analyses produced in the policy planning process as well.

The reason intelligence analysis did not have influence here is not because of cognitive bias or political bias but because the intelligence assessments were redundant. In this case, Wolfowitz suggests that intelligence agencies do not have any intrinsic advantage in terms of their ability to assess this kind of uncertainty. As he put it in terms of the 1989 NIE, "It would be totally unreasonable to expect an NIE at that time to have predicted what (Saddam Hussein) was going to do. I do not think Saddam himself knew what he was going to do. It is clear that most of the leaders of the Arab world, who had a very large stake in predicting what he was going to do, had no sense of what was coming."[53] Given this level of uncertainty and the significant consequences involved, Wolfowitz suggested that "you would have to conclude this (the Iraqi invasion of Kuwait) was a serious possibility. After all, we were dealing in a world where ten percent possibility was something we might plan for and, in fact, we did. That it turned out to be a hundred percent possible was not foreseen."[54]

What Wolfowitz is suggesting is that policymakers had already considered the prospect of Iraqi invasion of Kuwait and were taking it seriously prior to intelligence assessments that said such an eventuality was unlikely. While an intelligence analyst or an observer at the time might have attributed this policymaker disregard of intelligence analysis to cognitive biases expecting or perhaps even desiring war with Iraq, history has subsequently shown that different interpretations are possible from the same information and that sometimes international actors are more threatening than intelligence analysts expect them to be. The duplication of analysis in both the intelligence analysis and policy domains led to a differential in assessment. The policymakers chose to act on their own more alarmist interpretation, which in this case appears to have been the more accurate one. This may be a case where the independent, objective intelligence assessments were incorrect relative to assessments that policymakers either acquired from other sources or contingency plans they were developing for themselves.

YUGOSLAVIA (1990)

Another case of strategic intelligence analysis that did not influence policy was the 1990 NIE that predicted Yugoslavia would collapse into violence and

ultimately fall apart.[55] As Gregory Treverton has said, this NIE "predicted Yugoslavia's tragedy with a prescience that is awe inspiring . . . . (The NIE) concluded that Yugoslavia's breakup was inevitable. The breakup would be violent, and the conflict might expand to spill into adjacent regions. . . . this analysis actually predicted that future."[56] But, as Treverton goes on to say, "Yet so far as I can tell, the document had no effect (on policy). None." A 2003 case study written by Thomas Shreeve for the Intelligence Community's Case Method Program comes to the same conclusion.[57]

A standard interpretation of this failure of accurate intelligence analysis to influence decision-making would attribute this to the cognitive preconceptions of policymakers. Shreeve implies this is the case when he says that the NIE's assessment "was also fundamentally inconsistent with what US policymakers wanted to happen in the former Yugoslavia."[58] As Treverton suggests, "The senior levels of the Bush Administration's foreign policy machine were preoccupied with other issues, so being told of one more disaster lurking in the wings was unwelcome information. It was news they did not want to hear. Hoping that Yugoslavia might somehow stay together was *convenient*."[59] The implication is that they rejected the warning due to a combination of cognitive biases and political predispositions.

But a different interpretation is possible based on the duplication of analysis in both intelligence and policy domains. As Treverton suggests, some policy officials "recall agreeing that any breakup of Yugoslavia was bound to be violent, indeed extremely violent. Thus, for them the estimate's foreboding was on the mark but not news."[60] A senior member of the National Security Council staff agrees with this: "The NIE wasn't 'news' for those of us who had been following developments there. It was not a surprise."[61] It was not a surprise because they had come to much the same conclusions. State Department reporting was already highlighting how nationalistic forces were putting pressure on the political stability of the country and leading to pressures to fracture.[62] The reason it appears that the intelligence analysis did not matter was because the assessment it contained was redundant.

Intelligence analysts do not like it when their assessments fail to produce changes in policy. Shreeve quotes a former Deputy National Intelligence Officer for Eastern Europe criticizing the policy response to the warning. As he said, "The United States simply stopped caring about Yugoslavia . . . If Yugoslavia had fallen apart without bloodshed, we would have seen no US interest at all. It is only atrocities that catch our attention."[63] But as John Gannon points out, "it is important to remember that the break-up was not in fact inevitable. . . . In retrospect, analysts may not appreciate that their certainty was not entirely justified."

The negative outcome—the violent dissolution of Yugoslavia—happened not because policymakers ignored the intelligence analysis or failed to appreciate that it might happen but rather because they failed to implement policies that prevented that outcome. Why did they fail? Perhaps, as Shreeve points out, their time, attention, energy and resources were being devoted to the Middle East and to addressing the Iraqi invasion of Kuwait.[64] Or perhaps, as a result of the end of the Cold War, Yugoslavia's strategic importance was much less than it used to be. Or perhaps policy officials thought there was nothing they could do, so they did not do very much. Shreeve quotes a US government official as saying that policymakers believed there was "nothing they could do." Brent Scowcroft, the National Security Advisor at the time, said much the same thing.[65] The US Ambassador to Yugoslavia found this to be frustrating and tried to "prevent the NIE from becoming a 'self-fulfilling prophecy'" by pushing for other policy outcomes which in the end failed as well.

Contrary to the prevailing explanation, this NIE was not disregarded due to policymaker commitments or cognitive biases. Instead, its conclusions were the same as those of other policy assessments, making it redundant in the decision-making process. That some conclude it was ignored because it did not produce a change in policy is based on an inappropriate normative expectation that intelligence analysis will be both a precursor to and foundation for policy. In this case, policy failed not because it ignored the intelligence analysis but rather because the policymakers could not come up with a policy that would prevent the negative outcome.

TERRORIST THREAT BEFORE 9/11 ATTACKS

Another case where strategic intelligence analysis did not significantly influence or change policy for similar reasons was strategic assessment of the threat from al-Qaeda before the 9/11 terrorist attacks.

In 1995 and 1997 two NIEs had been produced on the terrorist threat, but neither of these analytic products appears to have had any impact on decision-making. The 9/11 Commission Report said that the 1995 NIE "warned that this danger would increase over the next several years" and "predicted future terrorist attacks against the United States—and in the United States."[66] This NIE said that the greatest threat "stemmed from the network of Islamist groups that had formed during the jihad against the Soviet Union in Afghanistan" and that they were looking at targets in both Washington, DC and New York City with "civil aviation as a vulnerable and attractive target."[67] There are no indications that this NIE led to any changes to counterterrorist policy. Nor is there any evidence that the NIE produced in 1997—"The Foreign Terrorist Threat in the US: Revisiting Our 1995 Estimate"—had any impact on decision-making either.[68]

The reason these NIEs appear not to have had much influence on policy was not because they were disregarded or ignored by policymakers but rather because the Clinton administration already appreciated the threat posed by al-Qaeda and was in the process of implementing policies to ramp up counterterrorism efforts. By the time the 1995 NIE was produced, decision-makers were already sensitized to the threat of terrorism and had decided to address the terrorist threat through Presidential Decision Directive 39 (PDD-39)—"US Policy on Counterterrorism"—which, according to the 9/11 Commission Report, "said that the United States should 'deter, defeat and respond vigorously to all terrorist attacks on our territory and against our citizens.'"[69]

Unfortunately, these counterterrorism policies were ineffective to the point that "officers at all levels questioned the effectiveness of the most active strategy the policymakers were employing to defeat the terrorist enemy."[70] Even Richard Clarke, the strongest proponent of more robust counterterrorist policy, "admits that his policy advice, even if it had been accepted immediately (in 2000) and turned into action, would not have prevented 9/11."[71] This statement from Clarke is significant, demonstrating that the national security decision-maker most responsible for coordinating counterterrorist policy before 9/11 did not believe that even the most robust of planned policies were adequate for addressing the threat.

This failure of the Clinton administration to respond effectively to the terrorist threat is not a result of either inadequate intelligence analysis or disregard of intelligence analysis but rather because constraints on policy prevented them from being able to act effectively. As a general observation, Michael Herman—a former chairman of the British Joint Intelligence Committee, and professor at Oxford University—has said, "Even if intelligence points to what should be done it may be impossible to do it; the best warnings of attack may lead to no action if there is nothing that can be done."[72] This can help explain the failure of pre-9/11 counterterrorism policies. As Joshua Rovner and Austin Long suggest, "Elected officials from both parties were unwilling to take the unpalatable but necessary steps that, with hindsight, might have stopped bin Laden. This is the real . . . failure of September 11."[73]

A surface-level evaluation consistent with the conventional explanation for policy disregard of intelligence analysis could attribute the Clinton administration's failure to be receptive to intelligence analysis warning them of the threat from al-Qaeda to a hope that current counterterrorism policies were effective and succeeding. As with the Yugoslavia case, such a belief would have been convenient and consistent with both policy preferences and cognitive biases. But the reality is more complicated. Policy analysis of the threat of terrorism led to the initiation of more robust counterterrorism policies, while intelligence analysis (the NIEs) that continued to highlight the threat-provided assessments that were redundant. Similar to the Yugoslavia case, the primary policy failure associated with the 2001 attacks was not due to a failure of intelligence analysis or policy disregard of intelligence analysis but rather because policymakers did not implement policies that would have prevented the negative outcome.

IRAQ WAR (2003)

The Iraq War also demonstrates the limited influence that strategic intelligence analysis can have on American foreign policy. For example, strategic intelligence analysis which had limited influence on policy include the 2002 NIE on Iraq's weapons of mass destruction and the two 2003 NIC assessments on the likelihood of postwar problems.[74]

That the 2002 NIE on Iraqi WMD failed to influence policy should not be a surprise; it was not requested by the Bush administration but rather by Congress. While it stimulated debate in the halls of Congress, there is no evidence that the 2002 NIE had any impact on the process of making the decision to go to war in Iraq. As Mark Lowenthal—the Assistant Director of Central Intelligence for Analysis and Production and Vice Chairman of the NIC at the time the NIE was produced— has said, this NIE "had virtually no effect on anyone's decision about whether to go to war."[75]

The 2002 NIE assessment that Iraq possessed WMD was not influential because it was consistent with intelligence assessments that had been produced over the past ten years. That this assessment was communicated with greater certainty and confidence than may have been justified is a problem, but even a more nuanced, accurate assessment would have concluded that Iraq probably possessed WMD.[76] The reason this NIE did not have any obvious influence on decision-making is because its conclusions were already known and incorporated into policy planning. As a result, their findings were consistent with the analyses of policymakers, thus making their findings redundant.

As for the two 2003 national intelligence assessments, Paul Pillar has criticized the Bush administration for its failure to incorporate pessimistic assessments of postwar outcomes from two 2003 National Intelligence Council products into its deliberative process. As he pointed out, the Bush administration "went to war without requesting—and evidently without being influenced by—any strategic-level intelligence assessments on any aspect of Iraq."[77] Per the conventional explanation for the lack of influence of intelligence analysis, perhaps the national security leadership chose to ignore these warnings due to a desire not to consider the possibility of a negative outcome along combined with its commitment to a policy of military invasion.

Alternatively, perhaps these 2003 intelligence assessments did not influence policy: while they warned that potentially serious problems could develop in Iraq as a result of the invasion, these kinds of warnings were incorporated into and addressed in the policy planning process. As President Bush has said that efforts were taken to prepare for the postwar period and provide security after Saddam, but at the same time "we were aware of our limitations."[78] That the Bush administration decided to invade despite the warnings from intelligence analysts does not necessarily indicate that the warnings were ignored. Instead, as occurred in the case of Yugoslavia and counterterrorism policies before 9/11, efforts were made to address the problems, but those efforts were not effective in preventing the negative outcome.

This limited influence of strategic intelligence analysis on policy has received a lot of criticism because, as previously established, for those who possess normative expectations that policymakers should rely on intelligence analysis in their decision-making processes, when decisions are made that disregard intelligence analysis it can be perceived as indicative of a corrupted decision-making process.

But rather than attribute the lack of influence of intelligence analysis to policymaker cognitive bias and political predisposition, a much simpler explanation is that the Bush administration decided that the risk of inaction had a greater chance of hurting national interest than the possible costs of action taken to protect national security. In retrospect this decision may have been mistaken given the combination of inaccurate intelligence on Iraqi possession of WMD and the postwar problems that resulted. That policymakers chose to rely on what in retrospect appear to have been less accurate analyses over more accurate analyses is tragic but not necessarily indicative of a corrupted decision-making process.

EVALUATING THE CASES TOGETHER

In all of these cases, strategic intelligence analysis did not influence American foreign policy and was not used by policymakers to create more effective policy. The key component in evaluating these cases is looking at the differential between intelligence and policy analysis.

In these cases, accurate intelligence analysis was rejected in favor of inaccurate policy analysis, (Iraq War 2003 NIE), or inaccurate intelligence analysis was rejected by policymakers in favor of more accurate policy analysis (Persian Gulf War). Interestingly, one important finding is that intelligence analysis (regardless of accuracy) can be the same as policy analysis, thus potentially increasing decisionmaking confidence in their own interpretation but producing no appreciable effect on policy and making it appear as if the intelligence analysis were ignored (Yugoslavia; 9/11; Iraq War 2002 NIE).

Contrary to the conventional explanation for policymakers' disregard of intelligence analysis, for the most part intelligence analysis was not disregarded due to policymaker cognitive impairment or political possession. Instead, policymakers relied on their assessment of the situation, or other alternative assessments, within a broader context of more and varied strategic interests and policies. As a result, the intelligence analysis provided was frequently redundant. When there was a difference between intelligence and policy assessments, decisionmaker receptivity frequently depended on the degree to

which they believed they could effectively address the threat or were willing to act. For the most part, the more willing or able they were to act, the more receptive and responsive they appeared to be to the intelligence analysis.

One key question is what policymakers should do with intelligence assessments warning of possible negative outcomes. In some cases, such warnings may be wrong; a case of crying wolf. In other cases, the potential for a negative outcome may exist but its likelihood may be exaggerated. In other cases the intelligence analysis warning might be accurate. And in other cases, warning may not be provided. As a result, decision-makers know that there is high variability in terms of accuracy of assessment. As decision-makers have the responsibility of deciding what to do, sometimes that means acting not based on the expert intelligence analysts' assessment of the most likely outcome but instead to prevent a lower likelihood but high-impact outcome. Other times, they either cannot or will not do what is necessary to prevent the negative outcome. But in the face of accurate warnings from intelligence analysts, a negative outcome or policy failure alone in and of itself does not indicate that the policymakers disregarded or ignored the intelligence analysis due to cognitive limitations or political preferences. Instead, it could just as easily indicate limitations to or failure of policy than rejection of the intelligence analysis.

IMPROVING THE INFLUENCE OF INTELLIGENCE ANALYSIS ON POLICY

The two different explanations for policymaker disregard of intelligence analysis produce radically different sets of policy recommendations. According to the predominant explanation—where policy disregard of intelligence analysis is due to the political commitments and cognitive impairments of those in power—there is little that can be done to solve this problem. Immerman in particular is quite pessimistic, suggesting that the influence of intelligence analysis on decision-making "is likely to be slight so long as the makers of that policy remain cognitively impaired and politically possessed."[79] Pillar is just as pessimistic that no solutions can be found for policymakers' cognitive impairment but pins his hopes for modest improvements on "structural solutions" that "might help to counteract the effects of that impairment" such as more formal policy processes and fewer political appointees.[80] By way of contrast, in the alternative explanation presented here—where the problem of policy disregard of intelligence analysis is due to the duplication of the assessment process in both the intelligence and policy domains—there are many possible ways to increase the positive influence of intelligence analysis on policymaking.

One way to improve the positive influence of intelligence analysis on policy would be to ensure that the intelligence analyst provides knowledge and expertise that the policymaker might have difficulty acquiring on his or her own. There is already a large and growing literature by intelligence professionals that accepts—and in some cases explicitly acknowledges—that their analytic input is frequently redundant, but its influence can be improved by identifying the specific and unique contributions that they can make to the policy process.[81] Whether that unique value added consists of history, language, culture, or some other kind of contribution depends on the nature of the question asked and the informational requirement of the policymaker. More generally, this approach taken by working professionals takes into account the duplicative nature of the assessment function and actively tries to work around its limitations.

In addition, intelligence analysts can increase the influence of the intelligence analysis on policy by being as transparent as possible in terms of the reliability of its sources, progression of its logic and argumentation, reflection of the analysts' confidence in its conclusions, and incorporating structured analytic techniques as a framework for providing decision-makers with an understanding of the social scientific underpinnings of the process.[82] This helps in increasing policy receptivity over past practice where intelligence analysis "made the call" in a way that was not transparent about how the judgment was made. When that happened, policymakers had the option of accepting or rejecting the entirety of the analysis. But with transparency in the production of intelligence analysis, decision-makers can decide whether to accept the evidence, logic, argument, or judgment of the analyst, or use it as a way to check or challenge their own judgments. Functionally, this changes the evaluative metric of influence from a bifurcated "accept or reject" to variants of partially accepted or partially rejected based on the degree to which the decision-maker finds the logic, argument, conceptual framework, or supporting information compelling and useful

(or not). This will lead to increased influence of intelligence analysis on policymaking as decision-makers take from the intelligence analysis the parts they find useful rather than solely the bottom-line judgment.

Another way to improve the potential influence of intelligence analysis on decision-making is to institutionalize mechanisms for the integration of both intelligence and policy perspectives in mutual assessments. As a way to do this, some have recommended that the US government explore the value of the British Joint Intelligence Committee's simultaneous assessment process.[83] James Steinberg, a former Deputy National Security Advisor, has also recommended the integration of intelligence and policy perspectives at the level of the National Security Council.[84] Interestingly, this approach existed in the past in the form of reports produced by the National Security Council Staff during the Nixon, Ford, and Carter administrations.[85] In these reports "intelligence frequently was merged with policy data in the . . . writing process."[86] Recreating this kind of product line would provide the US government with a vehicle to bring intelligence and policy assessments together in the same product.

Another way to improve the influence of intelligence analysis on policy is to improve the quality and rigor of policymaker assessments. Harold Ford said that improvement will rest on "the caliber, cooperativeness, and integrity" of policymakers.[87] As Richard Betts suggested in the 1970s, each decision-maker "should have a Special Assistant for Rigor Enforcement" to help them use intelligence assessments effectively in their decision-making processes.[88] But this may be an ideal solution and part of a much larger discussion about how to improve the policy-making and implementation process writ large.

Finally, it is important to revisit the assumption that strategic intelligence analysis should influence national level decision-making in a direct and obvious way. Intelligence analysis involves description, explanation, evaluation, and forecasting, and much of this effort is devoted to helping the government learn more over time.[89] Perhaps the primary influence that strategic intelligence analysts have is not on the highest levels of policy on the biggest issues of the day, but rather on the working-level bureaucrats throughout government who in the aggregate ensure that the government learns about threats and problems over time. As Betts has said, "Direct influence at the top is not the principal criterion for utility of finished analyses; as in any sort of educational process, the indirect and untraceable forms of influence—percolating through mid-level officials and special assistants in line agencies, or through other members of the intelligence community—can be just as important."[90] Perhaps too much emphasis is placed on the value that intelligence analysis has on high policy. Instead, what may matter more is how intelligence analysis shapes understandings and interpretations at the working levels of government, which is much more difficult to measure and evaluate than changes in strategic policy.

In the end, much of the difficulty between intelligence and policy can be attributed not to any malfunction or dysfunction in the process itself, but rather the duplication of function at different levels of responsibility within the overall decision-making process. Intelligence collection is obviously valued by all parties. It provides insight into the capabilities, intentions, and activities of adversaries and competitors. But the contributions of intelligence analysis—which substantially overlaps the functions of the decisionmakers and their staffs—is much more difficult to establish. The contention advanced here is that intelligence and security studies researchers are currently asking and answering the wrong question. Rather than explaining why decision-makers ignore intelligence analysis, it is more important to first address the empirical question of how decision-makers actually use intelligence analysis. Instead of assuming that decision-makers will, or should, rely on the intelligence analysis they are provided with to make their decisions, perhaps it is more important to explain why they should incorporate intelligence analysis into decision-making and exactly how they should do so.

The author would like to thank Richard Betts, Brent Durbin, Matthew Hughes, Robert Jervis, Jennifer Kibbe, Genevieve Lester, Mark Neocleous and Mark Stout for their help with this paper. Earlier versions of this paper were presented at the 2013 ISA and 2014 APSA conferences.

QUESTIONS FOR FURTHER DISCUSSION

1. Do scholars overestimate the impact of intelligence on policy formulation?
2. Do intelligence analysts spend most of their time telling policymakers what they already know?
3. Will policymakers pay attention to analysis of emerging issues that are not at the top of policy agendas?
4. Do you think the issues identified by Marrin reflect policymakers' inability or unwillingness to take action in response to the analysis and warning they receive from intelligence professionals?

ENDNOTES

1. Immerman, *Intelligence and Strategy*, 7.
2. Pillar, *Intelligence and U.S. Foreign Policy*, 96–120.
3. Hilsman, *Intelligence and Policy-Making in Foreign Affairs*, 23–24.
4. Wasserman, "The Failure of Intelligence Prediction," 164.
5. Kent, *Estimates and Influence*, 11–21.
6. Hughes, *The Fate of Facts*; Handel, *The Politics of Intelligence*; Harkabi, *The Intelligence-Policymaker Tangle*, 125–131; Gates, "The CIA and American Foreign Policy," 215–230.
7. Hilsman, *Intelligence and Policy-Making in Foreign Affairs*, 23–24.
8. Hilsman, Intelligence and Policy-Making in Foreign Affairs, 23–24.
9. Adams, *War of Numbers*; Goodman, *Failure of Intelligence*; Pillar. *Intelligence, Policy, and the War in Iraq*.
10. Cline, *Policy Without Intelligence*, 121–135.
11. Kerr, *The Track Record*, 35–54.
12. Immerman, *Intelligence and Strategy*, 2–3. Jervis, "Why Intelligence and Policymakers Clash"; Pillar, *Intelligence and U.S. Foreign Policy*, 18–204; Rovner, *Fixing the Facts*. Also see George Poteat, *The Intelligence Gap*, as cited in Betts, *Analysis, War, and Decision*, 81.
13. Ford, "The U.S. Government's Experience," 50.
14. *National Estimates: An Assessment of the Product and the Process. Intelligence Monograph.* Center for the Study of Intelligence. Central Intelligence Agency. April 1977, 35–36.
15. Examples include the lack of influence of intelligence assessment on: German military decision-making in World War I; American, Soviet, and German military decision-making in World War II; Soviet and East German decision-making during the Cold War; American decision-making during the Vietnam War; Israeli decision-making before the Yom Kippur War; American decision-making before 9/11; and American decision-making before and during the Iraq War. For the lack of influence in other domains, see: Ratcliffe, *Intelligence-led Policing*, 263–282; Bernhardt, *Consumer versus Producer*, 19–26; Bernhardt, *Intelligence versus Policy*, 24–28.

16. Marrin, "Intelligence Analysis and Decisionmaking," 133.

17. Pillar, *Intelligence, Policy, and the War in Iraq*, 15–27.

18. Fingar, *Reducing Uncertainty*, Omand, *Securing the State*, 23–24; Marrin, *Intelligence Analysis Theory*, 821–846.

19. Kent, *Strategic Intelligence for American World Policy*, 206.

20. Rovner, "Fixing the Facts," 26–29.

21. May, *Strange Victory*, 458–459. May attributes the general decision-making framework to Vickers, *Art of Judgment*. Also see May and Zelikow, *Seven Tenets*, 4.

22. Kent, *Strategic Intelligence for American World Policy*, 202.

23. Davis, "Intelligence Analysts and Policymakers," 1014.

24. Petersen, *The Challenge for the Political Analyst*, 51.

25. Gates, *An Opportunity Unfulfilled*, 37–38.

26. Petersen, *The Challenge for the Political Analyst*, 51–52.

27. Jervis, *Strategic Intelligence and Effective Policy*, 172.

28. Forbush, Chase, and Goldberg, *CIA Intelligence Support for Foreign and National Security Policy Making*, 3.

29. Russell, *Sharpening Strategic Intelligence*, 92.

30. Ford, The US Government's Experience, 50–51.

31. Gates, "The CIA and American Foreign Policy," 221.

32. Kent, *Strategic Intelligence for American World Policy*, 199.

33. Knorr, *Foreign Intelligence and the Social Sciences*, 23.

34. Heuer, *Psychology of Intelligence Analysis*, 62.

35. Heuer, *Psychology of Intelligence Analysis*, 60.

36. Armstrong, "Ways to Make Analysis Relevant but Not Prescriptive," 37–43.

37. Kendall, "The Function of Intelligence," 550.

38. Betts, "American Strategic Intelligence," 257.

39. Jervis, "Why Intelligence and Policymakers Clash," 204 .

40. "The Problem of Objectivity and Integrity" in Kent, *Strategic Intelligence for American World Policy*, 195–201.

41. Kent, *Strategic Intelligence for American World Policy*, 182.

42. Hilsman, Intelligence and Policy-Making in Foreign Affairs, 12–13.

43. Kent, *Strategic Intelligence for American World Policy*, 203–205.

44. Gates, *The CIA and American Foreign Policy*, 227.

45. Dahl, "Why Won't They Listen?," 70. Referencing Lowenthal, "Grant vs. Sherman," 198.

46. Wasserman, "The Failure of Intelligence Prediction," 165.

47. Dahl, "Why Won't They Listen?," 68–90.

48. Frantz and Waas, "CIA Failed to See Iraq's Attack Plans."

49. Foer and Ackerman, "The Radical: What Dick Cheney Really Believes."

50. Russell, "CIA's Strategic Intelligence in Iraq," 194.

51. Foer and Ackerman, "The Radical: What Dick Cheney Really Believes."

52. Wolfowitz, Comments, 78.

53. Wolfowitz, Comments, 78.

54. Wolfowitz, Comments, 78–79.

55. National Intelligence Estimate (NIE) 15–90: "Yugoslavia Transformed," October 1990.

56. Treverton. "Reshaping National Intelligence," 177.

57. Shreeve. "The Intelligence Community Case Method Program," 327–340.

58. Shreeve, "The Intelligence Community Case Method Program," 327.

59. Treverton, "Reshaping National Intelligence," 177.

60. Treverton, "Reshaping National Intelligence," 178.

61. Shreeve, "The Intelligence Community Case Method Program," 338.

62. Shreeve, "The Intelligence Community Case Method Program," 336–339.

63. Shreeve, "The Intelligence Community Case Method Program," 338.

64. Shreeve, "The Intelligence Community Case Method Program," 336–339.

65. Shreeve, "The Intelligence Community Case Method Program," 338

66. *The 9/11 Commission Report: Final Report of the National Commission on Terrorist Attacks Upon the United States* (New York: Norton, 2004), p. 341 (henceforth *9/11 Commission Report*).

67. Pillar, "A Scapegoat is Not a Solution."

68. Marrin. "The 9/11 Terrorist Attacks," 197.

69. Marrin, "The 9/11 Terrorist Attacks, "185, 197; *9/11 Commission Report*, 101.

70. National Commission on Terrorist Attacks Upon the United States. Staff Statement No. 7: Intelligence and Policy. 11. 2004. This comment was not duplicated in the *9/11 Commission Report*.

71. *9/11 Commission Report*, 348; Clarke, *Against All Enemies*, 238.

72. Herman, *Intelligence Power in Peace and War*, 141.

73. Rovner, Long, and Zegart. "Correspondence: *How Intelligent Is Intelligence Reform?*", 203.

74. US National Intelligence Council. *NIE: Iraq's Continuing Programs for Weapons of Mass Destruction*; US National Intelligence Council. *Regional Consequences of Regime Change in Iraq*; US National Intelligence Council. *Principal Challenges in Post-Saddam Iraq*.

75. Lowenthal, "The Real Intelligence Failure?," B01.

76. Betts, *Enemies of Intelligence*, 122.

77. Pillar. "Intelligence, Policy, and the War in Iraq"

78. Bush, *Decision Points*, 248–249.

79. Immerman, "Intelligence and Strategy," 23.
80. Pillar, *Intelligence and US Foreign Policy,* 317–330.
81. Petersen, "The Challenge for the Political Analyst," 51–56, Kerbel and Olcott, "The Intelligence-Policy Nexus," 1–13, Petersen, "What I Learned in 40 Years of Doing Intelligence Analysis," 13–20; Wilder, "An Educated Consumer is Our Best Customer," 23–31.
82. Davis, "The Challenge of Managing Uncertainty," 35–42.
83. The Twentieth Century Fund Task Force, *In From the Cold,* 11; Andrew, "An Agenda for Future Research," 225; Brown et al., "Preparing for the 21st Century."
84. Steinberg, "The Policymaker's Perspective," 88–89.
85. Marrin and Davies, "National Assessment by the National Security Council Staff 1968–80," 644–673.
86. Hulnick and Brammer. *The Impact of Intelligence on the Policy Review and Decision Process,* 9.
87. Ford, "The US Government's Experience," 52.
88. Betts, "Analysis, War, and Decision," 83–84.
89. Marrin, "Intelligence Analysis Theory."
90. Betts, "Policy-Makers and Intelligence Analysts," 185–186.

BIBLIOGRAPHY:

Adams, Samuel A. *War of Numbers: An Intelligence Memoir.* Hanover, NH: Steerforth, 1994.

Andrew, Christopher. "An Agenda for Future Research."' In *Eternal Vigilance? 50 Years of the CIA,* edited by Rhodri Jeffreys-Jones and Christopher Andrew, 224–233. London: Frank Cass and Co., 1997.

Armstrong, Fulton T. "Ways to Make Analysis Relevant but Not Prescriptive." *Studies in Intelligence* 46, no. 3 (2002): 37–43.

Bernhardt, Douglas. "Consumer versus Producer: Overcoming the Disconnect between Management and Competitive Intelligence." *Competitive Intelligence Review* 10, no. 3 (1999): 19–26.

Bernhardt, Douglas. Intelligence versus Policy: Healthy Tension or Lost Cause?" *Competitive Intelligence Review* 12, no. 4 (July/August 2009): 24–28.

Betts, Richard K. "American Strategic Intelligence: Politics, Priorities, and Direction." *Intelligence Policy and National Security,* edited by Robert L. Pfaltzgraff, Jr. and Uri Ra'anan, 245–267. Macmillan, 1981.

Betts, Richard K. "Analysis, War, and Decision: Why Intelligence Failures Are Inevitable." *World Politics* 31, no. 2 (October 1978): 61–89.

Betts, Richard K. *Enemies of Intelligence: Knowledge and Power in American National Security.* New York: Columbia University Press, 2007.

Betts, Richard K. "Policy-makers and Intelligence Analysts: Love, Hate or Indifference?" *Intelligence and National Security* 3, no. 1 (January 1988): 184–189.

Brown, Harold, et al. Preparing for the 21st Century: An Appraisal of US Intelligence, 'The Need for Policy Guidance'.

Bush, George W. *Decision Points.* New York: Crown, 2010.

Clarke, Richard A. *Against All Enemies: Inside America's War on Terror.* New York: Free Press, 2004.

Cline, Ray S. "Policy Without Intelligence." *Foreign Policy* 17 (Winter 1974–1975): 121–135.

Dahl, Erik J. "Why Won't They Listen? Comparing Receptivity Toward Intelligence at Pearl Harbor and Midway." *Intelligence and National Security* 28, no. 1 (2013): 68–90.

Davis, Jack. "Intelligence Analysts and Policymakers: Benefits and Dangers of Tensions in the Relationship." *Intelligence and National Security* 21, no. 6 (2006): 999–1021.

Davis, Jack. "The Challenge of Managing Uncertainty: Paul Wolfowitz on Intelligence-Policy Relations." *Studies in Intelligence* 39, no. 5 (1996): 35–42.

Fingar, Thomas. *Reducing Uncertainty: Intelligence Analysis and National Security.* Stanford, CA: Stanford Security Studies, 2011.

Foer, Franklin, and Spencer Ackerman. "The Radical: What Dick Cheney Really Believes." *The New Republic,* December 1–8, 2003.

Forbush, Ramsey, Gary Chase, and Ron Goldberg. "CIA Intelligence Support for Foreign and National Security Policy Making." *Studies in Intelligence* 20, no.1 (Spring 1976).

Ford, Harold P. "The U.S. Government's Experience with Intelligence Analysis: Pluses and Minuses." *Intelligence Analysis and Assessment.* Frank Cass and Co., 1996. 34–53.

Frantz, Douglas, and Murray Waas. "CIA Failed to See Iraq's Attack Plans, Gates Says : Intelligence: Agency told Bush in 1989 that Hussein Would Not Strike for Two to Three Years." *Los Angeles Times,* May 9, 1992.

Gates, Robert M. "An Opportunity Unfulfilled: The Use and Perceptions of Intelligence at the White House." *The Washington Quarterly* (Winter 1989): 35–44.

Gates, Robert M. "The CIA and American Foreign Policy." *Foreign Affairs* 66, no. 2 (Winter 1987–1988): 215–230.

Goodman, Melvin A. *Failure of Intelligence: The Decline and Fall of the CIA.* Lanham, MD: Rowman & Littlefield, 2008.

Handel, Michael I. "The Politics of Intelligence." *Intelligence and National Security* 2, no. 4 (October 1987): 5–46.

Harkabi, Yehoshafat. "The Intelligence-Policymaker Tangle." *Jerusalem Quarterly* 30 (Winter 1984): 125–131.

Herman, Michael. *Intelligence Power in Peace and War.* Cambridge, UK: Cambridge University Press, 1996.

Heuer, Richards. *Psychology of Intelligence Analysis.* Washington, DC: Center for the Study of Intelligence. 1999.

Hilsman, Roger. "Intelligence and Policy-Making in Foreign Affairs." *World Politics* (April 1953): 1–45.

Hughes, Thomas L. *The Fate of Facts in a World of Men,* Headline Series No. 233. New York: Foreign Policy Association, 1976.

Hulnick, Arthur S., and Deborah Brammer. *The Impact of Intelligence on the Policy Review and Decision Process.* Washington, DC: Central Intelligence Agency, Center for the Study of Intelligence. 1980.

Immerman, Richard H. "Intelligence and Strategy: Historicizing Psychology, Policy and Politics." *Diplomatic History* 32, no. 1 (January 2008): 1–23.

Jervis, Robert. "Strategic Intelligence and Effective Policy." *Security and Intelligence in a Changing World: New Perspectives for the 1990s.* 1991. 165–181.

Jervis, Robert. "Why Intelligence and Policymakers Clash." *Political Science Quarterly* 125, no. 2 (Summer 2010).

Kendall, Willmoore. "The Function of Intelligence." *World Politics,* 1, no. 4. (July 1949): 542–552.

Kent, Sherman. *Strategic Intelligence for American World Policy.* Hamden, CT: Archon, 1949.

Kerbel, Joshua, and Anthony Olcott. "The Intelligence-Policy Nexus." *Studies in Intelligence.* 54, no. 4 (December 2010): 1–13.

Kerr, Richard J. "The Track Record: CIA Analysis from 1950 to 2000." In *Analyzing Intelligence: Origins, Obstacles, and Innovations,* edited by Roger Z. George and James B. Bruce, 35–54. Washington, DC: Georgetown University Press, 2008.

Knorr, Klaus E. *Foreign Intelligence and the Social Sciences.* Research Monograph No. 17. Center of International Studies, June 1, 1964. Princeton, NJ: Woodrow Wilson School of Public and International Affairs.

Lowenthal, Mark M. "Grant vs. Sherman: Paradoxes of Intelligence and Combat Leadership." In *Paradoxes of Strategic Intelligence: Essays in Honor of Michael I. Handel,* edited by Richard K. Betts and Thomas G. Mahnken. New York: Routledge, 2003.

Lowenthal, Mark M. "The Real Intelligence Failure? Spineless Spies." *Washington Post,* May 25, 2008, B01.

Marrin, Stephen. "Intelligence Analysis and Decisionmaking: Methodological Challenges." *Intelligence Theory: Key Questions and Debates,* edited by P. Gill, S. Marrin, and M. Phythian, 131–150. London: Routledge, 2008.

Marrin, Stephen. "Intelligence Analysis Theory: Explaining and Predicting Analytic Responsibilities." *Intelligence and National Security* 22, no. 6 (December 2007): 821–846.

Marrin, Stephen. "The 9/11 Terrorist Attacks: A Failure of Policy Not Strategic Intelligence Analysis." *Intelligence and National Security* 26, no. 2 (2011): 182–202.

Marrin, Stephen, and Philip H. J. Davies. "National Assessment by the National Security Council Staff 1968–80: An American Experiment in a British Style of Analysis?" *Intelligence and National Security* 24, no. 5 (2009): 644–673.

National Commission on Terrorist Attacks Upon the United States. *The 9/11 Commission Report: Final Report of the National Commission on Terrorist Attacks Upon the United States.* New York: Norton, 2004.

National Commission on Terrorist Attacks Upon the United States. Staff Statement No. 7: Intelligence and Policy. 11. 2004.

Omand, David. *Securing the State.* C. Hurst, 2010.

Petersen, Martin. "The Challenge for the Political Analyst: Advice from a DI Careerist." *Studies in Intelligence* 47, no. 1 (2003): 51–56.

Petersen, Martin. "What I Learned in 40 Years of Doing Intelligence Analysis for US Foreign Policymakers." *Studies in Intelligence* (2011): 13–20.

Pillar, Paul R. "A Scapegoat is Not a Solution." *New York Times,* June 4, 2004.

Pillar, Paul R. *Intelligence and U.S. Foreign Policy: Iraq, 9/11, and Misguided Reform.* Columbia University Press, 2011.

Pillar, Paul R. "Intelligence, Policy, and the War in Iraq." *Foreign Affairs* 85, no. 2 (March-April 2006): 15–27.

Poteat, George. "The Intelligence Gap: Hypotheses on the Process of Surprise." *Intelligence Studies Notes* 3 (Fall 1976).

Ratcliffe, Jerry H. "Intelligence-led Policing." *Environmental Criminology and Crime Analysis,* edited by R. Wortley, L. Mazerolle, and S. Rombouts, 263–282. Cullompton, UK: Willan, 2008.

Rovner, Joshua. *Fixing the Facts: National Security and the Politics of Intelligence.* Ithaca, NY: Cornell University Press. 2011.

Rovner, Joshua, Austin Long, and Amy Zegart. "Correspondence: *How Intelligent Is Intelligence Reform?*" *International Security* 30, no. 4 (2006): 196–208).

Russell, Richard L. "CIA's Strategic Intelligence in Iraq." *Political Science Quarterly* 117, no. 2 (Summer 2002): 191–207.

Russell, Richard L. *Sharpening Strategic Intelligence: Why the CIA Gets It Wrong and What Needs to Be Done to Get It Right.* Cambridge, UK, and New York: Cambridge University Press, 2007.

Shreeve, Thomas W. "The Intelligence Community Case Method Program: A National Intelligence Estimate on Yugoslavia." In *Intelligence and the National Security Strategist*, edited by Roger Z George and Robert D. Kline, 327–340. Lanham, MD: Rowman & Littlefield Publishers, 2006.

Steinberg, James B. "The Policymaker's Perspective: Transparency and Partnership." In *Analyzing Intelligence: Origins, Obstacles and Innovations*, edited by Roger George and James Bruce, 88–89. Washington, DC: Georgetown University Press. 2008.

The Twentieth Century Fund Task Force on the Future of U.S. Intelligence. *In From the Cold: The Report of the Twentieth Century Fund Task Force on the Future of US Intelligence.* New York: Twentieth Century Fund Press, 1996.

Treverton, Gregory F. *Reshaping National Intelligence in an Age of Information.* Cambridge, UK: Cambridge University Press. 2001.

US Central Intelligence Agency. *National Estimates: An Assessment of the Product and the Process.* Intelligence Monograph April 1977. Washington, DC: Center for the Study of Intelligence. Central Intelligence Agency.

US National Intelligence Council. *Intelligence Community Assessment: Principal Challenges in Post-Saddam Iraq.* Washington, DC: US National Intelligence Council, 2003.

US National Intelligence Council. *Intelligence Community Assessment: Regional Consequences of Regime Change in Iraq.* Washington, DC: US National Intelligence Council, 2003.

US National Intelligence Council. *National Intelligence Estimate (NIE) 15–90: Yugoslavia Transformed.* Washington, DC: US National Intelligence Council, 1990.

US National Intelligence Council. *National Intelligence Estimate (NIE): Iraq's Continuing Programs for Weapons of Mass Destruction.* Washington, DC: US National Intelligence Council, 2002.

Wasserman, Benno. "The Failure of Intelligence Prediction." *Political Studies* 8, no. 2 (1960): 164.

Wilder, Dennis. "An Educated Consumer is Our Best Customer." *Studies in Intelligence* (2011): 23–31.

Wolfowitz, Paul. "Comments to Douglas J. MacEachin's 'The Tradecraft of Analysis.'" In *US Intelligence at the Crossroads: Agendas for Reform*, edited by Roy Godson, Ernest R. May, and Gary Schmitt, 63–85. National Strategy Information Center, 1995.

From Stephen Marrin, "Why Strategic Intelligence Analysis has limited Influence on American Foreign Policy," *Intelligence and National Security* 32: 6 (October 2017): 725–742. Reproduced by permission.

IV

INTELLIGENCE AND THE POLICYMAKER

Barnado: "Sit down awhile,
And let us once again assail your ears,
That are so fortified against our story . . . ."
—SHAKESPEARE, *Hamlet*, 1.1.31–33

Policymakers—elected officials, career civil servants, and senior military officers—have an extraordinarily important part to play in the intelligence cycle. They are the individuals who must develop or change policy in response to the estimates and reporting produced by the intelligence community. Without effective communication among policymakers and intelligence analysts and managers, there is simply no way to put intelligence to good use in making and conducting foreign or defense policy.

LINES OF COMMUNICATION

Although the September 11 tragedy is reshaping the lines of communication between the intelligence community and policymakers, intelligence managers and analysts direct most of their efforts toward five clients within the U.S. government. First and foremost is the president and his immediate staff. The relationship with this client is crucial and is often handled personally by the Director of National Intelligence (DNI). Occasionally, when the issues are important or the topics under consideration are complex or highly technical, the DNI (or, prior to 2005, the DCI) will bring analysts to the White House or the old Executive Office Building to brief the president or members of his staff. In the past, some DCIs were not particularly welcome at the White House, but most have served as the Chief Intelligence Officer to the president.

Second, the intelligence community maintains close links with the National Security Council (NSC), which supports the president in his conduct of U.S. foreign and defense policy. The NSC is staffed by military officers, political appointees, career civil servants, and intelligence professionals who are experts on various issues and regions. The intelligence community supports the NSC as it works to coordinate foreign and defense policy across a variety of government agencies and the military services and as it monitors policy implementation.

Third, intelligence managers and analysts have traditionally forged relationships with political appointees and senior career civil servants throughout the Defense and State departments. In the Defense Department, the intelligence community focuses on providing information to the civilians within the Office of the Secretary of Defense and the military officers who fill the ranks of the Joint Staff. These contacts within cabinet departments and with the Joint Staff are important because these individuals make recommendations that are used by top staffers directly supporting the president in the formulation of national policy. These officials also make sure their own organizations work faithfully to implement policy generated by senior members of the administration. In the aftermath of September 11, interaction is also increasing with the Departments of Justice, Commerce, Treasury, Agriculture, and Homeland Security, under the guidance of the DNI.

Fourth, the intelligence community interacts with individual members of Congress, congressional committees, and their staffs. In this role, intelligence managers provide not only finished intelligence to elected officials but also information related to congressional oversight of the activities of the intelligence community (Lowenthal 2006).

The intelligence community also is a great contributor to the *interagency process,* a system of consultations between mid-level officials over the formulation and conduct of foreign and defense policy. All organizations with a vested interest in the policy at hand are asked to arrive at a consensus that they can support. The interagency process can be cumbersome because it must accommodate multiple players with a variety of interests and because it gives tremendous power to holdouts—organizations that demand specific concessions to move forward with policy. The interagency process thus affects the intelligence community in two ways: (1) by the policies that flow from the interagency process and (2) by contributing intelligence materials that influence the nature of the interagency debate. Because they share the same long-term perspective on policy, career civil servants and intelligence professionals often have more common positions with each other in interagency debates than they do with the political appointees who face severe time constraints in terms of achieving their objectives.

THE ROLE OF POLICYMAKERS

Policymakers obviously need to use intelligence to advance national objectives, but they also play an important part in other functions of the intelligence cycle. Policymakers often have a great deal to say when it comes to setting intelligence requirements—that is, identifying topics that should be of interest to the intelligence community when it comes to collecting data and producing finished intelligence. Policymakers generally leave the technical and often arcane process of collecting information to intelligence professionals, although they sometimes intervene if intelligence operations pose grave political or military risks. The U-2 reconnaissance program attracted the attention of senior officials because of the risks of using aircraft to overfly Soviet or Cuban territory in the late 1950s and early 1960s. Policymakers can also turn to the intelligence community with specific requests for information that help them devise policy or political positions, a process that can lead to frustration if policymakers hold unrealistic expectations about intelligence capabilities. Policymakers tend to think that experts and information on just about everything reside somewhere within the intelligence community, an expectation that ignores budgetary and bureaucratic reality (Lowenthal, 2006). The risk of intelligence politicization also looms large if policymakers begin to see intelligence as simply another weapon in partisan politics.

The intelligence community would not exist if it were not for policymakers' need to make foreign and defense policy. But intelligence managers sometimes are wary of policymakers and worry about sharing too much sensitive intelligence. There is always a risk that officials will leak classified information to the media. Officials "leak" for a variety of reasons (see chapter 13). Sometimes they leak classified information to score political points by bolstering their position or damaging the position of their opponents. Sometimes they leak information to focus government or public attention on a problem they believe is being overlooked. Sometimes they leak information because they like to feel important; journalists might even be expected to return a favor by putting a positive news spin on one's pet policy or by writing a favorable story about one's performance in office. Most of the time, the information that is leaked is of transient importance. However, some leaked information can cause grave damage to national security or destroy the effectiveness of intelligence programs created at enormous expense. A September 1971 *Washington Post* article written by Jack Anderson is a case in point. Anderson wrote that U.S. intelligence organizations, in Operation

GUPPY, were intercepting telephone calls made by Politburo members from their limousines as they drove around Moscow (Anderson 1973). Soon after the report, the transmissions ceased. What is maddening from the perspective of the intelligence community is the fact is that these "leakers" are rarely if ever identified, reprimanded, or prosecuted for releasing classified information. Most intelligence officials probably would wish that Anderson had not written the story, but they are most critical of the government official (who of course might have been a member of the intelligence community) who gave Anderson the piece of information in the first place.

Occasionally, the president and his closest advisers decide to reveal classified information as part of a deliberate effort to build public and international support for national policy. Today, the public has almost come to expect that U.S. administrations will present their case using classified information—radio intercepts, pictures taken from reconnaissance satellites, or even agent reports. Although the president is within his rights to authorize the use of classified material in a public forum to support national policy, members of the intelligence community consider this type of action to be a mixed blessing. They recognize the enormous impact that classified information can have on public opinion, but they worry that using current intelligence in this way can compromise sources and methods. In other words, revealing classified information provides clear indications to opponents about how the intelligence community collects and analyzes data. Even though it might seem unlikely that publicly revealing a reconnaissance photo can do lasting damage, revelations of classified data can have a cumulative effect. Over time, those targeted by the intelligence community can build a good picture of how information is gathered and analyzed, allowing them to identify and rectify vulnerabilities that were being exploited for the purposes of intelligence collection. Intelligence managers and analysts focus on these long-term consequences when classified data are made public. They tend to worry that their future ability to collect and analyze information is being mortgaged to meet today's political demands.

INTELLIGENCE FOR THE POLICYMAKER

The relationship between the intelligence community and policymakers also varies in terms of the nature of the information supplied to senior officials. *Warning intelligence* informs policymakers about direct and immediate threats to national security or the impending failure of foreign policy. To produce warning intelligence, however, someone has to designate exactly what needs to be monitored. Intelligence analysts would prefer for policymakers to give them a list of people, places, or things that should be watched closely, while policymakers would rather deliver blanket orders to the intelligence community to take all necessary steps to avoid being surprised. If a warning needs to be delivered, analysts then face the problem of getting busy policymakers to pay attention to what at first glance might appear to be some minor disturbance (after all, warnings of potential disasters always appear less threatening than actual disastrous events). Sometimes, analysts face the opposite problem: They have to communicate to policymakers that signs of impending danger are overblown. Analysts have to place alarming news or diplomatic reporting in an analytical or historical context, and sometimes they have to convince policymakers not to overreact to events that appear threatening. Warning intelligence also works best when standard procedures are in place to communicate quickly and credibly to senior officials. Given the difficulty of getting people to pay attention to disturbing information, it also helps to have some sort of feedback mechanism in place so that analysts can be assured that their warnings have been received and understood.

Policymakers also rely on the intelligence community for *current intelligence*. Compared with other finished intelligence products, current intelligence—the *National Intelligence Daily* (NID) and *President's Daily Brief* (PDB)—resembles newspaper reporting. Working on the NID is a lot like working as a journalist at a major newspaper or television network. The NID and PDB are best thought of as classified newspapers (although they are now generally available in electronic formats), with feature articles and shorter "news stories" about important current and upcoming events. Analysts involved in the production of this current intelligence face many challenges, especially those created by competing news organizations. Given the advent of global news networks, Internet communications, and satellite television phones, current intelligence can be easily "scooped" by global media outlets, much to the chagrin of intelligence analysts. Instead of trying to beat the news cycle (an impossible task given the fact that cable news networks are monitored in offices throughout the government), intelligence analysts comment on the veracity of media stories or provide additional insights based on classified information. Current intelligence is unlikely to tell policy experts new information about their specific fields of expertise, but it does provide them with a body of knowledge about events that are affecting other parts of the government.

Analysts also conduct *basic research*—major research products that can take months to complete. They undertake these "term papers" to gain expertise or to respond to specific questions raised by policymakers. Basic research helps analysts place current events in their correct historical or political context and provides them with the background needed to identify and trace the impact of obscure issues that can undermine well-crafted policies. Unless policymakers ask for these basic research reports directly, however, they are unlikely to read them and often respond negatively to inboxes that seem to be filled with an endless stream of detailed intelligence reports. When it comes to intelligence, policymakers value brevity and relevance. The challenge for intelligence managers is to make sure that basic research is delivered to policymakers who would be interested in the report (i.e., individuals who already are experts in the field addressed by the research).

Intelligence estimates—the National Intelligence Estimates (NIEs), for example—are formal intelligence reports produced by the entire intelligence community to support key policy decisions. These estimates require close coordination with policy agendas because they attempt to single out and explore the key issues on which some policy hinges. To be useful, these estimates have to be closely coordinated with policy agendas, a situation that requires policymakers to provide the intelligence community with the lead time necessary to perform the analysis. Accusations about politicization of the intelligence process are most likely to emerge with intelligence estimates, because they are directly linked to issues of political or policy importance.

Finally, policymakers, to the consternation of intelligence professionals, sometimes request raw intelligence—agent reports, reconnaissance photographs, or intercepted communications—so that they can evaluate these materials themselves. Dissemination of this kind of information is risky from the perspective of intelligence managers, because it can easily compromise the sources or methods used to collect and analyze raw intelligence. But it is the timing of these requests that is especially disconcerting to intelligence professionals; the requests usually occur in moments of crisis, when information flows increase and critical decisions have to be made on short notice. When it matters most, policymakers or senior military commanders want to serve as their own chief intelligence analysts; they want to view raw data to make up their own minds about its meaning. But policymakers rarely have the expertise or knowledge to place raw intelligence in its proper context or to judge the authenticity or accuracy of the information, and a crisis is a poor time to attempt to develop that skill set. The best policymakers and senior officers resist the urge to serve as their own chief intelligence analyst and instead bombard analysts and managers with a series of questions to assess the degree to which they are confident in their assessments (Hulnick 1986).

GETTING OVER THE ROUGH SPOTS

One important perspective that separates career intelligence officers from policymakers who are political appointees is a different perception of the time available to accomplish the tasks before them. Political appointees are under pressure to show results quickly, or at least to demonstrate some progress on vexing issues before the next election. Intelligence professionals tend to see policy cycles in a longer perspective. In the rush to gain results, policymakers want support from the rest of the "career bureaucracy" to gain their policy objectives quickly. By contrast, intelligence analysts are less interested in the success of a specific policy per se and more interested in preserving the long-term effectiveness of the relationship between the intelligence and policy communities; they are likely to cry foul if they are pressured to supply intelligence to be used as ammunition in the political fray.

This difference in perspectives about time constraints and objectives creates several rough spots in the relations between elected officials and intelligence professionals. Policymakers want clear recommendations from the intelligence community and complain when finished intelligence tends to survey the range of possible future contingencies and policy outcomes. When intelligence analysts hedge their bets, policymakers suspect some sort of bias, especially when the reservations voiced by analysts conflict with policymakers' preferences. Policymakers, especially those with minimal government experience, often know little about how intelligence estimates are developed. Without knowing the individuals responsible for the analysis, they are sometimes not sure of how seriously to take various finished intelligence reports. As a result, they are reluctant to accept intelligence judgments that conflict with their preferences, which are of course the very findings that should enter into the policy formulation process. The intelligence community sometimes exacerbates this problem by carefully choosing the language used in estimates to suggest subtle differences in the confidence it has in key findings. These subtle variations are often lost on policymakers who know little of the distinctions that are being made. Additionally, policymakers are unlikely to wade through stacks of current intelligence reports and research papers in search of relevant material and often become frustrated by the need to cull through mountains of paperwork to get to a few useful nuggets of information (Hulnick 1986).

When dealing with policymakers, analysts also encounter their own problems. It is difficult to monitor the twists and turns in the debate over policy to guarantee that intelligence reports and estimates are relevant. Standardized intelligence products do little to address the concerns or needs of individual policymakers and are often ignored. Policymakers will also ignore information if it fails to address the issue filling their inbox at a given moment. If left to their own devices, policymakers tend to ask for opinions about policy options, advice that is beyond the purview of intelligence managers and analysts (Hulnick 1986).

THE READINGS

In the selections that follow, our contributors shed light on the relationship between policymakers and the intelligence community. Jack Davis addresses the sources of tension in relations between intelligence analysts and policymakers and various criticisms voiced by both parties about the behavior of their counterparts. In response to this criticism, Davis develops a series of best practices for both policymakers and analysts that can help steer them away from many of the pitfalls that can complicate their relationship and the development of effective policy.

In "Tribal Tongues: Intelligence Consumers, Intelligence Producers," Mark M. Lowenthal, a former senior official in the U.S. intelligence community and now a well-known intelligence educator, suggests that even though policymakers and intelligence professionals are on the same team, they do not always follow the same playbook. He describes how different organizational pressures and bureaucratic cultures shape the way policymakers and intelligence professionals view their roles and relationships, creating a gap that is often difficult to bridge in practice. Lowenthal also makes the key observation that policymakers can greatly influence the quality and timeliness of the intelligence they receive, even though they are often unaware of the way they shape intelligence inputs into the policy-making process.

The final selection consists of an extract from the final report of the Aspin-Brown Commission (1996). It emphasizes the necessity for policymakers to provide guidance to intelligence officers with respect to the informational needs of those holding high office. The report underscores that "intelligence agencies cannot operate in a vacuum" (p. 29).

10. INTELLIGENCE ANALYSTS AND POLICYMAKERS

JACK DAVIS

In this thoughtful overview of the tensions that complicate the relationship between intelligence analysts and policymakers, Jack Davis notes that at the heart of most problems is a shared judgment: criticism is politically motivated. His list of best practices is intended to steer the interaction between officials and analysts onto more productive paths.

This chapter is occasioned by public interest in reported tensions between Central Intelligence Agency (CIA) analysts and policy-making officials of the administration of President George W. Bush regarding the significance of ties between the Saddam Hussein regime and Al Qaeda terrorists, an important factor in the U.S. decision to invade Iraq in 2003. No evaluation of the latter case is provided. The chapter addresses, instead, general patterns of tensions between intelligence analysts and policy officials, in order to provide a context for public assessment of the Iraq-Al Qaeda incident when the public record is more complete as well as provide enhanced understanding of similar future instances of tension.

Over the years, most of the tens of thousands of written and oral assessments produced by CIA analysts in an effort to support the policy-making process have been received by policy officials with either appreciation or silence. Many of the assessments are in response to policy-maker tasking, usually a sign of expectation of useful insights. Many consist of briefings and exchanges via telephone or teleconferencing, where the fact that policy officials invest the time to elicit and discuss analysts' assessment of an important national security issue is testimony to the value the officials expect to receive. Many assessments, as to be expected considering the volume of production, miss the mark for the targeted officials in terms of relevancy, timing, or fresh insights, and thus evoke no reaction.

That said, tensions in the relationship between CIA intelligence analysts and administration policy makers are a common occurrence—an essentially normal by-product of the two camps' distinctive professional missions. The analyst's professional commitment is to assess national security issues without bias for or against the outcomes sought by the incumbent presidential administration; the policy maker's professional commitment is to articulate, advocate, and advance the administration's national security agenda.

Often, the resultant tension in the relationship helps both camps to deal more effectively with the challenges of analytic and policy-making uncertainty that usually attend complex national security issues. Under policy-maker criticism or questioning of judgments, analysts tend to revisit their initial views of the soundness of assumptions about what drives the issue and the implications of incomplete, ambiguous, and contradictory evidence. In response, policy officials often are moved to recalculate the elements of their own assessments of threats to and opportunities for advancing U.S. interests.

At times, though, tensions take a turn that does not serve well sound analysis effective policy making, or the national interest; charges of *politicization*, or analytic distortion to support or undermine a policy initiative, issue forth from one or both camps. These cases usually arise when policy officials repeatedly reject the analysts' studied interpretative judgments on the status of or outlook for a complex national security issue, especially when such judgments are seen to complicate policy initiatives that are politically important to an administration.

If tensions are a normal occurrence, and their elimination both impractical and unwise, recommendations of ground rules to enhance benefits and curb dangers would seem called for. But first one should make a closer assessment of the roots and branches of the tensions.

Tensions in analyst–policy maker relations in the United States can be traced back at least to the establishment in 1941, under the auspices of the Office of Strategic Services (OSS), of the first bureaucratically independent cadre of intelligence analysts. Sherman Kent, who later played a major role in setting professional standards for CIA analysis, came away from his World War II experience in the OSS with the conviction that relations between producers and consumers of intelligence assessments are not naturally harmonious, despite the common goal of advancing U.S. national security interests. Kent did not much change his views about inherent strains in the relationship during his years of analytic service with the CIA (1951–67).

Why not harmonious? The character of the policy issue at stake, personalities in both camps, the degree of contention about policy direction among administration leaders, and the role of Congress as a third party to the policy-making process from time to time have contributed to the onset and intensity of analysts' policy maker tensions. The underlying constant, though, is the aforementioned difference in perspective on professional mission between the producers of intelligence analysis and their policy-making clients.

criticism, even though they are aware of gaps and other flaws in their information.

Regarding prediction of future developments, where unexpected intermediate events can throw seemingly sound forecasts off course, analysts also have confidence in their expertise and work ethic, and they take pride in their belief in the independence of their judgments from policy and political influences.

Concerted public criticism of flawed analytic performance on major national security issues spawns intervals of analytic humility for the DI as an organization, its leaders, and usually the analysts directly involved. But for the most part, confidence, even overconfidence, in substantive judgments is a staple of the analyst's environment. Especially the more experienced DI analysts tend to see themselves as the best informed on the issues they follow as well as the most objective national security professionals in the U.S. government. Over the decades, on many issues they probably have been.

Analysts vary in their experiences with and attitudes toward policy officials. That said, a common first reaction to criticism of their assessments by policy officials is to suspect that either politics or the critics' lack of requisite substantive expertise is at work. Digging in at the heels in defense of the original assessment at times follows. Probably more often, the analysts undertake a reappraisal of their assumptions, evidence, and argumentation, though a substantial change in judgments does not necessarily result.

THE ANALYSTS' PERSPECTIVE

CIA analysts are concentrated in the Directorate of Intelligence (DI), which takes pride in its organizational independence from the President, the Secretaries of State and Defense, and the other policy makers its intelligence assessments are intended to serve. The conceit that DI assessments are free of policy and political influence or bias comes across in the slogans by which the analysts and their leaders usually define their professional mission: *objective analysis, carrying truth to power, telling it like it is.*

Over the decades, on many critical and controversial national security issues—for example, Soviet strategic arms, the Vietnam War, Central American insurgencies—considerable substantive expertise, much sweat equity, and tough-minded assessment of assumptions and evidence have gone into the analysts' Interpretation of past and ongoing events. The usual bureaucratic result was and is a readiness among analysts to defend key judgments against

THE POLICY MAKER'S PERSPECTIVE

Policy officials, for their part, also vary in their experiences with and attitudes toward CIA analysts. A good number of career policy officials over the decades have considered the DI analysts on their accounts not only the best informed among the governmental community of intelligence analysts, but also the quickest to respond to requests for analytic assistance. This subset of policy officials also appreciates that CIA assessments, unlike those issued by analysts in policy-making departments, are rarely skewed to support a party to the bureaucratic politics that usually colors the policy-analysis process on national security issues.

The tendency among officials closest to the president runs differently. These essentially political appointees, because of their own partisan cast, can be quick to attribute partisan motivation to CIA analysts. Especially when a political party has been out of power for some years, newly appointed Republican officials tend to see the Agency as dominated by holdover liberal Democrats, whereas new Democratic officials tend to see the strong influence of Republican conservatives. Many top-level appointees have served in previous presidential administrations and have requisite confidence in their own analytic skills and substantive knowledge of the issues. Some carry over from previous service critical views of the competence of Agency analysts as well as of their perceived propensity to an antiadministration bias.

Regarding professional mission, both career officials and political appointees see themselves as action officers as well as policy analysts. Their job is to get accomplished their vision of the president's national security agenda—the goals, strategies, and tactics that emerge from policy analysis.

Unlike intelligence professionals, policy officials are little pained by a merger of an administration's interests in domestic U.S. politics and foreign policy goals. As a rule, to policy officials, especially presidential appointees, government is politics as well as policy. The merger of policy and political advocacy at times requires building a "yes case" or a "no case" amidst inconclusive evidence of the soundness of a policy initiative and the uncertain implications for policy success of daily developments involving, for example, U.S. diplomatic or military campaigns.

This does not mean administration officials are ready to ignore CIA assessments that, say, would give political opponents in Congress ammunition to criticize policy. Often policy officials will ask analysts to "unpack" their assessment, revealing what is fact and what is opinion, or they will call for a briefing and an exchange of views either to enlighten or to leverage analysts.

In sum, at root, tensions, when they occur, represent a collision between the analyst's mission-driven belief that policy-maker criticism of carefully crafted assesments reflects politics or limited substantive command of issues and the policy official's mission driven belief that CIA assessments that complicate a well-deliberated initiative reflect antiadministration bias or poor analysis.

THE ANALYTIC BRANCHES OF TENSION: OPINIONS, FACTS, EVIDENCE

Though difficult to untangle in actual cases of analyst—policy maker tensions, separating the varieties of analytic production into three branches—opinions, facts, and evidence—serves to clarify both the character of strains in the relationship and potential ground rules for managing tensions.

Regarding estimative judgments or opinions on issues of high uncertainty (for example, multiyear projections of political developments in unstable foreign countries, or prediction of the outcome of protracted U.S. military and diplomatic engagements in violence-prone regions), even well-informed policy makers at times gain insights from intelligence analysts' well-argued estimative judgments.

But when analysts' bottom-line judgments are seen as implicit criticism of and potentially harmful to policy agendas, administration officials are prone to dismiss them as "opinions."

Secretary of Defense Donald Rumsfeld, in an October 24, 2002, press briefing, went to great lengths to define the limits of the analysts' opinions in such circumstances: "If you think about it, what comes out of intelligence is not fixed, firm conclusions. What comes out are a speculation, an analysis, probabilities, possibilities, estimates. Best guesses."[1] Further, policy officials claim, often with justification, that the opinions regarding future developments spawned by policy analysis are sounder than analysts' opinions, if only because they are able to take fuller account of the weight of carrots and sticks the United States may be ready to deploy.

More than once, policy officials have let it be known, in particular, that they are little interested in whether analysts think U.S. initiatives will succeed. The analyst's main job, according to critics, is to provide assessments that enable policy analysts to reach sound judgments about what actions to take to implement policy, despite the uncertainty that fogs complex world events. The analyst's focus should be on strengths and weaknesses of foreign players, their tendencies, motivations, and risk calculations that would help policy officials identify potential dangers and U.S. leverage points.

Regarding facts, tensions are infrequent and usually involve competing methods of determining facts. Here a fact is defined as something concrete and reliably detected and measured: what a foreign adversary said in a recorded speech or intercepted conversation, as opposed to what he or she meant or actually intends to do.

A prominent official once observed, regarding facts, that policy makers are like surgeons. "They don't last long if they ignore what they see once they cut the patient open."[2]

When policy officials are hesitant to accept as fact a condition or development reported by analysts that could complicate political goals or policy implementation, they tend to challenge the sources and methods the analysts relied on in their determination of facts. During military engagements, for example, military officials have preferred to determine battlefield damage to the enemy as recorded in post-flight reports by U.S. pilots, and to dismiss the analyst's usually more modest calculations of damage that were based on, say, overhead imagery.

The most noteworthy tensions between CIA analysts and policy officials usually are over differences about the meaning of available evidence—that is, differences over what to conclude about something knowable but not conclusively known to either intelligence or policy professionals.

On the issues that give rise to major tensions, first, there are gaps in information because of secrecy and collection limitations. Second, the available evidence reflects a body of reporting parts of which are of questionable reliability and are contradictory and ambiguous. Concerning, for example, the dispute between CIA analysts and prominent administration officials over Saddam Hussein's regime's connection to the U.S. war on terror: What will history show the burden of the evidence to have been regarding the nature of Iraq's prewar ties to Al Qaeda terrorists—a minor or major threat to U.S. interests?

Regarding the meaning of inconclusive evidence, former CIA Director and Cabinet member William Casey (1981–87), in a dispute with analysts over the Soviet role in International terrorism, set forth his standard for keeping a policy-sensitive issue on the table: "Absence of evidence is not evidence of absence."[3] In effect, if a development or relationship is plausible, analysts cannot prove a negative to the satisfaction of officials with minds and agendas of their own.

In disputes with analysts about the meaning of inconclusive evidence, policy makers can insist on raising as well as lowering the bar of proof regarding judgments that could have a negative impact on their agendas. Once, when an analyst averred that reliable evidence had become available that indicated a suspected development that undermined an administration policy initiative was "almost certainly taking place," a policy critic retorted that the analyst "couldn't get a murder-one conviction in an American court with [his] evidence."[4]

THE CRITIC'S CHALLENGES TO DI TRADECRAFT

Policy officials have been generous in spelling out the elements of their criticism of Agency analysis. In doing so, the officials at times were motivated principally to improve the quality of support they receive for the demanding task of policy analysis and implementation. At times, the motivation also included an effort to defang or discredit politcally unhelpful assessments. And at times the objective was to shape an intelligence deliverable into a tool that would lend political support to administration policy.

It is worth noting that policy officials who have been generally complimentary of the analyst's performance as well as those long dissatisfied with performance table similar criticisms.

Part of the analyst–policy maker tension in evaluating evidence reflects a difference in professional attitude toward odds. To an analyst, the judgment that the evidence indicates that a development favorable to U.S. interests is unlikely usually means the odds against the existence or emergence of the development at issue are roughly 4 to 1. Given such odds, the busy analyst as a rule is ready to go forward with his or her assessment and move on to the next assignment.

In contrast to a policy maker with an agenda to advance, the same starting odds of roughly 1 in 5 can make it promising as well as politically necessary to stay on the case. Moreover, on politically important issues the official will not overlook the prospect that the analyst's pessimistic judgment could be off base because, first, they are insufficiently informed about the current state and potential fluidity of foreign forces at play, and, second, because do not appreciate the impact on developments of U.S. carrots and sticks, if a policy initiative gathers backing.

The reluctance of critical policy officials to rely on what they see as unhelpful assessments on issues important to an administration goes beyond professionally necessary "positive thinking" on their part. Critics also point out what they see as systemic weaknesses in the analyst's tradecraft (i.e., analytic methodologies).

First, since cognitive bias is pervasive, analysts, like all observers, tend to see more quickly and vividly what they expect to see and, conversely, tend not to see and properly credit information that would undermine their prior judgments. Critics contend that analysts delude themselves if they think they are exempt from this so-called confirmation bias because of their claims to "objectivity."

Critics have made this point over the decades in defending requests that analysts take another look at their interpretation of the evidence regarding the rate of success of the strategic hamlet program in Vietnam (1960s), the seriousness of Soviet plans for winning a nuclear war (1970s), the battlefield successes of U.S.-backed insurgents in Nicaragua (1980s), and after September 11, 2001, the significance of Iraqi-Al Qaeda connections to the war on terror.

The analyst's phrase "we have no evidence that *X* exists" is judged particularly unhelpful by those officials dedicated to either blunting the threat or seizing the policy opportunity in question. The critics note that analysts rarely admit they have no evidence that *X* does not exist. Besides, one critic averred, "policy-making is not [done] in a court of law."[5] A similar criticism is that analysts are too tied to the specific reports that reach their "inbox" and do not take sufficient account of the inherent aggressiveness, ruthlessness, and duplicity of U.S. adversaries.

Policy-making critics also complain that analyst training and incentives place too much emphasis on "straight line, single outcome" analysis on complex and uncertain issues. Critics say this "make the call" approach is both unhelpful to sound decision making and prone to error.

Former Deputy Secretary of Defense Paul Wolfowitz, long a critic of Agency analysts, observed in an interview conducted in 1994 that analysts' assertiveness in the face of uncertainty can turn an Agency assessment on complex issues into a weapon for one policy-making camp to use against another. In contrast, by tabling alternative interpretations, analysts would provide a tool useful to all participants in policy debates and decision making.

Further, the critics aver that, especially when policy stakes are high, analysts should expend much more effort evaluating what they don't know and why they don't know it before issuing estimative judgments downplaying dangers on which policy officials are focused. For example, could gaps in information that lead analysts to discount the likelihood of potentially harmful developments of concern to U.S. officials be caused by denial and deception (D&D) operations, or inadequate U.S. collection, or flawed assumptions about which pathways and relationships an adversary is pursuing to effect the feared development?

The 1999 report of a commission chaired by the former Secretary of Defense Donald Rumsfeld, after noting past intelligence failures on timely detection of foreign ballistic missile developments, cautioned analysts not to be quick to conclude that absence of evidence indicated absence of vigorous weapons programs by potentially hostile countries. The report, instead, charged analysts with pursuing alternative plausible explanations for "particular gaps in a list of [program] indicators."[6]

In truth, policy officials may prize the analyst who can come quickly to a crisp conclusion on issues surrounded by uncertainty that supports their agenda. But policy officials who see CIA judgments as obstacles to their agenda are themselves quick to connect the make-the-call culture to the analyst's record of analytic failures from the Cuban missile crisis to the Iraqi invasion of Kuwait.

Perhaps most important, according to the critics, it is the duty of responsible policy officials to ask probing questions; to insist on critical review of the evidence; to send analysts back to the drawing board for another look; in effect, to pull any loose thread in an unhelpful intelligence assessment.

Secretary of Defense Rumsfeld in his October 24, 2002, press briefing referred to the importance of engagement and criticism: "to the extent there's no feedback coming from . . . a user of intelligence, then one ought not expect that the level of competence . . . on the part of people supplying the intelligence will be as good . . . as if there's an effective interaction."[7] Granted, political overtones often color these criticisms. But in tradecraft terms they represent reasonable standards for policy officials to levy on analysts charged with providing distinctive value added to U.S. policy-making efforts.

DEFINING PROFESSIONAL AND UNPROFESSIONAL ANALYSIS

The doctrinal basis for a response to criticism by administration officials should reflect definitions of professional and unprofessional standards for intelligence analysts as agents both of the national interest and of the policy-making process. Thus, a definition of analytic professionalism should posit as equally important standards both *objectivity* (defined as tough-minded evaluation of evidence and other sound analytic practices) and *utility* (defined as distinctive data and insights policy officials find useful for managing threats to and opportunities for advancing U.S. interests).

Neither objectivity without utility, nor utility without objectivity, would meet the test of the author's following definition: The mission of intelligence analysts is to apply in-depth substantive expertise, all-source information, and tough-minded tradecraft to produce assessments that provide distinctive value-added to policy clients' efforts to protect and advance

U.S. security interests. The analyst's long-held standard of analytic objectivity has helped to promote an institutional ethic of pursing independence from all biases, including policy and political influences, in making judgments in the face of substantive uncertainty. But studies, including those commissioned by the Agency, indicate that *substantive biases* (experience-based mindsets) are all but essential for effectiveness in an environment of high-volume production and tight deadlines. In such circumstances, the effect on production of an "open mind" is akin to the burden of an "empty mind." In addition, *cognitive biases* (especially seeking confirmation for experience-based assumptions amidst inconclusive evidence) in effect are hardwired mental traits.

Pursuit of the defined mission regarding objectivity, then, comes down to an effort to minimize bias by critical review of the assumptions driving the analyst's mindset and of the adequacy of the available evidence to draw any meaningful judgment, and, if so, the content of the judgment.

Also to fulfill the defined professional mission, analytic deliverables must be seen by policy officials to have utility as they define their professional agenda, which, as previously indicated, is to posit and enact an administration's politically colored policy agenda. The analysts who would produce an assessment with high potential for utility to the policy-making process can no more ignore the political context in which their clients operate than they can ignore where the latter are on their learning curves (e.g., how much background information is needed) and decision-making cycles (e.g., planning stage or implementation stage).

To take account of the politics of policy making is not a license for intelligence professionals, as analysts, to become policy makers, or their speech-writers or spear carriers. But if an analyst is not close enough to the process to feel the political pressures affecting policy making, he or she probably is not close enough to produce professionally crafted deliverables that provide distinctive value added.

Thus, there will always be a danger that analysts, in constructing their written assessments and oral commentary, will introduce a policy or political slant—either deliberately or through disregard of analytic standards. Analysts have done so in the past, and likely will do so from time to time in the future.

A politicized and therefore unprofessional assessment can be defined as an analytic deliverable that reflects either (1) the analyst's motivated effort to skew building-block assumptions, evaluation of the

evidence, and bottom-line judgments to support—or oppose—a specific policy, political entity, or general ideology, or (2) a conspicuous disregard for analytic standards that produces unmotivated but similarly distorted outputs that could affect the policy-making process.

From the policy makers' agenda-oriented perspective it makes little difference whether what they see as analytic bias is motivated or unmotivated. One senior official, for example, complained that every assessment that indicated or implied that an administration initiative was flawed constituted analytic policy making, because it provided ammunition for Congress to oppose funding the initiative.

As long as policy-makers' criticism of the objectivity, soundness, or utility of analysis reflects a legitimate tradecraft concern, they are not necessarily putting pressure on analysts to engage in unprofessional behavior. Policy officials have the license to change the intelligence question in search of insights in addition to those embedded in the analyst's initial assessment, to ask that assumptions and evidence be examined more thoroughly, and to request customized follow-on assessments. That is part of their job description, whether they are seeking fresh insights or analytic support for their established views.

Thus, it is not unprofessional behavior for analysts, on their own or when requested, to provide assessments that set out to make the case for an alternative view to their unit's agreed interpretations of ambiguous evidence of ongoing developments and estimative projections of complex trends. The only professional requirements are that such efforts at, say, devil's advocacy, be clearly labeled and vested with appropriate analytic standards for crafting a challenge to the mainline views on an issue embedded with substantive uncertainty.

Additionally, it is not unprofessional behavior for an analyst, when requested to address matters clarifying tactical policy options for dealing with specific threats to and opportunities for an established general policy. The key to sound "action" or "implementation" analysis is for the analyst to identify plausible initiatives and evaluate them in cost-benefit terms, and for the policy makers to choose what course to pursue and bear responsibility for their decisions.

Finally, for a manager to tighten tradecraft standards on a politically sensitive policy issue before an analyst's assessment goes forward under a corporate DI seal is not necessarily a signal of unprofessional behavior. Painful to the analyst, yes. Politicization of his assessment, no.

Analysts and their managers and leaders must be vigilant in identifying, deterring, and decrying unprofessional assessments as herein defined; when engaged in analysis, they are and must remain intelligence professionals, not policy or political aides—or critics. If an analytic cadre is to deserve its vaunted organizational independence, it must be ready to hold its ground, in the name of the national interest, against pressures for politicization, no matter the source, the intensity, or the circumstances.

But analysts must also take seriously the "cry wolf" danger of levying charges of politicization whenever their authority to control the key judgments of an assessment is abridged.

More to the point, if ever teamwork must prevail over turf warfare and over the individual analyst's sense of entitlement to determine what "call" to make on a matter of substantive uncertainty, it is when the analytic corps is constructing assessments on politically contentious policy issues. Over the decades, many analysts who have made adjustments to initial assessments that maintained objectivity while enhancing utility have felt the sting of colleagues' unreasonable charges of politicization.

THE ANALYST'S RESPONSE TO POLICY-MAKER CRITICISM: BEST PRACTICES

The challenge for analysts, then, is to turn tensions to professional advantage by maintaining rigorous analytic tradecraft standards while enhancing the utility of their assessments to policy makers. Despite a popular reputation for flawed performance, CIA analysts regularly meet this demanding standard. To turn on its head an observation on policy success and failure attributed to President Kennedy after the 1961 Bay of Pigs debacle: Analytic failures draw a thousand critics; analytic successes are orphans.[8]

Call them "ground rules," call them "best practices," lessons can be learned from both failures and successes, and recommendations made for how analysts should respond to policy-maker criticism. The underlying concept behind the recommendations that follow is that analysts carry the heavier burden of managing tensions in policy-maker relations in a manner that advances the national interest. The main reason is that the policy-making camp is the more powerful of the two. Policy officials have many alternative sources to Agency analysts for information and insight, including their own staffs and departmental analytic organizations; the academic, research, and business communities; the media and the Internet. In contrast, Agency analysts have no comparable alternative market that would justify the large size of their cadre and high volume of production of assessments. Congress demands and receives a steady stream of oral briefings from Agency analysts but is rarely seen as an equal to administration officials as a client for written assessments.

The central theme of the recommendations is that analysts are professionally required to take the tradecraft elements of policy-maker criticism seriously, no matter how much they may perceive that the politics of policy advocacy also are at play. Analysts, thus, should respond to criticism with a reassessment not only of the argumentation and judgments of the original assessment but also of whether it provided utility or distinctive value for the policy-making community. The goal is to take tradecraft issues off the table, so to speak, in an effort to isolate and then defuse any politically motivated elements of policy-maker criticism.

First, become expert on the policy maker's world. Analysts should commit to learning as much about the U.S. policy-making process and their key policy-making clients as, say, a national security correspondent for a major newspaper or other media outlet is expected to command. Analysts, starting from year one, have to spend quality time analyzing how Washington works, warts and all, even if this slows down the pace of grasping how Baghdad, Beijing, or Buenos Aires work. In particular, analysts should understand their client's role as action officer as well as policy analyst. This investment will enable analysts to role-play the policy clients who have criticized an assessment, not to mortgage analytic integrity but to evaluate tradecraft performance through a different set of eyes.

Second, become accomplished at understanding and managing substantive uncertainty. Analysts are taught and are generally aware that their judgments on complex issues are based on thoughtful but fallible assumptions that in turn color their evaluation of fragmentary, contradictory, ambiguous, and otherwise inconclusive evidence. They have been cautioned about mindset and confirmation bias. Yet the norm is to rely on these powerful but vulnerable mental processes to get their assessments out under tight deadlines, and with a confident judgment.

Usually the resultant assessment holds up well against both the expectations of policy-making clients and the subsequent course of events. Usually, But what to do when a policy official conveys doubts or outright criticism?

Here, without being too quick to jettison original argumentation and judgment, the analysts should move from passive to active awareness of the limitations of their analytic craft. More active attention to the perils of analysis amidst substantive uncertainty entails taking a more thorough accounting of plausible alternative explanations and outcomes that were discarded or downplayed during the crafting of the assessment that drew criticism.

Casual re-examination of an assessment by its author and production unit to take the measure of alternatives at times is helpful, but the process of "talking about alternatives" is prone toward defense rather than critical evaluation of the original argumentation. More structured and externalized challenges to the assessment hold greater promise of fresh insights that either strengthen confidence in, or point to useful modifications of, the assessment that drew criticism.

Tested approaches to alternative or challenge analysis include devil's advocacy, key assumptions check, quality of information review, and argument mapping. A more experimental technique, known as analysis of competing hypotheses, tests which of several plausible explanations for a complex event or trend stands up best against a battery of relevant information.

Third, become adept at role-playing. At times, as indicated, analysts will be well positioned to prepare a professional response to criticism by undertaking an open-minded assessment of the *policy critic's paradigm* (i.e., mental model) on a contentious issue. However colored by political considerations it may at first seem to the analysts, deconstruction will help identify the critic's assumptions, evaluation of evidence, and calculations of likelihood. Once this information is at hand, the analysts may see a path toward revision of their own assessment that both protects objectivity and enhances utility.

Fourth, lean forward professionally with action analysis. Analysts should not hesitate to respond to criticism about unhelpful analysis by changing the question from the one they initially believed should be addressed to one policy critics call for—again a posssible path to both objectivity and utility. Often the shift, as previously indicated, is from what is the most likely interpretation of an event or relationship or the most likely future path of development, to depiction of the direct and indirect leverage the United States has to reduce dangers and seize opportunities.

In most cases, analysts can be professionally comforted by assuming savvy administration officials, despite a politically required public optimism, know their policy initiative is facing heavy obstacles, even before the CIA assessment elaborated the point. What is now in demand are intelligence insights for doing something about the obstacles.

An analyst once tabled an assessment that placed emphasis on the general political dynamics in country Z, including both domestic reform tendencies promoted by the United States and a deliberate show of independence from Washington on certain international issues. The word came back that the high-level U.S. official who had asked for the assessment "wanted to leverage the president of country Z, not love him."[9]

Fifth, master techniques for evaluating inconclusive evidence. More deliberate analyst attention to evaluating evidence on contentious policy issues is another promising avenue for stripping tradecraft complaints from policy-maker criticism of analytic performance. Careful consideration of alternative meanings of gaps in information, especially regarding suspected programs to develop weapons of mass destruction (WMD), can help build credibility with critics.

Analysts can organize and asssess what is known and unknown to determine, for existance, whether the gaps in expected indicators more likely represent limited U.S. collection and substantial D&D, an innovative approach to WMD development, or nonexistence of a concerted development effort. The aforementioned analysis of competing hypotheses is well suited to provide an externally structured (that is, minimally subjective) competition to see which explanation is the most and least compatible with available related information.

Sixth, use estimative terminology carefully. Analysts have a professional obligation in maintaining integrity while supporting the policy-making process to avoid compounding substantive uncertainty with linguistic confusion. This is essential to managing tensions on sensitive issues. To deter both misunderstanding and manipulation of judgments, analysts should avoid vague estimative phrases such as "real possibility" and "good chance." Though not without risk of an exaggerated precision, analysts should aim to set boundaries to key judgments (e.g., "we judge the likelihood of *development Z* to be low—on the order of 10 to 20 percent"). On controversial issues analysts should also avoid nonfalsifiable judgments such as "it is possible," "suggests that," and "according to reports." They should provide instead an evaluation of the authenticity, adequacy in terms of completeness and consistency, and significance of the evidence. And when no confident judgment can be made, analysts should say so directly.

As previously indicated, policy officials tend to stick to initiatives even against long odds. An assessment that calculates an estimated probability of a development at, say, roughly 80 percent is making transparent a roughly 1-in-5 prospect of being wrong. An assessment that develops the longshot case using plausible alternative assumptions and evaluations of the evidence, as well as the analyst's preferred 4-in-5 prospect can serve professionally to provide distinctive value added to policy-maker criticis without sacrifice of analytic integrity.

Seventh, be responsive to criticism but not at the cost of objectivity. As long as an analytic unit believes it has done its homework in evaluating evidence and in considering alternative explanations and projections, it should stand by its estimative judgments even if policy-maker criticism persists or intensifies. But the unit should also work to ensure continued access to and credibility with critical clients by varying the focus and perceived utility of its deliverables. Analysts should consider the following "1-3-1" approach to an issue of critical policy import on which they are engaged in producing nearly daily assessments.

- Once a week, issue an assessment that features a net judgment, whether or not the one favored by policy officials. Include a credible accounting of the impact of recent developments and reports.
- Several times a week, put the net judgment approach aside and employ action analysis to address tactical dangers and policy opportunities on which direct and indirect U.S. leverage could be applied.
- Once a week, change the question via the tradecraft of alternative analysis, in order for both analysts and policy makers to examine the issue from another angle, for example: *what-if analysis* (what policy makers would see, if the likelihood of development X increased), *risk-benefit analysis* (the adversary's estimated calculations affecting its motivation for and ability to engage in development X), and *if-then analysis* (implications of the advent of the high-impact, low-probability development regarding X).

Finally, what of the danger that analysts' efforts to curb their own substantive and cognitive biases will generate deliverables that provide unwarranted support to the clients' biases and political agenda while weakening respect for the production unit's professional judgment?

There may be no win-win answer to the vulnerability of unintended consequences of attempts at professional accommodation of the tensions attending policy-maker criticism of analysis. Policy makers, for example, have been known to tear off the cover page (literally and figuratively) explaining the main view of the analysts and the context for presenting an alternative view—and then citing the latter as the Agency's judgment.

But avoidance of the initiatives recommended above for professional accommodation of criticism and instead countering policy-maker exaggeration of certitude with analyst exaggeration will help neither camp. As a rule, a blending of deliverables that indicates an openness toward alternative interpretations with regular affirmation of what analysts believe to be sound, if vulnerable, judgments will protect analytic professionalism, maintain credibility with and access to the policy clients, and best serve the national interest.

Analysts and production units unsure of how to proceed when confronted with policy-maker criticism with political overtones should engage the Agency's Ombudsman for Politicization and other detached veteran practitioners for help in identifying the best professional response. Agency training courses that include case studies on managing tensions would also help prepare analysts and managers for their initial exposure to friction with their policy-maker clients.

Largely as a result of internal as well as external reviews of flawed analytic performance regarding judgments about Iraqi WMD arsenals and programs under the Saddam Hussein regime, many recommendations for dealing with criticism of analysis by policy officials similar to those outlined above have been adopted or reinforced as tradecraft doctrine by CIA's senior leadership. As this chapter was written (March 2006) the difficult tranformation from doctrine to practice was under way.

POLICY MAKER PREROGATIVES— AND THEIR LIMITS

The preceding two sections of the chapter addressed: (1) analysts' professional prerogative to stick to their best judgment after testing it for soundness, no matter the intensity of policy-maker criticism; (2) their obligation to mitigate tensions via alternative means of support to policy clients, such as action analysis; and (3) the breach of professionalism entailed in both deliberate and unintentional politicization of analysis.

What about the rights and wrongs of the admittedly more powerful policy-making camp? The national interest is best served when the two camps work together to combine sound intelligence analysis with sound policy analysis. That said when the two camps clash, what are the prerogatives of policy officials and what actions should be considered a breach of their professional obligations?

The questions and answers that follow are an attempt by the author, long an observer of the relationship but a member of the analytic camp, to set ground rules for policy officials that would enhance the benefits and temper the dangers of tensions in analyst-policy maker relations.

1. *Are policy makers entitled professionally to reach, publicize, and act upon estimative judgments that diverge from intelligence assessments on a national security issue?*

Yes. As indicated throughout this chapter, intelligence analysis, especially inherently fallible interpretative and predictive analysis, is an input to and not a substitute for policy analysis. Policy makers as analysts take account of other providers of information and judgment, and also bring their own, often considerable, experience, insights, and biases to the difficult tasks of policy formulation and implementation, for which they must take ultimate responsibility.

2. *Are policy officials professionally entitled to ask intelligence analysts to take another look at their estimative judgments (e.g., to review assumptions, evidence, and argumentation)?*

Yes. Policy makers are commissioned to devise, promote, and enact the president's national security agenda. They know when a policy consensus is taking shape and the time for action is approaching on issues, despite intelligence assessments that sound a caution. Yet officials, especially those with an appreciation for the distinctive role of intelligence analysis, hesitate to ignore intelligence findings and estimative judgments that call into question the underpinnings for U.S. initiatives. One response in these circumstances is to ask analysts to go back to the drawing board. Furthermore, from the point of view of the national interest, well-articulated

criticism of analysis is much preferable to inadequate guidance for the execution of intelligence deliverables and scant attention to the assessments once delivered.

3. *Are policy makers professionally entitled to urge analysts to review and revise their confidence levels in analytic judgments?*

Yes. For the same, usually healthy, reasons, one analyst or intelligence agency challenges another's conclusions on whether a shrouded current relationship or indeterminate future development is *nearly certain, probable,* or *unlikely,* policy makers may ask analysts to rethink their degree of confidence in a judgment. Once again, the answer assumes estimative judgments are inherently subject to error and that policy makers' criticism of analysis is more useful to sound performance than their ignoring of analysis. Needless to say, intelligence analysts are professionally bound to stick to judgments on probability that survive their critical review; and intelligence professionals must take care not to allow the pressure of a process of repeated requests for revision to move the bottom line further toward one supportive of policy than the analysts' tradecraft would justify.

4. *Are policy makers professionally entitled to ask analysts to provide well-argued alternatives to their studied bottom-line judgments (e.g., devil's advocacy)?*

Yes. Policy officials are at least as wary of the consequences of policy failure as analysts are of intelligence failure. They are professionally entitled to task analysts to use their skills and resources to present for consideration alternative or multiple views of a complex and uncertain issue. At times a call for, say, devil's advocacy may be a caution against the perils of groupthink, especially in cases in which policy makers agree with the analysts' judgments. At times the policy maker's motive will be to move Agency analysis to closer alignment with his or her own thinking. As long as rigorous analytic tradecraft norms are adhered to for whatever form of alternative analysis is solicited, and the analyst's preferred bottom-line judgment is firmly attached to the deliverable, intelligence professionals should welcome the opportunity for customized service to their policy making counterparts.

5. *Are policy makers professionally entitled to ask analysts to change the question they address (say, from whether a development is likely, to how it might occur)?*

Yes. Once an administration adopts an initiative, policy makers tend to move forcefully into their action-officer mode and have limited interest in analysts' views, based on the latter's reading of the evidence, on whether the policy is likely to succeed, much less whether the policy was wise to undertake. Policy officials have a job to do—to make the policy work. They are professionally entitled to ask intelligence analysts to provide action or implementation analysis—that is, expert assessment of opportunities for moving the policy forward and of specific dangers to be avoided, taking account of insights into the adversary's strengths, weaknesses, and "game plan."

6. *Are policy makers professionally entitled to seek analytic judgments from sources other than CIA and other U.S. professional intelligence organizations?*

Yes. No matter how strongly intelligence professionals would prefer otherwise, policy officials, in pursuit of their policy-making and political goals, have a right to rely on whatever sources of information and insight they choose, either to supplement or to substitute for the support they get from intelligence professionals. This includes use of business, academic, and other nongovernmental sources; their own staffs, whether configured as a policy-making or intelligence unit; and also, as has happened, foreign intelligence services. Policy makers, in short, are entitled to reap the benefits of as complete and varied a set of substantive inputs as they can command as they undertake the arduous task of managing an uncertain and often perilous national security issue. If policy makers use different sources of analytic support simply because they want more cordial answers than those provided by intelligence professionals, then the policy officials must bear the burdens of self-deception, policy failure, and political censure when such outcomes prove to be the case.

7. *Are policy makers professionally entitled to attribute to intelligence analysts judgments that overstate or understate analysts' confidence levels?*

No. Once a studied, clear, and (if challenged) revisited statement of likelihood regarding a development, relationship, threat, or opportunity is established by Agency analysts, policy officials can attribute it to intelligence in order to buttress their own views, or reject it in favor of their own alternative statement of likelihood. But they do not have the

authority to attribute to intelligence professionals an estimative judgment the latter do not hold.

8. *Are policy makers professionally entitled to force analysts to alter their best estimative judgments?*

No. As already acknowledged, policy officials are entitled professionally to reject intelligence assessments and reach and promote their own estimative judgments (Question 1, above), and are also entitled to urge analysts to rethink and recast Agency intelligence judgments (Question 3, above). That clarified, under no circumstances are policy officials professionally entitled to force intelligence analysts to change estimative judgments. Obviously, there are risks to treating as inviolate intelligence judgments that are contrary to policy preferences. Events may prove the analysts to be wrong. Congressmen may complicate the funding and execution of an administration's strategy and tactics by using intelligence findings and estimative judgments to block or modify policy initiatives. Unauthorized leaks to the media of intelligence positions may create an untimely public debate over policy. These circumstances can cause a run-up in immediate costs ranging from embarrassment of the administration to the thwarting of what history may judge to have been a sound policy initiative. But the long-term costs to the integrity and morale of intelligence professionals of forcing them to change their judgments will likely cause much greater harm to the national interest by weakening a vital arm of the national security establishment.

9. *Are policy officials professionally entitled to use the media to criticize intelligence analysts' competence, in an effort to protect an administration from congressional and public criticism of a policy initiative?*

No. As argued in this chapter, policy officials are entitled, indeed encouraged, to criticize through government channels either a specific body of analysis or intelligence tradecraft generally. Furthermore, as policy professionals, they are entitled to raise publicly their criticism of analysis as long as it is couched in analytic terms and is not, in effect, a politically motivated *ad hominem* attack. That is, as policy professionals, they are not entitled to criticize publicly a careful body of intelligence work and the credentials of the analysts who produced it merely to relieve themselves of the burden of credible defense of their own contrary judgments. In principle, nearly all parties to the uniquely American system for making national security policy proclaim the value of maintaining the integrity of intelligence analysis. A practice of trying to leverage a congressional vote or public debate on a policy initiative by criticizing the credentials of analysts who produce uncongenial analysis undermines the principle.

10. *Are policy officials professionally entitled to apply pressure on Agency leaders to remove from a production unit a manager or analyst responsible for assessments with judgments policy makers see as biased, wrong, or otherwise unhelpful?*

No. Analysts and their managers should be judged by Agency leaders solely in terms of professional credentials and adherence to analytic tradecraft norms, including good-faith efforts to respond to tradecraft criticisms by policy officials through the various means outlined earlier in this chapter (e.g., key assumptions check, devil's advocacy). The challenge of reaching sound analytic judgments amidst the perils generated by substantive complexity and uncertainty should not be compounded by a requirement for "political correctness" or fears about job security.

11. *Are policy officials professionally entitled to request Agency analysts to engage in policy advocacy, for example, to produce a "white paper" that is released as an intelligence product?*

No. Agency analysts may assist by providing information for the production of a white paper, but this and other formats of policy advocacy must be issued under the seal of a policy-making department or staff. The role of Agency analysts is to provide analytic support to policy planning and implementation by administration officials—and not to make, advocate, or criticize policy. Again, the long-term importance to the national interest for Agency analysis to be and be seen as a source of substantive objectivity as well as policy utility far outweighs any short-term political advantage gained from using an adulterated form of intelligence analysis to gain public or congressional support for a policy initiative.

CONCLUDING THOUGHTS

What about enforcement of these or any other set of ground rules aimed at moderating tensions in analyst–policy maker relations? U.S. experience has shown that presidents and their inner circles from time to time will play by their own rules. Agreed prerogatives and constraints and authoritative calls of "foul" might

nonetheless serve well over the long haul, if only to evoke second thoughts about ignoring a transparent set of rules for improving both intelligence analysis and national security policy making.

Presidential administrations already have an instrument in place for monitoring the adequacy and quality of intelligence analysis, along with all other intelligence functions. The President's Foreign Intelligence Advisory Board (PFIAB) is well situated, both to help shape the ground rules and to monitor for analyst compliance. Over the decades, PFIAB members—former administration officials, members of Congress, and military and business leaders—collectively have commanded formidable knowledge about analysts and policy makers. And as a rule, PFIAB staff reports on analytic performance have been noted for both independence and insight.

For the Agency, the Ombudsman for Politicization has served since the early 1990s to educate new analysts about professional standards, to monitor for politicization, and to counsel analysts about the concerns they raise on the issue. Over the years, the Ombudsman, selected by and serving at the pleasure of the Director for Intelligence, has been a highly qualified former intelligence manager serving part-time as an independent contractor.

The following recommended changes relating to the Ombudsman are intended to strengthen both the educational and protection functions, including by participation in shaping ground rules and more active monitoring for compliance on the part of policy officials as well as intelligence professionals.

- Change the position name to Ombudsman for Analytic Professionalism (OAP). The professional obligations for analysts in the management of tensions involve more than the avoidance of policy or political bias.
- Provide the OAP with a small staff. The rise in importance to U.S. national security of countering weapons proliferation and terrorism—issues on which conclusive evidence will be a rarity—is likely to increase tensions over the meaning of available information and thus the demands on the OAP.
- To ensure the independence of and enhance analyst confidence in the OAP, have the newly instituted Director of National Intelligence nominate and Congress confirm the title holder to serve a fixed term of five years.
- To help hold policy makers as well as analysts accountable in their management of tensions, require the OAP to provide the intelligence oversight

committees of Congress with periodic reports on the compliance of both camps with agreed ground rules.

This chapter, by design, has mentioned Congress only briefly, although it is the third side of the triangle that constitutes the U.S. system for making and implementing national security policy. Yet for any set of ground rules for governing analyst–policymaker relations to have a lasting impact, Congress, on its own or in response to public demand, must take action to promote and monitor such an initiative. The goal, one last time, would be to ensure that the inevitable tensions between Agency analysts and administration officials are managed to the benefit of the national interest.

QUESTIONS FOR FURTHER DISCUSSION

1. Given their professional missions, why is there acrimony between analysts and policymakers?
2. Does a policymaker have the right to question analysts about their findings?
3. Should analysts ever make their estimates public to force policymakers to accept them?
4. Should policymakers have the right to alter questions put to analysts after receiving a discouraging estimate?

ENDNOTES

All statements of fact, opinion, or analysis expressed are those of the author and do not reflect the official positions or views of the CIA or any other U.S. government agency. Nothing in the contents should be construed as asserting or implying U.S. government authentication of information or Agency endorsement of the author's views. The material has been reviewed by the CIA to prevent the disclosure of classified information.

1. Quoted in "Rumsfeld on New DoD Intelligence Team," *Early Bird* (newsletter), Department of Defense (October 25, 2002), available at http://www.defenselink .mil/news/Oct2002/t10242002_t1024sd.htm.
2. Author's interview with Paul Wolfowitz, "Paul Wolfowitz on Intelligence-Policy Relations," *Studies in Intelligence* 39 (Langley, VA: Central Intelligence Agency, 1996).
3. Author's interview with CIA analysts present when the remark was made at CIA Headquarters, Langley, VA, in 1982, cited in Jack Davis, *Tensions in Analyst-Policymaker Relations: Opinions, Facts, and Evidence*, Occasional Papers, CIA, Kent Center 2 (2003), p. 3.

4. Comment made to the author in April 1980, CIA Headquarters, Langley, VA, cited in Davis, "Tensions," p. 3.
5. Author's interview with Paul Wolfowitz, "Paul Wolfowitz."
6. Intelligence Side Letter [to Congress and the Director of Central Intelligence], Report of the Commission to Assess the Ballistic Missile Threat to the United States (March 18, 1999).
7. Quoted in "Rumsfeld on New DoD Intelligence Team," *Early Bird.*
8. *Editor's note:* After the Bay of Pigs failure in 1961, President Kennedy observed, "There is an old saying that victory has a hundred fathers and defeat is an orphan," cited in Arthur M. Schlesinger, Jr., *A Thousand Days: John F. Kennedy in the White House* (Boston: Houghton Mifflin, 1965), p. 289.
9. Author's recollection of a 1973 incident, cited in Davis, "Tensions," p. 6.

NOTE ON SOURCES

The views on and of policy officials are based on remarks made at press conferences and in unclassified statements in reports by governmental commissions, media interviews, and discussion forums. Note, for example, the following publications that are available on the CIA website (http:// www.cia.gov). Note also, the unclassified source cited for the evaluation of and recommendations for analysts by the Missile Commission, chaired by Donald Rumsfeld.

BIBLIOGRAPHY

Armstrong, Fulton T. "Ways to Make Analysis Relevant But Not Prescriptive," *Studies in Intelligence* 46 (2002).

Davis, Jack. "[Ambassador Robert Blackwill] A Policymaker's Perspective on Intelligence Analysis," *Studies in Intelligence* 38 (1995).

———. "Paul Wolfowitz on Intelligence-Policy Relations," *Studies in Intelligence* 39 (1996).

Report of the Commission to Assess the Ballistic Missile Threat to the United States: Intelligence Side Letter [to Congress and the DCI], March 18, 1999.

The views on and of intelligence analysts and on the analyst-policy maker relationship generally are based on the following unclassified publications that, unless otherwise indicated, are available on the CIA website (http:// www.cia.gov).

Davis, Jack. *Analytic Professionalism and the Policymaking Process: Q&A on a Challenging Relationship*, Occasional Papers, CIA, Kent Center, Volume 2, No. 4 (2003).

———. "Combating Mindset," *Studies in Intelligence* 36 (1992).

———. *Improving CIA Analytic Performance: Analysts and the Policymaking Process,* Occasional Papers, CIA, Kent Center, Volume 1, No. 2 (2002).

———. *Improving CIA Analytic Performance: DI Analytic Priorities,* Occasional Papers, CIA, Kent Center. Volume 1, No. 3 (2002).

———. *Sherman Kent's Final Thoughts on Analyst–Policymaker Relations,* Occasional Papers, CIA, Kent Center, Volume 2, No. 3 (2003).

———. *Tensions in Analyst-Policymaker Relations: Opinions, Facts, and Evidence,* Occasional Papers, CIA, Kent Center, Volume 2, No. 2 (2003).

———. "Facts, Findings, Forecasts, and Fortune-telling." In *Intelligence and the National Security Strategist: Enduring Issues and Challenges,* ed. Roger Z. George and Robert D. Kline (Washington, DC: CIA, 2004).

Heuer, Richards J., *Psychology of Intelligence Analysis.* (Washington, DC: CIA, 1999).

11. TRIBAL TONGUES: INTELLIGENCE CONSUMERS, INTELLIGENCE PRODUCERS

MARK M. LOWENTHAL

Lowenthal suggests that the bureaucratic cultures of the policymaking and intelligence communities often form a significant barrier when it comes to the relationship between the consumers and producers of intelligence. Both policymakers and intelligence professionals are preoccupied with the demands of their own positions and tend to believe that their motivations and objectives are shared by everyone. "Tribal Tongues" offers many insights into the way policymakers and intelligence professionals view the real world around them.

In the aftermath of the Cold War and the Gulf War there has been much soul-searching in the executive and Congress concerning the organization and role of the intelligence community: How should it be organized? Which issues should it be covering? What are the emerging issues that should be addressed now? These are of course important questions. But they tend to by-pass more fundamental issues within the intelligence community that are of a more permanent—and thus, perhaps—more important nature because they deal with how the community functions and fulfills its role on a daily basis. One of these is the relationship between the intelligence consumers and the intelligence producers.

Most analyses of the U.S. intelligence process pay lip service to the consumer-producer relationship. Although occasional serious forays on the subject exist, such as Thomas Hughes's *The Fate of Facts in the World of Men*,[1] most either ignore or downplay the importance of this relationship as a significant shaper of intelligence *throughout* the so-called intelligence process, starting with collection and ending with its final consumption.

A major problem is that the consumer-producer relationship resembles that of two closely related tribes that believe, mistakenly, that they speak the same language and work in the same manner for agreed outcomes. Reality, when viewed from either perspective, suggests something wholly different. Indeed, one is often reminded of George Bernard Shaw's quip about Britons and Americans being divided by a common tongue.

WE ALL WANT THE SAME THING

Most policymakers (i.e., consumers) work on the assumption of basic support throughout the government for their various policy initiatives, including support by the intelligence community. The first problem lies in the very word *support*. For policymakers, this means a shared and active interest and, if necessary, advocacy. This runs counter, however, to the intelligence community's long-standing position not to advocate any policy. Rather, the intelligence community tends to see itself, correctly or not, as a value-free service agency, although at its upper levels the line begins to blur.

Second, the intelligence community, like all other parts of the permanent government bureaucracy, has a "we/they" view of its political masters. The intelligence community is part of the *permanent* government; those making policy are politically driven *transients*, even when nominated from within the professional ranks of agencies. Indeed, with the exception of the uniformed military, nowhere else in the entire foreign policy and defense apparatus can there be found as many career officials at such senior levels as in the intelligence community. They can sometimes be found at the level equivalent to deputy secretary and clearly predominate at and below the level equivalent to assistant secretary.

Compounding this professional versus political, "we/they" conflict is the fact that consumers can and do advocate policy initiatives that run athwart intelligence community preferences. For example, the political demands for visibly intrusive arms-control monitoring methods, regardless of their minimal contribution to verification, pose real dangers for counterintelligence. The need to go public with information in order to justify policy initiatives or to brief foreign officials in order to build international support for policies often poses dangers to intelligence sources and methods. Such confrontations must often be resolved at the cabinet level and, although there will be some cutting and pasting to accommodate intelligence concerns, the overall policy will generally prevail. This is as it should be within the U.S. system of government. At the same time, it deepens the "we/they" syndrome.

Finally, the two groups have very different interests at stake. A successful policy is what the consumers were hired to create and execute. The intelligence community's reputation however, rests less on the success of any policy than on its ability to assist in the formation of that policy and to predict potential outcomes—both good and bad. The producers are only vulnerable if the policy is perceived as failing because the intelligence support was in some way lacking. Ironically, the intelligence community is rarely given credit if the policy succeeds. In part, this is a self-fulfilling outcome given the distance the producers cultivate from the process; in part, it is the natural bureaucratic phenomenon of scrambling for honors.

THE VALUE OF A FREE COMMODITY: PRICELESS OR WORTHLESS?

Intelligence products arrive in the consumers' limousines, pouches, and in boxes every morning and evening. They are part of the established routine. These products are, for their readers, basically cost-free subscriptions that were never ordered and never have to be paid for, perks of the job. High-level policy consumers have no real sense of either budgetary or mission/manpower cost to their departments or agencies for the very existence of these products, even if some of the products come from entities that they control. Thus, the secretary of defense will rarely be faced with a significant trade-off between required intelligence programs for the Defense Intelligence Agency and the National Security Agency versus next year's weapons procurement, nor will the secretary of state have to juggle the Bureau of Intelligence and Research's budget against prospective embassy closings.

Intelligence production, for the consumers, exists somewhere beyond their ken, as if unseen gnomes labor to produce the papers that magically arrive. If the analyses are good, all the better; if they are not, consumers are unlikely to advocate redirecting some of their resources to improving them.

Moreover, the very regularity with which these products appear has a lulling effect. The standard items—the *National Intelligence Daily*, the *Secretary's Morning Summary*—are essentially newspapers. Anyone who has read yesterday's edition or watched last night's 11:00 p.m. news can predict what is likely to be covered in this morning's edition. Indeed, while these publications are all lumped together as part of the "current intelligence" emphasis of the intelligence community, in reality they represent items that can safely be given to customers the next day. They are not urgent warnings or long-awaited breakthroughs, items that scream "read me now." Rather, they are part of the daily routine.

To break through this lulling effect, intelligence has to be able to prove to its consumers that it brings "value added" to the steady drone of information, analysis, and opinion that comes from both within and beyond the intelligence community. But one bureau or agency's memo looks much like another's, unless you bother to read them and assess them. How do you assure that, if only one will be read, it's yours? In reality, the unstated value added that intelligence producers bring is their sources. But, for very good reasons, raw intelligence is rarely presented to consumers. The intelligence is given context and comment, analysis that again makes it look like everyone else's.

How does the producer break out of this trap? One way is simply packaging, designing products that *do* scream for attention when there is a truly important piece of intelligence or a fastbreaking event about which the producers know first. The second is establishing a track record, although this still depends on whether the consumer reads intelligence analyses and remembers who was right and who was wrong.

In the end, consumers incur no real and regular penalty for ignoring this daily flow of information. In managing their day, high-level consumers establish methods to cut down on reading extraneous material. At the very highest levels, a large portion of daily intelligence products probably falls into this category. These consumers assume that their subordinates will read what they must within their areas of responsibility and that truly urgent items will come to their attention.

CONSUMER BEHAVIORS THAT MATTER

In reality, the intelligence consumer does more than just consume. He or she is not some eager, expectant eye and mind waiting at the end of the intelligence process. The consumer helps set the agenda, from intelligence priorities, to collection, to format.

AGENDA

Consumers have their own sets of priorities and preferences, issues in which they are deeply interested, those in which they must take an interest by their nature, and those they would just as soon ignore. If they bother to communicate these preferences to the intelligence producers (a rare enough occurrence), and the producers respond accordingly, then the entire intelligence process has already been influenced. Although producers will not cease to try to cover all the issues that *they* believe are important, only those intelligence officers with a taste for abuse and a desire to be ignored will try to force these on an unwilling consumer. This can put producers in an awkward position, especially if the subject in question is one they feel quite strongly deserves attention. It can also run athwart the intelligence community's "warning function," namely, the requirement that it look ahead for issues—especially sleepers—that have the potential to become grave concerns.

COLLECTION

The most senior consumer, the president, can also determine what gets collected and what does not for reasons of policy beyond the preferences of the intelligence producers. The U.S. policy in the shah's Iran of having no contact with the mullahs,[2] or President Jimmy Carter's termination of U-2 flights over Cuba, both come to mind.

"WHAT DON'T I KNOW?"

To the producer, the ideal consumer is one who knows what he doesn't know. Unfortunately, this quality can be hard to come by. It is understandable that senior officials dislike admitting areas of ignorance within their fields of responsibility. Those who do, however, have a clear advantage, especially if they are willing to take steps, among them requested analyses and briefings, to remedy the situation. Similarly, it is important for the consumers to distinguish between what they must know, what they'd like to know, and what is simply enjoyable but unnecessary. Failure to do this well, and continually, can lead to one of two traps—either consuming too much time on some subjects or too little on others. Given the primacy of time management, this should be a crucial skill for the harried consumer. Once this skill is acquired, and its results communicated to the producers, it again establishes priorities and agendas.

DEALING WITH UNCERTAINTY

Neither producers nor consumers like intelligence gaps. At best they are annoying; at worst they can be both crucial and frightening. They do exist, however, and are often responsible for uncertainties in estimates and analyses. As strange as it may seem, such uncertainties appear to be very difficult to convey, at least in English. "If/then" constructions can become long laundry lists covering all the possibilities, without regard to likelihood; "on the one hand/on the other hand" often creates octopuses of sentences—too many hands spoil the analyses. The absence of an easily used subjunctive really hurts.

Unfortunately, consumers often interpret these very real problems of limited sources and uncertain outcomes as pusillanimity on the part of producers. "They have a best guess," consumers suppose, "they're just hedging so they won't be wrong." The inability on the part of producers to convey adequately the cause and nature of uncertainty and ambiguity tends to alienate a largely dubious audience.

"SHOOTING THE MESSENGER"

This consumer behavior is as old as recorded history—if the messenger brings bad news, kill him. Unfortunately, it still happens. The messenger is not killed; he is first berated and then, on subsequent occasions, ignored. In part this consumer behavior stems from the darker side of the "we all want the same thing" syndrome. Once consumers have figured out that they and their intelligence people do *not* all necessarily want the same thing, they become suspicious of the producers. Do they have their own agenda for their own dark reasons? If they are not actively supporting me are they working against me? Unfortunately, the delivery of "bad news," usually some piece of intelligence or an analysis that questions preferred or ongoing policies, fits this more paranoid view all too well.[3]

What, however, is the producer's alternative? Suppress the intelligence and risk having the consumer blindsided or even badly embarrassed, a sure blow to credibility? Better to err on the side of caution and risk opprobrium, knowing full well that this, too, can harm credibility. Either way, the outcome largely rests on the intelligence's reception by the consumers, on their maturity, experience, and willingness to be challenged by people who are not a threat to their policies.

THE CONSUMER AS ANALYST

Consumers are, by and large, a self-confident group. They have achieved fairly exalted and responsible positions through either the trial by fire of long professional careers or through the hurly-burly of private enterprise or partisan politics. No matter the route, they assume that it is not just connections and luck that have brought them to their current positions. This self assurance is all to the good, although it can lead to some aberrant behavior.

The first such behavior has to do with issues of long standing regarding which the consumer believes that he or she knows as much, if not more, than the intelligence analysts. Certainly, assistant secretaries of state for Europe, the Near East, and so on, are likely to have spent a large portion of their professional careers on these issues, and they probably know some of the key players in the region on a personal basis. Interestingly, the same perception eventually takes hold of senior officials dealing with Soviet issues, regardless of their previous experience. At least two factors are at work here. First, the long-standing nature of the U.S. rivalry with the Soviets lends an air of familiarity, whether deserved or not. Second, after about two years in office, the average secretary of state has met with his Soviet counterpart more than half a dozen times and probably feels he has greater insight into Soviet thinking than do "ivory tower" analysts who have only seen the Soviet Union from 150 miles up.[4] The recent upheaval in the Soviet Union and Eastern Europe may have tempered the first attitude, now that the familiar signposts of relations have gone. This probably results, however, in increased emphasis on the second attitude, the value of high-level, face-to-face contacts over analysis by those more remote from events.

For this type of reaction the "value-added" question becomes paramount. What can the producer bring to the issue that is new, insightful, and useful?

Here, the natural inclination, if not necessity, to hedge analyses works against the producer and only serves to reinforce the prejudice of the consumer.

The second "consumer-as-analyst" behavior manifests itself during those periods of intense activity usually misnamed crises. Suddenly, the premium for current intelligence rises dramatically; consumers will often cry out for the "raw intelligence." There is the sudden assumption that at moments like these, trained intelligence analysts will somehow get in the way, that they will, perhaps inadvertently, distort the incoming information. Ideally, the intelligence officers should resist, offering to come back in several minutes with some sort of analysis or context along with the raw intelligence. Quite simply, consumers are probably less well suited at these moments to serve as their own analysts. Their ability to assess objectively and dispassionately what is happening is usually inverse to the importance of the issue, its intensity, and the amount of time they have been dealing with it. This is not to say that consumers have nothing of analytical value to bring to the process, including during crises. They should not, however, act to cut off the contributions of professional expertise. At worst, they will get an alternative point of view that they are always free to reject.[5]

THE ASSUMPTION OF OMNISCIENCE

For the United States as a global power, it is difficult to find many issues or regions that are not of at least some minimal interest. For the consumer this translates into the erroneous assumption that somewhere in the labyrinths of the intelligence community there is at least one analyst capable of covering each issue that comes along.

The source of this assumption is most likely a conceit derived from the expectation that U.S. interests must be matched by U.S. capabilities, that intelligence managers must know that *all* bases should be covered. Interestingly, this runs counter to the often heard criticism (and accepted folk wisdom) that the intelligence community has traditionally spent too much time and effort on the Soviet target, to the disadvantage of less sexy albeit no less important issues.

Unfortunately, there is no safe way for the producers to correct the assumption of omniscience. The intelligence community is loath to admit that it is not true and is fearful of the criticism that will ensue if this is discovered. Yet, in a world of unlimited issues and limited intelligence resources gaps are unavoidable. How resources are allotted either to close or to allow gaps remains a murky process based on past experience and known or—more likely—perceived consumer interest. Too often this process degenerates into a debate over the size of the intelligence budget, raising the suspicion among consumers (and congressional overseers) that cries of insufficient coverage are in reality pleas for more resources that will be redirected to areas that the intelligence community sees fit. Were the producers, however, to address the issue forthrightly and ask consumers, say down to the assistant secretary level, for a list of issues that had to be covered and those that could be given shorter shrift, it is unlikely that they would get consensus. Here again the "free commodity" issue is at work, only now consumers would be asked to give up something that they had always received, even if they had never had any great use for it.

Inevitably, one of the issues that has long been considered below the threshold will suddenly require attention. With a little luck there may be an analyst somewhere who has at least passing familiarity with it. This is the moment when the producers hope to shine, to prove the "value added" they bring to the process. If they succeed, however, they also reinforce the omniscience assumption, which sooner or later will be found, painfully, to be false.

THE ABSENCE OF FEEDBACK

Intelligence consumers have neither the time nor the inclination to offer much feedback on what they are getting or not getting. This stems from several sources. First, the throwing of bouquets is not a habit in government nor should it be expected.[6] Second, there is rarely enough time. As soon as one problem is solved or crisis ended, it is time to move on to the next. But the absence of feedback enforces the producers' image of top consumers as "black holes," into which intelligence is drawn without any sense of the reception or effect. The result is to deny the producers any guidance as to how they are doing.

At the same time, it must be admitted that, despite calls on their part for feedback, many in the intelligence community are quite content with the status quo. They do not favor "report cards"; they fear that they will only hear the negative and not receive any praise; they are concerned lest feedback becomes a means by which consumers would try to affect the content of intelligence to elicit greater support for policies. None of this needs to happen if the feedback process is honest and regularized.

There also would be genuine benefits. The intelligence community is made up of analysts who largely enjoy their work and who believe, as individuals, that the issues they cover are worthy of attention. At the working level, however, they exist in relative isolation, without any reference point as to how well their work fulfills its purported purposes among the consumers. Analysts will continue to work on what they believe to be relevant and important unless or until consumers offer guidance as to preferences, needs, and style. In short, producers need to be told how best to shape their products and focus for the consumers, but the initiative for doing so remains with the consumers.[7]

Feedback is also an area where Congress, in its oversight role, can be helpful. Congress has, in the past, reviewed important policy issues for which intelligence was a major factor and has offered objective assessments of the quality of intelligence and the uses to which it was put by consumers. The Senate Select Committee on Intelligence, for example, offered a critique of the famous Team A– Team B competitive Soviet analysis and called the exercise worthwhile but flawed in its execution. This same committee also found that President Jimmy Carter's release of Central Intelligence Agency analysis of Soviet oil prospects was largely driven by his own political needs.[8] Similarly, the House Permanent Select Committee on Intelligence offered a scathing review of intelligence on Iran prior to the fall of the shah. The same committee's review of intelligence prior to the Mariel exodus from Cuba concluded that U.S. surprise on that occasion was not due to lack of intelligence warnings.[9]

Such a service is quite useful and can be done by Congress objectively and without partisan rancor. However, the two Select Committees on Intelligence also have limits on their time and cannot provide this sort of review regularly. Congress is an intelligence consumer as well, although it is not privy to the full extent of the analyses that flow to policymakers in the executive. Thus, Congress can supplement feedback from consumers but cannot fully substitute for it.

PRODUCER BEHAVIORS THAT MATTER

Just as the consumer does more than consume, the producers do more than simply collect, analyze, and produce. Their behavior also affects the product and the perceptions held by the consumers.

CURRENT VERSUS LONG-TERM INTELLIGENCE

All intelligence agencies, managers, and analysts are constantly tugged between the need for current intelligence and the desire to write longterm intelligence. Thomas Hughes portrayed the struggle as one of "intelligence butchers" (current intelligence, done in short, sharp chops of material) versus "intelligence bakers" (long-term intelligence, done in prolonged melding and blending). As cute as Hughes's model is, it gives the mistaken impression that the choice of which type of intelligence to emphasize lies with the producers. This tends not to be so. Rather, it is the very nature of how foreign and defense policy is handled by consumers that drives the choice. Intelligence producers claim not to be bothered by this consumer preference for current intelligence, but this too is not entirely correct.

Current intelligence (i.e., tonight, tomorrow, this week) will always dominate. That is the very nature of the U.S. policy process. It is very "now" oriented, creating a series of difficult choices among issues all crying for attention. Indeed, there is very little sense of completion, because each issue laid to rest has too many successors waiting for attention as well. The drive of current events even tends to distort the notion of "long-term" analysis, which becomes the next ministerial meeting, the next arms-control round, the next summit, next year's budget process at best.

Much lip service is given by both producers and consumers to the need for long-term intelligence. Yet nothing in their daily lives indicates what use they would make of such intelligence if it existed. For consumers it would represent luxury items, things to be read when or if the press of current business allowed. For producers it would mean just a chance to be more wrong at a greater distance from the events—a constant concern.

Some will argue that the intelligence community already produces long-term analyses in the form of the National Intelligence Estimates (NIEs). But what is the function of the NIEs? In theory they represent the best judgment of the entire intelligence community on major issues, as conveyed by the director of central intelligence to the president. Some NIEs are done at the request of consumers, most often a fast-track or Special NIE (SNIE, pronounced "snee"). Other NIEs are done at the suggestion of an intelligence organization or are initiated by national intelligence officers, who perceive a need among consumers.

But beyond their impressive name and theoretical status, do NIEs really influence long-term policies? Or are they, in the scathing words of the House Permanent Select Committee on Intelligence, "not worth fighting for"?[10] It is difficult to find many NIEs that have substantially influenced ongoing policy debates. Various intelligence agencies participate earnestly in the NIE game largely to keep track of their brethren and to preserve their own points of view. NIEs are important simply because they exist and not because of any great value that they regularly add to the process. More often they serve either as data bases for budget justifications (in the case of the annual NIE on Soviet programs) or as the source of self-serving and often misleading quotations for use by consumers during policy debates.

Although both producers and consumers constantly cry out for more long-term and less current intelligence, it remains unclear that the outcry has any substance beyond a general and unsubstantiated belief that, if it were produced, long-term intelligence would give greater coherence to policy.

PORTRAYING UNCERTAINTY

One of the most difficult problems that producers face on a daily basis is the need to portray uncertainty. Every issue that is analyzed has gaps, unknown areas, competing plausible outcomes. As much as producers would like to be able to predict with finality, they both know that it is rarely possible and tend to write so as to cover, at least minimally, less likely outcomes so as not to be entirely wrong.

Portraying this in writing can be difficult. In the absence of a widely used subjunctive tense, producers use other techniques: "perhaps, although, however, on the one hand/on the other hand, maybe." There is nothing intrinsically wrong with any of these, although their net effect can be harmful for several reasons.

First, their use becomes habitual, creating written safety nets that allow the producers to keep all their bets covered. Second, and perhaps more important, they strike the consumer, especially with repetition, as "weasel words," efforts by the producers to avoid coming down on one side or another of any issue.

Producers do not spend enough time or effort explaining why these uncertainties remain. Consumers, being thus uninformed, tend to revert to their omniscience syndrome and see pusillanimity instead.

THE PERCEIVED PENALTY
FOR CHANGING ESTIMATES

Producers do not like to be wrong, but they realize they are fallible. They also, however, do not like having to make changes in estimates, fearful of the cost to their credibility with the consumers. Wide swings are especially anathema; better to adjust one's estimates gradually, to bring the consumers along slowly to the new view. Thus, if for years the estimate has said "*T* is most likely," and producers now believe that "*Z* is most likely," few will want to jump directly from *T* to *Z*. Instead, they would rather move slowly through *U, V, W, X* and *Y,* preparing the consumer for the idea that *Z* is now correct.

In this case, the perception may be worse than the reality. Most consumers, if properly prepared as to why there is a change (new data, new sources, new models, and so on), are likely to accept it unless changes become so regular a phenomenon as to raise serious questions.[11] Again, it is largely an issue of communications, of adequately explaining the uncertainties inherent in any estimate and the factors that have led to the change. Unfortunately, the outcome is so dreaded that the process rarely takes place.

MIRACLES VERSUS SAINTS

One of the necessary premiums put on all intelligence writing (with the exception of some NIEs) is brevity. Less is more when dealing with overly busy readers. Unfortunately, this runs counter to the desire burning within nearly every analyst to tell as much of the story as possible, to give the reader background, context and, in part, to show off. (For example: "You can't really understand the FMLN insurgency in El Salvador unless you go back to the Spanish land grants of the sixteenth century." A plausible point, but not an analysis that any busy reader is likely to read.)

Analysts tend not to err on the side of brevity. It becomes, therefore, the task of the intelligence production managers to edit material down to a suitable length. Analysts must be admonished to "just tell the miracles, and not the lives of all the saints involved in making them happen."

The miracles versus saints problem, however, also poses a difficult managerial decision. Analysts cannot write about the miracles with any facility until they have mastered the lives of the saints. Managers therefore have to be flexible enough to allow their analysts the time to study, and even to write about the saints, if only for use in background papers sent to other analysts. But this time must not be allowed to conflict with ongoing demands for written products, including those about the very miracles in question. It's a tough call, but one that has a payoff later on.

JADED VERSUS NAIVE

Given a choice between appearing jaded or naive on a given subject, the average intelligence professional will choose to appear jaded at least nine times out of ten. No one wants to appear to be the new kid on the block. Instead, analysts act as though they have seen it all and done it all before. This is especially troublesome in group meetings with peers, where appearances matter.

What this means, in terms of analysis, is that few situations are treated as being truly new, regardless of their nature. But some situations *are* new or different and do require analysis that has not been done before. A nuclear power plant blows up catastrophically; the Chinese sell intermediate-range ballistic missiles; or the Soviet Union allows its East European satellites to remove their Communist governments. By taking the jaded approach analysts force themselves, first of all, to play catch-up to situations that are ongoing, having initially wasted time playing them down. Moreover, they allow themselves to appear less than perspicacious before their consumers and now must spend time explaining away their previous stance, for which there may be little justification beyond mind-set.

The fix here is apparently simple—approach issues with a more open mind. But how can this be implemented? It cannot be institutionalized or even easily taught. It largely depends on production managers who continually ask skeptical questions, forcing their analysts to rethink. It is not easy, but it is achievable.

"COVERING THE WORLD"

This is the producers' version of the agenda issue. At most times there will be more issues crying out for attention than resources available to cover them all adequately. Producers, however, do not want to let any one of these issues slip, in part out of concern that they will choose the wrong ones and not be ready if they become more important or if consumer interest is suddenly piqued. Interestingly, this behavior on the part of producers only reinforces the consumers' belief in the intelligence community's omniscience. Feedback from consumers is an essential ingredient in making choices. If this is absent, however, then the intelligence producers must decide, knowing they cannot cover everything. They must also be able to distinguish, which they sometimes do not, between issues genuinely requiring serious attention and those that do not. They may also find as noted earlier, that there are important issues that consumers do not want to address. Here, the producers are torn, their professional responsibilities and best judgment at odds with the political realities. Overall, producers tend to side with covering more than less.

REPORTING "NO CHANGE"

Although the intelligence community cannot cover everything, it does keep track of more issues than most of its consumers can or want to deal with. Because of the limits on space in written products and the consumers' time, much goes unreported. But a second filtering process also takes place. On issues that are not "front burner" but are still of some interest, analysts will choose not to report developments or, more significantly, the lack of developments. The absence of activity is taken to mean the absence of any need to report.

There is value, however, to reporting periodically (admittedly at long intervals) on these issues and nondevelopments. If the analysts or managers know that the Rumanian nuclear program is of interest but that nothing new has happened in the last six months, there is nothing wrong with reporting that to consumers. What is the effect of such a report? First, it shows the consumer that the producers are alert, that they are tracking areas of interest beyond the self-evident. Second, it allows consumers to check off that issue on their mental lists. They can assume, probably correctly, that the producers will alert them to any change. For the moment, they need not worry about it. There is, however, a cost to such reporting, in that it tends to reinforce the consumers' omniscience assumption. Still, the net effect remains a positive one, albeit infrequent.

THE ABSENCE OF SELF-ANALYSIS

This is the flip side of the absence of consumer feedback. Like everyone else in the government, intelligence analysts and officials are busy people. As soon as one crisis ends they move on to the next with very little reflection on what worked and what did not. Nor do they spend much time trying to sort out why certain analyses in certain situations work well and others do not, why warnings and indicators flag proper attention in some cases but not others, why the synergism of collection resources works for this topic or region and not for that.

Admittedly, genuine critical self-examination is difficult. The payoff for having it done more regularly, not by "outside" reviewers in the intelligence community but by the analysts and their supervisors themselves, is a much clearer insight into their institutional behaviors and processes that can greatly improve their work and their ability to serve the consumers.

CONCLUSION

The production and use or disuse of intelligence as part of the policy process is the net result of several types of mind-sets and behavior within and between two groups that are more disparate than most observers realize. Moreover, the disparity is more likely to be appreciated by one group, the intelligence producers, than it is by the intelligence consumers. As argued here, the consumers play a much greater role *throughout* the intelligence process and at all stages in that process than is customarily realized. Certain aspects of the gap between these two groups will never be bridged. Other aspects, like the issue of supporting policy, *should* never be bridged. Nonetheless, there remains much that can be done—even within current structures and processes—to improve communications between the two groups. The views expressed in this article are the author's and not attributable to any government agency.

QUESTIONS FOR FURTHER DISCUSSION

1. What accounts for the differences in perspectives between the permanent government and the political government?
2. What is the "value-added" problem faced by intelligence analysts and managers?
3. Why is it so difficult to correct a mistaken estimate?
4. How should the intelligence community report on "non-developments"?

ENDNOTES

1. Thomas Hughes, *The Fate of Facts in the World of Men* (New York: Foreign Policy Association, 1976).
2. See Gary Sick, *All Fall Down* (New York: Penguin Books, 1985), pp. 36, 64, 91, 104–105.

3. Needless to say, not all paranoia is unjustified. There have undoubtedly been instances in which intelligence analysts have tried to work against policies with which they disagreed. Most analysts, however, and certainly their senior supervisors know the severe penalty for being caught in such a compromising position and would most often prefer to avoid it, even at the risk that the policy will go forward. Most often, the cost to future credibility far outweighs the value of stopping one specific policy initiative.

4. During the first U.S.-Soviet ministerial meeting of the Bush administration, the deputy national security adviser, Robert Gates, who has spent a considerable part of his intelligence career as a Soviet analyst, was in Moscow for the first time. President Mikhail Gorbachev reportedly kidded Gates, asking him if the Soviet Union looked different from the ground than it did from satellites.

5. There is evidence that President George Bush, perhaps reflecting his past tenure as director of central intelligence, has a predilection for "raw traffic" and that he liked to sort out differences among reporting on his own without a sifting by lower-level analysts. See Andrew Rosenthal, "White House Aims to Sharpen Role in Panama Plots," *New York Times*, October 13, 1989, p. A-8; and Maureen Dowd, "2-Summit Plan Reflects Bush Style: Intense (Relaxed) Personal Diplomacy," *New York Times*, November 6, 1989, p. A-14.

6. Feedback is so rare that, when it occurs, the effect can often be comical. When one senior official noted his pleasure over a piece of intelligence analysis, the initial reaction among those responsible was, first, elation, quickly followed by doubts. Was this memo so good, they wondered, or was it that all of the others that received no such notice were so bad?

7. The President's Foreign Intelligence Advisory Board (PFIAB), a group of outside experts that reviews both intelligence analysis and operations, provides such guidance. It was PFIAB, for example, that suggested the Team A-Team B competitive analysis. However, PFIAB meets infrequently, reportedly once a month, and remains somewhat removed from the daily needs of producers. It cannot substitute entirely for direct producer feedback.

8. See Senate Select Committee on Intelligence, *The National Intelligence Estimates AB Team Episode Concerning Soviet Strategic Capability and Objectives and The Soviet Oil Situation: An Evaluation of CIA Analyses of Soviet Oil Production*, 95th Cong., 2d sess. 1978.

9. See House Permanent Select Committee on Intelligence, *Iran: Evaluation of U.S. Intelligence Performance Prior to November 1978*, 96th Cong., 1st sess., 1979, and *Cuban Emigres: Was There a U. S. Intelligence Failure?* 96th Cong., 2d sess., 1980.

10. See House Permanent Select Committee on Intelligence, *Iran*.

11. There have been cases, however, in which wide swings did hurt credibility. In the mid-1970s U.S. intelligence estimates of the portion of Soviet gross national product devoted to defense went from 6 to 7 percent in the mid-1970s to 10 to 15 percent, leading some consumers to question the validity of the new estimates as well. Critics in Congress suspected that the change was created to support the Ford administration's larger defense budget. See John W. Finney, "Soviet Arms Outlay May Be Bigger Slice of Pie Than Once Thought," *New York Times*, February 23, 1976, p. 13, and "U.S. Challenged on Arms Estimate," *New York Times*, March 8, 1976, p. 11. When the intelligence community repeated its estimate a year later, this threatened to discomfit the plans of the new Carter administration, which was in the midst of its review of Presidential Review Memorandum #10 on U.S. strategy. In drawing up PRM-10, Carter administration officials purposely excluded some of the premises that they saw driving the new estimates. See Hedrick Smith, "Carter Study Takes More Hopeful View of Strategy of U.S.," *New York Times*, July 8, 1977, p. A-1.

From Mark M. Lowenthal, "Tribal Tongues: Intelligence Consumers, Intelligence Producers," *Washington Quarterly* 15 (Winter 1992): 157–168. Reprinted by permission of the publisher (Taylor & Francis Ltd, http://www.informaworld.com).

12. THE NEED FOR POLICY GUIDANCE

ASPIN-BROWN COMMISSION

It is said that policymakers get the intelligence they deserve. Without specific requests from senior policy officials, the intelligence community is left to its own devices when it comes to selecting intelligence requirements and targets. As the Aspin-Brown Commission noted, the intelligence community is sometimes left without any guidance. This is especially the case when the National Security Council reconstitutes itself with the change of administrations; during this period, senior officials are diverted from their normal duties of conducting routine oversight and helping to establish desired intelligence requirements and targets. The Commission recommended dedicated committees, lodged in the NSC, to set long-term intelligence needs and to evaluate intelligence priorities periodically in the face of a changing strategic landscape.

Intelligence agencies cannot operate in a vacuum. Like any other service organization, intelligence agencies must have guidance from the people they serve. They exist as a tool of government to gather and assess information, and if they do not receive direction, chances are greater that resources will be misdirected and wasted. Intelligence agencies need to know what information to collect and when it is needed. They need to know if their products are useful and how they might be improved to better serve policymakers. Guidance must come from the top. Policymaker direction should be both the foundation and the catalyst for the work of the Intelligence Community.

The drafters of the National Security Act of 1947 understood the importance of such guidance in creating the National Security Council (NSC).[1] The NSC was created to coordinate the policies and functions of the departments and agencies of the Government relating to all aspects of national security, including the intelligence function.

Since then, each Administration has created its own structure and procedures to meet the policy objectives and management styles of the President and his senior advisers responsible for national security. Historically, intelligence information has made significant contributions to the substantive work of the NSC, whatever its structure; but where top-level guidance for intelligence requirements and policies is concerned, the role of the NSC and its staff has varied.

In some Administrations, formal NSC committees composed of cabinet-level officials have been established to provide guidance on intelligence matters. Such committees have been supported by a small professional staff within the NSC. In other Administrations, the national security advisor has delegated most intelligence issues to a senior member of the NSC staff. In some Administrations, the NSC principals and/or staff have taken an active and consequential role in providing guidance on intelligence matters; in others, they have served principally to coordinate the intelligence response during times of crises.

INTELLIGENCE AS AN NSC FUNCTION FROM THE NIXON ADMINISTRATION TO THE PRESENT

President Richard M. Nixon took office in 1969 and created an NSC structure shortly thereafter. Not until 1971, however, did his Administration create an "Intelligence Committee," one of the four top committees within the NSC responsible for providing policy guidance on national security issues. In addition, the NSC structure during the Nixon Administration contained a separate committee to approve and coordinate covert actions (the 40 Committee).

In 1975, the blue-ribbon "Commission on the Organization of the Government For the Conduct of Foreign Policy" (the Murphy Commission) reviewed this structure and found it largely ineffective. The Murphy Commission recommended that the NSC Intelligence Committee "should be actively used as the principal forum for the resolution, short of the President, of the differing perspectives of intelligence consumers and producers, and should meet frequently for that purpose."

In 1976, almost two years into his presidency, President Gerald R. Ford issued a new Executive Order on intelligence, abolishing the existing NSC structure on intelligence and creating in its place a "Committee on Foreign Intelligence" (CFI). This new Committee was composed of the Director of Central Intelligence, the Deputy Secretary of Defense for Intelligence, and the Deputy Assistant to the President for National Security Affairs. The Administration directed this committee to "control budget preparation and resource allocation" for national intelligence, as well as to establish priorities for collection and production. The Executive Order spelled out several specific tasks the CFI should accomplish, among them giving direction on the relationship between tactical and national intelligence and providing "continuing guidance to the Intelligence Community in order to ensure compliance with policy direction of the NSC."

This structure proved short-lived. President Ford remained in office less than a year thereafter, and his successor, President Jimmy Carter, immediately replaced the existing NSC apparatus with a two-committee structure consisting of a Policy Review Committee (PRC) and a Special Coordinating Committee (SCC). Depending upon the subject matter under consideration, the PRC would be chaired by, and composed of, different Administration officials, including the DCI when it addressed intelligence issues. The SCC was chaired by the National Security Advisor, and addressed the review and policy considerations of special activities, including covert action.

In 1978, President Carter provided more specific guidance on intelligence matters and issued a separate Executive Order on intelligence. It stipulated that the PRC, when dealing with intelligence matters, would be responsible for the establishment of requirements and priorities for national foreign intelligence, review of the intelligence budget, and the periodic review and evaluation of intelligence products. It was also charged with submitting an annual report on its activities to the NSC.

Three years later when he assumed office, President Ronald Reagan abolished the Carter NSC structure without creating a separate standing committee on intelligence, relying instead on a separate element on the NSC staff. He also signed Executive Order 12333, a broad statement of intelligence responsibilities and policies, which provided that the NSC "shall act as the highest Executive Branch entity that provides review of, guidance for, and direction to the conduct of all national foreign intelligence, counterintelligence, and special activities, and attendant policies and programs."

Later, as part of a reorganization of the NSC staff, a series of "Senior Interagency Groups" (SIGs) were created, one of which dealt with intelligence. Chaired by the DCI, the "SIG-I" was chartered to establish requirements and priorities for national foreign intelligence and review the program and budget for national intelligence as well as proposals for sensitive operations.

In 1989, President George Bush eliminated the Reagan NSC structure, and returned to a two-Committee structure, consisting of a "Principals Committee" and a "Deputies Committee." The Principals Committee was chaired by the National Security Advisor; the Deputies Committee, by his Deputy. A separate staff office coordinated intelligence programs.

Two years into the Administration, the NSC conducted the first in-depth review of intelligence requirements. The document that instituted the review, known as "National Security Review-29," noted that "senior policy makers traditionally have neglected their critical role in setting intelligence priorities and requirements." It produced a lengthy list of government-wide intelligence requirements, but it failed to assign priorities in a way that usefully guided collection efforts or the allocation of resources.

In 1993, President Bill Clinton took office. He retained the "Principals Committee/Deputies Committee" structure to coordinate major foreign policy issues and created a system of "Interagency Working Groups" to handle more routine issues. A separate staff office coordinated intelligence activities. In April, 1995, a new presidential directive was issued which, for the first time, stated in priority order what a President considered to be his intelligence requirements and established a working group of mid-level policy officials to review more regularly intelligence policies and requirements.

SHORTCOMINGS OF THE PAST

The Commission sees several shortcomings in the historical process described above. The institutional role played by the NSC in providing guidance and direction for intelligence activities has varied widely. Often substantial lapses occur at the change of Administrations when there is no guidance at all. As a result, a consistent level of guidance concerning appropriate roles for intelligence, as well as the guidance establishing requirements and priorities for collection and analysis, has, all too often, been missing.

In practice, the NSC's structures created to perform such functions often have foundered. Senior officials, such as cabinet secretaries or their deputies, who represent their respective departments and agencies at NSC-level meetings, usually have little or no background in intelligence and are inundated by the press of other duties. Intelligence is too often viewed as a support function that is "someone else's responsibility." Subordinates are increasingly sent to meetings in place of principals, and meetings become progressively less frequent. As a result, a true "consumer driven" intelligence process has never fully evolved within the NSC, regardless of the Administration in office.

The Commission believes the NSC as an institution should provide clearer guidance for intelligence, through regular tasking and a better organizational framework for handling intelligence issues. Several close allies visited by the Commission during its inquiry have effective mechanisms at the senior levels of governments to ensure that their intelligence agencies receive timely, ongoing guidance from the political level. In Great Britain, for example, a Cabinet-level office known as the Joint Intelligence Committee (JIC) brings together senior British policymakers and intelligence officials on a weekly basis. The JIC, functioning since 1936, is responsible for setting intelligence priorities on an ongoing basis, and for producing a weekly intelligence summary. Members include the principal producers and consumers of intelligence. While clearly the work and value of structures such as the JIC are facilitated where the government is considerably smaller than the U.S. Government and principally staffed by career civil servants, the Commission believes the concept embodied in the JIC can also be made to work in the United States.

WHAT NEEDS TO BE DONE

The Commission recognizes that every President must be free to use and structure the National Security Council as he or she sees fit, including the performance of its statutory role to provide direction to the Intelligence Community. From the Commission's standpoint, however, the particular structure decided upon by a president is less important than a clear and consistent understanding and implementation of the roles it should perform. Even when Administrations change, the functions of the NSC should not. Top-level direction to intelligence agencies would be greatly strengthened by a more institutionalized role for the NSC, one that is not rewritten every two or four years. The more the role of the NSC varies, the more difficult it is to develop and sustain working relationships that provide clear, frequent direction for intelligence and guidance for its collection and analytic efforts.

In the view of the Commission, the institutional role played by the NSC structure should include setting the policy guidelines for intelligence activities, stating what the intelligence agencies are expected to do and what they should not do. The NSC structure should clarify, for example, whether intelligence agencies should collect economic intelligence or analyze intelligence on the environment, whether they perform analysis of publicly-available information, and what rules should govern intelligence-gathering where allied and friendly governments are concerned.

The institutional role of the NSC also should include providing guidance for ongoing intelligence collection and analysis, to say what is needed and when, clarifying what is helpful and not helpful. What are the issues on the "front burner" for the President and other policymakers? What information would fill a void? On what subjects is intelligence adding little of value? Where does intelligence have access to information that would be of considerable value, but is not being collected?

It should also be the institutional role of the NSC (but not the NSC staff by itself) to assess, from time to time, the performance of the Intelligence Community in satisfying their substantive needs as policy makers, reporting its conclusions, as appropriate, to the President.

In the section that follows, the Commission proposes a two-tier NSC structure for carrying out these roles. It is intended as a model for this and future Administrations.

Whatever NSC structure may be adopted for intelligence, however, it must not interfere with the direct reporting relationship between the President and the Director of Central Intelligence, which must be preserved. The importance to the intelligence function of having a strong relationship between the

President and the DCI cannot be overemphasized. The Commission was consistently told by former DCIs that where their relationship was strong, it had repercussions across the entire Government, including the Congress, giving vitality and purpose to the whole enterprise. Conversely, where the relationship was weak, it took a heavy toll on the esprit and influence of the Intelligence Community.

3-1. The Commission recommends the establishment within the National Security Council of a "Committee on Foreign Intelligence" (CFI), chaired by the Assistant to the President for National Security Affairs and including the Director of Central Intelligence, the Deputy Secretary of State and the Deputy Secretary of Defense. The Chair should invite other senior officials to attend as may be appropriate given the meeting agenda.

The CFI should meet at least semiannually and provide guidance to the DCI for the conduct of intelligence activities, to include establishing overall requirements and priorities for collection and analysis. Appropriate NSC staff should formulate the agendas and supporting materials for these meetings, with NSC members and their staffs providing such assistance as may be required. The CFI should report annually to the President on its activities.

3-2. The Commission recommends that a "Consumers Committee" be established as a subordinate element of the CFI. This Committee should be chaired by the Deputy Assistant to the President for National Security Affairs and should include senior representatives at the Undersecretary level of the parent CFI members as well as senior representatives of other principal intelligence producers and consumers within the Government, e.g., the Secretaries of Commerce and Treasury, the U.S. Trade Representative. The Consumers Committee should meet at least monthly and provide continuous, ongoing guidance with respect to the priorities for intelligence collection and analysis to meet the needs of the Government. The Consumers Committee should monitor and periodically report to the CFI with respect to how well the Intelligence Community is meeting the needs of consumers, identifying gaps and shortcomings where appropriate. The NSC staff should be responsible for formulating the agendas and supporting materials for each meeting, with NSC members and their staffs providing such assistance as may be required.

The Commission opted for this bifurcated approach for several reasons. The Commission believes that the major overarching issues in the intelligence area are best left to a small group, consisting of the principal cabinet officers who are responsible for, and the users of, intelligence. The Commission believes such a group should be chaired by the National Security Advisor because he can approach the issues from the viewpoint of the President and has responsibility for coordinating national security matters on his behalf.

However, it is unrealistic to expect such a senior group to play an active role in setting ongoing requirements and priorities for intelligence-gathering and analysis. This function necessarily requires more frequent meetings and must be carried out at a lower level of representation. Membership should be at a high enough level so that the participant can represent the policies of his or her agency or department, but also at a level where the participant can be a regular attendee at the monthly meetings. Whoever may be designated, however, should have or be able to obtain a grasp of the overall intelligence requirements and priorities of the department or agency they represent.

The Commission believes that a forum outside the Intelligence Community (but including a representative of the Intelligence Community) should evaluate the substantive contributions made by the intelligence agencies. Hence, this role is suggested for the Consumers Committee. This is a function that the NSC has not performed in the past but is needed for the effective operation of the Intelligence Community.

Finally, the Commission does not contemplate that either the CFI or its subordinate Consumers Committee would perform oversight or management functions. The DCI would continue to report to the President and not to either of these committees. The function of both bodies would be to provide guidance to the Director of Central Intelligence and, through him, to the Intelligence Community as a whole. If disagreements arose which could not be resolved inside the NSC structure, each cabinet-level official would retain the right to appeal to the President.

THE PRESIDENT'S FOREIGN INTELLIGENCE ADVISORY BOARD

While not a part of the NSC structure, the President has another body at his disposal to provide advice on intelligence matters—the President's Foreign Intelligence Advisory Board (PFIAB). First created by

Executive Order in 1961, the PFIAB is charged with advising the President with respect to the quality, quantity, and adequacy of intelligence collection, analysis, counterintelligence, and other activities.[2] The PFIAB is also authorized to assess the adequacy of management, personnel and organizational arrangements in the intelligence agencies. Composed of private citizens, usually with some government experience, the number of PFIAB members has varied from one Administration to another.[3]

Historically, the PFIAB often has produced insightful and critical reports. Early boards were instrumental in analyzing and promoting the technical developments of the 1960s which revolutionized intelligence gathering. In the last several years, the PFIAB has looked at issues such as personnel practices within intelligence agencies and intelligence-sharing with multinational organizations.

The Commission supports the continuation of the PFIAB but believes that its role would be enhanced and its contributions more significant if it sought to perform functions that are not being performed elsewhere, either by the NSC or within the Intelligence Community itself. The Commission has noted in the course of its inquiry that very little thought is given by the Intelligence Community to the future, to finding creative technical or managerial solutions to the problems of intelligence or focusing on long-term issues and trends. By virtue of its membership, the PFIAB appears uniquely positioned to serve this function by bringing to bear the experience and expertise of the private sector and respected former government officials. Presidents must ensure that persons appointed to the Board have the qualifications necessary to perform this role and an adequate staff capability to support them.

QUESTIONS FOR FURTHER DISCUSSION

1. What are the problems that have troubled the National Security Council's effort to guide the intelligence community?

2. Do you think that the National Security Council should be the government organization charged with evaluating the intelligence community's support to policymakers? If not, who should?

3. What might account for the conclusion that intelligence managers rarely focus on the long-term trends and issues facing the intelligence community?

4. Do you think the risks of politicization will increase if the policymakers spend more time evaluating the usefulness of intelligence?

ENDNOTES

1. The statutory members of the NSC are the President, the Vice President, the Secretary of State, and the Secretary of Defense. Secretaries and Deputy Secretaries of other Executive departments may also serve on the NSC at the pleasure of the President. The present NSC includes the Secretary of the Treasury, the U.S. Ambassador to the United Nations, the U.S. Trade Representative, the Assistant to the President for National Security Affairs, the Assistant to the President for Economic Policy, and the Chief of Staff to the President.

    The Chairman of the Joint Chiefs is principal military adviser to the NSC and may attend and participate in NSC meetings. The Director of Central Intelligence also may attend and participate.

    The NSC is served by a staff headed by the Assistant to the President for National Security Affairs (who is often referred to as the National Security Advisor). The composition and organization of the NSC staff are left to the discretion of the President.

2. The PFIAB replaced an earlier "President's Board of Consultants on Foreign Intelligence Activities" that had been created by President Eisenhower in 1956. The PFIAB was disbanded in 1977 by President Carter but reconstituted by President Reagan in 1981.

3. The current Executive Order governing the PFIAB, E.O. 12863 (Sept. 13, 1993), limits membership to 16 individuals.

Reprinted from the Commission on the Roles and Capabilities of the United States Intelligence Community (the Aspin-Brown Commission), *Preparing for the 21st Century: An Appraisal of U.S. Intelligence* (Washington, D.C.: U.S. Government Printing Office, March 1, 1996): 29–35.

V

THE DANGER OF INTELLIGENCE POLITICIZATION

Hamlet: "Do you see yonder cloud that's almost in shape of a camel?"
Polonius: "By th' mass and 'tis, like a camel indeed."
Hamlet: "Methinks it is like a weasel."
Polonius: "It is backed like a weasel."
Hamlet: "Or, like a whale?"
Polonius: "Very like a whale."

—SHAKESPEARE, *Hamlet*, 3.2.378–384

Intelligence politicization is a complex phenomenon. The literature on intelligence suggests that politicization occurs when intelligence analysis is either deliberately or inadvertently skewed to give policymakers the results they want, not the unvarnished truth about the situation at hand. For intelligence analysts and managers, politicization is considered a mortal sin, a fundamental violation of their commitment to provide policymakers with honest answers and estimates. The U.S. intelligence community is supposed to be isolated from the political fray so that analysts and managers can tell policymakers the truth without fear of recrimination, no matter how unpleasant or politically damaging the truth might be to policymakers. The grand bargain within the intelligence community is that analysts will not meddle in politics and policy, and policymakers will not ask or force analysts to "cook the books" to guarantee that analysis supports their policy or political preferences.

Sherman Kent is the intelligence professional best known for championing this separation of intelligence analysis from policy. He was a historian in charge of the CIA's Office of National Estimates. In his writings, published in the immediate postwar period, Kent warned that it would be a mistake for analysts to get too close to policymakers because their analysis would inevitably be influenced by policymakers' political agendas. Above all, Kent (1949) argued that analysts have to maintain their objectivity if their estimates are to have any value. Intelligence professionals often champion Kent's view of the importance of analytical objectivity because it empowers them to pursue their intellectual and analytical interests to their logical—and sometimes even illogical—conclusions. Much in the same way that academic freedom empowers intellectuals to champion unpopular causes or to offer unpleasant observations about contemporary society, isolating analysts from policymakers allows intelligence professionals to set their own research agendas. From the viewpoint of intelligence professionals, Kent's emphasis on objectivity and analytical detachment makes perfect sense. After all, who is better able to set research agendas than analysts themselves?

Too much analytical detachment or too little interaction between analysts and policymakers, however, virtually guarantees that finished intelligence will fail to address the issues that fill policymakers' inboxes. Forced to focus on issues of immediate importance, policymakers simply ignore "academic" analyses (i.e., anything that fails to address the problems that preoccupy them). Repeated complaints that intelligence lacks relevance has led to calls for the production of "actionable" intelligence, estimates that policymakers will find useful in developing and executing current policy. This view is most closely associated with Robert Gates, a former Director of Central Intelligence. Gates and his supporters believe that relevance, not just objectivity, should govern intelligence production and that intelligence managers should shape finished intelligence so that it meets the needs of policymakers. According to those who embrace this perspective, intelligence managers, by interacting closely with policymakers and with a view of all intelligence assets, can create relevant finished intelligence from a variety of sources. The intelligence manager, not the analyst, would create the questions addressed in finished intelligence and sometimes even shape the answers. In a speech to analysts at the CIA in 1992, Gates explained what amounted to a revolutionary vision of the future of intelligence production:

> Unwarranted concerns about politicization can arise when analysts themselves fail to understand their role in the process. We do produce a corporate product. If the policymaker wants the opinion of a single individual, he can (and frequently does) consult any of a dozen outside experts on any given issue. Your work, on the other hand, counts because it represents the well-considered view of an entire directorate and, in the case of National Estimates, the entire intelligence community. Analysts . . . must discard the academic mindset that says their work is their own. (quoted in Betts 2002, 64)

It appeared to many analysts that Gates's vision of actionable intelligence guaranteed that intelligence would be politicized. If intelligence managers tailored intelligence analysis to meet policymakers' agendas, managers could be expected to generate a series of leading questions that would produce answers supporting existing political or policy preferences.

What is the correct balance between objective and actionable intelligence? How detached or engaged should analysts be in the policymaking process? These questions are generating much debate among academics, elected officials, and intelligence professionals. Although the most effective balance between these two positions depends on the issues at stake, the personalities involved, and the bureaucratic and political climate, it does appear that the debate itself becomes most acute at times of policy failure or when the intelligence community is out of step with changing political realities.

SOURCES OF POLITICIZATION

Although politicization can take a variety of forms, scholars focus on three ways in which the production of finished intelligence can be corrupted by undue policy or political influence. First, analysts can be directly pressured to emphasize findings that support the policies and preferences of officials or to ignore issues that could cause political or personal embarrassment. Sometimes this pressure comes in direct requests to support existing policy. Because they are viewed by most observers as inherently credible and not influenced by the wishes of officials, intelligence findings can be used to terminate political debate or to gain political support. Thus, this type of politicization is best viewed as corruption of the intelligence process because intelligence analysts are considered politically detached observers and are supposed to stand above the political fray and provide honest estimates. By contrast, other sources of politicization are produced by human frailty or organizational pathologies, not the direct manipulation of the intelligence process for political gain.

Charges that the intelligence production has been subjected to direct manipulation for political reasons emerged in the immediate aftermath of the Second Gulf War, when conclusive evidence supporting administration claims that Saddam Hussein had an active program to produce weapons of mass destruction (WMD) and a large stockpile of these weapons failed to materialize. Critics of the Bush administration claimed that "worst-case thinking," if not outright manipulation, dominated the interpretation of every scrap of evidence collected about Iraqi weapons programs and that most of this spin was concocted by administration officials looking to justify military actions against the kleptocracy that ruled in Iraq. Although some members of the intelligence community have suggested that the intelligence picture was far less conclusive than many administration officials suggested, most seem to stand by their general assessments of Iraq's overall desire to acquire and possess chemical, biological, and nuclear weapons. It is up to future historians to tell us whether the cup was really "half full," "half empty," or "completely drained" in terms of Iraq's chemical, biological, or nuclear capability and exactly who was responsible for "overselling" the Iraqi WMD threat.

Second, senior officials and officers sometimes give subtle and not-so-subtle cues to intelligence managers and analysts about the kinds of analyses they welcome or abhor. If intelligence consumers fawn over or reward analysts who provide them with encouraging reports but dismiss, berate, or punish analysts who bring them disconcerting news, they will send a powerful signal to analysts everywhere. Analysts will line up to provide consumers with positive estimates but shrink from the prospect of reporting bad news. Given the nature of senior leadership—only the most intractable problems and disputes are resolved at the top of the bureaucratic hierarchy—it takes an exceptional official to welcome the receipt of another negative report and to thank the bearer of bad news. Exceptional leaders cultivate a reputation for demanding the unvarnished truth from their staffs, and they make sure that not just the bearers of good news are recognized for outstanding efforts.

An interesting example of this second type of politicization occurred during the Vietnam War. General William C. Westmoreland, commander of U.S. Military Assistance Command, Vietnam (MACV), had asked his command historian to produce a study of sieges throughout history to generate some insights into the North Vietnamese effort to overwhelm the U.S. Marine firebase at Khe Sanh, which was located just below the demilitarized zone that separated North from South Vietnam. The command historian was asked to study the matter and to deliver a briefing to the MACV staff. After describing various battles that had occurred throughout history,

the historian concluded that the news was not good for the Marines: Most besieged fortresses fell because the attacker retained mobility. Needless to say, the news shocked the officers present at the briefing. When it concluded, Westmoreland thanked the historian for his report and turned to the staff, saying that now that they had heard the worst-case assessment, he would no longer tolerate anyone thinking, planning, or acting as if the siege of Khe Sanh would end in defeat. Whatever his motives, Westmoreland virtually guaranteed that whoever was in that room that day would think twice before bringing the boss bad news in the future.

Third, analysts can skew their estimates to advance their professional interests, attack their personal or professional rivals, or simply advance their careers. They can ignore negative trends or mistakes, especially if they are about to transfer into another organization or receive a promotion. It is better to leave one's position on a high note than to draw negative attention to problems that can jeopardize an otherwise positive record, especially at critical times. No news is always good news to those in charge of running a large organization; deciding not to rock the bureaucratic boat rarely damages one's career prospects. Politicization in this sense is really a form of careerism: Analysts or intelligence managers place a greater emphasis on enhancing their job prospects than on fulfilling their responsibilities. Sometimes conflict between professional responsibilities and personal interests occurs when analysts' findings call into question the performance or policies of their home organization or institution. Making senior officials aware of analyses that undermine the preferences or priorities of one's home institution is fraught with professional danger, and few people will persevere in the face of opposition from virtually everyone they encounter in the workplace.

John McCone's performance as director of the Central Intelligence Agency in the months leading up to the Cuban missile crisis provides an outstanding example of someone who did not allow concerns about his interests and reputation to get in the way of his responsibilities. During the summer of 1962, a consensus emerged among CIA analysts that it was unlikely that the Soviets would place offensive missiles in Cuba, and this finding was reported officially to policymakers in Special National Intelligence Estimate (SNIE) 85-3-62, "The Military Buildup in Cuba." McCone, however, became increasingly concerned about the possibility that the United States might suffer some sort of intelligence failure related to Cuba, as the Soviets attempted to shroud their activities on the island in secrecy. Despite the CIA's official estimate, an estimate that was reported to the most senior officials in the Kennedy administration, McCone pushed agency analysts to repeatedly reassess their judgments about Soviet activities in Cuba. McCone was less concerned about his reputation or his agency's track record for being correct and more interested in preventing the president from being caught by surprise by some nefarious scheme (Usowski 1988).

INTELLIGENCE AS POLITICS?

Politicization is a charge often leveled when intelligence estimates actually support one political position over another. In other words, when analysts "hit their mark" and produce timely finished intelligence that addresses matters of national importance and debate, charges are sometimes raised that someone has unduly influenced the intelligence process or that analysts are following their own policy or political agenda at the expense of objectivity. According to Richard Betts:

> For issues of high import and controversy, any relevant analysis is perforce politically charged, because it points to a policy conclusion. Various disputes—about which elements of information are correct, ambiguous, or false; which of them are important, incidental, or irrelevant; in which context they should be understood; and against which varieties of information pointing in a different direction they should assess—are in effect, if not in intent, disputes about which policy conclusion stands or falls. (Betts 2002, 60)

Because intelligence estimates are inherently credible, individuals who oppose findings that are adverse to their political position have to attack the objectivity of the intelligence process, not the inherent validity of the analysis. After all, few people have access to the classified materials used to develop intelligence estimates, so it is difficult for most observers to validate the intelligence community's findings

through independent analysis. Ironically, when intelligence estimates have a political impact and help shape policy—the very goal of the intelligence community—some people interpret that effect as evidence that the process must have been corrupted to serve political ends.

A variation of this phenomenon occurs when analysts themselves cry foul when their estimates are ignored by policymakers. This situation usually occurs when analysts warn policymakers of impending policy failure or indicate that past estimates were inaccurate and in need of significant revision. There are a variety of reasons, however, that policymakers might choose not to act on specific estimates. They might have information from other sources that provides different perspectives on current issues, or they might believe the effort to utilize the intelligence by changing policy might create more problems than solutions. In this sense, analysts break the grand bargain inherent in the relationship between the intelligence community and policymakers by going public in an effort to use estimates to shape policy.

THE READINGS

In the selections that follow, the authors explore politicization in its various forms. In the first selection, James J. Wirtz describes the tensions and pressures that shape relationships between intelligence professionals and policymakers. He describes the normative theories that influence discussions of the intelligence-policy nexus, focusing on the "ideal" types of relationships depicted by these theories and their prescriptions for avoiding politicization. Wirtz also describes how the information revolution is creating new challenges for existing theory, breaking down barriers between analysts and officials, and creating competing sources of information and analysis that threaten to overshadow finished intelligence products.

In the second selection, Joshua Rovner explores the possible benefits that might accrue from "politicization," that is, the manipulation of intelligence estimates to suit the policy preferences of decision makers.

13. THE INTELLIGENCE-POLICY NEXUS

JAMES J. WIRTZ

Although there is no consensus on how intelligence professionals and policymakers can avoid the risks of politicization, there are competing ideas about the proper intelligence-policy nexus at the heart of government. One approach strives to maintain distance between analysts and the officials they serve, while the other strives to make analysis relevant to current policy concerns. As the information revolution continues to transform the ways in which policymakers and analysts interact, however, new challenges and opportunities are beginning to characterize the intelligence-policy nexus.

INTRODUCTION

The intelligence-policy nexus is a critical part of modern government. Policy makers rely on intelligence professionals for data about broad international trends and their potential consequences, information about the intentions and capabilities of friends and foes alike, and specific warnings needed to avert disaster. Intelligence managers and analysts look to the policy establishment for their raison d'être. The intelligence community exists solely to provide policy makers with the information and analysis needed to formulate effective public policies. Few relationships in government are as symbiotic as the intelligence-policy nexus. One might thus expect that it would be relatively easy for intelligence professionals and policy makers to maintain smooth and productive working relations. Yet, few relationships are as challenging or produce as much controversy as the interaction between policy makers and intelligence professionals. The modus vivendi that governs their work is fragile, and disagreements that originate deep within the bureaucracy can easily find their way into tomorrow's headlines. The accusation that the Bush administration manipulated finished intelligence to support the decision to launch a preventive war against Iraq in 2003, for example, is the latest contentious issue in the history of the intelligence-policy nexus in the United States.

A variety of problems can emerge to bedevil relations between the intelligence and policy-making communities. The best-known pathology, politicization, occurs when policy makers place overt or subtle pressure on intelligence analysts and managers to produce intelligence estimates that support current political preferences or policies. Other issues, however, have received far less attention in the literature on intelligence. For example, there is no consensus about what constitutes best practices when it comes to intelligence-policy interaction, which can lead to acrimony as intelligence managers attempt to institute reforms. The information revolution also is creating new points of friction as intelligence analysts and policy makers interact using informal channels of communication, creating new challenges for those charged with monitoring the contents of finished intelligence—formal written reports that reflect a deliberate judgment made by analysts.

This chapter explores the tensions and pressures that shape interaction between intelligence professionals and policy makers as they go about the business of informing, making, and executing foreign and defense policy. The first section describes the two normative theories that offer competing explanations of how relations between intelligence professionals and policy makers should be organized. It also explores the intelligence pathologies that can emerge if either of these theories is applied with too much stringency. The second section explores the origins and consequences of politicization. The third section examines how the information revolution is transforming the relationship between analysts and officials, producing benefits as well as unintended consequences. Although technology has always shaped the intelligence cycle—setting intelligence requirements, collecting data, analyzing information and producing finished intelligence, and communicating information to people who can put it to good use—the information revolution might actually be altering the intelligence-policy nexus, creating an entirely new dynamic in relations between the intelligence and policy-making communities.

A THEORY OF THE INTELLIGENCE-POLICY NEXUS?

Two normative theories animate the debate about best practices in the intelligence-policy nexus. One, most closely associated with the work of Sherman Kent, focuses on ensuring the independence of intelligence analysts when it comes to providing information to policy makers.[1] Kent's thinking, which shaped the formation and early evolution of the U.S. intelligence community, identifies the importance of political and policy detachment when it comes to producing relevant and effective finished intelligence. The other operational framework, most closely associated with the reforms instituted in the mid-1980s by then Director of Central Intelligence Robert M. Gates, focuses on providing "actionable" intelligence, information of immediate and direct use to policy makers.[2] To produce actionable intelligence, analysts have to maintain close working relationships with policy makers, literally looking into officials' inboxes to make sure finished intelligence addresses important policy issues of the day. These frameworks appeal to different groups within the government, produce specific benefits, and exhibit unique intelligence pathologies.

THE KENT APPROACH

Sherman Kent's approach to the intelligence-policy nexus is based on the premise that effective intelligence is independent intelligence. Analysts must maintain their distance from current policy and policy makers to prevent their reports from being shaped by their customers' preferences. In Kent's view, intelligence managers and analysts should be free to set intelligence requirements and production plans for finished intelligence products, deciding which projects best support policy makers. This approach guards against politicization because it

creates real procedural and even physical barriers that prevent policy makers from influencing the questions addressed and answers presented in finished intelligence. Analysts often champion this model of the intelligence-policy nexus because it provides them with the intellectual freedom to pursue their interests within the relatively broad guidelines created by intelligence managers.

At the core of the Kent approach is a grand bargain between policy makers and intelligence professionals. The intelligence community is master of its own house, but analysts and intelligence managers must avoid becoming embroiled in political decisions or commenting publicly or even privately on current policy or political issues. This division of responsibility is especially important because it gives intelligence analysts a special cachet in the U.S. political system, where the intelligence community is often seen as an objective source of information that is beyond the reach of partisan influence. Intelligence professionals take this bargain seriously. The organizational culture of the Central Intelligence Agency (CIA), for instance, reinforces this bargain through formal and informal norms and rules against political or policy commentary in the products produced by the Agency. Finished intelligence analysis also is scrubbed clean of policy content or obvious political bias that might have inadvertently crept into the work of analysts.

The strength of Kent's approach is that it preserves the independence of analysts by separating the intelligence community from the overt pressure or organizational and interpersonal incentives that can shape intelligence to conform to current policy or the personal and political biases of policy makers. Yet, by creating a strong barrier against politicization, Kent's prescriptions can separate intelligence too completely from policy makers, leading to other problems. For instance, policy makers are "inbox driven": They only have the time and energy to deal with their areas of responsibility or issues of immediate importance. Thus, weighty research papers offering reviews of broad issue areas or regions are likely to be ignored by policy makers. Those who are not responsible for the issues or regions covered will not read the paper, while those with a professional interest in the topic will seek more detailed analyses. Similarly, in-depth reports are likely to be ignored by most policy makers who have no responsibility for the issue surveyed. Without a good understanding of the issues that preoccupy specific policy makers, high-quality finished intelligence might be viewed as useless by intelligence consumers because it covers the wrong topics, arrives too late to be of use, lacks the proper level of detail, or addresses the wrong facet of the problem at hand. In fact, without some sort of collaboration between analysts and policy makers, the arrival of timely, relevant, and useful finished intelligence would depend on luck.

Organizational pathologies also can emerge if intelligence managers and analysts become too detached from the needs of policy makers. Analysis can take on a life of its own as the personal or bureaucratic agendas of intelligence professionals begin to take precedence over the needs of their consumers. For instance, critics charged that the CIA's Office of Soviet Analysis (SOVA), especially its division specializing in the study of the Soviet economy, became increasingly scholastic as the Cold War progressed. Because the command economies of the Communist bloc had little in common with those of the capitalist West, the CIA was forced to create an entirely new academic discipline to understand Soviet economic performance and capability.[3] Promising academics were recruited from the best graduate schools and given specialized training, journals were founded to cultivate new methodologies and to provide a forum for theoretical debate, and analysts worked hard to gain insights into Soviet economic performance, a state secret of the Communist regime in Moscow. As analysts sought to sharpen their methodological skills and improve the sophistication of their theories, however, they began to lose sight of the big picture, especially the fundamental question that suggested itself to policy makers in the early 1980s. Could the Soviet command economy compete over the short term with the capitalist economies of the West, or was the regime in Moscow built upon an economic house of cards?

ACTIONABLE INTELLIGENCE

When Robert Gates, then Deputy Director for Analysis at the CIA, became frustrated with the unwillingness of CIA analysts to provide intelligence to meet the specific requirements of administration officials, actionable intelligence was born. Under Gates's system, analysts might have been asked, for example, when—not if—the Soviet economy would collapse. Intelligence professionals cried foul, noting that by posing specific and pointed questions, Gates was attempting to shape the analysis to suit the expectations of policy makers. In response, Gates suggested that he was trying to make analysts less academic so that they would produce relevant and timely finished intelligence that responded to the needs of administration officials.

The core assumption behind actionable intelligence is that analysts must be aware of the needs of policy makers and that intelligence managers have an obligation to task analysts so that they produce useful intelligence for their clientele. According to Gates:

> My view has been all along from the very beginning of my career—and perhaps due to the fact that I have served on the National Security Council—that the Intelligence community has to be right next to the policymaker, that [the analyst] has to be at his elbow—that he has to understand what is on his mind. He has to understand what his future concerns are. He has to understand what his agenda is. He has to understand some of the initiatives that he is thinking about taking. He has to be willing to ask the policymaker what he's working on, or what came of his last conversation with a world leader so that the intelligence can be made relevant; so that the Director, or the office director, or what can go back and give guidance to the analysts.[4]

From this perspective, policy makers already have a reasonable idea of what they need—information to help them implement their policies. Most of the support they require from the intelligence community is largely technical in nature: demographic, geographic, political, economic, and military data about the issue at hand and how allies and adversaries are responding to U.S. policies. Some observers have even noted that as crises emerge, policy makers should communicate with analysts directly to increase the flow of information and the timeliness of analysis. Under these circumstances, analytic debates within the intelligence community are counterproductive and actually reduce the confidence policy makers have in finished intelligence. When the chips are down, officials want information they can use to solve problems, not competitive analysis designed to highlight various theoretical or methodological approaches to the issues of the day.[5] In fact, some policy makers have discovered that the intelligence community can actually serve as an extension of their office staff, providing a ready source of analysis and information tailored to meet their personal interests and agendas.[6]

In reality, much of the finished intelligence produced by analysts takes the form of actionable intelligence: The information supplied to policy makers often is matter-of-fact data about what is occurring in a specific part of the world, the state of a foreign economy or industry, or the capability of a weapons system. Moreover, elected officials usually enter office with a pre-existing worldview and policy agenda; they look to the intelligence community to help them implement their policies. If intelligence professionals fail to recognize this political and policy reality, they risk becoming irrelevant.

Nevertheless, following the Gates model too closely can create its own set of problems. There is a possibility that policy makers will pose biased questions to the intelligence community to guarantee that analysis favorable to their positions will emerge, or that they will fail to pose the correct questions, leading to an incomplete understanding of the challenges they face. If analysts also concentrated only on actionable intelligence, they might lack the time to conduct the independent, in-depth research needed to uncover threats and trends not on current policy agendas. When they initially took office, for instance, members of the Bush administration had not placed Al Qaeda on the top of their foreign and defense policy agendas. Instead, they were more concerned with improving Russian-American relations, deploying a U.S. missile defense system, and reducing U.S. military commitments overseas. It was up to the intelligence community to increase the salience of the terrorist threat to the United States among senior officials.

Normative theory and practice thus highlight the competing priorities that animate the intelligence-policy nexus. Analysts need some leeway, unconstrained by the preference of policy makers or even intelligence managers, to pursue their hunches and interests, regardless of current political or policy preferences. Without this freedom, policy makers would lack independent information and insight into current and emerging international issues. For their analysis to be relevant and timely, however, intelligence professionals must possess a keen awareness of policy makers' current interests and responsibilities. What policy makers require is information and finished intelligence reports that address the issues found in their inboxes. They also would benefit from long-term research that highlights emerging problems before they become crises or sources of embarrassment.

POLITICIZATION

Politicization, the effort of policy makers to shape intelligence to conform to their policy or political preferences, can emerge in both overt and subtle

ways. Although the term suggests that intelligence analysts are victims when policy makers manipulate intelligence to suit their needs, intelligence professionals can themselves politicize intelligence when they allow bureaucratic or personal incentives to influence their estimates and reports. Intelligence managers and analysts can "pander" to policy makers by presenting them with information and analysis that meets their expectations and confirms their chosen policies. Intelligence estimates also can appear to be politicized when they are effective, that is, when they actually have a policy or political impact.

Overt politicization occurs when policy makers deliberately pressure analysts to produce estimates that support their policies or to shape the intelligence cycle to confirm current policy or political preferences. The act of deliberately shaping intelligence estimates would have to be driven by expediency or desperation because policy makers run a grave risk by preventing accurate, if unpleasant, information and finished intelligence from informing national policy. In extreme cases of politicization, senior officers or policy makers can even retaliate against analysts for providing them with information that contradicts their existing beliefs or plans. In the days leading up to Operation Market Garden, the Allied airborne-armor operation to seize the Rhine River crossings in September 1944, Major Brian Urquhart, Chief of Intelligence for the British I Airborne Corps, detected signs that Nazi armored divisions were actually bivouacked in Arnhem, that last objective of the Allied advance. When Urquhart relayed to his superiors this information, which called into question the feasibility of the entire operation, he was visited by a senior medical officer who placed him on sick leave.[7]

Overt politicization, however, is difficult to keep concealed, because analysts and intelligence managers will go to great lengths to resist what they believe are illegitimate efforts to influence their finished intelligence reports. In the aftermath of the Vietnam War, for instance, Samuel Adams, a former CIA analyst who helped develop estimates of enemy troop strength during the war, charged that senior intelligence officials and military officers deliberately suppressed his findings because they gave the Viet Cong greater strength than had been reported in previous intelligence estimates. The controversy over the incident only increased in the aftermath of the conflict, and became the subject of a CBS news documentary and libel litigation between General William C. Westmoreland (retired), who was the former head of the Military Assistance Command in Vietnam and CBS.[8] Some controversies boil over even more quickly. Following the second Gulf War, accusations emerged that the members of the George W. Bush administration had tried to undermine the credibility of Ambassador Joseph Wilson, who investigated reports that Iraqi agents had attempted to purchase yellowcake, a nuclear material, from Niger. Wilson had turned in a memo to intelligence officials in February 2002, explaining why the alleged Iraqi activity was probably a hoax. When the president claimed in his 2003 State of the Union Address that Iraq had sought uranium in Africa, Wilson went public in a July 6, 2003, editorial in the *New York Times*, stating that the Bush administration knowingly lied about the status of Iraq's nuclear program. In retaliation, Bush administration officials allegedly "outed" Valerie Plame, Wilson's wife, effectively ending her career as a clandestine CIA officer.[9]

Although they make headlines, charges that policy makers deliberately engage in politicization are relatively rare. Instead, policy makers and intelligence managers can shape analysis in more subtle, and sometimes even inadvertent, ways. Those who bring positive news can be rewarded with praise in front of colleagues, whereas those who bring unwelcome information can be chastised or criticized in front of their coworkers. "Positive" estimates are more likely to be rewarded with promotions, increases in pay, or sublime inducements important to bureaucrats—a larger office, new furniture, travel. "Negative" estimates are unlikely to be rewarded; in fact those with an eye for finding potential trouble in a generally positive situation are often avoided by policy makers whose workday is often spent responding to a never-ending series of crises, problems, or complaints. Loss of access to policy makers can take the form of *bureaucratic death*, a situation in which intelligence officials are no longer invited to important meetings because of their history of providing contradictory or discouraging reports.[10] Only the smartest and toughest policy makers encourage their staffs to take steps to avoid sending inadvertent signals to subordinates and intelligence managers to prevent analysis from being shaped to meet their expectations or to emphasize the positive aspects of every situation. Indeed, some observers have noted that the ability to literally pressure subordinates to provide honest assessments is a key to success in politics and war.[11]

Without knowing it, however, efforts to encourage analysts to provide their honest opinion can have unintended consequences. During the Vietnam War, for example, General Westmoreland was provided with a negative assessment of his command's ability to hold the marine position at Khe Sanh, the findings of an estimate that he had personally requested. After hearing the report, which was delivered to his entire staff, he thanked the analysts for their best estimate and then stated that he would no longer tolerate gloomy evaluations of the marine's prospects at Khe Sanh. Years later, Westmoreland's chief of intelligence, Major General Philip Davidson (retired) remarked that he had never heard a negative prediction for the outcome at Khe Sanh. In what was an apparent effort to bolster morale, Westmoreland had told his command that he no longer wanted negative reports about the situation at Khe Sanh. It is not surprising that his staff complied.[12]

When intelligence has an effect on important foreign and defense policy debates, charges of politicization often emerge. Ironically, when intelligence analysts offer timely and relevant estimates to policy makers, they are sometimes accused of meddling in political affairs because their reports have an impact, favoring one side in a political dispute over another. As issues become increasingly a matter of heated partisan politics or less focused on technical issues, the role played by intelligence analysts as neutral purveyors of information and analysis increases. Moreover, if the finished intelligence in question was not backed by a clear analytical consensus, there always will be intelligence "dissenters" ready to take their case to elected officials or the media. As Richard Betts has noted, this is exactly the situation that emerged in the controversy over enemy strength during the Vietnam War: The effort to shape an analytical consensus spilled over into acrimony that lasted for years and became a matter of public and political debate.[13]

THE INFORMATION REVOLUTION AND THE INTELLIGENCE POLICY NEXUS

The information revolution has broken down barriers of space and time by virtually eliminating the costs of communication, even at intercontinental distances. The computer and the Internet have provided individuals with an ability to organize and analyze information that was unheard of only a few decades ago. The Internet itself is a positive-sum institution: The more people who have access to the Internet and this virtually free means of communication, the more powerful the tool becomes for all concerned.[14] The real power of new computing and communication architectures is that they can potentially allow people everywhere and anywhere to find and interact with each other in real time.

As with any technology, the information revolution contains its own embedded ideology, so to speak: People will find that it should be employed in a particular way, regardless of the intentions of its designers. In fact, the inventor of a machine is often unaware of the logic inherent in the technology he or she is creating. Gutenberg was a Catholic, but his printing press made the Protestant reformation possible because printing facilitated the dissemination of competing ideas (i.e., heresy).[15] The automobile transformed America—dispersing extended families and building suburbs and new American cultures.[16] The automobile's effects, however, were perceived only when the transformation of society was well under way.

The information revolution also is transforming society. It is an egalitarian technology that breaks down social, economic, political, and bureaucratic barriers and allows people direct access to each other's very personal "inboxes," for the most part facilitating frank communication even across hierarchical organizations. At the same time, the information revolution also documents human interaction as it channels not just formal, but informal, communication into what amounts to official or corporate records. In a sense, people have to convert private interactions into a public record to participate in the information revolution, but they seem to accept this as the price of entry for using the new technology.

Because we use information revolution technologies on a daily basis, we often overlook the subtle and even not so subtle changes it is bringing to everyday life or well-understood bureaucratic practices. In terms of the intelligence-policy nexus, for example, the information revolution has reframed the opportunities for interaction between intelligence analysts and policy makers in ways that are not well captured by either the Gates or Kent frameworks. The barriers to interaction assumed by the Kent model, which are supplied by intelligence managers or by the process of crafting formal intelligence estimates, are completely broken down by the information revolution. Policy makers and their staffs can now easily communicate on a daily basis directly with analysts. It is increasingly difficult for analysts to stand above the fray of politics or policy if they are bombarded with a barrage of questions about current policy, calls for data, or requests for commentary or supplemental information about media coverage of some international event.

Moreover, as the volume of this informal interaction between policy makers and analysts increases, it can begin to drown out the message carried by the formal estimates offered by intelligence organizations. Because of the sheer volume of interaction between analysts and policy makers, it also might be nearly impossible for intelligence managers to monitor this informal communication, and any effort to restrict analysts' access to this communication technology would be resisted on both personal and professional grounds. The information revolution has created a new medium for interaction between analysts and policy makers that, by its very nature, flies in the face of the norms suggested by Kent's framework.

Policy makers' access to analysts is so great that it can overwhelm them, degrading their ability to provide significant actionable intelligence called for by the Gates model. It might be difficult for individuals outside of government or the military to understand, but as members of a "service industry," intelligence analysts must place the immediate needs of administration officials ahead of other important professional or organizational objectives. Questions or requests for information, no matter how trivial, must receive a prompt and complete response. Additionally, because service is part of the ethos of the intelligence community, performance metrics are focused on measuring responsiveness to policy makers' demands, not the quality or thoroughness of the response given or the opportunity costs created by setting aside long-term research projects. Because everyone within the policy-making and intelligence communities is virtually free to task analysts, intelligence managers are no longer able to set production priorities or timelines. In fact, because managers are judged by the same production metric as analysts, they have little incentive to intervene in informal communications to protect analysts from being endlessly besieged with questions by policy makers.

The information revolution offers more opportunities for intelligence analysts to interact with officials while making it increasingly difficult for analysts to hold their attention. Because policy makers have ready access to nongovernmental sources of information provided by twenty-four-hour cable television and Internet news services, intelligence analysts have to hold the attention of policy makers by providing catchy titles to reports that exaggerate the importance or the certainty underlying estimates. The Silberman-Robb Commission, which investigated the intelligence community's account of Iraq's weapons of mass destruction program prior to the second Gulf War, found that the

President's Daily Brief (PDB)—a tightly held piece of finished intelligence that is read by a few select senior officials on a daily basis—suffered from various flaws and created several problems.[17] PDBs tended to contain bold statements and judgments that were probably intended to engage the reader but failed to convey a sense of the qualifications, judgments, or assumptions that were embedded in the analysis. Commissioners were concerned that a daily exposure to PDB briefings might "create, over time, a greater perception of certainty about their judgments than is warranted." Questions posed to PDB briefers are answered in future PDBs or in a Senior Executive Memorandum, which are distributed to all those who receive the PDB. Commissioners believed that the volume of reporting that could be produced by a question of clarification, for example, could create a false impression among PDB recipients that the president was intensely interested in a subject, thereby shaping priorities and policy.[18]

The commissioners also searched in vain for evidence of politicization in the intelligence community's reporting on Iraqi weapons of mass destruction programs. What they uncovered, however, was evidence of the impact of the information revolution—especially the breakdown of hierarchy. The CIA Ombudsman for Politicization told the commissioners, for example, that analysts on Iraqi issues worked under more "pressure" than any other analysts in the history of the CIA. For months they were required to provide enormous amounts of both formal and informal reporting directly to the highest officials in the U.S. government. These officials also questioned analysts directly about their work to explore the assumptions and data that were used. Policy makers are justified in asking these types of questions, regardless of their motivations, but the fact that senior officials apparently scrutinized analysts directly probably affected subsequent analysis. Analysts also were under pressure "to answer the mail quickly," which in itself can be detrimental to calm contemplation of complicated issues.[19] Cutting and pasting is not a measured reassessment of first principles or even secondary assumptions, and it unfortunately occurs when timeliness takes precedence over depth in the information age.

CONCLUSION

Intelligence reform is cyclical. Sometimes scholars and other observers warn that analysts are too detached from policy makers' concerns and are producing finished intelligence that is dated or irrelevant. At other times, concerns about politicization emerge; observers worry that intelligence analysts and managers are no longer serving as an independent source of information for policy makers and that the intelligence cycle has been corrupted by all sorts of political or bureaucratic considerations. Since the early 1980s, the pendulum has been swinging in favor of producing "actionable" intelligence, but in the aftermath of a series of intelligence setbacks leading up to and following the September 11, 2001, terror attacks, observers have had second thoughts about the status of the U.S. intelligence community. Intelligence reform, based on organizational change, is the order of the day.

It is extraordinarily difficult to strike a balance between detachment and responsiveness in the intelligence-policy nexus. As Betts noted, fixing one type of intelligence problem only exacerbates other types of problems.[20] For instance, providing all available information to analysts would overwhelm them; by contrast, restricting the flow of information creates the risk that they will not receive critical bits of information needed to make sense of emerging threats. Because the correct balance of detachment and responsiveness depends upon the specific issue or problem confronting intelligence analysts and policy makers, it is virtually impossible ex ante to fine-tune the intelligence-policy nexus.

In a sense, those interested in intelligence reform are addressing a moving target. The proper balance in the relationship between intelligence professionals and policy makers is shaped by external and internal factors. Externally, the changing threat environment and issue agenda create different types of challenges for the intelligence community. Reporting on developments within nation states requires different collection and analytical capabilities than does reporting on terrorist networks or superempowered individuals. Internally, new communication and information processing capabilities—combined with the way analysts and policy makers actually use these novel capabilities—are creating new modes of interaction within the intelligence-policy nexus. It might be too early to sound the death knell for the Kent and Gates models, but in the future it will probably become increasingly difficult to capture the reality of the intelligence-policy nexus within these competing theoretical frameworks.

QUESTIONS FOR FURTHER DISCUSSION

1. What factors drive intelligence analysts and policymakers to collaborate?
2. Should intelligence reforms strive to maintain distance between analysts and the officials they serve or strive to make analysis responsive to current policy concerns?
3. How is the information revolution changing the relationship between analysts and policymakers?
4. Will the information revolution increase the risks of politicization of intelligence?

ENDNOTES

1. Sherman Kent, *Strategic Intelligence for American World Policy* (Princeton: Princeton University Press, 1946).
2. H. Bradfor Westerfield, "Inside Ivory Bunkers: CIA Analysts Resist Managers' 'Panderin'—Part II," *International Journal of Intelligence and Counterintelligence* 10 (Spring 1997), pp. 19–54; Richard K. Betts, "Politicization of Intelligence: Costs and Benefits," *Paradoxes of Strategic Intelligence*, eds. Richard K. Betts and Thomas Mahnken (London: Frank Cass, 2003), pp. 59–79.
3. David M. Kennedy, *Sunshine and Shadow: The CIA and the Soviet Economy* (Cambridge: Harvard University, JFK Case Program, 1991).
4. Gates quoted in Westerfield, "Inside Ivory Bunkers."
5. William Odom, *Fixing Intelligence: For a More Secure America* (New Haven, CT: Yale University Press, 2003).
6. Jack Davis, "A Policymaker's Perspective on Intelligence Analysis," *Studies in Intelligence* 39 (1995), pp. 7–15.
7. Sir Brian Urquhart, who was Under-Secretary-General of the United Nations (UN) from 1974 to 1986, played a leading part in the development of UN peacekeeping operations throughout the Cold War. Urquhart was eventually knighted for his service to the United Nations.
8. James J. Wirtz, "Intelligence to Please? The Order of Battle Controversy During the Vietnam War," *Political Science Quarterly* 106 (Summer 1991), pp. 239–63.
9. "Then & Now: Joseph Wilson," CNN, 19 June 2005, available at http://www.cnn.com/2005/US/03/07/CNN25.tan.wilson/index.html.
10. Mark Lowenthal, *Intelligence: From Secrets to Policy* (Washington, DC: CQ Press, 2003), p. 148.
11. Eliot Cohen, *Supreme Command* (New York: Free Press, 2002).
12. Phillip Davidson, Interview II by Ted Gittinger, June 30, 1982, Oral History Collection, LBJ Library, Austin, Texas, pp. 23–24; and William C. Westmoreland, *A Soldier Reports* (Garden City, NY: Doubleday, 1976), p. 338.
13. Betts, pp. 73–74.
14. Bill Gates, *The Road Ahead* (New York: Penguin, 1996).
15. Printing increased literacy because it provided common people with something to read. Without printing, Martin Luther could not have encouraged people to read the Bible themselves.
16. George F. Kennan, *Around the Cragged Hill* (New York: W. W. Norton, 1994).
17. Commission on the Intelligence Capabilities of the United States Regarding Weapons of Mass Destruction, "Report to the President of the United States," 31 March 2005.
18. Ibid., pp. 160–81.
19. Ibid., pp. 187–89.
20. Richard Betts, "Analysis, War, and Decision: Why Intelligence Failures Are Inevitable," *World Politics*, 21 (October 1968), pp. 61–89.

14. IS POLITICIZATION EVER A GOOD THING?

JOSHUA ROVNER

Politicization is the manipulation of intelligence estimates to reflect policy preferences. Policymakers are guilty of politicization if they compel intelligence agencies to alter their conclusions in ways that are politically convenient or psychologically comforting. Intelligence officials are guilty of politicization if they shape their estimates to reflect their own beliefs and preferences. At first glance politicization appears to be an unalloyed hazard: manipulating estimates seems to make bad intelligence inevitable. Nonetheless, some observers argue that under certain circumstances politicization can be a good thing, or at least a necessary risk. Intelligence officials should be willing to take that risk if the alternative means isolating themselves from the policy process and sacrificing any possible influence over policymakers' judgment. They also should be willing to tone down their conclusions on major issues, or withhold estimates on minor ones, in order to avoid offending policymakers. This kind of 'soft politicization' does not mean outright pandering, but it does constrain intelligence leaders from being blunt about estimates that are frankly at odds with policy beliefs and preferences. This chapter evaluates the possible benefits of politicization and tests it against the historical record. It concludes that politicization—even soft politicization—undermines the quality of threat assessment and does lasting damage to intelligence-policy relations.

Politicization is the attempt to manipulate intelligence estimates so that they reflect policy preferences.[1] Policymakers are guilty of politicization if they directly or indirectly compel intelligence agencies to alter their conclusions in ways that are politically convenient or psychologically comforting. Intelligence officials are guilty of politicization if they shape their estimates to reflect their own beliefs and preferences.

At first glance politicization appears to be an unalloyed hazard: manipulating intelligence seems to make bad assessments inevitable. Well-known cases of politicization have led to badly skewed estimates and have poisoned intelligence—policy relations for years after the fact. In the United States, politicization during the Vietnam War and during the period of *détente* with the Soviet Union led to wildly inaccurate estimates. It also exacerbated mutual stereotypes on both sides of the divide, reinforcing policymakers' belief that intelligence agencies were obstacles to policy implementation,

and reinforcing intelligence officials' belief that policy-makers were meddling bullies. Nonetheless, some observers argue that under certain circumstances politicization can be a good thing, or at least a necessary risk. Intelligence officials should be willing to take that risk if the alternative means isolating themselves from the policy process and sacrificing any possible influence over policymakers' judgment. They also should be willing to tone down their conclusions on major issues, or withhold estimates on minor ones, in order to avoid needlessly offending policymakers. This kind of 'soft politicization' does not mean outright pandering, but it does constrain intelligence leaders from being blunt about estimates that are frankly at odds with policy beliefs and preferences.

This article evaluates the possible benefits of politicization. The first section provides an overview of the logic in favor of soft politicization. The second section tests it against the historical record. The last section considers some implications for the theory of intelligence-policy relations and the broader relationship between intelligence and strategy.

WHY POLITICIZATION MIGHT BE USEFUL

I have argued elsewhere that politicization is almost always bad. The manipulation of intelligence leads to profoundly inaccurate and misleading assessments, and it also damages the long-term quality of intelligence-policy relations.[2] But many other commentators, intelligence scholars and practitioners alike, have argued that politicization should be treated as a comparatively minor concern. The greater danger is that intelligence officials will steer clear of the policy world in order to avoid being politicized, thus rendering intelligence irrelevant to strategy and policy. If this is true, then the *fear* of politicization is much more dangerous than politicization itself, because overwrought concerns about policy meddling will cause intelligence to lose its purpose.[3]

In a similar vein, scholars have argued that arguments against politicization are based on a stylized version of intelligence-policy relations that bears little resemblance to reality. Stephen Marrin notes that the so-called intelligence cycle, a linear model in which objective intelligence estimates are delivered in advance of policy decisions, is at odds with the messier business of policymaking.[4] This means that attempts to preserve the autonomy of intelligence in order to prevent politicization are essentially attempts to uphold a fiction. Moreover, policymakers have particular insights that intelligence officials should not ignore. The intelligence community should avoid the habit of assuming that their estimates will suffer if they are informed by policy considerations; some effort to invest policy beliefs into estimates might actually yield a more accurate and useful product. However, this would require intelligence leaders to accept the discomfiting notion that they should modify their estimates in response to policy feedback, even if this increases the risk of politicization.

Richard Betts goes further by arguing that a little politicization is probably necessary and sometimes even good. Many intelligence officials have agreed, and some have even admitted watering down estimates in order to husband political capital with their policy counterparts. To be clear, Betts does not approve of bending to blatant attempts to manipulate intelligence. Backing down in response to this kind of arm twisting is unacceptable because it corrupts the intelligence process: 'The irrevocable norm must be that policy interests, preferences, or decisions must *never* determine intelligence judgments'.[5] But the situation is more complicated when policymakers engage in a more indirect form of politicization by sending subtle signals about the direction of desired estimates. These cases are almost always controversial. While intelligence officials sometimes view indirect pressure as an insidious form of manipulation, policymakers reply that their signals are wholly appropriate. If they do not criticize draft estimates, they argue, intelligence runs the risk of intellectual sclerosis. It is difficult to navigate the thin line between constructive criticism and improper meddling, Betts concludes, but is an unavoidable task for intelligence officials who must respond to legitimate policy concerns while simultaneously protecting the integrity of analysts.

Betts emphasizes that intelligence-policy relations are iterative. Intelligence officials seek to create an enduring role for intelligence in the policy process, and they may have good reasons to fear that picking fights over small issues today might cost them access to policymakers in the future. Incautious dealings with leaders are likely to prove counterproductive. If intelligence officials deliver estimates that bluntly challenge policy expectations, they might soon find themselves out of the policy loop. Softening the language of estimates is one way to avoid this fate; another is to withhold estimates altogether. 'Outright pandering clearly crosses the line', Betts argues. 'But what about a decision simply not to poke a policymaker in the eye, to avoid confrontation, to get a better hearing for a negative view by softening its presentation when a no-compromise argument would be certain to provoke anger and rejection?'[6]

Betts's argument also suggests a rationale for appointing pliable intelligence chiefs whose views are well known and similar to those of policymakers. The use of what I call 'manipulation-by-appointment' can be harmful if it encourages groupthink and discourages debate.[7] On the other hand, policymakers might be wise to appoint like-minded intelligence officials in order to foster long-term collaboration. The alternative—appointing strong willed and potentially combative intelligence chiefs—might lead to fractious intelligence-policy relations punctuated by intense disputes and characterized by mutual mistrust. Manipulation-by-appointment might lead to a little politicization some of the time, but that is a small price to pay to ensure long-term harmony.

THE EFFECTS OF SOFT POLITICIZATION

Some intelligence officials have clearly acted according to this logic, softening estimates or stifling controversial views in order to protect their access to policymakers. In early 1963, for example, Director of Central Intelligence (DCI) John McCone insisted that the Board of National Estimates (BNE) revise its pessimistic appraisal of progress in the Vietnam War. This was a surprising turnabout for McCone, who had previously shared the Board's pessimism. One reason for his action was the need to restore the intelligence community's reputation among policymakers after the failure to predict that the Soviet Union would place nuclear missiles on Cuba in 1962. According to Harold Ford, his decision was 'almost certainly'

> directly related to the heavy fire he was taking at the time from the White House, and particularly from the President's Foreign Intelligence Advisory Board (PFIAB), for having released so mistaken an NIE that preceding September on a subject so crucial for US security interests. It (now the BNE) was asking him to issue a definitive NIE on Vietnam that differed sharply from the views of the leading presidential advisors and their staffs. Going against so many senior decision-makers without taking a second look would certainly not endear him to the White House or impress a skeptical PFIAB.[8]

McCone already had a strained relationship with the Kennedy administration. A well-known conservative, his appointment was a sop to congressional Republicans following the Bay of Pigs debacle and the forced resignation of DCI Allen Dulles. Though McCone's presence might have helped White House relations on the Hill, his relationship with the president was destined to be chilly. The failure to anticipate the Cuban Missile Crisis exacerbated the problem for McCone, even though he had bucked the prevailing view of the intelligence community and personally warned that the Soviet Union was becoming bolder in the fall of 1962.[9] Not surprisingly, he was wary of challenging policy beliefs just a few months later. To do so might mean permanently losing touch with the White House.

DCI Richard Helms found himself in a similar position a few years later, when the intelligence community once again challenged optimistic administration beliefs about progress in Vietnam. Military officers believed that the Vietcong (VC) numbered somewhere between 200,000 and 300,000 and that its end strength and manpower reserves were declining. In late 1966, however, Central Intelligence Agency (CIA) analysts began criticizing the official order of battle (O/B) because it failed to include part-time fighters and civilians who assisted the VC. Leaving these groups out meant that the official estimate presented a misleading portrait of the size, capabilities, and resiliency of the enemy. Indeed, the CIA's revised order of battle found that the enemy was perhaps twice as large as the military estimate. Much of the dispute between the military and the CIA had to do with legitimate methodological differences, but the political implications of the growing order of battle controversy were clear. If the intelligence community published an NIE with a much higher estimate of the size of the enemy, then the administration's optimistic public claims would ring hollow. After a meeting in June 1967, military and intelligence officials appeared to reach a compromise: the official NIE would include both estimates and divide them by category. This would provide a comprehensive picture for policymakers and allow them to judge the merits of including part-time civilian fighters in the order of battle.

The split estimate, however, was unacceptable to the White House. The Johnson administration wanted to present a unified position on the war and worried about the public fallout from apparent differences of opinion over such a fundamental issue. It also worried about its own credibility, given its ongoing public relations campaign to demonstrate progress in the war. White House staffers soon began to lean on intelligence officials to simply accept the standing order of battle. In his memoirs, Helms complained about White House staffers who 'frequently challenged our work with infuriating suggestions that we "get on the team"—that is, trim our reporting to fit policy'.[10] Nonetheless, he swallowed his professional pride and bent to policy pressure. In September, while CIA and military representatives were meeting in Saigon in another attempt to resolve the dispute, he ordered his subordinates to accept the military estimate rather than continuing the fight. Helms believed that while the O/B had important implications, it was a minor issue compared to the looming interagency controversy over the efficacy of strategic bombing, and he did not want to waste his political capital when it would be badly needed later. As he put it later, 'because of broader considerations we had to come up with agreed figures, that we had to get this O/B question off the board, and that it didn't mean a damn what particular figures we agreed to'.[11]

Helms also bent to pressure from the Nixon administration. In 1969, the White House was pushing Congress to approve funding for a new missile defense system. It argued that Soviet gains in missile technology, specifically the deployment of the SS-9 intercontinental ballistic missile (ICBM), required a network of defenses to protect US land-based Minuteman ICBMs from a preemptive Soviet first strike. The White House argued that the SS-9 was equipped with multiple independently targeted re-entry vehicles (MIRVs), which would greatly increase its lethality against the Minuteman force, because the landing pattern of incoming re-entry vehicles (RVs) could be programmed to match the distribution of Minuteman launch sites.[12] Soviet technical gains also had ominous implications for Soviet motives. While standing intelligence estimates concluded that Moscow was improving its arsenal to achieve strategic parity and stabilize deterrence, the administration worried that it sought strategic superiority by achieving the means to deliver a disarming first strike. Throughout the spring and summer it pressured Helms to make changes to the annual NIE on Soviet strategic capabilities and intentions, and enlisted Helms in public briefings before Congress. According to a senior CIA official, Henry Kissinger 'beat up' on Helms and the Chairman of the Board of National Estimates after he learned that they disagreed with the administration view. 'Look', he warned, 'the president of the United States and the secretary of defense have said the following. Now, are you telling me that you're going to argue with them?'[13] Kissinger repeatedly used his close relationship with the president to remind intelligence officials that Richard Nixon was unhappy with their obstinacy. In June he told a group of senior intelligence officials that his '"most important client" wanted the facts separated from the judgments and identified as such'. One witness recalled that Kissinger was 'pretty unhappy' about the CIA's conclusions about Soviet intentions: 'He kept saying he didn't want to influence our judgments—but!'[14]

Sustained pressure from the White House and the Pentagon caused Helms to back down. Despite opposition from CIA analysts, and despite his own suspicion that the White House position was 'tainted' by its determination to push Safeguard through the Senate, he removed language from the final version of the NIE that contradicted administration statements. He worried that prolonging the fight over the SS-9 would undermine any hope of ensuring the CIA's place in the policy process. Drawing a line in the sand would only make the administration cynical about the Agency's real intentions, causing it to view intelligence as an obstacle rather than an asset. Other controversies were sure to arise, Helms reasoned, and intelligence needed to retain a modicum of objectivity and political independence if it was to play a positive role. As he wrote later:

> I was not prepared to stake the Agency's entire position on this one issue—in an average year CIA was making some sixty estimates, very few of which ever reached the President's level of concern. I was convinced we would have lost the argument with the Nixon administration, and that in the process the Agency would have been permanently damaged.[15]

More recently, there is some evidence that DCI George Tenet sought to package intelligence in ways that satisfied the White House after it became clear that the Bush administration was committed to war in Iraq. Public and congressional skepticism about the rationale for war caused the administration to ratchet up its rhetoric on Iraqi nuclear, biological, and chemical weapons. Although reliable information on the current status of Iraqi weapons programs was scarce, Tenet sought to restore the reputation of the intelligence community in the White House after the 9/11 terrorist attacks, and was willing to help the administration make its public case for war. During a meeting in December, for instance, deputy director John McLaughlin presented a dry overview of the murky intelligence on Iraqi activities. The president was unhappy. 'Nice try', he said to McLaughlin. 'I don't think this is quite—it's not something that Joe Public would understand or gain a lot of confidence from'. At this point Tenet stepped in to support his deputy, assuring Bush that the intelligence was solid and that he would help create a more compelling presentation for the White House. According to *Washington Post* reporter Bob Woodward, Tenet told the president that the case against Iraq was a 'slam dunk'. The DCI denied using the phrase, but acknowledged later that he agreed to declassify intelligence that would make public statements more convincing. The result was an estimate of Iraqi capabilities that was much more certain and unequivocal than previous assessments, despite the fact that the underlying data remained patchy and ambiguous.[16]

Were these decisions necessary to preserve healthy intelligence-policy relations? The historical record suggests not. I have found nothing to suggest that DCI McCone's temporary optimism on Vietnam helped him get back in the good graces of the White House, and he soon returned to his pessimistic stance. His relationship with administration officials continued to deteriorate, and by the time he left office in 1964, it had become dysfunctional. And if McCone thought he was buying political capital by supporting the White House, he soon found out he was wrong. In June 1964 the Office of National Estimates (ONE) delivered two analyses that took aim at the prevailing domino theory and the strategic assumptions that underwrote an activist vision of containment. These analyses constituted a frontal attack on the administration's grand strategy and its views on Vietnam. Both were ignored.[17]

What about DCI Helms's decision to pull the CIA back from the fight over the Vietnam order of battle? Did his decision increase his personal standing with President Lyndon Johnson so that future intelligence estimates might inform future strategy and policy decisions? Recall that Helms' action was predicated on the expectation that the CIA would become involved in an ever-deepening controversy over strategic bombing. The Tet Offensive in January 1968 changed the political calculus for President Johnson, however, meaning that the anticipated fight over strategic bombing was far less intense than it might have been. For this reason, it is impossible to tell whether or not Helms capitalized on his decision to acquiesce to the Military Assistance Command, Vietnam (MACV). On the other hand, there is circumstantial evidence that Helms believed that his decision bought political capital with the president. Immediately after the controversy ended, he sent Johnson a remarkable eyes-only memo arguing that the consequences of withdrawing from Vietnam were manageable. It is possible that he would not have been so candid if he had continued to fight on behalf of CIA's order of battle estimate, but it is unknown if Johnson took this analysis seriously. It is certainly possible that Helms' memo provided additional rationale for Johnson's decision to begin de-escalating the war the following year, but the fact that the White House continued to pursue the attrition throughout 1967 suggests that it had very little impact.[18] The Tet Offensive was the shock that finally forced Johnson to reconsider his strategy, and during the period of reassessment he was swayed less by his own staff than by the so-called 'wise men', a group of advisors outside the government.[19] Nonetheless, it is certainly possible that Johnson remembered the Helms memo, and this case is the clearest example I have found that supports the argument about the benefits of soft politicization.

Helms's willingness to bend to pressure from the Nixon administration was no help at all. Despite his willingness to assist the administration with Congress during the SS-9 controversy, Helms was pushed out of the decision-making process. Indeed, Nixon never really wavered in his view that the intelligence community as an obstacle to policy implementation rather than an asset. The president fired Helms in late 1972, a casual dismissal that exasperated the normally staid intelligence chief.[20] The administration dissolved the Board of National Estimates one year later.

George Tenet's attempt to mollify the Bush administration also backfired. Rather than restoring good relations with the White House, the relationship sunk to a new low. It became clear soon after the US invasion in 2003 that Iraq possessed no stockpile of chemical, biological, or nuclear weapons. While critics blamed the administration for launching a war on false pretenses, the administration blamed the intelligence community for providing bad estimates of Iraqi capabilities. A short time later, the president's Weapons of Mass Destruction (WMD) Commission published a scathing report on the shortcomings of intelligence before the war. Unsurprisingly, intelligence analysts were furious at the White House, but they were equally livid at Tenet for failing to stand up to policy pressure. Tenet, like Helms, believed that soft politicization was necessary to maintain productive relations with policymakers. He was just as wrong as his predecessor.

Betts offers two other examples in support of the logic of soft politicization. In April 1970, the ONE wrote an analysis of possible consequences of an invasion of Cambodia. Aware the operation was already in the works, and conscious of the already fragile reputation of the intelligence community, Helms decided to withhold the estimate rather than circulate it to policymakers. Betts also notes that that the draft 'did not contain blockbuster conclusions that forcefully invalidated the president's reasons for deciding to invade'.[21] Given the direction of policy and the vulnerability of the intelligence community at the time, Helms' decision might seem prudent. But while the memo may not have contained any blockbusters, it did include a prescient warning about the pending invasion: to deny base areas and sanctuaries in Cambodia would require heavy and sustained bombing and large numbers of foot soldiers which could only be supplied by the United States and South Vietnam. Such an expanded allied effort could seriously handicap the communists and raise the cost to them of prosecuting the war, but, however successful, it probably would not prevent them from continuing the struggle in some form.[22]

The implications were ominous. According to the ONE, the invasion would require a protracted and substantial military footprint, and it would not compel the enemy to stop fighting. Put another way, an invasion would create precisely the same strategic problems in Cambodia that already existed in Vietnam. Betts is almost certainly correct that the estimate would not have stopped the administration from acting. (The invasion was scheduled to begin only 13 days after Helms received the draft.) But withholding important estimates based on the assumption that policymakers are set in their ways is a recipe for strategic myopia, and the White House would have been well served to reconsider its plans, especially given the enormous domestic upheaval that followed the Cambodian invasion. It is also worth noting that Helms had *already* pandered to the White House during the SS-9 affair in order to avoid a needless confrontation with policymakers. The fact that he faced the same dilemma less than a year later suggests the futility of this approach, as does the continued deterioration of intelligence-policy relations in the early 1970s.

Betts also cites an intelligence—policy controversy that arose during the first Gulf War. Military leaders hoped that a large scale preliminary bombing campaign would erode Iraqi tank capabilities and ease the US-led ground offensive. Commanders became increasingly eager to start the ground phase after several weeks of bombing, and they cited military intelligence reports about extensive damage to Iraqi armor in order to convince policymakers to give them the green light. CIA analysts disputed those reports, however, and they implied that much more bombing was necessary to reach predetermined attrition rates. General Norman Schwarzkopf, the overall US commander in the Gulf, believed that civilian analysts were improperly encroaching on military matters, and feared that their analysis would make him a scapegoat if the invasion failed. Ultimately he had nothing to fear. Policymakers accepted the original damage assessments, partly because they did not want to undermine senior military leaders in the field, and US conventional

superiority quickly turned the tank war into a rout. Post-war investigations found that the CIA's estimates were more accurate, but it was not clear at the time that the CIA had a better method for calculating attrition rates.[23]

Should intelligence officials have withheld their findings? Did they risk ruining their relations with the first Bush administration by challenging military estimates? To be sure, some policymakers were not happy about the CIA's intervention, including then-Secretary of Defense Dick Cheney, who was reminded of ferocious disputes between intelligence and the military during the Vietnam War.[24] The resignation of DCI William Webster shortly after the war also led to speculation that the White House was disappointed in performance of the intelligence community. But President George H.W. Bush lavishly praised intelligence in public and private, suggesting that the CIA's challenge did not affect its relationship with policymakers. When asked about the CIA's performance during Webster's retirement announcement, he admitted:

> we all got criticism. CIA got a little; Defense Department got a little; we took on some water over here. But the result was superb, and the intelligence was outstanding, and the community performed fantastically . . . I have no complaints whatsoever about the quality of our intelligence.[25]

It is also worth considering the episode from another direction. Suppose that CIA officials stifled their analysts so as to avoid damaging its relationship with policymakers. Suppose further that Iraqi divisions performed better in the war, destroying American tanks in large numbers. One can only imagine the recriminations against intelligence officials for withholding such a critical assessment.

IMPLICATIONS

This overview presented above is a first cut at the notion that there is such a thing as 'good' politicization. Although I remain skeptical, there are good reasons to take a harder look at the historical record because of the stakes involved in this issue. Knotty methodological issues also require attention. For example, a selection effect might lead us to undercount cases in which soft politicization succeeded in maintaining healthy intelligence-policy relations. Historical studies are more likely to focus on breakdowns rather than on periods of healthy working relations because there is not a lot to write about in the later cases. Indeed, decisions to soft-peddle or withhold estimates might never see the light of day. And even if we can locate such cases, measuring the impact on policymakers will require tricky counter-factual reasoning. Not only must we assess whether intelligence-policy relations profited by the decision to withhold discomfiting conclusions, but also whether they would have deteriorated if intelligence officials had been forthcoming.

There are at least two possible approaches to this problem. One is to work backwards from periods of generally harmonious intelligence-policy relations and look for instances in which intelligence chiefs used soft politicization in order to remain in the good graces of their policy bosses. Alternatively, we might look for periods of time in which estimates correlated with policy preferences, and look at policymakers' view of intelligence. Did they believe intelligence played an important role in decision-making during these periods? Did they value intelligence primarily because it helped overcome political or bureaucratic roadblocks to policy implementation? Or did they lose respect for intelligence officials for simply kowtowing? Also, did intelligence officials express satisfaction with their policy counterparts? And were intelligence analysts confident that their work mattered, or did they fear that their bosses were pandering to policymakers?

Certainly more work is needed on these questions, because the proposed distinction between good and bad politicization has important implications for intelligence and policy officials. If it is true that softening estimates or withholding bad news is necessary to maintain healthy relations, then intelligence officials are justified in treating policymakers with kid gloves, and leaders are justified in seeking out deferential advisors. But what if there is little supporting evidence for the benefits of instrumental politicization, as my research suggests? If this is the case, then intelligence officials who soft-pedal their views will risk the quality of estimates without any realistic hope of improving intelligence-policy relations. Politicized intelligence tends to present conclusions with an unrealistic sense of certainty even when the underlying information is incomplete or unreliable. This has the effect of amplifying analytical errors by discouraging re-assessment; intelligence agencies are bureaucratically disinclined from objective reassessments after they stake out strong and unequivocal positions. Analytical errors are inevitable whether intelligence is politicized or not, but such errors are extremely difficult to correct after politicization occurs.

Intelligence-policy relations suffer in the ugly aftermath of politicization. Intelligence officials accuse policymakers of bullying, policymakers accuse intelligence chiefs of craven obstructionism, and the result is that intelligence becomes increasingly irrelevant to the policy process. Even soft politicization can have this effect. Intelligence officials may believe that softening conclusions will curry favor with policymakers, but it might also lead to cynicism among analysts, which will subsequently reinforce policy suspicions about intelligence. In extreme cases policymakers will be wary of any estimate that challenges their views. Analysts' fear of policy manipulation will increase in the meantime, causing them to retreat behind institutional walls to protect their work from being corrupted. The result is what Sherman Kent called 'the sickness of irresponsibility', which is precisely the opposite of what well-intentioned intelligence officials hope to achieve through soft politicization.[26]

Another danger is that policymakers will overreact to estimates that confront their own views. Long stretches of soft politicization may accustom them to intelligence that supports their beliefs and preferences. A sudden change in intelligence might cause them to suspect that intelligence is no longer interested in supporting policy but is actively opposing it. Alternately, they might fall victim to familiar psychological problems associated with incorporating dissonant information. Individuals typically struggle with news that contradicts their preexisting beliefs. Rather than viewing such news objectively and reassessing their own beliefs, they are likely to ignore it or manipulate the new information so that it fits into their worldview. A prior pattern of watering down contrary estimates may contribute to this problem by reinforcing policy beliefs and expectations. The irony is that if soft politicization bolsters such beliefs, it may leave intelligence unable to persuade policymakers at key moments. Estimates that contradict policy views might be treated like any other piece of dissonant data. Soft politicization may be self-defeating.

There are also a number of related implications for intelligence and strategy. First, policymakers are likely to trust their own sources as intelligence-policy relations deteriorate. This is not necessarily a bad thing if their sources are knowledgeable and forthright, but it can be a very bad thing if their sources are motivated by rigid ideological beliefs. In the Iraq case, for instance, the desire to topple the Ba'ath regime seems to have blinded administration advisors to the profoundly flimsy knowledge about what was actually happening inside Iraq. Administration officials complained at the time that intelligence estimates were murky, and turned to unreliable sources like Iraqi exile groups for more unequivocal and damning evidence of Saddam's activities.[27] But this was because the underlying information *was* murky, and better intelligence-policy relations might have caused the White House to ask why this was so. Second, engaging in soft politicization means that intelligence officials are deliberately withholding details that might challenge policy beliefs. Near-term strategic decisions are more vulnerable to cognitive biases and wishful thinking under these conditions. Finally, in the worst-case scenario soft politicization will encourage strategic inertia, especially if it sets off the negative feedback loop described above. Policymakers who increasingly rely on a narrow circle of confidants (or worse, sycophants) and who indulge in wishful thinking are likely to be incapable of changing course even in the face of mounting evidence that their strategy is misguided.

QUESTIONS FOR FURTHER DISCUSSION

1. Do policymakers really want analysts to soft-pedal their estimates and analysis?
2. What actions can policymakers take to stop "soft politicization"?
3. Should intelligence officials make compromises to preserve their access to policymakers?
4. Should the intelligence community make policymakers aware of competing estimates or analytic disputes?

ENDNOTES

1. The views here are the author's alone.
2. Joshua Rovner, *Fixing the Facts: National Security and the Politics of Intelligence* (Ithaca, NY: Cornell University Press 2011).
3. See especially Gregory F. Treverton, *Reshaping National Intelligence for an Age of Information* (Cambridge, UK: Cambridge University Press 2001) pp.185–202.
4. Stephen Marrin, 'Intelligence Analysis and Decision-Making: Methodological Challenges' in Peter Gill, Stephen Marrin and Mark Phythian (eds.) *Intelligence Theory: Key Questions and Debates* (London: Routledge 2009).
5. Richard K. Betts, *Enemies of Intelligence: Knowledge & Power in American National Security* (New York: Columbia University Press 2007) p.75, italics in original.
6. Ibid., p.79.
7. Rovner, *Fixing the Facts*, pp.30–1.
8. Harold P. Ford, *CIA and the Vietnam Policymakers: Three Episodes, 1962–1968* (Washington, DC: Center for the Study of Intelligence 1998) p.18. Ford cites an internal CIA study of McCone that came to the same conclusion.
9. Christopher Andrew, *For the President's Eyes Only: Secret Intelligence and the American Presidency from Washington to Bush* (New York: HarperCollins 1995) pp. 283–4.
10. Richard Helms with William Hood, *A Look over My Shoulder: A Life in the Central Intelligence Agency* (New York: Ballantine Books 2003) p.328.
11. Michael Hiam, *Who the Hell are We Fighting? The Story of Sam Adams and the Vietnam Intelligence Wars* (Hanover, NH: Steerforth Press 2006) p.119.
12. US intelligence first became aware of the SS-9 in 1964, but there was no consensus about the purpose of such a large missile. Its enormous throw-weight made it a candidate for MIRVs, but its poor accuracy undermined the benefits of multiple warheads. In addition, some analysts believed that the size of the missile was simply intended for propaganda value. John Prados, *The Soviet Estimate: U.S. Intelligence Analysis and Soviet Strategic Forces* (Princeton, NJ: Princeton University Press 1982) pp.204–5.
13. Kirsten Lundberg, 'The SS-9 Controversy: Intelligence as Political Football', Case Program, John F. Kennedy School of Government, 1989, pp.11–12.
14. Jeffrey T. Richelson, *The Wizards of Langley: Inside the CIA's Directorate of Science and Technology* (Boulder, CO: Westview Press 2001) p.150.
15. Helms, *A Look Over My Shoulder*, pp.387–8.
16. Bob Woodward, *Plan of Attack* (New York: Simon & Schuster 2004) pp.247–50; and George Tenet with Bill Harlow, *At the Center of the Storm: My Years at the CIA* (New York: HarperCollins 2007) pp.359–63. On CIA efforts in the aftermath of 9/11, see Tenet, *At the Center of the Storm*, pp.175–89. See also Jeffrey Goldberg, 'Woodward vs. Tenet', *The New Yorker*, 21 May 2007.
17. Rovner, *Fixing the Facts*, ch.4.
18. In his memoir, Robert McNamara implies that Johnson did not find it persuasive. Robert McNamara, *In Retrospect: The Tragedy and Lessons of Vietnam* (New York: Random House 1995) pp.291–5.

19. George C. Herring, *America's Longest War: the United States and Vietnam, 1950–1975*, 2nd ed. (New York: McGraw Hill 1986) p.206.

20. The president and White House Chief of Staff H.R. Haldeman had agreed to let Helms stay on until March 1973, when he would reach the CIA's mandatory retirement age. Without warning, however, Nixon publicly introduced his replacement on 2 February. When Helms asked Haldeman what happened to their agreement, the chief of staff shrugged: 'Oh, I guess we forgot.' Helms, *A Look over My Shoulder*, pp.409–12.

21. Betts, *Enemies of Intelligence*, p.80.

22. Senate Select Committee to Study Governmental Operations with Respect to Intelligence Activities (Church Committee), *Final Report* (Washington, DC: Government Printing Office 1976), bk. I, pp.80–1. Betts cites the Church Committee as a source but leaves out its main conclusion: 'For whatever combination of reasons, in the spring of 1970 prior to the Cambodian incursion, the DCI did not provide senior policymakers formally with a national intelligence memorandum which argued that the operation would not succeed in thwarting the North Vietnamese effort to achieve control in Indochina'.

23. Betts, *Enemies of Intelligence*, pp.80–1. On later investigations into the episode, see Richard L. Russell, 'CIA's Strategic Intelligence in Iraq', *Political Science Quarterly* 117/2 (2002) pp.201–4.

24. Rick Atkinson, *Crusade: The Untold Story of the Persian Gulf War* (New York: Houghton Mifflin 2003) p.347.

25. Remarks Announcing the Resignation of William H. Webster as Director of the Central Intelligence Agency and a News Conference, 8 May 1991; in John T. Woolley and Gerhard Peters (eds.), *The American Presidency Project*, <http://www.presidency.ucsb.edu/ws/?pid=19563> (accessed 15 January 2012). See also Andrew, *For the President's Eyes Only*, p.526.

26. Sherman Kent, *Strategic Intelligence and American Foreign Policy* (Princeton, NJ: Princeton University Press 1949) pp.205–6.

27. On policy responses to intelligence estimates before the war, see Rovner, *Fixing the Facts*, pp.142–55.

Joshua Rovner (2013) "Is Politicization Ever a Good Thing?", *Intelligence and National Security*, 28:1, 55–67, DOI: 10.1080/02684527.2012.749065. Reprinted with permission of the publisher.

PART

VI

COVERT ACTION

Hamlet: ". . . And there put on him
What forgeries you please . . ."
—SHAKESPEARE, *Hamlet*, 2.1.19–20

Covert action (CA) may be defined as those activities carried out by national governments or other organizations, such as terrorist groups, to secretly influence and manipulate events abroad. Congress offered a formal definition in the Intelligence Authorization Act of 1991 (Public Law No. 102-88, 105 Stat. 441): "An activity or activities of the United States Government to influence political, economic, or military conditions abroad, where it is intended that the role of the United States Government will not be apparent or acknowledged publicly." The emphasis is on indirect, nonattribution, clandestine operations; the role of the government or other entity engaged in covert action is neither apparent nor publicly acknowledged (Godson 1996; Prados 1986; Treverton 1987).

This approach to advancing one's interests is also sometimes referred to as the "Third Option"—between sending in the Marines, on the one hand, and relying on the diplomatic corps to achieve one's goals, on the other hand. The use of military force is "noisy" and likely to draw a quick reaction from adversaries, as well as stir up criticism at home, while diplomacy can be notoriously slow and often ineffectual. Thus, covert action has a special appeal to

some policy officials; with this tool, they can move rapidly and in relative quiet, avoiding lengthy debate over tactics and broader objectives (hence, another euphemism for CA: the "quiet option"). Covert action has the added advantage of usually costing less, whether measured in blood or treasure, than a major military buildup.

THE EVOLUTION OF COVERT ACTION IN THE UNITED STATES

The use of covert action is older in the United States than the nation itself, having been used extensively by the colonial insurgents during the Revolutionary War (Knott 1996). The revolutionaries secretly urged France to aid the war effort by providing the colonial rebels with covert arms, and General George Washington initiated a campaign of propaganda against his British military adversaries. Soon after the founding of the new nation, President Thomas Jefferson secretly supplied arms to insurgents in Tripoli as a means for fermenting a coup against the unfriendly throne of the Bashaw, and President James Madison authorized paramilitary operations against the Spanish in Florida. During the Civil War, the North and the South both used covert actions for spreading propaganda and supplying arms to sympathizers.

Not until World War II, though, did the United States begin to carry out covert actions in a more concerted manner. President Franklin D. Roosevelt established an Office of Strategic Services (OSS) to engage not only in espionage but also in the sabotage of bridges and railroad tracks in Germany, the dissemination of propaganda, and the support of resistance groups. Although the OSS was disbanded after the war, President Harry S. Truman understood the importance of intelligence—Pearl Harbor had taught him—and he created the Central Intelligence Agency (CIA, or "the Agency") in 1947. The statutory language of the National Security Act of that year left open the possibility that the new Agency might be called on to engage in operations beyond the collection of intelligence. Without mentioning covert action explicitly, the law stated that the CIA had authority to "perform such other functions and duties related to intelligence affecting the national security as the National Security Council may from time-to-time direct."

The immediate challenge of the Soviet Union and its avowed intent to spread Communism far and wide turned the Truman administration toward this ambiguous phrase in the National Security Act. The administration interpreted the language broadly as an invitation to unleash the CIA to fight against Soviet expansion and the activities of other Communist countries and movements. In the late 1940s and early 1950s, secret funding went to pro-Western labor unions, political parties, and publishers in Europe; anti-Communist dictators in Latin America; and pro-Western factions in Asia, Africa, and the Middle East. By the end of the 1960s, the Agency had hundreds of operations under way around the world. During the major overt wars in Korea (1950–1953) and Vietnam (1964–1975), the budgets grew for CIA paramilitary or secret warlike operations in those nations.

When the United States withdrew from the unpopular war in Vietnam, funding for covert action began a downward slide, accelerated by the attempted misuse of the CIA by the Nixon administration during the Watergate affair in 1973–1974 and by investigative disclosures in 1975 that the Agency had spied on American citizens and tried to subvert the democratically elected president of Chile (Salvador Allende). When President Jimmy Carter entered office in 1977, the CIA's covert action budget had fallen to less than 5 percent of the Agency's funding (in contrast to over 50 percent during the Vietnam War). President Carter kept the budget at that level initially, but following the Soviet invasion of Afghanistan in 1979, he increased the funding for covert action sixfold.

When the Reagan administration came into power, this secret instrument of foreign policy entered its heyday. The Reagan Doctrine, a term coined by the media, entailed an all-out covert struggle led by the CIA against Communist partisans around the world—especially in Nicaragua and Afghanistan but also in El Salvador, Angola, Cambodia, and Eastern Europe, and against the Soviet Union itself.

The Iran-contra scandal (1987), in which the Reagan administration resorted to covert actions in Iran and Nicaragua without proper reporting to Congress and in defiance of a law (the Boland Amendment) strictly prohibiting such operations in Nicaragua, discredited the CIA generally and covert action in particular. The budget for CA dropped to its lowest levels since the opening months of the Cold War: less than 1 percent of the Agency's annual budget (Johnson 1996). The funding remained at this level throughout the first Bush administration and rose modestly when the Clinton administration turned to the CIA for help with its foreign policy woes in Haiti, Africa, and the Balkans.

It would take the terrorist attacks against the United States on September 11, 2001, to really stimulate the covert action budget, which began a rapid rise in the name of combating world terrorism. The use of CIA paramilitary operations against the Taliban regime in Afghanistan, in tandem with overt military operations by the indigenous Northern Alliance and U.S. bombing missions, opened a new chapter in America's reliance on covert action. Events in Afghanistan in 2001–2002 pointed to a successful triple-threat formula for the accomplishment of U.S. foreign policy objectives: a combination of pinpoint bombing, local allied insurgents, and paramilitary operations conducted by the CIA and Pentagon Special Forces. This formula was applied in Iraq in 2003, although in the context of a much larger overt U.S. invasion force in this second Persian Gulf War. From 2003 through 2018, the United States turned to an extensive use of CIA covert action to combat global terrorism, especially in the Middle East, Southwest Asia, and North Africa (Johnson 2017). Drone attacks, using Hellfire and other types of missiles, became the most lethal form of CIA covert action.

THE METHODS OF COVERT ACTION

Covert action takes four forms, often used in conjunction with one another: propaganda (psychological warfare operations, or "psy ops"), political operations, economic operations, and paramilitary (PM) operations—with the last including assassination as a subset. These activities are estimated to have accounted for 40, 30, 10, and 20 percent, respectively, of the total number of covert actions during the Cold War (Johnson 1989). Paramilitary operations were, however, (and continue to be) by far the most expensive and controversial form of CA.

PROPAGANDA

During the Cold War, the open instrument of U.S. propaganda was the United States Information Agency (USIA), which released, through American embassies abroad, a vast amount of information about the United States and its objectives. As a supplement to this overt flow of information, the CIA (following presidential directives) inserted comparable, often identical, themes into secret media channels around the world. As with the USIA releases, the CIA's propaganda was in almost all cases (98 percent) accurate, if partial to the policies of the United States; about 2 percent of the propaganda was false ("black").

Indigenous agents ("media assets") secretly working for the CIA in foreign countries—journalists, radio and television commentators, op-ed and magazine writers, book authors—expressed "their" views through local media channels. Yet the material was often written verbatim for them in their native tongues by propaganda specialists in the Operations Directorate at CIA Headquarters in Langley, Virginia. Local audiences understandably looked on these seemingly homegrown sources of information—their own newspapers—as far more credible than USIA press releases. In return for these services, the media assets would receive cash payments and travel stipends from their local CIA "case officer," who normally operated out of the American embassy in the nation's capital. During the height of the Cold War, the CIA made 70 to 80 insertions into various media outlets each day—a great tidal wave of information flowing secretly from Agency headquarters into hundreds of hidden channels around the globe.

In tightly controlled totalitarian regimes where it was difficult (if not impossible) to recruit local media assets, the CIA relied on infiltrating propaganda. Such efforts could be quite primitive, including the lofting of air balloons to carry speeches, magazines, books, and transistor radios into forbidden territories where—thanks to these airborne deliveries—a deprived citizenry might have the opportunity to read about the outside world. Most of the balloons aimed at the U.S.S.R. crash-landed in that empire's vast expanse, with unknown but probably negligible effects. The CIA also dispatched airplanes to drop leaflets over isolated regimes or transmitted radio broadcasts (sometimes from makeshift stations in remote jungles). Most successful were the radio transmissions directed toward the Soviet Union and other adversaries, especially those conducted by Radio Free Europe (RFE) and Radio Liberty (RL), operating in Munich initially under the auspices of the CIA, until their secret ties with intelligence were leaked to the press in the early 1970s, at which point the U.S. government provided overt funding for the radio stations. Supporters credit these stations with having helped to sustain hope behind the Iron Curtain among dissident groups and slowly, but steadily, abetting the erosion of support for the Communist Party in Moscow and Eastern Europe. Critics are less sure that they contributed much to the fall of the Soviet Union.

Although the CIAs secret propaganda operations against the Soviet Union and China during the Cold War have been praised by some in the United States and Europe, its operations in the developing world have been subjected to widespread criticism. The best known and most controversial example is Chile during the 1960s (Treverton 1987). In the Chilean presidential election of 1964, the CIA spent $3 million to mar the reputation of Salvador Allende, the Socialist candidate with suspected ties to Moscow. On a per capita basis, this amount was equivalent to the expenditure of $60 million in a U.S. presidential election at the time, a staggering level of funding likely to decide the outcome of a presidential election whether in Chile or the United States. The CIA managed to thwart Allende's election in 1964, but he persevered and in 1970 won the presidency in a free and open election.

The CIA then turned to a range of propaganda and other covert actions designed to destroy Allende's regime. The Agency poured $3 million into the country to support anti-Allende secret propaganda between 1970 and 1973, in the form of press releases, radio commentary, films, pamphlets, posters, leaflets, direct mailings, paper streamers, and vivid wall paintings conjuring images of Communist tanks and firing squads that would supposedly soon become a part of life in Chile. Printing hundreds of thousands of copies, the CIA blanketed the country, which is predominantly Catholic, with an anti-Communist pastoral letter written many years earlier by Pope Pius XI. The effect was to substantially weaken the Allende government.

Another successful CIA propaganda operation took place in Central America in 1954. The Agency set up a radio station in the mountains of Guatemala. Local media assets began to broadcast the fiction that a revolution had erupted and that the people of Guatemala were joining the movement in large numbers; meanwhile, other CIA recruits began a march against the pro-Communist dictator Jacobo Arbenz. With a speed that surprised even the CIA instigators, the reports became something of a self-fulfilling prophecy, and the hapless Arbenz, panicked by the mythical prospect of the masses storming his palace, resigned before a shot was fired. This bloodless coup was a heady experience for covert action advocates, coming only seven years after the establishment of the CIA and on the heels of a similar victory in Iran (though one that relied on clandestine political maneuvering as well as propaganda). It began to seem as though the world could be transformed toward a pro-Western orientation by Madison Avenue public relations techniques, secretly applied.

Despite these early successes, the CIA's use of propaganda has had its share of critics. Early in the Cold War, the CIA funded the National Student Association inside the United States as part of its propaganda operations. The purpose was to encourage young Americans to travel abroad and counter Soviet efforts at manipulating international student conferences. Critics were enraged, though, by this trespassing of the CIA into the activities of groups within the United States, an activity strictly prohibited by the Agency's founding statute. The specter of influencing American audiences, not just foreign countries, arose again when it became public that the CIA was sponsoring the publication of anti-Communist books written by Soviet defectors as well as U.S. authors. The idea of American students and writers on the payroll of a secret intelligence agency struck civil libertarians

as beyond the pale. So did the revelation that the CIA had journalists on its payroll. The estimates ranged from three dozen, conceded by the Agency, to over 400 alleged by investigative reporters. Furthermore, it came to light that the CIA had secretly encouraged its U.S. media assets to write negative reviews of books published by American authors critical of the Agency. Some of George Orwell's worst fears appeared to have come true in the United States.

Troublesome, too, was the notion of "blowback" or "replay": the insertion of propaganda abroad only to have it waft back to U.S. audiences by way of American correspondents innocently reading CIA media plants in foreign newspapers and reporting this information to American readers. Critics raised doubts as well about the propriety of placing secret propaganda into the media outlets of fellow democracies. The USSR and Communist China, yes, because their citizens had no access to accurate information about the world, their masters had no compunction about manipulating their own media, and the regimes were hostile toward the United States. But Denmark, France, and Germany seemed a different story—at least for critics, if not for the CIA's Operations Directorate.

Sometimes the Agency's propaganda operations looked as though they had been crafted by an imaginative descendent of Franz Kafka. As a means for discrediting Fidel Castro of Cuba, one CIA plan (according to the public testimony of an intelligence officer before a U.S. Senate investigating committee in 1975) consisted of

> spreading the word that the Second Coming of Christ was imminent and that Christ was against Castro [who] was anti-Christ. And you would spread this word around Cuba, and then on whatever date it was, that there would be a manifestation of the thing. And at that time—this is absolutely true—and at that time just over the horizon there would be an American submarine which would surface off of Cuba and send up some starshells. And this would be the manifestation of the Second Coming and Castro would be overthrown. (Church Committee 1975b)

The CIA called this operation "Elimination by Illumination." Fortunately, someone in the higher reaches of the Agency had the good sense to cancel this absurd exercise before it was attempted.

As one might expect, other nations carry out propaganda operations, too (and all the other forms of covert action). For instance, Russia is widely known to have tried to influence the 2016 presidential election by placing anonymous pro-Trump and anti-Clinton messages in social media targeted at the American electorate.

POLITICAL COVERT ACTION

Governments also carry out covert actions—or "special activities," as the United States likes to clothe the concept in its official and (rare) public references to the subject—of a political nature. Secret payments to friendly foreign politicians and bureaucrats are one example. Critics scorn this method as nothing less than bribery to advance America's national interests around the world. Advocates, however, prefer a more sanguine interpretation: not bribery, but rather stipends for the advancement of global democracy—what British intelligence officers in Her Majesty's Secret Service refer to affectionately as "King George's cavalry."

According to the public record, during the Cold War the CIA's political sponsorships included political parties, individual politicians, or dictators in (from a longer, mostly classified list) Italy, Jordan, Iran, Ecuador, El Salvador, Angola, Chile, West Germany, Greece, Egypt, Sudan, Suriname, Mauritius, and the Philippines. The secret funds were used to win the favor of influential government officials, to help win elections for pro-Western factions (Italy was a heated electoral battleground in the early days of the Cold War), to recruit and build parties and regimes opposed to Communism, and to strengthen labor unions in opposition to Communist Party takeovers (again, Italy and the rest of Europe were pivotal).

Propaganda and political covert action are meant to work hand-in-glove, and sometimes both are subsumed under the "political" label. Some offices in the CIA's Operations Directorate take on the attributes of a political campaign headquarters, with intelligence officers engaged in the mass production of brochures, speeches, placards, campaign buttons, and bumper stickers (never mind that campaign buttons look a little out of place on tribal warlords or that some of the developing countries where the bumper stickers are sent may have only a few automobiles). Their common purpose during the Cold War was to persuade important foreign officials to turn a favorable eye toward the United States and away from the Soviet Union—or, more recently, away from adversaries such as Saddam Hussein in Iraq or the global network of al-Qaeda terrorist organizations. In this sense, the Cold War and the era since may be thought of as a subterranean political struggle between the United States and its enemies abroad, in which intelligence organizations have waged a clandestine war to win the hearts and minds of people around the world and to place into government positions men and women of an ideological persuasion compatible with America's interests.

ECONOMIC COVERT ACTION

Another weapon in a nation's arsenal of clandestine operations is the use of subversion against an adversary's means of economic production. During its campaign to ruin Allende, the CIA provided financial support to factions within Chile for the purposes of encouraging strikes—especially against the trucking industry—that would plunge the regime into commercial chaos. Earlier, during the Kennedy administration, the CIA planned to undermine Soviet-Cuban relations by lacing 14,125 bags of sugar bound from Havana to Moscow with an unpalatable (though harmless) chemical substance. At the eleventh hour, a White House aide learned of the proposal and, deeming it excessive, put a stop to it (Wicker 1966).

In the conduct of economic covert action, foreign currencies may be counterfeited, the world price of trading commodities depressed (especially harmful to one-crop economies, as in the case of Cuba's reliance on sugarcane), harbors mined to discourage commercial shipping (carried out by the Johnson and Nixon administrations against North Vietnam and by the Reagan administration against the Marxist regime in Nicaragua), electrical power lines and oil-storage tankers dynamited (again, North Vietnam and Nicaragua), oil supplies contaminated (North Vietnam), and even clouds seeded in an effort to disrupt weather patterns over the enemy's territory (in North Vietnam, to no effect).

Today, a prime target of economic dislocation is an adversary's computer systems. With skillful hacking ("cyberwarfare"), a nation's or group's financial transactions can be left in disarray, its bank assets stolen, its communications hopelessly tangled, its electric grid disabled, and its military command-and-control capabilities frozen—an electronic assault that could be at least as dislocating as a military attack.

PARAMILITARY COVERT ACTION

While some of the covert actions we've mentioned earlier can be quite devastating (such as the mining of harbors), paramilitary or warlike operations are usually the most extreme and controversial forms of a nation's secret foreign policy. They can involve large-scale "secret" warfare—something of an oxymoron, since the extensive use of military force against an adversary does not stay secret for long, as the "quiet option" soon becomes noisy (an overt-covert action). The CIA's Special Operations Group (SOG), a subsidiary of its Operations Directorate, sponsored many guerrilla wars during the Cold War. From 1963 to 1973, the Agency backed the Hmong (Meo) tribes of North Laos in a war against the Communist Pathet Lao, who served as puppets of North Vietnam. The two sides fought to a draw, before the United States finally withdrew from the struggle. From the public record alone, it is clear that the CIA has also supported pro-Western insurgents in Ukraine, Poland, Albania, Hungary, Indonesia, China, Oman, Malaysia, Iraq, the Dominican Republic, Venezuela, North Korea, Bolivia, Thailand, Haiti, Guatemala, Cuba, Greece, Turkey, Vietnam, Afghanistan, Angola, and Nicaragua.

In these operations, the CIA's main role was to provide advice and weaponry. Anti-Communist dissidents during the early stages of the Cold War became the beneficiaries of a wide range of arms shipments from the United States, compliments of the CIA, including high-powered rifles, suitcase bombs, fragmentation grenades, rapid-fire machine guns, 64-mm antitank rockets, .38-caliber pistols, .30-caliber M-l carbines, .45-caliber submachine guns, tear-gas grenades, and supplies of ammunition. When the Reagan administration came into office, it funneled through the CIA a reported $3 billion worth of weaponry to anti-Soviet fighters in Afghanistan (the *mujahideen,* or "soldiers of god"). Among the weapons were sophisticated shoulder-held Stinger and Blowpipe missiles capable of bringing down Soviet bombers. This "secret" supply of armaments to the *mujahideen* is said to have been an important consideration in Moscow's decision to withdraw from its losing "Vietnam" war in Afghanistan.

Since the end of the Cold War, the CIA has provided substantial amounts of arms and financial support to a new list of pro-US factions, especially in the Middle East, the Balkans, and South Asia. Recipients have included the Iraqi National Congress, an umbrella group of insurgents opposed to Saddam Hussein's regime; opponents of Serbian expansion in Bosnia and Kosovo; and the Northern Alliance, along with other anti-Taliban factions, following the 2001 terrorist attacks against the United States that were widely thought to have been masterminded by al-Qaeda cells based in Afghanistan. In the 2002–2003 war to root out al-Qaeda and Taliban forces from Afghanistan, the CIA introduced the use of unmanned aerial vehicles (UAVs) such as the Predator, equipped with cameras and Hellfire missiles to spot and quickly eliminate enemy forces—the newest (highly lethal) approach to paramilitary operations.

As part of its paramilitary operations, the CIA is extensively involved in the training of foreign soldiers to fight on behalf of U.S. interests. These programs have entailed the training of foreign soldiers for guerrilla warfare, as well as counterterrorism. The CIA's military advisers for such purposes are often borrowed from the Department of Defense (DoD) and given nonofficial battlefield gear, a conversion known by insiders as "sheepdipping." The CIA's paramilitary program includes support to the Department of Defense in the development of the Pentagon's own unconventional warfare capability, known as Special Operations (or "Special Ops" for short) and carried out by elite Special Forces. For example, the CIA has provided armaments to the DoD for covert sales abroad. Some of the weapons sold to Iran by the Defense Department in the notorious arms-sale scandal of 1986–87 (the Iran-contra affair) had their origin in the CIA's paramilitary arsenal.

Moreover, the CIA provides training for military and police units in the developing world, particularly security personnel responsible for the protection of their nation's leaders. Among the skills taught at Camp Perry, the Agency's training facility in Virginia, are lessons in how to protect communications channels and the techniques of "executive driving" (designed to impart spin-away steering skills for maneuvering an automobile through terrorist roadblocks).

During those rare moments when the United States is not involved in the support of paramilitary wars in one place or another (as in the early years of the Carter administration), the CIA's Special Operations Group bides its time by carrying out training operations for its own personnel and by maintaining its military hardware (including a small navy and air force). Above all, SOG is kept busy in its added responsibility to provide support for intelligence collection operations, especially in remote regions like the mountains of Afghanistan and Pakistan, where U.S. paramilitary officers have recently developed geographic expertise and contacts with local warlords.

ASSASSINATION PLOTS

A special category within the realm of paramilitary operations is the assassination of individual foreigners—needless to say a subject fraught with controversy. This option has gone by a number of euphemisms, used in hushed tones within the government of the United States: "executive action," "terminate with extreme prejudice," or "neutralize." At one time during the Cold War, proposals for assassination were screened by a special unit within the CIA called the "Health Alteration Committee." (Its counterpart in the Soviet Union was the KGB's "Department of Wet Affairs.")

Fidel Castro was America's prime target for assassination during the Kennedy administration, although none of the plots against him succeeded. Another target for "health alteration" during the Kennedy years was Patrice Lumumba, the Congolese leader. Members of a rival Congolese faction beat the CIA to the punch, however, and murdered Lumumba for their own political reasons related to an internal power struggle. Recent research suggests that the CIA may have been involved in delivering Lumumba into the hands of his assassins (Weissman 2010).

In 1976, soon after the U.S. Senate revealed the CIA's involvement in international murder plots, President Gerald R. Ford signed an executive order against this practice. The wording of the order, endorsed by his successors, reads: "No person employed by or acting on behalf of the United States Government, shall engage in, or conspire to engage in assassination." While honored most of the time, when America is involved in an authorized overt war—one supported by a majority vote in each chamber of Congress—the executive order has been waived.

Most recently, the United States has been involved in congressionally authorized overt wars in Iraq and Afghanistan, as well as against al-Qaeda and its Taliban supporters in Afghanistan, Pakistan, and elsewhere. The executive order against assassination has been waived in these struggles. The Iraqi leader Saddam Hussein was regularly a target in the Second Persian Gulf War that began in 2003; but as in the First Persian Gulf War (1990–1991), when he

was also targeted, he proved elusive. Eventually, U.S. troops discovered him hiding in a hole in the ground near his hometown. They arrested him, and then he was subsequently tried by an Iraqi tribunal and hanged. Added to the current list of people to be captured or assassinated by the United States military and CIA paramilitary forces are extremist Taliban, as well as al-Qaeda members in the Middle East, Africa, and Southwest Asia. Recently Afghan narcotics dealers, who are frequently complicit in terrorist activities, have been added to the targeting list.

Since the end of the Cold War, the CIA (in cooperation with the U.S. Air Force) has developed and fielded its most deadly paramilitary weapon: unmanned aerial vehicles (UAVs), such as the Predator and its more muscular counterpart, the Reaper. Both drones are armed with surveillance cameras, as well as Hellfire or other types of missiles. These systems are controlled remotely from sites in Afghanistan and Pakistan (for the takeoffs and landings), as well as from locations in the United States (for the targeting and killing phases of flight). Cruising at low altitudes, the UAV cameras identify target and provide instant "analysis" before the missiles are released by their remote operators thousands of miles away. The Predator and the Reaper have become the most lethal instruments of CIA paramilitary covert action.

Target mistakes are made, compounded by the fact that Taliban and al-Qaeda terrorists often seek refuge in mosques, schools, and other locations where innocent civilians may be inadvertently struck by the UAV missiles, even though the CIA and the Pentagon (which controls its own fleet of drones for use on the battlefield) take pains to avoid this "collateral damage." The drone attacks remain controversial because they occasionally result in civilian deaths and are unpopular among may Pakistani citizens, who view the flights as a violation of their nation's sovereignty—just as many Pakistanis criticized the Navy's surprise commando raid in 2011 that led to the killing of the al-Qaeda leader Osama bin Laden in Abbottabad, a city just thirty-five miles from Islamabad, the capital of Pakistan.

Exactly who should be on the CIA "kill" list has been a controversial subject. Originally, the Patriot Act of 2001 stipulated that only those enemies involved in the 9/11 attacks were legitimate targets for retaliation. Since then, and without further legislative guidelines, the target list has expanded. For instance, a US-born cleric by the name of Anwar al-Awlaki, reportedly hiding in Yemen where he was considered an Al Qaeda recruiter, was placed on the CIA assassination list, even though he has never been convicted in a court of law (for an account, see Shane 2015). Further, it is unclear if he had actually been involved in plots against the United States. If he had, al-Awlaki could arguably be considered a legitimate target; however, if he was limiting himself to making speeches against the United States, he would have been just one of hundreds (perhaps thousands) of radicals in the Middle East and Southwest Asia who have advocated *jihad* against Western "infidels."

Without any judicial review, the Obama administration concluded in secret that al-Awlaki was indeed involved in terrorism against the United States, most notably in his alleged support of the so-called underwear bomber, Umar Farouk Abdulmutallah, a Nigerian man who had tried unsuccessfully to detonate a bomb hidden in his undergarments as he flew on a Christmas Day flight to Detroit in 2009. In response, al-Awlaki barely escaped a U.S. drone strike in May of 2011. Then in September of that year, a CIA drone managed to kill him and an aide (also an American). Two weeks later, a drone strike struck down al-Awlaki's son, another American citizen. In an earlier drone attack in 2002, a Predator missile incinerated an automobile in a Yemeni desert that carried six passengers suspected of being al-Qaeda affiliates. All six perished. One turned out to have been an American citizen—again, a person never brought to trial. Such events raise serious questions about due process, as well as the need to establish the identities of targets beyond the shadow of a doubt before pulling the trigger on a Hellfire missile.

At present the procedures for developing assassination target lists lack clarity and sufficient oversight. Reportedly, this decision to place an individual on a target list requires the approval of the U.S. ambassador to the target country, as well as the CIA chief of station, the Director of the Agency's National Clandestine Service, the Director of the CIA (D/CIA), and the Director of National Intelligence (DNI, an office established in 2004). If the target is an American citizen, attorneys in the Department of Justice must also approve. Moreover, at least some of the members and staff of the two congressional intelligence committees are reportedly briefed on the targeting.

In 2012, the Attorney General said publicly that assassinations may take place against American citizens who are planning an imminent attack against the United States or who are engaged in operations that take place on traditional battlefields. According to the AG, no prior judicial review of any kind would be necessary. In response, critics argued that at least a more formal congressional review should take place; and perhaps the judicial branch of government should be part of this decision making, too. A special court, similar to the one established in 1978 to review wiretap requests (the Foreign Intelligence Surveillance or FIS Court), could be established to evaluate requests for assassinations—especially when American citizens are the prospective targets.

A BALANCE SHEET

Since the outbreak of the Cold War and the establishment of the CIA in 1947, covert action has exercised a fascination on most presidential administrations. But what have been the results? This question may be answered according to practical outcomes and ethical considerations. With respect to practicalities, a further distinction must be made between the short-term and long-term consequences of covert action.

The practical results have been mixed. Sometimes covert action has led to stunning successes for the United States, at least in the short term. In Europe in the immediate aftermath of World War II (particularly in Greece and Italy), in Iran (1953), in Guatemala (1954), and less spectacularly throughout Latin America in the 1950s, covert action played a major role in thwarting Communist and Marxist political leaders and movements—often sponsored openly or covertly by the USSR. In the short run, the CIA also chalked up notable successes in Laos (1963–1973), Afghanistan (1982–1988), Panama (1989, toppling the corrupt dictator General Manuel Antonio Noriega), and Afghanistan and Iraq (2001–2003).

Yet, the lasting value of some of these "victories" (that is, the long-term consequences) has been questionable. Iran is hardly a close friend of the United States today; Guatemala and Panama are as poor and repressive as ever; the first Afghanistan intervention brought the Taliban regime to power, which in turn supported the al-Qaeda terrorist organization; and the second Afghanistan and Iraq interventions are unlikely to have brought global terrorism to a halt (although in Afghanistan it took a useful step in that direction). Earlier there were the Bay of Pigs fiasco, the madcap plots to dispatch Fidel Castro (exploding cigars, secret powders designed to make his charismatic beard fall out), the pouring of millions of dollars into the sinkhole of the Angolan civil war, and the Iran-contra scandal and its dismissal of the Constitution. Along the way came the CIA's abandonment of temporary allies in a string of anti-Communist paramilitary operations, including the freedom fighters in Hungary and at the Bay of Pigs, the South Vietnamese who aided the CIA and ended up buried in cemeteries throughout Saigon as the United States fled Indochina, the Meo tribesmen in Laos, the Khambas in Tibet, the Nationalist Chinese in Burma, and the ever-suffering Kurds.

On practical grounds, perhaps the best conclusion one can draw based on the empirical record is that covert action (like overt economic sanctions or aerial bombing) sometimes succeeds and sometimes fails. Its chances seem best when the objectives are limited, when strong opposition groups already exist within a target nation or group, and, in the case of paramilitary operations, when it is aided and abetted by overt precision bombing by the U.S. Air Force, along with assistance from elite DoD Special Forces on the ground.

THE READINGS

This section opens with a chapter by historian Michael Grow. He lays out the story of CIA covert actions in Chile during the 1970s, aimed at ridding that nation of its socialist leader, Salvador Allende. This covert action was particularly controversial, because Allende had been chosen by the people of Chile in a fair, open, and democratic presidential election.

In the second article of this section, Former Senator Frank Church (D, Idaho), who in 1975 led a searing investigation into legal violations of the intelligence agencies, argues that the covert action instruments of the CIA during the Cold War were "put to the service of reactionary and repressive regimes that can never, for long, escape or withstand the volcanic forces of change." A strong critic of most covert actions during the Cold War, Senator Church nonetheless saw a potential role for this approach, say, if a timely clandestine intervention were able to avert a nuclear holocaust or if covert action might aid the people of another nation in their struggle against an unpopular Marxist regime.

Elke Schwarz explores the role of drones, or Unmanned Aerial Vehicles (UAVs), in America's struggle against global terrorism. Drone attacks have become the most lethal form of covert action carried out by the CIA in its counterterrorism activities. Schwarz is skeptical about the long-range value of drone attacks as a counterterrorism measure.

Finally, on the controversial question of assassinations, Bruce D. Berkowitz examines the arguments for and against sending CIA officers on missions to murder individuals considered anathema to America's global interests.

15. COVERT ACTION IN CHILE, 1970

MICHAEL GROW

During the Johnson and Nixon Administrations, officials were often led in their foreign policy decisions by the mantra "ABC"—"Anybody But Communists." This provoked the Nixon Administration to escalate CIA covert actions against a left-leaning presidential candidate (and later president) Salvador Allende in Chile. This essay explores the rationales for the covert intervention, as well as the CIA's methods.

President Nixon was enraged. When Ambassador Edward Korry entered the Oval Office on October 13, 1970, to discuss U.S.-Chilean relations with the president, Nixon was slamming his fist into the palm of his hand and fuming, "That sonofabitch, that sonofabitch!" The "sonofabitch" in question, Nixon quickly explained, was "that bastard Allende"—a profane reference to the newly elected president of Chile, Salvador Allende.[1]

Nixon had ample reason to dislike Allende. The new Chilean president was, after Fidel Castro, one of Latin America's most prominent Marxist political leaders. Allende and Castro were close friends and fellow revolutionaries. Allende, however, rejected the Cuban model of insurrectionary violence and armed struggle as a strategy for socialist revolution in Chile. Instead, he was committed to pursuing a peaceful, democratic "road to socialism" in his country—a *vía parlamentaria*, or "parliamentary path," in which Chile's Marxist forces would first mobilize mass-based electoral support to win power democratically and then, once in control of the government, use constitutional processes and legislative enactments in the congress to construct a socialist society. The end result, Allende promised, would be a uniquely Chilean experience—a socialist revolution carried out in a framework of "democracy, pluralism, and liberty." If his revolutionary strategy succeeded, he believed, Chile would become a "second model of the transition to a socialist society," a peaceful, democratic alternative to the Soviet, Chinese, and Cuban models.[2]

Allende's commitment to the *vía parlamentaria* spanned some four decades. A founding member of Chile's Socialist Party in 1932, minister of health in a Popular Front government during World War II, and a senator in the Chilean congress from 1945 to 1970, he had spent his entire political career as "a normal, democratic politician" working for socialist change from within Chile's traditional institutional structures.[3] Now, with his electoral victory in the 1970 presidential election, he had an historic opportunity to make his vision of a nonviolent, democratic Marxist revolution in Chile a reality.

Not all of Allende's supporters shared their leader's commitment to parliamentary democracy, however. Allende had campaigned for the presidency as the candidate of Unidad Popular (Popular Unity, or UP), a heterogeneous and fractious electoral coalition of leftist parties consisting of Chile's Socialists and Communists along with four smaller organizations. The Chilean Communist Party—generally regarded as "the largest, best-organized, and most disciplined of its kind in Latin America"—was pursuing the *vía parlamentaria* largely for reasons of tactical opportunism. Following orthodox Leninist strategy, the Communists had for years been embarked on a "long march through the institutions," participating in Chile's democratic political system in the hope of gaining power and introducing revolutionary changes without resorting to armed insurrection or civil war. The Communists viewed their participation in the 1970 Unidad Popular electoral coalition as an appropriate strategy for the party during a preliminary "national-democratic stage" of the revolution—when the Communists, in alliance with other "popular forces" and "progressive" sectors of "the bourgeoisie," would win power electorally and implement broad reforms, attacking, weakening, and isolating Chile's capitalist elites in preparation for a full transition to socialism and the eventual establishment of a Soviet-style "dictatorship of the masses."[4]

Ironically, a majority of Allende's own Socialist Party was skeptical of the peaceful, parliamentary road to socialism and believed instead that a true socialist revolution could ultimately be achieved only through a process of revolutionary violence that would destroy socialism's capitalist enemies. During the mid-1960s, the party's leadership had fallen under the control of radicals, "mainly Trotsky-ites," who looked to the Cuban revolution as their source of political inspiration. A 1967 party congress declared that "revolutionary violence is inevitable and legitimate" and that "peaceful and legal forms of struggle are limited instruments of action" in a political process that inevitably would end in armed struggle. Party radicals accepted the Socialists' participation in the 1970 Unidad Popular electoral coalition for tactical reasons, but they made no secret of their belief that, if elected, Allende would at some point have to abandon "bourgeois legalism and constitutionality" and mobilize the working classes and popular masses for a decisive revolutionary assault on Chile's entrenched elites.[5] Indeed, at the time of Allende's election, many Socialist radicals openly supported the guerrilla-warfare tactics of the Movimiento de Izquierda Revolucionaria (Movement of the Revolutionary Left, or MIR), an organization of ultraleft Marxist militants that was carrying out a campaign of bombing attacks, hijackings, bank robberies, and illegal land seizures throughout the country.[6] Whether Allende would be able to control the radical elements in his own coalition when the peaceful road to socialism turned bumpy remained problematical as he prepared for his November 1970 inauguration.

Some of Allende's political opponents even questioned the depth of *his* commitment to democratic processes. Both outgoing president Eduardo Frei of the center-left Christian Democratic Party and Jorge Alessandri, the defeated 1970 candidate of the conservative National Party, expressed fears that if Allende found the *vía pariamentaria* blocked by centrist and right-wing forces in the Chilean congress, he might, under pressure from his radical-left supporters, suspend constitutional procedures and resort to authoritarian governance. To allay such concerns, Allende agreed prior to his inauguration to abide by a new constitutional "statute of democratic guarantees" that reaffirmed his commitment to preserve "the norms of pluralistic constitutional democracy."[7] Less reassuring, however, was the president-elect's proposed plan to replace Chile's traditional two-house legislature with a unicameral "assembly of the people" that would be empowered to select Chile's supreme-court judges and supervise the nation's judicial system. Given the pivotal role that Chile's courts would play in sanctioning any socialist reform initiatives passed by the congress, Allende's proposal only increased the fears of his political opponents that under his presidency Chilean democracy might mutate into an increasingly totalitarian system.[8]

Salvador Allende was no friend of the United States. Like the Guatemalan and Cuban revolutionaries before him, he ascribed his country's under development and poverty to an exploitative "symbiotic alliance" that Chile's upper-class oligarchy had forged with U.S. private investors. Unidad Popular's basic "Program" (which in effect served as Allende's 1970 campaign platform) explicitly blamed Chile's problems on "the imperialists and the ruling class," "reactionary interests, both national and foreign," and the "large-scale capitalists, both native and foreign" who "totally controlled" the country. Together, the UP Program claimed, "Imperialist capital and a privileged group of less than 10 per cent of the population monopolize half the national income," condemning the majority of Chile's citizens to deprivation and poverty. Chile was poor, the Program charged, because it was "a capitalist country, dependent upon imperialism, and dominated by sectors [of society] allied to foreign capital." The solution, according to the Program, was "to end the rule of the imperialists, of the monopolies, of the landed oligarchy, and to begin the construction of socialism."[9] As Allende's first minister of economy, Pedro Vuskovic, put it shortly after taking office, the whole purpose of state control was "to destroy the economic bases of imperialism and the ruling class by putting an end to the private ownership of the means of production."[10]

"Imperialism," of course, was a UP synonym for "U.S. economic domination." In 1970, U.S. corporations had more than $1 billion of capital invested in Chile, the bulk of it in the mining and communications industries. Allende and his followers were convinced that this "imperialist" capital had milked unconscionably large profits from the country—profits that by their calculations were "equivalent to twice the amount of capital invested" in Chile in its entire history.[11] Allende's socialist remedy was state ownership of Chile's economic infrastructure and resources, and his highest and most immediate priority was the nationalization of Chile's U.S.-owned copper industry. Copper was "the single dominant element in Chilean economic life"—"Chile's bread," in local parlance. Copper exports generated approximately three fourths of the country's foreign-exchange earnings and a substantial percentage of the Chilean government's revenues. The industry, however, was dominated by three U.S.-based copper companies—Anaconda, Kennecott, and Cerro—which together accounted for nearly 80 percent of the country's annual production. Allende charged that the U.S. companies were reaping excess profits from their Chilean operations; by his calculations, they had repatriated more than $4 billion in profits on initial investments of "no more than $30 million," leaving far too little money behind to finance economic development or social progress. As one of his supporters put it, the U.S. companies "pulled the treasure from the earth, took it home, and left us the hole." From Allende's perspective, nationalization of the copper industry was the key to "controlling our economic destiny" and "winning our second independence." It would restore Chilean control over Chile's own resources and in the process provide his government with the financial resources to build "a strong internal market" and "raise the standard of living of the masses." Unidad Popular's Program promised financial compensation to the owners of all expropriated properties, but if—as seemed likely—Allende factored his estimates of the copper companies' "excess" profits into his compensation figures, the copper companies could easily end up *owing* Allende's government hundreds of millions of dollars after their expropriation.[12]

In his foreign-policy pronouncements, Allende frequently drew a distinction between his hostility to "imperialistic" foreign capital and his desire for harmonious relations with the U.S. government. During the 1970 election campaign, he promised to adopt an independent, nonaligned foreign policy that would maintain relations "with all . . . countries regardless of their ideological or political position, based upon respect for self-determination and the interests of the people of Chile." After his election, he went out of his way to assure Washington that his government, although Marxist, posed no threat to the United States. Immediately following his swearing-in ceremony, he informed the head of the visiting U.S. inaugural delegation that although his government intended to nationalize the copper industry and other U.S.-owned enterprises, he nevertheless hoped to have "the best possible relations with the United States" and that U.S. security would "never be endangered by Chile or by anything that happens there." Even though "the interests of the United States and the interests of Latin America" had "nothing in common," he stated a few weeks later, Chile wanted "to maintain cordial and cooperative relations with all nations in the world and most particularly with the United States." Shortly thereafter, he publicly reaffirmed that "we will never do anything against the United States or contribute to injuring its sovereignty."[13]

The public record was nonetheless replete with less comforting statements. Allende had long advocated Chile's withdrawal from the Rio Pact—the U.S.-led hemispheric security system that he contemptuously characterized as "one cat and twenty mice"—and he regularly disparaged the Organization of American States and other manifestations of inter-American collaboration. During a July 1970 campaign speech, he allegedly referred to the United States as "public enemy number one" in the Western Hemisphere. His Unidad Popular campaign platform conveyed strong tones of anti-Americanism. Among other things, the UP Program promised that Allende's government would resist "any form of Pan-Americanism," reject the OAS as "the tool and agency of North American imperialism," and "revise, denounce and cancel" all "treaties of reciprocal assistance and mutual aid" between Chile and the United States; it also expressed Unidad Popular's "solidarity with the Cuban Revolution" and condemned "North American aggression in Vietnam."[14] Allende himself was an outspoken supporter of Castro's Cuba. Although he rejected insurrectionary violence as a revolutionary strategy in Chile, he nevertheless praised the Cuban revolution as "a revolution for all of Latin America" that had "shown the way for the liberation of all our peoples." In the aftermath of the Bay of Pigs debacle, he publicly condemned U.S. "aggression against Cuba" as "an aggression against the small nations of the world, against Latin America, and against Chile." He played a prominent role in helping Castro establish the Organización Latino América de Solidaridad, a Havana-based "mini-Comintern" created in 1966 to promote the spread of Marxist insurrections in the hemisphere, and served as the organization's first president.[15] Secretly, meanwhile, Allende was functioning as a longtime "confidential contact" of the Soviet KGB, providing information on political conditions in Chile and neighboring countries as a self-avowed "friend of the Soviet Union" and receiving "personal subsidies" of up to $50,000 from the Politburo for his services.[16]

All in all, Allende's Marxist revolutionary agenda, nationalistic designs on U.S. investment capital, anti-imperialist rhetoric, close association with Castro's Cuba, and secret collaboration with Soviet intelligence made it highly unlikely that the immediate future of U.S.-Chilean relations would be either "cordial" or "cooperative" as he prepared to begin his presidency.

Richard Nixon was not the first U.S. president to regard Salvador Allende as an enemy. In 1962, four years after Allende had lost the 1958 presidential election by less than three percentage points, the Kennedy administration mounted a covert campaign to prevent him from winning Chile's next presidential election, in 1964. According to U.S. ambassador Korry, "The Kennedys utilized every means—illegal and unconstitutional as well as legitimate—to defeat . . . Allende." Between 1962 and 1964, the CIA spent nearly $4 million on some fifteen covert action projects in Chile. Some of the money helped to finance the campaign of the center-left Christian Democrats and their candidate Eduardo Frei, whose opposition to communism was, by his own definition, unalterable and whose international orientation was, in his words, irrevocably with the West. Much of the rest was used to fund "a massive anti-communist propaganda campaign" designed, in Thomas Powers' words, "to scare the living daylights out of Chileans at the prospect of a victory by Allende." CIA-generated campaign materials depicted Chile's Socialists as "nakedly Stalinist," while Agency-produced "posters of Russian tanks in the streets of Budapest and of Cubans in front of Castro's firing squads proliferated on Chilean walls." In the end, Frei's landslide victory in the 1964 election owed at least a partial debt to the CIA-induced atmosphere of fear that helped to polarize Chile's voters during the campaign.[17]

The Nixon administration, by contrast, was notably lax in its response to Allende's 1970 presidential bid. During 1969, embassy and CIA proposals for new covert operations to block Allende elicited no action by Nixon's National Security Council. Instead, preoccupied with serious international crises

elsewhere and lulled into complacency by Chilean polls that showed conservative candidate Alessandri well in the lead, the White House failed to focus on the Chilean political situation until well into 1970. In late March, a small "spoiling" operation, modeled on the 1964 CIA propaganda campaign, was approved, with funding that eventually totaled some $435,000. But, according to Henry Kissinger, Nixon's national security adviser, this U.S. "token effort" was "much too little . . . far too late" and was carried out "in only the most minimal and ineffectual fashion." By August, as the Chilean election campaign entered its final phase and Kissinger finally began to "focus on the dangers" inherent in the situation, he was appalled to discover "that nothing further could now be done before the election."[18]

Allende's dramatic election victory on September 4, 1970, left Washington in a state of stunned surprise, Kissinger recalls; "Nixon was beside himself" and desperate to do "something, *anything*, that would reverse the previous neglect." Over the course of the next eleven days, in an atmosphere that Kissinger describes as frantic and frenzied, the White House hastily improvised a two-track strategy of covert initiatives designed to prevent Allende from taking office. In Track I, U.S. officials in Chile were ordered to secretly promote a constitutional coup d'état. Because Allende had won only a 36 percent plurality in the three-candidate presidential contest, he faced a congressional runoff election on October 24 in which the Chilean congress would choose between Allende and the runner-up candidate Alessandri. The Nixon administration's Track I strategy consisted of various plans to prevent Allende's election in the congress. One option (the "Frei reelection gambit") involved the bribing of Chilean congressmen to vote for Alessandri, who would immediately resign the presidency, forcing a new election in which the popular Frei—constitutionally barred from succeeding himself in office—would be free to run for a second term. Another Track I option consisted of applying pressure on Frei to "voluntarily yield power to an interim military regime" prior to Allende's confirmation, again opening the way to fresh elections, which Frei would presumably win.[19]

Track II took form on September 15 when Nixon ordered CIA director Richard Helms to instigate a military coup in Chile that would "prevent Allende from taking power or . . . unseat him" if he took office. According to Helms' oft-quoted notes from the meeting, the president recognized that there was probably only a one-in-ten chance of success, but he was determined to "save Chile" and was "not concerned [with the] risks involved." Nixon indicated that he was prepared to make "$10,000,000 available, more if necessary." Helms was instructed to assign the "best men we have" to the project, and to "make the [Chilean] economy scream," presumably as a pressure tactic to prod Chile's armed forces into moving against Allende. As Helms later testified, "The President came down very hard that he wanted something done, and he didn't much care how." Within days of the September 15 meeting, the CIA found itself under "constant . . . continual pressure . . . from the White House" to accomplish its assigned mission.[20]

In the end, however, Nixon's two-track strategy turned out to be "a real-life 'Mission Impossible'"—primarily because neither Frei nor any of Chile's key military officers would go along. As a result, Allende was confirmed as president-elect by the Chilean congress on October 24 and duly inaugurated on November 3.[21] Having failed to block the Chilean Marxist's accession to power, the Nixon administration then settled into a public policy of "cool but correct" behavior toward Allende's government combined with a covert program of economic destabilization designed to wreak havoc on Allende's socialist experiment and force the Chilean military to oust him. That Janus-like policy remained in effect until September 1973, when Chile's armed forces overthrew Allende's government in a bloody military coup that left Allende dead in the presidential palace.[22]

Any number of authors have attributed Nixon's Chilean intervention to economic motives. According to Seymour Hersh, "There is compelling evidence that Nixon's tough stance against Allende in 1970 was principally shaped by his concern for the future of the American corporations whose assets, he believed, would be seized by an Allende government." In his efforts to deny Allende the presidency, Hersh concludes, "Nixon was primarily protecting the interests of his corporate benefactors."[23] James Petras and Morris Morley characterize Nixon's interventionism as the effort of an imperial state to defend the interests of U.S.-based multinational corporations in Chile.[24] Allende and his advisers had said as much while they were still in office. In a 1972 speech to the UN General Assembly, Allende charged that his country was the victim of serious U.S. "aggression . . . designed to take revenge on the Chilean people for its decision to nationalize its copper." A 1973 internal

report prepared by Allende's government also attributed Nixon's hostility to his anger at Allende's nationalization of the copper industry. "What the United States cannot accept," the report concluded, "is the existence of a government like Popular Unity that can decide to nationalize without indemnification, using legal methods that paralyze the U.S. capacity to respond."[25]

The available evidence, however, is less "compelling" than economic interpretations would suggest. That U.S. companies lobbied the administration to intervene in Chile in 1970 is beyond dispute. In April, the board chairman of Anaconda Copper and a group of worried U.S. business leaders offered the State Department $500,000 to assist in financing anti-Allende campaign efforts. In July and September, senior officials of the International Telephone & Telegraph Company, a corporation with Chilean investments totaling $150 million, offered the CIA up to $1 million to help block Allende's accession to power. (International Telephone & Telegraph officials warned the White House that their company would be "in deep financial trouble" if it lost its Chilean holdings.)[26] Meanwhile, the administration's own intelligence assessments were predicting that Allende's election would lead to "harsh measures against U.S. business interests in Chile," resulting in "tangible economic losses" for the United States.[27] Nixon later acknowledged that he was aware of Allende's plans to expropriate U.S.-owned property at the time that he ordered the CIA to instigate a military coup.[28]

Nevertheless, no conclusive evidence has yet emerged that the intervention was based on Nixon's concern for the welfare of U.S. investors in Chile. Kissinger has categorically denied that economic factors played a role in the White House's policy formulations. "Nationalization of American-owned property was not the issue," he wrote in his memoirs; "the Nixon Administration did not view our foreign policy interests through the prism of the financial concerns of American companies." Colleagues have described Kissinger's own attitude toward U.S. businesses overseas as "contemptuous"—"He never gave a shit about the business community," one recalled.[29] Nor did administration officials accept any corporate financial support for the intervention effort; every private offer to contribute funds was quickly rejected as inappropriate.[30]

Nixon and Kissinger themselves, in their few public references to Chile, consistently defined their concerns in terms of U.S. national security. In his memoirs, Kissinger states categorically that "Our concern with Allende was based on national security, not on economics."[31] Nixon, in a 1977 television interview with journalist David Frost, recalled that in 1970 he considered "a leftwing dictatorship" in Chile to be a threat to "our security interests."[32] More specifically, both Nixon and Kissinger defined their security fears in terms of geopolitical "falling dominos." "I don't mean that [an Allende government] was an immediate threat," Nixon told Frost, "but I mean that if you let one go, you're going to have some problems with others. . . . Now we had one country in the Western Hemisphere, Cuba, that is, exporting revolution, and we didn't want another one, Chile, doing it." "Months before Allende came to power," Nixon recalled, "an Italian businessman came to call on me in the Oval Office and he said 'If Allende should win the election in Chile, and then you have Castro in Cuba, what you will in effect have in Latin America is a red sandwich, and eventually it will all be red.' And that's what we confronted."[33] Kissinger, in his memoirs, describes Allende as

> not merely an economic nuisance or a political critic but a geopolitical challenge. Chile bordered Peru, Argentina, and Bolivia, all plagued by radical movements. As a continental country, a militant Chile had a capacity to undermine other nations and support radical insurgency that was far greater than Cuba's, and Cuba has managed to do damage enough. If Chile had followed the Cuban pattern, Communist ideology would in time have been supported by Soviet forces and Soviet arms in the southern cone of the South American continent.[34]

Nixon's and Kissinger's retrospective public explanations conflict sharply, however, with the views of their own security analysts at the time. In August, Ambassador Korry had informed Washington that the U.S. embassy in Santiago was "unable to identify any vital U.S. security interests in Chile. The fall of Chile to Marxist totalitarianism," he wrote, "cannot . . . be considered a threat to the nation in military terms." Three days after Allende's election, the administration's interdepartmental Group for Inter-American Affairs—made up of representatives from the CIA, the State Department, the Department of Defense, and the White House—reported that the United States had "no vital national interests within Chile," that "the world military balance of power would not be significantly altered by an Allende government," and that an Allende-led Chile would not pose "any likely threat to the peace of the region." It would be "hard to argue" that Allende constituted "a mortal threat to the U.S.," the National Security Council's chief Latin American specialist advised Kissinger a week later.[35] A National Intelligence Estimate prepared in July concluded that although Allende would attempt to take Chile "a long way down the Marxist-Socialist road" during a six-year term in office, he would first have to surmount a long list of powerful domestic obstacles, "such as Chile's security forces, the Christian Democratic Party, some elements of organized labor, the Congress, and the Catholic Church."[36]

The intelligence community specifically discounted any likelihood that Allende's government would attempt to subvert its Andean neighbors and trigger a domino effect in South America. A CIA intelligence memorandum produced shortly after Allende's electoral victory predicted that the new Chilean president would be "cautious in providing assistance to extremists" in neighboring countries because of his "fear of provoking a military reaction in his own country." The memorandum also concluded that "the degree to which [foreign] revolutionary groups would be allowed to use Chile as a base of operations would be limited" because the Chilean Communist Party—Allende's partner in the Unidad Popular coalition—was opposed to "violence-prone groups."[37] Meanwhile, the U.S. embassy was continuing to assure Washington that an Allende government would pose no direct security threat to the region or to the United States. "Chile is really an island" isolated from its neighbors by geography, Ambassador Korry reported on September 5, the day after the election. Furthermore, Korry pointed out, "There is no country on earth that is so far from the two super-powers and Red China." Chile "is not Poland nor is it Mexico," he wrote, and "it will not require any massive commitment from anyone." Nor would the Soviet Union take advantage of Allende's victory to "expand its base" of influence in Chile, the ambassador informed Washington; instead, the Soviets would "move with caution" and not let Chile become "another Cuban drain of Moscow's resources."[38] Kissinger's off-the-cuff quip to reporters that Chile was "a dagger pointed at the heart of Antarctica" suggests that, despite his "official" explanations for the public record, the national security adviser may have privately shared his security bureaucracy's skepticism that an Allende-led Chile was a threat to U.S. security.[39]

In actuality, Nixon's hatred of Allende—and the U.S. intervention that resulted—can best be understood in the context of the goals that Nixon had set for his presidency. In direct contrast to his immediate predecessor in the White House, Nixon intended to achieve presidential greatness in the realm of foreign policy. He personally regarded himself as an expert in international affairs and confided to friends that he considered his life "dedicated to great foreign policy purposes." According to historian Melvin Small, Nixon also understood that politically "a president enjoyed considerable freedom of action in international relations and that the chances of achieving successes there were far greater than in trying to resolve intractable domestic problems." "I've always thought this country could run itself domestically without a President," he told an interviewer a year before his election; "All you need is a competent Cabinet to run the country at home. You need a President for foreign policy." He also thought the stakes were higher in international politics. "The American economy is so strong it would take a genius to ruin it," he later observed, "whereas one small mistake in foreign policy could blow up the world."[40]

Nixon entered office with an ambitious—even visionary—objective for his presidency: to lead the United States out of the draining environment of Cold War confrontation and into "a new era of peaceful coexistence with the communist world." Negotiations with the Soviet Union would produce a détente based on the concept of "linkage," in which Soviet political and military restraint in such international trouble spots as Vietnam, Berlin, and the Middle East would be rewarded with U.S. cooperation on issues of vital interest to the Soviet Union, such as strategic arms limitation, increased access to Western food and technology, and recognition of existing boundaries in Eastern Europe. Normalization of relations with Communist China would place the United States in "a balancing position" vis-à-vis the two leading communist bloc powers, providing the Nixon administration with "a great strategic opportunity" to construct a more stable and peaceful world. The "subtle triangle of relations between Washington, Peking, and Moscow" that would result would first enable Nixon to end the Vietnam War, by giving his administration the increased bargaining leverage that would induce the Soviets and Chinese to apply pressure on Hanoi to "moderate its requirements for a cease-fire." The broader long-term result would be a more stable international balance of power—a new multipolar "global equilibrium" based, in Kissinger's

words, on mutual restraint and "even eventual cooperation" among the major world powers.[41] If his grand design worked, Nixon—the quintessential U.S. cold warrior—would establish an historical legacy for himself as one of the twentieth-century's great peacemakers.

The vision proved easier to conceptualize than to implement. In the twenty months between Nixon's inauguration and Salvador Allende's election, the administration's efforts to give birth to a new international "structure for peace" ended mainly in what Nixon characterized as miscarriages. The communist world greeted the new administration with intransigence and acts of military aggression. In February 1969, a month after Nixon's inauguration, the North Vietnamese launched what he described as "a small-scale but savage offensive into South Vietnam." In April, North Korea shot down an unarmed U.S. EC—121 reconnaissance aircraft over the Sea of Japan, killing all thirty-one crew members. That summer, Hanoi bluntly rejected Nixon's offer to negotiate a speedy end to the Vietnam War; in rebuffing Nixon's conciliatory proposals, Ho Chi Minh "blamed the United States for the war, reiterated his determination to settle for nothing less than full independence of his country, and called for a complete U.S. withdrawal from Vietnam." For their part, the Soviets displayed little interest in "linkage"-induced behavior modification; in his memoirs, Kissinger criticizes them for refusing to reduce tensions in the Middle East or Berlin and for failing to assist the United States in its efforts to disengage from Vietnam. By October 1969, Nixon was complaining that Moscow had done "nothing to help" settle the war in Vietnam except to arrange for an oblong negotiating table at the Paris peace talks.[42]

The year 1970 brought more international crises. In March, the Soviets began a dramatic expansion of their military presence in the Middle East, pouring combat forces and advanced armaments into Egypt in support of the Nasser regime's military buildup along the Egyptian-Israeli frontier. In early September, fighting broke out in Jordan when radical Palestinian refugees, backed by pro-Soviet Syria, attempted to overthrow the moderate, pro-Western government of King Hussein. Nixon captured the tension of the moment in his memoir *RN*:

> One thing was clear. We could not allow Hussein to be overthrown by a Soviet-inspired insurrection. If it succeeded, the entire Middle East might erupt in war; the Israelis would almost certainly

take pre-emptive measures against a Syrian-dominated radical government in Jordan; the Egyptians were tied to Syria by military alliances; and Soviet prestige was on the line with both the Syrians and the Egyptians. Since the United States could not stand idly by and watch Israel being driven into the sea, the possibility of a direct U.S.-Soviet confrontation was uncomfortably high. It was like a ghastly game of dominoes, with a nuclear war waiting at the end."[43]

Simultaneously, halfway across the world, U.S. U-2 spy planes were producing evidence that a Soviet nuclear submarine base was under construction in Cienfuegos, Cuba; when completed, Kissinger informed Nixon, the base would mark "a quantum leap in the strategic capability of the Soviet Union against the United States."[44] Then, on September 4, the election returns from Chile presented the administration with yet another crisis situation.

For Nixon and Kissinger, the international crises of 1969–1970 represented "different facets of a global Communist challenge." Both men believed that communists respected only "power and strength" and that Soviet foreign policy was predicated on a relentless probing for points of international weakness. Now, the White House concluded, Moscow was probing "in several directions at once" in order to test the credibility of U.S. power under Nixon's stewardship. North Korea's shoot-down of the EC-121 was, in Kissinger's words, "a test of the new administration's decisiveness." The Jordanian crisis was "yet another test of U.S. resolve." And the construction of the Soviet submarine base in Cuba was also "part of a process of testing under way in different parts of the world."[45]

Above all, the administration looked upon the Vietnam War as a *decisive* test of U.S. global credibility—and the one that would determine the success or failure of Nixon's international grand design. According to Melvin Small, "Nixon and Kissinger were . . . certain that how the United States ended the war in Vietnam would influence upcoming negotiations with the Russians and Chinese. Relations with the communists could not be stabilized unless the United States left Vietnam with dignity." Kissinger had been warning since 1966 that a U.S. defeat at the hands of a "third-class Communist peasant state" like North Vietnam would "strengthen" America's enemies, "demoralize" her allies, "lessen the credibility" of the United States throughout the world, and tempt other countries to shift their alignments to the communist bloc.[46] In his memoirs, Kissinger writes that it was crucial for the

United States to avoid the perception of having been "routed" in Vietnam:

> As the leader of democratic alliances we had to remember that scores of countries and millions of people relied for their security on our willingness to stand by allies. . . . No serious policymaker could allow himself to succumb to the fashionable debunking of "prestige" or "honor" or "credibility." For a great power to abandon a small country to tyranny simply to obtain a respite from our own travail seemed to me . . . profoundly immoral and destructive of our efforts to build a new and ultimately more peaceful pattern of international relations. We could not revitalize the Atlantic Alliance if its governments were assailed by doubt about American staying power. We would not be able to move the Soviet Union toward the imperative of mutual restraint against the backdrop of capitulation in a major war. We might not achieve our opening to China if our value as a counterweight seemed nullified by a collapse that showed us irrelevant to Asian security. Our success in Middle East diplomacy would depend on convincing our ally of our reliability and its adversaries that we were impervious to threats of military pressure or blackmail.[47]

Kissinger's views mirrored those of the president. "I am utterly convinced that how we end this war will determine the future of the U.S. in the world," Nixon told several top advisers in July 1970. "We can maintain the American position in Europe and Asia if we come out well."[48]

Nixon interpreted the North Vietnamese military offensive of February 1969 as "a deliberate test, clearly designed to take the measure of me and my administration at the outset." He immediately responded by ordering the secret bombing of Vietnamese communist sanctuaries in Cambodia as a demonstration to Hanoi that his administration was "different and tougher" than its predecessors.[49] A year later, in April 1970, he told a national television audience that his controversial decision to widen the war by deploying U.S. ground forces into Cambodia was designed to put

> the leaders of North Vietnam on notice that . . . we will not be humiliated. We will not be defeated. . . .
>
> If, when the chips are down, the world's most powerful nation, the United States of America, acts like a pitiful, helpless giant, the forces of

totalitarianism and anarchy will threaten free nations and free institutions throughout the world. . . .

If we fail to meet this challenge, all other nations will be on notice that despite its overwhelming power the United States, when a real crisis comes, will be found wanting.[50]

Allende's election victory was seen in the White House as yet another communist challenge to U.S. interests—the latest in an accelerating series of communist "tests" of U.S. power under Nixon's leadership. Nixon recalled in his memoirs that "America was being tested in the fall of 1970—by war in Vietnam; by the threat of war in the Middle East; by the introduction of threatening nuclear capabilities in Cuba. In Chile the test was just as real, although much subtler." According to Kissinger, "We were faced simultaneously with a civil war in Jordan, a Soviet attempt to build a submarine base in Cuba, and the coming to power of Allende in Chile. It was at once *the most dangerous and decisive period of the new administration*".[51] "The Chilean election results," Kissinger continued,

came in just as Moscow and Cairo were rejecting our protests of Middle East cease-fire violations; Jordan feared an imminent move by Iraqi troops against the King; a Soviet naval force was steaming toward Cuba. By September 8, the day the Chilean developments were first discussed by an interagency committee, several airplanes had just been hijacked in the Middle East and the Soviet flotilla was nearing the port of Cienfuegos. Six days later, on September 14, when Chile was next considered, the Jordan situation had deteriorated, and Cuban MiGs intercepted a U-2 flight seeking to photograph Cienfuegos and the mission had to be aborted. In the weeks that followed, our government pondered Chilean events not in isolation but against the backdrop of the Syrian invasion of Jordan and our effort to force the Soviet Union to dismantle its installation for servicing nuclear submarines in the Caribbean. The reaction must be seen in that context.[52]

From Nixon's and Kissinger's perspective, the Soviets were now probing for new weak points in the Western Hemisphere. If they encountered "mush," they would proceed; if they encountered "steel," they would withdraw. The administration felt that it had to demonstrate its steel in Chile. The United States could not be "found wanting." The stakes were too high.[53]

Most immediately, a Marxist-led Chile would further erode the unity of the United States' hemispheric alliance system. According to Kissinger, Allende's government would represent "a permanent challenge to our position in the Western Hemisphere," while Nixon worried that the Chilean election would have "profound implications . . . for the inter-American system."[54]

But the implications extended far beyond Latin America. At the time of Allende's election, the administration was preparing for a new round of peace talks with North Vietnamese representatives in Paris, and Nixon was finalizing secret plans to withdraw 150,000 U.S. troops from Vietnam over the next several months. He feared that if the United States passively accepted the establishment of a new Marxist state in its own hemisphere, Hanoi would have even less reason to believe that the new president was "tougher" than his predecessors or that the United States had the strength of will to remain in Vietnam "for the duration." Why, then, would the North Vietnamese agree to a negotiated settlement of the war? More broadly still, why would Soviet and Chinese leaders agree to "mutual restraint," détente, or rapprochement with a "pitiful, helpless giant" that could no longer maintain hegemony in its Latin American sphere of influence? Ambassador Korry later acknowledged that the Nixon administration's "number one" concern in Chile was its fear, "at a time that we were about to . . . begin the scale down and withdrawal from Vietnam, and . . . launch new initiatives with Moscow and Peking, that for the United States to act indifferent to the disappearing of a democracy, of a unique democracy in what was viewed throughout the world as its back yard, could have a significant effect on those who made policy in the Soviet Union and the People's Republic of China."[55] The principal concern in Washington, Korry told Senator Frank Church, was

the probability that the governments in Moscow and Peking would misread US indifference in Chile. . . . At the time of the Chilean election campaign, the US [was] engaged in the reordering of its relations with the USSR and the PRC. I speculated to and in Washington that if the US did nothing to sustain a democracy of the caliber of Chile . . . then either or both of the two major Communist powers might conclude that the US disasters in Indochina, the subsequent demoralization within the US and abandonment in Chile—in our own hemisphere—taken together with the evident crises in Western Europe at that time, signified a general Western collapse in the offing. They might, I said, adopt the analysis of the leadership of Allende's own Socialist Party—that the US was incapable of defending its interests and, as the leader of the Socialist Party, Sr. Altamirano, kept emphasizing in Chile, the collapse of the US would be hastened by kicking it hard and often.[56]

The administration's "number two" concern, according to Korry, was the "certain effect" that Allende's Chilean model would have on political trends in Western Europe. Kissinger in particular was worried about the growing strength of communist parties in Italy and France. He feared that the successful example of a freely elected Marxist coalition government in Chile would encourage the "Eurocommunists" to seek political alliances with Socialists and Christian Democrats in upcoming elections and gain control of the Italian or French government as members of leftist popular-front coalitions. If communists came to power in Italy or France, Kissinger believed, the consequences would be devastating for the West's position in the Cold War and for the Nixon administration's goal of achieving peaceful coexistence. "The world balance of power," he wrote in 1969, "depends on our ability to deny the resources and manpower of Western Europe to an aggressor," while any "true relaxation in [East-West] tensions presupposes Western unity." In his view, there was "no doubt that a Communist breakthrough to power or a share of power in one country will have a major psychological effect on the others, by making Communist parties seem respectable, or suggesting that the tide of history in Europe is moving in their direction. . . . [T]he accession to power of Communists in an allied country would represent a massive change in European politics . . . [and] would have fundamental consequences for the structure of the postwar world as we have known it and for America's relationship to its most important alliances." According to political scientist Robert H. Johnson, "Kissinger argued that the military strength of NATO would be 'gravely weakened' because governments containing Communists would have to be excluded from discussions of classified subjects, [and] because they would seek to weaken NATO defense efforts. . . . With NATO weakened, member countries would be forced to accommodate to Soviet power and 'massive shifts against us would occur.'" In short, from Kissinger's perspective, "Allende's

success would have had implications . . . for the future of Communist parties in Western Europe, whose policies would inevitably undermine the Western Alliance." "The political evolution of Chile," he remarked soon after Allende's victory, "is a very serious matter for the national security interests of the United States because of its effects in France and Italy."[57]

Ambassador Korry shared "the conviction that were the U.S. to act indifferently to [Chile's] fate . . ., the effects would be devastating in other countries where a communist party had meaningful political influence or where ultra-Marxist-Leninists might play a significant role. I had in mind not only, or even primarily, Latin America," the ambassador recalled; "Chile seemed to share Western European political structure and outlook, so I spoke then to Washington of France, Italy, Spain—even Japan."[58]

Kissinger worried that the Chilean model of a democratic road to Marxist revolution could also have a harmful effect on Latin American politics. One of his staff assistants later recalled that "Henry saw Allende as being a far more dangerous threat than Castro. If Latin America ever became unraveled, it would never happen with a Castro. Allende was a living example of democratic social reform in Latin America. All kinds of cataclysmic events rolled around, but Chile scared him. He talked about Eurocommunism the same way he talked about Chile early on. Chile scared him."[59]

According to another aide, "Henry thought that Allende might lead an anti-U.S. move in Latin America more effectively than Castro, just because it *was* the democratic route to power."[60] It was this aspect of the Chilean situation that the U.S. intelligence community found to be the most worrisome. An interagency intelligence assessment produced three days after the Chilean election warned that although the United States had "no vital national interests within Chile," an Allende government "would . . . create considerable political and psychological costs. . . . Hemispheric cohesion would be threatened by the challenge that an Allende government would pose to the [Organization of American States], and by the reactions that it would create in other countries." "An Allende victory," the assessment concluded, "would represent a definite psychological set-back to the U.S. and a definite psychological advance for the Marxist idea."[61] Nixon personally underscored the dangerous effect that the Chilean model could have on international politics when, three days after Allende's inauguration, he told the National Security Council: "Our main concern in Chile is the prospect that [Allende] can consolidate himself and the picture projected to the world will be his success."[62]

The available evidence suggests, then, that the United States intervened in Chile in 1970 not for reasons of economic self-interest or military defense but because the Nixon administration viewed Salvador Allende as a dangerous challenge to its international credibility and strategic goals. The White House believed that it had to respond aggressively to what it regarded as a new communist "test" in Chile if it hoped to end the Vietnam War "with honor" and persuade the Soviets and Chinese to participate in a new global "structure for peace." The administration feared that a perception of U.S. weakness in Chile would damage its credibility in the eyes of communist bloc governments and hinder its "efforts to build a new and ultimately more peaceful pattern of international relations." "If . . . we are accommodating" to Allende, Kissinger told his Senior Review Group shortly after Unidad Popular's election victory, "we risk giving the appearance of weakness or of indifference to the establishment of a Marxist government in the Hemisphere." "If [Allende] is inaugurated," Korry advised from Santiago, "the United States has admitted its impotence." The communist world respected "power and strength," not impotence, and as Kissinger put it, *displays of American impotence in one part of the world . . . would inevitably erode our credibility in other parts of the world.*" In the national security adviser's evocative metaphor, the administration simply could not afford to look like "a sort of mother hen clucking nervous irrelevancies from the sidelines"—especially not in the middle of its "most dangerous and decisive period" in office.[63]

Administration officials likewise believed that the mere example of an Allende government could disrupt the East-West balance of power and endanger their plans to forge a more stable relationship with the communist bloc. In their view, the Chilean model had the capability of undermining the Western Alliance—first by fueling the political momentum of communist parties in Western Europe, with potentially disastrous consequences for NATO, and second by damaging the inter-American system, eroding "hemispheric cohesion," and possibly leading to Latin America's eventual "unraveling." Nixon and Kissinger believed that a "true relaxation in [Cold War] tensions" required "Western unity"—because communists compromised only when confronted by strength. There consequently could be little hope for successful negotiations with Moscow, Beijing, or Hanoi if the U.S. alliance system appeared to be falling apart in Western Europe and Latin America. To an administration that already considered itself under assault from communist "tests" and "challenges," Allende's government was an unacceptable threat to the stable new international system that Nixon was seeking to construct as his great historical legacy.

There was also a domestic political dimension to the intervention. More primal even than Nixon's hope for great achievements in international affairs was his desire to be a two-term president. As one of his presidential biographers writes, "Nixon began to think about his second term almost as soon as he took office" in 1969. Kissinger recalls that "Nixon had three goals" as he entered the White House: "to win [reelection in 1972] by the biggest electoral landslide in history; to be remembered as a peacemaker; and to be accepted by the 'Establishment' as an equal."[64]

From the start, Nixon understood that his reelection prospects hinged on his ability to extricate the United States from Vietnam. Domestic opposition to the war had forced Lyndon Johnson to abandon plans to seek a second full term in 1968, and Nixon was already being warned as he entered office that he too would be a one-term president unless he found a way to end the war quickly. His early reliance, however, on military escalation to push Hanoi toward a negotiated settlement not only failed to achieve the desired result—it triggered massive and increasingly violent antiwar protests at home. By mid-1970, the White House was literally besieged by antiwar demonstrators, and the president and his advisers found themselves embroiled in what they regarded as a virtual civil war in the United States. In September, when Chile added itself to the list of the administration's worries, Nixon's public-approval rating dropped below 50 percent for the first time in his twenty months as president. It was clear, he told Kissinger, that the war in Vietnam was "sapping his domestic support and therefore had to be ended before 1972."[65]

In the days leading up to his decision to intervene in Chile, Nixon was focusing heavily on his 1972 reelection strategy. On September 12, 1970, according to White House Chief of Staff H. R. Haldeman, the president ordered his aides to "gear everything to '72, reelection and winning Congress." According to Haldeman, Nixon spent the morning of September 15—the day he ordered the intervention—working on his "basic political approach" to reelection in 1972.[66]

Chile complicated his plans. A Marxist takeover of a second Latin American country would increase the already embattled president's political vulnerability. Nixon had built his political career on what Kissinger characterizes as "a tough, occasionally strident anti-Communism"; from his 1946 campaign for the House of Representatives onward, he had routinely accused his campaign opponents of weakness in combating communism. He believed that the reason he had lost the 1960 presidential election was because, as he wrote in his memoirs, "Kennedy conveyed the image . . . that he was tougher on Castro and communism than I was"; according to Kissinger, "Nixon was determined that no one would ever be able to make this charge again." During the early 1960s, he had heaped criticism on the Kennedy administration for its handling of Cuba—for having "goofed an invasion [and] given the Soviets squatters' rights in our backyard." Thanks to Kennedy's policies, he charged in 1963, "Cuba is western Russia, and the rest of Latin America is in deadly peril."[67] Now, in 1970, Nixon feared that it was payback time—the Democrats would blame him for having "lost Chile," for having been "asleep at the wheel" "on his watch."[68] To make matters worse, he knew that he was exceedingly vulnerable to such charges. Throughout 1969 and early 1970, his administration had taken no action to prevent Allende's election, despite recommendations from Korry and the CIA that covert anti-Allende blocking efforts should be initiated. According to Kissinger, the reason Nixon was "beside himself" when he received the news of Allende's election victory was because "for over a decade he had lambasted Democratic administrations for permitting the establishment of Communist power in Cuba. And now what he perceived—not wrongly—as another Cuba had come into being during his own Administration. . . . This explains the virulence of his reaction and his insistence on doing something, *anything*, that would reverse the previous neglect."[69]

The National Security Council reinforced Nixon's political concerns. On November 3, 1970—the day Allende was inaugurated—it warned that "the U.S. Congress and knowledgeable sectors of the public will follow with interest the political course which Chile takes internally and its attitudes and actions with regard to the United States. . . . As the actions of the Allende government become more overtly

hostile to U.S. interests . . . we may expect adverse reaction by some sectors of the U.S. public, press, and Congress to the 'establishment of another communist government in the hemisphere.'" Failure on the administration's part "to take any steps" against Allende, the NSC concluded, "would leave the initiative in his hands, discourage opposition to Allende in Chile, weaken our hemisphere leadership, and create serious problems with public and Congressional opinion in the United States."[70] The following morning, Kissinger defined the danger in terms that went to the heart of Nixon's fears. "Chile," the national security adviser told White House aide Dwight Chapin, "could end up being the worst failure in our administration—'our Cuba' by 1972."[71]

And so Richard Nixon intervened in Chile because he viewed Allende's Unidad Popular government as a threat not only to his foreign-policy goals but to his domestic political ambitions as well. It was this dual nature of the threat that Ambassador Korry highlighted in his September 5 cable to Washington informing the administration of Allende's election victory. "Chile," he wrote, "voted calmly to have a Marxist-Leninist state, the first nation in the world to make this choice freely and knowingly. . . . It will have the most profound effect on Latin America and beyond; we have suffered a grievous defeat; the consequences will be domestic and international. . . ." According to Kissinger, Nixon underlined the italicized sentence on his copy of Korry's cable.[72]

Finally, Nixon's decision to intervene was also influenced by the lobbying efforts of Allende's Chilean political enemies. A few days after Allende's election, Agustin Edwards, Chile's "most powerful businessman," called on Ambassador Korry in Santiago and asked whether the United States intended to "do anything militarily—directly or indirectly" to block Allende's accession to power. Korry's answer was no. Edwards then traveled to Washington, D.C., on what a Nixon administration official later described as "a last-minute effort" to recruit U.S. support for a plan to prevent Allende from taking office. In the United States, the wealthy Chilean capitalist—whose business empire included the conservative El Mercurio publishing chain, Chile's largest granary, a major poultry business, and a Pepsi Cola bottling plant—was the houseguest of PepsiCo chairman Donald Kendall, one of Nixon's "closest friends and largest campaign contributors." On September 14, Kendall visited the White House and personally conveyed

Edwards' thoughts on the Chilean political situation to Nixon. The following morning, September 15, Edwards was granted a one-hour breakfast meeting with Kissinger and Attorney General John Mitchell and a separate meeting with CIA director Richard Helms. Although the details of his conversations with Nixon's senior advisers remain classified, he likely warned them that Allende was "a Soviet dupe" who would transform Chile into "another Cuba." The suggested courses of action that he urged the U.S. government to consider bore a striking resemblance to the Track I and Track II covert operations that the administration subsequently implemented. A few hours after the meetings, Nixon ordered the intervention—and Edwards' input clearly had a significant impact on his decision to do so. Helms later testified that he had the "impression" that the president took action on the fifteenth "because of Edwards' presence in Washington and what he heard from Kendall about what Edwards was saying about conditions in Chile and what was happening there." Kissinger goes further, stating frankly that Nixon was "triggered into action . . . by Augustin [sic] Edwards . . . who had come to Washington to warn of the consequences of an Allende takeover."[73]

Edwards' lobbying activities were by no means an isolated phenomenon. Korry recalls being "propositioned by key Chileans anxious to involve the United States in hair-brained plots" against Allende. He later told a Senate subcommittee that "there were a great many Chileans who wanted the United States to do their bidding, a great many, and who were very active in Washington, who tried to manipulate the pressures on me in Chile. And in certain instances . . . they were very successful, indeed." "There were Chileans very anxious to involve us," he reiterated later in his testimony—"so many Chileans that were trying to entrap us, one way or another in this thing."[74]

Korry also mentions a "provocative" and "highly inflammatory" anti-Allende letter that outgoing president Frei sent to Nixon "the week before" September 15.[75] The impact of the letter is unclear, but Frei subsequently played a significant role in shaping Nixon's policy toward Chile after Allende was sworn in as president. On November 3, the day of Allende's inauguration, the National Security Council produced an "Options Paper on Chile" that outlined several alternative courses of action available to the United States in dealing with Allende's government. Option D called for the Nixon administration to "maintain an outwardly

correct but adversary posture, [and] adopt without delay economic, political and diplomatic measures designed to prevent Allende from consolidating his position." "This option," the NSC paper noted, "reflects the reported evaluation of the situation by ex-President Frei . . . that Chile is dead, without any future except as a fully Marxist state, and that the only miracle that might save it would be the incapacity of the government to handle the economic situation."[76] Option D became the basis of U.S. policy toward Chile from 1971 to the military coup of September 1973 that destroyed Allende and his Unidad Popular government.

Quietly, behind the scenes, Chile's political and economic elites worked to instigate a U.S. intervention and helped conceive the program of U.S. economic destabilization that contributed to Allende's eventual demise. Richard Nixon ordered the U.S. intervention in Chile because he believed that core elements of his presidential agenda—a reduction in Cold War tensions, an honorable withdrawal from Vietnam, reelection in 1972—were at stake, but Allende's Chilean opponents played an influential background role in the affair.

QUESTIONS FOR FURTHER DISCUSSION

1. How would you evaluate the seriousness of the threat to the United States posed by Allende?
2. What advice did Henry Kissinger offer the president of the United States for dealing with Allende?
3. What forms of covert action did the CIA resort to in its efforts to discredit Allende?
4. How relevant today are the kinds of covert actions used by the United States in the 1970s against Allende?

ENDNOTES

1. Thomas Powers, *The Man Who Kept the Secrets: Richard Helms and the CIA* (New York: Pocket, 1979), 294.
2. Paul E. Sigmund, *The Overthrow of Allende and the Politics of Chile, 1964–1976* (Pittsburgh: University of Pittsburgh Press, 1977), 131, 147; Robert J. Alexander, *The Tragedy of Chile* (Westport, CT: Greenwood, 1978), 137–143.
3. Sigmund, *Overthrow of Allende*, 24; Mark Falcoff, *Modern Chile, 1970–1989: A Critical History* (New Brunswick, NJ: Transaction, 1989), 44.
4. Sigmund, *Overthrow of Allende*, 88–89; Falcoff, *Modern Chile, 1970–1989*, 26–30; Julio Faúndez, *Marxism and Democracy in Chile: From 1932 to the Fall of Allende*

(New Haven, CT: Yale University Press, 1988), 165, 167–169, 171, 191–192, 194–195; Alexander, *The Tragedy of Chile,* 133–137.

5. Falcoff, *Modern Chile, 1970–1989,* 31; Robert Moss, *Chile's Marxist Experiment* (Newton Abbot, UK: David & Charles, 1973), 49; Faúndez, *Marxism and Democracy in Chile,* 164–171, 196–197; Paul E. Sigmund, *The United States and Democracy in Chile* (Baltimore: Johns Hopkins University Press, 1993), 33; Sigmund, *The Overthrow of Allende,* 140. Also see the revealing assessment of former Allende supporter Roberto Ampuero, "Thirty Years On, a Chilean Laments 'We All Killed Allende,'" *Washington Post,* 7 September 2003.

6. Sigmund, *The Overthrow of Allende,* 63, 84, 93.

7. Ibid., 112, 118–120; Faúndez, *Marxism and Democracy in Chile,* 188–189. Specifically, the "statute of democratic guarantees" guaranteed "the free functioning of political parties, trade unions, private education, and the mass media and the independence of the armed forces from political control" (Sigmund, *The United States and Democracy in Chile,* 49).

8. Sigmund, *The Overthrow of Allende,* 111; Faúndez, *Marxism and Democracy in Chile, 193.*

9. "The Programme of Unidad Popular," in *Chile's Road to Socialism,* ed. Joan E. Garces, trans. J. Darling, introduction by Richard Gott (Harmondsworth, UK, and Baltimore: Penguin, 1973), 23–24, 27, 29–30.

10. Moss, *Chile's Marxist Experiment,* 59.

11. Sigmund, *The United States and Democracy in Chile,* 58; Allende, "The Programme of Unidad Popular," 25.

12. U.S. House of Representatives, *United States and Chile during the Allende Years, 1970–1973: Hearings before the Subcommittee on Inter-American Affairs of the Committee on Foreign Affairs, July 1, 1971–September 18, 1974,* 92nd Cong., 1st sess. (Washington, DC: Government Printing Office, 1975), 375, 405, 408, 546; address by Salvador Allende, *Official Records of the United Nations General Assembly,* Twenty-Seventh Session, 2,096th Plenary Meeting, 4 December 1972, 2; Armando Uribe, *The Black Book of American Intervention in Chile* (Boston: Beacon, 1975), 21; "The Programme of Unidad Popular," 25; Jacques Zylberberg and Miguel Monterichard, "An Abortive Attempt to Change Foreign Policy: Chile, 1970–3," in *Why Nations Realign: Foreign Policy Restructuring in the Postwar World,* ed. K. J. Holsti (London: Allen & Unwin, 1982), 191. As president, Allende quickly nationalized the U.S. copper companies and arrived at a compensation figure that, after "excess profits" had been deducted from the book value of the companies' Chilean holdings, left the copper companies owing the Chilean government nearly $400 million. Sigmund, *The United States and Democracy in Chile,* 61–62.

13. Sigmund, *The Overthrow of Allende,* 131; F. Parkinson, *Latin America, the Cold War, and the World Powers, 1945–1973* (Beverly Hills and London: Sage, 1974), 239; "The Programme of Unidad Popular,"49; Uribe, *The Black Book of American Intervention in Chile,* 74, 76, 78; James Petras and Morris Morley, *The United States and Chile: Imperialism and the Overthrow of the Allende Government* (New York: Monthly Review Press, 1975), 178n13; Zylberberg and Monterichard, "An Abortive Attempt to Change Foreign Policy: Chile, 1970–3," 180.

14. Parkinson, *Latin America, the Cold War,* 64n69, 196; Jan Knippers Black, *United States Penetration of Brazil* (Philadelphia: University of Pennsylvania Press, 1977), 7; U.S. Senate, Select Committee on Intelligence Activities, *Intelligence Activities: Hearings before the Select Committee to Study Governmental Operations with Respect to Intelligence Activities,* vol. 7: *Covert Action,* 94th Cong., 1st sess. (Washington, DC: Government Printing Office, 1976), 33, 116 (hereafter cited as Senate Hearings, *Intelligence Activities*); Sigmund, *The Overthrow of Allende,* 131; "The Programme of Unidad Popular," 49–50.

15. Falcoff, *Modern Chile, 1970–1989,* 46; Brian Loveman and Thomas M. Davies Jr., eds., *The Politics of Antipolitics: The Military in Latin America,* 3rd rev. ed. (Wilmington, DE: Scholarly Resources, 1997), 129; William Sater, *Chile and the United States: Empires in Conflict* (Athens: University of Georgia Press, 1990), 133 (also quoted in Stephen G. Rabe, *The Most Dangerous Area in the World: John F. Kennedy Confronts Communist Revolution in Latin America* [Chapel Hill: University of North Carolina Press, 1999], 111); Faúndez, *Marxism and Democracy in Chile,* 170; Alexander, *The Tragedy of Chile,* 140–141.

16. Christopher Andrew and Vasili Mitrokhin, *The World Was Going Our Way: The KGB and the Battle for the Third World* (New York: Basic, 2005), 69–70, 72, 75.

17. Sigmund, *The Overthrow of Allende,* 24–25, 44, 53; Edward Korry, "The Sell-Out of Chile and the American Taxpayer," *Penthouse,* March 1978, 72; U.S. Senate, Select Committee on Intelligence Activities, *Covert Action in Chile 1963–1973: Staff Report,* 94th Cong., 1st sess. (Washington, DC: Government Printing Office, 1975), 14–17 (hereafter cited as Senate, *Covert Action in Chile, 1963–1973*); Powers, *The Man Who Kept the Secrets,* 285.

18. Senate, *Covert Action in Chile, 1963–1973,* 20–22; Henry Kissinger, *White House Years* (Boston: Little,

Brown, 1979), 662–669; Powers, *The Man Who Kept the Secrets*, 291; Seymour M. Hersh, *The Price of Power: Kissinger in the Nixon White House* (New York: Summit, 1983), 266. Also see Christopher Andrew, *For the President's Eyes Only: Secret Intelligence and the American Presidency from Washington to Bush* (New York: Harper-Collins, 1995), 370–371; and Falcoff, *Modern Chile, 1970–1989*, 204–207.

19. Peter Kornbluh, *The Pinochet File: A Declassified Dossier on Atrocity and Accountability* (New York: New Press, 2003), chap. 1; Kissinger, *White House Years*, 670–672; Senate, *Covert Action in Chile, 1963–1973*, 23–26; U.S. Senate, Select Committee to Study Governmental Operations with Respect to Intelligence Activities, *Alleged Assassination Plots Involving Foreign Leaders: An Interim Report* (Washington, DC: Government Printing Office, 1975), 231–234 (hereafter cited as Senate, *Alleged Assassination Plots*); Gregory F. Treverton, *Covert Action: The Limits of Intervention in the Postwar World* (New York: Basic, 1987), 104.

20. Kornbluh, *The Pinochet File*, chap. 1; Senate, *Alleged Assassination Plots*, 225–229, 231–235; Senate, *Covert Action in Chile, 1963–1973*, 23, 25–26. One U.S. official present at the September 15 meeting described Nixon as "frantic." Stephen Kinzer, *Overthrow: America's Century of Regime Change from Hawaii to Iraq* (New York: Henry Holt, 2005), 172. A special CIA task force was created to carry out Track II. Its assignment consisted of a "three-part program": "a. Collect intelligence on coup-minded officers; b. Create a coup climate by propaganda, disinformation, and terrorist activities intended to provoke the left to give a pretext for a coup; [and] c. Inform those coup-minded officers that the U.S. Government would give them full support in a coup short of direct U.S. military intervention" (Senate, *Alleged Assassination Plots*, 234).

21. Hersh, *The Price of Power*, 277; Senate, *Covert Action in Chile, 1963–1973*, 26; Kornbluh, *The Pinochet File*, 29.

22. Kornbluh, *The Pinochet File*, chap. 2; Senate, *Covert Action in Chile, 1963–1973*, 26–28; Mark Falcoff, "Kissinger and Chile: The Myth That Will Not Die," *Commentary*, November 2003, 41–49.

23. Hersh, *The Price of Power*, 270, 296.

24. Petras and Morley, *The United States and Chile*, viii–ix.

25. *Address by Salvador Allende*, Official Records of the United Nations General Assembly, *4 December 1972*, 3; Uribe, The Black Book of American Intervention in Chile, 144–145.

26. Treverton, *Covert Action*, 161–162; Hersh, *The Price of Power*, 266–268, 276; Senate, *Covert Action in Chile, 1963–1973*, 12; U.S. Senate, Committee on Foreign Relations, Subcommittee on Multinational Corporations, *Multinational Corporations and United States Foreign Policy: Hearings on the International Telephone and Telegraph Company and Chile, 1970–71*, 93rd Cong., 1st sess., March 20–April 2, 1973, pt. I, 21–22 (hereafter cited as Senate, *ITT Hearings*).

27. *Senate*, Covert Action in Chile, 1963–1973, 45; *Senate*, Alleged Assassination Plots, 229.

28. *New York Times*, 26 May 1977, B6.

29. Henry Kissinger, *White House Years*, 656; Kissinger, *Years of Upheaval* (Boston: Little, Brown, 1982), 376; Hersh, *The Price of Power*, 270; Roger Morris, *Uncertain Greatness: Henry Kissinger and American Foreign Policy* (New York: Harper & Row, 1977), 241.

30. *Hersh, The Price of Power, 266, 268, 276; Senate*, Covert Action in Chile, 1963–1973, 12. Although it turned down ITT funds for anti-Allende operations, the CIA advised the company on how to pass money to Allende's opponent Alessandri and his National Party. According to a subsequent Senate investigation, "Eventually at least $350,000 was passed by ITT to [Alessandri's] campaign. A roughly equal amount was passed by other U.S. companies; the CIA learned of this funding but did not assist in it" (Senate, *Covert Action in Chile 1963–1973*, 13). Danish historian Poul Jensen offers an economic interpretation of a different stripe. Jensen places Nixon's Chilean intervention within the context of a severe balance-of-payments crisis that was threatening to deplete U.S. gold reserves in 1969–1970. Because U.S. foreign-exchange earnings were heavily dependent on "remitted income . . . from direct US overseas investments," Jensen writes, Allende's determination to nationalize foreign capital would—by eliminating the $100 million in income that U.S. corporations in Chile remitted each year to the U.S. domestic economy—have made a bad situation considerably worse. Nixon responded to the growing balance-of-payments deficits by establishing the Overseas Private Investment Corporation (OPIC), a new "government insurance company" that provided U.S. foreign investors with insurance coverage to protect their investments in the event of expropriation. By late 1970, according to Jensen, more than $310 million of U.S. investment capital in Chile was protected by OPIC expropriation insurance, even though the corporation had available less than $70 million in financial reserves to meet its expropriation-insurance commitments worldwide. Administrators were openly warning that a series of large-scale nationalizations in Chile would be "catastrophic" for their corporation. And if successful expropriations in Chile stimulated a wave

of nationalizations throughout Latin America and the Third World, Jensen concludes, the "harmful economic effects" on the United States would obviously be "even greater." Nevertheless, even Jensen is forced to admit that there is no actual evidence that the White House officials who ordered the Chilean intervention had any "awareness of" or "interest in . . . the particular consequences of the expected Chilean nationalizations for OPIC." See Poul Jensen, *The Garotte: The United States and Chile, 1970–1973* (Aarhus, Denmark: Aarhus University Press, 1988), 450–460, 464–466, 474, 484–485, 487, 495.

31. Kissinger, *White House Years,* 656.

32. *New York Times,* 25 May 1977, B6.

33. Ibid. Nixon repeated his "Italian businessman" anecdote in *RN: The Memoirs of Richard Nixon* (New York: Grosset & Dunlap, 1978), 490.

34. Kissinger, *Years of Upheaval,* 376.

35. Edward M. Korry, "Contingency Paper ('Fidelism without Fidel')," August 1970, 23, reproduced in "Chile in the Archives of the USA (1970): Documents from the Former U.S. Ambassador to Chile Edward M. Korry (1967–1971)," *Estudios Públicos* (Centro de Estudios Públicos, Santiago, Chile), no. 72 (1998), www.cepchile.cl/dms/archivo_1147_316/rev72_korrydocing.pdf; Senate, *Alleged Assassination Plots,* 229; Kornbluh, *The Pinochet File,* 8, 11.

36. Senate, *Covert Action in Chile, 1963–1973,* 44.

37. Ibid., 47.

38. Korry to Rogers, 5 September 1970, 4, in *Chile and the United States: Declassified Documents Relating to the Military Coup, 1970–1976,* National Security Archive Electronic Briefing Book no. 8, http://www.gwu.edu/~nsarchiv/NSAEBB/NSAEBB8/nsaebb8.htm.

39. Paul E. Sigmund, "Crisis Management: Chile and Marxism," in *United States Policy in Latin America: A Quarter Century of Crisis and Challenge, 1961–1986,* ed. John D. Martz (Lincoln: University of Nebraska Press, 1988), 158; Treverton, *Covert Action,* 173.

40. Melvin Small, *The Presidency of Richard Nixon* (Lawrence: University Press of Kansas, 1999), 59–60.

41. Ibid., 60–65, 97; John Lewis Gaddis, *Strategies of Containment: A Critical Appraisal of Postwar American National Security Policy* (New York: Oxford University Press, 1982), chaps. 9–10; Kissinger, *White House Years,* 124–130, 135–136, 163–165, 191–192; Nixon, *RN,* 341–349.

42. Nixon, *RN,* 380, 406; Kissinger, *White House Years,* 143–147, 159–161, 278, 283, 313; Michael A. Genovese, *The Nixon Presidency: Power and Politics in Turbulent Times* (Westport, CT: Greenwood, 1990), 116; Jeffrey Kimball,

Nixon's Vietnam War (Lawrence: University Press of Kansas, 1998), 116, 118, 171.

43. Kissinger, *White House Years,* chaps. 14–15; Nixon, *RN,* 483.

44. Kissinger, *White House Years,* chap. 16; Stephen E. Ambrose, *Nixon: The Triumph of a Politician, 1962–1972* (New York: Simon & Schuster, 1989), 381. Also see Nixon, *RN,* 485–486.

45. Kissinger, *White House Years,* 118–119, 162, 316, 570, 594; Walter Isaacson, *Kissinger: A Biography* (New York: Simon & Schuster, 1992), 292; Nixon, *RN,* 485, 490; Hersh, *The Price of Power,* 251.

46. Small, *The Presidency of Richard Nixon,* 65; Kimball, *Nixon's Vietnam,* 38, 62, 72; Isaacson, *Kissinger,* 120. Also see H. R. Haldeman, *The Ends of Power* (New York: Times Books, 1978), 98–99.

47. Kissinger, *White House Years,* 228.

48. Kimball, *Nixon's Vietnam,* 225.

49. Nixon, *RN,* 380; Kimball, *Nixon's Vietnam,* 136.

50. Public Papers of the Presidents of the United States: Richard Nixon, 1970 *(Washington, DC: Government Printing Office, 1971),* 408–409.

51. Nixon, *RN,* 490; Kissinger, *White House Years,* 593 (emphasis added). According to Kissinger, "The Nixon Administration had told Moscow many times that we were prepared for a period of mutual restraint and conciliation. In the autumn of 1970 Moscow chose to test whether this willingness reflected indecision, domestic weakness due to Vietnam, or the strategy of a serious government" (ibid., 652).

52. Kissinger, *White House Years,* 654.

53. Nixon, *RN,* 490. In Kissinger's view, "None" of the "three major crises" that "descended upon the Administration" in September 1970—Jordan, Cienfuegos, or Chile—"could have succeeded without Communist impetus or encouragement" (Kissinger, *White House Years,* 594).

54. Kissinger, *White House Years,* 656; Petras and Morley, *The United States and Chile,* 39.

55. Kimball, *Nixon's Vietnam,* 173, 182–183, 230; William Buckley, "U.S. Policies in Chile under the Allende Government: An Interview with Former Ambassador Edward Korry," in *Chile: The Balanced View,* ed. Francisco Orrego Vicuña (Santiago: University of Chile Institute of International Studies, 1975), 294.

56. Korry to Senator Frank Church, 23 October 1975, in Senate Hearings, *Intelligence Activities,* 118–119.

57. Buckley, "U.S. Policies in Chile under the Allende Government," 294; Kissinger, *White House Years,* 102–103, 388, 657, 920–922; Gerry Argyris Andrianopoulos, *Kissinger and Brzezinski: The NSC and the*

Struggle for Control of US National Security Policy (New York: St. Martin's, 1991), 21–22; Robert H. Johnson, *Improbable Dangers: U.S. Conceptions of Threat in the Cold War and Beyond* (New York: St. Martin's, 1994), 66; Ricardo Israel, *Politics and Ideology in Allende's Chile* (Tempe: Arizona State University Center for Latin American Studies, 1989), 157. Kissinger's concern about the link between the "Chilean model" and Eurocommunism may have been well founded. Robert Alexander writes that "European Communists, especially those of Italy and France, were keeping a close eye on the Unidad Popular experiment. . . . In both Italy and France, the Communist parties ha[d] for some time been seeking an alliance with Socialists—and in Italy's case, even with Christian Democrats—which would permit them to return to the government of those countries, at least as junior partners" (Alexander, *The Tragedy of Chile*, 136). Mark Falcoff reports that "a group of Italian sympathizers told Allende shortly after his election, 'If you can show in Chile that a second road to socialism is possible. . ., then the next country to advance along that road will be Italy, and very soon others in Latin America, and later, in one or two generations, half the world" (Falcoff, *Modern Chile, 1970–1989*, 2). Allende's foreign minister, Clodomiro Almeyda, later recalled that "the victory of a clearly anti-imperialist, socialist political force in an important Latin American country changed the balance of power on the continent, and was inevitably linked to the general political process in Latin America and the hemisphere. This in turn had ramifications, at least to some extent, in the world political arena where the East-West conflict overshadowed . . . every event. Indeed, important actors in the *Unidad Popular* had participated in that world conflict and saw the Chilean experience in a larger context" (Clodomiro Almeyda Medina, "The Foreign Policy of the Unidad Popular Government," in *Chile at the Turning Point: Lessons of the Socialist Years, 1970–1973*, ed. Federico G. Gil, Ricardo Lagos E., and Henry A. Landsberger (Philadelphia: Institute for the Study of Human Issues, 1979), 76.

58. Korry to Church, Senate Hearings, *Intelligence Activities*, 118.

59. Hersh, *The Price of Power*, 270.

60. Morris, *Uncertain Greatness*, 241 (emphasis in original).

61. Senate, *Alleged Assassination Plots*, 229n3; Kornbluh, *The Pinochet File*, 8.

62. Quoted in Kornbluh, *The Pinochet File*, 79, 119.

63. Kissinger, *White House Years*, 129, 664, 668n678. Kissinger later observed that "the *appearance* of inferiority—whatever its actual significance—can have serious political consequences" (Gaddis, *Strategies of Containment*, 288; emphasis in original).

64. Small, *The Presidency of Richard Nixon*, 67; Kissinger, *Years of Upheaval*, 1187.

65. George C. Herring, *America's Longest War: The United States and Vietnam, 1950–1975*, 3rd ed. (New York: McGraw-Hill, 1996), 245; Kimball, *Nixon's Vietnam*, 118, 216–217, 229–230; Small, *The Presidency of Richard Nixon*, 67; Isaacson, *Kissinger: A Biography*, 287; Kissinger, *White House Years*, 969. That Nixon had inherited the domestic political turmoil over U.S. involvement in Vietnam that had driven Johnson from the presidency became evident during his 1969 inaugural parade when the incoming president's limousine was pelted by "a barrage of sticks, stones, beer cans, and what looked like firecrackers" by crowds of antiwar demonstrators (Nixon, *RN*, 366).

66. H. R. Haldeman, *The Haldeman Diaries: Inside the Nixon White House* (New York: Putnam's, 1994), 192–194. "Richard Nixon was a full-time politician," White House domestic affairs counsel John Ehrlichman later wrote. "At home and abroad, every day of the week and whatever the occasion, he (and we) looked after the politics" (John Ehrlichman, *Witness to Power: The Nixon Years* [New York: Pocket, 1982], 288).

67. Kissinger, *White House Years*, 126, 634; Ambrose, *Nixon: The Triumph of a Politician*, 19–20.

68. Ambrose, *Nixon: The Triumph of a Politician*, 378. One of Kissinger's National Security Council aides said of the administration's interventionist motives: "It was the 'who-lost-Chile' syndrome" (Morris, *Uncertain Greatness*, 241).

69. Kissinger, *White House Years*, 671 (emphasis in original).

70. National Security Council, "Options Paper on Chile (NSSM97)," 3 November 1970, 3, 5, in *Chile and the United States: Declassified Documents Relating to the Military Coup, 1970–1976*.

71. Memorandum, Chapin to H. R. Haldeman, 4 November 1970, in File 66-6, "National Security Council, 9–1–70 to 11–4–70," White House Central Files, Subject Files, Confidential Files, 1969–1974, box 14, Nixon Presidential Materials Project, U.S. National Archives, College Park, MD. Also quoted in Kornbluh, *The Pinochet File*, 80.

72. Kissinger, *White House Years*, 653. The full text of Korry's cable can be found in *Chile and the United States: Declassified Documents Relating to the Military Coup, 1970–1976*.

73. Peter Kornbluh, "The *El Mercurio* File: Secret Documents Shine New Light on How the CIA Used a Newspaper to Foment a Coup," *Columbia Journalism Review,* September–October 2003, 14, 16–17; Kinzer, *Overthrow,* 170–172, 177; Israel, *Politics and Ideology in Allende's Chile,* 171; Hersh, *The Price of Power,* 266; Sigmund. *The United States and Democracy in Chile,* 50, 55, 83; Korry, "The Sell-Out of Chile and the American Taxpayer," 88; *Washington Post,* 28 November 1975, A4; Powers, *The Man Who Kept the Secrets,* 291–292, 299; Ambrose, *Nixon: The Triumph of a Politician,* 378; Jensen, *The Garotte,* 244; Senate, *Alleged Assassination Plots,* 228nl; Kissinger, *White House Years,* 673. For Edwards' extensive ties to the CIA, see Hersh, *The Price of Power,* 260; Senate, *Covert Action in Chile 1963–1973,* 19, 22, 29; Korry, "The Sell-Out of Chile and the American Taxpayer," 114.

74. Senate Hearings, *Intelligence Activities,* 29; Senate, *ITT Hearings,* 292, 305.

75. Jensen, *The Garotte,* 491, 596nl51.

76. National Security Council, "Options Paper on Chile (NSSM 97)," 3 November 1970, 17, in *Chile and the United States: Declassified Documents Relating to the Military Coup, 1970–1976.*

16. COVERT ACTION: SWAMPLAND OF AMERICAN FOREIGN POLICY

SENATOR FRANK CHURCH

The chairman of the Senate Intelligence Committee that investigated intelligence abuses in 1975–76 finds in the excesses of the CIA abroad the symptoms of an illusion of American omnipotence that entrapped and enthralled the nation's presidents throughout the Cold War. Writing in the middle of the Cold War, the Senator saw no place for bribery, blackmail, abduction, or assassination in America's relations with the rest of the world.

Two hundred years ago, at the founding of this nation, Thomas Paine observed that "Not a place upon earth might be so happy as America. Her situation is remote from all the wrangling world." I still believe America remains the best place on Earth, but it has long since ceased to be "remote from all the wrangling world."

On the contrary, even our internal economy now depends on events far beyond our shores. The energy crisis, which exposed our vulnerable dependence upon foreign oil, made the point vividly.

It is also tragic but true that our own people can no longer be made safe from savage destruction hurled down upon them from the most hidden and remote regions on Earth. Soviet submarines silently traverse the ocean floors carrying transcontinental missiles with the capacity to strike at our heartland. The nuclear arms race threatens to continue its deadly spiral toward Armageddon.

In this dangerous setting, it is imperative for the United States to maintain a strong and effective intelligence service. On this proposition we can ill-afford to be of two minds. We have no choice other than to gather, analyze, and assess—to the best of our abilities—vital information on the intent and prowess of foreign adversaries, present or potential. Without an adequate intelligence-gathering apparatus, we would be unable to gauge with confidence our defense requirements; unable to conduct an informed foreign policy; unable to control, through satellite surveillance, a runaway nuclear arms race.

"The winds and waves are always on the side of the ablest navigators," wrote Gibbon. Those nations without a skillful intelligence service must navigate beneath a clouded sky.

With this truth in mind, the United States established, by the National Security Act of 1947, a Central Intelligence Agency to collect and evaluate intelligence, and provide for its proper dissemination within the government. The CIA was to be a clearing house for other U.S. intelligence agencies, including those of the State Department and the various military services. It was to be an independent, civilian intelligence agency whose duty it was, in the words of Allen Dulles, CIA Director from 1953–1961:

> To weigh facts, and to draw conclusions from those facts, without having either the facts or the conclusions warped by the inevitable and even proper prejudices of the men whose duty it is to determine policy and who, having once determined a policy, are too likely to be blind to any facts which might lend to prove the policy to be faulty.

"The Central Intelligence Agency," concluded Dulles, "should have nothing to do with policy." In this way, neither the President nor the Congress would be left with any of the frequently self-interested intelligence assessments afforded by the Pentagon and the State Department to rely upon.

In its efforts to get at the hard facts, the CIA has performed unevenly. It has had its successes and its failures. The CIA has detected the important new Soviet weapons systems early on; but it has often over-estimated the growth of the Russian ICBM forces. The CIA has successfully monitored Soviet adherence to arms control agreements, and given us the confidence to take steps toward further limitations; but it has been unable to predict the imminence of several international conflicts, such as the 1973 Arab-Israeli War. In a word, though it deserves passing marks for its intelligence work, the CIA has certainly not been infallible.

While one may debate the quality of the agency's performance, there has never been any question about the propriety and necessity of its involvement in the process of gathering and evaluating foreign intelligence. Nor have serious questions been raised about the means used to acquire such information, whether from overt sources, technical devices, or by clandestine methods.

What has become controversial is quite unrelated to intelligence, but has to do instead with the so-called covert operations of the CIA, those secret efforts to manipulate events within foreign countries in ways presumed to serve the interests of the United States. Nowhere are such activities vouchsafed in the statutory language which created the Agency in 1947, "No indication was given in the statute that the CIA would become a vehicle for foreign political action or clandestine political warfare," notes Harry Howe Ransom, a scholar who has written widely and thought deeply about the problems of intelligence in modern society. Ransom concludes that "probably no other organization of the federal government has taken such liberties in interpreting its legally assigned functions as has the CIA."

The legal basis for this political action arm of the CIA is very much open to question. Certainly the legislative history of the 1947 Act fails to indicate that Congress anticipated the CIA would ever engage in covert political warfare abroad.

The CIA points to a catch-all phrase contained in the 1947 Act as a rationalization for its operational prerogatives. A clause in the statute permits the Agency "to perform such other functions and duties related to intelligence affecting the national security as the National Security Council may, from time to time, direct." These vague and seemingly innocuous words have been seized upon as the green light for CIA intervention around the world.

MALIGNANT PLOTS

Moreover, these interventions into the political affairs of foreign countries soon came to overshadow the Agency's original purpose of gathering and evaluating information. Just consider how far afield we strayed.

For example:

- We deposed the government of Guatemala when its leftist leanings displeased us.
- We attempted to ignite a civil war against Sukarno in Indonesia.
- We intervened to restore the Shah to his throne in Iran, after Mossadegh broke the monopoly grip of British Petroleum over Iranian oil.
- We attempted to launch a counter-revolution in Cuba through the abortive landing of an army of exiles at the Bay of Pigs.
- We even conducted a secret war in Laos, paying Meo tribesmen and Thai mercenaries to do our fighting there.

All these engagements were initiated without the knowledge or consent of Congress. No country was too small, no foreign leader too trifling, to escape our attention.

- We sent a deadly toxin to the Congo with the purpose of injecting Lumumba with a fatal disease.
- We armed local dissidents in the Dominican Republic, knowing their purpose to be the assassination of Trujillo.
- We participated in a military coup overturning the very government we were pledged to defend in South Vietnam; and when Premier Diem resisted, he and his brother were murdered by the very generals to whom we gave money and support.
- We attempted for years to assassinate Fidel Castro and other Cuban leaders. The various plots spanned three Administrations, and involved an extended collaboration between the CIA and the Mafia.

Whatever led the United States to such extremes? Assassination is nothing less than an act of war, and our targets were leaders of small, weak countries that could not possibly threaten the United States. Only once did Castro become an accessory to a threat, by permitting the Soviets to install missiles on Cuban soil within range of the United States.

And this was the one time when the CIA called off all attempts against his life.

The roots of these malignant plots grew out of the obsessions of the Cold War. When the CIA succeeded the Office of Strategic Services of World War II, Stalin replaced Hitler as the Devil Incarnate. Wartime methods were routinely adopted for peacetime use.

In those myopic years, the world was seen as up for grabs between the United States and the Soviet Union. Castro's Cuba raised the specter of a Soviet outpost at America's doorstep. Events in the Dominican Republic appeared to offer an additional opportunity for the Soviets and their allies. The Congo, freed from Belgian rule, occupied the strategic center of the African continent, and the prospect of Soviet penetration there was viewed as a threat to U.S. interests in emerging Africa. There was a great concern that a communist takeover in Indochina would have a "domino effect" throughout Asia. Even the lawful election in 1970 of a Marxist president in Chile was still seen by some as the equivalent of Castro's conquest of Cuba.

In the words of a former Secretary of State, "A desperate struggle [was] going on in the back alleys of world politics." Every upheaval, wherever it occurred, was likened to a pawn on a global chessboard, to be moved this way or that, by the two principal players. This led the CIA to plunge into a full range of covert activities designed to counteract the competitive efforts of the Soviet KGB. Thus, the United States came to adopt the methods and accept the value system of the "enemy." In the secret world of covert action, we threw off all restraints. Not content merely to discreetly subsidize foreign political parties, labor unions, and newspapers, the Central Intelligence Agency soon began to directly manipulate the internal politics of other countries. Spending many millions of dollars annually, the CIA filled its bag with dirty tricks, ranging from bribery and false propaganda to schemes to "alter the health" of unfriendly foreign leaders and undermine their regimes.

Nowhere is this imitation of KGB tactics better demonstrated than in the directives sent to CIA agents in the Congo in 1960. Instructions to kill the African leader Lumumba were sent via diplomatic pouch, along with rubber gloves, a mask, syringe, and a lethal biological material. The poison was to be injected into some substance that Lumumba would ingest, whether food or toothpaste. Before this plan was implemented, Lumumba was killed by Congolese rivals. Nevertheless, our actions had fulfilled the prophesy of George Williams, an eminent theologian at the Harvard Divinity School, who once warned, "Be cautious when you choose your enemy, for you will grow more like him."

ALLENDE "UNACCEPTABLE"

The imperial view from the White House reached its arrogant summits during the Administration of Richard Nixon. On September 15, 1970, following the election of Allende to be President of Chile, Richard Nixon summoned Henry Kissinger, Richard Helms, and John Mitchell to the White House. The topic was Chile. Allende, Nixon stated, was unacceptable to the President of the United States.

In his handwritten notes for this meeting, Nixon indicated that he was "not concerned" with the risks involved. As CIA Director Helms recalled in testimony before the Senate Committee, "The President came down very hard that he wanted something done, and he didn't care how." To Helms, the order had been all-inclusive. "If I ever carried a marshal's baton in my knapsack out of the Oval Office," he recalled, "it was that day." Thus, the President of the United States had given orders to the CIA to prevent the popularly elected President of Chile from entering office.

To bar Allende from the Presidency, a military coup was organized, with the CIA playing a direct role in the planning. One of the major obstacles to the success of the mission was the strong opposition to a coup by the Commander-in-Chief of the Chilean Army, General Rene Schneider, who insisted that Chile's constitution be upheld. As a result of his stand, the removal of General Schneider became a necessary ingredient in the coup plans. Unable to get General Schneider to resign, conspirators in Chile decided to kidnap him. Machine guns and ammunition were passed by the CIA to a group of kidnappers on October 22, 1970. That same day General Schneider was mortally wounded on his way to work in an attempted kidnap, apparently by a group affiliated with the one provided weapons by the CIA.

The plot to kidnap General Schneider was but one of many efforts to subvert the Allende regime. The United States sought also to bring the Chilean economy under Allende to its knees. In a situation report to Dr. Kissinger, our Ambassador wrote that:

> Not a nut or bolt will be allowed to reach Chile under Allende. Once Allende comes to power we shall do all within our power to condemn Chile

and the Chileans to utmost deprivation and poverty, a policy designed for a long time to come to accelerate the hard features of a Communist society in Chile.

The ultimate outcome, as you know, of these and other efforts to destroy the Allende government was a bloodbath which included the death of Allende and the installation, in his place, of a repressive military dictatorship.

Why Chile? What can possibly explain or justify such an intrusion upon the right of the Chilean people to self-determination? The country itself was no threat to us. It has been aptly characterized as a "dagger pointed straight at the heart of Antarctica."

Was it to protect American owned big business? We now know that I.T.T. offered the CIA a million dollars to prevent the ratification of Allende's election by the Chilean Congress. Quite properly, this offer was rejected. But the CIA then spent much more on its own, in an effort to accomplish the same general objective.

Yet, if our purpose was to save the properties of large U.S. corporations, that cause had already been lost. The nationalization of the mines was decided well before Allende's election; and the question of compensation was tempered by insurance against confiscatory losses issued to the companies by the U.S. government itself.

No, the only plausible explanation for our intervention in Chile is the persistence of the myth that communism is a single, hydraheaded serpent, and that it remains our duty to cut off each ugly head, wherever and however it may appear.

Ever since the end of World War II, we have justified our mindless meddling in the affairs of others on the ground that since the Soviets do it, we must do it, too. The time is at hand to re-examine that thesis.

Before Chile, we insisted that communism had never been freely chosen by any people, but forced upon them against their will. The communists countered that they resorted to revolution because the United States would never permit the establishment of a communist regime by peaceful means.

In Chile, President Nixon confirmed the communist thesis. Like Caesar peering into the colonies from distant Rome, Nixon said the choice of government by the Chileans was unacceptable to the President of the United States.

The attitude in the White House seemed to be: If—in the wake of Vietnam—I can no longer send the Marines, then I will send in the CIA.

WHAT HAVE WE GAINED?

But what have we gained by our policy of consummate intervention, compared to what we have lost?

- A "friendly" Iran and Indonesia, members of the OPEC cartel, which imposes extortionate prices on the Western World for indispensable oil?
- A hostile Laos that preferred the indigenous forces of communism to control imposed by Westerners, which smacked of the hated colonialism against which they had fought so long to overthrow?
- A fascist Chile, with thousands of political prisoners languishing in their jails, mocking the professed ideals of the United States throughout the hemisphere?

If we have gained little, what then have we lost? I suggest we have lost—or grievously impaired—the good name and reputation of the United States from which we once drew a unique capacity to exercise matchless moral leadership. Where once we were admired, now we are resented. Where once we were welcome, now we are tolerated, at best. In the eyes of millions of once friendly foreign people, the United States is today regarded with grave suspicion and distrust.

What else can account for the startling decline in American prestige? Certainly not the collapse of our military strength, for our firepower has grown immensely since the end of World War II.

I must lay the blame, in large measure, to the fantasy that it lay within our power to control other countries through the covert manipulation of their affairs. It formed part of a greater illusion that entrapped and enthralled our Presidents: the illusion of American omnipotence.

Nevertheless, I do not draw the conclusion of those who now argue that all U.S. covert operations must be banned in the future. I can conceive of a dire emergency when timely clandestine action on our part might avert a nuclear holocaust and save an entire civilization.

I can also conceive of circumstances, such as those existing in Portugal today, where our discreet help to democratic political parties might avert a forcible take-over by a communist minority, heavily subsidized by the Soviets. In Portugal, such a bitterly-unwanted, Marxist regime is being resisted courageously by a people who earlier voted 84 percent against it.

But these are covert operations consistent either with the imperative of national survival or with our traditional belief in free government. If our hand were exposed helping a foreign people in their struggle to be free, we could scorn the cynical doctrine of "plausible denial," and say openly, "Yes, we were there—and proud of it."

We were there in Western Europe, helping to restore democratic governments in the aftermath of World War II. It was only after our faith gave way to fear that we began to act as a self-appointed-sentinel of the status quo.

Then it was that all the dark arts of secret intervention—bribery, blackmail, abduction, assassination—were put to the service of reactionary and repressive regimes that can never, for long, escape or withstand the volcanic forces of change.

And the United States, as a result, became ever more identified with the claims of the old order, instead of the aspirations of the new.

The remedy is clear. American foreign policy, whether openly or secretly pursued, must be made to conform once more to our historic ideals, the same fundamental belief in freedom and popular government that once made us a beacon of hope for the downtrodden and oppressed throughout the world.

QUESTIONS FOR FURTHER DISCUSSION

1. Why is Senator Frank Church so critical of U.S. covert actions?
2. Does Church see any need for covert action at all in the conduct of American foreign policy?
3. Against what kinds of nations was covert action directed by the United States, according to Senator Church?
4. What kinds of covert action, if any, do you think are morally acceptable for the United States, and under what conditions?

17. PURSUING PEACE: THE STRATEGIC LIMITS OF DRONE WARFARE

ELKE SCHWARZ

Since the 9/11 terrorist attacks against the United States, national security officials in Washington, DC, have searched for ways to defeat the global terrorist threat. The use of unmanned aerial vehicles (UAVs or drones) soon became the chief weapon of choice to seek out and destroy terrorist targets. This essay reminds readers that the use of drones for counterterrorism has its limits and that this method has been dogged by ethical controversies—especially related to the capacity of UAVs to inadvertently kill innocent civilian bystanders.

TAKING STOCK

For more than a decade now unmanned aerial vehicles (UAVs), more commonly known as "drones," have influenced the strategic approach to the US-led war on terrorism. In 2009, when Leon Panetta, then Director of the CIA, declared that drones are "the only game in town,"[1] he made clear how central drones would be not only to the US response to terrorism but also to the future of warfare more broadly. The ethos that underlies contemporary drone warfare goes at least as far back as the 1980s, when President Ronald Reagan yielded to his more hawkish advisors and signed the controversial National Security Decision Directive (NSDD) 138, thereby helping to institute an active and preventive approach to fighting terrorists (which included the "pre-emptive neutralisation of anti-American terrorist groups.")[2] Hitherto, this approach had been met with strict moral indignation. However, it was the advent of drone technology in particular that facilitated a large-scale rolling out of preemptive strikes against suspected global terrorists as the apparent "go-to" strategy in the war on terrorism.[3] With superior intelligence, surveillance, and reconnaissance capabilities, as well as an ability to take care of much of the F3EA (find, fix, finish, exploit, and analyze) targeting cycle, drones, at first glance, would appear to be the ideal instruments for the CIA's attempts to counter terrorism through targeted killings. Their value and wisdom as effective tools in the struggle against terrorism remain, however, strongly contested.

In a memorandum issued by President Obama on the legal and policy frameworks that inform the use of military force (including targeted killings), he reiterated that his administration considered the lethal drone strategy a viable and effective way to address terrorist threats across the globe. The sixty-six-page-long document emphasized that targeted killing decisions were subject to a conscientious process; however, the memo neither included any further information about the basis of these processes nor gave an elaboration as to what the foundations are for the government's assessment that the use of drones for targeted killings was indeed legal. Furthermore, the overall criteria for a lethal kill decision remain obscure in light of the "broad-brush approach" adopted in the memorandum, meaning that we still know little about the practices of target selection and kill decisions, and by extension their ethical, political, and strategic implications.[4] Finally, the memo failed to establish why the government considered the practice of targeted killing effective in eliminating terrorism; there was no empirical or analytical support given for this assertion. In relation to the clandestine CIA program, the rationale for strategic choices was even more opaque; and with very limited information available on the processes, targets, number of strikes and resulting deaths, it is very difficult to assess the value of the US drone program. What we do know is that drone strikes have proliferated in Afghanistan, Iraq, Somalia, Yemen, and Pakistan since 2004, as have terrorist attacks in

240

these same countries, during the same timespan. A cursory glance at the relevant statistics paints a bleak picture with significantly higher rates of terrorism incidences in all key regions of increased lethal drone use.[5] While correlation is of course not causation, the wisdom of using drones as one of the essential tools for fighting terrorism is at the very least put into question by the data we have on outcomes to date. If the goal is to attain peace (or the absence of violence) in regions marred by terrorism, then a reconsideration of strategy might be warranted.

In the absence of transparency around contemporary drone operations, assessing the viability and wisdom of their use in targeted killing and counterterrorism initiatives requires a turn to theory. The first and most important point, in my view, is that we avoid the trap of thinking about drones as a simple extension of conventional airpower. Instead, we must situate drones within a broader assemblage of technologies, paying particular attention to the sometimes-unintended practices that this 'assemblage' enables. Lacking the space to dissect this assemblage in its entirety, I will focus here on some of the broad strategic limits inscribed into the drone as a techno-scientific weapon system of war. In particular, I will highlight three strategic aspects for which drone technology is of limited service: (1) the production of intelligence about socially complex networks and societies; (2) the application and use of soft or smart power; and (3) the attainment of a medium- to long-term goal of peace.

KNOWLEDGE/POWER/VIOLENCE

A crucial part of the targeted killing program is the identification of relevant targets. The erstwhile criterion of only targeting "high value" individuals, which were known by name and position in a specific terrorist organization (as first instituted by George W. Bush), has long been replaced by a practice that sees individuals placed on "kill lists" not simply because of who they are but also for what they *appear* to be doing. In latter instance, previously unknown and unidentified individuals are marked as potentially dangerous and placed on a kill list for so-called "signatures strikes," on the basis of observed patterns in their behavior. This process entails a combination of human intelligence (HUMINT) and signals intelligence (SIGINT), but SIGINT is the more relevant component in this context. The role of SIGINT is to feed massive amounts of data into what is known as the "disposition matrix," which is integral to imputing

terrorist intent. However, the nature of the data collection process (to which the drone is instrumental) is such that in order to yield any relevant and actionable results, the definition of "what a terrorist is" must be broad. Without a single well-defined profile for a terrorist to work with, the only way that pattern-of-life analysis can identify the signature of terrorist activity is by taking a broad view of what kinds of patterns constitute a terrorist signature. As Jutta Weber has argued, in the end it is the fear of "failing to spot potential suspects" that provides the criteria for the algorithms that in turn determine who might be a suspect. "Accordingly, more and more data are included in watch and kill lists," says Weber, and more and more individuals are identified as potential terrorists.[6]

What is evident here is a kind of strategic fallacy: an attempt to eliminate all and every possible danger using a mode of SIGINT-enhanced warfare that by necessity produces ever-new categories of danger. And these new categories of danger produce new conflicts, because each quantitatively produced "terrorist" must be met with the same response as the high value named terrorists of old.[7] Thus, the greater the reliance on SIGINT (and the thinner the knowledge of social and cultural practices on the ground), the more unreliable this knowledge becomes as a foundation for eliminating or neutralizing real threats. This matters in particular when we consider that deep grievances (such as the unjustified death of a loved one) often spawn new acts of retributive violence. Killing people "based on meta-data"[8] brings forth new problems of a social, cultural, or political nature, which are invisible to data-driven modalities of killing.

This serves as an important reminder that sound strategic decisions require an understanding of different types of power in order to overcome an enemy or produce an outcome in one's interest. Power is multidimensional, and effective strategies—including foreign policy strategies—typically draw on a variety of tools on a continuum of power running from "hard" to "soft." Granted, there are many different perceptions of what power is, and it remains a contested concept. Scholars typically distinguish between force and influence, but as Joseph Nye notes, "From a policy point of view we are interested in the ability to produce preferred outcomes." [9] In the context of the US drone war, then, an analysis of *what* the preferred outcome is and *how* this can be achieved is required.

This is a simple and somewhat obvious point. However, it requires that we recognize the limitations to drone technology as a facet of power. Drones are good at a number of things, including the collection of vast amounts of data, the capacity to hover over territories for long periods of time, the ability to do so stealthily, and the precision with which targets can be reached. In this sense they are a powerful material tool. But if with this tool we identify and unnecessarily kill the wrong individuals (or indeed civilians), drones may in fact have counter-productive consequences and fail to achieve a preferred outcome. In other words, the data-driven logic of drones lacks the capacity to wield anything other than hard, material power and possibly diminishes relational power. Drones cannot, by virtue of their make-up and design, produce modalities of power that adhere to a more nuanced understanding of soft power capabilities.

Nye makes a further, important distinction between power as a material resource and power to achieve an outcome, calling the latter 'smart power'.[10] Smart power, too, cannot be exercised through by a powerful technological resource such as the drone; a sound cost-benefit analysis should take into consideration the wider spectrum of power, particularly in preventive warfare.[11] At present, it is this dominant reliance on power as a resource, and power as hard power that underpins the continuing use of armed drones in counter-terrorism warfare, despite the fact that the United States does not seem to be winning the war on global terrorism. Again, this might be an obvious point; however, it bears thinking through as geographies of drone warfare continue to expand,[12] turning more and more territories into zones of war, rather than zones of peace.[13]

If we are critical of the credo that "power grows out of the barrel of a gun" and take seriously General Stanley McChrystal's assessment that "the whole point of war is to take care of people, not just to kill them," then an understanding of what violence can and cannot achieve is important in the strategic assessment of drone warfare.[14] Unlike power, conceptions of violence have been somewhat undertheorized in scholarship and particularly in military studies. To address this, we will draw briefly on Hannah Arendt's seminal work *On Violence*. For Arendt, violence and power are two distinct categories that should be treated as such. Violence can denote, in fact, a certain lack of power, for example, in an uprising against a sovereign, the sovereign use of military power against his people is, for Arendt, an indicator of a lack of otherwise persuasive power over the people. The core characteristic of violence is its instrumental nature, which permits its use only in situations of self-defense and struggle against oppression. It can break an injustice, but it cannot bring forth long-term political goals. In other words, violence can be a tactical military means, but it can never serve to strategically bring about a political end. Here it is worth quoting Arendt at length:

> Violence, being instrumental in nature, is rational to the extent that it is effective in reaching the end that must justify it. And since when we act we never know with any certainty the eventual consequence of what we are doing, violence can remain rational only if it pursues short-term goals . . . If goals are not achieved rapidly, the result will be not merely defeat but the introduction of the practice of violence in the whole body politic.[15]

This relationship between violent means and the ends they seek to achieve is central to any assessment of targeted killing. When we defend targeted killing, we misunderstand violence as a productive force and fail to recognize the unpredictability of the actual ends or outcomes it will produce. Instead, most discourses on the effectiveness of drone warfare focus on the short term, tactical effects of leadership decapitation. There is no doubt that such tactical successes are important aspects of the counter-terrorism effort; but they must fit within a wider strategy of ridding contemporary zones of war or conflict of terrorism, which requires a more complex approach to knowledge, power, and the use of violent means. This, as McChrystal knows, is the danger of the CIA's clandestine approach: "If you go back in history, I can't find a covert fix that solved a problem long term."[16]

QUESTIONS FOR FURTHER DISCUSSION

1. How would you appraise the use of drones by the United States against suspected terrorist targets overseas? What if the target was known to be an American citizen? What if the target were walking the streets of Los Angeles rather than hiding in a Yemeni desert?

2. Do you agree or disagree with the views of General McChrystal on the uses of covert warfare?

3. How do you address the argument that covert drone warfare is superior to overt conventional land warfare, since drones only kill a few people while large ground invasions often lead to the death of thousands of people, including many non-combatants?

4. How do you think the use of drones as military and paramilitary weapons will evolve, as used by the United States and other nations?

ENDNOTES

1. Leon E. Panetta, 'Director's Remarks at the Pacific Council on International Policy', *CIA News & Information*, 18 May 2009. Available at <https://www.cia.gov/news-information/speeches-testimony/directors-remarks-at-pacific-council.html/>. Accessed 12 December 2016.

2. Markus Gunneflo, *Targeted Killing: A Legal and Political History* (Cambridge: Cambridge University Press, 2016), p. 111. See also: Jeffrey David Simon, *The Terrorist Trap: America's Experience with Terrorism* (Bloomington: Indiana University Press, 2001).

3. Christopher J. Fuller, "The Eagle Comes Home to Roost: The Historical Origins of the CIA's Lethal Drones Programme," *Intelligence and National Security* 30, no. 6 (2015), 769–792.

4. Alex Moorhead and Rahma A. Hussein, 'What's Actually New in the New Drone Strike & Military Force Disclosure?' *Just Security*, 6 December 2016. Available at https://www.justsecurity.org/35330/whats-drone-strike-military-force-disclosures/. Accessed 12 December 2016.

5. For statistics on drone strikes, see data from *The Bureau of Investigative Journalism*, *The Long War Journal*, or the *New America Foundation*, each of which show variations in numbers but similarities in trends. For data on terrorist attacks see the *Global Terrorism Database* and *Chicago Suicide Attack Database*.

6. Jutta Weber, "Keep Adding: On Kill Lists, Drone Warfare and the Politics of Databases," *Environment and Planning D: Society and Space*, OnlineFirst, 30 December 2015, 5.

7. Ibid., 17.

8. General Michael Hayden, former director of the NSA and the CIA, confirmed that people are killed based on meta-data not in the United States but on foreign soil. See David Cole, "We Kill People Based on Meta-data," *New York Review of Books*, 10 May 2014. Available at http://www.nybooks.com/daily/2014/05/10/we-kill-people-based-metadata/. Accessed 12 December 2016

9. Joseph Nye, "Power and Foreign Policy," *Journal of Political Power* 4, no.1 (2011), 9–24, at 11.

10. Ibid., 12.

11. Jennifer Taw, 'Preventive Force: The Logic of Cost and Benefit', in *Preventive Force: Drones, Targeted Killing, and the Transformation of Contemporary Warfare*, ed. Kerstin Fisk and Jennifer Ramons (New York: New York University Press, 2016), 33–58.

12. Charlie Savage, Eric Schmitt, and Mark Mazzetti, "Obama Expands War with Al Qaeda to Include Shabab in Somalia," *New York Times*, 27 November 2016. Available at http://www.nytimes.com/2016/11/27/us/politics/obama-expands-war-with-al-qaeda-to-include-shabab-in-somalia.html?_r=2/. Accessed 12 December 2016.

13. Michael Walzer, "Just and Unjust Targeted Killing and Drone Warfare," *Daedalus* 145, no. 4 (2016), 12–24.

14. General Stanley McChrystal, "Generation Kill: A Conversation with Stanley McChrystal," *Foreign Affairs*, March/April 2013. Available at https://www.foreignaffairs.com/interviews/2013-02-11/generation-kill/. Accessed 12 December 2016.

15. Hannah Arendt, *On Violence* (Orlando, FL: Harcourt, Brace, 1970), 79–80.

16. McChrystal, "Generation Kill."

From Elke Schwarz, "Pursuing Peace: The Strategic Limits of Drone Warfare," *Intelligence and National Security*, June 2017 (Volume 32, No. 4) 422–425. Reproduced by permission from Taylor & Francis.

18. ASSASSINATION AS AN INSTRUMENT OF AMERICAN FOREIGN POLICY

BRUCE D. BERKOWITZ

One of the more extreme and morally questionable forms of paramilitary covert action is the assassination plot against a foreign leader. This essay examines the use of this method from a legal, practical, and ethical perspective.

Soon after the September 11 terrorist attacks on New York and Washington, U.S. officials announced that they had evidence linking Osama bin Laden to the attacks. As Americans began to recover from their initial shock, many of them asked, "Why don't we just get rid of the guy?"

The terrorist tragedy reopened one of the most controversial issues in national security policy: assassination. Few topics raise more passion. Yet, despite the intense emotions assassination raises, assassination rarely gets the kind of dispassionate analysis that we routinely devote to other national security issues. That is what I will do here. When it comes to assassination, four questions are key: What is it? Is it legal? Does it work? And when, if ever, is assassination acceptable?

WHAT IS IT?

One reason assassination—or, for that matter, banning assassination—provokes so much disagreement is that people often use the term without a precise definition and thus are really arguing about different things. One needs to be clear. Depending on the definition, one can be arguing about activities that are really quite different.

For example, is killing during wartime assassination? Does assassination refer to killing people of high rank, or can anyone be the target of assassination? Does it matter if a member of the armed forces, a civilian government official, or a hired hand does the killing? Depending on the definition, killing a military leader during a bombing raid might be "assassination" but killing a low-level civilian official with a sniper might not.

For what it is worth, the *Merriam-Webster Dictionary* defines *assassination* by referring to the verb *assassinate*, which is defined as "to injure or destroy unexpectedly and treacherously" or "murder by sudden or secret attack usually for impersonal reasons." In other words, assassination is murder—killing a person—using secrecy or surprise. Assassination stands in contrast to murder without surprise (e.g., a duel). Also, assassination is not murder for personal gain or vengeance; assassinations support the goals of a government, organization, group, or cause.

Although people associate assassinations with prominent people, strictly speaking, assassination knows no rank. Leaders are often the targets of state-sponsored assassination, but history shows that generals, common soldiers, big-time crime bosses, and low-level terrorists have all been targets, too. Also, it does not seem to matter how you kill the target. It does not matter if you use a bomb or a booby trap; as long as you target a particular person, it's assassination.

For our purposes, assume that assassination is "deliberately killing a particular person to achieve a military or political objective, using the element of surprise to gain an advantage." We can call such a killing "sanctioned assassination" when a government has someone carry out such an action—as opposed to, say, "simple assassination," killing by an individual acting on his own. Then the question is, should we allow the United States to sanction such activities? And, if we allow the government to sanction assassination, when and how should do it?

244

IS IT LEGAL?

You might be surprised to learn that there are no international laws banning assassination. The closest thing to a prohibition is the 1973 Convention on the Prevention and Punishment of Crimes Against Internationally Protected Persons, Including Diplomatic Agents. This treaty (which the United States signed) bans attacks against heads of state while they conduct formal functions, heads of government while they travel abroad, and diplomats while they perform their duties.

The Protected Persons Convention was intended to ensure that governments could function and negotiate even during war. Without it, countries might start a war (or get drawn into one) and then find themselves unable to stop because there was no leader at home to make the decision to do so and because their representatives were getting picked off on their way to cease-fire negotiations.

But other than these narrow cases, the Protected Persons Convention says nothing about prohibiting assassination. Even then it applies only to officials representing bona fide governments and "international organizations of an intergovernmental character." So presumably the convention shields the representatives of the United Nations, the World Trade Organization, the International Red Cross, and, probably, the PLO. It does not protect bosses of international crime syndicates or the heads of terrorist groups such as Al Qaeda.

Another treaty that some might construe as an assassination ban is the Hague Convention on the "laws and customs" of war. The Hague Convention states that "the right of belligerents to adopt means of injuring the enemy is not unlimited." (This was a bold statement in 1907, when the convention was signed.)

The Hague Convention tried to draw a sharp line between combatants and noncombatants; combatants were entitled to the convention's protections but were also obliged to obey its rules. For example, the Hague Convention tried to distinguish combatants by requiring them to wear a "fixed distinctive emblem recognizable at a distance." Wear the emblem while fighting, and you are entitled to be treated as a POW if captured; fail to follow the dress code, and you might be hanged as a mere bandit.

Alas, maintaining this definition of a "combatant" proved a losing battle throughout the twentieth century. Guerrilla warfare transformed civilians into soldiers. Strategic bombing transformed civilians into targets. Headquarters staff, defense ministers, and civilian commanders in chief today are all more likely to wear suits than uniforms. Teenage paramilitary soldiers in Liberia are lucky to have a pair of Levis to go along with their AK-47s, let alone fatigues or insignia. That is why, practically speaking, a "combatant" today is anyone who is part of a military chain of command.

Yet the Hague Convention may be more interesting not for what it prohibits but for what it permits. The closest the convention comes to banning assassination is when it prohibits signatories from killing or wounding "treacherously individuals belonging to the hostile nation or army." But when it refers to "treachery," it is referring to fighting under false pretenses (e.g., flying the enemy's flag or wearing his uniform to lure him to death). The Hague Convention specifically permits "ruses of war." Snipers, land mines, deception, camouflage, and other sneaky tactics are okay. In fact, one might even argue that, since the convention prohibits *indiscriminate* killing, state-sanctioned assassination—the most precise and deliberate killing of all—during war is exactly what the treaty calls for.

The third international agreement that is relevant to assassination is the Charter of the United Nations, which allows countries to use military force in the name of self-defense. If a country can justify a war as "defensive," it can kill any person in the enemy's military chain of command that it can shoot, bomb, burn, or otherwise eliminate. And it can use whatever "ruses of war" it needs to get the job done. As a result, the main legal constraints on sanctioned assassination other than domestic law, which makes murder a crime in almost all countries, are rules that nations impose on themselves.

The U.S. government adopted such a ban in 1976, when President Ford—responding to the scandal that resulted when the press revealed CIA involvement in several assassinations—issued Executive Order 11905. This order prohibited what it called "political assassination" and essentially reaffirmed an often-overlooked ban that Director of Central Intelligence Richard Helms had adopted for the CIA four years earlier. Jimmy Carter reaffirmed the ban in 1978 with his own Executive Order 12036. Ronald Reagan went even further in 1981; his Executive Order 12333 banned assassination in toto. This ban on assassination remains in effect today.

Even so, there has been a disconnect between our policy and practice. The United States has tried to kill foreign leaders on several occasions since 1976, usually as part of a larger military operation.

For example, in 1986, U.S. Air Force and Navy planes bombed Libya after a Libyan terrorist attack against a nightclub frequented by American soldiers in Berlin. One of the targets was Muammar Qaddafi's tent. During Desert Storm in 1991, we bombed Saddam Hussein's official residences and command bunkers. After the United States linked Osama bin Laden to terrorist bombings of U.S. embassies in Kenya and Tanzania in 1998, we launched a cruise missile attack at one of his bases in Afghanistan.

In each case, U.S. officials insisted that our forces were merely aiming at "command and control" nodes or at a building linked to military operations or terrorist activities. In each case, however, the same officials admitted off the record that they would not have been upset if Qaddafi, Saddam, or bin Laden had been killed in the process.

More recently, according to press reports, presidents have also approved so-called lethal covert operations—operations in which there is a good chance that an unfriendly foreign official might be killed. For example, the press reported a CIA-backed covert operation to topple Saddam in 1996 that probably would have killed him in the process, given the record of Iraqi leadership successions (no one has left office alive). After the September 11 terrorist strikes on New York and Washington, former Clinton officials leaked word to reporters that the CIA had trained Pakistani commandos in 1999 to snatch bin Laden. Given the record of such operations, bin Laden would likely not have survived.

In short, the unintended result of banning assassinations has been to make U.S. leaders perform verbal acrobatics to explain how they have tried to kill someone in a military operation without really trying to kill him. One has to wonder about the wisdom of any policy that allows officials to do something but requires them to deny that they are doing it. We would be better off simply doing away with the prohibition, at least as it applies to U.S. military operations.

DOES IT WORK?

The effectiveness of assassination has depended much on its objectives. Most (but not all) attempts to change the course of large-scale political and diplomatic trends have failed. Assassination has been more effective in achieving small, specific goals.

Indeed, past U.S. assassination attempts have had great difficulty in even achieving the minimal level of success: killing the intended target. According to the available information, *every* U.S. effort to kill a high-ranking official since World War II outside a full-scale war has failed. This record is so poor that it would be

hard to find an instrument of national policy that has been less successful in achieving its objectives than assassination (although price controls or election reform may come in a close second).

According to the Church Committee investigations of the 1970s, the CIA supported assassins trying to kill Patrice Lumumba of the Congo in 1961 and repeatedly tried to assassinate Fidel Castro between 1961 and 1963. In addition, American officials were either privy to plots or encouraged coups that caused the death of a leader (Rafael Trujillo of the Dominican Republic in 1961, Ngo Dinh Diem of South Vietnam in 1963, General Rene Schneider of Chile in 1970, and, later, President Salvador Allende in 1973). And, as noted, in recent years the United States has tried to do away with Qaddafi, Saddam, and bin Laden.

What is notable about this record is that it is remarkably free of success. Castro, Qaddafi, Saddam, and (at least at this writing) bin Laden all survived. (As this is being written, U.S. forces are hunting bin Laden as part of the larger war against the Taliban in Afghanistan.) What is more, Qaddafi continued to support terrorism (e.g., the bombing of Pan Am flight 103). Saddam has managed to outlast the terms of two presidents who wanted to eliminate him (George Bush and Bill Clinton), while continuing to support terrorism—and developing weapons of mass destruction.

One might have predicted this dismal record just by considering why American leaders have resorted to the assassination option. More often than not, assassination is the option when nothing seems to work but officials think that they need to do *something*. When diplomacy is ineffective and war seems too costly, assassination becomes the fallback—but without anyone asking whether it will accomplish anything.

This seems to have been the thinking behind the reported U.S. covert operation to eliminate Saddam in the mid-1990s. Despite a series of provocations—an assassination attempt against former president George Bush, violence against Shi'ite Muslims and Kurds, and violations of U.N. inspection requirements—the Clinton administration was unwilling to wage a sustained, full-scale war against him. Diplomacy was also failing, as the United States was unable to hold together the coalition that won Desert Storm. Covert support to Saddam's opponents in the military was the alternative. It was an utter failure.

True, some other countries have been more successful in that they have killed their target. For example, after the terrorist attack on Israeli athletes in the 1972 Munich Olympics, Israeli special services tracked down and killed each of the Palestinian guerrillas who took part (they also killed an innocent Palestinian in a case of mistaken identity). In 1988 Israeli commandos killed Khalil Al-Wazir, a lieutenant of Yasser Arafat's, in a raid on PLO headquarters in Tunisia. More recently, Israel has killed specifically targeted Palestinian terrorist leaders—for example, Yechya Ayyash, who was killed with a booby-trapped cell phone.

Other countries have also attempted assassinations with some degree of tactical success. During the Cold War, the KGB was linked to several assassinations. Most recently, the Taliban regime in Afghanistan was suspected of being involved in the assassination of Ahmed Shah Massoud, the leader of the Northern Alliance opposition.

But even "successful" assassinations have often left the sponsor worse off, not better. The murder of Diem sucked the United States deeper into a misconceived policy. The assassination of Abraham Lincoln (carried out by a conspiracy some believe to have links to the Confederate secret service) resulted in Reconstruction. German retribution against Czech civilians after the 1942 assassination of Nazi prefect Reinhard Heydrich by British-sponsored resistance fighters was especially brutal. The 1948 assassination of Mohandas Gandhi by Hindu extremists led to violence that resulted in the partition of India.

In short, assassination has usually been unreliable in shaping large-scale political trends the way the perpetrators intended (though the assassination of Yitzhak Rabin by a Zionist extremist in 1995 may be the exception). When it accomplishes anything beyond simply killing the target, it is usually by depriving an enemy of the talents of some uniquely skilled individual. For example, in 1943 U.S. warplanes shot down an aircraft known to be carrying Admiral Isoroku Yamamoto—the architect of Japan's early victories in the Pacific. His loss hurt the Japanese war effort. The same could be said of the loss of Massoud to the Northern Alliance.

The problem is, picking off a talented individual is almost always harder than it looks. One paradox of modern warfare is that, although it is not that hard to kill many people, it can be very difficult to kill a particular person. One has to know exactly where the target will be at a precise moment. This is almost always hard, especially in wartime.

SHOULD WE DO IT, AND IF SO, HOW?

This is the most complex issue, of course. The morality of sanctioned assassination depends mainly on whether and when one can justify murder. Most religions and agnostic philosophies agree that individuals have the right to kill in self-defense when faced with immediate mortal danger. This principle is codified in American law. And, as we have seen, even international law seems to allow killing—even killing specific individuals—when it can be justified as armed self-defense.

Although most Americans do not like the idea of deliberate killing, they do not completely reject it, either. Most would agree that their government should be allowed to kill (or, more precisely, allow people to kill in its behalf) in at least two situations.

One situation is when a police officer must eliminate an immediate threat to public safety—for example, shooting an armed robber or apprehending a suspect who has proven dangerous in the past and who resists arrest. The other situation is when soldiers go to war to defend the country from attack. In addition, many—but not all—Americans believe that the government should be allowed to kill in the case of capital crimes.

It is probably not a coincidence that the U.S. Constitution also envisions these three—and only these three—situations in which the federal government might take a life: policing, going to war, and imposing capital punishment. Logically, then, assassination must fit into one of these three tracks. Assassination can be considered a police act, in which case it must follow the rules for protecting accused criminals. Or it can be considered a military act, in which case it must follow the rules that control how the United States wages war. Or it can be considered capital punishment, in which case it must follow the rules of due process.

Given this, when would we want to allow government to kill a particular foreign national? Clearly we should not use assassination as a form of de facto capital punishment. Unless the intended target presents a clear and immediate threat, there is always time to bring a suspect to justice, where we could guarantee due process. Similarly, although police should be able to protect themselves and others while making an arrest, we would not want police to pursue their targets with the expectation that they would routinely kill them.

The only time we should consider assassination is when we need to eliminate a clear, immediate, lethal threat from abroad. In other words, assassination is a military option. We need to understand it as such because the United States will face more situations in which it must decide whether it is willing, in effect, to go to war to kill a particular individual and how it will target specific individuals during wartime. Two factors make this scenario likely.

First, technology often makes it hard for one *not* to target specific people. Weapons are so accurate today that, when one programs their guidance systems, you aim not just for a neighborhood, or a building in the neighborhood, but for a particular *room* in a particular building. In effect, even bombing and long-range missile attacks have become analogous to sniping. You cannot always be sure you will hit your target—just as snipers often miss and sometimes hit the wrong target—but you still must aim at specific people.

Second, the nature of the threats we face today will likely require us to target specific individuals. Terrorist organizations today use modern communications to organize themselves as worldwide networks. These networks consist of small cells that can group and regroup as needed to prepare for a strike. This is how the bin Laden organization has operated. Seeing how successful these tactics have been, many armies will likely often adopt a similar approach. To defeat such networked organizations, our military forces will need to move quickly, find the critical cells in a network, and destroy them. This inevitably will mean identifying specific individuals and killing them—in other words, assassination.

But when we do so, we should be clear in our own minds that, when the United States tries to assassinate someone, we are going to war—with all the risks and costs that war brings. These include, for example, diplomatic consequences, the danger of escalation, the threat of retaliation against our own leaders, the threat of retaliation against American civilians, and so on.

Because assassination is an act of war, such activities should always be considered a military operation. American leaders need to resist the temptation to use intelligence organizations for this mission. Intelligence organizations are outside the military chain of command. Intelligence operatives are not expected to obey the rules of war and thus are not protected by those rules. At the same time, intelligence organizations are also not law enforcement organizations. In many situations, having intelligence organizations kill specific individuals looks too much like a death sentence without due process.

Indeed, there is reason to question whether intelligence organizations are even technically qualified for assassination. In every publicly known case in which the CIA has considered killing a foreign leader, the agency has outsourced the job. In most cases, it has recruited a foreign intelligence service or military officials with better access. In some of the attempts to kill Castro, the CIA recruited Mafia hit men. Even in the more recent reported cases of lethal covert actions, foreigners would have done the actual killing. It is hard to maintain control and quality when you subcontract assassination-services—as the record shows.

The United States did not ask for the threats we currently face, and killing on behalf of the state will always be the most controversial, most distasteful policy issue of all. That is why we need to use blunt language and appreciate exactly what we are proposing. Sugarcoating the topic only hides the tough issues we need to decide as a country. But if we do need to target specific people for military attack, it is important that we get it right.

QUESTIONS FOR FUTHER DISCUSSION

1. What exactly is meant by the term assassination and has the CIA engaged in such activities?
2. What are the legal arguments for and against assassination plots?
3. Does assassination help a nation achieve its foreign policy goals?
4. What are the ethical arguments that surround this controversial topic?

VII

COUNTERINTELLIGENCE

Polonius: "Your bait of falsehood takes this carp of truth . . ."
—SHAKESPEARE, *Hamlet*, 2.1.60

Although it was never directly mentioned in the National Security Act of 1947, America's secret agencies quickly adopted a second intelligence mission in support of their primary mission of intelligence collection and analysis: namely, the protection of America's secrets from espionage by hostile, and sometimes even friendly, foreign powers. This mission is known as *counterintelligence* (Church Committee 1976; Godson 1996; Johnson 1987; Zuehlke 1980). The purpose of counterintelligence (CI) is to uncover and thwart foreign intelligence operations directed against the United States, especially infiltration by foreign agents.

Defined more formally, counterintelligence is the

knowledge needed for the protection and preservation of the military, economic, and productive strength of the United States, including the security of the Government in domestic and foreign affairs against or from espionage, sabotage, and all other similar clandestine activities designed to weaken or destroy the United States. (Commission on Government Security 1957, 48–49)

Or in a more recent definition found in Executive Order 13470, signed in 2008 by President George W. Bush, counterintelligence is "information and activities to identify, receive, exploit, disrupt, or protect against espionage."

As Jennifer E. Sims puts it, "Counterintelligence is traditionally understood to include operations designed to block, disrupt, or destroy the intelligence operations of an adversary" (Sims and Gerber 2009, 21). Counterintelligence specialists wage nothing less than a secret war against antagonistic intelligence services and terrorist organizations—the latter task a subsidiary of CI known as *counterterrorism* (CT). As a CI expert noted in testimony before the Church Committee (1975a, 163): "In the absence of an effective U.S. counterintelligence program, [adversaries of democracy] function in what is largely a benign environment."

THE CONCERNS OF COUNTERINTELLIGENCE

Over the years, the United States has faced numerous adversaries, from British Redcoats and Barbary Pirates in the early days to the Soviet Red Army and Al Qaeda terrorists in the modern era. In the midst of the Cold War, over 1,000 Soviet officials were on permanent assignment in the United States, according to FBI figures (Church Committee 1975a, 163). Among them, the FBI identified over 40 percent as members of the KGB or GRU, the Soviet civilian and military intelligence units. Estimates on the number of unidentified intelligence officers lurking in the United States raised this figure to over 60 percent of the Soviet "diplomatic" representation, and some defector sources have estimated that 70–80 percent of Soviet Embassy officials in Washington, D.C., and Soviets assigned to the United Nations in New York City had intelligence connections of one kind or another.

The opening of American deepwater ports to Russian ships in 1972 gave the Soviet intelligence services "virtually complete geographic access to the United States," a counterintelligence specialist testified before the Church Committee. In 1974, for example, over 200 Soviet ships with a total crew complement of 13,000 officers and men called at 40 deepwater ports in the United States. Various exchange groups provided additional opportunities for Soviet intelligence gathering within the United States. Some 4,000 Soviets entered the United States as commercial or exchange visitors on an annual basis during the latter decades of the Cold War, and the FBI identified over 100 intelligence officers among the approximately 400 Soviet students who attended American universities during this period as part of an East-West student exchange program. In addition, in the 1970s, the United States experienced a sharp increase in the number of Soviet immigrants to the United States, along with a rise in East-West commercial exchange visitors. Recently, the co-chair of a joint investigative committee on intelligence expressed shock at the FBI estimates on the number of suspected Al Qaeda terrorists and sympathizers who continued to move about inside the United States after the September 11, 2001, attacks (Pelosi 2002). Russian and Chinese spying inside the United States continues unabated, never mind that the Cold War ended in 1991 (Sims and Gerber 2009, 2–3).

Foreign intelligence agents have attempted to recruit U.S. executive branch personnel and congressional staff members. They have also tried to steal secrets in America regarding weapons systems as well as commercial activities and strategies (Johnson 1989). The most elusive counterintelligence threat has been from "illegal" agents, who have no easily detectable contacts with their intelligence service. The problem of "illegals" is summarized by the FBI as follows:

> The illegal is a highly trained specialist in espionage tradecraft. He may be a [foreign] national and/or a professional intelligence officer dispatched to the United States under a false identity. Some illegals [may be] trained in the scientific and technical field to permit easy access to sensitive areas of employment.
>
> The detection of . . . illegals presents a most serious problem to the FBI. Once they enter the United States with either fraudulent or true documentation, their presence is obscured among the thousands of legitimate emigrés entering the United States annually. Relatively undetected, they are able to maintain contact with [their foreign masters] by means of secret writing, microdots, and open signals in conventional communications that are not susceptible to discovery through conventional investigative measures. (Church Committee 1976, 164)

The espionage activities of nations and terrorist cells against the territory of the United States, as well as its citizens, troops, diplomats, and interests abroad, are extensive and relentless, especially by the Soviet Union during the Cold War and today by an assortment of "rogue nations" and terrorist organizations—not to mention Russia, China, and even traditional America allies such as France. To combat these threats, America's counterintelligence officers have developed sophisticated investigative techniques to obtain information about adversaries (at home and abroad) and to guard the U.S. intelligence agencies. The task is difficult technically; moreover, the targeting of counterintelligence operations can raise sensitive legal and ethical questions at home. "U.S. counterintelligence programs, to be both effective and in line with traditional American freedoms," a CIA official told the Church Committee (1975a, 164),

> must [on the one hand] steer a middle course between blanket, illegal, frivolous and unsubstantiated inquiries into the private lives of U.S. citizens, and [on the other hand] excessive restrictions which will render the Government's counterintelligence arms impotent to protect the nation from foreign penetration and covert manipulation.

COUNTERINTELLIGENCE AS A PRODUCT: INFORMATION ABOUT "THE ENEMY"

Counterintelligence is both a product and an activity. The product is reliable information about all hostile foreign intelligence services and other threats, such as Al Qaeda cells within the United States. It is necessary to understand the organizational structure of the enemy, its key personnel, its methods of recruitment and training, and the details of specific operations. The efforts of intelligence services through the world to conceal such information from one another, through various security devices and elaborate deceptions, create what former CIA Chief of Counterintelligence James Angleton (borrowing a line from the poet T. S. Eliot) referred to as a "wilderness of mirrors."

COUNTERINTELLIGENCE AS AN ACTIVITY: COUNTERESPIONAGE AND SECURITY

As an activity, CI consists of two matching halves: counterespionage and security. *Counterespionage* (CE) is the offensive, or aggressive, side of counterintelligence. It involves identifying specific adversaries and developing detailed knowledge about the operations they are planning or conducting. Counterespionage personnel must then attempt to block these operations by infiltrating the hostile service, an operation known as a "penetration," and by using sundry forms of manipulation. Ideally, as in jujitsu, the thrust of the hostile operation is turned back against the enemy.

Security is the passive, or defensive, side of counterintelligence. It entails putting in place static defenses against all hostile and concealed operations aimed at the United States, regardless of who might be attempting to carry them out. Security defenses include screening and clearance of personnel and establishment of programs to safeguard sensitive intelligence information—in a phrase, the administration of security controls. The objectives are to defend the personnel, installations, and operations against enemy intelligence services and terrorists (Prunckun 2012).

Among the specific defensive devices used for information control by counterintelligence officers are security clearances (consisting of thorough inquiries into the backgrounds of job candidates), polygraphs, locking containers, security education, document accountability, censorship, camouflage, and codes. Grim-faced uniformed guards with German shepherds patrol the electrified fences at the CIA's headquarters, and, inside, polygraph experts administer tests of loyalty to all new recruits and, periodically for seasoned intelligence officers, cross-examine them on whether they have had any associations with foreigners. The polygraph has produced uneven results. Several traitors have been able to fool the machines,

among them Aldrich H. Ames, a Russian recruit at the heart of the CIA (discovered in 1994 and now in prison for life). On occasion, though, polygraph sessions have uncovered treasonous behavior, and not long ago they even elicited a confession from a nervous would-be employee that he had murdered his wife and buried her body in his backyard.

Beyond armed guards and watchdogs, devices for physical security include fences, lighting, general systems, alarms, badges, and passes. The control of a specific area relies on curfews, checkpoints, and restricted zones. As a CIA counterintelligence officer has observed (Church Committee 1975a, 166), the security side of counterintelligence "is all that concerns perimeter defense, badges, knowing everything you have to know about your own people," while the counterespionage side "involves knowing all about foreign intelligence services—their people, their installations, their methods, and their operations—so that you have a completely different level of interest."

COUNTERINTELLIGENCE AS ORGANIZATION

At the CIA, the Office of Security is responsible for protecting that agency's personnel and installations, while counterespionage operations are largely the preserve of the Operations Directorate and its CI staff (which has personnel overseas using official or nonofficial cover). To combat terrorism more effectively, DCI William J. Casey established a Counterterrorism Center (CTC) in 1986. Despite its preponderance of CIA personnel, the center has 24 officers from a dozen other agencies, including the FBI and the Department of State (the two most important links); the Department of Defense; the Secret Service; the Department of Energy; the Bureau of Alcohol, Tobacco and Firearms; the Naval Investigative Service; the Federal Aviation Agency (another vital participant in this mission); the National Security Agency; the Immigration and Naturalization Service; and, most recently, the new Department of Homeland Security.

A senior officer in the center has remarked:

The whole concept behind the CTC was to bring elements from all four [CIA] Directorates together and put them under one single chain-of-command, so that we'd have all the necessary resources together to tackle the problem. In addition, we brought in these detailees from outside [the CIA], so that we'd have a very close relationship with the intelligence community. These people can pick up a secure [telephone] line and cut through the bureaucratic thickets that we normally face. (Johnson 2000, 177)

The 1993 bombing of the World Trade Center in New York City and the 1995 bombing of a federal building in Oklahoma City, as well as bombings at the U.S. embassies in Kenya and Tanzania in 1998, led Congress to fund expansively those agencies combating terrorism, including the CTC (even though it did not deal with U.S. domestic terrorism—exclusively the FBI's preserve, until the 9/11 attacks). After September 11, 2001, the steady funding for counterterrorism became a flood. Despite funding and sophisticated organizations, some forms of terrorism are nearly impossible to stop, such as a suicide attack carried out by an individual or a group prepared to die in the cause (as happened against Egyptian President Anwar Sadat in 1979, the U.S. Marine base in Lebanon in 1983, and the Israeli Embassy in Buenos Aires in 1992, and with the events of September 11, 2001).

In combating terrorism, the CTC has worked closely with the Nonproliferation Center (both located at the CIA), since each has a mandate to curb the use of dangerous weapons against mass populations. Both centers have concluded that a terrorist organization is more likely to use biological or chemical weapons against the United States, or a radioactive "dirty" bomb, rather than a fission or fusion nuclear device. The NPC concentrates on the supply side of the weapons problem, trying to stem the flow of weapons at the origins of production and distribution; the CTC focuses on the demand side, frustrating terrorist groups from acquiring weapons or weapons material (uranium, plutonium, or chemical-biological substances) in the first place.

The most important defense against terrorism is information about its likely occurrence, so that law enforcement officials can intercede before an attack takes place. To this end, the perfection of HUMINT and other collection methods stands at the top of the CTC's priorities—especially the infiltration of terrorist organizations or the wooing of a defector from the enemy's camp. These are difficult tasks, as modern terrorist organizations are sophisticated, tightly controlled, and acutely aware of the CTC's aspirations.

In growing frustration over the failure of the CTC and the FBI to adequately share counterterrorism information with each other both before and after the 9/11 attacks on the United States, President George W. Bush established a new Terrorist Threat Integration Center (TTIC) in 2003. As the president said in his State of the Union Address that year, the purpose of the TTIC was "to merge and analyze all threat information in a single location." Continued the president: "In order to better protect our homeland, our intelligence agencies must coexist like they never had before." The TTIC incorporates the CIA and FBI counterterrorism units along with representatives involved in counterterrorism from throughout the government. The precise structure and mission of the TTIC remains foggy, however, and riven with bureaucratic bickering—much like the new Department of Homeland Security (with its obvious interest in counterintelligence matters). Among the confusions was how the TTIC would relate to the CIA's Counterterrorism Center, which has a comparable mission.

THE PENETRATION AND THE DOUBLE AGENT

Several kinds of operations exist within the rubric of counterespionage (the more aggressive side of counterintelligence). One, however, transcends all the others in importance: the *penetration*, or, in the common vernacular, the "mole." Since the primary goal of counterintelligence is to contain the intelligence services and saboteurs of the enemy, it is desirable to know his plans in advance and in as much detail as possible. This logical, but challenging, objective may be achieved through a high-level infiltration of an adversary's intelligence service or government, or of a terrorist cell. As DCI John McCone observed in 1963 during the Cold War, "Experience has shown penetration to be the most effective response to Soviet and Bloc [intelligence] services" (Church Committee 1975a, 167).

Furthermore, a well-placed infiltrator in a hostile intelligence or terrorist camp may be better able than anyone else to determine whether one's own service has been penetrated by an outsider. A former director of the Defense Intelligence Agency (DIA) has emphasized that the three principal programs used by the United States to meet, neutralize, and defeat hostile penetrations are penetrations of America's own, the security screening and clearance of personnel, and efforts to physically safeguard sensitive intelligence information (Carroll Report of 1964, cited by the Church Committee 1976, 167).

Methods of infiltrating the opposition service take several forms. Usually the most effective and desirable penetration is recruitment of an agent-in-place. He or she is already in the employment of an enemy intelligence service or a terrorist group. Ideally, the agent-in-place will be both highly placed and susceptible to recruitment by the United States. The prospective recruit—say, a Pakistani diplomat at the U.N. with suspected ties to remnants of the Taliban regime in Afghanistan (and, therefore, possible ties to Al Qaeda)—is approached and asked to work for "the government" of the United States (in fact, the CIA or the FBI). Various inducements may be used to entice the recruit. Money is the most popular bait since the Cold War, while during the Cold War foreigners—notably disaffected individuals inside the intelligence services of the Soviet Bloc—would sometimes spy for the United States purely out of a sense of anti-communist ideology or disenchantment over the misdirection of communism by Joseph Stalin and other Soviet dictators. The importance of money as a trigger for treason in the post–Cold War era was recently illustrated in the United States. In 2003, Brian P. Regan, an intelligence analyst with access to spy satellite technology and a $100,000 credit card debt, was convicted of plotting to sell to Iraqi officials the coordinates of U.S. satellite targeting in the Persian Gulf region.

If recruitment is successful, an agent-in-place operation can be highly fruitful, since the agent is presumably already trusted within his or her organization and will have unquestioned access to key secret documents. Jack E. Dunlap, who worked at and spied on the National Security Agency in the 1960s, is a well-known example of a Soviet agent-in-place within the U.S. intelligence service during the Cold War. His handler was a Soviet Air Force attaché at the Soviet Embassy in Washington. A single penetration can be an intelligence gold mine, as were Kim Philby (inside MI6, British foreign intelligence), Aldrich H. Ames (CIA), Robert P. Hanssen (FBI) for the Soviet Union, and Col. Oleg Penkovsky (KGB) for the United States.

Another method of infiltration is the double agent. Double agents, however, are costly and time-consuming, and they are risky, because the loyalty of the agent remains a question mark, with double-crosses being commonplace. The running of double agents involves much pure drudgery with few dramatic results, as new information must be constantly and painstakingly checked against existing files. Moreover, passing credible documents back to the enemy to ensure the credibility of the double agent can be a major undertaking. The operations must appear plausible to the adversary, so, to make fake papers seem realistic the genuine article must be provided now and again. In this process, classified documents must be cleared—typically a slow and contentious activity, since intelligence agencies are reluctant to release any classified information to an outsider. "This means letting a lot of good stuff go to the enemy, without much in return," complained a CIA counterintelligence officer to a Senate Committee (Church Committee 1976, 168).

To accomplish each of these tasks, hard work, careful planning, and considerable staff resources are necessary. The extraordinary staffing requirements of double-agent operations restricted the capacity of the British to run many of them during World War II—only approximately 150 for the entire period of the war and no more than about 25 at any one time—even though the task was eased significantly by the ability of the British to read German secret ciphers throughout most of the war (Masterman 972).

THE DEFECTOR

Almost as good as the agent-in-place, and less troublesome to manage than the double agent, is the "defector with knowledge." In this case the challenge consists of a skillful interrogation and validation of the defector's bona fides (as usual), but without the worrisome, ongoing requirement to provide the agent with a credible mix of false and genuine documents along with other logistical support. Although an agent-in-place is preferable because of the ongoing useful information he or she can provide, often an agent-in-place does not want to accept the risk of staying in place—especially in nations where the security is sophisticated and the execution of traitors swift and often painful. The agent's usual preference is to defect to safety in the United States. As a result, agents-in-place are harder to come by in tightly controlled totalitarian regimes with robust counterintelligence services of their own; defection is more likely. In contrast, agents-in-place are more easily recruited in the developing nations, where sophisticated security that might discover them is often lacking.

Defectors recruited overseas by the CIA are occasionally brought to the United States and resettled if they are considered highly important (that is, someone likely to provide valuable ongoing information or someone who has already provided vital information and now seeks exfiltration to avoid capture and execution in his or her own country). The FBI is notified, and after the CIA completes its interrogation,

FBI counterintelligence officers may interrogate. Terrorists captured in the United States are normally interrogated first by the FBI, then by the CIA; the process is vice versa for terrorists captured abroad. Sometimes the bona fides of a defector remain in dispute for many years, as in the case of Yuri Nosenko, who defected from the U.S.S.R. soon after the assassination of President John F. Kennedy in 1963. The FBI viewed Nosenko as a legitimate defector; the CIA's chief of counterintelligence worried, however, that Nosenko was really a false defector, sent to the United States to sow disinformation.

THE DECEPTION OPERATION

The penetration (mole) or double agent is closely related to another important counterespionage method: the *deception operation*. Simply stated, the deception is an attempt to give the enemy a false impression about something, causing him to take action contrary to his own interests. Fooling the Germans into a believing that D-Day landings would occur in the Pas de Calais rather than in Normandy is a classic example of a successful deception operation during World War II.

Deception is related to penetration, because U.S. agents-in-place operating within foreign intelligence agencies or terrorist groups can serve as an excellent channel through which misleading information can flow to the enemy. So moles and double agents can serve as both collectors of intelligence and instruments of deception. In another illustration of an approach to deception, the CIA might allow a hostile foreign penetration into its own intelligence service and then carefully feed false information through him or her back to the enemy.

OTHER COUNTERINTELLIGENCE TECHNIQUES

Counterespionage operations also include surreptitious surveillance of various kinds (for instance, audio, mail, physical, and "optical"—that is, photography), as well as interrogation (sometimes keeping the subject incommunicado until his or her bona fides are verified). Part and parcel of the CE trade are decoding of secret messages sent by an adversary to a mole, trailing suspected agents, observing "dead drops" (the exchange of material, such as secret documents or instructions, between a spy and his handler), and photographing individuals entering opposition embassies or at other government locations. At the Arlington Cemetery funeral of CIA officer Richard Welch in

1975, Eastern European diplomats were discovered among the media corps snapping photographs of CIA officers (and their automobile license plates) who were attending the burial service. Since the focus of offensive counterintelligence is disruption of the enemy service, provocation can be an important element of counterespionage, too. This approach involves harassment of an adversary, such as publishing the names of his agents or sending a troublemaking false defector into his midst who is in reality an agent provocateur.

COUNTERINTELLIGENCE AND RESEARCH

Good research is critical to effective counterintelligence. It involves amassing encyclopedic knowledge on suspected foreign spies, including American citizens associated (wittingly or unwittingly) with hostile intelligence services or terrorist organizations. Such research can step over the line of protected civil liberties in the United States unless care is taken by the intelligence agencies to honor the law and the rights of citizens.

Counterintelligence officials also have a responsibility for preparing guidelines regarding interrogation of defectors. The matter of counterintelligence interrogation methods has been controversial, raising the question of what techniques should be permissible in a democracy. In 2003, the CIA captured in Pakistan Kahlid Sheikh Mohammed (known as KSM, for short, by U.S. counterintelligence officers), the suspected mastermind of the Pentagon and World Trade Center attacks two years earlier. Immediately, media accounts around the world (including in the United States) speculated that he might be mistreated—even tortured—by his CIA handlers. Officials within the CIA responded that no brutal force would be used, not least because psychological pressure was considered more effective. Former CIA officers speculated that the Al Qaeda strategist would be subjected to sleep deprivation; if he cooperated, he would be given rewards, such as good food, rest, and a television. They conceded, though, that while there would be no stretching on the rack, the captured terrorist might be forced to sit or stand in awkward or painful positions for hours at time—"torture lite." Only subsequently did it come to light that KSM was waterboarded, a harsh form of interrogation that simulates the sense of drowning in water. It remains a matter of intense dispute whether this extreme counterintelligence method achieves results, but one conclusion is widely accepted: In the court of world opinion, torture harms America's reputation for fair play and ethical behavior (Johnson 2007c).

The line between acceptable and unacceptable interrogation techniques is not well defined and in the light of the savage 9/11 attacks is apt to be smudged by interrogators who may be angry about past attacks as well as concerned about the possibility of another sudden strike against the United States unless warning information is extracted quickly from the subject. "There was a before 9/11 and there was an after 9/11," Cofer Black, the head of the CIA's Counterterrorism Center, has said. "After 9/11, the gloves came off" (Harden 2003, A1). Abu Zubaydah, another top Al Qaeda leader captured in Pakistan after the September 11, 2001, attacks, was on painkillers because of a pistol shot to the groin; until he began to cooperate, interrogators held back his full medication. Reports suggest that other Al Qaeda suspects have been chained, naked and hooded, to the ceiling; routinely kicked to keep them awake; and shackled so tightly that blood flow is halted. Most alarming are charges that two Al Qaeda prisoners were killed during interrogation at a U.S. military base in Afghanistan, beaten to death with blunt instruments (Campbell 2003, 1). If the assertion is proved true, the interrogators would be subject to U.S. civil and military prosecutions. Those being interrogated can also be threatened with the prospect that they will be turned over to a government allied with the United States that is known to have a decidedly malevolent approach to interrogation and few, if any, laws on the subject (Egypt, for example).

Counterintelligence officials also study such subjects as use of proprietary companies by foreign intelligence services or terrorist cells, and the organization and methods of those who practice terrorism. Further, they analyze defector briefs and, if they suspect that internal classified documents have been compromised, they help ascertain who had access and what secrets might have been lost (a process called "damage assessment").

COUNTERINTELLIGENCE AND LIAISON

Liaison among U.S. counterintelligence services, at home and abroad, is vital as well, as no single CI organization can do its job alone. The relationship among CI units is especially important for the United States, because counterintelligence—with all its intricacies and deceptions—requires close coordination among agencies and sharing of records; yet, traditionally, the American intelligence "community" has

been organizationally fragmented. Thus, a liaison system to overcome these centrifugal forces is crucial. This need for coordination is especially important between CIA and FBI counterintelligence units, since the CIA has foreign jurisdiction and the FBI domestic, but they must jointly monitor the movements of foreign spies who travel in and out of these two jurisdictions. Sometimes this coordination has suffered spectacular failures. In 1970, for example, FBI Director J. Edgar Hoover terminated formal liaison with the CIA and all other CI units in the government because of a disagreement over how to handle a particular East European defector. Far more tragically, the FBI and the CIA proved unable to share information effectively about the whereabouts of Al Qaeda terrorists just prior to the attacks against the World Trade Center and the Pentagon in 2001, losing track of two known to be inside the United States weeks before the attacks.

Liaison with foreign intelligence services overseas can undergo strain, too. Each nation fears that the intelligence services of its allies have been infiltrated by hostile agents and, therefore, that the ally should not be given sensitive information. Nonetheless, cooperation does take place, since all intelligence services seek information and—with precautions—will take it where they can get it, if the information is useful.

COUNTERINTELLIGENCE AND ACCOUNTABILITY

The counterintelligence mission is among the most secretive of all intelligence activities—the heart of the onion. Its tight compartmentalization makes proper supervision a challenge for lawmakers and executive overseers. The most disquieting chapter in U.S. counterintelligence occurred during the 1960s when America's secret agencies began to spy at home, against the very people they had sworn to protect (Johnson 1985). In the midst of the Cold War, the CIA generated a data bank on 1.5 million U.S. citizens, almost all of whom were simply exercising their First Amendment rights to dissent against the war in Vietnam. Many had their mail intercepted and read, their telephones tapped, their day-to-day activities monitored. The NSA intercepted every cable sent overseas or received by Americans. The FBI carried out 500,000 investigations of so-called subversives (again, mainly Vietnam War dissenters, plus civil rights activists and even Klan members were added to the "enemies list"), without a single case ending in a court conviction.

During this period, FBI agents wrote anonymous letters meant to incite violence among African Americans. The Bureau's counterintelligence program, labeled "Cointelpro," involved not only spying on but harassing civil rights activists and Vietnam War dissidents, in an attempt to fray or break family and friendship ties. A campaign to wreck America's civil rights movement stood at the center of Cointelpro.

The overzealous pursuit of counterintelligence threatened the very foundations of American democracy, undermining basic U.S. laws and the constitutional right to free expression. Only when the CIA's transgressions leaked to the press in 1974, triggering a congressional inquiry, did these illegal operations by the CIA, the FBI, the NSA, and military intelligence units come to a halt. Counterintelligence—so vital to the nation's security—had strayed, and Americans were again reminded of Madison's warning (etched on the walls of the Library of Congress) that "power, lodged as it must be in the hands of human beings, is ever liable to abuse." A democracy cannot remain free without having strong accountability over its counterintelligence corps. The proper balance between security and civil liberties was tested again after the 9/11 attacks, when the George W. Bush Administration initiated warrantless wiretaps against American citizens inside the United States and critics cried foul, perceiving this privacy intrusion as a violation of the Foreign Intelligence Surveillance Act of 1978.

THE READINGS

In the first selection in this part of the book, Paul J. Redmond brings his long experience in CIA counterintelligence (CI) to bear on the question of defending America's secrets. He examines several cases in which the CI defenses of the United States failed abysmally.

Next, Stan A. Taylor and Daniel Snow review the motivations of 139 American traitors during the Cold War, as well as how they were unmasked. The authors found money to be the most prevalent motive for treason, although during the 1950s some Americans spied for the Soviet Union out of attraction to communist ideology. With respect to the post–Cold War era, Taylor and Snow note that treason continues and that materialism remains the primary motivation. As for improvements in capturing spies, the authors give considerable credit to the establishment of better electronic surveillance procedures in the United States as a result of the passage of the Foreign Intelligence Surveillance Act in 1978.

The final selection is drawn from a Senate Select Committee on Intelligence report on the discovery in 1995 of a Soviet mole in the CIA: Aldrich Hazen Ames, the most devastating counterintelligence failure in the history of the Agency. The damage caused by Ames's treachery, and how counterintelligence officials finally tracked him down, are the subjects of this fascinating, if disheartening, report.

19. THE CHALLENGES OF COUNTERINTELLIGENCE

PAUL J. REDMOND

A former Chief of CIA Counterintelligence and one of the leading investigators in the hunt to find the Russian mole inside the CIA (Aldrich Ames) explores the difficulties of guarding America's secrets against the prying eyes of hostile intelligence services.

1. COUNTERINTELLIGENCE DEFINITIONS

Counterintelligence, known in the trade as "CI," is a complex, controversial subject that is hard to define. Only at the strategic level are there reasonably consistent definitions of counterintelligence. According to the current, official U.S. government definition: "Counterintelligence means information gathered and activities conducted to identify, deceive, exploit, disrupt or protect against espionage, other intelligence activities, sabotage or assassination conducted for or on behalf of foreign powers, organizations or persons or their agents, or international terrorist organizations or activities."[1] A former senior counterintelligence officer of the KGB's First Chief Directorate[2] defines CI as "special activities of security organizations authorized and directed by the government to protect the State and its citizens against espionage, sabotage and terrorism."[3]

The Russians also have an institutional definition for counterintelligence or *kontrrazvedka*—"State agencies granted special powers in the fight against the intelligence services (*razvedka*) of other states and the subversive activity of organizations and individuals used by those services. Counterintelligence is one of the instruments in the hands of the political authorities of the state" (Mitrokhin 2002).

As is the case with the Russians, a British definition of counterintelligence includes countersubversion—". . . protection of national security against threats from espionage, terrorism and sabotage from the activities of foreign powers and from activities intended to overthrow or undermine parliamentary democracy by political industrial or violent means."[4]

While these strategic definitions are mostly in agreement in that they mention espionage, sabotage, and terrorism, they encompass a wide diversity of activity, a variety of professional skills, and a range of tactical purposes and means. As a former national counterintelligence executive observed, "Across the profession, there are vast differences in understanding of what counterintelligence means, and how it is done, and even the basic terminology it employs" (Van Cleave 2008). CI means different things to different organizations and intelligence officers, and encompasses a wide continuum of activities from analysis of observed events through the aggressive operational activity of mounting deception operations, from conduct of espionage investigations to the intensely personal, clandestine activity of recruiting and securely managing human sources among the enemy—without simultaneously being deceived.

The U.S. military, which runs "offensive" counterintelligence operations against the enemy, places CI under the overall umbrella of "force protection."[5] The FBI, which is part of the U.S. Department of Justice and is the "lead" U.S. agency in the field, does engage in operational CI activity but it tends to emphasize CI as a law enforcement activity, counterespionage, or the identification and successful prosecution of spies.

The Central Intelligence Agency embraces under the rubric of counterintelligence a very wide variety of activities. They include the recruitment and management of sources within foreign intelligence services; "asset validation" to prevent the opposition from deceiving the U.S. intelligence community by running sources they actually control; the maintenance of good operational "tradecraft" to prevent the opposition from uncovering American intelligence-collection operations; analysis of the capabilities and intentions of the foreign intelligence opposition; and counterespionage operations with the FBI. To other national security or defense agencies not engaged in operational intelligence activities but rather consumers and analysts of intelligence information or custodians/producers of other sorts of national-security data, counterintelligence means primarily programs to prevent the enemy from stealing secrets. Agencies such as the United States Department of Homeland Security actually engaged in government operations have to design programs to protect not only sensitive technical programs and intelligence data but also to defend, at the tactical level, against terrorist organizations suborning employees to facilitate the infiltration of terrorists and/or weapons into the United States.

The end of the Cold War brought even more complications to the definition and conduct of counterintelligence by the United States. While U.S. intelligence agencies tried, with an almost complete lack of success, to run deception operations against the Warsaw Pact during the Cold War, counterintelligence meant mostly counterespionage against the efforts of the Soviet Union, its allies and, to a lesser degree, China to steal secrets. The break-up of the Soviet Union mostly eliminated the espionage activity by the states of Eastern Europe but Russia and China have remained counterintelligence threats. Moreover, a host of new ones have emerged including "non-State actors" such as terrorist organizations and the drug cartels. The post-9/11 era has further complicated matters by raising the bureaucratic and operational issues of the relationship between counterterrorism and counterintelligence, not to mention the perennial conundrum of defining and coping organizationally with the overlapping roles of counterintelligence and security. The intersection of the roles of CI and security leads, in turn, to the question of where the CI function should reside within an organization. Further confounding the definition of CI the advent of the "cyber" era has raised the issue of "cyber CI" and how a national defense entity protects itself against attacks on its databases, electronically controlled operations, and digital communications.

Even the basic terminology of CI is not universally shared. Different intelligence/security services within the same government use different words. The German Federal Intelligence Service (BND) uses the term "Gegenspionage" which, translated literally, means "the countering of espionage," but the internal security service, Federal Office for the Protection of the Constitution, BfV, uses the term "Spionageabwehr" which means "counter espionage."[6] In English, "counterintelligence" is even spelled differently: "counterintelligence," "counter intelligence" and "counter-intelligence."[7]

The various organizational positions and levels of status and influence within government agencies that the CI function occupies also reflect the complexity of the subject. Perhaps because of Russia's Byzantine cultural heritage and the conspiratorial roots of the Bolsheviks, the external part of KGB, the First Chief Directorate and its successor organization the SVR, places tremendous emphasis on CI. It maintains an entire organization, Directorate K, in Moscow. The SVR also has a CI career track and a CI section, referred to as Line KR, within each residency.[8] Except temporarily in the aftermath of spy scandals and major operational failures, the CIA historically has put less emphasis on CI. Although it has not established a separate CI operations officer track within the National Clandestine Service, it does have career CI officers at CIA Headquarters and some posted abroad. Perhaps most curiously, during the latter part of the Cold War, the head of CI in one European service also had as his duties legislative and public affairs.

This diversity of approach is also reflected in CI's relationship to the security function in various organizations. In the U.S. National Security Agency, the functions are fully merged in the Associate Directorate for Security and Counterintelligence. From the Edward Lee Howard spy case[9] the CIA learned the painful lesson that lack of internal communication can lead to disaster. In this instance, there had been no effective sharing of information among the Directorate of Operations, Office of Security, and Office of Medical Services. As a result, the CIA as an institution did not recognize Howard as a CI threat. At the CIA, counterintelligence and security are still separate organizations, but the interchangeability of personnel appears to make for effective cooperation.

In addition to the complexity of the subject, one other factor makes CI hard to discuss in public. It is probably the most arcane and certainly among the most secret, conspiratorial, and "sensitive" of intelligence activities. Thus, it is a very hard subject to describe to the "uncleared" reader in anything but the abstract. The following discussion of the multifarious aspects of CI endeavors to overcome this difficulty by describing situations and cases. In the interests of security and ease of getting publication clearance, some of these cases have been "sterilized," but the writer hopes they remain faithful to the lessons they reveal.

Regardless of the complexity of the subject, the diversity of the functions and activities it encompasses, and the "spooky" nature of the business, one basic rule must apply to counterintelligence: "all things in moderation." Because there was a belief that the Soviets had penetrated the CIA, during the 1960s and early 1970s CI reigned supreme, paralyzing operations against the Warsaw Pact by assuming that the KGB knew of and controlled all operations. During the tenure of DCI William Colby in the mid-1970s, there was a reaction to this mindset that destroyed CI at the CIA and led to spies in the Agency going undetected and the flowering of opposition-controlled cases. These two periods represent a typical sine wave of either too much or too little CI in the U.S. intelligence community. The waves oscillate in radical reaction to the previous peak, rarely staying in the moderate range required to deal rationally with the hard issues of counterintelligence.

2. THE VARIOUS ASPECTS OF COUNTERINTELLIGENCE

2.1 COUNTERINTELLIGENCE AS COUNTERESPIONAGE

"Catching spies," or counterespionage, which is the detection and neutralization of human spies, is probably the first thing that comes to mind when the general public thinks of "counterintelligence." It is also the easiest to describe since there are many well-documented, important spy cases. This is indeed a very important aspect of CI. During the Cold War, the Warsaw Pact and its allies such as Cuba had spectacular success in penetrating every U.S. government agency engaged in national security (except apparently the Coast Guard), most defense contractors, and the U.S. Congress. An informal historical review of Cold War spy cases shows that at any one time there were at least seven significant spies working for the enemy in the U.S. national security establishment.

During that tense era in international affairs, four spy cases alone could have given the Soviet Union a decisive advantage if war had broken out. The Walker spy case in the U.S. Navy[10] provided cryptographic key material and encryption equipment design data enabling the KGB to read over a million messages,

which would have allowed the Russians virtually to neutralize the deterrence of the American submarine-based missile systems. The Clyde Conrad spy ring[11] provided the Soviets, via the Hungarian military intelligence service, the details of the U.S. Army's operational plans and communications in Western Europe, which could have provided the Warsaw Pact a decisive advantage in a ground war in Western Europe. Robert Hanssen, who worked for both the KGB and GRU[12] off and on for about twenty years before his arrest in 2001, passed the Soviets enough documentary data to neutralize U.S. efforts to continue a viable democratic government in time of a nuclear war. Aldrich Ames, an equally notorious spy who worked for the KGB for about nine years until he was arrested in 1994, compromised nearly all the CIA's human sources working against the Soviet Union in the mid-1980s.

These four spy cases capture the spectrum of ways in which espionage cases begin. The Ames case resides at the end of the spectrum that is hardest to pursue, empirical indications that there is a problem—secrets are getting to the opposition—but no clues as to how. In the mid-1980s, the KGB started, in a rather rapid-fire manner, to arrest CIA's Soviet sources. After a period of analysis, false trails, and inattention to the problem, a joint CIA-FBI examination of the very large number of officers aware of the compromised cases produced a small number of people on whom to concentrate. This process eventually focused on Ames, chronologically linking his operationally approved contacts with a Russian in the Washington embassy to financial transactions. When combined with some suggestive source reporting, this effort enabled the FBI to mount a very skillful investigation culminating in his arrest.

The Ames episode represents the extreme difficulty of pursuing a case when the only way to attack the problem is massive analysis of the people aware of the cases compromised. So-called knowledge ability or "bigot lists" are a farce in the U.S. government. Even in the rare cases where good records actually exist, they are almost useless because hundreds of employees can know about an operation. The FBI found in the mid-1980s they could not pursue the compromise of a Soviet source because about 250 people at one field office alone had knowledge of the operation (Bromwich 1997). On the other hand, non-American CI officers can have an easier time both in protecting their operations and investigating losses. Knowledgeable CI professionals in the U.S. government estimate that fewer than ten KGB officers knew the identities of

Ames and Hanssen, and a former senior Greek intelligence officer recently stated to the media that only three of his colleagues knew the identity of Steven Lalas, a State Department communications officer who spied for the Greeks from 1977 to 1993.[13]

So-called lead information is helpful in starting and pursuing an espionage investigation in direct proportion to its specificity. Multiple CIA human sources in three different Warsaw Pact intelligence services provided information over many years that the Hungarian Military Intelligence Service had a very valuable source in the U.S. Army's V Corps in Germany. Through one human asset involved in the actual processing of the product but not knowledgeable about the source, the CIA was even able to inform the Army of specific documents passed and the disturbing fact that amendments to operational plans were occasionally reaching the Red Army Headquarters in Moscow before they were issued to U.S. forces. Eventually, after many years and a massive investigation based on a large accumulation of diverse lead material, plus some good luck, the Army was able to identify Clyde Conrad (and a net of associate spies) as the source. Conrad was subsequently arrested and successfully prosecuted by the Federal Republic of Germany. The CIA had multiple sources reporting on the case. However, because of excellent compartmentation within the Warsaw Pact intelligence services, no single source had more than a few small pieces of the puzzle. As a consequence this very damaging operation ran for many years before enough information accumulated to allow the U.S. Army investigators to focus on Conrad.

While "lead information" is much more valuable than a well-founded suspicion of a CI problem, the pursuit of leads can be extraordinarily difficult and fraught with the potential for mistakes. For years the CIA and FBI fruitlessly pursued lead information from the 1960s indicating that a CIA officer had volunteered to provide information on the Agency's operations in the USSR. Many years later during the course of the intensive research which led to the Aldrich Ames spy case, it became clear that this "old lead" from a Soviet intelligence source was his garbled version of a U.S.-controlled volunteer, a walk-in to a Soviet installation in the United States. In the early 1980s, the CIA received from two separate, well-placed KGB officers similar information that a CIA "communicator" had an operational meeting with the KGB in a North African city during a particular time period. The Agency and the FBI chased that "lead" for years until it became clear, following his arrest, that John Walker was the person the Soviets met on that occasion. At that time, senior and middle-grade KGB officers apparently assumed all communicators worked for the CIA.

The Walker spy case illustrates how empirical data pointing to a CI problem and general lead information is not enough to unearth a spy. During the 1970s and early 1980s, Navy flag officers had expressed anger and extreme frustration that Soviet electronic collection ships seemed to appear regularly at just the right places and times to conduct intercept operations during U.S. naval maneuvers, particularly in the Mediterranean. This was an obvious indication that the Soviets somehow had insight into U.S. operational planning. During this period the CIA did disseminate one CI report from a Soviet intelligence officer who alleged that the USSR had achieved massive success in reading U.S. Navy communications. Even if these two straws in the wind had been considered together, which they probably were not, they did not provide a sufficient basis to attack the problem. The start of the case had to wait until the best kind of lead came along, the specific identification of a spy by a source or, as in this case, a "snitch." Walker's former wife, apparently drunk, called an FBI office to say her husband was a spy; the FBI acted on the lead and Walker was eventually arrested. Often the problem with pursuing snitch leads is persuading superiors to take them seriously, as happened in a case involving another KGB penetration of the U.S. Navy, when security authorities discounted the statement of a discontented wife that her husband was a spy and his espionage career thus ran four years longer than it should have.

Two other cases illustrate the supreme value of specific source information, the other end of the continuum from purely empirical indicators of a CI problem. Resourceful and persistent operational work by the FBI, with help from the CIA, led to source reporting unambiguously identifying Robert Hanssen as a spy (Risen 2003, A1). Likewise, the KGB defector Vitaliy Sergeyevich Yurchenko[14] provided enough specific information to enable the CIA within minutes to identify former employee Edward L. Howard as a KGB asset.

Other factors also play a role in starting espionage investigations. Through the security/polygraph process the CIA has identified individuals who had been directed to apply for employment by foreign intelligence services and most recently, apparently by terrorist organizations.[15] The espionage investigation of Jonathan Pollard[16] was started because of the alertness and CI consciousness of a fellow employee. While the KGB, with its massive resources, caught

U.S. spies in the USSR through surveillance of CIA officers, only rarely have Western security services had similar success.

Defectors represent a special case as sources of spy leads. Historically, they have been gold mines for data in starting investigations; but once the excitement of their defection is over, they have told all that they know and attention toward them lags, they often start to make up stories. During the effort, which led to Ames's identification as a spy, a defector from the then KGB's internal security component, the Second Chief Directorate (now FSB), concocted a story for his American handler about the recruitment of a CIA officer in Moscow. It turned out that he made up the story to retain the attention of the CIA and FBI. All espionage investigations should view all spy leads with skepticism, at least initially, and they should judge leads on Oscar Wilde's principle that "the truth is rarely pure and never simple."

Another maxim which applies to counterespionage and CI in general is "your CI capability is only as good as your records." Leads to spies are more often than not ambiguous and fragmentary. CI analysis has been described as trying to do a monocolor jigsaw puzzle with pieces fitting in multiple places or not at all, or more simply, the archaeological reconstruction of shards from a broken pot. Records in the form of formal data in storage or, as was the case in the two examples cited below, institutional memory, are invaluable in resolving leads. In the mid-1980s, a European service obtained from a source in a Warsaw Pact intelligence service the detailed description for a dead drop site that the source knew only had been cased and written up for an important spy. Investigation and surveillance of the site proved fruitless. Several years later, a CIA source in another country identified a spy who was connected to the dead drop site, thus reinforcing the evidence against the spy and resolving the original lead. The connection was made only because the intelligence officers involved happened to remember the original dead drop data, not because there were organized holdings of such information.

Another case where institutional memory played a major role involved an informal discussion between a CIA officer and a senior member of a European service. The subject was lead information to KGB penetrations in the U.S. computer industry, where the principal spies had European and South Asian connections. The Western European officer noted the leads "sounded" similar to information acquired from a completely different source several years earlier. He went home and confirmed his suspicions from his service's rather good records and the CIA eventually found similar data residing in the proverbial shoe box under a desk. The connection of the data considerably expanded and refined the investigation. It is hoped that the advent of the cyber era and "link analysis" is now being used to correlate leads and identify spies more systematically. However, data processing and manipulation should not be viewed as a substitute for professional expertise gained by career CI professionals with years of experience. The two CIA officers who played the major role in identifying Aldrich Ames as a spy followed their instincts in focusing on him as a candidate and, using their vast knowledge and experience, were even able to accurately construct, from fragmentary data before his arrest, a significant part of his KGB meeting plan.

2.2 COUNTERINTELLIGENCE AS "ASSET VALIDATION"

The vetting of sources or "asset validation" usually, and too narrowly, is applied to human sources by American intelligence services. This counterintelligence function is at the very heart of all human collection operations and it should be applied also to technical collection and SIGINT operations.[17] It is critically important to determine to the degree possible that the source is not a fabricator or under opposition control. The disastrous CURVEBALL source, who reinforced the Bush administration's predisposition to believe Iraq had a weapons-of-mass-destruction program, is a classic example. He was a source of German intelligence that was dealing with the Pentagon's Defense Humint Service (DHS), and he was never properly vetted until after his data were used to support the invasion of Iraq. It is equally critical to determine, if possible, whether a source may be under the control of the opposition and thus used to provide disinformation or lure officers out onto the street for a contact, where they can be apprehended and noisily declared persona non grata.

During the Cold War, the Warsaw Pact and its allies enjoyed spectacular success in running controlled cases against the CIA. During much of the Cold War, *all* the "sources" the CIA was running against Cuba were controlled by its intelligence service. With a very small number of possible exceptions, the same parlous state of affairs existed in the operations against East Germany. The KGB, unlike most Western intelligence services, reflexively favored running controlled cases and mounted many "dangle" operations.[18] The same conspiratorial mindset that motivated the KGB to attempt many controlled operations led them, as a matter of course, not to trust their own sources. Thus they engaged intensively, one might say obsessively, in testing and validation. In the mid-1980s American CI officers were amazed to learn that a former U.S. military officer was still the subject of elaborate testing by the KGB about ten years after he started working for the Soviets and had been of enough value to meet personally with a KGB general and directorate chief.

It is clear that the Warsaw Pact's success in running cases against American intelligence was at least partly a function of American naïveté, lack of professionalism, and the refusal of officers to believe their case could be a fabricator or controlled by the opposition, particularly when promotions were involved. It must be emphasized, however, that asset validation is a very difficult task, particularly when the source is handled in a "denied area"[19] and there are few, if any, other sources of "collateral" information on which to rely for comparison. Most Western intelligence sources in denied areas are "met" only briefly for a very quick passage of information or are handled impersonally by dead drops or clandestine electronic communications. There is no regular opportunity for personal meetings and the type of systematic debriefing that can identify and pursue issues related to the source's validity. In the absence of any sources of its own within the opposition service to warn them, Western services running cases in denied areas have had to rely on the value of the intelligence provided, corroboration of its validity by other sources, if available, and the operational circumstances surrounding the case—particularly how it started.

This is a very complicated, difficult business. It is not a science. In one Warsaw Pact country in the 1970s, an individual purporting to be an officer of the internal security service volunteered by note to the CIA. He was handled impersonally by dead drop over many years and provided valuable information concerning his services plans to run controlled cases against the CIA and other operations against the U.S. embassy. He even warned of an impending ambush by the internal security service. Because he had been of established value, CIA CI officers were stunned to learn, at the end of the Cold War, that the case had been controlled from the beginning. It appears that his country's internal security service, taking the long view so alien to Western services, was trying to establish him as a contingency asset for a major disinformation operation in the future. It is noteworthy that the only doubts about the case were expressed by the initial case officer who picked up the first dead drop. He observed people in the area and expressed the view that they might have been surveillants. This case reinforces the informal maxim of some CI officers: "the answer (to the validity of the case) always resides in the first 10–15 pages of the file."

A source in another Eastern European country had been providing valuable, validated military R&D data for many years when his handling officer was ambushed by the security service when meeting the asset on the street in the capital. CI officers at the CIA assumed the source had been compromised because of a mistake on his or the Agency's part and only learned to their amazement after the Cold War that the case had been controlled all along. The Eastern European service had been running the case for years to have something "on the shelf" to use against the CIA, should the need arise. As the chief of the service said, he did not care that they were passing valuable information because it hurt only the Russians, not his own country.

Three other cases illustrate another aspect of how the validation of sources is not easy and a decision to declare a case controlled should not be made lightly. At the height of U.S.-Soviet tensions in the 1960s, an East European intelligence official living behind the iron curtain volunteered to American intelligence and started providing CI information on Warsaw Pact spies in the West. While the information appeared to have potential, CI officers began doubting his bona fides when he also began suggesting that Western intelligence officers travel into other Eastern European countries to recruit senior communist intelligence officers whom he believed to be disaffected. Given the Cold War atmosphere and the operational conditions then prevailing behind the iron curtain, such suggestions were ludicrous. Some CI officers, not unreasonably, concluded that he was a controlled case trying to lure the CIA into an operational fiasco in Eastern Europe. Nonetheless, the CIA and an allied service continued to run the case and he turned out to be the one of the most valuable sources of CI information in history. It became clear over time that the individual was mentally unstable and his outlandish operational suggestions were the result of his ignorance of life on the other side of the iron curtain and his assumption that Western services were as powerful as those in the Soviet Bloc.

The Soviet engineer who started volunteering by note during a period when timid management precluded the Agency from replying to his overtures is another example illustrating the need to persevere despite well-founded, in fact compelling, doubts. Because of the CIA's passivity over a considerable period of time, the engineer eventually out of frustration pounded on the trunk of the car of a U.S. diplomat who was filling his tank at one of the diplomatic gas stations in Moscow, an area very well covered by KGB surveillance, both static and mobile. The combination of this suicidal means of volunteering, plus the obscurity and initially incomprehensible nature of the data provided, logically led officers at the CIA to believe he was a controlled case, until knowledgeable engineers and experts in the DOD determined that his production was extraordinarily valuable. That case turned out to be the most significant run by the CIA against the USSR during the Cold War.

Another case involved risk taking. The CIA had been running a source in Europe who returned to Moscow with the expectation of being assigned to an office with access to a veritable gold mine of military information. After his return home, a source provided the CIA enough information to make it clear that the KGB had learned something of the operation but was apparently following an investigative avenue that probably would not lead quickly to this potentially superb source. He eventually signaled for a contact and CI officers had to calculate the odds on whether the KGB had found him and was setting the Agency up for an ambush. Based on a seat-of-the-pants assessment of known KGB investigative intentions, the likelihood of a huge payoff in intelligence product, plus a lot of hope, the CIA decided to make the contact. It came off without incident and produced a massive amount of very valuable intelligence.

The in-place source or defector who does not tell you all he knows, either to protect himself or to apply future leverage, is another challenge to asset validation. The most famous such case is Alexander Orlov, a senior Bolshevik intelligence officer, who defected in Canada in 1938 because he thought he was about to be assassinated as part of the Great Purge. He knew the identities of most of the important spies working for the Soviets in the West, including the high-level penetrations of the British government; but he did not reveal this information, having sent a message to Stalin via the head of Bolshevik intelligence saying that he would tell all if anything happened to himself or his family. The only effective way to get a full debriefing from a source inclined to hold back is to subject him to an officer with an in-depth, intimidating knowledge of the subject matter and good human-relations skills. When the principal CIA case officer handling Colonel Oleg Penkovskiy[20] first met him in a hotel room in London, he asked him whether so-and-so (by first name and patronymic) had issued him the dreary sack of a suit he was wearing. So-and-so was the apparatchik who issued civilian clothing to Soviet military intelligence officers traveling abroad. The intimate knowledge on the part of the CIA officer would have sufficiently impressed Penkovskiy and created enough rapport to minimize any inhibitions.

While it depends on disciplined attention to detail, great expertise, unbiased analysis, healthy skepticism, and sense of conspiracy, asset validation, like counterespionage, is not a science or a bureaucratic exercise. It is an art which is aided greatly by an experiential, intuitive understanding, in other words, "feel." One noteworthy case involved an engineer who volunteered in Moscow with plans for a new Soviet aircraft. The initial approach of this would-be source and data provided simply did not "feel" right to the CI officers examining it in Washington. There was simply something "off" about his "presentation." When overhead satellite coverage imaged an aircraft on a runway which resembled the volunteer's reporting, some CI officers asked "How much plywood and balsa wood did it take to build that fake?" The volunteer did turn out to be controlled. On the other side of the coin, similarly skeptical officers were on too many other occasions successfully fooled by the KGB, which resulted in the loss of operational techniques, noisy persona non grata declarations, and some successful disinformation operations.

The vetting of SIGINT information and sources, and the product of other technical collection operations, is one of the most difficult and perhaps the most controversial aspect of "asset validation." The SIGINT practitioners stand on the assertion, "SIGINT never lies." SIGINT is often based on cryptanalytic successes or major technical collection breakthroughs and it is almost impossible for intelligence officers to gain enough access to the operations to make independent judgments about the sources. SIGINT, as now practiced in the West, presents a fertile area for the opposition to engage in deception and disinformation operations.

3. COUNTERINTELLIGENCE AS DISINFORMATION OPERATIONS

The section above on source vetting described the difficulties of determining whether a human source is valid. This section looks at the issue from the other side: the purposes and techniques of running operations against the opposition, in order to control their activities, misinform them, trap them, or get them to reveal their operational techniques and capabilities. In the early 1920s, the State Political Directorate (OGPU) of the Soviet Union penetrated existing, anti-Communist organizations. Instead of eliminating them, it co-opted and expanded them into an organization that had the operational name, "The Trust." This control enabled the OGPU effectively to neutralize a large part of the opposition to the Bolsheviks.

During World War II deception and disinformation played a vital role in operations against Germany. Prior to the Normandy invasion in 1944, the British used apprehended Nazi spies, along with a massive disinformation campaign involving the creation of an entirely fictitious Allied army corps, to persuade the Germans that the invasion would be directed against the Pas de Calais, not Normandy. The success of this operation was, of course, founded on superb British CI operations, which identified and neutralized all Nazi sources in Great Britain, thus eliminating any sources still working for the Germans who could have cast doubt on the information provided by those under British control. The British were also greatly aided in this effort by excellent intelligence on German reactions to the deception campaign afforded by successful decryption of German military communications. Another spectacular World War II success involved an elegant, if macabre, operation in which the British arranged to have float ashore in Spain the perfectly documented corpse of an ostensibly drowned British officer carrying fake war plans. The corpse successfully misled the Germans into thinking the allies intended to invade Sardinia and Greece instead of Sicily. In this operation, the British illustrated their skill at disinformation, counterintelligence, and attention to detail, by using the corpse of an individual who had died of pneumonia, a cause of death that apparently displays pathological signs similar to drowning.[21]

After receiving data from Aldrich Ames on almost all CIA's human source operations against the USSR in 1985, the KGB, apparently under pressure from the Soviet leadership, quickly started arresting these sources, which ran the risk of alerting CIA to a CI problem and jeopardizing Ames. To mitigate this risk, the KGB CI Directorate conducted a number of disinformation operations to try to explain away the compromises of the American sources. In the summer of 1985, a KGB officer working for the CIA in Africa who was compromised by Ames went on home leave carrying operational directions to a dead drop containing a large number of rubles, which he planned to spend while on vacation. He did not return from home leave. Instead the CIA received information from a source in Europe that the officer had been arrested picking up the dead drop in Moscow. At about the same time, the CIA and FBI received essentially the same story about this compromise from another KGB source. After Ames was identified as a spy, it became clear that the KGB knew that both the sources were working for the Americans and, to protect Ames, used them as unwitting vehicles to misinform U.S. Intelligence before they found ways to lure the officers back to the USSR.

The United States intelligence community has not distinguished itself in running controlled sources against the opposition. While the U.S. military allegedly had success in running "perception management" operations against Iraq before operation Desert Storm, the American effort during the Cold War was consistently unsuccessful. The U.S. military policy is that "Offensive Counterintelligence Operations" (OFCO) are run to protect and enhance national security. The Defense Intelligence Agency subscribes to the following succinct objectives of double agent operations as summarized from the book, *The Double-Cross System* by Sir John C. Masterman. The objectives are: 1. Control the adversary's espionage system and by doing so, in effect make him work for you. 2. Identify, neutralize or suppress new agents and spies. 3. Obtain information on the personnel and methods of the adversary service. 4. Secure access to adversary codes and ciphers. 5. Gain evidence of the adversary's intentions. 6. Influence the enemy's operational intentions. 7. Systematically deceive the enemy (Masterman 1972). Item 5 represents a very important example where "counter" intelligence can greatly assist "positive" intelligence. Considerable insight into an adversary's policies and intentions can be gained from knowing the thrust and focus of his intelligence-collection activities.

In its own operations and in cooperation with the military services, the FBI has sought to convince the opposition of a dangle's value in an effort to induce hostile intelligence services to handle the operation in the United States, which would give the Bureau very valuable information on how they operate in America. The CIA, with very rare exceptions, has not tried to run controlled operations; rather it has served merely to coordinate such operations run abroad by other agencies.

The lack of U.S. success in this area during the Cold War is at least partly attributable to the KGB's success in penetrating U.S. intelligence. Ames and Hanssen, complemented by other lesser-known sources in the military, provided the KGB with detailed information on the double-agent program, all the doctrine, the complete "play book" of operational techniques and many, if not all, the specific operations. The apparent success of deception operations against Iraq prior to Desert Storm bespeaks a salutary improvement in the U.S. CI posture, because it shows Saddam Hussein did not have the valuable sources within the U.S. intelligence establishment enjoyed by the KGB.

4. COUNTERINTELLIGENCE AS OPERATIONAL TRADECRAFT

In any organization engaged in intelligence collection, the imposition of the highest possible standards of operational security, or tradecraft, is a critical counterintelligence function, particularly in the intelligence services of Western democracies. Unless the discipline of good operational security is forcefully imposed on the average American case officer,[22] the default will be sloppy or non-existent tradecraft. Putative sources will be met in the dining room of a posh hotel literally next to the U.S. embassy. Operational failures will be explained away by the case officer's statement that he was using "semi-clandestine" tradecraft, and officers operating in alias abroad will call home on cell phones. In the early twenty-first century the use of sloppy tradecraft presents the U.S. intelligence community with a daunting and critical challenge. An entire generation of new American case officers is getting its initial, formative, "on-the-street" experience in the war zone of Iraq, meeting sources with armed and sometimes armored military or paramilitary escorts or within fortress compounds. This sort of "tradecraft" bears no resemblance to the clandestine operational activities required to recruit and manage human sources elsewhere.

5. COUNTERINTELLIGENCE AS THE RECRUITMENT AND RUNNING OF CI SOURCES

The very best way to engage in counterintelligence activities is to have a valid source, or preferably sources, in the opposition service who can tell you what spies they have, or are trying to develop, in your government or defense industries; what technical, cyber, or disinformation operations they are running or plan to mount; and what they are doing to detect and negate your own intelligence collection operations. The acquisition of such sources is a controversial subject. It is a

fact that most of the productive counterintelligence sources acquired by the West during the Cold War were volunteers. Armchair media and academic experts advocate a passive approach, denigrating the use of resources to pursue actively the recruitment of foreign intelligence officers. This approach ignores a significant fact. Many of the volunteers acted only after, and probably as a result of, exposure to, and cultivation by, American intelligence officers. In addition, to get the most from a source requires cultural understanding and great substantive expertise, which cannot be learned from a file, book, movie, or television series, and can be gained only by close, long-term engagement with the opposition.

Unfortunately, the best example of an extraordinarily productive counterintelligence human source is FBI Special Agent Robert Hanssen, who volunteered to and worked for the KGB and GRU off and on for about twenty-one years. Over his spy career Hanssen informed the Soviets/Russians of human-source operations the CIA and KGB were running against the Soviet Union/Russia; some truly exquisite and productive technical and SIGINT collection operations; details of the double-agent program; and, of signal importance, full details of the FBI's counterintelligence program and operations against the Russians. This latter body of data gave the KGB/SVR an enormous advantage in acquiring and managing sources in the United States.

6. COUNTERINTELLIGENCE: DEVELOPING ISSUES AND CHALLENGES

Much of the material used above to describe the various aspects of counterintelligence is of Cold War vintage. Even though that body of historical data continues to shed light on the modalities of CI, several new factors and issues must be taken into account, not least the role of counterterrorism.

6.1 COUNTERINTELLIGENCE AND COUNTERTERRORISM

The practical goals of counterintelligence and counterterrorism (CT) are identical: the identification and neutralization of secret organizations engaged in secret operations to attack the United States and its allies. However, the difference in the nature of the threats has caused U.S. bureaucracies to separate the functions, particularly at the CIA and the FBI. Counterintelligence professionals thus face the challenge of ensuring that all the rules and standards of their discipline, such as operational security/tradecraft, asset validation, and counterespionage, are observed in the CT arena.

Since the Cold War never led to a military clash between the superpowers, the CI emphasis was on uncovering and neutralizing espionage, that is, on the stealing of secrets. The United States and some of its allies are now engaged in shooting wars and it must defend against sabotage and terrorist attacks both by state and "nonstate" entities. Therefore CI must work to protect not just secrets, but installations, operations, communications, and data storage as well as people. Today a hostile intelligence entity might be just as likely to be planning to kill or kidnap a U.S. official as to recruit him as a spy. Civilian CI officers should recognize the increasing relevance of the U.S. Department of Defense's concept of "force protection," which includes CI in a broad program of security disciplines to protect people, facilities, equipment, and operations.

6.2 COUNTERINTELLIGENCE: THE CYBER THREAT AND DENIGRATION OF COMPARTMENTATION

The so-called cyber threat has recently been described as the "new frontier" of counterintelligence. The cyber era has greatly complicated the work of counterintelligence officers. It is now much easier for an insider to steal vast amounts of national security information simply by downloading data onto devices such as thumb drives or to insert "malware" into networks to facilitate data exfiltration from remote platforms when plain hacking has been unable to penetrate the network.

There exists at the human, professional, and management levels a mutual disaffinity between CI officers and the "computer people." The former are mostly the proverbial "social science majors" who are not computer experts and who, by experience, think in terms of human spies. The latter, by technical training and experience, are motivated to create the smoothest flow of data to as many people as quickly as possible. The technical approach is best illustrated by Deputy Defense Secretary Paul Wolfowitz's statement that "the U.S. intelligence system needs to be adapted to the information age . . . we must emphasize speed of exchange and networking to push information out to people who need it, when they need it, wherever they are" (Inside the Pentagon 2002).

The complications for CI created by the onset of the computer age are being exacerbated by the post-9/11 conventional wisdom that failure "to connect the dots" led to that disaster. The 9/11 Commission Report emphasized the need to change the "mindset" in the intelligence community from "need to know" to "need to share" (Director of National Intelligence 2008, 6). The Director of National Intelligence, Vice Admiral J.M. McConnell (Ret.), and his Associate Director and Chief Information Officer Major General (Ret.) Dale Meyerrose, took the policy a step further by decreeing that "need to share" would become "responsibility to provide" (Director of National Intelligence 2008, 9). Regardless of the lip service paid to security and statements about "managing risk," this new policy will inevitably lead to a further breakdown in compartmentation, as more and more networks are interconnected, easing the work of spies and making the work of identifying and neutralizing them more difficult.

In addition to the understandable tendency of the computer people to speed the widest possible dissemination of data and the post-9/11 mindset to do away with "need to know," the American tendency to think mostly in terms of technical solutions comes into play in the issues facing counterintelligence. The National Counterintelligence Executive has recently emphasized that ". . . computer architecture and the soundness of electronic systems" are a key CI issue (Warrick and Johnson, 2008, A1A). Professional CI officers thus face three major challenges. One is to remind management that people are always involved, whether as an insider spy or as an opposition intelligence officer attacking U.S.-national-security organizations through electronic means. The second challenge is that CI professionals must learn enough about data processing and networks to communicate and work effectively with information management officers. Only with this basic knowledge can CI officers force a rational balance between information flow and dissemination and the need to find technical ways sensibly to restrict data and to establish techniques and procedures quickly to identify the inevitable hostile activity within and among networks. This issue presents intelligence officers with the third challenge: to inculcate CI awareness into the professional culture of information-technology professionals, who alone have the expertise to design the necessary policies and systems.

6.3 COUNTERINTELLIGENCE: LAW ENFORCEMENT AND NATIONAL SECURITY

Another dysfunction similar to that between CI officers and computer experts exists between CI officers and law enforcement. Counterintelligence officials are intent on protecting national security by identifying and neutralizing threats posed by hostile intelligence entities. Law enforcement officers at the U.S. Department of Justice (DOJ) are almost exclusively focused on making successful prosecutions, with the result that once the arrest of a spy is imminent or has taken place, CI considerations are not allowed to come into play. For instance, in one recent case, DOJ prosecutors included in the charging documents all of the considerable body of data known to have been passed to the opposition by the spy in order to intimidate him into accepting a plea agreement. While that ploy succeeded, CI officers were greatly hampered doing a damage assessment because the spy and his lawyer quickly figured out precisely what the government knew and refused, despite the terms of a plea agreement, to expand on its knowledge.

In another instance, CI officers gained personal access to a foreign intelligence officer who had been handling a minor spy in the United States. That officer, in effect, volunteered to help the CI officers but the government chose to go ahead with an arrest and well-publicized prosecution, which eliminated any chance the officer would help U.S. authorities identify other spies the foreign intelligence service was running against the United States. Another incident involved a technical collection operation uncovered by outstanding CI work. Law enforcement officers at the management level would not even consider using the still-secret discovery for a possible disinformation operation. Rather, they insisted on a public announcement of the find and a noisy expulsion of a foreign intelligence office. American CI professionals face the challenge of stimulating discussion at the National Security Council level to determine whether national security issues can be given equal importance to prosecutorial considerations in such cases.

QUESTIONS FOR FURTHER DISCUSSION

1. What means are used to protect a nation's secrets against adversarial intelligence services?
2. Which of the several counterintelligence approaches is most desirable to uncover moles within one's own intelligence services?
3. Does counterintelligence pose risks to a nation's civil liberties?
4. How would you evaluate torture, extraordinary rendition, and warrantless wiretaps as methods to enhance counterintelligence effectiveness?

ENDNOTES

1. Executive Order 12333, Sec. 3.5, as amended on July 31, 2008.
2. The First Chief Directorate was the foreign intelligence arm of the Soviet KGB, and is now named the SVR.
3. Colonel General Oleg Danilovich Kalugin, former Chief of Directorate K (Counterintelligence) of the KGB First Chief Directorate, October 2008.
4. British Security Service Act of 1989.
5. Defined as "[p]reventive measures taken to mitigate hostile actions against Department of Defense Personnel (to include family members), resources, facilities, and critical 'information." Joint Publication 1–02, Department of Defense Dictionary of Military and Associated Terms, a 0073, amended through October 17, 2008.
6. Dr. Dirk Doerrenberg, former Director of Counterintelligence for the BfV, December 2008.
7. The terms counterintelligence and CI will be used interchangeably in this chapter.
8. The Russian intelligence representation abroad, the equivalent of a CIA "station" is called a "residency."
9. Howard, a former CIA case officer, was identified in 1985 as spying for the KGB, and escaped to the USSR where he subsequently died.
10. John Walker, a U.S. Navy Communicator, started working for the KGB in 1968 and along with his brother, son, and a friend spied for the Soviets for about seventeen years.
11. Conrad, a retired U.S. Army Sergeant, was arrested in 1988 as part of a spy net in the U.S. Army, which by that time had existed for seventeen years.
12. The GRU is the Russian military intelligence service.
13. Statement by retired General Nikolaos Gryllakis, former head of Greek security. Undated translation/transcription of Greek television show, "Fakeli" (files).
14. Vitaliy Sergeyevich Yurchenko, a senior KGB counterintelligence officer, defected to the CIA in Rome in August 1985 and redefected to the USSR three months later.
15. The prospect of a polygraph examination has also deterred existing spies from applying to CIA for employment or accepting an assignment there.
16. Jonathan Pollard, a U.S. Navy civilian intelligence analyst, was arrested in 1985 for spying for Israel.
17. SIGINT or signals intelligence is one of the many examples of "int" terminology including MASINT, IMINT, and HUMINT imposed on the U.S. government by the Department of Defense. Some civilian, professional intelligence officers prefer "human espionage" to HUMINT.
18. "Dangle" is the term of art for an individual controlled by a CI service who is put in the way of a

hostile service, making himself as attractive as possible in the hope the service will take him on as an agent, a "double agent." The American media, displaying their usual ignorance of the intelligence business, have taken to describing spies such as Aldrich Ames and Robert Hanssen as "double agents," apparently because they were employees of intelligence organizations. They should be labeled spies or penetrations.

19. "Denied area" is an intelligence term of art describing an extremely hostile operational environment with heavy surveillance.

20. Penkovskiy was a Soviet military intelligence officer who worked for the United States and Great Britain from 1960 lo 1962.

21. This operation is described in the 1956 movie, *The Man Who Never Was.*

22. The term "case officer" has been used to designate the operations officer who manages a human source or, in a broader sense, the officer in charge of a technical collection project. Under the influence of Washington-based personnel professionals, this title apparently has been replaced by the bureaucratic term "core collector."

REFERENCES

Bromwich, M. R. 1997. *Office of the Inspector General Department of Justice Report, A Review of the FBI's Performance in Uncovering the Espionage Activities of Aldrich Hazen Ames.* Unclassified Executive Summary (April 21).

Director of National Intelligence. 2008. *United States Intelligence Community Information Sharing Strategy* (February 22).

Inside the Pentagon. 2002. *Deputy Defense Secretary Backs New Approach to Processing Intelligence* (September 26).

Masterman, J. C. 1972. *The Double-Cross System in the War of 1939 to 1945.* New Haven, Conn.: Yale University Press, 1972.

Mitrokhin, V. I., ed. 2002. *KGB Lexicon, The Soviet Intelligence Officer's Handbook.* London: Frank Cass.

Risen, J. 2003. "Jailing in Russia Is a Reminder that Spy Wars Still Smolder," *New York Times* (June 16): A1.

Van Cleave, M. 2008. "Meeting Twenty-First Century Security Challenges 2008 The NCIX and the National Counterintelligence Mission: What Has Worked, What Has Not and Why." *Washington Post* (April 3): A1.

Warrick, J., and C. Johnson, 2008. "Chinese Spy 'Slept' in U.S. for Decades." *Washington Post* (April 3): A1.

Reprinted with permission from Paul Redmond "The Challenges of Counterintelligence," in Loch K. Johnson, ed., *The Oxford Handbook of National Security Intelligence* (New York: Oxford University Press, 2010): 537–554.

20. COLD WAR SPIES: WHY THEY SPIED AND HOW THEY GOT CAUGHT

STAN A. TAYLOR AND DANIEL SNOW

Why do some people commit treason against their own country? Taylor and Snow examine this question and find that the answer is usually simple enough: for money. They note, too, that the United States has become somewhat more effective in catching American traitors, as a result of improvements in electronic surveillance procedures.

The purpose of this study is to ask why certain Americans decided to betray their country and how it is that they were caught. While the general intelligence literature has grown rapidly, not much has been written about traitors as a class or group.[1] Several books have been written about Soviet citizens who have betrayed their government, particularly about those who have defected to the West.[2] And a fair amount has been written about specific Americans who have betrayed their government, particularly the famous cases.[3] But beyond the well known cases, often little exists except one or two short newspaper articles on specific traitors. And as a *category*, very little has been written about Americans who have betrayed their government and revealed classified information to other states.[4]

For this research, we created a database consisting of 139 Americans who have been *officially* charged with spying against their government. We have attempted to include all who either began their treason or were caught during or immediately after the Cold War.[5] To the best of our knowledge, this is a fairly complete list. Obviously, undetected traitors are not included and we have also left out moles or penetration agents—foreign agents who have entered America legally or illegally and have attempted to penetrate national security organizations—unless they acquired US citizenship and were caught. We have relied solely on public information and realize that this may not present the entire picture. But more information is publicly available than is generally realized. We collected information about 40 variables associated with each case. These variables included: date of birth, date of arrest, personal habits (gambling, drinking, and drug habits), sexual preferences, how they were recruited, and a range of other variables. . . .[6]

WHY THEY SPIED

MODELS OF ESPIONAGE

Some scholars have developed highly sophisticated models which, they believe, explain espionage.[7] These models consider various psychological attributes, situational factors, and behavioral chains, coupled with insight from several academic disciplines. Others adopt rather simple models.[8] Nearly all such attempts to explain espionage, however, focus on two areas: factors associated with the individual and factors associated with the situation. No single explanation adequately explains treason nor any other human action. Even the most treasonous of individuals must have access to classified information before it can be pilfered. And only a small percentage of those who do have access to classified information (fewer than .001 percent) ever commit treason.[9]

Our research suggests that nearly all motivations can be grouped into four categories—money, ideology, ingratiation, and disgruntlement. Of these four, money and disgruntlement appear to be growing in importance and ideology and ingratiation appear to be waning (see Figure 20.1)[10]. We also consider a few additional, and probably idiosyncratic, variables which we believe cannot be overlooked, especially when combined with other motives.

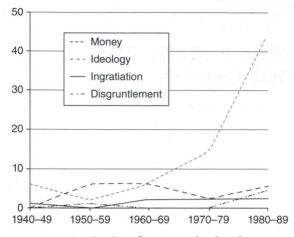

FIGURE 20.1 Motivations for treason by decade.

MONEY

Money appears to be the most prevalent motive for betrayal in recent American history. William Webster, when he was Director of Central Intelligence (DCI), told a reporter that he had not known of a traitor since 1986 who had been motivated by anything beyond money.[11] "It was a truism of the 1980s that ideology was out; materialism was in."[12]

Our data reveal that financial gain has been the primary motivation in 55.4 percent of all cases of Cold War espionage, by far the single most prevalent motive. This counts those whose intent was to get money even though they may have been arrested before any money changed hands. When linked with secondary factors (disgruntlement, ideology, etc.) money was the motive in 62.6 percent of the 139 cases. Seventy-one percent of enlisted personnel were motivated *solely* by money. Until military pay raises in the early 1980s, pay for low ranking military personnel was traditionally meager and many of our cases turned to espionage merely to pay outstanding debts or to allow them to live more stylishly.[13] Rather than turn to family, friends, or banks for loans, they turned to the KGB or related services.

It is difficult to know precisely how much money was involved in each case. Unless the foreign intelligence services revealed how much they paid, or unless the captured spy kept careful records of his or her payments, many dollar amounts are estimates. From what is known, it appears that 17 were paid between $10,000 and $100,000, seven were paid between $100,000 and $1,000,000, and four were paid over $1,000,000.[14] The recent American traitor Aldrich Ames typifies this financial motive. Ames related that he "felt a great deal of financial pressure"

and that it was stress from this pressure that led him to conceive "a scam to get money from the KGB."[15] The scam got out of hand and Ames continued to betray his country. His reports to the KGB cost at least ten human lives, compromised scores of intelligence operations, and earned him at least $1,397,300.[16] Ames' vulnerability to monetary temptation is revealed in the crass "Publisher's Clearinghouse"-like document given him by his Russian handlers. This piece of paper tallied the money and prizes available to him for his continuing service. . . .

The prevalence of avarice in these cases is remarkable. Thomas Patrick Cavanagh was sentenced to life imprisonment on 23 May 1985 for his involvement in espionage. Cavanagh was an engineer for Northrop Corporation who was working on what was called "quiet" radar techniques. Facing serious financial crises, he contacted what he thought was a KGB agent and offered him information for $25,000. As was often the case in our research, the "KGB agent" was an FBI undercover agent and Cavanagh was arrested. His explanation is typical of many of those who were trying to get into the espionage business for monetary gain. Cavanagh matter-of-factly suggested that since he did not know how to rob a bank, he instead offered classified documents to a foreign country. "There was this piece of paper. I thought it might be worth $25,000. I took the avenue of least resistance. I didn't have the foggiest idea of how to rob a bank."[17]

William Bell was arrested in 1981 for providing classified information about sensitive technologies being developed at Hughes Aircraft to Polish intelligence. After being arrested, Bell was asked if he supported or had sympathies for the Polish government. "No" he replied, "Mr Zacharski [his Polish handler] had found a fool who needed money. I had a weak spot. He took advantage of me."[18]

The prevalence of financial motivation may reflect increasing materialism and greed, but it also says something about recruitment techniques. All intelligence officers are taught to involve money as quickly as possible when dealing with potential or actual assets. When money is exchanged and a receipt is signed, the semblance of a contract is created. A reporting relationship based on ideology, revenge, or other motives is not entirely under the control of the case officer and is less stable.

IDEOLOGY

Conventional wisdom suggests that while most Soviet citizens betrayed their country for ideological reasons, Americans have done so solely for money.

As with most conventional wisdom, this generalization is not entirely true. In fact, all traitors, regardless of national origin, have reacted to somewhat similar changing social circumstances. Many early traitors in the West appeared to be motivated by ideological considerations—at least to the degree that anyone acts on single motivation. In Britain, all of the members of the Cambridge ring (Philby, Burgess, Maclean, Blunt, and Cairncross) were attracted to communism early in life. In the United States, the Rosenbergs, Klaus Fuchs, Alger Hiss, and Lauchlin Curry, as well as the much later Larry Wu-Tai Chin, had all been at one time members of the Communist Party.[19]

But after the famous atomic spies cases in the early 1950s, the number of Americans who spied for ideological reasons dropped dramatically. And those that do appear are not the typical cases of communist sympathizers. Several international events seem to be responsible for this trend—revelations about the horrors of Stalin were verified in the 1950s and Soviet violence in Hungary and other Eastern European countries did much to disabuse ideological communists in the West of the purity of the Soviet version of Marxism.

Ultimately, it appears, capitalist materialism prevailed over Marxist materialism—when historical and dialectical materialism failed, avarice was always ready to step in. On both sides of the Iron Curtain, money came to replace beliefs as a motive for betrayal. While Oleg Penkovsky risked his life in the late 1950s and early 1960s to betray what he believed was an evil political system, Victor Belenko, who flew his MiG-25 from the Soviet Union to Hokkaido in 1976, was more anxious to escape his dreary family life and line his pockets with large sums of money.[20]

In about 23.7 percent of 139 cases, we find ideology to be a primary motive. Even in these cases, other motives were apparent. For example, the Chinese-American, Larry Wu-Tai Chin, who joined the Communist Party in China in 1942 seems to illustrate the allure of money more than the allure of ideology. Chin may have begun as an agent-in-place for the Chinese communists, but the longer he lived in the West, the more he continued his espionage in order to maintain his rather opulent life style.

Jonathan Jay Pollard and Anne Henderson-Pollard also illustrate this shading of motives. The Pollards originally contacted Israeli military personnel and agreed to pass information Jonathan would obtain from the US Navy. Pollard's Zionist sympathies seem to have prompted his original betrayal, but, as with Chin, before long Pollard was attracted to the $30,000 per year he was promised by his Israeli contacts.

But over the last 15 years, ideology has almost disappeared as a motive. Only six individuals appear to have entered into espionage for ideological reasons since 1980, five of whom appear to have been motivated *solely* by ideological considerations. Thomas Dolce (who actually began spying in late 1979) wanted to support the white-dominated South African government; Glenn Souther developed Marxist leanings while in college; Jeffrey Carney spied for East Germany, essentially because of his anti-American feelings; Michael Moore wanted to defect to the USSR while serving as an American seaman in the Philippines; Frederick Hamilton's desire to end the perennial border dispute between Peru and Ecuador led him to give US electronic intercepts to Ecuadorian officials; and Robert Kim, a naturalized US citizen born in South Korea, appears to have been a mole. In fact, Hamilton appears to be the only *purely* ideologically motivated traitor to enter into espionage since 1984, and he was motivated by a commitment to peace rather than to a Cold War ideology.

INGRATIATION

Ingratiation becomes a motive when information is betrayed to foreign sources in order to fulfill friendship or love obligations or in order to make favorable impressions on someone whose approval is desired. In our database, ingratiation figured as the primary motive in eight, or 5.8 percent, of the cases. This is not enough cases to allow broad conclusions, but it does appear that ingratiation is declining as a motive. Ingratiation, especially sexually motivated ingratiation, may be a relic of the Cold War.

The use of same- or opposite-sex "honey traps" to attract and, if necessary, blackmail potential traitors has been a favorite theme of novelists and scriptwriters, but has been little understood and vastly overrated by them. In our database, there are only four cases of betrayal brought on by blackmail and they are spread over many years—1951, 1960, 1970, and 1984. Ingratiation's effectiveness may be judged by the handful of spies who were motivated by it. Though there is no publicly-available evidence to support it, we believe that if we had a record of every KGB, or related service, attempt to attract a potential traitor through some variety of friendship, the list would be much longer than it is in our database which counts only those who succumbed and were caught.

The case of the only FBI agent ever arrested for treason illustrates this motive. Richard Miller was recruited by the FBI in 1963 and served in New York, Puerto Rico, Florida, and California. In 1981 he was given a counterintelligence position in the Los Angeles FBI office. His past performance had been far from stellar and he had been suspended twice for weighing more than FBI guidelines allowed. Moreover, his marriage was disintegrating. After a series of extra-marital affairs, in May 1984 Miller met Svedana Ogorodnikov, who described herself to Miller as a KGB major. Miller became emotionally and sexually involved with her. Miller was arrested on 2 October 1984 and, after three separate trials, was convicted of espionage. Miller argued throughout the trials that he was trying to ingratiate himself with Ogorodnikov for counterintelligence purposes, but two different judges and even a member of Miller's family believed that the KGB had capitalized on Miller's emotional needs and compromised his career through seduction.[21]

Ingratiation's decline probably results from several developments. One is the end of the Cold War. Clearly, if Soviet and East European secret service defectors are to be believed, various forms of seduction were part of the KGB espionage arsenal.[22] One prominent Soviet defector suggested that compromise and coercion based on various levels and types of friendship were techniques in which KGB officers were well-trained.[23] Moreover, seductions and sexual affairs now can have graver medical consequences than they did for much of the Cold War. Also, the instability of the international system and the fast pace of technological developments make long-term spy operations less useful. Effective and efficient intelligence operations today require short-time success and do not allow long-term development of relationships. Finally, the role of sex in espionage has always attracted more attention than it merited. American secret services have found that happy and well-adjusted family men and women make better agents than those who are sexually promiscuous, emotionally impaired, and susceptible to blackmail.[24]

DISGRUNTLEMENT

Like money, disgruntlement is a motive of growing importance. By disgruntlement we refer to the sense of personal dissatisfaction that stems from feelings of being overlooked, overworked, and under-appreciated. No cases of disgruntlement occurred in the 1940s, and virtually none occurred in the 1950s. However, as the military and defense industry grew, the likelihood of disgruntled employees

taking revenge against their employers by betraying secrets also grew. Disgruntlement has grown in importance in the last five years.[25] Disgruntlement was the primary motive in 2.9 percent of our 139 cases. People entrusted by their government with classified information are given a unique ability to exact revenge on that government if it offends them.

If we consider those who, though not completely disgruntled, were not entirely "gruntled" (to borrow from Oscar Wilde), then disgruntlement becomes a more prevalent motive. Disgruntlement comes from a variety of sources. Often, disgruntled because of low pay, individuals have attempted to supplement their income through selling information. We classified these cases as motivated by disgruntlement rather than by greed. In other cases, dissatisfaction with their treatment would lead individuals to treason. The case of Daniel Walter Richardson illustrates the latter point. Richardson was described in reports as a mediocre soldier, and in August 1987 was demoted from tank instructor to tool room manager for his chronic tardiness. Shortly after, he called the Soviet embassy in Washington and offered to sell them defense information. The FBI intercepted this call and, posing as the KGB, was able to stage a meeting with Richardson. At this meeting, Richardson turned over a training manual and circuitry from an M-l tank. Richardson illustrates disgruntlement leading to a desire for revenge and followed by an attempt to sell secrets for money.

Other cases illustrate this pattern. Allen John Davies left the Air Force in 1984 as a result of poor job performance. Two years later he tried to get revenge by attempting to sell classified information to Soviet agents. A disgruntled ex-CIA employee, Edwin G. Moore, followed a similar path. Unhappy about his failure to be promoted in the CIA, Moore collected ten boxes of classified documents and attempted to sell them to Soviet diplomats in Washington.

There is an interesting parallel between disgruntlement as a motive for espionage and disgruntlement as a motive for leaking classified or confidential information. Leaking is virtually a national pastime in Washington. Hardly a week passes without some public revelation of information that was meant to be confidential or private. Every president since Eisenhower has complained about the debilitating and discouraging effects of leaking. One in-depth study of several cases of unauthorized leaks revealed that disgruntlement and revenge are the primary motives of such leaking.[26]

OTHER FACTORS

Other factors account for the remaining 12.2 percent of our cases. As with more common motives, when combined with other motives these miscellaneous factors figure in a larger percentage of espionage cases. But as a sole or primary motivation, they are rare. Some, however, deserve comment.

One under-appreciated motive is fantasy. We were surprised by the number of spies who appear to have developed an addiction to the mystique of espionage. We call this the "James Mitty" syndrome because it combines the allure of a James Bond lifestyle with a Walter Mitty sense of fantasy.

Two cases illustrate this motivation. William Kampiles was a young man who was so attracted to the life of espionage that he sought a position with the CIA's Directorate of Administration in March 1977 and was assigned to cable. When he did not get selected as a case officer in the Directorate of Operations, he concocted a plan through which he thought he could prove to his bosses that he had all of the skills necessary to be a case officer. Seeing a classified document left lying on a filing cabinet one night, he stole it, fled to Greece, and eventually sold it to the Soviet Embassy.[27] His logic was that as soon as he was hired by the KGB, he could confess to the CIA and become a double agent.

Jeffery Loring Pickering was convicted of espionage in 1983 and was described as a person who fantasized about espionage. Even in the many cases where money, disgruntlement, or ideology was the primary motive, we were surprised to notice the large number of cases where an obsession with excitement and intrigue, or a fascination with spying, blended and shaded with other motives.

Though closely related to disgruntlement, a desire to bolster one's ego or self-importance also played a role in some cases. For example, Samuel Loring Morison was hired as an analyst for the Navy Intelligence Support Center (NISC) in 1974. Described by his peers as an "oddball genius" and an "eccentric patrician," Morison considered himself to be above many of the rules that governed the handling of sensitive information. In 1978, two years after he was hired by the NISC, Morison became involved with Jane's Defense Weekly as a part-time editor. Morison regularly pushed the security limits until, in 1984, he provided Jane's with three secret US satellite-photos of a Soviet submarine under construction. Jane's published the pictures, revealing some of the resolution capabilities of the ultrasecret KH-11 spy satellite. Morison's principle motivation for doing this was to impress his higher-ups at Jane's.

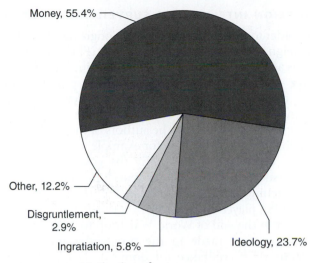

FIGURE 20.2 Motivations for treason.

Kinship was a factor in several cases. In the famous Walker case, John Walker involved both his brother and his son. Kinship even played a factor in the demise of the Walker ring—it was his former wife who reported John's spying to the FBI. The Pollard case involved kinship ties, Edward Howard's escape required his wife's complicity, and Aldrich Ames' wife was also convicted of spying.

In summary, people enter into treason for a variety of reasons and any attempt to classify risks oversimplification since every human being is unique and no human act is ever motivated by a single factor. However, the cases in our database suggest that avarice, disgruntlement (including job dissatisfaction, desires to harm to one's employer and alienation), ideology, and ingratiation explain the overwhelming number of cases of treason (see Figure 20.2, p. 273). The next question, however, is how they are caught.

HOW THEY GOT CAUGHT

Many counterintelligence methods are closely guarded. But one can imagine that they are somewhat similar to crime detection methods. Known foreign intelligence service officers in the United States are kept under close surveillance and embassies and other buildings, particularly those of hostile states, are monitored. It is widely suspected that telephone calls and correspondence with certain embassies and individuals might also be monitored. But until 1978, one of the most frequently used law enforcement techniques for detecting criminal behavior was not available to the intelligence community. That technique was electronic surveillance.

FOREIGN INTELLIGENCE SURVEILLANCE ACT

In order to address that problem, Congress passed the Foreign Intelligence Surveillance Act (FISA) in 1978. This act established warrant-like procedures to authorize electronic surveillance of foreign powers and their agents.[28] The effect of FISA on the detection and conviction of American traitors has been overlooked by intelligence scholars. The authors of the most thorough study yet published, for example, conclude that they "cannot determine" why the government was more successful in the 1980s than it had been earlier in catching espionage attempts.[29] Our data suggest that FISA played a major role in this development.

From the end of World War II up to 1978, many changes were made to the procedures governing electronic surveillance for domestic criminal purposes. But the procedures for authorizing the collection of electronic surveillance for national security purposes remained the same—presidential authorization. Although presidents believed they had extremely broad powers to authorize warrantless electronic surveillance for national security purposes, that practice suffered from two significant problems. First, there were many abuses. Presidents and other senior government officials could order electronic surveillance and place entities of foreign governments located in the United States or their agents, as well as US persons suspected of spying for these entities, under the most intrusive of electronic surveillance techniques without court issued warrants. These techniques, especially when conducted against US persons, exceeded the "unreasonable search and seizure" and "probable cause" requirements of the Fourth Amendment. But, as long as national security was invoked, senior government officials were willing to overlook constitutional niceties and condone this questionable behavior.

Second—and from a counterintelligence point of view, perhaps more serious—the evidence obtained through arguably illegal monitoring techniques was often rejected by American courts.[30] Thus, many who engaged in treason against the United States found evidence against them either rejected by courts or found decisions against them overturned by higher courts. Aware of this latter fate, the Federal Bureau of Investigation (FBI) became reluctant to use evidence obtained in this manner in courts.

A series of lower court decisions between 1971 and 1977 accepted the Executive's argument that warrantless national security-related electronic surveillance could lawfully be authorized by the President or...the Attorney General....In several cases, however, surveillances were found to be unlawful when courts retrospectively disagreed with the judgments of Executive officials as to whether national security, rather than law enforcement, objectives were being served by warrantless electronic surveillance.[31]

Moreover, the government became reluctant to seek normal surveillance warrants through open court procedures for three reasons. First, to do so might result in unwanted "publicity about the secret information and [establish] the fact of its loss."[32] To convince a regular court to issue a warrant required publicly proving the significance of that information, a task which often could not be done without revealing other classified information relating to it. Second, purchased secret information is often viewed suspiciously by the government that buys it. That government does not know whether it is false information made up just to make a sale, misinformation given purposely to mislead it, or valuable secret information which might enhance its national security. Corroboratory information revealed in an open warrant procedure tends to confirm the veracity and importance of the purloined information. And, third, and perhaps most importantly, to reveal enough information to obtain a warrant in an open court might compromise the sources and methods through which the information was obtained.

FISA changed all of this. It created a special court procedure that is "consistent with the 'reasonable search' requirement of the Fourth Amendment."[33] Under FISA, the Department of Justice was not bound by the traditional "probable cause" standard required to obtain warrants in normal criminal cases. Yet, at the same time, it was bound by specified procedures which protected civil liberties by banning electronic surveillance of Americans merely on the order of a government official under a loosely defined national security standard.

[FISA] established comprehensive legal standards and procedures for the use of electronic surveillance to collect foreign intelligence and counter-intelligence within the United States. The Act provided the first legislative authorization for wiretapping and other forms of electronic surveillance for intelligence purposes against foreign powers and foreign agents in this country. It created the Foreign Intelligence Surveillance Court comprised of seven federal district judges, to review and approve surveillances capable of monitoring United States persons who are in the United States.[34]

In general, FISA has been supported both by law enforcement agencies as well as by most civil libertarians. Evidence obtained under FISA has been accepted in courts as long as it satisfied the foreign intelligence and counterintelligence requirements of the act and as long as the procedural requirements of the act were met. Perhaps the most thorough constitutional justification of FISA can be found in *United States v. Duggan* (743 F.2d 59[2d Cir. 1984]) where both Fourth and Fifth Amendment challenges to this kind of electronic surveillance were addressed by the court.[35]

FISA allows the government to obtain a court order authorizing electronic surveillance, but to do so in a non-public setting which protects national security information and intelligence methods from foreign scrutiny. The problems of the earlier warrant procedure were overcome while at the same time American citizens were assured that their government could not "spy" on them capriciously.

RECORD OF FISA

The record of FISA is good and may say more about the increase in successful espionage prosecution in recent years than other explanations. For example, "between 1965 and 1974, an average of 177 warrantless national security surveillances were approved annually by the Attorney General."[36] The FISA Court, by contrast, approved an annual average of 530 surveillances between 1980 and 1994 (see Table 20.1).

Given the length of time necessary to put together a solid court case for treason, the surge of espionage cases in 1984 and 1985 may be attributable to the impact of the FISA court. It is also obvious why 1984 is often referred to as "The Year of the Spy" and the 1980s as "The Decade of the Spy." In the Ames case, for example, the FBI was searching for a penetration agent in the CIA as early as 1987. After dropping the investigation in 1989, they began again in 1991 and identified Ames as the traitor in March 1993, but did not arrest him until February 1994. Even after learning that Ames was the long sought KGB agent-in-place, it took nearly a year to complete the evidence necessary for a trial.[37]

Until all of the classified information relating to the detection and arrest of each case is made public, it is difficult to document the precise contribution of the FISA legislation. But the raw numbers do suggest that FISA made a significant difference in the government's ability to detect and prosecute traitors. Clearly, the Carter administration's decision to prosecute espionage more vigorously also contributed to the

TABLE 20.1   FOREIGN INTELLIGENCE SURVEILLANCE ACT COURT-SURVEILLANCE ORDERS ISSUED

Year	FISA Orders Issued
1979 (partial year)	207
1980 (first full year)	319
1981	431
1982	475
1983	583
1984	635
1985	587
1986	573
1987	512
1988	534
1989	546
1990	598
1991	593
1992	484
1993	511
1994	575

Source: United States Senate Select Committee on Intelligence and Administrative Office of the US Court System.

higher arrests in the mid-1980s, but that new vigor would not have been possible without FISA.

Excluding those who defected and were not caught, from 1945 to 1977, 23 percent of the detected spies were caught during their first attempt at espionage, suggesting that many continued their espionage for longer periods of time. From 1978 to date, however, 38 percent have been caught in their first foray into espionage. This probably reflects not only increasing skills on the part of counterintelligence agents, but also the role of FISA in making electronic surveillance more available and usable in court.

PHYSICAL SEARCHES

To make matters even worse for traitors, Congress recently adopted legislation creating FISA-like procedures covering physical searches, a category that was explicitly left out of the 1978 FISA Act. In 1980, then Attorney-General Benjamin Civiletti asked that requests for national security-related physical search authorizations also be considered under FISA. A few physical search authorizations were actually approved by the FISA court even though the original legislation was specifically limited to electronic surveillance. Several earlier attempts to include physical searches under the FISA procedures failed.

In 1981, however, the Reagan administration convinced the USA court that it had no authority to approve applications for physical searches. It is somewhat ironic that "the only government request that the FISA Court has ever rejected was done at the insistence of the Executive Branch itself."[38]

Following Aldrich Ames's arrest in 1994, however, both public opinion and the mood of Congress changed regarding physical searches. Physical searches are now under the FISA procedures and the government can obtain court orders authorizing access to phone records, banking information, and other personal data by following the procedural requirements of FISA.[39] Prior to this change, it was easier to tap a telephone than to obtain telephone records.

FAULTY TRADECRAFT

In any discussion of why spies are caught, one often overlooked motive deserves mention. After reading as much data as was available about our 129 cases, we are amazed at the poor level of tradecraft, even abject stupidity, displayed in many cases. This is especially apparent among one-time-sellers, but even among those with some understanding of tradecraft, foolish blunders played a significant role in their eventual detection. One worries, in fact, that an especially acute spy with good tradecraft might be very difficult to catch. But even spies with some tradecraft skills (Walker, Howard, and Ames, for example) made foolish mistakes, perhaps stemming from feelings of overconfidence, which often betrayed them. Since 1976, at least 16 of the spies in our database telephoned or walked into the Soviet Embassy and asked if they would like to buy some secrets. In every case the FBI, who had intercepted the calls, met these would-be spies, bought what they had to offer, and then arrested them. In one case, the budding traitor threw a package of classified material with a note in it asking for money over the wall of the Soviet Embassy. The Soviets thought it was a bomb and called the Washington fire department who came and collected the material. Aldrich Ames, one of the most recent traitors, paid $540,000 cash for a home while earning a $62,000-a-year salary. Robert Haguewood walked into a bar and started talking to a stranger on an adjacent stool about his desire to sell classified information to the Soviets. The man was an off-duty policeman. Time and time again, these spies would engage in activities that any thinking person would avoid.

INTELLIGENCE AFTER THE COLD WAR

Some have wondered whether clandestine intelligence gathering and counterintelligence activities are needed in the post-Cold War world. Senator Daniel Patrick Moynihan, former member of the Senate Intelligence Committee, has introduced legislation that would assign most of the CIA's current functions to State, Defense, and other government departments and change the focus of most intelligence gathering operations to open sources.[40] Less draconian is the proposal of former CIA director Stansfield Turner, who has proposed significant shifts in priorities in the US intelligence community. Admiral Turner believes that economic intelligence ought to be the primary goal of the intelligence community, and that it should reorganize its efforts to reflect that new priority.[41]

Others, however, might remind us of Lord Palmerston's adage, first expressed in the House of Commons in 1848, that there are no eternal enemies and there are no eternal friends, there are only eternal interests. If that is the case, then all states will continue to gather information about other states, and all states will try to protect against that collection. Even without the Soviet challenge, intelligence gathering will continue and counterintelligence efforts will still be necessary. In fact, the collection of both open- and denied-source information may be more important now than it was during the Cold War.

Stanley Hoffmann once said that as the "physics of power declines, the psychology of power rises."[42] That is, as the material elements of power become less capable of shaping and determining events, then perceptions and images become more important. And as perceptions and images become more important, then what Joseph Nye calls "soft power" becomes more important.[43] With the end of the Cold War, the eggs of power—particularly nuclear weapons—have become relatively less important. But that merely forces attention to the hens that make that power possible—the economies and social and political developments of other states.

This logic suggests that all nations will continue to collect clandestine intelligence information and that all nations will need to protect against that activity through counterintelligence efforts. What has changed is the nature of the intelligence desired. Strategic intelligence—information about abilities and intentions of hostile or potentially hostile states—is still important. But information about general social, economic, and political conditions of states has become perhaps even more significant. What used to be called non-strategic intelligence may be the new strategic intelligence.[44] In the information age, information, indeed, may be the principle commodity of international relations.

The recent case of Aldrich Ames, who may be the most damaging traitor in all American history, suggests two conclusions. First, treason is still possible, even after the Cold War. Ames began his treason in 1991, and continued to sell classified information to non-Communist Russia even after the Soviet Union collapsed in 1989. He was identified as a Russian asset in March 1993, but not arrested until February 1994.[45] His activities were celebrated in Moscow, but will be condemned in the United States for years to come.[46] Within the last 15 years, we know of attempts by France, Israel, Japan, Germany, and South Korea to gather denied information about the United States.

Second, while some isolated cases of ideologically motivated treason may still be found, most recent treason has been motivated by cupidity and avarice. Knowing how difficult it is to change institutional directions, one can only speculate whether the profile of traitors that existed during the years that James Angleton headed the CIA's counterintelligence efforts made it more or less difficult to identify non-ideological traitors. Angleton headed counterintelligence efforts over the very two decades during which our data suggest ideology was declining and other motives were becoming more important. Clearly, current counterintelligence profiles must pay more attention to the kinds of motivations we have discussed.[47] As a thoughtful reviewer of an earlier version of this article suggested, it may have been difficult for the CIA to find people like Ames when it was searching for people like Philby.

QUESTIONS FOR FURTHER DISCUSSION

1. What are the primary motivations that lead people to spy against their own nation? How would you describe what these individuals have in common, if anything?
2. How have these motivations changed over time, and why?
3. How has the United States caught those engaged in treason?
4. How can one balance the needs of counterintelligence and security, on the one hand, and civil liberties, on the other hand? Has the Foreign Intelligence Surveillance Act achieved this balance when it comes to wiretaps?

ENDNOTES

1. The prolific writer Rebecca West published one of the early and interesting books on treason. In her *The Meaning of Treason* (NY: Viking 1946) and *The New Meaning of Treason* (ibid. 1964), West discusses some specific British traitors during World War II. Her Epilogue in both volumes is a good introduction to the concept of ideological treason. See also Chapman Pincher, *Traitors* (London: Penguin 1988) for a more lengthy discussion of treason.

2. See e.g., Gordon Brook-Shepherd, *The Storm Petrels: The First Soviet Defectors, 1928–1938* (London: Weidenfeld 1977) and the same author's *The Storm Birds: Soviet Postwar Defectors* (NY: Harcourt Brace Jovanovich 1989). The best bibliography for both first- and second-hand accounts of Soviet defectors and Western agents-in-place is Raymond G. Rocca and John J. Dziak, *Bibliography on Soviet Intelligence and Security Services* (Boulder, CO: Westview 1985).

3. See e.g., John Barron, *Breaking the Ring: The Bizarre Case of the Walker Family Spy Ring* (Boston: Houghton Mifflin 1987), Wolf Blitzer, *Territory of Lies: The Exclusive Story of Jonathan Jay Pollard* (NY: Harper & Row 1989), and Robert Lindsey, *The Falcon and the Snowman* (NY: Simon & Schuster 1979).

4. Of the recent books, Theodore R. Sarbin *et al.* (eds.) *Citizen Espionage: Studies in Trust and Betrayal* (Westport, CT . Praeger 1994) is, by far, the best generally available trade book. The Defense Personnel Security Research Center, created by the Dept. of Defense in the wake of several security breaches in 1984 and 1985 and located at Monterey, California, has published several reports, primarily for use within the defense community. See, for example, Susan Wood and Martin F. Wiskoff, *Americans Who Spied Against Their Country Since World War II* (Monterey, CA: Def. Pers. Security Res. Center). See also, Thomas B. Allen and Norman Polmar, *Merchants of Treason* (NY: Delacourt 1988), Ronald Kessler, *Spy vs. Spy: Stalking Soviet Spies in America* (NY: Scribner's 1988), Pincher, *Traitors* (note 1), and Robert J. Lamphere and Tom Shachtman, *The FBI-KGB War: A Special Agent's Story* (NY: Random House 1986). Most of these works are somewhat anecdotal and earlier works consider only a few cases.

5. Several deified databases obviously exist; however, we have had access to none of them. By far the best and most thorough analysis of espionage cases is Wood and Wiskoff, *Americans Who Spied* (note 4). Their database was created from unclassified information; however, their study was conducted under government

contract and they had cooperative personnel at all of the intelligence agencies with whom they dealt. Their database included cases through 1990, while ours includes cases through 1996. As a contracted study, their report was not as widely distributed as it should have been. But any student of treason should obtain it. No research on American traitors would be possible were it not for the valuable contributions made by the Defense Personnel Security Research Center and the Dept. of Defense Security Institute. The latter's *Recent Espionage Cases* is the only data available on some spies. Our rather narrow definition of traitor as *an* American citizen who was charged with treason caused us to omit several early ideological spies whose prosecution was considered too sensitive by the government. For example, we have not included William Weisband, an NSA spy, because he was charged only with failing to report to a grand jury even though he was a known spy. We have not included cases of economic espionage in our database unless the traitor was charged by the government under espionage acts. We did not include the case of two Connecticut company executives who sold carbon-carbon technologies and equipment to Indian defense-related organizations. They were convicted of violating export laws, but were not charged with espionage. Similar cases are discussed in Peter Schweizer, *Friendly Spies: How America's Allies Are Using Industrial Espionage to Steal Our Secrets* (NY: Adantic Monthly Press 1993).

6. On 11 July 1995 the National Security Agency released communications relating to the Rosenberg case which could not have been made public at the time without compromising sensitive collection techniques. See David Kahn, "VENONA Messages and Atomic Bomb Espionage," in *World Intelligence Review* (formerly *Foreign Intelligence Literary Scene*) 14/2 (1995) p. l and Lamphere and Shachtman, *FBI-KGB War* (note 4).

7. See e.g., the excellent article by Carson Eoyand, "Models of Espionage," in Sarbin, *Citizen Espionage* (note 4) Ch. 4.

8. See e.g., the MICE model (motivation, ideology, compromise or coercion and ego) first described by KGB defector Stanislav Levchenko, *On The Wrong Side: My Life in the KGB* (Washington, DC: Pergamon-Brassey's 1988).

9. Herbig accepts the figure of 3 million Americans holding security clearances in the 1980s. See Katherine L. Herbig, "A History of Recent American Espionage," in Sarbin, *Citizen Espionage* (note 4) p. 45. Approximately 30 were charged with espionage during the same time period.

10. Joseph P. Parker and Martin F. Wiskoff, *Temperament Constructs Related to Betrayal of Trust* (Monterey, CA: Def. Pers. Security Res. Center 1991) p. 50.

11. "US Finds it Difficult to Catch Spies Who Sell Out For Cash, Not Ideology," *Wall Street Journal*, 30 June 1986, p. 26, quoted in Sarbin, *Citizen Espionage* (note 4) p. 51.

12. Herbig, "A History of Recent American Espionage" (note 9) p. 51.

13. See ibid. p. 53.

14. Wood and Wiskoff, *Americans Who Spied* (note 4) p. 55.

15. The quotation is from an FBI transcript interview with Ames and is reported in US Congress, Senate, Select Committee on Intelligence, *An Assessment of the Aldrich H. Ames Espionage Case and Its Implications for U.S. Intelligence*, S. Rpt. 103–90, 103d Cong., 2d sess. (Washington, DC: 1994) p. 11.

16. See US Senate, *An Assessment of the Aldrich H. Ames Case* (note 15) p. 39. *U.S. News & World Report*, 6 March, 1995, p. 50, claims Ames' revelations could have resulted in 30 deaths.

17. *The San Francisco Examiner*, 21 June 1987, p. l. Also cited in Herbig (note 9) p. 54.

18. United States, Senate, Select Committee on Intelligence, *Meeting the Espionage Challenge: A Review of United States Counterintelligence and Security Programs*, Report 99–522, 98th Cong., 2d sess. (Washington, DC, 1986), p. 118.

19. For many of the insights in this section, I am indebted to Herbig (note 9).

20. John Barron, *MIG Pilot: Lt. Victor Belenko's Final Escape* (NY: Reader's Digest Press 1980) is the most complete account of Belenko's delivery of the Soviet Foxbat jet fighter into Western hands.

21. Most of the information on Richard Miller is taken from articles in the *Los Angeles Times* by William Overend published on 24 Oct. 1985, 7 Nov. 1985 and 15 July 1986. Mr. James McQuivey also interviewed Miller's son Paul in 1991 and used that interview in a class case study of Miller that is in the authors' possession.

22. "The use of sex to lure and entrap potential agents is known to be a technique of Soviet and bloc intelligence services," according to George C. Constantinides, *Intelligence and Espionage: An Analytical Bibliography* (Boulder, CO: Westview 1983) p. 292. But Constantinides rightly discredits David Lewis' *Sexpionage: The Exploitation of Sex by Soviet Intelligence* (NY: Harcourt Brace 1976) for being based on "a potpourri of fact, rumor, and speculation," p. 292.

23. Levchenko, *On the Wrong Side* (note 8).

24. Joseph P. Parker and Martin F. Wiskoff, *Temperament Constructs Related to Betrayal of Trust* (Monterey, CA: 1991), pp. 32–35.
25. Herbig (note 9) p. 50.
26. See Martin Linsky, *How the Press Affects Federal Policymaking: Six Case Studies* (NY: Norton 1986).
27. Kampiles sold for $3,000 a technical manual for the KH-11, an overhead reconnaissance satellite, a highly classified US secret. This satellite, the capabilities of which were unknown to the Soviets, provided real-time photographs in high resolution. Had Kampiles known the significance of his information, he could have sold the manual at a considerably higher price.
28. Public Law 95-511. This legislation passed Congress as S. 1566. Electronic surveillance refers to wire taps, television monitoring, hidden microphones, electronic tracing devices, and other electronic means to gather evidence. S. 1566 did not address the question of physical searches.
29. Wood and Wiskoff, *Americans Who Spied* (note 4) pp. A12 and A13.
30. Americo R. Cinquegrana, "FISA: A Reformist Success Story," in *Foreign Intelligence Literary Scene* 8/6 (1989) p. 2.
31. Ibid. p. 2.
32. Herbig (note 9) p. 64. The case of William Weisband, mentioned in note 5 above, illustrates this principle. Had Weisband been caught after passage of FISA, prosecution would have been possible.
33. US Senate, *Foreign Intelligence Surveillance Act of 1978*, Report No. 95–701, 95th Cong., 2d sess. (Washington, DC: 1978) p. 9.
34. US Senate, *The Foreign Intelligence Surveillance Act of 1978: The First Five Years*, Report 98–660, 98th Cong., 2d sess. (Washington, DC 1984) p. l.
35. FISA has survived unscathed over 20 challenges in various court cases. See, for example, *United States v. Fahey*, 540 F. Supp. 1306, 1314 (E.D.N.Y. 1982), *United States v. Megahey*, No. 83–1313, 2d cir. 8 Aug. 1984, and *United States v. Belfied*, 692 F. 2d 141 (D.C. Cir. 1982). These and other cases are discussed in United States Senate, Foreign Intelligence Surveillance Act (note 34).
36. Cinquegrana, "FISA" (note 30).
37. US Senate, *Assessment of the Aldrich H. Ames Case* (note 15).
38. Cinquegrana (note 30) p. 12.
39. This is contained in Section 303 of S. 2056. See, United States, Senate, Select Committee on Intelligence, *The Counterintelligence and Security Enhancements Act of 1994*, Report 103–296, 103d Cong. 2d sess. (Washington, DC 1994) p. 8.
40. Moynihan explained the rationale for his legislation on Public Television's *MacNeil/Leher News Hour* on 13 Feb. 1995: The text of this discussion is available on Lexis/Nexis, 15 Feb. 1995.
41. Stansfield Turner, "Intelligence for a New World Order," *Foreign Affairs* 70 (Fall 1991), pp. 151–152.
42. Stanley Hoffmann, "Perceptions, Reality, and the Franco-American Conflict," in John C. Farrell and Asa P. Smith (eds.), *Image and Reality in World Politics* (NY: Columbia UP 1967) p. 58.
43. Joseph S. Nye, Jr., "Soft Power," *Foreign Policy* No. 80 (Fall 1990), pp. 153–171.
44. In 1976 and 1977, the Senate Intelligence Committee, on the urging of then member Senator Adlai Stephenson, III, undertook a lengthy study of so-called non- strategic intelligence—general information about the social, economic, and political conditions within the Soviet Union. In the wake of criticism of the intelligence community for its failure to see more clearly the pending collapse of the Soviet Union in 1989, the strategic importance of general social, economic, and political information now seems more apparent.
45. Literally hundreds of newspsaper and magazine articles have been written about the Ames case. Undoubtedly, scores of books will follow, not to mention TV miniseries and movies. But the best brief official record is found in United States Senate, *An Assessment of the Aldrich H. Ames Espionage Case* (note 15).
46. It appears his KGB managers even sent him photographs of the "beautiful land" on which his country house (dacha) would be located when he had to end his treason. See "The Cold War's Last Spy," U.S. *News and World Report*, 6 March 1995, p. 59.
47. Angleton continues to have supporters and detractors. Perhaps the most objective review of the literature about Angleton can be found in "Of Moles and Molehunters: A Review of Counterintelligence Literature, 1977–92" written by Cleveland C. Cram and published as an intelligence monograph by the CIA's Center for the Study of Intelligence in 1993.

From Stan A. Taylor and Daniel Snow, "Cold War Spies: Why They Spied and How They Got Caught," *Intelligence and National Security* 12 (April 1997): 101–125. Reprinted by permission of the publisher (Taylor & Francis Ltd, http://www.informaworld.com).

21. TREACHERY INSIDE THE CIA

SENATE SELECT COMMITTEE ON INTELLIGENCE

In 1994, the U.S. Senate Select Committee on Intelligence (SSCI) conducted an investigation into one of America's most damaging counterintelligence failures: the treachery of Aldrich H. Ames inside the Central Intelligence Agency. This chapter provides a look at the Committee's findings.

In the end, regardless of what the Committee may recommend or what Congress may enact, fundamental change will come only if the Director of Central Intelligence, supervisors at all levels, and the employees of the CIA bring it about. The Committee intends to monitor the Agency's progress in this regard, but the leadership must come from within.

The Committee undertook its inquiry not for the purpose of assessing individual blame—which is the exclusive responsibility of the Executive branch—but rather to learn what had gone wrong and to evaluate the institutional lessons to be learned from the Ames case. Nevertheless, the Committee believes that the recent actions taken by the Director of Central Intelligence, R. James Woolsey, against past and current CIA officials implicated in the Ames case warrant comment.

On March 10 of this year, Director Woolsey appeared before the Committee in closed session to outline his interim responses to the Ames case. One area for reform which was cited by the Director was "management accountability." According to the Director: "[T]o my mind, this is very much at the heart of the entire matter." The Committee strongly shares this view.

Despite the CIA Inspector General's recommendation that 23 current and former CIA officials be held accountable for the Agency's failure to prevent and detect Ames' espionage activities, Director Woolsey chose only to issue letters of reprimand to 11 individuals—7 retired and 4 current Agency employees. None of the individuals cited by the Inspector General was fired, demoted, suspended or even reassigned as a result of this case. In response to what was arguably the greatest managerial breakdown in the CIA's history, the disciplinary actions taken by the Director do not, in the collective experience and judgment of the Committee, constitute adequate "management accountability."

All Committee Members believe that the Director's disciplinary actions in this case are seriously inadequate and disproportionate to the magnitude of the problems identified in the Inspector General's report. It is clear, given the immense national security interests at stake, that there was "gross negligence"—both individually and institutionally—in creating and perpetuating the environment in which Ames was able to carry out his espionage activities for nine years without detection.

The Committee is concerned about the message that Director Woolsey's mild disciplinary actions will send to the overwhelming majority of CIA employees who are dedicated, conscientious, patriotic, and hard-working professionals, many of whom are exposed daily to risk and hardship. For the current employees who were faulted by the Inspector General for their role in the Ames case to remain in their grades and positions falls far short of the level of accountability expected by the Committee. Indeed, in the wake of the Director's decision, many professionals within the Intelligence Community have contacted the Committee to register the same sentiment.

As this report documents, the failures evident in the Ames case were numerous and egregious. While it might be argued that the majority of individuals cited by the Inspector General were guilty of acts of omission rather than commission, the seriousness of these omissions cannot be overstated. The failures of the individuals cited by the Inspector General led to the loss of virtually all of CIA's intelligence assets targeted against the Soviet Union at the height of the Cold War. Ten of these agents were executed. The inability of the CIA to get to the bottom of these losses in a timely way was itself a significant management failure.

If there is not a higher standard of accountability established by DCIs, then a repeat of the Ames tragedy becomes all the more likely. Management accountability within the Intelligence Community should be no less than the highest levels found elsewhere in the Executive branch. Director Woolsey's actions do not meet this standard.

Having noted in strong terms the magnitude of CIA's failures, the Committee would be remiss not to point out what went right. A traitor, responsible for heinous acts of espionage, was identified and convicted. He has been imprisoned for life. In the end, this was accomplished by the work of a small group of CIA and FBI personnel who took part in what became a long and arduous inquiry—for some, lasting almost nine years. At least one member of this group appears to have pushed from the very beginning to get to the bottom of the 1985 compromises. It was his impetus that eventually put the investigation back on track in 1991. Over time, the scope and pace of the investigation had taken many twists and turns, some caused by the KGB and some by internal factors beyond the control of the investigators themselves. The commentary which follows is not intended to diminish in any way what was ultimately accomplished by this dedicated group of investigators and analysts.

Finally, the Committee notes that its recommendations are based upon the situation that pertained through early 1994. Director Woolsey has promulgated some new policies since then and has announced his intention to institute still others. While the Committee believes in general that stronger measures are needed, it is too early to pass judgment on the Director's recent actions.

THE FAILURE TO "FIX" PAST COUNTERINTELLIGENCE PROBLEMS

The counterintelligence function at the CIA is weak and inherently flawed. Despite repeated internal and external reports which have recognized a longstanding cultural problem with the counterintelligence function, CIA managers have, judging from the Ames case, failed to fix it.

In particular, the Committee was struck by the number of internal and external studies undertaken after 1985—which became known as the "Year of the Spy" following the exposure of spies John Walker, Ronald Pelton, Edward Lee Howard, and Jonathan Pollard—which pointed out the systemic and deeply-rooted problems in the CIA's conduct of counterintelligence.

As summarized by the recent report of the CIA Inspector General, these internal and external reports over the years focused on common themes:

> That a counterintelligence career was held in low esteem at the CIA and did not attract high caliber officers. This was, in part, because officers gained promotions by agent recruitments, not by analyzing problems in recruitment operations;

> That there was an ambiguous division of responsibility for counterintelligence among CIA offices;

> That counterintelligence information was not being shared properly among CIA components; and

> That CIA was reluctant to share counterintelligence information fully and in a timely manner with the FBI (IG Report, pp. 16–22)

The poor state of counterintelligence at the CIA in the mid-1980s can be explained in part by the reaction to the so-called "Angleton era." James Angleton had been the head of the Counterintelligence Staff of the CIA from 1954 until 1974 (when he was involuntarily retired by DCI William Colby). He became convinced that the KGB had penetrated the CIA. Accordingly, Angleton was suspicious of virtually every Soviet agent who was recruited by the CIA and suspicious of every CIA officer responsible for such recruitment. On occasion, his suspicions led to CIA officers being fired without adequate justification.

While several of the officers who had been unjustly fired were later compensated, the counterintelligence function was effectively undermined by the negative reaction to Angleton's relentless pursuit of spies, particularly within the Soviet-East European (SE) Division of the Directorate of Operations, which had the principal responsibility for recruiting Soviet agents for the CIA.

In addition, there appears to have been an excessive focus within the Directorate on the recruitment of intelligence sources to the exclusion of counterintelligence concerns. Few officers wanted to go into counterintelligence because promotions and recognition came from successful recruitments, not from questioning, or identifying problems with, ongoing operations. Further, there was an image of a "corporate elite" constructed among these officers which led them to dismiss too readily the possibility of a spy among them.

By all accounts, these attitudes were prevalent within the Directorate of Operations at the time Ames sabotaged the Agency's Soviet operations in the summer of 1985, and they greatly contributed to management's failure to focus upon the CIA employees who had had access to the compromised cases (as explained in detail below).

The CIA made some efforts to address these shortcomings after "the Year of the Spy." In 1988, the head of the counterintelligence staff was made an "Associate Deputy Director" in the Directorate of Operations, and was double-hatted as the head of a new Counterintelligence Center (CIC). The CIA and FBI also signed a new Memorandum of Understanding (MOU) in 1988, which provided, at least on paper, for improved sharing of information in counterintelligence cases.

But these new bureaucratic "trappings" for the counterintelligence function did not overcome the fundamental problems which continued to be cited in reports issued in the 1990s. Despite the formation of a "lead office" for counterintelligence and the 1988 MOU with the FBI, the sharing of counterintelligence information between CIA components and with the FBI continued to be a serious problem, as was clearly evident in the Ames case.

In conclusion, the Committee finds that, despite repeated internal and external reports which recognized a longstanding cultural problem in the counterintelligence function, the CIA failed to implement adequate solutions. Indeed, the Committee believes the fundamental problems persist.

RECOMMENDATION NO. 1: The Director of Central Intelligence should revise the CIA's strategy for carrying out the counterintelligence function. The Director should institute measures to improve the effectiveness of counterintelligence to include (1) establishing as a requirement for promotion among officers of the Directorate of Operations, service in a counterintelligence or counterintelligence-related position during their careers; (2) establishing incentives for service in a counterintelligence position; (3) instituting effective and comprehensive counterintelligence training for all officers of the Directorate of Operations and for appropriate officers assigned elsewhere in the CIA; and (4) ensuring adequate access to ongoing foreign

intelligence operations by those charged with the counterintelligence function. The Committee will make this a "special interest area" for purposes of oversight until it is satisfied the weaknesses noted above have been adequately addressed.

THE FAILURE TO DEAL WITH SUITABILITY PROBLEMS

As the Ames case all too clearly demonstrates, the CIA Directorate of Operations is too willing to dismiss, deny, or ignore suitability problems demonstrated by its officers.

From the outset of his career at the CIA, Ames demonstrated serious suitability problems which, over the years, should have led his supervisors to reassess his continued employment. These problems included drunkenness, disregard for security regulations, and sloppiness towards administrative requirements. In the years immediately before he began to commit espionage and during the rest of his career, his supervisors were aware of his personal and professional deficiencies, but did not make his problems part of his official record, nor act effectively to correct them. Despite his recognized unsuitability, there is little evidence that his assignments, activities, or access to sensitive information were in any way limited as a result.

Prior to Ames's assignment to the counterintelligence staff of the SE Division in 1983, his supervisor in Mexico City sent a message to CIA headquarters recommending that Ames be counseled for alcohol abuse when he returned. While Ames's supervisor recognized a chronic problem, the message to headquarters apparently stemmed from an incident which occurred at an official reception at the U.S. Embassy where Ames was drunk and became involved in a loud argument with a Cuban official. On another occasion, Ames was involved in a traffic accident in Mexico City and was so drunk he could not answer police questions nor recognize the U.S. Embassy officer sent to help him. In fact, based upon recent interviews with his colleagues, Ames was notorious for long, alcoholic lunches, often slurring his speech when he returned to the office. None of this behavior prompted any serious effort to correct the problem while Ames was overseas, or when he later returned to CIA headquarters.

In April 1983, when CIA headquarters asked Ames's supervisors in Mexico City whether Ames qualified for a staff position in another Latin American country, they recommended against it, citing his alcohol problem, his failure to do financial accountings, and his generally poor performance. Nevertheless, six months later, when a former supervisor of Ames requested him to fill a position in the SE Division at headquarters—the most sensitive element of the Directorate of Operations—there is no indication that Ames' alcohol problem or poor performance were ever noted. Indeed, Ames was placed in a position which provided him access to the identities of virtually all of the Soviet intelligence officers by the CIA without his new supervisors being aware of the problems he had had in Mexico City.

The alcohol abuse counseling that Ames ultimately did receive upon his return to headquarters amounted to one conversation with a counselor, who, according to Ames, told him that his case was not a serious one when compared to many others in the Directorate of Operations.

In 1983, during the assignment in Mexico City, Ames also began an extra-marital relationship with a Colombian national, Rosario Casas Dupuy (hereinafter "Rosario"), herself a recruited asset of the CIA. Over time, the seriousness of their relationship became apparent to several of Ames's colleagues, but this never led to any action by Ames's supervisors, despite the fact that CIA regulations prohibit sexual relationships with recruited assets and require that reports of "close and continuing" relationships with foreign nationals be submitted by employees. Despite the security implications of this relationship, the violation of Agency regulations was ignored.

In fact, Ames did not file an official report concerning his relationship with Rosario until April 1984, four months after she came to the United States to live with him. Indeed, it appears that until their marriage in August 1985, Ames (still married to his first wife) and Rosario continued to live together, without any perceptible concern being registered by the CIA. While the counterintelligence staff recommended in February 1985, that in view of the anticipated marriage, Ames be moved to a less sensitive position, nothing changed. Ames continued in the same position.

While his alcohol problem abated during this assignment to the SE Division—at least as a matter of attracting official attention—it resurfaced during his assignment in Rome. He was known among colleagues for his long, alcoholic lunches, for sleeping at his desk, for often slurred speech, and generally as a marginal performer. On one occasion, after an Embassy reception, he was so drunk that he passed out on a street and awakened in a hospital. While his

supervisor was unhappy, this incident did not become part of Ames' record, nor does it appear that this episode led to counseling or any serious reevaluation of Ames' fitness for continued service. Indeed, the same supervisor extended Ames' tour in Rome for a third year.

Over his career, Ames repeatedly demonstrated carelessness and disdain for security requirements. In 1975, while on his way to meet a CIA source in New York, Ames left a briefcase of classified materials identifying the source on a subway train. Although the briefcase was ultimately recovered, it might well have compromised the source's relationship with the CIA. In the fall of 1984, he brought Rosario to CIA housing where CIA undercover officers were staying, in violation of security regulations. In August 1985, he took her to the safe house where the Soviet defector Yurchenko was being debriefed, again in violation of security procedures. In Rome, he was known to prepare classified reports at home. During his assignments at CIA headquarters between 1989 and 1994, he was occasionally found in other CIA offices where he had no reason to be, and with materials he had no reason to have.

He was equally negligent throughout his career in complying with the administrative requirements imposed on officers of the Directorate of Operations, such as submitting financial accountings for the cases he was handling.

Despite these and other incidents, Ames never received a single official reprimand during his 31-year career at the CIA. Indeed, most of the incidents and shortcomings which have come to light since Ames was arrested were never made a matter of official record. Once on board, his fitness to serve in the Directorate of Operations was never reevaluated.

The Committee appreciates that intelligence officers of the Directorate of Operations are often placed in jobs and situations with stresses and strains that far exceed those of the average government employee. But these positions also demand self-control and personal discipline. Particularly in overseas assignments, it may be impossible to separate an intelligence officer's private life from his or her public, official one. A single misstep can prove his undoing or that of other officers.

It is the Committee's perception, which the Ames case confirms, that the Directorate of Operations has been far too willing to dismiss or ignore flagrant examples of personal misconduct among its officers. Excessive drinking and extra-marital relationships with sources have all too often been seen as part of the job, rather than as indicators of problems. Security concerns are too often dismissed as the bureaucratic whining of small-minded administrators. All too often an officer who has been through training, gone through the polygraph examination, and had an overseas assignment, is accepted as a "member of the club," whose fitness for assignments, promotions, and continued service becomes immune from challenge.

Director Woolsey, in a recent speech, said that the "culture" of the directorate must be changed. The Committee shares that view. Such change will not come solely by changing regulations or personnel. It will come only when supervisors at every level of the directorate take seriously their responsibilities as managers. Personal misconduct should be documented. Officers who do not meet acceptable standards of personal behavior should not be assigned to sensitive positions nor qualify for supervisory positions. Personal shortcomings should be factored into consideration of promotions and bonus awards. While officers with personal problems should be given an opportunity, as well as appropriate assistance, to rehabilitate themselves, failing that, their employment with the directorate, if not with the Agency itself, should be terminated.

RECOMMENDATION NO. 2: The Director of Central Intelligence should ensure that where evidence of suitability problems comes to the attention of supervisors, it is made a matter of official record and factored into the consideration of assignments, promotions, and bonus awards; that efforts are made to counsel and provide assistance to the employee where indicated, and, if the problem persists over time, the employment of the individual is terminated. The Committee will make this a "special interest area" for purposes of oversight until it is satisfied these policies have been instituted and are being observed within the Directorate of Operations.

RECOMMENDATION NO. 3: The Director of Central Intelligence should, in particular, take prompt and effective action to deal with what appears to be a widespread problem of alcohol abuse by ensuring that CIA employees experiencing such problems are identified and are put into effective counseling and/or treatment. During this period, these employees should be suspended from their duties until they have demonstrated to a qualified professional their fitness to return to service. Should their problems continue, their employment should be terminated.

RECOMMENDATION NO. 4: The Director of Central Intelligence should institute, consistent with existing legal authority, an "up or out" policy for employees of the CIA, similar to that of the Foreign Service, without waiting for the report required by section 305 of the Intelligence Authorization Act for Fiscal Year 1995, pertaining to the Intelligence Community as a whole. Chronically poor performance should be grounds for dismissal from the Agency. If the Director decides not to institute such a policy and does not provide a persuasive rationale to the Committee for his decision, the Congress should enact legislation requiring such a policy during the next Congress.

RECOMMENDATION NO. 5: The Director of Central Intelligence should review and revise the performance appraisal reporting system of the CIA, to include a review of the factors upon which employees are rated and the grading system which now exists, to institute a system which reflects more accurately job performance. Where supervisors are concerned, their rating should include an assessment of how well they have supervised the performance and development of their subordinates.

THE FAILURE TO COORDINATE EMPLOYEES' OPERATIONAL ACTIVITIES

The Ames case provides a striking example of CIA supervisors failing to critically evaluate the contacts of an operations officer—with known personal shortcomings and in an extremely sensitive position—with Soviet officials in 1984 and 1985. Further, the fact that Ames virtually ceased submitting reports of such contacts, in violation of standard Agency procedures, never became known to his SE Division supervisors or made part of his official record.

In 1984, while occupying a position within the SE Division which gave him access to the identities of Soviet agents working with the CIA and FBI, Ames, with the approval of his immediate supervisor, began making contacts with Soviet Embassy officials in Washington, D.C. According to testimony received by the Committee, it was not infrequent that Directorate of Operations Officers at CIA headquarters were asked to "help out" other CIA elements that had responsibility for establishing relationships and maintaining contacts with foreign individuals located in the Washington area.

The Committee has been advised that Ames's senior supervisors in the SE Division were unaware that he was having these meetings and would have disallowed them had they known.

In any event, to permit a person in Ames's position, and someone with the personal and professional shortcomings already noted, to meet alone with Soviet Embassy officials substantially increased the risk of the disaster that eventually occurred. It provided Ames with an opportunity that he otherwise may not have had, or may have had difficulty in contriving on his own.

After June 1985, after his espionage activities had begun, Ames repeatedly failed to submit reports of his contacts with Soviet officials. While his failure prompted complaints from the FBI, the CIA element that Ames was supporting failed to bring this to the attention of his supervisors in the SE Division, nor was it reflected in his official record. Again, had Ames' SE Division supervisors been aware of his failure to file these reports, it may have alerted them to a possible problem. Since the advancement of Directorate of Operations officers depends upon their official reporting, the failure to file such reports should have suggested something was amiss.

A similar failure occurred during his assignment in Rome. While his supervisor was aware that he was meeting alone with Soviet officials in Rome (one of whom was Ames' KGB contact), Ames explained his failure to file reports of such meetings on the basis that he had obtained little worthwhile information. This apparently was enough to satisfy the supervisor.

RECOMMENDATION NO. 6: The Director of Central Intelligence should revise the policies and procedures governing the operational activities of CIA officers to ensure that these activities are better supervised, controlled, coordinated, and documented.

THE FAILURE TO APPLY A STRUCTURED METHODOLOGY TO THE INVESTIGATION OF INTELLIGENCE COMPROMISES

The most puzzling deficiency in the Ames case was the failure, in the wake of the 1985–86 compromises, to aggressively investigate the possibility that CIA had been penetrated by a KGB spy.

Certainly by the fall of 1986, the CIA was aware that it had suffered a disaster of unprecedented proportions which was not explained by the defection of Edward Lee Howard. Within a matter of months, virtually its entire stable of Soviet agents had been imprisoned or executed. In the days of the Cold War, Soviet operations represented the Agency's principal *raison d'etre*. There were no operations which had greater importance to its mission. The CIA was left virtually to start from scratch, uncertain whether new operations would meet the same fate as its old ones.

To be sure, these compromises involved extremely sensitive agents. There was a need for discretion in terms of how the matter was handled. But this does not explain or excuse the Agency's tentative, tepid response. Initially, some CIA officers could not believe that the KGB would "roll up" all of CIA's sources at once if the KGB had a source in the CIA who was still in place. Taking some comfort that new operations appeared to be surviving, some believed the problem had gone away. But this in no way explains the seeming lack of urgency to get to the bottom of what had gone so drastically wrong.

The obvious place to begin would have been with the CIA employees who had had access to the information which had been compromised. At least one official in the SE Division made a strong plea to his supervisors at the time that they needed to "investigate it, not study it." But this did not happen. The CIA task force created in October 1986, undertook what was largely an analytical review of the compromised cases. The task force did oversee an Office of Security review of personnel who had served in Moscow, but no broader examination was made of all CIA officers who had had access to the compromised cases. No systematic effort was made to identify and investigate problem employees and their activities, as was eventually done in 1991–92.

Later, the CIA came to suspect that the KGB was running ploys against them, purposely suggesting reasons for the compromises other than a penetration of the CIA itself. Even then, however, any sense of urgency was lacking. CIA analysts waited for things to happen, for more information to surface. They continued to analyze and conjecture. There was no clear sense of purpose, no clear methodology, and no clear sense of what was required to get to the bottom of the compromises.

In a related counterintelligence investigation of a report suggesting that the KGB may have recruited a source in a particular office in the CIA, a CIA investigator conducted a systematic investigation of over 90 employees who were assigned to that office. The inquiry took more than year. But investigators did not conduct the same type of inquiry of the CIA employees who had had access to the information that was actually compromised in 1985 until 1991–1992.

The FBI was officially brought into the case in October 1986, when the CIA learned that two sources recruited by the FBI had been compromised. But the two agencies worked their investigations separately, despite the likelihood that the compromises were caused by the same source (whether it be human or technical).

While the FBI and CIA task forces regularly exchanged information on the compromises and on the progress of their respective analyses, they never performed a systematic assessment, together, of the CIA employees who had had access to the compromised information, until mid-1991.

Why CIA management during the 1986–1991 period did not attach more importance or urgency to getting to the bottom of the 1985 compromises is incomprehensible to the Committee. While CIA Director William Casey and Deputy Director for Operations (DDO) Clair George, who were in office at the time the compromises occurred, reportedly regarded them as "a huge problem," the Agency's response was to create a 4-person team to analyze the problem. No one believed there was a basis for bringing in investigators from the FBI at this juncture, apparently because CIA was unable to pin responsibility on a particular CIA employee.

While Casey and George became deeply enmeshed in the Iran-contra scandal in the fall of 1986 and spring of 1987, this circumstance does not explain, in the view of the Committee, why a problem so close to the heart of the CIA's mission was not given more attention by senior management. Indeed, once Casey and George departed the scene, it does not appear that their successors—either as DCI or as DDO—gave the inquiry any particular emphasis or priority. DCI William Webster, his deputy Robert M. Gates, and the new DDO Richard Stolz were briefed on the compromises in 1988, but did not delve deeply into either the nature of the problem (which was now several years old) or what the Agency was doing to resolve it.

Due to the extraordinary sensitivity of this inquiry, there was only one junior investigator from the Office of Security assigned to the case from 1985 until 1991. He was responsible for investigating all counterintelligence leads and reports coming in which involved CIA employees. After he began to develop information regarding Ames' unexplained affluence in the fall of 1989, he was diverted from this investigation for a nine-month period, first for training and then to handle other leads. There was no one else assigned to pick up the Ames leads. Nor was consideration given to having the FBI pick up the leads, despite the fact that the information now focused upon a particular CIA employee within the United States.

While the Committee believes that the investigator in question made a good faith effort to work the leads he was given, he was essentially self-trained and, because of the compartmented nature of the investigation, was given very little help and guidance. Overworked and overloaded, he did not use all of the investigative techniques he might have utilized to get at Ames' financial situation. Indeed, the statutory authority invoked by the CIA in 1992 to obtain access to Ames' bank records was available to the Agency in 1989. Had this authority been utilized at the time information was received concerning Ames's unexplained affluence, it might well have led to his detection at a much earlier stage. The investigator also apparently made no effort to develop information regarding Ames's unexplained affluence during his assignment in Rome. Efforts to verify the financial condition of Ames's in-laws in Bogota were shoddy and ineffective, producing inaccurate information which supported rather than exposed Ames's contrived explanation.

The Committee does not think it fair to hold the investigator assigned to the case solely responsible for these failures. CIA managers simply failed to assign enough investigators to such an important task and failed to provide them with sufficient legal and administrative support to ensure that all appropriate avenues would be explored and all appropriate investigative authorities utilized. Since the professional investigative expertise of the FBI was effectively spurned during this period, insufficient resources and expertise were brought to bear on the case.

The Committee believes that those in charge of the CIA during the 1986–1991 period—Director William Casey, Acting Director and later Deputy Director Robert Gates, Director William Webster, and Deputy Director and later Acting Director Richard Kerr—must ultimately bear the responsibility for the lack of an adequate investigative response to the 1985 compromises. Whatever they may have personally understood the situation to be, they were in charge. It was their responsibility to find out what was being done to resolve the 1985 compromises. Based upon the information available to the Committee, they failed to do so.

Their failure is especially disheartening when one realizes that the information developed in August 1992, which finally focused the investigation on Ames—correlating his bank deposits in 1985 and 1986 with his meetings with Soviet officials—was available to investigators since 1986. Unfortunately, no one asked for it, even when alerted to Ames's unexplained affluence in October 1989.

Although the 1985–86 compromises represented a unique situation for the CIA, the Ames case demonstrates the lack of a clear *modus operandi* for dealing with situations where intelligence sources are known to have been compromised.

RECOMMENDATION NO. 7: The Director of Central Intelligence should establish procedures for dealing with intelligence compromises. At a minimum, these procedures should entail a systematic analysis of all employees with access to the relevant information and, if suspects are identified, provide an investigative methodology to determine whether there is evidence of unexplained affluence, unreported travel, unreported contacts, or other indicators of possible espionage. This type of systematic analysis should begin when a known compromise occurs, not after CIA has eliminated the possibility of a technical penetration, or after CIA has narrowed the range of possible suspects to one or two employees. Analysis and investigation should be undertaken on the basis of access and opportunity, and should not be delayed waiting for evidence on culpability.

RECOMMENDATION NO. 8: Pursuant to section 811 of the Intelligence Authorization Act for Fiscal Year 1995, the FBI should be notified immediately of any case where it is learned that an intelligence source has been compromised to a foreign government, regardless of whether the CIA believes at the time that there is a basis for an FBI counterintelligence or criminal investigation of a particular employee or employees. The CIA should also coordinate with the FBI subsequent investigative actions involving employees potentially involved in the case in order not to prejudice later criminal or counterintelligence activities of the FBI and in order to benefit from the investigative assistance and expertise of the FBI.

RECOMMENDATION NO. 9: The Director of Central Intelligence should require that all employees assigned as counterintelligence investigators have appropriate training, experience, and supervision which ensures, at a minimum, such investigators will be familiar with, and know how to utilize, the investigative authorities available to the CIA and the FBI.

RECOMMENDATION NO. 10: CIA management must ensure that adequate analytical and investigative resources are assigned to counterintelligence cases, and that other kinds of staff assistance (e.g., legal support, administrative support) are made available. In turn, those involved in these cases must ensure that their needs are communicated to their supervisors. The Inspector General of the CIA should periodically assess the counterintelligence cases of the CIA to ensure that adequate resources are being afforded to particular cases.

RECOMMENDATION NO. 11: The status of significant counterintelligence investigations must be regularly briefed to senior Agency officials, including the Director of Central Intelligence. Such briefings should include an explanation of the resources and expertise being brought to bear upon a particular case.

THE FAILURE TO EXPEDITE THE INQUIRY AFTER 1991

The period after the CIA and FBI decided to join forces in June 1991—compared with the period between 1985 and 1991—was relatively intense and focused. For the first time, investigators conducted a systematic review of the CIA employees who had had access to the compromised information, and there was an intensive, productive effort to link Ames and other priority suspects to the compromises.

Yet even during this phase, the investigation took an inordinate amount of time and was plagued by past inefficiencies. The joint investigative unit still had only four people (two from each agency); and there was still a lone CIA investigator working with them. While members of the joint investigative unit did obtain support from the CIA Office of Security and the FBI Washington Metropolitan Field Office, they were still but a few people carrying an extraordinarily demanding workload.

In August 1991, the joint investigative unit developed a list of 29 CIA employees for priority scrutiny. Ames was at the top of the list.

Yet the first letters to go out to financial institutions requesting access to Ames's financial records did not go out until June 1992, almost 10 months later.

In August 1992, when investigators correlated the records of Ames's bank deposits with what was known about Ames's 1985 meetings at the Soviet Embassy, the joint investigative unit suspected they had their man. When they learned in October of Ames's Swiss bank accounts, their suspicions were confirmed.

But according to the Inspector General's report, this crucial information was not presented to FBI headquarters until January 1993. It was explained to the Committee that the joint investigative unit was looking at possible suspects in addition to Ames. But this still does not explain why significant information pertaining to Ames was not passed contemporaneously to the FBI, particularly given the presence of two FBI agents on the joint investigative unit.

On the basis of the work of the joint investigative unit—which culminated in the March 1993 Skylight/playactor report—the FBI assembled an investigative team and tasked the team members to acquaint themselves with the facts. The FBI began an intensive investigation of Ames shortly thereafter. The Committee was advised in the course of its investigation that FBI headquarters had determined that the earlier information developed on Ames by the joint investigative unit did not meet the standards for an intensive FBI investigation. The Committee believes, however, that there was ample evidence by October 1992, to reasonably suggest that Ames was acting in 1985 (and thereafter) as an agent of the Soviet Union. The FBI's hesitation resulted in a six-month delay before the FBI began to apply the full array of its investigative capabilities against Ames. Once applied, they produced impressive results. Indeed, the FBI investigative team from the Washington Metropolitan Field Office, together with the CIA, did a superb job in bringing the investigation to a successful conclusion.

RECOMMENDATION NO. 12: The Director of the FBI should ensure that adequate resources are applied to counterintelligence cases involving the CIA and other federal agencies, and that FBI headquarters is apprised immediately of significant case developments which could form the basis for the FBI's opening an intensive counterintelligence investigation.

RECOMMENDATION NO. 13: The Attorney General and the Director of the FBI should review the FBI's guidelines for the conduct of counterintelligence investigations to determine whether clearer guidance is needed in determining whether a subject of a counterintelligence inquiry is acting as an agent of a foreign power.

FAILURE TO RESTRICT THE ASSIGNMENTS AND ACCESS TO SUSPECTS IN COUNTERINTELLIGENCE CASES

The Ames case reveals glaring weaknesses in the CIA's procedures for dealing with the career assignments of employees who are under suspicion for compromising intelligence operations. The CIA failed to restrict Ames's assignments and access even after information surfaced in 1989 which indicated Ames was a possible counterintelligence problem.

In September 1989, after a poor tour in Rome, which was known to the managers in the SE Division,

his SE superiors allowed Ames to return to the SE Division and assigned him to the office supporting to all Soviet and East European operations in Europe, a position affording him broad access to sensitive information. He remained assigned to the SE Division until August 1990. During this period, investigators learned about Ames's unexplained affluence and developed information regarding several large bank deposits and a particularly large currency exchange. Yet none of this appears to have had any bearing on Ames's continued assignment or access during this period.

In fact, at the end of this assignment, notwithstanding his own poor performance record (he was then ranked 3rd from the bottom among 200 officers in his rating group), Ames was appointed to serve on a promotion board for mid-level CIA operations officers. This assignment gave him access to the personnel records of an entire class of mid-level CIA operations officers.

In October 1990, SE Division managers reassigned Ames to the Counterintelligence Center (CIC) because he had performed poorly and they wanted him out of the Division. Apparently, supervisors in the CIC knew Ames was a poor performer and were aware that questions had been raised about his unexplained affluence. Yet they believed they could manage the problem. After his arrest, these officials recognized that Ames' position had given him access to data which identified virtually every double agent operation controlled by the United States. It is unclear how or why this access was permitted. It is clear that despite the security concerns raised about Ames, his CIC supervisors did not ascertain or evaluate the extent of his access at the time.

In April 1991, while Ames was assigned to the CIC, the Office of Security carried out an updated background investigation of Ames. The results of this investigation were evaluated and shared with the investigator assigned to the special task force. Reflecting interviews with his co-workers in Rome and his Arlington, Virginia neighbors, the investigation produced information that Ames had frequent contacts in Rome with Soviet and East European officials not fully explained by his work requirements, frequently violated security regulations by leaving his safe open and doing classified work at home, and lived far beyond his CIA salary in both Rome and Arlington. (One of those interviewed went so far as to say that he would not be surprised if Ames were a spy.)

Inexplicably, the CIA security officer who reviewed the investigative report evaluated it as "raising no CI concerns" and the task force investigator assigned to the case did not regard the report as providing any new information. Ames retained his security clearance and his job in the Counterintelligence Center, and no further action was taken to follow-up on the information developed in this report. Indeed, the special task force members viewed the investigative report, together with the favorable results of the April 1991 polygraph, as giving Ames "a clean bill of health."

In September 1991, despite having been "booted out" of the SE Division a year earlier, and despite the special task force inquiry then underway, Ames was allowed to return to the SE Division to conduct a special study of the KGB. While the study itself did not call for particularly sensitive access, Ames once again was given access to the personnel and records of the SE Division.

In December 1991, he was assigned to the Counternarcotics Center (CNC) where he remained until his arrest in 1994. This apparently was the first assignment made on the basis of the security concerns about Ames. But due to the sensitivity of the investigation into the 1985–86 compromises, CNC senior managers were not told of the investigation or the suspicions about Ames until the beginning of the FBI's intensive investigation in 1993. Even then, there was little or no effort made to evaluate and control the extent of Ames' access to classified information. Indeed, investigators later learned that Ames had computer access to a vast range of classified information that did not pertain to counternarcotics. Moreover, when a computer upgrade was installed in November 1993, it provided Ames with the capability to "download" vast quantities of information onto computer discs which he could take out of the building. Fortunately, Ames was arrested before he was able to pass these discs to his KGB handlers. But the fact that he was provided this capability at all at a time when his arrest was imminent is indicative of the CIA's lack of attention to this security problem.

RECOMMENDATION NO. 14: The Director of Central Intelligence should establish procedures to inform current and prospective supervisors about employees under suspicion in counterintelligence cases. While the need to protect the secrecy of the investigation is essential, as well as the need to protect the employees themselves from unfair personnel actions, the assignment of employees under suspicion without frank consultations at the supervisory level increases the likelihood of serious compromises and leads to conflict between CIA elements.

RECOMMENDATION NO. 15: The Director of Central Intelligence should issue procedures to require, in any case in which an employee is under suspicion for espionage or related activities, that a systematic evaluation be made of the employee's access to classified information, and that appropriate and timely actions be taken to limit such access. While care must obviously be taken to ensure that such actions do not tip off the employee that he or she is under suspicion, the failure to evaluate the access of an employee in these circumstances may eventually result in damage that might have been prevented.

RECOMMENDATION NO. 16: The Director of Central Intelligence should establish more stringent criteria for CIA employees serving on promotion and assignment boards, which, among other things, prevent the appointment to such panels of employees with poor performance records or records of suitability problems.

DEFICIENCIES IN SECURITY PROCEDURES

The Ames case demonstrated numerous deficiencies in the CIA's use of the polygraph, its control over classified documents and materials, and its coordination of security and counter-intelligence functions.

THE POLYGRAPH

Ames was able to pass polygraph examinations in 1986 and 1991 with relative ease. Although deeply involved in espionage activities, he was able to answer questions such as whether he worked for a foreign intelligence service, or had contacts with foreign nationals which he failed to report, without showing signs of deception.

The CIA Inspector General's report faults the 1986 examination, finding that the examiner was "too chummy" with Ames. When Ames showed a slight reaction to a question asking whether he had ever been "pitched," i.e., asked to work for a foreign intelligence service, the examiner appeared to readily accept his explanation that he was concerned about being "pitched" in his upcoming assignment in Rome.

The 1991 polygraph examination, according to the Inspector General's report, was deficient in that the examiners (there were two separate sessions) were not sufficiently familiar with the existing information on Ames' unexplained affluence, or with the information developed in the April 1991 background investigation of Ames. The examination was also deficient in that the investigator assigned to the special task force had not participated directly in the examination process, and there had been no prior planning in terms of how the CIA would handle the situation if Ames suddenly made damaging admissions.

According to Ames's debriefings, he did not take drugs or use any particular technique to pass the polygraph examinations. Acting on the advice of the KGB, he tried only to be cooperative and stay as calm as he could. Since he was acquainted with how polygraph examinations were conducted, he also was able to manipulate the process to prevent a "problem" from arising.

If Ames's account is true, it seems to indicate problems beyond those cited by the Inspector General's report, i.e. that examiners should be better informed and prepared. Indeed, it suggests that the CIA's reliance on the results of polygraph examinations needs to be far more circumspect than in the past.

RECOMMENDATION NO. 17: The Director of Central Intelligence should tighten polygraph procedures to make the polygraph more useful. Such procedures should include random examinations instead of exams at regular intervals, with little or no prior notice, and variations in the polygraph technique. These procedures should also ensure that polygraph examinations involving employees under suspicion are carefully planned and constructed, and that appropriate prior notification is made to the Federal Bureau of Investigation if such cases have potential criminal implications. In addition, the Director should review the policies applicable to the training, supervision, and performance appraisal of polygraph examiners to ensure that polygraph examinations are conducted in a professional manner and produce optimum results.

RECOMMENDATION NO. 18: The Director of Central Intelligence should institute a fundamental reevaluation of the polygraph as a part of CIA's security program. As the Ames case demonstrates, the polygraph cannot be relied upon with certainty to detect deception. This necessarily puts far more reliance on other aspects of the security process, e.g., background investigations, supervisory reporting, psychological testing, financial reporting, etc. The DCI's review should also include a reevaluation of the use of inconclusive polygraph test results. Even where the polygraph does indicate deception, such information is often useless unless damaging admissions are also obtained from the subject. The Committee believes that if an employee with access to particularly sensitive information does not make such admissions but continues to show deception to relevant questions after adequate testing, there should

be additional investigation of the issues in question to attempt to resolve them. Should such investigation fail to do so, the CIA should have the latitude, without prejudice to the employee, to reassign him or her to less sensitive duties.

CONTROL OF CLASSIFIED DOCUMENTS AND MATERIALS

The Ames case also demonstrated gaps in the control of sensitive classified information. Ames was able—without detection—to walk out of CIA headquarters and the U.S. Embassy in Rome with bags and envelopes stuffed with classified documents and materials. Many of the classified documents he passed to his KGB handlers were copies of documents that were not under any system of accountability. Ames did not even have to make copies of them. In his last job in the Counter narcotics Center at the CIA, Ames was able to "download" a variety of classified documents onto computer discs and then simply remove them to his home. When he attended a conference in Turkey in 1993, he brought a lap-top computer to do work in his hotel room. This apparently raised no security concern among those familiar with the incident. He was also able to visit offices he had no reason to be in, and gain access to information he had no business seeing.

In the late 1970s, the CIA instituted a policy calling for random and unannounced spot-checks of personnel leaving Agency compounds. But the policy was discontinued soon thereafter due to the inconvenience caused to those subject to such searches.

Ames recounted later that his KGB handlers were amazed at his ability to gain access to sensitive operations and take large bundles of classified information out of CIA offices without arousing suspicion, a sad commentary on the laxness of security at the CIA.

RECOMMENDATION NO. 19: The Director of Central Intelligence should reinstate the policy making persons leaving CIA facilities subject to random searches of their person and possessions, and require that such searches be conducted unannounced and periodically at selected locations. Such searches should be conducted frequently enough to serve as a deterrent without unduly hampering the operation of the facilities involved.

RECOMMENDATION NO. 20: The Director of Central Intelligence should institute computer security measures to prevent employees from being able to "download" classified information onto computer diskettes and removing them from CIA facilities. In addition, existing policies for the introduction, accountability, dissemination, removal, and destruction of all forms of electronic media should be reevaluated. The ability of the CIA's security managers to "audit" specific computer-related functions in order to detect and monitor the actions of suspected offenders should be upgraded.

RECOMMENDATION NO. 21: The Director of Central Intelligence should institute a policy requiring employees to report to their supervisor any instance in which a CIA employee attempts to obtain classified information which the CIA employee has no apparent reason to know. In turn, supervisors should be required to report to the CIA Counterintelligence Center any such case where a plausible explanation for such a request cannot be ascertained by the supervisor.

RECOMMENDATION NO. 22: The Director of Central Intelligence should institute new policies to improve the control of classified documents and materials within the CIA. In particular, the Directorate of Operations should undertake an immediate and comprehensive review of its practices and procedures for compartmenting information relating to clandestine operations to ensure that only those officers who absolutely need access can obtain such information. Further, the Directorate should establish and maintain a detailed, automated record of the access granted to each of its employees.

COORDINATION OF SECURITY AND COUNTERINTELLIGENCE

The Ames case demonstrated a serious division between security and counterintelligence activities in the CIA. Even though an investigator from the Office of Security (OS) participated in the investigation of the 1985–86 compromises under the auspices of the Counterintelligence Center (CIC), he failed to coordinate properly with OS with respect to Ames' 1991 polygraph examination. OS had initiated a background investigation of Ames in March 1991, but went ahead with the polygraph in April without the benefit of the background investigation. As it turned out, the background investigation provided significant information about Ames that was largely ignored by the investigator assigned to the CIC in light of Ames's passing the polygraph examination.

Citing senior security officials, the Inspector General's report noted there had always been a "fault line" in communications between the CIC and its predecessors, and the OS. The CIC had not always shared information regarding its counterintelligence investigations and had failed to make use of OS's investigative expertise. Indeed, the search to find the cause of the 1985 compromises might have moved more quickly from analysis to investigation if there had been better coordination between security and counterintelligence.

The Inspector General's report also found "a gradual degradation" of the resources and authority given the security function since 1985, concluding that "this degradation has adversely affected the Agency's ability to prevent and deter activities such as those engaged in by Ames. . . ." The Committee shares the view that this decline has been too great, too precipitous. The Committee had recommended an increase in personnel security funding for the CIA and other agencies for Fiscal Year 1995, but was unable to sustain its initiative due to the lack of interest shown by the agencies involved.

Responding to the continuing problem of CIA offices failing to share pertinent information on CIA personnel with one another, Director Woolsey recently created a new Office of Personnel Security that combines elements of the old Office of Personnel, the Office of Medical Services, and the Office of Security. While this consolidation may facilitate the sharing of information regarding suitability problems, it may also hamper the exchange of counterintelligence information from the CIC and may further dilute the security function, particularly the expertise of security investigators.

The Committee believes that the personnel security function should be preserved with a separate office. Routine monitoring of Agency employees from a security perspective remains an important function and one that must be accomplished without carrying a presumption that persons are under suspicion. An effective personnel security program would deter potential traitors, limit the burden on counterintelligence investigators and result in faster, more effective counterintelligence investigations.

RECOMMENDATION NO. 23: The Director of Central Intelligence should reexamine the decision to combine the Office of Security with the other elements of the CIA's new personnel center, and should ensure sufficient funding is provided to the personnel security function in Fiscal Year 1995 and in future years. The Director should also clarify the relationship between security and counterintelligence, specifying their respective functions and providing for effective coordination and cooperation between them.

FAILURE TO ADVISE THE OVERSIGHT COMMITTEES

The CIA failed to notify the congressional oversight committees in any meaningful way of the compromises of 1985–1986, as required by applicable law.

Indeed, in the hearings held annually on counterintelligence matters and in numerous staff briefings on the subject from 1985 until 1994, the massive compromises of 1985–86 were never once mentioned by representatives of the CIA or the FBI.

Based upon the recollections of individuals, there were two occasions when the 1985–86 compromises were alluded to in discussions with Members or staff of the Senate Select Committee on Intelligence (SSCI). The first mention came during a staff visit to Moscow in December 1988. The second occurred in 1992 during a visit to Moscow by two Members of the Committee. But on each occasion, the information provided was fragmentary and anecdotal and did not specifically address what was being done by the CIA about the problem. Informal staff efforts to follow-up on each of these conversations were put off by the CIA.

The Committee strongly believes that both the CIA and the FBI had an obligation to advise the oversight committees at the time of the 1985–86 compromises. Section 502 of the National Security Act of 1947 specifically requires intelligence agencies to report to the oversight committees "any significant intelligence failure." The compromises of 1985–86 resulted in a virtual collapse of CIA's Soviet operations at the height of the Cold War. According to the SE Division officers memorandum of November, 1986, the evidence was at that point "overwhelming" and clearly indicated a problem of disastrous proportions. The oversight committees were responsible for funding the activities of the Directorate of Operations. They should have been formally notified pursuant to section 502 of the National Security Act of 1947.

THE NEED FOR CONTINUED FOLLOW-UP

Many of the problems identified by the Committee are deep-seated and pervasive, and will not be solved easily or quickly. Yet these problems are too important and too integral to the functioning of an agency with important national security responsibilities not to merit continuing and intensive scrutiny by both CIA managers and the congressional oversight committees.

While the Committee intends to make the CIA's response to this report an area of "special oversight interest" in the years ahead, the Committee also directs the Inspector General of the CIA to provide the Committee, through the Director of Central Intelligence, with a report no later than September 1, 1995, and annually thereafter, on the CIA's progress in responding to the recommendations contained in this report and to the continuing counterintelligence and security challenges that the CIA faces.

QUESTIONS FOR FURTHER DISCUSSION

1. What was Aldrich Ames's motivation for spying against the United States from inside the CIA?
2. How was Ames apprehended? Why did it take so long?
3. Do you think other instances of treason could happen inside the government today? What are the best approaches to prevent this from happening again?
4. Why has counterintelligence often been the neglected stepchild among intelligence activities?

Reprinted from "An Assessment of the Aldrich H. Ames Espionage Case and Its Implications for U.S. Intelligence," *Staff Report*, Select Committee on Intelligence, U.S. Senate, 103d Cong., 2d. Sess. (November 1, 1994): 53–72.

VIII

ACCOUNTABILITY AND CIVIL LIBERTIES

Hamlet: "Come, come, and sit you
down, you shall not budge,
You go not till I set you up a glass
Where you may see the inmost part of you."
—SHAKESPEARE, *Hamlet*, 3.4.17–20

Virtually every nation in the world has a secret intelligence apparatus, whether this apparatus consists of just a few agents in key foreign capitals (if the nation is poor) or a vast network of humans and machines for spying around the world (if the nation is affluent). By collecting information from abroad and by engaging in the companion activities of counterintelligence and covert action, an intelligence establishment can help provide a shield against external threats—what President George H. W. Bush, a former Director of Central Intelligence (DCI), liked to call the nation's "first line of defense."

THE SPECIAL CASE OF INTELLIGENCE

In most nations, intelligence agencies are treated as exceptions from the rest of government. They are cloaked in secrecy, allowed exceptional access to policymakers, and given leeway to get the job done—even if that means breaking laws overseas (which is almost always the case) and engaging in unsavory activities that would be deemed inappropriate for other government agencies. From the beginning, the United States embraced this laissez-faire philosophy for intelligence activities, even as its leaders sought to "bind down" the rest of the government "with the chains of the Constitution" (as Thomas Jefferson described the theory of checks and balances in his draft of the Kentucky Resolutions in 1798). The Founders well understood the dangers from abroad to the new republic and were willing to grant broad discretionary powers to America's intelligence officers as they endeavored to protect the nation from foreign threats.

As the United States matured and its intelligence service expanded in the aftermath of World War II, this hands-off philosophy continued. The Cold War against the Communist world required a strong and flexible intelligence shield; in the nuclear age, a nation may not survive another surprise attack like the one that shook the nation at Pearl Harbor in 1941. A top secret study group reported to the Eisenhower administration in 1954 that

we are facing an implacable enemy whose avowed objective is world domination by whatever means and at whatever cost. There are no rules in such a game. Acceptable norms of human conduct do not apply. We must develop effective espionage and counterespionage services. We must learn to subvert, sabotage and we must destroy our enemies by more clear, more sophisticated and more effective methods than those used against us. (Church Committee 1976, 9)

In light of these hostile conditions, the CIA and its fellow agencies would have to be set loose to fight the Communists. If the United States were to win this ideological battle, often fought "in the back alleys of the world" (as Secretary of State Dean Rusk often described this hidden side of the Cold War), America's intelligence agencies would have to be as tough and as effective as anything the Soviet Union could field.

This is not to say the CIA was without supervision, even in this warlike climate (however "cold"). Most of its activities were approved by the White House and were reported, in broad outline at least, to small oversight subcommittees in the House and Senate. The approvals were highly discretionary, however, allowing DCIs broad scope to fill in the details in this struggle against Communism; and reporting to Congress was usually sketchy, perfunctory, and frequently rebuffed. "No, no, my boy, don't tell me," a leading Senator overseer, Democrat John Stennis of Mississippi, told DCI James R. Schlesinger in 1973 when he tried to provide a full accounting of the CIA's operations abroad. "Just go ahead and do it, but I don't want to know!" (Johnson 2000, 202).

Model democracy or not, the United States would follow the practice of other nations—democracies and dictatorships alike—in placing the secret agencies outside the normal framework of governmental supervision. If Americans were to be secure, a hostile world demanded no less.

AN ABRUPT CHANGE OF PHILOSOPHY

In 1975, this philosophy of intelligence exceptionalism changed dramatically, a rare occurrence in this or any other government. The shift resulted not from any sudden sea change in world affairs; that would not happen until the dissolution of the Soviet Empire in 1991. Rather, the stimulus arose from revelations at home regarding alleged abuses of power by the CIA (Johnson 1980, 1985, 1989, 2018; Smist 1994). Looking into charges of malfeasance published by the *New York Times*, government investigators uncovered a startling number of transgressions during this season of inquiry known as the "Year of

Intelligence" (or what many intelligence officers recall more ruefully as the "Intelligence Wars").

The horrors that emerged from the investigations included assassination plots against foreign leaders; illegal mail openings, wiretaps, and interception of international cable traffic; intelligence files on over a million American citizens; improper drug experiments and unlawful sequestering of dangerous chemicals and biological materials; a master spy plan to conduct surveillance against Vietnam war dissenters in the United States; intelligence infiltration into a wide range of groups in American society, from universities to religious and media organizations; incitement of violence against African American groups; and covert actions abroad aimed not just at autocracies but at democratically elected regimes as well.

The effects of this breathtaking catalog of secret government excesses were profound. From then on, America's support for a muscular, unbound intelligence capability would have to compete with another value long central to the rest of America's government: liberty—safeguarding the American people against the power of their own government and not only foreign governments. Beginning in 1975, the nation's leaders undertook an unprecedented experiment to balance security and liberty with respect to its secret agencies. In contrast, most other democracies continued to shelter their intelligence services under a special status outside the purview of parliamentary overseers.

THE EXPERIMENT IN ACCOUNTABILITY UNFOLDS

In the United States, reformers shed the traditional exceptionalism bestowed on intelligence in favor of a new kind of experiment in an intelligence partnership between the legislative and executive branches. America's intelligence agencies could be subjected to the norms of rigorous accountability, a hallmark of constitutional government (Currie 1998; Snider 1997). This era of enhanced supervision, following thirty years of benign neglect by Congress, began with the establishment of three new oversight panels: a Senate Select Committee on Intelligence (SSCI, in 1976), a White House Intelligence Oversight Board (IOB, 1976), and a House Permanent Select Committee on Intelligence (HPSCI, 1977).

The congressional committees have authority to hold hearings on intelligence matters, whether routine or in response to charges of impropriety; to scrutinize annual budgets line by line; to inspect intelligence facilities at home and abroad; to draft intelligence legislation; and, in the Senate, to conduct confirmation hearings on nominations for the office of D/CIA, DNI, and other top intelligence managers. On behalf of the president, the IOB carries out special inquiries into allegations of abuse.

The thoroughness with which these groups pursue their duties depends on how much media attention is focused on claims of wrongdoing, as well as on the philosophy of members toward the concept of intelligence accountability (for some, an oxymoron). Among the members of these three panels, a few have expressed the view that intelligence should return to its status as a special case, with only the lightest supervision from Capitol Hill. They join the chorus of anti-reformers inside and outside the government who look on the new oversight as an exercise in "micromanagement"—too many legislative fingers clumsily probing into delicate intelligence operations that require quickness, skill, and secrecy for success.

Republican Barry Goldwater of Arizona provides an example of the anti-reformist view. Ironically having risen to the chairmanship of the Senate Intelligence Committee, whose creation he opposed, the Senator opined in 1982: "When it comes to covert operations, it would be best if they [the CIA's leaders] didn't have to tell us anything." The antireformers complain, too, that legislators cannot be trusted with the nation's secrets; loquacious by nature, politicians will invariably babble—perhaps inadvertently, or even on purpose if they oppose a secret operation (a "leak item veto"). Senator Goldwater viewed his own legislative chamber as a place with "more leaks than the men's room at Anhauser-Busch" (Johnson 1996, 52).

In rebuttal, pro-reformers are quick to recite the litany of abuses uncovered in 1975 that led to new oversight in the first place. They echo James Madison's warnings about the corrupting nature of power and the need to have "ambition counteract ambition" (*Federalist Paper* No. 51), pitting one branch of government against another. They dismiss the micromanagement criticism, noting that—despite the tightened supervision—secret operations have moved swiftly forward when necessary. They argue, too, that leaks from Capitol Hill (as opposed to the executive branch) have been few and insignificant.

The very existence of this debate over intelligence reform raises eyebrows in most countries. Leaders overseas, even in fellow democracies, find it difficult to understand why the United States would intentionally seek to handicap its intelligence agencies—just as they failed to understand why Americans insisted on pursuing the Watergate investigation in 1974, at the expense of discrediting their own government and driving an incumbent president from office in shame.

Even at home, the experiment has hardly been a smooth evolution toward some golden means of accountability agreed on by everyone. On the contrary, it has been characterized by fits and starts. Among the enduring features have been an executive order prohibiting assassination plots against foreign leaders (1976); a Foreign Intelligence Surveillance Act (1978), which establishes judicial safeguards against overzealous wiretaps for purposes of national security; strict reporting requirements, which force the secret agencies to keep Congressional overseers informed of intelligence operations and the discovery of abuse inside their high walls; persistent questioning by lawmakers and staff that requires intelligence managers to explain and defend their budgets and programs; and expectations on Capitol Hill that intelligence reports will be shared with the Congressional intelligence committees on the same footing as executive officials.

More contentious has been the question of when the intelligence agencies should inform Congress about their operations, especially controversial covert actions designed to manipulate foreign governments. Should the reports come before or after these operations are launched? After demanding "prior notification" in a 1980 statute, lawmakers retreated somewhat (under pressure from President George H. W. Bush in 1991) to the current prescription of prior reporting in most cases but with an escape hatch for the president of a couple of days delay in times of emergency. Any delay, though, must be fully explained to the two oversight committees at the time the report is sent to Congress. This strikes most people as a sensible compromise and is a good illustration of the constructive debate on intelligence between the legislative and executive branches of government that has gone on since 1975.

BALANCING LIBERTY AND SECURITY: AN UNFINISHED STORY

The current equilibrium between liberty and security in the intelligence domain has failed to satisfy everyone. On the reform side, some have called for the abolition of the CIA, particularly in light of its failure to predict the U.S.S.R.'s disintegration in 1991 (although it did better in tracking the Soviet decline, especially the economic dimension, than is usually acknowledged). On the antireform side, the criticism of legislative micromanagement continues, with commentators advocating a repeal of the assassination prohibition; the unprecedented use of the Peace Corps as a cover for CIA officers abroad; the adoption of media, academic, and clerical credentials by intelligence officers; and more aggressive participation in coups d'état against regimes deemed unfriendly to the United States—all activities deemed inappropriate by reformers in 1975 (Johnson 2002). A central goal of the antireformers remains dismantlement of the three oversight panels, removing what they see as undue constraints on the intelligence agencies.

Even those not on the extreme fringes of this debate have raised troubling questions about the success of the experiment. At times the secret agencies have simply ignored Congress and the IOB, as if the new oversight rules were so much flotsam in the wake of the ship of state as it plows through the turbulent seas of international affairs. During the Iran-contra affair of the Reagan administration (a full decade into the new oversight), the staff of the National Security Council (NSC) bypassed Congress to raise secret funds for its covert actions in Nicaragua from foreign potentates and private citizens within the United States, making a mockery of Congress' power of the purse and, therefore, of constitutional government. Officers of the CIA and the NSC staff also lied to legislative investigators about their involvement in the affair. When the less-than-forthright nature of his testimony became clear, one high-ranking CIA officer proffered this gloss: he had been "technically correct, if specifically evasive." This is not exactly the sort of comity the new spirit of intelligence partnership and accountability was meant to engender.

The CIA also failed to inform legislative overseers of its ties to Col. Julio Roberto Alpirez in Guatemala, an unsavory agent charged with murder. Further, the National Reconnaissance Office (NRO) misled legislators about major cost overruns in its new headquarters buildings, as well as the NRO's improper accumulation of unspent appropriated funds. Although less serious than the blow struck against democratic procedures by the Iran-contra affair, neither of these cases did anything to nurture the bonds of trust and cooperation between the branches that are so vital for accountability to succeed.

More recently, the NSA has been the cause of much concern about the proper degree of intelligence accountability in the United States. In 2005, the *New York Times* revealed that, soon after the 9/11 attacks, the George W. Bush administration had bypassed the Foreign Intelligence Surveillance (FIS) Court warrant procedures for wiretaps. It took several years for this secret violation of the law to leak to the *Times*, and even then the newspaper sat on the story for a year at the administration's request; but when finally published, the revelation caused a stir in Washington and throughout the country. After much debate (and anger expressed by some lawmakers for being left in the dark about this violation), Congress finally moved in 2008 to restore the procedures of the 1978 FISA law, with some modifications to take into account modern technological advances in telephone and electronic communications.

Then, in 2013, another NSA scandal broke, this time as a result of documents leaked to *The Guardian* (a British publication) by a young NSA contractor by the name of Edward J. Snowden, an employee of the Booz Allen Hamilton Corporation (one of several giant private-sector companies with government intelligence contracts). These highly classified documents, shared with other newspapers as well, revealed that the NSA was gathering telephone "metadata" on millions of American citizens—though not the content of the messages, which still required a FIS Court warrant. Nevertheless, the volume of data collected on who was calling whom, how often, and when was staggering, This dragnet approach to intelligence collection inside the United States vacuumed into NSA computers more information than had ever been gathered before about Americans by one of their government agencies.

The documents leaked by Snowden revealed, as well, that the NSA had increasingly close ties with Microsoft, Facebook, Google, Apple, and other high-tech companies for the purposes of collecting similar metadata on the use of social media by U.S. citizens (a program called PRISM by the NSA). Such information could reveal to government officials the political leanings and other personal beliefs of individual citizens. In the past, information on citizens gathered by America's secret agencies had been misused for political purposes, as in the case of the FBI's COINTELPRO operations. Critics wondered why the NSA could not gather metadata just on suspected terrorists, rather than conducting a fishing expedition against just about everyone who uses a cell phone or the Internet. Officials at the NSA had few convincing answers and conceded in public hearings that they had exaggerated the usefulness of these programs in fighting terrorism.

On another front, the use of torture as a counter-terrorism tool by the CIA, the Senate Select Committee on Intelligence (SSCI) decided in March of 2009 (at long last, critics would complain) to initiate a staff investigation into the Agency's interrogation practices. Prodded by public calls for a "truth commission" to examine torture and rumors of other brutal acts levied against terrorist detainees, as well as upset by the unauthorized destruction of the interrogation tapes, the SSCI voted 14-to-1 in favor on a formal inquiry. The lone holdout was Republican Senator Saxby Chambliss from Georgia. After Chambliss retired from the Senate, the new SSCI Vice Chairman, Republican Kit Bond from Missouri, withdrew Republican support on the committee for the inquiry, using the excuse that the Department of Justice had just launched a criminal investigation into possible CIA counterintelligence abuses. This DoJ probe, he argued, made it impossible for the SSCI staff to interview Agency personnel, since Agency director Leon Panetta had excused his officers from having to testify twice and possibly place themselves in legal jeopardy. "The GOP pulled out early when the threat of prosecutions of participants in the program went live," recalls a senior Republican staffer on SSCI.[1] The DoJ inquiry eventually concluded that the Agency had committed no prosecutable offenses.

Yet in its files SSCI already had troves of interviews and oral histories with key Agency personnel knowledgeable about the interrogation methods, including a session with DCI George Tenet on the subject. Moreover, the SSCI and CIA staffs had engaged in continuous back-and-forth discussions about the report as it was being prepared, which in themselves amounted to a large number of "interviews." It is not as if the Agency's views on the matter were unknown. Chairwoman of the Committee Dianne Feinstein (Democrat, California) attempted to convince the Republicans to stick with the committee's investigation but to no avail. As a SSCI Democratic staffer recalled to me, "We asked the Republicans to join in the investigation and at first they said yes. Then it became so political."[2] The truth of the matter: the GOP did not want to be viewed as hobbling the CIA in an age of terrorist threats: thus, Republicans on the committee opted out. Democratic staff members

who also have respect for what the CIA does (but were concerned about interrogation excesses) soldiered on, poring over 6.3 million pages of Agency documents. In December of 2012, the committee approved the Democratic staff report (at 6,700 pages with 38,000 footnotes—probably the most thorough accountability study ever produced by a congressional panel on a single intelligence activity) by a vote of 9 to 6: eight Democrats and one lonely member of the GOP, independent-minded Olympia Snowe (Maine), against a half-dozen Republicans.

In 2017, both the Senate and the House Intelligence Committees opened inquiries into the question of whether Russia had attempted to manipulate the U.S. presidential election of 2016, including the possibility that the victorious Donald Trump GOP team had colluded with Russian intelligence agents in defeating Democratic candidate Hillary Clinton—a potentially explosive line of inquiry and difficult new territory for lawmakers on the congressional oversight committees. In May of 2017, early into the inquiry, President Trump fired FBI Director James B. Comey, raising questions among observers about the propriety of dismissing the FBI chief while his organization was investigating the White House. The firing reminded some commentators of the "Saturday Massacre" when President Richard M. Nixon dismissed government officials who were investigating rumors about the Watergate cover-up.

. . . .

While the intelligence agencies have occasionally transgressed against both the spirit and the letter of the law behind the new oversight, Congress, too, has been far from perfect in meeting its responsibilities. Some members and staff have been dedicated overseers, trying to strike a balance between liberty and security. They have pored over intelligence budgets and asked probing questions of intelligence officials during open and closed hearings. Others, though, have been distracted, perhaps less interested in the subject, facing a tough reelection bid, or simply true believers in the pre-1975 philosophy of laissez-faire for the secret agencies. Keeping the balance has required the devotion of at least a few individuals willing to dedicate the necessary time to maintain the eternal vigilance that is the price of liberty, and usually there have been a few lawmakers so disposed—but not many. Particularly important have been the attitudes of the chairs of the House and Senate intelligence committees, and that has been a mixed record: some have been dynamic overseers while others have been rather passive (Johnson 2018).

A QUALIFIED SUCCESS

With the major exception of Iran-*contra*—an appalling lapse in accountability from which, presumably, the nation has learned some lessons—the watchdogs on the oversight panels have been sufficient in number and commitment to make the experiment a qualified success. That is, unless one believes that secret agencies ought to be abolished or, at the opposite extreme, that they should be given the broad leeway they once enjoyed. Although the current state of intelligence accountability is still imperfect and subject to ongoing debate and adjustment (like democracy itself), most government officials and observers agree that it represents a workable balance between the two important values of security and liberty.

Certainly most people who have closely examined the subject value the contribution made by secret agencies to America's security. During the Cold War, the eyes and ears of these agencies helped keep a third world war at bay by providing a reasonably clear understanding of Soviet military capabilities and activities. Indeed, the modern espionage capabilities of both superpowers greatly reduced anxieties and the likelihood of hair-trigger responses on either side of the Iron Curtain. Moreover, no one wants to see a return to the abuses of power by the secret agencies that were revealed to the American people by the Church Committee during the Year of Intelligence.

Close followers of intelligence issues also understand that the key to a stronger U.S. intelligence capability lies not in upsetting the current oversight arrangements that were so carefully hammered out on the anvil of experience by bipartisan majorities over the years since 1975. Rather, improved performance will require organizational and attitudinal changes within the executive branch. The needed reforms include, above all, further strengthening of the DNI's authority over community-wide budgets and appointments. Otherwise, the intelligence "community" will remain a collection of tribal fiefdoms with little interest in working together and sharing information.

Even more important to the success of American intelligence will be a willingness on behalf of policymakers to clarify their precise intelligence needs to the secret agencies in a timely fashion, then listen with an open mind to the findings of these agencies. This seemingly simple and obvious requirement has, nonetheless, become the Achilles heel of American intelligence—especially the problem of listening. All too often policymakers have shunted aside accurate intelligence that failed to conform with their preconceptions or ideological preferences or, worse still, have exaggerated the intelligence they have received in order to bolster their policy arguments. This charge has been made by critics of the administrations of President George W. Bush and U.K. Prime Minister Tony Blair with respect to the possible existence of weapons of mass destruction in Iraq in 2003. Both are said to have hyped the threat to gain public support for a military invasion.

AN IMMUTABLE PRINCIPLE FOR DEMOCRACIES

A free government must maintain security from foreign and internal threats or it will not survive, but it must have liberty at home as well. A true democracy depends on both. In his memoir, former DCI Robert M. Gates (1996) writes:

> Some awfully crazy schemes might well have been approved had everyone present [in the White House] not known and expected hard questions, debate, and criticism from the Hill. And when, on a few occasions, Congress was kept in the dark, and such schemes did proceed, it was nearly always to the lasting regret of the presidents involved. (p. 559)

Here is another reminder of the necessity for checks on the use of executive power—especially secret executive power. Accountability is a tenet of free government that remains as valid today as it did when it animated the thinking of the Founders and the writing of the American Constitution over 200 years ago.

THE READINGS

In the first selection, Gregory F. Treverton spells out the importance of bringing the intelligence agencies into the normal framework of American government, facing the rigors of accountability just like the more open agencies have always experienced. He refers to the new intelligence oversight as an "uncompleted experiment" and notes that the new procedures, though certainly an improvement on the overlook approach of an earlier era, are still "no guarantee against stupid presidential decisions" (such as the Iran-*contra* affair).

In the next chapter, a former legal counsel in the CIA, Frederic F. Manget, examines the role of the third branch of government in intelligence matters: the judiciary. He reports that the federal courts have not been shy to assert their authority over the intelligence agencies when individual rights may have been jeopardized by intelligence operations. In such cases, judges routinely require intelligence officials to visit the courthouse and explain their activities—another safeguard for liberty envisioned by the Founders when they created the judicial branch of government.

In the following selection, Loch K. Johnson offers a history of the Church Committee investigation in 1975, which opened a Pandora's box of domestic intelligence abuses against the civil liberties of citizens in the United States. The safeguards against future intelligence improprieties established by the committee "have endured," Johnson argues, "and, on most occasions, they have brought greater sobriety to the conduct of intelligence operations at home and abroad. Someone beyond the walls of the secret agencies is now steadily watching their activities; would-be violators of the public trust know they might be caught—a vital check on abuse." Johnson's study of intelligence abuses uncovered in the mid-1970s is a reminder of how this dark stain on the U.S. intelligence ledger came about as a result of the fear of Communism that gripped the nation during the Cold War (see also Johnson 2018).

Fear has frequently been the reason the government has occasionally tilted too far toward security at the expense of liberty: the fear of the Japanese that led President Franklin D. Roosevelt to authorize the internment of Japanese American citizens during World War II; the fear of Communists that produced the witch hunts of the House Un-American Activities Committee and, later, of Senator Joseph McCarthy; the fear of student dissent that led to CIA spying at home during the Vietnam War; the fear of civil rights activists that inspired the FBI's COINTELPRO; and the fear of terrorism that could now lead to the trampling of civil liberties for Arab Americans and other minorities in the search for al-Qaeda supporters inside the United States. Of course, Japanese sabotage was a legitimate concern during the World War II, just as Communism was during the Cold War. Moreover, some students broke the law during the Vietnam War era, even robbing banks and murdering bank guards to support their radical activities. But there are lawful ways to deal with criminal acts without resorting to mass internment, congressional hearings guided less by evidence than innuendo, illegal surveillance, secret harassment of citizens, and jailing of terrorist suspects without legal counsel or formal charges. The goal is to maintain security while preserving democracy, but not to become a totalitarian state in the process.

Finally, this part ends with a series of expert viewpoints on the implications of the major leak in 2013 of National Security Agency documents by an intelligence staff consultant Edward J. Snowden. These electronic files indicated that in the aftermath of the 9/11 attacks the NSA was involved in warrantless wiretapping against American citizens, despite the Foreign Intelligence Surveillance Act of 1978 (FISA) that requires warrants for such purposes. This was a controversial issue for the NSA at the time the wiretaps were ordered by the George W. Bush administration.

22. INTELLIGENCE: WELCOME TO THE AMERICAN GOVERNMENT

GREGORY F. TREVERTON

For most of America's history, intelligence agencies were treated differently from the rest of the government. Their operations were considered too sensitive for normal procedures. Yet when the intelligence agencies were accused in 1974 of abusing their powers by engaging in spying at home, reformers argued that the time had come to bring the dark side of government more into the sunlight of stricter accountability. Treverton examines the merits of viewing intelligence organizations as a regular part of America's government, as subject to constitutional safeguards as any other department or agency.

Congress was deeply engaged in intelligence at the beginning of the Republic: in 1775 the Second Continental Congress set in motion covert operations to secure French supplies for Washington's army. The next year Thomas Paine, the first congressional "leaker," was dismissed for disclosing information from the Committee of Secret Correspondence. For the next century and a half, however, the congressional role lapsed. A disengaged America had little need for foreign intelligence, and for the first thirty years after World War II the preeminence of the president and the imminence of the cold war induced Congress to leave intelligence to the executive, for better or worse.

Events of the 1970s changed that. Since then, the role of Congress in intelligence matters has increased dramatically, and the intelligence community has become like the rest of the government. In the intelligence agencies' relations with Congress, especially, they are coming to resemble the Agriculture or Commerce departments. The House and Senate Intelligence committees have become, like other committees on Capitol Hill, the patrons as well as the overseers of "their" government agencies.

Intelligence officials are finding, as have other members of the executive branch before them, that congressional patrons who control purse strings are also tempted to tell them how to run their business. For their part, members of Congress find secret oversight politically awkward. In the words of Republican Senator William Cohen, then vice-chairman of the Senate Intelligence Committee: "It's not exactly a Faustian bargain, . . . But if we wish to have access, we are bound."[1]

The paradox of secret oversight by the branch of government meant to be characterized by open debate is sharpest in the realm of covert action. There, intelligence officials are tempted to see their congressional overseers as potential leakers, while the overseers fear being misled or deceived or becoming responsible, in secret, for covert actions they cannot easily stop even if they oppose them.

Yet the oversight process has not worked badly even for covert action; ironically, the recent Iran-contra debacle is testimony to that judgment even as it also testifies to the limits whereby process can impose wisdom on the making of American public policy. This grappling over secret *operations* gets the headlines; as a vexing constitutional question, it merits them.

However, covert action is only a small part of oversight, and despite the publicity accorded it, the balance between executive and Congress in the making of foreign policy is probably more affected by a related change: Congress now receives virtually the same intelligence *analysis* as the executive. One senior Central Intelligence Agency (CIA) official described the agency as "involuntarily poised equidistant between the executive and legislative branches."[2] Asking whether intelligence agencies can serve both masters is shorthand for a wider question about the implications of intelligence joining an American government in which the fault lines sometimes divide along the executive-legislative gap but often cut across it.

"PLAUSIBLE DENIAL" AND THE "BUDDY SYSTEM"

Since its first serious investigations of intelligence in the mid-1970s, Congress has become steadily more involved in secret operations. Its most recent investigations into the Iran-contra affair, however, testify to the continuing puzzles, constitutional and procedural. These questions run through all of foreign affairs but are sharper in the realm of intelligence.

The investigations in the mid-1970s began very much in the shadow of Watergate; the press was full of intimations that intelligence agencies had acted outside the law, beyond the ken of Congress and the control even of presidents. Democratic Senator Frank Church, the chairman of the Senate investigating committee, likened the CIA to a "rogue elephant on the rampage."[3] In the event, the committees did not find much evidence of rogue elephants in the CIA or other agencies involved in foreign intelligence, like the National Security Agency or the Defense Intelligence Agency.[4]

Yet the committees did find a troubling looseness in the control of covert action. Part of the problem was CIA abuse of so-called plausible denial, a practice intended to protect the American government, a practice also abused by Oliver North and John Poindexter during the arms sales to Iran in the 1980s. A second part of the problem was a kind of "buddy system" in which oversight consisted of informal conversations between the director of central intelligence (DCI) and a few senior members of Congress. Neither plausible denial nor the buddy system emerged because the CIA had broken free of its political masters. Rather, they emerged because that was how successive administrations and Congress had wanted it.

In 1975, testifying before the Senate committee—often called the "Church committee" after its chairman—about charges that the CIA had tried to kill Fidel Castro, former DCI Richard Helms was vivid in describing plausible denial and almost plaintive in drawing its implications:

> It was made abundantly clear . . . to everybody involved in the operation that the desire was to get rid of the Castro regime and to get rid of Castro . . . the point was that no limitations were put on this

injunction . . . one . . . grows up in [the] tradition of the time and I think that any of us would have found it very difficult to discuss assassinations with a President of the U.S. I just think we all had the feeling that we're hired out to keep those things out of the Oval Office.[5]

If he had ever thought he would later have to testify before Congress about what he had done, Helms reflected, he would have made sure that his orders were clear and in writing.

By their own testimony, not a single member of the National Security Council (NSC) outside the CIA knew of, much less authorized, those plots.[6] Even inside the CIA, officials spoke with each other about these operations only in riddles. And if they spoke of them at all with those outside the CIA charged with approving covert operations, they did so indirectly or in circumlocutions. Thus, in 1975 the Church committee spent hours trying to unravel whether terse references in documents to "disappear" or "direct positive action" or "neutralize" referred to assassination. It could not be sure. And that was precisely the point of plausible denial. Those CIA officials who spoke in circumlocutions could feel they had done their duty as they understood it. Their political superiors could understand what they would, ask for more information if they desired, but also forebear from asking. If things went awry, they could, if they chose, disclaim knowledge and do so more or less honestly.

These effects of plausible denial are extreme in the instance of the Cuban assassination plots, but similar effects ran through covert actions of the 1950s and 1960s. Dean Rusk, who served Presidents Kennedy and Johnson as secretary of state, observed that he routinely knew little of CIA operations: "I never saw a budget of the CIA, for example."[7] Of thousands of covert action projects between 1949 and 1968, only some 600 received consideration outside the CIA by the National Security Council body then charged with reviewing covert operations.

For its part, the American Congress was more interested in making sure the CIA had what it needed in the fight against communism than in overseeing its operations. The fate of several congressional initiatives for improving oversight that came to naught in these early years is eloquent testimony to the mood of the time and the temper of Congress. In early 1955 Democratic Senator Mike Mansfield, later chairman of the Foreign Relations Committee, introduced a resolution calling for a joint oversight committee. The resolution had thirty-five cosponsors. It also had the strong opposition not only of the executive but also of the "club" of senior senators. In hearings on the resolution, Mansfield elicited the following comment from Senator Leverett Saltonstall, the ranking Republican on the Armed Services Committee:

> It is not a question of reluctance on the part of the CIA officials to speak to us. Instead, it is a question of our reluctance, if you will, to seek information and knowledge on subjects which I personally, as a Member of Congress and as a citizen, would rather not have, unless I believed it to be my responsibility to have it because it might involve the lives of American citizens.[8]

In April 1956 the resolution was voted down, 59–27, with a half dozen cosponsors voting against it.

The debate did, however, result in the creation of formal CIA subcommittees in both Armed Services committees. Yet the buddy system remained largely unchanged. Allen Dulles, the near legend, was DCI until the Bay of Pigs fiasco in 1961; relaxed and candid with senior members, he had their absolute trust. In the Senate Armed Services Committee, Senator Richard Russell appointed to the formal subcommittee those senators with whom he had been meeting informally on CIA matters—Saltonstall and Harry Byrd. Later he added Lyndon Johnson and Styles Bridges. When, in 1957, the Appropriations Committee formed a subcommittee for the CIA, its members were Russell, Byrd, and Bridges. They both authorized and appropriated, often at the same meeting. Most CIA business continued to be conducted as before—by Dulles and Russell, meeting informally.

THE CLIMATE CHANGES

The Bay of Pigs marked the end of an era for the CIA. It was a stunning defeat for an agency known only for success. Dulles and his deputy, Richard Bissell, were eased out of their jobs. Yet neither executive procedures for, nor congressional oversight of, intelligence changed all that much.

A decade later, with the big expansion in covert action in Asia as the war in Vietnam heated up, the executive branch undertook somewhat more formal procedures. For instance, the NSC body charged with reviewing covert action (after 1970 called the 40 committee) considered operations in Chile on 23 separate occasions between March 1970 and October 1973, the period surrounding the presidency of Salvador Allende. Still, in numbers, most covert action projects continued not to be

approved by anyone outside the CIA. By the early 1970s only about a fourth of all covert actions came before the NSC review body.[9]

During the 1960s more committees of Congress were receiving more information from the CIA than in the early days; however, about clandestine operations the CIA did not often volunteer information and Congress did not often ask. The role of Congress had not moved from receiving information to overseeing operations. In 1961 after the Bay of Pigs, and again in 1966, Democratic Senator Eugene McCarthy attempted unsuccessfully to revive the idea of a CIA oversight committee.

Watergate and Chile, coming on the heels of the war in Vietnam, changed all that. So did the passing of a congressional generation and the enacting of internal reforms that dispersed authority away from committee chairmen. The buddy system, smooth and private, had depended on a handful of congressional barons. Thus, as a former CIA director of congressional liaison put it, "When Chairmen Russell, [Carl] Hayden, [Mendel] Rivers, and [Carl] Vinson retired between 1965 and 1971, CIA's congressional constituency retired with them."[10] Or as William Colby, the DCI at the time of the first congressional investigations, later recalled:

> There had been a time when the joint hearing held by the Senate's intelligence subcommittees would have been deemed sufficient [to end the matter]. Senators with the seniority and clout of [John] McClellan and [John] Stennis then could easily have squelched any demands for further action on the part of their junior colleagues. But this was no longer the case.[11]

Congress's disinclination to ask about secret operations was the first change. Neither reticence nor deference were hallmarks of the congressional class of 1974, elected as Watergate played out on the nation's television screens. Congress passed the Hughes-Ryan act of 1974, the operative paragraph of which reads:

> No funds appropriated under the authority of this or another Act may be expended by or on behalf of the [CIA] for operations in foreign countries, other than activities intended solely for obtaining necessary intelligence, unless and until the President finds that each such operation is important to the national security of the United States and reports, in a timely fashion, a description and scope of such operation to the appropriate committees of the Congress.[12]

From the verb "finds" came the noun "finding"—a written document bearing the president's signature. As was often the case, Congress sought to change the pattern of executive action not by making specific decisions but rather by changing the process by which decisions were made. The Hughes-Ryan act was intended to end the abuse of plausible denial displayed in the Cuban assassination plots, which seemed to have confused procedures within the executive—and deluded Congress—more than it protected anyone.

Hughes-Ryan required the president to put his name and his reputation on the line. It was meant to ensure that there would be no future wrangles such as those over assassinations. Covert actions, wise or stupid, would reflect presidential decision; there would be no doubt that someone was in charge. It also meant that members of Congress would find it harder to assert that they had been kept in the dark. Less often could they speechify in professed ignorance of covert action. The "appropriate committees" now became six: the Intelligence subcommittees of Armed Services and Appropriations in both houses plus the Foreign Affairs and Foreign Relations committees.

TENDING THE "GOVERNMENT'S" SECRETS

A year later Congress established the Church Committee and a parallel investigating committee in the House, chaired by New York Democrat Otis Pike. Those committees, the Church Committee in particular, represented an innovation in constitutional relations between the executive and Congress.[13] At the heart of the wrangling between the committees and the Ford administration over access to classified documents lay a constitutional issue: were those secret documents, written and classified by the CIA or State, the property of the executive only? Or were they the "government's" documents, to which Congress should have access on terms decided by it and which could be declassified by its decision as well as that of the executive? Popular usage mirrors ambiguity about what constitutes "the government," particularly in foreign affairs. Constitutionally, Congress is a coequal branch of the government, yet people often speak of "the government" more narrowly to refer to a particular administration in power.

The committees did not resolve the question of who controlled documents. In the nature of the system, they could not. But Congress and the executive did move a long way toward the view that even in matters of clandestine operations. Congress has

its own right to the "government's" secret documents and that it bears the responsibility that goes with that right.

The Ford administration was a grudging partner in adjusting the constitutional bargain. A few in the administration, Colby foremost among them, believed the changes were fundamentally correct; others felt that, given the public mood, the administration simply had no choice. The administration had something of a dual approach to the Church Committee. At one level, that of executive prerogatives in foreign affairs, it was opposed to the investigation and its results. It held, thus, that publication of an interim report on assassinations was not only wrong but also a mistake that would harm the reputation of the United States. At another level, however, it was prepared to work with the committee, particularly to protect intelligence sources and methods. In that regard the administration and the committee shared an interest; the committee had no reason to want to endanger intelligence methods or agents' lives. In the case of the assassination report, the issue boiled down to whether the committee would publish the names of some thirty-three CIA officers. The administration argued that publishing the names would tarnish reputations and might, in one or two instances, endanger the individuals in question. Colby even took the issue to district court.

In the end, the committee and the administration reached a sensible compromise. The committee agreed to delete the names of twenty of the officers, required for neither the substance nor the credibility of the report. The remaining names were left in. Most were those of senior officers and were already in the public domain. The committee felt, moreover, that senior officials should be held publicly accountable for their actions. Like most compromises, it pleased neither side fully but was one with which both could live.[14]

In seeking to establish its position, the Church committee was assiduous about leaks. Not a single secret worth mention got out.[15] The same could not be said of the Pike Committee, whose entire final report leaked into the press in 1976 after the fall House had voted not to release it until the president certified that it did not contain information that would harm U.S. intelligence activities.[16]

When the House, like the Senate, later decided to establish a permanent intelligence committee, the Pike Committee experience, which had created acrimony not only between the committee and the administration but within the House as well, was much on the House's collective mind. As one sophisticated former staffer observed: "The message from the House was clear: no more fiascos. The new . . . committee would have to stay in line; the honor of the House was at stake."[17]

The House did not agree to a permanent committee until 1977, a year after the Senate. The vote was closer—227–171 in the House, compared with 75–22 in the Senate; and the House committee was granted less autonomy and control over classified information. For instance, the Senate committee was authorized to disclose classified information over the president's objection, while in the House that right rested with the full body. The House committee was also smaller and more partisan—13 members, nine of them Democrats, in a House of 435, compared with 15, eight Democrats, in a Senate of 100. The House Democrats were chosen by the Speaker, not the majority caucus, evidence of a desire to retain control. By contrast, the Senate committee, following the relatively bipartisan approach of the Church Committee, made the ranking minority member the vice-chairman, a unique arrangement in Congress.

Initially, the two congressional investigations resulted only in two new permanent oversight committees, increasing the number of congressional overseers of intelligence from six committees to eight, albeit ones with more access to information. Yet the institutional legacy of permanent select committees in each house of Congress has turned out to be an important one. The committees established the principle of rotating memberships, limiting tenures to six years in the House and eight in the Senate, to broaden their representation within Congress, thus guarding against a recurrence of the buddy system in image or in fact.

Reflecting their different lineages, the Senate committee was initially more self-confident in its approach to oversight. A cadre of members and staff from the Church committee moved to the new permanent committee, while the House started afresh, staffed mostly by ex-intelligence officials. Over time, however, the House staff, though smaller and divided along partisan lines, acquired the reputation of being more professional, especially in those aspects of oversight that seldom find their way into headlines—budgets, collection systems, and intelligence products.

Over time, too, the committees were stamped by the styles and personalities of their chairmen as well as by the character of their parent bodies. The House committee was chaired in the 1980s by Edward Boland and Lee Hamilton, members of experience and stature in the legislature by comparison with their counterparts on the Senate side, Republican David Durenberger and Democrat Patrick Leahy. The Republican ascendance to control of the Senate in 1980 not only brought new young senators to control of the committee, but also shifted the focal point for congressional scrutiny of secret operations to the House. And it frayed cooperation between the two committees.

By the latter half of the 1980s, with the Democrats again in control of the Senate, the Senate committee reflected its parent body in being less partisan than the House. Its Democrats were mostly moderates, senators like David Boren, Sam Nunn, and Ernest Hollings, who had few counterparts on the House committee. Some of those moderate Democrats, especially southerners, were attracted to the Intelligence Committee as a way to become active in foreign affairs without acquiring the liberal taint of the Foreign Relations Committee.

The Carter administration, disinclined from the start to resort to covert action, found its intelligence relations with Congress easy. It first pressed the House to establish a permanent intelligence committee, then cooperated with Congress in passing the Intelligence Oversight Act of 1980, the most important law in the realm of covert action. The act cut back the executive's reporting requirements for covert action to the two Intelligence committees; eight committees were too unwieldy for both executive and Congress, and virtually invited executive charges of being "too leaky." At the same time, however, the act charged the two committees with informing other relevant committees, especially Foreign Affairs, Foreign Relations, and the two Appropriations committees. It also made clear that Congress wanted to be notified of all covert actions, not just those carried out by the CIA; secret executive recourse to other agencies, in particular the military, was denied.

Congress also tiptoed toward prior notification of covert action; the "timely fashion" of the Hughes-Ryan act, which allowed notification after the fact (within twenty-four hours came to be the understanding), became "fully and currently informed," including "any significant anticipated intelligence activity" in the 1980 act. Yet notifying Congress still was not a "condition precedent to the initiation" of covert action. And the act gave the president another escape hatch, for in emergencies he was permitted to limit notice to eight members—the chairmen and ranking minority members of the Intelligence committees, the Speaker and minority leader of the House, and the majority and minority leaders of the Senate—the "gang of eight" or the "eight wise men," depending on the describer's inclinations.

THE "COVERT" WAR IN CENTRAL AMERICA

The tussle between executive and Congress, which had been restrained when operators and overseers shared the view that the covert instrument should be used sparingly, grew more passionate with the surge of covert actions in the 1980s. The Reagan administration came into office determined to make covert assistance to "freedom fighters" around the world a key element of its global pressure on the Soviet Union. Strikingly, in light of what came later, Reagan's executive order 12333 gave the CIA full responsibility for covert actions except in time of war or by specific presidential instruction.[18]

With the new administration, however, attitudes changed more than directives or procedures. One congressional staffer referred to men like NSC staffer Lieutenant Colonel Oliver North as "field grades," people eager for action, long on energy, but short on political savvy. William Miller, the staff director of both the Church committee and the first permanent Senate Intelligence Committee, observed that the CIA and its sister agencies were led in the late 1970s by people who had been through the experience of investigation and reform. They were "so immersed in the constitutional questions that they could recite chapter and verse. Questions of law and balance occurred naturally to them." By contrast, the Reagan leadership was dominated by "advocates, people who were always trying to get around the roadblocks, who were looking for a way to get it done."[19]

In Central America, the long reign of the Somoza family in Nicaragua had come to an end in 1979, bringing to power the regime's armed opponents, the Sandinista National Liberation Front, in uneasy partnership with a range of civilian opposition groups. Early in its tenure, the Reagan administration charged that the Sandinistas were becoming a base for Cuban and Soviet subversion in the region and, specifically, that they were shipping arms to guerrilla opponents of the U.S.-supported government of El Salvador. At first, the Sandinistas were confronted primarily by remnants of Somoza's hated National Guard who had found sanctuary in Honduras, but over time several of the Sandinistas'

original allies fell out with the government. One of them opened a new anti-Sandinista front operating out of Costa Rica.

Congressional opposition to the administration's course in Nicaragua grew in direct proportion to the breakdown in congressional-executive relations. The administration sought to unite the Sandinistas' armed opponents—dubbed the contras—and to support them. Yet the purpose of that covert support seemed a moving target, which suggested to Congress either confusion or deception. In November 1981 President Reagan signed National Security Council Decision Directive 17 proposing to build a force of contras to interdict arms shipments from Nicaragua to the rebels in El Salvador. However, the directive, when turned into a finding, contained language—"engage in paramilitary . . . operations in Nicaragua, and elsewhere"—that seemed to permit almost anything.[20] The congressional Intelligence committees first made clear in their classified reports on the CIA budget that they opposed covert efforts to overthrow the Sandinista government or Nicaragua. Then, at the end of 1982, they put that language, as the Boland amendment, publicly into the appropriations bill. Named for Edward P. Boland, then chairman of the House Intelligence Committee it stipulated that no money could be used "for the purpose of overthrowing the Government of Nicaragua or provoking a military exchange between Nicaragua and Honduras."[21]

The aims of America's covert intervention remained in dispute while the war intensified, especially as the CIA opened a second front in Costa Rica. In response, Boland and the House shifted their focus from appropriations to authorization, proposing not to limit covert action in Nicaragua but to end it. The House voted to do so in July 1983. However, the Senate Intelligence committee, with the Republicans in the majority, was prepared to approve more money if the administration would be precise about its objectives. The administration "thoroughly scrubbed" a new finding, which was signed in September 1983.[22]

In October the House again voted to end the contra program but at year's end the House-Senate conference compromised, accepting the revised presidential finding, which expanded the American aim from halting arms flows from Nicaragua to pressuring the Sandinistas to negotiate with their neighbors. However Congress capped funding at $24 million, enough for one year's operations, thus requiring the administration to return to Congress before the end of the fiscal year if it wanted the program to continue.[23]

Any limited American objective seemed less plausible after revelations early the next year that the CIA itself had mined Nicaraguan harbors. The mining, a new phase in the covert war, was itself an act of war and one that threatened the shipping of both American allies and the Soviet Union. The operation was approved by the president in the winter, probably in December 1983.[24] The Sandinistas protested on January 3, 1984, that the contras were laying mines in Nicaraguan harbors, and the rebel leaders, who plainly had no capacity to lay mines on their own, finally learned their lines and announced on January 8 that they would do so.

On January 31, 1984, DCI William Casey met with the House Intelligence Committee and mentioned the mining, though the meeting was primarily about releasing further funds for the overall contra project. The House committee apparently did not share its information with its Senate colleagues, although the CIA may have briefed several members of the Senate committee and its staff. The Senate, however, was pushing toward its February recess, and the administration twice asked for a delay so that Secretary of State George Shultz could also attend. As a result, a full briefing of the Senate committee was delayed, and many, perhaps most, members remained unaware of the operation, especially of the direct CIA role in it.

Casey first met with the full Senate Intelligence committee on March 8, for over an hour, but this meeting too dealt primarily with authorizing the release of funds, over which the Intelligence committee was fighting a jurisdictional battle with Appropriations. Only one sentence dealt with the mining, and it, like the rest of the briefing, was delivered in Casey's inimitable mumble.[25] Many on the committee did not learn of the mining until a month later, and then almost by accident.

Casey nodded toward the letter of the law with his brief reference, but the episode angered even Senator Barry Goldwater, the Republican committee chairman and a man not known for his opposition to covert action. He had not understood the reference. When he learned about the mining operation, once the committee staff received a full briefing on April 2, he was furious. His letter to Casey, which leaked into the press, was notable for its unsenatorial prose as well as for its displeasure: "It gets down to one, little, simple phrase: I am pissed off!"[26] In the wake of this episode, the Senate committee moved toward the House's position, and Congress cut off further covert assistance with a second Boland amendment enacted into law in October 1984, thus rejecting the president's request for $21 million more.

By the end of 1984 the House of Representatives had voted three times against paramilitary aid, only to have the operation rescued by House-Senate conferences. Yet despite these losses, the Reagan administration was succeeding in framing the debate on its own ground. Americans' deep ambivalence—their fears of U.S. involvement competed with their distaste for the Sandinistas—left covert support standing as a "middle option," cheap in money and American blood, and hard for members of Congress, even Democrats, to vote against lest they be branded "soft on communism" by a popular president.

In early 1985 President Reagan again asked for aid to the contras, this time for $14 million. The House again voted down the aid after a sharp debate. However, when Sandinista leader Daniel Ortega unwisely journeyed to Moscow just after the vote, those Democrats who had voted against covert aid looked soft and foolish. They responded by enacting economic sanctions, largely symbolic, against Nicaragua. In August 1985 Congress compromised on $27 million in "nonmilitary" aid to the contras; this was not to be administered by the CIA, and the agency was barred from direct contact with the contras or assistance in their training. Congress did not restore CIA funding for this purpose until October 1986.

This off-again, on-again funding, deeply frustrating to those in the Reagan administration most committed to the contras, bred circumventions of the congressional restrictions—efforts suspected in press accounts as early as the spring of 1985. The second Boland amendment applied to the CIA, the Defense Department, and "any other agency or entity involved in intelligence."[27] Some in the administration felt it did not prevent the NSC staff or other officials from seeking aid from other sources. By early 1984, as the $24 million ran out, the president directed the NSC staff, in the words of national security adviser Robert McFarlane, "to keep the contras together 'body and soul.'" Casey and other officials began to approach governments ranging from Israel to Brunei to Saudi Arabia and quietly canvassed private sources in the United States, South Korea, Taiwan, and Latin America. That private support totaled some $34 million during the period of the aid cutoff.[28]

By May 1984, when the congressional appropriation ran out, Oliver North, the NSC staff's deputy director for political-military affairs, had become coordinator of the private support, dubbed "the Enterprise" by those involved. In October when Congress barred any CIA involvement, the agency issued a "cease and desist" order to its stations. Nevertheless, about a dozen CIA officers remained involved in North's operation, apparently construing his role to signify White House authorization. By the fall of 1985, North was overseeing the shipping of privately purchased arms to the contras and the construction of a secret airfield in Costa Rica. North, who also called his operation "Project Democracy," relied on a network of conservative organizations and ex-military men, one of whom, retired general Richard V. Secord, was also a key conduit for arms sales to Iran.

In the fall of 1986 a Beirut newspaper published a bizarre account of a secret mission to Iran the previous May by former national security adviser McFarlane. The account, which first seemed another piece of partisan Middle East nonsense, turned out to be true. McFarlane's delivery of U.S. weapons to Iran was part of a sequence running back to August 1985. The first two shipments had been made by Israel, through middlemen, with U.S. approval and assurance that depleted Israeli stocks would be replenished. The operation, also managed day to day by North, was so closely held that even the CIA was at first cut out, though Casey himself was central. Critical meetings were held with no analytic papers prepared beforehand and no record of decisions kept afterward.

North sought and received CIA help in November 1985 when, in a comedy of errors, Secord could not get one shipment through Portugal to Israel. When he heard of the CIA involvement, John McMahon, the agency's deputy director, angrily barred any further CIA involvement without a presidential finding. The next month the president signed one finding to provide retroactive approval for the shipments; the new national security adviser, Admiral John Poindexter, destroyed that finding a year later because, he later testified, it would have been embarrassing to the president.[29]

The president approved another finding on January 17, 1986, "to establish contact with moderate elements within and outside the Government of Iran by providing these elements with arms, equipment and related materiel." However, the accompanying background paper, prepared by North, was explicit about the link to getting U.S. hostages out of Lebanon:

> This approach . . . may well be our only way to achieve the release of the Americans held in Beirut. . . . If all of the hostages are not released after the first shipment of 1,000 weapons, further transfers would cease.[30]

In February, American arms were first shipped directly from the United States by the CIA to Israel for transfer to Iran. Three other shipments were made, the last in late October. In all, some 2,000 TOW anti-tank weapons, as well as other weapons and spare parts were sold to Iran. Three U.S. hostages were released, but three more were taken during the course of the operation.

The strange tale became more bizarre when it was revealed that the profits of the Iranian arms sales had been diverted to support the Nicaraguan contras. The arms had been sold to Iran for nearly $16 million more than the CIA had paid the Pentagon for them. In a scheme masterminded by North, the profits were then laundered through Swiss bank accounts, to be drawn on by the contras. When the scheme was revealed, North was fired, and his boss, Poindexter resigned.

The story unfolded first through an executive investigating panel, named by the president in December 1986 and chaired by former Senator John Tower. Then Congress began a joint Senate-House investigation in January 1987, which treated the nation to the spectacle of public testimony by the central figures, most notably Oliver North, through the hot summer of 1987. The focus of both investigations was narrowly the diversion of profits from the Iran arms sales to the contras: had the president authorized or known of it? This charge remained unproven. The investigations, however, did what Congress had been unable, in part unwilling, to do before—unravel the trail of private support for the contras.

The narrow initial focus broadened further through the criminal trials of McFarlane, North, and Poindexter. McFarlane, distraught to the point of breakdown by what had been done, pleaded guilty to lying to Congress. North, the loyal soldier to the end, asserted his innocence; he was found guilty of destroying documents and other charges but not of deceiving Congress. North's light sentence reflected the discrediting of what had been the administration's primary defense, one accepted by the

Tower panel: that the wrongdoing was the result of a small cabal centered on North. North plainly was central, but just as plainly the circle of those involved was wider than the administration wanted to acknowledge.

SOURCES OF TENSION:
EXTERNAL AND INTERNAL

The sources of tension in the intelligence role of Congress are displayed in this history. They are both external and internal to Congress. The houses of Congress not only share a distrust of the executive, no matter which party is in power, but they are also jealous of each other. The two Intelligence committees do not automatically share information, as is apparent in the case of the mining of Nicaragua's harbors. Working together is all the harder if, as in this case, there is both disagreement on the merits and partisan division: Democrats controlled the House, Republicans the Senate from 1980 until 1986. In December 1985, during the time CIA assistance was cut off, the Intelligence committees did approve some money for "communications" and "advice" to the contras, subject to conditions negotiated with the committees. There then ensued an exchange of letters suggesting that the two chairmen were uncertain—or disagreed—over what was permitted and what was proscribed.[31]

Moreover, despite their authority, the Intelligence committees do not monopolize oversight of covert operations. Because covert actions are foreign policy, the Foreign Affairs and Foreign Relations committees have an interest in their authorization; because they cost money, the Appropriations committees have their stakes. The tracks of both sets of jurisdictional battles are visible in the Nicaraguan episode.

However, the sharper tensions arise between Congress and the executive. Even with good will in both branches, congressional overseers have to get deeply into the details of ongoing operations, which is hard for them and uncomfortable for covert operators in the executive branch. Critical details can fall between the cracks: it may be that Senate committee members, like Goldwater, simply were not paying attention when Casey mumbled about the mining. Even their staffs are hard-pressed to keep up with the details of forty-odd covert actions. As one staffer close to the process put it: "How can you know which detail will jump up and bite you? Things move fast.

How long did the mining take from beginning to end? A few weeks."[32]

For members, oversight remains something of an unnatural act. They are not hard to interest in intelligence; the lure of secrecy and the mystique of covert operations are a powerful tug on their attentions. At the beginning of the One-hundredth Congress in 1987, 60 members of the House signed up for four openings on the Intelligence Committee. Given rotating memberships, chairs can come quickly; Republican Senator Dave Durenberger became chairman of the Senate committee after only six years. Still, the assignment is one among many, whatever its fascination. Members have little political reason to become involved, still less to take responsibility for particular operations. Politicians' temptation to use their special access to information on morning talk shows competes uneasily with the disciplines of committee membership. Sometimes the special access is, in political terms, more a burden than an asset; as Senator Daniel K. Inouye, the first chairman of the permanent Senate Intelligence Committee, observed, in words not much different from Saltonstall's thirty years before: "How would you like to know a very, very high official of a certain government was on our payroll?"[33]

On balance, members have resolved the contest between responsibility and self-promotion or credit taken in favor of the former. The temptations of the latter are always there, and the dividing line is fine, but the penalties for being seen to traverse it are high: recent incidents demonstrate both these points. In early 1987 Senator Patrick Leahy, the chairman of the Senate Intelligence Committee, was forced to resign his chairmanship after leaking an unclassified but not yet released version of the committee's Iran-contra report. His action was unwise, but by the standard applied to Leahy, the executive branch would be depopulated. In 1988 House Speaker Jim Wright told a reporter that he had "received clear testimony from CIA people that they have deliberately done things to provoke an overreaction on the part of the Government in Nicaragua."[34] He was not the first to characterize American policy in that way, he later denied he had leaked secret testimony, and the incident was later overshadowed by his other ethical problems. But at the time, invoking the CIA as the source was enough to earn him a storm of criticism.

Iran-contra provides most graphic testimony to the tensions in the congressional role when the committees confront a determined president, especially if they themselves are of divided mind. Administrations, especially one as committed to covert operations as the Reagan administration, are bound to want the flexibility of broad, general findings that give the CIA room to adapt to changing circumstances. Congress is almost equally bound to be wary of signing a blank check, particularly when the administration is committed. McGeorge Bundy, who ran the NSC review committee for the Kennedy and Johnson administrations, emphasized by understatement in 1975 the difficulty reviewers outside the CIA confront:

> I think it has happened that an operation is presented in one way to a committee . . . and executed in a way that is different from what the committee thought it had authorized.[35]

Norman Mineta, a charter member of the House Intelligence Committee, put his frustration more colorfully in speaking of the executive: "They treat us like mushrooms. Keep us in the dark and feed us a lot of manure."[36]

At more than one point in the Iran-contra affair, administration officials deceived Congress. The January 1986 arms sales finding was explicit: do not tell Congress. The congressional overseers did not find out about the operation until the following autumn—not "fully and currently informed" by anyone's definition. Earlier, the Intelligence committees responded to press accounts that the ban on aid to the contras was being circumvented. In August 1985, for instance, the House asked the administration about North's activities. The response drafted by McFarlane and North and signed by the former, said that at no time did I or any member of the National Security Council staff violate the letter or spirit of the restrictions.[37]

That is outright deception, even granting some ambiguity in the wording of the ban. Did the wording mean no administration official could seek other sources of aid? If so, how could Congress enforce the ban? Its means were limited, as they are in more normal cases. Even if the committees are united in their opposition to an operation, they cannot easily stop it, for if the administration is determined to proceed it can fund the operation for a year from the CIA Contingency Reserve.[38] Congress has in two cases resorted to public legislation banning covert action—the Boland amendments and the 1976 Clark-Tunney amendment on Angola. These were signs that it did not trust the administration, or its designated overseers of covert action, or both.

In the instance of aid to the contras, however, Congress's will was also limited. In part, it was reluctant to take on a popular president even on a controversial issue. The reluctance is customary in relations between the executive and Congress, even if the president is less popular than Reagan; unless the president is plainly out of step with the American people, members of Congress do not like to confront the presidency. The House Intelligence Committee, like its parent body, was sharply divided over aid to the contras; in later votes, whichever side captured a group of thirty-odd swing votes, mostly Democratic and mostly conservative southerners, carried the day. The Senate although wavering, probably had a consistent majority favoring aid in principle.

In those circumstances, it is perhaps less surprising that the committees were halfhearted in inquiring into violations of the ban that their later, retrospective investigations framed the issues narrowly or that Congress breathed an audible sigh of relief that Reagan had left the presidency by the time new revelations during the trials of his former aides might have raised questions of impeachment.

LIMITS TO THE SYSTEM

Aid to the contras was as divisive within the Intelligence committees as it was in the nation, but almost every other covert action has elicited a near consensus, even within the House committee. The congressional overseers have been informed of the covert action and recorded their views; presidents cannot lightly ignore those views, especially if they are held by senior committee members in both parties. Lest the president miss the point, the committees can take a formal vote to underscore their view. More than once, apparently, such votes have induced a president to rescind approval of an operation.[39]

In other cases the committees have said, in the words of one staff member, "Hey, do you know how risky that is?"[40] Hearing an affirmative response, they have let the program go ahead despite their doubts. They did so in the case of Angola, letting the administration resume covert aid to Jonas Savimbi's UNITA (Union for the Total Independence of Angola, in its Portuguese acronym) in 1986 to the tune of some $15 million a year; they did so in that case despite the fact that Lee Hamilton, the House Intelligence committee chairman, took his personal opposition to the House floor.

The Reagan administration wanted to make use of covert action much more frequently than did its predecessor, and the oversight committees, reflecting the mood of Congress and probably of the American people as well, assented to that expansion of covert action. The centerpiece of the Reagan program was aid to the resistance in Afghanistan, begun under the Carter administration, which came to total more than a half billion dollars a year by 1986. Indeed, Congress was if anything ahead of the executive, appropriating unrequested additional money for the resistance in 1983 and pressing the administration to deliver more sophisticated weaponry.

In a sense the system "worked" even in the instance of arms sales to Iran. In deciding to sell, the president pursued a policy that was opposed by his secretaries of state and defense and about which he was afraid to inform the congressional oversight committees. Those should have been warning signals aplenty that the policy was unwise.

If presidents are determined to do something stupid, they will find someone, somewhere, to do it.

In seeking to circumvent the requirements of process, the president, it appears, also set himself up for deception. It was he who was not told when the Iran and contra operations crossed. Keeping Congress in the dark also encouraged looseness within the executive, just as it did a quarter century earlier in the CIA's attempted assassinations of Fidel Castro. North and Poindexter mistakenly construed plausible denial after their own fashion, much the same as Helms and his colleagues had, keeping their president ignorant in order to protect him. Although convinced the president would approve the use of proceeds from the Iranian arms sales for the contras as an "implementation" of his policy, Poindexter "made a very deliberate decision not to ask the President" so that he could "insulate [him] from the decision and provide some future deniability."[41]

When the president's closest advisers become the operators, the president loses them as a source of detached judgment on the operations. They become advocates; not protectors of the president (even if he does not quite realize his need for protection). So it was with McFarlane and Poindexter; once committed, they had reason to overlook the warning signals thrown up by the process. Excluding Congress also excluded one more "political scrub," one more source of advice about what most Americans would find acceptable.

In circumventing the ban on aid to the contras, the Reagan administration's approach to Congress was more one of contempt than of exclusion. An isolated act or two of aiding the contras would have been a close call, given the ambiguity of the ban. But close congressional votes do not excuse establishing "the Enterprise." Poindexter and North were explicit in their later testimony before Congress: "I simply did not want any outside interference," and "I didn't want to tell Congress anything," they said, respectively.[42]

"The Enterprise" is the most troubling piece of the entire story, one the congressional investigations paused over far too briefly. It was an attempt to escape congressional oversight entirely, to construct a CIA outside the American government. As North put it: "Director Casey had in mind . . . an overseas entity that was . . . self-financing, independent of appropriated monies."[43] The idea was dangerous, but the price the administration eventually paid for it was high. If covert actions are to be undertaken, they should be done by the agency of government constructed to do them—the Central Intelligence Agency. It has both the expertise and the accountability.

INFORMATION AND THE BALANCE OF POWER

Disputes over secret operations between Congress and the executive have grabbed the headlines, yet the day-to-day balance of power between the two branches has been more affected by the sharply increased availability of intelligence analysis to Congress. This latter change has coincided with the tug-of-war over operations and so has been obscured by it. However, Congress now receives nearly every intelligence item the executive does. In this way, too, the intelligence agencies are coming to have a more customary relationship with Congress, but one that is more awkward for them than for the Agriculture or Commerce departments.

Intelligence agencies, the CIA in particular, were conceived as servants of their executive masters. It bears remembering that *the* intelligence issue in the early postwar period was not operations; rather it was avoiding another Pearl Harbor. That problem was what to do about fragmented intelligence that could neither sort out signals of warning from surrounding "noise" nor make the warning persuasive to senior officials of government. This problem, along with the balkanized way the separate armed services had fought World War II, begat the National Security Council. It also begat the sequence of efforts to coordinate American intelligence, beginning with the Central Intelligence Group in 1946.

Congress was a promoter of these changes but essentially a bystander to them. As in other areas of government, it used laws to shape processes in the executive branch. Long after it had tried to centralize and formalize the intelligence process in the executive, it left its own oversight of intelligence and its role in receiving intelligence information informal and fragmented. Changing congressional attitudes toward operations both coincided with and produced an altered view of intelligence products. If Congress was to know about and judge covert operations, it was logical to assess them in light of the intelligence premises on which they were based.

Some numbers suggest the extent of the change over the past decade. Virtually everything the CIA produces goes to the two Intelligence committees, and most also goes to the Foreign Affairs, Foreign Relations, Armed Services, and Appropriations committees. All eight committees receive the CIA "newspaper," the National Intelligence Daily (NID). The CIA alone sends some 5,000 reports to Congress each year and conducts over a thousand oral briefings.[44] By contrast, CIA records show only twenty-two briefings to Congress (on topics other than covert action) about Chile in the decade 1964–74.[45] Overall, the CIA gave perhaps a hundred briefings a year to Congress in the mid-1970s.[46]

What is true of CIA analyses is also the case in varying degrees for the products of other intelligence agencies. Just as the Intelligence committees get a biweekly list of new CIA publications, they receive indexes from the Defense Intelligence Agency (DIA), along with the DIA daily summary.[47] The National Security Agency provides weekly summaries of signals intelligence. Committee staffers can get access to "raw" intelligence, like defense attache or CIA agent reports, by special request, although in the most sensitive cases these must be made by the committee chairman to the DCI. People move in both directions from committee staffs to intelligence community analyst jobs, and occasionally committee staffers get friendly calls from intelligence community analysts suggesting that they ask for a particular item.

The change is marked enough without overstating it. Because intelligence is available on Capitol Hill does not mean it is read. Congress is an oral culture, while written products are the intelligence analyst's predilection. If they read, members of Congress, like their counterparts in the executive, will turn to the *New York Times* and *Washington Post* before they pick up the NID. The committees, especially the Intelligence committees, are tightly compartmented in their handling of classified material, which means that getting access to some intelligence is at least a bother. And since knowledge is power and access prestige, Hill staffers who receive intelligence may hold it, not share it.

The people within the intelligence community who conduct the briefings or write the reports are analysts, not operators. They are more professorial than conspiratorial in temperament. They work for the CIA's Directorate of Intelligence, not its Directorate of Operations, and they tell their neighbors openly that they work for the CIA or for the State Department's Bureau of Intelligence and Research or the Pentagon's DIA.

They get much of their information about foreign governments the same way academics do, through reading periodicals or transcripts of media monitored openly by the Foreign Broadcast Information Service. In addition they have access to two sets of secret sources—diplomatic cables sent by State Department officers abroad and raw intelligence, such as agent reports produced by the CIA's Directorate of Operations or foreign communications monitored secretly by the National Security Agency.

The change is dramatic for these analysts, many of whom had never dealt with Congress before a decade ago and all of whom have been steeped in a professional culture that separates intelligence from policy lest the former be biased or politicized through contact with the latter. When the subject is technical and, preferably, out of the limelight, briefing Congress is a welcome chance to educate another set of consumers. Yet the analysts recognize that members of Congress, like executive officials, seldom are disinterested consumers of information. They seek it as leverage, often to be used against the executive that is the analysts' ostensible master. If the subject is politically hot, like Central America in the 1980s, the experience is painful, the sense of being manipulated keen.

CONGRESS AS LEVER OR ALLY?

Sometimes Congress listens to intelligence analysis when the executive will not. In such cases, benefits and risks are two sides of the same coin. In June 1987, Representative Duncan Hunter smashed a Toshiba radio-cassette player on the steps of the Capitol. The purpose of his stunt was attention: Toshiba and a Norwegian firm had deliberately sold the Soviet Union milling equipment that would make Soviet submarines quieter, hence harder to track. Hunter charged that the $17 million sale might "cost the West $30 billion to regain the superiority we lost."[48] The Toshiba bashing was the culmination of a series of events in which the CIA's Technology Transfer Assessment Center (TTAC) had, in effect, hawked its analyses around Washington.

The story began not with TTAC but with a disaffected Japanese employee who took the story of the Toshiba sale to COCOM, the Paris-based export control organization comprising the NATO allies and Japan. Staffers at COCOM, however, accepted Toshiba's word that it had sold only permitted technology. The employee then took his story to the U.S. embassy in Tokyo, which put him in touch with TTAC. The first stop for TTAC was the State Department, which made a diplomatic "demarche" to Japan. Like most such demarches, it was, however, brushed off for want of hard information. Moreover, the State Department looked askance at TTAC: TTAC's desire to control the issue left its colleagues at State's Bureau of Intelligence and Research feeling cut out, and policy officials at State were nervous about the repercussions of the issue on relations with two allies. Yet the tradition of CIA independence, plus TTAC's control of the issue, made it difficult for State to influence what TTAC said.

The next stop was the Defense Department, where Undersecretary Fred Iklé, a willing listener, agreed to take the issue up in his forthcoming trip to Japan. For Iklé the issue was one among several, not primary, and his trip produced little more than the demarche. But Iklé's office, briefed by TTAC and now with a better case in hand, in turn briefed Senator Jake Gam, a kindred hard-liner on technology transfer. At about the same time, December 1986, mention of this "major technology transfer" appeared in classified written briefings to the two Intelligence committees. Word was spreading.

Within two months the issue was public. First it went again to COCOM, where this time TTAC briefed representatives of the fifteen member nations. As Japan and Norway responded, Washington buzzed with rumors of a big new case. In late February the House Armed Services seapower subcommittee was briefed on the issue, and the next month, at hearings on the omnibus trade bill, Iklé's deputy, Richard Perle, referred obliquely to an export control violation he "could go into in a classified hearing." A week later the conservative *Washington Times* broke the story, quoting unnamed officials "outside the government."

From then on, TTAC did not lack audiences; it had more than it wanted. Members of Congress outbid each other in proposals for retaliating against the wrongdoers, especially Toshiba, for Norway had acted to defuse the issue by admitting guilt and working with the United States. In the end, the weight of other interests at play in U.S.-Japanese relations began to be felt, and congressional leaders cooperated with the executive in enacting sanctions against Toshiba that, while sounding tough, were relatively mild.

The kind of interaction with Congress reflected in the Toshiba affair was uncharted water. On one hand, Guy DuBois, the principal TTAC analyst, sought to hold to the traditional line between intelligence and policy: "Once you state a position, how that position affects policy . . . is not your business."[49] On the other hand, DCI Casey had given TTAC a mandate that was more than providing information; it was to be a player in a quasi-prosecutorial process. In that sense, its information was to be nearly self-implementing: if it could prove guilt then that would frame the response. Congress was not the principal prosecutor, but telling it was a way to make sure someone paid attention.

The Toshiba case coincided with William Webster's arrival as DCI, replacing the late William Casey; plainly, Webster's main mission was repairing relations with Congress after Iran-contra. "To Webster," the TTAC analyst recalled, "Congress has an insatiable appetite and to the extent we can, we satisfy it." Moreover, "if a Congressman finds out that you decided not to be completely forthcoming," the credibility of the CIA could be damaged. The CIA's role, however, was not simply responding to congressional requests: "If they ask a stupid question, tell them it's stupid, then tell them what the smart question is and answer it."

It is still rare for Congress to be the lead consumer of intelligence. Most of the time Congress's effect is indirect. Since Congress will also know what the executive knows, executive officials are prudent to pay attention to intelligence lest they be skewered by Congress for the failure. Consider the contrast between the fall of the shah of Iran in 1978 and the departure from the Philippines of President Ferdinand Marcos in 1986.[50] The experience with the shah had taught policy officials in both the executive and Congress not to dismiss unwelcome news about Marcos, nor to assume, as they had about the shah, that Marcos knew his politics better than Washington did. That the Philippine opposition—moderate, Catholic, and U.S.-educated—was both much more accessible to intelligence collection and much more acceptable than Iran's mullahs made the lesson easier to learn.

The Philippine crisis moved more slowly than the Iranian, beginning in earnest with the assassination of opposition leader Benigno Aquino on the airport tarmac in Manila as he returned from the United States in August 1983. The intelligence community concluded that if Marcos had not ordered the assassination, it almost certainly had been done on his behalf. From then on the Philippines was on the congressional agenda almost as much as it was on that of the executive. The contrast with Iran could hardly be sharper; a 1979 House Intelligence committee postmortem on the Iran case contains not a single reference to Congress.[51]

The State Department worried about Congress in the instance of Toshiba, but in the instance of the Philippines the East Asia "mafia" in the executive—including State, Defense, and the NSC—welcomed congressional pressure as a way to persuade *their bosses*, not least the president, that Marcos might have to go. An August 1985 Senate Intelligence Committee report concluded that "the Marcos government is unlikely to pursue the changes necessary to stop the economic hemorrhaging, to slow or halt the insurgency or to heal the major lesions that are infecting the political process."[52] Later in the year, the links between Congress and the executive were tightened when one Senate Foreign Relations Committee staffer moved to the intelligence community to be national intelligence officer for East Asia and the Pacific.

Another Senate Foreign Relations Committee staff member described the interaction:

> The people in the State Department were using us, the Foreign Relations Committee, to get their point across in the White House. They were delighted when (Chairman Richard] Lugar decided to write a letter, not to Marcos but to the President of the United States. In other words, we laid it right on the President; We shifted our focus from the President of the Philippines to the President of the United States.

In November 1985, Marcos called a snap election for February 1986. The opposition managed to unite to name Aquino's widow, Corazon, as its presidential candidate. In December 1985 the intelligence community was still predicting a narrow Marcos victory, but by January 1986 it labeled the election too close to call, and on the eve of the vote it actually predicted an Aquino victory while also betting that Marcos would fix the results if need be. On January 30 President Reagan announced a bipartisan mission of U.S. election observers, cochaired by Lugar.

The effect of Congress's access to intelligence was most evident in the crunch. Most of the U.S. observers witnessed fraud by the ruling party, but as late as February 11, as votes trickled in, Reagan commented that the United States was concerned about both violence and "the possibility of fraud, although it could have been that all of that was occurring on both sides," a quote that so pleased Marcos that he had it shown over and over on Philippine television.[53]

At this point, the intelligence community was told, in effect, to put up or shut up. It responded with convincing proof of massive fraud by Marcos's party. Thus the administration had to act in the knowledge that Congress would soon have the same proof. Its options—to ride out the storm with Marcos, for instance—were correspondingly constrained. By February 15 the White House had dropped the "fraud on both sides" line, and on the 17th Lugar called for Marcos to resign.

Judgments about whether the sharing of intelligence with Congress creates more consensus or less, let alone whether it produces wiser policy or more foolish, are hard to make and inevitably subjective. In retrospect, if the departure of Marcos is regarded as a success, the fact that Congress knew what the executive did seems to have contributed to that success. Unwise options were foreclosed, and senior officials, especially the president, had to see the election as it was, not as they might wish it to be: Congress was watching. At the end, sharing intelligence about what Marcos had done in stealing votes made a compelling case and was enough to produce consensus.

In the case of Nicaragua, however, if shared intelligence produced a more enlightened debate, it surely did not produce consensus. This issue, like so many others, turned not on what the Sandinistas did but what their actions meant, implied, or portended. On those latter questions, even good intelligence assessments are seldom convincing. Officials in the executive and Congress disagreed, unsurprisingly, despite looking at the same data and reading the same analyses of it.

So far, there is little evidence of analysts cutting their cloth to suit congressional consumers. However, it may simply be that the congressional role is new. A cynic would say that analysts always hedged their bets, and critics would argue that analysts feel the most formidable pressures to change assessments from their bosses in the executive branch. Analysts did not soften the news in the Philippines even though it was unwelcome to some in the administration; nor did TTAC hold back in the Toshiba case because the State Department did not much like its assessment (and Congress liked it too much). In the heat of the debate over Nicaragua, the House Intelligence Committee, while generally praising intelligence community performance, certainly did not feel it had been pandered to—quite the contrary.[54]

THE SPECIAL CASE OF VERIFICATION

The more direct role of intelligence agencies in the political process is especially apparent in battles over arms control verification. Since the Senate must ratify treaties, verification is plainly an issue for Congress. Treaty supporters and opponents, as well as those who seek a way out by voting against the treaty without being labeled against arms control, all use verification as an argument. In the process they seek, understandably, to push decisions about what is finally a political issue—whether existing monitoring arrangements provide for adequate verification—onto the technical intelligence agencies, which in turn want, again understandably, to confine their role to describing those monitoring arrangements.

Verification was not an issue during the debate over SALT I in 1972, but charges of Soviet violations of that treaty, as well as the much more ambitious aims of SALT II, raised the issue five years later. Accordingly, in 1977 the Senate Foreign Relations Committee asked the Intelligence Committee for a thorough review of monitoring capabilities. The report was relatively sanguine. It appeared verification would not, after all, be a stumbling block in the ratification debate.[55]

Then, in March 1979 the United States lost access to monitoring facilities in Iran. Verification returned to the agenda, especially for the fence sitters, prominent among whom was Senator John Glenn, who said he could not support the treaty until the lost capabilities were replaced. The Intelligence Committee's final report, released on the eve of the floor debate, distinguished between the treaty's numerical limits and many of its qualitative constraints that could be monitored with high confidence, and several qualitative limits for which confidence was relatively low.[56]

Opponents zeroed in on the low-confidence provisions, while supporters pointed to the committee judgment that the treaty itself would enhance America's ability to monitor the treaty limits. The ratification vote boded to be a close-run thing, due largely to verification issues, but the whole debate was rendered moot by the Soviet invasion of Afghanistan. President Carter withdrew the treaty from Senate consideration.

In 1988 the Senate Intelligence Committee's unanimous judgment was decisive in removing verification as an issue in the discussion over the Intermediate Nuclear Forces (INF) treaty.[57] The treaty itself both embodied the most elaborate verification arrangements ever negotiated and simplified verification by eliminating weapons systems entirely, not merely reducing them in number. In its report approving the INF treaty, the committee explicitly opened the debate on a future strategic arms treaty by observing that strategic reductions would be far more demanding to monitor than those in the INF treaty.

The committee report also sought to protect the intelligence community by noting that verification is not simple, nor does it alone settle whether a treaty is desirable; a bad treaty that can be verified is still a bad treaty. It also distinguished carefully between monitoring and verification—the former an intelligence community responsibility, the latter a judgment by the executive of whether Soviet behavior as reported by the community is compatible with the treaty.[58]

CLIENTS AND PATRONS

Yet another sign that the intelligence community has joined the American government is that the institutional relations that have grown up between intelligence agencies and their congressional overseers have come to resemble those between domestic agencies and their congressional committees. Although the committees can be sharply critical of their agencies—witness covert actions or particular "intelligence failures"—in general the interests of the overseers and those overseen run parallel. The creation of the two intelligence oversight committees was thus the best thing that ever happened to the intelligence community, even if the heat of specific disputes sometimes has obscured that fact for intelligence officials.

The committees and their staffs have created a pool of people knowledgeable about intelligence and able to serve as advocates throughout the two chambers. By the time both new committees had been formed, in 1977, only 3 percent of House and 20 percent of Senate incumbents had served on the then-existing oversight subcommittees of Appropriations and Armed Services. Ten years later the percentages were 8 and 43. Over the period between 1980, when the Intelligence committees became the budget authorizers for intelligence, and 1986, the CIA budget more than doubled, growing faster than the defense budget. The total budget for the intelligence community nearly tripled, reaching close to $20 billion.[59]

Indeed, the committees have been accused of becoming as much protectors of the intelligence community as overseers—a risk that runs through all relations between Congress and executive agencies. It is true that the base of knowledge among members and staff does build understanding. The difference between the congressional investigations of intelligence in the mid-1970s and the Iran-contra panel was, for better or worse, striking: the latter was narrow, disciplined, and, Oliver North excepted, boring, with no visible sentiment for ending covert operations, much less for dismantling the CIA.

The bulk of the increase in the intelligence budget has gone for expensive satellites and other technical collection systems, where the role of Congress and the link to arms control have been central. The fall of the shah underscored the need for better human intelligence and analysis, and the closing of the Iranian monitoring sites showed just how fragile U.S. technical collection could be. As members of the Intelligence committees came to know what U.S. intelligence can do, they naturally became sympathetic to what more it could do with more money. That was particularly the case in monitoring arms control, for if judgments about verification are subjective, those about monitoring are less so: if existing systems provide 50 percent confidence in monitoring some aspect of Soviet weaponry, the argument that an additional system would increase the confidence to 80 percent can be relatively straightforward.

For example, in its report on the INF treaty, the Senate Intelligence Committee prefaced its positive judgment about verification with this statement on behalf of new technical collection systems needed to verify a future strategic arms treaty: "The Committee feels that this potential gap between intelligence capabilities and intelligence requirements must be appreciated by Members of the Senate."[60] As is typical of the multifaceted relations between committees and agencies, the committee apparently had in mind not only systems the intelligence community eagerly sought, but also ones about which it had doubts.

Other cases of congressional involvement, departures in the realm of intelligence, also look more familiar in the domestic sweep of executive-congressional relations. A good example is counterintelligence. Early in the Reagan administration the breaking wave of spy scandals elicited a number of dramatic proposals from political officials in and around the White House. Most of these ideas were judged excessive or unwise by career counterintelligence professionals; the Senate Intelligence Committee came to share that judgment, and careerists and Congress cooperated in beating back the proposals.

Later in the administration, concern remained high, fed by evidence that the new U.S. embassy in Moscow was riddled with eavesdropping devices. By then, cooler heads had come to the fore in the White House, and the Senate committee now sided with them about counterintelligence even as Congress and the White House were at loggerheads over aid to the contras.[61] The committee became a player in the administration debate, siding with those who proposed to take strong measures (the FBI and part of the CIA) against those who worried that Soviet retaliation could hinder America's ability to run foreign policy (State and the CIA's espionage managers). Liberals on the committee were persuaded to the FBI view both because they came to believe the administration was not doing enough and because they wanted to demonstrate that their attitude toward the intelligence agencies was not purely negative, that they could say "yes" as well as "no."

Joining the government means pluses and minuses for the intelligence community that are familiar from the experience of domestic agencies. For instance, for most of its history the CIA was better at understanding foreign governments than its own. One congressional staffer described Clair George, the CIA director of congressional affairs during the contra affair and a career clandestine service officer, as a man convinced that "Washington was a foreign country and he was the station chief in hostile terrain, mounting operations against the Congress."[62] Joining the American government provides both sympathetic guides to and experience in reconnoitering that terrain.

The negative side is also familiar: the more "your" congressional committees know, the more able they are to help you, but also the more they are tempted to tell you how to do your business. The Intelligence committees have been voracious requirers of reports even if, like other committees, they receive more than they can digest. Like other committees, they have also been tempted to "micromanage"; the line between oversight and management can blur, especially perhaps if the subject to be managed is exciting.

To be sure, micromanagement is relative, and the intelligence budget is not subject to anything like the intrusions of, say, the Armed Services committees into the defense budget. The CIA, for instance, has all training lumped under a single budget line item. Still, the CIA is coming to look like other agencies of government, for good and ill. Simple aging has made it more bureaucratic in any case, but congressional oversight has abetted that tendency. Projects conceived one year do not get approved until the next. Even minor operations require major paperwork. And despite renewed fondness for covert action on the part of American administrations, CIA officers retain an anxious eye on their political masters outside the executive; no one wants to be a subject of the next congressional investigation. The CIA is becoming more cautious; its officers want authorization in writing. On balance, the caution is a benefit, but it has come at some cost to the entrepreneurial spirit of the CIA.

OPEN QUESTIONS

The process of intelligence becoming a more ordinary part of the government is an uncompleted experiment. It is not, however, reversible. It was inevitable that the intelligence community would come to resemble the rest of the government as the conditions that spawned it as an exception changed: the waning of the deepest fears of the cold war, the loss after the Bay of Pigs of the CIA's image of mastery, the tarnishing of the presidency by Watergate, and the rise of investigative journalism. Perhaps the most important changes are internal to Congress, for intelligence oversight had been the quintessential working of the congressional club. When age removed those few committee chairmen from Congress, and reform meant that they would not be replaced, intelligence's relation to Congress was bound to change.

In 1954 when news of the covert operation to overthrow Guatemala's President Jacobo Arbenz leaked out, it was the leak that was discredited, not the operation. In *Time's* overheated prose, the revelations were "masterminded in Moscow and designed to divert the attention . . . from Guatemala as the Western Hemisphere's Red problem child."[63] Not so three decades later, not even if the initial leak was in Beirut in Arabic.

The government that intelligence has joined is a divided one, its divisions institutionalized. The executive-legislative division is the most obvious but not always the most important. In areas like agriculture or commerce, for instance, it is taken for granted that, whether particular observers like it or not, executive agencies and congressional committees serve essentially the same domestic constituencies. Those agencies and committees then contend within their respective arenas against representatives of other constituencies.

Intelligence analysis, by contrast, represents no conventional domestic interest groups. It is a source of advice about foreign countries. Offering advice within a single branch is political enough. Whether the intelligence community can sustain its credibility in offering advice across two branches, often in sharp contention remains to be seen. Congress may come to feel it wants its own intelligence analysts, as it came into another area of advice, the budget, to feel it required its own budgeteers, the Congressional Budget Office. A Congressional Intelligence Office does not seem imminent, however. It would ensue, if it did only from a bitter conflict between the executive and Congress. Nor is there a stream of congressional action whose shape and deadlines would argue for an in-house intelligence service comparable to the one that exists for the budget.

Yet it is instructive, and perhaps a little fearsome, to contemplate, now that Congress and intelligence analysts are acquainted, just how perfect they are for each other. The lives of foreign policy officials in the executive are dominated by their in-boxes; for them, analysis is a nuisance unless they can be sure it will support their predilections. Moreover, when assistant secretaries average not much more than a year in tenure, neither they nor intelligence analysts have much incentive, or much opportunity, to take the measure of each other.

By contrast, members of Congress, and still more their staffs are not so driven by their in-boxes. Their quest to signify means a hunt for information and for issues, just what intelligence analysts have to offer. And career paths in Congress and intelligence fit together neatly, most members are, in effect, elected for life if they choose and the tenures of their senior staffers are much longer than those of assistant secretaries.

Arrangements linking Congress to intelligence analysis are portentous but will change only gradually, for the most part out of the spotlight and out of the headlines. The focal point of conflict between the two branches will remain covert operations. There, in the nature of both constitutional and political reality, the conflict cannot be resolved, for it runs to the heart of foreign policy: balancing the responsibility of Congress with the primacy of the president.

The 1988 debate over when Congress would be notified of covert actions is illustrative of that fact. On its face the debate seemed almost trivial: both sides agreed that normally the president should inform the committees of a covert action in advance if possible, within a day or so of its start; and so the debate was over whether the forty-eight-hour requirement would be binding or not. Both sides cited examples to suit their preferences: proponents of a mandatory requirement cited arms sales to Iran, opponents, an offer by Canada during the Carter administration to help in smuggling U.S. hostages out of Iran but only if the U.S. Congress were not notified.[64]

Like most debates about intelligence, the argument was about not only the powers of the president but also about where to strike the balance between expediency and accountability. Over the past two decades the balance has moved toward accountability, and in one sense the Iran-contra affair can be seen as confirmation that the evolution has worked tolerably well. Yet there can be no full resolution to the dilemma, for secret operations inescapably raise the trade-off between democratic, thus open, process and effective, hence secret, foreign policy.

Observers fearful that increased congressional involvement poses a risk to secrecy have proposed combining the separate House and Senate committees into one joint intelligence committee. The idea of a joint committee, however, is misdirected. While a single committee might give the president less

justification for excluding Congress as "too leaky," Congress has not been leaky, certainly not by comparison with the executive.

The disadvantage of having two committees is the risk of miscommunication: witness the mining of the Nicaraguan harbors. Yet given the institutional jealousies of the two houses, the advantages of two committees—their different personalities, different priorities, and a greater claim to credibility in their respective houses—outweigh that risk. Moreover, the greatest risk to oversight is that the overseers will become co-opted. So it was by all accounts with an earlier joint committee, the Joint Atomic Energy Committee. Having two points of oversight, and even a certain amount of competition between them, reduces the chance that the overseers will become only the patrons of those they oversee.

Congress neither desires nor is able to approve every covert action in advance. Apart from constitutional questions, the process is simply too slow: Congress's instruments are blunt. One way to increase congressional control over controversial operations would be to require the Intelligence committees to approve any withdrawal from the CIA Contingency Reserve. That would be uncomfortable for the committees in that it would put them more directly on the line in the eyes of their congressional colleagues, but it would at least spare them the discomfort of having to choose between silent opposition to an operation and public exposure of it.

When administrations feel secrecy is at a premium, they can resort to informing only the "gang of eight," a procedure that had been used only once by mid-1988.[65] Had relations between Casey and the committees been better, the Reagan administration might have done so in the instance of Iranian arms sales. That would not necessarily have resulted in wiser policy, for it is conceivable that the gang of eight would have been seduced down the path from geostrategic interests to releasing hostages just as the president was. But the subsequent debate would then have been about the wisdom of the policy, not about whether Congress was deceived.

In the future, major covert actions will be overt, as was aid to the contras or to the resistance in Afghanistan. The controversy over them will spill into public, even if they are not propelled there by the executive. If some options are thereby foreclosed, at least the choices will be openly debated. Administrations will have to make evident how those covert programs support coherent public policies. And because major covert actions will not remain secret, presidents will be well advised, before the fact, to ask themselves whether the covert action could bear the test of disclosure: would it still seem sensible once it were public?

The views of congressional overseers will give the president a good indication of what the public would think if it knew of the operation. If the administration is out of step with what the public will accept, as in the case of arms sales to Iran, it may learn that in advance, rather than being punished by Congress after the fact. If the public is divided or confused, as with aid to the contras, the administration probably can have its way. This process is about the best we can do. It is, as Iran-contra testifies, no guarantee against stupid presidential decisions or the resulting public scandals.

QUESTIONS FOR FURTHER DISCUSSION

1. What does Treverton mean when he writes: "Welcome to the American Government"?
2. What have been the main sources of tension between Congress and the executive branch over intelligence activities?
3. How optimistic is Treverton—and are you—about the chances of successful congressional accountability for intelligence operations?
4. Have lawmakers become too meddlesome when it comes to sensitive intelligence activities, or have they provided a valuable safeguard against the abuse of secret power?

ENDNOTES

1. Quoted in Susan F. Rasky, "Walking a Tightrope on Intelligence Issues," *New York Times*, October II, 1988, p. A26.
2. Quoted in "Taking Toshiba Public," Case C15–88–858.0, Harvard University, Kennedy School of Government, 1988, p. 5.
3. At a press conference at the Capitol, July 19, 1975, quoted in Gregory F. Treverton, *Covert Action: The Limits of Intervention in the Postwar World* (Basic Books, 1987), p. 5.
4. The committees did find some rogue elephants in domestic intelligence activities, especially those of the Federal Bureau of Investigation.
5. *Alleged Assassination Plots Involving Foreign Leaders*, An Interim Report of the Senate Select Committee to Study Governmental Operations with Respect to Intelligence Activities, S. Rept. 94–465, 94 Cong. 1 sess. (Government Printing Office, 1975), p. 149. (Hereafter cited as *Assassination Report.*)
6. See *Assassination Report*, p. 108ff.
7. Richard B. Russell Library Oral History No. 86, taped by Hughes Gates, February 22, 1977, University of Georgia, Athens, Georgia, cited in Loch K. Johnson, *America's Secret Power: The CIA in a Democratic Society* (Oxford University Press, 1989), p. 108.
8. Quoted in "History of the Central Intelligence Agency," in *Supplementary Detailed Staff Reports on Foreign and Military Intelligence*, bk. 4, *Final Report*, S. Rept. 94–755, Senate Select Committee to Study Governmental Operations with Respect to Intelligence Activities, 94 Cong. 2 sess. (GPO, 1976), p. 54.
9. *Covert Action in Chile, 1963–1973*, Committee Print, Senate Select Committee to Study Governmental Operations with Respect to Intelligence Activities, 94 Cong. 1 sess. (GPO, 1975), pp. 41–42.
10. David Gries, "The CIA and Congress: Uneasy Partners," *Studies in Intelligence* (September 1987), p. 77. This is an unclassified article in a CIA journal. In the original, "Vinson" is rendered "Vincent," a typographical error that is, perhaps, inadvertent testimony to just how foreign the Congress was to the CIA.
11. William Colby and Peter Forbath, *Honorable Men: My Life in the CIA* (Simon and Schuster, 1978), pp. 402–03.
12. Officially, Foreign Assistance Act of 1974, sec. 32 (88 Stat. 1804).
13. For an intriguing account of the Senate Select Committee, see Loch K. Johnson, *A Season of Inquiry: The Senate Intelligence Investigation* (University Press of Kentucky, 1985).
14. For instance, Colby regards the outcome as "not unreasonable." See Colby and Forbath, *Honorable Men*, p. 429.
15. The Church committee was more often the victim of leaks than the perpetrator. See Johnson, *Season of Inquiry*, pp. 206–07.
16. It was published by the *Village Voice* as "The CIA Report the President Doesn't Want You to Read," February 16 and 23, 1976.
17. Loch Johnson, "The U.S. Congress and the CIA: Monitoring the Dark Side of Government," *Legislative Studies Quarterly*, vol. 5 (November 1980), pp. 491–92.
18. The order was printed in *New York Times*, December 5, 1981, pp. 18–19.
19. Interview, January 16, 1986.

20. This account is drawn primarily from the subsequent congressional investigation, *Report of the Congressional Committees Investigating the Iran-Contra Affair with Supplemental, Minority, and Additional Views*, H. Rept. 100–400, S. Rept. 100–216, 100 Cong. 1 sess. (GPO, 1987) (hereafter cited as *Iran-Contra Affair*); and from the earlier *Report of the President's Special Review Board* (known as the Tower commission after its chairman, former Senator John Tower) (GPO, 1987). (Hereafter cited as *Tower Commission*.) The NSC documents are quoted in *Washington Post*, March 10, 1982.

21. *Report of the Select Committee on Intelligence, U.S. Senate, Jan 1, 1983 to Dec. 31, 1984*, S. Rept. 98–665, 98 Cong. 2 sess. (GPO, 1984), pp. 4–5. (Hereafter *Intelligence Report*.)

22. The phrase is Oliver North's, quoted in *Iran-Contra Affair*, p. 3.

23. 23 The House-Senate conference report spoke of Nicaragua "providing military support (including arms, training, and logistical, command and control, and communications facilities) to groups seeking to overthrow the Government of El Salvador." See *Intelligence Report*, pp. 6–7.

24. See Stephen Kinzer, "Nicaraguan Says No Mines Are Left in Nation's Ports," *New York Times*, April 13, 1084, p. A1; Philip Taubman, "How Congress Was Informed of Mining of Nicaragua Ports," *New York Times*, April 16, 1984, p. A1; and Bernard Gwenzman, "C.I.A. Now Asserts It Put Off Session with Senate Unit," *New York Times*, April 17, 1984, p. A1. See also the account in *Intelligence Report*, p. 4ff.

25. Interviews with Intelligence Committee staff members, January 1987.

26. The letter was dated April 9; see Joanne Omang and Don Oberdorfer, "Senate Votes, 84–12, to Condemn Mining of Nicaraguan Ports," *Washington Post*, April 11, 1984, p. A16.

27. *Iran-Contra Affair*, p. 41.

28. The quote and the estimate are both from *Iran-Contra Affair*, pp. 37 and 4, respectively.

29. *Iran-Contra Affair*, p. 7.

30. The finding is printed in *Tower Commission*, pp. B60, B66 (emphasis in the original).

31. *Tower Commission*, p. III-22.

32. Interview, January 9, 1986.

33. As quoted in "Overseeing of C.I.A. by Congress Has Produced Decade of Support," *New York Times*, July 7, 1986, p. A10.

34. Quoted in Susan F. Rasky, "Walking a Tightrope," *New York Times*, October 11, 1988, p. A26.

35. Quoted in Johnson, *America's Secret Power*, p. 125.

36. Quoted in Martin Tolchin, "Of C.I.A. Games and Disputed Rules," *New York Times*, May 14, 1984, p. A12.

37. *Iran-Contra Affair*, p. 123.

38. Interview with CIA officials, August 1986 and January 1987.

39. One reported instance was an operation in Suriname in early 1983. See Philip Taubman, "Are U.S. Covert Activities Best Policy on Nicaragua?" *New York Times*, June 15, 1983, p. A1.

40. Interview, January 9, 1987.

41. Testimony before the Iran-Congress investigation, quoted in *Iran-Contra Affair*, p. 271.

42. *Iran-Contra Affair*, p. 19.

43. *Iran-Contra Affair*, p. 333.

44. Robert M. Gates, "The CIA and American Foreign Policy," *Foreign Affairs*, vol. 66 (Winter 1987–88), p. 224; and Gries, "The CIA and Congress," p. 78.

45. *Coven Action in Chile*, p. 49.

46. "Taking Toshiba Public," p. 5.

47. The information in this paragraph derives from interviews with congressional staffers conducted principally in September 1988.

48. "Taking Toshiba Public," p. 1.

49. This and subsequent quotes from DuBois are from "Taking Toshiba Public."

50. The source for this account is W. E. Kline, "The Fall of Marcos," Case C16–88-868.0, Harvard University, Kennedy School of Government, 1988.

51. See *Iran: Evaluation of U.S. Intelligence Performance Prior to November 1978*, Committee Print, Subcommittee on Evaluation of the House Permanent Select Committee on Intelligence, 96 Cong. 1 sess. (GPO, 1979).

52. This and the following quote are from "The Fall of Marcos," pp. 18–19.

53. "The Fall of Marcos," p. 20.

54. See *U.S. Intelligence Performance on Central America: Achievements and Selected Instances of Concern*, Committee Print, Subcommittee on Oversight and Evaluation of the House Permanent Select Committee on Intelligence, 97 Cong. 2 sess. (GPO, 1982).

55. See Stephen J. Flanagan, "The Domestic Politics of SALT II: Implications for the Foreign Policy Process," in John Spinier and Joseph Nogee, eds., *Congress, the Presidency and American Foreign Policy* (Pergamon Press, 1981), pp. 63–64.

56. *Principal Findings on the Capabilities of the U.S. to Monitor the SALT II Treaty*, Committee Print, Senate Select Committee on Intelligence, 96 Cong. 1 sess. (GPO, 1979).

57. *The INF Treaty Monitoring and Verification Capabilities,* S. Rept. 100–318, Senate Select Committee on Intelligence, 100 Cong. 2 sess. (GPO, 1988).

58. *INF Treaty,* S. Rept. 100–318, p. 5.

59. Numbers of members and the CIA budget are from Gries, "The CIA and Congress," p. 78. The total intelligence community budget is an estimate, compiled from interviews and published sources.

60. *INF Treaty,* S. Rept. 100–318, p. 3.

61. See, for instance, *Meeting the Espionage Challenge: A Review of United States Counterintelligence and Security Program,* S. Rept. 99–522, Senate Select Committee on Intelligence, 99 Cong. 2 sess. (GPO, 1986).

62. Interview, January 18, 1987.

63. *Time,* February 8, 1954, p. 36.

64. *Intelligence Oversight Act. of 1988,* H. Rept. 100–705, 100 Cong. 2 sess. (GPO, 1988), pt. 1, pp. 56–57. See also Dick Cheney, "Covert Operations: Who's in Charge," *Wall Street Journal,* May 3, 1988. However, a subsequent investigation by the Senate Intelligence Committee left doubt that the Canadian example actually happened.

65. *Intelligence Oversight Act of 1988,* H. Rept. 100–705, p. 11.

23. INTELLIGENCE AND THE RISE
OF JUDICIAL ACCOUNTABILITY

FREDERIC F. MANGET

Throughout most of the history of U.S. intelligence, the secret agencies were different from the rest of the government in an important way. They had little to no oversight exercised over them by entities outside their walls. This was especially true when it came to congressional and judicial accountability. In the mid-1970s, Congress changed this through the establishment of permanent oversight committees in both of its chambers. At the same time, President Gerald R. Ford established an Intelligence Oversight Board in the Office of the Presidency. As Frederic Manget points out in this piece, now the judicial branch of government has also gotten into the intelligence act.

1. INTRODUCTION

Intelligence and law enforcement occupy different worlds, but they are parallel worlds that have common dimensions. The differences are legion. Missions, cultures, tools, histories, authorities, restrictions, and resources, not to mention theory and practice, are so often incompatible that wise and experienced managers of the two worlds have often thrown their hands skyward and told their troops, "Just muddle through!"

On closer examination, however, there are enough similarities or at least points of congruity that hope for a grand unified field theory continues to exist. For example, ask any major Western intelligence service or national police force what their significant missions are and each would answer: Stop terrorists. Catch spies. Block narcotics trafficking. Smash weapons smuggling. At the highest levels of government-policy execution, intelligence and law enforcement may be viewed as different aspects of national power (among others) to be applied to problems or threats to national interests. There may be two mules pulling that load, but they should be heading in roughly the same direction and held in tentative harmony by the harness and the mule driver. . . .

Law enforcement seeks to subject those violating criminal laws to justice. Prosecutions establish a description of a past criminal act in a trial proceeding and judges and juries impose judgment. Evidence

for and against a defendant is the end use of law enforcement information. An accused person is entitled to protections and rules of process based on the basic compact between the people and the government, such as the Constitution of the United States. Law enforcement must engender enough evidence to prove guilt beyond a reasonable doubt, and the accused are presumed to be innocent. Openness, transparency, and fairness are the essential hallmarks of the Western notion of criminal justice.

Detectives and intelligence officers may both collect and analyze information, but they are different. Detectives try to meet specific and long-established legal standards of probable cause, beyond a reasonable doubt, or preponderance of the evidence. Intelligence does not provide evidence or proof, and it is hardly ever certain. It deals with threat-based national security imperatives and foreign entities that take countermeasures and build denial and deception operations into a wilderness of mirrors (Lowenthal 4–7).

Intelligence looks at the world as it finds it, in order to provide estimates of what is happening and what will happen to policymakers so that their decisions will be better informed. Intelligence seeks a best guess of what reality may be. Protection of secret sources and methods is a fundamental aspect of intelligence, and the discovery of the prosecution's information required by criminal proceedings is anathema. There is always reasonable doubt. Corroboration is the best hope for a piece of intelligence information, not proof. The violation of other nations' espionage laws is the heart of human intelligence activities. Treason, betrayal, compromise, deception, seduction, double-dealing, and theft are tools of the trade (Baker 36–40).

2. FROM MANY, ONE

The post–World War II experience in the United States, however, has been the convergence of the two worlds. America's experiment with centralized, all-source, independent, and civilian intelligence began in 1947 with the creation of the Central Intelligence Agency. It was a creature of public statutory law, the National Security Act of 1947, enacted by a democratic process and subject to the historical American preference for checks and balances in government. The act specifically prohibited CIA from having law enforcement powers or internal security functions.

That prohibition remains unchanged in the National Security Act today (section 403–4a(d)(1)). It reflects the deep uneasiness surrounding the creation of the CIA based upon fears that a unified intelligence and police force would tend toward abuses associated with Nazi Germany and the Soviet Union's centralized security and espionage apparatuses. It also stemmed from the resistance of the powerful and long-established federal law enforcement agency, the Federal Bureau of Investigation, with its own mission, political support, history, and culture (Riebling).

There were many aspects of this policy of separation of intelligence and law enforcement. The CIA could not arrest anyone or issue subpoenas. The CIA could not conduct electronic surveillance inside the United States (EO12333 section 2.4(a)). Intelligence community agencies could not collect foreign intelligence by acquiring information concerning the domestic activities of U. S. persons. Representatives of intelligence-community agencies could not joint or otherwise participate in any organizations within the United States without disclosing their intelligence affiliation, except according to procedures approved by the attorney general (Civiletti 13–15).

On the other hand, the FBI could not conduct espionage overseas. It had to coordinate in advance with the CIA its intelligence-related activities and contacts with foreign liaison and security services. Foreign intelligence information that resulted from grand jury proceedings could not be shared with the intelligence community. Prosecutors could not pass to non-law enforcement officials any foreign intelligence

information resulting from criminal wiretap surveillance. The separation was reflected in the organization of the FBI, the CIA, and the Department of Justice and was referred to in shorthand as the "wall" (Hulnick 1997, 269).

Even from this beginning, however, the wall developed a number of one-way and two-way mirrors. Although the CIA had no law enforcement powers, it could support law enforcement activities. This became settled in intelligence law, both in executive orders (EO 12333 section 2.6) and statute (National Security Act section 403–5a). In 1997 a specific and explicit law enforcement authority for the intelligence community was added to the National Security Act. Upon the request of a law enforcement agency, elements of the intelligence community may collect information outside the United States about individuals who are not United States persons, even if the law enforcement agency intends to use the information collected for purposes of a law enforcement investigation.

Other parts of the National Security Act were added that required that other federal agencies disclose to the Director of Central Intelligence foreign intelligence acquired in the course of a criminal investigation (National Security Act section 403–5b(a)(1)). Law enforcement agencies were later authorized by statute to share with the intelligence community any foreign intelligence information that was formerly withheld under the prohibition on disclosing information from a grand-jury proceeding (Collins 1261). Intelligence agencies were also allowed to obtain access to electronic, wire, or oral interception information that had been generated by a criminal investigation authorized under Title III of the U.S. criminal code (PATRIOT Act).

The FBI's overseas activities also expanded. The Department of Justice opined in 1989 that the FBI has the authority to override customary or other international law in its extraterritorial law enforcement activities. The FBI could investigate and arrest fugitives in another state without the consent of the host government (OLC Opinion 195). Supreme Court cases contributed to this trend. One held that an extradition treaty was not the exclusive means by which the United States could take custody of a suspect in a foreign country in which he had been apprehended by persons acting on behalf of the United States without regard to the treaty's provisions (*U.S. v. Alvarez-Machain* 1992, 655).

Another held that the Fourth Amendment requirement that government searches be "reasonable" does not apply to the search and seizure of property in a foreign country owned by a nonresident alien who has no significant voluntary connection with the United States (*U.S. v. Verdugo-Urquidez* 1990, 259). In addition, the Ames spy case in the mid-1990s led to a reorganization of U.S. counterintelligence lanes in the road between the FBI and the intelligence community. A new statutory provision required intelligence agencies to immediately advise the FBI of any information indicating that classified information may have been disclosed in an unauthorized manner to a foreign power or agent of a foreign power, which is a potential crime under several U.S. laws (IAA FY 95 section 402a). It also required prior coordination and consultation between the agencies for any further actions they might take. In the mid-1990s, the FBI vigorously expanded the mission of the legal attaches attached to U.S. embassies to enhance cooperation with foreign law enforcement agencies, many of whom also had internal security and intelligence functions as well.

Much of this convergence of worlds occurred because of the convergence of targets. Both intelligence agencies and law enforcement agencies were directed to bring their rapidly overlapping methods to bear on the same individuals, organizations, and activities. The crime of espionage always had both a foreign intelligence and a criminal law aspect, leading to overlapping FBI and CIA counterintelligence activities that created a history of both friction and effective joint spy-catching. The Intelligence Identities Protection Act was specifically added to the U.S. criminal code to address a gap in the espionage and related crimes that seem to allow publication of the true identities of U.S. intelligence officers serving under cover. In the 1970s, the U.S. created and expanded a number of other extraterritorial crimes. Violations of U.S. domestic criminal law could now be committed outside the territory of the United States by foreign nationals. These included aircraft hijacking and piracy, weapons proliferation (notably chemical and biological weapons), international narcotics trafficking, and organized crime. The U.S. later added terrorism and related crimes and borderless offences such as the cybercrimes of computer hacking and sabotage.

This resulted in a critical need to reconcile the intelligence imperative for secrecy with law enforcement's requirement for fair trials. As a result, the U.S. amended the procedures by which information is introduced into criminal trial processes. The Classified Information Procedures Act (C1PA) was enacted in 1980 to address the problem of greymail. Greymail is the risk that a defendant will publicly disclose classified information that could damage national security interests of the United States. Prior to the passage of CIPA, when criminal procedure rules required that the defendant have access to classified materials, the government had to make an uninformed guess as to what would ultimately be disclosed in the trial and how much damage would occur. CIPA is meant to mitigate that uncertainty while keeping the essence of those basic criminal processes required by long-held notions of a fair trial in an adversarial judicial system.

CIPA is procedural rather than substantive, and thus does not affect the outcome of whether classified information must be disclosed to the defendant or used in a public proceeding. It does, however, limit the threat of ambush that dogged prosecutors in earlier cases. CIPA requires notice of what classified information the defense intends to use. It allows for the court to hear in camera (in chambers, not in a public courtroom) and ex parte (only one party—the government—is present) presentations in order to review classified information and determine if it must be disclosed in order to ensure a fair trial or otherwise meet criminal due process, discovery, and evidentiary requirements. It also allows the government to propose unclassified substitutions for classified information that would give the defendant the same ability to put on a defense as would the use of the original classified information. The court also has the ability under CIPA to fashion sanctions, including dismissal, in cases where the government refuses to disclose the classified information at issue.

The government can use CIPA procedures to get evidentiary rulings from the court on the classified information in advance of public hearings or trials. Once those evidentiary rulings are made, the government then can assess the risk of proceeding with the prosecution and any resulting damage to intelligence interests that might occur. The defendant still has the substantive rights to demand discovery and proof, but the government can make a more rational and informed decision. Intelligence officers cannot act with one eye looking over their shoulder at a theoretical future prosecution of someone, somewhere, for some crime that might threaten some intelligence source or method, to be determined at some future time. All of the criminal procedure requirements that are second nature to law enforcement agents—Miranda warnings, search warrants, chain of custody integrity—would seriously hamper intelligence collection (Fredman 1998).

CIPA processes have been challenged by numerous defendants on the grounds that they violate fair-trial notions of due process under the Constitution, but the law is settled that CIPA successfully—if slowly and painfully—holds both Constitutional law enforcement rules and intelligence equities in a reasonable and lawful balance.

Issues related to surveillance also led to another area in which law enforcement and intelligence community components had to develop statutory rules of engagement to reconcile different needs. In 1978 the Foreign Intelligence Surveillance Act (FISA) was enacted to establish a court to hear government applications for orders authorizing electronic surveillance (and later, unconsented physical searches) directed at foreign powers and agents of foreign powers, rather than potential criminals or criminal evidence.

Searches by the U.S. government are constrained by the Fourth Amendment of the Constitution, which requires that searches be reasonable and in most cases authorized by a judicial search warrant. (Hall) The issue that arose was whether information gathered as foreign intelligence could be used as evidence by law enforcement authorities to convict a criminal defendant. FISA required robust secrecy and entirely ex parte hearings and application procedures, a rarity in criminal proceedings.

For many years, the legal reasoning in a seminal espionage case controlled the approach of the U.S. government in counterintelligence activities (U.S. vs. Truong 1980). In the 1970s, U.S government counterintelligence uncovered a U.S. Information Agency employee (Humphrey) who was giving classified diplomatic information to a Vietnamese citizen (Truong) who then passed it to North Vietnamese officials who were negotiating with U.S. representatives in Paris. The FBI, using a national security rationale rather than a criminal standard under Title III, bugged Truong's apartment and tapped his phone over the course of a number of months. At some point in the foreign counterintelligence surveillance, prosecutors from the Department of Justice began to take an active part in directing the surveillance.

When the issue arose of whether the incriminating evidence surfaced by the surveillance could be admitted in evidence in the criminal case against Humphrey and Truong, the court opined that so long as the primary purpose of the surveillance was collection of information relating to activities of a foreign power, the resulting information could be used in the criminal case. But at some point during the surveillance of Truong, the primary purpose changed and became collection of information to support a prosecution. The court noted that the involvement of the law enforcement officers determined the shift in the primary purpose of the collection, and thus information collected under foreign intelligence rules could not be used for criminal trial purposes after the change of primary purpose. The "primary purpose" test was adopted by a number of other federal circuits in cases where issues of surveillance arose, and it was the basis of relationships between law enforcement and intelligence agencies and their rules of engagement, lanes in the road, and tribal encounters for over twenty years.

The wall finally came tumbling down in 2002. The Foreign Intelligence Surveillance Court of Review (the appellate court for decisions made by the Foreign Intelligence Surveillance Court, or FISC, which authorizes FISA searches and surveillance), convened for the first time in history to hear an appeal brought by the U.S. government from a FISC surveillance order imposing a number of restrictions on the government based upon the wall and the primary purpose test. The FISC opinion stated that it could approve FISA surveillance applications only if the government's objective is not primarily directed toward criminal prosecution of the foreign agents for their foreign intelligence activity.

The Court of Review did not agree. It said that at some point in the 1980s (". . . the exact moment is shrouded in historical mist") the Department of Justice applied the pre-FISA Truong analysis to FISA without justification (In re Sealed Case 2002). There is now no need to find a primary purpose of either national security intelligence collection or acquisition of information about a crime in order to pass any wall established by FISA. The end of the wall is reflected in every major recent review of U.S. intelligence policy and organization, which all call for increased information sharing, unity of command and control, and removal of barriers to joint and complementary action among elements of the U.S. government.

This convergence of law enforcement and intelligence missions and activities has not reconciled the underlying bases for each sphere of activity, however. For example, foreign intelligence surveillance differs markedly from that in criminal investigations. In the criminal context, the Fourth Amendment reasonableness requirement usually requires a showing of probable cause and a warrant. But that is not universal.

The central requirement is one of reasonableness. The probable cause standard is peculiarly related to criminal investigations and is often unsuited to determining reasonableness of other searches (*Board of Education v. Earls* 2002, 828). The Supreme Court has repeatedly opined that in situations involving "special needs" that go beyond a routine interest in law enforcement, a warrant is not required. The Court has found no warrant requirement in circumstances in which the government faces an increased need to be able to react swiftly and flexibly or when there are at stake interests in public safety beyond the interests in ordinary law enforcement, such as response to an emergency beyond the need for general crime control (In re Sealed Case 2002, 745–46).

Foreign intelligence collection, especially related to a threat to public safety, has many of the characteristics of a special need. The executive branch of the U.S. government has consistently taken the position that foreign intelligence collection is far removed from ordinary criminal law enforcement. Methodology and rules for criminal searches are ". . . inconsistent with the collection of foreign intelligence and would unduly frustrate the President in carrying out his foreign intelligence responsibilities . . . (W)e believe that the warrant clause of the Fourth Amendment is inapplicable to such (foreign intelligence) searches" (Gorelick 1994, 63).

There are thus significant distinctions between searches undertaken for ordinary law enforcement purposes and those done for intelligence purposes (Howell 145–147) (Kris).

Foreign intelligence surveillance may be undertaken without probable cause to believe that a crime has been committed. The surveillance may be of considerable duration and scope. Its purpose is to gather information about the intentions and capabilities of foreign governments or organizations, rather than to obtain admissible evidence of a crime. Yet, foreign intelligence gained through a wiretap may be used as evidence in a criminal prosecution. The Department of Justice has ongoing concerns that the increasing blur between law enforcement and intelligence activities will lead to the avoidance of criminal law protections by disguising a criminal investigation as an intelligence operation, where less stringent restraints apply to the government.

Counterintelligence in particular raises many of the difficult issues. Only a small percentage of all counterintelligence cases can be considered for successful prosecutions. Investigations of foreign intelligence agents are seldom conducted from the outset as they would be if eventual prosecution were expected. Many counterintelligence professionals believe that prosecutions should never be brought against hostile foreign agents because it would only result in their replacement by other unknown agents whose activities would not come to the attention of the U.S. counterintelligence community.

The convergence of targets and especially the need to meet international terrorist threats caused a recent reorganization of the intelligence and law enforcement communities. The Department of Homeland Security created in 2002 has components that are deeply rooted in law enforcement and policing authorities, such as customs, border patrol, and immigration. Yet it also has several components that are part of the intelligence community, including an office of intelligence analysis and even part of the Coast Guard. The FBI has created a new National Security Service from its former counterintelligence and counterterrorism elements, all under an executive assistant director reporting to the new Director of National Intelligence (DNI). The Department of Justice has a new National Security Division that combines the intelligence policy (the Office of Intelligence Policy Review), counterespionage, and counterterrorism components of the Department under a new Assistant Attorney General for national security. In 2002, the Counterintelligence Enhancement Act called for the creation of the National Counterintelligence Executive (NCIX) to be the head of U.S. counterintelligence and develop government-wide counterintelligence policies and plans. The NCIX is now under the new DNI, created by the Intelligence Reform and Terrorism Prevention Act of 2004 (IRTPA). New DNI centers such as the National Counterterrorism Center (NCTC), which often replicated previous DCI centers, were created to bring together, or "fuse," intelligence, law enforcement, and related efforts directed at joint targets. The organizational hallmark of these centers was widespread and rapid sharing of information and personnel.

This convergence should not mask the fundamental differences between the two worlds, however. The United States continues to be wary of combining the powers and authorities of intelligence and law enforcement regimes. (Thompson 6) Intelligence activities require secrecy, swiftness, and latitude for success. Law enforcement activities require openness, painstaking and often slow diligence, and strict adherence to complicated legal rules of engagement for success. The authorities and restrictions for each activity have been tailored to meet the unique characteristics of each and maintain an acceptable level of checks and balances by maintaining the real differences between the two areas. For example, in 1991 rules for authorizing and conducting covert actions, and notifying Congress of such actions, were codified and added as Title V of the National Security Act of 1947, as amended. The general definition of covert action had several exceptions, one of which was "traditional law enforcement activities" or support to them.

The legislative history of Title V contains descriptions of traditional law enforcement activities, which include those conducted by the FBI to apprehend, or otherwise cooperate with foreign law enforcement authorities to apprehend those who have violated U.S. laws or the laws of other nations. It also includes activities of other U.S. government agencies (such as DEA) that assist other countries, with their consent, in the destruction or interdiction of narcotics supplies or products in those countries. "Routine support" is specifically described as not a "backdoor instrument of covert action" (Senate Report No. 102–85, 47–48).

This distinction is important because if an action of the U.S. government falls within the definition of "covert action," then a number of requirements must be met to lawfully authorize it, all of which would be unreasonably burdensome for law enforcement goals to be efficiently met. It is a clear indication that for many purposes, the differences between intelligence and law enforcement should be maintained and the policy of the United States is to separate the two.

An additional and still-current wall between intelligence and law enforcement is the restriction on direct involvement by the military in domestic law enforcement. Most of the agencies in the intelligence community are located within the Department of Defense (DOD). Since the immediate aftermath of the Civil War, the DOD has been largely prohibited from participating in civilian law enforcement by *posse comitatus* statutes, with the recent exception of the authority to assist law enforcement counternarcotics activities. But military personnel may still not be involved in the arrest and detention of suspects (Doyle 1995).

There is current interest in reviving proposals to create an agency whose operations would overlap in the middle between intelligence and law enforcement. Commentators have raised the British domestic security service MI-5 as a possible model. It would carry out an intelligence function separate from the law enforcement mission now owned by the FBI and the Department of Homeland Security. It would be directed toward collection and analysis of intelligence related to threats within the United States, and to the disruption and prevention of such threats, whether domestic, foreign, or international in nature. Reconciling a domestic intelligence service with traditional foreign intelligence and domestic law enforcement, and ensuring that civil-liberties interests are not unduly affected in an area where American public is wary, would be highly challenging.

Other issues arose as the world shrank, as well. These issues included oversight by different sets of congressional committees with varying agendas. Judiciary, intelligence, and defense committees are separate and different areas of responsibility. Even though there is some effort to have sufficient "crossover" membership on all concerned committees, there is still significant overlap, underlap, and opacity, all enveloped by the fog of legislation.

Coordination of intelligence and law enforcement activities is a perennial if not a daily issue. In the late 1980s, there were investigations into two international banks, the Bank of Credit and Commerce International (BCCI) and Banca Nazionale del Lavoro (BNL) who were alleged to have laundered money for criminal enterprises. The investigations revealed that the CIA had acquired information about possible crimes committed by the banks but had not made the information available to the Justice Department. Most observers concluded that there was no effort by the CIA to protect either of the banks or hide the information from the Justice Department, but congressional committees recommended that procedures be established to ensure that relevant information about international criminal activity collected by the intelligence community would be made available to law enforcement, while still protecting intelligence sources and methods (Snider et al. 1994).

As a result of the bank scandals, the Joint Task Force on Intelligence and Law Enforcement was established in 1993. It was comprised of senior attorneys from CIA and the Justice Department, and it made a number of recommendations to improve information sharing, coordination, and the management of data searches and retrieval. One was the creation of a Joint Intelligence-Law Enforcement Working Group (JICLE) which began operations in 1994. Although JICLE has faded into the bureaucratic graveyard, it is an example of the continuing efforts to bridge the gap between intelligence and law enforcement operations by establishing methods to keep channels of communication open and operating.

3. WE DON'T NEED NO STINKIN' BADGES

When intelligence activities relate to collection of information, they are governed by rules significantly different than those that apply to law enforcement activities targeting the exact same information. Intelligence information comes into the criminal process in two major ways. One is when intelligence collection results in information that may be useful for the prosecution in developing its case in chief. Law enforcement agencies routinely receive a great deal of information in disseminated intelligence reports that is for lead purposes only and remains classified and under the general control of the originating intelligence agency. Law enforcement agencies may use it to develop their own independently acquired information, but not as evidence to be introduced in a public court proceeding. If the lead-purpose information is important enough for the prosecutors to want to use it as evidence, then the clash of civilizations and cultures is joined.

Most intelligence information is fragmentary, nebulous, riddled with alternative meanings, and related to "proximate reality," rather than truth. It is an incomplete mosaic at best. If it were not, it would be news or history, not intelligence. Concepts such as the general ban on hearsay testimony or the best evidence rule, which are central trial procedure concepts in the United States, cannot be reconciled with the intelligence concepts of compartmentation, need to know, and protection of sources and methods so that they will continue to generate intelligence. Chain of custody issues and search warrants are not part of intelligence tradecraft. "Beyond a reasonable doubt" is a concept alien to intelligence collection or analysis.

Intelligence information also enters the criminal justice system because of the prosecution's efforts to comply with discovery rules requiring the disclosure to the defense of certain types of information. Federal discovery obligations apply not only to law enforcement agencies but also to other government agencies that are aligned with the prosecution. Alignment occurs when another agency becomes an active participant in the investigation or prosecution of a particular case. Alignment is significant in counterterrorist and weapons-proliferation cases because

of the extensive cooperation between intelligence and law enforcement agencies in those areas.

The most important discovery rules are the constitutional requirements of the *Brady* and *Giglio* cases, Federal Rule of Criminal Procedure (FRCrP) 16, and the Jencks Act. *Brady* requires the government to disclose to the defendant any evidence that is material to the guilt or punishment of the accused (*Brady v. Maryland* 1963). *Giglio* requires the same discovery for evidence material to the impeachment of a government witness (*Giglio v. U.S.* 1972). FRCrP 16 obligates the government to disclose any relevant written or recorded statement of the defendant within the custody or control of the government, and any documents or tangible objects that are material to the defense, belong to the defendant, or are intended for use in the government's case in chief. The Jencks Act requires the government to disclose any statements of government witnesses within its possession that relate to the witnesses' testimony.

Prosecutors generally conduct a prudential search of intelligence community files prior to indictment because they have objective, articulable factors justifying the conclusion that the files probably contain classified information that may have an impact upon the government's decision whether to seek an indictment, and what crimes and defendants should actually be charged. The prudential search includes a search for Brady and other information that would be the subject of the government's post-indictment discovery obligations.

Intelligence agency files must be reviewed in a particular criminal case based on several factors. The first is whether the intelligence agency has been an active participant in the investigation or prosecution of a case. If so, alignment generally results and the agency's files are subject to the same requirements of search and disclosure as the files of the prosecuting attorney or lead agency (usually the FBI). If the defendant makes an explicit request that certain files be searched, and there is a non-trivial prospect that the examination of those files will yield material exculpatory information, then courts usually also require a file review.

In addition, if prosecutors acquire information that suggests the defendant may have had, or as part of his defense at trial will assert that he has had, contacts with an intelligence agency, then some limited review by the affected agency is almost always done. In such cases, a positive defense of acting pursuant to public authority under FRCrP 12.3 may be implicated. Such a defense is based upon the notion that if a defendant thought he was acting under a lawful and authorized directive by the government, he would not have the required mental state of knowingly violating a criminal law. In those circumstances, determining the existence and extent of any contact between a defendant and an intelligence agency becomes important to the prosecution's case.

If the prosecution is required by these discovery rules to examine the voluminous holdings of the intelligence community, it is a serious drain on law enforcement and prosecution resources. If the prosecution is required by these discovery rules to disclose intelligence information to the defendants, their attorneys, clerks, secretaries, experts, and other defense team personnel, then the risk to the sources of the information expands greatly. And if these process rules allow the defendants to disclose the information in open court in order to have a fair chance to put on their defenses, then the damage is no longer potential but actual. CIPA allows the government to calculate and understand in advance the risk of going forward with a prosecution, but it does not change the fundamental rules of criminal process.

A typical CIPA case involves classified information surfacing either from the defendant's own knowledge or from discovery obligations of the U.S. government to allow defense counsel to search or use such information. The court usually convenes a pretrial conference to attempt to resolve as many issues as possible. It then enters a protective order requiring appropriate security procedures and limited access to the classified information, including in some cases even prohibiting defense counsel from discussing some matters with the defendants themselves. The defense is required to notify the government under section 5 of CIPA of what classified information the defense intends to disclose. The government then attempts to challenge disclosure of the classified information based upon the regular procedural objections to evidence (everything from not material to hearsay). The government then tries to minimize damage by proposing unclassified summaries or substitutions for any classified information that the court rules may be disclosed by the defense. There is a provision for an interlocutory (pre-verdict) appeal of court rulings, and a range of sanctions the court can use if the government does not allow the defense to disclose the classified information. CIPA has been in effect for almost thirty years, without significant amendment, and the general view of the U.S. government is that it has achieved its purpose.

Individuals in custody also create immediate conflicts between intelligence and law enforcement. The criminal law system in Anglo-American jurisdictions (among others) wants those in jeopardy of criminal penalties to have a level playing field. Fundamental notions of what is fair include those explicitly set out in the Constitution: the Fifth Amendment right against self-incrimination, and the Sixth Amendment right to legal counsel. Assuming the U.S. government has lawful grounds for incarcerating individuals other than to try them on criminal charges (such as holding enemy prisoners of war), application of such basic elements of criminal law would raise tremendous barriers to acquiring information about future threats. The Miranda warning of the right to remain silent and to have an attorney appointed and paid for by the state would end almost any conceivable intelligence interrogation.

The status of detainees of the U.S. government in military custody at Guantanamo Bay and other locations overseas has created an epic clash over how the U.S. criminal system should treat them. As this is written, the first of the military-commission proceedings are beginning. The U.S. Supreme Court has held that the detainees have a right to petition federal civilian courts for writs of habeas corpus to challenge their detentions. Habeas corpus is a long-time staple of the criminal law system that allows convicted federal prisoners another venue to allege they are being wrongfully held, other than a strict appellate review. Use of the military criminal law system under either the Uniform Code of Military Justice (UCMJ) or the laws of war does not reconcile the fundamentally different ends of intelligence and law enforcement. The UCMJ largely follows the civilian Federal Rules of Criminal Procedure, including a version of CIPA.

The Supreme Court has also opined that Common Article 3 of the Geneva Conventions apply to such detainees (*Hamdan v. Rumsfeld* 2006). Article 3 states that prisoners of war may not be forced to provide any information except name, rank, and serial number. They may be asked for and even volunteer more information, but no physical or mental torture or any other form of coercion may be inflicted on prisoners of war to secure from them information of any kind whatever. Prisoners of war who refuse to answer may not be threatened, insulted, or exposed to unpleasant or disadvantageous treatment of any kind. They also cannot be denied regular visits from the Red Cross and packages from home (FM 27–10 para. 93).

Other issues arise when intelligence agencies provide direct assistance to law enforcement organizations. The circumstances under which a defendant is rendered to a court of competent jurisdiction may become litigated if the defense raises the *Toscanino* exception to the *Ker-Frisbie* doctrine. The *Ker-Frisbie* doctrine (based on two seminal cases) holds that a trial court will not bar a trial based upon the conditions under which the defendant is brought before the court (*Ker v. Illinois* 1886; *Frisbie v. Collins* 1952). Even if the defendant is taken into custody and transported before the court in some manner that is arguably unlawful, the court will not dismiss the case so long as the defendant can expect a fair trial before that particular court. *Toscanino* was a Second Circuit decision that created an exception to the *Ker-Frisbie* doctrine (*U.S. v. Toscanino* 1974). The court in *Toscanino* said that if the conduct of government agents who rendered the defendant to the court's jurisdiction was so outrageous as to shock the conscience of the court, then the court would at least hear defense motions to dismiss based upon those conditions.

If an intelligence agency supplies resources of equipment, personnel, or technical assistance for a clandestine exfiltration or delivery of a prisoner, then it is possible that the conditions of the operation could be litigated. Disclosure of intelligence sources, methods, and sensitive operational activities would be likely to be an issue in such litigation. There has not been much historical success in raising the *Toscanino* defense, but it has been raised.

Press reporting has also described renditions of individuals by the U.S. government to a number of foreign jurisdictions, where the individuals then become subject to those other nations' law enforcement systems. The renditions are described as clandestine and do not involve formal extradition procedures that are a staple of many treaties involving public law enforcement jurisdictional proceedings. Press reports also describe claims by a number of individuals that they were delivered to law enforcement authorities who tortured or otherwise abused them. It is not difficult to imagine the difficulties in avoiding such circumstances or defending against spurious claims if secret intelligence resources are involved in such transport.

4. GO DIRECTLY TO JAIL. DO NOT PASS GO. DO NOT COLLECT $200

Enforcement of criminal laws is also a significant limitation on the ability of the intelligence establishment to conduct particular activities. There is no comprehensive and universal legal principle that exempts intelligence agencies from substantive criminal prohibitions. Intelligence activities that might implicate a U.S. criminal statute have to be reviewed one by one.

Intelligence agencies have special authorities that allow them to lawfully conduct activities that could be unlawful if conducted by other federal agencies or private individuals or organizations. Much of the authority granted to intelligence agencies is based upon the need for secrecy and the fact that most intelligence activities are directed at foreign governments, organizations, and individuals. International law principles and treaties relating to extradition of criminal suspects have established long-held norms about how to treat those accused of espionage and related crimes. Such crimes have at their base clandestine actions by national governments that are recognized and accepted by customary international law and formal conventions. Accordingly, such crimes are deemed "political" crimes and are not subject to extradition agreements.

A related concept is that of diplomatic immunity, in which certain diplomats are beyond the reach of the criminal laws of any nation except their own. The only sanction in such instances is not a law enforcement penalty, but rather the diplomatic one of expulsion from the territory of the host nation (the declaration of the status of persona non grata). Intelligence officers with diplomatic immunity thus do not have a get-out-of-jail-free card issued by the law enforcement authorities, but they do have a free ticket home.

This latitude for action based upon special authorities is limited when a specific criminal prohibition applies. For example, in the current executive order that is a presidential charter for the U.S. intelligence community, there is a section that states: "*Consistency With Other Laws*. Nothing in this Order shall be construed to authorize any activity in violation of the Constitution or statutes of the United States." Further, the intelligence authorization acts passed (until recently) on a near-annual basis contained similar language.

The National Security Act uses similar language to limit the use of covert action (National Security Act Title V). It establishes by statute the authority of the president to use clandestine means to influence political, economic, or military conditions abroad, where it is intended that the role of the U. S. government will not be apparent or acknowledged publicly. The definition of covert action specifically excludes traditional law enforcement activities. In order to authorize a covert action, the president must issue a finding that meets certain requirements in the act. The act states, however: "A finding may not authorize any action that would violate the Constitution or any statute of the United States."

This limit on intelligence activities created a grey area in which government officials thrash around trying to reconcile law enforcement requirements with intelligence authorities. Some U.S. criminal statutes are so broadly worded that a specific exemption has been explicitly included to prevent otherwise authorized intelligence activities from being at least arguably covered by the prohibitions. For example, under Title 18 of the U.S. criminal code, it is a crime to intercept electronic communications. Since intercepting electronic communications is the basic function of signals intelligence (SIGINT), a large portion of the intelligence community would be affected. Accordingly, the drafters exempted from the definition of the crime electronic surveillance within the United States that is covered by FISA, as well as the acquisition of foreign intelligence information from international or foreign communications (18 U.S.C. sections 2511(2)(e)-(f) (2005)).

Cybercrime, in the form of fraud and related actions in connection with unauthorized access or damage to computer systems, also contains a specific intelligence and law enforcement exemption (18 U.S.C. section 1030(f)(2005)). Other statutes are broadly worded but not extraterritorial in application. Activities conducted abroad that do not involve U.S. persons or property or have a sufficient nexus with the territory of the United States may not be crimes.

Other criminal laws, however, are in fact clearly intended to apply to the activities of the U.S. government. For example, if possession of a biological or chemical weapon does not fall within the exceptions in the criminal statutes implementing the Biological and Chemical Weapons Conventions (relating to the purpose of the possession), intelligence agencies would be violating the law (18 U.S.C. sections 175(c), 229F(7) (2005)). The federal crime of torture specifically refers to persons "acting under the color of law," meaning those acting on behalf of an official governmental entity. Torture is an extraterritorial federal crime and may not be authorized by any federal intelligence, military, or law enforcement official (18 U.S.C. sections 2340–2340A (2005)).

Unclear language in some criminal statutes and different circumstances that have expanded the reach of others create problems for intelligence agencies and their employees. In some statutes there is neither a specific exemption for otherwise authorized intelligence activities nor a clear intent to extend the criminal law to cover such activities. Wire and mail fraud statutes state that "whoever" obtains money or property by means of false representations and uses the mail, telephone, radio, or television to do so will be committing a federal crime (18 U.S.C. sections 1341, 1343 (2005)). There is no specific exclusion for otherwise lawful and authorized intelligence activities. "Whoever" seems all-inclusive. If defrauding includes acquiring secrets of foreign persons and organizations by subterfuge or deceit, intelligence activities might be arguably included. In light of intelligence needed by the U.S. national security policymakers, that would be absurd.

Another example is the crime related to provision of support to terrorists or terrorist groups. It applies to, "whoever knowingly provides material support or resources to a foreign terrorist organization, or attempts or conspires to do so" (Antiterrorism and Effective Death Penalty Act section 303). There is no intelligence exception in the text of the statute. There is no discussion of intelligence activities in the legislative history and no explicit expression of congressional intent to include or exclude intelligence activities from the definition of the crime.

On its face, that language would prohibit an intelligence agency and its employees from providing money or equipment to assist a human asset in establishing his bona fides in order to penetrate a terrorist organization. Precluding the federal government itself from taking steps to fight international terrorism defies both logic and the statutory purposes expressed in legislative report language. Providing material support to a terrorist organization in order to penetrate and defeat it brings the intelligence world—where all is not as it seems in many circumstances—into conflict with a law enforcement system that is premised upon constitutional and common law requirements of clarity, proof beyond a reasonable doubt, fairness, and lines between right and wrong.

Other examples demonstrate the difficulty of using a law enforcement system to impose limits on foreign intelligence activities. Intelligence agencies deploy officers and assets in the field under various types of cover. Cover protects their personal safety and their affiliation with the United States government. It requires ruses, deception, false-flag persona, and misrepresentation. In the U.S. criminal code, however, "(w)hoever falsely and willfully represents himself to be a citizen of the United States shall be fined under this title or imprisoned not more than three years, or both." Such an act is a felony. There is no exception for intelligence activities. According to the strict statutory language, a non-U.S. citizen working for the CIA cannot say that he is a U.S. citizen to anyone who is a potential intelligence source.

In these circumstances, principles of statutory interpretation of criminal laws are the only way to reconcile statutory intent with statutory language. The most significant principle stems from the *Nardone* case, which states that criminal laws of general applicability should not be interpreted to apply to actions of the government as sovereign unless there is specific language to that effect (*Nardone v. U.S.* 1937, 384). Other rules of interpretation also require looking to the reasons for enactment of the statute and the purpose to be gained by it, and construing the statute in the manner which is consistent with such purpose. A statute should not be read literally where such a reading is contrary to its purposes.

The difficulty with reliance on such rules is that *Nardone* is not universal in its reach and each set of circumstances requires examination of the specific facts involved. Advance review by legal counsel for intelligence agencies can help insulate intelligence officers from exposure. Intelligence agency employees proceed at their own peril when they carry out operations over the objections of agency counsel that are based upon potential criminal liability. Yet in grey areas, employees could be subject to criminal investigations for actions taken under the stress, danger, and critical time pressures experienced in the field. A criminal investigation has highly serious effects upon individuals and organizations, even if no charges or other sanctions are ever brought after years go by.

Subjecting intelligence activities to advance legal review for potential criminal activities and producing legal opinions in coordination with the appropriate criminal law enforcement elements of the Department of Justice is burdensome, slow, and inefficient. The Department of Justice dislikes and resists formal declinations of prosecution. Intelligence activities that raise such a risk are simply avoided.

The use of "dirty" assets also creates the same dangers. Sources of certain intelligence information may be individuals who have committed crimes even though their actions took place completely overseas. This can occur in areas such as terrorism, narcotics trafficking, and weapons proliferation. Law enforcement wants to convict them or use them to convict others. Intelligence wants to use them to collect information that will remain secret. This conflict is ancient, as illustrated by the famous Biblical passage describing Joshua's battle at Jericho. Joshua sent two men to spy on Jericho, and Rahab the "harlot" hid them, lied to Jericho authorities, and deceived all around her in assisting the Israelites. Continuing to use human assets to collect intelligence after information surfaces tying them to a crime significantly increases the likelihood that a successful criminal case cannot be brought against them without seriously risking intelligence equities. In such a case it is very difficult to serve both intelligence and criminal interests.

Concerns with criminal statutes also led to the passage of Title XI of the National Security Act. It creates a statutory-interpretation presumption that domestic U.S. laws implementing international treaties and conventions would not make unlawful otherwise lawful and authorized intelligence activities, absent express statutory language to the contrary. Title XI recognizes that it would be exceedingly difficult for the Departments of State and Justice to ensure that every new transnational criminal convention and its implementing legislation contain a specific exemption for intelligence activities. Trying to address issues of espionage, covert action, and other unacknowledged national state activities in an international convention would be close to impossible. Public discussion necessary to adopt such agreements would be very damaging to the clandestine activities that the agreements sought to protect. As a result, it was imperative to craft this rule of statutory interpretation to make congressional intent manifest when it otherwise was silent.

Secrecy has not shielded intelligence agencies from scrutiny under criminal law standards, either. All components of the U.S. intelligence community are required by executive order and presidential direction to report possible violations of federal, criminal laws by employees, and certain specified federal criminal laws by any other persons, according to procedures developed between the attorney general and the intelligence organization involved.

In 1982, the then-serving attorney general and director of central intelligence promulgated such procedures for CIA. They require the CIA's General Counsel (currently a Senate-confirmed, presidential appointment) to report to the Criminal Division of the Department of Justice and the FBI any information that an Agency employee may have violated any federal crime, and any information that any person may have committed any of a list of serious federal offenses such as those involving intentional inflic-tion or threat of death or serious physical harm, espi-onage, or perjury or false statements. Crimes reporting under those procedures is extensive. In addition, in the late 1980s Congress created a statutory Inspector General for CIA. The Inspector General's duties in-clude investigating possible violations of federal crim-inal laws that involve programs or operations of CIA, and reporting any such information to the attorney general.

Law enforcement can be a profound deterrent to intelligence activities, either advertently or inadver-tently. Criminal law can bar actions of even the President of the United States. It is unlikely that gov-ernment employees will be found guilty of a crime if they are carrying out in good faith what is other-wise a lawful activity, since they would not have the *mens rea*, or guilty mind, necessary for a crime to be proven. Nevertheless, the threat of a criminal inves-tigation itself can be a punishing and debilitating experience for both the individuals and their agen-cies, often lasting years in duration.

Intelligence issues also create problems for prose-cutions when they arise in almost any part of a crimi-nal case. This is especially notable in prosecutions in two areas of high interest and significance to both law enforcement and intelligence agencies. Espionage prosecutions by their nature involve someone who has had access to classified national security informa-tion. Such defendants already have knowledge about the government's case against them without any dis-covery or chance for the government to minimize the risk of disclosure of sensitive information through the CIPA process. The case in chief will almost always involve a high risk that other sensitive information will have to be revealed to achieve a conviction, thus multiplying in ways difficult to evaluate the damage already caused by the defendant.

This significant additional hurdle for the prose-cution also arises when an employee of the intelli-gence community is charged with crimes other than espionage. Typically these charges involve either some type of violation of anti-corruption ethics laws or more often, violations of perjury laws or prohibi-tions of false statements to Congress or others (such as inspector generals) investigating some aspect of intelligence activities. The problem is multiplied when independent counsel prosecutors operate without the usual check on prosecutorial discretion that operates when the executive branch agencies decide on whether the damage of going forward with a prosecution greatly outweighs the likelihood of

achieving a significant conviction for a major crime. This dilemma arose most notably during the exis-tence of the statutory independent counsel created to minimize possible conflicts of interest arising when the Department of Justice prosecutes senior U.S. gov-ernment officials (such as the Iran-Contra prosecu-tions). The statute creating the independent counsel was not renewed by Congress after it expired, but the appointment of quasi-independent special counsels by the attorney general continues.

Terrorism cases raise an additional problem for the prosecution. Terrorist acts and the activities of terrorist organizations have at their base a violent attack on the United States or its citizens and their property anywhere in the world. The national secu-rity and intelligence elements of the U.S. govern-ment expend enormous efforts to prevent such attacks. Law enforcement contributes to that pre-emption in a number of significant ways, but fun-damentally law enforcement actions are geared toward capturing those committing crimes in the past and amassing evidence to prove their guilt beyond a reasonable doubt. If a potential terrorist has not yet committed a terrorist act, the prevention role of the intelligence community prevails and the retribution role of the law enforcement community has to stand to the side, often to its future detriment in criminal trials.

In addition, the special authorities of the intelli-gence community have given rise to a number of in-stances in which defendants assert the "CIA defense." It is a variation of the defense of public authority, in which a defendant essentially argues that if he in fact did the acts as charged by the prosecution, he was authorized to do so by the government itself (FRCrP 12; *U.S. v. Rosenthal* 1986, 1235–1237; *Smith v. U.S.* 1984, 432) Because the intelligence community operates in secrecy and in fact is lawfully authorized to do certain activities that would be criminal viola-tions if conducted by private entities, the CIA de-fense can be a significant weakness in a prosecution. If allowed under the rules of criminal procedure, a defendant may demand much more discovery from the intelligence community, including testimony by intelligence officials, and thus expand the greymail danger. It may also raise doubts in the minds of jurors who have the generally widespread exposure of the public to Hollywood notions of the CIA and other intelligence agencies having roving bands of desperados with licenses to kill, all being directed by sinister conspirators to hide the aliens in New Mexico at all costs.

5. THE WORLD IS FLAT, EXCEPT WHEN IT IS ROUND

The post–World War II expansion of international law enforcement is creating new challenges and problems for intelligence services. Increasingly, some nations are advocating universal jurisdiction, in which certain of their criminal laws may be applied to individuals with no connection to the country seeking to try them. Jurisdiction generally has been restricted to the territory of a particular nation or to its citizens. Universal jurisdiction would allow a national of Kenya to be tried in Belgium for certain crimes (such as crimes against humanity or genocide) committed against Kenyans in Kenya. Other principles of international law have also expanded the ability of a state to prosecute conduct that occurs outside its territory (the protective principle, the objective territorial principle, the national principle, and especially the passive personality principle, which allows a state to prosecute someone for crimes against nationals of that state; *U.S. v. Bin Laden* 2000).

Demands for war-crimes trials have also led to the creation of international institutions under the purview of the United Nations or the NATO Alliance. A number of international criminal tribunals were created to deal with charges against individuals in the former Yugoslavia, Rwanda, and Sierra Leone, for example. The International Criminal Court (ICC) was also established by international convention as an ongoing venue for such charges to be heard.

The trial of two alleged Libyan intelligence operatives for the destruction of Pan Am Flight 103 over Scotland was a hybrid legal proceeding demonstrating the high cost of international joint ventures involving both law enforcement and intelligence. The trial was held at The Hague, but the law applied was Scots law and the court was composed of Scots judges. There was an extensive and costly trial, which involved the first time in history that a CIA officer testified in a foreign criminal proceeding. The split verdict left many participants unsatisfied with the result and the resources it took to translate a vast, multinational intelligence and law enforcement effort to identify those responsible for the terrorist act into a judicial proceeding bound by rules of fairness, individual rights, and certainties needed for convictions.

The problems associated with intelligence and law enforcement under domestic criminal statutes and systems is multiplied exponentially when foreign nations attempt joint prosecutions under notions of international criminal laws that are often vague and enforced in widely varying ways (e.g., "crimes against humanity," or "genocide.") Intelligence information is very likely to become an issue in such situations as the executive agencies of the involved governments direct collection and analysis against potential defendants who are also targets of intense foreign and defense policy interest. By agreement with the prosecutors, such agencies establish procedures for the tribunal proceedings minimizing exposure of intelligence sources and methods. The sources and methods may be at risk because information in the case could reveal highly sensitive information ranging from direct evidence of criminal acts and intent (SIGINT intercepts of conversations of defendants discussing the alleged crimes) to the location of wanted individuals sought by police departments (unmanned aerial vehicle electro-optical imagery of cars or houses where such individuals might be located). Exposure of such information to foreign nationals involved in the prosecution or defense of war crimes would significantly increase the risk of any participating nation's intelligence secrets being exposed. At best, international law is imprecise, uncertain, and dependent upon actions of foreign nations and foreign courts. Criminal law enforcement, by contrast, requires precision, clarity, and predictability if it is to have political legitimacy.

6. CONCLUSION: TOMORROW IS ANOTHER DAY

At the end of the day, the most pressing issues in the intersection of intelligence and law enforcement will probably involve a balance between the parts of the two worlds that are irreconcilable. In certain areas, intelligence equities should and will prevail, and in other areas law enforcement will be the prime actor. In the grey area where the two imperatives overlap, mission managers will have to further their own goals while devoting reasonable efforts to avoid impeding the other's mission.

The most pressing issue is the creation of a domestic intelligence organization separate from law enforcement and foreign intelligence establishments. It is driven by the most dangerous threat facing the United States: nuclear weapons in the hands of suicidal terrorists such as al-Qaida, who would use them. The authorities, rules of engagement, restrictions, safeguards, oversight, and resources for such an intelligence organization would have to be established in a balance of national security interests with privacy and other civil liberties.

A second issue is the extent to which traditional notions of due process in the United States' law enforcement system hamper or otherwise significantly restrict the intelligence community in its primary roles of producing foreign intelligence and supporting military operations. The right to remain silent does not apply to a suicide bomber bent on destroying a city (Posner 2006).

Another issue relates to the appropriate use of the armed forces. Restrictions on military involvement with domestic civilian law enforcement or even military operations against an enemy inside the United States may be out of date.

In addition, military law enforcement (including military commissions and the enforcement of the laws of war) differs from civilian law enforcement. The current effort to try non-state actors and unlawful combatants detained by the United States in the war on terrorism by military commissions has led to litigation and confusion in heroic proportions, and that is not over yet (Hamdan).

A further issue is the extent to which technical means of conducting surveillance have advanced to such a degree that they intrude on Americans' long-held notions of the acceptable boundary between government scrutiny and citizens' privacy. Reasonable expectations of privacy that grew out of many years of uncomplicated police work enforcing domestic criminal laws may not be appropriate for the effective prevention of unidentified foreign terrorists. The recent debate regarding amendments to FISA underscored the deep wariness many Americans have about any extension of foreign intelligence collection by intrusive means inside the United States or outside the United States when the target of the collection is a U.S. person.

These issues are part of a seamless web and each issue affects the others, for the most part. What is clear is that immediate post–World War II notions of the differences between one side of the border of the United States and the other do not fit the world as we find it. Where, in fact, is cyberspace?

The divide between national security and law enforcement is, ". . . carved deeply into the topography of American government" (Carter et al. 1998, 82). Intelligence and law enforcement will continue to co-exist more or less peacefully, but there are continuing issues that probably have no better solution than the professionals of both worlds, and their policy making masters, act in well-informed and well-intentioned ways to support and deconflict their activities and missions. The different cultures and narratives of each community are significant and important (Best). They affect the view that each has of the other and of themselves. That affects the ability of managers to manage them, overseers to watch them, and ultimately the ability of the U.S. government to succeed in their areas of operation.

As one commentator noted, FBI officers are from Mars, from Fordham, from the football team, from the Boy and Girl Scouts, from off the street. CIA officers are from Venus, from Yale, from the tennis team, from the front row in class where they always raise their hands, from a book-lined study, from academe (Gorman 2003).

Muddling through is part of the job.

QUESTIONS FOR FURTHER DISCUSSION

1. Do you think there is a proper role for the judicial branch in the supervision of intelligence activities?
2. Which organizations do you think provide the best safeguards against the misuse of secret power by the CIA and other intelligence agencies: the National Security Council, the Office of the DNI, the Congress, the courts, or the media?
3. What kinds of intelligence activities are covered by the FISA Court?
4. What are some reasons why the court system may not provide a strong check on the executive branch when it comes to intelligence operations?

REFERENCES

Antiterrorism and Effective Death Penalty Act, Pub. L. No. 104–132, no Stat. 1214.

Authority of the Federal Bureau of Investigation to Override Customary or Other International Law in the Course of Extraterritorial Law Enforcement Activities, 13 Op. Ofc. Legal Counsel 195 (1989).

Baker, S. A. 1994–95. Should Spies Be Cops? *Foreign Policy* 97 (Winter): 36.

Best, R. A., Jr. 2001. *Intelligence and Law Enforcement: Countering Transnational Threats to the U.S.* Washington, D.C.: Congressional Research Service.

Board of Education v. Earls. 536 U.S. 822 (2002).

Brady v. Maryland, 373 U.S. 83 (1963).

Carter, A., J. Deutch, and P. Zelikow. 1998. Catastrophic Terrorism: Tackling the New Danger. *Foreign Affairs* (November–December).

Civiletti, B. R. 1983. Intelligence Gathering and the Law. *Studies In Intelligence.* Center for the Study of Intelligence 27, no. 2 (Summer): 13.

Classified Information Procedures Act, as amended, 18 U.S.C.A. app. 3 sections 1–16.

Collins, J. M. 2002. *And the Walls Came Tumbling Down: Sharing Grand Jury Information with the Intelligence Community under the USA PATRIOT Act*, 39 American Criminal Law Review 1261.

Commission on Intelligence Capabilities of the U.S. Regarding Weapons of Mass Destruction (WMD Commission). 2005. *Report to the President.*

Commission on Roles and Capabilities of the U.S. Intelligence Community (Aspin-Brown Commission). 1996. *Preparing for the 21st Century: An Appraisal of U.S. Intelligence.*

Doyle, C. 1995. *The Posse Comitatus Act & Related Matters: The Use of the Military to Execute Civilian Law,* Congressional Research Service Report 95–964 S (September 12).

Executive Order 12333. (EO 12333).

Federal Rules of Criminal Procedure. (FRCrP).

Foreign Intelligence Surveillance Act, as amended. (FISA).

Fredman, J. 1998. Intelligence Agencies, Law Enforcement, and the Prosecution Team. *Yale Legal and Policy Review* 16:331.

Frisbie v. Collins, 342 U.S. 519 (1952).

Funk, W. *Electronic Surveillance of Terrorism: The Intelligence/Law Enforcement Dilemma—A History*, 11 Lewis & Clark L. Rev. 1099 (2007).

Giglio v. United States, 405 U.S. 150 (1972).

Gorelick, J. S. 1994. *Amending the Foreign Intelligence Surveillance Act: Hearings Before the House Permanent Select Comm. on Intelligence*, 103d Cong, 2d Sess., 62.

Gorman, S. 2003. FBI, CIA Remain Worlds Apart. *National Journal* (August 1).

Hall, J. W. 2000. Search and Seizure. 3rd ed., section 36.7.

Hamdan v. Rumsfeld, 126 S. Ct. 2749 (2006).

Hamdi v. Rumsfeld, 542 U.S. 507 (2004).

Howell, B. A., and D. J. Lesemann. 2007. Symposium, *Protecting the Nation at the Expense of Individuals? Defining the Scope of U.S. Executive Power at Home and Abroad in Times of Crisis: FISA's Fruits in Criminal Cases: An Opportunity for Improved Accountability*, 12 UCLA Journal of International Law & Foreign Affairs 145 (2007).

Hulnick, A. S. 1997. Intelligence and Law Enforcement. *International Journal of Intelligence and Counterintelligence* 10 (Fall): 269.

In re Scaled Case No. 02–001, 310 F.3d 717 (FISA Ct. Rev. 2002).

Intelligence Authorization Act for Fiscal Year 1995, 50 U.S.C. section 402a (2005).

Johnson, L. K., *and* J. J. Wirtz. 2008. *Intelligence and National Security: The Secret World of Spies.* 2nd ed. New York: Oxford University Press.

Ker v. Illinois, 119 U.S. 436 (1886).

Kris, D. S., and J. D. Wilson. *National Security Investigations & Prosecutions* §§ 2.9–2.15 [2008 loose-leaf].

Lowenthal, M. M. 2006. *Intelligence: From Secrets to Policy.* 3rd ed. Washington D.C.: CQ Press.

Manget, F. F. 2006. Intelligence and the Criminal Law System. *Stanford Law and Policy Review* 17:415.

Nardone v. United States, 302 U.S. 379 (1937).

National Commission on Terrorist Attacks upon the U.S. 2004. *9/11 Commission Report.*

National Security Act of 1947, as amended.

Posner, R. A. 2006. *Not a Suicide Pact: The Constitution in a Time of National Emergency.* New York: Oxford University Press.

Riebling, M. 2002. *Wedge: The Secret War between the FBI and the CIA.* New York: Touchstone.

Senate Select Committee on Intelligence and House Permanent Select Committee on Intelligence, Joint Inquiry Into Intelligence Community Activities Before and After the Terrorist Attacks of September 11, 2001, Senate Report No. 107–351, House Report No. 107–792 (2d Sess. 2002).

Smith v. United States, 592 F. Supp. 424 (E.D. Va. 1984).

Snider, L. B., E. Rindskopf, and J. Coleman. 1994. *Relating Intelligence and Law Enforcement: Problems and Prospects.* Washington: Consortium for the Study of Intelligence.

Thompson, B. G. 2006. *The National Counterterrorism Center: Foreign and Domestic Intelligence Fusion and the Potential Threat to Privacy*, 6 PGH Journal of Technology Law and Policy, 6.

United States v. Alvarez-Machain, 504 U.S. 655 (1992).

United States v. Bin Laden, 92 F. Supp. 2d 189 (S.D.N.Y. 2000).

United States v. Rosenthal, 793 F.2d 1214 (11th Cir. 1986).

United States v. Toscanino, 500 F.2d 267 (2d Cir. 1974), *reh'g denied*, 504 F.2d 1380 (2d Cir. 1974).

United States v. Truong, 629 F.2d 908 (4th Cir. 1980), cert, denied, 454 U.S. 1144 (1982).

United States v. Verdugo-Urquidez, 494 U.S. 259 (1990).

U.S. Department of Army, Field Manual 27–10, The Law of Land Warfare (1956). (FM 27–10).

USA PATRIOT Act (United and Strengthening America by Providing Appropriate Tools Required to Intercept and Obstruct Terrorism Act of 2001). Pub. L. No. 107–56, 115 Stat. 272.

From Frederic F. Manget, "Intelligence and the Rise of Judicial Intervention" in Loch K. Johnson, ed., *Handbook of Intelligence Studies* (New York: Routledge, 2007): 329–342. Reproduced by permission of Taylor and Francis Books UK.

24. CONGRESSIONAL SUPERVISION OF AMERICA'S SECRET AGENCIES: THE EXPERIENCE AND LEGACY OF THE CHURCH COMMITTEE

LOCH K. JOHNSON

A former assistant to Senator Frank Church, who led the Senate inquiry into alleged CIA abuses of power in 1975, Johnson reviews the experiences of that investigation and gauges the contribution made by the Church Committee to the search for a proper balance between security against America's enemies and the civil liberties of its own citizens.

KEEPING AN EYE ON THE HIDDEN SIDE OF GOVERNMENT

For purposes of gathering and interpreting information from around the world, the United States created thirteen major agencies during the Cold War, known collectively as the "intelligence community" and led by a Director of Central Intelligence (DCI). Seven of the agencies have a predominantly military mission and are within the jurisdiction of the Defense Department (among them, the National Security Agency or NSA, which gathers signals intelligence); five are associated with civilian departments, such as the Federal Bureau of Investigation (FBI) within the Justice Department; and one, the Central Intelligence Agency (CIA), stands alone as an independent entity answerable directly to the president (Lowenthal 1992; Richelson 1999). Together, these agencies comprise the largest cluster of information-gathering organizations in American history, and rivalled in world history only by the intelligence apparatus of the Soviet Union during the Cold War and Russia today.

Concealed from public scrutiny, America's intelligence agencies pose a major challenge to the idea of government accountability in a democratic society (Ransom 1970, 1975; Johnson 1986). This essay examines the failure of legislative supervisors to hold the intelligence community in check during the Cold War, leading to a significant erosion of civil liberties in the United States. It explores as well the prerequisites necessary to lessen the probability of the further abuse of power by the secret agencies.

A CONCEPTUAL FRAMEWORK

An extensive literature exists on the subject of congressional control over administrative agencies, commonly referred to as legislative oversight (e.g., Aberbach 1990; Ogul 1976; Scher 1963). As Spence notes (1997), positive theorists and quantitative empiricists have pointed to the capacity of lawmakers to shape the environment of agency decision making in such a way as to align bureaucrats toward the goals of oversight committees on Capitol Hill. For instance, Calvert, McCubbins, and Weingast (1989), as well as McCubbins *et al.* (1989), maintain that executive agencies are essentially "hard-wired" at their statutory inception to honor legislative intentions (*ex ante* control). Moreover, they posit, lawmakers have potent sanctions that may be used to punish rogue bureaucratic behavior, notably the power of the purse to reduce funding for recalcitrant agencies (*ex post* control).

Theorists emphasize as well that organized interest groups provide an added safeguard to assist lawmakers in thwarting errant bureaucrats who fail to uphold original legislative mandates. Lobbyists set off "fire alarms" to alert members of Congress when agencies have violated expected norms (McCubbins and Schwartz 1984). Media reporting on agency activities can serve a similar function. Moreover, lawmakers and their staff can engage in "police patrolling," that is, a more active and direct monitoring of agency activities through persistent hearings and less formal dialogues with agency personnel.

Yet, in contrast to these roseate theories on the efficacy of legislative oversight, a more extensive body of research that stretches over four decades of scholarly reporting offers quite a different impression. From this point of view, lawmakers have engaged in oversight only sporadically and halfheartedly (Bibby 1968; Ransom, 1970, 1977; Dodd and Schott 1979, 170–184; Johnson 1994). This failure of accountability has stemmed chiefly from a lack of motivation among members of Congress to immerse themselves in oversight activities, such as hearings and detailed budget reviews. For lawmakers, greater political advantage lies in the passage of legislation, where credit-claiming—vital to re-election—is more visible to constituents (Mayhew 1986).

Further, representatives have often been reluctant to become involved in (and, thus, responsible for) controversial agency decisions; better to keep a distance from potential trouble (Walden 1970). Information asymmetries have contributed as well to the failure of oversight, giving agencies room to maneuver as lawmakers remain unaware of informal rules, internal memoranda, and private deals struck inside the vast domains of the executive departments (Spence 1997, 200).

THE SPECIAL CASE OF INTELLIGENCE

With respect to the intelligence agencies, the limited relevance of the safeguards heralded by the positivists and quantitative empiricists is manifest. In the first place, the statutory rules established for the secret agencies by the National Security Act of 1947 (50 U.S.C. 401) are broadly worded and often ambiguous. In one clause, for instance, this statute grants the CIA with authority to "perform such other functions and duties related to intelligence affecting the national security as the President or the National Security Council may direct . . ."—not exactly a tight legislative leash.

As for the appointment power, it is true that lawmakers have closely examined the credentials of some DCI nominees, rejecting a handful over the years in hotly debated hearings (as with the donnybrook over the failed nomination of Anthony Lake during the Clinton Administration). Yet, the Office of DCI is notoriously weak. The DCI is head of the CIA, but exercises only marginal control over the dozen

other agencies in the community. Their separate chiefs have extensive discretionary authority and are seldom subjected to the kind of legislative scrutiny directed toward DCI nominations (Johnson 2000).

Fire alarms set off by lobbyists or by media reporters are unreliable, too. Few interest groups exist in this policy domain, and those that do (the Boeing corporation, for instance, which manufactures surveillance satellites) are rarely able to discuss whatever grievances they may have in public, given the classified nature of their work. And as Dana Priest, the *Washington Post's* correspondent with an intelligence beat, has remarked (2003), the "high walls" of the intelligence agencies make it very difficult to report on intelligence activities. These walls are important to protect the nation's secrets from foreign spies; however, they have the effect, too, of isolating the intelligence agencies from the normal processes of legislative accountability envisioned in the Constitution (Article I), the *Federalist Papers* (e.g., No. 51), and various Supreme Court opinions (among the most famous, Justice Brandeis's comments in *Myers v. U.S.*, 272 U.S. 52 [1926]).

Police patrolling by Congress itself has been minimal, resulting from the lack of motivation by lawmakers in all policy domains, alluded to earlier. Specifically with respect to intelligence, members of Congress made it clear during the early stages of the Cold War that they were content to rely on the intelligence professionals to take care of business, with limited congressional supervision. The House and the Senate maintained small oversight subcommittees on the Armed Services and Appropriations Committees, but they met only infrequently and the questioning was typically brief if not perfunctory. One of the overseers, Leverett Saltonstall (D, Massachusetts), said on the floor of the Senate in 1956 that he was hesitant to "obtain information which I personally would rather not have, unless it was essential for me as a member of Congress to have it. . . ." (Holt 1995, 211).

Intelligence enjoyed a special dispensation since the days of the American Revolution (Knott 1996). The sense was that secret operations were too sensitive to be treated as normal government activities. The intelligence agencies would have to be kept apart; whether fighting Barbary pirates in the early days or communists during the Cold War, the nation would have to rely on the good intentions and sound judgment of its spymasters and professional intelligence officers.

The results of this "hands off" approach to intelligence supervision are probed here, using the methodologies of archival research, interviews with government officials, and participant observation as a scholar-in-residence on Capitol Hill. Lord Acton's venerable aphorism provides a working hypothesis: "Power corrupts and absolute power corrupts absolutely." To which he might have added, "especially secret power."

AN AWAKENING

In 1974, a pivotal year in American politics, the nation had just withdrawn from the war in Vietnam and the ensuing Watergate scandal produced the first ever resignation of a president, Richard M. Nixon. It was a time of great turmoil and the confidence of Americans in their institutions of government began to plummet. Coming on top of these jarring experiences, the *New York Times* accused the CIA of spying at home.

In December, the newspaper's allegations produced a firestorm of public outrage (Colby 1978). Congressional offices received thousands of letters from citizens across the country. "Watergate might only be a prelude" to an even deeper assault on democracy, worried a constituent from Minnesota—a common theme in these mailings (Mondale 1975). A feeling of anger and dismay spread through the Congress. "To whom are the intelligence -agencies responsible?" the fiery orator John Pastore (D, Rhode Island) demanded to know as he introduced a resolution calling for an investigation. On January 21, 1975, senators voted overwhelmingly in support of the resolution (Johnson 1986). The House launched its own inquiry as well, and, not to be left behind, so did the White House under the leadership of President Gerald R. Ford (Smist 1994). If the Orwellian charges were true, something had to be done.

The formal name of the investigative panel created by the Senate was the "Special Select Committee to Investigate Intelligence Activities," known less formally as the "Select Committee on Intelligence" or simply the Church Committee after its chairman, Frank Church (D, Idaho), with whom I served as a special assistant during the 16-month inquiry. A veteran of the Senate (elected at age 32, almost two decades earlier) and an expert on foreign affairs, Church was drawn chiefly to the accusation in the *Times* that dealt with CIA excesses overseas. Most of the others on the eleven-member panel were more concerned about the charges of domestic spying, particularly the next ranking Democrat Walter F. Mondale (Minnesota). Church asked him to lead a

special subcommittee looking into this aspect of the Committee's investigation. The four additional Democrats on the Committee were Philip Hart of Michigan, Walter "Dee" Huddleston of Kentucky, Robert Morgan of North Carolina, and Gary Hart of Colorado. The Republican members included John Tower of Texas, Howard Baker of Tennessee, Barry Goldwater of Arizona, Charles Mathias of Maryland, and Richard Schweiker of Pennsylvania.

The charges of intelligence abuse came as a shock to lawmakers. This is not to say that they were unaware of problems that had cropped up in the intelligence community from time to time. Earlier reports had surfaced that the FBI kept extensive data banks on U.S. citizens, for example, and rumors were rife in the nation's Capitol about the personal files kept by Bureau Director J. Edgar Hoover on government officials, used to "encourage" their support of his programs and budgets (Ungar 1975). Yet, despite occasional revelations about intelligence improprieties (and dismay over the CIA's disastrous Bay of Pigs operation in 1961), no efforts toward reform had managed to gain the support of a majority in either chamber of Congress. Certainly none of the members of Congress serving in 1974 had ever suggested that America's secret agencies might be engaged in widespread spying against the very people they had sworn to protect (although in 1947 a few of their predecessors had expressed fears about this possibility when Congress passed the CIA's founding statute).

The paths of spies and lawmakers had seldom crossed. The FBI enjoyed the most frequent presence on Capitol Hill, having learned early the skills of legislative lobbying. Its officers came across as dedicated, hardworking public servants engaged in catching bank robbers, white-collar criminals, and Soviet spies. The drumbeat message from the Bureau was straightforward: its legitimate law enforcement and counterintelligence duties helped keep thugs, terrorists, and foreign agents at bay and deserved the approbation of the American people (Kessler 2003).

Moreover, lawmakers comforted themselves in the thought that both chambers had intelligence oversight subcommittees within the jurisdictions of the Armed Services and Appropriations Committees. These panels were supposed to monitor the nation's intelligence activities on behalf of the Congress, freeing the vast majority of lawmakers from concern—and culpability (Barrett 1998). Hence, when the allegations of abuse came to light in 1974, the public and their representatives in Washington were taken aback.

MANDATE FOR REFORM

The scope of the Church Committee investigation was staggering. The Senate Watergate Committee had taken over a year to examine just that single event; during the next eight months, Congress expected the Church Committee to probe a multitude of alleged intelligence abuses that had taken place over the past quarter century. Members of the Committee would eventually have to seek an additional eight-month extension to complete their work. As the Committee started up, it confronted one frustration after another, for the executive branch did its best to slow the pace of the inquiry. Compliance with the Committee's documents request would take time, the White House argued; the Committee would have to be patient. It seemed like the same old stonewalling that had plagued the Senate during its Watergate inquiry.

Slowly, however, the Church Committee managed to uncover revealing documents during the summer of 1975 and, at last, was prepared to hold public hearings in September. The initial focus was a master spy plan prepared for President Nixon by a young White House aide from Indiana by the name of Tom Charles Huston. Despite laws to the contrary (not to mention the first amendment to the Constitution), the so-called Huston Plan recommended using the nation's secret agencies to spy on Vietnam War dissenters. Huston and the intelligence chiefs who signed onto the Plan, including DCI Richard Helms and FBI Director Hoover, portrayed the United States as a nation under siege by student radicals. The document revealed, as Mondale observed during the hearings (U.S. Senate 1975), an "enormous, unrestricted paranoid fear about the American people."

The executive branch had concluded, wrongly, that the youthful dissenters were agents of Moscow. As a result, the United States would have to move outside the framework of the Constitution and the law; the legal system had become too confining in the struggle against the Soviet Union, itself unrestrained by a Bill of Rights. The enemy was sinister and lawless, so, the United States would have to become that way, too. Fire would have to be fought with fire. Yet, as Huston conceded in testimony before the Committee (U.S. Senate 1975), his spy plan raised the risk that the secret agencies would "move from the kid with a bomb to the kid with a picket sign, and from the kid with the picket sign to the kid with the bumper sticker of the opposing candidate. And you just keep going down the line."

The Committee's chief counsel, Frederick A. O. Schwarz, Jr. (grandson of the toy manufacturer) saw this chilling declension as the most important insight to emerge from the inquiry. "Government," he concluded (Schwarz 2000), "is going—inevitably and necessarily, I submit—to keep on going down that line, once it departs from suspected violation of the law as the only legitimate ground to investigate Americans."

The Huston Plan was just the first of many jolts to the Committee as it opened a Pandora's box of wrongdoing. One abuse after another came tumbling out as lawmakers and staff investigators shined a light into the hidden recesses of government (U.S. Senate 1976). Looking over the shoulder of the Church Committee, the American public discovered:

- The FBI had created files on over 1 million Americans and carried out over 500,000 investigations of "subversives" from 1960–74, without a single court conviction.
- NSA computers had monitored every cable sent overseas, or received from overseas, by Americans from 1947–75.
- The Internal Revenue Service had allowed tax information to be misused by intelligence agencies for political purposes.
- FBI agents had conducted a campaign to incite violence among African-Americans.
- An FBI counterintelligence program ("Coin-telpro") had harassed civil rights activists and Vietnam war dissidents, in an attempt to fray and often break apart family and friendship ties.

COINTELPRO

Senators on the Church Committee found Cointelpro deeply troubling. With its spying at home (Operation CHAOS), the CIA had also acted in a manner inconsistent with American laws and values; but Cointelpro stunned lawmakers, for it went beyond even domestic spying. Internal Bureau documents revealed that from 1956 to 1971 the FBI had carried out smear campaigns against individuals and groups across the country, simply because they had expressed opposition to the war in Vietnam, criticized the slow pace of the civil rights movement, or (quite the opposite) advocated racial segregation. The attacks were directed against people in all walks of life and of various political persuasions; the expansive hatred of the Bureau's leaders embraced black leaders and white supremacists alike, with critics of the war in Vietnam thrown in for good measure. As Mondale recalled, "no meeting was too small, no group too insignificant" to escape the FBI's attention (2000).

Among the thousands of Cointelpro victims was Dr. Anatol Rapoport, a gifted social scientist at the University of Michigan. He attracted the Bureau's attention because of his criticism of the war in Indochina and his "suspicious" origins (he had been born in Russia shortly before his parents immigrated to America early in the twentieth century). The FBI's agent in charge for the Ann Arbor area, responding to top secret directives from Bureau headquarters, set out to "neutralize" Professor Rapoport—a term used by the FBI to mean the harassment of an individual as a means for curbing his or her dissent. The Bureau mailed anonymous letters to senior administrators at the University, as well as to prominent citizens in Ann Arbor and throughout the state, claiming without a shred of evidence that Rapoport was, if not a communist, then at least an apologist for communism and a troublemaker. The letters were typically signed "a concerned citizen" or "a concerned taxpayer."

The Bureau also placed informants in Rapoport's classrooms to report on his "subversive" activities. He was to be embarrassed, discredited, and spied upon in whatever imaginative ways the FBI's special agent could devise. These pressures, whose underlying source Rapoport never comprehended (Rapoport 1975), eventually led him to resign from the University of Michigan and take up a faculty post at the University of Toronto. The FBI had won. Although he remained a critic of the war in Vietnam, Cointelpro had damaged Rapoport's career, drained him emotionally, strained his family and professional ties, and drove him from this country.

White supremacists also failed to fit into Hoover's Procrustean bed of conformity. The FBI sent another of its poisonous letters, this time written in Southern slang, to a wife of a Ku Klux Klan member, intimating that her husband was having an affair with another woman. The Klan, the -women's liberation movement, socialists, the New Left, antiwar and civil right activists—all became enemies of the Republic whom the Bureau set out secretly to destroy (U.S. Senate 1976). In the Twin Cities, an FBI *agent provocateur* encouraged striking taxi drivers to construct a bomb for use in their battle against local teamsters; in California, a Bureau office boasted in a memorandum back to headquarters:

> Shootings, beatings, and a high degree of unrest continues to prevail in the ghetto area of southeast San Diego. Although no specific counterintelligence action can be credited with contributing to this overall situation, it is felt that a substantial amount of the unrest is directly attributable to this program.

One day in the middle of the Committee's inquiry, a staff aide came across Hoover's "Personal & Confidential" files at FBI Headquarters in Washington, D.C. (Gittenstein 2000). Most of the files had been destroyed by the Director's assistant, Johnny Moore, who started burning the papers in reverse alphabetical order after Hoover died. Moore had gotten to "C" before being discovered and stopped by Bureau officials. In "B" was a file labeled "Black Bag Jobs." It contained documents that proved Hoover had wiretapped Dr. Martin Luther King, Jr., the famed civil rights leader, without the benefit of a court order. When the Church Committee investigator presented lawmakers with this and related papers, even the more sceptical among them began to realize: "My god, Hoover really did these things!"

Soft-spoken, bearded Philip Hart was one of the most influential members of the Committee (one of the Senate's three office buildings is now named after him). His struggle with cancer prevented him from attending most Committee meetings, but he found the strength to come to the opening hearing on the FBI. Hundreds of people filled the ornate Senate Caucus Room, site of famous investigations into the sinking of the Titanic, the Pearl Harbor attack, Joseph McCarthy's witch-hunt, and the recent Watergate scandal. With his frail body bent over the Committee bench, Hart listened intently to testimony from witnesses about Cointelpro. When it came time for him to speak, the cavernous hall fell silent as reporters and tourists strained to hear his weakened voice. He recalled that he had been sceptical when his own family of political activists had complained about how the FBI was trying to discredit opposition to the war in Vietnam. With his words cracking in emotion, Hart conceded that they had been right all along; he had been wrong to defend the Bureau. Not a soul stirred in the Caucus Room as he continued:

> As a result of my superior wisdom in high office, I assured them they are on pot—it just wasn't true. [The FBI] wouldn't do it. What you have described is a series of illegal actions intended to deny certain citizens their first amendment rights, just like my children said.

It was the most poignant moment in the Committee's inquiry.

TARGETING REVEREND KING

Nor were lawmakers apt to forget other key FBI documents unearthed by the Committee. The most shocking to the Committee's members was an anonymous letter written by the Bureau, accompanied by a tape recording. As King travelled around the country, FBI agents had followed him and placed listening devices in his hotel room, recording compromising romantic liaisons. The Bureau then mailed the letter and tape to King in 1964, 34 days before he was to receive the Nobel Prize for Peace. In a ploy interpreted as an attempt by the FBI to push King into taking his own life, the letter read (U.S. Senate 1976):

> King, there is only one thing left for you to do. You know what it is. You have just 34 days in which to do it. (The exact number has been selected for a specific reason.) It has a definite practical significance. You are done. There is but one way out for you. You better take it before your filthy, abnormal fraudulent self is bared to the nation.

A month later, the Bureau sent a copy of the tape recordings to Mrs. King, who joined her husband in denouncing the blackmail attempt.

The goal of wrecking the civil rights movement stood at the heart of Cointelpro and the efforts to ruin Rev. King were relentless. All the elements of the Bureau's dark side came together as it directed its full surveillance powers against him. In tandem with the blackmail attempt, the Bureau initiated whispering campaigns to undermine the moral authority of the civil rights leader, and sent anonymous letters to newspapers that questioned his patriotism. The purpose, according to an FBI document, was to knock King "off his pedestal" (U.S. Senate 1976). Like Professor Rapoport, he would be "neutralized." Hoover pressured his subordinates to either rewrite their field reports on King, falsely labelling him the pawn of a Soviet agent—or else lose their jobs.

In 1964, the FBI bugged King's hotel suite at the Democratic National Convention, along with rooms occupied by delegates of the Mississippi Freedom Democratic Party, using this information to disrupt civil rights activists at the convention. Further, the Bureau blocked King from receiving honorary degrees, tried unsuccessfully to keep him from meeting with the Pope, planted an attractive female *agent provocateur* on his staff, and supplied friendly reporters with a stream of prurient stories about his private life (U.S. Senate 1976).

The Bureau continued to harass King until his final days. Committee investigators assigned to examine the case brooded darkly about the possibility of a Bureau set up to end the life of the civil rights leader. They wondered if, on a fateful trip to Memphis, King might have been "encouraged" by FBI media leaks to abandon plans to stay in a white-owned hotel and move instead to the less secure, black-owned Lorraine Hotel. The Committee never found any evidence to support this theory, but close associates of the slain civil rights leader continue to harbor suspicions about FBI and local law enforcement complicity in King's assassination (Pepper 2003). Andrew Young, for example, points to the quick removal of potential evidence from the murder scene, even the cutting down of bushes across the street from the Lorraine near the area where the fatal shots were fired (Young 2000). After King's death, when lawmakers began to consider whether his birthday should be made a national holiday, the FBI developed plans to brief selected members of Congress on how to stop the proposal.

During hearings into the King case, Senator Mondale asked the Committee's chief counsel, Schwarz: "Was there any evidence at any time that [the FBI] was suspicious that [Dr. King] was about to or had committed a crime?" The answer was "no." Mondale asked further: "Was he ever charged with fomenting violence? Did he ever participate in violence?" Again the answer was "no." Mondale considered King the nation's greatest civil rights hero, an apostle of non-violence at a time in American history when there were tremendous pressures to use violence. King was a man of the cloth, acting from a deep sense of conviction—only to be treated by the FBI as a common criminal. "There is nothing in this case that distinguishes that particular action from what the KGB does with dissenters in that country [the U.S.S.R.]," he said in disgust during a Committee hearing (U.S. Senate 1976). He concluded: "I think it is a road map to the destruction of American democracy."

Schwarz remembers being "shocked" by the attacks on King:

> Here was a peaceful civil rights leader whom I admired as much as anybody in our history, and the FBI was trying to get him to commit suicide. The bureau called the Southern Christian Leadership Conference a black hate organization. The words were all upside down. (2000)

When the Attorney General in the Ford Administration, Edward H. Levi, former dean of the law school at the University of Chicago, came before the Church Committee, Mondale—who had evolved into the Committee's leading interrogator on matters of domestic intelligence—asked him what he intended to do about cleaning up the FBI mess. The AG's answers were far from what Committee members, most of whom had gone to law school and two of whom (Mondale and Morgan) had served as state attorneys general, expected to hear from the nation's chief law enforcement officer and a noted constitutional scholar. Levi sought unprecedented authority for the Bureau to act against a group or individual, before a crime was committed—the same slippery slope that had led to Cointelpro in the first place. He seemed to have forgotten that the job of the FBI was to focus on actual or suspected violations of the law, not just the expression of ideas. Levi had assumed the role of the Bureau's protector, while Mondale had taken on the role of the Committee's leading defender of civil liberties. A collision was inevitable.

Mondale suggested to the AG that his guidelines were "vaguely defined" and that, if they were not strengthened and codified into law, they "would be swept away as quickly as a sand castle is overrun by a hurricane" (U.S. Senate 1976). The temperature in the Senate Caucus Room rose as the two men confronted each other across the green-baize hearing table. When Levi resorted to an evasive answer, Mondale stared at him and said, "Well, I think that kind of arrogance is why we have trouble between the executive and the legislative branch." Levi replied, "I apologize to Senator Mondale if I appeared arrogant. I thought that someone else was appearing arrogant, but I apologize."

Mondale had put the AG on notice: the Committee was not going to be a push over; it would strenuously defend the liberties of American citizens. Despite this public confrontation, Mondale and Levi soon met privately and placed behind them any bad feelings, agreeing to work together in the crafting of FBI guidelines that would be acceptable both to the Committee and to the Justice Department. It was an important turning point in the investigation that led to constructive negotiations between the branches over proper guidelines for Bureau activities.

A WIDENING GYRE OF ABUSE

As the investigation unfolded, the Church Committee discovered just how far the violations of public trust had extended to the CIA and military intelligence units as well. For instance:

- The CIA had opened the mail to and from selected American citizens, which generated 1.5 million names stored in the Agency's computer bank (Operation CHAOS). No one was immune, not

Leonard Bernstein, not John Steinbeck, not Arthur Burns; even Richard Nixon had made the CIA's "watch list."
- Army intelligence units had conducted investigations against 100,000 U.S. citizens during the Vietnam war era.
- The CIA had engaged in drug experiments against unsuspecting subjects, two of whom had died from side effects.
- The CIA had manipulated elections even in democratic regimes like Chile.
- The CIA had infiltrated religious, media, and academic organizations inside the United States.
- The CIA had plotted failed assassination attempts against Fidel Castro of Cuba and Patrice Lumumba, among other foreign leaders.

The CIA's assassination plots and drug experiments were as unacceptable to the Church Committee as the FBI's Cointelpro operations had been. The CIA had even resorted to the recruitment of mafia mobsters to assist in the plots against Castro.

In Joseph Conrad's *Heart of Darkness*, the protagonist Marlow discovers in the jungles of central Africa the savagery that had befallen upon his once civilized companion, Mr. Kurtz. Isolated in a primitive setting, Kurtz had succumbed to a steady moral deterioration. In the last hours of his life, he peered into his own soul and, confronting the decay, cried out in despair: "The horror! The horror!" The allegory suited the secret agencies. Removed from the rest of democratic society, they had descended into a primordial underworld, using methods deemed necessary to combat foreign enemies, then turning these dark arts against citizens at home whose only crime had been to express beliefs that the White House or the intelligence chiefs found objectionable. In this crusade, the secret agencies had adopted some of the tactics of the repressive regimes they opposed. To argue that the United States had to abandon liberty in the name of security was to say that the nation had to become more like its enemies in order to protect itself from them—a pernicious doctrine that the Committee rejected out of hand.

How could the intelligence community have strayed so far from its rightful duties and into this heart of darkness? The answer stemmed in part from the paranoia engendered by the Cold War, even though—as acknowledged by William Sullivan (1975), the top FBI agent in charge of Cointelpro—there were not enough communists in the United States to carry the smallest precinct in New Hampshire, let alone take over the country. Sullivan told the Committee that the secret agencies had been caught up in an anti-communist tide that swept aside safeguards against the misuse of power (just as, today, a war against global terrorism in the wake of the 9/11 attacks against the United States holds the danger of eroding civil liberties at home, especially for law-abiding Arab-Americans). As Sullivan recalled, during the FBI's operations against Rev. King,

> No holds were barred. We have used [similar] techniques against Soviet agents. [The same methods were] brought home against any organization against which we were targeted. We did not differentiate. This is a rough, tough business. (U.S. Senate 1976)

He added that never once had he heard a discussion about the legality or constitutionality of any aspect of the FBI's internal security program. His explanation: "We were just naturally pragmatic."

During the Committee's public hearings on the NSA and its interception of cables sent to and from U.S. citizens (Operation SHAMROCK), a revealing exchange took place between Senator Mondale and the NSA's deputy director, Benson Buffham (U.S. Senate 1975):

MONDALE: Were you concerned about its legality?
BUFFHAM: Legality?
MONDALE: Whether it was legal.
BUFFHAM: In what sense? Whether that would have been a legal thing to do?
MONDALE: Yes.
BUFFHAM: That particular aspect didn't enter into the discussion.
MONDALE: I was asking you if you were concerned about whether that would be legal and proper.
BUFFHAM: We didn't consider it at the time, no.

It was a response echoed by other agency representatives during the hearings. One of the Committee members asked Clark Clifford, who had helped to draft the charter for the CIA in 1947 and served as secretary of defense during the Johnson Administration, about constitutional protections against abuses. He replied, "Well, that was a different time when we could afford that."

Criticism of the intelligence agencies was widely considered unpatriotic. They had to be given broad discretionary powers if they were to be successful in subduing America's adversaries at home and abroad. As a consequence, the secret agencies took on the features of a political police, growing increasingly autonomous, insulated, and aggressive. As William W. Keller has written (1989, 154), the intelligence community became "a state within the state, which would not be bound by the constraints of the constitutional order."

Responsibility for the abuses did not fall on the intelligence community alone. Presidents of both parties used the secret agencies to spy on political adversaries. Lawmakers were derelict, as well, for permitting the growth of an inadequately supervised security state. Intelligence scholar Harry Howe Ransom has drawn the proper conclusion (1984, 21): the Congress had become "a sleeping watchdog." James R. Schlesinger, DCI in 1973, remembers his initial briefing to the small Senate oversight subcommittee of that day (1993). As he began his briefing, John Stennis (D, Mississippi) interrupted the DCI: "No, no my boy, don't tell me. Just go ahead and do it, but I don't want to know."

William Sullivan of the FBI testified about another influence that contributed to the lawlessness that gripped the intelligence agencies (U.S. Senate 1976). "During World War Two, we had grown up topsy-turvy," he said, "when legal matters were secondary to achieving victory against the Nazis. This mentality carried over easily into the new war against the communists." During the course of its inquiry, the Committee came across a telling top secret document that had been prepared for President Dwight D. Eisenhower (U.S. Senate 1976, 9). A key passage advised that in the war against communism:

> . . . hitherto acceptable norms of human conduct do not apply. If the U.S. is to survive, long-standing American concepts of "fair play" must be reconsidered . . . we must learn to subvert, sabotage, and destroy our enemies by more clear, more sophisticated and more effective methods than those used against us.

The underlying philosophy reminded Schwarz (2000), the Committee counsel, of Macbeth's words: inevitably, the invention returns home "to plague the inventor."

The FBI's skillful lobbying of lawmakers further warded off serious oversight. So did its clever promotion of a favorable public relations image, as with the television show *The FBI Story*, which starred the dashing actor Efrem Zimbalist, Jr. The FBI censored the program's scripts and CBS beamed the program into millions of living rooms each week during the 1960s. Self-promotion helped the Bureau gain remarkable popularity and independence, free from congressional probes and detailed laws to guide its activities (Ungar 1975).

Hannah Arendt's ever lingering "banality of evil" (1973) entered the picture, too. When asked by the Committee how he could have brought himself to participate in the Cointelpro operations, William Sullivan replied (U.S. Senate 1976):

> I was so inured and accustomed to any damn thing I was told to do, I just carried it out and kept my resentment to myself. I was married and trying to buy a house with a big mortgage and raise a family.

The Church Committee came to the conclusion that the overwhelming majority of the men and women in the nation's intelligence agencies had consistently carried out their assignments with integrity and devotion to the law and constitutional principles. Some had given their lives in the defense of liberty. America owed its freedom in part to their dedication in the struggle against those who wish to harm the United States. Yet some intelligence officers had clearly overstepped the boundaries of law and propriety, and the Committee felt impelled to adopt measures that would help protect citizens against future abuses.

STEPS TOWARD REFORM

The initial congressional response to the CIA's domestic spying was to pass the Hughes-Ryan Act on December 31, 1974 (22 U.S.C. 2422). This statute, which marks the beginning of the new era of intelligence accountability, required the president to review and authorize (in a "finding") every important CIA covert action, then report to Congress on those he had approved. Prior to the Hughes-Ryan law, pinning down responsibility for covert action was, observed Mondale during the Church Committee inquiry, "like nailing jello to a wall." With this statute in place, there would be no more plausible denial; no more vanishing paper trails. It was the first attempt since the creation of the CIA to place meaningful limits on its activities.

The Congress then began its formal investigations, with probes by the Church Committee in the Senate and the Pike Committee in the House (led by Otis Pike, D, New York, and concentrating on the quality of intelligence reporting, as opposed to the Church Committee focus on charges of abuse). Along with the inquiry conducted by the White House (the Rockefeller Commission, led by Vice President Nelson Rockefeller), the congressional committees did much to educate the American people on the importance of more meaningful intelligence supervision.

In May 1976, the Church Committee presented 96 proposals for reform of domestic intelligence alone, many of which were adopted by the Congress. The most significant, affecting both domestic and foreign intelligence, was the creation of a permanent Senate Select Committee on Intelligence (SSCI). As Mondale noted at the time (1976), "If there is one lesson that our Committee felt above all must be learned from our study of the abuses which have been reported, it has been the crucial necessity of establishing a system of congressional oversight." The Senate had put into place a potentially effective standing committee, equipped with a large and experienced professional staff, devoted to monitoring the secret agencies day-by-day and reviewing their programs and budgets with a fine-tooth comb.

The creation of an intelligence oversight committee in the Senate was not an easy task, opposed as it was by the White House, the intelligence agencies, and even a few members of the Church Committee on the Republican side (Tower, Goldwater, and Baker). In floor debate on the proposal, Church and Mondale stressed the necessity of providing the new committee with annual budget authorization, realizing that without the power of the purse as leverage over the intelligence community no form of accountability would succeed. Opponents introduced a number of weakening amendments; but, one-by-one, they were defeated and on May 19, 1976, by a vote of 72 to 18, the Senate created the new intelligence oversight committee. It was a remarkable achievement. Institutional inertia normally carries the day in the Congress, yet the Church Committee had been able to bring about a major power shift. Responsibility for supervision of the intelligence agencies would be largely removed from the jurisdiction of the Armed Services Committee and given the closer attention it warranted.

Not to be left behind, President Ford set up an Intelligence Oversight Board (IOB) in the White House in 1976, and (also by executive order in the same year) he prohibited further assassination plots against foreign leaders. In 1977, the House established an intelligence oversight committee of its own, patterned after the Senate model and designated the House Permanent Select Committee on Intelligence (HPSCI).

Many of the reforms advanced by the Church Committee and eventually adopted were of a technical nature, dealing with FBI investigative methods and how they should be employed without violating the civil liberties of American citizens. Others were broader, including the recommendation that the CIA clarify and sharply limit its ties to U.S. journalists. The Committee proposed a single eight-year term limit on the directorship of the FBI; no more imperial czars like Hoover, who served an incredible forty-eight years in that capacity. The Congress eventually settled on a ten-year term. The Committee recommended as well that the Office of Professional Responsibility (OPR), established in reaction to the Watergate scandal, be given legal status, thereby providing it firmer footing to probe allegations of abuse inside the intelligence agencies. During the Carter Administration, the President bestowed upon Vice President Walter Mondale extensive responsibilities over intelligence issues, especially with respect to the FBI and domestic intelligence matters. In turn, Mondale and the new AG, Griffin Bell of Georgia, relied upon OPR to oversee intelligence activities (Mondale 2000; Bell 1982). The attorneys in OPR were expected to investigate fully any allegations of intelligence misconduct, reporting their findings and conclusions to the Vice President and the AG.

Since the Carter years OPR has been less actively involved in intelligence oversight, as its responsibilities broadened to investigate charges of misconduct across the policy board. Its attorneys are expected as well as to represent the government in litigation and to provide legal advice to the AG, which places OPR in a "precarious position in the Justice Department because it threatens the prerogatives of the prosecuting divisions. . . ." (Elliff 1979). Contributing to OPR's demise as a vigorous intelligence overseer has been the fact that no president and or vice president since the Carter years have been as focused on questions of intelligence accountability as were Jimmy Carter and Walter Mondale. The creation of an inspector general at the Department of Justice has further diminished the influence of OPR. Nevertheless, the Office has played a useful mediating role at times between the FBI and the prosecuting divisions in the Justice Department (Elliff 1979, 169); and it has conducted some important investigations into charges of wrongdoing in the Department, including an inquiry into alleged financial improprieties by FBI Director William Sessions during the Reagan Administration (Kessler 2002, 277–283).

The Church Committee also proposed that all non-consensual electronic surveillance, mail-opening, and unauthorized entries be conducted only with the authority of a judicial warrant, instead of allowing the White House and the intelligence agencies to use such invasive tools at their own discretion. Further, the Committee stressed that the threshold for FBI investigations should be sufficiently high to ensure that only groups with a record of violence would be targeted for intelligence gathering; and the Committee took a strong stand, in addition, against the conduct of intelligence operations inside the United States by the CIA or any other foreign-oriented component of the intelligence community. In 1978, as urged by the Church Committee, Congress passed the Foreign Intelligence Surveillance Act (FISA; 50 U.S.C. 1801–1811), which provided for a special FISA court to review wiretap requests. The third branch of government, too, was now firmly in the business of intelligence oversight.

THE LEGACY OF THE CHURCH COMMITTEE

Soon after the investigation, historian Henry Steele Commager observed (1976, 32) that the indifference of the intelligence agencies to constitutional restraint was "perhaps the most threatening of all the evidence that [emerged] from the findings of the Church Committee." The inquiry was able to focus citizen awareness on this threat, creating a foundation of public support indispensable for the reform measures subsequently adopted by Congress and the executive branch. Legislators laid out the facts for the American people—a difficult and important duty in itself—about the extent of lawlessness that had overtaken the secret agencies. The Committee was unable to plumb to the depths of every intelligence abuse; it did not have time enough. Rather it laid out key findings that pointed to a pattern of wrongdoing, without trying to probe every specific allegation. This public airing proved thorough enough to bring about a sea change in attitudes throughout the intelligence community.

The Committee's central conclusion was clear and important: the law works. In every case where the secret agencies had violated the law, the Committee demonstrated how U.S. security objectives could have been achieved through legal means. As the Committee emphasized, security and liberty were compatible values in a democracy; it was possible to defend the nation without becoming a police state. Thoughtful intelligence officers began to understand how the unlawful activities of their agencies had actually interfered with the nation's legitimate intelligence and counterintelligence duties.

The Committee made it clear as well that the principle of accountability was valid even with respect to the hidden side of government—indeed, there most especially. The Senate and House intelligence oversight committees would now stand guard as watchmen to America's civil liberties, replacing the small and ineffectual subcommittees that the nation had relied upon before, only to see fail. Today as the nation's spymasters plan their secret operations, they must take into account the likely reactions of two full committees of elected representatives. This new relationship has strengthened the intelligence community by better defining its limits and responsibilities, and by tying the secret agencies closer to the values and beliefs of the American people and their surrogates in Congress. The resulting higher level of professionalism among the intelligence agencies has helped to restore public confidence and respect in their activities, a primary objective of the Church Committee.

The Committee conveyed to the American people that the Senate would stand up for their constitutional rights. "'We can't slide back into the days of J. Edgar Hoover'—that was the message delivered by the Committee through its promulgation of guidelines and recommendations," recalls John Elliff, the Committee's top staff aide for the FBI side of the inquiry (2000). William E. Colby, DCI during the investigation, wrote afterward that the Church Committee had shed light on the boundaries "within which [the intelligence community] should, and should not, operate" (1976, 11). The current DCI, George Tenet, himself a former SSCI staff director, has similarly stated that the new oversight procedures represent ". . . our most vital and direct link to the American people—a source of strength that separates us from all other countries of the world" (1997).

DISCUSSION AND CONCLUSION

The importance of establishing intelligence oversight committees in the Senate and the House cannot be overemphasized. The protection of freedom requires daily attention; someone has to be continuously on guard. That "someone" in the world of intelligence now includes two permanent, well-staffed committees that concentrate exclusively on intelligence activities, not (as earlier) small, feckless subcommittees that occasionally reviewed the nation's secret operations as an adjunct to their principal duties. Robert M. Gates, a career intelligence officer and DCI under the first President Bush, has come to this conclusion about the new era of intelligence oversight (1997, 559):

> . . . some awfully crazy schemes might well have been approved had everyone present not known and expected hard questions, debate, and criticism from the Hill. And when, on a few occasions, Congress was kept in the dark, and such schemes

did proceed, it was nearly always to the lasting regret of the presidents involved.

Here was the most vital result of the Church Committee's work: the establishment of safeguards to ensure that lawmakers are able to provide a check against abuses by the secret, not just the more open, agencies of government. This is not to say that the Church Committee created a fool-proof system of intelligence accountability. The Iran-*contra* affair of 1986–87 served as a reminder that even robust legislative safeguards are no guarantee against the misuse of power by determined conspirators in the executive branch (Cohen and Mitchell 1988). That scandal led to a further tightening of oversight procedures, however, including the creation of a CIA Office of Inspector General directly answerable to Congress (Kaiser 1994; Currie 1998).

The best assurance against future abuse lies, as the ancient philosophers realized, in the selection of individuals of the highest integrity for positions of power. Then, lawmakers and their staff on the oversight committees must maintain close watch over intelligence budgets and programs, posing detailed questions in hearings and probing fearlessly into any activities that seem untoward. Outside the executive branch, only Congress has the authority to insist on access to intelligence documents and testimony; if elected representatives lapse into complacency, the secret agencies will again drift toward autonomy and the arrogance that isolation breeds.

Even now there are signs that some have failed to learn this lesson of American democracy. A senior official in the Association of Retired Intelligence Officers opined in the wake of Iran-*contra* that those who had lied to legislators during that affair were right to have done so, since sensitive intelligence operations are none of Congress's business (cited in Turner 1991). In 1994, Senate overseers learned that the National Reconnaissance Office (NRO, a component of the intelligence community that builds and manages spy satellites) had run up $159 million in cost overruns for the construction of its new headquarters in Virginia, without properly informing lawmakers (*New York Times* 1994); and, in 1995, the CIA failed to report, as required by law, on its questionable ties to a suspected murderer in the Guatemalan military (*New York Times* 1996). Just in the past two years, DCI Tenet resisted a probe by lawmakers on a special Senate-House Joint Committee of Intelligence into the failure of the intelligence community to warn the nation of the 9/11 attacks (see, e.g., Lewis 2002). The second

Bush White House has stonewalled efforts by a commission to further investigate this subject and related weaknesses in U.S. security (Johnson 2003).

This backsliding emphasizes the need for renewed attention to the question of intelligence accountability. Still, these episodes notwithstanding, the safeguards set up by the Church Committee and the Ford Administration in 1976 have endured and, on most occasions, they have brought greater sobriety to the conduct of intelligence operations at home and abroad. Someone beyond the walls of the secret agencies is now steadily watching their activities; would be violators of the public trust know they might be caught—a vital check on abuse.

This nation must have strong and effective intelligence agencies; America's security depends on it. Yet that power has to remain within the framework of the Constitution, not relegated to some dark outside realm. This is all the more true in an age where the methods of spying are far more sophisticated than in the era of J. Edgar Hoover. Breaches of faith will occur again; such is the nature of the human condition. It is imperative, however, that responsible officials remain ever vigilant in their protection of lawful political activities, ensuring that citizens do not become the target of secret intimidation by the intelligence community. The constitutional right to free expression must remain the lynchpin of American democracy.

With the safeguards established in 1976, citizens of the United States are far less likely to suffer abuse at the hands of the secret agencies than during the earlier years of benign neglect. The effectiveness of the safeguards will continue to depend on the resolve of lawmakers to carry out their duties of accountability with fresh resolve, with a willingness to engage in day-to-day "police patrolling," and with a determination to preserve liberty at home even in the face of global terrorism.

QUESTIONS FOR FURTHER DISCUSSION

1. What triggered the Church Committee investigation in 1975?
2. What were the strengths and weaknesses of the Church Committee inquiry?
3. How has intelligence in the United States changed as a result of the Church Committee's probe?
4. What do you make of the argument that the Church Committee weakened American intelligence and made the nation vulnerable to the intelligence mistakes that were made in 2001 (9/11) and 2002–2003 (Iraq)?

REFERENCES

Aberbach, Joel D. 1990. *Keeping a Watchful Eye: The Politics of Congressional Oversight*. Washington, D.C.: The Brookings Institution.

Arendt, Hannah. 1973. *The Origins of Totalitarianism*. New York: Harcourt.

Barrett, David M. 1998. Glimpses of a Hidden History: Sen. Richard Russell, Congress and Early Oversight of the CIA. *International Journal of Intelligence and Counterintelligence* 11 (3): 271–99.

Bell, Griffin B., with Ronald J. Astrow. 1982. *Taking Care of the Law*. New York: Morrow.

Bibby, John F. 1968. Congress' Neglected Function. In *The Republican Papers*, edited by Melvin R. Laird, 477–488. New York: Anchor.

Calvert, Randall, Mathew D. McCubbins, and Barry R. Weingast. 1989. A Theory of Political Control and Agency Discretion. *American Journal of Political Science* 33 (3): 588–611.

Cohen, William S., and George J. Mitchell. 1988. *Men of Zeal: A Candid Inside Story of the Iran-Contra Hearings*. New York: Viking.

Colby, William E. 1976. After Investigating U.S. Intelligence. *New York Times*, February 26.

———. with Peter Forbath. 1978. *Honorable Men*. New York: Simon and Schuster.

Commager, Henry Steele. 1976. *Intelligence: The Constitution Betrayed*. New York Review of Books, September 30.

Currie, James. 1998. Iran-Contra and Congressional Oversight of the CIA. *International Journal of Intelligence and Counterintelligence* 11 (2): 185–210.

Dodd, Lawrence, and Richard Schott. 1979. *Congress and the Administrative State*. New York: Wiley.

Elliff, John T. 1979. *The Reform of FBI Intelligence Operations*. Princeton: Princeton University Press.

———. 2000. Author's telephone interview: April 14.

Gates, Robert M. 1997. *From the Shadows*. New York: Simon and Schuster.

Gittenstein, Mark. 2000. Author's telephone interview: April 14.

Holt, Pat M. 1995. *Secret Intelligence and Public Policy*. Washington, D.C.: CQ Press.

Johnson, Loch K. 1986. *A Season of Inquiry*. Lexington: University Press of Kentucky.

———. 1994. Playing Ball with the CIA: Congress Supervises Strategic Intelligence. In *Congress, the Executive, and the Making of American Foreign Policy*, edited by Paul E. Peterson, 49–73. Norman: University of Oklahoma Press.

———. 2000. *Bombs, Bugs, Drugs, and Thugs: Intelligence and America's Quest for Security*. New York: New York University Press.

———. 2003. Author's interviews with members and staff of the Kean Commission, Washington, D.C.: January–March.

Kaiser, Frederick M. 1994. Impact and Implications of the Iran-contra Affair on Congressional Oversight of Covert Action. *International Journal of Intelligence and Counterintelligence* 7 (2): 205–234.

Keller, William W. 1989. *Liberals and J. Edgar Hoover: Rise and Fall of a Domestic Intelligence State.* Princeton: Princeton University Press.

Kessler, Ronald. 2003. *The Bureau: The Secret History of the FBI.* New York: St. Martin's.

Knott, Stephen F. 1996. *Secret and Sanctioned: Covert Operations and the American Presidency.* New York: Oxford University Press.

Lewis, Neil. 2002. Senator Insists C.I.A. Is Harboring Iraq Reports. *New York Times,* October 4.

Lowenthal, Mark. 1992. *U.S. Intelligence: Evolution and Anatomy,* 2nd edition. Washington, D.C.: Center for Strategic and International Studies.

Mayhew, David. 1986. *The Electoral Connection.* New Haven: Yale University Press.

McCubbins, Mathew D., and Thomas Schwartz. 1984. Congressional Oversight Overlooked: Police Patrols and Fire Alarms. *American Journal of Political Science* 28 (1): 165–179.

———. Roger G. Noll, and Barry R. Weingast. 1989. Structure and Process, Politics and Policy: Administrative Arrangements and the Political Control of Agencies. *Virginia Law Review* 75 (3): 431–482.

Mondale, Walter F. 1975. Personal archives. (Church Committee), Minneapolis.

———. 1976. Personal archives (Church Committee), Minneapolis.

———. 1996. Unsigned editorial, August 18.

———. 2000. Author's interview, Minneapolis: February 17. *New York Times.* 1994. Unsigned editorial, May 19.

Ogul, Morris S. 1976. *Congress Oversees the Bureaucracy: Studies in Legislative Supervision.* Pittsburgh: University of Pittsburgh Press.

Pepper, William F. 2003. *An Act of State.* Verso, London.

Priest, Dana. 2003. Remarks, Panel on Congress, Intelligence and Secrecy During War, Woodrow Wilson Center, May 9, Washington, D.C.

Ransom, Harry Howe. 1970. *The Intelligence Establishment.* Cambridge: Harvard University Press.

———. 1975. Secret Intelligence Agencies and Congress. *Society* 123(2): 33–38.

———. 1977. Congress and the Intelligence Agencies. In *Congress Against the President,* edited by Harvey C. Mansfield, 153–166. New York: Praeger.

———. 1984. CIA Accountability: Congress As Temperamental Watchdog. Paper, American Political Science Association Annual Convention, September 1, Washington, D.C.

Rapoport, Anatole. 1975. Author's interview, Toronto: September 21.

Richelson, Jeffrey T. 1999. *The U.S. Intelligence Community,* 4th edition. Boulder; Westview Press.

Scher, Seymour. 1963. Conditions for Legislative Control. *Journal of Politics* 25 (3): 526–551.

Schlesinger, James R. 1994. Author's interview, Washington, D.C.: June 16.

Schwarz, Frederick A. O., Jr. 2000. Author's interview, New York City: April 27.

Smist, Frank, Jr. 1994. *Congress Oversees the United States Intelligence Community,* 2nd ed. Knoxville: University of Tennessee Press.

Spence, David. 1997. Agency Policy Making and Political Control: Modeling Away the Delegation Problem. *Journal of Public Administration Research and* Theory 7 (2): 199–219.

Sullivan, William. 1975. Author's interview, Boston: September 21.

Tenet, George. 1997. Remarks, Panel on Does America Need the CIA? Gerald R. Ford Library, November 19, Ann Arbor, Michigan.

Turner, Stansfield. 1991. Purge the C.I.A. of K.G.B. Types. *New York Times,* October 2.

Ungar, Sanford. 1975. *FBI.* Boston: Atlantic Monthly Press.

U.S. Congress. 1987. Report on the Iran-*Contra* Affair. *Senate Select Committee on Secret Military Assistance to Iran and the Nicaragua Opposition and House Select Committee to Investigate Covert Arms Transactions with Iran.* S. Rept. 100–216 and H. Rept 100–433, November.

U.S. Senate. 1975. Hearings. *Select Committee to Study Governmental Operations with Respect to Intelligence Activities* (Church Committee), 94th Cong., 2d. Sess., September–December.

———. 1976. Final Report. *Select Committee to Study Governmental Operations with Respect to Intelligence Activities* (Church Committee). S. Rept. 94–755, 95th Cong., 1st. Sess., May.

Walden, Jerrold L. 1970. The C.I.A.: A Study in the Arrogation of Administrative Power. *George Washington Law Review* 39 (3): 66–101.

Young, Andrew. 2000. Author's interview, Minneapolis: June 6.

25. FORUM ON THE IMPLICATIONS OF THE SNOWDEN LEAKS OF NSA DOCUMENTS

LOCH K. JOHNSON, RICHARD J. ALDRICH AND CHRISTOPHER MORAN, DAVID M. BARRETT, GLENN HASTEDT, ROBERT JERVIS, WOLFGANG KRIEGER, ROSE MCDERMOTT, SIR DAVID OMAND, MARK PHYTHIAN, WESLEY K. WARK

In 2014, the journal *Intelligence and National Security* assembled some intelligence experts to discuss the implication of the leaks provided to the media by Edward J. Snowden, who purloined some 1.7 million documents from the National Security Agency while serving there as an outside consultant. The views of these experts are presented in this chapter. In public opinion polls, some people seemed to view Snowden as a hero for exposing a NSA warrantless wiretapping program against U.S. citizens, while others saw him as a traitor to the United States for revealing sensitive (indeed, top secret) intelligence operations.

INTRODUCTION

Loch K. Johnson

In 2013, the National Security Agency (NSA) in the United States became embroiled in controversy—again. Its questionable use of wiretaps (Operation MINARET) and its improper reading of international cables sent and received by Americans over decades (Operation SHAMROCK) had been revealed by the Church Committee in 1976; and, in 2005, the *New York Times* disclosed that the NSA had been wiretapping selected American citizens without a warrant, contrary to the Foreign Intelligence Surveillance Act of 1978.

In this most recent scandal, the NSA hired Edward J. Snowden to help with some of its computer work. At the time of his hiring in 2013, Snowden—a twenty-nine-year-old high school dropout from suburban Maryland and a former CIA computer specialist—was under contract as a data specialist with the giant defense firm Booz Allen Hamilton. In his short stint with the NSA, Snowden reportedly stole over a million classified documents from the agency's computers. He leaked many of these documents over the next year to American and British journalists, as a protest against what he viewed as improper surveillance

methods used by the NSA against American and British citizens. The stolen documents also revealed that the NSA had been wiretapping the communications of some leading U.S. allies, including the cellphone of German Chancellor Angela Merkel. She was not pleased to learn about this intrusion. "Surveillance Revelations Shake U.S.-German Ties," observed a *New York Times* headline. Nor were other Europeans happy about the revelations of widespread NSA surveillance against them.

Before releasing the first of his documents, Snowden fled the United States in search of a safe haven, first in Hong Kong and then (when other options fell through) to Russia. The leaks revealed that the NSA had been gathering "metadata" (the records of telephone numbers dialed and the duration of calls) on about a third of all the telephone calls made by American citizens, both inside the United States and with parties overseas; moreover, the agency was collecting data on the use of social media by U.S. citizens. The appropriateness of this "dragnet" or "bulk collection" method of intelligence gathering, and against Americans no less, became a topic of heated national debate in 2013, spilling over into 2014. It appeared that the NSA preferred a vacuum-cleaner approach to electronic surveillance, while its critics advocated a more pinpointed targeting of individuals based on a standard of probable cause that they might be involved in terrorist activities.

Central to the debate stood the question of whether or not Snowden was a patriot for disclosing to the public a questionable intelligence program or a traitor for his unauthorized disclosure of classified information—much of it going beyond the metadata program that he claimed had justified his actions. The retiring NSA Director, General Keith B. Alexander, called the Snowden leaks "the greatest damage to our combined nations' intelligence systems that we have ever suffered." In contrast, his replacement in 2014, Admiral Michael S. Rogers, deplored the leaks but downplayed their damaging, saying that there was no indication "the sky is falling." [These quotes are from David E. Sanger, "Sky Isn't Falling After Snowden, N.S.A. Chief Says," *New York Times* (June 30, 2014), p. A1.] The *Times* had noted earlier that none of the secret agencies had presented "the slightest proof that his disclosures really hurt the nation's security" ("Edward Snowden, Whistle-Blower," unsigned editorial, January 2, 2014, p. A18).

In June of 2014, the U.S. House enacted legislation—the USA Freedom Act—to trim back on the breath of the NSA metadata program, although not to ban it altogether. The Senate was expected to take up the measure in the summer of 2014. Shortly before the House passed the bill, the editors of Intelligence and National Security asked some members of its Editorial Board to comment on the implications of the Snowden leaks. I would like to take this opportunity to thank the participants for their thoughtful contributions, under a short deadline. Below, in alphabetical order, are their responses.

REMARKS

Richard J. Aldrich, with co-author Christopher Moran

The main significance of Edward Snowden relates more to the decline of secrecy than the decline of privacy. The U.K. and U.S. governments are increasingly concerned by large-scale and unauthorized releases of classified documents facilitated by disaffected officials who are often described as "whistle-blowers." Governments invest considerable resources in protecting secrets and, in the United States, the annual cost of classification is estimated at $11 billion. Yet we know little about elite attitudes toward secrecy and its opponents. We need to reflect on this notable lacuna at a time when legislators are urgently reviewing these issues which increasingly connect science and security.

In June 2013, Snowden leaked remarkable details of several highly classified U.S./U.K. mass surveillance programs to the press, sparking an international furor. He was vilified and applauded in equal measure. Officials in London and Washington regard these latest disclosures as the most serious breach in government security for several decades. The media have framed this episode around surveillance and civil liberties, focusing upon "the end of privacy." Certainly, there has been a degree of moral panic, with governments allegedly able to monitor every aspect of our digital lives. However, it is our contention that the nature of privacy has in fact changed little over the last decade and instead these developments denote a "crisis of secrecy." The real issue is not government looking at us, but us looking at government.

Information and communications technology is central to this process. Ten official whistle-blowers have come to public attention in the last decade, beginning with the GCHQ [the British counterpart of the NSA] employee Katherine Gun in 2003. However, since 2010, websites such as WikiLeaks have deployed anonymizing software to allow officials to release large collections of documents, in collaboration with several mainstream newspapers. In November 2010, the website leaked more than 250,000 U.S. diplomatic cables, exposing the frank views of officials on a wide range of current international issues. As Heather Brooke, the journalist who exposed the U.K. parliamentary expenses scandal, observed in the wake of this event: "The data deluge is coming."

Scholars now need to interrogate the nature of state secrecy in the United States and the United Kingdom in the early twenty-first century. We need to discover how disaffected government employees and contractors are using new technology to challenge secrecy, and how officials are responding to the present crisis of secrecy. We need to ask whether we are on the brink of what David Brin described as "The Transparent Society," in which it will be increasingly difficult for governments to safeguard classified information. In the 1970s, Daniel Ellsberg required twenty-four hour access to photocopiers in order to leak the "Pentagon Papers," but now disgruntled officials can release entire archives of secret material with a pen drive.

Perhaps the most substantial challenge that government now confronts is a cultural one around new forms of oversight and accountability. Internet activists and digital whistle-blowers claim that their purpose is a new form of horizontal regulation secured through the democratization of information. In the "Twitter age," the use of blogs and social networks are allowing journalists to mount lengthy investigations that rival those of elected bodies. Deep investigation of government security activity may be passing from formally constituted commissions and committees toward a version of global civil society, characterized by NGOs, civil rights lawyers, journalists, and regional bodies such as the Council of Europe.

There are attendant regulatory questions for parliaments and assemblies. Both the United States and Europe are investigating the entire question of "Whistle-blower Protection," raising important normative issues around where the line should be drawn between the public right to know and the right of civil servants to offer confidential advice to ministers. Snowden has placed officials in Whitehall and Washington on notice, and new conventions around what remains of secrecy will need to be put in place.

REMARKS

David M. Barrett

It was inevitable, I suppose, when the story broke about Edward Snowden's conveyance of thousands of National Security Agency documents to journalists, that I would compare it to the first time NSA was "outed." I had researched and, in 2009, published a scholarly article on how two young American employees of NSA—Bernon Mitchell and William Martin—had defected to the Soviet Union in 1960 and revealed many ethically and legally questionable activities of the Agency. With NSA as one of its main tools, the U.S. government had spied not just on the Soviet Union, but on allies, and had even monitored communications going in and out of the United States. Congressional oversight of NSA was entirely lacking, Mitchell and Martin said that they had gone to a member of Congress with their information about the Agency's activities and seen no concrete results; so they traveled secretly to Moscow and held a "tell all" press conference that was extensively reported by American and international news media. Then they settled down to their new lives in a place that turned out not to be the workers' paradise they had expected.[1] I was struck by the equal combination of naïveté and arrogance that led them to do what they thought was the idealistic thing. They thought the United States had been uniquely unjust in its foreign policies and intelligence activities, and they wished to alert American citizens and the world to these things. But in 1960 America, there was virtually no sympathy for the two young men. Harry Truman said, "They ought to be shot," and few thought the former president's statement to be out of line.

Snowden seems the same—naïve and arrogant, but also wishing to do good. As he told one interviewer, "Sometimes to do the right thing you have to break a law. And the key there is in terms of civil disobedience, you have to make sure that what you're risking, what you're bringing on to yourself does not serve as a detriment to anyone else, it doesn't hurt anybody else."[2]

Snowden claims that the United States and its people have not been hurt by his actions, but how can he possibly know that? Did it serve the interests of the American people for the government of China to learn (from the *New York Times*, relying on documents from Snowden) that NSA hacked into the servers of the Chinese telecom company, Huawei?[3] I doubt it. On the contrary, foreign governments and groups have obviously learned much about U.S. intelligence that they should not know.

I know from experience that the U.S. government stupidly, wastefully, and illegally keeps half-century-old (or even older) documents secret. I am not inclined to sympathize with absurd government classification policies. But Snowden's documents are not old or irrelevant to current international politics. Had he limited his release of documents to some small number showing that the NSA was collecting data on communications of ordinary Americas, I would have some sympathy and respect for him. The trove he turned over, however, is vast and the benefit to governments and groups hostile to the United States seems obvious.

There can be no doubt, though, that Snowden's revelations have led many in Congress, the judiciary, and the executive branch, to pay more attention to NSA. That, I hope, will be for the good. Early in 2014, the *New York Times* editorialized, "He may have committed a crime to do so [that is, reveling information and exposing intelligence abuses], but he has done his country a great service. It is time for the United States to offer Mr. Snowden a plea bargain or some form of clemency."[4]

I think that, with Mr. Snowden, we have a very mixed bag. Some good and probably some very bad results have come out of his actions. Perhaps if he comes back to the United States and faces the legal process (without a guarantee of clemency), I might develop the slightest respect and sympathy for him. In the meantime, I'll stick with the highly imperfect elected officials and judges rather than a naïve and arrogant young man to decide what intelligence agencies should do or not do, and what we should know about them.

REMARKS

Glenn Hastedt

Just over one year ago secret documents taken by NSA contractor Edward Snowden began appearing in the press. In the months that followed virtually all aspects of NSA's program have been debated. Perhaps no debate has been as emotional as that over Snowden's motives and actions. Representative John Boehner (Republican, Ohio), the Speaker of the House, identified him as a "traitor." Democrat Senator Dianne Feinstein from California, chair of the Senate Select Committee on Intelligence, said Snowden committed "an act of treason." The American Civil Liberties Union characterized Snowden as a patriot.

Assessing the long-term significance of Snowden's leaking of secret intelligence information to the media requires moving beyond characterizations such as these to focus on the underlying context within which his actions took place. The most commonly debated question is whether Snowden should be considered a whistleblower. As used in the media Snowden is a whistleblower, since his release of the NSA documents brought attention to a highly controversial secret government program and promoted public debate over its merits. From a legal perspective Snowden is not a whistleblower. As defined in legal statutes and policy directives, whistleblowing refers to the lawful disclosures of wrongdoing made through appropriate channels to those who can correct them and includes channels for bringing them to the attention of Congress. From this perspective whistle-blower protection neither refers to nor covers unlawful communications.

Too often the debate over Snowden's actions begins and ends here. This is unfortunate since the question of whether Snowden is a whistleblower or if he stole and leaked information has greater long-term significance. We can begin to grasp these implications by employing three core concepts introduced by Albert Hirschman: exit, voice, and loyalty.[5]

To exit is to leave an organization and cut one's ties to it. Most often this is done in silence. Voice is whistleblowing; it is protest from within, designed to alert organizational officials of a failing in need of correction. Loyalty is to remain in an organization and support it out of a sense of commitment to its mission. Together, they define the set of options individuals must choose from if they feel their organization is not performing as it should. These options do not exist in isolation from one another. Without the possibility of exit, loyalty loses much of its meaning. Without loyalty, exit is a costless strategy for someone disaffected by organizational policies and products. Loyalty postpones exit and in the process can activate voice. Yet, voice can be overdone and hinder rather than promote organizational reform if it produces a backlash within the organization. It may also be routinized to the point where it loses its ability to promote change.

Three points are particularly noteworthy in looking at the dynamics and consequences of exit, voice, and loyalty for the Snowden case. First, complete exit is impossible when the organizational product is a public good. One cannot walk away from the consequences of intelligence failures or secret electronic surveillance. In these cases, exit is unlikely to be a silent departure but one that takes on an accusatory tone whose charges, in Hirschman's words, are "unanswerable." Snowden's intelligence leaks fit this category very well, as evidenced by the often tortured defense put forward by NSA officials and supporters.

Second, loyalty's ability to activate voice over exit increases with an individual's depth of identity and commitment to an organization. One should not expect to see contractors evidence the same depth of loyalty as career employees. The increasing reliance on contractors to perform intelligence functions thus raises a warning sign, as it may contribute to the existence of an organizational environment that supports exit and future leaks.

Third, in making calculations as to whether to exit or use one's voice, individuals rely heavily on past experience. Snowden is not the first to select exit and leak secret intelligence. He pointedly noted that those who had gone before him had been "destroyed by the experience." The accuracy of this assessment is of less significance than the fact that Snowden believed it to be true and guided his decision-making. Future potential Snowdens may not act as copycats, but they will be watching closely both his fate and those of intelligence officers who exercise voice over exit.

REMARKS

Robert Jervis

To ask whether Edward Snowden is a traitor or a hero is to pose the question crudely, but it does take us to central issues.

We should try to separate motives from effects, although the two overlap and neither are entirely knowable at this point. It seems clear that Snowden did not seek to harm the American national interest, at least as he saw it. He was not moved by financial gain and did not owe his allegiance to another country or to a cause associated with one. Although he may have been moved at least in part by the desire to be in the spotlight, given the price he knew he would pay even the harshest critic would be hard pressed to deny that his main motive was to change what he saw as disastrous American policies. Of course, it is also true that ideologically motivated spies like Alger Hiss and the Rosenbergs were serving what they saw as the American interest, believing that not only the Soviet Union but U.S. citizens would be better off if the former country were strengthened. Snowden perhaps wanted to strengthen the other countries' abilities to protect themselves against American intrusions, but this is hardly the same thing.

In his desire to change American policy, Snowden more closely resembles Daniel Ellsberg, who calculated that revealing the deceptions of the Kennedy and Johnson administrations would allow President Nixon to renounce the war. Unfortunately, he badly misjudged Nixon's beliefs and values, although the release may have slightly accelerated the erosion of public support for the war. Furthermore, while critics argued that this massive loss of secrets would damage American diplomacy, as far as we can tell this did not happen. Among other things, this raises the question of whether the United States and other countries need to keep as many documents secret as they do.

The effect of Snowden's releases have been much greater. The most credible claim that Snowden is a hero rests on the fact that, unlike Ellsberg, he has produced a change in policy. In the wake of the releases, President Barack Obama called for a national dialogue on surveillance; but he disingenuously failed to acknowledge the fact that such a conversation was only possible because of what Snowden did. Although the public was divided, a presidential commission called for reforms; and some, but not all of them, appear likely to be enacted into law. Once Congress understood what the government was doing, it declared that we had drawn the balance between security and civil liberties wrong; and the president, who had sponsored the old policy, agreed. If this does not make Snowden a hero, it certainly makes the label of traitor a bad fit.

Of course, critics say that the new restrictions were not necessary to protect our rights and have left us less secure. This may be so, but two objections are obvious. First, the value of the extensive domestic surveillance has never been demonstrated; and, second, the current policy was arrived at through a more open and democratic process than was the earlier one.

The related argument that Snowden's revelations have destroyed a set of extremely valuable tools by making them public may be correct, but is also subject to twin rebuttals. First, the remaining tool kit is rather full; and, second, our adversaries probably always assumed that we listened to everything that we could. Indeed, they probably think that we still are, irrespective of what any new laws and regulations may say.

What of Snowden's revelations about foreign spying? Although creating some frictions with allies, I suspect that the changes will be even less because there was little that the United States was doing that was really unusual, something that foreign leaders knew despite the domestic political incentives that led them to express outrage. It is not quite clear why Snowden revealed these activities if his concern was with domestic spying, however.

This brings me to my final point: I have spoken of "Snowden's" revelations, but he delegated the choice of what to make public to the journalists to whom he entrusted the secrets. It is as though Snowden did not trust his own judgment, and perhaps he was correct; and here he displayed a degree of self-awareness unusual for either a traitor or a hero.

REMARKS

Wolfgang Krieger

No other country in Europe has reacted more drastically to the Snowden affair than Germany. The NSA issue has rested on the front burner of national affairs for over a year now, and there are no signs of it going away soon. The German press serves an almost daily diet of reports on Uncle Sam's sneaky ways of gathering vast amounts of Germany's private, political, and business data. Edward Snowden became an instant hero. No one wished to discuss the moral and political downside of his betrayal of government secrets.

When Chancellor Angela Merkel failed to calm things down and to deflect attention away from the "NSA scandal," she gave the go-ahead to establish a parliamentary commission of inquiry into U.S. spying operations against "innocent Germans" and their political leadership (including Merkel's mobile phone). Several German ministers were dispatched to Washington "to clarify matters" and to negotiate (in vain as it turned out) a "no-spying agreement." Then, in early May of 2014, Merkel herself paid a visit to President Obama, officially to discuss the Ukrainian crisis, but NSA was no doubt mentioned as well. This was viewed on the German side, and presumably by Obama, as a gesture of "let's be friends again."

Yet the Snowden affair continues to burden German-American relations. Pessimists even think it could wreck them for good. Not since the missile crisis of the 1980s has the German-American partnership had so little public support among Germans. To be sure, most of the harsh criticism of NSA snooping comes from the far left, particularly from neo-Communists, who have a strong electoral foothold in the former communist parts of Germany. But the harm done by the NSA affair reaches very far into the mainstream of the political spectrum, including Chancellor Merkel's own political party.

The second observation concerns Snowden's allegations that the Bundesnachrichtendienst or BND, as well as Germany's domestic intelligence services, were (and still are) part of the NSA snooping systems: sharing data, internet tracking software, and all the rest of NSA's tool box and collection methods. While the German services claim to work 100 percent according to what is allowed by German laws, the public seems to have little confidence in such assurances. In sharp contrast to the public support given by President Obama to the NSA, the Merkel government has left German intelligence services to fight for themselves. No public support. No backing. No public statement to explain what few people seem to know: namely, that intelligence exchanges across national borders are a matter for the political masters to decide, not for the services themselves.

Thirdly, there is the political fallout in relation to cybersecurity. While neighboring France and Britain have launched huge programs to build up reactive and proactive cyber capabilities, Germany has merely a small coordinating unit which is so weak that even the budget control office has recently criticized its inefficiency. The Snowden leaks should have alerted Germany to her massive deficits in cybersecurity; but the opposite is likely to happen, because the political leadership will not dare inject more money into intelligence now.

Finally, we need to look at Germany's role in the fight against Islamist terrorist and Wahhabi movements in the Middle East (Syria and Iraq in particular), in Central Asia (think of the imminent withdrawal from Afghanistan), and in parts of Africa (to say nothing about the ongoing Iranian nuclear issue and the Ukrainian crisis). Germany will now be much less willing to follow American leadership in tackling any of these issues. Her willingness to deploy her military forces in any of the foreseeable crisis scenarios has sharply declined. Her programs to improve the mobility and firepower of her crisis intervention forces are in limbo. The ongoing debates about developing or buying armed drones are unlikely to produce any results: this is because armed intervention is now even more strongly associated with "American imperialism" and its ugly hidden face, the NSA. Between them, NSA and Snowden have badly damaged transatlantic relations and the worst part of it may still lie ahead.

REMARKS

Rose McDermott

The security implications of Edward Snowden's leak of enormous amounts of classified information remain unclear and indeed may never be fully known. However, the political fallout has been extensive and continuing. Regardless of the effect, much of the commentary has concentrated on speculation regarding Snowden's motives. And indeed, this attention itself is not independent of political motivation; if Snowden's motives were pure, he can more easily be seen as a brave patriot seeking to reveal heinous hidden aspects of U.S. national security policy. If they can be shown to be more personally or financially motivated, then he can more easily be dismissed as a traitorous coward who betrayed national trust and placed lives and careers at risk. Of course, the motive and the consequences need not be logically linked, and yet they often remain intertwined in public and political perception.

Yet the greatest likelihood is more complex. Specifically, it is almost impossible upon observation not to categorize Edward Snowden as a prototypical narcissistic personality disorder, in which a person given to excessive vanity becomes preoccupied to the point of obsession with his or her own personal prestige and importance. As long as everyone goes along with telling them how wonderful they are, everything is fine; but once someone pricks the person's narcissistic wound, they commonly lash out against those who fail to sufficiently appreciate them, by their own estimation, by trying to demonstrate their superior value and power. However, his actions may nonetheless have inspired an important public debate about the rights to privacy and the limits of surveillance in a democratic society that were perhaps long overdue in the wake of the extensive expansions of government infiltration into the lives of private citizens with the Patriot Act, which was passed quickly after the devastating attacks of 9/11.

Two narratives have dominated in the discussion of Snowden, as nicely detailed by Jay Epstein in the *Wall Street Journal* on May 9, 2014. The first casts him as a whistleblower who made enormous personal sacrifices to expose corrupt American government surveillance programs. This is the version that has received the most attention and endorsement. The second suggests that Snowden was perhaps too clever and that he was a spy who engaged in espionage for foreign governments for personal profit. After all, why else would the Russians take him in and pay his bills? Never mind that he may be useful to Putin as a post-hoc annoyance in a period of escalating international tension, displayed in places such as Crimea unrelated to Snowden. But a third narrative appears more plausible, if less dramatic. Snowden is a narcissist who seeks attention and did not get as much of it as he wanted in his relatively low-level job (or at least lower than he claimed). From this perspective, he did what he did to get exactly what he got: a lot of acclaim and attention. From this vantage point, it is noteworthy that every time his story almost begins to fall off the front page, he gives a new interview or engages in some new activity that brings him front and center on the national stage once again.

Snowden's supporters compare his behavior to similar actions taken by such heroic figures as Daniel Ellsberg, who released the Pentagon Papers to Seymour Hersh at the *New York Times* in 1971. These papers documented the extensive history of American involvement in Vietnam and in particular revealed secret incursions and bombings in Cambodia and Laos that had not been revealed either by Congress or the American public. Ellsberg was charged with conspiracy, espionage, and theft of government property, although all of these charges were dropped in the course of a subsequent investigation. Importantly, Ellsberg was an extremely credible scientist. His doctoral dissertation in economics from Harvard in decision science examined the phenomenon of ambiguity aversion. He demonstrated the ways that individual choice violates the expectations of utility theory, a relationship eponymously named "The Ellsberg Paradox." As important as his release of the Pentagon Papers may have been to the history of American foreign policy, Ellsberg's most important and enduring contribution to society is likely to derive from the many consequences of his delineation of the paradox named after him.

Another analogous case can be found in the example of Joe Darby, the young reservist stationed in Iraq who revealed the disks that held images of American soldiers engaged in torture against prisoners in the Abu Ghraib prison in 2004. After encountering resistance to his concerns within the chain of military command, Darby turned the disks over to Seymour Hersh, who by then had moved to the *New Yorker* magazine. The images horrified the American public and led to investigations and examinations of the torture and abuse uncovered at the prison. Darby was ostracized by his community for his actions, although he did not suffer any legal consequences.

Snowden's case is unlike the Ellsberg or Darby examples, both of which represent genuine whistleblowing in their attempt to expose secret government malfeasance ostensibly conducted on behalf of the American public without their knowledge. While some of what Snowden stole remains sealed, the vast majority of what has been revealed does not relate to government surveillance. But this does not mean that his motive was espionage. Rather, his motive can much more parsimoniously be explained as resulting from his unrelenting and unquenchable desire for attention, regardless of the kind or source.

The debate surrounding the release of Snowden's leaked documents has inspired a healthy discussion about the limits of government surveillance on domestic citizens, although frankly most Americans are only too willing to offer up unlimited forms of personal information and data on a wide variety of social media platforms, and seem less concerned than perhaps they should be about the extent and capacity of government interference in their public and private lives. However, good effects need not necessarily derive from noble motives. Ironically, although it is perhaps too snide to suggest, the likely true significance of Snowden's motives, like that which surrounds public shooters, rests in the revelation of the inadequacy of mental health care in this country.

REMARKS

Sir David Omand

Three challenges face the intelligence communities of the democracies.

First, the challenge of meeting insistent demands for secret intelligence: for example to counter the threats to cybersecurity and provide actionable intelligence about the identities, associations, location, movements, financing, and intentions of dictators, terrorists, insurgents, and cyber-, narco-, and other criminal gangs.

Secondly, the challenge of harnessing the ability in the digital age to supply intelligence about suspects: for example by accessing communications, social media, and digital databases of personal information.

Thirdly, the challenge of achieving that intelligence mission while applying the safeguards needed to ensure ethical behavior in accordance with modern views of human rights, including respect for personal privacy.

Like some elementary experiment in mechanics, the resultant of these three forces—of demand, of supply and of public attitudes—will determine the future path of our intelligence communities. Into that forcefield blunders the idealistic Edward Snowden, the information campaigners Laura Poitras and Glenn Greenwald, plus a posse of respectable journalists. In the United States, the federal government's collection and storage by the NSA of the Americans' digital metadata of U.S. citizens, secretly authorized under s.215 of the Patriot Act, is exposed.[6] President Obama is obliged to admit to the program; and Congress is currently legislating to regulate it.[7]

Snowden might therefore be regarded by some as a U.S. whistleblower, although he did not exhaust his remedies before going public, and he did not have to steal so many secrets (including British intelligence secrets) to make his main case.[8] So perhaps he scores half a point as a U.S. whistleblower.

Now turn to the United Kingdom. It turns out there is no secrecy scandal over interception by GCHQ. The independent U.K. Interception Commissioner, who was one of the nation's most senior judges, reports to Parliament that everything GCHQ does is properly authorized, and legally properly justified, including under Article 8 of the European Human Rights convention regarding personal privacy.[9] But the media alleges that GCHQ is using its links to the NSA to evade the constraint of U.K. law. Not true, says the commissioner. It turns out that the media did not explain that the United Kingdom uses a strict legal definition of "communications data," not the much looser concept of "metadata" obtained from Internet and social media use.[10] Accessing browsing history or other detailed digital metadata, whether from U.S. or U.K. sources, is for British analysts equivalent to accessing "content," and they have to have the relevant U.K. warrant.

Furthermore, the media fall into the category error that has crept into much of the recent public debate of not distinguishing bulk access by computers to the Internet—which the United States and United Kingdom certainly do have—and so-called mass surveillance, which they do not conduct. Mass surveillance implies observers, human beings who are monitoring the population. As the U.K. Interception Commissioner confirms, no such mass surveillance by takes place by GCHQ; it would be unlawful.

Thus, Snowden has not exposed any British wrongdoing—the only justification for whistleblowing that involves betraying serious confidences. A Vodaphone global survey in fact credits the United Kingdom with having the best practice in interception safeguards.[11] Snowden himself said: "Not all spying is bad. The NSA and the rest of the U.S. intelligence community is exceptionally well positioned to meet our intelligence requirements through targeted surveillance—the same way we've always done it—without resorting to the mass surveillance of entire populations." Targeted surveillance is only what is conducted by the U.K. intelligence agencies. They will continue to need to examine individual cases for which there are warrants; for example, jihadist extremists from the U.K. who are fighting in

Syria and Iraq and who may return to the United Kingdom as hardened and dangerous terrorists.

Finally, we have to recognize the damage Snowden's revelations have done to our security. The newspapers may have redacted the stories they printed to remove obvious dangers; but they did not understand where the real sensitivities lay in exposing the nature of the coverage of the authorities, allowing terrorists and criminals to alter their behavior—as they undoubtedly have—and in compromising the relationships with Internet companies, making it harder to obtain targeted intelligence on key suspects.

REMARKS

Mark Phythian

It has long been an accepted principle that, as CIA analyst Ray Cline once put it: "There is no way to be on top of intelligence problems unless you collect much more extensively than any cost-accounting approach would justify . . . You might think you could do without most of what is collected; but in intelligence, in fact, as in ore-mining, there is no way to get at the nuggets without taking the whole ore-bearing compound."[12] The Snowden leaks detail how this principle has been applied in 21st-century U.S. intelligence collection and expose the ethical tensions it can generate.

The Cold War environment in which Ray Cline operated and the contemporary one are different in key respects. The contemporary intelligence environment is scarred by the experience of the 9/11 terrorist attacks; haunted by the belief that collecting more information would have resulted in better dot-connection and prevention. While 9/11 provided the impetus to collect more, technological advances since then have made the goal of gathering all electronic communications seem feasible. Encouraged by a security industry with such close ties to the intelligence/security bureaucracy that they are not always easily distinguishable, it has emerged as a realistic aim. However, the Snowden leaks expose the extent to which this wide-ranging surveillance, while solely justified by reference to the potential terrorist threat, has had much broader targets: step forward Angela Merkel. The prevalence of diplomatic and economic espionage aimed at third countries and international organizations is a striking feature of the leaks.

This points us toward the fact that the picture of global electronic communications collection provided by Snowden is not complete; it is extensive but one dimensional. The complete picture would be more complex and multidimensional, featuring a wide range of actors engaging in a global electronic "great game"—competing to collect information to the extent that their self-definitions of national security, alliance commitments, and technological capabilities make necessary or feasible. Only snapshots of this wider picture emerge from the leaks; for example, that Israel is regarded as the third most aggressive intelligence service acting against the United States and that France targets the U.S. Department of Defense. Nevertheless, we should not lose sight of the existence of this broader "great game."

Public trust has been a notable casualty of the Snowden revelations—trust in technology providers, in intelligence providers, in government—and greater levels of resistance can be expected from providers and individuals in future. This, in turn, reflects the democratic deficit exposed by Snowden. There is a risk that aspects of intelligence are treated as a disfiguring birthmark on the democratic body politic, carefully concealed and never discussed. Yet, informed public debate is essential to democratic legitimacy here. This debate needs to consider what "security" means and involves before it can consider the options for providing it and the price worth paying for it; in particular, whether attempted universal collection justifies the invasion of personal space that it involves. The conclusion of the President's Review Group on Intelligence and Communications Technologies that, contrary to the view offered by the NSA, this global dragnet approach to collection "was not essential to preventing [terrorist] attacks,"[13] reinforces the need for public debate.

Admiral Stansfield Turner once said that the ethics of intelligence rested on whether actions could be defended before the public if exposed.[14] Reactions to the Snowden leaks suggest that mass electronic surveillance has failed the "Turner Test." But the Snowden revelations also expose the limits of the "Turner Test" itself. The practices revealed were linked to understandings of national security; but the targets were also international, and it is international as well as national public opinion that has been galvanized as a result, both at mass and elite levels. The decision of Germany's federal prosecutor to open an investigation into the Merkel phone tapping is simply one of the most prominent expressions of this. In the twenty-first century, intelligence actions clearly need to be justifiable in normative terms beyond the water's edge. In this regard, it has been suggested that principles of proportionality and last resort should, and do, provide ethical guides for intelligence. The Snowden revelations suggest, however, that these guides have been of only limited relevance, if any, with regard to electronic intelligence collection.

REMARKS

Wesley K. Wark

Edward Snowden will be tried in many "courts" and ultimately in the most merciless—the court of history. The verdict on Snowden will depend on the milieu and may well prove elastic, depending on what more we learn about his motivations, his illicit gathering of information from sensitive U.S. intelligence databases, his sharing of such information with media groups and possibly others, evidence of harm done and intelligence capabilities compromised, and a complex weighing of the balance between motivation, methods, harm and the public interest.

Whatever badge we stick to Mr. Snowden (and his media collaborators) may in itself not matter very much and certainly will be dwarfed by the issue that he has called our attention to. That issue is the practice and future of global electronic surveillance by state intelligence agencies. The ultimate verdict(s) regarding Edward Snowden the man will pale in significance alongside the verdict(s) on global surveillance.

Of course, the verdict on global SIGINT surveillance is not yet in. Once rendered, it will neither be absolute nor universal. But it is easy to predict where the verdict will be made, who the verdict will affect, and what its broad contours should be. The verdict on the future of global surveillance will be shaped by American responses and will have to embrace significant change: this is because the status quo has been made untenable and because any prohibitionist stance would be dangerous, and, in a global sense, ultimately self-defeating. Because this is America and not, say, China or Russia, the verdict on the future of global surveillance after Snowden will be hammered out in a democratic political space. Because this is America, a world power, the verdict will have to take account of the sensitivities of close allies and friends. Because this is America, with a vested interest in sustaining the American export of "soft power," it will also have to pay attention to the American image, both at home and abroad.

American-led global electronic surveillance will have to be curtailed. This will be the real "Snowden verdict." The United States has lost credibility, especially around its defense of the principles of a free and open Internet. The United States has angered its friends, in Europe and elsewhere. American businesses in the vast telecommunications and info-data sectors have or will lose global customers. At home in the United States, the Snowden revelations have stirred fierce debate around the protection of privacy and the legitimacy of surveillance.

The degree to which American-led global surveillance will be curtailed, and the precise measures to be taken, remain to be seen, although a start has been made, under pressure, by the Obama administration. What needs greater clarity are the principles around which the recalibration of global surveillance should take place.

Four such principles should be uppermost:

1. necessity
2. proportionality
3. legitimacy
4. privacy

Figuring out the necessity of global electronic surveillance means a better aligning of signals intelligence capabilities with legitimate, top-of-the-list security threats. It means much greater attention being paid to signals intelligence tasking and much closer monitoring of signals intelligence payoffs. It means a system of targeted global electronic surveillance that is not driven by technological capabilities nor by misleading haystack metaphors and "collect it all" machismo.

Proportionality represents an additional layer of calculation to complement necessity. Getting proportionality right means creating a system in which the risks and rewards of any particular intelligence collection effort can be carefully weighed: not just in the context of possible outcomes but also in the post-Snowden light of "what if it comes out?" Some intelligence games are just not worth the candle.

Legitimacy might be the hardest principle for intelligence agencies to swallow. But the NSA and its partners have to recognize that their long-term viability rests not in their machines and algorithms but in their ability to convince their own publics that what they do is not just legal (especially when legal can be hard to pin down) but also right.

Privacy might be the most surprising principle of all. But the Snowden revelations have re-awakened a deep concern in democratic polities about over-reaching surveillance and have intersected with a renewed concern, in the age of digital living and ubiquitous information flows, with privacy protections. Future global electronic surveillance will have to pay much greater attention to domestic (and maybe even international) privacy rights.

As the United States grapples with post-Snowden change, those states such as Canada, whose own signals intelligence agency, the Communications Security Establishment Canada, is closely tied to the NSA and its surveillance practices, though the "Five Eyes" partnership, watch and wait. For Canadians, this is both a hopeful and a distressing reality. Hopeful in the sense that we can anticipate a kind of recalibration of U.S.-led global surveillance which might accord with our own principles and interests; distressing in that it reveals that Canada, enmeshed in its dependency on the NSA, and suffering problems of endemic secrecy, inadequate laws, poor accountability, hands-off political leadership, and an ill-informed public, cannot make independent headway in coming up with our own, applied Snowden verdict on global surveillance.

QUESTIONS FOR FURTHER DISCUSSION

1. Did Edward Snowden's revelations make him a hero or a traitor in your view, or perhaps something in between?
2. Could Snowden have chosen another pathway to disclose what he thought was an illegal spy program, one less controversial that would not have required him to flee the United States?
3. What would likely happen to Snowden if he returned to U.S. soil today? What would be your decision if you were an American judge required to determine punishment for him—or no punishment at all—in light of the documents he stole and released to the media?
4. What are your thoughts on the merits of the NSA intelligence-collection programs that Snowden found anathema?

ENDNOTES

1. "Secrecy, Security, and Sex: The NSA, Congress, and the Martin-Mitchell Defections." International Journal of Intelligence and Counterintelligence 22, no. 4 (Winter 2009): 699–729.

2. Transcript, Interview of Snowden by Brian Williams, NBC News. Aired May 28, 2014; accessed at: http://www.twitlonger.com/show/n_1s203lc].
3. "N.S.A. Breached Chinese Servers Seen as Security Threat," New York Times (March 22, 2014), p. A1.
4. "Edward Snowden, Whistle-Blower," New York Times (January 2, 2014), p. A18.
5. Albert Hirschman, Exit, Voice, and Loyalty (Cambridge: Harvard University Press, 1970).
6. The program was secretly authorized under s.215 of the Patriot Act. The Congressional Oversight Committee was given a misleading answer by DNI Jim Clapper when Senator Wyden asked him directly whether such activity was carried out.
7. The President's statement of 17 January 2014 on his Review of Signals Intelligence of can be found at http://www.whitehouse.gov/the-press-office/2014/01/17/remarks-president-review-signals-intelligence.
8. He is known to have stolen 58,000 highly classified intelligence documents from GCHQ, the equivalent of the U.S. NSA, that were shared with the NSA.
9. Sir Anthony May, Annual Report, 8 April 2014, available at http://www.iocco-uk.info/
10. A GCHQ analyst can find out under the rules for communications data that the suspect accessed Google—but not the questions asked; that the suspect accessed Amazon but not what was purchased; the email address to which an email was sent but not what is in the title of the message and not the message itself; if they want to access more detailed metadata whether from U.S. or U.K. sources they have to have the relevant Secretary of State warrant.
11. Vodaphone, Law Enforcement Disclosure Report 2014, accessible at http://www.vodafone.com/content/dam/sustainability/2014/pdf/operating-responsibly/vodafone_law_enforcement_disclosure_report.pdf
12. From Cline's Secrets Spies and Scholars (1976), quoted in Charles E. Lathrop, The Literary Spy (New Haven, CT: Yale University Press, 2004), p. 41.
13. The President's Review Group on Intelligence and Communications Technologies, The NSA Report: Liberty and Security in a Changing World (Princeton, NJ: Princeton University Press, 2014), p. 57.
14. Stansfield Turner, Secrecy and Democracy: The CIA in Transition (Boston, MA: Houghton Mifflin, 1985), p. 178.

From an INS Special Forum [Loch K. Johnson (ed.), Richard J. Aldrich and Christopher Moran, David M. Barrett, Glenn Hastedt, Robert Jervis, Wolfgang Krieger, Rose McDermott, Sir David Omand, Mark Phythian, and Wesley J. Wark], entitled "Implication of the Snowden Leaks," Intelligence and National Security, 29/6 (December 2014): 793–810. Used with permission of Taylor & Francis.

IX

INTELLIGENCE ACTIVITIES IN THE AFTERMATH OF THE 9/11 AND WMD INTELLIGENCE FAILURES

Polonius: "Hath there been such a time, I'd fain
know that,
That I have positively said ''Tis so,'
When it proved otherwise?"
King: "Not that I know."

—SHAKESPEARE, *Hamlet*, 2.2.153–155

The September 11, 2001 terrorist attacks on the World Trade Center and the Pentagon and the failure of the U.S. intelligence agencies and key allied governments to assess accurately the status of Iraq's programs to develop weapons of mass destruction (WMD) on the eve of the Second Gulf War were transformational events for the U.S. intelligence community. Both events are widely considered to be intelligence failures, but more recent explanations of what went wrong are beginning to emerge. The history of these events highlights how the limits of intelligence collection and analysis, politics, and the interaction between intelligence professionals and policymakers led, in the 9/11 instance, to lethargy in the face of an acute threat posed by Islamic fundamentalists. In the WMD example, in contrast, the intelligence and policy communities displayed a strong interest and examined the available data at

length. The 9/11 case suggests that the U.S. government fell victim to a fundamental intelligence mistake— failing to respond to valid threat indicators prior to the terrorist attacks. The government then made quite a different error in the WMD case, reaching the conclusion that Iraq was in the process of restarting its prohibited weapons program.

THE SEPTEMBER 11 ATTACKS

When the Islamic terrorist organization al-Qaeda used civilian airliners to attack the World Trade Center and the Pentagon, many observers believed that the U.S. intelligence community had failed to generate the warnings needed to stop the terrorist group before it could strike. Because of the devastating effects of the attacks, many assumed that the intelligence mistakes leading up to 9/11 were complete and total. In fact, the intelligence community had been tracking Islamic fundamentalists for years and had generated a steady stream of estimates about the possibility of terrorist attacks directed against U.S. forces and interests overseas, as well as against the American homeland itself. The intelligence community recognized that al-Qaeda had emerged from the remnants of U.S.-supported *mujahideen* fighters, who had successfully battled Soviet forces occupying Afghanistan. The community also recognized that, in the aftermath of the Soviet defeat, some of these "holy warriors" had gravitated toward Osama bin Laden, a Saudi financier who had built a reputation as a construction expert in Afghanistan. Bin Laden's motivations and rhetoric changed over time, but initially his anger seemed to have been directed toward what he believed was a corrupt Wahabi regime in Saudi Arabia. The American military presence in the Persian Gulf and Saudi Arabia, necessitated by the need to pressure Baghdad to end its WMD programs following the first Gulf War, only fueled Bin Laden's hatred of the Saudi Royal Family and the United States. Emboldened by its victory over the Soviets, al-Qaeda did not shy away from directly attacking the remaining superpower: the United States.

By the mid-1990s, the CIA had identified Bin Laden not only as an advocate of violence but also as someone who was willing to organize and direct attacks against U.S. interests. By 1998, he had become increasingly public about his intentions, issuing a *fatwa* and holding press conferences in which he called for attacks against Americans. In August 1998, al-Qaeda attacked U.S. embassies in Nairobi in Kenya and Dar es Salaam in Tanzania. In 2000, after a failed attempt to attack the USS *The Sullivans*, his followers launched a suicide attack against the USS *Cole*, moored in the Gulf of Aden off the coast of Yemen. This attack produced 50 American casualties and nearly sank the ship. Bin Laden talked openly about his ambitions, which were codified in an insightful article published by *Foreign Affairs* (Rashid 1999).

As the threats posed by al-Qaeda became realities, U.S. officials were confronted, too, with a series of warnings that the United States was not prepared or organized to meet the challenge of international terrorism. Findings from no less than 11 major commissions and studies addressed the topic of intelligence reform. Several of these studies offered recommendations to improve coordination between the FBI and the rest of the intelligence community. Reform was needed to eliminate the wall that

separated U.S. law enforcement officers from intelligence officials, a division that made it difficult to respond to terrorist networks that crossed domestic and international boundaries. A report issued in 2000 by the National Commission on Terrorism, for example, proposed clarifying the FBI's authority to investigate terrorist groups; allowing the CIA access to Bureau informants linked to terrorist organizations; placing terrorism high on the agendas of officials at the CIA, FBI, and NSA; and establishing new procedures for the quick dissemination of terrorist information to national security officials (Hart-Rudman 2001). Few of these recommendations, however, were acted upon. When al-Qaeda operatives infiltrated the United States prior to September 11, 2001, they effectively exploited the seam running between the intelligence community and domestic law enforcement agencies.

U.S. officials and organizations were slow to respond to the emerging threat posed by al-Qaeda, as well as to warnings that the U.S. government was poorly organized to meet the threat posed by transnational terrorist networks. Long accustomed to dealing with the menace of a Warsaw Pact conventional assault across what was then the inter-German border, or the prospect of a strategic nuclear exchange with the Soviet Union, officials and organizations were late in understanding the rising menace of international terrorism and how it was beginning to exploit the communication and transportation networks made possible by the information revolution and globalization. Mass-casualty terrorism was recognized as a possibility, but policymakers and scholars alike debated whether such extreme violence would actually be carried out by terrorist organizations, or even whether non-state actors were capable of creating high-casualty events. Most observers concluded that the 1993 attack on the World Trade Center by Islamic fundamentalists and the 1996 Aum Shinrikyo sarin attack on the Tokyo subway were failures. Some analysts also argued that launching a mass-casualty incident could easily rebound to the detriment of a terrorist organization, mobilizing governments and publics alike to undertake increasingly harsh and effective measures to eradicate the masterminds of terrorism and their supporters.

By the time President Bill Clinton left office, intelligence analysts had developed an increasingly alarming picture of al-Qaeda's international reach and ambitions to wreak havoc on the United States. Rocked by scandal and afflicted by chronic handwringing—Attorney General Janet Reno repeatedly warned that al-Qaeda might retaliate if attacked—the Clinton administration failed to translate its growing recognition of the threat into effective action. When President George W. Bush arrived in Washington to begin his term of office, his staff (with its own foreign policy agenda) seemed slow to recognize the looming threat. Here al-Qaeda might have enjoyed a lucky break: Preparations for the 9/11 attacks roughly corresponded to the change of administrations in Washington, a time when the effectiveness of the U.S. government is reduced. Al-Qaeda was able to capitalize on the fact that a new team was in the White House, busy moving in and holding its first meetings. The threat of transnational terrorism was rising to the top of the Bush administration's agenda by the late summer of 2001, but by then it was too late.

THE IRAQ WMD ESTIMATE

In the aftermath of the 9/11 attacks, debate about the possibility of mass-casualty terrorism was laid to rest, and a new threat came into sharp focus: WMD terrorism. All eyes focused on Iraq and the possibility that Saddam Hussein's regime had restarted its program to develop nuclear weapons following the ejection of UN Special Commission (UNSCOM) inspectors in the late 1990s. Many feared that the interests of Saddam and al-Qaeda might coincide, leading to an alliance of convenience that could make Bin Laden's often-stated interest in WMD a reality. With this nightmarish, if somewhat far-fetched, scenario in the background, the Bush administration apparently made the political decision that the risk of living with an Iraq armed with WMD outweighed the risk of taking direct action to bring about regime change in Iraq. Support for this decision was provided by the October 2002 Iraqi Weapons of Mass Destruction National Intelligence Estimate (NIE). Although the judgments of this NIE were heavily qualified (the estimate went into some detail about the limitations of its conclusions and the data used in reaching them), it was seen by most policymakers within the U.S. government as evidence that Saddam had again embarked on the path of obtaining nuclear weapons. Subsequent findings now suggest that the 2002 NIE was off the mark. No significant WMD programs were uncovered following the American and British invasion of Iraq in March 2003 that began the Second Gulf War and drove Saddam's Ba'athist regime from power. But by the time the weaknesses of the 2002 NIE were clear, the die had been cast.

The origins of the intelligence community's overestimate of Iraq's WMD capability probably can be found in its underestimation of Iraq's nuclear capabilities that became apparent following the First Gulf War (1990–1991). Information obtained by U.S. forces in the immediate aftermath of that war, data gleaned from UNSCOM inspections, and the revelations of Hussein Kamil (Saddam's son-in-law, who for a time defected to the West) settled first-order questions about the suspected Iraqi WMD program: Saddam seemed to be interested in all types of WMD. With justification, the intelligence community concluded that information available to it before the First Gulf War really was just the tip of the iceberg, and at least until the mid-1990s, more data became available that painted an increasingly vivid picture of Iraq's previous WMD efforts. What emerged was a policy-intelligence consensus about Iraq's WMD: Saddam Hussein would do everything in his power to obtain mass-casualty weapons, and the full extent of Iraq's WMD program was being concealed by the regime. New data generally confirmed worst-case estimates of Iraq's WMD capability. This estimate and the baseline data used to assess Iraq's WMD programs did not significantly change beliefs inside the Bush administration and most agencies in the intelligence community until the aftermath of the Second Gulf War, although UN weapons inspectors and a few elements inside the U.S. intelligence community raised doubts before the U.S.-led invasion in 2003.

A turning point for most analysts in the American intelligence community came with the ejection of UNSCOM inspectors in the late 1990s. Analysts concluded that the Iraqi regime, no longer hamstrung by the threat of detection by UNSCOM, would be able to restart its WMD programs and, given Saddam's objectives, probably *would* restart its WMD programs. What analysts failed to take into account, however, was that the Iraqi regime had been subjected to nearly a decade of international sanctions, UNSCOM inspections, continuous overflights, and concerted preventive attacks (the First Gulf War and Operation Desert Fox) intended to destroy, disrupt, and dissuade further efforts to produce, store, train with, or equip a large-scale WMD arsenal. These actions had a profound effect on the ability and will of the Iraqi regime to continue its WMD programs. Nevertheless, Saddam Hussein and his henchmen continued to create suspicion that nefarious activities might be taking place beyond the view of the prying eyes of the United States and allied intelligence agencies. Without a true "net assessment" to evaluate the full effect of international policies against Iraq—and there is no agency in the U.S. government that evaluates the overall success of U.S. foreign and defense policy—developments in Iraq tended to be judged with an eye toward Iraq's past capabilities, which were based on data gathered in the early 1990s and reflected the status of Iraq's programs in the 1980s.

If Western analysts were going to accurately assess the changing nature of Iraq's WMD program and current capabilities, they needed to step outside this policy-intelligence consensus about Iraqi behavior (a problem similar to the one faced by Israeli analysts prior to the Yom Kippur War in 1973). This type of assessment is extraordinarily difficult, because analysts would have to abandon their own policy-analytical-historical context to evaluate available information in a detached way. The U.S. intelligence community failed to undertake this reassessment of Iraq's weapons policies and capabilities; no one in the government of the United States attempted to reassess the underlying assumptions behind the Iraq estimate of October 2002. No one realized that the policy-intelligence consensus was no longer falsifiable, because most of the positive—as well as the negative—evidence, quite possibly manipulated by Iraqi denial and deception operations, suggested the presence of a clandestine Iraqi nuclear program. If matters look cut and dried to intelligence analysts, suspicions should have been raised that results might have been a little *too* cut and dried. This did not occur, however, in terms of the Iraq NIE. Indeed, there were no "intelligence dissenters" to that document—individuals who objected to the consensus and tried to make their opinions known. No one inside the U.S. government stepped forward effectively to object to the data, analysis, or conclusions contained in the Iraq NIE—although behind the scenes some officials in the Department of State intelligence service (Intelligence and Research, or INR), in the Energy Department intelligence unit, and in Air Force intelligence did raise objections but without success. By and large, the NIE was considered to be rather ho-hum.

THE READINGS

The readings in this section examine these two intelligence-policy failures. The first selection is excerpted from the 9/11 Commission Report. Chaired by Thomas H. Kean and Lee H. Hamilton, the commission produced a document that offers a riveting account of the events leading up to the September 11 tragedy. The report should be read in its entirety by everyone but especially by students who were too young in 2001 to absorb the full shock of the events of that dark day. The sections of the Commission Report that we present here contain its recommendations for overcoming the organizational weaknesses of the U.S. government revealed on 9/11. They also highlight the global threat posed by the rise of transnational terrorist networks and outline a national strategy to meet that threat. The report also offers reforms needed to make effective defense, homeland security, and intelligence a reality.

The second reading, written by Amy B. Zegart, confronts the problem of organizational and management failures in the intelligence community as major explanations for the 9/11 and Iraqi WMD intelligence failures. Her work is known for its criticism of the government for not reforming its institutions adequately to protect the nation—what she refers to as "adaptation failure." She laments the outcome of reform efforts in 2004, which "left the secretary of defense with greater power, the director of national intelligence with little, and the Intelligence Community even more disjointed."

In the third article, co-editor James J. Wirtz looks at intelligence challenges presented by the rise of the terrorist organization known as ISIS, a brutal non-state terrorist organization that has been able to exploit social media as a means for recruiting new members to *jihadism* around the world.

Next, a prominent CIA intelligence analyst, Paul R. Pillar, puts the Iraqi WMD issue under a microscope. He finds deeply troubling instances of the misuse of intelligence, including the cardinal sin: the politicization of information by policy officials to suit their own political objectives. He offers a set of sensible reforms that, if adopted, would improve the way in which intelligence is treated in Washington, DC.

Finally, James Burch examines intelligence in various democracies. He evaluations the state of intelligence accountability in these nations; and, further, assesses whether the establishment of a domestic intelligence agency in the United States is viable for meeting the asymmetric threats of the twenty-first century.

26. 9/11 INTELLIGENCE FAILURE

KEAN COMMISSION

The 9/11 Commission, chaired by former New Jersey Republican Governor Thomas H. Kean and former U.S. Representative Lee H. Hamilton (D, Indiana), produced an influential account of the events surrounding the September 11, 2001, Al Qaeda attacks on the World Trade Center and the Pentagon. The report achieved best-selling status and remains a valuable research document on global terrorism. Our selection from the report identifies the nature of the terrorist threat facing the United States, the organizational reforms needed to meet this challenge, and national strategies that the commissioners believed should be adopted to keep terrorism at bay.

WHAT TO DO? A GLOBAL STRATEGY (REFLECTING ON A GENERATIONAL CHALLENGE)

Three years after 9/11, Americans are still thinking and talking about how to protect our nation in this new era. The national debate continues.

Countering terrorism has become, beyond any doubt, the top national security priority for the United States. This shift has occurred with the full support of the Congress, both major political parties, the media, and the American people.

The nation has committed enormous resources to national security and to countering terrorism. Between fiscal year 2001, the last budget adopted before 9/11, and the present fiscal year 2004, total federal spending on defense (including expenditures on both Iraq and Afghanistan), homeland security, and international affairs rose more than 50 percent, from $354 billion to about $547 billion. The United States has not experienced such a rapid surge in national security spending since the Korean War.[1]

This pattern has occurred before in American history. The United States faces a sudden crisis and summons a tremendous exertion of national energy. Then, as that surge transforms the landscape, comes a time for reflection and revaluation. Some programs and even agencies are discarded; others are invented or redesigned. Private firms and engaged citizens redefine their relationships with government, working through the processes of the American republic.

Now is the time for that reflection and reevaluation. The United States should consider *what to do*—the shape and objectives of a strategy. Americans should also consider *how to do it*—organizing their government in a different way.

DEFINING THE THREAT

In the post-9/11 world, threats are defined more by the fault lines within societies than by the territorial boundaries between them. From terrorism to global disease or environmental degradation, the challenges have become transnational rather than international. That is the defining quality of world politics in the twenty-first century.

National security used to be considered by studying foreign frontiers, weighing opposing groups of states, and measuring industrial might. To be dangerous, an enemy had to muster large armies. Threats emerged slowly, often visibly, as weapons were forged, armies conscripted, and units trained and moved into place. Because large states were more powerful, they also had more to lose. They could be deterred.

Now threats can emerge quickly. An organization like al Qaeda, headquartered in a country on the other side of the earth, in a region so poor that electricity or telephones were scarce, could nonetheless scheme to wield weapons of unprecedented destructive power in the largest cities of the United States.

In this sense, 9/11 has taught us that terrorism against American interests "over there" should be regarded just as we regard terrorism against America "over here." In this same sense, the American homeland is the planet.

But the enemy is not just "terrorism," some generic evil.[2] This vagueness blurs the strategy. The catastrophic threat at this moment in history is more specific. It is the threat posed by *Islamist* terrorism—especially the al Qaeda network, its affiliates, and its ideology.[3]

Usama Bin Ladin and other Islamist terrorist leaders draw on a long tradition of extreme intolerance within one stream of Islam (a minority tradition), from at least Ibn Taymiyyah, through the founders of Wahhabism, through the Muslim Brotherhood, to Sayyid Qutb. That stream is motivated by religion and does not distinguish politics from religion, thus distorting both. It is further fed by grievances stressed by Bin Ladin and widely felt throughout the Muslim world—against the U.S. military presence in the Middle East, policies perceived as anti-Arab and anti-Muslim, and support of Israel. Bin Ladin and Islamist terrorists mean exactly what they say: to them America is the font of all evil, the "head of the snake," and it must be converted or destroyed.

It is not a position with which Americans can bargain or negotiate. With it there is no common ground—not even respect for life—on which to begin a dialogue. It can only be destroyed or utterly isolated.

Because the Muslim world has fallen behind the West politically, economically, and militarily for the past three centuries, and because few tolerant or secular Muslim democracies provide alternative models for the future, Bin Ladin's message finds receptive ears. It has attracted active support from thousands of disaffected young Muslims and resonates powerfully with a far larger number who do not actively support his methods. The resentment of America and the West is deep, even among leaders of relatively successful Muslim states.[4]

Tolerance, the rule of law, political and economic openness, the extension of greater opportunities to women—these cures must come from within Muslim societies themselves. The United States must support such developments.

But this process is likely to be measured in decades, not years. It is a process that will be violently opposed by Islamist terrorist organizations, both inside Muslim countries and in attacks on the United States and other Western nations. The United States finds itself caught up in a clash *within* a civilization. That clash arises from particular conditions in the Muslim world, conditions that spill over into expatriate Muslim communities in non-Muslim countries.

Our enemy is twofold: al Qaeda, a stateless network of terrorists that struck us on 9/11; and a radical ideological movement in the Islamic world, inspired in part by al Qaeda, which has spawned terrorist groups and violence across the globe. The first enemy is weakened, but continues to pose a grave threat. The second enemy is gathering, and will menace Americans and American interests long after Usama Bin Ladin and his cohorts are killed or captured. Thus our strategy must match our means to two ends: dismantling the al Qaeda network and prevailing in the longer term over the ideology that gives rise to Islamist terrorism.

Islam is not the enemy. It is not synonymous with terror. Nor does Islam teach terror. America and its friends oppose a perversion of Islam, not the great world faith itself. Lives guided by religious faith, including literal beliefs in holy scriptures, are common to every religion, and represent no threat to us.

Other religions have experienced violent internal struggles. With so many diverse adherents, every major religion will spawn violent zealots. Yet understanding and tolerance among people of different faiths can and must prevail.

The present transnational danger is Islamist terrorism. What is needed is a broad political-military strategy that rests on a firm tripod of policies to

- attack terrorists and their organizations;
- prevent the continued growth of Islamist terrorism; and
- protect against and prepare for terrorist attacks.

MORE THAN A WAR ON TERRORISM

Terrorism is a tactic used by individuals and organizations to kill and destroy. Our efforts should be directed at those individuals and organizations.

Calling this struggle a war accurately describes the use of American and allied armed forces to find and destroy terrorist groups and their allies in the field, notably in Afghanistan. The language of war also evokes the mobilization for a national effort. Yet the strategy should be balanced.

The first phase of our post-9/11 efforts rightly included military action to topple the Taliban and pursue al Qaeda. This work continues. But long-term success demands the use of all elements of national power: diplomacy, intelligence, covert action, law enforcement, economic policy, foreign aid, public diplomacy, and homeland defense. If we favor one tool while neglecting others, we leave ourselves vulnerable and weaken our national effort.

Certainly the strategy should include offensive operations to counter terrorism. Terrorists should no longer find safe haven where their organizations can grow and flourish. America's strategy should be a coalition strategy, that includes Muslim nations as partners in its development and implementation.

Our effort should be accompanied by a preventive strategy that is as much, or more, political as it is military. The strategy must focus clearly on the Arab and Muslim world, in all its variety.

Our strategy should also include defenses. America can be attacked in many ways and has many vulnerabilities. No defenses are perfect. But risks must be calculated; hard choices must be made about allocating resources. Responsibilities for America's defense should be clearly defined. Planning does make a difference, identifying where a little money might have a large effect. Defenses also complicate the plans of attackers, increasing their risks of discovery and failure. Finally, the nation must prepare to deal with attacks that are not stopped.

MEASURING SUCCESS

What should Americans expect from their government in the struggle against Islamist terrorism? The goals seem unlimited: Defeat terrorism anywhere in the world. But Americans have also been told to expect the worst: An attack is probably coming; it may be terrible.

With such benchmarks, the justifications for action and spending seem limitless. Goals are good. Yet effective public policies also need concrete objectives. Agencies need to be able to measure success.

These measurements do not need to be quantitative: government cannot measure success in the ways that private firms can. But the targets should be specific enough so that reasonable observers—in the White House, the Congress, the media, or the general public—can judge whether or not the objectives have been attained.

Vague goals match an amorphous picture of the enemy. Al Qaeda and its affiliates are popularly described as being all over the world, adaptable, resilient, needing little higher-level organization, and capable of anything. The American people are thus given the picture of an omnipotent, unslayable hydra of destruction. This image lowers expectations for government effectiveness.

It should not lower them too far. Our report shows a determined and capable group of plotters.

Yet the group was fragile, dependent on a few key personalities, and occasionally left vulnerable by the marginal, unstable people often attracted to such causes. The enemy made mistakes—like Khalid al Mihdhar's unauthorized departure from the United States that required him to enter the country again in July 2001, or the selection of Zacarias Moussaoui as a participant and Ramzi Binalshibh's transfer of money to him. The U.S. government was not able to capitalize on those mistakes in time to prevent 9/11.

We do not believe it is possible to defeat all terrorist attacks against Americans, every time and everywhere. A president should tell the American people:

- No president can promise that a catastrophic attack like that of 9/11 will not happen again. History has shown that even the most vigilant and expert agencies cannot always prevent determined, suicidal attackers from reaching a target.
- But the American people are entitled to expect their government to do its very best. They should expect that officials will have realistic objectives, clear guidance, and effective organization. They are entitled to see some standards for performance so they can judge, with the help of their elected representatives, whether the objectives are being met.

ATTACK TERRORISTS AND THEIR ORGANIZATIONS

The U.S. government, joined by other governments around the world, is working through intelligence, law enforcement, military, financial, and diplomatic channels to identify, disrupt, capture, or kill individual terrorists. This effort was going on before 9/11 and it continues on a vastly enlarged scale. But to catch terrorists, a U.S. or foreign agency needs to be able to find and reach them.

NO SANCTUARIES

The 9/11 attack was a complex international operation, the product of years of planning. Bombings like those in Bali in 2003 or Madrid in 2004, while able to take hundreds of lives, can be mounted locally. Their requirements are far more modest in size and complexity. They are more difficult to thwart. But the U.S. government must build the capacities to prevent a 9/11-scale plot from succeeding, and those capabilities will help greatly to cope with lesser but still devastating attacks.

A complex international terrorist operation aimed at launching a catastrophic attack cannot be mounted by just anyone in any place. Such operations appear to require

- time, space, and ability to perform competent planning and staff work;
- a command structure able to make necessary decisions and possessing the authority and contacts to assemble needed people, money, and materials;
- opportunity and space to recruit, train, and select operatives with the needed skills and dedication, providing the time and structure required to socialize them into the terrorist cause, judge their trustworthiness, and hone their skills;
- a logistics network able to securely manage the travel of operatives, move money, and transport resources (like explosives) where they need to go;
- access, in the case of certain weapons, to the special materials needed for a nuclear, chemical, radiological, or biological attack;
- reliable communications between coordinators and operatives; and
- opportunity to test the workability of the plan.

Many details ... illustrate the direct and indirect value of the Afghan sanctuary to al Qaeda in preparing the 9/11 attack and other operations. The organization cemented personal ties among veteran jihadists working together there for years. It had the operational space to gather and sift recruits, indoctrinating them in isolated, desert camps. It built up logistical networks, running through Pakistan and the United Arab Emirates.

Al Qaeda also exploited relatively lax internal security environments in Western countries, especially Germany. It considered the environment in the United States so hospitable that the 9/11 operatives used America as their staging area for further training and exercises—traveling into, out of, and around the country and complacently using their real names with little fear of capture.

To find sanctuary, terrorist organizations have fled to some of the least governed, most lawless places in the world. The intelligence community has prepared a world map that highlights possible terrorist havens, using no secret intelligence—just indicating areas that combine rugged terrain, weak governance, room to hide or receive supplies, and low population density with a town or city near enough to allow necessary interaction with the outside world. Large areas scattered around the world meet these criteria.[5]

In talking with American and foreign government officials and military officers on the front lines fighting terrorists today, we asked them: If you were

a terrorist leader today, where would you locate your base? Some of the same places come up again and again on their lists:

- western Pakistan and the Pakistan-Afghanistan border region
- southern or western Afghanistan
- the Arabian Peninsula, especially Saudi Arabia and Yemen, and the nearby Horn of Africa, including Somalia and extending southwest into Kenya
- Southeast Asia, from Thailand to the southern Philippines to Indonesia
- West Africa, including Nigeria and Mali
- European cities with expatriate Muslim communities, especially cities in central and eastern Europe where security forces and border controls are less effective

In the twentieth century, strategists focused on the world's great industrial heartlands. In the twenty-first, the focus is in the opposite direction, toward remote regions and failing states. The United States has had to find ways to extend its reach, straining the limits of its influence.

Every policy decision we make needs to be seen through this lens. If, for example, Iraq becomes a failed state, it will go to the top of the list of places that are breeding grounds for attacks against Americans at home. Similarly, if we are paying insufficient attention to Afghanistan, the rule of the Taliban or warlords and narcotraffickers may reemerge and its countryside could once again offer refuge to al Qaeda, or its successor.

RECOMMENDATION: The U.S. government must identify and prioritize actual or potential terrorist sanctuaries. For each, it should have a realistic strategy to keep possible terrorists insecure and on the run, using all elements of national power. We should reach out, listen to, and work with other countries that can help.

We offer three illustrations that are particularly applicable today, in 2004: Pakistan, Afghanistan, and Saudi Arabia.

PAKISTAN

Pakistan's endemic poverty, widespread corruption, and often ineffective government create opportunities for Islamist recruitment. Poor education is a particular concern. Millions of families, especially those with little money, send their children to religious schools, or madrassahs. Many of these schools are the only opportunity available for an education, but some have been used as incubators for violent extremism. According to Karachi's police commander, there are 859 madrassahs teaching more than 200,000 youngsters in his city alone.[6]

It is hard to overstate the importance of Pakistan in the struggle against Islamist terrorism. Within Pakistan's borders are 150 million Muslims, scores of al Qaeda terrorists, many Taliban fighters, and—perhaps—Usama Bin Ladin. Pakistan possesses nuclear weapons and has come frighteningly close to war with nuclear-armed India over the disputed territory of Kashmir. A political battle among anti-American Islamic fundamentalists, the Pakistani military, and more moderate mainstream political forces has already spilled over into violence, and there have been repeated recent attempts to kill Pakistan's president, Pervez Musharraf.

In recent years, the United States has had three basic problems in its relationship with Pakistan:

- On terrorism, Pakistan helped nurture the Taliban. The Pakistani army and intelligence services, especially below the top ranks, have long been ambivalent about confronting Islamist extremists. Many in the government have sympathized with or provided support to the extremists. Musharraf agreed that Bin Ladin was bad. But before 9/11, preserving good relations with the Taliban took precedence.
- On proliferation, Musharraf has repeatedly said that Pakistan does not barter with its nuclear technology. But proliferation concerns have been long-standing and very serious. Most recently, the Pakistani government has claimed not to have known that one of its nuclear weapons developers, a national figure, was leading the most dangerous nuclear smuggling ring ever disclosed.
- Finally, Pakistan has made little progress toward the return of democratic rule at the national level, although that turbulent process does continue to function at the provincial level and the Pakistani press remains relatively free.

Immediately after 9/11, confronted by the United States with a stark choice, Pakistan made a strategic decision. Its government stood aside and allowed the U.S.-led coalition to destroy the Taliban regime. In other ways, Pakistan actively assisted: its authorities arrested more than 500 al Qaeda operatives and Taliban members, and Pakistani forces played a leading part in tracking down KSM, Abu Zubaydah, and other key al Qaeda figures.[7]

In the following two years, the Pakistani government tried to walk the fence, helping against al Qaeda

while seeking to avoid a larger confrontation with Taliban remnants and other Islamic extremists. When al Qaeda and its Pakistani allies repeatedly tried to assassinate Musharraf, almost succeeding, the battle came home.

The country's vast unpoliced regions make Pakistan attractive to extremists seeking refuge and recruits and also provide a base for operations against coalition forces in Afghanistan. Almost all the 9/11 attackers traveled the north-south nexus of Kandahar–Quetta–Karachi. The Baluchistan region of Pakistan (KSM's ethnic home) and the sprawling city of Karachi remain centers of Islamist extremism where the U.S. and Pakistani security and intelligence presence has been weak. The U.S. consulate in Karachi is a makeshift fortress, reflecting the gravity of the surrounding threat.[8]

During the winter of 2003–2004, Musharraf made another strategic decision. He ordered the Pakistani army into the frontier provinces of northwest Pakistan along the Afghan border, where Bin Ladin and Ayman al Zawahiri have reportedly taken refuge. The army is confronting groups of al Qaeda fighters and their local allies in very difficult terrain. On the other side of the frontier, U.S. forces in Afghanistan have found it challenging to organize effective joint operations, given Pakistan's limited capabilities and reluctance to permit U.S. military operations on its soil. Yet in 2004, it is clear that the Pakistani government is trying harder than ever before in the battle against Islamist terrorists.[9]

Acknowledging these problems and Musharraf's own part in the story, we believe that Musharraf's government represents the best hope for stability in Pakistan and Afghanistan.

- In an extraordinary public essay asking how Muslims can "drag ourselves out of the pit we find ourselves in, to raise ourselves up," Musharraf has called for a strategy of "enlightened moderation." The Muslim world, he said, should shun militancy and extremism; the West—and the United States in particular—should seek to resolve disputes with justice and help better the Muslim world.[10]
- Having dome close to war in 2002 and 2003, Pakistan and India have recently made significant progress in peacefully discussing their long-standing differences. The United States has been and should remain a key supporter of that process.
- The constant refrain of Pakistanis is that the United States long treated them as allies of convenience.

As the United States makes fresh commitments now, it should make promises it is prepared to keep, for years to come.

RECOMMENDATION: If Musharraf stands for enlightened moderation in a fight for his life and for the life of his country, the United States should be willing to make hard choices too, and make the difficult long-term commitment to the future of Pakistan. Sustaining the current scale of aid to Pakistan, the United States should support Pakistan's government in its struggle against extremists with a comprehensive effort that extends from military aid to support for better education, so long as Pakistan's leaders remain willing to make difficult choices of their own.

AFGHANISTAN

Afghanistan was the incubator for al Qaeda and for the 9/11 attacks. In the fall of 2001, the U.S.-led international coalition and its Afghan allies toppled the Taliban and ended the regime's protection of al Qaeda. Notable progress has been made. International cooperation has been strong, with a clear UN mandate and a NATO-led peacekeeping force (the International Security Assistance Force, or ISAF). More than 10,000 American soldiers are deployed today in Afghanistan, joined by soldiers from NATO allies and Muslim states. A central government has been established in Kabul, with a democratic constitution, new currency, and a new army. Most Afghans enjoy greater freedom, women and girls are emerging from subjugation, and 3 million children have returned to school. For the first time in many years, Afghans have reason to hope.[11]

But grave challenges remain. Taliban and al Qaeda fighters have regrouped in the south and southeast. Warlords control much of the country beyond Kabul, and the land is awash in weapons. Economic development remains a distant hope. The narcotics trade—long a massive sector of the Afghan economy—is again booming. Even the most hardened aid workers refuse to operate in many regions, and some warn that Afghanistan is near the brink of chaos.[12]

Battered Afghanistan has a chance. Elections are being prepared. It is revealing that in June 2004, Taliban fighters resorted to slaughtering 16 Afghans on a bus, apparently for no reason other than their boldness in carrying an unprecedented Afghan weapon: a voter registration card.

Afghanistan's president, Hamid Karzai, is brave and committed. He is trying to build genuinely national institutions that can overcome the tradition of allocating powers among ethnic communities. Yet even if his efforts are successful and elections bring a democratic government to Afghanistan, the United States faces some difficult choices.

After paying relatively little attention to rebuilding Afghanistan during the military campaign, U.S. policies changed noticeably during 2003. Greater consideration of the political dimension and congressional support for a substantial package of assistance signaled a longer-term commitment to Afghanistan's future. One Afghan regional official plaintively told us the country finally has a good government. He begged the United States to keep its promise and not abandon Afghanistan again, as it had in the 1990s. Another Afghan leader noted that if the United States leaves, "we will lose all that we have gained."[13]

Most difficult is to define the security mission in Afghanistan. There is continuing political controversy about whether military operations in Iraq have had any effect on the scale of America's commitment to the future of Afghanistan. The United States has largely stayed out of the central government's struggles with dissident warlords and it has largely avoided confronting the related problem of narcotraficking.[14]

RECOMMENDATION: The President and the Congress deserve praise for their efforts in Afghanistan so far. Now the United States and the international community should make a long-term commitment to a secure and stable Afghanistan, in order to give the government a reasonable opportunity to improve the life of the Afghan people. Afghanistan must not again become a sanctuary for international crime and terrorism. The United States and the international community should help the Afghan government extend its authority over the country, with a strategy and nation-by-nation commitments to achieve their objectives.

- This is an ambitious recommendation. It would mean a redoubled effort to secure the country, disarm militias, and curtail the age of warlord rule. But the United States and NATO have already committed themselves to the future of this region—wisely, as the 9/11 story shows—and failed half-measures could be worse than useless.
- NATO in particular has made Afghanistan a test of the Alliance's ability to adapt to current security challenges of the future. NATO must pass this test. Currently, the United States and the international community envision enough support so that the

central government can build a truly national army and extend essential infrastructure and minimum public services to major towns and regions. The effort relies in part on foreign civil-military teams, arranged under various national flags. The institutional commitments of NATO and the United Nations to these enterprises are weak. NATO member states are not following through; some of the other states around the world that have pledged assistance to Afghanistan are not fulfilling their pledges.

- The U.S. presence in Afghanistan is overwhelmingly oriented toward military and security work. The State Department presence is woefully understaffed, and the military mission is narrowly focused on al Qaeda and Taliban remnants in the south and southeast. The U.S. government can do its part if the international community decides on a joint effort to restore the rule of law and contain rampant crime and narcotics trafficking in this crossroads of Central Asia.[15]

We heard again and again that the money for assistance is allocated so rigidly that, on the ground, one U.S. agency often cannot improvise or pitch in to help another agency, even in small ways when a few thousand dollars could make a great difference.

The U.S. government should allocate money so that lower-level officials have more flexibility to get the job done across agency lines, adjusting to the circumstances they find in the field. This should include discretionary funds for expenditures by military units that often encounter opportunities to help the local population.

SAUDI ARABIA

Saudi Arabia has been a problematic ally in combating Islamic extremism. At the level of high policy, Saudi Arabia's leaders cooperated with American diplomatic initiatives aimed at the Taliban or Pakistan before 9/11. At the same time, Saudi Arabia's society was a place where al Qaeda raised money directly from individuals and through charities. It was the society that produced 15 of the 19 hijackers.

The Kingdom is one of the world's most religiously conservative societies, and its identity is closely bound to its religious links, especially its position as the guardian of Islam's two holiest sites. Charitable giving, or *zakat*, is one of the five pillars of Islam. It is broader and more pervasive than Western ideas of charity—functioning also as a form of income tax, educational assistance, foreign aid, and

a source of political influence. The Western notion of the separation of civic and religious duty does not exist in Islamic cultures. Funding charitable works is an integral function of the governments in the Islamic world. It is so ingrained in Islamic culture that in Saudi Arabia, for example, a department within the Saudi Ministry of Finance and National Economy collects zakat directly, much as the U.S. Internal Revenue Service collects payroll withholding tax. Closely tied to zakat is the dedication of the government to propagating the Islamic faith, particularly the Wahhabi sect that flourishes in Saudi Arabia.

Traditionally, throughout the Muslim world, there is no formal oversight mechanism for donations. As Saudi wealth increased, the amounts contributed by individuals and the state grew dramatically. Substantial sums went to finance Islamic charities of every kind.

While Saudi domestic charities are regulated by the Ministry of Labor and Social Welfare, charities and international relief agencies, such as the World Assembly of Muslim Youth (WAMY), are currently regulated by the Ministry of Islamic Affairs. This ministry uses zakat and government funds to spread Wahhabi beliefs throughout the world, including in mosques and schools. Often these schools provide the only education available; even in affluent countries, Saudi-funded Wahhabi schools are often the only Islamic schools. Some Wahhabi-funded organizations have been exploited by extremists to further their goal of violent jihad against non-Muslims. One such organization has been the al Haramain Islamic Foundation; the assets of some branch offices have been frozen by the U.S. and Saudi governments.

Until 9/11, few Saudis would have considered government oversight of charitable donations necessary; many would have perceived it as interference in the exercise of their faith. At the same time, the government's ability to finance most state expenditures with energy revenues has delayed the need for a modern income tax system. As a result, there have been strong religious, cultural, and administrative barriers to monitoring charitable spending. That appears to be changing, however, now that the goal of violent jihad also extends to overthrowing Sunni governments (such as the House of Saud) that are not living up to the ideals of the Islamist extremists.[16]

The leaders of the United States and the rulers of Saudi Arabia have long had friendly relations, rooted in fundamentally common interests against the Soviet Union during the Cold War, in American hopes that Saudi oil supplies would stabilize the supply and price of oil in world markets, and in Saudi hopes that America could help protect the Kingdom against foreign threats.

In 1990, the Kingdom hosted U.S. armed forces before the first U.S.-led war against Iraq. American soldiers and airmen have given their lives to help protect Saudi Arabia. The Saudi government has difficulty acknowledging this. American military bases remained there until 2003, as part of an international commitment to contain Iraq.

For many years, leaders on both sides preferred to keep their ties quiet and behind the scenes. As a result, neither the U.S. nor the Saudi people appreciated all the dimensions of the bilateral relationship, including the Saudi role in U.S. strategies to promote the Middle East peace process. In each country, political figures find it difficult to publicly defend good relations with the other.

Today, mutual recriminations flow. Many Americans see Saudi Arabia as an enemy, not as an embattled ally. They perceive an autocratic government that oppresses women, dominated by a wealthy and indolent elite. Saudi contacts with American politicians are frequently invoked as accusations in partisan political arguments. Americans are often appalled by the intolerance, anti-Semitism, and anti-American arguments taught in schools and preached in mosques.

Saudis are angry too. Many educated Saudis who were sympathetic to America now perceive the United States as an unfriendly state. One Saudi reformer noted to us that the demonization of Saudi Arabia in the U.S. media gives ammunition to radicals, who accuse reformers of being U.S. lackeys. Tens of thousands of Saudis who once regularly traveled to (and often had homes in) the United States now go elsewhere.[17]

Among Saudis, the United States is seen as aligned with Israel in its conflict with the Palestinians, with whom Saudis ardently sympathize. Although Saudi Arabia's cooperation against terrorism improved to some extent after the September 11 attacks, significant problems remained. Many in the Kingdom initially reacted with disbelief and denial. In the following months, as the truth became clear, some leading Saudis quietly acknowledged the problem but still did not see their own regime as threatened, and thus often did not respond promptly to U.S. requests for help. Though Saddam Hussein was widely detested, many Saudis are sympathetic to the anti-U.S. insurgents in Iraq, although majorities also condemn jihadist attacks in the Kingdom.[18]

As in Pakistan, Yemen, and other countries, attitudes changed when the terrorism came home.

Cooperation had already become significant, but after the bombings in Riyadh on May 12, 2003, it improved much more. The Kingdom openly discussed the problem of radicalism, criticized the terrorists as religiously deviant, reduced official support for religious activity overseas, closed suspect charitable foundations, and publicized arrests—very public moves for a government that has preferred to keep internal problems quiet.

The Kingdom of Saudi Arabia is now locked in mortal combat with al Qaeda. Saudi police are regularly being killed in shootouts with terrorists. In June 2004, the Saudi ambassador to the United States called publicly—in the Saudi press—for his government to wage a jihad of its own against the terrorists. "We must all, as a state and as a people, recognize the truth about these criminals," he declared, "[i]f we do not declare a general mobilization—we will lose this war on terrorism."[19]

Saudi Arabia is a troubled country. Although regarded as very wealthy, in fact per capita income has dropped from $28,000 at its height to the present level of about $8,000. Social and religious traditions complicate adjustment to modern economic activity and limit employment opportunities for young Saudis. Women find their education and employment sharply limited.

President Clinton offered us a perceptive analysis of Saudi Arabia, contending that fundamentally friendly rulers have been constrained by their desire to preserve the status quo. He, like others, made the case for pragmatic reform instead. He hopes the rulers will envision what they want their Kingdom to become in 10 or 20 years, and start a process in which their friends can help them change.[20]

There are signs that Saudi Arabia's royal family is trying to build a consensus for political reform, though uncertain about how fast and how far to go. Crown Prince Abdullah wants the Kingdom to join the World Trade Organization to accelerate economic liberalization. He has embraced the *Arab Human Development Report*, which was highly critical of the Arab world's political, economic, and social failings and called for greater economic and political reform.[21]

Cooperation with Saudi Arabia against Islamist terrorism is very much in the U.S. interest. Such cooperation can exist for a time largely in secret, as it does now, but it cannot grow and thrive there. Nor, on either side, can friendship be unconditional.

RECOMMENDATION: The problems in the U.S. Saudi relationship must be confronted, openly. The United

States and Saudi Arabia must determine if they can build a relationship that political leaders on both sides are prepared to publicly defend—a relationship about more than oil. It should include a shared commitment to political and economic reform, as Saudis make common cause with the outside world. It should include a shared interest in greater tolerance and cultural respect, translating into a commitment to fight the violent extremists who foment hatred.

PREVENT THE CONTINUED GROWTH OF ISLAMIST TERRORISM

In October 2003, reflecting on progress after two years of waging the global war on terrorism, Defense Secretary Donald Rumsfeld asked his advisers: "Are we capturing, killing or deterring and dissuading more terrorists every day than the madrassas and the radical clerics are recruiting, training and deploying against us? Does the US need to fashion a broad, integrated plan to stop the next generation of terrorists? The US is putting relatively little effort into a long-range plan, but we are putting a great deal of effort into trying to stop terrorists. The cost-benefit ratio is against us! Our cost is billions against the terrorists' costs of millions."[22]

These are the right questions. Our answer is that we need short-term action on a long-range strategy, one that invigorates our foreign policy with the attention that the President and Congress have given to the military and intelligence parts of the conflict against Islamist terrorism.

ENGAGE THE STRUGGLE OF IDEAS

The United States is heavily engaged in the Muslim world and will be for many years to come. This American engagement is resented. Polls in 2002 found that among America's friends, like Egypt—the recipient of more U.S. aid for the past 20 years than any other Muslim country—only 15 percent of the population had a favorable opinion of the United States. In Saudi Arabia the number was 12 percent. And two-thirds of those surveyed in 2003 in countries from Indonesia to Turkey (a NATO ally) were very or somewhat fearful that the United States may attack them.[23]

Support for the United States has plummeted. Polls taken in Islamic countries after 9/11 suggested that many or most people thought the United States was doing the right thing in its fight against terrorism; few people saw popular support for al Qaeda; half of those surveyed said that ordinary people had a favorable view of the United States. By 2003, polls showed that "the bottom has fallen out of support for America in most of the Muslim world. Negative views of the U.S. among Muslims, which had been largely limited to countries in the Middle East, have spread. . . . Since last summer, favorable ratings for the U.S. have fallen from 61% to 15% in Indonesia and from 71% to 38% among Muslims in Nigeria."[24]

Many of these views are at best uninformed about the United States and, at worst, informed by cartoonish stereotypes, the coarse expression of a fashionable "Occidentalism" among intellectuals who caricature U.S. values and policies. Local newspapers and the few influential satellite broadcasters—like al Jazeera—often reinforce the jihadist theme that portrays the United States as anti-Muslim.[25]

The small percentage of Muslims who are fully committed to Usama Bin Ladin's version of Islam are impervious to persuasion. It is among the large majority of Arabs and Muslims that we must encourage reform, freedom, democracy, and opportunity, even though our own promotion of these messages is limited in its effectiveness simply because we are its carriers. Muslims themselves will have to reflect upon such basic issues as the concept of jihad, the position of women, and the place of non-Muslim minorities. The United States can promote moderation, but cannot ensure its ascendancy. Only Muslims can do this.

The setting is difficult. The combined gross domestic product of the 22 countries in the Arab League is less than the GDP of Spain. Forty percent of adult Arabs are illiterate, two-thirds of them women. One-third of the broader Middle East lives on less than two dollars a day. Less than 2 percent of the population has access to the Internet. The majority of older Arab youths have expressed a desire to emigrate to other countries, particularly those in Europe.[26]

In short, the United States has to help defeat an ideology, not just a group of people, and we must do so under difficult circumstances. How can the United States and its friends help moderate Muslims combat the extremist ideas?

RECOMMENDATION: The U.S. government must define what the message is, what it stands for. We should offer an example of moral leadership in the world, committed to treat people humanely, abide by the rule of law, and be generous and caring to our neighbors. America and Muslim friends can agree on respect for human dignity and opportunity. To Muslim parents, terrorists like Bin Ladin have nothing to offer their children but visions of violence and death. America and its friends have a crucial advantage—we can offer these parents a vision that might give their children a better future. If we heed the views of thoughtful leaders in the Arab and Muslim world, a moderate consensus can be found.

That vision of the future should stress life over death: individual educational and economic opportunity. This vision includes widespread political participation and contempt for indiscriminate violence. It includes respect for the rule of law, openness in discussing differences, and tolerance for opposing points of view.

RECOMMENDATION: Where Muslim governments, even those who are friends, do not respect these principles, the United States must stand for a better future. One of the lessons of the long Cold War was that short-term gains in cooperating with the most repressive and brutal governments were too often outweighed by long-term setbacks for America's stature and interests.

American foreign policy is part of the message. America's policy choices have consequences. Right or wrong, it is simply a fact that American policy regarding the Israeli-Palestinian conflict and American actions in Iraq are dominant staples of popular commentary across the Arab and Muslim world. That does not mean U.S. choices have been wrong. It means those choices must be integrated with America's message of opportunity to the Arab and Muslim world. Neither Israel nor the new Iraq will be safer if worldwide Islamist terrorism grows stronger.

The United States must do more to communicate its message. Reflecting on Bin Ladin's success in reaching Muslim audiences, Richard Holbrooke wondered, "How can a man in a cave out communicate the world's leading communications society?" Deputy Secretary of State Richard Armitage worried to us that Americans have been "exporting our fears and our anger," not our vision of opportunity and hope.[27]

RECOMMENDATION: Just as we did in the Cold War, we need to defend our ideals abroad vigorously. America does stand up for its values. The United States defended, and still defends, Muslims against tyrants and criminals in Somalia, Bosnia, Kosovo, Afghanistan, and Iraq. If the United States does not act aggressively to define itself in the Islamic world, the extremists will gladly do the job for us.

- Recognizing that Arab and Muslim audiences rely on satellite television and radio, the government has begun some promising initiatives in television and radio broadcasting to the Arab world, Iran, and Afghanistan. These efforts are beginning to reach large audiences. The Broadcasting Board of Governors has asked for much larger resources. It should get them.
- The United States should rebuild the scholarship, exchange, and library programs that reach out to young people and offer them knowledge and hope. Where such assistance is provided, it should be identified as coming from the citizens of the United States.

AN AGENDA OF OPPORTUNITY

The United States and its friends can stress educational and economic opportunity. The United Nations has rightly equated "literacy as freedom."

- The international community is moving toward setting a concrete goal—to cut the Middle East region's illiteracy rate in half by 2010, targeting women and girls and supporting programs for adult literacy.
- Unglamorous help is needed to support the basics, such as textbooks that translate more of the world's knowledge into local languages and libraries to house such materials. Education about the outside world, or other cultures, is weak.
- More vocational education is needed, too, in trades and business skills. The Middle East can also benefit from some of the programs to bridge the digital divide and increase Internet access that have already been developed for other regions of the world.

Education that teaches tolerance, the dignity and value of each individual, and respect for different beliefs is a key element in any global strategy to eliminate Islamist terrorism.

RECOMMENDATION: The U.S. government should offer to join with other nations in generously supporting a new International Youth Opportunity Fund. Funds will be spent directly for building and operating primary and secondary schools in those Muslim states that commit to sensibly investing their own money in public education.

Economic openness is essential. Terrorism is not caused by poverty. Indeed, many terrorists come from relatively well-off families. Yet when people lose hope, when societies break down, when countries fragment, the breeding grounds for terrorism are created. Backward economic policies and repressive political regimes slip into societies that are without hope, where ambition and passions have no constructive outlet.

The policies that support economic development and reform also have political implications. Economic and political liberties tend to be linked. Commerce, especially international commerce, requires ongoing cooperation and compromise, the exchange of ideas across cultures, and the peaceful resolution of differences through negotiation or the rule of law. Economic growth expands the middle class, a constituency for further reform. Successful economies rely on vibrant private sectors, which have an interest in curbing indiscriminate government power. Those who develop the practice of controlling their own economic destiny soon desire a voice in their communities and political societies.

The U.S. government has announced the goal of working toward a Middle East Free Trade Area, or MEFTA, by 2013. The United States has been seeking comprehensive free trade agreements (FTAs) with the Middle Eastern nations most firmly on the path to reform. The U.S.-Israeli FTA was enacted in 1985, and Congress implemented an FTA with Jordan in 2001. Both agreements have expanded trade and investment, thereby supporting domestic economic reform. In 2004, new FTAs were signed with Morocco and Bahrain, and are awaiting congressional approval. These models are drawing the interest of their neighbors. Muslim countries can become full participants in the rules-based global trading system, as the United States considers lowering its trade barriers with the poorest Arab nations.

RECOMMENDATION: A comprehensive U.S. strategy to counter terrorism should include economic policies that encourage development, more open societies, and opportunities for people to improve the lives of their families and to enhance prospects for their children's future.

TURNING A NATIONAL STRATEGY INTO A COALITION STRATEGY

Practically every aspect of U.S. counterterrorism strategy relies on international cooperation. Since 9/11, these contacts concerning military, law enforcement, intelligence, travel and customs, and financial matters have expanded so dramatically, and often in an ad hoc way, that it is difficult to track these efforts, much less integrate them.

RECOMMENDATION: The United States should engage other nations in developing a comprehensive

coalition strategy against Islamist terrorism. There are several multilateral institutions in which such issues should be addressed. But the most important policies should be discussed and coordinated in a flexible contact group of leading coalition governments. This is a good place, for example, to develop joint strategies for targeting terrorist travel, or for hammering out a common strategy for the places where terrorists may be finding sanctuary.

Presently the Muslim and Arab states meet with each other, in organizations such as the Islamic Conference and the Arab League. The Western states meet with each other in organizations such as NATO and the Group of Eight summit of leading industrial nations. A recent G-8 summit initiative to begin a dialogue about reform may be a start toward finding a place where leading Muslim states can discuss—and be seen to discuss—critical policy issues with the leading Western powers committed to the future of the Arab and Muslim world.

These new international efforts can create durable habits of visible cooperation, as states willing to step up to their responsibilities join together in constructive efforts to direct assistance and coordinate action.

Coalition warfare also requires coalition policies on what to do with enemy captives. Allegations that the United States abused prisoners in its custody make it harder to build the diplomatic, political, and military alliances the government will need. The United States should work with friends to develop mutually agreed-on principles for the detention and humane treatment of captured international terrorists who are not being held under a particular country's criminal laws. Countries such as Britain, Australia, and Muslim friends, are committed to fighting terrorists. America should be able to reconcile its views on how to balance humanity and security with our nation's commitment to these same goals.

The United States and some of its allies do not accept the application of full Geneva Convention treatment of prisoners of war to captured terrorists. Those Conventions establish a minimum set of standards for prisoners in internal conflicts. Since the international struggle against Islamist terrorism is not internal, those provisions do not formally apply, but they are commonly accepted as basic standards for humane treatment.

RECOMMENDATION: The United States should engage its friends to develop a common coalition approach toward the detention and humane treatment of captured terrorists. New principles might draw upon Article 3 of the Geneva Conventions on the law of armed conflict. That article was specifically designed for those cases in which the usual laws of war did not apply. Its minimum standards are generally accepted throughout the world as customary international law.

PROLIFERATION OF WEAPONS OF MASS DESTRUCTION

The greatest danger of another catastrophic attack in the United States will materialize if the world's most dangerous terrorists acquire the world's most dangerous weapons. . . . [A]l Qaeda has tried to acquire or make nuclear weapons for at least ten years. . . . [O]fficials worriedly discuss[ed], in 1998, reports that Bin Ladin's associates thought their leader was intent on carrying out a "Hiroshima."

These ambitions continue. In the public portion of his February 2004 worldwide threat assessment to Congress, DCI Tenet noted that Bin Ladin considered the acquisition of weapons of mass destruction to be a "religious obligation." He warned that al Qaeda "continues to pursue its strategic goal of obtaining a nuclear capability." Tenet added that "more than two dozen other terrorist groups are pursuing CBRN [chemical, biological, radiological, and nuclear] materials."[28]

A nuclear bomb can be built with a relatively small amount of nuclear material. A trained nuclear engineer with an amount of highly enriched uranium or plutonium about the size of a grapefruit or an orange, together with commercially available material, could fashion a nuclear device that would fit in a van like the one Ramzi Yousef parked in the garage of the World Trade Center in 1993. Such a bomb would level Lower Manhattan.[29]

The coalition strategies we have discussed to combat Islamist terrorism should therefore be combined with a parallel, vital effort to prevent and counter the proliferation of weapons of mass destruction (WMD). We recommend several initiatives in this area.

Strengthen Counterproliferation Efforts

While efforts to shut down Libya's illegal nuclear program have been generally successful, Pakistan's illicit trade and the nuclear smuggling networks of Pakistani scientist A. Q. Khan have revealed that the spread of nuclear weapons is a problem of global dimensions. Attempts to deal with Iran's nuclear program are still underway. Therefore, the United States should work with the international community to develop laws and an international legal regime with universal jurisdiction to enable the capture, interdiction, and prosecution of such smugglers by any state in the world where they do not disclose their activities.

Expand the Proliferation Security Initiative

In May 2003, the Bush administration announced the Proliferation Security Initiative (PSI): nations in a willing partnership combining their national capabilities to use military, economic, and diplomatic tools to interdict threatening shipments of WMD and missile-related technology.

The PSI can be more effective if it uses intelligence and planning resources of the NATO alliance. Moreover, PSI membership should be open to non-NATO countries. Russia and China should be encouraged to participate.

Support the Cooperative Threat Reduction Program

Outside experts are deeply worried about the U.S. government's commitment and approach to securing the weapons and highly dangerous materials still scattered in Russia and other countries of the Soviet Union. The government's main instrument in this area, the Cooperative Threat Reduction Program (usually referred to as "Nunn-Lugar," after the senators who sponsored the legislation in 1991), is now in need of expansion, improvement, and resources. The U.S. government has recently redoubled its international commitments to support this program, and we recommend that the United States do all it can, if Russia and other countries will do their part. The government should weigh the value of this investment against the catastrophic cost America would face should such weapons find their way to the terrorists who are so anxious to acquire them.

RECOMMENDATION: Our report shows that al Qaeda has tried to acquire or make weapons of mass destruction for at least ten years. There is no doubt the United States would be a prime target. Preventing the proliferation of these weapons warrants a maximum effort—by strengthening counterproliferation efforts, expanding the proliferation Security Initiative, and supporting the Cooperative Threat Reduction program.

TARGETING TERRORIST MONEY

The general public sees attacks on terrorist finance as a way to "starve the terrorists of money." So, initially, did the U.S. government. After 9/11, the United

States took aggressive actions to designate terrorist financiers and freeze their money, in the United States and through resolutions of the United Nations. These actions appeared to have little effect and, when confronted by legal challenges, the United States and the United Nations were often forced to unfreeze assets.

The difficulty, understood later, was that even if the intelligence community might "link" someone to a terrorist group through acquaintances or communications, the task of tracing the money from that individual to the terrorist group, or otherwise showing complicity, was far more difficult. It was harder still to do so without disclosing secrets.

These early missteps made other countries unwilling to freeze assets or otherwise act merely on the basis of a U.S. action. Multilateral freezing mechanisms now require waiting periods before being put into effect, eliminating the element of surprise and thus virtually ensuring that little money is actually frozen. Worldwide asset freezes have not been adequately enforced and have been easily circumvented, often within weeks, by simple methods.

But trying to starve the terrorists of money is like trying to catch one kind of fish by draining the ocean. A better strategy has evolved since those early months, as the government learned more about how al Qaeda raises, moves, and spends money.

RECOMMENDATION: Vigorous efforts to track terrorist financing must remain front and center in U.S. counterterrorism efforts. The government has recognized that information about terrorist money helps us to understand their networks, search them out, and disrupt their operations. Intelligence and law enforcement have targeted the relatively small number of financial facilitators—individuals al Qaeda relied on for their ability to raise and deliver money—at the core of al Qaeda's revenue stream. These efforts have worked. The death or capture of several important facilitators has decreased the amount of money available to al Qaeda and has increased its costs and difficulty in raising and moving that money. Captures have additionally provided a windfall of intelligence that can be used to continue the cycle of disruption.

The U.S. financial community and some international financial institutions have generally provided law enforcement and intelligence agencies with extraordinary cooperation, particularly in supplying information to support quickly developing investigations. Obvious vulnerabilities in the U.S. financial system have been corrected. The United States has been less successful in persuading other countries to adopt financial regulations that would permit the tracing of financial transactions.

Public designation of terrorist financiers and organizations is still part of the fight, but it is not the primary weapon. Designations are instead a form of diplomacy, as governments join together to identify named individuals and groups as terrorists. They also prevent open fundraising. Some charities that have been identified as likely avenues for terrorist financing have seen their donations diminish and their activities come under more scrutiny, and others have been put out of business, although controlling overseas branches of Gulf-area charities remains a challenge. The Saudi crackdown after the May 2003 terrorist attacks in Riyadh has apparently reduced the funds available to al Qaeda—perhaps drastically—but it is too soon to know if this reduction will last.

Though progress apparently has been made, terrorists have shown considerable creativity in their methods of moving money. If al Qaeda is replaced by smaller, decentralized terrorist groups, the premise behind the government's efforts—that terrorists need a financial support network—may become outdated. Moreover, some terrorist operations do not rely on outside sources of money and may now be self-funding, either through legitimate employment or low-level criminal activity.[30]

PROTECT AGAINST AND PREPARE FOR TERRORIST ATTACKS

In the nearly three years since 9/11, Americans have become better protected against terrorist attack. Some of the changes are due to government action, such as new precautions to protect aircraft. A portion can be attributed to the sheer scale of spending and effort. Publicity and the vigilance of ordinary Americans also make a difference.

But the President and other officials acknowledge that although Americans may be safer, they are not safe. Our report shows that the terrorists analyze defenses. They plan accordingly.

Defenses cannot achieve perfect safety. They make targets harder to attack successfully, and they deter attacks by making capture more likely. Just increasing the attacker's odds of failure may make the difference between a plan attempted, or a plan discarded. The enemy also may have to develop more elaborate plans, thereby increasing the danger of exposure or defeat.

Protective measures also prepare for the attacks that may get through, containing the damage and saving lives.

TERRORIST TRAVEL

More than 500 million people annually cross U.S. borders at legal entry points, about 330 million of them noncitizens. Another 500,000 or more enter illegally without inspection across America's thousands of miles of land borders or remain in the country past the expiration of their permitted stay. The challenge for national security in an age of terrorism is to prevent the very few people who may pose overwhelming risks from entering or remaining in the United States undetected.[31]

In the decade before September 11, 2001, border security—encompassing travel, entry, and immigration—was not seen as a national security matter. Public figures voiced concern about the "war on drugs," the right level and kind of immigration, problems along the southwest border, migration crises originating in the Caribbean and elsewhere, or the growing criminal traffic in humans. The immigration system as a whole was widely viewed as increasingly dysfunctional and badly in need of reform. In national security circles, however, only smuggling of weapons of mass destruction carried weight, not the entry of terrorists who might use such weapons or the presence of associated foreign born terrorists.

For terrorists, travel documents are as important as weapons. Terrorists must travel clandestinely to meet, train, plan, case targets, and gain access to attack. To them, international travel presents great danger, because they must surface to pass through regulated channels, present themselves to border security officials, or attempt to circumvent inspection points.

In their travels, terrorists use evasive methods, such as altered and counterfeit passports and visas, specific travel methods and routes, liaisons with corrupt government officials, human smuggling networks, supportive travel agencies, and immigration and identity fraud. These can sometimes be detected.

Before 9/11, no agency of the U.S. government systematically analyzed terrorists' travel strategies. Had they done so, they could have discovered the ways in which the terrorist predecessors to al Qaeda had been systematically but detectably exploiting weaknesses in our border security since the early 1990s.

We found that as many as 15 of the 19 hijackers were potentially vulnerable to interception by border authorities. Analyzing their characteristic travel documents and travel patterns could have allowed authorities to intercept 4 to 15 hijackers and more effective use of information available in U.S. government databases could have identified up to 3 hijackers.[32]

Looking back, we can also see that the routine operations of our immigration laws—that is, aspects of those laws not specifically aimed at protecting against terrorism—inevitably shaped al Qaeda's planning and opportunities. Because they were deemed not to be hona fide tourists or students as they claimed, five conspirators that we know of tried to get visas and failed, and one was denied entry by an inspector. We also found that had the immigration system set a higher bar for determining whether individuals are who or what they claim to be—and ensuring routine consequences for violations—it could potentially have excluded, removed, or come into further contact with several hijackers who did not appear to meet the terms for admitting short-term visitors.[33]

Our investigation showed that two systemic weaknesses came together in our border system's inability to contribute to an effective defense against the 9/11 attacks: a lack of well-developed counterterrorism measures as a part of border security and an immigration system not able to deliver on its basic commitments, much less support counterterrorism. These weaknesses have been reduced but are far from being overcome.

RECOMMENDATION: Targeting travel is at least as powerful a weapon against terrorists as targeting their money. The United States should combine terrorist travel intelligence, operations, and law enforcement in a strategy to intercept terrorists, find terrorist travel facilitators, and constrain terrorist mobility.

Since 9/11, significant improvements have been made to create an integrated watchlist that makes terrorist name information available to border and law enforcement authorities. However, in the already difficult process of merging border agencies in the new Department of Homeland Security—"changing the engine while flying" as one official put it[34]—new insights into terrorist travel have not yet been integrated into the front lines of border security.

The small terrorist travel intelligence collection and analysis program currently in place has produced disproportionately useful results. It should be expanded. Since officials at the borders encounter travelers and their documents first and investigate travel facilitators, they must work closely with intelligence officials.

Internationally and in the United States, constraining terrorist travel should become a vital part of counterterrorism strategy. Better technology and training to detect terrorist travel documents are the most important immediate steps to reduce America's vulnerability to clandestine entry. Every stage of our border and immigration system should have as a part of its operations the detection of terrorist indicators on travel documents. Information systems able to authenticate travel documents and detect potential terrorist indicators should be used at consulates, at primary border inspection lines, in immigration services offices, and in intelligence and enforcement units. All frontline personnel should receive some training. Dedicated specialists and ongoing linkages with the intelligence community are also required. The Homeland Security Department's Directorate of Information Analysis and Infrastructure Protection should receive more resources to accomplish its mission as the bridge between the frontline border agencies and the rest of the government counterterrorism community.

A BIOMETRIC SCREENING SYSTEM

When people travel internationally, they usually move through defined channels, or portals. They may seek to acquire a passport. They may apply for a visa. They stop at ticket counters, gates, and exit controls at airports and seaports. Upon arrival, they pass through inspection points. They may transit to another gate to get on an airplane. Once inside the country, they may seek another form of identification and try to enter a government or private facility. They may seek to change immigration status in order to remain.

Each of these checkpoints or portals is a screening— a chance to establish that people are who they say they are and are seeking access for their stated purpose, to intercept identifiable suspects, and to take effective action.

The job of protection is shared among these many defined checkpoints. By taking advantage of them all, we need not depend on any one point in the system to do the whole job. The challenge is to see the common problem across agencies and functions and develop a conceptual framework—an architecture— for an effective screening system.[35]

Throughout government, and indeed in private enterprise, agencies and firms at these portals confront recurring judgments that balance security, efficiency, and civil liberties. These problems should be addressed systemically, not in an ad hoc, fragmented way. For example:

What information is an individual required to present and in what form? A fundamental problem, now beginning to be addressed, is the lack of standardized information in "feeder" documents used in identifying individuals. Biometric identifiers that measure unique physical characteristics, such as facial features, fingerprints, or iris scans, and reduce them to digitized, numerical statements called algorithms, are just beginning to be used. Travel history, however, is still recorded in passports with entry-exit stamps called cachets, which al Qaeda has trained its operatives to forge and use to conceal their terrorist activities.

How will the individual and the information be checked? There are many databases just in the United States—for terrorist, criminal, and immigration history, as well as financial information, for instance. Each is set up for different purposes and stores different kinds of data, under varying rules of access. Nor is access always guaranteed. Acquiring information held by foreign governments may require painstaking negotiations, and records that are not yet digitized are difficult to search or analyze. The development of terrorist indicators has hardly begun, and behavioral cues remain important.

Who will screen individuals, and what will they be trained to do? A wide range of border, immigration, and law enforcement officials encounter visitors and immigrants and they are given little training in terrorist travel intelligence. Fraudulent travel documents, for instance, are usually returned to travelers who are denied entry without further examination for terrorist trademarks, investigation as to their source, or legal process.

What are the consequences of finding a suspicious indicator, and who will take action? One risk is that responses may be ineffective or produce no further information. Four of the 9/11 attackers were pulled into secondary border inspection, but then admitted. More than half of the 19 hijackers were flagged by the Federal Aviation Administration's profiling system when they arrived for their flights, but the consequence was that bags, not people, were checked. Competing risks include "false positives," or the danger that rules may be applied with insufficient training or judgment. Overreactions can impose high costs too—on individuals, our economy, and our beliefs about justice.

- A special note on the importance of trusting subjective judgment: One potential hijacker was turned back by an immigration inspector as he tried to enter the United States. The inspector relied on intuitive experience to ask questions more than he relied on any objective factor that could be detected by "scores" or a machine. Good people who have worked in such jobs for a long time understand this phenomenon well. Other evidence we obtained confirmed the importance of letting experienced gate agents or security screeners ask questions and use their judgment. This is not an invitation to arbitrary exclusions. But any effective system has to grant some scope, perhaps in a little extra inspection or one more check, to the instincts and discretion of well trained human beings.

RECOMMENDATION: The U.S. border security system should be integrated into a larger network of screening points that includes our transportation system and access to vital facilities, such as nuclear reactors. The President should direct the Department of Homeland Security to lead the effort to design a comprehensive screening system, addressing common problems and setting common standards with systemwide goals in mind. Extending those standards among other governments could dramatically strengthen America and the world's collective ability to intercept individuals who pose catastrophic threats.

We advocate a system for screening, not categorical profiling. A screening system looks for particular, identifiable suspects or indicators of risk. It does not involve guesswork about who might be dangerous. It requires frontline border officials who have the tools and resources to establish that people are who they say they are, intercept identifiable suspects, and disrupt terrorist operations.

THE U.S. BORDER SCREENING SYSTEM

The border and immigration system of the United States must remain a visible manifestation of our belief in freedom, democracy, global economic growth, and the rule of law, yet serve equally well as a vital element of counterterrorism. Integrating terrorist travel information in the ways we have described is the most immediate need. But the underlying system must also be sound.

Since September 11, the United States has built the first phase of a biometric screening program, called US VISIT (the United States Visitor and Immigrant Status Indicator Technology program). It takes two biometric identifiers—digital photographs and prints of two index fingers—from travelers. False identities are used by terrorists to avoid being detected on a watchlist. These biometric identifiers make such evasions far more difficult.

So far, however, only visitors who acquire visas to travel to the United States are covered. While visitors from "visa waiver" countries will be added to the program, beginning this year, covered travelers will still constitute only about 12 percent of all noncitizens crossing U.S. borders. Moreover, exit data are not uniformly collected and entry data are not fully automated. It is not clear the system can be installed before 2010, but even this timetable may be too slow, given the possible security dangers.[36]

- Americans should not be exempt from carrying biometric passports or otherwise enabling their identities to be securely verified when they enter the United States; nor should Canadians or Mexicans. Currently U.S. persons are exempt from carrying passports when returning from Canada, Mexico, and the Caribbean. The current system enables non-U.S. citizens to gain entry by showing minimal identification. The 9/11 experience shows that terrorists study and exploit America's vulnerabilities.
- To balance this measure, programs to speed known travelers should be a higher priority, permitting inspectors to focus on greater risks. The daily commuter should not be subject to the same measures as first-time travelers. An individual should be able to preenroll, with his or her identity verified in passage. Updates of database information and other checks can ensure ongoing reliability. The solution, requiring more research and development, is likely to combine radio frequency technology with biometric identifiers.[37]
- The current patchwork of border screening systems, including several frequent traveler programs, should be consolidated with the US VISIT system to enable the development of an integrated system, which in turn can become part of the wider screening plan we suggest.
- The program allowing individuals to travel from foreign countries through the United States to a third country, without having to obtain a U.S. visa, has been suspended. Because "transit without visa" can be exploited by terrorists to enter the United States, the program should not be reinstated unless and until transit passage areas can be fully secured to prevent passengers from illegally exiting the airport.

Inspectors adjudicating entries of the 9/11 hijackers lacked adequate information and knowledge of the rules. All points in the border system—from consular offices to immigration services offices—will need appropriate electronic access to an individual's file. Scattered units at Homeland Security and the State Department perform screening and data mining: instead, a government-wide team of border and transportation officials should be working together. A modern border and immigration system should combine a biometric entry-exit system with accessible files on visitors and immigrants, along with intelligence on indicators of terrorist travel.

Our border screening system should check people efficiently and welcome friends. Admitting large numbers of students, scholars, businesspeople, and tourists fuels our economy, cultural vitality, and political reach. There is evidence that the present system is disrupting travel to the United States. Overall, visa applications in 2003 were down over 32 percent since 2001. In the Middle East, they declined about 46 percent. Training and the design of security measures should be continuously adjusted.[38]

RECOMMENDATION: The Department of Homeland Security, properly supported by the Congress, should complete, as quickly as possible, a biometric entry-exit screening system, including a single system for speeding qualified travelers. It should be integrated with the system that provides benefits to foreigners seeking to stay in the United States. Linking biometric passports to good data systems and decisionmaking is a fundamental goal. No one can hide his or her debt by acquiring a credit card with a slightly different name. Yet today, a terrorist can defeat the link to electronic records by tossing away an old passport and slightly altering the name in the new one.

Completion of the entry-exit system is a major and expensive challenge. Biometrics have been introduced into an antiquated computer environment. Replacement of these systems and improved biometric systems will be required. Nonetheless, funding and completing a biometrics-based entry-exit system is an essential investment in our national security.

Exchanging terrorist information with other countries, consistent with privacy requirements, along with listings of lost and stolen passports, will have immediate security benefits. We should move toward real-time verification of passports with issuing authorities. The further away from our borders that screening occurs, the more security benefits we gain. At least some screening should occur before a passenger departs on a flight destined for the United States. We should also work with other countries to ensure effective inspection regimes at all airports.[39]

The international community arrives at international standards for the design of passports through the International Civil Aviation Organization (ICAO). The global standard for identification is a digital photograph; fingerprints are optional. We must work with others to improve passport standards and provide foreign assistance to countries that need help in making the transition.[40]

RECOMMENDATION: The U.S. government cannot meet its own obligations to the American people to prevent the entry of terrorists without a major effort to collaborate with other governments. We should do more to exchange terrorist information with trusted allies, and raise U.S. and global border security standards for travel and border crossing over the medium and long term through extensive international cooperation.

IMMIGRATION LAW AND ENFORCEMENT

Our borders and immigration system, including law enforcement, ought to send a message of welcome, tolerance, and justice to members of immigrant communities in the United States and in their countries of origin. We should reach out to immigrant communities. Good immigration services are one way of doing so that is valuable in every way—including intelligence.

It is elemental to border security to know who is coming into the country. Today more than 9 million people are in the United States outside the legal immigration system. We must also be able to monitor and respond to entrances between our ports of entry, working with Canada and Mexico as much as possible.

There is a growing role for state and local law enforcement agencies. They need more training and work with federal agencies so that they can cooperate more effectively with those federal authorities in identifying terrorist suspects.

All but one of the 9/11 hijackers acquired some form of U.S. identification document, some by fraud. Acquisition of these forms of identification would have assisted them in boarding commercial flights, renting cars, and other necessary activities.

RECOMMENDATION: Secure identification should begin in the United States. The federal government should set standards for the issuance of birth certificates and sources of identification, such as driver's licenses. Fraud in identification documents is no longer just a problem of theft. At many entry points to vulnerable facilities, including gates for boarding aircraft, sources of identification are the last opportunity to ensure that people are who they say they are and to check whether they are terrorists.[41]

STRATEGIES FOR AVIATION AND TRANSPORTATION SECURITY

The U.S. transportation system is vast and, in an open society, impossible to secure completely against terrorist attacks. There are hundreds of commercial airports, thousands of planes, and tens of thousands of daily flights carrying more than half a billion passengers a year. Millions of containers are imported annually through more than 300 sea and river ports served by more than 3,700 cargo and passenger terminals. About 6,000 agencies provide transit services through buses, subways, ferries, and light-rail service to about 14 million Americans each weekday.[42]

In November 2001, Congress passed and the President signed the Aviation and Transportation Security Act. This act created the Transportation Security Administration (TSA), which is now part of the Homeland Security Department. In November 2002, both the Homeland Security Act and the Maritime Transportation Security Act followed. These laws required the development of strategic plans to describe how the new department and TSA would provide security for critical parts of the U.S. transportation sector.

Over 90 percent of the nations $5.3 billion annual investment in the TSA goes to aviation—to fight the last war. The money has been spent mainly to meet congressional mandates to federalize the security checkpoint screeners and to deploy existing security methods and technologies at airports. The current efforts do not yet reflect a forward-looking strategic plan systematically analyzing assets, risks, costs, and benefits. Lacking such a plan, we are not convinced that our transportation security resources are being allocated to the greatest risks in a cost-effective way.

- Major vulnerabilities still exist in cargo and general aviation security. These, together with inadequate screening and access controls, continue to present aviation security challenges.
- While commercial aviation remains a possible target, terrorists may turn their attention to other modes. Opportunities to do harm are as great, or greater, in maritime or surface transportation. Initiatives to secure shipping containers have just begun. Surface transportation systems such as railroads and mass transit remain hard to protect because they are so accessible and extensive.

Despite congressional deadlines, the TSA has developed neither an integrated strategic plan for the transportation sector nor specific plans for the various modes—air, sea, and ground.

RECOMMENDATION: Hard choices must be made in allocating limited resources. The U.S. government should identify and evaluate the transportation assets that need to be protected, set risk-based priorities for defending them, select the most practical and cost-effective ways of doing so, and then develop a plan, budget, and funding to implement the effort. The plan should assign roles and missions to the relevant authorities (federal, state, regional, and local) and to private stakeholders. In measuring effectiveness, perfection is unattainable. But terrorists should perceive that potential targets are defended. They may be deterred by a significant chance of failure.

Congress should set a specific date for the completion of these plans and hold the Department of Homeland Security and TSA accountable for achieving them.

The most powerful investments may be for improvements in technologies with applications across the transportation modes, such as scanning technologies designed to screen containers that can be transported by plane, ship, truck, or rail. Though such technologies are becoming available now, widespread deployment is still years away.

In the meantime, the best protective measures may be to combine improved methods of identifying and tracking the high-risk containers, operators, and facilities that require added scrutiny with further efforts to integrate intelligence analysis, effective procedures for transmitting threat information to transportation authorities, and vigilance by transportation authorities and the public.

A LAYERED SECURITY SYSTEM

No single security measure is foolproof. Accordingly, the TSA must have multiple layers of security in place to defeat the more plausible and dangerous forms of attack against public transportation.

- The plan must take into consideration the full array of possible enemy tactics, such as use of insiders, suicide terrorism, or standoff attack. Each layer must be effective in its own right. Each must be supported by other layers that are redundant and coordinated.
- The TSA should be able to identify for Congress the array of potential terrorist attacks, the layers of security in place, and the reliability provided by each layer. TSA must develop a plan as described above to improve weak individual layers and the effectiveness of the layered systems it deploys.

On 9/11, the 19 hijackers were screened by a computer-assisted screening system called CAPPS. More than half were identified for further inspection, which applied only to their checked luggage.

Under current practices, air carriers enforce government orders to stop certain known and suspected terrorists from boarding commercial flights and to apply secondary screening procedures to others. The "no-fly" and "automatic selectee" lists include only those individuals who the U.S. government believes pose a direct threat of attacking aviation.

Because air carriers implement the program, concerns about sharing intelligence information with private firms and foreign countries keep the U.S. government from listing all terrorist and terrorist suspects who should be included. The TSA has planned to take over this function when it deploys a new screening system to take the place of CAPPS. The deployment of this system has been delayed because of claims it may violate civil liberties.

RECOMMENDATION: Improved use of "no-fly" and "automatic selectee" lists should not be delayed while the argument about a successor to CAPPS continues. This screening function should be performed by the TSA, and it should utilize the larger set of watchlists maintained by the federal government. Air carriers should be required to supply the information needed to test and implement this new system.

CAPPS is still part of the screening process, still profiling passengers, with the consequences of selection now including personal searches of the individual and carry-on bags. The TSA is dealing with the kind of screening issues that are being encountered by other agencies. As we mentioned earlier, these screening issues need to be elevated for high-level attention and addressed promptly by the government. Working through these problems can help clear the way for the TSA's screening improvements and would help many other agencies too.

The next layer is the screening checkpoint itself. As the screening system tries to stop dangerous people, the checkpoint needs to be able to find dangerous items. Two reforms are needed soon: (1) screening people for explosives, not just their carry-on bags, and (2) improving screener performance.

RECOMMENDATION: The TSA and the Congress must give priority attention to improving the ability of screening checkpoints to detect explosives on passengers. As a start, each individual selected for special screening should be screened for explosives. Further, the TSA should conduct a human factors study, a method often used in the private sector, to understand problems in screener performance and set attainable objectives for individual screeners and for the checkpoints where screening takes place.

Concerns also remain regarding the screening and transport of checked bags and cargo. More attention and resources should be directed to reducing or mitigating the threat posed by explosives in vessels' cargo holds. The TSA should expedite the installation of advanced (in-line) baggage-screening equipment. Because the aviation industry will derive substantial benefits from this deployment, it should pay a fair share of the costs. The TSA should require that every passenger aircraft carrying cargo must deploy at least one hardened container to carry any suspect cargo. TSA also needs to intensify its efforts to identify, track, and appropriately screen potentially dangerous cargo in both the aviation and maritime sectors.

THE PROTECTION OF CIVIL LIBERTIES

Many of our recommendations call for the government to increase its presence in our lives—for example, by creating standards for the issuance of forms of identification, by better securing our borders, by sharing information gathered by many different agencies. We also recommend the consolidation of authority over the now far-flung entities constituting the intelligence community. The Patriot Act vests substantial powers in our federal government. We have seen the government use the immigration laws as a tool in its counterterrorism effort. Even without the changes we recommend, the American public has vested enormous authority in the U.S. government.

At our first public hearing on March 31, 2003, we noted the need for balance as our government responds to the real and ongoing threat of terrorist attacks. The terrorists have used our open society against us. In wartime, government calls for greater powers, and then the need for those powers recedes after the war ends. This struggle will go on. Therefore, while protecting our homeland, Americans should be mindful of threats to vital personal and civil liberties. This balancing is no easy task, but we must constantly strive to keep it right.

This shift of power and authority to the government calls for an enhanced system of checks and balances to protect the precious liberties that are vital to our way of life. We therefore make three recommendations.

First, to open up the sharing of information across so many agencies and with the private sector, the

President should take responsibility for determining what information can be shared by which agencies and under what conditions. Protection of privacy rights should be one key element of this determination.

RECOMMENDATION: As the President determines the guidelines for information sharing among government agencies and by those agencies with the private sector, he should safeguard the privacy of individuals about whom information is shared.

Second, Congress responded, in the immediate aftermath of 9/11, with the Patriot Act, which vested substantial new powers in the investigative agencies of the government. Some of the most controversial provisions of the Patriot Act are to "sunset" at the end of 2005. Many of the act's provisions are relatively noncontroversial, updating America's surveillance laws to reflect technological developments in a digital age. Some executive actions that have been criticized are unrelated to the Patriot Act. The provisions in the act that facilitate the sharing of information among intelligence agencies and between law enforcement and intelligence appear, on balance, to be beneficial. Because of concerns regarding the shifting balance of power to the government, we think that a full and informed debate on the Patriot Act would be healthy.

RECOMMENDATION: The burden of proof for retaining a particular governmental power should be on the executive, to explain (a) that the power actually materially enhances security and (b) that there is adequate supervision of the executive's use of the powers to ensure protection of civil liberties. If the power is granted, there must be adequate guidelines and oversight to properly confine its use.

Third, during the course of our inquiry, we were told that there is no office within the government whose job it is to look across the government at the actions we are taking to protect ourselves to ensure that liberty concerns are appropriately considered. If, as we recommend, there is substantial change in the way we collect and share intelligence, there should be a voice within the executive branch for those concerns. Many agencies have privacy offices, albeit of limited scope. The Intelligence Oversight Board of the President's Foreign Intelligence Advisory Board has, in the past, had the job of overseeing certain activities of the intelligence community.

RECOMMENDATION: At this time of increased and consolidated government authority, there should be a board within the executive branch to oversee adherence to the guidelines we recommend and the commitment the government makes to defend our civil liberties.

We must find ways of reconciling security with liberty, since the success of one helps protect the other. The choice between security and liberty is a false choice, as nothing is more likely to endanger America's liberties than the success of a terrorist attack at home. Our history has shown us that insecurity threatens liberty. Yet, if our liberties are curtailed, we lose the values that we are struggling to defend.

SETTING PRIORITIES FOR NATIONAL PREPAREDNESS

Before 9/11, no executive department had, as its first priority, the job of defending America from domestic attack. That changed with the 2002 creation of the Department of Homeland Security. This department now has the lead responsibility for problems that feature so prominently in the 9/11 story, such as protecting borders, securing transportation and other parts of our critical infrastructure, organizing emergency assistance, and working with the private sector to assess vulnerabilities.

Throughout the government, nothing has been harder for officials—executive or legislative—than to set priorities, making hard choices in allocating limited resources. These difficulties have certainly afflicted the Department of Homeland Security, hamstrung by its many congressional overseers. In delivering assistance to state and local governments, we heard—especially in New York—about imbalances in the allocation of money. The argument concentrates on two questions.

First, how much money should be set aside for criteria not directly related to risk? Currently a major portion of the billions of dollars appropriated for state and local assistance is allocated so that each state gets a certain amount, or an allocation based on its population—wherever they live.

RECOMMENDATION: Homeland security assistance should be based strictly on an assessment of risks and vulnerabilities. Now, in 2004, Washington, D.C., and New York City are certainly at the top of any such list. We understand the contention that every state and city needs to have some minimum infrastructure for emergency response. But federal homeland security assistance should not remain a program for general revenue sharing. It should supplement state and local resources based on the risks or vulnerabilities that merit additional support. Congress should not use this money as a pork barrel.

The second question is, Can useful criteria to measure risk and vulnerability be developed that assess all the many variables? The allocation of funds should be based on an assessment of threats and vulnerabilities. That assessment should consider such factors as population, population density, vulnerability, and the presence of critical infrastructure within each state. In addition, the federal government should require each state receiving federal emergency preparedness funds to provide an analysis based on the same criteria to justify the distribution of funds in that state.

In a free-for-all over money, it is understandable that representatives will work to protect the interests of their home states or districts. But this issue is too important for politics as usual to prevail. Resources must be allocated according to vulnerabilities. We recommend that a panel of security experts be convened to develop written benchmarks for evaluating community needs. We further recommend that federal homeland security funds be allocated in accordance with those benchmarks, and that states be required to abide by those benchmarks in disbursing the federal funds. The benchmarks will be imperfect and subjective; they will continually evolve. But hard choices must be made. Those who would allocate money on a different basis should then defend their view of the national interest.

COMMAND, CONTROL, AND COMMUNICATIONS

The attack on 9/11 demonstrated that even the most robust emergency response capabilities can be overwhelmed if an attack is large enough. Teamwork, collaboration, and cooperation at an incident site are critical to a successful response. Key decisionmakers who are represented at the incident command level help to ensure an effective response, the efficient use of resources, and responder safety. Regular joint training at all levels is, moreover, essential to ensuring close coordination during an actual incident.

RECOMMENDATION: Emergency response agencies nationwide should adopt the Incident Command System (ICS). When multiple agencies or multiple jurisdictions are involved, they should adopt a unified command. Both are proven frameworks for emergency response. We strongly support the decision that federal homeland security funding will be contingent, as of October 1, 2004, upon the adoption

and regular use of ICS and unified command procedures. In the future, the Department of Homeland Security should consider making funding contingent on aggressive and realistic training in accordance with ICS and unified command procedures.

The attacks of September 11, 2001 overwhelmed the response capacity of most of the local jurisdictions where the hijacked airliners crashed. While many jurisdictions have established mutual aid compacts, a serious obstacle to multi-jurisdictional response has been the lack of indemnification for mutual-aid responders in areas such as the National Capital Region.

Public safety organizations, chief administrative officers, state emergency management agencies, and the Department of Homeland Security should develop a regional focus within the emergency responder community and promote multi-jurisdictional mutual assistance compacts. Where such compacts already exist, training in accordance with their terms should be required. Congress should pass legislation to remedy the long-standing indemnification and liability impediments to the provision of public safety mutual aid in the National Capital Region and where applicable throughout the nation.

The inability to communicate was a critical element at the World Trade Center, Pentagon, and Somerset County, Pennsylvania, crash sites, where multiple agencies and multiple jurisdictions responded. The occurrence of this problem at three very different sites is strong evidence that compatible and adequate communications among public safety organizations at the local, state, and federal levels remains an important problem.

RECOMMENDATION: Congress should support pending legislation which provides for the expedited and increased assignment of radio spectrum for public safety purposes. Furthermore, high-risk urban areas such as New York City and Washington, D.C., should establish signal corps units to ensure communications connectivity between and among civilian authorities, local first responders, and the National Guard. Federal funding of such units should be given high priority by Congress.

PRIVATE-SECTOR PREPAREDNESS

The mandate of the Department of Homeland Security does not end with government; the department is also responsible for working with the private sector to ensure preparedness. This is entirely appropriate, for the private sector controls 85 percent of the critical infrastructure in the nation. Indeed, unless a terrorist's target is a military or other secure government facility, the "first" first responders will almost certainly be civilians. Homeland security and national preparedness therefore often begins with the private sector.

Preparedness in the private sector and public sector for rescue, restart, and recovery of operations should include (1) a plan for evacuation, (2) adequate communications capabilities, and (3) a plan for continuity of operations. As we examined the emergency response to 9/11, witness after witness told us that despite 9/11, the private sector remains largely unprepared for a terrorist attack. We were also advised that the lack of a widely embraced private-sector preparedness standard was a principal contributing factor to this lack of preparedness.

We responded by asking the American National Standards Institute (ANSI) to develop a consensus on a "National Standard for Preparedness" for the private sector. ANSI convened safety, security, and business continuity experts from a wide range of industries and associations, as well as from federal, state, and local government stakeholders, to consider the need for standards for private sector emergency preparedness and business continuity.

The result of these sessions was ANSI's recommendation that the Commission endorse a voluntary National Preparedness Standard. Based on the existing American National Standard on Disaster/Emergency Management and Business Continuity Programs (NFPA 1600), the proposed National Preparedness Standard establishes a common set of criteria and terminology for preparedness, disaster management, emergency management, and business continuity programs. The experience of the private sector in the World Trade Center emergency demonstrated the need for these standards.

RECOMMENDATION: We endorse the American National Standards Institute's recommended standard for private preparedness. We were encouraged by Secretary Tom Ridge's praise of the standard, and urge the Department of Homeland Security to promote its adoption. We also encourage the insurance and credit-rating industries to look closely at a company's compliance with the ANSI standard in assessing its insurability and creditworthiness. We believe that compliance with the standard should define the standard of care owed by a company to its employees and the public for legal purposes. Private-sector preparedness is not a luxury; it is a cost of doing business

in the post-9/11 world. It is ignored at a tremendous potential cost in lives, money, and national security.

HOW TO DO IT? A DIFFERENT WAY OF ORGANIZING THE GOVERNMENT

As presently configured, the national security institutions of the U.S. government are still the institutions constructed to win the Cold War. The United States confronts a very different world today. Instead of facing a few very dangerous adversaries, the United States confronts a number of less visible challenges that surpass the boundaries of traditional nation-states and call for quick, imaginative, and agile responses.

The men and women of the World War II generation rose to the challenges of the 1940s and 1950s. They restructured the government so that it could protect the country. That is now the job of the generation that experienced 9/11. Those attacks showed, emphatically, that ways of doing business rooted in a different era are just not good enough. Americans should not settle for incremental, ad hoc adjustments to a system designed generations ago for a world that no longer exists.

We recommend significant changes in the organization of the government. We know that the quality of the people is more important than the quality of the wiring diagrams. Some of the saddest aspects of the 9/11 story are the outstanding efforts of so many individual officials straining, often without success, against the boundaries of the possible. Good people can overcome bad structures. They should not have to.

The United States has the resources and the people. The government should combine them more effectively, achieving unity of effort. We offer five major recommendations to do that:

- unifying strategic intelligence and operational planning against Islamist terrorists across the foreign-domestic divide with a National Counterterrorism Center;
- unifying the intelligence community with a new National Intelligence Director;
- unifying the many participants in the counterterrorism effort and their knowledge in a network-based information-sharing system that transcends traditional governmental boundaries;
- unifying and strengthening congressional oversight to improve quality and accountability; and
- strengthening the FBI and homeland defenders.

UNITY OF EFFORT ACROSS THE FOREIGN-DOMESTIC DIVIDE

JOINT ACTION

Much of the public commentary about the 9/11 attacks has dealt with "lost opportunities." ... These are often characterized as problems of "watchlisting," of "information sharing," or of "connecting the dots." ... [T]hese labels are too narrow. They describe the symptoms, not the disease.

In each of our examples, no one was firmly in charge of managing the case and able to draw relevant intelligence from anywhere in the government, assign responsibilities across the agencies (foreign or domestic), track progress, and quickly bring obstacles up to the level where they could be resolved. Responsibility and accountability were diffuse.

The agencies cooperated, some of the time. But even such cooperation as there was is not the same thing as joint action. When agencies cooperate, one defines the problem and seeks help with it. When they act jointly, the problem and options for action are defined differently from the start. Individuals from different backgrounds come together in analyzing a case and planning how to manage it.

In our hearings we regularly asked witnesses: Who is the quarterback? The other players are in their positions, doing their jobs. But who is calling the play that assigns roles to help them execute as a team?

Since 9/11, those issues have not been resolved. In some ways joint work has gotten better, and in some ways worse. The effort of fighting terrorism has flooded over many of the usual agency boundaries because of its sheer quantity and energy. Attitudes have changed. Officials are keenly conscious of trying to avoid the mistakes of 9/11. They try to share information. They circulate—even to the President—practically every reported threat, however dubious.

Partly because of all this effort, the challenge of coordinating it has multiplied. Before 9/11, the CIA was plainly the lead agency confronting al Qaeda. The FBI played a very secondary role. The engagement of the departments of Defense and State was more episodic.

- Today the CIA is still central. But the FBI is much more active, along with other parts of the Justice Department.
- The Defense Department effort is now enormous. Three of its unified commands, each headed by a four-star general, have counterterrorism as a primary mission: Special Operations Command, Central Command (both headquartered in Florida), and Northern Command (headquartered in Colorado).
- A new Department of Homeland Security combines formidable resources in border and transportation security, along with analysis of domestic vulnerability and other tasks.
- The State Department has the lead on many of the foreign policy tasks. . . .
- At the White House, the National Security Council (NSC) now is joined by a parallel presidential advisory structure, the Homeland Security Council.

So far we have mentioned two reasons for joint action—the virtue of joint planning and the advantage of having someone in charge to ensure a unified effort. There is a third: the simple shortage of experts with sufficient skills. The limited pool of critical experts—for example, skilled counterterrorism analysts and linguists—is being depleted. Expanding these capabilities will require not just money, but time.

Primary responsibility for terrorism analysis has been assigned to the Terrorist Threat Integration Center (TTIC), created in 2003, based at the CIA headquarters but staffed with representatives of many agencies, reporting directly to the Director of Central Intelligence. Yet the CIA houses another intelligence "fusion" center: the Counterterrorist Center that played such a key role before 9/11. A third major analytic unit is at Defense, in the Defense Intelligence Agency. A fourth, concentrating more on homeland vulnerabilities, is at the Department of Homeland Security. The FBI is in the process of building the analytic capability it has long lacked, and it also has the Terrorist Screening Center.[43]

The U.S. government cannot afford so much duplication of effort. There are not enough experienced experts to go around. The duplication also places extra demands on already hard-pressed -single-source national technical intelligence collectors like the National Security Agency.

COMBINING JOINT INTELLIGENCE AND JOINT ACTION

A "smart" government would *integrate* all sources of information to see the enemy as a whole. Integrated all-source analysis should also inform and shape strategies to collect more intelligence. Yet the Terrorist Threat Integration Center, while it has primary responsibility for terrorism analysis, is formally proscribed from having any oversight or operational authority and is not part of any operational entity, other than reporting to the director of central intelligence.[44]

The government now tries to handle the problem of joint management, informed by analysis of intelligence from all sources, in two ways.

- First, agencies with lead responsibility for certain problems have constructed their own interagency entities and task forces in order to get cooperation. The Counterterrorist Center at CIA, for example, recruits liaison officers from throughout the intelligence community. The military's Central Command has its own interagency center, recruiting liaison officers from all the agencies from which it might need help. The FBI has Joint Terrorism Task Forces in 84 locations to coordinate the activities of other agencies when action may be required.
- Second, the problem of joint operational planning is often passed to the White House, where the NSC staff tries to play this role. The national security staff at the White House (both NSC and new Homeland Security Council staff) has already become 50 percent larger since 9/11. But our impression, after talking to serving officials, is that even this enlarged staff is consumed by meetings on day-to-day issues, sifting each day's threat information and trying to coordinate everyday operations.

Even as it crowds into every square inch of available office space, the NSC staff is still not sized or funded to be an executive agency. . . . [S]ome . . . problems . . . arose in the 1980s when a White House staff, constitutionally insulated from the usual mechanisms of oversight, became involved in direct operations. During the 1990s Richard Clarke occasionally tried to exercise such authority, sometimes successfully, but often causing friction.

Yet a subtler and more serious danger is that as the NSC staff is consumed by these day-to-day tasks, it has less capacity to find the time and detachment needed to advise a president on larger policy issues. That means less time to work on major new initiatives, help with legislative management to steer needed bills through Congress, and track the design and implementation of the strategic plans for regions, countries, and issues. . . .

Much of the job of operational coordination remains with the agencies, especially the CIA. There DCI Tenet and his chief aides ran interagency meetings nearly every day to coordinate much of the government's day-to-day work. The DCI insisted he did not make policy and only oversaw its implementation. In the struggle against terrorism these distinctions seem increasingly artificial. Also, as the DCI becomes a lead coordinator of the government's operations, it becomes harder to play all the position's other roles, including that of analyst in chief.

The problem is nearly intractable because of the way the government is currently structured. Lines of operational authority run to the expanding executive departments, and they are guarded for understandable reasons; the DCI commands the CIA's personnel overseas; the secretary of defense will not yield to others in conveying commands to military forces; the Justice Department will not give up the responsibility of deciding whether to seek arrest warrants. But the result is that each agency or department needs its own intelligence apparatus to support the performance of its duties. It is hard to "break down stovepipes" when there are so many stoves that are legally and politically entitled to have cast-iron pipes of their own.

Recalling the Goldwater-Nichols legislation of 1986, Secretary Rumsfeld reminded us that to achieve better joint capability, each of the armed services had to "give up some of their turf and authorities and prerogatives." Today, he said, the executive branch is "stove-piped much like the four services were nearly 20 years ago." He wondered if it might be appropriate to ask agencies to "give up some of their existing turf and authority in exchange for a stronger, faster, more efficient government wide joint effort."[45] Privately, other key officials have made the same point to us.

We therefore propose a new institution: a civilian-led unified joint command for counterterrorism. It should combine strategic intelligence and joint operational planning.

In the Pentagon's Joint Staff, which serves the chairman of the Joint Chiefs of Staff, intelligence is handled by the J-2 directorate, operational planning by J-3, and overall policy by J-5. Our concept combines the J-2 and J-3 functions (intelligence and operational planning) in one agency, keeping overall policy coordination where it belongs, in the National Security Council.

RECOMMENDATION: We recommend the establishment of a National Counterterrorism Center (NCTC), built on the foundation of the existing Terrorist Threat Integration Center (TTIC). Breaking the older mold of national government organization, this

NCTC should be a center for joint operational planning and joint intelligence, staffed by personnel from the various agencies. The head of the NCTC should have authority to evaluate the performance of the people assigned to the Center.

- Such a joint center should be developed in the same spirit that guided the military's creation of unified joint commands, or the shaping of earlier national agencies like the National Reconnaissance Office, which was formed to organize the work of the CIA and several defense agencies in space.

  NCTC—Intelligence. The NCTC should lead strategic analysis, pooling all-source intelligence, foreign and domestic, about transnational terrorist organizations with global reach. It should develop *net* assessments (comparing enemy capabilities and intentions against U.S. defenses and countermeasures). It should also provide warning. It should do this work by drawing on the efforts of the CIA, FBI, Homeland Security, and other departments and agencies. It should task collection requirements both inside and outside the United States.
- The intelligence function (J-2) should build on the existing TTIC structure and remain distinct, as a national intelligence center, within, the NCTC. As the government's principal knowledge bank on Islamist terrorism, with the main responsibility for strategic analysis and net assessment, it should absorb a significant portion of the analytical talent now residing in the CIA's Counterterrorist Center and the DIA's Joint Intelligence Task Force—Combatting Terrorism (JITF-CT).

  NCTC—Operations. The NCTC should perform joint planning. The plans would assign operational responsibilities to lead agencies, such as State, the CIA, the FBI, Defense and its combatant commands, Homeland Security, and other agencies. The NCTC should not direct the actual execution of these operations, leaving that job to the agencies. The NCTC would then track implementation; it would look across the foreign-domestic divide and across agency boundaries, updating plans to follow through on cases.[46]
- The joint operational planning function (J-3) will be new to the TTIC structure. The NCTC can draw on analogous work now being done in the CIA and every other involved department of the government, as well as reaching out to knowledgeable officials in state and local agencies throughout the United States.
- The NCTC should not be a policymaking body. Its operations and planning should follow the policy direction of the president and the National Security Council.

  NCTC—Authorities. The head of the NCTC should be appointed by the president, and should be equivalent in rank to a deputy head of a cabinet department. The head of the NCTC would report to the national intelligence director, an office whose creation we recommend below, placed in the Executive Office of the President. The head of the NCTC would thus also report indirectly to the president. This official's nomination should be confirmed by the Senate and he or she should testify to the Congress, as is the case now with other statutory presidential offices, like the U.S. trade representative.
- To avoid the fate of other entities with great nominal authority and little real power, the head of the NCTC must have the right to concur in the choices of personnel to lead the operating entities of the departments and agencies focused on counterterrorism, specifically including the head of the Counterterrorist Center, the head of the FBI's Counterterrorism Division, the commanders of the Defense Department's Special Operations Command and Northern Command, and the State Department's coordinator for counterterrorism.[47] The head of the NCTC should also work with the director of the Office of Management and Budget in developing the president's counterterrorism budget.
- There are precedents for surrendering authority for joint planning while preserving an agency's operational control. In the international context, NATO commanders may get line authority over forces assigned by other nations. In U.S. unified commands, commanders plan operations that may involve units belonging to one of the services. In each case, procedures are worked out, formal and informal, to define the limits of the joint commander's authority.

The most serious disadvantage of the NCTC is the reverse of its greatest virtue. The struggle against Islamist terrorism is so important that any clear-cut centralization of authority to manage and be accountable for it may concentrate too much power in one place. The proposed NCTC would be given the authority of planning the activities of other agencies. Law or executive order must define the scope of such line authority.

BOX 26.1

Consider this hypothetical case. The NSA discovers that a suspected terrorist is traveling to Bangkok and Kuala Lumpur. The NCTC should draw on joint intelligence resources, including its own NSA counterterrorism experts, to analyze the identities and possible destinations of these individuals. Informed by this analysis, the NCTC would then organize and plan the management of the case, drawing on the talents and differing kinds of experience among the several agency representatives assigned to it—assigning tasks to the CIA overseas, to Homeland Security watching entry points into the United States, and to the FBI. If military assistance might be needed, the Special Operations Command could be asked to develop an appropriate concept

for such an operation. The NCTC would be accountable for tracking the progress of the case, ensuring that the plan evolved with it, and integrating the information into a warning. The NCTC would be responsible for being sure that intelligence gathered from the activities in the field became part of the government's institutional memory about Islamist terrorist personalities, organizations, and possible means of attack.

In each case the involved agency would make its own senior managers aware of what it was being asked to do. If those agency heads objected, and the issue could not easily be resolved, then the disagreement about roles and missions could be brought before the National Security Council and the president.

The NCTC would not eliminate interagency policy disputes. These would still go to the National Security Council. To improve coordination at the White House, we believe the existing Homeland Security Council should soon be merged into a single National Security Council. The creation of the NCTC should help the NSC staff concentrate on its core duties of assisting the president and supporting interdepartmental policymaking.

We recognize that this is a new and difficult idea precisely because the authorities we recommend for the NCTC really would, as Secretary Rumsfeld foresaw, ask strong agencies to "give up some of their turf and authority in exchange for a stronger, faster, more efficient government wide joint effort." Countering transnational Islamist terrorism will test whether the U.S. government can fashion more flexible models of management needed to deal with the twenty-first-century world.

An argument against change is that the nation is at war, and cannot afford to reorganize in midstream. But some of the main innovations of the 1940s and 1950s, including the creation of the Joint Chiefs of Staff and even the construction of the Pentagon itself, were undertaken in the midst of war. Surely the country cannot wait until the struggle against Islamist terrorism is over.

"Surprise, when it happens to a government, is likely to be a complicated, diffuse, bureaucratic thing. It includes neglect of responsibility, but also responsibility so poorly defined or so ambiguously delegated that action gets lost."[48] That comment was made more than 40 years ago, about Pearl Harbor. We hope another commission, writing in the future about another attack, does not again find this quotation to be so apt.

UNITY OF EFFORT IN THE INTELLIGENCE COMMUNITY

In our first section, we concentrated on counterterrorism, discussing how to combine the analysis of information from all sources of intelligence with the joint planning of operations that draw on that analysis. In this section, we step back from looking just at the counterterrorism problem. We reflect on whether the government is organized adequately to direct resources and build the intelligence capabilities it will need not just for countering terrorism, but for the broader range of national security challenges in the decades ahead.

THE NEED FOR A CHANGE

During the Cold War, intelligence agencies did not depend on seamless integration to track and count the thousands of military targets—such as tanks and missiles—fielded by the Soviet Union and other adversary states. Each agency concentrated on its specialized mission, acquiring its own information and then sharing it via formal, finished reports. The Department of Defense had given birth to and dominated the main agencies for technical collection of intelligence. Resources were shifted at an incremental pace, coping with challenges that arose over years, even decades.

[T]he resulting organization of the intelligence community . . . is outlined [in Box 26.2].

The need to restructure the intelligence community grows out of six problems that have become apparent before and after 9/11:

- *Structural barriers to performing joint intelligence work.* National intelligence is still organized around the collection disciplines of the home

BOX 26.2 MEMBERS OF THE U.S. INTELLIGENCE COMMUNITY

- Office of the Director of Central Intelligence, which includes the Office of the Deputy Director of Central Intelligence for Community Management, the Community Management Staff, the Terrorism Threat Integration Center, the National Intelligence Council, and other community offices
- The Central Intelligence Agency (CIA), which performs human source collection, all-source analysis, and advanced science and technology

National Intelligence Agencies

- National Security Agency (NSA), which performs signals collection and analysis
- National Geospatial–Intelligence Agency (NGA), which performs imagery collection and analysis
- National Reconnaissance Office (NRO), which develops, acquires, and launches space systems for intelligence collection
- Other national reconnaissance programs

Departmental Intelligence Agencies

- Defense Intelligence Agency (DIA) of the Department of Defense
- Intelligence entities of the Army, Navy, Air Force, and Marines
- Bureau of Intelligence and Research (INR) of the Department of State
- Office of Terrorism and Finance Intelligence of the Department of Treasury
- Office of Intelligence and the Counterterrorism and Counterintelligence Divisions of the Federal Bureau of Investigation of the Department of Justice
- Office of Intelligence of the Department of Energy
- Directorate of Information Analysis and Infrastructure Protection (IAIP) and Directorate of Coast Guard Intelligence of the Department of Homeland Security

---

agencies, not the joint mission. The importance of integrated, all-source analysis cannot be overstated. Without it, it is not possible to "connect the dots." No one component holds all the relevant information.

- By contrast, in organizing national defense, the Goldwater-Nichols legislation of 1986 created joint commands for operations in the field, the Unified Command Plan. The services—the Army, Navy, Air Force, and Marine Corps—organize, train, and equip their people and units to perform their missions. Then they assign personnel and units to the joint combatant commander, like the commanding general of the Central Command (CENTCOM). The Goldwater-Nichols Act required officers to serve tours outside their service in order to win promotion. The culture of the Defense Department was transformed, its collective mind-set moved from service-specific to "joint," and its operations became more integrated.[49]
- *Lack of common standards and practices across the foreign-domestic divide.* The leadership of the intelligence community should be able to pool information gathered overseas with information gathered in the United States, holding the work—wherever it is done—to a common standard of quality in how it is collected, processed (e.g., translated), reported, shared, and analyzed. A common set of personnel standards for intelligence can

create a group of professionals better able to operate in joint activities, transcending their own service-specific mind-sets.

- *Divided management of national intelligence capabilities.* While the CIA was once "central" to our national intelligence capabilities, following the end of the Cold War it has been less able to influence the use of the nation's imagery and signals intelligence capabilities in three national agencies housed within the Department of Defense: the National Security Agency, the National Geospatial-Intelligence Agency, and the National Reconnaissance Office. One of the lessons learned from the 1991 Gulf War was the value of national intelligence systems (satellites in particular) in precision warfare. Since that war, the department has appropriately drawn these agencies into its transformation of the military. Helping to orchestrate this transformation is the under secretary of defense for intelligence, a position established by Congress after 9/11. An unintended consequence of these developments has been the far greater demand made by Defense on technical systems, leaving the DCI less able to influence how these technical resources are allocated and used.
- *Weak capacity to set priorities and move resources.* The agencies are mainly organized around what they collect or the way they collect it. But the priorities for collection are national. As the DCI makes hard choices about moving resources, he

or she must have the power to reach across agencies and reallocate effort.

- *Too many jobs.* The DCI now has at least three jobs. He is expected to run a particular agency, the CIA. He is expected to manage the loose confederation of agencies that is the intelligence community. He is expected to be the analyst in chief for the government, sifting evidence and directly briefing the President as his principal intelligence adviser. No recent DCI has been able to do all three effectively. Usually what loses out is management of the intelligence community, a difficult task even in the best case because the DCI's current authorities are weak. With so much to do, the DCI often has not used even the authority he has.

- *Too complex and secret.* Over the decades, the agencies and the rules surrounding the intelligence community have accumulated to a depth that practically defies public comprehension. There are now 15 agencies or parts of agencies in the intelligence community. The community and the DCI's authorities have become arcane matters, understood only by initiates after long study. Even the most basic information about how much money is actually allocated to or within the intelligence community and most of its key components is shrouded from public view.

The current DCI is responsible for community performance but lacks the three authorities critical for any agency head or chief executive officer: (1) control over purse strings, (2) the ability to hire or fire senior managers, and (3) the ability to set standards for the information infrastructure and personnel.[50]

The only budget power of the DCI over agencies other than the CIA lies in coordinating the budget requests of the various intelligence agencies into a single program for submission to Congress. The overall funding request of the 15 intelligence entities in this program is then presented to the president and Congress in 15 separate volumes.

When Congress passes an appropriations bill to allocate money to intelligence agencies, most of their funding is hidden in the Defense Department in order to keep intelligence spending secret. Therefore, although the House and Senate Intelligence committees are the authorizing committees for funding of the intelligence community, the final budget review is handled in the Defense Subcommittee of the Appropriations committees. Those committees have no subcommittees just for intelligence, and only a few members and staff review the requests.

The appropriations for the CIA and the national intelligence agencies—NSA, NGA, and NRO—are then given to the secretary of defense. The secretary transfers the CIA's money to the DCI but disburses the national agencies' money directly. Money for the FBI's national security components falls within the appropriations for Commerce, Justice, and State and goes to the attorney general.[51]

In addition, the DCI lacks hire-and-fire authority over most of the intelligence community's senior managers. For the national intelligence agencies housed in the Defense Department, the secretary of defense must seek the DCI's concurrence regarding the nomination of these directors, who are presidentially appointed. But the secretary may submit recommendations to the president without receiving this concurrence. The DCI cannot fire these officials. The DCI has even less influence over the head of the FBI's national security component, who is appointed by the attorney general in consultation with the DCI.[52]

COMBINING JOINT WORK WITH STRONGER MANAGEMENT

We have received recommendations on the topic of intelligence reform from many sources. Other commissions have been over this same ground. Thoughtful bills have been introduced, most recently a bill by the chairman of the House Intelligence Committee Porter Goss (R-Fla.), and another by the ranking minority member, Jane Harman (D-Calif.). In the Senate, Senators Bob Graham (D-Fla.) and Dianne Feinstein (D-Calif.) have introduced reform proposals as well. Past efforts have foundered, because the president did not support them; because the DCI, the secretary of defense, or both opposed them; and because some proposals lacked merit. We have tried to take stock of these experiences, and borrow from strong elements in many of the ideas that have already been developed by others.

RECOMMENDATION: The current position of Director of Central Intelligence should be replaced by a National Intelligence Director with two main areas of responsibility: (1) to oversee national intelligence centers on specific subjects of interest across the U.S. government and (2) to manage the national intelligence program and oversee the agencies that contribute to it.

First, the National Intelligence Director should oversee *national intelligence centers* to provide all source analysis and plan intelligence operations for the whole government on major problems.

- One such problem is counterterrorism. In this case, we believe that the center should be the intelligence entity (formerly TTIC) inside the National Counterterrorism Center we have proposed. It would sit there alongside the operations management unit we described earlier, with both making up the NCTC, in the Executive Office of the President. Other national intelligence centers—for instance, on counterproliferation, crime and narcotics, and China—would be housed in whatever department or agency is best suited for them.
- The National Intelligence Director would retain the present DCI's role as the principal intelligence adviser to the president. We hope the president will come to look directly to the directors of the national intelligence centers to provide all-source analysis in their areas of responsibility, balancing the advice of these intelligence chiefs against the contrasting viewpoints that may be offered by department heads at State, Defense, Homeland Security, Justice, and other agencies.

Second, the National Intelligence Director should manage the national intelligence program and oversee the component agencies of the intelligence community. (See Figure 26.1.)[53]

- The National Intelligence Director would submit a unified budget for national intelligence that reflects priorities chosen by the National Security Council, an appropriate balance among the varieties of technical and human intelligence collection, and analysis. He or she would receive an appropriation for national intelligence and apportion the funds to the appropriate agencies, in line with that budget, and with authority to reprogram funds among the national intelligence agencies to meet any new priority (as counterterrorism was in the 1990s). The National Intelligence Director should approve and submit

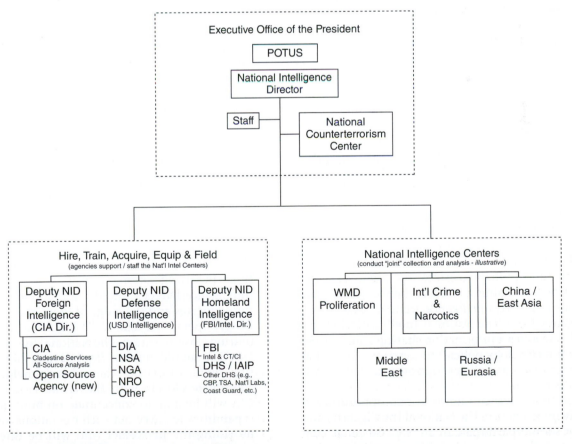

FIGURE 26.1 Unity of effort in managing intelligence.

nominations to the president of the individuals who would lead the CIA, DIA, FBI Intelligence Office, NSA, NGA, NRO, Information Analysis and Infrastructure Protection Directorate of the Department of Homeland Security, and other national intelligence capabilities.[54]

- The National Intelligence Director would manage this national effort with the help of three deputies, each of whom would also hold a key position in one of the component agencies.[55]
  - Foreign intelligence (the head of the CIA).
  - Defense intelligence (the under secretary of defense for intelligence).[56]
  - Homeland intelligence (the FBI's executive assistant director for intelligence or the under secretary of homeland security for information analysis and infrastructure protection).

    Other agencies in the intelligence community would coordinate their work within each of these three areas, largely staying housed in the same departments or agencies that support them now.

Returning to the analogy of the Defense Department's organization, these three deputies—like the leaders of the Army, Navy, Air Force, or Marines—would have the job of acquiring the systems, training the people, and executing the operations planned by the national intelligence centers.

And, just as the combatant commanders also report to the secretary of defense, the directors of the national intelligence centers—e.g., for counterproliferation, crime and narcotics, and the rest—also would report to the National Intelligence Director.

- The Defense Department's military intelligence programs—the joint military intelligence program (JMIP) and the tactical intelligence and related activities program (TIARA)—would remain part of that department's responsibility.
- The National Intelligence Director would set personnel policies to establish standards for education and training and facilitate assignments at the national intelligence centers and across agency lines. The National Intelligence Director also would set information sharing and information technology policies to maximize data sharing, as well as policies to protect the security of information.
- Too many agencies now have an opportunity to say no to change. The National Intelligence Director should participate in an NSC executive committee that can resolve differences in priorities

among the agencies and bring the major disputes to the president for decision.

The National Intelligence Director should be located in the Executive Office of the President. This official, who would be confirmed by the Senate and would testify before Congress, would have a relatively small staff of several hundred people, taking the place of the existing community management offices housed at the CIA.

In managing the whole community, the National Intelligence Director is still providing a service function. With the partial exception of his or her responsibilities for overseeing the NCTC, the National Intelligence Director should support the consumers of national intelligence—the president and policymaking advisers such as the secretaries of state, defense, and homeland security and the attorney general.

We are wary of too easily equating government management problems with those of the private sector. But we have noticed that some very large private firms rely on a powerful CEO who has significant control over how money is spent and can hire or fire leaders of the major divisions, assisted by a relatively modest staff, while leaving responsibility for execution in the operating divisions.

There are disadvantages to separating the position of National Intelligence Director from the job of heading the CIA. For example, the National Intelligence Director will not head a major agency of his or her own and may have a weaker base of support. But we believe that these disadvantages are outweighed by several other considerations:

- The National Intelligence Director must be able to directly oversee intelligence collection inside the United States. Yet law and custom has counseled against giving such a plain domestic role to the head of the CIA.
- The CIA will be one among several claimants for funds in setting national priorities. The National Intelligence Director should not be both one of the advocates and the judge of them all.
- Covert operations tend to be highly tactical, requiring close attention. The National Intelligence Director should rely on the relevant joint mission center to oversee these details, helping to coordinate closely with the White House. The CIA will be able to concentrate on building the capabilities to carry out such operations and on providing the personnel who will be directing and executing such operations in the field.

- Rebuilding the analytic and human intelligence collection capabilities of the CIA should be a full-time effort, and the director of the CIA should focus on extending its comparative advantages.

RECOMMENDATION: The CIA Director should emphasize (a) rebuilding the CIA's analytic capabilities; (b) transforming the clandestine service by building its human intelligence capabilities; (c) developing a stronger language program, with high standards and sufficient financial incentives; (d) renewing emphasis on recruiting diversity among operations officers so they can blend more easily in foreign cities; (e) ensuring a seamless relationship between human source collection and signals collection at the operational level; and (f) stressing a better balance between unilateral and liaison operations.

The CIA should retain responsibility for the direction and execution of clandestine and covert operations, as assigned by the relevant national intelligence center and authorized by the National Intelligence Director and the president. This would include propaganda, renditions, and nonmilitary disruption. We believe, however, that one important area of responsibility should change.

RECOMMENDATION: Lead responsibility for directing and executing paramilitary operations, whether clandestine or covert, should shift to the Defense Department. There it should be consolidated with the capabilities for training, direction, and execution of such operations already being developed in the Special Operations Command.

- Before 9/11, the CIA did not invest in developing a robust capability to conduct paramilitary operations with U.S. personnel. It relied on proxies instead, organized by CIA operatives without the requisite military training. The results were unsatisfactory.
- Whether the price is measured in either money or people, the United States cannot afford to build two separate capabilities for carrying out secret military operations, secretly operating standoff missiles, and secretly training foreign military or paramilitary forces. The United States should concentrate responsibility and necessary legal authorities in one entity.
- The post-9/11 Afghanistan precedent of using joint CIA-military teams for covert and clandestine operations was a good one. We believe this proposal to be consistent with it. Each agency would concentrate on its comparative advantages in building capabilities for joint missions. The operation itself would be planned in common.
- The CIA has a reputation for agility in operations. The military has a reputation for being methodical and cumbersome. We do not know if these stereotypes match current reality; they may also be one more symptom of the civil-military misunderstandings. . . . It is a problem to be resolved in policy guidance and agency management, not in the creation of redundant, overlapping capabilities and authorities in such sensitive work. The CIA's experts should be integrated into the military's training, exercises, and planning. To quote a CIA official now serving in the field: "One fight, one team."

RECOMMENDATION: Finally, to combat the secrecy and complexity we have described, the overall amounts of money being appropriated for national intelligence and to its component agencies should no longer be kept secret. Congress should pass a separate appropriations act for intelligence, defending the broad allocation of how these tens of billions of dollars have been assigned among the varieties of intelligence work.

The specifics of the intelligence appropriation would remain classified, as they are today. Opponents of declassification argue that America's enemies could learn about intelligence capabilities by tracking the top-line appropriations figure. Yet the top-line figure by itself provides little insight into U.S. intelligence sources and methods. The U.S. government readily provides copious information about spending on its military forces, including military intelligence. The intelligence community should not be subject to that much disclosure. But when even aggregate categorical numbers remain hidden, it is hard to judge priorities and foster accountability.

UNITY OF EFFORT IN SHARING INFORMATION

INFORMATION SHARING

We have already stressed the importance of intelligence analysis that can draw on all relevant sources of information. The biggest impediment to all-source analysis—to a greater likelihood of connecting the dots—is the human or systemic resistance to sharing information.

The U.S. government has access to a vast amount of information. When databases not usually thought of as "intelligence," such as customs or immigration information, are included, the storehouse is immense. But the U.S. government has a weak system for processing and using what it has. In interviews around the government, official after official urged us to call attention to frustrations with the unglamorous "back office" side of government operations.

In the 9/11 story, for example, we sometimes see examples of information that could be accessed—like the undistributed NSA information that would have helped identify Nawaf al Hazmi in January 2000. But someone had to ask for it. In that case, no one did. Or . . . the information is distributed, but in a compartmented channel. Or the information is available, and someone does ask, but it cannot be shared.

What all these stories have in common is a system that requires a demonstrated "need to know" before sharing. This approach assumes it is possible to know, in advance, who will need to use the information. Such a system implicitly assumes that the risk of inadvertent disclosure outweighs the benefits of wider sharing. Those Cold War assumptions are no longer appropriate. The culture of agencies feeling they own the information they gathered at taxpayer expense must be replaced by a culture in which the agencies instead feel they have a duty to the information—to repay the taxpayers' investment by making that information available.

Each intelligence agency has its own security practices, outgrowths of the Cold War. We certainly understand the reason for these practices. Counterintelligence concerns are still real, even if the old Soviet enemy has been replaced by other spies.

But the security concerns need to be weighed against the costs. Current security requirements nurture over classification and excessive compartmentation of information among agencies. Each agency's incentive structure opposes sharing, with risks (criminal, civil, and internal administrative sanctions) but few rewards for sharing information. No one has to pay the long-term costs of overclassifying information, though these costs—even in literal financial terms—are substantial. There are no punishments for *not* sharing information. Agencies uphold a "need-to-know" culture of information protection rather than promoting a "need-to-share" culture of integration.[57]

RECOMMENDATION: Information procedures should provide incentives for sharing, to restore a better balance between security and shared knowledge.

Intelligence gathered about transnational terrorism should be processed, turned into reports, and distributed according to the same quality standards, whether it is collected in Pakistan or in Texas.

The logical objection is that sources and methods may vary greatly in different locations. We therefore propose that when a report is first created, its data be separated from the sources and methods by which they are obtained. The report should begin with the information in its most shareable, but still meaningful, form. Therefore the maximum number of recipients can access some form of that information. If knowledge of further details becomes important, any user can query further, with access granted or denied according to the rules set for the network—and with queries leaving an audit trail in order to determine who accessed the information. But the questions may not come at all unless experts at the "edge" of the network can readily discover the clues that prompt to them.[58]

We propose that information be shared horizontally, across new networks that transcend individual agencies.

- The current system is structured on an old mainframe, or hub-and-spoke, concept. In this older approach, each agency has its own database. Agency users send information to the database and then can retrieve it from the database.
- A decentralized network model, the concept behind much of the information revolution, shares data horizontally too. Agencies would still have their own databases, but those databases would be searchable across agency lines. In this system, secrets are protected through the design of the network and an "information rights management" approach that controls access to the data, not access to the whole network. An outstanding conceptual framework for this kind of "trusted information network" has been developed by a task force of leading professionals in national security, information technology, and law assembled by the Markle Foundation. Its report has been widely discussed throughout the U.S. government, but has not yet been converted into action.[59]

RECOMMENDATION: The president should lead the government-wide effort to bring the major national security institutions into the information revolution. He should coordinate the resolution of the legal, policy, and technical issues across agencies to create a "trusted information network."

- No one agency can do it alone. Well-meaning agency officials are under tremendous pressure to update their systems. Alone, they may only be able to modernize the stovepipes, not replace them.

- Only presidential leadership can develop government-wide concepts and standards. Currently, no one is doing this job. Backed by the Office of Management and Budget, a new National Intelligence Director empowered to set common standards for information use throughout the community, and a secretary of homeland security who helps extend the system to public agencies and relevant private-sector databases, a government-wide initiative can succeed.

- White House leadership is also needed because the policy and legal issues are harder than the technical ones. The necessary technology already exists. What does not are the rules for acquiring, accessing, sharing, and using the vast stores of public and private data that may be available. When information sharing works, it is a powerful tool. Therefore the sharing and uses of information must be guided by a set of practical policy guidelines that simultaneously empower and constrain officials, telling them clearly what is and is not permitted.

"This is government acting in new ways, to face new threats," the most recent Markle report explains. "And while such change is necessary, it must be accomplished while engendering the people's trust that privacy and other civil liberties are being protected, that businesses are not being unduly burdened with requests for extraneous or useless information, that taxpayer money is being well spent, and that, ultimately, the network will be effective in protecting our security." The authors add: "Leadership is emerging from all levels of government and from many places in the private sector. What is needed now is a plan to accelerate these efforts, and public debate and consensus on the goals."[60]

UNITY OF EFFORT IN THE CONGRESS

STRENGTHEN CONGRESSIONAL OVERSIGHT OF INTELLIGENCE AND HOMELAND SECURITY

Of all our recommendations, strengthening congressional oversight may be among the most difficult and important. So long as oversight is governed by current congressional rules and resolutions, we believe the American people will not get the security they want and need. The United States needs a strong, stable, and capable congressional committee structure to give America's national intelligence agencies oversight, support, and leadership.

Few things are more difficult to change in Washington than congressional committee jurisdiction and prerogatives. To a member, these assignments are almost as important as the map of his or her congressional district. The American people may have to insist that these changes occur, or they may well not happen. Having interviewed numerous members of Congress from both parties, as well as congressional staff members, we found that dissatisfaction with congressional oversight remains widespread.

The future challenges of America's intelligence agencies are daunting. They include the need to develop leading-edge technologies that give our policymakers and warfighters a decisive edge in any conflict where the interests of the United States are vital. Not only does good intelligence win wars, but the best intelligence enables us to prevent them from happening altogether.

Under the terms of existing rules and resolutions the House and Senate intelligence committees lack the power, influence, and sustained capability to meet this challenge. While few members of Congress have the broad knowledge of intelligence activities or the know-how about the technologies employed, all members need to feel assured that good oversight is happening. When their unfamiliarity with the subject is combined with the need to preserve security, a mandate emerges for substantial change.

Tinkering with the existing structure is not sufficient. Either Congress should create a joint committee for intelligence, using the Joint Atomic Energy Committee as its model, or it should create House and Senate committees with combined authorizing and appropriations powers.

Whichever of these two forms are chosen, the goal should be a structure—codified by resolution with powers expressly granted and carefully limited—allowing a relatively small group of members of Congress, given time and reason to master the subject and the agencies, to conduct oversight of the intelligence establishment and be clearly accountable for their work. The staff of this committee should be nonpartisan and work for the entire committee and not for individual members.

The other reforms we have suggested—for a National Counterterrorism Center and a National Intelligence Director—will not work if congressional oversight does not change too. Unity of effort in executive management can be lost if it is fractured by divided congressional oversight.

RECOMMENDATION: Congressional oversight for intelligence—and counterterrorism—is now dysfunctional. Congress should address this problem. We have considered various alternatives: A joint committee on the old model of the Joint Committee on Atomic Energy is one. A single committee in each house of Congress, combining authorizing and appropriating authorities, is another.

- The new committee or committees should conduct continuing studies of the activities of the intelligence agencies and report problems relating to the development and use of intelligence to all members of the House and Senate.
- We have already recommended that the total level of funding for intelligence be made public, and that the national intelligence program be appropriated to the National Intelligence Director, not to the secretary of defense.[61]
- We also recommend that the intelligence committee should have a subcommittee specifically dedicated to oversight, freed from the consuming responsibility of working on the budget.
- The resolution creating the new intelligence committee structure should grant subpoena authority to the committee or committees. The majority party's representation on this committee should never exceed the minority's representation by more than one.
- Four of the members appointed to this committee or committees should be a member who also serves on each of the following additional committees: Armed Services, Judiciary, Foreign Affairs, and the Defense Appropriations subcommittee. In this way the other major congressional interests can be brought together in the new committee's work.
- Members should serve indefinitely on the intelligence committees, without set terms, thereby letting them accumulate expertise.
- The committees should be smaller—perhaps seven or nine members in each house—so that each member feels a greater sense of responsibility, and accountability, for the quality of the committee's work.

The leaders of the Department of Homeland Security now appear before 88 committees and subcommittees of Congress. One expert witness (not a member of the administration) told us that this is perhaps the single largest obstacle impeding the department's successful development. The one attempt to consolidate such committee authority, the House Select Committee on Homeland Security, may be eliminated. The Senate does not have even this.

Congress needs to establish for the Department of Homeland Security the kind of clear authority and responsibility that exist to enable the Justice Department to deal with crime and the Defense Department to deal with threats to national security. Through not more than one authorizing committee and one appropriating subcommittee in each house, Congress should be able to ask the secretary of homeland security whether he or she has the resources to provide reasonable security against major terrorist acts within the United States and to hold the secretary accountable for the department's performance.

RECOMMENDATION: Congress should create a single, principal point of oversight and review for homeland security. Congressional leaders are best able to judge what committee should have jurisdiction over this department and its duties. But we believe that Congress does have the obligation to choose one in the House and one in the Senate, and that this committee should be a permanent standing committee with a nonpartisan staff.

IMPROVE THE TRANSITIONS BETWEEN ADMINISTRATIONS

In ... the transition of 2000–2001, ... the new administration did not have its deputy cabinet officers in place until the spring of 2001, and the critical subcabinet officials were not confirmed until the summer—if then. In other words, the new administration—like others before it—did not have its team on the job until at least six months after it took office.

RECOMMENDATION: Since a catastrophic attack could occur with little or no notice, we should minimize as much as possible the disruption of national security policymaking during the change of administrations by accelerating the process for national security appointments. We think the process could be improved significantly so transitions can work more effectively and allow new officials to assume their new responsibilities as quickly as possible.

- Before the election, candidates should submit the names of selected members of their prospective transition teams to the FBI so that, if necessary, those team members can obtain security clearances immediately after the election is over.

- A president-elect should submit lists of possible candidates for national security positions to begin obtaining security clearances immediately after the election, so that their background investigations can be complete before January 20.
- A single federal agency should be responsible for providing and maintaining security clearances, ensuring uniform standards—including uniform security questionnaires and financial report requirements, and maintaining a single database. This agency can also be responsible for administering polygraph tests on behalf of organizations that require them.
- A president-elect should submit the nominations of the entire new national security team, through the level of under secretary of cabinet departments, not later than January 20. The Senate, in return, should adopt special rules requiring hearings and votes to confirm or reject national security nominees within 30 days of their submission. The Senate should not require confirmation of such executive appointees below Executive Level 3.
- The outgoing administration should provide the president-elect, as soon as possible after election day, with a classified, compartmented list that catalogues specific, operational threats to national security; major military or covert operations; and pending decisions on the possible use of force. Such a document could provide both notice and a checklist, inviting a president-elect to inquire and learn more.

ORGANIZING AMERICA'S DEFENSES IN THE UNITED STATES

THE FUTURE ROLE OF THE FBI

We have considered proposals for a new agency dedicated to intelligence collection in the United States. Some call this a proposal for an "American MI-5," although the analogy is weak—the actual British Security Service is a relatively small worldwide agency that combines duties assigned in the U.S. government to the Terrorist Threat Integration Center, the CIA, the FBI, and the Department of Homeland Security.

The concern about the FBI is that it has long favored its criminal justice mission over its national security mission. Part of the reason for this is the demand around the country for FBI help on criminal matters. The FBI was criticized, rightly, for the overzealous domestic intelligence investigations

disclosed during the 1970s. The pendulum swung away from those types of investigations during the 1980s and 1990s, though the FBI maintained an active counterintelligence function and was the lead agency for the investigation of foreign terrorist groups operating inside the United States.

We do not recommend the creation of a new domestic intelligence agency. It is not needed if our other recommendations are adopted—to establish a strong national intelligence center, part of the NCTC, that will oversee counterterrorism intelligence work, foreign and domestic, and to create a National Intelligence Director who can set and enforce standards for the collection, processing, and reporting of information.

Under the structures we recommend, the FBI's role is focused, but still vital. The FBI does need to be able to direct its thousands of agents and other employees to collect intelligence in America's cities and towns—interviewing informants, conducting surveillance and searches, tracking individuals, working collaboratively with local authorities, and doing so with meticulous attention to detail and compliance with the law. The FBI's job in the streets of the United States would thus be a domestic equivalent, operating under the U.S. Constitution and quite different laws and rules, to the job of the CIA's operations officers abroad.

Creating a new domestic intelligence agency has other drawbacks.

- The FBI is accustomed to carrying out sensitive intelligence collection operations in compliance with the law. If a new domestic intelligence agency were outside of the Department of Justice, the process of legal oversight—never easy—could become even more difficult. Abuses of civil liberties could create a backlash that would impair the collection of needed intelligence.
- Creating a new domestic intelligence agency would divert attention of the officials most responsible for current counterterrorism efforts while the threat remains high. Putting a new player into the mix of federal agencies with counterterrorism responsibilities would exacerbate existing information-sharing problems.
- A new domestic intelligence agency would need to acquire assets and personnel. The FBI already has 28,000 employees; 56 field offices, 400 satellite offices, and 47 legal attaché offices; a laboratory, operations center, and training facility; an existing network of informants, cooperating

defendants, and other sources; and relationships with state and local law enforcement, the CIA, and foreign intelligence and law enforcement agencies.

- Counterterrorism investigations in the United States very quickly become matters that involve violations of criminal law and possible law enforcement action. Because the FBI can have agents working criminal matters and agents working intelligence investigations concerning the same international terrorism target, the full range of investigative tools against a suspected terrorist can be considered within one agency. The removal of "the wall" that existed before 9/11 between intelligence and law enforcement has opened up new opportunities for cooperative action within the FBI.

- Counterterrorism investigations often overlap or are cued by other criminal investigations, such as money laundering or the smuggling of contraband. In the field, the close connection to criminal work has many benefits.

Our recommendation to leave counterterrorism intelligence collection in the United States with the FBI still depends on an assessment that the FBI—if it makes an all-out effort to institutionalize change—can do the job. . . . [W]e have been impressed by the determination that agents display in tracking down details, patiently going the extra mile and working the extra month, to put facts in the place of speculation. In our report we have shown how agents in Phoenix, Minneapolis, and New York displayed initiative in pressing their investigations.

FBI agents and analysts in the field need to have sustained support and dedicated resources to become stronger intelligence officers. They need to be rewarded for acquiring informants and for gathering and disseminating information differently and more broadly than usual in a traditional criminal investigation. FBI employees need to report and analyze what they have learned in ways the Bureau has never done before.

Under Director Robert Mueller, the Bureau has made significant progress in improving its intelligence capabilities. It now has an Office of Intelligence, overseen by the top tier of FBI management. Field intelligence groups have been created in all field offices to put FBI priorities and the emphasis on intelligence into practice. Advances have been made in improving the Bureau's information technology systems and in increasing connectivity and information sharing with intelligence community agencies.

Director Mueller has also recognized that the FBI's reforms are far from complete. He has outlined a number of areas where added measures may be necessary. Specifically, he has recognized that the FBI needs to recruit from a broader pool of candidates, that agents and analysts working on national security matters require specialized training, and that agents should specialize within programs after obtaining a generalist foundation. The FBI is developing career tracks for agents to specialize in counterterrorism/counterintelligence, cyber crimes, criminal investigations, or intelligence. It is establishing a program for certifying agents as intelligence officers, a certification that will be a prerequisite for promotion to the senior ranks of the Bureau. New training programs have been instituted for intelligence-related subjects.

The Director of the FBI has proposed creating an Intelligence Directorate as a further refinement of the FBI intelligence program. This directorate would include units for intelligence planning and policy and for the direction of analysts and linguists.

We want to ensure that the Bureau's shift to a preventive counterterrorism posture is more fully institutionalized so that it survives beyond Director Mueller's tenure. We have found that in the past the Bureau has announced its willingness to reform and restructure itself to address transnational security threats, but has fallen short—failing to effect the necessary institutional and cultural changes organization-wide. We want to ensure that this does not happen again. Despite having found acceptance of the Director's clear message that counterterrorism is now the FBI's top priority, two years after 9/11 we also found gaps between some of the announced reforms and the reality in the field. We are concerned that management in the field offices still can allocate people and resources to local concerns that diverge from the national security mission. This system could revert to a focus on lower-priority criminal justice cases over national security requirements.

RECOMMENDATION: A specialized and integrated national security workforce should be established at the FBI consisting of agents, analysts, linguists, and surveillance specialists who are recruited, trained, rewarded, and retained to ensure the development of an institutional culture imbued with a deep expertise in intelligence and national security.

- The president, by executive order or directive, should direct the FBI to develop this intelligence cadre.

- Recognizing that cross-fertilization between the criminal justice and national security disciplines is vital to the success of both missions, all new agents should receive basic training in both areas. Furthermore, new agents should begin their careers with meaningful assignments in both areas.
- Agents and analysts should then specialize in one of these disciplines and have the option to work such matters for their entire career with the Bureau. Certain advanced training courses and assignments to other intelligence agencies should be required to advance within the national security discipline.
- In the interest of cross-fertilization, all senior FBI managers, including those working on law enforcement matters, should be certified intelligence officers.
- The FBI should fully implement a recruiting, hiring, and selection process for agents and analysts that enhances its ability to target and attract individuals with educational and professional backgrounds in intelligence, international relations, language, technology, and other relevant skills.
- The FBI should institute the integration of analysts, agents, linguists, and surveillance personnel in the field so that a dedicated team approach is brought to bear on national security intelligence operations.
- Each field office should have an official at the field office's deputy level for national security matters. This individual would have management oversight and ensure that the national priorities are carried out in the field.
- The FBI should align its budget structure according to its four main programs—intelligence, counterterrorism and counterintelligence, criminal, and criminal justice services—to ensure better transparency on program costs, management of resources, and protection of the intelligence program.[62]
- The FBI should report regularly to Congress in its semiannual program reviews designed to identify whether each field office is appropriately addressing FBI and national program priorities.
- The FBI should report regularly to Congress in detail on the qualifications, status, and roles of analysts in the field and at headquarters. Congress should ensure that analysts are afforded training and career opportunities on a par with those offered analysts in other intelligence community agencies.

- The Congress should make sure funding is available to accelerate the expansion of secure facilities in FBI field offices so as to increase their ability to use secure email systems and classified intelligence product exchanges. The Congress should monitor whether the FBI's information-sharing principles are implemented in practice.

The FBI is just a small fraction of the national law enforcement community in the United States, a community comprised mainly of state and local agencies. The network designed for sharing information, and the work of the FBI through local Joint Terrorism Task Forces, should build a reciprocal relationship, in which state and local agents understand what information they are looking for and, in return, receive some of the information being developed about what is happening, or may happen, in their communities. In this relationship, the Department of Homeland Security also will play an important part.

The Homeland Security Act of 2002 gave the under secretary for information analysis and infrastructure protection broad responsibilities. In practice, this directorate has the job to map "terrorist threats to the homeland against our assessed vulnerabilities in order to drive our efforts to protect against terrorist threats."[63] These capabilities are still embryonic. The directorate has not yet developed the capacity to perform one of its assigned jobs, which is to assimilate and analyze information from Homeland Security's own component agencies, such as the Coast Guard, Secret Service, Transportation Security Administration, Immigration and Customs Enforcement, and Customs and Border Protection. The secretary of homeland security must ensure that these components work with the Information Analysis and Infrastructure Protection Directorate so that this office can perform its mission.[64]

HOMELAND DEFENSE

At several points in our inquiry, we asked, "Who is responsible for defending us at home?" Our national defense at home is the responsibility, first, of the Department of Defense and, second, of the Department of Homeland Security. They must have clear delineations of responsibility and authority.

We found that NORAD, which had been given the responsibility for defending U.S. airspace, had construed that mission to focus on threats coming from outside America's borders. It did not adjust its focus even though the intelligence community had gathered intelligence on the possibility that terrorists might turn to hijacking and even use of planes as missiles. We have been assured that NORAD has now embraced the full mission. Northern Command has been established to assume responsibility for the defense of the domestic United States.

RECOMMENDATION: The Department of Defense and its oversight committees should regularly assess the adequacy of Northern Command's strategies and planning to defend the United States against military threats to the homeland.

The Department of Homeland Security was established to consolidate all of the domestic agencies responsible for securing America's borders and national infrastructure, most of which is in private hands. It should identify those elements of our transportation, energy, communications, financial, and other institutions that need to be protected, develop plans to protect that infrastructure, and exercise the mechanisms to enhance preparedness. This means going well beyond the preexisting jobs of the agencies that have been brought together inside the department.

RECOMMENDATION: The Department of Homeland Security and its oversight committees should regularly assess the types of threats the country faces to determine (a) the adequacy of the government's plans—and the progress against those plans—to protect America's critical infrastructure and (b) the readiness of the government to respond to the threats that the United States might face.

We look forward to a national debate on the merits of what we have recommended, and we will participate vigorously in that debate.

QUESTIONS FOR FURTHER DISCUSSION

1. How is the threat posed by Al Qaeda different from the threats posed by nation-states?
2. Do you think the recommendations proposed by the commissioners represent an effective response to the challenge posed by weapons of mass destruction in the hands of terrorists?
3. What do you think will be the main challenges faced by the National Counterintelligence Center in trying to coordinate an effective federal government response to transnational terrorist networks?
4. Why did the commissioners conclude that the U.S. intelligence community was badly organized to combat international and domestic terrorism?

ENDNOTES

1. For spending totals, see David Baumann "Accounting for the Deficit," *National Journal*, June 12, 2004, p. 1852 (combining categories for defense discretionary, homeland security, and international affairs).
2. White House press release, "National Strategy for Combating Terrorism," Feb. 2003 (online at <www.whitehouse.gov/news/releases/2003/02/20030214-7.html>).
3. "Islamist terrorism is an immediate derivative of *Islamism*. This term distinguishes itself from *Islamic* by the fact that the latter refers to a religion and culture in existence over a millennium, whereas the first is a political/religious phenomenon linked to the great events of the 20th century. Furthermore Islamists define themselves as 'Islamiyyoun/Islamists' precisely to differentiate themselves from 'Muslimun/Muslims.' . . . Islamism is defined as an Islamic militant, antidemocratic movement, bearing a holistic vision of Islam whose final aim is the restoration of the caliphate." Mehdi Mozaffari, "Bin Laden and Islamist Terrorism," *Militaert Tidsskrift*, vol. 131 (Mar. 2002), p. 1 (online at <www.mirkflem.pup.blueyonder.co.uk/pdf/islamistterrorism.pdf>). The Islamist movement, born about 1940, is a product of the modern world, influenced by Marxist-Leninist concepts about revolutionary organization. "Islamists consider Islam to be as much a religion as an 'ideology,' a neologism which they introduced and which remains anathema to the ularnas (the clerical scholars)." Olivier Roy, *The Failure of Political Islam*, trans. Carol Volk (Harvard Univ. Press, 1994), p. 3. Facing political limits by the end of the 1990s, the extremist wing of the Islamist movement "rejected the democratic references invoked by the moderates; and as a result, raw terrorism in its most spectacular and destructive form became its main option for reviving armed struggle in the new millennium." Gilles Kepel, *Jihad: The Trail of Political Islam*, trans. Anthony Roberts (Harvard Univ. Press, 2002), p. 14.
4. Opening the Islamic Conference of Muslim leaders from around the world on October 16, 2003, then Malaysian prime minister Mahathir Mohamad said: "Today we, the whole Muslim ummah [community of believers] are treated with contempt and dishonour. Our religion is denigrated. Our holy places desecrated. Our countries are occupied. Our people are starved and killed. None of our countries are truly independent. We are under pressure to conform to our oppressors' wishes about how we should behave, how we should govern our lands, how we should think even."

He added: "There is a feeling of hopelessness among the Muslim countries and their people. They feel that they can do nothing right. They believe that things can only get worse. The Muslims will forever be oppressed and dominated by the Europeans and Jews." The prime minister's argument was that the Muslims should gather their assets, not striking back blindly, but instead planning a thoughtful, long-term strategy to defeat their worldwide enemies, which he argued were controlled by the Jews. "But today the Jews rule the world by proxy. They get others to fight and die for them." Speech at the Opening of the Tenth Session of the Islamic Summit Conference, Oct. 16, 2003 (online at <www.oicsummit2003. org.my/speech_03 .php>).

5. CIA map, "Possible Remote Havens for Terrorist and Other Illicit Activity," May 2003.

6. For the numbers, see Tariq interview (Oct. 20, 2003).

7. For Pakistan playing a key role in apprehending 500 terrorists, see Richard Armitage testimony, Mar. 23, 2004.

8. For Pakistan's unpoliced areas, see Tasneem Noorani interview (Oct. 27, 2003).

9. Pakistanis and Afghanis interviews (Oct. 2003); DOD Special Operations Command and Central Command briefings (Sept. 15–16, 2004); U.S. intelligence official interview (July 9, 2004).

10. Pervez Musharraf, "A Plea for Enlightened Moderation: Muslims Must Raise Themselves Up Through Individual Achievement and Socioeconomic Emancipation," *Washington Post*, June 1, 2004, p. A23.

11. For a review of ISAF's role, see NATO report, "NATO in Afghanistan," updated July 9, 2004 (online at <www .nato.int/issues/afghanistan>).

12. United States Institute of Peace report, "Establishing the Rule of Law in Afghanistan," Mar. 2004, pp. 1–3 (online at <www.usip.org/pubs/specialreports/srll7.html>).

13. For the change, see Lakhdar Brahimi interview (Oct. 24, 2003); U.S. officials in Afghanistan interview (Oct. 2003). For the request that the United States remain, see Kandahar province local leaders interview (Oct. 21, 2003). For the effect of the United States leaving, see Karim Khalili interview (Oct. 23, 2003).

14. Some have criticized the Bush administration for neglecting Afghanistan because of Iraq. Others, including General Franks, say that the size of the U.S. military commitment in Afghanistan has not been compromised by the commitments in Iraq. We have not investigated the issue and cannot offer a judgment on it.

15. Even if the U.S. forces, stretched thin, are reluctant to take on this role, "a limited, but extremely useful, change in the military mandate would involve intelligence sharing with civilian law enforcement and a willingness to take action against drug warehouses and heroin laboratories." United States Institute of Peace report, "Establishing the Rule of Law in Afghanistan," Mar. 2004, p. 17.

16. For barriers to Saudi monitoring of charities, see, e.g., Robert Jordan interview (Jan. 14, 2004); David Aufhauser interview (Feb. 12, 2004).

17. For the Saudi reformer's view, see Members of *majles al-shura* interview (Oct. 14, 2003).

18. Neil MacFarquhar, "Saudis Support a Jihad in Iraq, Not Back Home," *New York Times*, Apr. 23, 2004, p. Al.

19. Prince Bandar Bin Sultan, "A Diplomat's Call for War," *Washington Post*, June 6, 2004, p. B4 (translation of original in *Al-Watan*, June 2, 2004).

20. President Clinton meeting (Apr. 8, 2004).

21. For Jordan's initiatives, see testimony of William Burns before the Subcommittee on the Middle East and Central Asia of the House International Relations Committee, Mar. 19, 2003 (online at <www.house .gov/international_jrelations/108/burn0319.htm>). For the report, see United Nations Development Programme report, *Arab Human Development Report 2003: Building a Knowledge Society* (United Nations, 2003) (online at <www.miftah.org/Doc/Reports/ Englishcomplete2003.pdf>).

22. DOD memo, Rumsfeld to Myers, Wolfowitz, Pace, and Feith, "Global War on Terrorism," Oct. 16, 2003 (online at <www.usatoday.com/news/washington/ executive/rumsfeld-memo.htm>).

23. For the statistics, see James Zogby, *What Arabs Think: Values, Beliefs, and Concerns* (Zogby International, 2002). For fear of a U.S. attack, see Pew Global Attitudes Project report, *Views of a Changing World: June 2003* (Pew Research Center for the People and the Press, 2003), p. 2. In our interviews, current and former U.S. officials dealing with the Middle East corroborated these findings.

24. For polling soon after 9/11, see Pew Research Center for the People and the Press report, "America Admired, Yet Its New Vulnerability Seen as Good Thing, Say Opinion Leaders; Little Support for Expanding War on Terrorism" (online at <http://peoplepress.org/ reports/print.php3?ReportID=145>). For the quotation, see Pew Global Attitudes Project report, "War With Iraq Further Divides Global Publics But World Embraces Democratic Values and Free Markets," June 3, 2003 (online at <www.pewtrusts.com/ideas/ ideas_item.cfm?content_item_id=1645&content_ type_id=7>).

25. For the Occidentalist "creed of Islamist revolutionaries," see, e.g., Avishai Margalit and Ian Buruma, *Occidentalism: The West in the Eyes of Its Enemies* (Penguin Press, 2004).

26. We draw these statistics, significantly, from the U.S. government's working paper circulated in April 2004 to G-8 "sherpas" in preparation for the 2004 G-8 summit. The paper was leaked and published in *Al-Hayat*. "U.S. Working Paper for G-8 Sherpas," *Al-Hayat*, Feb. 13, 2004 (online at <http://english .daralhayat.com/Spec/02-2004/Article-20040213-ac4 0bdaf-c0a8-01ed004e-5e7ac897d678/story.html>).

27. Richard Holbrooke, "Get the Message Out," *Washington Post*, Oct. 28, 2001, p. B7; Richard Armitage interview Jan. 12, 2004.

28. Testimony of George Tenet, "The Worldwide Threat 2004; Challenges in a Changing Global Context," before the Senate Select Committee on Intelligence, Feb. 24, 2004.

29. U.S. Department of Energy Advisory Board. report, "A Report Card on the Department of Energy's Nonproliferation Programs with Russia," Jan. 10, 2001, p. vi.

30. For terrorists being self-funded, see United Nations report, "Second Report of the [UN] Monitoring Group, Pursuant to Security Council Resolution 1390," Sept. 19, 2002, p. 13.

31. For legal entry, see White House report. Office of Homeland Security, "The National Strategy for Homeland Security," July 2002, p. 20 (online at <www .whitehouse.gov/homeland/book/index.html>). For illegal entry, see Chicago Council on Foreign Relations task force report, *Keeping the Promise: Immigration Proposals From the Heartland* (Chicago Council on Foreign Relations, 2004), p. 28.

32. The names of at least three of the hijackers (Nawaf al Hazmi, Salem al Hazmi, and Khalid al Mihdhar) were in information systems of the intelligence community and thus potentially could have been watchlisted. Had they been watchlisted, the connections to terrorism could have been exposed at the time they applied for a visa or at the port of entry. The names of at least three of the hijackers (Nawaf al Hazmi, Salem al Hazmi, and Khalid al Mihdhar), were in information systems of the intelligence community and thus potentially could have been watchlisted. Had they been watchlisted, their terrorist affiliations could have been exposed either at the time they applied for a visa or at the port of entry. Two of the hijackers (Satain al Suqami and Abdul Aziz al Omari) presented passports manipulated in a fraudulent manner that has subsequently been associated with al Qaeda. Based on our review of their visa and travel histories, we believe it possible that as many as eleven additional hijackers (Wail al Shehri, Waleed al Shehri, Mohand al Shehri, Hani Hanjour, Majed Moqed, Nawaf al Hazmi, Hamza al Ghamdi, Ahmed al Ghamdi, Saeed al Ghamdi, Ahmed al Nami, and Ahmad al Haznawi) held passports containing these same fraudulent features, but their passports have not been found so we cannot be sure. Khalid al Mihdhar and Salem al Hazmi presented passports with a suspicious indicator of Islamic extremism. There is reason to believe that the passports of three other hijackers (Nawaf al Hazmi, Ahmed al Nami, and Ahmad al Haznawi) issued in the same Saudi passport office may have contained this same indicator; however, their passports have not been found, so we cannot he sure.

33. Khallad Bin Attash, Ramzi Binalshibh, Zakariya Essabar, Ali Abdul Aziz Ali, and Saeed al Ghamdi (not the individual by the same name who became a hijacker) tried to get visas and failed. Kahtani was unable to prove his admissibility and withdrew his application for admission after an immigration inspector remained unpersuaded that he was a tourist. All the hijackers whose visa applications we reviewed arguably could have been denied visas because their applications were not filled out completely. Had State visa officials routinely had a practice of acquiring more information in such cases, they likely would have found more grounds for denial. For example, three hijackers made statements on their visa applications that could have been proved false by U.S. government records (Hani Hanjour, Saeed al Ghamdi, and Khalid al Mihdhar), and many lied about their employment or educational status. Two hijackers could have been denied admission at the port of entry based on violations of immigration rules governing terms of admission— Mohamed Atta overstayed his tourist visa and then failed to present a proper vocational school visa when he entered in January 2001; Ziad Jarrah attended school in June 2000 without properly adjusting his immigration status, an action that violated his immigration status and rendered him inadmissible on each of his six subsequent reentries into the United States between June 2000 and August 5, 2001. There were possible grounds to deny entry to a third hijacker (Marwan al Shehhi). One hijacker violated his immigration status by failing to enroll as a student after entry (Hani Hanjour); two hijackers overstayed their terms of admission by four and eight months respectively (Satam al Suqami and Nawaf al Hazmi). Atta and Shehhi attended a flight school (Huffman Aviation)

that the Justice Department's Inspector General concluded should not have been certified to accept foreign students, see DOJ Inspector General's report, "The INS' Contacts with Two September 11 Terrorists: A Review of the INS's Admissions of Atta and Shehhi, its Processing of their Change of Status Applications, and its Efforts to Track Foreign Students in the United States," May 20, 2002.

34. John Gordon interview (May 13, 2004).

35. For a description of a layering approach, see Stephen Flynn, *America the Vulnerable: How the U.S. Has Failed to Secure the Homeland and Protect Its People From Terrorism* (HarperCollins, 2004), p. 69.

36. The logical and timely rollout of such a program is hampered by an astonishingly long list of congressional mandates. The system originated in the Illegal Immigration Reform and Immigrant Responsibility Act of 1996 and applied to all non-U.S. citizens who enter or exit the United States at any port of entry. Pub. L. No. 104–208, 110 Stat. 3009 (1996), § 110. The Data Management Improvement Act of 2000 altered this mandate by incorporating a requirement for a searchable centralized database, limiting the government's ability to require new data from certain travelers and setting a series of implementation deadlines. Pub. L. No. 106–215, 114 Stat. 337 (2000), § 2(a). The USA PATRIOT Act mandated that the Attorney General and Secretary of State "particularly focus" on having the entry-exit system include biometrics and tamper-resistant travel documents readable at all ports of entry. Pub. L. No. 107–56, 115 Stat. 272 (2001), § 1008(a). In the Enhanced Border Security and Visa Entry Reform Act, Congress directed that, not later than October 26, 2004, the attorney general and the secretary of state issue to all non-U.S. citizens only machine-readable, tamper-resistant visas and other travel and entry documents that use biometric identifiers and install equipment at all U.S. ports of entry to allow biometric authentication of such documents. Pub. L. No. 107–173, 116 Stat. 543 (2002), § 303(b). The Act also required that increased security still facilitate the free flow of commerce and travel. Ibid. § 102(a)(1)(C). The administration has requested a delay of two years for the requirement of tamper-proof passports. Testimony of Thomas Ridge before the House Judiciary Committee, Apr. 21, 2004 (online at <www.dhs.gov/ dhspublic/ display?theme=45&content=3498&print=true>). Program planners have set a goal of collecting information, confirming identity, providing information about foreign nationals throughout the entire immigration system, and ultimately enabling each point in the system to assess the lawfulness of travel and any security risks.

37. There are at least three registered traveler programs underway, at different points in the system, designed and run by two different agencies in the Department of Homeland Security (outside the U.S.VISIT system), which must ultimately be the basis for access to the United States.

38. For the statistics, see DOS report, "Workload Statistics by Post Regions for All Visa Classes," June 18, 2004. One post-9/11 screening process, known as Condor, has conducted over 130,000 extra name-checks. DOS letter, Karl Hofmann to the Commission, Apr. 5, 2004. The checks have caused significant delays in some cases but have never resulted in visas being denied on terrorism grounds. For a discussion of visa delays, see General Accounting Office report, "Border Security: Improvements Needed to Reduce Time Taken to Adjudicate Visas for Science Students and Scholars," Feb. 2004. We do not know all the reasons why visa applications have dropped so significantly. Several factors beyond the visa process itself include the National Security Entry-Exit Registration System, which requires additional screening processes for certain groups from Arab and Muslim countries; the Iraq war; and perhaps cyclical economic factors. For the cost to the United States of visa backlogs, see National Foreign Trade Council report, "Visa Backlog Costs U.S. Exporters More Than $30 Billion Since 2002, New Study Finds," June 2, 2004 (online at <www.nftc .org/newsflash/newsflash.asp?Mode=View&article id=1686&Category=All>).

39. These issues are on the G-8 agenda. White House press release, "G-8 Secure and Facilitated Travel Initiative (SAFTI)," June 9, 2004 (online at <www .whitehouse.gov/news/releases/2004/06/20040609-51 .html>). Lax passport issuance standards are among the vulnerabilities exploited by terrorists, possibly including two of the 9/11 hijackers. Three models exist for strengthened prescreening: (1) better screening by airlines, such as the use of improved document authentication technology; (2) posting of border agents or inspectors in foreign airports to work cooperatively with foreign counterparts; and (3) establishing a full preinspection regime, such as now exists for travel to the United States from Canada and Ireland. All three models should be pursued, in addition to electronic prescreening.

40. Among the more important problems to address is that of varying transliterations of the same name. For example, the current lack of a single convention for

transliterating Arabic names enabled the 19 hijackers to vary the spelling of their names to defeat name-based watchlist systems and confuse any potential efforts to locate them. While the gradual introduction of biometric identifiers will help, that process will take years, and a name match will always be useful. The ICAO should discuss the adoption of a standard requiring a digital code for all names that need to be translated into the Roman alphabet, ensuring one common spelling for all countries.

41. On achieving more reliable identification, see Markle Foundation task force report, *Creating a Trusted Information Network for Homeland Security* (Markle Foundation, 2003), p. 72 (online at <www.markle.org>).

42. General Accounting Office report, *Mass Transit: Federal Action Could Help Transit Agencies Address Security Challenges,* GAO-03–263, Dec. 2002 (online at <www.gao.gov/new.items/d03263.pdf>).

43. The Bush administration clarified the respective missions of the different intelligence analysis centers in a letter sent by Secretary Ridge, DCI Tenet, FBI Director Mueller, and TTIC Director Brennan to Senators Susan Collins and Carl Levin on April 13, 2004. The letter did not mention any element of the Department of Defense. It stated that the DCI would define what analytical resources he would transfer from the CTC to TTIC no later than June 1, 2004. DCI Tenet subsequently told us that he decided that TTIC would have primary responsibility for terrorism analysis but that the CIA and the Defense Intelligence Agency would grow their own analysts. TTIC will have tasking authority over terrorism analysts in other intelligence agencies, although there will need to be a board to supervise deconfliction. George Tenet interview (July 2, 2004). We have not received any details regarding this plan.

44. "TTIC has no operational authority. However, TTIC has the authority to task collection and analysis from Intelligence Community agencies, the FBI, and DHS through tasking mechanisms we will create. The analytic work conducted at TTIC creates products that inform each of TTIC's partner elements, as well as other Federal departments and agencies as appropriate." Letter from Ridge and others to Collins and Levin, Apr. 13, 2004.

45. Donald Rumsfeld prepared statement, Mar, 23, 2004, p. 20.

46. In this conception, the NCTC should plan actions, assigning responsibilities for operational direction and execution to other agencies. It would be built on TTIC and would be supported by the intelligence community as TTIC is now. Whichever route is chosen, the scarce analytical resources now dispersed among TTIC, the Defense Intelligence Agency's Joint Interagency Task Force—Combatting Terrorism (JITF-CT), and the DCI's Counterterrorist Center (CTC) should be concentrated more effectively than they are now.

The DCI's Counterterrorist Center would become a CIA unit, to handle the direction and execution of tasks assigned to the CIA. It could have detailees from other agencies, as it does now, to perform this operational mission. It would yield much of the broader, strategic analytic duties and personnel to the NCTC. The CTC would rely on the restructured CIA (discussed in the next section) to organize, train, and equip its personnel.

Similarly, the FBI's Counterterrorism Division would remain, as now, the operational arm of the Bureau to combat terrorism. As it does now, it would work with other agencies in carrying out these missions, retaining the JITF structure now in place. The Counterterrorism Division would rely on the FBI's Office of Intelligence to train and equip its personnel, helping to process and report the information gathered in the field.

The Defense Department's unified commands—SOCOM, NORTHCOM, and CENTCOM—would be the joint operational centers taking on DOD tasks. Much of the excellent analytical talent that has been assembled in the Defense Intelligence Agency's JITFCT should merge into the planned NCTC.

The Department of Homeland Security's Directorate for Information Analysis and Infrastructure Protection should retain its core duties, but the NCTC should have the ultimate responsibility for producing net assessments that utilize Homeland Security's analysis of domestic vulnerabilities and integrate all source analysis of foreign intelligence about the terrorist enemy.

The State Department's counterterrorism office would be a critical participant in the NCTC's work, taking the lead in directing the execution of the counterterrorism foreign policy mission.

The proposed National Counterterrorism Center should offer one-stop shopping to agencies with counterterrorism and homeland security responsibilities. That is, it should be an authoritative reference base on the transnational terrorist organizations: their people, goals, strategies, capabilities, networks of contacts and support, the context in which they operate, and their characteristic habits across the life cycle of operations—recruitment, reconnaissance, target selection, logistics, and travel. For example, this Center would offer an integrated depiction of groups like al Qaeda or Hezbollah worldwide, overseas, and in the United States.

The NCTC will not eliminate the need for the executive departments to have their own analytic units. But it would enable agency-based analytic units to become smaller and more efficient. In particular, it would make it possible for these agency-based analytic units to concentrate on analysis that is tailored to their agency's specific responsibilities.

A useful analogy is in military intelligence. There, the Defense Intelligence Agency and the service production agencies (like the Army's National Ground Intelligence Center) are the institutional memory and reference source for enemy order of battle, enemy organization, and enemy equipment. Yet the Joint Staff and all the theater commands still have their own J-2s. They draw on the information they need, tailoring and applying it to their operational needs. As they learn more from their tactical operations, they pass intelligence of enduring value back up to the Defense Intelligence Agency and the services so it can be evaluated, form part of the institutional memory, and help guide future collection.

In our proposal, that reservoir of institutional memory about terrorist organizations would function for the government as a whole, and would be in the NCTC.

47. The head of the NCTC would thus help coordinate the operational side of these agencies, like the FBI's Counterterrorism Division. The intelligence side of these agencies, such as the FBI's Office of Intelligence, would be overseen by the National Intelligence Director we recommend later in this chapter.

48. The quotation goes on: "It includes gaps in intelligence, but also intelligence that, like a string of pearls too precious to wear, is too sensitive to give to those who need it. It includes the alarm that fails to work, but also the alarm that has gone off so often it has been disconnected. It includes the unalert watchman, but also the one who knows he'll be chewed out by his superior if he gets higher authority out of bed. It includes the contingencies that occur to no one, but also those that everyone assumes somebody else is taking care of. It includes straightforward procrastination, but also decisions protracted by internal disagreement. It includes, in addition, the inability of individual human beings to rise to the occasion until they are sure it is the occasion—which is usually too late. . . . Finally, as at Pearl Harbor, surprise may include some measure of genuine novelty introduced by the enemy, and some sheer bad luck." Thomas Schelling, foreword to Roberta Wohlstetter, *Pearl Harbor: Warning and Decision* (Stanford Univ. Press, 1962), p. viii.

49. For the Goldwater-Nichols Act, see Pub. L. No. 99-433, 100 Stat. 992 (1986). For a general discussion of the act, see Gordon Lederman, *Reorganizing the Joint Chiefs of Staff: The Goldwater-Nichols Act of 1986* (Greenwood, 1999); James Locher, *Victory on the Potomac: The Goldwater-Nichols Act Unifies the Pentagon* (Texas A&M Univ. Press, 2003).

50. For a history of the DCI's authority over the intelligence community, see CIA report, Michael Warner ed., *Central Intelligence; Origin and Evolution* (CIA Center for the Study of Intelligence, 2001). For the Director's view of his community authorities, see DCI directive, "Director of Central Intelligence Directive 1/1: The Authorities and Responsibilities of the Director of Central Intelligence as Head of the U.S. Intelligence Community," Nov. 19, 1998.

51. As Norman Augustine, former chairman of Lockheed Martin Corporation, writes regarding power in the government, "As in business, cash is king. If you are not in charge of your budget, you are not king." Norman Augustine, *Managing to Survive in Washington: A Beginner's Guide to High-Level Management in Government* (Center for Strategic and International Studies, 2000), p. 20.

52. For the DCI and the secretary of defense, see 50 U.S.C. § 403–6(a). If the director does not concur with the secretary's choice, then the secretary is required to notify the president of the director's nonconcurrence. Ibid. For the DCI and the attorney general, see 50 U.S.C. § 403–6(b)(3).

53. The new program would replace the existing National Foreign Intelligence Program.

54. Some smaller parts of the current intelligence community, such as the State Department's intelligence bureau and the Energy Department's intelligence entity, should not be funded out of the national intelligence program and should be the responsibility of their home departments.

55. The head of the NCTC should have the rank of a deputy national intelligence director, e.g., Executive Level II, but would have a different title.

56. If the organization of defense intelligence remains as it is now, the appropriate official would be the under secretary of defense for intelligence. If defense intelligence is reorganized to elevate the responsibilities of the director of the DIA, then that person might be the appropriate official.

57. For the information technology architecture, see Ruth David interview (June 10, 2003). For the necessity of moving from need-to-know to need-to-share, see James Steinberg testimony, Oct. 14, 2003. The Director still has no strategy for removing information-sharing barriers and—more than two years since 9/11—has only appointed a working group on the subject. George Tenet prepared statement, Mar. 24, 2004, p. 37.

58. The intelligence community currently makes information shareable by creating "tearline" reports, with the nonshareable information at the top and then, below the "tearline," the portion that recipients are told they can share. This proposal reverses that concept. All reports are created as tearline data, with the shareable information at the top and with added details accessible on a system that requires permissions or authentication.

59. See Markle Foundation Task Force report, *Creating a Trusted Information Network for Homeland Security* (Markle Foundation, 2003); Markle Foundation Task Force report, *Protecting America's Freedom in the Information Age* (Markle Foundation, 2002) (both online at <www.markle.org>).

60. Markle Foundation Task Force report, *Creating a Trusted Information Network,* p. 12. The pressing need for such guidelines was also spotlighted by the Technology and Privacy Advisory Committee appointed by Secretary Rumsfeld to advise the Department of Defense on the privacy implications of its Terrorism Information Awareness Program. Technology and Privacy Advisory Committee report, *Safeguarding Privacy in the Fight Against Terrorism* (2004) (online at <www.sainc .com/tapac/TAPAC_Report_Final_5-1004.pdf>). We take no position on the particular recommendations offered in that report, but it raises issues that pertain to the government as a whole—not just to the Department of Defense.

61. This change should eliminate the need in the Senate for the current procedure of sequential referral of the annual authorization bill for the national foreign intelligence program. In that process, the Senate Armed Services Committee reviews the bill passed by the Senate Select Committee on Intelligence before the bill is brought before the full Senate for consideration.

62. This recommendation, and measures to assist the Bureau in developing its intelligence cadre, are included in the report accompanying the Commerce, Justice and State Appropriations Act for Fiscal Year 2005, passed by the House of Representatives on July 7, 2004. H.R. Rep. No. 108–576, 108th Cong., 2d sess. (2004), p. 22.

63. Letter from Ridge and others to Collins and Levin, Apr. 13, 2004.

64. For the directorate's current capability, see Patrick Hughes interview (Apr. 2, 2004).

Reprinted from The 9/11 Commission (the Kean Commission), *Final Report of the National Commission on Terrorist Attacks Upon the United States* (New York: Norton, July 2004): 361–428.

27. SPYING BLIND

AMY B. ZEGART

Government activities take place in an organizational setting. Professor Zegart is an expert on organizational behavior, and she applies this public administration approach to the study of intelligence agencies. She rebukes officials for their failure to embrace reform proposals that would help correct the deep-seated flaws in the institutional design of U.S. intelligence.

What's needed for the fix is known. But is it accepted? Not generally. And is it well on the way to getting implemented? Not at all. Can we say we're really on the way to remedying the problems that got us into the deep shit we're in? The answer is no. But we have to. There is no other way.

—*Former senior intelligence official*[1]

History suggests that transformative change rarely occurs during ordinary times. Instead, dramatic departures from the past often require a large external shock—a tragedy, catastrophic failure, scandal, or focusing event that challenges conventional wisdom and exposes the dangers of the status quo. Examples abound. The Civil War led to ratification of the Thirteenth, Fourteenth, and Fifteenth Amendments of the U.S. Constitution. The Great Depression produced Roosevelt's New Deal. World War II gave rise to the CIA, the United Nations, and the Marshall Plan. The Cuban missile crisis of 1962 ushered in an era of détente between the United States and the Soviet Union. By this reasoning, the adaptation failure of U.S. intelligence agencies before 9/11 may not be surprising. But adaptation failure after 9/11 is. If ever we would expect to find a catalyst for major change, the worst terrorist attack in U.S. history should be it. As one senior government official remarked, "You can talk about how we missed watchlisting two guys, that information sharing wasn't what it should have been, that there were cultural differences between the FBI and CIA. But find me a time when the world went to war without a galvanizing event."[2]

Yet nearly six years after 9/11, the Intelligence Community's most serious deficiencies remain. In this chapter, I examine the missed opportunities to overhaul the U.S. Intelligence Community since the attacks, the current state of intelligence capabilities, and prospects for the future. Such assessments are always incomplete. Only a rearview mirror in a distant future will reveal how many plots al Qaeda hatched, how many were stopped, and what U.S. capabilities, policies, and actions made a difference. And that's to say nothing of what new enemies may emerge. As one former intelligence official ruefully noted, "By the time we master the al Qaeda problem, will al Qaeda be the problem?"[3] International politics is rife with uncertainty.

Nevertheless, two things are already clear: 9/11 was not enough to jolt U.S. intelligence agencies out of their Cold War past, and future adaptation—to terrorism or any other threat—is unlikely. The nature of organizations, rational self-interest, and the fragmented federal government make intelligence agencies exceptionally impervious to reform, even after catastrophic failure. Adaptation is not impossible, but it is close.

ADAPTATION FAILURE SINCE 9/11

There have been two rounds of opportunities to transform U.S. intelligence agencies since 9/11. The first lasted a little more than a year. Between the attacks and December 2002, Congress and the president passed the USA PATRIOT Act, created the Department of Homeland Security, and the Congressional Intelligence Committees launched their Joint Inquiry of

9/11. What policymakers did not do was tackle intelligence overhaul. In the nation's darkest hour, when prospects for intelligence reform were brightest, elected officials chose to place their energies elsewhere. As we shall see, this was no accident; incentives and institutional fragmentation created strong pressures for President Bush and congressional leaders to avoid rather than confront the Intelligence Community's worst problems.

Round two began in July 2004, when the convergence of an extraordinary set of circumstances thrust intelligence reform back onto the political agenda. Again, a sudden turn of events raised the possibility of dramatic change. And again, it was not enough. Although Congress attempted to pass a major restructuring of the Intelligence Community, the 2004 reform bill was obstructed by the same forces that had thwarted reform for decades: bureaucratic resistance, tepid presidential support, and opposition from key congressional committee chairmen who stood to lose and had the power to resist. The Intelligence Reform and Terrorism Prevention Act of 2004 started with high hopes but ended up producing only modest changes.

ROUND ONE: AVOIDING REFORM, 2001 TO 2002

On the evening of September 11, 2001, with smoke still billowing from the Pentagon, congressional leaders gathered on the Capitol steps. Standing shoulder to shoulder, Democrats and Republicans expressed a newfound bipartisanship and a determination to fight terrorism. They then burst into a spontaneous chorus of "God Bless America." Several days later, the *New York Times* wrote that Washington was experiencing a "disaster-driven level of bipartisan civility not seen here in decades."[4] The moment seemed ripe for a major transformation of U.S. intelligence agencies.

Nobody seized the opportunity. Inside Congress, the House and Senate Intelligence Committees decided to investigate the terrorist attacks before considering reform legislation.[5] After twelve expert reports and hundreds of recommendations urging extensive intelligence reforms during the previous ten years, Congress's intelligence watchdog committees announced that they needed to study the issues more. Meanwhile, the White House spent the first forty-five days after 9/11 pressing for the USA PATRIOT Act, which granted the FBI and other law enforcement agencies a number of authorities that had

been proposed and scuttled in previous years.[6] In the aftermath of tragedy, both the White House and Congress settled for a quick fix. "The administration wanted to look like they were doing something . . . but there was no effort to connect the contributing factors of 9/11 and what the PATRIOT Act would solve,"[7] noted one congressional staffer. Others agreed. "Everyone wants to do something," said one former FBI official. "It's human dynamics. Logic and common sense are not a part of the formula."[8] Six weeks after 9/11, the new law sailed through Congress with astonishing speed and little debate. Only a single senator, Russ Feingold (D-WI), voted against it.[9] As the FBI official noted, "If you're a member of Congress, following a tragedy like 9/11, are you going to vote against the PATRIOT Act?"[10] (emphasis his).

In the following year, the president and Congress missed three more chances to reform the U.S. Intelligence Community. The first came in November 2001, when General Brent Scowcroft delivered a classified report to the White House urging radical overhaul.[11] Scowcroft was no ordinary messenger. He had served as national security advisor to two presidents (Gerald Ford and George H. W. Bush), was considered one of the best informed and most well respected foreign policy officials in Washington, and had recently been appointed chairman of the President's Foreign Intelligence Advisory Board. Scowcroft's report, moreover, had been requested by President Bush himself in May 2001, four months before September 11, as an independent, comprehensive review of U.S. intelligence capabilities.[12] Now, eight weeks after the attacks, Scowcroft turned in his recommendations. They were bold. He urged stripping the three largest defense intelligence agencies from the Pentagon—the National Reconnaissance Office, which builds and runs spy satellites; the National Security Agency, which intercepts signals communications; and the National Imagery and Mapping Agency, which handles imagery and mapping[13]—and placing them directly under the control of the director of cental intelligence.[14] The idea was to give the director of central intelligence real power "to direct" the entire Intelligence Community, "not plead and cajole," said one former official familiar with the report.[15]

Pentagon reaction was swift and lethal: Secretary of Defense Donald Rumsfeld hated the idea.[16] As one former intelligence official paraphrased, "Rumsfeld says 'No fucking way.' He tells Scowcroft to put it into the wastepaper basket."[17] The proposal quickly died.

The next opportunity came in June 2002, when President Bush proposed the creation of a Department of Homeland Security. The move signaled a major policy reversal for the president, who had initially preferred integrating homeland security efforts in a small White House office rather than creating a massive new cabinet department. But with pressure mounting on Capitol Hill to do more, with congressional midterm elections just months away, and with Senator Joe Lieberman's democratic homeland security department bill gaining momentum in Congress, the president had to act fast. On June 6, he abruptly announced a proposal to merge twenty-two different agencies, including the Coast Guard, Customs Service, Immigration and Naturalization Service, Federal Emergency Management Agency (FEMA) and the recently created Transportation Security Administration, into a new homeland security department. "Employees of this new agency," the president announced in a nationally televised address, "will come to work every morning knowing their most important job is to protect their fellow citizens."[18] It would be the largest government reorganization since the 1940s.

Once more, intelligence reform was not a major part of the plan. The overriding purpose of the Homeland Security Department was identifying and protecting critical U.S. targets from terrorist attack, improving emergency response to disasters, and integrating border patrol functions, not revamping the U.S. intelligence system. Although the president's proposal included an intelligence division within the new department, its role was limited and its capabilities weak. The Homeland Security Department's Information Analysis and Infrastructure Protection (IAIP) division was an analysis shop only, charged with analyzing foreign and domestic terrorism threat reporting and assessing U.S. vulnerabilities. It had no power to collect intelligence. It had no tasking authority over other agencies. And it had no ability to knock bureaucratic heads together. Rather than integrating the CIA, FBI, and other intelligence agencies, IAIP was beholden to them for information.[19] Moreover, it was housed outside the DCI's control and inside a behemoth new department whose consolidation was expected to take years.[20] With twenty-two human resource service centers,[21] more than eighty different financial management applications,[22] and 170,000 employees whose jobs ranged from inspecting plants to distributing hurricane relief supplies, the Department of Homeland Security was not likely to produce crack intelligence analysis any time soon. Many feared, in the words of one counterterrorism official, that DHS "[wouldn't] know its ass from its elbow."[23]

Even without intelligence reform in the mix, the homeland security bill proved contentious. By the summer of 2002, business as usual was already returning to Washington. Agencies targeted for absorption in the new department, as well as the congressional committees that oversaw them, began slicing and dicing the president's proposal to protect their own pieces. Secretary of Health and Human Services Tommy G. Thompson launched a campaign behind the scenes to keep units rather than cede them to DHS. "Make sure this doesn't happen!" he told one of his deputies.[24] In Congress, turf trumped party loyalty; Republican-led committees in the House picked apart virtually every aspect of the president's bill. The Judiciary Committee voted against moving the Secret Service to the new department, and also voted to split the Immigration and Naturalization Service in half, moving only part of it to DHS. The Transportation and Infrastructure Committee voted to keep FEMA and the Coast Guard out entirely. The Ways and Means Committee agreed to let the Customs Service move only if the Treasury Department retained management authority over it. In addition, a bitter partisan feud erupted, with Democrats pressing to extend federal employment protections to homeland security workers and Republicans blasting them during an election season for being soft on national security. In the end, it took extensive lobbying (including an unprecedented joint visit to Congress by the administration's top four cabinet officers, Secretary of State Colin Powell, Defense Secretary Donald Rumsfeld, Attorney General John Ashcroft, and Treasury Secretary Paul O'Neill), some bitter wrangling, and the help of the Republican leadership in Congress—which established a special nine-member panel to write the House bill and stacked it with administration supporters who overruled committee votes—to secure passage of the Homeland Security Act of 2002.[25]

No sooner had the ink dried than the president circumvented DHS's new intelligence directorate. On January 28, 2003, just days after swearing in Tom Ridge as the first Secretary of Homeland Security, Bush announced the creation of a new Terrorist Threat Integration Center (TTIC) in his State of the Union address. TTIC ("T-TIC") would report directly to the director of central intelligence and would be responsible for terrorism threat analysis, the same functions that had been assigned to the Homeland Security Department's Information Analysis and Infrastructure

Protection Directorate. Ridge was stunned. His deputies were furious. "It was as if the White House created us and then set out to marginalize us," one later recalled.[26] Confusion was rampant. Senators Susan Collins (R-ME) and Joseph Lieberman (D-CT), the chair and ranking members of the Senate Homeland Security and Governmental Affairs Committee, quickly held hearings[27] where they demanded "critically important information about the structure of the Terrorist Threat Integration Center, and how it and other key agencies would share responsibility for the collection, analysis, and dissemination of terrorism-related intelligence."[28] Nearly a year later, little had been settled. "The very fact of TTIC's creation," noted a Markle Foundation expert task force in December 2003, "has caused confusion within the federal government and among state and local governments about the respective roles of TTIC and the DHS."[29]

In short, fourteen months after September 11, the president and Congress passed a major homeland security bill which failed to remedy any of the organizational shortcomings in U.S. intelligence that had left the United States so vulnerable to terrorist attack. The Homeland Security Act of 2002 did not integrate the Intelligence Community, improve human intelligence, change agency incentives and cultures to enhance information sharing, reform the FBI, or match intelligence resources against priorities. What's more, before any ribbons were cut, DHS's intelligence directorate was stripped of its primary function. The Homeland Security Department's Information Analysis and Infrastructure Protection directorate was weak by design and undermined before it ever began.

The fourth and final opportunity for intelligence reform occurred in December 2002, when the Congressional Joint Inquiry issued its final report about the September 11 attacks. The report's nineteen recommendations included establishing a powerful new director of national intelligence, revamping the intelligence priority process, and considering whether a new domestic intelligence agency should replace the FBI. But by then, the momentum for reform was gone. As former Bush Deputy Homeland Security Advisor Richard Falkenrath observed, the report's recommendations "were ignored."[30] Intelligence reform went nowhere for the next year and a half.

THE LIMITS OF CATASTROPHE

In each of these four episodes, crisis was not enough. During the first year after 9/11, lawmakers went 0 for 4 on intelligence reform. These failures were not for lack of information or urgency. Days after the attacks, as the president and Congress rushed to draft the USA PATRIOT Act, reports were already surfacing about more far-reaching problems in the Federal Bureau of Investigation.[31] In November, at the very moment Defense Secretary Donald Rumsfeld was trashing Scowcroft's sweeping intelligence reform plan behind closed doors, even the *New York Times* editorial page was calling for "radical change."[32] And throughout the fall of 2002 as Bush administration officials lobbied for a new Department of Homeland Security, the House and Senate Intelligence Committees' Joint Inquiry released staggering details about the Intelligence Community's failures leading up to the 9/11 attacks.[33] "[T]he Community made mistakes prior to September 11 and the problems that led to those mistakes need to be addressed and to be fixed," declared Joint Inquiry Staff Director Eleanor Hill.[34] But problems weren't fixed. Intelligence deficiencies were everywhere in the headlines but nowhere on the political agenda.

This was more than a case of bad luck or timing. A track record that poor with tragedy so recent and reforms so urgently needed suggests something more systematic at work. Closer examination reveals that the same enduring realities that prevented adaptation before 9/11 stymied adaptation afterward.

In the weeks following the attacks, elected officials faced strong pressure to do something. But they responded to this pressure in ways that maximized electoral returns and minimized political costs. For the House and Senate Intelligence Committees, this meant investigating what went wrong rather than pushing massive legislative overhaul. Studying the problem had the advantage of demonstrating fast action and resolve without triggering opposition and almost certain defeat by the Congressional Armed Services Committees. As one congressional intelligence staffer bitterly complained in the spring of 2002, "we suck at getting things done. . . . We're a subcommittee of armed services. They swallow our bills."[35]

The same logic explains why 9/11 prompted the president and Congress to pass the PATRIOT Act instead of instituting more sweeping changes to the FBI and the rest of the Intelligence Community. Throwing together old proposals to enhance the FBI's legal authorities was far easier than mandating new and far-reaching changes inside the bureau. Increasing investigatory powers was an FBI crowd pleaser. Demanding that agents do their jobs in fundamentally different ways was quite another matter.

The PATRIOT Act made improvements and headlines without making tough choices or raising the hackles of the FBI. From the perspective of executive branch officials and members of Congress, the new law was an ideal response to 9/11. From a national security perspective, it was a squandered opportunity to do more.

Rational self-interest and structural fragmentation also led the president to dismiss reform recommendations from the very intelligence study he had requested. When General Scowcroft submitted his intelligence restructuring plan in November 2001, Secretary of Defense Rumsfeld vehemently opposed it and the president quickly scrapped it. This should not be surprising. Turf-conscious Defense Department officials had been rejecting the same types of reforms for years, and for years presidents had capitulated to their demands, concluding that intelligence reform was not worth the fight. The post-9/11 period was no different. If anything, the costs of intelligence reform may have been even higher: With the onset of military operations in Afghanistan, the president could ill-afford to pick a fight with the Pentagon and its supporters on Capitol Hill.

It should also come as no surprise that when pressure finally forced the president to reorganize the government, he took the path of least resistance. For months, Bush had opposed the creation of a new homeland security department, changing his mind only when it appeared that a democratic bill might pass Congress without his support. Including intelligence reform would have made a difficult government reorganization bill impossible. As it was, the president had to fight hard to win.

Instead, like so many presidents before him, Bush settled for a lower cost approach to intelligence reform: using his unilateral powers of office to mitigate a handful of problems where the odds of success were high and the opposition weak. From September 2001 to August 2004, the president studiously avoided getting embroiled with the Defense Department, opting instead to direct more minor changes through executive orders and announcements. The most significant of these were an executive order tasking the U.S. attorney general with improving coordination of terrorist tracking efforts—an initiative that was still floundering four years later—and the establishment of TTIC.[36] From the president's vantage point, such changes were far more attractive than the alternatives. The Terrorist Threat Integration Center, for example, could be stood up overnight with staff from existing agencies. It could report directly to the director of central intelligence rather than another cabinet official. It required no approval from congressional committees or their powerful chairmen. It posed no serious threat to the Pentagon. And it usurped the power of the one department incapable of fighting back—the Department of Homeland Security, which had not yet opened for business. Like his predecessors, President Bush calculated the costs and benefits of his alternatives. He chose intelligence solutions that were easy and quick instead of difficult and permanent. Catastrophic failure was not enough to alter incentives and institutional realities.

ROUND TWO: THE REFORM THAT WASN'T, 2004

Intelligence reform appeared all but dead until July 2004, when three factors suddenly converged: Director of Central Intelligence George Tenet resigned; the Senate Intelligence Committee issued a scathing report criticizing prewar intelligence assessments of Iraq's weapons of mass destruction,[37] and the 9/11 Commission released its final report.

Together, these three events temporarily suspended the enduring realities that normally impede legislative reform. While bureaucrats ordinarily fiercely oppose such changes, Tenet's resignation removed the Intelligence Community's staunchest and most public defender. During the summer and fall of 2004, as the 9/11 Commission and 9/11 families' groups took aim at U.S. intelligence agencies, there was no public face to defend them. At the same time, the Senate Intelligence Committees Iraq report momentarily shifted the electoral incentives for members of Congress. During ordinary times, most legislators have little reason to champion intelligence reform, while lawmakers serving on the Armed Services Committees have every reason to block it. But the Senate report was released in the middle of a national election campaign with a tight presidential race, and it linked intelligence failures to an issue that was then gripping the nation: whether legislators had voted to authorize the war in Iraq based on flawed intelligence.[38] Questions about intelligence failures and the Iraq War dogged congressional candidates on the campaign trail everywhere from New York to Nebraska. Intelligence reform was no longer about abstract organizational charts, but about how to avoid making mistakes that were costing American soldiers their lives.

Finally, the 9/11 Commission and the 9/11 families' organizations served as powerful interest groups, lobbying lawmakers and using public media to press their reform agenda. Between July 22, when the commission released its final report, and December 10, 2004, two days after Congress passed the Intelligence Reform and Terrorism Prevention Act, the commission and the families received more national television news coverage than the war in Iraq.[39] These were the first intelligence reform interest groups in U.S. history, and they were powerful forces for change. In interviews, several officials involved in post-9/11 intelligence reform efforts said that the families and the commission were crucial. "It was the kind of ultimate pressure," said one.[40]

Even with all of these advantages, however, the intelligence reform bill was nearly derailed and ultimately diluted by the same forces that had defeated similar efforts for years: vigorous opposition from the Defense Department and prodefense lawmakers on the Congressional Armed Services Committees, and tepid support by the president. Rational incentives and structural fragmentation once again led to disappointment. The 2004 Intelligence Reform and Terrorism Prevention Act produced only modest changes.

THE PENTAGON: "TRASHING EVERYTHING"

In the fall of 2004, just like the 1992 and 1996 reform episodes, Defense Department officials savaged legislative proposals to create a powerful new director of national intelligence and streamline the Intelligence Community—two of the principal recommendations of the 9/11 Commission—because these changes threatened to undermine Pentagon control over defense intelligence agencies and the lion's share of the intelligence budget. According to Republican Representative Christopher Shays (R-CT), Secretary of Defense Donald Rumsfeld "just trashed everything about the national intelligence director," in private meetings on Capitol Hill.[41] Other lawmakers from both parties issued similar assessments. One Democrat described Rumsfeld as someone who "was not at all enthusiastic about intelligence reform."[42] Another Republican angrily noted, "the Pentagon for months was working behind the scenes to derail the bill."[43]

The Pentagon's public campaign was equally damaging. Representative Jane Harman (D-CA), the ranking Democrat of the House Intelligence Committee and one of the chief architects of the 2004 reform bill, later remarked, "No one missed the big fights when we were doing the intel reform law with the Pentagon. If any of you missed it, I'm not sure what planet you were on."[44] One key salvo came on October 21, when General Richard Myers, chairman of the Joint Chiefs of Staff, delivered a bombshell letter to House Armed Services Committee Chairman Duncan Hunter (R-CA). In the letter, Myers opposed giving the proposed director of national intelligence strong budgetary authorities over intelligence agencies housed in the Pentagon, arguing that only a Pentagon-controlled budget would ensure sufficient "support to the warfighters."[45] It was a move taken right out of the Defense Department's intelligence reform opposition playbook. In 1992 and 1996, when intelligence reform bills started gathering momentum in Congress, senior defense officials used similar arguments in similar letters sent to Congressional Armed Services Committee chairmen. Both times, the letters helped deliver death blows to the bills.[46]

Although supporting the warfighter proved to be an effective public relations argument, it was a red herring: in reality, nothing in the proposed reforms threatened to disrupt the military chain of command. The real threat was to Pentagon dominance over intelligence collection agencies, a dominance that had over time gutted the Intelligence Community's ability to produce strategic intelligence that anticipated threats and sought to keep warfighters off the battlefield in the first place. Senator Pat Roberts (R-KS), chairman of the Senate Intelligence Committee, drove the point home on national television. Appearing on the November 21, 2004 edition of *Fox News Sunday*, Roberts declared, "I want to point something out. You know, I'm a former Marine. There are no ex-Marines. I am a former Marine, all right? I serve on the Armed Services Committee." His voice grew louder and his tone more angry as he continued: "No bill that I have seen . . . had anything to do with doing any harm to tactical intelligence in regards to that warfighter in the field . . . . There is no reason, if we do intelligence reform, that these agencies we are talking about, these so-called combat support agencies, will not continue to support the warfighter. Nobody is against that."[47]

Despite such rebuttals, intelligence reform still made little headway. As in earlier efforts, Pentagon opposition in 2004 had powerful allies on the House and Senate Armed Services Committees and other prodefense lawmakers who feared diminishing their own jurisdictions if intelligence reform succeeded. Opposition from House Armed Services Committee Chairman Duncan Hunter (R-CA) and House Judiciary Chairman James Sensenbrenner

(R-WI) grew so strong that on November 20, House Speaker Dennis Hastert (R-IL) pulled the intelligence reform bill from floor consideration. Senator Susan Collins (R-ME), one of the champions of intelligence reform, called November 20 "the weakest moment" in the 2004 reform battle.[48]

THE PRESIDENT: "GET THIS THING OFF OUR BACKS"

The 2004 intelligence reform bill also drew lukewarm public support from the president. "The president was not engaged," declared one democratic lawmaker. "For a long time the White House was in denial about the failure."[49] In press reports and interviews, officials and staffers in both parties agreed.[50] As one former Republican official put it, "The president . . . did absolutely nothing to stop Defense Department lobbying and did not engage after that time. . . . It was less the White House feeling the compulsion to do something. It was, 'Get this thing off our backs.'?"[51] Here, too, rational self-interest was to blame. President George W. Bush, like all presidents since Harry Truman, knew that successful intelligence reform required battling, and defeating, his own Department of Defense. Former Senator Gary Hart (D-CO) described the persistence of presidential reluctance this way:

> Imagine the president sitting in the room with a secretary of defense, Harry. The director of central intelligence says, "Mr. President, I cannot do my job unless I have authority over the entire range of intelligence." That's going to require Secretary of Defense. Harry down the table there to give up his intelligence agencies. I'm asking you to introduce legislation to get this to happen." Harry down the table is going to say, "Mr. President, if you do that, you'll destroy the Pentagon." That's just the kind of conversation that goes on.[52]

Congress ultimately passed the Intelligence Reform and Terrorism Prevention Act in December 2004, which created a new director of national intelligence and National Counterterrorism Center, among other changes. However, Pentagon opposition forced lawmakers to weaken substantially the new intelligence chief's legal authorities over two vital levers: control over budgets and personnel across the Intelligence Community. As one former official put it, "the language is fuzzy on both. . . . You're right back to cajoling, wheedling, trying to get cooperation."[53]

A LACK OF PROGRESS REPORT

Six years after the World Trade Center and Pentagon attacks, the U.S. Intelligence Community's worst problems endure. Although legislative, executive, and internal agency initiatives have made many changes to U.S. intelligence agencies, most have created halting progress. Some have made matters worse. None could be declared successes yet. In March 2005, three and a half years after 9/11, the Commission on the Intelligence Capabilities of the United States regarding Weapons of Mass Destruction (the Silberman-Robb Commission) released a report about another intelligence failure: analysis of Iraqi weapons of mass destruction in the run-up to the 2003 Iraq War. The commission found that the Intelligence Community was "dead wrong in almost all of its pre-war judgments."[54] The commission also found the causes of failure to be systemic. Despite the "laudable steps" taken to improve U.S. intelligence agencies, the commission noted that, "we believe that many within those agencies do not accept the conclusion that . . . the Community needs fundamental change if it is to confront the threats of the 21st century." The commission pointedly noted that time and time again, others had targeted the "same fundamental failings," without success. "The Intelligence Community is a closed world," the commission noted, "and many insiders admitted to us that *it has an almost perfect record of resisting external recommendations*" (emphasis theirs).[55]

WHO'S IN CHARGE?

The 9/11 Commission found that before September 11, "the intelligence community's confederated structure left open the question of who really was in charge of the entire U.S. intelligence effort."[56] This is still the case today, despite the creation of the director of national intelligence with the passage of the Intelligence Reform and Terrorism Prevention Act of 2004. Indeed, instead of enhancing coordination and centralization, the 2004 legislation has triggered a scramble for turf that has left the secretary of defense with greater power, the director of national intelligence with little, and the Intelligence Community even more disjointed. Many intelligence experts and officials believe that John Negroponte, who became the first director of national intelligence in April 2005, succeeded only in adding yet another bureaucratic layer to an already fragmented system.[57] When Negroponte abruptly announced his resignation in January 2007, his staff had already ballooned to 1,500 people, prompting outcries from members of Congress. "I don't see the leadership," noted Senator Dianne Feinstein (D-CA) in a Senate Intelligence Committee hearing. "What I see . . . is the growth of a bureaucracy over there. And it concerns me very much."[58]

Since 9/11, Pentagon dominance has grown rather than diminished. Details of Defense Department intelligence programs are classified, but public reports suggest an ever-widening expansion of units and activities that often duplicate existing capabilities in other agencies and are not well overseen by either the DNI or Congress. In 2002, the Defense Department quietly and successfully lobbied Congress to pass legislation consolidating Pentagon intelligence activities under a new position, undersecretary of defense for intelligence. In the words of former senior intelligence official John Gannon, the move added "more heft to what already was the IC's thousand pound gorilla."[59] The undersecretary of defense, Stephen Cambone, who served until 2007, dramatically increased the number of clandestine teams conducting secret counterterrorism operations and collecting information abroad—activities that had traditionally been performed by the CIA.[60] He also expanded Pentagon intelligence activities at home, transforming a small unit called the Counterintelligence Field Activity (CIFA)—which was created in 2002 to protect U.S. military installations from terrorist attack—into a sprawling agency with a 1,000-member staff, nine directorates, and wide-ranging responsibilities that include conducting terrorism investigations of Americans inside the United States.[61] By 2005, CIFA had the authority to give orders to approximately 4,000 Army, Air Force, and Navy investigators in the United States, in addition to its own staff, making its counterterrorism investigatory ranks equal to the FBI's.[62] One former senior defense intelligence official described CIFA's evolution this way: "They started with force protection from terrorists, but when you go down that road, you soon are into everything . . . where terrorists get their money, who they see, who they deal with."[63]

None of these activities came at the behest of Director Negroponte. Instead, from 2005 to 2007, the nation's first director of national intelligence labored unsuccessfully to exercise the powers he had on paper. For example, although the intelligence reform act gave the DNI power to transfer personnel across different agencies—a measure deemed critical for integrating the Community—within months of the new law, Secretary Rumsfeld issued a Defense Department directive that required Pentagon "concurrence" for any personnel transfers affecting defense intelligence agencies.[64] In October 2006, Representative Jane Harman (D-CA) blasted Secretary of Defense Rumsfeld, calling him "the best bureaucratic infighter in the history of America," and complained that "finding a way to outsmart" Rumsfeld on intelligence reform was "a high art" that had "not been mastered."[65]

Other agencies have resisted central management from the director of national intelligence as well. Between 2005 and 2006, a bureaucratic food fight erupted over the division of staffing and responsibilities between the CIA's Counterterrorist Center and the DNI's new National Counterterrorism Center. According to one DNI official, during the summer of 2005, even when DNI staffers requested additional parking at CIA headquarters, the CIA turned them down. "Nothing's changed," complained the official. "CIA still thinks they're in charge. They don't get that we *own* those parking spaces."[66]

In interviews, intelligence officials from a variety of agencies expressed grave concerns about the DNI's ability to forge the Intelligence Community into a coherent whole.[67] "The DNI," one noted, "is turning out to be nothing more than another layer on top of sixteen organizations."[68] Another issued an even more negative assessment. "The American public has been sold a bill of goods," he said. "When the next attack happens, an awful lot of people will say, 'How could this happen? We created a DNI.'?"[69] Even the DNI's creators share these concerns. In February 2006, Senator Susan Collins (R-ME), one of the chief architects of the 2004 intelligence reform bill, noted, "Director Negroponte has battles to fight within the bureaucracy, and particularly with the Department of Defense. DOD is refusing to recognize that the director of national intelligence is in charge of the intelligence community."[70] In April 2006, the House Intelligence Committee warned that the DNI was heading down the path toward becoming "another layer of large, unintended and unnecessary bureaucracy."[71] Committee Chairman Peter Hoekstra (R-MI) described the report as a "shot across the bow."[72] Ranking member Jane Harman (D-CA), another key player in the creation of the DNI, was even more critical. "The concept behind intelligence reform," she said on national television, "was to create a unified command structure . . . not a bureaucracy. We've said that Mr. Negroponte should stop calling himself ambassador. He's a director. In order to change cultures, you have to lead. You have to make some people mad at you. You have to send new signals."[73]

Instead of sending new signals, however, Negroponte resigned nine months later, leaving the top two DNI posts vacant at the same time. His departure led many to worry that turnover would further bog down the slow pace of reform. "I am deeply troubled by the timing of this announcement and the void of leadership at the top of our Intelligence Community," said Senate Intelligence Committee Chairman Jay Rockefeller (D-WV). "The leadership of the Intelligence Community is too important."[74] By March 2007, the Intelligence Community was in the full throes of leadership transition, with a new secretary of defense, a new undersecretary of defense for intelligence, a new director of national intelligence, a vacant deputy DNI slot, and a CIA leadership team that had been in place less than a year.

Information sharing and analysis, two critical shortcomings raised in the wake of 9/11, have not improved much and in some cases have gotten worse. In 2003, President Bush established the Terrorist Threat Integration Center to provide a hub for analyzing terrorism-related intelligence across the Community. TTIC confused the lines of authority at first, until the 2004 intelligence reform bill expanded the agency's mission and renamed it the National Counterterrorism Center (NCTC). Today, NCTC is widely considered to be one of most successful improvements in U.S. intelligence. Different agency officials now sit in the same room and draft collective analytic reports about terrorism. The Center also has developed a classified counterterrorism Web site, NCTC Online, which provides synthesized terrorism intelligence to policymakers, analysts, and a number of other consumers across the U.S. government.[75]

All that sounds good. Now consider this: Because NCTC's analysts have varying levels of security clearances and come from different agencies, they still see different pieces of information.[76] Most U.S. intelligence agencies have no experience conducting all-source analysis, so the personnel they assign to NCTC are learning on the job. As one senior government official put it, "Eleven organizations sent people to NCTC. Only two of them sent people who knew what they were doing."[77] Officials still resist sharing information with colleagues assigned from other agencies even when the rules allow it.[78] Fusing intelligence is done by humans, not computers; information is stored on nearly thirty separate, incompatible information networks. To access them all, NCTC analysts must use more than a half dozen different computers stacked underneath their desks. "It's a little scary,"

noted Senator Mike DeWine (R-OH) in a May 2006 Senate Intelligence Committee hearing. "[I]t's like we have duct-taped our systems together. Surely we can do better than this."[79]

This is the shining example. Information sharing in other parts of the Intelligence Community is far more problematic. In 2005 the Silberman-Robb Commission wrote that, "No shortcoming of the Intelligence Community has received more attention since the September 11 attacks than the failure to share information." Yet, despite "literally dozens" of Intelligence Community information sharing initiatives, including executive guidelines and statutory requirements, the commission found that only "minor advances" had been made.[80] The commission urged that the new director of national intelligence make improving the Community's information management system a top priority.[81]

The president quickly responded, appointing a career intelligence official named John Russack to develop a Community-wide information sharing system in June 2005. But Russack was initially given only a two-person staff to do the job.[82] He left seven months later. In December 2005, the 9/11 Commission's Public Discourse Project issued a report card assessing implementation of its recommendations. Information sharing efforts received a D.[83] In July 2006, another expert task force, this time from the Markle Foundation, concluded that improvements had been made, but found "turf wars and unclear lines of authority," officials who "still cling" to old ways of doing business, and a diminishing sense of commitment and determination to improve information sharing.[84] "[A]lmost five years since the terrorist attacks of September 11," the report concluded, "systematic, trusted information sharing remains more of an aspiration than a reality."[85] In January 2007, the Intelligence Community's chief information officer, Major General Dale Meyerrose, offered a similarly discouraging progress report. "The policy that's in place took three years to write, four years to coordinate, and we've not touched it in five," he told the Senate Intelligence Committee. Although Meyerrose noted that his office had been working hard to improve information sharing for over a year and that he expected to produce a series of proposals soon, he underscored that "most of the sharing issues we face are cultural and process rather than technology."[86]

Strategic analysis has not fared any better. In March 2005, the Silberman-Robb Commission found that the pressure to respond to current events was still driving out big picture thinking. "The Intelligence

Community we have today is buried beneath an avalanche of demands for 'current intelligence,'?" the commission noted.[87] While it found the "pressing need" to meet the tactical demands of military and other requirements necessary, the commission made clear that inattention to strategic analysis posed grave long-term consequences.[88] "Across the board," the commission wrote, "the Intelligence Community knows disturbingly little about the nuclear programs of many of the world's most dangerous actors. In some cases, it knows less now than it did five or ten years ago."[89]

A year later, strategic intelligence again topped the list of unresolved problems. At his May 2006 confirmation hearings to become CIA director, General Michael Hayden singled out rebuilding strategic intelligence as one of the agency's greatest challenges and his top priorities. "We must set aside talent and energy to look at the long view and not just be chasing our version of the current news cycle," Hayden declared, or else the United States would "be endlessly surprised." Hayden bluntly told the committee that doing so would not be easy because of the natural pressures to put current demands ahead of long-term needs. "I actually think it might be worse now than it has been historically," he said, noting that the twenty-four-hour news cycle as well as the operations tempo in Afghanistan, Iraq, and the war on terror have "suck[ed] energy into doing something into the here and now."[90] Outside the hearings, other intelligence officials echoed the theme. John McLaughlin, who served as the CIA's deputy director and then acting director, complained in May 2006 that the demand for instant information had made CIA analysts "the Wikipedia of Washington."[91] Carl W. Ford, Jr., a veteran intelligence official who served in both the CIA and State Department, was even more critical: "We haven't done strategic analysis for so long that most of our analysts don't know how to do it anymore," he told a reporter. Without "fundamental changes" in analysis, Ford noted, "we will continue to turn out the $40 billion pile of fluff we have become famous for."[92]

HUMAN INTELLIGENCE

The CIA's human intelligence capabilities have also made little progress since September 11. The reason: to date, the agency's approach to improving human intelligence has focused primarily on increasing the number of spies rather than improving quality or dramatically increasing nontraditional recruitment models to penetrate terrorist groups. In November 2004, the president issued a memorandum that directed the CIA to expand its spy ranks by 50 percent.[93] The agency responded, tripling the number of trained clandestine case officers from 2001 to 2006.[94] But to many intelligence veterans, this was precisely the wrong approach: success requires fewer and better spies operating differently, not more of the same.[95] "The conditions of looking for human intelligence are so different from the Cold War that just more money and more people doesn't guarantee you anything," said former CIA bin Ladin Unit Chief Michael Scheuer.[96] In interviews, several other clandestine case officers agreed. Here's how one CIA veteran described the problem:

> The core element to our business is access. In the Cold War, we wanted to recruit against bureaucracies, and so we were on the diplomatic circuit, we were out there, and that gave us access. We need access, somehow, we need to figure out how do you get access to people that are not on the diplomatic circuit. That's the enemy, that's where they are, that's their battlefield, that's their environment. We need to be in that environment. And we're not going to get there if we sit in the green zone in Baghdad. . . . The whole terrain has shifted, and we still, we haven't shifted with it, except to say, "we want to get back to basics."[97]

"If we were really serious about this," said another, "we would have said the NOC (nonofficial cover) is our primary model of how case officers are deployed. And the exception will be somebody sitting inside an embassy, writing telegrams. But we have never, ever even come close to that position. We have never even contemplated that."[98] John MacGaffin, a thirty-one-year veteran of the CIA's clandestine service, put it more bluntly: "Fifty percent more gets you to 'Stupid.' You'll get 50 percent more of what you've got now."[99]

THE FBI

The FBI has attempted the most ambitious changes, with perhaps the most disappointing results. Since 2001, the bureau has made counterterrorism its top priority; hired roughly 1,000 new special agents;[100] doubled its analyst corps;[101] created Field Intelligence Groups to integrate law enforcement and intelligence operations in the field offices; begun training some special agents alongside CIA clandestine case officers to enhance the bureau's human intelligence capabilities;[102] consolidated intelligence, counterterrorism, and counterintelligence functions into a single National Security

Branch run by a senior FBI official; and undertaken a massive technology modernization campaign.[103] Interviews with several FBI officials in 2006 and 2007 emphasized the same theme: the FBI is trying to transform itself. As one special agent put it, "We get it. We get it. We really do."[104]

Nevertheless, old law enforcement priorities and attitudes have been slow to change.[105] In 2005, forty-seven of the fifty-six field office heads still came from the Criminal Division.[106] Until 2007, newly hired special agents still received more time for vacation than counterterrorism training.[107] And analysts were still being given secretarial tasks. A 2005 Justice Department survey of more than 800 FBI analysts (two-thirds of the total employed by the FBI at the time)[108] found that on average, analysts were spending only half their time actually doing analysis.[109] Other duties commonly included answering phones, escorting visitors, and collecting the trash.[110] In personal interviews, one FBI analyst who had previous experience as a translator and analyst in another intelligence agency recalled having to spend a week watching repair workers so that FBI office security would not be compromised. One said he was required to work nights and weekends operating the switchboard and escorting the cleaning crew. Another told Justice Department officials that, "A lot of my job doesn't require a college education."[111] Twenty-seven percent of analysts surveyed said that the FBI's special agents—who dominate the bureau—"rarely" or "never" understood what capabilities they had or what functions they were supposed to be performing.[112] Field interviews by the Congressional Research Service and others confirmed the persistence of the old cops-and-robbers culture. As one special agent-in-charge put it, the special agents, not analysts, "will always be the center of the universe."[113]

Changing this law enforcement culture has proven particularly vexing.[114] In May 2006, one FBI official was caught short when asked by a reporter whether FBI agents really wanted to work in the bureau's new National Security Branch, which is the heart of the FBI's counterterrorism, counterintelligence, and intelligence activities. "Not really," the official admitted. "[Agents] say to me, 'Hey, I joined up to arrest people.'"[115] Another FBI official put it this way. "We are working for a better corporate sense of how we employ our resources. We are trying to turn ourselves into an organization that is intelligence driven which has historically been operations driven . . . [but] it's a huge evolutionary process. . . . It's like shifting the direction of an aircraft carrier in mid-stream. . . . Every

day it's a battle."[116] Even FBI Director Robert Mueller admitted that one of the bureau's most important continuing challenges is ensuring that "the persons who do not wear the badge and the gun have the equal respect" of others in the FBI. "We're developing that," Mueller noted in January 2007, but added, "We're not where we need to be."[117] In March 2007, the bureau's own Web site still classified FBI employees as either special agents or "professional support staff"—a term that lumped analysts together with secretaries, auto mechanics, janitors, and all other bureau employees.[118]

According to FBI officials, 2006 marked the beginning of a radical transformation in how FBI field offices used intelligence analysis.[119] Dubbed "domain awareness," the new initiative no longer held field office heads responsible for pursuing specific cases. Instead, the special agents-in-charge [SACs] of all fifty-six U.S. field offices were evaluated based on how well they understood the threats to their geographic jurisdictions, how well they identified information gaps surrounding key issues, and how well they devised programs to fill them. "This has been really over the last year a very dramatic shift in how we're approaching problems," noted FBI intelligence directorate chief Wayne Murphy in 2007. He added:

> If a year ago, I asked an SAC to define for me how they understood a particular problem, the way they defined their understanding was framed in terms of how many cases they had. What we've worked to do, and I think successfully, is to create a methodological approach to say you can't say you understand a problem if you define it by what you already know about it. You understand a problem if you have indices to understand it, you've investigated whether it's just smoke or whether there's really a fire there, and you've taken steps to close those knowledge gaps.[120]

As the above description suggests, the domain awareness initiative requires a better understanding of and respect for intelligence analysis. Importantly, however, FBI analysts remain only notional partners in this effort; bureau rules still mandate that senior positions in the field, including the top spot in every U.S. field office, be staffed by FBI special agents—or in the words of one bureau official, the people who "carry guns and risk their lives."[121] These rules mean that analysts must still do battle from below, convincing their special agent superiors that chasing information has as much value as chasing suspects. As one analyst put it, despite progress in domain awareness, "outreach to our own agency" remains an ongoing frustration.[122] John Gannon, a respected senior intelligence official who spent twenty-four years working with the FBI in various positions—including the CIA's analytic branch chief, chairman of the National Intelligence Council, and staff director of the House Homeland Security Committee—offered a more pessimistic assessment. "If you go to the Defense Intelligence [Agency or] if you're CIA," he told the Senate Intelligence Committee in January 2007, "you have analytic structures where any analyst who is working in those organizations can look right up the chain of command to the director, and it is all analytic managers who are reviewing the process and applying rigor to what is done. And ultimately, that analytic system can challenge the agent culture." But, he quickly added, "I don't think that can ever happen out of the FBI system as it is."[123]

Efforts to improve the bureau's antiquated technology systems have been even more feckless. In February 2005, Director Mueller announced he was scrapping the bureau's Trilogy technology modernization program—at the cost of nearly $200 million—because it did not work.[124] A new system, named Sentinel, is now underway. It is expected to cost an additional $425 million and will not be fully operational until 2009. In May 2006, four and a half years after 9/11, the Justice Department's Inspector General testified that, "the FBI still does not have a modern, effective case management records system."[125] Director Mueller himself called the technology modernization program his "greatest frustration." Reflecting on the bureau's continued technology weaknesses in early 2007, he noted:

> I would love to be able to go out and get a contractor and say, "okay, come in and fix it." Part of the problem is that you have to change your business practices, as well. We've probably had the same business practices in place for ninety-eight years of our existence. And one of the things you do *not* want to do is just tell the technologists to go ahead and change it without changing your business practices. We're in that process. If there's one area of impatience that I have, it's that area [emphasis his].[126]

These and other developments have led to a series of increasingly dire prognoses. In March 2005, the Silberman-Robb Commission noted with concern that the FBI's transformation into an intelligence organization "is still in doubt."[127] In December 2005, the 9/11 Commission issued more alarming warnings. "Reforms are at risk from inertia and complacency," the commission declared in its report card.

"[T]hey must be accelerated or they will fail."[128] And in May 2006, John Gannon issued this stark assessment to the Senate Judiciary Committee:

> The salient fact is that, approaching five years after 9/11, we still do not have a domestic intelligence service that can collect effectively against the terrorist threat to the homeland or provide authoritative analysis of that threat. It is not enough to say that these things take time. It could not be clearer from the Intelligence Community's experience over the past 25 years that it is extraordinarily difficult to blend the families of intelligence and law enforcement, and that the Bureau's organizational bias toward the latter for deep-seated historic reasons—is powerful and persistent.[129]

Although Gannon had argued for some time that the FBI was the right agency to develop a domestic intelligence capability after 9/11, by the spring of 2006 he had given up. "[W]atching the FBI struggle with its new national intelligence mandate and recalling earlier interagency 'culture wars' in my career," Gannon declared, "I have changed my mind. I now doubt that the FBI, on its present course, can get there from here."[130]

MAKING HEADLINES MORE THAN PROGRESS

Instead, it is fair to say that U.S. intelligence agencies since 9/11 have made more headlines than progress. The CIA has been an agency in turmoil. In September 2004, former House Intelligence Committee Chairman Porter Goss succeeded George Tenet as CIA Director.[131] His twenty-month tenure was steeped in controversy. Several senior agency officials quit in protest over Goss's weak management and fierce personality clashes with Goss's management team, who were viewed as overly partisan. Then, in May 2006, Goss announced his surprise resignation amidst revelations that one of his closest aides, Kyle "Dusty" Foggo, was under investigation in a corruption probe linked to former Congressman Randy "Duke" Cunningham (R-CA). It was a scandal made for the movies, with press reports that Foggo had attended poker parties with prostitutes in—of all places—the Watergate Hotel.

News headlines throughout 2005, 2006, and 2007 were also full of revelations about the Intelligence Community's secret activities and the ensuing political furor over their legality and publication. In November 2005, the *Washington Post* reported the existence of a top secret system of foreign CIA prisons or "black sites" that were being used to hold and interrogate some of the most important al Qaeda detainees.[132] One month later, the *New York Times* revealed that the National Security Agency had been wiretapping phone calls between parties in the United States and foreign countries, including American citizens suspected of al Qaeda connections—all without court warrants.[133] The NSA wiretapping program ignited a political firestorm about the program's legality, the security risks of revealing it, and whether White House, Justice Department, and intelligence officials had properly briefed members of Congress. Then in May 2006, *USA Today* reported that the National Security Agency had also secretly collected the domestic telephone records of millions of Americans and was mining the data to find clues of terrorist threats.[134] When General Michael Hayden appeared before the Senate Intelligence Committee for his CIA director confirmation hearings on May 18, scandal, not reform, was the main topic of conversation. As Committee Chairman Pat Roberts (R-KS) noted at the opening of the hearing, "the public debate in regard to your nomination has been dominated not by your record as a manager or your qualifications, the needs of the CIA, its strengths and its weaknesses and its future, but rather the debate is focused almost entirely on the presidentially authorized activities of another agency."[135] Finally, in March 2007 a Justice Department inspector general report found that the FBI had improperly used provisions of the PATRIOT Act to gather telephone, bank, and other information about American citizens. Bipartisan outrage erupted on Capitol Hill, with Democratic committee chairmen vowing to hold more hearings.[136]

ADAPTATION IN PERSPECTIVE

Some will argue that the assessment above is unduly harsh. The overwhelming consensus in Washington is that while much work remains, U.S. intelligence agencies are making progress. Scores of officials whose names are not known and whose work goes unheralded have dedicated their professional careers to one goal: getting the right information into the right hands to protect American lives. The steady refrain is that talented officials are working hard, and that we are safer now than before. As one FBI official remarked, "What bugs me the most is that the public believes the FBI is not an organization with truly dedicated people who want to make a

difference. They are not here to make a lot of money. They do it for very altruistic reasons. The public often loses sight of that."[137]

Yes, tremendous effort has been expended, individuals have made extraordinary sacrifices, and improvements have been made. But some perspective is in order. Effort often does not translate into performance. And progress is not the same as success. The question is not whether the CIA and FBI are better equipped than they were on September 10, 2001—certainly a low standard. Nor is it whether the CIA and FBI have smart and dedicated officials; they always have. The question is whether these two agencies, and the rest of the U.S. Intelligence Community, have adapted to the point where they now stand a reasonable chance of preventing the next catastrophe. The evidence is not encouraging.

It is often said that change takes time. But it is now sixteen years since the end of the Cold War and the U.S. Intelligence Community is still struggling to develop the rudimentary building blocks to combat terrorism. History is filled with examples where more was accomplished in far less time. Twelve years after the Soviet Union stunned the world by launching Sputnik, the first satellite, the United States landed a man on the moon and won the space race. In 1945, just four years after Japan's surprise attack decimated much of the Pacific fleet at Pearl Harbor, the United States had built a fighting force that had crossed two oceans and defeated both Germany and Japan.[138] Within two years of the end of World War II, American leaders had helped create the United Nations and launched the Marshall Plan to rebuild Europe. And in 1787, it took less than one hundred working days to draft the U.S. Constitution.[139]

Yet here we are. Although al Qaeda has not attacked the U.S. homeland since 9/11, there is little evidence to suggest that effective intelligence is the reason. As one Congressional Intelligence Committee lawmaker noted in the fall of 2005, "We still stink at collecting. We still stink at analysis . . . all the problems we set out to correct are still there."[140]

CONCLUSION

This chapter's argument can be summed up in two words: Organization matters. The structures, cultures, and incentives of U.S. intelligence agencies critically influence what they do and how well they do it. Structures create capabilities and jurisdictions, determining who performs which tasks by what authority at what level of competence. Culture has an invisible but powerful hold, coloring how intelligence officials view the world and their role in it. Incentives unavoidably give greater weight to certain issues, jobs, and interests, encouraging some activities more than others. Individual leadership also plays a vital role in the policy process. Too often, however, discussion of foreign policy success and failure treats individuals as the only important factors, ignoring the powerful organizational forces in the background. Although organization alone cannot guarantee good policy outcomes, it can significantly affect what gets done, and how well. At the dawn of the Cold War, Senator Henry M. "Scoop" Jackson (D-WA) underscored the importance of getting the organizational basics right, noting, "Organization by itself cannot assure a strategy for victory in the cold war. But good organization can help, and poor organization can hurt."[141] Decades later, the 9/11 Commission, the Silberman-Robb Commission, and the House and Senate Intelligence Committees all confronted a radically different enemy but came to the same conclusion.

Criticizing U.S. intelligence agencies is nothing new. As early as 1948, the *New York Times* castigated a newly created CIA as "one of the weakest links in our national security."[142] The stakes, however, have never been higher. The spread of weapons of mass destruction, the information revolution, and the rise of transnational terrorist networks have changed the old rules and realities of international relations. For the first time in history, great power does not bring security. It is now the weak who threaten the strong. And it is intelligence, not military might, which provides the first and last line of defense. The United States' ability to protect itself hinges on whether U.S. intelligence agencies built for a different enemy at a different time can adapt. Many obstacles stand in the way. The crux of the problem lies in the enduring realities of American politics, and success requires finding ways to overcome them.

QUESTIONS FOR FURTHER DISCUSSION

1. How have institutional matters affected the performance of America's secret agencies?
2. Is it likely that institutional reforms in the intelligence community prior to the 9/11 attacks would have prevented this disaster?
3. How would you go about improving the relationship between the FBI and the CIA, both with quite different bureaucratic cultures?

4. Do you share Professor Zegart's pessimism about the intelligence reforms of 2004? How could the Intelligence Reform and Terrorism Prevention Act of 2004 be amended to achieve the outcomes she desires?

ENDNOTES

1. Interview, November 2006.
2. Interview, March 2007.
3. Interview, February 2006.
4. Adam Clymer, "A Nation Challenged: The Political Parties; Disaster Forges a Spirit of Cooperation in a Usually Contentious Congress," *New York Times*, September 20, 2001, p. B3.
5. Interviews with four congressional staffers, April 2002 and October 2005.
6. The PATRIOT Act included three provisions that President Clinton had tried, but failed, to pass in the mid-1990s: "roving wiretaps," which enabled the FBI to obtain a single court warrant for multiple telephone and communications devices used by a single terrorism suspect rather than requiring separate court orders for each device; expanded FBI access to telephone and other records in terrorism cases; and lower restrictions governing the FBI's use of "pen registers" or "trap and trace" devices to monitor the identities of those sending and receiving communication in terrorism cases. For a discussion of the statutory changes President Clinton sought but never won, see President William Clinton, "President's Statement on Antiterrorism Bill Signing," April 24, 1996, Clinton Materials Project (National Archives). http://clinton6.nara.gov/1996/04/1996–04–24-president-statement-on-antiterrorism-bill-signing.html (accessed February 3, 2006); *Congress and the Nation*, vol. IX (1993–96) (Washington, DC: Congressional Quarterly Press), pp. 727–33. For an analysis of the provisions of the PATRIOT Act, see Charles Doyle, "The USA Patriot Act: A Legal Analysis," *Congressional Research Service Report RL 31377*, April 15, 2002.
7. Interview, October 2005.
8. Interview, July 2006.
9. In the House, 357 representatives voted in favor of the PATRIOT Act, while 66 voted against it.
10. Interview, July 2006.
11. Walter Pincus, "Rumsfeld Casts Doubt On Intelligence Reform: Changes Suggested by Presidential Panel," *Washington Post*, April 9, 2002, p. A17; interview with former government official, November 2005. This report was the first of two classified reviews of U.S. intelligence led by Scowcroft.

12. Walter Pincus, "Rumsfeld Casts Doubt On Intelligence Reform: Changes Suggested by Presidential Panel," *Washington Post*, April 9, 2002, p. A17.

13. In 2003 the National Imagery and Mapping Agency was renamed the National Geospatial-Intelligence Agency.

14. Walter Pincus, "Rumsfeld Casts Doubts On Intelligence Reform: Changes Suggested by Presidential Panel," Washington Post, April 9, 2002, p. A17.

15. Interview, November 2005.

16. Spencer Ackerman, "Small Changes," *New Republic*, December 13, 2004, p. 12; interview with former government official, October 2005; interview with former government official, November 2005.

17. Spencer Ackerman, "Small Change," *New Republic*, December 13, 2004, p. 12.

18. "Remarks by the President in Address to the Nation," June 6, 2002, Office of the Press Secretary, the White House, available at http://www.whitehouse.gov/news/releases/2002/06/20020606-8.html (accessed July 18, 2006).

19. President George W. Bush, "A Bill to Establish a Department of Homeland Security," submitted to Congress June 18, 2002, available at http://www.whitehouse.gov/news/releases/2002/06/20020618-5.html (accessed July 19, 2006).

20. See fox example, Government Accountability Office, *Department of Homeland Security: A Comprehensive and Sustained Approach Needed to Achieve Management Integration*, GAO 05–139, March 16, 2005.

21. Amelia Gruber, "Squeezing Services," *Government Executive Magazine*, March 1, 2005, available at http://www.govexec.com/features/0305-01/0305-01sls4.htm (accessed July 18, 2006).

22. Todd Datz, "From the Ground Up," *CSO Magazine*, March 1, 2004.

23. Quoted in Michael Crowley, "Bush's Disastrous Homeland Security Department," *New Republic*, March 15, 2004, p. 17.

24. Susan B. Glasser and Michael Grunwald, "Department's Mission was Undermined from Start," *Washington Post*, December 22, 2005, p. A01.

25. *The Homeland Security Act of 2002*: Public Law 107–296, 107th Cong., 2nd sess., November 25, 2002.

26. Quoted in Susan B. Glasser and Michael Grunwald, "Department's Mission was Undermined from Start," *Washington Post*, December 22, 2005, p. A01.

27. "Consolidating Intelligence Analysis: A Review of the President's Proposal to Create a Terrorist Threat Integration Center," Senate Committee on Homeland Security and Governmental Affairs, 108th Cong., 1st sess., February 14, 2003 and February 26, 2003.

28. Press release, "Senator Collins Receives Answers on Terrorist Threat Integration Center: Satisfied with Response, but Concerned by Its Delay," April 20, 2004, Senate Committee on Homeland Security and Governmental Affairs.

29. Task Force on National Security in the Information Age, Markle Foundation, *Creating a Trusted Network for Homeland Security: Second Report of the Markle Foundation Task Force*, December 2003, p. 3.

30. Richard A. Falkenrath, "The 9/11 Commission Report: A Review Essay," *International Security* 29, 3 (Winter 2004–05): 172.

31. Joby Warrick, Joe Stephens, Mary Pat Flaherty, and James V. Grimaldi "FBI Agents Ill-Equipped to Predict Terror Acts," *Washington Post*, September 24, 2001, p. A01.

32. Editorial, "The Spy Puzzle," *New York Times*, November 4, 2001, p. 12.

33. These were: "Joint Inquiry Staff Statement, Part I," HPSCI and SSCI hearing, 107th Cong., 2nd sess., September 18, 2002; "The Intelligence Community's Knowledge of the September 11 Hijackers Prior to September 11, 2001," 107th Cong., 2nd sess., September 20, 2002; "The FBI's Handling of the Phoenix Electronic Communication and Investigation of Zacarias Moussaoui Prior to September 11, 2001," HPSCI and SSCI hearing, 107th Cong., 2nd sess., September 24, 2002; "Counterterrorism Information Sharing with Other Federal Agencies and with State and Local Governments and the Private Sector," HPSCI and SSCI hearing, 107th Cong., 2nd sess., October 1, 2002; "Joint Inquiry Staff Statement: Proposals for Reform within the Intelligence Community," HPSCI and SSCI hearing, 107th Cong., 2nd sess., October 3, 2002; "Joint Inquiry Staff Statement: Hearing on the Intelligence Community's Response to Past Terrorist Attacks Against the United States from February 1993 to September 2001," HPSCI and SSCI heating, 107th Cong., 2nd sess., October 8, 2002; "Joint Inquiry Staff Statement," HPSCI and SSCI hearing, 107th Cong., 2nd sess., October 17, 2002. The staff statements were submitted in open hearings which also featured testimony by senior government officials, key intelligence personnel, and outside experts.

34. Eleanor Hill, "Joint Inquiry Staff Statement, Part I," HPSCI and SSCI hearing, 107th Cong., 2nd sess., September 18, 2002.

35. Interview, April 2002.

36. TTIC later became the National Counterterrorism Center.

37. Senate Select Committee on Intelligence, *US. Intelligence Community's Prewar Intelligence Assessments on Iraq*, 108th Cong., 2nd sess., July 9, 2004.

38. Senate Select Committee on Intelligence, *U.S. Intelligence Community's Prewar Intelligence Assessments on Iraq,* 108th Cong., 2nd sess., July 9, 2004.

39. Analysis from based on full text LexisNexis searches of ABC, CBS, NBC, CNN, Fox News, MSNBC, CNBC, and *The News Hour with Jim Lehrer* between July 22, 2004 and December 10, 2004.

40. Interview, November 2005.

41. Quote in Philip Shenon and Douglas Jehl "House Proposal Puts Less Power in New Spy Post," *New York Times,* September 25, 2004, p. Al.

42. Interview, October 2005.

43. Interview, October 2005. See also comments made by Representative Jane Harman and Senator Pat Roberts, *Fox News Sunday,* November 21, 2004.

44. Representative Jane Harman, Intelligence Reauthotization News conference with members of the House Permanent Select Committee on Intelligence, March 30, 2006. Harman went on to say that she believed the law had overcome Pentagon objections and provided adequate statutory budget authority to the DNI, but needed more vigorous leadership to be effective.

45. Myera's letter can be found in Intelligence Reform and Terrorism Prevention Act of 2004 Conference Report, *Congressional Record* S11939–S12010, appendix. Available at www.fas.org/irp/congress/2004_cr/sl20804 .html (accessed February 22, 2006).

46. Letter from Richard Cheney to Senator Les Aspin, March 17, 1992, available at http://www.fas.org/irp/congress/1992_cr/cheney1992.pdf (accessed February 16, 2006); letter from Deputy Secretary of Defense John White to Senate Armed Services Committee Chairman Strom Thurmond (R-SC), April 29, 1996, described in Walter Pincus, "Panels Continue Impasse on Intelligence," *Washington Post,* June 7, 1996, p. A21.

47. Pat Roberts, *Fox News Sunday,* November 21, 2004.

48. Quoted in Walter Pincus, "Intelligence Bill Clears Congress," *Washington Post,* December 9, 2004, p. A4.

49. Interview, October 2005.

50. Interviews with four officials, October 2005 and November 2005. See also Mary Curtius, "Intelligence Reform Looks Like a Lame Duck for Now," *Los Angeles Times,* November 12, 2004, p. A24; Charles Babington and Mike Allen, "White House View of Stalled Bill in Doubt," *Washington Post,* November 24, 2004, p. A4; Michael Isikoff and Bleanor Clift, "Intel Reform: Did Bush Push. Hard?" *Newsweek,* December 6, 2004, p. 6; Julie Hirschfield Davis, "Intelligence Reform in Limbo," *Baltimore Sun,* November 23, 2004, p. 1A; Elisabeth Bumiller and Philip Shenon, "Bush Urged to Get Pentagon In Step on Intelligence Bill," *New York Times,* November 23, 2004, p. A20.

51. Interview, November 2005.

52. Interview, May 2004.

53. Interview, November 2005.

54. Letter from the Honorable Laurence H. Silbmeran and The Honorable Charles S. Robb to the president, March 31, 2005, reprinted in *Silberman-Robb Commission Report,* preface.

55. *Silbeman-Robb Commission Report,* p. 6.

56. *9/11 Commission Report,* p. 93.

57. Walter Pincus, "Some Lawmakers Doubt DNI Has Taken Intelligence Reigns," *Washington Post,* February 2, 2006, p. A09; interview with Congressional Intelligence Committee member, October 2005; interview with former CIA official, February 2006. See also Richard A. Posner, *Countering Terrorism* (Oxford: Rowman & Littlefield, 2006); Scott Shane, "In New Job, Spymaster Draws Bipartisan Criticism," *New York Times,* April 20, 2006, p. A1; John Lehman, "Are We Any Safer?" *Proceedings of the U.S. Naval Institute,* September 2006.

58. Senate Select Committee on Intelligence, "Progress Made on Intelligence Reform" 110th Cong., 1st sess., January 23, 2007.

59. John Gannon, written testimony submitted to the Senate Judiciary Committee, hearing on FBI oversight, 109th Cong., 2nd, sess., May 2, 2006.

60. Eric Schmitt, "Clash Foreseen Between CIA and Pentagon," *New York Times,* May 10, 2006, p. A1.

61. Barton Gellman and Dafna Linzer, "Pushing the Limits of Wartime Powers," *Washington Post,* December 18, 2005, p. A01.

62. Walter Pincus, "Pentagon's Intelligence Authority Widens; Fact Sheet Details Secretive Agency's Growth from Focus on Policy to Counterterrorism," *Washington Post,* December 19, 2005, p. A10.

63. Quote in Walter Pincus, "Pentagon's Intelligence Authority Widens; Fact Sheet Details Secretive Agency's Growth from Focus on Policy to Counterterrorism," *Washington Post,* December 19, 2005, p. A10.

64. Eric Schmitt, "Clash Foreseen between CIA and Pentagon," *New York Times,* May 10, 2006, p. A1.

65. Jane Harman, Remarks at the Second Annual Rand/Terrorism Early Warning Group Conference, Santa Monica, CA, October 19, 2006. Secretary Rumsfeld announced his resignation on November 8, one day after Democrats regained control of both the House and Senate in the 2006 midterm elections.

66. Interview, July 2005.

67. Interviews with six current and former intelligence officials, October 2005, November 2005, and February 2006.

68. Interview, May 2006.

69. Interview, February 2006.

70. Quote in Scott Shane, "Year into Revamped Spying, Troubles and Some Progress," *New York Times*, February 28, 2006, p. A12.

71. House Permanent Select Committee on Intelligence, Intelligence Authorization Act for Fiscal Year 2007, 109th Cong., 2nd sess., April 6, 2006, Report 109–411.

72. Quote from *Fox News Sunday*, April 23, 2006.

73. Ibid.

74. Press release, office of Senator Jay Rockefeller, January 4, 2007, available online at http://www.senate.gov/rockefeller/news/2007/pr010407a.html (accessed March 9, 2007).

75. Admiral John Scott Redd, Director, National Counterterorism Center, "Statement for the Record," Senate Foreign Relations Committee hearing, 109th Cong., 2nd sess., June 13, 2006.

76. Michael Isikoff and Daniel Klaidman, "Look Who's Not Talking—Still," *Newsweek*, April 4, 2005, p. 30.

77. Interview, March 2007.

78. Michael Isikoff and Daniel Klaidman, "Look Who's Not Talking—Still," *Newsweek*, April 4, 2005, p. 30.

79. Senator Mike DeWine, Hearing on the Nomination of General Michael Hayden to be the director of CIA, SSCI, 109th Cong 2nd sess., May 18, 2006. See also comments on NCTC by former Acting CIA Director John McLaughlin, Council on Foreign Relations Meeting, "Intelligence Support to the Military," Washington, DC, April 4, 2006; Helen Fessenden, "The Limits of Intelligence Reform," *Foreign Affairs* 84, 6 (November–December 2005), pp. 106–20.

80. *Silberman-Robb Commission Report*, p. 320.

81. Ibid. pp. 320–21. Information sharing with state and local agencies is worse. See Richard Falkenrath, "Prepared Statement of Testimony before the Senate Committee on. Homeland Security and Governmental Affairs," 109th Cong., 2nd sess., September 12, 2006.

82. Shane Harris and Greta Wodele, "Bureaucracy Hinders 9/11 Commission. Recommendations," *National Journal*, January 13, 2006.

83. *Final Report on 9/11 Commission Recommendations,* 9/11 Public Discourse Project, December 5, 2005, available at www.9–11.pdp.org (accessed December 5, 2005), p. 3.

84. Zoe Baird and James Barksdale, chairmen, Markle Foundation Task Force on National Security in the Information Age, *Mobilizing Information to Prevent Terrorism: Accelerating Development of a Trusted Information Sharing Environment,* July 2006, p. 7.

85. Ibid., p. 1.

86. Testimony of Major General Dale Meyerrose, associate director of National Intelligence and chief information officer, Senate Select Committee on Intelligence, "Progress Made on Intelligence Reform," 110th Cong., 1st sess., January 23, 2007.

87. *Silberman-Robb Commission Report*, p. 5.

88. Ibid.

89. Ibid.

90. Testimony of Michael Hayden, Senate Select Committee on Intelligence, "Hearing on the Confirmation of General Michael B. Hayden to become Director of the Central Intelligence Agency," 109th Cong., 2nd sess., May 18, 2006.

91. Quoted in Tim Weiner, "Langley, We Have a Problem," *New York Times*, May 14, 2006, Week in Review, section 4, p. 1.

92. Quoted in Tim Weiner, "Langley, We Have a Problem," *New York Times*, May 14, 2006, Week in Review, section 4, p. 1.

93. Office of the Press Secretary, the White House, "Memorandum for the Director of Central Intelligence," November 23, 2004, available at www.wlhitehouse.gov/news/releases/2004/11/print/20041123–5.html (accessed February 8, 2006). See also hearing of the House Select Committee on Homeland Security, Subcommittee on Intelligence, Information Sharing, and Terrorism Risk Assessment, 109th Cong., 2nd sess., May 10, 2006; U.S. Government Accountability Office, "Information Sharing: The Federal Government Needs to Establish Policies and Processes for Sharing Terrorism-Related and Sensitive but Unclassified Information," GAO-06-385, March 17, 2006.

94. Mark Mazzetti, "CIA Making Rapid Strides for Regrowth," *New York Times*, May 17, 2006, p. A1.

95. Interviews with four former clandestine officials, December 2004 and June 2005; interview with member of Congressional Intelligence Committee, October 2005; Siobhan Gorman, "Fewer Better Spies Key to Intelligence Reform, Former Official Says," *National Journal*, March 18, 2005.

96. Quoted in Siobhan Gorman, "Fewer Better Spies Key to Intelligence Reform, Former Official Says," *National Journal*, March 18, 2005.

97. Interview, December 2004.

98. Interview, December 2004.

99. Quoted in Siobhan Gorman, "Fewer Better Spies Key to Intelligence Reform, Former Official Says," *National Journal*, March 18, 2005.

100. Federal Bureau of Investigation, "The FBI Work-force by the Numbers," www.fib.gov/page2/aug04/workforce082504.htm (accessed February 10, 2006).

101. Testimony of Director Robert Mueller, House Appropriations Subcommittee on Science, State, Justice and Commerce and Related Agencies, 109th Cong., 1st sess., September 14, 2005.

102. Interview with FBI official October 2006; interview with former CIA official, November 2006.

103. The National Security Branch was created in September 2005. For more see the FBI's Web site at http://www.fbi.gov/hq/nsb/nsb_faq.htm (accessed July 25, 2006).

104. Interview, October 2006. Six other current FBI officials expressed similar views in interviews conducted during the fall of 2006.

105. Chitra Ragavan, "Fixing the FBI," *U.S. News and World Report*, March 28, 2005, pp. 19–30; *Silberman-Robb Commission Report*, pp. 451–57; hearing of the House Appropriations Subcommittee on Science, State, Justice and Commerce and Related Agencies, 109th Cong., 1st sess., September 14, 2005.

106. *Silberman-Robb Commission Report*, p. 453.

107. In early 2007, the bureau added three more weeks of national security training to its eighteen-week new agent training program. Interview with senior law enforcement official, March 2007; testimony of John S. Pistole, deputy director of the FBI, Senate Select Committee on Intelligence, "Intelligence Reform," 110th Cong., 1st sess., January 23, 2007.

108. Office of the Inspector General, Audit Division, U.S. Department of Justice, *The Federal Bureau of Investigation's Efforts to Hire, Train, and Retain Intelligence Analysts*, Audit Report 05–20, May 2005, p. 116.

109. Ibid., p. 64.

110. Ibid., pp. x–xi, *Silberman-Robb Commission Report*, p. 455; hearing of the House Appropriations Subcommittee on Science, State, Justice and Commerce and Related Agencies, 109th Cong., 1st sess., September 14, 2005; testimony of Glenn A. Fine, Inspector General, U.S. Department of Justice, Senate Judiciary Committee hearing, "FBI Oversight," 109th Cong., 2nd sess., May 2, 2006.

111. Office of the Inspector General, Audit Division, U.S. Department of Justice, *The Federal Bureau of Investigation's Efforts to Hire, Train, and Retain Intelligence Analysts*, Audit Report 05–20, May 2005, p. 86.

112. Ibid., p. xi.

113. Quote in testimony by Todd Masse, House Appropriations Subcommittee on Science, State, Justice and Commerce and Related Agencies, 109th Cong., 1st sess., September 14, 2005.

114. For an excellent discussion of the differences between law enforcement and intelligence cultures, see Richard A. Posner, *Countering Terrorism* (Oxford: Rowman & Littlefield, 2006), chapter 5.

115. Quoted in Jeff Stein, "FBI Under the Gun," *CQ Weekly*, May 1, 2006, p. 1152.

116. Interview, October 2006.

117. Interview, January 2007.

118. Available at http://www.fbi.gov/aboutus/faqs/faqsone.htm (accessed March 8, 2007).

119. Interview with Robert Mueller, January 2007; interview with Wayne Murphy, February 2007; interview with two FBI special agents, October 2006.

120. Interview, February 2007.

121. Interview, October 2006.

122. Interview, October 2006.

123. Testimony before the Senate Select Committee on Intelligence, "Intelligence Reform," 110th Cong., 1st sess., January 25, 2007.

124. U.S. Department of Justice, "The Federal Bureau of Investigation's Management of the Trilogy Information Technology Modernization Project," pp. 27–30; Senate Appropriations Subcommitee on Commerce, Justice, and State, the Judiciary, and Related Agencies, "FBI Information Technology Modernization," hearing, 109th Cong., 1st sess., February 3, 2005; Jonathan Krim, "FBT Rejects Its New Case File Software: Database Project Has Cost Nearly $170 Million," *The Washington Post*, January 14, 2005, p. A05.

125. Glenn A. Fine, Inspector General, United States Department of Justice, testimony before the Senate Judiciary Committee, "FBI Oversight," 109th Cong., 2nd sess., May 2, 2006.

126. Interview, January 2007.

127. *Silberman-Robb Commission Report*, p. 454.

128. *Final Report on 9/11 Commission Recommendations*, 9/11 Public Discourse Project, December 5, 2005, available at www.9–11.pdp.org (accessed December 5, 2005), p. 3.

129. John Gannon, written testimony submitted to the Senate Judiciary Committee, hearing on "FBI Oversight," 109th Cong., 2nd. sess., May 2, 2006.

130. Ibid.

131. Goss was effectively demoted three months later when Congress passed the Intelligence Reform and Terrorism Prevention Act, which established the director of national intelligence.

132. Dana Priest, "CIA Holds Terror Suspects in Secret Prisons," *Washington Post*, November 2, 2005, p. A1.

133. James Risen and Eric Lichtblau, "Bush Lets U.S. Spy on Callers without Courts," *New York Times*, December 16, 2005, p. A1.

134. Leslie Cauley, "NSA has Massive Database of Americans' Phone Calls," *USA Today*, May 11, 2006, p, 1A. Note: significant details of this original report were subsequently recanted, although the program was verified by additional sources in other reports. See Frank Ahrens and Howard Kurtz, "USA Today Takes Back Some of NSA Phone-Records Report," *Washington Post*, July 1, 2006, p. A02. The call records do not include contents of the conversations.

135. Senator Pat Roberts, hearing on the nomination of General Michael Hayden to be director of the CIA, Senate Select Committee on Intelligence, 109th Cong., 2nd. sess., May 18, 2006.

136. Quoted in David Stout, "F.B.I. Head Admits Mistakes in Use of Security Act," *New York Times*, March 10, 2007, p. A1.

137. Interview, October 2006.

138. The Silberman-Robb Commission first made this comparison, p. 452.

139. National Archives, "Constitution of the United States: Questions and Answers," http://www.archives.gov/national-archives-experience/charters/constitution_q_and_a.html (accessed July 25, 2006).

140. Interview, October 2005.

141. Henry M. Jackson, "How Shall We Forge a Strategy for Survival?" Address before the National War College (April 16, 1959), in Karl F. Inderfurth and Loch K. Johnson, eds., *Decisions of the Highest Order: Perspectives on the National Security Council* (Pacific Grove, CA: Brooks/Cole, 1988), pp. 78–81.

142. Hanson W. Baldwin, "Intelligence—I; One of the Weakest Links in Our Security, Survey Shows—Omissions, Duplications," *New York Times*, July 20, 1948, p. 6.

28. INTELLIGENCE AND THE GLOBAL STRUGGLE AGAINST ISIS

JAMES J. WIRTZ

Developing an accurate estimate of the threat posed by the Islamic State of Iraq and Syria created significant challenges for intelligence analysts. Not only did the new actor adopt different goals from its predecessor, Al Qaeda in Iraq, it harnessed new social media outlets to recruit young people from around the world by offering excitement, romance and a way to escape the bane of adolescence, overbearing parents. Al Qaeda was highly deliberate in conducting its operations and selective in its recruiting; the Islamic State encourages all sympathizers to commit mayhem in their communities.

Intelligence failures can take many forms and can have many causes. When using the term "intelligence failure," however, it is important to be specific about what intelligence analysts and organizations have failed to do or to predict. Indeed, the term "intelligence failure" generally denotes an absence of a timely warning about the occurrence of a discrete event. In other words, if intelligence analysts fail to estimate what is about to occur, where and when it will occur, and why it is occurring (and to provide that estimate to policymakers in time for them to take appropriate action) then the label "intelligence failure" is likely to be used to characterize recent events.

Because of a lack of comprehensive data, it is impossible to judge definitively how well intelligence agencies actually succeed at this demanding task: the literature on intelligence failure selects on the dependent variable, so to speak. Failures rather than successes gain the lion's share of attention from scholars, practitioners, officials, and the public alike. Nevertheless, intelligence analysts sometimes get it right. On the eve of the Battle of Midway during World War II, naval intelligence analysts and officers accurately estimated that Midway would be the target of a Japanese attack, and actually positioned the U.S. fleet to launch a devastating carrier air strike against the Japanese force nearing Midway.[1] In October 1962, U.S. intelligence analysts, after first predicting such an eventuality was unlikely,[2] detected the Soviet deployment of medium-range and intermediate-range ballistic missiles in Cuba, providing the John F. Kennedy administration with enough warning to take constructive action. Such "moments of splendid" to use Sherman Kent's phrase, are admittedly rare, but they do in fact occur.[3]

By contrast, general warnings of deteriorating conditions that are not accompanied by discreet event predictions are not enough to prevent analysts from being accused of responsibility for an "intelligence failure." In the weeks leading up to Pearl Harbor, for example, the Franklin D. Roosevelt administration was aware that Japanese-American relations had reached a nadir. Naval officers and intelligence analysts actually expected some sort of Japanese military action in the Far East and had even expressed profound misgivings about forward deploying the U.S. fleet to Pearl Harbor, a move that they believed left the fleet vulnerable and badly positioned to respond to the outbreak of hostilities in the Pacific.[4] Similarly, in the days before the September 11, 2001 terrorist attack on the World Trade Center and Pentagon, the U.S. intelligence community delivered a strategic warning to the White House. The highly classified and community-wide product, the President's Daily Brief (PDB), stated that al-Qaeda had expressed interest in hijacking commercial airliners. Excerpts of the August 6, 2001 PDB, published in the 9/11 Commission report, also made it clear that al-Qaeda operatives were quite active in the United States.[5] Nevertheless, despite the fact that the system was indeed "blinking red" in December 1941 and September 2001, Pearl Harbor and 9/11 are today synonymous with the term "intelligence failure" in the annals of the intelligence studies literature.

So what is exactly meant by labeling the U.S. intelligence community's response to the rise of Islamic State in Iraq and the Levant (ISIL) in 2013 and early 2014 as an "intelligence failure"? The chapter posits that the so-called ISIL intelligence failure indeed has much in common with the events leading up to both Pearl Harbor and the 9/11 attacks. On the one hand, both intelligence and press reports provided accurate and timely warning of a deteriorating security situation within Iraq produced by what was believed to be a resurgence of al-Qaeda. On the other hand, the intelligence community, and the press for that matter, failed to anticipate the political-military shock that placed ISIL at the forefront of U.S. domestic politics and international diplomacy: the June 2014 fall of Mosul and the collapse of the Iraqi Army. This was an especially alarming turn of events: approximately 1,500 ISIL fighters prevailed over a 30,000-man Iraqi force that simply disintegrated after years of U.S. training and material support. In other words, the intelligence community managed to issue some strategic warnings about the deteriorating military situation in Iraq, but it failed to provide a compelling estimate of the true nature of the emerging threat or to warn policymakers about how it would likely manifest. Not surprisingly, the term "intelligence failure" now surrounds the rise of ISIL.

Nevertheless, if one explores this so-called intelligence failure, one can begin to understand the hurdles faced by the intelligence community in developing an accurate and timely estimate of ISIL and a nuanced reassessment of exactly what the intelligence community failed to understand about the rise of the Islamic State. To offer this reassessment, the chapter will first suggest that there were several unique elements about ISIL, which represented a departure from the "al-Qaeda" model of international terrorism. It will also focus on the structural constraints inherent in the U.S. intelligence community that made "ISIL" a difficult target. The chapter will then offer some concluding observations about the so-called ISIL intelligence failure and how it might constitute a harbinger of things to come.

THE ISIL ESTIMATE

In the twenty-first century, both experts and average citizens have a detailed and generally horrifying image of ISIL, whose rank and file routinely and gleefully commit and digitize unmentionable atrocities against Shia, "sheikists," Christians, Yazidis, apostates, prisoners of war, and even their own members suspected of disloyalty. In 2014, for instance, *Newsweek* magazine provided an impressive and rather strange list of ISIL's opponents: Salafis, Arab oil sheiks, Shiites, the governments and militaries of the United States, Iran, Iraq, Syria and Turkey, Hamas, Hezbollah, and al-Qaeda.[6] Indeed, the list of ISIL's opponents continues to grow and now includes the Lebanese Army, the Kurdistan Worker's Party, the Islamic Front (rebel groups in Syria allied with al-Qaeda) and the Free Syrian Army. Nevertheless, it is important not to allow hindsight to guide one's judgments about the intelligence community's assessments of ISIL. Various aspects of ISIL were actually rather unique on the world stage, combing to create what amounts to a new type of non-state actor. The elements that made ISIL unique also made it a difficult target for the U.S. intelligence community.

THE LACK OF NET ASSESSMENT

The origins of ISIL can be traced back to the chaos and anarchy that gripped Iraq in the aftermath of the Second Gulf War and the fall of the Ba'athist regime in Baghdad. Coalition Provisional Authority (CPA) Proclamations Number 1 and Number 2, which banned the Ba'ath Party and dismantled the Iraqi Army in May 2003, left approximately the top 1 percent of the personnel in the Iraqi government and military outside the new Iraqi government (around 20,000 individuals). CPA 1 and 2 did not destabilize the situation on the ground in Iraq, but its impact was amplified by the fact that the Iraqi army literally "self-demobilized" rather than face the brunt of the international coalition arrayed against it during the Second Gulf War. Iraq's defeat and the initial decisions made by the CPA abruptly changed the political balance in Iraq. Specifically, Saddam Hussein's government and officer corps was dominated by Sunnis and in the aftermath of the war this leadership was left adrift in a country now dominated by a Shia majority. L. Paul Bremer, the top civilian administrator of the CPA, noted that the U.S. government had little real choice in the matter of "De-Baathification":

> 80% of the population, the Kurds and the Shia, were very clear about the likely results of our recalling the army. Each had heard rumors that some American soldiers favored recalling Saddam's army. The Kurdish leaders—Masoud Baranzi and Jalal Talabani—told me if you recall the army, we Kurds will secede from Iraq. The secession of the Kurds from Iraq then or today or in the future will, in my view, bring on a major regional war. It will start civil war in Iraq. But it would also likely bring on a major regional war because neither the Iranians nor the Turks could tolerate an independent Kurdistan. The Shia leaders said they interpreted these rumors as showing our intention to install "Saddamism without Saddam." The Shias had been cooperating with the Coalition following guidance from Grand Ayatollah Ali al-Sistani. So the political arguments against recalling the army were even stronger than the practical arguments.[7]

Bremer notes that the U.S. response to this dilemma was to create a new Iraqi army. But this was politically impossible (and as events would show, unrealistic) to re-mobilize Ba-athist Iraqi units.[8]

Although Bremer is correct to note that De-Baathification was limited in scope, the political and security impact of postwar policies greatly curtailed the ability of Sunni personnel to participate in Iraq's new government and security forces. In 2003, for instance, the CPA formed the Iraqi Governing Council, whose membership was allocated along sectarian lines. The decision, according to Isaac Kfir, "heightened sectarianism, as representation was based on quotas that only reinforced the simmering age-old divisions, instead of being meritocratic."[9] In hindsight, it is clear that these disenfranchised individuals constituted a disgruntled group that would be politically and ethnically attracted to a Suni-centric, anti-Shia ideology—the kind of ideology advanced by ISIL. What is not clear in hindsight, however, is the hurdle that the U.S. intelligence community would have to overcome to make the connection between De-Baathification and the rise of ISIL. The community would have had to engage in a "net assessment" to identify the second- and third-order risks created by De-Baathification. In other words, they would have had to make a deliberate estimate of how U.S. policy was producing unintended and unwanted consequences. Organizational culture, however, leaves the U.S. intelligence community incapable of conducting this type of net assessment.

Two normative theories, reflected in the culture of analysts, make it difficult to conduct a net assessment as a routine part of the analytical process. One, most closely associated with the work of Sherman Kent, focuses on ensuring the independence of intelligence analysts when it comes to providing information to policymakers. Kent's thinking, which shaped the formation and early evolution of the U.S. intelligence community, identifies the importance of political and policy detachment when it comes to producing relevant and effective finished intelligence. The strength of Kent's approach is that it preserves the independence of analysts by separating the intelligence community from the overt pressure or organizational and interpersonal incentives that can shape intelligence to conform to current policy or the personal and political biases of policy makers.[10] Yet, by creating a strong barrier against politicization, Kent's prescriptions can separate intelligence too completely from policymakers. In this framework, policy assessment is beyond the scope of the intelligence community. The other operational framework, most closely associated with the reforms instituted in the mid-1980s by then Director of Central Intelligence Robert M. Gates, focuses on providing "actionable" intelligence, which is information of immediate use to policymakers. To produce actionable intelligence, analysts have to maintain close working relationships with policymakers, literally looking into officials' inboxes to make sure finished intelligence addresses important policy issues of the day.[11] Nevertheless, following the Gates model too closely can create its own set of problems. There is a possibility that policymakers will pose biased questions to the intelligence community to guarantee that analysis favorable to their positions will emerge; there is also the possibility that they will fail to pose the correct questions, leading to an incomplete understanding of the challenges they face. By following the Gates model, the only way that the U.S. intelligence community would have linked the growth of ISIL to De-Baathification is if they were directly asked that question by senior officials. It is hard to believe that, barring some extremely dire set of circumstances, policymakers would deliberately task the U.S. intelligence community to assess the role of U.S. postwar policy in terms of the rise of sectarian violence in Iraq.

ISIL was a particularly difficult target for the U.S. intelligence community because an accurate estimate of the origins of the movement would have needed to recognize the impetus it received from U.S. policy. An accurate assessment, *ceteris paribus*, would have amounted to a critique of a decade's worth of American policy vis-à-vis Iraq. In terms of organizational culture, this sort of assessment is largely beyond the capability of the U.S. intelligence community. Indeed, other weak or misleading assessments produced by the U.S. intelligence community have been tied to the absence of a net assessment (i.e., a failure to account for the impact of U.S. policy on an unfolding situation). The failure of the Central Intelligence Agency to foresee the fall of the Shah or the fact that U.S. policy had stymied Saddam Hussein's efforts to acquire WMD are cases in point.[12] In any event, without this net assessment, it was impossible to develop an accurate estimate of the potential scope and appeal of ISIL. U.S. policy made ISIL appealing to more than true radicals: It made it appealing to Sunnis who were politically disenfranchised following the Second Gulf War.

AN IDEOLOGICAL TWIST: ISIL IS NOT AL-QAEDA

As Erik Dahl's contribution to the volume makes clear, beginning in mid-2013, the intelligence community repeatedly sounded the tocsin when it came to deteriorating conditions in Iraq. These estimates, however, primarily focused on the growing strength and activity of al-Qaeda in Iraq (AQI), a Sunni-based organization inspired by the exploits of Osama Bin Laden, which would eventually morph into ISIL. In hindsight, it is clear that ISIL embraced a different political agenda than al-Qaeda; indeed, it was a completely different animal. ISIL and al-Qaeda are different organizations with different goals that operate different ways and pose different threats. As a result, just warning about an increasing "al-Qaeda like" threat in Iraq tended to mischaracterize the real danger posed by the nascent ISIL. And, as Dahl's commentary demonstrates, there was nothing in the intelligence reporting that suggested that something fundamentally different from al-Qaeda was about to emerge out of the chaos of the Syrian civil war and political unrest in Iraq. Dahl's chapter demonstrates that the intelligence community did in fact notice that things were indeed heating up in Syria and Iraq; what they failed to note was that the very nature of the threat was changing.

Admittedly, experts debate the finer points about al-Qaeda's objectives and operational style, but it is possible to characterize the organization and its objectives in a general way to highlight some important differences between al-Qaeda and ISIL. Al-Qaeda was ultimately about influencing events within the Muslim world, especially Saudi Arabia. Nevertheless, by 1997 Bin Laden turned his attention to non-Muslim states in an effort to drive Western influence from the Middle East, leaving targeted regimes unable to resist the "internal Jihad" that would follow. To undertake this strategy, al-Qaeda employed a centrally controlled, hierarchical organization that specialized in finely crafted operations mostly directed against transportation targets.[13] The organization employed the Internet to communicate to operatives and to disseminate its message to a global audience, but it was cautious when it came to vetting recruits and disseminating operationally sensitive information. It utilized trained and apparently "cleared" operatives who evidenced relatively sophisticated tradecraft. Al-Qaeda also operated a sort of "franchise system," lending its stamp of approval to local and regional organizations but apparently only after the new franchisees agreed to take a degree of guidance from al-Qaeda Central.[14] And, as Bruce Hoffman has recently noted, Bin Laden remained engaged in all facets of the al-Qaeda operation until his demise in 2011, despite reports suggesting he was "out of sync" or disengaged from al-Qaeda and its affiliates around the world.[15]

Before his death, Bin Laden had crafted a strategy for al-Qaeda Central and its affiliates. According to U.S. military intelligence, Bin Laden had apparently articulated a strategy for al-Qaeda to continue to preserve its traditional goals while taking steps to preserve itself in the face of U.S. pressure:

- attriting and enervating America so that a weakened United States would be forced out of Muslim lands and therefore have neither the will nor the capability to intervene;
- taking over and controlling territory, creating the physical sanctuaries and save havens that are al-Qaeda's lifeblood;
- declaring "emirates" in these liberated lands that would be safe from U.S. and Western intervention because of their collective enfeeblement.[16]

In a remarkably prescient analysis, Hoffman identifies what in hindsight are the origins of ISIL, which emerged when AQI applied Bin Laden's strategy to the deteriorating security situations in Iraq and Syria:

> Syria has . . . long been an Al Qaeda *idée fixe*. . . . that country has even more of the characteristics of the same type of perfect *jihadi* storm than Afghanistan possessed three decades ago: widespread support among the Arab world, the provision of financial assistance from wealthy Gulf supporters, a popular cause that readily attracts foreign volunteers, and a contiguous border facilitating the movements of these fighters into and out of the declared battle space.[17]

Syria also offers a base in the Arab heartland, and offered AQI and opportunity to do battle with the "hated Shi'a apostate Alawite minority" in the country.[18]

In hindsight this "perfect jihadi storm" began to build by mid-2012. First, with the death of Bin Laden, al-Qaeda's efforts to centrally direct its franchisees seems to have lost traction, freeing affiliates to act more independently. Second as AQI and other al-Qaeda allies (e.g., the Syrian rebel organization Japhat al Nusra il-Ahli al Shaam) attempted to exploit conditions in Syria. They escalated their operations and began to enjoy success. Third, to better exploit these opportunities, a new organization, ISIL, began to displace AQI and to embrace different objectives and strategies. ISIL embraced a patently sectarian strategy that captured disaffected Sunnis and directed them against Shia and Alawites. Fourth, ISIL also shifted to "internal Jihad," by at least initially focusing on the establishment of its own safe haven in territory formerly controlled by Syria and Iraq. Fifth, ISIL began to recruit disenfranchised, disillusioned, and marginalized youth not just from Arab countries but from the entire world. In other words, unlike al-Qaeda central, ISIL did not focus on developing trained and vetted operatives for complex operations but instead welcomed all sorts of fellow travelers and adventure seekers to fill an emerging army. ISIL reportedly even set up training camps for youth in Ninewa province in Iraq and Aleppo and Raqqah in Syria to bolster its ranks with children taken from captured territory.[19] Needless to say, al-Qaeda central never resorted to this sort of tactic to increase the number of its operatives.

Viewed in this manner, ISIL again posed a difficult target for the U.S. intelligence community.

An accurate estimate of the threat posed by ISIL involved more than just an assessment of growing numbers of fighters or growing combat capability (i.e., the ability to deploy crew-served weapons or field relatively large military units). An accurate estimate would have needed to account for the opportunities presented by the death of Bin Laden and the chaos of the Syrian civil war, the impact of a shift to internal jihad, a sectarian strategy, and a change in recruiting preferences. The real intelligence challenge did not involve recognizing that the potential for death and destruction was increasing: The intelligence community actually sounded that warning. Instead, it was to understand that AQI was being displaced by ISIL and that these organizations were fundamentally different entities. And, once again, the U.S. intelligence community would have benefited from a net assessment that would have focused on the externalities created by the death of Osama Bin Laden.[20]

These issues were in fact acknowledged by an intelligence scholar/practitioner working in the Office of the Director of National Intelligence. When asked if the rise of ISIL represented a failure on the part of the U.S. Intelligence Community, he responded with the question, "When do you give it a name?"[21] In other words, ISIL represented a departure among violent non-state actors. It was difficult to anticipate because its whole was greater than the sum of its contributing parts and enabling factors. It was new and different, making it difficult to define until it actually existed.

ISIL IS NOT A "NORMAL" CLANDESTINE ACTOR

In the years immediately following the 9/11 terrorist attacks, scholars were particularly interested in searching for clandestine links between different types of non-state actors. There was a fear that criminal networks, black marketers and money laundering operations, smugglers, grassroots political or ethnic movements, proliferation entrepreneurs, or terrorist groups might somehow collaborate by sharing services, networks, or personnel for mutual advantage.[22] This type of collaboration was neither unknown nor unprecedented. In 1993, for instance, a Chinese narcotics organization in New York City linked up with a human-trafficking operation and branched into smuggling illegal immigrants into California by transferring paying clients from ocean-going vessels to smaller fishing boats near San Francisco and Moss Landing.[23] What was of special concern was the use of similar drug-smuggling networks to move terrorists or weapons of mass destruction across international borders. In other words, there was a fear that multifaceted organizations would emerge when different types of non-state actors pooled resources and communication and logistical networks.

ISIL is different in this regard. It is a multifaceted, entrepreneurial enterprise that exploits opportunities by pursuing a variety of objectives simultaneously. It is not a network of different non-state actors (i.e., the traditional fear); but instead it is a non-state actor that undertakes multiple activities that in the past required specialized entities. For instance, it can be characterized as a political movement to create its own state. Alternatively, it can be characterized as a commercial operation intended to exploit black market trade, especially by selling the oil production under its control. It also can be characterized as a sectarian movement, exploiting Sunni hostility toward Shia and other minority groups (Christians, Yazidis, etc.) in areas under its control. Sometimes, it appears to be a way for disenfranchised Ba'athists to gain political control over local areas. More recently, it has branched out into a global terrorist network that uses operatives or self-radicalized individuals to carry our relatively unsophisticated but deadly attacks on Western targets in revenge for Western kinetic operations against its forces in the areas that it controls. It could even be characterized as a youth movement, reaching out to disaffected adolescents who seek liberation from local constraints (i.e., their parents).

ISIL also possess an especially dangerous threat because it is the first terrorist organization that exploited Internet-enabled social media for its own nefarious purposes. Al-Qaeda Central rode the rails of the Information revolution and globalization to undertake precision strikes at intercontinental ranges, but ISIL used social media such as Twitter and Facebook, platforms that emerged around 2006, to communicate highly personalized messages to young people around the world. These messages were framed to appeal to young people and speak a language that young people best understand. They offered the prospect of adventure, romance, and escape from the constraints of overbearing parents: the type of message that has a universal appeal to a key demographic. German

intelligence officials, for example, have reported that almost 700 people had left Germany to join ISIL, many of which were characterized as "normal teens."[24] ISIL uses a host of new media that incorporate types of audio and visual messaging that are easy for teenagers to understand but are often incomprehensible to most adults. Indeed, many adults are completely unfamiliar with even the "Apps" used to communicate to young people. According to Kathleen Bouzis:

> The group utilizes numerous communication platforms including Snapchat, Kik, Twitter, ASK.fm, Facebook, Youtube, Whatsapp, and others. Its multiplatform social media messaging targets a broad recruitment audience in at least 23 languages and is part of the reason for ISIL's estimated 31,500 fighters. ISIL has also reached out to computer-savvy youth hacking networks that have conducted pro-ISIL attacks on over two hundred websites. These hacks included banners that read "I love you ISIS" and are targeted at seemingly arbitrary websites such as the University of New Brunswick Student Union.[25]

For individuals whose significant reality exists in cyberspace, not in the physical reality of everyday life, social media takes on a special importance that displaces family, friends, school, the workplace, etc. In other words, ISIL's appeal is to the young and impressionable audience that "lives" in cyberspace, an appeal that has more to with the discontents of adolescence than the exigencies of jihad. Social media provides the group with an especially potent recruiting tool. This audience and this tool simply did not exist in the years preceding the 9/11 attacks. At least in its international manifestation, ISIL might in fact be best characterized as a youth movement—a sort of pied piper to restless adolescents everywhere.

An accurate estimate of the threat posed by ISIL would have required an assessment of how a new technology, "social media," could be innovatively employed by a non-state actor to open new communication and recruitment strategies, broadening its base of international support. ISIL can thus be seen as a form of technological surprise in the sense that it pioneered an innovative application of an emerging technology. Although the political use of social media—tweets, false news stories, and personalized political messages delivered by anyone with access to a Facebook account—was obviously unheard of before 2007, in the aftermath of the 2016

U.S. Presidential election, it is now a fixture in our social reality. ISIL pioneered the use of this new media to increase its appeal to a global youth audience.

THEORETICAL MUSINGS

In his recent edited volume on the impact of intelligence organizations since 1945, Paul Maddrell and his contributors offer an important observation about the ability of intelligence organizations to warn policymakers about untoward events.[26] Intelligence organizations and the policymakers they serve tend to operate within a common view of the world that channels analysis along relatively narrow paths. If unfolding events fit within scope of this analytical and policy consensus, then intelligence agencies often provide useful and relevant analysis to policymakers. If unfolding developments are beyond this shared consensus, however, then it is unlikely that intelligence analysts will be able to provide timely warning to policymakers. Failures of omission and commission lie behind this observation. Questions that need to be addressed might never be raised by analysts or policymakers because they seem irrelevant to this shared consensus. And if discordant analysis somehow manages to emerge from intelligence agencies, it is likely to be altered to fit the shared consensus or ignored as an irrelevant outlier. A government culture that is shaped by bureaucratic, social, and political influences inevitably places some limits on what the intelligence agencies understand and address. When a threat suddenly emerges from outside these frames of common consensus and expectation, they can be difficult to recognize. ISIL was just such a threat.

The preceding analysis suggests several factors that made ISIL a difficult target for the U.S. intelligence community. First, a net assessment would have greatly facilitated an accurate estimate of the threat posed by ISIL, but the U.S. government, not to mention the U.S. intelligence community, lacks a formal mechanism to evaluate not only the success or failure of U.S. policy but to determine if U.S. policy is producing externalities that are leading to a deteriorating international situation. Admittedly, the impact of De-Baathification on the security situation in Iraq remains a hotly debated topic. Nevertheless, it appears that the U.S. intelligence community did not directly address how disenfranchising thousands of Sunnis might bolster AQI and inflame sectarian tensions in Iraq. Ironically, the "fundamental attribution error" (i.e., "we had no

choice") echoes in the explanations offered by policymakers for the possible link between the rise of AQI/ISIL and De-Baathification. Similarly, the death of Osama Bin Laden in 2011 was touted as a great success for U.S. counter-terrorism policy. Nevertheless, questions about unintended consequences (i.e., the impact on al-Qaeda franchisees) never seemed to be entertained. *Everyone* seems to have forgotten that no government policy is universally good or bad but instead represents a mix of positive and negative effects. The idea that the U.S. government would have undertaken a net assessment to better understand the externalities created by the death of Osama Bin Laden, even in hindsight, appears farfetched. The question itself was beyond the intelligence consensus, and the intelligence community rarely conducts this type of net assessment. In other words, if net assessment was critical to the ISIL estimate, the occurrence of an "intelligence failure" appears to be overdetermined.

Second, as other contributors to the volume note, the rise of ISIL contained a theological and religious component, which is difficult to detect and assess within the U.S. intelligence consensus. The separation of church and state in the American political context runs deep, restricting the ability of the U.S. intelligence community to monitor the way theological differences influence Islamic fundamentalists. Mark Stout, for instance, has noted that this failure to understand the interaction between Islam and terrorism slowed an accurate appreciation of al-Qaeda:

> This prejudice against religion manifested itself in the IC no less than in the rest of the government. Lt. Gen. James Clapper, who had led the DIA [Defense Intelligence Agency] from 1991 to 1996, recalls no discussion of religion whatsoever during that time. For its part the CIA [Central Intelligence Agency] "veered toward 'hard fact' reporting (names, dates, places and the like) creating an environment in which consideration of the divine did not fit comfortably. The result was that analysts tended to address terrorism either through ethnic or national lenses (despite the fact that this enemy explicitly denigrated such distinctions) or simply focused on the tactical mechanics of the problem. In essence, the IC projected its self-image onto the enemy. . . .[27]

Because an accurate estimate of the menace posed by ISIL required a nuanced appreciation of theological or ideological differences between ISIL and al-Qaeda, developing this estimate was something that did not easily fit within U.S. intelligence culture. As Stout notes, stark assessments of the interaction between Islam and terrorism, which were admittedly not particularly nuanced, were injected into intelligence debates by outsiders four-years after the September 11, 2001 terror attacks.[28] Because its operational style and agenda find their roots in theological differences with other Islamic fundamentalists, ISIL posed a difficult target for those operating within the U.S. intelligence consensus.

Third, although Americans launched the information revolution, rushing to exploit the opportunities created by the impact of Moore's Law on everyday life, they take both a "technical" and rather "utopian" view of the impact of emerging technology on the human condition. In the view of the creators of the information revolution, new technologies are supposed to drive a steady improvement in the human condition as they increase productivity, disseminate best practices, and empower individuals at the expense of bureaucracies and governments.[29] Outside of this rather positive-sum view of technology, however, Americans, along with other proponents of the information revolution, are slow to focus on the externalities created by said revolution or to envision the social, political, and strategic impact of this new technology.[30] Other strategic and intelligence cultures now appear far more adept at estimating the broad societal, political impact of the information revolution and are more adept at exploiting the new possibilities created by the emergence of cyberspace.[31] In other words, grasping that social media could have a profound impact on politics and society is not necessarily the forte of the U.S. intelligence community. Recognition that there is an "Information Revolution 2.0" underway is now entering our collective consciousness but only after other groups—ISIL in particular—recognized the true political and social opportunities created by this new technology. Although it appears counterintuitive, the ISIL intelligence failure might be based on a failure to assess properly the impact of technology on society.

CONCLUSION

There is an old saying among analysts that comes to mind when one offers judgments about the performance of the U.S. intelligence community against ISIL: "there is no such thing as a policy failure, only intelligence failure." In other words, regardless of the performance of intelligence analysts,

they will be blamed when policymakers encounter a policy setback. With that said, it really is impossible to tell what, if anything, went wrong inside the U.S. intelligence community until a complete accounting is made of the classified warnings and estimates that accompanied the rise of ISIL. The U.S. intelligence community might have issued detailed and profound warnings about the nature and implications of the rise of ISIL without having any discernible impact on U.S. policymakers. This sort of situation is not unprecedented. Prior to the Nazi invasion of the Soviet Union, national intelligence agencies, diplomats and even foreign governments provided a string of detailed and compelling warnings to the Soviet government with no real effect. Sometimes, policy is impervious to intelligence.

More realistically, however, the rise of ISIL constituted a very modern and maddening conundrum to the U.S. intelligence community. It emerged out of a complex interaction of theological debate, sectarianism, opportunism, and technological innovation that produced a new type of non-state actor on the world stage. It represented an abrupt and dangerous departure from conventional wisdom, from policy expectations, from what was considered to be socially, politically and strategically possible. ISIL constituted an abrupt change. In fact it was the speed of this change, not necessarily the transformation of AQI to ISIL, that made the ISIL estimate so difficult. And because the pace of change in international affairs continues to accelerate, the ISIL "intelligence failure" might in fact be a harbinger of things to come.

QUESTIONS FOR FURTHER DISCUSSION

1. How would "net assessment" have warned of the possible rise of ISIS?
2. How are non-state actors exploiting social media?
3. Is it fair to say that the rise of ISIS was accompanied by an intelligence failure?
4. Do you think senior intelligence managers have ever used Snapchat?

ENDNOTES

1. Gordon W. Prange with Donald M. Goldstein and Katherine V. Dillon, *Miracle at Midway* (New York: Penguin Books 1982).
2. The Central Intelligence Agency Special National Intelligence Estimate 85-3-62 dated 19 September 1962 stated that the Soviet Union was unlikely to deploy

ballistic missiles to Cuba because such a move would be deemed as too risky by the Kremlin. See James J. Wirtz, "Organizing for Crisis Intelligence: Lessons from the Cuban Missile Crisis," in James G. Blight and David A. Welch (eds.) *Intelligence and the Cuban Missile Crisis* (London: Frank Cass, 1998), pp. 120-149; and Peter S. Usowski, ""John McCone and the Cuban Missile Crisis: A Persistent Approach to the Intelligence-Policy Relationship," *International Journal of Intelligence and Counterintelligence* Vol. 2. No. 4 (Winter 1988), pp. 547-576.

3. In the words of Sherman Kent, collecting photographic evidence of Soviet efforts to deploy missiles in Cuba was a "moment of splendid," Kent quoted in Loch Johnson, *National Security Intelligence* (Cambridge: Policy 2012), p. 50.

4. Navy officers wanted the Pacific fleet to return to the West Coast to prepare for war and believed that the lack of facilities at Pearl Harbor made forward deployment a hollow deterrent that only served to give the American public a false sense of confidence in U.S. defenses in the Pacific. When its commander, Admiral J.O. Richardson, failed to convince his superiors to reposition the fleet in California, he penned a message to President Franklin D. Roosevelt that led to his relief: "The senior officers of the Navy do not have the trust and confidence in the civilian leadership of this country that is essential for a successful prosecution of a war in the Pacific," see George W. Baer, *One Hundred Years of Sea Power: The U.S. Navy, 1890-1990* (Stanford: Stanford University Press, 1994), p. 151.

5. *9/11 Commission Report*, pp. 261-262. https://9-11 commision.gov/report/911Report.pdf

6. Kurt Eichenwald, "ISIS's Enemy List: 10 Reasons the Islamic States is Doomed," *Newsweek* September 8, 1014. http://www.newsweek.com/2014/09/19/isiss-enemy-list-10-reasons-islamic-state-doomed-268953.html

7. Interview with L. Paul Bremer, "De-Baathification and Dismantling the Iraqi Army," *Moments in Diplomatic History*. http://adst.org/2016/01/de-baathification-and-dismantling-the-iraqi-army/

8. Bremer retells a story that demonstrates that it indeed might have been impossible to reconstitute the Iraqi army: "In the spring of 2004, the Marines were trying to subdue violence in the western city of Fallujah. The commanding general of the Marines decided, apparently on his won, to recall a brigade of the old Iraqi Army there. . . . The recall of this single brigade caused a political crisis in Baghdad and among Iraqis

everywhere. Several Iraqi ministers resigned or threatened to resign. Several members of the Governing Council tendered their resignations . . . . Worse when the recalled brigade was sent by the Marines into Fallujah, instead of helping to restore order, the entire unit went over to the enemy itself and had to be disbanded," Ibid.

9. Isaac Kfir, "Social Identity Group and Human (In)Security: The Case of Islamic State in Iraq and the Levant (ISIL)," *Studies in Conflict and Terrorism* 38:1, p. 238.

10. Sherman Kent, *Strategic Intelligence for American World Policy* (Princeton: Princeton University Press, 1946).

11. H. Bradford Westerfield, "Inside Ivory Bunkers: CIA Analysts Resist Mangers' 'Pandering'—Part II," *International Journal of Intelligence and Counterintelligence* 10 (Spring 1997), pp. 19–54; Richard K. Betts, "Politicization of Intelligence: Costs and Benefits," *Paradoxes of Strategic Intelligence*, eds. Richard K. Betts and Thomas Mahnken (London: Frank Cass, 2003), pp. 59–79.

12. James J. Wirtz, "The Art of the Intelligence Autopsy," *Intelligence and National Security* Volume 29, Issue 1 2014, pp. 1-8.

13. Rohan Gunaratna and Aviv Oreg, "Al Qaeda's Organization Structure and its Evolution," *Studies in Conflict and Terrorism* 33:12, pp. 1043-1078.

14. Under pressure from the international coalition arrayed against it, Al-Qaeda Central, according to Isaac Kfir, came to promote franchises aimed at instill[ing] its ideology and agenda. It became "more identified with an ideology rather than operating as a traditional, hierarchical, terrorist organization, committing acts of terror." Kfir, p. 233.

15 Bruce Hoffman, "Al Qaeda's Uncertain Future," *Studies in Conflict and Terrorism* 36:8, p. 639.

16. U.S. Special Operations Command 2012 Intelligence Estimate quoted by Hoffman, pp. 640-641.

17. Hoffman, p. 644.

18. Ed Husain, "Syria; Why al Qaeda is Winning," *National Review Online*, 23 August 2012. Available at http://www.nationalreview.com/articles/314685/syria-why-al Qaeda-winning-ed-husain

19. Kathleen Bouzis, "Countering the Islamic State: U.S. Counterterrorism Measures," *Studies in Conflict and Terrorism* 38:10, p. 887.

20. This was the issue that set Bruce Hoffman's pen to paper in early 2013 – the possibility that Al-Qaeda Central, to say nothing about its franchisees, might have not been terminally damaged by Bin Landen's death, see Hoffman.

21. Author interview September 20, 2016.

22. James Russell and James Wirtz (eds), *Globalization and WMD Proliferation: Terrorism, Transnational Networks and International Security* (New York: Routledge, 2007).

23. Richard C. Paddock and Katherine Edwards, "300 Illegal Chinese Immigrants Arrested: Smuggling Boats try to take Refugees ashore South of San Francisco. It is the third Foiled attempt in three weeks," *Los Angeles Times* June 3, 1993. http://articles.latimes.com/1993-06-03/news/mn-42768_1_san-francisco

24. Florian Flade, Carolin George and Per Hinrichs, "Why 2 'Normal' Teens Joined ISIS," OZY.com www.ozy.com/true-story/why-2-normal-teens-joined-isis/61629

25. Bouzis, p. 888.

26. Paul Maddrell (ed.), *The Image of the Enemy: Intelligence Analysis of Adversaries Since 1945* (Washington, D.C.: Georgetown University Press, 2015).

27. Mark Stout, "American Intelligence Assessments of the Jihadists, 1989-2011, in Paul Maddrell (ed.), *The Image of the Enemy: Intelligence Analysis of Adversaries Since 1945* (Washington, D.C.: Georgetown University Press, 2015). p. 263.

28. Stout, p. 264.

29. Bill Gates, The Road Ahead (New York: Penguin, 1996); Mark Tovey (ed.), *Collective Intelligence: Creating a Prosperous World At Peace* Oakton, Virginia: Earth Intelligence Network, 2008,

30. James J. Wirtz, *"Blogging in the World Cafe,"* International *Journal of Intelligence & Counterintelligence* Vol. 22, No. 2 Summer 2009, pp. 357-359.

31. Dima Adamsky, *The Culture of Military Innovation: The Impact of Cultural Factors on the Revolution in Military Affairs in Russia, the US and Israel* (Stanford: Stanford University Press, 2010); and James J. Wirtz, "The Russian Integration of Cyber Power into Grand Strategy," in Kenneth Geers (ed.) *Cyber War in Perspective: Russian Aggression Against Ukraine* (Tallinn: NATO Cooperative Cyber Defence Centreof Excellence. 2015), pp. 29-38.

From James J. Wirtz, "When do You Give it a Name? Theoretical Observations about the ISIS Intelligence Failure," in Feisal al-Istrabadi and Sumit Ganguly, eds. *The Future of ISIS: Regional and International Implications* (Washington, D.C.: The Brookings Institution, 2018): 67–85. Reprinted with permission.

29. INTELLIGENCE, POLICY, AND THE WAR IN IRAQ

PAUL R. PILLAR

The purpose of intelligence is to provide decision-makers with reliable, timely, actionable information that might illuminate the policy choices before them. That entire *raison d'état* is destroyed when the decision-makers (or intelligence officers) twist the information to suit policy needs (or career-advancement opportunities)—the "politicization" of intelligence that is taboo but all too often a reality. Former CIA analyst Paul Pillar traces the unfortunate emergence of the politicization phenomenon during the buildup to the invasion of Iraq in 2003.

A DYSFUNCTIONAL RELATIONSHIP

The most serious problem with U.S. intelligence today is that its relationship with the policymaking process is broken and badly needs repair. In the wake of the Iraq war, it has become clear that official intelligence analysis was not relied on in making even the most significant national security decisions, that intelligence was misused publicly to justify decisions already made, that damaging ill will developed between policymakers and intelligence officers, and that the intelligence community's own work was politicized. As the national intelligence officer responsible for the Middle East from 2000 to 2005, I witnessed all of these disturbing developments.

Public discussion of prewar intelligence on Iraq has focused on the errors made in assessing Saddam Hussein's unconventional weapons programs. A commission chaired by Judge Laurence Silberman and former Senator Charles Robb usefully documented the intelligence community's mistakes in a solid and comprehensive report released in March 2005. Corrections were indeed in order, and the intelligence community has begun to make them.

At the same time, an acrimonious and highly partisan debate broke out over whether the Bush administration manipulated and misused intelligence in making its case for war. The administration defended itself by pointing out that it was not alone in its view that Saddam had weapons of mass destruction (WMD) and active weapons programs, however mistaken that view may have been.

In this regard, the Bush administration was quite right: its perception of Saddam's weapons capacities was shared by the Clinton administration, congressional Democrats, and most other Western governments and intelligence services. But in making this defense, the White House also inadvertently pointed out the real problem: intelligence on Iraqi weapons programs did not drive its decision to go to war. A view broadly held in the United States and even more so overseas was that deterrence of Iraq was working, that Saddam was being kept "in his box," and that the best way to deal with the weapons problem was through an aggressive inspections program to supplement the sanctions already in place. That the administration arrived at so different a policy solution indicates that its decision to topple Saddam was driven by other factors—namely, the desire to shake up the sclerotic power structures of the Middle East and hasten the spread of more liberal politics and economics in the region.

If the entire body of official intelligence analysis on Iraq had a policy implication, it was to avoid war—or, if war was going to be launched, to prepare for a messy aftermath. What is most remarkable about prewar U.S. intelligence on Iraq is not that it got things wrong and thereby misled policymakers; it is that it played so small a role in one of the most important U.S. policy decisions in recent decades.

A MODEL UPENDED

The proper relationship between intelligence gathering and policymaking sharply separates the two functions. The intelligence community collects information, evaluates its credibility, and combines it with other information to help make sense of situations abroad that could affect U.S. interests. Intelligence officers decide which topics should get their limited collection and analytic resources according to both their own judgments and the concerns of policymakers. Policymakers thus influence which topics intelligence agencies address but not the conclusions that they reach. The intelligence community, meanwhile, limits its judgments to what is happening or what might happen overseas, avoiding policy judgments about what the United States should do in response.

In practice, this distinction is often blurred, especially because analytic projections may have policy implications even if they are not explicitly stated. But the distinction is still important. National security abounds with problems that are clearer than the solutions to them; the case of Iraq is hardly a unique example of how similar perceptions of a threat can lead people to recommend very different policy responses. Accordingly, it is critical that the intelligence community not advocate policy, especially not openly. If it does, it loses the most important basis for its credibility and its claims to objectivity. When intelligence analysts critique one another's work, they use the phrase "policy prescriptive" as a pejorative, and rightly so.

The Bush administration's use of intelligence on Iraq did not just blur this distinction; it turned the entire model upside down. The administration used intelligence not to inform decision-making, but to justify a decision already made. It went to war without requesting—and evidently without being influenced by—any strategic-level intelligence assessments on any aspect of Iraq. (The military made extensive use of intelligence in its war planning, although much of it was of a more tactical nature.) Congress, not the administration, asked for the now-infamous October 2002 National Intelligence Estimate (NIE) on Iraq's unconventional weapons programs, although few members of Congress actually read it. (According to several congressional aides responsible for safeguarding the classified material, no more than six senators and only a handful of House members got beyond the five-page executive summary.) As the national intelligence officer for the Middle East, I was in charge of coordinating all of the intelligence community's assessments regarding Iraq; the first request I received from any administration policymaker for any such assessment was not until a year into the war.

Official intelligence on Iraqi weapons programs was flawed, but even with its flaws, it was not what led to the war. On the issue that mattered most, the intelligence community judged that Iraq probably was several years away from developing a nuclear weapon. The October 2002 NIE also judged that Saddam was unlikely to use WMD against the United States unless his regime was placed in mortal danger.

Before the war, on its own initiative, the intelligence community considered the principal challenges that any post-invasion authority in Iraq would be likely to face. It presented a picture of a political culture that would not provide fertile ground for democracy and foretold a long, difficult, and turbulent transition. It projected that a Marshall Plan-type effort would be required to restore the Iraqi economy, despite Iraq's abundant oil resources. It forecast that in a deeply divided Iraqi society, with Sunnis resentful over the loss of their dominant position and Shiites seeking power commensurate with their majority status, there was a significant chance that the groups would engage in violent conflict unless an occupying power prevented it. And it anticipated that a foreign occupying force would itself be the target of resentment and attacks—including by guerrilla warfare—unless it established security and put Iraq on the road to prosperity in the first few weeks or months after the fall of Saddam.

In addition, the intelligence community offered its assessment of the likely regional repercussions of ousting Saddam. It argued that any value Iraq might have as a democratic exemplar would be minimal and would depend on the stability of a new Iraqi government and the extent to which democracy in Iraq was seen as developing from within rather than being imposed by an outside power. More likely, war and occupation would boost political Islam and increase sympathy for terrorists' objectives—and Iraq would become a magnet for extremists from elsewhere in the Middle East.

STANDARD DEVIATIONS

The Bush administration deviated from the professional standard not only in using policy to drive intelligence, but also in aggressively using intelligence to win public support for its decision to go to war. This meant selectively adducing data—"cherry-picking"—rather than using the intelligence community's own analytic judgments. In fact, key portions of the administration's case explicitly rejected those judgments. In an August 2002 speech, for example, Vice President Dick Cheney observed that "intelligence is an uncertain business" and noted how intelligence analysts had underestimated how close Iraq had been to developing a nuclear weapon before the 1991 Persian Gulf War. His conclusion—at odds with that of the intelligence community—was that "many of us are convinced that Saddam will acquire nuclear weapons fairly soon."

In the upside-down relationship between intelligence and policy that prevailed in the case of Iraq, the administration selected pieces of raw intelligence to use in its public case for war, leaving the intelligence community to register varying degrees of private protest when such use started to go beyond what analysts deemed credible or reasonable. The best-known example was the assertion by President George W. Bush in his 2003 State of the Union address that Iraq was purchasing uranium ore in Africa. U.S. intelligence analysts had questioned the credibility of the report making this claim, had kept it out of their own unclassified products, and had advised the White House not to use it publicly. But the administration put the claim into the speech anyway, referring to it as information from British sources in order to make the point without explicitly vouching for the intelligence.

The reexamination of prewar public statements is a necessary part of understanding the process that led to the Iraq war. But a narrow focus on rhetorical details tends to overlook more fundamental problems in the intelligence-policy relationship. Any time policymakers, rather than intelligence agencies, take the lead in selecting which bits of raw intelligence to present, there is—regardless of the issue—a bias. The resulting public statements ostensibly reflect intelligence, but they do not reflect intelligence analysis, which is an essential part of determining what the pieces of raw reporting mean. The policymaker acts with an eye not to what is indicative of a larger pattern or underlying truth, but to what supports his case.

Another problem is that on Iraq, the intelligence community was pulled over the line into policy advocacy—not so much by what it said as by its conspicuous role in the administration's public case for war. This was especially true when the intelligence community was made highly visible (with the director of central intelligence literally in the camera frame) in an intelligence-laden presentation by Secretary of State Colin Powell to the UN Security Council a month before the war began. It was also true in the fall of 2002, when, at the administration's behest, the intelligence community published a white paper on Iraq's WMD programs—but without including any of the community's judgments about the likelihood of those weapons being used.

But the greatest discrepancy between the administration's public statements and the intelligence community's judgments concerned not WMD (there was indeed a broad consensus that such programs existed), but the relationship between Saddam and al Qaeda. The enormous attention devoted to this subject did not reflect any judgment by intelligence officials that there was or was likely to be anything like the "alliance" the administration said existed. The reason the connection got so much attention was that the administration wanted to hitch the Iraq expedition to the "war on terror" and the threat the American public feared most, thereby capitalizing on the country's militant post-9/11 mood.

The issue of possible ties between Saddam and al Qaeda was especially prone to the selective use of raw intelligence to make a public case for war. In the shadowy world of international terrorism, almost anyone can be "linked" to almost anyone else if enough effort is made to find evidence of casual contacts, the mentioning of names in the same breath, or indications of common travels or experiences. Even the most minimal and circumstantial data can be adduced as evidence of a "relationship," ignoring the important question of whether a given regime actually supports a given terrorist group and the fact that relationships can be competitive or distrustful rather than cooperative.

The intelligence community never offered any analysis that supported the notion of an alliance between Saddam and al Qaeda. Yet it was drawn into a public effort to support that notion. To be fair, Secretary Powell's presentation at the UN never explicitly asserted that there was a cooperative relationship between Saddam and al Qaeda. But the presentation was clearly meant to create the impression that one existed. To the extent that the intelligence community was a party to such efforts, it crossed the line into policy advocacy—and did so in a way that fostered public misconceptions contrary to the intelligence community's own judgments.

VARIETIES OF POLITICIZATION

In its report on prewar intelligence concerning Iraqi WMD, the Senate Select Committee on Intelligence said it found no evidence that analysts had altered or shaped their judgments in response to political pressure. The Silberman-Robb commission reached the same conclusion, although it conceded that analysts worked in an "environment" affected by "intense" policymaker interest. But the method of investigation used by the panels—essentially, asking analysts whether their arms had been twisted—would have caught only the crudest attempts at politicization. Such attempts are rare and, when they do occur (as with former Undersecretary of State John Bolton's attempts to get the intelligence community to sign on to his judgments about Cuba and Syria), are almost always unsuccessful. Moreover, it is unlikely that analysts would ever acknowledge that their own judgments have been politicized, since that would be far more damning than admitting more mundane types of analytic error.

The actual politicization of intelligence occurs subtly and can take many forms. Context is all-important. Well before March 2003, intelligence analysts and their managers knew that the United States was heading for war with Iraq. It was clear that the Bush administration would frown on or ignore analysis that called into question a decision to go to war and welcome analysis that supported such a decision. Intelligence analysts—for whom attention, especially favorable attention, from policymakers is a measure of success—felt a strong wind consistently blowing in one direction. The desire to bend with such a wind is natural and strong, even if unconscious.

On the issue of Iraqi WMD, dozens of analysts throughout the intelligence community were making many judgments on many different issues based on fragmentary and ambiguous evidence. The differences between sound intelligence analysis (bearing in mind the gaps in information) and the flawed analysis that actually was produced had to do mainly with matters of caveat, nuance, and word choice. The opportunities for bias were numerous. It may not be possible to point to one key instance of such bending or to measure the cumulative effect of such pressure. But the effect was probably significant.

A clearer form of politicization is the inconsistent review of analysis: reports that conform to policy preferences have an easier time making it through the gauntlet of coordination and approval than ones that do not. (Every piece of intelligence analysis reflects not only the judgments of the analysts most directly involved in writing it, but also the concurrence of those who cover related topics and the review, editing, and remanding of it by several levels of supervisors, from branch chiefs to senior executives.) The Silberman-Robb commission noted such inconsistencies in the Iraq case but chalked it up to bad management. The commission failed to address exactly why managers were inconsistent: they wanted to avoid the unpleasantness of laying unwelcome analysis on a policymaker's desk.

Another form of politicization with a similar cause is the sugarcoating of what otherwise would be an unpalatable message. Even the mostly prescient analysis about the problems likely to be encountered in postwar Iraq included some observations that served as sugar, added in the hope that policymakers would not throw the report directly into the burn bag, but damaging the clarity of the analysis in the process.

But the principal way that the intelligence community's work on Iraq was politicized concerned the specific questions to which the community devoted its energies. As any competent pollster can attest, how a question is framed helps determine the answer. In the case of Iraq, there was also the matter of sheer quantity of output—not just what the intelligence community said, but how many times it said it. On any given subject, the intelligence community faces what is in effect a field of rocks, and it lacks the resources to turn over every one to see what threats to national security may lurk underneath. In an unpoliticized environment, intelligence officers decide which rocks to turn over based on past patterns and their own judgments. But when policymakers repeatedly urge the intelligence community to turn over only certain rocks, the process becomes biased. The community responds by concentrating its resources on those rocks, eventually producing a body of reporting and analysis that, thanks to quantity and emphasis, leaves the impression that what lies under those same rocks is a bigger part of the problem than it really is.

That is what happened when the Bush administration repeatedly called on the intelligence community to uncover more material that would contribute to the case for war. The Bush team approached the community again and again and pushed it to look harder at the supposed Saddam-al Qaeda relationship—calling on analysts not only to turn over additional Iraqi rocks, but also to turn over ones already examined and to scratch the dirt to see if there might be something there after all. The result was an intelligence output that—because the question being investigated was never put in context—obscured rather than enhanced understanding of al Qaeda's actual sources of strength and support.

This process represented a radical departure from the textbook model of the relationship between intelligence and policy, in which an intelligence service responds to policymaker interest in certain subjects (such as "security threats from Iraq" or "al Qaeda's supporters") and explores them in whatever direction the evidence leads. The process did not involve intelligence work designed to find dangers not yet discovered or to inform decisions not yet made. Instead, it involved research to find evidence in support of a specific line of argument that Saddam was cooperating with al Qaeda—which in turn was being used to justify a specific policy decision.

One possible consequence of such politicization is policymaker self-deception. A policymaker can easily forget that he is hearing so much about a particular angle in briefings because he and his fellow policymakers have urged the intelligence community to focus on it. A more certain consequence is the skewed application of the intelligence community's resources. Feeding the administration's voracious appetite for material on the Saddam-al Qaeda link consumed an enormous amount of time and attention at multiple levels, from rank-and-file counterterrorism analysts to the most senior intelligence officials. It is fair to ask how much other counterterrorism work was left undone as a result.

The issue became even more time-consuming as the conflict between intelligence officials and policymakers escalated into a battle, with the intelligence community struggling to maintain its objectivity even as policymakers pressed the Saddam-al Qaeda connection. The administration's rejection of the intelligence community's judgments became especially clear with the formation of a special Pentagon unit, the Policy Counterterrorism Evaluation Group. The unit, which reported to Undersecretary of Defense Douglas Feith, was dedicated to finding every possible link between Saddam and al Qaeda, and its briefings accused the intelligence community of faulty analysis for failing to see the supposed alliance.

For the most part, the intelligence community's own substantive judgments do not appear to have been compromised. (A possible important exception was the construing of an ambiguous, and ultimately recanted, statement from a detainee as indicating that Saddam's Iraq provided jihadists with chemical or biological training.) But although the charge of faulty analysis was never directly conveyed to the intelligence community itself, enough of the charges leaked out to create a public perception of rancor between the administration and the intelligence community, which in turn encouraged some administration supporters to charge intelligence officers (including me) with trying to sabotage the president's policies. This poisonous atmosphere reinforced the disinclination within the intelligence community to challenge the consensus view about Iraqi WMD programs; any such challenge would have served merely to reaffirm the presumptions of the accusers.

PARTIAL REPAIRS

Although the Iraq war has provided a particularly stark illustration of the problems in the intelligence-policy relationship, such problems are not confined to this one issue or this specific administration. Four decades ago, the misuse of intelligence about an ambiguous encounter in the Gulf of Tonkin figured prominently in the Johnson administration's justification for escalating the military effort in Vietnam. Over a century ago, the possible misinterpretation of an explosion on a U.S. warship in Havana harbor helped set off the chain of events that led to a war of choice against Spain. The Iraq case needs further examination and reflection on its own. But public discussion of how to foster a better relationship between intelligence officials and policymakers and how to ensure better use of intelligence on future issues is also necessary.

Intelligence affects the nation's interests through its effect on policy. No matter how much the process of intelligence gathering itself is fixed, the changes will do no good if the role of intelligence in the policy-making process is not also addressed. Unfortunately, there is no single clear fix to the sort of problem that arose in the case of Iraq. The current ill will may not be reparable, and the perception of the intelligence community on the part of some policymakers—that Langley is enemy territory—unlikely to change. But a few steps, based on the recognition that the intelligence-policy relationship is indeed broken, could reduce the likelihood that such a breakdown will recur.

On this point, the United States should emulate the United Kingdom, where discussion of this issue has been more forthright, by declaring once and for all that its intelligence services should not be part of public advocacy of policies still under debate. In the United Kingdom, Prime Minister Tony Blair accepted a commission of inquiry's conclusions that intelligence and policy had been improperly comingled in such exercises as the publication of the "dodgy dossier," the British counterpart to the United States' Iraqi WMD white paper, and that in the future there should be a clear delineation between intelligence and policy. An American declaration should take the form of a congressional resolution and be seconded by a statement from the White House. Although it would not have legal force, such a statement would discourage future administrations from attempting to pull the intelligence community into policy advocacy. It would also give some leverage to intelligence officers in resisting any such future attempts.

A more effective way of identifying and exposing improprieties in the relationship is also needed. The CIA has a "politicization ombudsman," but his informally defined functions mostly involve serving as a sympathetic ear for analysts disturbed by evidence of politicization and then summarizing what he hears for senior agency officials. The intelligence oversight committees in Congress have an important role, but the heightened partisanship that has bedeviled so much other work on Capitol Hill has had an especially inhibiting effect in this area. A promised effort by the Senate Intelligence Committee to examine the Bush administrations use of intelligence on Iraq got stuck in the partisan mud. The House committee has not even attempted to address the subject.

The legislative branch is the appropriate place for monitoring the intelligence-policy relationship. But the oversight should be conducted by a nonpartisan office modeled on the Government Accountability Office (GAO) and the Congressional Budget Office (CBO). Such an office would have a staff, smaller than that of the GAO or the CBO, of officers experienced in intelligence and with the necessary clearances and access to examine questions about both the politicization of classified intelligence work and the public use of intelligence. As with the GAO, this office could conduct inquiries at the request of members of Congress. It would make its results public as much as possible, consistent with security requirements, and it would avoid duplicating the many other functions of intelligence oversight, which would remain the responsibility of the House and Senate intelligence committees.

Beyond these steps, there is the more difficult issue of what place the intelligence community should occupy within the executive branch. The reorganization that created the Office of the Director of National Intelligence (DNI) is barely a year old, and yet another reorganization at this time would compound the disruption. But the flaws in the narrowly conceived and hastily considered reorganization legislation of December 2004—such as ambiguities in the DNI's authority—will make it necessary to reopen the issues it addressed. Any new legislation should also tackle something the 2004 legislation did not: the problem of having the leaders of the intelligence community, which is supposed to produce objective and unvarnished analysis, serve at the pleasure of the president.

The organizational issue is also difficult because of a dilemma that intelligence officers have long discussed and debated among themselves: that although distance from policymakers may be needed for objectivity, closeness is needed for influence. For most of the past quarter century, intelligence officials have striven for greater closeness, in a perpetual quest for policymakers' ears. The lesson of the Iraq episode, however, is that the supposed dilemma has been incorrectly conceived. Closeness in this case did not buy influence, even on momentous issues of war and peace; it bought only the disadvantages of politicization.

The intelligence community should be repositioned to reflect the fact that influence and relevance flow not just from face time in the Oval Office, but also from credibility with Congress and, most of all, with the American public. The community needs to remain in the executive branch but be given greater independence and a greater ability to communicate with those other constituencies (fettered only by security considerations, rather than by policy agendas). An appropriate model is the Federal Reserve, which is structured as a quasi-autonomous body overseen by a board of governors with long fixed terms.

These measures would reduce both the politicization of the intelligence community's own work and the public misuse of intelligence by policymakers. It would not directly affect how much attention policymakers give to intelligence, which they would continue to be entitled to ignore. But the greater likelihood of being called to public account for discrepancies between a case for a certain policy and an intelligence judgment would have the indirect effect of forcing policymakers to pay more attention to those judgments in the first place.

These changes alone will not fix the intelligence-policy relationship. But if Congress and the American people are serious about "fixing intelligence," they should not just do what is easy and politically convenient. At stake are the soundness of U.S. foreign-policy making and the right of Americans to know the basis for decisions taken in the name of their security.

QUESTIONS FOR FURTHER DISCUSSION

1. What is "broken" about the intelligence-policymaking process, according to Pillar?
2. What are the "varieties of politicization"?
3. What is your critique of Pillar's suggestions for reform?
4. What options does an intelligence analyst have if he or she thinks intelligence is being misused by a policymaker?

30. INTELLIGENCE AND HOMELAND SECURITY

JAMES BURCH

Homeland security expert James Burch takes a look at intelligence organizations in democratic regimes, comparing America's intelligence reforms with efforts to improve intelligence activities in fellow open societies. He focuses on the potential value of a domestic intelligence agency in the United States.

OVERVIEW

The safest place in the world for a terrorist to be is inside the United States. . . . As long as terrorists don't do something that trips them up against our laws, they can do pretty much all they want.

—*Brent Scowcroft, former National Security Advisor*[1]

Several paradigms were altered on 9/11. The U.S. intelligence community, largely focused on state actors, now faced the threat posed by elusive terrorists. The community also had to address the asymmetry posed by the terrorists' use of unconventional and relatively unsophisticated methods to inflict loss of life and damage—a more complex intelligence task. Lastly, due to terrorist disregard for national borders, laws, and transnational financing, the United States had to change its concept of foreign versus domestic intelligence.[2]

The area of domestic intelligence raises several issues. First, law enforcement and intelligence operate in different worlds—one seeks to prosecute, the other to gather information.[3] Second, with the development of multiple state fusion centers and the creation of additional organizations focused on intelligence, there is a corresponding increase in bureaucratization. This adds to the challenge of sharing information. Lastly and perhaps most importantly, there are issues concerning the protection of civil liberties and effective oversight.

The challenge in developing a viable domestic intelligence capability for the United States centers on how to organize these capabilities optimally within the larger U.S. intelligence framework, how to ensure streamlined information sharing between foreign intelligence and the multitude of law enforcement agencies, and how best to implement oversight mechanisms to protect civil liberties and ensure accountability of intelligence operations. *Organizational mechanisms, information sharing,* and *oversight* are the three critical components to instituting an effective domestic intelligence capability.

One of the proposed constructs to meet these organizational and information sharing challenges is to create a domestic intelligence agency. The United States is unique among Western or highly industrialized countries in that it does not possess one. This paper examines the feasibility, suitability, and acceptability of instituting a domestic intelligence agency in the United States from the viewpoint of organization, information sharing, and oversight. It will assess the domestic intelligence organizations of three countries that possess liberal democratic institutions—the United Kingdom's Military Intelligence 5 (MI5), the Australian Security Intelligence Organisation (ASIO), and India's Intelligence Bureau (IB)—to determine their relative effectiveness in countering terrorism, identify their strengths and shortfalls, and determine applicable policy recommendations for the United States.

Specific criteria are used to establish a measure of assessment for a domestic intelligence agency. In this case, the criteria are derived from the Geneva Centre for the Democratic Control of Armed Forces (DCAF), which partners with countries to promote governance and determine recommendations that promote government reform. Examples of some criteria are the subordination of intelligence to national laws, effective coordination, and oversight.

Examining countries with similar democratic institutions, threats, and (in the case of Australia and India) geographic scope will result in identifying key factors for instituting an effective domestic intelligence capability for the United States. This examination will also determine whether current intelligence reform policies are targeting perceived intelligence shortfalls and offer additional recommendations. It will also determine whether the establishment of a domestic intelligence agency is feasible, acceptable, and suitable to meeting the asymmetric threats of the 21st century.

INTRODUCTION

Al Qaeda conducted a devastating strike on 9/11 by using airliners as weapon of mass destruction (WMD). In terms of scale, it incurred a relatively small cost to create billions of dollars' worth of damage.[4] The psychological impact was also devastating and prompted a massive response and reorganization of the U.S. government to combat this threat.[5] Part of this reorganization was a close examination of the Federal Bureau of Investigation (FBI). A Congressional inquiry into 9/11 revealed several FBI shortcomings:

- "The FBI's decentralized structure and inadequate information technology made the Bureau unable to correlate the knowledge possessed by its components. The FBI did not gather intelligence from all its many cases nation-wide to produce an overall assessment of al Qaeda's presence in the United States."
- "Many FBI field offices had not made counterterrorism a top priority and they knew little about al Qaeda before September 11."
- The FBI also did not inform policymakers of the extent of terrorist activity in the United States. "Although the FBI conducted many investigations, these pieces were not fitted into a larger picture."[6]

These findings highlighted a domestic intelligence gap and, as a result, have led to several larger governmental initiatives and internal FBI reforms. Another organizational alternative is to create a domestic intelligence agency to focus solely on domestic intelligence and collection. Supporters of a domestic intelligence agency have proposed this alternative as the best method to address the domestic intelligence gap effectively. In attempting to address this gap, however, there are additional issues. First, there are opposing viewpoints as to whether the domestic intelligence apparatus should remain within and tied to the FBI versus establishing it as an independent entity. Second, the creation of another bureaucracy raises concerns about the effectiveness of information sharing. Third, an increased focus on domestic intelligence leads to concerns about civil liberties and oversight. Examining the domestic intelligence structures of the United Kingdom, Australia, and India in terms of these three issues can assist in determining the applicability of those structures and offer implementation considerations for the United States.

Advocates for a separate domestic intelligence agency point to several advantages. The first is a symbolic one: the creation of such an agency would emphasize the government's commitment to preventing another catastrophic attack.[7] As Mark Lowenthal states, "several issues spill over into the domestic realm—economies, narcotics, crime, and terrorism—thus curtailing the activities of much of the intelligence community . . ."[8] A domestic intelligence agency would also focus directly on these domestic-foreign terrorism nexus' issues and afford greater precision to developing and categorizing the domestic threat. Creating an agency strictly focused on this mission could more directly address the domestic intelligence gap as compared to the higher organizational and bureaucratic changes that have been implemented since 9/11. Second, there is inherent competition between law enforcement and intelligence for resources and focus. Harry Ransom highlighted this competitive tension when referring to CIA intelligence and operations: "The ill advised marriage of intelligence collection-analysis-estimates with covert action has further complicated role theory."[9] Advocates for a domestic intelligence agency argue that the FBI's intelligence function will always take a secondary role to its law enforcement responsibilities due to the focus on "making cases" and the preponderance of the FBI's leadership coming from law enforcement.[10] Combining two missions that operate in different worlds and possess different challenges under one organization contributes to operational ineffectiveness.

Lastly, it is much easier to recruit, perform undercover work, and take advantage of the loyal Muslim base in the United States.[11] As one FBI official noted before a Congressional inquiry, "foreign governments often knew more about radical Islamist activity in the United States than did the U.S. Government because they saw this activity as a threat to their own existence."[12] The development of a domestic intelligence baseline to categorize the terrorist threat in terms of cells, planning efforts, and underlying support networks would directly support investigatory efforts. For the advocates, a renewed focus by a domestic intelligence agency dedicated to developing these intelligence resources in the United States would directly support prevention efforts.

Despite the advantages, there is also considerable opposition. Opponents counter that the addition of another organization adds another layer of bureaucracy, making it harder to overcome the already-obscured relationship between law enforcement and intelligence.[13] Creating another agency, while having the merit of focusing on intelligence issues, does not address the larger problem of information sharing outside of its organization.[14] As Eric Taylor states, "added bureaucracies will only cause agile terrorist groups glee as they outmaneuver sluggish government attempts to counter them."[15]

There is also the potential abuse of civil liberties and danger of politicization. U.S. intelligence agencies historically have had limited roles in internal security.[16] Letting an organization pursue an aggressive domestic intelligence agenda could lead to the domestic spying abuses similar to those of the 1950s and 1960s.[17] The potential for such abuse will also increase the scrutiny of the executive branch, which could lead to a backlash similar to the Church and Pike Committee recommendations.[18] There is also the danger of politicization. As Ransom asserts, ". . . politicization is inherent in the production of intelligence because information is crucial to gaining and preserving political power."[19] A domestic intelligence agency has the unique potential of becoming politicized. As Ransom further states, the CIA was insulated from partisan politics from 1947 to 1967 because, "a foreign policy consensus prevailed, secrecy normally expected by an intelligence agency was maintained and congressional knowledge and monitoring of intelligence operations was very limited."[20] Those sets of circumstances do not exist today.

The arguments for developing a domestic intelligence agency center on its prevention activities, the organization's unity of purpose, and the recruitment of intelligence sources. The reasons for not implementing are the additional layers of bureaucracy that do not facilitate information sharing, the potential abuse of civil rights, and the danger of politicization. The challenge and key task is to determine how to organize domestic intelligence efforts, how

to facilitate information sharing, and how to protect against potential abuses in the U.S.

Democracies, by their nature, are faced with a conflicting dilemma regarding terrorism. As Benjamin Netanyahu, the former Prime Minister of Israel, states:

> The governments of free societies charged with fighting a rising tide of terrorism are thus faced with a democratic dilemma: If they do not fight terrorism with the means available to them, they endanger their citizenry; if they do, they appear to endanger the very freedoms which they are charged to protect.[21]

This dilemma lies at the center of the public debate. Richard A. Posner, a noted jurist, identifies two issues. The first is where to draw the line between security and liberty; the second is which controls are necessary to prevent any law enforcement or intelligence agency from crossing the line leading to potential civil rights abuses.[22] As Posner further notes, public safety and personal liberty are both constitutional values.

The challenge is to devise a system that balances law enforcement and intelligence equities, allows for information sharing, and ensures effective oversight and accountability of intelligence activities. The Geneva Centre for the Democratic Control of Armed Forces (DCAF) offers some benchmarks:

- Domestic intelligence and collection are subject to national laws.
- The separation of foreign and domestic intelligence requires an effective coordination of collection.
- Coordination is performed by an executive branch entity.
- Joint assessments are undertaken ideally by an independent body.
- Executive, legislative, and judicial branches exercise oversight.[23]

Examining the United Kingdom's Military Intelligence 5 (MI5), the Australian Security Intelligence Organisation (ASIO), and the Indian Intelligence Bureau (IB) in terms of these benchmarks can offer ideas and insight into implementation challenges for improving homeland security intelligence in the United States. Each of the countries is similar in that they possess democratic institutions. Australia and India are more similar to the United States in that both possess a federalist-type structure with the sharing of power between the federal government and state or provincial institutions. This distinction is considerably less in the United Kingdom. Additionally, India—the world's largest democracy—can be compared more readily with the United States in terms of the scope of domestic intelligence challenges. Other specific intelligence similarities and challenges include:

- The refocus of the British, Australian, and Indian intelligence on transnational terrorism and internal security issues since 9/11.
- The reorganization of the British, Australian, and Indian intelligence communities through creation of special task forces and assessment bodies focused on terrorism.
- The passage of strong anti-terror legislation and the subsequent debate over internal security and civil liberties.

There are, however, significant differences. The United Kingdom, Australia, and India possess parliamentary systems where the power of the executive is divided between the head of state and head of government. The head of government, in this case the prime minister, is also reliant on the support of the legislative branch or parliament. This support is expressed through a vote of confidence or no confidence. The distinction and separation between the executive and legislative branches of government is much clearer in the United States. Other differences include those of language and culture within India versus the United States, the United Kingdom, and Australia. The ethnic differences in India have resulted in significant and recurring sectarian violence since its independence in 1947. The United Kingdom has also faced a similar issue with regard to the Irish Republican Army (IRA). Simply put, a relationship exists between countries with significant internal stability problems and the nature of the oversight mechanisms they possess. Specific differences include:

- The United Kingdom is much smaller geographically than the United States. Additionally, the United Kingdom and Australia are island nations with fewer border control and security issues than the United States or India.
- Indian geography—its scale and proximity to terrorist safe havens in Afghanistan, Iran, Pakistan, and the Kashmir—coupled with its much larger population and significant Muslim minority leads to greater internal security issues beyond the scale of the United Kingdom, Australia, and the United States.

Considering the similarities and differences, there is value in assessing the effectiveness of the United Kingdom's MI5, Australia's ASIO, and India's IB. The applicability of their practices will be assessed by using the DCAF's benchmarks and utilizing the following criteria:

- *Feasible*: Task can be accomplished with forces and resources.
- *Suitable*: Will mission be accomplished if tasks are carried out successfully?
- *Acceptable*: Results are politically supportable.[24]

THE UNITED KINGDOM'S SECURITY SERVICE BRANCH—MILITARY INTELLIGENCE 5 (MI5)

We're always trying to improve our intelligence gathering but these groups operate in an immensely secretive way, it is very, very difficult often to track down exactly what they're doing. . . .
—*Tony Blair, Prime Minister of the United Kingdom*[25]

ORGANIZATION

The MI5, also known as the Security Service, is the United Kingdom's domestic intelligence agency. It is responsible for responding to a wide range of security threats that include terrorism, counterintelligence, weapons of mass destruction, and organized crimes. MI5 falls under the Home Ministry, which has no precise U.S. equivalent.[26] The Security Service is one of three tier-one intelligence organizations. The Secret Intelligence Service, or MI6, focuses on foreign intelligence and the Government Communications Headquarters (GCHQ) is responsible for communications intercept and code breaking efforts.[27]

MI5 is chartered to conduct domestic surveillance operations against a wide variety of targets, but it does not possess independent arrest powers.[28] The philosophy behind this organizational relationship is to force MI5 to work hand-in-hand with the various fifty-six police forces in the United Kingdom, particularly the Metropolitan and provincial Special Branches (SB).[29] As Peter Chalk states, "The Special Branch structure is the primary instrument through which intelligence is translated into operational activity and prosecutions."[30]

Despite the terrorist attacks in London (2005), the MI5 can point to credible successes. Former Director of MI5 Dame Eliza Manningham-Buller has stated that MI5 is tracking approximately 200 radical groups and over 1,600 individuals who are actively supporting or linked to terrorist activities focused on the United Kingdom—whether domestically or in foreign areas.[31] Given MI5's size, the scope of these numbers would suggest a high degree of coordination, precision, and fidelity between Britain's foreign intelligence community, its assessment bodies, and law enforcement entities.[32]

STRATEGIC OUTLOOK

The United Kingdom has a history of combating terrorists, particularly in its long struggle against the IRA. As a result, MI5 has an established tradition of conducting domestic intelligence operations to include electronic surveillance, recruitment, and infiltration of terrorist groups. It also has a well established working relationship with law enforcement.

The events of 9/11 fundamentally shifted the focus of the United Kingdom's intelligence apparatus. Islamic terrorism is now identified as the number one threat.[33] MI5's intelligence functions are part of a greater government counterterrorism strategy known as CONTEST. The overarching aim of this strategy is to reduce the risk of terrorism through pursuit of four strategic approaches or lines of operation: *prevent*, *pursue*, *protect*, and *prepare*.[34] Intelligence gathering and disrupting terrorist activities are identified as two integral components under pursuit activities. MI5 performs a unique service to support these two lines of operation.[35]

INFORMATION SHARING

MI5 serves as an assessment agency as well as a collection entity. Its analysis directly supports the United Kingdom's Joint Intelligence Committee (JIC), which serves as the government's focal point for intelligence prioritization and assessment.[36] The JIC also provides regular assessments to ministers and other senior officials.[37] The establishment of the Joint Terrorism Analysis Centre (JTAC) in June 2003 (under the supervision of MI5) brings analysts from the respective intelligence agencies under one umbrella to facilitate the sharing of intelligence and breaking down of cross-agency barriers.[38] Underneath the JTAC structure, the various Special Branches have pooled their resources to develop Regional Intelligence Cells that share responsibilities and support further information sharing.[39]

Although the United Kingdom has a highly-evolved intelligence structure with a long tradition of conducting domestic intelligence, there have been several instances of information-sharing shortfalls.

MI5 has been criticized for not providing warning of the Bali attacks in October 2002, the Mombasa attack in November 2002, and failing to pass specific intelligence regarding the shoe bomber, Richard Reid.[40]

The development of a strategic intelligence architecture and information sharing policies is a relevant issue for the United States. Information sharing remains a problematic issue despite the United Kingdom's well-established intelligence mechanisms, clearly defined missions and roles, and assessment organs. An examination of the U.S. intelligence architecture and information sharing practices—a key 9/11 shortfall—is critical and uniquely relevant particularly given the numerous changes, reorganizations, and reforms within the U.S. intelligence community. An assessment of these changes is necessary particularly as the events of 9/11 move further into the past.

OVERSIGHT

The authority of Britain's Cabinet structure from a majority in the House of Commons affords the Prime Minister greater latitude on national security and intelligence matters.[41] Although the *Security Service Act of 1989* codified MI5's rules, missions, and functions, the intelligence and security services were largely exempt from the scrutiny of Parliament and the public until the passing of the *Intelligence Services Act of 1994*.[42] As a result of this legislation, Parliament's Intelligence and Security Committee (ISC) now reviews the budget, administration, and policy of all three intelligence agencies.[43] Its legislative oversight function, however, is much more limited than the U.S. congressional committee system.[44]

Executive oversight is also exercised by the ISC, which consists of nine members of parliament from various political parties. The ISC reports directly to the prime minister and is charged with producing an annual report on intelligence activities.[45] This committee operates within Britain's "ring of secrecy," which is bounded by the *Official Secrets Act*.[46] The *Official Secrets Act* allows the British government to exercise, in effect, prior restraint with respect to any disclosure of information that can be deemed harmful to the national interest.[47] Although the ISC is chartered with exercising oversight, its members are appointed by and answer directly to the prime minister—creating the potential for a conflict of interest. Additionally, despite the oversight mechanisms, MI5 continues to remain essentially a self-tasking organization requiring no separate approval before initiating a new operation.[48] There have also been instances of politicization, particularly during the 1980s when MI5 conducted counter-subversive operations against leftwing politicians and organizations whom Prime Minister Margaret Thatcher termed, "the Enemy Within."[49]

CONCLUSION

MI5's strengths lie in its ability to operate under a well-defined executive structure that utilizes an independent intelligence assessment umbrella and operates under a well-understood set of laws. The organization also has a long history of performing its internal security and domestic intelligence functions. The United Kingdom also possesses several highly-evolved mechanisms to coordinate the sharing of intelligence. Despite this structure, there have been several instances where MI5 did not share its intelligence. Effective intelligence sharing remains an issue. Although there are existing oversight mechanisms, the structure of the United Kingdom's oversight organs also inhibits significant legislative oversight of the intelligence process. Utilizing the DCAF benchmarks listed in Figure 30.1, the United Kingdom's strengths lie in its strong executive co-ordination and independent assessment process. Its domestic intelligence agency also operates under a well-defined set of national laws, although the effectiveness of information sharing remains an issue. Lastly, given the United Kingdom's oversight structure and MI5's past abuses, the oversight and accountability mechanisms that balance civil liberties versus public safety remain a potential area of concern. An assessment of information-sharing practices and oversight procedures—given the numerous changes within the U.S. intelligence community and the

recent FBI controversy on the handling and accountability of National Security Letters—is of particular relevance for the United States.

THE AUSTRALIAN SECURITY INTELLIGENCE ORGANISATION (ASIO)

> In the difficult fight against the new menace of international terrorism, there is nothing more crucial than timely and accurate intelligence.
> —*John Howard, Australian Prime Minister*[50]

ORGANIZATION

The Australian Security Intelligence Organisation (ASIO) serves as Australia's domestic intelligence organization. Similar to MI5, it is chartered to address a wide variety of threats.[51] ASIO works closely with the Australian Protective Service (APS), with both agencies falling under Australia's Attorney General.[52] ASIO is also one of three tier-one intelligence organizations. The Australian Secret Intelligence Service (ASIS) functions as the foreign intelligence entity while the Defence Signals Directorate (DSD) is focused on signals intelligence.[53]

Heavily influenced by the British philosophy of separating domestic intelligence and law enforcement powers, ASIO does not have independent arrest powers.[54] As such, ASIO must work closely with police entities particularly the APS—roughly equivalent to the FBI or the Royal Canadian Mounted Police (RCMP). The primary venue for APS-ASIO interaction is through the National Threat Assessment Centre, which serves as the focal point for collaboration with federal organizations and state police forces.[55]

STRATEGIC OUTLOOK

Australia does not have a long history of combating terrorists. It has not been plagued by an internal threat (like the United Kingdom by the IRA) or India's numerous internal security issues due to its linguistic and ethnic differences. Additionally, Australia has been largely isolated by the nature of its geography. As a whole, Australia has typically viewed its strategic threats in a foreign context and has prized international cooperation with its allies to deal with its security issues.

Despite its lack of internal threats, the Australian government has taken a serious and very thorough approach to internal security. It went through

DCAF BENCHMARKS	U.K.	Australia	India	U.S.
DOMESTIC INTELLIGENCE SUBJECT TO LAWS	◑			
COORDINATION OF DOMESTIC & FOREIGN INTELLIGENCE	◑			
EXECUTIVE BRANCH COORDINATING	●			
INDEPENDENT BODY CONDUCTING ASSESSMENTS	●			
OVERSIGHT MECHANISMS	◐			

● ←——————→ ○
Most Effective   Least Effective

FIGURE 30.1   DCAF benchmarks versus the U.K.

significant security preparations for the Sydney 2000 Olympic Games, which also highlighted the value of international cooperation.[56] The Australian government now recognizes Islamic terrorism as its highest threat priority and has committed significant resources to counterterrorism as a result of the 9/11 attacks and al Qaeda statements that identify Australia as a target.[57] ASIO's intelligence function operates as part of the government's four-pronged counterterrorism approach: *prevention, preparedness, response,* and *recovery.* Improving intelligence capacity, increasing the effectiveness of information sharing, seeking better detection capabilities, and improving law enforcement coordination are the overarching themes under prevention and preparedness.[58]

Despite the lack of a historical internal security threat or Australia's priority as a target for a terrorist attack, the ASIO can point to some success in categorizing and tracking domestic terrorist threats. Similar to the MI5, ASIO also has the reputation for thoroughness and developing precise intelligence. On November 18, 2005, Australian authorities foiled the activities of two terrorist cells. ASIO and Australian law enforcement agencies were able to prevent an attack possibly aimed at critical infrastructure as a result of an eighteen-month long investigation into individuals with possible linkages to al Qaeda and radical Kashmiri groups.[59]

INFORMATION SHARING

Like MI5, ASIO also serves as an analytic assessment agency. The Office of National Assessment (ONA) serves as Australia's premier strategic assessment organization. ONA, ASIO, ASIS, and DSD also enjoy close access to the prime minister's office.[60] The National Intelligence Group (NIG), which resides under ASIO, collates intelligence from multiple sources and disseminates products to governmental and law enforcement officials through Joint Intelligence Groups.[61] Executive coordination of domestic intelligence and other matters is accomplished through the National Security Committee of Cabinet (NSC) and the Secretaries' Committee on National Security (SCoNS). The NSC consists of senior policy makers while the SCoNS consists of department secretaries who, like those in the United Kingdom, are professional bureaucrats.[62]

Although Australia's intelligence system is modeled on the United Kingdom's, with domestic intelligence having to work closely with law enforcement entities, there have also been corresponding shortfalls in information sharing. ASIO's performance was also criticized for disregarding threat assessments from regional analysts regarding the Bali attack in 2002—an area directly under ASIO's concern.[63] Like the United Kingdom, Australia has a highly defined intelligence community; however, its track record on information sharing is an issue. Despite Australian and British similarities and the ability of their domestic intelligence agencies to possibly develop greater precision in categorizing the domestic threat, their information sharing problems remain a relevant issue for the United States.

OVERSIGHT

ASIO's statutory responsibilities are outlined in the *ASIO Act of 1979.* Although Australia is similar to the United Kingdom, there is a greater distinction between executive and legislative oversight roles. The *Intelligence Services Act of 2001* expanded the role of the Parliamentary Joint Committee on Intelligence and Security in overseeing Australia's intelligence apparatus.[64] The committee can initiate investigations or respond to requests from the Attorney General.[65] Australia's executive oversight is also more robust. The Inspector General of Intelligence and Security (IGIS) is an independent officer appointed by the Governor-General and located within the prime minister's office. This unique arrangement allows the IGIS to assist the government and parliament in oversight matters, but allows the office to act independently. The IGIS also enjoys total access to all intelligence and possesses the power of independent inquiry.[66] This oversight also includes access to case files, warrant powers, and financial records.

Although not a method of oversight, the Australian government also has an aggressive public outreach program. The federal government has established National Security Public Information Guidelines for all agencies engaged in national security issues to promote the public's understanding of the missions and threat. A National Security Public Information Campaign also seeks to encourage public vigilance. Security information is pushed via a variety of media to inform the Australian public of the government's efforts against terrorism and to create a safer environment.[67] These efforts directly support ASIO's efforts in engaging communities to derive community-based information conduits to support its assessments. This is in stark contrast to MI5's historical outlook regarding public engagement, which took the major step of instituting a public website only after 9/11.[68] Despite these

DCAF BENCHMARKS	U.K.	Australia	India	U.S.
DOMESTIC INTELLIGENCE SUBJECT TO LAWS	◗	●		
COORDINATION OF DOMESTIC & FOREIGN INTELLIGENCE	◗	◗		
EXECUTIVE BRANCH COORDINATING	●	●		
INDEPENDENT BODY CONDUCTING ASSESSMENTS	●	●		
OVERSIGHT MECHANISMS	◑	◑		

● ⟷ ○
Most Effective   Least Effective

FIGURE 30.2 DCAF benchmarks versus the U.K.-Australia.

strong oversight mechanisms, ASIO has also been criticized for heavy-handed and intrusive tactics in the past against leftwing groups.[69]

CONCLUSION

ASIO's strength, like MI5, lies in its ability to operate under a well-defined structure and an independent assessment umbrella. ASIO also has a long history in internal security and domestic intelligence. Despite possessing a highly-evolved information sharing structure, there have also been corresponding shortfalls in ASIO's information sharing performance. Lastly, Australia has robust executive and legislative oversight mechanisms, which although not possessing a perfect track record, are effective in overseeing the country's intelligence process. An examination of Australian oversight mechanisms and public outreach programs may offer some areas for improvement in the United States. When compared to the DCAF benchmarks in Figure 30.2, Australia's top strengths lie in its strong laws governing domestic intelligence, the ability of the executive body to coordinate intelligence, and its independent assessment capability. Similar to the United Kingdom, it also has faced some information sharing shortfalls and although it possesses a better-defined executive and legislative oversight process, there have been instances of past abuse.

THE INDIAN INTELLIGENCE BUREAU (IB)

> We are fully on board as far as the global war against terror is concerned. We will cooperate with everybody, bilaterally, regionally, at the global level, in the fight against terror.
> —Manmohan Singh, Prime Minister of India[70]

ORGANIZATION

The Intelligence Bureau (IB) functions as India's internal security agency.[71] One of the longest-functioning intelligence agencies, its roots can be traced back to the Imperial Intelligence Bureau, which served British interests in India.[72] It is chartered with a wide range of responsibilities spanning from combating terrorists and the separatist efforts of *Naxalists* (Indian Maoists) to critical infrastructure protection—particularly aviation security.[73] The IB falls under India's Ministry of Home Affairs although the Director of the IB can report to the Prime Minister on intelligence issues.[74] Unlike the United Kingdom and Australia, which possess separate foreign espionage and signals intelligence organizations, India's Research and Analysis Wing (RAW) oversees all of India's foreign intelligence.[75] Similar to MI5 and ASIO, the IB does not have independent arrest powers and must rely on federal and state law enforcement elements.

India has been hard-pressed to reform its intelligence apparatus. Following the eleven-week skirmish in 1999 with Pakistan, the Group of Ministers (GoM) initiated a major study of India's security and intelligence. This study, headed by former RAW director Girish Saxena, submitted numerous recommendations to streamline the intelligence process.[76] The Saxena Committee performed the first major review of Indian national security and intelligence since its independence in 1947.[77] For the IB, these initiatives included the development of an independent signals intelligence capability, an expansion of the IB's field presence by bolstering its Subsidiary Intelligence Bureaus (SIB) at the state level, implementation of Inter-State Intelligence Support Teams, development of Joint Task Forces for Intelligence (JTFIs), and a Multi Agency Centre (MAC) to electronically collate and database related intelligence.[78]

Despite its promise, most of the reforms have not been implemented—due largely to bureaucratic infighting. The Ministry of Home Affairs and the Ministry of Finance have disapproved the key elements recommended by the committee.[79] The development of the IB's signals intelligence capability has been stalled. The Finance Ministry has disapproved the IB's request for computer trained personnel to develop and maintain the MAC. Funding for the JTFIs and associated training has also been cut. This bureaucratic confrontation is attributable to the long-standing infighting between the Indian Administrative Service officers who dominate the Home ministry and the Indian Police Service officers who constitute the majority of the IB.[80] The inability of the Indian government to institute meaningful intelligence reforms, establish clear organizational mission roles and responsibilities, and manage the competitive tensions between different bureaucracies is of critical importance given the similarities of the U.S. intelligence community and its efforts to reform itself, institute organizational change, and establish a strategic approach to combating terrorism in a post-9/11 environment.

STRATEGIC OUTLOOK

India has faced many internal security problems since establishing its independence in 1947. Consisting of a multitude of ethnicities, languages, and particularly due to the partition of India and Pakistan, India has faced numerous acts of sectarian violence. In 1999, the hijacking of Indian Airlines flight 814 prompted calls for stronger anti-terrorism legislation. The subsequent events of 9/11 affected the Indian government's perception of the al Qaeda threat and provided an opportunity for parliamentarians to enact stronger legislation that addressed transnational terrorism and financing issues.[81] In 2002, the legislature, led by the nationalist Bharatiya Janata Party, passed *The Prevention of Terrorism Act (POTA)*—a strong anti-terror legislation similar to the United States, the United Kingdom, and Australia.[82] The legislation came under severe criticism and was later repealed in 2004 with the entrance of a new government under the opposing Congress party.[83] The July 2006 terrorist attacks in Mumbai have renewed the demands for more stringent anti-terrorism legislation.

Although the Indian government has recognized the threat posed by al Qaeda through its proximity to the Indian subcontinent, the government has been unable to articulate precisely its approach to combating terrorism. A key shortfall in the *POTA* legislation was that it lacked any linkage to a wider counterterrorism strategy and approach. As Swati Pandey states:

> For a counterterrorism law, lawmakers should consider the state's police capabilities, the legal system, and the political leanings of its population to make sure that the law will be successful. If these means are sufficient, then the goals of the law can be reached.[84]

The absence of political buy-in, unclear linkages between the legislation's intent and the actual capabilities of security forces, and poor existing oversight mechanisms result in a mismatch between the strategic vision and actual practice. The Indian government's approach has been erratic with limited consensus between political parties. These inconsistencies stem from India's longer-term inadequacy in managing national security. As B. Raman asserts, this is due to three factors:

> The absence of long-term thinking and planning are due to preoccupation with day-to-day crisis management and short-term compulsions, the inhibition of fresh thinking and a coordinated approach to national security issues due to the undue influence of narrow departmental mindsets, and the absence of a watchdog set-up, uninfluenced by departmental loyalties, to monitor the implementation of the national security decisions and remove bottlenecks.[85]

Given this framework and unlike MI5 and ASIO, the role of the IB is less clear. The IB clearly has many domestic intelligence functions. Conversely, unclear strategic guidance, obscured responsibilities, bureaucratic infighting, and extremely limited oversight mechanisms severely hamper its ability to execute its mission. The Indian shortfalls of translating strategic intent into coherent intelligence reform and community management are of paramount—*indeed critical*—importance for the United States as it attempts to redefine its intelligence apparatus in a post 9/11 environment.

INFORMATION SHARING

The challenges faced by the IB are also a reflection of the Indian national security apparatus. The Saxena Committee recommended the implementation of an Intelligence Coordination Group (ICG) and Technology Coordination Group (TCG) to work closely with the National Security Council Secretariat (NSCS) and the Joint Intelligence Committee (JIC).[86] These groups were intended to focus on resource allocation, annual reviews, national estimates, and executive oversight.[87]

Bureaucratic infighting has also plagued the information sharing and assessment process. The National Security Council (NSC), revived as part of the committee's recommendations, has been ineffective in orchestrating the various agencies towards a single purpose.[88] The NSC is rarely convened and does not have a dedicated staff structure to support this process.[89] Senior officials also state that there is little to no coordination between the IB, RAW, and the newly formed Defence Intelligence Agency (DIA).[90]

Although India's organizational structures are similar to the United Kingdom and Australia, they are not as developed or resourced. Bureaucratic infighting and the lack of strong executive direction have limited the IB's effectiveness. There is also an inherent instability in India's organizational approaches and processes to managing national security and intelligence functions.[91] Despite its responsibility for domestic intelligence, the IB has not been given the requisite tools to perform various responsibilities. As Praveen Swami, an Indian journalist noted for his coverage of Indian national security issues commented, "The head of the U.S.' Federal Bureau of Investigation can authorize the cash down purchase of millions of dollars of equipment, while the Director of India's Intelligence Bureau cannot authorize the purchase of a new desktop computer for his secretary."[92]

OVERSIGHT

The Saxena Committee also attempted to address oversight issues by defining India's different intelligence agency's missions and roles and to ensure executive oversight via the NSCS.[93] The inability to implement these reforms, particularly at the executive and assessment level, has resulted in little-progress. Additionally abuse of the *Official Secrets Act of 1923* prohibits national security issues from coming into the forefront of public debate.[94] As Sarath Ramkumar notes, "Top-level political appointees quickly become vigilant in seeking to preserve three main bureaucratic prerogatives of secrecy: control over preservation, control over custody and control over access."[95]

In the absence of a wider public debate, India's parliamentary members rarely discuss or understand the wider implications of India's intelligence issues.[96] In fact, the IB and the RAW are not formally accountable to the parliament.[97] The lack of an effective oversight structure leads to India's legislature being removed from the process. The Standing Committee on Home Affairs has received briefings on the IB's activities, but few of its members have a background in intelligence or are sufficiently staffed to exercise effective oversight.[98] Ramkumar offers the following insightful assessment of India's intelligence community:

> Intelligence agencies are not islands that exist outside executive control. The usefulness and the quality of intelligence is only as good as the government of the day requires. Any serious reforms

in the field of intelligence need an understanding of the precise role of intelligence agencies in serving the nation's national security interest.[99]

The lack of executive and legislative oversight mechanisms has resulted in the politicization of the IB. Most of the bureau's focus has been on political surveillance and election-related information gathering in support of the ruling party.[100] As one member of the National Security Advisory Board commented recently, "How can we expect the IB to function if a large part of its resources is directed at serving the ruling political party of the day?"[101]

Although the United Kingdom and Australia have suffered from oversight shortfalls, the Indian shortcomings in this area have hampered greater intelligence reforms. Understanding the linkage between implementing reform and oversight, given the challenge faced by the Indian government, is of unique importance for the United States. Improving the effectiveness of intelligence oversight—an identified 9/11 recommendation—serves to link the intent and vision of national strategy to the implementation of intelligence reforms.[102]

CONCLUSION

The IB has not been given the necessary tools and resources to fulfill its mission. Although the IB has a long history of performing its internal security function, the majority of its focus has been on political surveillance. Despite sound recommendations and higher-level organizational initiatives, bureaucratic infighting and petty competition have inhibited translating these initiatives into meaningful activities. Lastly, despite possessing definitive intelligence organizations and mandated assessment entities, the lack of strong executive direction and bipartisanship, weak legislative oversight, organizational instability, and ineffective resourcing have resulted in a listless national security and intelligence apparatus. These limitations, when compared to the DCAF benchmarks in Figure 30.3, display a marginal effectiveness. India's intelligence apparatus does not operate under a well-defined set of laws and coordination between intelligence agencies remains an endemic problem. Its independent assessment capability has not been properly resourced and bureaucratic infighting greatly inhibits the ability of the executive to coordinate and direct intelligence efforts. Lastly, India's almost total lack of executive and legislative oversight severely limits accountability and the ability to reform the system.

DCAF BENCHMARKS	U.K.	Australia	India	U.S.
DOMESTIC INTELLIGENCE SUBJECT TO LAWS	●	●	◐	○
COORDINATION OF DOMESTIC & FOREIGN INTELLIGENCE	◐	●	○	
EXECUTIVE BRANCH COORDINATING	●	●	◐	
INDEPENDENT BODY CONDUCTING ASSESSMENTS	●	●	◐	
OVERSIGHT MECHANISMS	◐	◐	○	

Most Effective ⟷ Least Effective

FIGURE 30.3 DCAF benchmarks versus the U.K.-Australia-India.

DOMESTIC INTELLIGENCE AGENCY: APPLICATION FOR THE UNITED STATES?

Proponents of a domestic intelligence agency highlight the importance of prevention, yet domestic intelligence agencies focused solely on information gathering and developing sources have not been proven to be more effective in preventing terrorist attacks. They may have a greater ability to develop better and more precise intelligence assessments on the nature of the domestic threat. The bombings in London (2005) and Mumbai (2006), however, highlight the point that not all attacks can be prevented. Additionally, the metrics for how many attacks have been prevented and where these agencies can cite unreported successes is absent due to their classified nature. By examining the United Kingdom, Australia, and India, it is evident that the challenges of coordinating intelligence, sharing information, and implementing oversight mechanisms are problematic and relevant issues for their domestic intelligence agencies.

ORGANIZATION

For the United States, intelligence coordination and assessment were highlighted as significant shortfalls after 9/11. Although the United States does not have an assessment apparatus as highly centralized and evolved as the United Kingdom or Australia, it has been recognized as a shortfall and steps have been taken to address this issue. The major change was the creation of the Department of Homeland Security with an intelligence charter. The U.S. government also adopted measures to implement

intelligence coordination and improve identified shortfalls through the creation of the Director for National Intelligence (DNI), the National Counter Terrorism Center (NCTC), and revamping the FBI's intelligence capability.[103] Calls for further FBI reforms have continued. As a result of further findings, the FBI consolidated many of its intelligence functions under the creation of the National Security Servicer.[104] Despite the creation of these new agencies and initiatives, the effectiveness of these organizations to implement and institutionalize intelligence reforms, manage resources, and develop strategic assessments as envisioned in the national strategy is questionable, particularly since these initiatives have occurred within a relatively short period of nearly six years after 9/11 and given similar Indian attempts over the last decade.

INFORMATION SHARING

As with the United Kingdom, Australia, and India, information sharing is a significant issue for the United States. This is recognized as a core issue in the *National Intelligence Strategy for the United States*.[105] Further measures have been taken to address this issue by creating the NCTC, instituting the DHS, reforming the FBI's headquarters, implementing Field Intelligence Groups (FIGs), and developing state intelligence fusion centers. The domestic intelligence challenge in the United States is similar to India's in terms of organization and the scope of the problem. Despite higher-level initiatives, the FBI continues to have a "law enforcement" mindset, is experiencing similar problems with implementing its information sharing technology, and is faced with coordinating with multiple state and local efforts.[106] The DHS has also been faced with similar bureaucratic hurdles. Additionally, there is no clear linkage or relationship between the NCTC and the numerous state and local fusion centers that have been created since 9/11.[107] As a result, the level of integration remains questionable. Despite the plethora of executive findings and directives, there are still significant bureaucratic hurdles and infighting to sharing information.

OVERSIGHT

Intelligence oversight remains an issue for the United States. Controversies such as the National Security Agency's (NSA) electronic surveillance and the Department of Defense's Counter Intelligence Field Activities (CIFA) monitoring of U.S. persons, the intelligence activities in Guantanamo, and the handling of National Security Letters remain at the forefront of the political debate. Intelligence initiatives have been undertaken since 9/11, but most of these efforts—particularly with regard to domestic intelligence—have received significant criticism due to ineffective implementation efforts and a lack of bipartisan buy-in. While oversight issues are also challenges for MI5, ASIO, and the IB, Australia seems to have a highly developed, resourced, and aggressive executive and legislative oversight component. A closer examination of Australia's oversight practices and mechanisms could yield practical lessons for the United States. Additionally, the United States needs to streamline and improve its legislative oversight process—a key recommendation of the 9/11 Commission—to ensure proper safeguards for civil liberties and accountability of intelligence operations.[108] Progress in this area has been tepid.

CONCLUSION

When compared to the DCAF benchmarks in Figure 30.4, the United States possesses a well-defined set of laws operating under a strong executive mechanism. These strengths are offset, however, by a weaker executive and legislative oversight process. Although U.S. oversight mechanisms limit the statutory ability of the FBI and other agencies to conduct domestic intelligence, there are still oversight shortfalls in terms of staffing, resources, and legislative access. As seen in the Indian case, limited oversight can also lead to poor implementation of intelligence initiatives. Although there have been numerous fact-finding commissions, such as the 9/11, the Commission on *Intelligence Capabilities of the United States regarding Weapons*

of Mass Destruction, and the numerous panels prior to 9/11, there has not been a strategic and bipartisan approach to overseeing and tracking the implementation and effectiveness of these reforms. Lastly, although steps have been taken to institutionalize the NCTC's independent assessment capability and fuse domestic and foreign intelligence, it is uncertain whether these steps are translating into positive action, whether they are truly combining with the efforts of the DHS or regional, state, or large metropolitan fusion centers, or whether an additional layer of bureaucracy has been added to an already heavily bureaucratized intelligence apparatus.

SUMMARY

Although domestic intelligence agencies possess several shortfalls in not being able to prevent terrorist attacks and have corresponding information-sharing shortfalls and oversight issues, these shortfalls do not address the entire scope of the problem. While domestic intelligence agencies may not be able to prevent all terrorist attacks, are they more successful in preventing most attacks? Do effective domestic intelligence agencies, solely focused on intelligence gathering and unencumbered by law enforcement responsibilities, possess a better ability to focus and develop precise intelligence? Without access to classified sources or performance measures, most literature would suggest that domestic intelligence agencies are more effective in developing intelligence through the penetration of terrorist cells and collation of other intelligence data.[109]

Additionally, the combination of law enforcement and intelligence functions under the FBI and the Attorney General, acting as the federal government's chief legal officer, has also led to civil rights abuses. Opponents to the creation of a domestic intelligence agency fail to recognize that the argument for separating domestic intelligence from law enforcement functions was precisely the reason for limiting the West German government's ability to exercise arbitrary power when it was reconstituted as a nation in the 1950s.[110] In other words, the German domestic intelligence apparatus was consciously separated from law enforcement responsibilities to prevent an abuse of power. Balancing civil rights and public safety remains a problematic issue for democracies whether they possess a domestic intelligence agency or not. Despite the arguments posed by the advocates for and opponents of having a domestic intelligence agency for the United States,

DCAF BENCHMARKS	U.K.	Australia	India	U.S.
DOMESTIC INTELLIGENCE SUBJECT TO LAWS	◑	●	◐	●
COORDINATION OF DOMESTIC & FOREIGN INTELLIGENCE	◑	●	○	◐
EXECUTIVE BRANCH COORDINATING	●	●	◐	◐
INDEPENDENT BODY CONDUCTING ASSESSMENTS	●	●	◐	◐
OVERSIGHT MECHANISMS	○	◑	◑	◐

● Most Effective ←→ ○ Least Effective

FIGURE 30.4 DCAF benchmarks versus U.K.-Australia-India-U.S.

an examination of MI5, ASIO, and the IB have shown that domestic intelligence agencies are not necessarily the solution to the domestic intelligence gap. They may possess a greater ability to better categorize threats and operate unencumbered by complicated and competing mission roles within one agency. In terms of the feasibility, suitability, and acceptability of implementing this organizational construct for the United States, it is *feasible* to develop a U.S. domestic intelligence agency if the resources and executive direction are applied to instituting this capability. The critical *feasibility* issue, however, is whether the United States can translate strategic guidance and direction into meaningful change, reform, and capability that mitigate the domestic intelligence gap—whether under a domestic intelligence agency or some other organizational construct. This is the clear lesson from India's attempt to reform the IB and institute larger intelligence reforms.

Suitability (whether the mission will be accomplished if the tasks are carried out successfully) is also contingent on the ability to translate strategic intent into meaningful change. The 9/11 Commission did not see a need to create a domestic intelligence agency *unless their other recommendations were not adopted*—to create an effective NCTC and Director of National Intelligence (DNI).[111] The effectiveness of the DNI to implement reform was questionable when 96 percent of the FBI's intelligence function fell *outside* of the DNI's purview.[112] Continued FBI reform attempts, as evidenced by reorganization efforts in 1998, 1999, 2000, and 2001, are indicative of organizational instability or resistance to change.[113] Organizational instability and resistance to change can also be applied to NSA. Additionally, the obstacles to creating a unified DHS are another indication of bureaucratic intransigence. The implementation of a strategic vision into reality is clearly a challenge that India has had to face. These shortfalls and others would indicate that current tasks and reforms are not being effectively implemented.

Like the United States, the United Kingdom, Australia, and India have been unable to prevent terrorist attacks. In the absence of definitively demonstrating that domestic intelligence agencies are better positioned to prevent most attacks, the single largest obstacle to implementing this organizational construct in the United States is cultural. Given the history and structure of the United States, it is probably still not *acceptable* to have a domestic intelligence agency. Although the political supportability was stronger after 9/11, most Americans do not like to

feel that they are being spied upon by their government or neighbors.[114] Additionally, as Kate Martin points out, "Nothing in the pre-September 11 law prevented the CIA from informing the FBI that the suspected terrorists had entered the United States, and nothing would have prevented the FBI from pursuing them."[115] The issue lies in the practical interpretation of these regulations. It was the inability to effectively put these regulations into practice that led to information-sharing shortfalls prior to 9/11. It is also the inability to effectively implement the post 9/11 regulations and intelligence initiatives through a bipartisan approach—such as the NSA monitoring program—that creates continued foreign-domestic information sharing gaps.

The central issue is not whether to have a combined law enforcement and intelligence organization versus a sole domestic intelligence agency. The issue is effective *organizational reform, information sharing,* and *oversight.*[116] Effective organizational change, information sharing, and oversight are not necessarily achieved through high-level organizational repositioning, implementing common information data systems, or passing new regulations for managing intelligence operations and reform. The absence of a significant terrorist attack in the United States since 9/11 is also not a good indicator that the intelligence apparatus is operating more efficiently. The creation of additional bureaucracies, an increased centralization of intelligence functions that inhibits the analysis of opposing alternatives, and the inability of the U.S. Congress to reform its oversight process may have actually led to greater drawbacks rather than progress. Although the United States has developed strategies and applied significant resources to address its weaker areas—such as the creation of the DNI to oversee the intelligence community, the NCTC to integrate domestic-foreign intelligence and develop assessments, and the professionalization of the DHS and the FBI's intelligence functions—there remains a level of uncertainty whether these initiatives have resulted in greater progress and meaningful transformation. This uncertainty continues to place the United States at risk. To address these information sharing and oversight uncertainties, the following actions are recommended:

- Assess the ability of the DNI to exercise leadership and management over the intelligence community in terms of controlling resources, implementing cross-organizational information sharing initiatives, and effecting reform consistent with the

National Intelligence Strategy for the United States. This is a clear lesson learned from similar Indian attempts to reform its intelligence community since the 1999 GoM findings.

- Capitalizing on the British and Australian strengths in developing strategic assessments and categorizing domestic threats, conduct an end-to-end organizational review of NCTC to analyze its performance compared to its stated mission, particularly its ability to support its domestic intelligence assessment within a *national* and not strictly federal context.
- Given the identified information-sharing shortfalls with countries possessing domestic intelligence agencies, conduct a review of information sharing and knowledge management policies to assess the applicability of current policies versus actual practice, most notably providing warning and the sharing of raw and unevaluated intelligence between organizations.[117]
- Review the FBI's and DHS's intelligence reform initiatives in terms of professionalization, information sharing, strategic focus, and resource allocation to determine if there is a continued law enforcement versus intelligence mindset, as evidenced by Indian bureaucratic infighting.
- Drawing from Australian strengths, reevaluate executive and congressional oversight mechanisms and reforms to identify duplicative functions, staffing, resources, and the ability to link strategic intent to implementation of intelligence reforms.

Merely implementing a U.S. domestic intelligence agency will not prevent further terrorist attacks. Although the domestic intelligence agencies of the United Kingdom, Australia, and to a lesser extent, India, have had their successes, they have also suffered the same shortcomings of the United States in terms of information sharing and oversight. Additionally, there have been numerous organizational changes and attempts at reform since 9/11. Only an in-depth appraisal of the DNI and NCTC's performance, the ability of intelligence and law enforcement organizations to share information, the FBI's progress at reforming itself, the implementation of the DHS as an organization with a domestic intelligence function, and the ability to provide effective oversight will determine whether the intelligence shortfalls identified in the congressional inquiry into the attacks on 9/11 have been addressed.[118]

QUESTIONS FOR FURTHER DISCUSSION

1. In what ways have domestic intelligence organizations and activities evolved recently in the United States?
2. How does Burch deal with the question of oversight for domestic intelligence operations?
3. What is Burch's view of domestic intelligence effectiveness in other lands?
4. What vulnerabilities do you think the United States continues to face in its homeland defenses? Would you be willing to see taxes increase if the money were spent toward improving homeland security against another 9/11 attack? What could be done to help ensure that the monies would not be misspent on pork barrel projects?

ENDNOTES

1. U.S. Congress, House, Permanent Select Committee on Intelligence and Senate Select Committee on Intelligence, *Report of the Joint Inquiry into the Terrorist Attacks of September 11, 2001*, 107th Congress, 2nd Session, December 2002, S. Rept. No. 107–531, H. Rept. No. 107–792, 244. http://www.fas.org/irp/congress/2002_rpt/911rept.pdf.
2. National Commission on Terrorist Attacks upon the United States, *The 9/11 Commission Report* (New York: W.W. Norton & Company, 2004), 353. The inability to manage and fuse foreign and domestic intelligence information was identified as a key shortfall.
3. Gregory F. Treverton, "Intelligence, Law Enforcement, and Homeland Security," *The Century Foundation* (January 8, 2002): 1. http://www.tef.org/Publications/HomelandSecurity/treverton-intelligence.pdf.
4. National Commission on Terrorist Attacks, *The 9/11 Commission Report*, 172. The estimate for al Qaeda's monetary cost to plan and execute the 9/11 attacks ranges from $400,000 to $500,000.
5. U.S. Congress, Senate, *Homeland Security Act of 2002*, Public Law 107–296, sec. 101 (2002), 13; http://fli.fiudlaw.com/ news.findlaw.com/hdocs/docs/terrorism/hsa2002.pdf. Section 101 established the Department of Homeland Security and reorganized several preexisting government agencies under it.
6. Permanent Select Committee on Intelligence, *Report of the Joint Inquiry*, 245.
7. Paul R. Pillar, "Intelligence," in *Attacking Terrorism: Elements of a Grand Strategy* (Washington, DC: Georgetown University Press, 2004), 134.

8. Mark W. Lowenthal, *Intelligence: From Secrets to Policy*, 3rd ed (Washington, DC: CQ Press, 2006), 234.

9. Harry Howe Ransom, "The Politicization of Intelligence," in *Strategic Intelligence: Windows Into a Secret World*, ed. Loch K. Johnson and James J. Wirtz (Los Angeles, CA: Roxbury Publishing Company, 2004), 175.

10. Harvey Rishikof, "The Role of the Federal Bureau of Investigation in National Security," in *Intelligence and National Security Strategist: Enduring Issues and Challenges*, ed. Roger Z. George and Robert D. Kline (New York: Rowan & Littlefield Publishers, Inc., 2006), 126: The Marlke Foundation, *Protecting America's Freedom in the Information Age: A Report of the Morkle Foundation Task Force* (October 2002), 21. http://www.markle.org/downloadahle_assets/nstf_full.pdf.

11. Michael Massing, "A War on Terrorism is Futile," in *Are Efforts to Reduce Terrorism Successful?*, ed. Lauri S. Friedman (New Haven, CT: Greenhaven Press, 2005), 25.

12. Permanent Select Committee on Intelligence, *Report of the Joint Inquiry*, 245.

13. Larry M. Wortzel, "Americans Do Not Need a New Domestic Spy Agency to Improve Intelligence and Homeland Security," *The Heritage Foundation*, no. 818 (January 10, 2003): 2. http://www.heritage.org/Rescarch/HomelandDefense/loader.cfm?url=/-commonspot/security/getfile.cfm&PageID=34700.

14. Erie R. Taylor, "The Department of Homeland Security May Make Americans Less Safe," in *Homeland Security*, ed. James D. Torr (New Haven, CT: Greenhaven Press, 2004), 64.

15. Ibid., 61.

16. Frederic R. Manget, "Another System of Oversight: Intelligence and the Rise of Judicial Intervention," in *Strategic Intelligence: Windows Into a Secret World*, ed. Loch K. Johnson and James J. Wirtz (Los Angeles, CA: Roxbury Publishing Company, 2004), 408.

17. B. Raman, *Intelligence: Past, Present, and Future* (New Delhi, India: Lancer Publishers & Distributors, 2002), 6.

18. Manget, "Another System of Oversight," 408; Rishikof, "The Role of the Federal Bureau of Investigation in National Security," 126.

19. Ransom, "The Politicization of Intelligence," 171.

20. Ibid., 175.

21. Benjamin Netanyahu, *Fighting Terrorism: How Democracies Can Defeat the International Terrorist Network* (New York: Farrar, Straus and Giroux, 1995), 30.

22. Richard A. Posner, *Remaking Domestic Intelligence* (Palo Alto, CA: Hoover Institution Press, 2005), 73.

23. Geneva Centre for Democratic Control of Armed Forces, "Intelligence Services and Democracy," no. 13, Geneva Centre for the Democratic Control of Armed Forces (DCAF) (April 2002): 3–13, http://www.dcaf.ch/_docs/WP13.pdf.

24. Department of Defense, *Joint Staff Officer's Guide* (Washington, DC: GPO, 2000), 4–87, G-75.

25. Tony Blair, "BBC Breakfast with Frost Interview," interview by Sir David Frost, *British Broadcasting Corporation (BBC)* (30 September 2001); http://news.bbc.co.uk/1/hi/programmes/breakfast_with_frost/ 1571541.stm.

26. Lowenthal, *Intelligence: From Secrets to Policy*, 291.

27. Frank Gregory, "Intelligence led Counter-terrorism: A Brief Analysis of the UK Domestic Intelligence System's Response to 9/11 and the Implications of the London Bombings of 7 July 2005," *Real Instituto Elcano de Estudios Internacionoles y Estraegeicos*, no. 94 (7 December 2005), 3; http://www.realinstitutoelcano.org/analisis/78l/Gregory781-v.pdf.

28. U.S. Congress, Senate, *Catching Terrorists: The British System versus the U.S. System*, Hearing Before a Subcommittee of the Committee on Appropriations, 109th Congress, and Session (September 14, 2006), 23; http://frwchgate.access.gpo.gov/cgi-bin/getdoc.cgi?dbname=109_senate_hearings&docid=f:30707.pdf.

29. Todd Masse, *Domestic Intelligence in the United Kingdom: Applicability of the MI5 Model to the United States* (Washington DC: The Library of Congress, 19 May 2003), 6; http://wwv.fas.org/irp/crs/RL31920.pdf.

30. Peter Chalk and William Rosenau, *Confronting the Enemy Within: Security Intelligence, The Police, and Counter-terrorism in Four Democracies* (Santa Monica, CA: RAND Corporation, 2004), 12. http://www.rand.org/pubs/monographs/2004/RAND_MG100.pdf.

31. Jane's Intelligence Digest, *Britain: Intelligence versus Terrorism* (London: Jane's Information Group, 2006), 1.

32. According to MI5, the Security Service currently employs approximately 2,800 persons. The organization as a whole has experienced targeted growth since 9/11. See MI5's website at www.mi5.gov.uk.

33. Her Majesty's Government, *Countering International Terrorism: the United Kingdom's Strategy*, CM6888 (July 2006), 16; http://www.mi5.gov.uk/files/pdf/ct_strategy.pdf.

34. Ibid., 2.

35. Ibid., 16.

36. U.S. Congress, Senate, *Catching Terrorists: The British System versus the U.S. System*, 22.

37. Chalk and Rosenau, *Confronting the Enemy Within*, 10.
38. Paul Tumelty, "An In-Depth Look at the London Bombers," *Terrorism Monitor* 3, no. 15 (July 28, 2005): 4; http://jamestown.org/terrorism/news/uploads/ter_003_015.pdf.
39. Gregory, "Intelligence led Counter-terrorism," 3.
40. Jim Dempsey, "Domestic Intelligence Agencies: The Mixed Record of the UK's MI5," *Center for Democracy and Technology* (27 January 2003), 2; http://www.cdt.org/security/usapatriot/030127mi5.pdf.
41. Masse, Domestic *Intelligence in the United Kingdom*, 6.
42. Chalk and Rosenau, *Confronting the Enemy Within*, 31; Gregory, "Intelligence led Counter-terrorism," 3.
43. U.S. Congress, Senate, *Catching Terrorists; The British System versus the U.S. System*, 28.
44. Lowenthal, *Intelligence: From Secrets to Policy*, 292–293.
45. Chalk and Rosenau, *Confronting the Enemy Within*, 14–15.
46. U.S. Congress, Senate, *Catching Terrorists: The British System versus the U.S. System*, 28.
47. Masse, *Domestic Intelligence in the United Kingdom*, 9. The doctrine of prior restraint was deemed unconstitutional in the United States in *New York Times v. United States (1971)*.
48. Chalk and Rosenau, *Confronting the Enemy Within*, 51, 53.
49. Ibid., 14.
50. John Howard, "Prime Minister's Address to the Nation," *Prime Minister of Australia News Room* (March 20, 2003), http://www.pm.gov.au/news/speeches/speech79.html.
51. Inspector-General of Intelligence and Security, annual report 2005–2006, 25 September 2006, File Reference 2005/125, 22 http://www.igis.gov.au/annuals/05–06/pdf/IGIS_AR_2005–06.pdf.
52. Nicholas Grono, "Australia's Response to Terrorism," *Studies in Intelligence*, 48, no. 1 (2004): 28; http://www.cia.gov/csi/studies/vol48no1/articleo3.html.
53. Australian Government, *Protecting Australia Against Terrorism 2006: Australia's National Counterterrorism Policies and Arrangements* (2006), 40–4l; http://www.dpmc.gov.au/publications/protecting_australia_2006/docs/paat_2006.pdf.
54. Director-General of Security, *ASIO Report to Parliament 2005–2006*, September 2006, Reference no. eAl004090, viii, 42; http://www.asio.gov.au/Publications/comp.htm. Under Australia's *ASIO Legislation Amendment Act 2006*, ASIO possesses special warrant powers to initiate questioning and detention for particular circumstances under the review of the Attorney General.
55. Australian Government, *Protecting Australia Against Terrorism 2006*, 40.
56. Grono, "Australia's Response to Terrorism," 27.
57. Australian Government, *Protecting Australia Against Terrorism 2006*, 8.
58. Ibid., 13.
59. Mark Thomson, *Jane's Terrorism & Security Monitor* (London: Jane's Information Group, 2006), 1.
60. Inspector-General of Intelligence and Security, *Annual Report 2005–2006*, 52.
61. Director-General of Security, *ASIO Report to Parliament 2005–2006*, 51.
62. Australian Government, *Protecting Australia Against Terrorism 2006*, 16.
63. Chalk and Rosenau, *Confronting the Enemy Within*, 49.
64. Australian Government, *Protecting Australia Against Terrorism 2006*, 42.
65. Chalk and Rosenau, *Confronting the Enemy Within*, 40.
66. Australian Government, *Protecting Australia Against Terrorism 2006*, 41–42.
67. Ibid., 24.
68. Gregoty, "Intelligence led Counter-terrorism," 4.
69. Chalk and Rosenau, *Confronting the Enemy Within*, 50.
70. Manmohan Singh, "Interview of Prime Minister Dr. Manmohan Singh," interview by Charlie Rose, *Charlie Rose Show* (21 September 2004), http://www.indian-embassy.org/pm/pin_charlie_rose_sep_21_04.html.
71. Jane's Intelligence Digest, *Jane's Sentinel Security Assessment: South Asia-India: Security and Foreign Forces* (London: Jane's Information Group, 2006), 29.
72. Maloy Krishna Dhar, *Open Secrets: India's Intelligence Unveiled* (New Delhi, India: Manas Publications, 2005), 11.
73. Ministry of Home Affairs, *Annual Report 2006–07* (Government of India: 2007), 28, 31–32; http://mha.nic.in/Annual-Reports/ar0607_Eng.pdf.
74. Sarath Ramkumar, "Intelligence Agencies: Need for Greater Attention by the Government," *Institute of Peace & Conflict Studies*, no. 579 (17 September 2001): 1; http://www.ipcs.org/newKashmirLevel2.jsp?action=showView&kValue=909&subCatID=null&mod=null.
75. Jane's Intelligence Digest, *Jane's Sentinel Security Assessment: South Asia—India: Security and Foreign Forces*, 28.
76. Rahul Bedi, "Indian intelligence gathering undermined by budget cuts," *Jane's Intelligence Review* (1 July 2004): 2.
77. Praveen Swami, "Handicapped Intelligence," *Frontline* 21, no. 14 (July 2004): 1; http//www.hinduonnet.com/fline/fl2114/stories/20040716001204900.htm.
78. Rahul Bedi, "Indian Security Shake Up," *Jane's Intelligence Review*, (4 May 2001): 2; Praveen Swami, "A New Intelligence Organisation," *Frontline* 19, no. 6 (March 2002): 2; http://www.hinduonnet.com/fline/fl1906/19061240.htm.

79. Praveen Swami, "Bureaucrats Kill Critical Intelligence Reforms," *The Hindu* (June 18, 2004): 1; http://www.hinduonnet.com/thehindu/2004/06/18/stories/2004061805171100.htm.

80. Bedi, "Indian intelligence gathering undermined by budget cuts," 2; Praveen Swami, "Stalled reforms," *Frontline* 20, no. 9 (April/May 2003): 5; http://www.hinduonnet.com/fline/fl2009/stories/20030509002108700.htm.

81. Swati Pandey, *Law and Counterterrorism: The Prevention of Terrorism Act in a Strategic Dimension*, Institute of Peace & Conflict Studies Research Papers (April 2004), 4; http://www.ipcs.org/IRP04.pdf.

82. Government of India, Parliament, *Prevention of Terrorism Act, 2002* (March 28, 2002), Bill No. 5-C of 2002; http://rajyasabha.nic.in/bills-ls-rs/5-c-2002.pdf.

83. Jane's Intelligence Digest, Jane's *Sentinel Security Assessment: South Asia—India: Security And Foreign Forces*, 39; Pandey, *Law and Counterterrorism*, 5. Pandey highlighted the use of the *POTA* legislation to target political opponents.

84. Pandey, *Law and Counterterrorism*, 9. See pages 9–12 for the importance of linking law to national strategy.

85. Raman, *Intelligence: Past, Present, and Future*, 358–359.

86. Saikat Datta, "There Are No Secrets Here," *New Delhi Outlook* (19 November 2006): 1; http://www.outlook-india.com. The Joint Intelligence Committee had merged with National Security Council Secretariat in 1998, but was reformed into its own separate entity.

87. Bhashyam Kasturi, "The Intelligence Secret," *Institute of Peace & Conflict Studies*, no. 589 (27 September 2001): 1; http://www.ipcs.org/newKashmirLevel2.jsp?action=showView&kValue=899&subCatID=null&mod=null; Bedi, "Failures prompt India to reform intelligence service," *Jane's Intelligence Review* (23 May 2001): 3.

88. Dhar, 15.

89. Bedi, "Failures prompt India to reform intelligence service," 7.

90. George Iype, "Why intelligence fails, and terrorists suceeed," *Rediff* (20 July 2006): 1; http://www.rediff.com/news/2006/jul/20george.htm.

91. U.S. Congress, Senate, *Catching Terrorists: The British System versus the U.S. System*, 23–24. Stability in organizational relationships and intelligence sharing processes is touted as a significant strength of the British system where these functions have been allowed to mature over time.

92. Swami, "Bureaucrats kill critical intelligence reforms," 2.

93. Kasturi, "The Intelligence Secret," 1.

94. Sarath Ramkumar, "Revamping of Intelligence Apparatus," *Institute of Peace & Conflict Studies*, no. 328 (22

February 2000): 1; http://www.ipcs.org/newKashmirLevel2.jsp?action=showView&kValue=641&subCatID=null&mod=null.

95. Ramkumar, "Intelligence Agencies: Need for greater attention by the government," 1.

96. Swami, "Handicapped Intelligence," 4.

97. Dhar, *Open Secrets: India's Intelligence Unveiled*, 83.

98. Swami, "Stalled reforms," 4.

99. Sarath Ramkumar, "KRC: Government's Success, but Intelligence Failure," *Institute for Peace & Conflict Studies*, no. 392 (30 July 2000): 2; http://www.ipcs.org/newKashmirLevel2.jsp?action=showView&kValue=1036&subCatID=null&mod=null.

100. Bedi, "India's security shake up," 2.

101. Saikat Datta, "War Below the Radar," *New Delhi Outlook* (31 July 2006): 1; http://www.outlookindia.com.

102. National Commission on Terrorist Attacks, *The 9/11 Commission Report*, 395.

103. U.S. Congress, Senate, *Intelligence Reform and Terrorism Prevention Act of 2004*. Public Law 108–458 (Washington DC: GPO, December 17, 2004), 3644; http://frwebgate.access.gpo.gov/cgi-bin/getdoc.cgi?dbname=l08_cong_public_laws&docid=f:pub1458.108.pdf. Section 101(a) established the Office of the DNI. The act also codified the NCTC. Congressional Research Service, *FBI Intelligence Reform Since September 11, 2001: Issues and Options for Congress* (Washington DC: The Library of Congress, August 4, 2004), 5–6; http://www.fas.org/irp/crs/RL32336.pdf.

104. Commission on the Intelligence Capabilities of the United States Regarding Weapons of Mass Destruction, *Report to the President of the United States* (Washington DC: GPO, March 31, 2005), 30; http://www.wmd.gov/report/wmd_report.pdf. The report specifically called for the consolidation of the FBI's counterterrorism and counterintelligence function under the Directorate of Intelligence. It also identified several other shortfalls with the FBI's progress in transforming its organizational culture and intelligence reforms. See Chapter 10 of the report for further details.

105. Office of the Director of National Intelligence, *The National Intelligence Strategy of the United States: Transformation through Integration and Innovation* (Washington, DC: GPO, October 2005), 1. The strategy highlights the necessity of integrating foreign and domestic intelligence efforts to eliminate the traditional gap in U.S. national security efforts.

106. Dhar, *Open Secrets: India's Intelligence Unveiled*, 13–14, 84–85. Dhar highlights these challenges for the Intelligence Bureau.

107. U.S. Congress, House, Committee on Homeland Security, *Statement of Kenneth Bouche, Colonel, Illinois State Police Regarding a Hearing on "State and Local Fusion Centers and the Role of DHS"* (September 7, 2006), 4; http://www. fas.org/irp/congress/2006_hr/ 090706bouche.pdf.

108. National Commission on Terrorist Attacks, *The 9/11 Commission Report*, 419.

109. The Markle Foundation, *Protecting America's Freedom in the Information Age*, 107.

110. U.S. Congress, Senate, *Catching Terrorists: The British System versus the U.S. System*, 37.

111. National Commission on Terrorist Attacks, *The 9/11 Commission Report*, 423.

112. Commission on the Intelligence Capabilities of the United States Regarding Weapons of Mass Destruction, 459. The DNI is chartered to exercise greater oversight since the creation of the National Security Service.

113. Posner, *Remaking Domestic Intelligence*, 37.

114. Pillar, "Intelligence," 134.

115. Kate Martin, "Domestic Intelligence and Civil Liberties," *SAIS Review* 24, no. 1 (Winter-Spring 2004): 12.

116. National Commission on Terrorist Attacks, *The 9/11 Commission Report*, 423.

117. Netanyahu, *Fighting Terrorism*, 138. Netanyahu highlights the sharing of basic, or raw, data versus the sharing of intelligence warning. He highlights the fact that basic data are often not shared between intelligence agencies of the same government due to the need to protect the information's source or from outright organizational jealousy.

118. Permanent Select Committee on Intelligence, *Report of the Joint Inquiry into the Terrorist Attacks of September 11, 2001*. This study identified many of the foreign-domestic intelligence sharing shortfalls, the inability of the intelligence community to provide assessments, and particularly the FBI's shortfalls in intelligence.

Reprinted with permission from James Burch, "A Domestic Intelligence Agency for the United States? A Comparative Analysis of Domestic Intelligence Agencies and Their Implications for Homeland Security," *Homeland Security Affairs* 3 (June 2007): 1–16.

INTELLIGENCE

A COMPARATIVE PERSPECTIVE

Hamlet: "... For every man hath business and desire
Such as it is ..."

—SHAKESPEARE, *Hamlet*, 1.5.130–131

Although most states, non-state actors, and even corporations have organizations that collect, analyze, and disseminate information, intelligence organizations are not all cut from the same mold. They often undertake different missions, have different capabilities, and are subjected to different types of public or governmental oversight. The U.S. intelligence community is not a typical national intelligence organization. It specializes in technical intelligence collection (e.g., electronic and photographic space surveillance), and it takes a "social science" approach to intelligence analysis. It is also governed by a strict normative and legal code of conduct that is supposed to distance intelligence work from domestic politics.

The United States also is a relative newcomer when it comes to running large intelligence organizations, although at moments of crisis the nation has usually found a way to recruit spies and organize their "take" to meet military and diplomatic needs. Other great powers—France, Great Britain, China, Russia—have long maintained competent and sometimes quite extensive intelligence organizations and operations. Additionally, smaller states—Israel and interwar Poland, for example—have developed highly capable intelligence organizations to offset powerful and threatening neighbors. In fact, it was Polish intelligence that gave the Allies in World War II their greatest asset. Polish mathematicians reproduced a German code machine, known as "Enigma," and using outmoded code "keys" supplied to them by French intelligence were able to read encoded Nazi radio traffic. The intelligence produced by Enigma, known as "Ultra," was closely guarded and highly valued by the Allies because it literally gave them the capability to read Nazi war plans before they were received by frontline commanders.

CLASSIFICATION AND COMPARISON OF ORGANIZATIONS

There is no commonly accepted scheme for separating intelligence agencies into categories, but scholars have used several variables to facilitate the comparative study of intelligence organizations. First, scholars classify national intelligence organization in terms of whether they perform covert actions, paramilitary operations, espionage, technical collection, military intelligence, political intelligence, or internal security and surveillance. They are also interested in determining which of these operations tends to dominate a state's approach to intelligence and who or which agency actually runs the overall intelligence operation. Sometimes states maintain separate organizations to undertake each intelligence function, and sometimes several or all functions are lumped together in a single organization. National priorities and resource constraints can also limit the scope of intelligence activities: Few states have the capability to launch reconnaissance satellites to observe their opponents from space or to monitor events in more than a few areas of special interest. Additionally, culture, history, and tradition shape intelligence organizations and national outlooks about the proper role of intelligence organizations in foreign, defense, and domestic policy.

Second, scholars often use an important distinguishing characteristic to classify national intelligence and security organizations. They look to see whether a division of responsibility exists between monitoring external threats and domestic security and surveillance. States that maintain this distinction between external and domestic activities have a greater likelihood of having professional intelligence organizations that are responsive to the rule of law and oversight by other government institutions and elected officials. By contrast, when domestic and external intelligence and security activities are undertaken by a single organization, most scholars believe that it is likely that intelligence will simply be used as an instrument of state terror to keep a ruling party, clique, or dictator in power. John Dziak (1988) has called this second type of intelligence institution the "counterintelligence state."

The counterintelligence state forms when the distinction between legitimate government and intelligence infrastructure vanishes and the resources of the state come to serve the interests of the ruling elite, which include intelligence functionaries. The counterintelligence state maintains a large intelligence-security force that is responsible for identifying and responding to both domestic and international threats to the regime. Left to its own devices, it often identifies broad and arbitrary domestic and foreign threats, placing virtually everyone not in the intelligence-security force under suspicion. These threats, in turn, justify calls for constant vigilance and the maintenance of a large surveillance and enforcement apparatus. The intelligence-security force is never accountable to the public. Instead, it protects the privileges of the members of the regime and security apparatus itself (Waller 1994). In the counterintelligence state, all political and social dissent is identified as a threat to national security and a crime against the state.

In the past, counterintelligence states have been linked to the influence of the "dead hand of ideology" on state security organizations. In other words, ideology itself predetermines domestic and international threats to the state or regime; the nature, source, or severity of the threats to the nation is not something open to discussion or analysis under these circumstances. Steven David (1999), however, has developed a theory of "omnibalancing" that can also account for the rise of the counterintelligence state. David stands traditional realist notions of security on their head by suggesting that for many states, internal threats—not the military threat posed by other states—preoccupy national leaders. In these situations, political dissidents, rival ethnic or religious factions, or state institutions themselves (such as the military) pose the greatest threat to regime survival. The intelligence-security force thus becomes the premier government institution; senior intelligence officials often find themselves at the top of the ruling regime.

Third, scholars are interested in the degree to which intelligence organizations exist as independent institutions within a government and the degree to which they are held accountable by other bodies for their activities and performance. The counterintelligence state represents an extreme situation when intelligence work, national policy, and what amounts to "oversight" are fused into a single entity. Intelligence organizations, however, are subjected to different amounts of scrutiny and enjoy varying degrees of autonomy. Some intelligence agencies face judicial or legislative oversight that requires detailed and highly classified information about their activities. Others are subjected to less public oversight: Intelligence managers might simply have to offer general reports to some executive authority. Of related interest is the degree to which intelligence work emerges as a recognized profession within a state and the history and culture that shapes the way intelligence organizations operate.

Fourth, intelligence institutions vary in terms of the degree to which they conduct scientific and technical intelligence. Some maintain highly effective programs to reverse-engineer captured weapons or other items of military or industrial significance. Some intelligence organizations focus on economic espionage—gathering corporate secrets, product designs, and research results—to support domestic enterprises. Not all intelligence organizations apply traditional social science methodology in intelligence analysis. Some rely on espionage alone or on commercially or publicly available information to gain insights into their opponent's motivations and behavior. The *Komitet Gosudarstvennoi Bezopasnosti* (KGB), for example, maintained a minimum analytic capability and relied on espionage for insights into current events. The KGB often delivered this raw intelligence directly to senior Soviet officials. This lack of analytical capability sometimes led to bizarre activities. In the weeks leading up to the Cuban Missile Crisis, Soviet agents fanned out across Washington trying to pick up bits of information about the Kennedy Administration's response to the Soviet decision to deploy long-range nuclear-armed missiles to Cuba. It was unlikely, however, that officials would be discussing Soviet missile deployments to Cuba—especially if the missiles remained, as the Soviets intended, hidden from the prying eyes of U S. reconnaissance capabilities. It is difficult to accept, but one of the world's largest intelligence organizations relied on overheard loose talk in D.C. bars and bistros as its primary mode of "analysis."

Fifth, scholars often classify intelligence organizations in terms of their collaborative activities—that is, the nature and intensity of their relationships with foreign intelligence agencies. Most intelligence organizations maintain formal and informal contacts with friendly and even rival intelligence agencies. These channels are used to backstop normal diplomatic communications by providing secure methods of transmitting sensitive information, to conform to or explain formal and public diplomatic positions, or to communicate when normal diplomatic relations have been severed. Among allied governments, collaboration among intelligence agencies can be highly extensive, and in some instances—such as the war on terrorism—it is actually crucial to success. Governments often decide to share classified information, and intelligence professionals are usually charged with delivering these materials. Sometimes personnel in friendly intelligence agencies cannot resist the opportunity to exploit existing lines of communication to penetrate other intelligence organizations. For instance, in the mid-1980s, Israeli intelligence officers used Jonathan Pollard, a U.S. intelligence analyst who volunteered to spy for Israel, to obtain classified U.S. information that was not granted through formal intelligence channels.

SOME EXAMPLES OF FOREIGN INTELLIGENCE SERVICES

This section provides more of an international perspective on intelligence studies, a field of inquiry that has been dominated by scholars engaged in research on spy agencies in the United States, the United Kingdom, Canada, Australia, and New Zealand: the so-called "Five Eyes" who worked together on a number of global intelligence activities. The citizens of these democracies have insisted that their governments conduct serious inquiries into periodic allegations of power abuse within their secret agencies. These probes have led to the declassification of thousands of documents related to their intelligence activities, which in turn has allowed scholars to research and write about these hidden organizations and at least some of the operations they have carried out over the years. Critics have complained, and properly so, that the field of study has become too Anglo-American in its focus; responding to this criticism, scholars are now trying to examine the uses and abuses of intelligence by nations outside the "Five Eyes" framework. Some excellent examples of this extended research net are presented in the next set of readings.

THE READINGS

In the selections that follow, our authors provide insights into the history, culture, and capabilities of the national intelligence communities they survey. Raymond Garthoff examines the state of Soviet intelligence before, during, and after the most frightening moment in the Cold War: the Cuban missile crisis of 1962. He notes the difficulties that both U.S. and Soviet intelligence agencies had in trying to determine during the international crisis the perceptions and objectives of leaders in the respective superpower camps: the Kremlin and the White House.

The second selection by Percy Cradock offers a nuanced assessment on the performance of the British intelligence community in the second half of the twentieth century. Intelligence professionals may help shape history; however, as Cradock observes, the march of events and the resulting record of intelligence failures and successes also determine the directions taken by a nation's spy services.

The section concludes with Wolfgang Krieger's study of Germany's leading intelligence agency, the *Bundesnachrichtendienst*. He comments on the close ties between the *BND* and the CIA, especially during the early days of the Cold War. Krieger explains how, today, the *BND* differs from other Western intelligence agencies in a number of respects.

31. SOVIET INTELLIGENCE AND THE CUBAN MISSILE CRISIS

RAYMOND L. GARTHOFF

The most dangerous moment of the Cold War occurred in October of 1962, when the world's two superpowers—the United States and the Soviet Union—confronted one another with teeth bared over the placement of Soviet nuclear missiles on the island of Cuba, just ninety miles from Florida. Intelligence played an important role during the crisis—particularly in alerting President John F. Kennedy to the presence of Soviet nuclear missilery so close to America's shores; but, as Garthoff relates, both U.S. and Soviet intelligence displayed disquieting limitations on their ability to understand the perceptions and likely decisions of leaders in both Moscow and Washington, DC.

Nikita Khrushchev gradually moved into a leading position in the collective leadership that took power following Stalin's death and became fully dominant by 1957, when he managed to oust a majority of Politburo members he labeled the "Anti-Party Group." The new leaders shared Stalin's Marxist-Leninist worldview but showed sharply varying readiness to consider departures in some areas of policy. Georgy Malenkov moved early to advocate mutual deterrence and peaceful coexistence, only to have Khrushchev ally himself with Vyacheslav Molotov and other conservatives to attack his initiatives and overwhelm him politically—albeit later to adopt those views as his own and the Communist Party line. Meanwhile, the American adversary cautiously sought to sound out the new Soviet leadership.

President Dwight Eisenhower, who had assumed office only six weeks before Stalin's death, was disinclined to take any initiative toward the Soviet Union. British prime minister Winston Churchill (again in that office), however, took the initiative by proposing publicly on May 11 that the Western leaders meet with the Soviet leaders at "the summit" (coining the term that would be used for decades thereafter). The Soviet leaders had an equivocal reaction.[1] Eisenhower himself was wary of such a meeting before the views of the new leaders in Moscow were clarified, believing public opinion could have excessive optimistic expectations. Eisenhower was, however, more ready than Secretary of State John Foster Dulles to test the Soviet position, and on April 16, 1954, in a speech called "The Chance for Peace," he set out four preliminary conditions that the Soviet leaders could meet to demonstrate their readiness to "strengthen world trust."[2] The four were signature of an Austrian peace treaty, release of World War II prisoners of war still held, an armistice in Korea, and steps to curb the arms race. Within two years, the first three of these were fully met, and the Soviet leaders had shown readiness to reach agreements in the fourth area by agreeing (in May 1955) in principle to reduce arms and accept inspection in Europe.

One of the new Soviet leaders took an initiative to recognize new imperatives of the nuclear age. On August 8, 1953, Georgy Malenkov, now the chairman of the Council of Ministers (prime minister), announced that the United States no longer had a monopoly on the hydrogen bomb, the Soviet Union having just held its first test of a partial thermonuclear bomb. But in seeking to present a step toward military equality with the United States, Malenkov again called for the peaceful resolution of any contested issues, stating that "we consider that there are no objective grounds for a clash between the United States and the USSR." Although not a departure from previous Soviet positions, it reemphasized the importance of peaceful resolution of differences with the main adversary.[3]

Then, in a significant departure from the previous Soviet position, a year after Stalin's death—on March 12, 1954—Malenkov declared that a world war in the nuclear age "would mean the end of world civilization," a statement echoing what President Eisenhower had stated on December 8, 1953. On the same day, his Politburo colleague Anastas Mikoyan added that nuclear weapons in Soviet hands served "as a means for deterring aggressors and for waging peace," for the first time explicitly ascribing a deterrent role for Soviet nuclear weapons. Malenkov's statement directly, and Mikoyan's indirectly, not only contradicted the logic of the Stalinist doctrine on inevitability of war but also were arguably not consistent with predictions of ultimate victory for socialism in the world.[4] These statements even raised the intriguing possibility that those issues had arisen while Stalin was still in power. Stalin, in his last theoretical pronouncement some six months before his death, had written that "some comrades," not identified, believed that "wars between capitalist countries have ceased to be inevitable. . . . These comrades are mistaken. . . . They say that the theories of Lenin that imperialism inevitably gives rise to war must be considered obsolete. . . . That is incorrect." Stalin also had continued to publicly display optimism as to the outcome of a nuclear world war, should one occur: "War with the USSR would certainly pose the question of the continued existence of capitalism itself"—but not, apparently, the existence of the Soviet Union.[5]

Malenkov's bold revisionism put him in a politically vulnerable position, and his opponents forced him a year later to retract his statement and used the issue to remove him from the post of chairman of the Council of Ministers in February 1955, although he (like Molotov) remained on the Politburo (Presidium). But the Twentieth Communist Party Congress in February 1956, most famously remembered for Khrushchev's denunciation of Stalin's crimes, revised Stalinist doctrine to conclude that "there is no fatal inevitability of war." And the Twenty-Second Communist Party Congress in 1961 fully embraced the Malenkov heresy: A nuclear war "would cause the complete destruction of the main centers of civilization and the annihilation of entire peoples. . . . A contemporary nuclear war, however one looks at it, can in no way be a factor that would accelerate the revolution and bring nearer the victory of socialism"; "only madmen could want such a catastrophe to happen."[6]

Recognition of the implications of a dawning nuclear age did not change the belief in Moscow (or Washington) of a continuing contest between the two main adversaries. But it did call for consideration of possible means of reducing tensions and the possibility of war, while continuing to prevent the adversary from threatening one's own security and to seek ways of achieving one's own objectives. As Khrushchev consolidated his authority within the leadership, not only was the inevitability of war in the nuclear age abandoned, but also at the same time (at the Twentieth Communist Party Congress) a significant new formulation to describe a possible, and desirable, relationship between the capitalist and socialist camps was unveiled: "peaceful coexistence." Peaceful coexistence did not mean an end to the Cold War, but it envisaged that the conflict between the two sides—a conflict the Soviet leaders still believed would eventually be won by socialism triumphant in the entire world—would be won by the ineluctable victory of "the working class" (which had power in the Soviet Union) over the capitalist rulers of the imperialist states. This victory would, however, as originally projected by Karl Marx, be historically destined rather than the result of war. Many in the West considered peaceful coexistence to be a propaganda slogan designed to mask continuing Soviet pursuit of world domination, but it was not. To be sure, it was used in propaganda, but its real significance was an ideologically sanctioned recognition of realism in the nuclear age.[7]

Khrushchev and other Soviet leaders continued to believe that Western leaders were hostile to the USSR and endorsed as a corollary of peaceful coexistence the maintenance of a strong Soviet nuclear and overall military deterrent in order to prevent Western resort to force. Although Soviet leaders embraced the idea that war was not inevitable and that military conflict with America should if possible be averted, war remained a deadly possibility if not prevented by diplomacy and military strength.

In response to interest on both sides in reducing tensions, the first East-West summit meeting since the Potsdam summit in July 1945 convened in Geneva in July 1955. Western leaders quickly saw that Khrushchev was the most important of the several Soviet leaders who attended, including the colorless Nikolai Bulganin, who had succeeded Malenkov as chairman of the Council of Ministers and was the nominal head of the Soviet delegation. Marshal Georgy Zhukov, minister of defense, who had recently been added to the party Presidium (as the Politburo was then called), was also included for the first time that a military member of the leadership played a political or diplomatic role. He had in 1946 visited the United States for a World War II victory celebration and been escorted by Gen. Dwight Eisenhower. So they met again.

Although no concrete agreements were reached, the Soviet leaders gained confidence, with Khrushchev in particular bolstered by a belief he had taken the measure of his foreign adversaries. He later stated that the meeting had convinced him and his colleagues that "our enemies probably feared us as much as we feared them" and that it was "an important breakthrough for us on the diplomatic front. We had established ourselves as able to hold our own in the international arena."[8] Ambassador Charles Bohlen believed that the Geneva summit led Khrushchev to conclude the West was not planning to attack the Soviet Union.[9] The now-declassified briefing papers prepared before the meeting by Foreign Ministry / KI analysts were professionally done (although they did not know about President Eisenhower's "Open Skies" proposal). The KI also had analysts on hand who worked with intelligence officers supplying intercepted communications during the conference.[10]

The Soviet leaders were always suspicious of American instigation of subversion in Eastern Europe, but they recognized that the internal crises in East Germany in 1953 and in Poland and Hungary in 1956 arose from domestic problems and did not fear direct Western intervention.

Khrushchev's aggressive diplomatic ventures owed nothing to intelligence; they resulted from his impetuous nature, faith in the political power of nuclear weapons, ideological view of world politics, and lack of understanding of the West. He gambled with nuclear brinkmanship in the Suez Crisis of 1956. Lacking appropriate means to aid Egypt, which had been led to expect Soviet support, Khrushchev publicized a Soviet message to the British and French governments warning that if they did not cease their intervention, nuclear missiles could strike their countries. The Soviets had no missiles deployed capable of such a strike, and Britain and France called off their intervention because of American insistence (and an acute financial crisis caused by absence of American support), not owing to Khrushchev's threat.[11] But judging from indications in internal Soviet discussions and the testimony of his son Sergei, Khrushchev believed that his threat had led to the Anglo-French withdrawal.[12]

In June 1957 Khrushchev definitively defeated his erstwhile colleagues in the post-Stalin collective leadership, who were subsequently branded "the anti-party group." Marshal Zhukov, whose support to Khrushchev had been important in defeating Malenkov, Molotov, and the other political rivals, publicly pledged support to the new Khrushchev party leadership "on behalf of the armed forces." But if Zhukov could pledge the support of the armed forces for one political leader, he might do so for another. In October, while Zhukov was on an official visit abroad, he was suddenly relieved of all his military and political posts, sharply criticized, and retired permanently from political life.[13]

At about the same time, Khrushchev's attraction to the use of nuclear bluff and blackmail was boosted by the USSR's first successful test of an intercontinental ballistic missile and orbiting of *Sputnik*, the first artificial satellite of Earth. The alarmed Western reaction to those developments magnified the strategic significance of Soviet entry into the missile age and encouraged Khrushchev to seek political advantages from the promise of strength even long before significant military capabilities were achieved. At one point, he talked about Soviet missiles being "turned out like sausages," with seeming disregard for the possibility that such threats might lead the other side to respond in kind.

In October 1957 Khrushchev spun a tale of a Turkish and NATO threat to intervene in Syria and announced military maneuvers, then claimed credit for forestalling a NATO attack on Syria that was never contemplated. In July 1958 the pro-Western king and prime minister of Iraq were killed and succeeded by a military dictator who was considered a threat by its neighbors. In response to their appeals for assistance, the United States landed troops in Lebanon and the United Kingdom in Jordan. The Soviet Union with fanfare announced military maneuvers in the Transcaucasus and Bulgaria and issued vague warnings against a Western intervention in Iraq that was never contemplated. Soon thereafter, in September 1958, Khrushchev again issued verbal threats as a supportive gesture to the Chinese communists, who were bombarding the Nationalist-held island of Quemoy, and claimed to have prevented an American intervention. In fact, the United States never contemplated such an intervention (nor did the Chinese leaders welcome this unsought "support"). But then his run of successful bluffs ran out.

Khrushchev's confidence became his nemesis in a crisis that he initiated in November 1958 when he called for the Western powers to withdraw their military and political presence from West Berlin, to convert it into a "free city," and to recognize the German Democratic Republic (East Germany). In messages to the Western powers soon after, the initiative was broadened to include a six-month deadline for signing a German peace treaty with both German states (constituting Western diplomatic recognition of East Germany, which the Western powers were not prepared to do). Khrushchev had important defensive objectives: to force Western recognition of East Germany, to stop the massive exodus of East Germans through West Berlin, and to curtail extensive Western intelligence operations mounted through Berlin. As he later put it, Berlin was "a bone in my throat," and he sought to remove it. He also had important offensive goals: to end a Western presence deep in Eastern Europe and to do so by coercive diplomacy in order to emphasize Soviet politico-military strength and weaken the political stature of the United States, West Germany, and NATO. He sought to shift the "correlation of forces" in the USSR's favor and saw West Berlin as a vulnerable Western pressure point.

The ensuing Berlin Crisis lasted four years, finally ending with no change in the city's status. Inept and damaging, Khrushchev's failed initiative stemmed entirely from his overconfidence in judging that the main adversary and its allies would acquiesce in such a political defeat. In launching the venture, Khrushchev had obtained the consent of his compliant colleagues without seeking any intelligence advice on possible Western reactions.[14] He was aware of budding American concern as to a possible "missile gap" favoring the USSR, and he may have thought he could play that US perception to his advantage. If so, the calculation failed. Although US concern about Soviet missile strength did grow during 1959–60 when Berlin was a focal point of US-Soviet confrontation and contributed to a sense of crisis, during 1961 it became clear to all that America actually had the lead in strategic missiles. By then Khrushchev realized that his Berlin ploy had become a liability rather than a lever and settled in August 1961 for cutting off westward emigration of East Germans (and sharply curtailing Western intelligence operations) by unilaterally building the infamous Berlin Wall.

What altered Khrushchev's view of America during the crisis was the firmness of the US and NATO stand, which was reported by Soviet intelligence, but also by a change in his own impressions of the United States and its leaders. His twenty-day visit to the United States in September 1959—the first ever by a Soviet leader—provided him with a partial corrective and broadening of his understanding of the United States. Upon his return to the Soviet Union, he publicly stated his belief that President Eisenhower "sincerely wishes to see the end of the Cold War." Khrushchev saw his reception in America (he received full honors as head of state although he did not hold that title) as according himself personally, and by extension the USSR, equality with President Eisenhower and the United States, in his eyes reflecting a major advance.

There had been unprecedented high-level visits on both sides in 1959 leading up to Khrushchev's visit and a planned return visit by President Eisenhower to the USSR. The two first deputy premiers of the USSR, Anastas Mikoyan and Frol Kozlov, came to the United States in January and July, and Vice President Richard Nixon visited Moscow in July and August. These were useful familiarization visits rather than vehicles for diplomatic negotiations, although Mikoyan did recommend to Eisenhower that the two sides work to "end the cold war."[15]

Intelligence had little influence on Khrushchev's basic views toward the United States. His political power allowed him to disregard intelligence he received or even not to consult his intelligence services, and he relied instead on his own limited direct observations and personal judgments. The KGB lacked high-grade sources of political intelligence on the main adversary that could correct Khrushchev's misperceptions. For example, KGB foreign intelligence reported extensively on events in 1960, but apart from such things as acquiring Western position papers prepared for the aborted May 1960 Paris summit, various Western diplomatic exchanges on Berlin and Germany, and a steady stream of documents and reports on NATO planning, there was nothing of note on high-level political decision making in Washington in the annual report covering 1960 sent to Khrushchev by the head of the KGB in early 1961.[16]

Khrushchev believed that CIA director Allen Dulles was responsible for sending the U-2 reconnaissance plane that was shot down after penetrating far into Soviet airspace on May 1, 1960. Thinking that President Eisenhower would not have authorized the flight, Khrushchev sought a propaganda dividend by suddenly producing the pilot, who had survived the event, and publicly suggesting that anti-Soviet American militarists and intelligence chiefs had been responsible for the flight. Rather than exonerating Eisenhower, however, the statement implied that the president did not control American government actions—a charge he could not let stand—and led him to assert publicly his own responsibility. When Eisenhower than refused to offer an apology that Khrushchev had demanded, Khrushchev canceled his participation in a planned Four Power summit already convening in Paris and called off the Eisenhower visit to the Soviet Union planned for June. This episode, marked by Soviet misperceptions and propaganda overreach, in effect suspended US-Soviet relations until the change of administration in Washington in January 1961.[17]

John F. Kennedy, Andrei Gromyko told Khrushchev, would be anti-Soviet like his father. KGB analysts on the other hand believed that he would try to moderate tensions. Both, however, thought that Kennedy believed in a missile gap in Soviet favor as he had highlighted in his election campaign and would therefore pursue a military buildup.[18] Khrushchev, eager to test the young new president's mettle over Berlin, sought an early meeting with him.

In a January 1961 speech before Kennedy's inauguration, Khrushchev made clear that war must be prevented, not only general nuclear war but also even local, limited, conventional wars involving the great powers. But he also seemed to promise stepped-up Soviet support for "wars of national liberation" in previously colonial territories such as South Vietnam, the Democratic Republic of the Congo, and Algeria, wars he depicted as just and inevitable, although not appropriate for direct great-power intervention. Kennedy and his advisers interpreted the speech as articulating a challenge the West had to meet. Khrushchev, who did not intend or see his remarks in that light, was (we now know) dismayed by the negative US reaction and felt personally rebuffed by Kennedy.[19]

The failed American landing of anti-Castro Cuban émigrés at the Bay of Pigs in April 1961 also affected Khrushchev's view of Kennedy. The Soviet leader believed that Kennedy had been inveigled into the venture by Allen Dulles and Secretary of the Treasury Douglas Dillon, holdover Republicans from the Eisenhower administration.[20] The move affected the very kind of newly liberated country Khrushchev had touted in his January speech. It also contributed to Khrushchev's perception of Kennedy as a young and inexperienced leader without a firm hand on foreign policy, a view not changed by their personal meeting in Vienna in June. On that occasion, Khrushchev tried to browbeat Kennedy, and the two leaders largely talked past one another in sterile debate fashion rather than resolving or clarifying their differences. Khrushchev's development of respect for Kennedy as an opponent would have to await subsequent events.

Khrushchev's and Kennedy's use of unofficial, off-the-record personal communication channels, which bypassed some bureaucratic filters and were unlikely to leak, bore mixed results in terms of building mutual understanding. Even before his inauguration, Kennedy had used a KGB officer posing as a Soviet newsman in Washington to pass a message that he would be firm but was willing to seek common ground on Berlin. In May he used a GRU officer ostensibly serving as an embassy press officer, Col. Georgy Bol'shakov, who became a conduit through White House press secretary Pierre Salinger and soon through the president's brother Robert. Although this channel was used to help defuse a crisis in Berlin later in 1961, Khrushchev abused it in 1962 to give Kennedy false assurances that the USSR would not send missiles to Cuba, thereby ending the arrangement. Kennedy nevertheless moved to establish another such channel in September 1963 through Col. Georgy Karpovich, a KGB officer, but it ended almost immediately with Kennedy's demise.[21]

Khrushchev sometimes benefited from concrete and verifiable intelligence information as he conducted his proactive, erratic diplomacy. Throughout the 1960s Soviet intelligence obtained good coverage of NATO planning, including policy discussions and concrete military plans for various contingencies concerning Berlin. For example, KGB chairman Aleksandr Shelepin was able in July 1961 to report to Khrushchev that NATO was preparing to deal with the Berlin Crisis as a military problem with serious contingency planning and also considering various possible sanctions against the USSR and East Germany. Stiff personal letters on US resolve sent by President Kennedy to the leaders of Britain, France, and West Germany as well as follow-up actions by Secretary of State Dean Rusk were all intercepted and rapidly reported to Moscow. Also, an American sergeant stationed at the Orly Armed Forces Crisis Center in Paris was handling, and copying for Moscow, all the NATO top-secret Live Oak military contingency planning documents for the Berlin Crisis, and there were multiple other penetrations of NATO.[22]

At the same time, Khrushchev was, according to his son, wary and dismissive of intelligence reports from vague, undisclosed sources and possible hostile misinformation, perhaps because he himself had authorized intelligence disinformation and deception measures.[23] In June 1960 the KGB had sent him a report that its chief in Washington had received information from "contact maintained with a [NATO] collaborator of the CIA" that "the Pentagon has prepared a plan for a preventive nuclear strike on the USSR while the USA has a preponderance of strategic arms." According to the cursory and ambiguous account we have on this report (the original document is not available), it would appear at most that allegedly someone was *proposing* consideration of a preventive strike while the United States had a clear strategic advantage, not that one was planned. There is no indication that this report received serious attention in Moscow.[24] In early 1962 a GRU report was said to describe a list of Soviet cities targeted by American missiles, ready for immediate launch if and when ordered.[25] Another GRU report in March 1962 stated that, "according to a source in the US national security bureaucracy," in June 1961 after the Vienna summit the Pentagon had given serious consideration to a nuclear strike on the USSR but had called it off after a Soviet nuclear weapons test in September showed that Soviet thermonuclear weapons were more advanced than Americans had previously believed.[26] Such alarmist reports may have sustained pre-existing suspicions in the minds of Soviet leaders, but they did not lead to serious consideration that America was ruled by leaders bent on radical gambles.

Khrushchev had decided long before that American leaders, specifically including Eisenhower and John Foster Dulles, and then Kennedy, were rational and did not intend to start a war or launch a surprise nuclear attack on the Soviet Union. He had earlier believed Kennedy and NATO would back down over Berlin, but in October 1961 he abandoned the idea of signing a separate peace treaty with East Germany (and also suspended earlier plans to send substantial arms, including air-defense missiles, to Cuba).[27] At a meeting of the Presidium (the renamed Politburo) on January 8, 1962, Khrushchev admitted to his colleagues that he had been wrong in believing that Kennedy would give in on Berlin, asserting that Kennedy was in a weaker position than he had thought and that leading capitalist circles were calling the tune on US policy. He also acknowledged that the Western Europeans had been more supportive of a strong Berlin stand than he had anticipated. In the future, he said, the USSR would still press on Berlin but without ultimatums.[28] Khrushchev's more sober views at the end of 1961 were probably also induced by an important October speech by Deputy Secretary of Defense Roswell Gilpatric asserting that the United States had such strategic superiority that it could respond to any Soviet attack with an even more powerful response than the initial Soviet attack (the USSR had only four intercontinental ballistic missile launchers operationally deployed at the time). Khrushchev made no riposte like his earlier bragging about Soviet missiles being "turned out like sausages," and indeed no Soviet challenge to Gilpatric's assertion was issued at all.

The earlier back-and-forth in the United States on missile gaps and the strategic balance had shown the importance of perceptions and the problematic nature of communicating information as to military capabilities and intentions. A potentially serious moment in October 1961 provides an example of how even tactical events can affect mutual understanding. Over the period October 22 to 28, a mini-crisis arose over the issue of Western access to East Berlin. East German guards at a sector-crossing point called "Checkpoint Charlie" refused to allow the American civilian deputy commandant to enter East Berlin without showing identification documents. US authorities misperceived this action as an attempt by Moscow to squeeze the West into indirect recognition of East German sovereignty in East Berlin and thus as a threat to the American presence and authority in West Berlin and to reciprocal rights of access to all parts of the city. Fearing the consequences of backing down, the United States brought in American troops to escort the official into East Berlin, and the East German guards withdrew. Eventually the Americans brought in tanks, including some with bulldozer attachments, to clear away obstacles that might be placed at the checkpoint, and the Soviets met this step by bringing in their own tanks. A stalemate with ten uncovered tank guns on each side pointing at the other ended only when President Kennedy contacted Khrushchev through Colonel Bol'shakov and suggested that if the Soviets withdrew their tanks, the Americans would do the same. This happened, the East Germans abandoned their identification demand, and the status quo ante was restored.[29]

The difference in American and Soviet interpretations of what had occurred was stunning. The American side, including President Kennedy, was satisfied the outcome meant the Soviet leadership had understood American determination and backed down. The United States had stood fast and won. Khrushchev, for his part, believed *he* had won. Unlike the Americans, he knew he had not instigated the credentials demand (the East Germans had done it on their own), and when the Americans introduced tanks, he thought they were using a contrived issue to challenge the recently established Berlin Wall. To him, the Soviet response had successfully rebuffed a major American initiative to use military force to intervene in the Soviet sphere. In his taped memoir, he says the outcome was "a great victory for us": "The West had tested our nerve by prodding us with the barrels of their [tank] cannons and found us ready to accept their challenge. They learned that they couldn't frighten us."[30]

Specific and accurate intelligence on the Soviet side played an important part in leading Khrushchev to his conclusion about the outcome. Soviet military intelligence had observed and photographed tanks *equipped with bulldozer attachments practicing* techniques to break down part of a replica Berlin Wall in a secluded wooded area of West Berlin. Gen. Lucius Clay, a hero of the 1948 Berlin confrontation who had recently been returned to Berlin as a symbol of steadfastness, had undertaken the exercise. Although no one in Washington was even aware of Clay's action, Khrushchev and the other Soviet leaders, thanks to Soviet intelligence reporting, had been fully informed about it. Little wonder that Khrushchev connected the American tanks at the checkpoint with possible actions directed at the wall. The lesson for intelligence, and for recipient use of intelligence, was that accurate information, while in general a good thing, can be wrongly interpreted. In this instance, US practice for a military contingency was misconstrued in Moscow as preparation for a hostile initiative.[31]

As was often the case throughout the Cold War, intelligence in the Checkpoint Charlie case was not up to the task of clarifying the intentions of the other side. Neither side had political intelligence on the other sufficient to provide reliable understanding of the other's initiatives. The problem of accurately communicating intentions, and the related problems of unintended communication of intentions and of communication of apparent but not real intentions, are all difficult and made yet more so by inability to know whether one's real intentions have been understood by an adversary when the communication is intended or whether inaccurate understanding of

one's intentions has inadvertently occurred. The situation becomes even more uncertain when secret intelligence conveys inaccurate information or when misinformation and deception are involved, and even accurate but partial intelligence can reinforce misperceptions or otherwise aggravate misunderstandings.

In some respects, Soviet intelligence can fairly be said to have played a positive role. Soviet and other Warsaw Pact espionage penetrations of NATO headquarters and NATO member countries were extensive during virtually all of the Cold War. Potentially most important for a war that fortunately never occurred, these disclosures of secret NATO political and military deliberations and decisions revealed thinking, plans, and decisions relating to a whole range of East-West relations. Although such information might on occasion be exploited for unilateral advantage, overall it conveyed in a way that open Western declarations could not the firmness of the Western position (in the case of Berlin, it contributed to the Soviet decision to drop ultimatums). It also provided evidence that NATO had no offensive plans for war against the Warsaw Pact—although Soviet intelligence remained suspicious that the United States had ultrasecret offensive war plans not shared with its NATO partners and thus not attainable by Soviet espionage against NATO and its member countries. On the whole, Warsaw Pact intelligence on NATO probably actually served basic Western interests.[32]

Regrettably, in some cases Soviet intelligence obtained information that was interpreted by intelligence analysts and military leaders as representing American and NATO offensive intentions. In the documentary intelligence provided to the West by Col. Oleg Penkovsky were assessments by Col. Gen. Semyon Ivanov, the chief of the Operations Directorate of the Soviet General Staff, of two major NATO field exercises held in 1959 and 1960. In both cases, although the exercises were announced to be for NATO defensive responses, the actual scenarios as reported to Moscow showed NATO forces launching nuclear strikes *before* the Warsaw Pact attack. Ivanov characterized the acknowledged defensive purposes as meant to mislead NATO publics and military officers and concluded that the exercises revealed intentions for NATO at some time to launch a surprise attack claiming it was a preemptive defensive response. Thus the Soviet military leadership was given top-secret intelligence analyses, buttressed with detailed facts, seeming to support US and NATO first-strike plans and intentions.[33]

Soviet intelligence reports often exaggerated the Western military threat through deductive reasoning based on assumptions of hostile intent rather than evidence. As we have noted, Soviet leaders often discounted such reports because they understood the bureaucratic impulses of those supplying them and had taken their own measure of Western leaders via direct contacts, an important positive factor that helped keep the Cold War cold.

As the Berlin Crisis wound down and the American edge in strategic military power grew, Soviet leaders became even more convinced that nuclear war had to be prevented. At the Twenty-Second Communist Party Congress in October 1961, the Communist Party of the Soviet Union (CPSU) replaced Lenin's party program of 1919 with a new one that confirmed the absolute need for peaceful coexistence in the nuclear age.[34]

This reaffirmation of a vitally important guideline did not, however, prevent Khrushchev from embarking on what would turn out to be his most dangerous foreign policy initiative, secretly deploying in Cuba nuclear-armed missiles that could at least temporarily shore up the weak Soviet strategic missile force in the strategic balance with the United States. The origin of this initiative was Khrushchev's misunderstanding of a remark made to his son-in-law and informal foreign affairs adviser, Aleksei Adzhubei, by President Kennedy. Meeting Adzhubei on November 25, Kennedy said that American concern over Castro's Cuba could be compared with Soviet concern over developments in Hungary in 1956 that had been settled in three days. Presumably he was trying to say that the United States wanted to handle Cuba less drastically than the USSR had dealt with the uprising in Hungary. Unfortunately, Khrushchev interpreted the comment as indicating that Kennedy thought he had a right to deal with Cuba quickly and forcefully (as indeed he had unsuccessfully tried to do earlier in the year). The Soviet leaders were well aware of the American program of subversion and sabotage in Cuba mounted after the Bay of Pigs fiasco, and they interpreted Kennedy's remark as warning them that he intended to act again to remove Castro and that they should not stand in the way.[35]

Khrushchev consequently revived a plan to provide arms to Cuba that he had suspended the previous fall, and in the spring of 1962 the Presidium first decided to send weapons to the Cuban armed forces and later decided also to include, under Soviet control and with Soviet protective forces, tactical nuclear weapons for defense of Cuba and strategic missiles with nuclear warheads capable of striking deep into the United States.[36] Khrushchev pushed through this reckless move with the support of the military establishment, believing that the deployment could be made secretly so he could present the United States and the world with a fait accompli in November 1962 after the US elections. He believed that Kennedy, however unhappily and reluctantly, would acquiesce in the deployment. Once again he miscalculated, overestimating (with no professional assessment) that US intelligence would not learn of the action until after the US election in November and underestimating his adversary's mettle. Once again he was compelled to retreat.[37] The only gains he achieved were a conditional American promise not to invade Cuba and an American statement (not made public) reaffirming its intention to remove its missiles from Turkey.

Khrushchev embarked on this gambit, as he had with Berlin, without seeking any intelligence assessment as to likely or possible American responses or other potential international developments, or as to whether the deployments could be successfully concealed. (Gromyko tried to raise questions about possible American reactions but fell silent when it became clear that Khrushchev did not want to hear them.) As for Soviet intelligence, it did not discover that the United States had known of the missile deployment for an entire week, during which time American leaders considered, decided upon, and prepared for a course of action. During the crisis, Soviet military intelligence did provide detailed data on the US military buildup and readiness for possible action, confirming American resolve. As for high policy, there was no intelligence information on either side from espionage or other means concerning the deliberations, decisions, and intentions of the leaders prior to or during the crisis. Thus, on crucial questions of perceptions and willpower, the leaders of the two adversaries had to consider and select their successive actions of public and private diplomacy to resolve the crisis virtually blindfolded.[38]

In later describing how the Cuban Missile Crisis had affected his understanding of the main adversary, Khrushchev said in the part of his taped memoirs kept confidential until the end of the Cold War: "Thanks to President Kennedy the United States began to weigh its words more carefully and take into account the Soviet Union's military strength. America began to understand that if it could not be friends with the Soviet Union, at least it should not incite conflict. For us, that was a big victory." He also said—in an acknowledgment of mutual deterrence—that the crisis was a "classic example" of the fact that if both sides "keep military strength at reasonable levels, we should be able to avoid war."[39] In a personal letter to Kennedy after the crisis, he wrote of mutual trust and claimed that there now was "a special relationship" between them.[40] Both Khrushchev and Kennedy, and even more importantly subsequent leaders on both sides throughout the Cold War, showed—if not an appreciation of "reasonable levels" of deterrents—a new, deeper understanding of the need for the adversaries not only not to resort to war in the nuclear age but also to conduct relations in such a way that the risk of war would not be raised. No more bluffing or ultimatums. Khrushchev's behavior in his remaining two years in office also showed an awareness of the need for each side to "weigh its words more carefully and take into account" the other side's military strength and "not incite conflict." Both his assessment of the main adversary and his recognition of the need for prudence in Soviet policy in dealing with it were importantly affected by the chastening experience of the crisis.

Following the Cuban Missile Crisis, the two adversaries sought to lessen tensions and reach agreements. President Kennedy took the initiative in breaking the ice with a major speech, "Toward a Strategy of Peace," on June 10, 1963, that set a new tone for US-Soviet relations. Kennedy called upon Americans to "reexamine our attitude toward the Soviet Union" and—in a reference to the importance of perceptions—"not to fall into the same trap as the Soviets, not to see only a distorted and desperate view of the other side, not to see conflict as inevitable, accommodation as impossible, and communication as nothing more than an exchange of threats." He even urged that Americans "reexamine our attitude to the cold war," calling for a "strategy of peace" and declaring that "we can seek a relaxation of tensions without relaxing our guard." Specifically he called for agreement on a direct communication link between Washington and Moscow and on a nuclear test ban.[41] Khrushchev told his advisers, and later Ambassador Harriman, that the speech was the best by an American president since Roosevelt, and years later senior Soviet diplomats told me the speech had had a great impact in Moscow. It serves as an example of the importance of leadership statements in affecting an adversary's understanding.

Khrushchev responded favorably less than a month later, and a ban on all nuclear tests except underground ones was reached before the end of July.[42] Agreements were also rapidly concluded on a bilateral "hotline" for crisis communications and on not placing nuclear weapons in outer space.[43] These agreements constituted significant opening steps toward lessening tensions, and both Khrushchev and Kennedy seemed ready to move further despite remaining doubts and opposition in both countries. Then Kennedy's assassination changed the political landscape. Khrushchev believed the act resulted from a conspiracy of right-wing American militarists and Texas oil barons and carried ominous implications for US policy.[44] He and his colleagues considered how best to establish relations with Kennedy's successor, but before Lyndon Johnson's election as president in his own right, Khrushchev was ousted.

QUESTIONS FOR FURTHER DISCUSSION

1. During this middle phase of the Cold War, which "int" did the Soviets seem to rely on most to track the activities of NATO members?
2. Why do you think Soviet intelligence had so little influence on President Nikita Khrushchev?
3. Why were alarmist reports from the KGB about the intentions of the United States so prevalent during these years?
4. In what manner was accurate intelligence about the United States often wrongly interpreted by Soviet spy agencies?

ENDNOTES

1. Zubok and Pleshakov, *Inside the Kremlin's Cold War*, p. 157.
2. Two days after Eisenhower's speech, which John Foster Dulles had not favored, Dulles followed it with a vintage "Cold War speech" championing the liberation theme rather than encouraging possible change in the Soviet Union. For background, see Raymond L. Garthoff, *Assessing the Adversary: Estimates by the Eisenhower Administration of Soviet Intentions and Capabilities* (Washington: Brookings Institution, 1991), pp. 6–8. The KI, however, instead of recognizing that Dulles was taking a harder line than Eisenhower, concluded that the stiff Dulles diatribe was intended to reinforce the Eisenhower speech rather than to undercut it. See Zubok, "Soviet Intelligence and the Cold War," p. 461.
3. "Speech of G. M. Malenkov," *Izvestiya*, August 9, 1953.
4. See "Speech of G. M. Malenkov," *Pravda*, March 13, 1954, and "Speech of A. I. Mikoyan," *Kommunist* (Yerevan), March 12, 1954. Malenkov's speech was almost

certainly prompted by a sobering account of future thermonuclear bombs and a real threat to world civilization prepared by Academician Igor Kurchatov, head of the Soviet nuclear weapons program, and discussed with Malenkov before it was officially submitted to him, Molotov, and Khrushchev on April 1, 1954, by Kurchatov's superior, Deputy Premier Vyacheslav Malyshev. Malenkov thus jumped the gun on a public recognition of this impending revolution in political-military affairs without adequate consideration of how his rivals, Khrushchev and Molotov, could and would use his daring initiative against him. Khrushchev completely embraced the Malenkov line after securing power, and Molotov was excluded from the leadership for continuing to hold Stalinist views on this and other matters. See Zubok, *Failed Empire*, pp. 124–27, on the Kurchatov memorandum.

5. I. V. Stalin, "Economic Problems of Socialism in the USSR," *Bol'shevik*, no. 18 (September 1952): pp. 18–19.

6. For a more complete analysis, see Raymond L. Garthoff, "The Death of Stalin and the Birth of Mutual Deterrence," *Survey* (London) 25, no. 2 (Spring 1980): pp. 10–16.

7. As late as the Moscow summit meeting of June 1988, Ronald Reagan reluctantly rejected a communiqué reference to "peaceful coexistence" proposed by Mikhail Gorbachev, after George Shultz and Frank Carlucci persuaded him to withdraw his initial readiness to include it. See Igor Korchilov, *Translating History: Thirty Years on the Front Lines of Diplomacy with a Top Russian Interpreter* (New York: Scribner, 1997), pp. 177–80.

8. Nikita Khrushchev, *Khrushchev Remembers*, ed. and trans. Strobe Talbott (Boston: Little, Brown, 1970), p. 400.

9. Bohlen, *Witness to History*, p. 389.

10. Zubok, *Failed Empire*, p. 107. The "Open Skies" proposal by President Eisenhower would have required exchanges of military information and reciprocal overflights by the United States and the USSR of the territory of the other to verify this military information. It was promptly rejected. See Garthoff, *Assessing the Adversary*, pp. 10–12.

11. See Aleksandr Fursenko and Timothy Naftali, *Khrushchev's Cold War: The Inside Story of an American Adversary* (New York: W. W. Norton, 2006), pp. 99–137.

12. Ibid., p. 130. See also Sergei Khrushchev, *Nikita Khrushchev and the Creation of a Superpower* (University Park: Penn State University Press, 2000), p. 211;

William Taubman, *Khrushchev: The Man and His Era* (New York: W. W. Norton, 2003), pp. 359–60; and Zubok and Pleshakov, *Inside the Kremlin's Cold War*, p. 191.

13. In August 1957, I personally visited the Ministry of Defense in Moscow and sought an interview with Marshal Zhukov. Two days later, I was called in by the colonel to whom I had given my request and got an answer. "The Marshal," he said, "has read your book [*Soviet Military Doctrine* (Glencoe, IL: Free Press, 1953)] and would very much have liked to talk to you but regrettably cannot do so in view of the press of his duties, military and political" (emphasis added). I was not surprised that Zhukov did not receive me, but I did find it interesting that even in such a minor matter he would not only respond to an unofficial approach by an American but also that he would go out of his way to emphasize his political role.

14. Georgy Kornienko, later first deputy foreign minister, serving in 1958 in the newly established Information (Evaluation) Service of the Central Committee (successor to the Small KI) headed by Ambassador Georgy Pushkin, informed me that he believed the inspiration for Khrushchev's initiative on Berlin stemmed at least in part from the fact that Pushkin had drawn Khrushchev's attention to a speech by Secretary of State John Foster Dulles in October 1958 comparing the importance of Quemoy to West Berlin and that thinking about that may have led Khrushchev to decide to push on Berlin. Paradoxically, Pushkin, a former ambassador to East Germany, argued strongly against any attempt to force the West out of Berlin.

15. See Memorandum of Conversation, "Mikoyan's Call on the President," January 17, 1959, p. 6.

16. An extensive summary of the annual report by the chairman of the KGB to Khrushchev on 1960, submitted on February 14, 1961, is provided in Vladislav M. Zubok, "Spy vs. Spy: The KGB vs. the CIA, 1960–1962," *Cold War International History Project Bulletin*, no. 4 (Fall 1994): pp. 22–24.

17. For an analysis of American assessment and policy in the Khrushchev period, see Garthoff, *Assessing the Adversary*.

18. See Fursenko and Naftali, *Khrushchev's Cold War*, pp. 339–40.

19. See Raymond L. Garthoff, *A Journey through the Cold War: A Memoir of Containment and Coexistence* (Washington: Brookings Institution, 2001), pp. 132–38; Michael Beschloss, *The Crisis Years: Kennedy and Khrushchev, 1960–1963* (New York: Edward Burlingame

Books / HarperCollins, 1991), pp. 60–61; and Christopher Andrew and Vasili Mitrokhin, *The World Was Going Our Way: The KGB and the Battle for the Third World* (New York: Basic Books, 2005), pp. 9–10.

20. See Fursenko and Naftali, *Khrushchev's Cold War*, pp. 348–49.

21. See ibid., pp. 341, 349–50, 403–4, 418–20, 462–63, and 530; and see academician A. A. Fursenko, "The Unusual Fate of Intelligence Officer G. N. Bol'shakov," *Novaya i noveishaya istoriya* (Modern and contemporary history), no. 4 (July/August 2005), pp. 92–101.

22. See Fursenko and Naftali, *Khrushchev's Cold War*, pp. 372–74, and Andrew and Gordievsky, *KGB*, pp. 460–62.

23. See Khrushchev, *Nikita Khrushchev and the Creation of a Superpower*, p. 535.

24. See Fursenko, "Unusual Fate of Intelligence Officer," p. 94, citing the archives of the Russian Foreign Intelligence Service (Sluzhba Vneshnei Razvedki, or SVR) but with no precise reference. Andrew and Mitrokhin, *Sword and the Shield*, p. 180, also discusses this report and states that the "collaborator" was a Western European NATO liaison officer with the CIA.

25. Fursenko, "Unusual Fate of Intelligence Officer," pp. 94–95.

26. Fursenko and Naftali, *Khrushchev's Cold War*, p. 424. A more far-reaching version of this GRU report appears in Andrew and Mitrokhin, *Sword and the Shield*, p. 182, without indication of its source. The latter account states that a decision to launch a nuclear attack had been made in June but canceled in September after the nuclear test. Such a decision, however, on its face is not credible: If a decision to attack had been made, or even if one were under consideration, indications of advances in nuclear tests (which could not be weaponized for a considerable time) would only have reinforced arguments for a preventive strike and not led to reversing such a decision or dropping one under consideration.

27. Fursenko and Naftali, *Khrushchev's Cold War*, pp. 396 and 427.

28. Ibid., pp. 412–16.

29. For a more full account and sourcing, see Raymond L. Garthoff, "The American-Soviet Tank Confrontation at Checkpoint Charlie," in *Mysteries of the Cold War*, ed. Steven J. Cimbala (Aldershot, UK: Ashgate, 1999), pp. 73–87.

30. Khrushchev, *Khrushchev Remembers*, pp. 459–60.

31. For discussion of this problem with respect to the Berlin contingency military planning in 1961, see Garthoff, *Journey through the Cold War*, pp. 127–31.

32. For a brief review of some such penetrations in 1961, including the findings of NATO (and American) "damage assessments" of a case in 1968 in which the author participated, and other evidence, see Garthoff, *Journey through the Cold War*, pp. 234–35. The United States sometimes passed secret information to NATO knowing that it would probably be acquired by Soviet and other Warsaw Pact intelligence agents, in cases where it wanted such information to go to Moscow and knew that the Soviet leaders often gave greater credence to information received from clandestine intelligence than from open sources. This was done because the United States wanted them to know in certain cases how much it knew about some of their activities and sometimes to let them know what the United States was planning or was prepared to do if necessary.

33. For a detailed account, see ibid., pp. 114–16. The author sought to have this information declassified, but that did not happen until after the end of the Cold War.

34. See Raymond L. Garthoff, *Soviet Military Policy: A Historical Analysis* (New York: Frederick A. Praeger, 1966), pp. 65–97 and 191–237, for the ideological foundation for this pragmatic conclusion.

35. Fursenko and Naftali, *Khrushchev's Cold War*, p. 420. See also Beschloss, *Crisis Years*, pp. 345–47 and 362.

36. Ibid., pp. 427–39, and see 443–507.

37. For an analytical summary of the Cuban Missile Crisis, see Garthoff, *Journey through the Cold War*, pp. 168–87. For the best overall account, see Michael Dobbs, *One Minute to Midnight: Kennedy, Khrushchev, and Castro on the Brink of Nuclear War* (New York: Alfred A. Knopf, 2008). Khrushchev's misadventure was scathingly criticized by the Chinese communists as both "adventurism" for deploying strategic missiles in Cuba and then "capitulationism" for taking them out.

38. On this general subject, see James G. Blight and David A. Welch, eds., *Intelligence and the Cuban Missile Crisis* (London: Frank Cass, 1999), especially the chapters on Soviet intelligence by Aleksandr Fursenko and Timothy Naftali, pp. 64–87, and on US intelligence by Raymond L. Garthoff, pp. 18–63.

39. Nikita Khrushchev, *Khrushchev Remembers: The Glasnost Tapes*, ed. and trans. Jerrold Schecter and Vyacheslav V. Luchkov (Boston: Little, Brown, 1990), p. 80.

40. Ibid., p. 180. The reference from the personal letter is cited by his son Sergei Khrushchev in *Nikita Khrushchev and the Creation of a Superpower*, p. 641.

41. "Toward a Strategy of Peace: Address by President Kennedy," June 10, 1963, in *Department of State Bulletin* 49, no. 1253 (July 1, 1963): pp. 2–6.

42. Regrettably, a comprehensive nuclear test ban eluded agreement, owing to a misunderstanding in informal discussions from which Khrushchev understood three on-site inspections per year to monitor an agreement would be acceptable, while the US position called for a minimum of seven, and both leaders had stretched to come even that close.

43. For discussion of these measures, see Garthoff, *Journey through the Cold War*, pp. 154–67.

44. Fursenko and Naftali, *Khrushchev's Cold War*, p. 530. They report that the KGB tried to find evidence to support this belief but without success—but also without excluding it.

Raymond L. Garthoff, "Khrushchev: Thaw and Crisis, 1954-64," in *Soviet Leaders and Intelligence* (Washington, D.C.: Georgetown University Press, 2015): 17–36. Reproduced with permission.

32. THE BRITISH EXPERIENCE WITH INTELLIGENCE

PERCY CRADOCK

In this essay, Cradock assesses the performance of British Intelligence since World War II. Weaved into this assessment is a description of the limits of intelligence and a discussion of how the changing national fortunes of Great Britain in the second half of the twentieth century transformed the role of intelligence in the formulation of foreign policy. Cradock concludes that British intelligence passed the ultimate test: it outperformed its competitors.

In judging the performance of any intelligence organization we need first to come to a realistic understanding of the limits to intelligence. There is too often an exaggerated idea of what it can achieve and a corresponding readiness to criticize anything short of omniscience. It is commonly assumed that the outside world is knowable and that it is the function of the intelligence officer to know it, and know it in advance. Inability to do so is a fault and results in what is called an intelligence failure. This view, in extreme form, would have it that foreign state secrets are out there and attainable. They are arcane admittedly, a set of sibylline books, and expensive or dangerous to acquire; but they are intelligible, given the key. The pages can then be read and their content passed to the policy-makers.

To recognize how far this is from the reality of foreign affairs, needs only a moment's reflection. International dealings, even confined to the present tense, are infinitely variable, an amalgam of the fears, ambitions, collusions and contentions of the great cast of states that make up the international community. Little that happens is thoroughly foreordained and planned. Miscalculations abound. Governments are commonly acted upon rather than acting. The "events, dear boy, events" of Harold Macmillan's celebrated remark crowd in upon them.

If this is the present, the future is even more contingent and uncertain. Some facts about other states may be established with reasonable accuracy: their economic resources, the number of their tanks, aircraft and missiles, even perhaps the intangibles, such as organization and morale. Such facts are necessary, but in themselves insufficient. They are what one eminent American analyst called the "secrets," hidden but knowable, as opposed to the "mysteries," by their nature impenetrable. But it is on this second, much more elusive, category that a view has to be formed if intelligence estimates are to do their work; on the thinking that drives policy, above all, on the intentions of governments. These are the true *arcana imperii*; and, short of some extraordinary stroke of luck, or genius, they are likely to remain obscure. Intelligence targets are commonly closed societies; and even where this is not so, the foreign leaders themselves often do not see their way clearly, or determine it long in advance, and in most cases still prefer to keep their cards hidden.

To attempt a reading here calls for qualities very different from those needed in the earlier, factual stages of enquiry: a capacity, based on a careful study of culture, history and practice, to enter into the mind of a foreign leader and speculate in a relatively informed way on his likely reactions in certain situations. Such predictive assessment goes well beyond pure analysis: the "hard intelligence" to hand is usually fragmentary or ambiguous; this is much more a work of imaginative transference and, as such, highly fallible.

With time and study it is usually possible to construct a working model of the other side which will serve as a guide to likely behaviour. But this too is not without its risks. The analyst readily becomes attached to his creation, to his picture of Stalin, or Mao or Saddam, and prone to reject any new or awkward reports which do not fit his assumptions. We all become attached to our own views. But in the end these are only hypotheses; and what seem rules built on careful observation and induction can easily be overridden in special cases. So, in the Cuban crisis of 1962, the hitherto sound principle that the Russians would not expose their strategic missiles outside Soviet territory proved highly misleading.

Given such conditions, all that we can do, while seeking by all means available to read a foreign state's intentions, is to accept that in the last resort intelligence is an attempt to know the unknowable and scale down our expectations accordingly.

This recognition has been made harder by one historical fact, the extraordinary success of Allied intelligence against the Axis in the Second World War. This has set all successors an impossible standard. In that irrecoverable golden age of Western intelligence, Sigint ensured that the enemy's military dispositions and often his strategic intentions were laid out before Allied leaders as on an illuminated screen. But there was nothing remotely similar in the post-war era. There were successes against Third World targets, but, although James Bamford states that Soviet military communications were readable for a while after the war, the West did not have access to Soviet communications which would have revealed strategic thinking.[1] There was never again going to be anything like the intercepted Japanese telegram of 12 June 1941, reporting Hitler's determination to have done with Russian communism and enabling the JIC Chairman to bring his committee to a confident prediction of an early full-scale German assault on the Soviet Union. By contrast, the JIC and CIA analysts of the next generation found themselves excluded from knowledge of the other side's councils and reduced to picking up fragments from outside the fortress, by studying Soviet externals, the leaders' statements and Russian behaviour in Turkey and Iran, and thereby slowly constructing a plausible sketch of their adversary.

Memories of the wartime achievement have bedevilled judgements of intelligence performance, by policy-makers and media alike, ever since, raising unreal expectations. But, in fairness, it is only the second-best, post-1945 standards, not those of Ultra or Magic, that can be applied to the Joint Intelligence Committee's work in the period under review.

As we have seen, the Committee successfully discharged its main post-war task of identifying the chief threat to British interests and predicting the form Soviet policies could be expected to take. The work was helped by the insights of the embassy in Moscow and, above all, by Soviet conduct in Eastern and South-Eastern Europe, in Iran and, finally, in Germany. The full portrait took time, up to 1947–8 when the vital ideological element was added, but it was to the life and immensely influential in shaping the course of British and Allied policy in the early post-war years.

The Committee was surprised by the speed of Soviet atomic development but correct in identifying Soviet strategic caution, perhaps the most important single judgement of the period. In the first major postwar crisis, the Berlin blockade, though the Committee gave no formal warning, there was widespread expectation of pressure on the city, and precise details of the Russian plans for strangulation were probably not a practical target.

In the Korean War, there was at first a shortage of intelligence in London because of policy differences with the Americans, though it must be said that even if US assessments had been available, they would probably have been misleading. For various reasons both allies were in the dark. On the issue of Chinese involvement, the Committee came close to the truth at several points but in the end failed to predict large-scale intervention. The Chiefs of Staff, however, working on the basis of JIC material, gave ample notice, to the Cabinet and to Washington, of the impending danger. The JIC was correct in seeing China as a largely independent actor, not just a Soviet puppet, the US view, and supported the Chiefs and the government in their ultimately successful efforts to bring United States strategy down to earth.

Suez was a policy rather than an intelligence failure. In the nature of things, the Committee's warnings made little impact, but they read well in retrospect: Nasser's determination to make the Canal work; his ability to do so; Soviet caution; the dangers of even coincidence (let alone collusion) with Israel; the overriding need for a short, sharp victory if there was to be a military campaign; the unpleasant consequences if that were not achieved; the risks to Nuri's regime in Iraq. What they failed to point out was the illusory nature of military victory in Egypt, even if that could be brought about, and the resilience and independence of Arab nationalism. In this and the undue emphasis on military rather than political and economic responses to the problems of the area the Committee was a creature of its time.

In the second Berlin crisis, the Committee accurately predicted the division of the city to meet the refugee efflux and Khrushchev's permission to Ulbricht to erect this new barrier. It took two years of high tension for the permission to be given: as often with strategic estimates, the outcome was foreseen but not the precise timing; and, on the policy side, despite the warning on the books, no contingency planning was undertaken. When eventually the Wall went up the East Germans achieved tactical surprise. The Allies were preparing for more dangerous situations, involving their own troops, and were nonplussed.

On Sino-Soviet relations, the JIC, like the CIA, was alive to the signs of dispute between the two communist giants and to the immense implications of such a rift. The problem here was getting the policymakers to pay attention. The British policy paper of 1960, postponing a Sino-Soviet split until a Russian conversion to democracy, was perhaps an extreme case, but illustrated well the reluctance of many Western politicians and advisers to believe that the Soviet and the Chinese governments could ever do anything so opposed to their best interests as to fall out (their best interests, of course, being defined in Western terms).

In the case of Cuba and Vietnam, the Committee, like Britain, was relegated to the sidelines. The Cuban crisis was sudden, and fast: the real emergency was over in a week; and the JIC had to make do with items of cold intelligence passed on by the CIA after the decisions had been taken on them. Vietnam was a slow tragedy and there was ample time to comment on its unfolding. The Committee identified many of the coming dangers but could not get beyond the role of a Greek chorus, bewailing events it might foresee but which it had no power to change. At the policy level, the picture was the same, the British Prime Minister seeking a larger role, but rebuffed, gently in the case of Cuba, brutally in the case of Vietnam.

In the smaller, purely British operations of Kuwait and Indonesian confrontation, there was plentiful intelligence, both strategic and tactical, and policy was well served and effective. In the case of Rhodesia, there was little surprise about the unilateral declaration of independence and the errors lay on the policy-making side, chiefly in the wishful thinking on the effect of sanctions. Finally, we return to East-West crises with Czechoslovakia in 1968, where, admittedly, there was uncertainty, even in the Kremlin, until the last moment, but which in the

end cannot be reckoned an intelligence, or policy, success. The failure probably lay in a misreading of the nature of Russian control in Eastern Europe and an underrating of the part pure violence played in the Soviet empire.

Given the perplexities and obscurities of the situation in each instance, this was a creditable performance. Where the JIC went wrong was usually in attributing rational motivation to the other side, most strikingly in the case of China in the Korean War. What I have called "the rational assumption" often appears in studies on intelligence as "mirror imaging" and is rightly condemned. But mirror imaging is usually the cruder form of the failing, the reasoning, "We would not do this, therefore they will not." Such thinking commits the serious error of disregarding the "otherness" of all foreign governments and the way in which what to us looks illogical or excessive may not be so in a foreign environment. So, in the Yom Kippur War of 1973, what Kissinger called "the notion of starting an unwinnable war to restore self-respect" had a strength for Sadat that the West, and Israel, failed to appreciate. So Russians and Chinese in their schism had very different ideas of what constituted their best interests from those entertained in Western capitals. And Mao's priorities for China in 1950 had a native consistency which only close acquaintance with him and his background could have disclosed.

At the same time, the analyst has a defence. In order to communicate with colleagues, ministers and allies he must follow rational procedures and modes of expression. Rationality is after all the condition of intelligent discourse; without it the world becomes arbitrary and unfathomable, my hunch against yours. It must also be assumed that the foreign leader—be it Stalin, Mao or Nasser—is doing the best for his country, as he sees it. The trap is in the last four words and in the tendency to set too narrow and domestic a standard, to overlook the differing views of rationality that can prevail in other political systems and cultures, and to forget the amount of emotion and unreason that can enter the most serious decisions. In the end the only safeguard is understanding of the other side and a consequent feel for their likely behaviour.

It is sometimes said that the Committee produced too varnished and unified judgements and gave the policy-maker no indication of the other interpretations that might be placed on the same facts. In Washington, by contrast, there were always a number of estimates to choose from. With limited resources Britain had to operate on a narrower front. Dissenting views were allowed in the Committee's papers, though differences were rarely deep and the permission was scarcely, if ever, invoked. But there were obvious dangers in offering a plurality of views or falling back into the old pre-war individualism. And failure to give a clear guide to ministers could be seen as an abdication of responsibility: the JIC had access to superior information; it owed them a judgement. And, provided the approach to that judgement was transparent, provided the agreed facts, the possible interpretations and the reasons for preferring one to another were clearly set out, the policymaker was able to follow the line of argument but in the end, if he felt strongly, free to diverge and come to another conclusion.

There was also a risk that the Committee, as an interdepartmental group, would produce only safe, uncontentious views and reflect only a low-level Whitehall consensus. Committees are by nature often dull and the JIC must have been often humdrum. Churchill, though a great man for unifying intelligence, shrank from the logical conclusion and did not think highly of the committee approach to truth. Writing of the prelude to the German invasion of Russia in 1941, he said, "I had not been content with this form of collective wisdom and preferred to see the originals myself . . . thus forming my own opinion sometimes at much earlier dates."[2]

It is true that in specific instances gifted individuals could, and did, outperform the JIC. Whether over a period the track record would have been so much better is less certain. The Committee itself would probably have forecast the German invasion of Russia as early as February 1941 if Cavendish-Bentinck had not had to carry the military with him. In any case the structure of government in Whitehall, the need to bring maximum expertise to bear on each issue, and the concern to escape prewar disarray ruled out any other approach. A price had to be paid for coordinated intelligence and the record shows that it was worth paying.

Ideally, intelligence and policy should be close but distinct. Too distinct and assessments become an in-growing, self-regarding activity, producing little or no work of interest to the decision-makers. The French lord in Shakespeare's *Henry V* who on the eve of Agincourt measures the exact distance between the English and the French tents, a matter of supreme indifference to the French leaders, is an early exponent of worthy but irrelevant research and

he has had many descendants. The analyst needs to be close enough to ministers to know the questions troubling them and he must not fight shy of tackling the major issues. In its earliest days the JIC had to pronounce on life-and-death matters: invasion of Britain or not; a German invasion of Russia or not; and so on; and modern practitioners must maintain the same level of courage, or presumption.

Too close a link and policy begins to play back on estimates, producing the answers the policymakers would like, as happened with Soviet intelligence. The analysts become courtiers, whereas their proper function is to report their findings, almost always unpalatable, without fear or favour.

The best arrangement is intelligence and policy in separate but adjoining rooms, with communicating doors and thin partition walls, as in cheap hotels.

But however well connected the analysts are, the transition from intelligence to policy is often an uncertain one. Policy conclusions are commonly inherent in estimates; but the decisions lie with ministers: they have the privilege of interpreting the facts differently or ignoring them altogether. At this stage the situation and its likely development are no longer the sole considerations; other factors, party politics, economic interests, public opinion, personal convictions and vanities, enter the equation and can prove decisive. It is also in the nature of government, with its day-to-day pressures and concern with immediate issues, that strategic warnings are not always acted upon. Cruder stimuli are usually required. The predictions are rarely categorical: coming events are described at best as "probable" or, more usually, "on balance likely." Departments are unwilling to embark on contingency planning except for the plainest threats. They lack the resources and the danger may not materialize. When Sir Alec Douglas-Home, Commonwealth Secretary at the time of Suez, was many years later asked why ministers had disregarded the warnings that the venture would go wrong, he said, "A warning is a different thing from it happening. You often get warnings of this sort and then the results are different."[3] Suez was an extreme case of ministerial blindness; but there is something in Home's answer: governments may be alive to a possibility without taking the remedial action the historian would like to have seen.

With the rare exception, such as the exhortation to rearmament during the Korean War, the Committee sedulously avoided policy recommendations. Its concern was with the first part of Cabinet papers, namely, what is the problem and how is it likely to develop? But the Joint Intelligence Organization was never a separate entity like the CIA; its staff were mainly seconded, not permanent; and the Committee members themselves met only for a limited time each week. Their connections with departments and policy remained close. This was particularly true in the case of the Chairman, who was also the senior Foreign Office official responsible for defence and security policy. In practice the JIC always stood in a close relationship, not only with the Chiefs of Staff, but also with senior ministers. How close depended in part on ministerial tastes and in part on the urgency of the international situation. It was inseparable from policy in the early Cold War years, in the assessment of the Soviet threat which prompted such responses as the Atlantic Alliance and the Marshall Plan. The Berlin blockade, the alarms of the Korean War and the fear of similar proxy attacks in Europe again made its assessments highly relevant and the policy arguments with the Americans over Korea were barely concealed behind the intelligence exchanges with Washington. Bevin's Cabinet papers and correspondence with Attlee over foreign policy show strong signs of JIC and Chiefs of Staff influence.

Over Suez, by contrast, there was a gulf between intelligence and policy, to the country's great cost. There was probably also a less intimate link with policy than in the past over the second Berlin crisis in 1958–61. Macmillan acted as his own Foreign Minister and evolved a highly individual approach to East–West relations. He put specific questions to the JIC, as over French progress toward nuclear weapons, and had JIC assessments on the UK deterrent as background to the decisions over Blue Streak and Polaris; but the policy style and structure were very much his own.

In 1964, as Harold Wilson takes over, we have the Cabinet Secretary, Burke Trend, telling him of the practice hitherto of submitting JIC papers and offering two examples, on North Vietnamese intentions and capabilities, and on the possible scale and nature of an attack on the UK in the event of a major war in the next four years. He asks whether he should proceed along these lines and is told "Yes."[4] Copies also go to the Foreign Secretary, the Commonwealth Secretary, the Defence Secretary and, in the case of the paper on a possible attack on the UK, the Home Secretary. We can also assume that the regular weekly survey of intelligence is sent round to the same addresses. But again, with exceptions, as in the case of estimates on Rhodesia, Wilson is probably not an avid reader of intelligence. His later obsession with the subject took a different form.

In fact, as we move into the 1960s there is an impression that the JIC assessments become less central to British foreign policy. There are a number of reasons. First, after Cuba the East–West confrontation becomes rather less acute. The Berlin blockade and the Korean War were direct challenges, occupying the centre of the stage. In the next decades, though the long-term threat persists, there are more international agreements regulating East–West competition. There is more caution, more time for the constructive work of diplomacy, most of it lying outside the Committee's remit.

The second reason is that Britain itself becomes less central in world affairs. Its power declines, not only in relation to the Soviet Union but also, even more critical, in relation to the United States. Beginning with the Eisenhower–Khrushchev meeting at Camp David in 1959, the Americans and the Russians develop the habit of meeting à *deux* to discuss East–West issues. Kennedy meets Khrushchev in Vienna in June 1961, Lyndon Johnson meets Kosygin at Glassboro in 1967. Britain is no longer needed as auxiliary or intermediary. The signing of the Partial Test Ban Treaty in August 1963 is the last time Britain occupies her old place at the top table.

The effect of superpower bilateralism is intensified by continuing British economic decline and the enforced retreat in 1968 from a worldwide to a predominantly European role. It is true of course that Britain is financially embarrassed throughout the period of this study. In Attlee's and Bevin's day the sudden withdrawal of Lend-Lease and the onerous American loan left little doubt about the true situation. But Britain was then one of the Big Three, a victorious power, with large and highly trained armed forces, vast tracts of territory still under its control and a sharp industrial advantage over other European economies. At the time of the Korean War US testimony shows how essential an element Britain was in American decision-making. By the late 1960s this situation has changed: the armies have melted away, the empire has been dismantled, but the economic troubles persist and intensify.

The decline brings an increasing element of pretence and posturing into British policy, an attempt to make up for declining material assets by manipulating the symbols of power, nuclear status, the special relationship, diplomatic finesse, the outer forms rather than the substance. The charade reflects a disturbing unwillingness to come to terms with the realities of Britain's new position. Macmillan, as a born showman, is rather better at the game than Wilson and in any case is luckier in having to face less acute economic pressures. The decreasing relevance of Britain is painfully demonstrated in Wilson's unsuccessful attempts to mediate over Vietnam.

But there is not only a decline in power; there is also a growing uncertainty of direction, the realzation by British governments that, with the success of European economic integration, the American alliance and the Commonwealth are no longer in themselves a sufficient basis for policy. The policy papers make the new dilemmas clear. A study in 1958 by a committee of Permanent Secretaries, entitled "The Position of the United Kingdom in World Affairs," is traditional in its priorities. Defeating Russian and Chinese efforts to dominate the world and preserving and strengthening the cohesion of the Commonwealth come first. Europe is well down the list: "We aim to strengthen our ties with Europe and are seeking to negotiate a European Free Trade Area. We support the North Atlantic Alliance as the bulwark against Soviet encroachment in Europe."[5]

But in 1960 there is a big change. The "Future Policy Study, 1960–70," provides the background to Macmillan's strategy in the 1960s. It is written by a Foreign Office team under Sir Patrick Dean (still JIC Chairman) and submitted to the Prime Minister via a steering committee chaired by Sir Norman Brook, the Cabinet Secretary. It recognizes the importance of the EEC, foreseeing it as "one of the three giants," along with the United States and the Soviet Union, by the year 1970, and acknowledges that it would seriously weaken Britain's own standing in the Commonwealth and the Atlantic Alliance, and the cohesion of the Alliance itself, if Britain found itself excluded from Europe; moreover that, as a relatively small economic power, the country would risk serious damage if it failed to establish a satisfactory association with the EEC. In its key section, entitled "The Balance between Our Friends," the paper enunciates as a basic rule of British policy that "we must never allow ourselves to be put in a position where we would have to make a final choice between the United States and Europe."[6]

In this new policy language we encounter in early form the persistent British belief that America or Europe involved an exclusive choice. It was in many ways a false dichotomy. It was not how the United States saw it: consistent American advice was that British influence in Washington would depend on

British influence in Europe. But it was the fear of successive British governments that Europe meant sacrifice, a fear reinforced by the fact that the approach to Europe had to be made at the same time as decisions on the future of the British deterrent which underlined the critical importance of the American link. In such a situation the principle of "no final choice" had its attractions. But it could only too readily become an excuse for putting off any thorough analysis of the future courses open to the country, a principle of evasion and indecision. Indeed it could be argued that Britain has remained in this state of suspended judgement on Europe ever since those days.

Britain's situation in the late 1960s, which was at the same time the source of its uncertainty and illusion, was eloquently defined by someone who was pre-eminently in a position to know, Sir Con O'Neil, the government's chief official negotiator with Europe, in a lecture delivered in 1972:

> Britain's experience had been different, or seemed different; and for a long time we misinterpreted it. The world still seemed our oyster, though in fact we lacked the power to open it. We had escaped defeat and occupation; we had been spared the collapse of our society and institutions. But we had not escaped exhaustion and diminution, the common lot of our European neighbours.[7]

Against this background of diminution and uncertainty, the influence of the Committee was bound to decline. But it retained its hold on the primary concern of any government, national security. So long as the Soviet Union posed the main threat to Western Europe its views would be certain to command attention. And so long as the outside world remained dangerous and unpredictable—sadly a permanent condition of international life—the Committee could never be disregarded. Middle East wars, oil crises, terrorist plots would provide a steady *raison d'être*. Moreover by then the post-Cold War security agenda was already beginning to appear in its assessments. The first papers on "The development of nuclear weapons by fifth countries" come in 1960; and the first intelligence from Northern Ireland of impending trouble from the IRA begins to arrive as early as December 1965.[8]

The Committee has also to be seen as an important element in US–UK relations. Britain was fortunate in being able to act on the outside world not only directly but also, on occasion, through the most powerful of proxies, the United States. As will have become apparent, this study is almost as much about

United States as about British estimates and policy. From the Second World War on there was a continuous intimate dialogue between the two governments about world affairs. All British governments sought as a cardinal objective to exert maximum influence in Washington. In Macmillan's definition of 1957 the British deterrent itself became largely an agent of influence. One very effective means of exercising this persuasion was the production of highly regarded intelligence estimates and their regular exchange with US counterparts. Fortunately, for most of the time the two sides agreed on the problem and the response. Where they differed always presented the most delicate choices for London between narrower British interests and the demands of solidarity with Washington. For better or worse, US–UK relations were always the key strand of British foreign policy.

As we look back over these first twenty to twenty-five years of the post-war era, the record of the JIC shows it as an important part of central government, intimately involved in the main crises of the period and exerting a powerful influence on foreign policy in Britain and even, to some extent, in America. It looks on the world coolly and realistically, with few illusions; the pretences and evasions are there, but they belong to the realm of policy. It has to its credit a number of accurate or enlightened forecasts of coming events, though like any body required to read the future, it has its share of mistakes. Its main merit, however, may lie less in individual assessments of greater or lesser accuracy than in the fact of its existence as a responsible and increasingly influential organization bringing together at manageable and less than Cabinet level the chief sources of knowledge on international affairs and engaging them in a continuous and forward-looking discussion and evaluation of the evolving scene. Thereby it contributed substantially to the ideal of efficient and prescient policy-making. Despite the best intentions, government is usually a hand-to-mouth affair. The Committee made it less so.

At a more basic level the achievement consists simply in the coordination of intelligence, giving Britain a critical advantage over competitors. In his memoirs in 1956 President Truman reflected that "if there had been something like co-ordination of information in the government it would have been more difficult, if not impossible, for the Japanese to succeed in the sneak attack on Pearl Harbor."[9] The same lack of co-ordination bedevilled American intelligence four years later in the Korean War and was similarly lamented in later inquests.

A final example. At the end of the Second World War the JIC conducted a study on "Why Germany lost the War?" The resulting paper gave as one of the reasons the fragmented state of German intelligence:

> Within the Abwehr [the principal German intelligence service] there was little or no centralised evaluation of intelligence, which was in itself nearly always derived from personal sources . . . reports were often rejected on internal grounds by the service ministries, who lacked the means of assessing the reliability of the information which they received.

In addition to the internal weakness of the Abwehr, the salient weakness of German Intelligence, and one of its main causes of failure, was the absence of any inter-service staff for the co-ordination and appreciation of intelligence. Both Keitel and Jodl have stated that no organisation comparable with the allied joint intelligence machinery was ever formed. Operational intelligence was supplied by each of the service ministries and by the Abwehr direct to the planning staff of OKW [the supreme command of the armed forces] where it was inadequately coordinated.[10]

This tells the whole story. Britain was very fortunate that, in those desperate days and for many years afterwards, in London such matters were distinctly better managed.

QUESTIONS FOR FURTHER DISCUSSION

1. Can good intelligence salvage bad policy?
2. To what extent is national military and economic strength related to a nation's effective collection and analysis of intelligence?
3. Can intelligence help compensate for a lack of military or economic resources?
4. Are policy prescriptions inherent in the conclusions of intelligence estimates?

ENDNOTES

1. James Bamford, *Body of Secrets: How America's NSA and Britain's GCHQ Eavesdrop on the World* (London, Century, 2001).
2. Churchill on committee work, quoted in R.V. Jones, *Most Secret War* (London, Hamish Hamilton, 1978).
3. Hennessy, *The Prime Minister*, p. 236.
4. PRO PREM 13/8, Minute by Sir Burke Trend, 24 October 1964.
5. PRO PREM 11/2321, of 5 June 1958, "The Position of the United Kingdom in World Affairs."

6. PRO CAB 129/100, FP (60) 1, "Study of Future Policy, 1960–1970," 24 February 1960.

7. Sir Con O'Neil, Stamp Memorial Lecture, 1972, quoted in David Hannay (ed.), *Britain's Entry into the European Community* (London, Frank Cass, 2000), p. xxii, Sir Con O'Neil's Report on the Negotiations of 1970–2.

8. Peter Rose, *How the Troubles Came to Northern Ireland* (London, Macmillan, 2000), p. 18.

9. Harry S. Truman, *Memoirs, Vol. 2: Years of Trial and Hope 1946–1953* (London, Hodder & Stoughton, 1956), p. 56.

10. PRO CAB 81/132, JIC (46) 33 of 20 October 1946.

33. GERMAN INTELLIGENCE IN THE SHADOW OF THE THIRD REICH

WOLFGANG KRIEGER

A prominent German scholar writes about the special nature of Germany's leading intelligence agency, the *Bundesnachrichtendienst*. Professor Krieger observes that the *BND* carries out both military and foreign espionage activities with a single agency, a model quite different from most other nations. Moreover, the *BND* it has only a limited role in the conduct of covert actions, although at times in its past it has been known to engage in disinformation campaigns as well as the secret supply of arms to rebel movements that favor regime change against autocracies. The history of the *BND* also reveals unusually close ties with the CIA, especially as the German spy agency was finding its legs during the early years of its existence.

1. INTRODUCTION

Germany's foreign intelligence service, the *Bundesnachrichtendienst* or *BND*, is marked by several peculiarities. The first one is its role as Germany's single foreign and military espionage agency. Unlike most other Western nations such as Britain, France, or the United States, Germany has no separate military intelligence service or services. Thus the *BND* integrates most functions of a military intelligence service, excepting only the protection of the German armed forces (Bundeswehr) from foreign espionage, which is organized in a separate institution, the MAD or Office for the Protection of the Armed Forces. After a considerable reshuffling of responsibilities in December 2007, the Bundeswehr retained some units for tactical reconnaissance but had to close down its Center for Military Information (ZNBw), which had provided the minister of defense with a separate capacity for the analysis of a wide range of security-related intelligence. Now the military depends entirely on the *BND* for all analysis and most intelligence gathering. These changes have produced serious doubts among the senior military, since the *BND* operates under the chancellor's office but employs a considerable number of military personnel among its staff of about six thousand.[1]

The second peculiarity is the absence within the *BND* of an acknowledged capacity for covert operations. This has been the official position since the end of the Cold War when the *BND* was finally put on a statutory basis.[2] It is a point of reference every time the activities of the *BND* come under fire either from the press or in the parliamentary oversight committee of the Bundestag (federal parliament) or both. But what does this mean in practice? Does the *BND* no longer provide secret funding for foreign political movements as it did, for example, in Spain and Portugal before they became democracies in the mid-1970s? Does it no longer engage in disinformation campaigns? Has it stopped its secret supplies of arms and other "forbidden" items to foreign governments and rebel movements?

There is little evidence either way. But since the Bundeswehr maintains an acknowledged capacity for clandestine operations, the need for tactical and strategic intelligence support is obvious. After the intelligence reforms of 2007 much of this support must come from the *BND*. In recent years these "special forces" of 1,100 soldiers have operated in former Yugoslavia, in Afghanistan, and elsewhere. They were established in 1996, after the 1994 crisis in Rwanda, when German nationals had to be rescued by Belgian special forces because Germany had no such capability.

While it is true that the *BND* law of 1990 contains no language referring to a capability for covert operations, it does not explicitly exclude them either. Indeed, that law deals essentially with the parameters for information management within the framework of data privacy rather than with the totality of the *BND*'s operational mandate. The latter is determined by the head of the chancellor's office, with the rank of cabinet minister, who is in charge of executive tasking and oversight of all three federal intelligence services. (The third one is the domestic service *BfV* described below.)

A third peculiarity has resulted from the historical origins of the *BND* during the early Cold War. In 1946, US military intelligence in Europe created a German intelligence unit under American operational control and staffed it with former Wehrmacht officers who had served in intelligence during the German war against the Soviet Union (Krieger 2007; Critchfield 2003). It became known by the name of its leader, former Wehrmacht general Reinhard Gehlen, who in 1956 became the first president of the *BND*. At the same time the majority of his staff was transferred to the new *BND*.

How did this peculiar metamorphosis happen? At the end of the war Gehlen had preserved a collection of files and materials that he put at the disposal of US army intelligence. He identified a large number of his former collaborators, held in POW camps all around western Germany, who were willing to work with American intelligence. After considerable head scratching they were given operational tasks. Gehlen's radio specialists proved particularly useful during the Berlin airlift because they could record and decipher Soviet tactical communications. Their work helped the Western Allied powers track Soviet military activities throughout eastern Germany. Thus the Americans knew that Stalin was not about to launch a surprise attack on them. Other parts of project RUSTY, as the Gehlen organization was called, debriefed German POWs returning from Soviet POW camps. Building up and maintaining a ground-level network of informers in the Soviet-occupied part of Germany was yet another task performed by RUSTY.

When the CIA was founded and eventually became operational in Europe the need for the Gehlen group became less obvious. The CIA hesitated until 1949 before taking charge of it. The CIA did so grudgingly at a moment when West German rearmament was on the horizon and when the United States was keen to influence the emerging German military structures in order to make sure a new German army would not position itself politically between Moscow and the West. Thus the Gehlen organization became a large waiting room in which suitable ex-Wehrmacht officers could be employed temporarily until the political battles over German rearmament were terminated. As it turned out, an agreed policy between Britain, France, and the United States had to wait until 1954.[3]

By the time the *BND* was established in 1956, as part of West German rearmament within the NATO framework, the Bonn government had already abandoned its previous efforts to build up a military intelligence organization from scratch and with people of its own choice. This choice was never explained to the German public, though it met with considerable criticism from the parliamentary opposition parties. It seems that at the time the numerous political battles over the armed forces left no time and energy for the government to develop a coherent policy on foreign and military intelligence. In this way Gehlen and his associates, who had been intelligence mercenaries for the Americans over a period of ten years, gave the Americans a unique intelligence asset of sorts deep inside the West German government. The last head of the *BND* to work for the Americans was Eberhard Blum, recruited in 1947. He retired in 1985.

2. EVOLUTION

By the time Reinhard Gehlen was appointed as the first "president" of the *BND*, in 1956, he had made a considerable effort to involve himself and his organization in the politics of the young Bonn republic. He understood perfectly well that his special ties to the Americans, indeed his subordination to the CIA, would not make him easily acceptable to a body of German politicians and government officials who were tired of having American, British, and French diplomats and military brass breathing down their necks.

Gehlen developed three avenues of influence into the German government apparatus. First, he hired a great number of senior ex-Wehrmacht officers irrespective of their lack of expertise in intelligence work. In this way he helped them make the transition from Allied POW camps to an eventual posting in the new German army, which the three foreign ministers had decided on at their New York meeting in September 1950, in the wake of the outbreak of the Korean War. Though the government of

Chancellor Konrad Adenauer had followed up on that decision by recruiting a small military staff to prepare for a German rearmament, that outfit was far too small to accommodate the large numbers of volunteers and of senior officers needed for an army of several hundred thousand soldiers. (Eventually, the three powers agreed on a ceiling of 495,000.) Based on currently available evidence it is not clear how hard Gehlen had to work in order to persuade his CIA overseers to keep all those officers out of the civilian German labor market. We only know it happened at a time when that market picked up sharply due to the economic boom triggered by west European and above all by American rearmament during the Korean War.

By the time the Bundeswehr's officer corps began to be built up in 1955 Gehlen had already established a network of loyalties inside it, which helped him achieve his desired goal of heading a single foreign and military intelligence service. After all, the first military chief of the Bundeswehr, General Adolf Heusinger, had been Gehlen's chief of intelligence analysis in 1948–1950. One of Gehlen's most trusted lieutenants, Colonel (later General) Gerhard Wessel, left the organization to pursue a career in the Bundeswehr, where he was instrumental in preventing the development of a separate intelligence capacity. He would later return to the *BND* as Gehlen's successor from 1968 to 1978.

The second avenue of influence was to build up a relationship with a key member of the chancellor's office, Hans Globke, for whom he provided a wide variety of information ranging from intelligence in the proper sense to "dirty linen" gathered under the cover of intelligence and counterintelligence. This gave Adenauer the opportunity to discredit political opponents at will and to keep his ministers and high officials under wraps. In addition, Gehlen provided regular briefings on the international security picture to the chancellor who received, however, additional briefings directly from CIA officials. Adenauer, who had never served in the military, was not easily impressed by military officers, above all not by Germans. It appears that he did not entirely succumb to Gehlen's charm offensive though he welcomed his sinister help. Some years later he developed an outright hostility toward Gehlen but failed to replace him.

Thirdly, Gehlen approached a number of members of the Bundestag (federal parliament), including opposition members. By giving them individual briefings, inviting them to the Pullach headquarters

and providing saucy information about various personalities in politics, journalism, and business, he developed a certain degree of loyalty. This was above all needed during the weeks when the federal budget was discussed in parliament. After all, even the most secret government activities needed funding which had to be approved by parliament. The Bundestag established a parliamentary oversight committee of sorts that consisted of the leaders of the parliamentary groups in the Bundestag. It did not, however, have a clearly defined mandate. Its rather infrequent meetings were initiated by the chancellor, who also took the chair. A small number of parliamentarians involved themselves in matters concerning the *BND*'s day-to-day workings, particularly in the selection of senior staff. Many others, particularly parliamentarians from the political left, were ill at ease with the *BND*, its legacy, and its chief. Given Gehlen's background it was to be expected that he would favor people with conservative political leanings over liberals or social democrats. Another issue of concern was the employment of former Nazis of various shades.

Gehlen had a rather peculiar way of selecting his staff. His preference was to hire young men from professional military families, including his own. He literally employed his own brothers, son, daughter, nieces and nephews, and of course his in-laws. The same hiring pattern was followed with respect to the female staff, most of them working as secretaries, translators, and other lower-grade office workers. In terms of pro-active counterintelligence, this was perhaps wise since the descendants of military families were usually imbued with a spirit of service to the German nation and with the kind of "manners" fit for the gentlemanly age of foreign intelligence. But it had its obvious drawbacks, too, since the sons of such well-known families could not easily work and live under a false identity. Eventually, starting in the 1960s, the *BND* began to recruit from a much wider social spectrum and with a preference for people who had the scientific or engineering backgrounds needed for mastering the new information technologies. Lawyers and journalists were also favored. As in other government agencies, women remained a rare sight in managerial and senior positions at least until the 1970s.

Scandals were frequent at the *BND* during the early years. They provided opportunities for parliament to investigate the policies of Gehlen and his successors. Among the most serious was the Felfe/Clemens case. Those two former SS officers began working for Gehlen in the early 1950s, presumably because of their expertise in police and counterintelligence work, particularly work directed against Communists, which they had acquired during the Nazi era. Both, however, had previously signed up with the KGB and were employed to misdirect and to subvert Western intelligence. The Soviets helped Heinz Felfe build up an alleged network of spies that produced masses of material, including what was believed to be an organizational picture of the Soviet military administration in Karlshorst (Berlin). Felfe was among Gehlen's favorites. He moved up to the position of chief of counterintelligence responsible for fighting Soviet penetration. By the time Felfe, Hans Clements, and their collaborators within the *BND* were arrested in November 1961 they had delivered many thousands of documents and microfilms to Moscow and had betrayed the identities of close to two hundred CIA and *BND* agents. They had thoroughly misled not only the *BND* but also the CIA.

After Felfe, Clemens, and their associates were imprisoned there remained the more general question of what to do about the other former SS people in the service of the *BND*. How many were there? Why had they not been recognized as special security risks?

These questions have not been fully answered even today. While many of those people were removed from Gehlen's payroll when his service became a German federal office in 1956 or later, it seems that a considerable number of them were retained on a freelance basis under the designation of "Y-Personal" (Waske 2009, 94). Their total number may have been around one hundred.[4]

A year later, in 1962, the *Spiegel* crisis rocked the West German republic. At the surface this crisis was about a press report allegedly containing defense secrets concerning the inadequacies of the Bundeswehr's training and armaments. This report was published by *Der Spiegel*, a newsweekly highly skeptical of NATO defense and nuclear policies. Some of the information in the article had been leaked by senior officials in the German defense department who had an axe to grind with their minister, Franz Josef Strauss. At the same time *Der Spiegel* was known to have good relations with the *BND*. In fact, the article had been submitted in advance to the *BND* to help with fact checking and to ascertain that no "real" secrets were to be disclosed.

Strauss and Chancellor Adenauer were upset that the *BND*, which was directly subordinate to the chancellor's office, should provide such assistance.

They started a legal investigation and had the editor and two of his senior journalists arrested for suspicion of treason. This created a public outcry. The freedom of the press seemed at stake, at least as far as the numerous political opponents of Adenauer and Strauss were concerned (Schoenbaum 1968).

Underneath that public quarrel was another one, this time concerning military intelligence. Strauss had been dissatisfied with the services rendered by the *BND* and wished to strengthen the Bundeswehr's intelligence capacities. To Gehlen and his people such plans had to be fought with all possible means, including disloyalty to the government. Adenauer, who suspected an American intrigue against him and his defense policy, scolded the US ambassador that "the US had burdened him with Gehlen." In the end, Strauss was fired and Gehlen remained in office though Adenauer from that point refused to be briefed by him. His successor, Ludwig Erhard (1963–1966), took little interest in intelligence, leaving Gehlen to carry on without much guidance from the government and with less control by the federal parliament (Waske 2009, 67–72).

By then the German press had discovered the *BND* as one of those Cold War institutions that responded badly to the public demands for social and political change. Those demands would ultimately explode in the student revolt of the 1960s. Apart from the simmering issue of "old Nazis" there was a growing debate on the *BND*'s "illegal" wire-tapping activities inside West Germany that, like Gehlen's "special files" on various political figures, were often targeted at "political trouble-makers." To be sure, the *BND* and the agencies responsible for domestic intelligence were acting in something like a legal vacuum left by the incomplete agreement between the Bonn government and the three Western victor powers. The latter reserved the right to carry out or to mandate such intrusions so long as there was no German law regulating interceptions. Eventually this situation was brought under control by legislation. In 1978 a special oversight committee for wire-tapping was established. It reported to the federal parliament and had to grant individual permissions in each case (Krieger 2009).

When the social democrats led by Willy Brandt first participated in the federal government in 1966 they began to focus not only on the *BND*'s spy work against them but also on its personnel management and on its operating procedures. An investigation was launched, headed by three senior personalities, which produced a long list of grave management failures as well as gross distortions of what the *BND* had been producing in terms of intelligence output during the 1960s. The "Mercker" report, submitted to the government in 1969, has not been fully released as of this writing. In retrospect, the most senior civil servant in the chancellor's office at the time, Karl Carstens, called it one of the most gripping documents he had ever read. (Carstens was federal president from 1979 to 1984.) One of the results of this investigation was a considerable strengthening of executive oversight and a number of sweeping reforms under Gehlen's successor Gerhard Wessel. The *BND* also revised its hiring practices in order to attract young people with a more moderate view of the Cold War ideologies. But finding suitable senior intelligence managers with a Social Democratic Party book turned out to be a tricky problem, even after Brandt became chancellor in 1969.

While it is relatively easy to trace the *BND*'s failures, particularly when moles were uncovered and tried before law courts, there is little in the way of solid material in the public domain to document the *BND*'s achievements. Only the massive collection effort against Soviet armed forces stationed in eastern Germany can now be traced in some detail from *BND* files released to the German federal archives. The bulk of this material relates to the days before the Berlin Wall was built in 1960-61. In those days it was still possible for *BND* agents to meet personally with many of their informants who were doing the donkey work of counting Soviet vehicles, recording their markings, and estimating the military personnel in each Soviet military facility (Wagner and Uhl 2007).

From these and other sources it seems reasonable to assume that throughout the Cold War eastern Germany was the *BND*'s main intelligence target, including of course the Soviet forces in place and their relations with other Warsaw Pact armed forces. Its expertise on Warsaw Pact conventional forces was superb and highly respected within NATO. As an offshoot a highly profitable relationship was formed with Israel based on the important fact that Israel was threatened by its Arab neighbors mostly with Soviet and other Warsaw Pact weaponry. After each of the Middle Eastern wars Israel shared with the Germans the captured Soviet equipment. Beyond comparing notes on the latest in Soviet weaponry, Israel and West Germany jointly developed equipment for their defense against those weapons systems (Shpiro 2004 and 2006). The *BND* also supported Israel in other ways, for example with false flag operations such as

those carried out by Israeli agent Wolfgang Lotz in Nasser's Egypt (Lotz, 1972).

While it is known that the *BND* had extensive networks in the Middle East and in Africa their purpose is much less clear. West Germany had no post-colonial ties in those parts of the world that could be compared to Britain's or France's. Neither was it in a position to distribute money and weapons on the scale of US intelligence, which competed directly with Soviet and Chinese influence. The Germans did, however, play an important role in supporting democratic forces in Spain and Portugal during the Franco and Salazar dictatorships. This support paid off nicely after the fall of those dictatorships in 1974–1975 when many of the beneficiaries moved into leadership positions. By contrast it is far from clear to what extent the *BND* was able to influence the struggle for democracy in Eastern Europe, leading up to the 1989 "springtime of nations." Since it was barred from having permanent stations in the Warsaw Pact countries it would appear such aid was likely to have been quite limited.

The end of the Cold War spelled much trouble for the *BND*. Among left-wing politicians there was an urge to abolish it along with other Cold War institutions. Joschka Fischer's Green Party even introduced an official motion to that effect in the Bundestag, just two years before Fischer became foreign minister. Instead of being closed down the *BND* was forced to reduce its staff. At the same time it was shaken by the discovery of several moles deep inside its senior staff. There followed a frantic mole hunt that even targeted Volker Foertsch, one of the *BND*'s most senior figures, who was the current chief of counterintelligence. This son of a Wehrmacht general had been recruited in 1957 and had climbed right to the top of the *BND* hierarchy. As it turned out Foertsch was fully cleared of all charges, but he took early retirement, partly because his case had been leaked to the press. Among the real moles was Gabriele Gast, uncovered in 1990, who had worked in the *BND* for seventeen years as a Soviet specialist and had been on intimate terms with the East German Stasi's foreign intelligence chief Markus Wolf, who acted as her control.

If press leaks are any indication of the *BND*'s internal troubles, the 1990s were a period of extreme frustration. The full extent of that crisis became apparent when the oversight committee of the Bundestag ordered a special inquiry. It was led by a retired federal judge who was given access to pertinent *BND* files. His report ("Schäfer-Bericht") uncovered a whole swamp of affairs inside the *BND*. It came to the conclusion that a considerable part of the service was malfunctioning largely because of bureaucratic infighting. Moreover, it had used dubious methods to identify those on the inside who might have passed confidential information to various journalists. Certain journalists were even brought to spy on their colleagues. Others were put under observation as if they had been suspected of major crimes, while in actual practice they only did their job as guaranteed by freedom-of-the-press legislation.

To add insult to injury, the parliamentary oversight committee released that classified report in May 2006 after deleting only the names of the victims but not their circumstantial identification in the text. Thus even a lay person could identify them by consulting the Internet about "journalist X, the well-known author of such and such a book," with the book's title freely supplied in the text. The Schäfer-Bericht was put on the Bundestag's website. It gained enormous popularity, not in the least because it appeared to confirm what critics had always suspected about the quality of the *BND*'s intelligence work.[5] Indeed, the *BND* leadership never even managed to identify the sources of those press leaks.

3. CURRENT ISSUES

Even twenty years after the Berlin Wall came down the *BND* is still in the process of adapting to the twin developments that dominate German security policy today. The first evolved as the German defense institutions changed from a large defensive force, with an enormous army of tanks and artillery, to a much smaller and more mobile crisis intervention force suitable for the new world of multinational crisis management, mostly far from Europe. The second is related to the focus on international terrorism, organized international crime, and WMD proliferation, which has largely replaced the intelligence work on Soviet armament and strategy during the Cold War, hitherto the *BND*'s main line of business.

While international terrorism and WMD concerns had long been on the *BND*'s agenda, the requirements for supporting an entirely new defense posture and policy were difficult to meet. For over twenty years Germany's armed forces (more precisely West Germany's) had not been a national force directed by a national government for national purposes but an element, albeit a very large one, of NATO-coalition defense forces under SACEUR. Therefore the *BND*, in terms of its military intelligence functions, did not have to provide any stand-alone strategic or tactical intelligence. Its job was rather to contribute to NATO intelligence. Since the 1990s, when German armed forces began to be deployed in various peacemaking missions, the lack of adequate intelligence support became apparent. German military units had to beg other nations' armies for intelligence. This was particularly embarrassing during the 1999 Kosovo War (Goebel 2000).

The Bundeswehr was understandably angry at this kind of intelligence failure. There followed an institutional battle over who could and should provide the newly required military intelligence. While the details of this battle have been carefully hidden from public view, it is obvious that the *BND* won. At the end of 2007 the Bundeswehr's office for military intelligence (ZNBw) was closed down. Of its 650 full-time posts, 270 were transferred to the *BND*. This decision was taken against the advice of many senior military leaders who had wished to enhance the existing ZNBw structure, making it into a fully functioning military intelligence service along the lines of the British model. Their proposal was turned down by the political leadership. The Bundeswehr only retained its strategic intelligence command (KSA), headquartered near Bonn in 2002. It comprises all mobile technical intelligence gathering and electronic warfare units. It is also responsible for satellite imagery derived from the five German SAR-Lupe mini-satellites. The KSA now has about 7,000 full-time posts, of which 10 percent are filled with civilians. This figure includes several hundred specialists inherited from the former ZNBw. The German navy has some additional capacities for intelligence gathering while on overseas mission. The related personnel are integrated with small naval infantry or marine units, another novelty of the sweeping military reforms.

One of the most surprising aspects of this bureaucratic saga is that all this happened under the "red-green" government of Chancellor Gerhard Schröder and his foreign minister Joschka Fischer. In 1998, soon after he came into office, Schröder appointed a new head of the *BND*. His somewhat surprising choice was a typical conservative German mandarin, August Hanning, who had loyally served Schröder's right-of-center predecessor Helmut Kohl. Schröder even took the most unusual step of travelling to the *BND* headquarters on the outskirts of Munich ("Pullach") in order to introduce the new boss to his staff. Hanning immediately announced the creation of a liaison staff of two hundred people in Berlin, the new seat of the German government and federal parliament as of 1999. In Bonn the *BND* liaison staff had been considerably smaller. A year later, Hanning announced that the entire analysis staff of one thousand people would be transferred to Berlin. All this happened well before 9/11 and the many changes it entailed for the intelligence community.

While several of Hanning's predecessors had tried without success to move the *BND* to the seat of the government, the Schröder government was now willing to accept it, albeit without stating its reasoning in public. Being so far from the seat of government shaped not only the *BND* but also its relations with the governments in Bonn. While one could well understand why Chancellor Adenauer had preferred to keep Gehlen's motley crew at arm's length, headquartered in Pullach some four hundred miles to the southeast of Bonn, that remoteness became increasingly absurd as the German federal bureaucracy matured. It made it nearly impossible for the *BND* to interact with the defense and foreign ministries at the working level. Yet every government, including Kohl's after German unification, refused to consider such a move. As to the reasons, one can only speculate. Perhaps Kohl did not wish to give the *BND* any special importance at a time when German unification had raised the specter of a more "assertive" Germany. Bringing the *BND* closer to the seat of political power might have been seen as a signal for a more independent German foreign and security policy.

While Kohl wished to be seen as a "good European," Schröder was quite willing to pursue a more assertive foreign policy. His refusal in 2002 to join the war coalition against Saddam Hussein's Iraq was the prime example of this new orientation and incidentally helped him win the 2002 German federal elections. It is therefore no mere coincidence that the decision for the complete transfer of the *BND* to Berlin was made in this context.

During a meeting of the cabinet committee for national security in April 2003, Hanning raised the issue of moving the *BND* headquarters to Berlin. After a brief debate the chancellor and his most senior ministers approved this proposal (Gujer 2006). This decision was made exactly at the moment when the American-British coalition forces had overcome Iraqi military resistance and looked like they had achieved their goals brilliantly. At that point it seemed likely that the two main victor powers would put the heat on their skeptical friends, such as Germany, and force them to shoulder "their share" of the post-Saddam clean-up—though without getting their hands on the most lucrative international contracts for rebuilding Iraq's infrastructure and oil industry. In that situation the Berlin government would either be submissive as Chancellor Kohl had been during the previous Iraq War, to which the Germans (along with the Japanese) had been forced to make a massive financial contribution. Or else, Berlin would pursue its assertive course of a more "national" foreign policy, contributing to world security only at times and in places of its own choosing. The obvious consequence of the latter course was to speed up the reforms of the German military and intelligence capabilities.

Admittedly, there is a danger of reading too much into this issue. Schröder and Hanning may simply have used a moment of intense uncertainty, when Germany's public attention was focused uncomfortably on the events in Iraq, to do what they had long intended to do. Moreover, Schröder's "opposition" to the Iraq War was much softer than it appeared. Throughout that war American armed forces were making full use of their bases, including their support and command structure on German territory, without the slightest complaint from Berlin. Some years later it was revealed that the *BND* actively supported US war operations, in part through two *BND* agents on the ground in Bagdad (and sheltered in the French embassy).

This clandestine support later became the focus of a parliamentary inquiry in which Chancellor Angela Merkel's foreign minister, Frank-Walter Steinmeier, was the chief target because he had been responsible for executive oversight of all federal intelligence activities during the Schröder government. In December 2008 his predecessor, Joschka Fischer, stepped out of retirement to testify before a parliamentary committee: "I gave the green light in early 2003." True or not, that statement does not entirely clear Steinmeier of the charges brought against him. Both he and Fischer resolutely denied that those *BND* agents did anything to support the American war effort. By contrast, US General James Marks, who had been working in military intelligence in Iraq at the time, strongly emphasized their "extreme usefulness" to American military operations.[6]

Apart from the usual political game in which the political opposition goes after a government minister, the political far left saw an opportunity to damage Steinmeier, who hoped to succeed chancellor Merkel after the September 2009 federal elections. At the same time those same parliamentarians wished to hurt the *BND* as an institution. The idea of having

3,000 *BND* staff or more inside the city of Berlin (of an expected total of 6,500) clearly made them uncomfortable. Meanwhile, work goes forward at a huge construction site just 700 yards north of the chancellery in Berlin where the *BND* hopes to reside by 2012.

The complete reorientation of the Bundeswehr has not only assigned an enhanced role to the *BND*. It has also made the Berlin-Potsdam area (once again!) into the new hub of German security policy. While the nominal seat of the ministry of defense remains located in Bonn, a new command center for overseas operations has been established near Potsdam. The ministry's Berlin headquarters is housed in the historic "Bendler Block," built in 1911–1914 as the seat of the imperial German navy. (On 20 July 1944 it was the site where some of the leaders of the attempted assassination of Hitler were shot, among them Colonel Claus von Stauffenberg.) Numerous other military institutions have been moved to that region as well. In 2004 the joint center for defense against terrorism (GTAZ) was set up in Berlin-Treptow. It brings together some 220 representatives from all German intelligence services, including those of the sixteen Länder (states) and their criminal-police offices, and the military and federal security agencies. In this way, a completely new security infrastructure has been built up in and around Berlin that deals both with the new overseas military engagements and the new concern with anti-terrorism, WMD proliferation, and international organized crime. Needless to say that the German intelligence services, including the *BND*, have a large stake in these new institutions.

Against this background it is easy to see why the *BND*'s relocation to Berlin has been essential to its institutional survival. Never again would it be sidestepped in big-time national-security decision-making as it had been in 1990, during the negotiations for German unification. That "tense non-relationship between Bonn and Pullach," as its former chief Hans-Georg Wieck has described it, would have to come to an end (Wentker 2008, 344). Neither would it rely on the erstwhile mantra that "modern communication makes it unnecessary to be physically close to the center of political decision-making" as argued by numerous opponents both within and outside the *BND*. "Pullach" is now history, even if the actual removal of all staff will take a few more years.

Aside from this external adaptation to a new security environment, the *BND* had to undergo an internal reshuffling of people and resources. The biggest

reform was undertaken in 2008. It essentially did away with the organizational separation of intelligence gathering and intelligence analysis, hitherto organized on each side in geographical and functional offices. The new scheme is essentially arranged by functions, leaving only two geographical departments. Intelligence support for current Bundeswehr missions now has a separate division, as do terrorism and proliferation. There are several divisions for dealing with intelligence-related technologies, including signals intelligence, which is organized in separate services in Britain, in the United States, and elsewhere, but not so in Germany. To underline the long-term nature of this restructuring, the *BND* chief now has a deputy director for institutional reforms. To emphasize the new responsibilities in operational military intelligence the second deputy director is a major-general from the Bundeswehr, while the third deputy director is a career diplomat. Previously the typical arrangement had been a military man as chief of intelligence gathering and a diplomat at the head of the analysis branch.

The combination of a physical relocation of headquarters and a fundamental organizational reform has produced much ill will inside the *BND*. The current *BND* leadership has lived through a number of crises that have found their expressions in the press and in the parliamentary oversight committee of the Bundestag, both usually acting in tandem. Relations with the oversight staff inside the chancellor's office are tense. Few senior politicians are willing to defend the *BND* against public criticism. Chancellor Merkel keeps a great distance, leaving her chief-of-staff and minister for special duties, Thomas de Mazière, to handle those matters. (His father had been one of the founding generals of the Bundeswehr.)

The still-inconclusive debates on the *BND*'s role during the 2003 Iraq war, mentioned above, are only one of several issues related to German-American relations in security matters. Another concerns the "extraordinary rendition" flights that the CIA routed through Germany (among many other countries) in order to subject suspected terrorists to intense questioning. In a June 2006 report the Council of Europe estimated that one hundred people had been kidnapped by CIA officers on EU territory. In a February 2007 report the number of rendition flights is put at 1,245.[7] So far no answer has been given by the German government to the many allegations made in this context, which obviously touch on the role of the *BND*.

Another "intelligence crisis" concerns the young Turkish-German Murat Kurnaz who was captured by the Americans in Pakistan shortly after the 9/11 terrorist attacks, and eventually kept at the Guantanamo Bay detention camp. In August 2006 he was released without being charged. (He features in the 2008 John le Carré novel *A Most Wanted Man*.) Why had the German authorities not tried to get Kurnaz freed much earlier even though intelligence contacts had indicated that he turned out to be "small fry"? What had been the role of German intelligence and police authorities?

To many in Germany, particularly (but by no means only) those on the political left, the Kurnaz case represents the submissive policies of Germany vis-à-vis the United States when it comes to security and intelligence issues. But there is also a deep concern with civil liberties in which the intelligence services, along with the police, figure prominently.

Like most countries, Germany responded to the 9/11 events with a wide range of new legislation granting all sorts of new special privileges to the security and intelligence community. They range from electronic surveillance, particularly related to Internet access and private use, to new police and judicial regulations concerning people suspected of planning terrorist acts or of supporting any type of associated organization. In this context the *BND* was given authority not only to acquire such information but especially to make such information available to law-enforcement agencies. Hitherto, such access had been very tightly regulated, based on the assumption that police work and intelligence should be kept very far apart. Now the new anti-terrorism policies call for a close cooperation between all government and law-enforcing agencies.

A similar change of doctrine occurred on the issue of separating domestic from foreign intelligence. In Germany, domestic intelligence is handled by a large number of agencies. At the federal level, the Bundesamt für Verfassungsschutz (BfV) or Federal Office for the Protection of the Constitution is the largest and best known. Headquartered in Cologne it has a staff of some 2,500. It acts in close cooperation with the sixteen related agencies run by the sixteen Länder that, taken together, have an estimated staff of 3,200, bringing the total staff employed in German domestic intelligence to about 5,700 (for a total population of 82 million).[8] Its main mission, apart from general counterintelligence work, is to track political extremism, both from left- and right-wing groups, as well as other organizations hostile to the principles and liberties laid down in the German constitution. Their major findings are summarized in published annual reports issued by all seventeen agencies and in various special reports. Their agents have no police powers (such as search and arrest). But they use clandestine methods and infiltrate spies into their target organizations or groups. Due to the activities of Palestinian terrorist groups as far back as the 1960s and 1970s—think of the attacks during the Munich Olympics in 1972—they have a long experience with terrorism from the Islamic world. Thus jihadist terrorism since the 1990s was no surprise to them.

To round off the picture of German intelligence we need to mention the Bundeskriminalamt (BKA) or Federal Criminal Police Office, headquartered in Wiesbaden (near Frankfurt/Main), and with a staff of 5,200, including 2,600 police officers. While it remains essentially a law-enforcement agency, comparable to the American FBI, combating major crime, including international organized crime, its mandate for fighting international terrorism was significantly enlarged in recent years. In 2004 the Schröder government even tried to transfer most of the BKA to Berlin in order to enhance the emerging new anti-terrorism center. However, the project raised a storm of political protest and had to be abandoned. According to the German constitution, police work essentially remains a prerogative of the Länder (states) while the federal government is restricted to auxiliary functions.

The Länder did not wish to see their constitutional position weakened, under the pretext of enhancing the institutional structures for combating international terrorism. They already feel uneasy about the expansion of the Bundespolizei (Bpol) or federal police, which had originally been established in 1951 as a border-control force, armed like light infantry units, and was subsequently transformed into a police force ready to deal with large-scale domestic threats to public order. Its total force of 39,000 police officers dwarfs the forces of any single Land (state). In 2005 its name was formally changed from "border police" to "federal police"—a clear message that the German federal government has enlarged its law-enforcement mandate.

Another aborted project was made public in May 2008. The ambition was to create a new intelligence organization for electronic surveillance, somewhat along the lines of the British GCHQ or the much larger American NSA (*Der Spiegel*, 19 May 2008, 30). It would have marked yet another post-9/11 step to give the German federal government more intelligence power and to tear down the walls between foreign and domestic intelligence. Even though the very powerful interior minister Wolfgang Schäuble proposed Cologne rather than Berlin as the site of such a "German NSA," his plan met with massive opposition from many sides. Apart from the ongoing battle between the federal level of government and the Länder, there is also a widely held belief among the German public that the security legislation and institutional changes made in the wake of 9/11 already pose a fundamental threat to civil liberties and must not be allowed to progress any further. At the same time, however, there is a deep fear that German intelligence agencies might be unable to bring the new post-9/11 threats under control. It seems therefore likely that Schäuble or his successor after the 2009 German federal elections will eventually revive the idea of a "German NSA." If not, the massive technological infrastructure needed will be allocated to several independent agencies, which would result in an inefficient use of an enormously expensive investment.

4. CONCLUSION

No crystal ball is needed to forecast that intelligence institutions at the level of the European Union are unlikely to replace national institutions any time soon (or ever). The chief concern among professionals is to improve cooperation at the working levels and to bring the new Eastern European EU members up to the level of performance of their much richer Western European neighbors. Standardization or at least interoperability of hardware and software is another major concern.[9]

The main challenge to Germany's new security and intelligence architecture is likely to come from two directions. The most troubling is the tense and nearly hopeless situation in some of the crisis zones where German soldiers are now deployed, particularly the southern ex-Yugoslav republics and Afghanistan. By contrast, jihadist terrorism is a better understood field where past experience and current expertise are applied successfully, even though success is not always certain. Unless a miracle happens, the Balkan operations and even more so the situation in Afghanistan are likely to bring a rude shock to the German public, torn as it is between the idealism of humanitarian intervention and crisis resolution on the one hand and "playing at little Switzerland" on the other. At fault are not Germany's new security institutions, her new Bundeswehr and a reformed (and relocated) BND, but

the frame of mind that got the Germans into those difficulties. In the view of this author no amount of institutional reform will fill the gap in realistic strategic thinking that has developed inside the liberal democracies, formerly called "the West," since the enthusiastic days of 1989 and 1990.

QUESTIONS FOR FURTHER DISCUSSION

1. How did the BND and the CIA come to be so close in the years after the Second World War?
2. Would it be sensible for the BND to have a fullblown covert action capability, like other major powers in the world? What has inhibited this development?
3. The Snowden leaks disclosed extensive efforts by the NSA to conduct electronic surveillance in Germany against suspected terrorists. To what extent are such operations condonable? Should they have been carried out only with the full knowledge of the German government in Berlin, and with the cooperation of the BND?
4. How close do you think the German and the US international threat assessments would correspond with one another? What would be the main differences, if any?

ENDNOTES

1. The precise reasons for these changes have never been made public. From private conversations with senior Bundeswehr officers one gets the impression that the military was simply overruled by the stronger institutional battalions of the chancellor's office.
2. The BND's name itself suggests that it only deals with "Nachrichten," which literally means "news" and is usually applied to press reporting. One is reminded of its predecessor, the "Abwehr," which literally means "defense" (against foreign espionage) while in reality it was a full-fledged foreign and military intelligence service with a considerable capacity for clandestine warfare and sabotage. The lack of a German word for "intelligence" (in the sense of secret information and operations) makes it easy to hide behind a screen of innocent terminology.
3. The West German border police (Bundesgrenzschutz), founded in 1951, was another "waiting room" for ex-Wehrmacht personnel.
4. See also Hachmeister's (2008) book review and letters concerning James Critchfield's book (*Partners at the Creation . . .*), in *Foreign Affairs* (November/December 2004); the figure of one hundred former SS men is

taken from the letter to the editor by ambassador Hans-Georg Wieck who headed the *BND* in 1985–90.

5. The text can be found on the following website: http://www.bundestag.de/aktuell/archiv/2006/pkg/index.html; see also "Die Schnüffler vom Dienst" in *Der Spiegel* (22 May 2006).

6. For details, see *Der Spiegel,* online international ed. (16 December 2008) "The Germans Were Invaluable to Us."

7. Supporting documentation is found in http://assembly.coe.int/Main.asp?link=/Documents/AdoptedText/ta06/ERES1507.htm.

8. This is my own estimate, based on rather incomplete published figures.

9. This consensus emerged from a conference of German intelligence experts held by the Friedrich-Ebert-Stiftung in Berlin on 8 April 2008. The proceedings will be published in 2009.

BIBLIOGRAPHY

Critchfield, J. 2003. *Partners at the Creation: The Men behind Postwar Germany's Defense and Intelligence Establishments.* Annapolis, Md.: Naval Institute Press.

Frankfurter Allgemeine Zeitung (daily).

Goebel, P., ed. 2000. *Von Kambodscha bis Kosovo: Auslandseinsätze der Bundeswehr seit Ende des Kalten Krieges.* Bonn: Report-Verlag.

Gujer, E. 2006. *Kampf an neuen Fronten: Wie sich der BND dem Terrorismus stellt.* Frankfurt am Main: Campus-Verlag.

Hachmeister, L. 2008. Weiße Flecken in der Geschichte des Bundesnachrichtendienstes. *Frankfurter Allgemeine Zeitung* (May 13): 50.

Krieger, W. 2007. US Patronage of German Postwar Intelligence. In *Handbook of Intelligence Studies,* ed. L. K. Johnson. London: Routledge.

———. 2009. Oversight of Intelligence: A Comparative Approach. In *National Intelligence Systems: Current Research and Future Prospects,* ed. G. F. Treverton and W. Agrell. New York: Cambridge University Press.

Lotz, W. 1972. *The Champagne Spy: Israel's Master Spy Tells His Story.* New York: St. Martin's Press.

Schoenbaum, D. 1968. *The Spiegel Affair.* Garden City, NJ.: Doubleday.

Shpiro, S. 2004. Know Your Enemy: West German–Israeli Intelligence Evaluation of Soviet Weapons Systems. *Journal of Intelligence History* 4, no. 1:14–29.

Shapiro, S. 2006. Cold War Radar Intelligence: Operation "Cerberus." *Journal of Intelligence History* 6, no. 2:53–64.

Der Spiegel (weekly).

Wagner, A., and M. Uhl. 2007. *BND contra Sowjetarmee: Westdeutsche Militärspionage in der DDR.* Berlin: Links-Verlag.

Waske, S. 2009. *Mehr Liaison als Kontrolle: Die Kontrolle des BND durch Parlament und Regierung, 1955–1978.* Wiesbaden, Germany: VS-Verlag.

Wentker, H. 2008. Die DDR in den Augen des BND (1985–1990): Ein Interview mit Dr. Hans-Georg Wieck. *Vierteljahrshefte für Zeitgeschichte* 56, no. 2:323–58.

Wolfgang Krieger, "The German Bundesnachrichtendienst (BND)," in Loch K. Johnson, ed., *The Oxford Handbook of National Security Intelligence* (New York: Oxford University Press, 2010): 790–805. Reproduced with Permission.

U.S. INTELLIGENCE LEADERSHIP, 1947–2018

DIRECTORS, NATIONAL INTELLIGENCE (DNIS)

2005–2007	John D. Negroponte
2007–2009	J. M. ("Mike") McConnell
2009–2010	Dennis C. Blair
2011–2017	James R. Clapper Jr.
2018–	Dan Coates

DIRECTORS, CENTRAL INTELLIGENCE (DCIS)

1947–1950	Rear Adm. Roscoe H. Hillenkoetter
1950–1953	Gen. Walter Bedell Smith
1953–1961	Allen W. Dulles
1961–1965	John A. McCone
1965–1966	Vice Adm. William F. Raborn Jr.
1966–1973	Richard Helms
1973	James R. Schlesinger
1973–1976	William E. Colby
1976–1977	George H. W. Bush
1977–1981	Adm. Stansfield Turner
1981–1987	William J. Casey
1987–1991	William H. Webster
1991–1993	Robert M. Gates
1993–1995	R. James Woolsey
1995–1997	John M. Deutch
1997–2004	George J. Tenet
2004–2005	Porter J. Goss

DIRECTORS, CENTRAL INTELLIGENCE AGENCY (D/CIAS)

2005–2006	Porter J. Goss
2006–2009	Gen. Michael V. Hayden
2009–2011	Leon E. Panetta

2011–2012	Gen. David Petraeus
2013–2017	John Brennan
2017–2018	Mike Pompeo
2018–	Gina Haspel

CHAIRS, SENATE SELECT COMMITTEE ON INTELLIGENCE (SSCI)

1976–1977	Daniel K. Inouye, Democrat, Hawaii
1977–1981	Birch Bayh, Democrat, Indiana
1981–1985	Barry Goldwater, Republican, Arizona
1985–1987	David Durenberger, Republican, Minnesota
1987–1993	David L. Boren, Democrat, Oklahoma
1993–1995	Dennis DeConcini, Democrat, Arizona
1995–1997	Arlen Specter, Republican, Pennsylvania
1997–2001	Richard C. Shelby, Republican, Alabama
2001–2003	Bob Graham, Democrat, Florida
2003–2006	Pat Roberts, Republican, Kansas
2006–2009	John D. Rockefeller IV, Democrat, West Virginia
2009–2015	Diane Feinstein, Democrat, California
2015–	Richard Burr, Republican, North Carolina

CHAIRS, HOUSE PERMANENT SELECT COMMITTEE ON INTELLIGENCE (HPSCI)

1977–1985	Edward P. Boland, Democrat, Massachusetts

1985–1987	Lee H. Hamilton, Democrat, Indiana	1995–1997	Larry Combest, Republican, Texas
1987–1989	Louis Stokes, Democrat, Ohio	1997–2004	Porter J. Goss, Republican, Florida
1989–1991	Anthony C. Beilenson, Democrat, California	2004–2006	Peter Hoekstra, Republican, Michigan
1991–1993	Dave McCurdy, Democrat, Oklahoma	2007–2011	Silvestre Reyes, Democrat, Texas
1993–1995	Dan Glickman, Democrat, Kansas	2011–2015	Mike Rodgers, Republican, Michigan
		2015–	Devin Nunes, Republican, California

THE ORGANIZATION OF THE U.S. INTELLIGENCE COMMUNITY

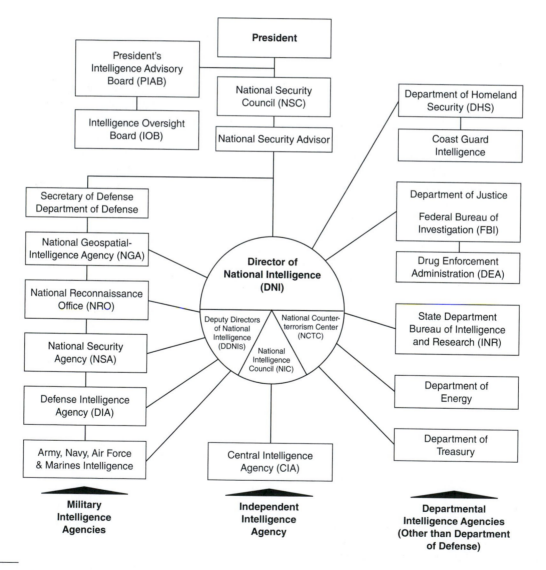

GLOSSARY

ABM	anti-ballistic missile	**CI**	counterintelligence
ADCI/A&P	assistant director of Central Intelligence/Analysis and Production	**CIA**	Central Intelligence Agency (the "Agency")
		CIC	Counterintelligence Center (CIA)
ADCI/C	assistant director of Central Intelligence/Collection	**CIG**	Central Intelligence Group (CIA)
		CINC	commander-in-chief (regional military commander)
AFIO	Association of Former Intelligence Officers	**CIPA**	Classified Information Procedures Act of 1980 (U.S.)
AFRICOM	Africa Command (U.S.)		
AG	Attorney General	**CMS**	Community Management Staff
AI	artificial intelligence	**CNC**	Crime and Narcotics Center (CIA)
A-12	U.S. spy plane	**CNO**	Chief of Naval Operations
ASIO	Australian Security Intelligence Organization	**COINTELPRO**	Counterintelligence Program (FBI)
		comint	communications intelligence
AWAC	airborne warning and control system (U.S. spy plane)	**CORONA**	codename for the first U.S. spy satellite system
		C/O	case officer (CIA)
BDA	battle damage assessment	**COS**	chief of station, the top CIA officer in the field
BMD	ballistic missile defense		
BW	biological weapons	**CSIS**	Canadian Security and Intelligence Service
CA	covert action	**CTC**	Counterterrorism Center (CIA)
CAS	Covert Action Staff	**CW**	chemical weapons
CB	chemical-biological		
CBW	chemical-biological warfare	**D**	Democrat
CE	counterespionage	**DA**	Directorate of Administration (CIA)
CENTCOM	Central Command (U.S.)	**DAS**	Deputy Assistant Secretary
C4I	command, control, computer, communications, and intelligence	**DBA**	dominant battlefield awareness
		DCIA or D/CIA	Director of the Central Intelligence Agency
CHAOS	code name for CIA domestic spying operation		
		DCI	Director of Central Intelligence

DDA	Deputy Director for Administration (CIA)	FISA	Foreign Intelligence Surveillance Act
DDCI	Deputy Director of Central Intelligence	FISC	Foreign Intelligence Surveillance Court
DDCIA	Deputy Director for the Central Intelligence Agency	FSB	Russian Federal Security Service
DDIC	Deputy Director for the Intelligence Community	GATT	General Agreement on Trade and Tariffs
DDI	Deputy Director for Intelligence	GEO	Geosynchronous Orbit
DDO	Deputy Director for Operations	geoint	geospatial intelligence
DDP	Deputy Director for Plans (CIA)	GOP	Grand Old Party (the Republican Party)
DDS	Deputy Director for Support (CIA)		
DDS&T	Deputy Director for Science and Technology	GRU	Soviet Military Intelligence
DD	Deputy Director for Support (CIA)	HEO	highly elliptical orbit
DEA	Drug Enforcement Administration	HPSCI	House Permanent Select Committee on Intelligence
DEC	Director's Environmental Center (CIA)	humint	human intelligence (espionage assets)
DHS	Department of Homeland Security		
DI	Directorate of Intelligence (CIA)	IC	intelligence community
DIA	Defense Intelligence Agency	ICBM	intercontinental ballistic missile
DIAC	Defense Intelligence Agency Center	ICS	Intelligence Community Staff
DIA/Humint	Defense Humint Service	IG	Inspector General
DMA	Defense Mapping Agency (part of NGA)	IM	Intelligence Memorandum
		imint	imagery intelligence (photography), now known as geoint
DO	Directorate of Operations (CIA), also known as the Clandestine Services	INR	Bureau of Intelligence and Research (Department of State)
DoD	Department of Defense	ints	intelligence collection methods (as in "sigint")
DoE	Department of Energy		
DoS	Department of State	IOB	Intelligence Oversight Board
DoT	Department of Transportation	IRTPA	Intelligence Reform and Terrorism Prevention Act (2004)
DMI	Director of Military Intelligence (proposed)	IT	information technology
DNI	Director of National Intelligence	I&W	indicators and warning
DP	Directorate of Plans (CIA), a DO precursor	JCS	Joint Chiefs of Staff
DS&T	Directorate for Science and Technology (CIA)	JIC	Joint Intelligence Committee (U.K.)
		JMIP	joint military intelligence program
DS	Directorate for Support (CIA, replacing the DA)	JROC	Joint Reconnaissance Operations Center
		JSOC	Joint Special Operations Command
elint	electronic intelligence		
E.O.	executive order	JSTARS	Joint Surveillance Target Attack Radar Systems
EOP	Executive Office of the President		
EPA	Environmental Protection Agency		
EURA	Office of European Analysis (CIA)	KGB	Soviet Secret Police and Foreign Intelligence: Committee for State Security
FAS	Federation of American Scientists		
FBI	Federal Bureau of Investigation	KH	Keyhole (satellite)

KJ	Key Judgment (NIE executive summaries)
LEO	low earth orbit
MAGIC	Allied code-breaking operations against the Japanese in World War II
masint	measurement and signatures intelligence
MI	military intelligence
MIA	missing in action
MIP	Military Intelligence Program
MIRV	multiple, independently targeted, re-entry vehicle
MI5	British Security Service
MI6	Secret Intelligence Service (SIS—United Kingdom)
MIT	Massachusetts Institute of Technology
MRBM	medium-range ballistic missiles
MRC	major regional conflict
MX	Missile Experimental (a component of U.S. nuclear deterrence)
NAFTA	North American Free Trade Agreement
NASA	National Aeronautics and Space Administration
NATO	North Atlantic Treaty Organization
NCPC	National Counterproliferation Center (for the DNI)
NCS	National Clandestine Service (formerly CIA's DO)
NCTC	National Counterterrorism Center (for the DNI)
NEOB	New Executive Office Building
NFIP	National Foreign Intelligence Program (now NIP)
NGA	National Geospatial-Intelligence Agency
NGO	non-governmental organization
NIA	National Imagery Agency (proposed)
NIC	National Intelligence Council
NID	*National Intelligence Daily*; also, National Intelligence Director (a variation of DNI)
NIE	National Intelligence Estimate
NIO	National Intelligence Officer
NIMA	National Imagery and Mapping Agency
NIP	National Intelligence Program
NIT	National Intelligence Topic
NOC	nonofficial cover
NPC	Nonproliferation Center (CIA)
NPIC	National Photographic Interpretation Center (part of NGA)
NRO	National Reconnaissance Office
NSA	National Security Agency
NSC	National Security Council
NTM	National Technical Means
OBE	overtaken by events
OC	official cover
ODNI	Office of the Director of National Intelligence
OMB	Office of Management and Budget
ONE	Office of National Estimates
OPEC	Organization of Petroleum Exporting Countries
osint	open-source intelligence
OSS	Office of Strategic Services
PDB	*President's Daily Brief*
PDD	Presidential Decision Directive
PFIAB	President's Foreign Intelligence Advisory Board (as of 2008, PIAB)
PIAB	President's Intelligence Advisory Board
PM ops	paramilitary operations
PNG	*persona non grata*
POW	prisoner of war
PRB	Publication Review Board (CIA)
PRC	People's Republic of China
R	Republican
radint	radar intelligence
RAF	Royal Air Force
RAND Corporation	a Washington, D.C. and California think tank
R & D	research and development
RMA	revolution in military affairs
RPG	rocket-propelled grenade
SAIS	School of Advanced International Studies (Johns Hopkins)
SAM	surface-to-air missile
secdef	Secretary of Defense

SHAMROCK	cryptonym for NSA domestic spying operations	**TSA**	Transportation Security Administration (U.S.)
sigint	signals intelligence	**TTAC**	Technological Transfer Assessment Center (CIA)
SDO	support to diplomatic operations		
SIG	Senior Intelligence Group	**TTIC**	Terrorist Threat Integration Center (White House)
SLBM	submarine-launched ballistic missile		
SMO	support to military operations		
SNIE	Special National Intelligence Estimate	**UAV**	unmanned aerial vehicle (drone)
		UK	United Kingdom
SOCMINT	social media intelligence	**U-2**	CIA spy plane
SOCOM	Special Operations Command	**UN**	United Nations
SOF	Special Operations Forces (DoD)	**UNSCOM**	United Nations Special Commission
SOG	Special Operations Group (CIA)		
SOVA	Office of Soviet Analysis (CIA)	**USAF**	United States Air Force
SR-21	U.S. spy plane	**USAID**	United States Agency for International Development
SSCI	Senate Select Committee on Intelligence		
		USC	United States Code (a statutory identification system)
START	Strategic Arms Reduction Treaty		
SVR	Russian Foreign Intelligence Service (post-Cold War)	**USIB**	United States Intelligence Board
		USSR	Union of Soviet Socialist Republics
TCA	Technical Collection Agency (proposed)	**USTR**	United States Trade Representative
techint	technical intelligence	**VX**	a deadly nerve agent used in chemical weapons
telint	telemetry intelligence		
TIARA	tactical intelligence and related activities	**WMD**	weapons of mass destruction

SELECT BIBLIOGRAPHY

Agrell, Wilhelm, and Gregory F. Treverton. 2015. *National Intelligence and Science: Beyond the Great Divide in Analysis and Policy*. New York: Oxford University Press.

Allen, Michael. 2013. *Blinking Red: Crisis and Compromise in American Intelligence After 9/11*. Washington, DC: Potomac Books.

Aid, Matthew M. 2009. *The Secret Sentry: The Untold History of the National Security Agency*. New York: Bloomsbury Press.

Aldrich, Richard J. 2002. *The Hidden Hand: Britain, America, and Cold War Secret Intelligence*. Woodstock, NY: Overlook Press, 2002.

Anderson, Jack. 1973. "How the CIA Snooped Inside Russia," *Washington Post* (December 10): B17.

Andrew, Christopher. 1995. *For the President's Eyes Only: Secret Intelligence and the American Presidency From Washington to Bush*. New York: HarperCollins.

———, and Visili Mitrokhin. 1999. *The Sword and the Shield: The Mitrokhin Archive and the Secret History of the KGB*. New York: Basic Books.

Aspin-Brown Commission. 1996. *Preparing for the 21st Century: An Appraisal of U.S. Intelligence*. Report of the Commission on the Roles and Capabilities of the United States Intelligence Community. Washington, DC: Government Printing Office.

Baer, Robert. 2002. *See No Evil: The True Story of a Gropund Soldier in the CIA's War on Terrorism*. New York: Three Rivers Press.

Bamford, James. 1984. *The Puzzle Palace*. Boston: Houghton Mifflin.

Bar-Joseph, Uri. 2005. *The Watchman Fell Asleep: The Surprise of Yom Kippur and its Sources*. Albany: State University of New York Press.

Barrett, David M. 2005. *The CIA and Congress: The Untold Story from Truman to Kennedy*. Lawrence: University Press of Kansas.

Batvinis, Raymond J. 2007. *The Origins of FBI Counterintelligence*. Lawrence: University Press of Kansas.

Beebe, Sarah Miller, and Randolph H. Pherson. 2012. *Cases in Intelligence Analysis: Structured Analytic Techniques in Action*. Los Angeles: CQ Press.

Berkowitz, Bruce, and Allen Goodman. 2000. *Best Truth: Intelligence in the Information Age*. New Haven, CT: Yale University Press.

Betts, Richard K. 1978. "Analysis, War and Decision: Why Intelligence Failures are Inevitable," *World Politics* 31(1): 61–89.

———. 2002. "Fixing Intelligence," *Foreign Affairs* 81 (January–February): 43–59.

———. 2007. *Enemies of Intelligence: Knowledge & Power in American National Security*. New York: Columbia University Press.

Bissell, Richard M., Jr., with Jonathan E. Lewis and Frances T. Rudlo. 1996. *Reflections of a Cold War*. New Haven, CT: Yale University Press.

Born, Hans, Loch K. Johnson, and Ian Leigh. 2005. *Who's Watching the Spies? Establishing Intelligence Service Accountability*. Washington, DC: Potomac Books.

Brown, Juanita, and David Isaacs. 2008. "The World Café: Awakening Collective Intelligence and Committed Action," in Mark Tovey (ed.), *Collective Intelligence: Creating a Prosperous World at Peace*. Oakton, VA: Earth Intelligence Network: 47–53.

Brugioni, Dino A. 1969. "The Unidentifieds," *Studies in Intelligence* (Summer): 1–20.

Burrows, William E. 1986. *Deep Black: Space Espionage and National Security*. New York: Random House.

Byrne, Malcolm. 2014. *Iran-Contra: Reagan's Scandal and the Unchecked Abuse of Presidential Power*. Lawrence: University Press of Kansas.

Campbell, Duncan. 2003. "Afghan Prisoners Beaten to Death," *The Guardian* (March 7): 1.

Central Intelligence Agency. 1983. *Fact Book on Intelligence*. Washington, DC: Central Intelligence Agency.

Church Committee (Select Committee to Study Governmental Operations with Respect to Intelligence Activities). 1975a. Declassified CIA memorandum, Committee files, U.S. Senate, 94th Cong., 2d Sess.

———. 1975b. "Alleged Assassination Plots Involving Foreign Leaders," *Interim Report. S. Rept. No. 94–465*. Washington, DC: U.S. Government Printing Office.

———. 1976. *Final Report, Sen. Rept. No. 94–755*, vol. 1. Washington, DC: U.S. Government Printing Office.

Cirincione, Joseph. 2000. "Assessing the Assessment: The 1999 National Intelligence Estimate of the Ballistic Missile Threat," *Nonproliferation Review* 7 (Spring): 125–137.

Cohen, William S., and George J. Mitchell. 1988. *Men of Zeal: A Candid Inside Story of the Iran-Contra Hearings*. New York: Viking.

Colby, William E., and Peter Forbath. 1978. *Honorable Men: My Life in the CIA*. New York: Simon & Schuster.

Commission on Government Security, *Report*. 1957. Washington, DC: U.S. Government Printing Office.

Cormac, Rory. 2018. *Disrupt and Deny: Spies, Special Forces, and the Secret Pursuit of British Foreign Policy*. Oxford: Oxford University Press.

———. and Richard J. Aldrich. 2018. "Grey is the New Black: Covert Action and Implausible Deniability," *International Affairs* 94/ 3 (May): 477–494.

Cradock, Percy. 2002. *Know Your Enemy: How the Joint Intelligence Committee Saw the World*. London: John Murray.

Crumpton, Henry A. 2012. *The Art of Intelligence; Lessons from a Life in the CIA's Clandestine Service*. New York: Penguin.

Currie, James. 1998. "*Iran-Contra* and Congressional Oversight of the CIA," *International Journal of Intelligence and Counterintelligence* 11 (Summer): 185–210.

Davis, Jack. 2007. "Strategic Warning: Intelligence Support in a World of Uncertainty and Surprise," in Loch K. Johnson (ed.), *Handbook of Intelligence Studies*. London: Routledge: 173–188.

Diamond, John. 2008. *The CIA and the Culture of Failure*. Stanford, CA: Stanford University Press.

Dover, Robert, Michael S. Goodman, and Claudia Hillebrand, eds. 2014. *Routledge Companion to Intelligence Studies*. New York: Routledge.

Garthoff, Raymond L. 2015. *Soviet Leaders and Intelligence: Assessing the American Adversary During the Cold War*. Washington, DC: Georgetown University Press.

Gates, Robert M. 1996. *From the Shadows*. New York: Simon & Schuster.

Gill, Peter, Stephen Marrin, and Mark Phythian, eds. 2009. *Intelligence Theory: Key Questions and Debates*. London: Routledge.

Godson, Roy S. 1996. *Dirty Tricks or Trump Cards: U.S. Covert Action and Counterintelligence*. Washington, DC: Brassey's, 1996.

Goldman, Jan, ed. 2006. *Ethics of Spying*. Lanham, MD: Scarecrow Press.

Graham, Bob, with Jeff Nussbaum. 2004. *Intelligence Matters*. New York: Random House.

Greenberg, Karen J. 2016. *Rogue Justice: The Making of the Security State*. New York: Crown.

Halpern, Samuel, and Hayden B. Peake, "Did Angleton Jail Nosenko?" *International Journal of Intelligence and Counterintelligence* 3 (Winter): 451–464.

Handel, Michael. 1977. "The Yom Kippur War and the Inevitability of Surprise," *International Studies Quarterly* 21, 3:461–501.

Harden, Toby. 2003. "CIA 'Pressure' on Al Qaeda Chief," *Washington Post* (March 6): A1.

Hart-Rudman Report. 2001. Commission on National Security/21st Century. Washington, DC.

Hastedt Glenn. 1986. "The Constitutional Control of Intelligence," *Intelligence and National Security* 1 (May): 255–271.

Hennessy, Peter. 2003. *The Secret State: Whitehall and the Cold War*. London: Penguin.

Herman, Michael. 1996. *Intelligence Power in Peace and War*. New York: Cambridge University Press.

Heuer, Richards J., Jr. 1999. *Psychology of Intelligence Analysis*. Washington, DC: Center for the Study of Intelligence.

———. 1981. "Strategic Deception and Counterdeception," *International Studies Quarterly* 25 (June): 294–327.

Heylighen, Francis. 2008. "The Emergence of a Global Brain," in Mark Tovey (ed.), *Collective Intelligence: Creating a Prosperous World at Peace*. Oakton, VA: Earth Intelligence Network: 305–314.

Hitz, Frederick P. 2004. *The Great Game: The Myth and Reality of Espionage*. New York: Knopf.Hughes, R. Gerald, Peter Jackson, and Len Scott, eds. 2008. *Exploring Intelligence Archives*. New York: Routledge.

Hoffman, David E. 2015. *The Billion Dollar Spy: A True Story of Cold War Espionage and Betrayal*. New York: Anchor Books/Penguin Random House.

Hulnick, Arthur S. 1986. "The Intelligence Producer-Policy Consumer Linkage: A Theoretical Approach," *Intelligence and National Security* 1(2): 212–233.

———. 1999. *Fixing the Spy Machine: Preparing American Intelligence for the Twenty-First Century*. Westport, CT: Praeger.

Jackson, Peter. 2007. A Look at French Intelligence Machinery in 1936. *Intelligence and National Security*, 22(4): 546-62.

Jackson, William R. 1990. "Congressional Oversight of Intelligence: Search for a Framework," *Intelligence and National Security* 5(2): 113–137.

Jeffreys-Jones, Rhodri. 1989. *The CIA and American Democracy*. New Haven, CT: Yale University Press.

———. 2013. *In Spies We Trust: The Story of Western Intelligence*. New York: Oxford University Press.

Jervis, Robert. 1986–87. "Intelligence and Foreign Policy," *International Security* 11 (Winter): 141–161.

———. 2010. *Why Intelligence Fails: Lessons from the Iranian Revolution and the Iraq War*. Ithica, NY: Cornell University Press.

Johnson, Loch K. 1980. "The U.S. Congress and the CIA: Monitoring the Dark Side of Government," *Legislative Studies Quarterly* 5 (November): 477–99.

———. 1985. *A Season Inquiry: The Senate Intelligence Investigation*. Lexington: University Press of Kentucky.

———. 1989. *America's Secret Power: The CIA in a Democratic Society*. New York: Oxford University Press.

———. 1996. *Secret Agencies: U.S. Intelligence in a Hostile World*. New Haven, CT: Yale University Press.

———. 2000. *Bombs, Bugs, Drugs, and Thugs: Intelligence and America's Quest for Security*, p. 177. New York: New York University Press.

———. 2001. "The CIA's Weakest Link," *Washington Monthly* 33 (July/August): 9–14.

———. 2004. "The Aspin-Brown Intelligence Inquiry: Behind the Closed Doors of a Blue Ribbon Commission," *Studies in Intelligence* 48 (Winter), pp. 1–20.

———. 2007. *Seven Sins of American Foreign Policy*. New York: Longman.

———. (ed.). 2007a. *Strategic Intelligence*, 5 Vols. Westport, CT: Praeger.

———. (ed.). 2007b. *Handbook of Intelligence Studies*. London: Routledge.

———. 2007c. "Educing Information: Interrogation: Science and Art, *Studies in Intelligence* 51 (December): 43–46.

———. 2007d. "An Introduction to the Intelligence Studies Literature," in Loch K. Johnson (ed.), *Strategic Intelligence: Understanding the Hidden Side of Government*. Westport, CT: Praeger: 1–20.

———. ed. 2010. *The Oxford Handbook of National Security Intelligence*. New York: Oxford University Press.

———. 2011. *The Threat on the Horizon: An Inside Account of America's Search for Security After the Cold War*. New York: Oxford University Press.

———. 2015. *American Foreign Policy and the Challenges of World Leadership: Power, Principle, and the Constitution*. New York: Oxford University Press.

———. 2015. *A Season of Inquiry Revisited: The Church Committee Confronts America's Spy Agencies*. Lawrence: University Press of Kansas.

———. ed. 2015. *Essentials of Strategic Intelligence*. Santa Barbara, CA: Praeger.

———. 2017. *National Security Intelligence: Secret Operations in Defense of the Democracies*, 2d ed. Cambridge, UK: Polity.

———. 2018 *Spy Watching: Intelligence Accountability in the United States*. New York: Oxford University Press.

Johnson, Paul. 1997. "No Cloak and Dagger Required: Intelligence Support to U.N. Peacekeeping," *Intelligence and National Security* 12 (October): 102–112.

Johnson, William R. 1987. *Thwarting Enemies at Home and Abroad: How to Be a Counterintelligence Office*. Bethesda, MD: Stone Trail Press.

Kaiser, Frederick M. 1992. "Congress and the Intelligence Community: Taking the Road Less Traveled," in Roger H. Davidson (ed.), *The Postreform Congress*. New York: St. Martin's Press: 279–300.

Kam, Ephraim. 1988. *Surprise Attack*. Cambridge: Harvard University Press.

Kent, Sherman. 1949. *Strategic Intelligence for American World Policy*. Princeton: Princeton University Press.

Kerr, Richard, Thomas Wolfe, Rebecca Donegan, and Aris Pappas. 2008. "Intelligence Collection and Analysis on Iraq: Issues for the U.S. Intelligence Community," in James P. Pfiffner and Mark Phythian (eds.), *Intelligence and National Security Policymaking on Iraq: British and American Perspectives*. Manchester, UK: Manchester University Press: 151–161

Kibbe, Jennifer. 2010. "Congressional Oversight of Intelligence: Is the Solution Part of the Problem?" *Intelligence and National Security* 25(1): 24–49.

Knott, Stephen F. 1996. *Secret and Sanctioned: Covert Operations and the American Presidency*. New York: Oxford University Press.

Kramer, Mark. 2002. "Oversight of Russian's Intelligence and Security Agencies: The Need for and Prospects of Democratic Control," PONARS Policy Memo 281, <http://www.csis.org/ruseura/ponars/policymemos/pm_0281.pdf>.

Kurlantzick, Joshua. 2016. *A Great Place to Have a War: America in Laos and the Birth of a Military CIA*. New York: Simon & Schuster.

LeCarré, John. 2016. *The Pigeon Tunnel*. New York: Penguin.

Lowenthal, Mark M. 2005. *U.S. Intelligence: Evolution and Anatomy*, 3rd ed. Westport, CT: Praeger.

———. 2017. *Intelligence: From Secrets to Policy*, 7th ed. Los Angeles, CA: Sage/CQ Press.

———. 2018. *The Future of Intelligence*. Cambridge, UK: Polity.

———. and Robert M. Clark, eds. 2016. *The 5 Disciplines of Intelligence Collection*. Los Angeles: Sage/CQ Press.

Malone, Thomas W. 2008. "What is Collective Intelligence and What will We Do About It?," in Mark Tovey (ed.), *Collective Intelligence: Creating a Prosperous World at Peace*. Oakton, VA: Earth Intelligence Network: 1–4.

Markle Foundation. 2002. *Protecting America's Freedom in the Information Age*. New York: Markle Foundation.

Marrin, Stephen. 2013. "Rethinking Analytic Politicization," *Intelligence and National Security* 28(1): 32–54.

Masse, Todd. 2006. *Homeland Security Intelligence: Perceptions, Statutory Definitions, and Approaches*. CRS Report for Congress. Order Code RL33616.

———. Siobhan O'Neil, and John Rollins. 2007. *Fusion Centers: Issues and Options for Congress*. CRS Report for Congress. Order Code RL34070.

Masterman, Sir John. 1972. *Double Cross System of the War of 1939–45*. New Haven, CT: Yale University Press.

May, Ernest R. 1992. "Intelligence: Backing Into the Future," *Foreign Affairs* 71 (Summer): 63–72.

Mazzetti, Mark. 2013. *The Way of the Knife: The CIA, A Secret Army, and a War at the Ends of the Earth*. New York: Penguin.

Medina, Carmen A. 2008. "The New Analysis," in Roger Z. George and James B. Bruce (eds.), *Analyzing Intelligence: Origins, Obstacles, and Innovations*. Washington, DC: Georgetown University Press: 238–248.

Miller, Russell A., ed. 2008. *U.S. National Security, Intelligence and Democracy: From the Church Committee to the War on Terror*. New York: Routledge.

Millis, John. 1998. Speech, Central Intelligence Retiree's Association, Langley, Virginia.

Moran, Christopher. 2015. *Company Confessions: Revealing CIA Secrets*. Biteback, London.

National Intelligence Council. 2000. *Global Trends 2015: A Dialogue About the Future with Nongovernmental Experts*. Washington, DC: Central Intelligence Agency.

Naylor, Sean. 2003. "The Lessons of Anaconda," *New York Times* (March 2): A13.

9/11 Commission. 2004. *Report*. New York: Norton.

Odom, William. 2003. *Fixing Intelligence*. New Haven, CT: Yale University Press.

Omsted, Kathryn. 1996. *Challenging the Secret Government: The Post-Watergate Investigations of the CIA and FBI*. Chapel Hill: University of North Carolina Press.

———. 2002. *Red Spy Queen: A Biography of Elizabeth Bentley*. Chapel Hill: University of North Carolina Press.

Pelosi, Nancy (D, California). 2002. Remarks to Loch K. Johnson, Athens, Georgia (November 26).

Perrow, Charles. 2005. "Organizational or Executive Failures?" *Contemporary Sociology* 34(2): 99–107.

Pfiffner, James P., and Mark Phythian (eds.). 2008. *Intelligence and National Security Policymaking on Iraq*. Manchester, U.K.: Manchester University Press.

Phythian, Mark, ed. 2013. *Understanding the Intelligence Cycle*. New York: Routledge.

Pillar, Paul R. 2011. *Intelligence and U.S. Foreign Policy*. New York: Columbia University Press.

Powers, Thomas. 1979. *The Man Who Kept the Secrets: Richard Helms and the CIA*. New York: Knopf.

Prados, John. 1986. *Presidents' Secret Wars: CIA and Pentagon Covert Operations Since World War II*. New York: Dial.

Prunckun, Hank. 2012. *Counterintelligence: Theory and Practice*. Lanham, Maryland: Rowman & Littlefield.

Ransom, Harry Howe. 1970. *The Intelligence Establishment*. Cambridge, MA: Harvard University Press.

Rashid, A. 1999. "The Taliban: Exporting Extremism," *Foreign Affairs* 78: 22–35.

Rheingold, Howard. 2008. "A Slice of my Life in my Virtual Community," in Mark Tovey, ed., *Collective Intelligence: Creating a Prosperous World at Peace*. Oakton, VA: Earth Intelligence Network: 173-200.Rheingold, Howard. 2008. "A Slice of Life in my Virtual Community," in Mark Tovey (ed.), *Collective Intelligence: Creating a Prosperous World at Peace*. Oakton, VA: Earth Intelligence Network: 173–200.

Richelson, Jeffrey. 2017. *The U.S. Intelligence Community*, 7th, ed. Boulder, CO: Westview Press.

Risen, James. 2006. *State of War: The Secret History of the CIA and the Bush Administration*. New York: Free Press.

Rizzo, John. 2014. *Company Man: Thirty Years of Controversy and Crisis in the CIA*. New York: Simon & Schuster.

Rockefeller Commission. 1975. *Report*. Washington, DC: Government Printing Office.

Rovner, Joshua. 2013. "Is Politicization Ever a Good Thing?" *Intelligence and National Security* 28(1): 55–67.

Russell, Richard L. 2007. *Sharpening Strategic Intelligence: Why the CIA Gets It Wrong and What Needs to be Done to Get It Right*. New York: Cambridge University Press.

Schelling, Thomas C. 1962. "Preface" to Roberta Wohlstetter, *Pearl Harbor: Warning and Decision.* Stanford, CA: Stanford University Press.

Schwarz, Frederick A. O., Jr. 1987. "Recalling Major Lessons of the Church Committee," *New York Times* (July 20): A25.

———. 2015. *Democracy in the Dark: The Seduction of Government Secrecy.* New York: New Press.

———. and Aziz Z. Huq. 2007. *Unchecked and Unbalanced: Presidential Power in a Time of Terror.* New York: The New Press.

Scott, Len. 2011. "Intelligence and the Risk of Nuclear War: Able Archer-83 Revisited," *Intelligence and National Security* 28(6): 759–777.

Scoville, Herbert. 1976. "Is Espionage Necessary for Our Security?" *Foreign Affairs* 54 (April): 482–495.

Senate Select Committee on Secret Military Assistance to Iran and the Nicaraguan Opposition and House Select Committee to Investigate Covert Arms Transactions with Iran. 1987. *Hearings and Final Report.* Washington, DC: Government Printing Office.

Shane, Scott. 2008. "A Spy's Motivation: For Love of Another Country," *New York Times* (April 20): Wk 3.

———. 2015. *Objective Troy: A Terrorist, a President, and the Rise of the Drone.* New York: Tim Duggan Books.

Sharp, David H. 2012. *The CIA's Greatest Covert Operation.* Lawrence: University Press of Kansas.

Shorrock, Tim. 2008. *Spies for Hire: The Secret World of Intelligence Outsourcing.* New York: Simon & Schuster.

Shulsky, Abram N., and Gary J. Schmitt. 1993. *Silent Warfare: Understanding the World of Intelligence,* 2nd rev. ed. Washington, DC: Brassey's.

Sims, Jennifer E., and Burton Gerber (eds.). 2005. *Transforming U.S. Intelligence.* Washington, DC: Georgetown University Press.

———. 2009. *Vaults, Mirrors, and Masks: Rediscovering U.S. Counterintelligence.* Washington, DC: Georgetown University Press.

Smist, Frank J., Jr. 1994. *Congress Oversees the United States Intelligence Community,* 2nd ed. Knoxville: University of Tennessee Press.

Snider, L. Britt. 1997. *Sharing Secrets With Lawmakers: Congress as a User of Intelligence.* Washington, DC: Central Intelligence Agency, Center for the Study of Intelligence.

———. 2008. *The Agency and the Hill: CIA's Relationship with Congress, 1946-2004.* Washington, D.C.: Center for the Study of Intelligence, Central Intelligence Agency.

Stanton, Doug. 2009. *Horse Soldiers.* New York: Scribner.

Steele, Robert D. 1999. "Relevant Information and All Source Analysis: The Emerging Revolution," *American Intelligence Journal* 19: 23–30.

———. 2001. *On Intelligence: Spies and Secrecy in an Open World.* Washington, DC: OSS International Press.

Stuart, Douglas T. 2008. *Creating the National Security State: A History of the Law That Transfored Amerca.* Princeton, NJ: Princeton University Press.

Theoharis, Athan G. 1978. *Spying on Americans: Political Surveillance From Hoover to the Huston Plan.* PhiladelphiA: Temple University Press.

———. (ed.). 2006. *The Central Intelligence Agency: Security Under Scrutiny.* Westport, CT: Greenwood Press.

Treverton, Gregory F. 1987. *Covert Action: The Limits of Intervention in the Postwar World.* New York: Basic Books.

———. 2001. *Reshaping National Intelligence for an Age of Information.* New York: Cambridge University Press.

Troy, Thomas F. 1991–92. "The 'Correct' Definition of Intelligence," *International Journal of Intelligence and Counterintelligence* 5 (Winter): 433–454.

Tsang, Steve, ed. 2007. *Intelligence and Human Rights in the Era of Global Terrorism.* London: Praeger Security International.

Turner, Michael A. 2005. *Why Secret Intelligence Fails.* Washington, DC: Potomac Books.

Turner, Stansfield. 1985. *Secrecy and Democracy: The CIA in Transition.* Boston: Houghton Mifflin.

———. 2005. *Burn Before Reading.* New York: Hyperion.

Usowski, Peter S. 1988. "John McCone and the Cuban Missile Crisis: A Persistent Approach to the Intelligence-Policy Relationship," *International Journal of Intelligence and Counterintelligence* 2 (Winter): 547–576.

Wallace, Robert, and H. Keith Melton, with Henry Robert Schlesinger. 2009. *Spycraft: The Secret History of the CIA's Spytechs, from Communism to Al-Qaeda.* New York: Penguin/Plum.

Waller, Michael J. 1994. *Secret Empire: The KGB in Russia Today.* Boulder, CO: Westview.

Warner, Michael. 2007. Sources and Methods for the Study of Intelligence. In Loch K. Johnson, ed. *Handbook of Intelligence Studies.* New York: Routledge: 17–27.

———. 2014. *The Rise and Fall of Intelligence: An International Security History.* Washington, D.C.: Georgetown University Press.

Weiner, Tim. 2007. *Legacy of Ashes: The History of the CIA.* New York: Doubleday.

Weissman, Stephen R. 2010. "An Extraordinary Rendition," *Intelligence and National Security* 25 (April): 198–222.

Westerfield, H. Bradford. 1995. *Inside CIA's Private World: Declassified Articles From the Agency's Internal Journal, 1995-1992.* New Haven, CT: Yale University Press.

Wicker, Tom, et al. 1966. "CIA Operations: A Plot Scuttled." *New York limes,* April 25: A1.

Wirtz, James J. 1989. "The Intelligence Paradigm," *Intelligence and National Security* 4(4): 829–837.

———. 1998. "Organizing for Crisis Intelligence: Lessons from the Cuban Missile Crisis," in James G. Blight and David A. Welch (eds.), *Intelligence and the Cuban Missile Crisis.* London: Frank Cass.

———. 1991. *Intelligence Failure in War: The American Military and the Tet Offensive.* Ithaca, NY: Cornell University Press.

———. 2008. "Hiding in Plain Sight: Denial, Deception, and the Non-State Actor," *The SAIS Review of International Affairs* 28(1): 55–63.

———. and Jon J. Rosenwasser. 2010. "From Combined Arms to Combined Intelligence: Philosophy, Doctrine and Operations," *Intelligence and National Security* 25(6): 725–743.

Wise, David. 1976. *The American Police State: The Government Against the People.* New York: Random House.

Wohlstetter, Roberta. 1962. *Pearl Harbor: Warning and Decision.* Stanford, CA: Stanford University Press.

Woolsey, R. James. 1993. Testimony, *Hearings,* U.S. Senate Select Committee on Intelligence, 103rd Cong., 2nd Sess.: March 6.

Zegart, Amy B. 2007. *Spying Blind: The CIA, the FBI, and the Origins of 9/11.* Princeton, NJ: Princeton University Press.

Zuehlke, Arthur A. 1980. "What is Counterintelligence?" in Roy S. Godson (ed.), *Intelligence Requirements for the 1980s: Counterintelligence.* Washington, DC: National Strategy Information Center.

NAME INDEX

SUBJECT INDEX

Abu Ghraib prison, 59–60, 356
Abwehr, 485, 496n2
accountability. *See* oversight and
    accountability
actionable intelligence, 186, 191–92,
    194, 195–96, 430
Afghanistan
    Al Qaeda in, 46, 49, 59, 61, 72, 212,
      368, 370
    covert action in, 208, 211, 214
    and drone warfare, 240
    intelligence failures in, 49
    Muslim views on U.S. in, 374
    and post-Third Reich German
      intelligence, 496
    Soviet occupation of, 70, 71, 208, 212,
      311, 315
    as terrorist sanctuary, 370–71
    U.S. assistance to, 370
    U.S. War in, 214
African Americans, covert action against,
    256, 294, 340, 341, 342–43
After the Empire (Todd), 83
Agranat Commission, 114
aircraft
    delivery of propaganda by, 209
    drones, 48–49, 54, 60–61, 208–9,
      212–15, 240–42, 334
    U-2 spy planes, 12, 13, 45, 49, 67, 114,
      152, 173, 224–25
Alamo Scouts, 9
Albania, 212
Al Jazeera, 373
Allied Translator and Interpreter Section, 9
all-source analysis
    and analysis of intelligence, 105
    and human intelligence, 66
    and integration of intelligence
      functions, 387
    and intelligence analyst-policymaker
      relationship, 161
    and intelligence collection process, 51
    and 9/11 Commission
      recommendations, 389, 391,
      393, 395

and open-source intelligence, 78, 84
and organization of post-9/11
    intelligence community, 417
and social media intelligence, 95
and structure of U.S. intelligence
    community, 4
al Qaeda
    in Afghanistan, 46, 49, 59, 61, 72,
      212, 368, 370
    agents and supporters within U.S.,
      250
    attacks before September 11th, 362
    as component of larger threat, 366
    and counterintelligence, 49–50, 255
    covert action against, 211, 214
    emergence as threat, 72, 192, 362, 366
    exploitation of technology, 76
    exploitation of U.S. weaknesses,
      378, 379
    fundraising, 371, 377
    as global threat, 365
    Hussein regime ties to, 157, 160–61,
      363, 440–42
    intelligence on, 75
    in Iraq, 431–32, 434, 435
    and ISIS, 428–29, 431–35
    open-source information on, 83
    and organization of post-9/11
      intelligence community, 421
    in Pakistan, 369
    in Saudi Arabia, 372–73
    and social media intelligence, 89
    and strategic intelligence analysis,
      142–43
    vulnerabilities of, 367
    WMDs and, 376
Al-Shabaab, 89
ambassadors, 27, 50, 142, 214. *See also*
    specific individuals
American Civil Liberties Union
    (ACLU), 353
analysis of intelligence
    all-source fusion in, 51
    as art, 479
    barriers to, 103–7, 110–12, 112–14

bureaucracy and, 106–7
client influence on, 175–78,
    441–42, 482
customized, value to policymakers,
    126–32
failures in, 46–47
faulty or incomplete data and, 54
and the intelligence cycle, 45–46, 54
isolation from collection, 55, 58
1-3-1 approach, 165
and organization of post-9/11
    intelligence community, 418
policymaker as final judge of, 188, 482
preconceptions and, 480
professional standards for, 161–63
research intelligence (in-depth
    studies), 47–48, 56–57, 154,
    176, 177
revisiting, 164–65, 166–67
secrets vs. mysteries, 48, 479
theory of, 109
uncertainty, methods of conveying,
    173, 176
volume of data and, 49, 54, 113
analyst-policymaker relationship
    analyst behavior and, 173–75, 175–78,
      441–42, 482
    best practices, 153, 163–66
    Gates' actionable intelligence
      paradigm for, 186, 191–92, 194,
      195–96
    information revolution and, 189,
      193–94, 195–96
    inherent challenges of, 189
    and intelligence–policymaker
      communication, 151–52
    Iraq War decision and, 440, 442
    Kent's isolation paradigm for, 185–86,
      190–91, 194, 195–96, 235
    policymaker prerogatives and limits,
      166–68
    proper balance in, 186, 195, 443,
      482–83
    reconciling different perspectives,
      154–55